Criminal Law

Criminal Law

Cases, Statutes, and Lawyering Strategies

FOURTH EDITION

David Crump
JOHN B. NEIBEL PROFESSOR OF LAW
UNIVERSITY OF HOUSTON LAW CENTER

John T. Parry
ASSOCIATE DEAN OF FACULTY
EDWARD BRUNET PROFESSOR OF LAW
LEWIS & CLARK LAW SCHOOL

CAROLINA ACADEMIC PRESS
Durham, North Carolina

ISBN   978-1-5310-1885-6
e-ISBN   978-1-5310-1886-3
LCCN   2020932552

Carolina Academic Press
700 Kent Street
Durham, North Carolina 27701
Telephone (919) 489-7486
Fax (919) 493-5668
www.cap-press.com

Printed in the United States of America

We dedicate this edition to the memory of our friends and coauthors Neil Cohen and Penny Pether.

David Crump
John Parry

Additional Dedications

From David Crump:
To Susanne.

From John Parry:
To my family

Summary of Contents

Contents

Table of Cases

Preface

We Wanted to Create a Different Kind of Criminal Law Casebook from those that are already on the market. But at the same time, we wanted a familiar organization, with all of the subjects that are part of a traditional casebook.

Traditional Organization and Coverage. This casebook contains all of the subjects that ought to be covered in a first course in Criminal Law. The elements of crimes, actus reus and mens rea receive thorough coverage. The basic crimes, including homicide, sexual assault (or rape), theft, and related offenses, are there. The book covers multiple party crimes and preparatory offenses. Sentencing receives a major chapter. And the justification and legality of the criminal law, including constitutional limits on crime definition and the relationship between crimes, harm, and morals, are all covered.

There is one important innovation in our organization. We have designed the book so that the professor can start the course either with homicide or with the elements of crimes. Various casebooks on the market reflect each of these starting points, but we believe ours is the only one consciously designed to provide the professor with a choice. Some of us, the authors, believe in starting with a concrete body of crime definitions, and this group prefers to begin with homicide. On the other hand, some of us prefer to begin with crime elements, or in other words, with the framework of mens rea, actus reus, circumstances, causation, and harm, before going to specific crimes. Either way makes sense, and either way is convenient with this casebook.

At the very beginning of the book, there is a short introductory chapter on "Fundamentals" that facilitates either the homicide-first or the elements-first approach. That chapter (Chapter 1) briefly provides tools for understanding the rest of the book. Chapter 2 (the first major chapter) is about homicide, and those who want to consider homicide first will proceed in that order. Chapter 3 covers elements of crimes, concentrating on mens rea and actus reus, and those who want that approach will skip from Chapter 1 to Chapter 3, and they will take up homicide, in Chapter 2, after Chapter 3. The book is set up so that either approach is easy.

Special Features: Introductions, Explanations, Current Cases, Statutes, Cutting-Edge Problems, Useful Notes, Newspaper Review Cases, and Simulation Exercises — All in a Compact Book. Traditional coverage and organization were important to us, but they definitely were not all that we wanted. Our casebook contains many features that are unusual, as well as some that are unique. We think that these features will enable the professor to do more for students: To develop the theoretical aspects of the subject in greater depth, while at the same time showing how Criminal Law really works. Here are some of the features that make this casebook special:

1. *Compactness.* This casebook is one of the shortest casebooks on the market. We achieved this feature by carefully editing the cases so that they contain the full background that is needed but so that unrelated material is excised. And we did the same with our introductions, explanations, notes, and problems. We wanted our materials to be lean and effective, and we worked hard to keep them concise.

2. *Cutting-Edge Problems.* A professor can use the problem method in teaching from our casebook, as well as using cases. Most chapters cover each important topic with problems that challenge the student to put together doctrines from groups of cases and to answer questions about current, controversial situations. The more advanced problems are based on real cases: reported decisions, newspaper articles, and cases that the authors handled. Each problem has a "tease" in its heading that alerts the reader to both the legal issues and the factual context.

3. *Current Cases, Carefully Edited.* This casebook emphasizes recent cases. We have tried, when possible, to use decisions from the 2000's, and failing that, we have preferred cases from the 1990's. Usually, recent cases exhibit various pedagogical advantages: more relevant situations, more current policy conflicts, and modern language. Students seem to appreciate cases that were decided after they were born, and we want students' interest to ascend to the highest level possible. Furthermore, it usually is not necessary to sacrifice the development of the law when using up-to-date cases, because the better examples of recent cases (the ones we have selected) usually summarize historical concerns when relevant, as well as the governing principles of today. We have not, however, concentrated only on recent cases. Sometimes a slightly older opinion is better, and then, that is the one we have put in the casebook. Also, there are some much older cases that still are foundations of the law: *M'Naghten's Case* in the insanity coverage; *Pinkerton v. United States* in the conspiracy and accomplice materials. Those cases are included, of course. But unless there were reasons to the contrary, we selected current cases.

4. *Reading Statutes: Assistance and Encouragement.* Our casebook encourages students to read statutes and concentrate on their elements, because criminal law is statutory in most states today. Chapter 1 explores the differences that this statutory basis makes. Later chapters contain problems that require students to break statutes down carefully into their elements. An appendix to the elements chapter (Chapter 3) develops the logic of statutes, as well as examples of interpretive methods. Excerpts from the Model Penal Code are contained in an Appendix ("Appendix A"); throughout the book, conspicuously formatted instructions direct the reader to study sections from the MPC corresponding to the subjects at hand. Experience shows that this casebook will prompt

students to concentrate on statutes and to read them with a different method than cases.

5. ***Introductions and Explanations.*** Class meetings are better if students have understood and absorbed the basics before they come to class. The professor need not spend valuable class time in establishing simple propositions, and everyone can advance to more interesting subjects: current issues, ambiguous situations, and lawyers' strategies. For this reason, our casebook introduces every subject with explanations of the underlying principles, the history, and the doctrinal ambiguities. Students need not rely solely on ancient cases to absorb the distinctions among larceny, false pretenses, and embezzlement; the cases are there, to illustrate the differences and to provide challenges, but so are the history and theory, explained in clear text. We have included the same kinds of explanations about the structures of homicide laws, the ingredients of actus reus, and the determinants of sentences; and in fact, we have tried to precede every important doctrine by a textual introduction with explanations.

6. ***Optional Simulation Exercises That Can Develop Strategic Thinking.*** Each coauthor of this book has had experience as a criminal lawyer. Some of us were defense lawyers, some were prosecutors, and some have practiced on both sides. We are familiar with the distinct kinds of thinking that guide lawyers in strategy decisions: in papering an indictment, for example, or in attacking it. A good criminal lawyer knows how to deconstruct an appellate opinion, but a good criminal lawyer also knows that case law is only the starting point. Decisions about strategy cannot be made solely from reading cases. For that reason, we have included twelve lawyering strategy puzzles that (for want of a better name) we have called "Simulation Exercises."

The Simulation Exercises call for various lawyering competencies. They range from attacking a Pre-Sentence Report to delivering a jury argument and from arguing a Motion for Judgment of Acquittal to drawing up a proposed court's charge. The Simulation Exercises are keyed to "Case Files," which contain materials based on actual cases. The Case files are available online. Please go online to https://caplaw.com/sites/cl4/. The Case Files feature murder, burglary, rape, and white-collar bank fraud charges. Students who use these Case Files will be exposed to the realities of Criminal Law. The homicide Case File, for example, reproduces police reports, an autopsy report, laboratory results, statements, and a confession. In designing these Simulation Exercises, we made sure to reflect a variety of chapters, from the homicide coverage to the sentencing materials, and we also wanted to develop differing lawyering activities, from document analysis and counseling to fact argument and negotiation.

We need to stress, however, that the Simulation Exercises are optional. A professor can decide to use none of them, simply by directing students to omit them. They appear at the ends of chapters and are not integral to the rest of the materials. We think many professors, however, will want to use several of them, and some professors may use them all. There is no substitute for the expanded awareness, newly developed abilities, and genuine excitement that students gain from successful use of these Simulations. Furthermore, students who perform the Simulations tend to understand the other materials in the book better, including the most highly theoretical coverages.

7. *"Newspaper" Review Cases.* Each major chapter contains a set of review problems at its end, requiring the student to put the chapter together and to apply the principles learned from it. Because students respond well to situations that are real, these problems are all based on recent reports from newspapers. Questions accompany each newspaper report to focus attention on doctrines relevant to the case. This is a powerful device for helping students to consolidate and apply what they have learned, and usually, the newspaper review problems are among the high points of a given chapter.

8. *Useful Notes, with Descriptive Headings.* The functions of notes that follow a case are to facilitate understanding of the case, to provide variations or new information, or to challenge students with targeted questions. We have tried our best to make our notes useful for these functions. In particular, we have tried to avoid what we call the "question cloud" method of writing notes: arrangements of disconnected questions that do not make their relationship to the surrounding materials clear.

We tried instead to target our notes so that they help develop understanding and retention. Every note begins with a brief but descriptive heading that tells what it is about. The notes are self-contained. We adopted the convention of explaining every case cited in the notes sufficiently to make it meaningful, without assuming that the student will do legal research to understand each note. Also, we tried to focus each note around one or two targeted questions, rather than producing "question clouds." In summary, we hope that we have written our notes so that they are useful.

Expanded Coverage: The Burden of Proof, Sentencing Law, Controlled Substances (Drugs), White Collar Offenses, Terrorism, Domestic Violence, Stalking, Plea Bargaining, Victims' and Survivors' Interests, Non-Criminal Crime Reduction, and Other Subjects. In addition to these special features, our casebook contains expanded coverage of subjects that many casebooks omit or treat only briefly. Here are some examples:

1. *More Extensive Coverage of the Requirement of Proof Beyond a Reasonable Doubt.* The burden of proof is a transforming aspect of the criminal law. It is possible, for example, for a legislature to enact a statute that "looks good" on paper but that is ineffective, because the crime it defines cannot be proved in court in accordance with the rigorous standard that controls criminal trials. Conversely, a well written statute is one that has been designed with the proof burden as a major consideration. Unfortunately, this phenomenon is not easy to understand. Students come to the Criminal Law course having already

heard the phrase, "beyond a reasonable doubt," but its meaning remains surprisingly elusive. The fictional crime shows or books that furnish most people's background knowledge rarely depend on proof standards, because fiction must reflect dramatic compression. Consequently, if the full implications of the burden of proof are not carefully developed, students will emerge from the course with poor understanding of either theory or reality. Therefore, we devote a chapter—not one of our longer chapters, but a serious chapter nonetheless—to the meaning and implications of the burden of proof. Students find this chapter fascinating, first because of counterintuitive examples of real crimes that remain unprovable, then because of the puzzles that accompany the definition of the burden of proof, next because of the ethical dilemma that the burden represents, and finally because each of the familiar types of evidence used to prove crimes exhibits serious flaws. All of these issues are treated compactly but meaningfully.

2. *Sentencing Law, as Well as Sentencing Philosophy.* We also provide expanded coverage to the law of sentencing. James Q. Wilson famously observed that in most criminal cases the real question is sentencing, not guilt or innocence. It follows that without serious attention to the law of sentencing, a casebook will produce only a partial exposure to Criminal Law even if its definition of crimes and defenses is sound. Most Criminal Law casebooks today, including this one, cover sentencing philosophy—deterrence, incapacitation, rehabilitation and retributive justice—but most contain little coverage of the law of sentencing. Our casebook certainly exposes students to sentencing philosophy, but it covers the law of sentencing, too. It develops the sentencing options that are available, such as probation, probation conditions, fines, incarceration, parole, diversion, clemency, and other variations, and it illustrates the legality and use of these options with cases and problems.

   We also wanted to include thorough coverage of the comparison between determinate and discretionary sentencing. Along with that, we wanted our casebook to contain coverage of the Federal Sentencing Guidelines, coverage that went beyond a note announcing their existence. Therefore, our coverage shows how the Guidelines work and allows students to learn how to compute a sentence under the Guidelines as well to interpret their ambiguities. The Guidelines are advisory today, but courts still must consult them, and most actual sentences comport with the Guidelines. Our aim is to produce students who not only understand sentencing philosophy, but also can argue about conditions of probation, propose an alternative sentence to a judge that will minimize incarceration, and understand the promises and perils of determinate models.

3. *Contraband: Controlled Substances (Drugs) and Other Prohibited Items.* A short and optional—but also important—chapter in this casebook covers crimes involving contraband such as drugs and weapons. These crimes are a major component of actual court dockets, and in some jurisdictions, they

are the biggest component. The law that governs these crimes is different in concept from the law that governs other kinds of crimes. For these reasons, our casebook exposes students to a typical statutory framework by including excerpts from the Uniform Controlled Substances Act, and we use problems or cases to explore the meaning and proof of crimes that include manufacturing, delivery, distribution, precursors, imitations, and possession. The chapter also includes materials that facilitate debate of the question whether criminalizing drugs is the best policy, as well as the impact of drug crimes on race and gender issues.

4. *Other Coverages: White Collar Offenses, Domestic Violence, Stalking, and Terrorism.* Another optional chapter includes brief but focused coverage of white collar offenses and of the features that make them different. It also explores solutions to the problems of domestic violence and stalking in a way that is compact but that will help students confront the real issues. Finally, the law of terrorism has expanded so that it is an appropriate subject of the Criminal Law course today. Our coverage of terrorism is short (it appears at the end of the chapter on contraband), but it shows students the statutory framework of criminal anti-terrorism laws, covers a selected variety of terrorism-related crimes, and highlights the due process and separation of powers challenges that face anyone trying to deal with anti-terrorism offenses.

5. *Perspectives: Non-Criminal Means of Crime Reduction, Victims' and Survivors' Interests, Plea Bargaining, Competencies in the Criminal Law, and the Personal Dimension.* Our casebook contains an optional chapter entitled "Perspectives," which explores other influences on the Criminal Law. First, the criminal sanction is expensive and heavy-handed, and good lawmakers of tomorrow will rely increasingly on other means of reducing crime. Our coverage ranges from regulatory methods to broken-windows theories to architectural design. Second, crime victims and survivors are no longer so neglected as they once were. Our coverage explores the claims and demands of crime victims and survivors and considers the implications. Third, most cases are settled by guilty plea agreements today, and a casebook that neglected this issue would be seriously incomplete. Our casebook describes the phenomenon, explores the underlying reasons, and considers safeguards and procedures for conviction by guilty plea. Fourth, the competencies needed for the practice of criminal law go far beyond the ability to read cases and statutes, and our coverage includes materials that describe and explore those competencies. Finally, it is not always easy for criminal lawyers (or for lawyers in any specialty) to find satisfaction and to live full lives, and we address this issue in Appendix B.

6. *Modular Construction: Selection and Omission of Optional Materials.* Few professors will want to use every one of our features or expanded coverages. Even with a compact book, the number of hours devoted to the Criminal Law course will not permit it. Therefore, we have designed this casebook with

frequent use of "modular construction": sections and chapters that are readily identifiable for either inclusion or omission. For example, extra materials about the logic of reading statutes are contained in an appendix to the chapter on crime elements. Our coverage of the mechanics of the Federal Sentencing Guidelines is concentrated at the end of the sentencing chapter. The Perspectives chapter and its five sections are set off separately, as is the chapter on contraband and terrorism. It should be easy for a professor to describe to students the parts of this casebook that are to be omitted or included.

A Classroom-Tested Book That Helps the Study of Criminal Law Become "Serious Fun." The fundamental ingredients of this casebook have been classroom-tested multiple times. Experience shows that the casebook can make the study of criminal law fascinating to students and, at the same time, help them expand their understanding of both the theory and the reality of the subject. We hope that you and your students will enjoy and benefit from it as much as we have enjoyed writing it.

* * *

David Crump, John B. Neibel Professor of Law, University of Houston Law Center

John T. Parry, Associate Dean of Faculty and Edward Brunet Professor of Law, Lewis & Clark Law School

Criminal Law

Chapter 1

Foundation Considerations: Statutes, Crimes, Proof, Processes, and Purposes

"The law of the realm cannot be changed but by Parliament."—Edward Coke, *Articuli Cleri* (1605)

"[People] are rewarded and punished not for what they do, but for how their acts are defined. This is why [they] are more interested in better justifying themselves than in better behaving themselves."—Thomas Szasz (American psychiatrist, 1920-), *The Second Sin*

§ 1.01 Introduction

The study of criminal law raises a number of important questions that you should consider now and return to throughout your course. They include:

- What actions should be dealt with by criminal laws as opposed to the civil justice processes or no legal process at all?

- Who should be criminally responsible for acts that violate criminal laws? People who are insane? Drunk? Careless? Acting involuntarily? What are the general principles?

- Why—and how to—punish people who violate criminal laws?

- What are the elements and policies of the basic crimes and defenses?

§ 1.02 Civil and Criminal Law

Both the civil and criminal justice systems provide mechanisms to deal with conduct deemed sufficiently harmful to merit redress through the legal system.

For example, assume that Drinker consumes 10 beers, gets in her car, and drives 60 m.p.h. the wrong way on a suburban street with a speed limit of 35 m.p.h. While rounding a corner, she loses control and smashes into an oncoming vehicle, killing the driver, Dedd, who was obeying all traffic laws at the time of the collision.

Drinker's carelessness may subject her to liability under both criminal law and civil (tort) law.

(1) *Two Systems: Crimes and Torts, In General.* The criminal and civil processes for redressing the harm Drinker caused may result in *both* a civil lawsuit (perhaps called "wrongful death") and a criminal prosecution (perhaps for a crime called vehicular homicide or criminally negligent homicide). The two "actions" are generally independent of one another.

(2) *Different Underlying Theories: Punishment and Compensation.* The fundamental difference between civil and criminal liability is their general approach. The primary purpose of the civil case is *compensation* for the wrongful conduct. For example, a civil court might find Drinker liable for Dedd's death and order that she pay Dedd's family $2 million in compensation for their loss.

The primary purpose of the criminal justice system is to *punish* the offender. If Drinker is convicted of, say, vehicular homicide, she could be sent to prison for a number of years. As noted below, punishment is said to serve a number of functions, such as reducing future criminality and providing justice.

The reliance on punishment raises many philosophical questions that are of less consequence in the civil arena. For example, many people believe that a person should be *punished* only if he or she is morally culpable for the conduct. Thus, some argue that people should not be punished if, for example, at the moment of the crime the person was insane or, in some contexts, drunk, mistaken, forced into committing a crime, or acting involuntarily.

(3) *Different Sanctions.* A punishment-oriented system uses far different sanctions than a compensation-focused one. The tort system will require the wrongdoer to pay money while the criminal justice system may mandate a loss of freedom.

Sometimes, however, the sanctions for the two appear to overlap. Often, for example, a criminal conviction leads to an order for the offender to make *restitution* to the victim as compensation for the harm.

(4) *Different "Victim."* A criminal case is conceptualized as a harm to the state, while the tort case is viewed as a harm to the victim. The victim is usually not even considered a formal "party" in the criminal case, although the recent rise of Victim's Rights laws has increased the victim's role in the case. Because the state is the formal victim in the criminal case, the case is brought by the state (the prosecutor), while the civil case is a "private" matter brought by the victim (here Dedd's family) against the wrongdoer (Drinker). Importantly, the state may proceed with the criminal prosecution even if the victim wants the case dropped.

(5) *Different "Style of the Case."* Because the criminal case is brought by the government, the case name ordinarily includes the name of the government and the defendant. The vehicular homicide illustration above may bear the name

State (or *Commonwealth* or *People* or *United States*) *v. Drinker*, depending on the jurisdiction.

(6) *Some Different Procedures.* Although there are many similarities in the procedures used in civil and criminal cases, there are also many differences. The precise distinctions are beyond the scope of this book, but you will study them in your Civil Procedure and Criminal Procedure courses. For our purposes, the primary distinction is that criminal cases provide the accused with more protections than are available in civil matters. The impact of these protections ranges from the defendant's right not to testify, to a higher burden of proof before the defendant can be found liable, to the provision of free defense counsel for indigent defendants.

§ 1.03 The Purposes of the Criminal Law: Why Criminalize? And Why Punish?

[A] Measuring Appropriate Sentences: The Theories That Guide the Criminal Sanction

Notes on Deterrence, Incapacitation, Rehabilitation, and Retributive Justice

(1) *Four Traditional Theories Underlying the Criminal Sanction.* Lawmakers often cite four theories in deciding what sentence should be imposed for violating a criminal law: (1) deterrence (both general and specific); (2) incapacitation; (3) rehabilitation; and (4) retributive justice. The first three theories are "Utilitarian," in that they use the criminal law to serve society's interests in reducing crime and protecting the public. The fourth factor, however, is "Kantian" or "retributive." Rather than considering the usefulness of the punishment to society, it considers moral blameworthiness.

(2) *Examples of Deterrence, Incapacitation, Rehabilitation, and Retributive Justice.*

(a) *Specific and General Deterrence.* If the goal of the criminal sanction against an embezzler is to "send a message" to this embezzler and to other citizens to persuade them to avoid this conduct, then the purpose is *deterrence*. ("Specific" or "special" deterrence punishes an offender in order to deter the same offender from future criminality, while "general" deterrence punishes this offender in order to deter other people who might consider committing similar crimes.)

(b) *Incapacitation.* On the other hand, in the case of a serial murderer with a long history of prior convictions, the goal more likely will be to separate the killer by lengthy incarceration from society, so as to protect people from the risk the offender poses. This theory is called *incapacitation*.

(c) *Rehabilitation.* Rehabilitation imposes punitive measures for the purpose of changing the offender's mental outlook so he or she will be reformed, ideally losing the desire to recidivate. Thus, for a misdemeanor offense of intoxicated driving, the sanction may focus on rehabilitating the offender, perhaps by assessing a sentence of probation with conditions requiring counseling and even medical treatment for alcoholism.

(d) *Retribution.* In all of these cases, and others, the factor of retributive justice, or proportionality to wrongdoing, may also be important. The defendant is punished because he or she *deserves* it. In some cases, retribution becomes the principal purpose of the criminal sanction, as when a court sentences a frail, elderly individual to a substantial prison term for a murder committed many years before, one that the individual is unlikely to repeat. Opponents of this theory argue that it is barbaric and inappropriate in an advanced society.

(3) *Conflict Among the Factors.* The four punishment theories often point in different directions. For example, if the embezzler receives a sentence of probation, without incarceration, we may preserve the hope of rehabilitation, but we may diminish the effect of deterrence—and disserve retributive justice. Reconciling these kinds of conflicts is a frequent issue.

United States v. Blarek [and Pellecchia]
7 F. Supp. 2d 192 (E.D.N.Y. 1998)

WEINSTEIN, DISTRICT JUDGE.

[Blarek and Pellecchia were convicted by a jury of conspiracy to commit racketeering and money laundering, based on their laundering of funds for a Columbian drug kingpin named Santacruz, who was a customer of their interior decorating business. In sentencing the defendants, Judge Weinstein had to consider the requirements of the "Federal Sentencing Guidelines," as well as evidence bearing on whether he should "depart" from the Guideline Sentence.

[On the one hand, Blarek and Pellecchia's money-laundering scheme was systematic, planned, years in duration, highly profitable, and involved large amounts of drugs, money, and underlings whom the defendants supervised. On the other hand, the defendants had no criminal records, they were otherwise law-abiding, they had been "lured into" beginning their participation by their Columbian customer before money laundering became a crime, and they used no weapons and engaged in no acts of violence (although presumably, they inferred that Santacruz did). The court considered the defendants "vulnerable" in prison, because they were lovers and because Pellecchia was HIV-positive.]

Four core considerations . . . have traditionally shaped American sentencing determinations: incapacitation of the criminal, rehabilitation of the offender, deterrence of the defendant and of others, and just deserts for the crime committed. *See, e.g., Harmelin v. Michigan,* 501 U.S. 957, 999 (1991) ("The federal and state criminal systems have accorded different weights at different times to the penological goals of retribution, deterrence, incapacitation, and rehabilitation.") (Kennedy, J., concurring). . . .

Ascertaining priorities among these potentially conflicting notions has long been a point of contention. . . . Somewhat oversimplifying, there are two basic camps. Retributivists contend that "just deserts" are to be imposed for a crime committed. Utilitarians, in their various manifestations, suggest that penalties need to be viewed more globally by measuring their benefits against their costs. . . . Implied in this debate are questions about our basic values and beliefs: Why do we impose punishment? Or is it properly to be named "punishment"? . . .

Two eighteenth and nineteenth century philosophers set the terms of the current . . . debate.

1. *Kant's Retributive Just Deserts Theory.* Immanuel Kant, born in East Prussia in 1724, is regarded by some as "one of the most important philosophers in Western culture." . . . Kant's anti-utilitarian thesis on criminal penalties is reflected in an oft-cited passage from his work, *The Metaphysical Elements of Justice*: "[P]unishment can never be used merely as a means to promote some other good for the criminal himself or for civil society, but instead it must in all cases be imposed on him only on the ground that he has committed a crime; for a human being can never be manipulated merely as a means to the purposes of someone else and can never be confused with the objects of the Law of things. . . ." It follows from this position that the sole justification for criminal punishment is retribution. . . . For Kant and his adherents, "[p]unishment that gives an offender what he or she deserves for a past crime is a valuable end in itself and needs no further justification." "It is not inflicted because it will give an opportunity for reform, but because it is merited." . . .

2. *Bentham's Utilitarian Theory.* Jeremy Bentham, an English philosopher born in 1748, advocated a far different, more prospective approach through his "Principle of Utility." For him, law . . . was intended to produce the "greatest happiness for the greatest number," a concept sometimes referred to as the "felicity calculus." . . . It was his view that punishment was sometimes essential to ensure compliance with public laws. . . . [Unlike Kant, however,] Bentham was not interested in criminal punishment as a way of avenging or canceling the theoretical wrong suffered by society. . . . Rather, a criminal sanction was to be utilized only when it could help ensure the greater good of society and provide a benefit to the community. . . . Under the Benthamite approach, [therefore,] deterring crime, as well as correction and reformation of the criminal, are primary aspirations of criminal law. . . .

[The Kantian and Benthamite philosophies conflict, and judges historically have struck compromises between them.] . . . Given these problems, it may make sense to continue to equivocate, oscillating between these poles, tempering justice with mercy, [and] just deserts with utility calculations, in varying pragmatic ways. . . .

Utility and Retribution Under Sentencing Guidelines. The Sentencing Guidelines, written by the United States Sentencing Commission pursuant to the Sentencing Reform Act, purport to [further the goals of] "deterrence, incapacitation, just punishment, and rehabilitation." [The Sentencing Guidelines use a point system to determine a "Guideline Sentence" for each offense and offender. They also allow judges to "depart" from Guideline Sentences. A later chapter of this book covers the Guidelines in greater depth.]

Total Computations. [Here, Judge Weinstein made the factual findings necessary under the Guidelines. Then, he determined the Guideline Sentences for these crimes:] [D]efendant Blarek's total offense level [is] 32, while defendant Pellecchia's is . . . 30. Blarek faces a [Guideline Sentence] of imprisonment of 121 to 151 months. Pellecchia faces 97 to 121 months' incarceration. . . .

Traditional and Statutory Sentence Rationales. [The next issue, however, is whether Judge Weinstein should depart from the Sentencing Guidelines. To decide this issue, the judge considered the four rationales discussed above.]

1. *Incapacitation.* Incapacitation seeks to ensure that "offenders . . . are rendered physically incapable of committing crime." . . . In the instant case, incapacitation is not an important factor. First, these defendants have no prior criminal record. . . . Second, their connection to the criminal world, Santacruz, is now deceased. Third, it does not appear that long term restriction is necessary to ensure that defendants do not reenter a life of crime. . . .

2. *Rehabilitation.* Rehabilitation is designed to instill "in the offender proper values and attitudes, by bolstering his respect for self and institutions, and by providing him with the means of leading a productive life. . . ." Neither of these men is wayward or in need of special instruction on the mores of civilized society. . . . This criterion, rehabilitation, therefore, is not one that is useful in assessing a penalty.

3. *Deterrence.* . . . General deterrence attempts to discourage the public at large from engaging in similar conduct. It is of primary concern in this case. . . . While it is not appropriate under just deserts views for defendants in famous cases to be treated more harshly . . . , simply for the sake of making an example of them, under a utilitarian view the notoriety of a particular defendant may be taken into account by sentencing courts provided the punishment is not disproportionate to the crime.

4. *Retribution.* Retribution is considered by some to be a barbaric concept, appealing to a primal sense of vengeance. It cannot, however, be overlooked as an appropriate consideration. When there is a perception on the part of the community that the courts have failed to sensibly sanction wrongdoers, respect for the law may be reduced. . . . Should punishment fail to fit the crime, the citizenry might be tempted to vigilantism. . . . It is important, therefore, that the imposition of a penalty in this case capture . . . the "worth" of defendants' volitional criminal acts. . . .

Individual Sentences. . . . The final task is weighing [these] considerations . . . , with particular emphasis on general deterrence and imposition of a punishment that can be viewed as deserved in light of the seriousness . . . of the crimes. While defendants have forfeited most of their property to the government . . . , and do deserve a downward departure from the Guidelines, a stiff fine to eliminate all their assets as well as a substantial period of incarceration is required. . . .

Blarek, whose actions indicate a somewhat greater culpability than do Pellecchia's, begins with a computed offense level of 32[, corresponding to a Guideline Sentence of about 10 to 12½ years]. [But because of the sentencing evidence and factors,] the sentence imposed should reflect a downward departure of six levels to offense level 26. Blarek is sentenced [within the Guideline range for level 26] to a concurrent term of 68 months' incarceration. A lesser or greater departure would not be appropriate in view of the facts and law. In addition, Blarek is fined a total of $305,186, which represents his approximate total net worth after his forfeiture of over $2,000,000 in cash and property to the government. . . . The maximum period of supervised release, three years, is imposed. . . .

Pellecchia's total offense level is computed at 30[, corresponding to a Guideline Sentence of about 8 to 10 years]. The sentence should reflect a downward departure of seven levels to offense level 23. This represents the same six level departure granted for defendant Blarek with an addition level of downward departure based upon defendant's health [he is HIV-positive] as well as his lesser culpability. . . . [This departure results in a reduced sentence of 48 months.] No fine has been imposed for Pellecchia since he [has] a negative net worth of over $100,000. . . . Three years of supervised release is ordered. . . . [These two sentences] follow statutory and case law mandates requiring these defendants to be treated harshly, primarily to deter others.

Notes and Questions

(1) *Money Laundering: Why Should We Make It a Crime?* Money laundering is made a crime by several federal statutes. It consists of "cleansing" money or disguising its source by putting illegally-obtained money into legitimate investments, then drawing out the money as if it had been earned legitimately.

Consider whether Retributive or Utilitarian reasoning would support the use of the criminal sanction against money laundering: *i.e.*, consider why money laundering should be a crime at all. The conduct does no direct harm to any person, and it is costly to enforce laws against it, because compliance itself is costly (financial institutions and their employees, for example, face heavy preventive burdens) and also, because it makes criminals out of many otherwise law-abiding individuals. But money laundering arguably does harm by facilitating other crimes, and it frustrates efforts to prevent crimes by seizing funds. Which of these considerations would appeal to a Retributivist and which to a Utilitarian?

(2) *Actual Sentences That Amounted to Roughly Half the Guideline Sentences: Do Judge Weinstein's Results Conform to the Four Sentencing Factors?* Blarek's Guideline Sentence would have been roughly 10 to 12½ years, but Judge Weinstein assessed only 5 years. Pellecchia's Guideline Sentence would have been roughly 8 to 10 years,

but the judge assessed 4 years instead. Do these sentences seem to reflect an appropriate resolution of the four traditional factors of deterrence, incapacitation, rehabilitation, and retributive justice? What about the Guideline Sentences (which would have been roughly double the actual sentences)?

[B] The Creation of Criminal Prohibitions: Harm, Morality, Symbolism, Legality, and Pragmatism

Notes on Defining Crimes: What Should (or Can) We Criminalize?

(1) *What Should Be Made Criminal?* There is probably little disagreement with the proposition that the criminal justice system should deal with offenses such as murder, arson, rape, and robbery. The issue for these crimes is how to define their outer limits. For example, should arson include a homeowner's burning of her own home, or should a person have to attempt a retreat before using deadly force to resist an attack? For less obvious harms, by contrast, there may be considerable debate over whether the conduct should be made criminal at all. Should a person be subject to criminal prosecution for spitting on a sidewalk, betting a few dollars with a friend on a football game, not wearing a motorcycle helmet, or smoking marijuana for pleasure or to dull the unpleasantness caused by chemotherapy?

A number of perspectives have evolved in addressing this important question.

(2) *Harm to Others as a Required Justification for Criminalization.* Some commentators have argued that the only proper purpose of defining crimes is to prevent harm to people other than the actor: harm that exceeds the incursion on liberty that results from the prohibition itself. This view was stated forcefully by John Stuart Mill. He argued that "other-directed harm" could be the proper subject of criminal legislation, but it was not legitimate for government to prohibit "self-directed harm"—to protect a person from that person's own actions. This view remains a major factor in criminal justice, although it is not the only approach.

(3) *Crime and Morality—Another View: The Hart-Devlin Debate.* British Judge Patrick Devlin argued instead that the paramount issue in defining crimes was the underlying public morality. That morality needed protection from violation, even by acts that caused no measurable harm to anyone. Thus, if "the [person] in the Clapham Omnibus" (today, we would say, "the person in the street") found certain conduct to be disgusting and immoral, that revulsion was at least one indicator to Lord Devlin that it was proper to criminalize the behavior. H.L.A. Hart eloquently opposed Devlin's views, arguing that even if the person in the Clapham Omnibus "gets sick" at certain conduct engaged in by the minority of the population, that revulsion is insufficient justification for criminalizing it. Later, near the end of this book, we shall consider the Hart-Devlin debate in greater depth.

(4) *Are Both Harm and Morals Relevant?* Many commentators would say that both Devlin and Hart are right, to a degree. And in fact, few philosophers would

deny that harm and morals are each relevant—to some degree, and at some point. Hart himself observed that it was more practical to define and enforce a criminal sanction if its purposes coincided with the public morality. His disagreement with Devlin went only to whether morality was a sufficient condition for criminalization, without demonstrable harm. And Devlin did not advocate the random criminalization of offenses against morals. In other words, the relationship between crime and morals, and crime and harm, is a matter of degree—and a matter of debate.

(5) *Other Constraints on Criminalization: Direct versus Indirect Harm.* In some instances, criminal law prohibits conduct that facilitates harm, even if it does not cause harm directly. A drunk driver commits a crime even if the driver makes it home safely, because the act has a sufficiently significant statistical connection to harm.

At some point, this factor—the remoteness of the conduct from the "real crime"—becomes relevant. Do we criminalize the conduct of a financial institution that suspects money laundering, but facilitates it indirectly, by maintaining accounts for ostensibly law-abiding customers? At each step away from a relatively direct harm, negative fallout from the decision to criminalize is likely to increase. And yet, the best way to prevent an object crime that causes harm may be to remove indirect factors that make the object crime possible. Thus, the decision whether to criminalize conduct is a balancing act. With respect to money laundering, this balance has convinced lawmakers to criminalize it in some contexts.

(6) *Legitimacy and Pragmatism as Constraints on Overcriminalization: The Example of Defining Harassment-Without-Threat as a Crime.* Another constraint is that crime definition must be reasonably specific. The Due Process Clauses of the U.S. Constitution require criminal statutes to use reasonably clear language so as to provide guidance to private persons and limit the discretion accorded law enforcement officials. Further, the need for specific language ensures that the crime does not include broad areas of innocent or valuable actions.

There is a pragmatic concern here: a desire not to criminalize too much, or not to sweep into prohibited areas wide swaths of normal, harmless behavior. And in extreme cases, there also is a concern for legitimacy: the problem, that is, that prevention of some kinds of harm would require such broad and vague prohibitions that the meaning of the law would become guesswork, in which instance the law may violate the Constitution. For example, harassment causes harm to the person who is the object of it. If a former spouse follows an ex-spouse, communicates frequently, and scares the ex-spouse out of her wits, there may appear to be strong justification for criminalizing that actor's conduct. Most states, however, have been unsuccessful in defining broad harassment crimes, with coverage sufficient to address the conduct of determined and resourceful harassers, without running afoul of the Constitution. We shall consider this issue further in later chapters.

(7) *Stigma, Symbolism, Resources, and the Availability of Other Alternatives.* Imagine that a State Education Agency discovers widespread cheating by teachers

and students on standardized tests that the Agency uses to assess student achievement, advance students, place children in gifted-and-talented classes, rate schools as "Exemplary" or "Adequate," and disburse funds. This cheating, in other words, causes real harm. Should the State define cheating on an examination as a crime? On the one hand, criminalization may generate deterrence, and the symbolism of labeling the harm as significant (that is, criminal) rather than trivial may seem justified. On the other hand, it is easy to imagine judges and police departments objecting that their resources already are stretched thin. Besides, the teachers can be fired, the students dismissed. These alternative remedies are not always easy, but they will consume fewer resources than criminal prosecutions. And then, there is the question whether it is really appropriate to stigmatize students by criminal conviction for this behavior? A decision to criminalize may appear justifiable, but on second thought, lawmakers may decide that the costs outweigh the benefits. Consider the problem that follows.

Problem 1A (The Decision to Criminalize): For a Motorcycle Helmet Law, Is the Issue Freedom — Or Is It Public Safety?

(1) *A Proposed Law Making a Second Helmet Offense a Serious Misdemeanor: What Will the Debate Sound Like?* From the serious faces in the West York House of Representatives that day, one would never have guessed the subject of debate. But a somber mood certainly accompanied the arguments, which pitted calls for "basic freedoms" against defenses of "the safety of our children." A controversial West York law already defined motorcycle riding without a helmet as a traffic-court misdemeanor, punishable by a fine of up to $100. But a bill authored by Representative Jane Goodheart proposed to put major teeth in the helmet law by making a second offense a "Class B misdemeanor," carrying a jail term of as much as six months. The existing law had been widely flouted by the Yuppie Pack, whose President, Butch Freebeard, passionately opposed the Goodheart bill increasing the penalty for noncompliance.

Freebeard argued, "It's a personal choice. Some of our members do wear helmets, and that's fine. But it ought to be up to them. We're not hurting anybody! It's not the State's business, it's the individual's. Have you ever tried wearing a helmet outside on a hundred-degree day? We have one member who has to commute to his job as a Building Manager in his pin-striped suit, he doesn't have a car, and if he wears a helmet, he has to take a shower after he gets there. Motorcycles are environmentally friendly, and they promote national security, by using only a fraction of the gasoline that most of you consume. But that's not the main reason why this is a bad, bad bill. Motorcycles are about freedom! In fact, members, you ought to repeal the law making it a violation not to wear a helmet in the first place, if you're real Americans! When the Yuppie Pack rallies out west on Interstate 73, we feel the breeze, taste the sun, smell the bluebonnets, and see the mountains. We can talk to each other, and it's pointless if you can't. Make us carry insurance, if you want to. Enforce the rules of the road as hard as you can; we're the Yuppie Pack, and we don't speed. But don't take our most basic freedoms away from us!"

Then, Officer Bart Crabapple of the West York Police Deparment told the House members, "I get sick and tired of stopping these bikers and having them sneer and say, 'I'll just pay the standard thirty-five dollar fine and be right back.' They don't think anything they want to do is against the law." But Judge J. Edgar Weary disagreed. "We have a hundred cases a day in my misdemeanor court now, and it's a cattle call. If you ladies and gentlemen keep passing laws that make everyone who spits on the sidewalk a criminal, we'll be overwhelmed. Besides, nobody's going to brand a young person as a criminal for this, or put them in jail for six months."

At last, Representative Goodheart stood up. "Butch Freebeard says it's an individual thing and none of the state's business. But when a guy without a helmet gets wiped off the road, it's the state that picks him up, transports him in an ambulance to the hospital, and furnishes his medical care. The state cleans the blood off the highway, and the state—and incidentally, it's not really 'the state,' it's us, those of us who abide by the helmet law—it's the state, or rather us, who pays welfare to that biker's spouse and children! The state furnishes the courts, and that's where the biker will sue the unfortunate driver who was involved in the accident, which wouldn't have hurt the biker if he merely had worn a helmet." The chamber fell silent, and Representative Goodheart's eyes glistened, as she held up an 18 by 24 blown-up photograph. "My beautiful son Stephen was nineteen when he left me that Tuesday morning, this past April. He never came back. He didn't wear a helmet. He listened to the propaganda spewed out by the likes of Butch Freebeard and that Yuppie Pack. The officer with the downcast eyes who knocked on my door an hour later said he was sorry—and I knew instantly. Stephen had lost control of his motorcycle and suffered eggshell fracturing and a subdural hematoma when he ran into a utility pole. The Yuppie Pack has created a climate that encourages this kind of thing, and they've made it attractive, glamorous, romantic, even though it's crazy dangerous! It's just wrong. It's the wrong message. We've got to change the culture, use some leadership, and make the law fit what law abiding people think! Vote for this bill, members, if you value the safety of our children!"

(2) *What Are the Arguments for and Against Criminalizing Helmetless Motorcycling?* These speakers have used informal language, but they also have touched on most of the philosophical and pragmatic arguments about criminalization that are mentioned in the notes above. Can you identify the argument that harm is a requirement for legitimacy, in these motorcycle-helmet debates? That public morality about helmet-wearing also matters? That inclusion of excessive amounts of harmless conduct should weigh against criminalization, even if there is some preventable harm that the law can address? That indirectness of harm dissipates support for the criminal sanction? That symbolism, in the form of widespread flouting of the existing helmet law, is important? That constraints on resources should constrain the definition of helmet crime? That stigma can be an argument against criminalization?

§ 1.04 Sources of Criminal Law:
The Primacy of Statutes

(1) *Criminal Law Is Mostly Statutory (and This Factor Makes a Difference)*. In most states today, criminal law is entirely or almost entirely statutory. If a statute cannot be read to prohibit a given action, that action is not usually a crime. Consistently with what Lord Coke said in the quotation that begins this chapter (although it said it in a somewhat different context), it generally takes the legislature to define an offense in most states. Federal law also relies on statutes to define criminal offenses. This statutory basis means that the starting point for almost all of the cases in this book will be a statute enacted by the state or federal legislature to define a criminal offense.

(2) *Many Sources of Criminal Law*. American criminal law comes primarily from statutes, but other sources remain important as well.

(a) *Common Law*. At one point, English criminal law was generally the product of the common law. The American colonies adopted the "common law system," including the crimes that had evolved through the common law.

Most American jurisdictions no longer recognize common law crimes or defenses. Instead, their criminal law is entirely statutory. As the psychiatrist, Dr. Szasz, said in the quotation at the beginning of this chapter, the issue is not whether there is something wrong in what the actor has done, but rather how the actor's conduct is defined by law.

A small minority of American jurisdictions use the common law as "gap fillers." If a statute addresses an issue, then the statute controls. But matters not covered by criminal statutes are still subject to prosecution under the common law crime dealing with the conduct. A few jurisdictions simply name some of their crimes in a statute and leave the actual definition of the crime to the common law process (*i.e.* courts provide the definition of the offense).

(b) *Other Sources: Military Law, Administrative Regulations, International Law, and Tribal Law*. Congress has created a military legal system that includes crimes and defenses occurring on military bases and similar locales. While these crimes are statutory, they are separate from the rest of federal criminal law. Military personnel and others who commit military crimes may be punished in a manner similar to civilian offenses. Trials occur in military courts, though some civilian judicial review is possible. Some statutes make it a crime to violate certain administrative regulations. International law also creates crimes, such as genocide. And in Native-American jurisdictions, tribal authority can define crimes.

(3) *The Model Penal Code (Appendix A) and Its Use Throughout This Book*. Before the Model Penal Code, every state had enacted statutes defining some crimes and defenses. These "criminal codes" developed piecemeal (often in response to a particular case that raised an issue) and were sometimes poorly drafted. The "Model Penal Code" ("MPC") was the result of nine years of work by a group of experts

working with the American Law Institute to provide a model for states to use in reforming their own criminal codes. Since its promulgation in 1962, it has been enormously—although unevenly—influential, and we shall refer to the MPC throughout this book. The necessary excerpts from the MPC appear in Appendix A.

(a) *State Criminal Codes.* Today perhaps two-thirds of the states have integrated penal codes influenced to greater or lesser degrees by the MPC. If you understand the MPC, you have a head start on comprehending both the structure and provisions of most state codes. Codes not based on the MPC tend to be continuations of the pre-code "piecemeal" approach.

(b) *Basic Structure of a Modern Penal Code.* Modern codes, based on the MPC, contain two parts: General and Special. The General Part provides rules that apply to all crimes, including burden of proof, basic definitions, guides to interpreting the code, general underlying policies, and defenses. The Special Part contains the elements of specific crimes, such as murder, theft, and sexual assault.

(c) *Federal Criminal Laws.* Unlike most states, the federal government has not enacted a comprehensive penal code despite years of efforts by reform-minded legislators. Federal criminal laws were added piecemeal over many years and vary from virtually primitive (federal homicide laws reflect a model developed in the late 1600s) to extremely well-written and effective. Most federal defenses are based in the common law, not statutes. *See, e.g., United States v. Leahy*, 473 F.3d 401, 405–07 (1st Cir. 2007) (discussing the development of common law defenses to the federal crime of being a felon in possession of a firearm).

(4) *How to Read a Statute.* Reading a statute is different from absorbing a court opinion. When you read an opinion, you can look for the important parts, and if you miss a string of words, you may still understand the case. A statute is different. If you let your eyes glaze over and you miss three or four words, you might miss a major issue. Statutes are dense; they need to be read word for word and broken down into their elements. The need to focus on each word of a statute also means that the court has less discretion to shape the law than it would if it were engaged only in common law reasoning.

(5) *The Fact That Statutes are Primary Does Not Make the Common Law Irrelevant.* Historically, our law of crimes originated in England under the common law, and statutes today continue to use common law terminology. For example, to consider what a murder statute means, you may have to understand the common law definition of murder as killing with "malice aforethought," because the legislatures of some states have inserted it into their statutes. Using common law definitions is one of the "interpretive principles" that are used to decipher statutes.

(6) *General Interpretive Principles, Such as the "Rule of Lenity" and the Concept of "Fair Import": What Do the Words Mean?* Since so much depends on relatively few words, there can be vigorous disagreement about what the words in a statute mean. Therefore, throughout this book we shall encounter rules for statutory

construction. One rule is the "Rule of Lenity." In the case that follows, the court says, "It is the policy of this state to construe a penal statute as favorably [leniently] to the defendant as its language and the circumstances of its application may reasonably permit. . . ." But the concept of "Fair Import" tells a court to read a statute in accordance with its plain or common meaning. In this same case, a state statute requires the courts to interpret crime definitions "according to the fair import of [their] terms, with a view to effect [their] objects and promote justice." Sometimes this idea of "Fair Import" clashes with the "Rule of Lenity." (So it is here.)

(7) As the cases below will demonstrate, the definition of the crime in a statute is critical. As you read these cases, consider why we depend on statutes to define the limits of criminal behavior and how courts decide legislative intent.

People v. Latour

2012 Cal. App. Unpub. LEXIS 8677 (Nov. 29, 2012)
(Unreported Decision)

This case contains a startling (but accurate) headline saying, "Robbery of a Bank Is Not a Crime."(!?)

Defendant and his nephew Marcus Zapata did, indeed, rob a bank. Specifically, "they entered a Wells Fargo Bank in Rocklin wearing masks and carrying guns. Zapata jumped over the teller counter and emptied Beaumont and Crivineau's cash drawers while defendant remained in the customer area. Zapata then jumped back over the counter, and he and defendant ran out of the bank and into a waiting car. . . . [A] high speed chase ensued. . . . [The robbers] were apprehended a short time later" and a jury convicted them of robbery of Wells Fargo Bank.

Ironically, on appeal, it was the prosecution that called for the defendant's acquittal. As the court put it, "The People say that 'Count 1, robbery against Wells Fargo Bank, should be reversed because a bank is not a person and cannot be susceptible to robbery under [the applicable statute].'" The problem had originated because the charging document had named "Wells Fargo Bank" as the victim. Instead, it should have named one of the tellers, Beaumont or Crivineau. The court pointed out that section 211 of the California Penal Code provided, "Robbery is the felonious taking of personal property in the possession of another, from his person or immediate presence, and against his will, accomplished by means of force or fear." Therefore, "[a]s the statute states, robbery is an offense against a person." The court concluded, "A bank is not a person; thus, defendant's conviction for robbery of Wells Fargo Bank cannot stand."

This misguided prosecution resulted because a prosecutor prepared the charging instrument erroneously, possibly from inadvertence or inexperience. But it resulted in the defendant's acquittal upon a serious charge, under circumstances in which, because of the constitutional prohibition against multiple jeopardy, the defendant probably could not be retried.

Notes and Questions

(1) *Couldn't the Court Have Found a Way to Affirm This Conviction?* The court asserts that the offense must be against a person, because the "statute states" that it must. But the statute does not precisely say this. Instead, it says that the offense consists of taking personal property from "another" (couldn't Wells Fargo qualify as "another"?), and it says that it must be taken from "his person or immediate presence" (wasn't the property, here, in Wells Fargo's "immediate presence?"), and that it must be taken "against his will" (wasn't the property taken against Wells Fargo's will?). See whether you can explain why the court did not interpret the statute so that the prosecution could be affirmed.

(2) *In Most States, Every Conviction Requires Conformity between All Statutory Elements and the Proof in the Record.* What does this odd case, *People v. Latour*, tell you about the statutory basis of the criminal law? Consider the case that follows, also.

United States v. Venegas-Vasquez

376 F. Supp. 3d 1094 (D. Ore. 2019)

MICHAEL H. SIMON, District Judge.

In this criminal case, the Court must decide whether a recipient of Deferred Action for Childhood Arrivals ("DACA"), who also was [at an earlier time] paroled [*i.e.,* allowed by permission] into the United States, may be prosecuted for violating a federal law that prohibits an alien who is illegally or unlawfully in the United States from possessing a firearm. Defendant Emmanuel Venegas-Vasquez ("Venegas-Vasquez") is charged with one count of violating 18 U.S.C. § 922(g)(5). That statute makes it unlawful for an alien who is "illegally or unlawfully in the United States" to possess a firearm or ammunition. Venegas-Vasquez contends that he was not illegally or unlawfully in the United States, and thus the indictment should be dismissed for failure to allege an element of the offense. Venegas-Vasquez relies upon two facts, which the Government does not dispute. First, in January 2015, United States Citizenship and Immigration Services ("USCIS") granted Venegas-Vasquez Deferred Action for Childhood Arrivals ("DACA") [by which the Government withheld prosecution of illegal entrants who entered as minors]. Second, in 2016, USCIS "paroled" Venegas-Vasquez into the United States, pursuant to . . . 8 U.S.C. § 1182(a)(9)(B)(iii). Based on these facts, Venegas-Vasquez argues that he was not illegally or unlawfully in the United States at the time the indictment alleges he was in possession of two firearms . . . . The Government responds by arguing that Venegas-Vasquez did not have legal or lawful status in the United States and that is all that is required under that element of § 922(g)(5). The Court concludes that § 922(g)(5)(A) is grievously ambiguous regarding whether the phrase "illegally or unlawfully in the United States" refers to either [illegal] presence or [illegal] status. . . . [T]he Court grants Defendant's motion to dismiss.

Background

Venegas-Vasquez is an alien citizen of Mexico. It is not disputed that Venegas-Vasquez unlawfully entered the United States as a child in 2001. Immigrations and Customs Enforcement ("ICE") records show that Venegas-Vasquez has applied for neither citizenship nor residence in the United States.

In September 2014, Venegas-Vasquez applied to USCIS under the DACA program [which withholds prosecution of certain aliens who entered as children]. On January 22, 2015, USCIS granted Venegas-Vasquez DACA, and renewed his DACA in January 2018. In January 2015, the USCIS also provided Venegas-Vasquez with an employment authorization card, allowing him to work in the United States. In February 2015, the Social Security Administration issued a social security number to Venegas-Vasquez. In addition, in March 2016, Venegas-Vasquez applied for permission to travel to Mexico to visit his family. USCIS authorized Venegas-Vasquez for parole back into the United States under § 212(d)(5) of the INA, and Venegas-Vasquez was paroled back into the United States in 2016. [However, his parole expired before this alleged offense.]

On May 26, 2017, police officers responded to two calls, one from Venegas-Vasquez' neighbor, who reported hearing gunfire, and another from Venegas-Vasquez' wife. Police arrived and took Venegas-Vasquez into custody. With Venegas-Vasquez' consent, the police searched his truck and found a loaded 9mm handgun and a loaded AK-47 style assault rifle. [A] federal grand jury indicted Venegas-Vasquez for one count of violating 18 U.S.C. § 922(g)(5).

Standards

... A pretrial motion to dismiss is appropriate if the motion involves a question of law as opposed to a question of fact. ... The question of law at issue in this pretrial motion is the meaning of the phrase "illegally or unlawfully in the United States" in 18 U.S.C. § 922(g)(5)(A) [i.e., whether it refers to "illegal presence" or "illegal status"].

Discussion

A. Statutory Interpretation and § 922(g)(5)

Section 922(g)(5) states that it shall be unlawful for any person "who being an alien— ... is illegally or unlawfully in the United States; ..." to possess in or affecting commerce, any firearm or ammunition. The statute provides no definitional guidance on what it means to be "illegally or unlawfully in the United States." ...

The statute does not expressly use the terms "present" or "presence;" nor does it use the terms "status" or "immigration status." Venegas-Vasquez emphasizes that by referring to individuals who are illegally or unlawfully *in the United States*, the focus of § 922(g)(5) is on the lawfulness of a person's physical presence in the United States, not their immigration status. In response, the Government emphasizes the lack of any mention of the word "presence" in the statute. The Supreme Court has cautioned that "we ordinarily resist reading words or elements into a statute that do not appear on its face." *Dean v. United States*, 556 U.S. 568, 572 (2009). The Court notes, however, that the word "in," which does appear in § 922(g)(5), is more naturally read to relate to physical or geographical presence, rather than a status . . . .

[T]he Court [now] considers the meaning of both "presence" and "status" under federal immigration law to analyze whether either term appropriately expresses the meaning of § 922(g)(5), and to analyze Venegas-Vasquez' argument that he was not unlawfully present, either because of his receipt of DACA or because [once earlier] he was paroled into the United States, or both.

B. Presence versus Status

The Ninth Circuit has noted that the "terms presence' and 'status' are terms of art in the scheme of federal immigration law, and they are not necessarily interchangeable." *Ariz. Dream Act Coal. v. Brewer*, 757 F.3d 1053, 1073 (9th Cir. 2014) (*Brewer I*). Under the INA, an alien is "unlawfully present in the United States if the alien is present in the United States after the expiration of the period of stay authorized by the Attorney General or is present in the United States without being admitted or paroled." . . .

Contrary to the Government's position, unlawful presence is not synonymous with unlawful status. Other Circuits, as well as the Board of Immigration Appeals, have noted that

> unlawful presence and unlawful status are distinct concepts in the argot of immigration specialists. It is entirely possible for aliens to be lawfully present (*i.e.*, in a "period of stay authorized by the Attorney General") even though their lawful status has expired.

Chaudhry v. Holder, 705 F.3d 289, 291 (7th Cir. 2013) (Wood, J). . . .

C. No Unlawful Presence Based on DACA

Venegas-Vasquez argues that he was not unlawfully present due to his receipt of DACA. It bears repeating that an alien is unlawfully present for the purposes of the INA "if the alien is present in the United States after the expiration of the period of stay authorized by the Attorney General or is present in the United States without being admitted or paroled." 8 U.S.C. § 1182(a)(9)(B)(iii). The Ninth Circuit has observed that the Department of Homeland Security ("DHS") "considers DACA recipients not to be unlawfully present in the United States *because their deferred action is a period of stay authorized by the Attorney General.*" *Brewer I*, 757 F.3d at 1059 (emphasis added). The Ninth Circuit also has made clear that "DACA recipients enjoy no formal immigration *status.*" *Id.* (emphasis added); *see also Ariz. Dream Act Coal. v. Brewer*, 855 F.3d 957, 968 (9th Cir. 2017) (*Brewer II*) ("DACA recipients . . . do not, and may never, possess formal immigration status."). . . .

The Court therefore concludes that Venegas-Vasquez was not "unlawfully present" because his deferred action is a period of stay authorized by the Attorney General. The Court also concludes, however, that Venegas-Vasquez has no formal immigration status based on his receipt of DACA. As a result, if "illegally or unlawfully in the United States" in § 922(g)(5) means or requires illegal or unlawful *presence*, then Venegas-Vasquez was not illegally or unlawfully in the United States, and the indictment must be dismissed. If, however, "illegally or unlawfully in the United States" means illegal or unlawful *immigration status*, then Venegas-Vasquez was illegally or unlawfully in the United States, and the indictment should not be dismissed.

The Court, however, also finds persuasive Venegas-Vasquez's argument concerning the legislative history of § 922. The legislative history of that statute indicates that Congress intended this criminal law to apply to individuals who could "not be trusted to possess a firearm without becoming a threat to society." 114 Cong. Rec. 14, 773 (1968). . . .

The Court agrees that the set of people Congress intended to prohibit from possessing firearms in § 922 is very different from the set of DACA recipients, who are required to report their address to the Government, who have intentionally revealed themselves to the Government through their DACA application, who are required to work and are therefore are not "living outside the law." and who cannot obtain DACA if they have been "convicted of [various] offenses, or otherwise pose[] a threat to national security or public safety." . . .

D. No Unlawful Presence Based on Parole

Venegas-Vasquez also argues that he was not unlawfully present in the United States because unlawful presence occurs "if the alien . . . is present in the United States without being admitted or paroled." 8 U.S.C. § 1182(a)(9)(B)(iii). Venegas-Vasquez argues, and the Court agrees, that because he was present in the United States after having been paroled into the United States on May 31, 2016, his presence in the United States was not "unlawful," at least for the purposes of 8 U.S.C. § 1182(a)(9)(B)(iii). The Government argues that because Venegas-Vasquez' grant of advanced parole had expired at the time of his alleged possession of firearms, he no longer was lawfully present. The Court, however, notes that "paroled" in 8 U.S.C. § 1182(a)(9)(B)(iii) is in the past tense and finds that Venegas-Vasquez was present in the United States after "being paroled." The Court thus concludes that Venegas-Vasquez was not unlawfully present in the United States under 8 U.S.C. § 1182(a)(9)(B)(iii).

E. Rule of Lenity

The Court concludes that Venegas-Vasquez' argument based on the rule of lenity is particularly persuasive. That rule "requires courts to limit the reach of criminal statutes to the clear import of their text and construe any ambiguity against the government." *United States v. Romm*, 455 F.3d 990, 1001 (9th Cir. 2006). . . .

Conclusion

The Court holds that the meaning of "illegally or unlawfully in the United States" in § 922(g)(5) is grievously ambiguous and uncertain and therefore that

Venegas-Vasquez is entitled to the benefit of the rule of lenity. The indictment against him is dismissed.

Notes and Questions

(1) *The Relevance of the Statute.* Notice that the court's reasoning depends entirely on the statute and its meaning. Thus, if the statute clearly had been applicable in cases in which the alien was of "unlawful status," the court would not have dismissed the indictment, as the judge says in Part C of the Discussion.

(2) *Is the Court's Reasoning Persuasive?* The court's reasoning based on DACA is vulnerable to the argument that the program is identified as a "deferral" of enforcement. Does a deferral of enforcement create lawful presence? The court's reasoning based on the defendant's earlier parole is vulnerable to the argument that the parole had expired and no longer applied. The court has arguments to support its contrary positions. Are they persuasive?

(3) *Analyzing Cases: The "IRAC" Method.* Consider for a moment a popular method for analyzing a case. Law students are often taught the "IRAC" method for analyzing cases and answering law school questions: (1) Can you identify the "Issue" in *Venegas-Vasquez*? (2) What "Rule(s)" does the court examine to address that issue? (3) What type of "Analysis" of the facts does the court do with that rule? In other words, what are the "facts" and how do they fit the "rule"? (4) What is the court's "Conclusion" regarding the issue?

(4) *"Formalism" (or "Literalism") versus "Instrumentalism" (or "Functionalism"): Should We Focus upon the Textually Defined Elements of the Statute, or on Its "Purpose" or "Intent"?* There is more than one way to approach statutory interpretation. One approach—"formalism"—extracts the elements set forth in the statute and compared the facts to those elements in a relatively rigorous manner. Formalism (sometimes called "literalism") is a relatively rigorous, piece-by-piece method of interpretation.

"Instrumentalism" (or "functionalism") is a very different approach. It seeks to discern the purpose, intent, or function of a statute and to apply it consistently with that purpose, intent, or function. This method reasons inductively or by analogy, so that the outcome depends on whether the facts are such that the statute was "meant" to apply to them.

Which method did the court use in *Venegas-Vasquez*?

(5) *"Strict Construction" vs. "Fair Import" in Statutory Construction.* "Strict construction" often is said to be a principle in the criminal law. Thus, some jurisdictions follow the approach that a criminal statute is to be read narrowly, so as to avoid criminalizing any conduct by too-broad implication. This idea is related to the Rule of Lenity, described earlier and applied in *Venegas-Vasquez*. The rationale for this rule is that the government, not the citizen, is responsible for drafting criminal statutes and should be penalized if the wording is so vague that citizens do not have fair notice of what the law proscribes.

Some jurisdictions, by contrast, expressly reject strict construction in favor of a more even-handed (but less defendant-friendly) view called "fair import." A California statute adopts that view and requires courts to follow the "fair import" of the words. If the federal government had a similar statute, what effect, if any, would it have had in *Venegas-Vasquez*?

(6) *What if a Court Ignores Relatively Clear Statutory Language?* Sometimes, courts ignore statutes, even in the face of clear language. Later courts then must decide whether to follow the statute, as they presumably should have done in the first place, or the erroneous judicial decision. Sometimes, a later court may correct the error.

Consider *State v. Sandoval*, 156 P.3d 60 (Or. 2007). Sandoval was convicted of intentional murder. The jury rejected his defense of self-defense after being instructed that Sandoval was required to retreat, if possible, before using deadly force in self-defense: "There must be no reasonable opportunity to escape to avoid the affray and there must be no other means of avoiding or declining the combat." The trial judge's instruction had been mandated by the state supreme court in *State v. Charles*, 647 P.2d 897 (Or. 1982). But the instruction had no obvious basis in the governing self-defense statute, which provides that a person "may use a degree of force which the person reasonably believes to be necessary for the purpose" and says nothing about retreat or escape. Sandoval argued that the trial court's instruction was erroneous. The state supreme court agreed, rejected its own *Charles* decision, and reversed the conviction:

> [T]he entire analytical flow of the *Charles* opinion is distinctly odd: The court did not examine the wording of [the statute] *at all*. Instead, the court set out the wording that the Oregon Criminal Law Commission had *proposed* to the legislature regarding the use of deadly force as part of the final draft of the proposed 1971 Criminal Code, which wording explicitly imposed a duty of retreat to avoid the necessity of using deadly force. Then, after noting that the 1971 legislature had *rejected* that wording, the court cited a view expressed in the Oregon Criminal Law Commission's Commentary to the 1971 Code to the effect that "the statute probably was not necessary" because of existing Oregon case law. Then, without discussing at all the fact that the Oregon legislature had adopted statutes on the subject, the court concluded, inexplicably, that "Oregon case law * * * controls the subject." ...

> Although ... it seems surprising that this court would attempt to answer the question presented in *Charles* without resort to the controlling criminal statutes, that is precisely what the *Charles* court did. ... We conclude, in short, that the legislature's intent is clear on the face of [the statute]: The legislature did *not* intend to require a person to retreat before using deadly force to defend against the imminent use of deadly physical force by another. It follows from the foregoing that the trial court erred in giving the instruction in question. [Reversed and remanded.]

§ 1.05 Two Types of Crime Elements: "Mens Rea" and "Actus Reus"

Notes on Mens Rea and Actus Reus

(1) *"Elements" of Crimes.* Crimes are composed of elements. Elements are the requirements that the prosecution must satisfy to prove that the defendant is guilty. The two primary types of ingredients for crimes are a *mental state* ("mens rea") and a *physical act* ("actus reus"). Other typical elements include attendant circumstances, causation, and result or harm—all of which are sometimes included as part of the actus reus. Some crimes contain only a few of these elements, while others contain all of them.

(2) *The Wrongful Mind: "Mens Rea."* Most criminal statutes require mental fault on the part of the defendant, which is to say, a criminal state of mind. This element at common law was called "mens rea," or the "wrongful mind." The law has invented a blizzard of terms to describe mens rea for different crimes: malice aforethought, intent, knowledge, recklessness, negligence, willfulness, premeditation, deliberation, scienter, "willful blindness," and others. To add one more complexity to the picture, there are some "strict liability" crimes. These offenses dispense with mens rea.

(3) *The Physical Elements: "Actus Reus."* The term, "actus reus," might be translated as "the wrongful act," but that literal interpretation is inadequate. The term really includes all of the physical elements of the crime, not just the defendant's act. For example, the crime of possessing cocaine involves more than just possessing a powder. The physical nature of that powder must be cocaine. An actus reus may be a positive act, such as hitting another person, or it may be a failure to act when there is a duty to do so. Consider the following case.

United States v. Zandi

769 F.2d 229 (4th Cir. 1985)

Murnaghan, Circuit Judge:

I

Hadi and Mehdi Zandi seek reversals of their convictions for possession of opium with intent to distribute on the following grounds: . . . the government failed to prove that the Zandis *possessed* the opium within the meaning of 21 U.S.C. §841(a)(1); [and] the government failed to prove that the Zandis had *knowledge* that opium was concealed within a package labelled "gift cloth". . . .

On October 26, 1983, Hadi and Mehdi were arrested at Dulles International Airport as they attempted to claim a package, which, on arrival from Pakistan, had been stored in a bonded customs warehouse. . . . [B]oth appellants were charged by the Government with importation of opium, 21 U.S.C. §952(a), and possession of opium with intent to distribute, 21 U.S.C. §841(a)(1). . . .

. . . The jury returned verdicts of not guilty on Count I (importation) and guilty on Count II (possession with intent to distribute) as to both defendants. The appellants were each sentenced to one year imprisonment and a three year special parole term.

II

Mehdi and Hadi are brothers who were living with their "Uncle Noory" in the United States. Appellants are Iranian citizens. Morteza Zandi is a brother of the appellants who, in 1982, fled Iran and went to Pakistan. While in Pakistan, Morteza received financial support from the appellants amounting to $10,000 by August 3, 1983.

On August 3, 1983, Mehdi called Morteza in Pakistan. Mehdi recorded the conversation. The brothers engaged in a rather cryptic discussion about a "box of presents" which was to be sent to the United States from Pakistan. The box was to be sent to a post office box number provided by Mehdi. Morteza requested that $3,000 be sent to him. . . . Hadi sent Morteza the requested sum.

On September 22, 1983, the manifest to the box referred to in the recorded conversation of August 3, 1983, was sent to a post office box of Uncle Noory's friend, Mohammed Ayat. The return address was a hotel in Pakistan at which Morteza had previously been a guest. The manifest indicated that the package contained "gift cloth." The package was addressed to "Kamran Divani KISA." The name of the shipper was false.

On October 24, 1983, after learning that the package had arrived at Dulles airport, the appellants went to pick it up. They paid $5.00 to obtain an airway bill receipt and a carrier's certificate. That same day, the appellants took the documents to Cosimano, Inc., in whose bonded warehouse at Dulles the package was being stored. Cosimano told them that they had to pay a $50.00 storage fee and a $20.00 after hours surcharge before receiving the package. Mehdi allegedly told Cosimano that he would come back the next day during normal hours in order to avoid the surcharge.

On October 25, 1983, Mehdi returned to the warehouse, paid the $50.00 storage fee, obtained the receipt for it and produced the airway bill and carrier's certificate. Mehdi then asked a warehouse employee to bring the package to the front office. She did so and informed Mehdi that a customs inspector was in the office ready to clear the package. Mehdi, however, left abruptly without obtaining possession of the package.

Mehdi's abrupt departure raised the suspicions of the warehouse staff. A customs inspector was promptly called. The inspector opened the package and discovered packets of opium. Some of the opium was removed and the box was resealed.

On October 26, 1983, Hadi and Mehdi drove to the warehouse to pick up the box. Mehdi stayed in the car while Hadi went inside to claim the package. Hadi presented the necessary documents to Cosimano. Cosimano had the box brought up to the front office. Hadi stated that he was picking up the package for his Uncle Noory. After Hadi was handed the package, he was asked by a custom's officer to open it for inspection. Hadi complied and assisted in the removal of articles from the box. During the inspection, the opium was discovered. Hadi was immediately arrested. Mehdi was then arrested in his car. . . .

III . . .

We . . . turn to the issue of whether there was sufficient evidence for a jury to conclude that the brothers had possession of the opium. Possession of a controlled substance with intent to distribute, as prohibited by 21 U.S.C. § 841(a)(1), may be either actual or constructive. Constructive possession exists when the defendant exercises, or has the power to exercise, dominion and control over the item. The appellants contend on appeal that they never had actual or constructive possession of the opium and that, therefore, their convictions must be reversed. According to the appellants, although they possessed the PIA Airway Bill, customs officials had complete control and dominion over the package and were directed by law not to release the package until it had been inspected. In rebuttal, the government argued 1) that the appellants had "constructive possession" of the drugs because they possessed the shipping documents which authorized the holders thereof to gain receipt of the goods and 2) that the mere fact government officials, pending customs clearance, had an inspection duty to perform before the Zandis could obtain full control of the drugs was not dispositive on the issue of constructive possession.

[We agree with the government and conclude that] the appellants acquired constructive possession of the opium when they acquired actual possession of the shipping documents. . . .

The appellants contend that even if they had constructive possession of the opium, the government failed to prove beyond a reasonable doubt that the brothers had knowledge that the package contained opium. . . . Knowledge, it is true, is an essential element of an offense under 21 U.S.C. § 841(a)(1). In determining whether there was sufficient evidence regarding "knowledge" to sustain the guilty verdicts, the court must consider whether any rational trier of fact could have found the existence of knowledge beyond a reasonable doubt. The Court must uphold the guilty verdict if there is substantial evidence viewed in the light most favorable to the government.

The government [proved] knowledge circumstantially. That is, the government [showed] that Morteza had access to plentiful and inexpensive opium in Pakistan, that Hadi and Mehdi sent Morteza money to Pakistan to help finance the drug transactions, and that Morteza and Mehdi had a mysterious telephone conversation regarding "gifts" being sent to the United States for later sale. The government also impressed upon the jury that Mehdi's and Hadi's false exculpatory statements at the time of their arrest were consistent with a guilty conscience. Although the jury was asked to proceed along a logical line involving several steps, a rational juror could certainly have found that the brothers had knowledge opium was in the package. [AFFIRMED.]

Notes and Questions

(1) *The Physical Elements of the Crime in Zandi.* As noted above, the physical elements of the crime—collectively called the actus reus—include the defendant's actual conduct, the result, relevant (or "attendant") circumstances, and causation. Try to describe the actus reus of the crime in *Zandi* (and remember that not all possible elements have to be present; it depends on the crime). Also, describe the evidence that supports each element.

(2) *The Mens Rea in Zandi.* Likewise, describe the guilty mind element and the evidence that supports it. (Note: the court talks about knowledge, but what is the actual crime?)

(3) *Variations on Zandi.* Consider what the result might be if the facts in *Zandi* were different in each of the following respects. (a) Customs officers discover the contraband at an early stage of the crime, and they arrest the Zandi brothers before they make any effort to retrieve the package or even know that it has arrived. (b) Their third brother Morteza, back in Pakistan, has pulled off a classic "buy-burn" by keeping his brothers' money but substituting powdered sugar instead of opium.

Problem 1B (Crime Elements): "You Mean, *Flying an Aircraft While Intoxicated* Isn't *a Crime?*"

(1) *A Problem Adapted from an Actual New York Case: Flying an Aircraft While Intoxicated, Charged as "Driving under the Influence."* Police officers summoned to a small regional airport in New York observed a single-engine aircraft turning with bizarre wobbles, dangerously close to inhabited buildings. The airplane finally swooped down and landed on the airport runway at such a steep angle that it bounced repeatedly. The officers promptly arrested the pilot, whose ten-year-old niece occupied the passenger seat. From what the officers saw, the pilot was highly intoxicated.

The prosecutor assigned to the case informed the officers that there was no New York statute that specifically addressed "flying while intoxicated." He suggested that the case be brought under the usual driving-under-the-influence statute. [Note that New York has since added a new section 7 to its air traffic law that now criminalizes flying while under the influence. *See* McKinney's N.Y. General Business Law § 245(7).—Eds.]

(2) *Driving under the Influence in New York.* The state charged the pilot with "driving under the influence." The relevant parts of this New York statute provided,

> No person shall operate a motor vehicle in the State of New York while the person's ability to operate such vehicle is impaired by the consumption of alcohol [or] while such person has .08 per centum or more of alcohol in the person's blood.

The statute also stated that it "shall apply upon public highways, private roads open to motor vehicle traffic, and parking lots capable of parking four motor vehicles." New York Vehicle & Traffic Law § 1192.

(3) *First, Identify All of the Elements.* What are the elements of the actus reus of driving while intoxicated under the New York statute, above? (Don't forget the very first one: The state must prove that *this* defendant was the one who "operated" the instrumentality: not difficult in this case, but difficult in some.) You should find at least seven (7) elements, two of which can be satisfied in alternate ways. Notice that there is no mens rea. Why might it make sense to create strict liability for this conduct?

(4) *Can the Pilot Be Convicted of Driving under the Influence?* Consider the statutory elements, and consider the evidence (the facts). Can the prosecution prove all the elements, here?

§ 1.06 The Requirement of Proof Beyond a Reasonable Doubt

United States v. Zandi

(excerpted above)

Reconsider the next-to-last paragraph of the excerpt from *Zandi*, above. Notice that the court refers to the requirement of "proof beyond a reasonable doubt that the brothers had knowledge that the package contained opium." The trial court was required to instruct the jurors that they must find proof of each element "beyond a reasonable doubt." The court also observes, however, that appellate review of the evidence does not re-weigh the evidence to decide whether the judges are convinced beyond a reasonable doubt. Instead, the issue is "whether any rational trier of fact [meaning, any reasonable juror] could have found the existence of [each element] beyond a reasonable doubt."

Notes and Questions

(1) *The Burden of Proof in Criminal Cases versus The Burden of Proof in Civil Cases.* The burden of proof in a civil case usually rests with the plaintiff, who must convince the trier of fact "by a preponderance of the evidence" (*i.e.*, more likely than not). Civil lawyers often explain this burden to juries by reference to a "fifty-one percent likelihood" or a "set of scales that tip just ever so slightly." But the burden on the prosecution in criminal cases is much higher: proof of each element of the crime "beyond a reasonable doubt." Can you explain why the criminal burden differs (and what practical differences the burden makes in a criminal case)?

(2) *The Substantive Impact of the Burden of Proof: A Transforming Aspect of the Criminal Law.* The government's high burden of proof in a criminal case can have a substantive impact on the definition of crimes. If the words used to define a crime are poorly chosen, it may be impossible for the prosecution to secure a conviction even when it appears the defendant should be punished. The burden of proof transforms the substantive criminal law by forcing lawmakers to define crimes carefully. Can you explain why?

(3) *Illustrating the Impact of the Beyond a Reasonable Doubt Standard: Proof of Knowledge.* Knowledge is an odd concept. Arguably, we know only that of which we are absolutely certain. But as philosophers called "skeptics" have demonstrated time and again, all human knowledge can be critiqued as uncertain. In a case in which the government must prove beyond a reasonable doubt that a defendant "knew" something (for example, that a package contained heroin and not another substance), how can the prosecution meet this high standard? This conundrum has led lawmakers to redefine "knowledge" as less than absolute certainty; mere "reasonable" or "substantial" certainty is sufficient to establish "knowledge." This redefinition is a transformation of the substantive law — influenced by the proof burden.

(4) *The Proof Standard in the Appellate Court.* Although the jury must decide whether the defendant is guilty "beyond a reasonable doubt," a different standard applies when appellate courts review a criminal conviction. An appellate judge must view the evidence "in the light most favorable to the government" and must affirm if any "rational trier of fact" could have found the elements of the crime beyond a reasonable doubt. This lenient appellate standard, which favors upholding the results of the trial, may at first blush seem inconsistent with the policy underlying the criminal law. Why does the law permit such a permissive approach for appellate courts?

Problem 1C (Proof Beyond a Reasonable Doubt): How Does the Burden of Proof Affect the Preceding Problem (Flying While Intoxicated)?

(1) *Reconsider Problem 1B, Above, in Light of the Burden of Proof.* As we saw in Problem 1B, convicting an intoxicated pilot under New York's driving-under-the-influence statute requires proof beyond a reasonable doubt of a large number of elements. Some of them require strained interpretation to cover the intoxicated pilot. And even if the judge holds that the legal definitions of the elements would, in general, allow them to be satisfied in this case, the jury still would have to find beyond a reasonable doubt that these particular facts fit the elements.

(2) *Can the State Convince a Jury, Beyond Reasonable Doubt, That the Pilot Operated a "Motor Vehicle"?* Some courts have held that an aircraft cannot be a "motor vehicle." Even if the New York courts think it is a sufficiently open question to allow a jury to consider whether an airplane qualifies, the pilot's defense attorney probably will argue forcefully to the jury, "An airplane's not like your car! And it's not a motor vehicle." The defense attorney might add, "And if you have a reasonable doubt about whether my client was driving a *'motor vehicle,'* you must acquit." How will this argument affect the case?

(3) *Can the State Convince a Jury, Beyond a Reasonable Doubt, That the "Operation" Occurred on a "Public Highway," or on a "Private Road Open to Motor Vehicle Traffic," or on a "Parking Lot"?* Consider how the requirement of proof beyond a reasonable doubt might affect the jury in deciding whether, by taxiing on the *runway,* the pilot operated the vehicle on a *"highway," "road,"* or *"parking lot,"* as is required by this statutory language.

(4) *Can the State Even Prove Beyond a Reasonable Doubt That the Pilot "Operated" the Aircraft on the Runway? Circumstantial Evidence.* The police officers who arrested the defendant can testify that the pilot *landed* the aircraft on the runway, but this testimony may not be enough, for technical reasons. Here is why: New York law requires a "voluntary act," and some cases indicate that landing an aircraft is involuntary (the pilot cannot choose not to come down). But didn't the pilot necessarily have to "operate" the aircraft while *taking off*, even if no one saw him do it? Does it matter that the pilot's niece was also aboard the aircraft?

(5) *Can the Prosecution Convince a Jury Beyond a Reasonable Doubt That the Pilot Was Impaired "by Alcohol"?* Imagine that the pilot did not take a blood alcohol test, and the source of impairment is unknown. It could have been illegal drugs, or for that matter prescription drugs. If the state charges the pilot under the statute it must prove impairment "by alcohol" beyond a reasonable doubt. Intoxication by drugs will not suffice. Can this element be proved?

(6) *How the Burden of Proof Influences Crime Definition.* Should this New York statute be rewritten? For example, consider the idea of defining "vehicles" broadly, to include "any conveyance." The "public highway" provision might be rewritten to become, "any public place." Instead of having separate provisions for intoxication by alcohol or drugs (which may require a prosecutor to guess which one applies), the statute could refer to impairment by reason of "the ingestion of any substance into the body." Some statutes outside New York already embody these ideas. Can you explain, then, the influence that the burden of proof should have upon a legislature, when it defines a crime such as driving under the influence?

§ 1.07 The Process of a Criminal Case: An Overview of Criminal Procedure

Myron Moskovitz
An Overview of the Criminal Courtroom Process

From *Cases and Problems in Criminal Procedure: The Courtroom* vii-x (6th ed. 2014) [Reprinted with permission of Carolina Academic Press]

[The study of how criminal cases proceed through the court system is often covered in a separate course on criminal procedure, as are the constitutional restrictions of police arrests, searches and interrogations. However, it is important in a basic criminal law course to have some understanding of how a criminal case is prosecuted and defended: *i.e.*, the adjudicative procedures associated with criminal law.]

[H]ere is a brief overview of the whole process in felony cases, as it usually operates in federal courts and most state courts.

Suppose the police believe that Dan has committed a series of four bank robberies. They arrest Dan and "book" him (write the charges and biographical data about Dan in a book), and they send a report of the case to the prosecutor's office ("United States Attorney" in the federal system, "District Attorney" in most states). The prosecutor considers the strength of the evidence against Dan and other factors in determining what charges to file, and then files a *complaint* against Dan in court. The complaint is similar to a complaint in a civil case. Each *count* (*i.e.*, each separate charge) in the complaint states that on a certain date, Dan committed certain acts which violated a specified penal statute, at a location within the jurisdiction of the court.

Within a few days, Dan will be *arraigned* before a magistrate of the court (who does not have as much authority as the judge who will later preside at the trial of the case). At the arraignment, the magistrate will read the charges to Dan and ask him to enter a *plea* of guilty, not guilty, not guilty by reason of insanity, or *nolo contendere* (*i.e.*, a default), to each charge. If Dan does not have a lawyer with him to advise him on what plea to enter, the magistrate will usually give Dan some time to hire one, or, if Dan is indigent, time to arrange for the services of a public defender. If Dan pleads guilty to any charge, the magistrate will sentence him or refer him to a judge for sentencing.

Suppose that, after consulting with counsel, Dan pleads not guilty to all charges. The magistrate will then set a date for a *preliminary hearing* (sometimes called a *preliminary examination*) to be held before the magistrate, unless Dan waives his right to a preliminary hearing. The magistrate will also consider whether Dan should be released on *bail* (or on his "own recognizance"), pending the preliminary hearing.

The preliminary hearing is intended to permit the magistrate to decide whether there is "probable cause" to hold Dan for trial on each count. This is a screening device, meant to save Dan the expense and anxiety of a trial on a weak case, and meant to save the courts the expense of a trial which is unlikely to lead to a conviction. At the preliminary hearing, the prosecutor will put on a somewhat skeletal case, with a minimum of witnesses—enough to show probable cause but not enough to let defense counsel see the whole prosecution case. The defense will seldom put on witnesses of its own, but will cross-examine prosecution witnesses in an effort to undermine probable cause and to try to "discover" as much of the prosecutor's case as possible, in preparation for trial.

. . . If the magistrate finds probable cause as to any charge which is a felony, she will "hold the defendant to answer" the charges at trial, and she will order the defendant "bound over" to the court for trial on these charges. The prosecutor will then file an *information* in the trial court. The information is similar to the complaint, setting out the remaining charges.

In federal court and in a few states, the prosecutor must obtain an *indictment* from a grand jury (unless Dan waives indictment, in which case an information may be filed). The grand jury may indict only if it finds probable cause to believe that Dan committed the crimes, based on evidence presented in secret by the prosecutor to the grand jury. (Defense counsel is not present before the grand jury, and no cross-examination of witnesses occurs.) Usually, if the prosecutor obtains the indictment before the date set for the preliminary hearing, the preliminary hearing will not be held, as the purpose of the preliminary hearing—to determine "probable cause"—will already have been served.

After the indictment or information is filed, Dan will be arraigned before a trial court judge, and Dan will enter a plea of guilty or not guilty to the remaining charges. If Dan pleads not guilty, the judge will set a date for the trial. The judge may also decide whether Dan should be released on bail pending trial. Before trial, both the prosecutor and defense counsel may be given certain rights to *discover* each other's cases—although these rights are much more limited than discovery rights in civil cases.

Before trial, defense counsel may file certain *pretrial motions*, such as motions for discovery and motions to suppress evidence which is the result of an illegal search or interrogation.

At any point in this process, but usually before the trial begins, the parties may engage in *plea bargaining*. Each defendant has a right to a *speedy trial* (*i.e.*, a trial which begins fairly soon after the arrest or indictment), but the prosecutor and the court do not have the resources to give a speedy trial to every defendant. So the prosecutor must induce most defendants to plead guilty. This is done by offering to dismiss or reduce some charges or to recommend certain sentences. Before accepting a guilty plea, the judge will make sure that the defendant knows what he has been promised and not promised, and that he is giving up the right to trial by jury on the charges.

At trial, if both parties agree, the case may be tried by the judge. Usually, however, the defendant demands a jury trial, as it is generally assumed that a group of lay people is less likely to convict than a "case-hardened" judge. In most cases, the jury's verdict must be unanimous, which makes it less likely that the prosecutor will obtain a guilty verdict from a jury.

The case begins with *voir dire*, the questioning of prospective jurors by the two lawyers and/or the judge. If any prospective juror displays improper bias, a lawyer may challenge that person "for cause," and if the judge finds improper bias, that person will be dismissed. Each lawyer also has a limited number of *peremptory challenges*, allowing the dismissal of several prospective jurors for any (almost) or no reason.

After the jury is selected and sworn, each lawyer may make an *opening statement* to the jury, summarizing the evidence to be presented. Then the prosecution puts on its witnesses, who are subject to cross-examination by the defense. When the prosecution rests its case, defense counsel may move for a *directed verdict* of acquittal, on the ground that the prosecution evidence, even if believed by the jury, does not show all of the elements of the crime(s) charged in the information or indictment. If such a motion is denied or not made, the defense then puts on its case, and its witnesses are subject to cross-examination by the prosecutor. The defendant has a constitutional right not to testify, but if he does testify, he too is subject to cross-examination by the prosecutor. When the defense rests, the prosecutor may introduce rebuttal evidence, and sometimes the defense may introduce surrebuttal evidence.

After each side rests its case, each attorney submits to the judge proposed *jury instructions*, containing the rules of law which apply to the case. Some of these instructions will be standard instructions taken from appellate court opinions and form books, and others will be devised by the lawyers. After hearing and ruling on any objections to proposed instructions, the judge will inform the lawyers as to which instructions will be given. Each lawyer then delivers a *summation* (sometimes called *closing argument*) to the jury. Because the prosecutor has the burden of proof (beyond a reasonable doubt), she will go first, then the defense lawyer will argue, and then the prosecutor is allowed a final rebuttal. Since each lawyer then knows what instructions the judge will give the jury, the lawyers will usually argue that the law contained in the instructions, when applied to the evidence heard by the jury, dictates a result favorable to that side.

After the summations, the judge reads the jury instructions to the jury. The jury then deliberates and returns with its verdict. If the jury is unable to decide any of the charges by the required majority (usually unanimity), the judge will declare a *mistrial* as to those charges and, if the prosecutor so requests, set the case for re-trial before a new jury. If the jury acquits the defendant, the defendant will be released and the case is over—the prosecutor has no right to appeal an acquittal. If the jury convicts the defendant on any charge, the jury is then discharged, in most cases. Usually, the jury plays no role in the next phase—sentencing—unless the jury convicted the defendant of a capital crime and the prosecutor is seeking the death penalty. [In some states, however, the defendant may elect to have the jury decide the sentence.]

Statutes control what the judge may consider in sentencing the defendant. Some statutes set low and high limits on the sentence, but allow the judge wide discretion as to any sentence within these limits (*e.g.,* "two to 10 years"). Such statutes often allow the judge to consider just about any factor in choosing the sentence. Other statutes confer the authority to select the actual sentence on some other board or agency. Some statutes set the sentence at specific terms of years, depending on certain factors the judge must find (*e.g.,* two years for a robber with no criminal record and who injured no one, six years for a robber with a record who injured someone, and four years for an in-between robber). Before sentencing the defendant, the judge will usually request a *pre-sentence report* from the court's probation department or similar agency. These officials will investigate the defendant's background and recommend a sentence to the judge. At the sentencing hearing, defense counsel may object to all or parts of the pre-sentence report, and may present evidence on the appropriate sentence. The sentence may also include a fine. In some cases, the judge may grant *probation* to the defendant, perhaps on the condition that the defendant serve a few months at a local jail.

After selecting the appropriate sentence for the defendant, the judge will enter a *judgment*, which states both the conviction and the sentence. From this judgment, defendant may file a *notice of appeal* to the appellate court which oversees the trial court. Filing this notice does not stay the sentence, and the defendant will have to seek a stay of the sentence and bail on appeal in order to avoid incarceration during the appeal.

A defendant will often obtain a new attorney on appeal, one who specialized in appellate work. The prosecutor often does the same. Copies of the pleadings and other documents are compiled (usually into a volume called the "clerk's transcript"). A court reporter's transcript of all of the oral testimony and argument is also prepared. Using these transcripts and any exhibits submitted as evidence at trial, the defendant's lawyer writes and files an "Appellant's Opening Brief," the prosecutor's attorney writes and files a "Respondent's Brief," and the defendant's lawyer then writes and files an "Appellant's Reply Brief." The appellate court then sets the case for oral argument, the case is argued, and it is submitted for decision. The appellate court then decides the case, usually issuing a written opinion, which may or may not be published in the official reports. The court may affirm the trial court judgment, reverse it (usually for retrial, but sometimes with instructions to dismiss certain charges), or modify it (*e.g.*, by reducing the sentence). If either side is unhappy with the appellate court's ruling, that party may seek review from the next highest court (usually the state supreme court or United States Supreme Court), but that court usually has discretion to grant or deny a hearing in the case.

An appeal must be based on the *record*—the transcripts and exhibits from the trial court—and no other evidence will be considered by the appellate court . . . .

If all else fails, Dan must pay his debt to society.

Notes and Questions

(1) *Discretion in the Process.* At many points in the process, there are decision-makers who have discretion to choose according to their own judgment. For example, a prosecutor has discretion to decline prosecution of a charge where there is minimally sufficient evidence or even when there is overwhelming evidence of all elements of the charge. When they do decide to bring charges, prosecutors have an enormous amount of discretion in choosing among various offenses and grades of offenses. Judges have wide discretion in sentencing in many jurisdictions, sometimes ranging from probation without incarceration all the way to life imprisonment. Should legal rules narrow this kind of discretion, and if so, how does one figure out the "right level" of discretion?

(2) *Screening Processes.* Preliminary hearings, grand juries, and other decision processes in some states are intended to perform screening functions to prevent inappropriate prosecutions. So are the prosecutor's discretion to decline prosecution and the judge's ongoing power to dismiss. After trial commences, the judge's

power to grant a directed verdict of acquittal is another screening device, and the judge has the same power after verdict (as does an appellate court). But is it possible that the existence of so many screeners diminishes the responsibility of each? A grand juror may not worry so much about probable cause since there will be another jury at trial, and the trial jury, in turn, may realize that the judge can correct (at least some) mistakes. Would it be better to reduce screening mechanisms to the minimum necessary and make decisionmakers more responsible?

(3) *Where the "Rubber Meets the Road" in Your Criminal Law Course: The Stages at Which Crime Definition Is Most Important.* Criminal procedure usually is a separate course. This casebook is centered, instead, on the law of crimes. But there are several key procedural points in the criminal process at which the precise definition of the crime, and its comparison to the facts in evidence, are most important. These include:

(a) *The Charging Decision*, when the prosecuting authority decides what crime to charge.

(b) *The Grand Jury or Preliminary Hearing*, at which the decisionmaker must decide whether there is probable cause to believe that the evidence satisfies all of the elements.

(c) *The Preparation of (or Attacks upon) the Indictment or Other Charging Instrument*, which usually must charge each element of the crime.

(d) *Jury Instructions*, which must explain all crime elements and the burden of proof.

(e) *Legal Review of the Sufficiency of the Evidence by Directed Verdict or Appeal*, which considers whether each element of the crime is proved by sufficient evidence.

Most of the cases in this book will involve one of these stages. In fact, most will involve just two procedural stages: (1) jury instructions and (2) the sufficiency of the evidence. Can you explain why?

§ 1.08 Simulation Exercise: Analyzing a Burglary Indictment Against a Defendant Who Wants to Plead Guilty

Simulation Exercise No. 1: *Investigating and Resolving the Case of* State v. Bates

(1) *What You Should Learn from This Problem, Which Is Based upon a Real Criminal Case.* This problem will require you to assume an actual lawyering role in a simulation based upon a real case. You will analyze the elements in a criminal statute, compare them to evidence, and use this analysis to negotiate resolution of the case, in exactly the way a criminal lawyer might. Please go online to https://caplaw.

com/sites/cl4/, then click on "Case File No. 1" to find the relevant documents for this exercise.

(2) *The Agreed Settlement of a Criminal Case Charged as a Burglary, Where Defendant Was Apprehended at the Scene.* This case is simple to describe but tricky to resolve. The defendant, John Ingalls Bates, has been indicted for burglary in the (imaginary) State of West York. Burglary is a third degree felony, punishable by "not less than two nor more than ten years in the West York Department of Criminal Justice" (prison). The evidence appears to show that the defendant and two friends entered a just-constructed home owned by an individual named Gerald Simpson, believing that no one was there. But Simpson was present. He pursued the three young men and apprehended Bates at the point of a shotgun.

Bates is seventeen years old and is a good candidate for probation. The defense lawyer has interviewed Bates, who admits, "I did it, and they caught me red-handed." He is spectacularly remorseful and frightened of a jury trial; he "just want[s] to tell the judge what I did and take my medicine." The prosecutor wants to handle this matter professionally, consistently with similar cases. Defendants without criminal records generally receive about five years probation (without confinement) for burglary in this jurisdiction.

(3) *Your Assignment: Simulate the Role of Either Prosecutor or Defense Lawyer, as Assigned by Your Professor, and Negotiate a Settlement (or Negotiated Plea), Using the Available Evidence and Applicable Laws (in an Appendix to This Book).* Your first step will be to read the applicable law. This imaginary state (West York) has adopted a set of "statutes," which are laws passed by the legislature, that follow the Model Penal Code (MPC). The MPC is a model set of statutes written by criminal law scholars, and excerpts are contained in Appendix A at the end of this book. The applicable crime definitions are in "Article 221: Burglary and Other Criminal Intrusion." You should locate Article 221 in the Appendix and read all of it (sections 221.0 through 221.2).

The key provisions are the first sentence of 221.1 ("burglary defined"), the last two sentences of 221.1(2) ("grading"), and the first two sentences of 221.2 ("criminal trespass"). Now, reconsider these key sections—and divide the definitions into elements. Thus, section 221.1 says that burglary is complete if (1) "a person" (2) "enters" (3) "a building or occupied structure" . . . [and more elements]. (You should complete this breakdown, numbering each element.) The penalty for burglary is indicated above, while criminal trespass is a "petty offense," punishable by "a fine not to exceed 500 dollars."

(4) *Comparison of the Statutory Elements to the Evidence.* Next, you should read "Case File No. 1," at https://caplaw.com/sites/cl4/. It contains the prosecutor's file. In West York, the defense lawyer also sees the state's file, because the prosecutor customarily makes it available if there are plea negotiations. Here, the file contains (1) an indictment (which corresponds to the burglary statute), (2) two police reports, and (3) a written statement (or "confession") signed by Bates. Consider these items

of evidence, and evaluate whether they prove each statutory element. In other words, can the state prove the crime it has charged?

In a real case, you also would conduct further investigation. Assume, however, that all sources agree with the state's file and provide nothing further. As for sentencing, Bates is seventeen, a high school senior with average grades, has no criminal record, and lives in a stable home.

(5) *The Proof Standard: Beyond a Reasonable Doubt.* There is a specific burden of proof in criminal cases. The prosecution must prove all elements "beyond a reasonable doubt." Therefore, reconsider the evidence and elements in light of this burden.

(6) *Finally, Negotiate an Appropriate Resolution (a Negotiated Sentence), Conforming to the Law, the Evidence, and the Duties of Counsel.* If your professor has designated your role as either defense lawyer or prosecutor, fulfill that role. If not, assume the following duties for this problem. If your last name begins with a letter between A and K (inclusive), function as prosecutor. If your last name begins with a letter between L and Z (inclusive), assume the role of defense lawyer. Come to class prepared to discuss the statutes, the evidence, and the roles of counsel.

Also, be prepared in class to negotiate a settlement (negotiated plea). You should be ready to suggest a concrete resolution, including sentence. For this exercise, reaching an actual settlement is important. In real life, you might not reach agreement in any given case.

(7) *Your Respective Duties as Prosecutor or Defense Counsel.* As prosecutor, you must do your part in enforcing the law. But you should advocate a sentence that is not excessive, and refrain from seeking conviction for any crime for which the defendant is not responsible. As defense lawyer, you must protect your client and minimize the sentence, while seeking your client's legitimate objectives. With regard to this last duty, assume that you have questioned Mr. Bates (and his parents), and he persists in his desire to plead guilty. (This would not be surprising to an experienced lawyer, because some clients insist on pleading guilty and are terrified by the idea of trial.) Now, please go online to https://caplaw.com/sites/cl4/, then click on "Case File No. 1."

Chapter 2

Homicide

"But if the act of killing, though intentional, be committed under the influence of passion . . . produced by an adequate or reasonable provocation . . . , then the law, out of indulgence to the frailty of human nature, . . . regards the offense as of a less heinous character than murder, and gives it the designation of manslaughter." — Christiancy, J., in *Maher v. People*, 81 Am. Dec. 781 (Mich. 1862).

"But evil is wrought by want of thought, / As well as want of heart!" — Thomas Hood (1799–1845), *The Lady's Dream*

§ 2.01 Starting with Homicide; Models of Homicide Laws

Notes on Starting the Study of Homicide Law

(1) *Why Should We Study Homicide Early in a Criminal Law Course?* The crime of homicide provides a window into many fundamental aspects of criminal law.

(2) *History, Grading, Elements, Statutes and Policy.* First, homicide law still shows its historic roots and is an excellent study in how vestiges of traditional laws are reflected in modern statutes. For example, ancient terms, such as "malice afore-thought," continue to govern the meaning of today's murder statutes in some states. Second, homicide presents an interesting example of grading of offenses. There are different degrees of homicide, including murder, manslaughter, and negligent homicide. The process of analyzing possible "pigeonholes" for a particular killing sheds light on how the law treats different degrees of personal responsibility.

Third, the interplay among statutes, decisional law, and fact-finders is complex in homicide laws. If you can master this process, you have skills that will be useful in other courses as well as the practice of law itself. Finally, as noted in the quotation from Judge Christiancy that begins this chapter, learning homicide law requires us to examine fundamental policies underlying criminal law and how we use it to influence human behavior.

(3) *Models of Homicide Law: The "Pennsylvania Pattern."* Different jurisdictions have different models for their homicide laws. As you examine each model, consider the pros and cons of its approach. We will focus on two models: the so-called "Pennsylvania model," so named because it was popularized in that state but

adopted in some form in some other jurisdictions. Then we will turn to the more modern approach represented by the Model Penal Code, which rejects some, but not all, of the principles embraced in the Pennsylvania approach. The following "map" of homicide law summarizes the substantive law of both approaches. It is only an outline, and you cannot understand everything from it. But it will provide a useful summary.

A Chart or "Map" of Homicide Law
(to Be Referred to Throughout the Chapter)

(A) The Pennsylvania Pattern (including, for example, California). The Pennsylvania pattern, which is generally followed by many other states, consists of these offenses:

(1) *first degree murder* (malice aforethought, and deliberate, premeditated killing or felony murder for some felonies) or

(2) *second degree murder* (killing with malice aforethought);

(3) *voluntary manslaughter* (passion killing);

(4) *involuntary manslaughter* (killing with gross negligence or during misdemeanor); and

(5) *vehicular manslaughter* (grossly negligent unlawful driving, often while intoxicated).

(B) The Model Penal Code (MPC). The Model Penal Code attempts to simplify and to use clearer language, and it has only one degree of murder:

(1) *murder* (causing death intentionally or knowingly — or with recklessness and extreme indifference to human life);

(2) *manslaughter* (killing committed recklessly or with extreme emotional disturbance — which includes what would be both voluntary and involuntary manslaughter under the Pennsylvania pattern); and

(3) *negligent homicide* (killing as result of gross deviation from the standard of a reasonable person).

We will develop these offenses in more detail below, but you should consult this "map" frequently during your study of this chapter, to keep an overview in mind.

Notes and Questions

(1) *What Do These Approaches Have in Common?* What do each of these models have in common? How are they different?

(2) *Reliance on Terms of Art.* Each of these models relies on terms of art to define the levels of homicide. The Pennsylvania approach refers to "malice aforethought." Do you know what that means, or are the terms used under the MPC approach clearer?

(3) *Why Grade Homicides at All?* Finally, you might be asking, "Why bother to have multiple levels of homicide?" There is a historical answer and a policy answer. Historically, the Pennsylvania system was adopted because originally, unlawful killings were capital offenses. Jurisdictions looked for ways to avoid the death penalty by distinguishing between the really bad homicides and the criminal, yet not so bad, homicides. The present-day answer is that the levels serve the policy of grading the seriousness of homicidal offenses to accommodate different sanctions for killers with different levels of moral responsibility.

§ 2.02 The Historical Requirement of Malice Aforethought for Murder

Note on the Meaning of Malice Aforethought: Neither "Malice" nor "Aforethought"

Historically, murder was defined as a killing with "malice aforethought." That term still survives in the Pennsylvania pattern of homicide laws. It was adopted in England as a way of determining which killers deserved the greatest punishment. A killing without malice aforethought was still a crime, but not as serious as one where malice aforethought was present.

Although malice aforethought was a common aspect of state homicide law for many years, today many jurisdictions have rejected the term as inaccurate and imprecise. States often try to define its meaning in their statutes. Below are California's homicide statutes.

California Penal Code

§ 187. Murder defined.

(a) Murder is the unlawful killing of a human being, or a fetus, with malice aforethought.

(b) [Section (b) exempts certain lawful abortions.]

§ 188. Malice, express malice, and implied malice defined.

Such malice may be express or implied. It is express when there is manifested a deliberate intention unlawfully to take away the life of a fellow creature. It is implied, when no considerable provocation appears, or when the circumstances attending the killing show an abandoned and malignant heart. . . .

§ 189. Murder; degrees.

All murder which is perpetrated by means of a destructive device or explosive, a weapon of mass destruction, knowing use of ammunition designed primarily to penetrate metal or armor, poison, lying in wait, torture, or by any other kind of willful, deliberate, and premeditated killing, or which is committed in the perpetration of, or attempt to perpetrate, arson, rape, carjacking, robbery, burglary, mayhem, kidnapping, train wrecking, or any act punishable under [certain other statutes], or any murder which is perpetrated by means of discharging a firearm from a motor vehicle, intentionally at another person outside of the vehicle with the intent to inflict death, is murder of the first degree. All other kinds of murders are of the second degree. . . .

To prove the killing was "deliberate and premeditated," it shall not be necessary to prove the defendant maturely and meaningfully reflected upon the gravity of his or her act.

§ 190. Punishment for murder. . . .

(a) Every person guilty of murder in the first degree shall be punished by death, imprisonment in the state prison for life without the possibility of parole, or imprisonment in the state prison for a term of 25 years to life. . . .

Except as provided [elsewhere], every person guilty of murder in the second degree shall be punished by imprisonment in the state prison for a term of 15 years to life. . . .

§ 192. Manslaughter; voluntary, involuntary, and vehicular.

Manslaughter is the unlawful killing of a human being without malice. It is of three kinds:

(a) Voluntary—upon a sudden quarrel or heat of passion.

(b) Involuntary—in the commission of an unlawful act, not amounting to felony; or in the commission of a lawful act which might produce death, in an unlawful manner, or without due caution and circumspection. This subdivision shall not apply to acts committed in the driving of a vehicle.

(c) Vehicular—[Subsection (c) covers various vehicular homicides, including by driving grossly negligently while performing an unlawful act, as well as by driving while under the influence of intoxicants; these vehicular homicides are defined as "vehicular manslaughter."]

§ 193. Voluntary manslaughter, involuntary manslaughter and vehicular manslaughter; punishment.

(a) Voluntary manslaughter is punishable by imprisonment in the state prison for three, six, or eleven years.

(b) Involuntary manslaughter is punishable by imprisonment . . . for two, three, or four years.

(c) Vehicular manslaughter is punishable as follows: [the sentence depends on the type of violation; lesser violations, by up to one year in county jail, greater by up to ten years in prison].

Notes and Questions

(1) *No Malice, No Murder.* As stated in § 187 and routinely in Pennsylvania-type homicide laws, murder is an unlawful killing of a human being with "malice

aforethought." A person who killed with malice was deemed very morally blame-worthy and meriting severe punishment. If a defendant kills without malice, what possible crime might there be?

(2) *"Malice Aforethought": A Misnomer.* The term "malice aforethought," though designed to distinguish the most blameworthy killers, is a misnomer, since it requires neither malice nor aforethought; the defendant does not have to act from hatred and does not have to think beforehand. In fact, some accidental killings qualify. But because the term is in the statute, it must be told to the jury, with lawyers having to explain to the jury that it does not mean what it appears to mean.

(3) *"Express" Malice (Intentional Killings).* The statute refers to "express" malice, which means that the killing is intentional. Thus, an intentional unlawful kill-ing qualifies as first or second degree murder, absent circumstances that reduce the grade of the crime. Intent can supply malice aforethought. But it is not the only way.

(4) *"Implied" Malice: Depraved-Heart Murder and Other Unintended Killings.* Malice aforethought can be found in some unintended killings deemed sufficiently grave to justify harsh treatment. The historical development of malice aforethought included "depraved heart" killings. The defendant's depraved heart (also phrased as "abandoned and malignant" heart) supplied an implied kind of malice afore-thought. No doubt it has occurred to you that the phrase "depraved heart" is vague, and indeed it is. But as Thomas Hood wrote, in the quotation that begins this chap-ter, "evil is wrought by want of thought /As well as want of heart!"

(5) *Still More Unintended Murders: Implied Malice from Commission of a Felony.* And as we shall see, the common law exhibited marvelous flexibility. It created other kinds of malice aforethought that did not require intent to kill. For example, a killing in the course of the commission of a felony could be treated as done with (implied) malice and therefore as murder, even if it was accidental, and so could a killing resulting from assault or resistance to an arrest.

(6) *Summary of Malice Aforethought Categories.* Recall that malice aforethought is required for both first and second degree murder. As the notes above indicate, traditionally the main categories of malice aforethought involve a killing with:

(a) Intent to kill (express malice),

(b) Intent to cause serious bodily injury,

(c) Depraved heart recklessness (gross carelessness), or

(d) During the commission of a felony (felony murder).

So, the elements of murder (first and second) in general under the statutes above are: (1) this defendant (2) unlawfully (3) killed (4) a human being or fetus (5) with malice aforethought. Is this a complete statement of the elements? (Actually, the "unlawfully" element is not an independent element, but just signals the absence of defenses such as self-defense.) First degree murder contains some additional ele-ments, particularly premeditation and deliberation, as discussed in the next note.

(7) *"Premeditation and Deliberation": Distinguishing Levels of Murder.* The Pennsylvania pattern involves "degrees" of murder. The division of murder into two degrees enabled Pennsylvania authorities to limit the death penalty to the "worst of the worst," those killers committing first degree murder. People convicted of second degree murder were spared the penalty of death.

(8) *Rough Definitions of Premeditation and Deliberation.* First degree murder often is distinguished by requiring the government to prove both "premeditation" and "deliberation." (There also are other ways to commit first degree murder.) Exactly what these terms mean varies with the state and with the court.

(9) *Is This Any Way to Define a Crime?* Malice aforethought does not mean malice aforethought, and premeditation and deliberation do not always mean what you would think premeditation and deliberation should mean. To jurors, this ancient terminology must be more than mildly confusing, especially since the judge will instruct them that the words mean something else. As you read the cases in this chapter, consider whether the terms are helpful or whether they should now be changed.

(10) *The Model Penal Code (and States that Follow It): Abandonment of the Malice-Aforethought and Premeditation-Deliberation Formulas.* The Model Penal Code ("MPC"), discussed in detail below, abandons these ancient formulas. The MPC is a set of model statutes drafted by the American Law Institute ("ALI"). The MPC uses more direct language than the Pennsylvania pattern. But first: the Pennsylvania pattern.

§ 2.03 The Pennsylvania Pattern: Defining Levels of Homicide

[A] Intentional Killings: Malice Aforethought and the Premeditation-Deliberation Formula

Commonwealth v. Carroll

194 A.2d 911 (Pa. 1963)

Reaffirmed, Commonwealth v. Jordan

65 A.3d 318 (Pa. 2013)

The defendant, Carroll, pleaded guilty generally to an indictment charging him with the murder of his wife, and was tried by a judge without a jury.... That court found him guilty of first degree murder and sentenced him to life imprisonment.... The only questions involved [on appeal] are thus stated by the appellant: (1) "Does not the evidence sustain a conviction no higher than murder in the second degree?" (2) "Does not the evidence of defendant's good character, together with the testimony of medical experts, including the psychiatrist for the Behavior

Clinic of Allegheny County, that the homicide was not premeditated or intentional, *require* the Court below to fix the degree of guilt of defendant no higher than murder in the second degree?"

The defendant married the deceased . . . when he was serving in the Army in California. Subsequently he was stationed in Alabama, and later in Greenland. During the latter tour of duty, defendant's wife and two children lived with his parents in New Jersey. Because this arrangement proved incompatible, defendant returned to the United States on emergency leave in order to move his family to their own quarters. On his wife's insistence, defendant was forced first to secure a "compassionate transfer" back to the States, and subsequently to resign from the Army . . . , by which time he had attained the rank of Chief Warrant Officer. Defendant was a hard worker, earned a substantial salary and bore a very good reputation among his neighbors.

[Earlier], decedent-wife suffered a fractured skull while attempting to leave defendant's car in the course of an argument. Allegedly this contributed to her mental disorder which was later diagnosed as a schizoid personality type. . . . She complained of nervousness and told the examining doctor "I feel like hurting my children." This sentiment sometimes took the form of sadistic "discipline" toward their very young children. . . . With this background we come to the immediate events of the crime.

. . . [D]efendant was selected to attend an electronics school in Winston-Salem, North Carolina, for nine days. His wife greeted this news with violent argument. Immediately prior to his departure for Winston-Salem, at the suggestion and request of his wife, he put a loaded .22 calibre pistol on the window sill at the head of their common bed, so that she would feel safe. [After the electronics school,] defendant returned home and told his wife that he had been temporarily assigned to teach at a school in Chambersburg, which would necessitate his absence from home four nights out of seven for a ten week period. A violent and protracted argument ensued at the dinner table and continued until four o'clock in the morning.

Defendant's own statement after his arrest details the final moments before the crime: "We went into the bedroom a little before 3 o'clock on Wednesday morning where we continued to argue in short bursts. Generally she laid with her back to me facing the wall in bed and would just talk over her shoulder to me. I became angry and more angry especially what she was saying about my kids and myself, and sometime between 3 and 4 o'clock in the morning I remembered the gun on the window sill over my head. I think she had dozed off. *I reached up and grabbed the pistol and brought it down and shot her twice in the back of the head.*" [When pressed on cross-examination defendant approximated that five minutes elapsed between his wife's last remark and the shooting.]

Defendant's testimony at the trial elaborated this theme. He started to think about the children, "seeing my older son's feet what happened to them. I could see the bruises on him and Michael's chin was split open, four stitches. I didn't know what to do. I wanted to help my boys. Sometime in there she said something in there, she called me some kind of name. I kept thinking of this. *During this time I either thought or felt—I thought of the gun, just thought of the gun.* I am not sure whether I felt my hand move toward the gun—I saw my hand move, the next thing—the only thing I can recollect after that is right after the shots or right during the shots I saw the gun in my hand just pointed at my wife's head. She was still lying on her back—I mean her side. I could smell the gunpowder and I could hear something—it sounded like running water. I didn't know what it was at first, didn't realize what I'd done at first. Then I smelled it. I smelled blood before. . . ."

> "Q. At the time you shot her, Donald, were you fully aware and intend to do what you did?

> "A. I don't know positively. All I remember hearing was two shots and feeling myself go cold all of a sudden."

Shortly thereafter defendant wrapped his wife's body in a blanket, spread and sheets, tied them on with a piece of plastic clothesline and took her down to the cellar. He tried to clean up as well as he could. That night he took his wife's body, wrapped in a blanket with a rug over it to a desolate place near a trash dump. . . . He was arrested the next Monday in Chambersburg where he had gone to his teaching assignment. . . .

. . . Murder in Pennsylvania was first authoritatively defined in the famous case of *Commonwealth v. Drum*, 58 Pa. 9, 15. "Murder . . . is defined as an *unlawful killing of another with malice aforethought, express or implied*." The legislature divided murder into two classifications, murder in the first degree and murder in the second degree; and provided that "(1) all murder perpetrated by poison or lying in wait; or by any other kind of wilful, deliberate [and] premeditated killing, or any murder which shall be committed in the perpetration of or attempt to perpetrate certain specified felonies [arson, rape, robbery, burglary, or kidnapping], is murder in the first degree and (2) every other kind of murder is murder in the second degree. . . ." [These provisions closely resemble California's law. The key requirements, then, are "malice aforethought," which is required for either degree of murder, and "deliberate and premeditated killing," which distinguishes first from second degree.]

"Malice express or implied is . . . the criterion and absolutely essential ingredient of murder. Malice in its legal sense exists not only where there is a particular ill will, but also whenever there is a wickedness of disposition, hardness of heart, wanton conduct, cruelty, recklessness of consequences and a mind regardless of social duty." Malice is [also] present if the defendant had an intent to do the deceased serious bodily harm.

The test of the sufficiency of the evidence—irrespective of whether it is direct or circumstantial—is whether accepting as true all the evidence upon which, if believed, the jury could properly have based its verdict, it is sufficient in law to prove beyond a reasonable doubt that the defendant is guilty of the crime charged. . . . It has become customary for a defendant in his argument before an Appellate Court to base his claims and contentions upon his own testimony or that of his witnesses even after a jury has found him guilty. This, of course, is basic error. After a plea or verdict of guilty, "we accept as true all of the Commonwealth's evidence upon which, if believed, the jury could have properly based its verdict."

. . . If we consider only the evidence which is favorable to the Commonwealth, it is without the slightest doubt sufficient in law to prove first degree. However, even if we believe all of defendant's statements and testimony, there is no doubt that this killing constituted murder in the first degree. Defendant first urges that there was insufficient time for premeditation in the light of his good reputation. This is based on an isolated and oft repeated statement in *Commonwealth v. Drum*, 58 Pa. 9, 16, that "no time is too short for a wicked man to frame in his mind his scheme of murder." Defendant argues that, conversely, a long time is necessary to find premeditation in a "good man." We find no merit in defendant's analogy or contention. As Chief Justice Maxey appropriately and correctly said in *Commonwealth v. Earnest*, 342 Pa. 544, 21 A.2d 38 (pages 549–550): "Whether the intention to kill and the killing, that is, the premeditation and the fatal act, were within a brief space of time or a long space of time is immaterial if the killing was in fact intentional, wilful, deliberate and premeditated. . . ."

Defendant further contends that the time and place of the crime, the enormous difficulty of removing and concealing the body, and the obvious lack of an escape plan, militate against and make a finding of premeditation legally impossible. This is a "jury argument"; it is clear as crystal that such circumstances do not negate premeditation. . . .

Defendant's most earnestly pressed contention is that the *psychiatrist's opinion* of what *defendant's state of mind must have been and was at the time of the crime*, clearly establishes not only the lack but also the legal impossibility of premeditation. Dr. Davis . . . testified that defendant was "for a number of years . . . passively going along with a situation which he . . . [was] not controlling and he . . . [was] not making any decisions, and finally a decision . . . [was] forced on him. . . . He had left the military to take this assignment, and he was averaging about nine thousand a year; he had a good job. He knew that if he didn't accept this teaching assignment in all probability he would be dismissed from the Government service, and at his age and his special training he didn't know whether he would be able to find employment. More critical to that was the fact that at this point, as we understand it, his wife issued an ultimatum that if he went and gave this training course she would leave him. . . . He was so dependent upon her he didn't want her to leave. He couldn't make up his mind what to do. He was trapped. . . ."

The doctor then gave *his opinion* that "rage", "desperation", and "panic" produced "an impulsive automatic reflex type of homicide. . . . as opposed to an intentional premeditated type of homicide. . . . Our feeling was that if this gun had fallen to the floor he wouldn't have been able to pick it up and consummate that homicide. And I think if he had to load the gun he wouldn't have done it. This is a matter of opinion, but this is our opinion about it."

There are three answers to this contention. First, . . . neither a judge nor a jury has to believe all or any part of the testimony of the defendant or of any witness. Secondly, the opinion of the psychiatrists was based to a large extent upon statements made to them by the defendant, which need not be believed and which are in some instances opposed by the facts themselves. Thirdly, a psychiatrist's opinion of a defendant's impulse or lack of intent or state of mind is, in this class of case, entitled to very little weight, and this is especially so when defendant's own actions, or his testimony or confession, or the facts themselves, belie the opinion. . . .

Defendant's *own statement* after his arrest, upon which his counsel so strongly relies, *as well as his testimony at his trial,* clearly convict him of first degree murder and justify the finding and sentence of the Court below. From his own statements and from his own testimony, it is clear that, terribly provoked by his allegedly nagging, belligerent and sadistic wife, *defendant remembered the gun, deliberately took it down, and deliberately fired two shots into the head of his sleeping wife.* . . . [I]f defendant's version is true, the remedy lies in a commutation by the Board of Pardons and not by a disregard of the law by the Courts. . . . There is no doubt that this was a wilful, deliberate and premeditated murder.

Notes and Questions

(1) *Should Mr. Carroll's Defense Lawyer Have Insisted on Trial by Jury?* The defendant waived a jury. Why? Perhaps his lawyer believed that the outcome was so clear that a rigorous application of the law of first degree murder would result in a lesser conviction because the government could not prove premeditation and deliberation. If so, the decision to waive a jury might seem reasonable. However, the conventional wisdom is, "Try your case to a jury — unless it's so hopeless that it's pointless to demand a jury, or the acquittal of your client [in this case of first degree murder] is so clear that a judge can't avoid it." Is this that kind of case?

(2) *What Would a Jury Have Done in this Case?* Once a jury finds malice aforethought, such as by finding that the defendant intentionally killed the victim, all that is required for reduction from first to second degree murder is that the jury finds a "reasonable doubt" about "premeditation" or "deliberation." Wouldn't twelve citizens be more likely than a judge to harbor a reasonable doubt about that?

(3) *What Is Meant by "Premeditation and Deliberation," and How Is It Different from Malice Aforethought?* The defense conceded that Carroll acted with malice aforethought. What does malice aforethought mean in this case? If it means that the defendant killed intentionally, how is that different from acting with premeditation?

(4) *How Long Does It Take to Premeditate?* Does premeditation refer to a particular thought process or length of time? If premeditation can arise "in an instant," as this court says, how do we distinguish between those intentional killings that qualify as second-degree murder, although committed with malice aforethought but lacking in premeditation, and those that should be punished as first-degree murder where premeditation is proven?

(5) *Are These Mushy, Confusing Misnomers a Useful Way to Instruct a Jury?* Consider whether terms like "malice" and "premeditation" are useful injury instructions, given that we must tell the jury they don't mean what they say. Is this a bad way to instruct a jury?

(6) *Consider Carroll While You Read the Next Case and Decide Whether The Verdicts Are Backwards.* The next case, *Anderson*, is a California Supreme Court decision, and it results in a holding of second degree murder in a case that seems more aggravated and more serious than *Carroll*. What accounts for the different outcomes?

People v. Anderson

447 P.2d 942 (Cal. 1968) (en banc)

TOBRINER, JUSTICE.

Defendant was indicted for the murder of Victoria Hammond, a 10-year-old girl, in 1962. [The jury convicted him of first degree murder and sentenced him to death but the death penalty was overturned because of a procedural error.]

We do not find it necessary to remand the case for a new penalty trial, however, because we conclude that the evidence is insufficient to support a verdict of first degree murder on the theory of either (a) premeditated and deliberate murder, or (b) murder committed during the perpetration or attempted perpetration of a [sexual act upon a child].

Defendant, a San Jose cab driver, had been living for about eight months with a Mrs. Hammond and her three children, Cynthia, aged 17, Kenneth, aged 13, and the victim, Victoria, aged 10. [On the day of the murder], . . . Mrs. Hammond left for work at 7:30 a.m., leaving only Victoria at home with the defendant. Defendant was still in bed. He had been home from work for the previous two days, during which time he had been drinking heavily, and apparently he did not go to work on the day of the murder. . . .

Kenneth testified that he arrived home from school at 3:30 p.m. on December 7. He found the front door locked, which was not unusual, so he went around to the back of the house and down to the basement. . . . In a short time he heard noise coming from upstairs in the house which sounded like boxes and other things being moved around, like someone was cleaning up. He then heard the shower water running. . . .

Kenneth testified further that he then came up from the basement and went to the back porch screen door. . . . [T]he defendant was wearing slacks only. . . . When Kenneth noticed the blood on the kitchen floor and asked defendant about it, the defendant told Kenneth that he had cut himself. This explanation apparently satisfied Kenneth, as he finished dressing and left the house sometime [thereafter]. Kenneth testified that no one else was at his house when he was there between 3:30 and 4 p.m. He further testified that about 6:30 he realized that he had forgotten his wallet and returned home. As he approached the front door, his mother came out and asked to see the cut on his arm, and Kenneth explained that he had no cut. His mother then asked defendant about the blood she had noticed and [said that] defendant told her that Victoria had cut herself, but that the mother should not worry, as the cut was not serious. After defendant told her that Victoria was at a friend's for dinner, the mother wanted to take Kenneth with her to get Victoria. Kenneth went back to his room to get a jacket. Because he had a "weird" feeling, he looked into Victoria's room. He found her nude, bloody body under some boxes and blankets on the floor near her bed. Kenneth ran out of the room screaming that defendant had killed her. Mrs. Hammond, after seeing Victoria's body, went next door to phone the police.

Mrs. Hammond testified that she returned home from work at 4:45 p.m. . . . Mrs. Hammond noticed blood on the couch in the living room, and when she asked defendant about it, he told her that Kenneth had cut himself playing with a knife and that he was at a teenage dance. Mrs. Hammond then went to the grocery store and returned about 5:30 p.m. She testified that at both times she arrived home defendant was drinking a highball. She also testified as to examining Kenneth's arm for a cut when he returned home for his wallet and as to defendant's subsequent explanation that Victoria had been cut, but not seriously. Mrs. Hammond discovered Victoria's body after Kenneth came out of Victoria's room. . . .

The arresting officer found Victoria's body on the floor near her bed. He found defendant's blood-spotted shorts on a chair in the living room, and a knife and defendant's socks, with blood encrusted on the soles, in the master bedroom. The evidence established that the victim's torn and bloodstained dress had been ripped from her, that her clothes, including her panties out of which the crotch had been ripped, were found in various rooms of the house, that there were bloody footprints matching the size of the victim's leading from the master bedroom to Victoria's room, and that there was blood in almost every room including the kitchen, the floor of which appeared to have been mopped.

The TV cameraman who covered the murder story for channel 11, the officer who drove defendant to the police station, and the officer who "observed" defendant for four hours at the station the night of December 7, 1962, all testified that defendant did not appear intoxicated. The officers who talked to defendant testified, however, that they smelled alcohol on his breath; a blood test taken at 7:45 p.m. indicated that the alcohol content in defendant's blood was .34 percent, which was more than necessary for an automobile driver to be classified as "under the influence."

Over 60 wounds, both severe and superficial, were found on Victoria's body. The cuts extended over her entire body, including one extending from the rectum through the vagina, and the partial cutting off of her tongue. Several of the wounds, including the vaginal lacerations, were post mortem. No evidence of spermatozoa was found in the victim, on her panties, or on the bed next to which she was found.

The prosecution contended that the murder was sexually motivated. The defendant, who pleaded not guilty and not guilty by reason of insanity, presented no defense whatsoever. The court instructed the jury on two theories of first degree murder, premeditated and deliberate murder, and murder committed in the perpetration or attempt to perpetrate [a sexual act upon a child]; second degree murder; and voluntary and involuntary manslaughter. The court also instructed the jury on diminished capacity due to voluntary intoxication and its relationship to second degree murder and manslaughter. The jury found the defendant guilty of murder in the first degree.

We must, in the absence of substantial evidence to support the verdict of first degree murder, reduce the conviction to second degree murder. The legislative definition of the degrees of murder leaves much to the discretion of the jury in many cases. That discretion, however, must have a sound factual basis for its exercise. . . .

Viewing the evidence in a light most favorable to the judgment, the first degree conviction must rest upon the following supporting proof: when Kenneth arrived home from school he found the doors locked, and when the police officers arrived to arrest defendant they found the shades in the front room down; defendant apparently had attempted to clean up the bloodstained kitchen, and had fabricated conflicting explanations of the blood that Kenneth noticed in the kitchen, the blood that Victoria's mother observed in the living room, and Victoria's absence on the evening of the killing; defendant had stabbed Victoria repeatedly and had inflicted a post mortem rectal-vaginal wound; bloodstains were found in several rooms of the house; Victoria's bloodstained and shredded dress was found under her bed next to which her nude body was discovered under a pile of boxes and blankets; Victoria's slip, with the straps torn off, was found under the bed in the master bedroom; the crotch was ripped out of Victoria's bloodsoaked panties; and the only bloodstained clothes of defendant's which were discovered were his socks and his shorts, from which facts the People argue that defendant was almost nude during the attack. . . .

. . . [A]lthough premeditation and deliberation maybe shown by circumstantial evidence, the People bear the burden of establishing beyond a reasonable doubt that the killing was the result of premeditation and deliberation, and that therefore the killing was first, rather than second, degree murder.

Given the presumption that an unjustified killing of a human being constitutes murder of the second, rather than of the first, degree, and the clear legislative intention to differentiate between first and second degree murder, we must determine in any case of circumstantial evidence whether the proof is such as will furnish a reasonable foundation for an inference of premeditation and deliberation. . . .

Recognizing the need to clarify the difference between the two degrees of murder . . . , we set forth standards . . . for the kind of evidence which is sufficient to sustain a finding of premeditation and deliberation. We then analyze representative cases, including those which the People argue require an affirmance here. In conclusion we demonstrate . . . that the kind of evidence from which a jury can reasonably infer that an accused wilfully, deliberately, and with premeditation killed his victim within the meaning of Penal Code section 189 is totally lacking here.

. . . [W]e have repeatedly pointed out that the legislative classification of murder into two degrees would be meaningless if "deliberation" and "premeditation" were

construed as requiring no more reflection than may be involved in the mere formation of a specific intent to kill. (Thus we have held that in order for a killing with
malice aforethought to be first . . . degree murder, "(t)he intent to kill must be . . .
formed upon a *pre-existing* reflection . . . (and have) been the subject of actual
deliberation or *forethought*. . . ." (*People v. Thomas, supra,* 156 P.2d 7, at p. 18.) We
have therefore held that "a verdict of murder in the first degree . . . is proper only if
the slayer killed as a result of careful thought and weighing of considerations; as a
deliberate judgment or plan; carried on coolly and steadily, (especially) according to
a *preconceived design.*"

The type of evidence which this court has found sufficient to sustain a finding
of premeditation and deliberation falls into three basic categories: (1) facts about
how and what defendant did prior to the actual killing which show that the defendant was engaged in activity directed toward, and explicable as intended to result
in, the killing—what may be characterized as "planning" activity; (2) facts about
the defendant's *prior* relationship and/or conduct with the victim from which the
jury could reasonably infer a "motive" to kill the victim, which inference of motive,
together with facts of type (1) or (3), would in turn support an inference that the
killing was the result of "a pre-existing reflection" and "careful thought and weighing of considerations" rather than "mere unconsidered or rash impulse hastily executed"; (3) facts about the nature of the killing from which the jury could infer that
the *manner* of killing was so particular and exacting that the defendant must have
intentionally killed according to a "preconceived design" to take his victim's life in a
particular way for a "reason" which the jury can reasonably infer from facts of type
(1) or (2).

Analysis of the cases will show that this court sustains verdicts of first degree
murder typically when there is evidence of all three types and otherwise requires at
least extremely strong evidence of (1) or evidence of (2) in conjunction with either
(1) or (3). . . .

. . . Here, . . . we do not have any evidence of either (1) any conduct by defendant
prior to the killing which would indicate that he was planning anything, felonious or otherwise, or (2) any behavior towards Victoria from which the jury could
reasonably infer that defendant had a "motive" or desire to sexually attack and/or
kill her. The evidence of (3), the manner of killing and the condition of the body,
is [such that] the only inference which the evidence reasonably supports in either
case is that the killing resulted from a "random," violent, indiscriminate attack
rather than from deliberately placed wounds inflicted according to a preconceived
design. . . .

. . . [T]he evidence suffices only to support a verdict of second degree murder.

[The Court also concluded that the evidence was insufficient to support a finding
of a specific intent to commit a sexual act upon a child or to sustain the first degree
conviction on that theory.]

[Reversed; reduced to second-degree murder.]

BURKE, JUSTICE (dissenting).

I dissent. The substantial circumstantial evidence presented in this case supports the verdict of the jury that the homicide was committed by defendant in his attempted performance or actual performance of lewd or lascivious acts upon the body of the child victim . . . and therefore constituted first degree murder . . . (Pen .Code, § 189).

The jury could reasonably infer from the evidence adduced that the underlying motive of the crime was sexual gratification: defendant chose a time when he was alone in the house with the little girl; the window blinds were down and the doors locked; he pursued the child throughout the house inflicting one wound after another; he ripped out the crotch of her panties; he tore her remaining clothes from her; he had removed his own clothes excepting his socks—there was no other logical explanation for the absence of other bloody male clothing and he took a shower immediately after the crime; furthermore, at one time during the assault he had the child on the bed as evidenced by the large bloodstain found in the center of the mattress; and, finally, a number of the wounds inflicted upon the child could be considered sexual in nature, particularly the thrust of the knife into her vagina, the cutting through to the anal canal and the numerous cuts and contusions of her private parts and thighs. . . .

. . . I [also] believe there is credible evidence from which the jury could find a premeditated homicide, *e.g.* the locking of the doors (whether before or after the actual killing is a matter of conjecture), the duration of the assault, the pursuit through many rooms with a quantity of blood being left in each room, the extensive stabbings many of which would have sufficed as fatal, the removal of the murder weapon from one room and the apparent repeated use of it in other rooms. [But] it is not necessary to rest the jury's determination of first degree murder on that ground since the evidence is substantial that the homicide was [committed during lewd acts upon a child].

In the instant case the question of whether the evidence showed that the defendant had the requisite intent to commit lewd acts upon the child victim was for the jury to determine from all the surrounding circumstances. In the face of the physical evidence produced in this case I submit it cannot be said that no reasonable ground was shown to support an inference that such intent existed. . . . I would affirm the judgment [of first degree murder]. . . .

Notes and Questions

(1) *Can an Intentional Killing That Is "Random, Violent, [and] Indiscriminate" Be Just as Blameworthy as a "Planned" One?* The Pennsylvania pattern usually makes the highest grades of homicide depend on one dimension: premeditation and deliberation, both requiring some degree of "planning" (at least in California). The California court downgrades Anderson's offense precisely because it finds this horrific crime was hasty, senseless, and ill-considered, or in the court's words, "random,

violent, [and] indiscriminate." But could a reasonable lawmaker just as well decide that an "indiscriminate" killing can be deserving of treatment as serious as some more deliberate ones, if not more so? Consider whether the Pennsylvania pattern, by making the highest grade depend so heavily on premeditation and deliberation, omits other factors that also might be important in categorizing a homicide as meriting the harshest punishment.

(2) *Formulas for Premeditation*. The *Anderson* court seems to suggest that the concept of premeditation can be equated to a formula that usually requires evidence of (1) planning activity; (2) motive; and (3) a method that shows pre-existing reflection, or some combination of these factors. Can premeditation be fitted into this formula, or is it a more fluid concept for jurors? If these had been the controlling factors in *Carroll*, would there have been enough evidence of premeditation?

(3) *How Much Juror Discretion is Desirable?* The premeditation formula is difficult to apply consistently because it is difficult to understand precisely. Is this a good thing? How much "discretion" should jurors have in distinguishing first degree from second-degree murders (what are the disadvantages of providing jurors with broad discretion)?

(4) *Criticisms of People v. Anderson*. The holding in *Anderson* has been the subject of much criticism. Which of the following criticisms, if any, have merit?

(a) *The Statute Is Poorly Drafted (It's the Legislature's Problem)*. One possibility is that the difference between first and second degree murder usually depends exclusively on "premeditation and deliberation." These terms are mushy and confusing. Furthermore, they fail to account for the possibility that a "random, violent, indiscriminate" killing can be serious enough to merit the law's strongest condemnation, because frenzied thoughtlessness is not a virtue. [In this view, the California Supreme Court did what it had to do and it faithfully carried out the judicial role, following the legislative command.]

(b) *The Court Failed to Evaluate the Evidence Properly*. Another view is that of the dissent. This argument maintains that the Court construed the evidence to fit its idiosyncratic preferences and did not defer to the jury. The issue is not whether the Court believes that the murder is first degree; it is whether the jury found it to be first degree and whether there is any reasonable way to sustain that finding. [In this view, the legislation is not the problem. The problem is that the Court usurped the function of the factfinder.]

(c) *Both of the Above: The Legislation Is Poorly Drafted and the Court Mishandled the Evidence*. Still another possibility is that the statute is misdrafted, but still it would have supported first degree here if only the Court had not mistreated the evidence.

(d) *None of the Above: Defending the Result in Anderson*. Still another view is that *Anderson* is rightly decided. A deliberate, planned crime, in this view, always is worse than a frenzied, indiscriminate one, no matter how brutal. And in this view, the Court correctly handled the evidence. Moreover, given that

Anderson faced the death penalty, the Court arguably found another way to take his mental status into account in deciding on the verdict.

(5) *Comparing Anderson and Carroll: Are They Backward?* If *Anderson* is rightly decided, is *Carroll* wrong? Many people think *Carroll* presents a more appealing case for reduction to second degree than *Anderson*. Is this right (are the two decisions backward)? If so, should Carroll have been convicted only of second degree, or should both be first degree (or both only second)?

(6) *The MPC Approach: No Degrees of Murder; Severity to Be Taken Account of at Sentencing.* Considerations such as these convinced the drafters of the MPC to eliminate degrees of murder. Under the MPC, discussed below, there is one kind of murder. This doesn't mean that differences in severity, including mental state, aren't important; they are taken into account at sentencing. This way, the entire variety of factors can influence the sentence of either a Carroll or an Anderson. Is this a better way?

(7) *Did the California Court Later Retreat from the Anderson Result?* In *People v. Perez*, excerpted below, the California Court upholds some of the reasoning in *Anderson* but limits the specific holding. In effect, the Court seems to adopt alternative (b) above: the problem with *Anderson*, if any, may have been that Court's treatment of the evidence. Is *Perez* consistent with *Anderson*, or does it change the law?

PEOPLE v. PEREZ, 831 P.2d 1159 (Cal. 1992), *reaffirmed by* **PEOPLE V. POTTS**, 436 P.3d 899 (Cal. 2019). This case involved a murder of a pregnant woman named Victoria by an acquaintance inside a home, accomplished by multiple stab wounds. The jury's verdict was first-degree murder. The court of appeals, following *Anderson*, reversed and reduced the grade to second degree. The California Supreme Court, through Justice Panelli, reinterpreted *Anderson* and reinstated the jury's finding of first-degree murder:

> In *People v. Anderson*, this court . . . identified three categories of evidence pertinent to the determination of premeditation and deliberation: (1) planning activity, (2) motive, and (3) manner of killing. . . . [The court] was attempting to do no more than catalog common factors that had occurred in prior cases. The *Anderson* factors . . . are not a sine qua non to finding first degree premeditated murder, nor are they exclusive. . . .
>
> [T]he evidence is sufficient to support the jury's findings of premeditation and deliberation. Evidence of [1] planning activity is shown by the fact that defendant did not park his car in the victim's driveway, he surreptitiously entered the house, and he obtained a knife from the kitchen. As to [2] motive, regardless of what inspired the initial entry and attack, it is reasonable to infer that defendant determined it was necessary to kill Victoria to prevent her from identifying him. . . . The [3] manner of killing is also indicative of premeditation and deliberation. The evidence of blood in

the kitchen knife drawer supports an inference that defendant went to the kitchen in search of another knife after the steak knife broke. This action bears similarity to reloading a gun. . . .

Justice Mosk dissented. He relied heavily on *Anderson*, reasoning that "the rule *of Anderson* is [not] satisfied here." As for the manner of killing, Justice Mosk concluded:

> [T]here is no substantial evidence that defendant employed a manner of killing the victim that reveals forethought and reflection. The record is weak as to "facts about the nature of the killing from which the jury could infer that the *manner* of killing was so particular and exacting that the defendant must have intentionally killed according to a preconceived design" to take his victim's life in a particular way for a "reason" which the jury can reasonably infer from facts of planning or motive. (*People v. Anderson, supra.*)

Notes and Questions

(1) *Perez's and Potts's Limitations on Anderson.* Is *Anderson* still good law after *Perez* and *Potts*? If so, how do these two cases modify or limit the holding in *Anderson*?

(2) *What Does the "Manner of Killing" Prove: Intent or Premeditation?* The court's opinion in *Perez* relies heavily on the "manner of killing." The manner of killing usually is enough to supply intent to kill. That is to say, use of a weapon in a way that is likely to kill indicates intent. But all that intent supplies is malice, *i.e.* murder, which could be second-degree. First-degree murder requires premeditation and deliberation, which is supposed to be something different. What is the difference between using manner of killing to prove intent and using it to prove premeditation? Has the court equated intent with premeditation or deliberation?

Problem 2A (Intentional Homicide Levels): The I-Dare-You-to-Kill-Him Murder

(1) *A Thoughtless, Inexcusable Killing—But Was Shorty's Conduct "Premeditated"?* This problem will require you to apply *Carroll, Anderson,* and *Perez* to explore the distinction between first- and second-degree murder. Two gang members, known as "Big Jim" and "Shorty," are sitting in a car waiting to do a drive-by shooting. They do not plan to kill anyone, just to leave a "calling card" by shooting up a rival's home. Suddenly, a stranger on a bicycle, unknown to either of them, approaches. Big Jim says to Shorty, "I dare you to kill this guy." Without hesitation, Shorty shoots and kills the cyclist. It appears that Shorty's conduct is a mere reaction, with no thought or purpose, and in fact Shorty is afraid of Big Jim and usually does what he tells him to do without question.

(2) *Thoughtless and Random, but Does That Mean This Crime is Less Culpable?* In a murder prosecution against Shorty, a jury would be offered the option of second-degree murder, a lesser crime. Recall that second degree murder requires malice aforethought but lacks premeditation and deliberation. Perhaps, under the Pennsylvania pattern, the thoughtless, bizarre nature of this murder it somehow less

culpable than first degree murder, at least as the statutory pattern defines it. Do you think this thoughtless killing is less morally blameworthy than a carefully planned one?

(3) *The Effect of the Burden of Proof.* The jury will be told, of course, to opt for second-degree murder if it has a "reasonable doubt" about premeditation or deliberation. This burden of proof will be a powerful factor inducing the jury to opt for the lesser crime. Can you explain why? (In fact, the prosecution will have great difficulty in proving this crime at all, at least without a confession. Big Jim is unlikely to be willing to testify, and without Big Jim's evidence, the crime may not be capable of being reconstructed accurately at all, much less proved as a first-degree murder.)

(4) *If the Jury Does Find Shorty Guilty of First-Degree Murder, Will the Court Be Able to Impose Judgment for That Offense?* After the *Anderson* case, imagine that the jury does find Shorty guilty of first degree murder. (It's possible, because of the flexibility in the concepts of premeditation and deliberation.) If it follows the California Supreme Court's holding, won't the trial court be forced to reduce the offense to second-degree (because planning and motive are conspicuously absent)? How does the later *Perez* case modify this conclusion, if at all?

[B] Translating the Law into Jury Instructions
Notes and Questions

The Position of the Jury: Like You, on Your First Day in Law School. If it is difficult for courts and law students to understand the standards for murder convictions, how can the legal system expect jurors to understand these concepts? The jury learns the law through jury instructions. Imagine how a juror must feel when confronted with a lengthy and internally contradictory charge. It may be reminiscent of your first day in law school when you worked hard to sort out even the matters that are obvious to you now: the positions of the parties, the issues, and the meanings of common legal terms. Are the jury instructions in the next case adequate to inform the jurors of the law to be applied?

People v. Conley
411 P.2d 911 (Cal. 1966)

[This excerpt contains a suggested charge to a jury in a California homicide case. Consider how well it does at distinguishing the crimes and possible verdicts at issue, in the minds of average jurors. Today's California charge is different (and arguably better) in some respects, but it still contains much of the same confusing and internal conflict.]

"Murder is the unlawful killing of a human being with malice aforethought.

"Such malice may be express or implied. It is express when there is manifested a deliberate intention unlawfully to take away the life of a fellow creature. It is implied when no considerable provocation appears, or when the circumstances attending the killing show an abandoned and malignant heart.

"The law prohibits acts highly dangerous to human life that cause serious injury or death unless legal cause or excuse is shown. Malice aforethought, either express or implied, is manifested by the doing of such an act by a person who is able to comprehend this prohibition and his obligation to conform his conduct to it. There is a presumption that the defendant was able to understand this prohibition but he may rebut the presumption by evidence of diminished capacity. . . . Malice does not require a pre-existing hatred or enmity toward the person injured.

"All murder perpetrated by any kind of willful, deliberate, and premeditated killing is murder of the first degree. [To be followed here by definitions of deliberation and premeditation as in customary instructions.]

"Murder of the second degree must be distinguished not only from murder of the first degree, but also from manslaughter. Manslaughter shortly will be defined for you, and you will note than an essential feature of that offense, which distinguishes it from murder, is that the killing be done without malice.

"If the unlawful killing of a human being is done with malice aforethought, but without deliberation and premeditation, that is, without the willful, deliberate and premeditated intent to take life that is an essential element of first degree murder, then the offense is murder in the second degree.

"The defendant has offered evidence that because of mental illness and intoxication he was unconscious. If you find that he was conscious of the shootings, but had substantially reduced mental capacity because of mental illness or intoxication, you must consider what effect, if any, this diminished capacity had on the defendant's ability to form any of the specific mental states that are essential elements of murder, which I have defined for you, or of manslaughter, which I will define shortly.

"Thus, if you find that the defendant killed [the victim] while conscious and with malice, you will return a verdict of murder. If you find that this murder was committed willfully, deliberately, and with premeditation, you will find the murder to be of the first degree. If you find, however, that the defendant's mental capacity was so diminished that he did not, or you have a reasonable doubt whether he did, premeditate, deliberate, or form an intent to kill, you will find the murder to be of the second degree.

"Premeditation, deliberation, an intent to kill, and malice must be present for the killing to be first degree murder.

"Malice is an essential element of either degree of murder. Therefore, if you find that the defendant did not harbor malice because of his diminished capacity, or have a reasonable doubt whether he harbored malice, you cannot find him guilty of a higher offense than manslaughter.

"Manslaughter is the unlawful killing of a human being without malice. Two kinds of manslaughter, the definitions of which are pertinent here, are:

"1. Voluntary manslaughter, an intentional killing in which the law, recognizing human frailty, permits the defendant to establish the lack of malice either by

"a. Showing provocation such as to rouse the reasonable [person] to heat of passion or sudden quarrel. When such provocation is shown, the law will presume that the defendant who acts in the heat of passion or on sudden quarrel, acts without malice. I instruct you that as a matter of law no such provocation was shown to exist at the time of the killing of [the victim] or,

"b. Showing that due to diminished capacity caused by mental illness, mental defect, or intoxication, the defendant did not attain the mental state constituting malice."

"2. Involuntary manslaughter is a killing in the commission of an unlawful act not amounting to a felony, or in the commission of a lawful act which might produce death, in an unlawful manner, or without due caution and circumspection.

"Thus, if you find that the defendant killed while unconscious as a result of voluntary intoxication and was therefore unable to formulate a specific intent to kill or to harbor malice, his killing is involuntary manslaughter. The law does not permit him to use his own vice as a shelter against the normal legal consequences of his act. An ordinary and prudent man would not, while in possession of a dangerous weapon, permit himself to reach such a state of intoxication as to be unconscious of his actions."

Notes and Questions

(1) *Simplify, Simplify, Simplify.* Can you think of a way to simplify these instructions for the jury and still keep them accurate and objective? Why do you think jury instructions are written in such a complicated manner? Note that they have to conform to statutory definitions.

(2) *Does It Matter Whether the Jury is Confused by the Instructions?* Consider the following two (opposite) possibilities: (a) The jury is unable to understand or agree on the meaning of a fundamental term in the court's instructions (such as "malice aforethought," because it does not remember that neither malice nor aforethought is required), and therefore it finds reasonable doubt in a serious case where jurists would agree that the crime is murder. (b) Alternatively, the jury focuses on ambiguous phraseology such as "abandoned and malignant heart." Even lesser or innocent homicides sometimes are committed by bad people who might be said to harbor "malignant hearts." Therefore, the jury convicts of murder when it would instead have returned a lesser (or not guilty) verdict if it had understood the law. Is there a way to reduce the risk of either possibility?

(3) *Is the Jury Like a "Roulette Wheel"?: Ambiguous Definitions Leading to Inconsistent Results.* If ten juries were to try a homicide case involving the same fact situation under the charge given above, how many might return verdicts of first-degree

murder, how many second-degree, and how many lesser degrees? Inconsistency due to differing jury understandings of crime definition can be a serious problem. In some cases, some trial lawyers see the jury as resembling a roulette wheel, particularly when the charge is clumsy.

(4) *The Function of Counsel: Voir Dire, Opening Statement, and Jury Argument.* Confusing crime definition in the jury instructions means harder work for trial lawyers. The prosecutor and defense lawyer can, through skillful use of jury argument, explain the instructions so that jurors understand them better. (They also may have opportunities to do so during *voir dire* or opening statement, although these opportunities may be more limited.) Of course, if one attorney is skillful and the other not, an imbalance may result, and thus a confusing jury charge makes outcomes depend significantly on the randomly distributed abilities of lawyers. Can you explain why?

[C] Voluntary Manslaughter: An Intentional Killing, but in the Heat of Passion

Notes on Voluntary Manslaughter

(1) *Voluntary Manslaughter as an Alternative to Murder.* So far, we have concentrated on the law of murder. But could the defendant instead be guilty of voluntary manslaughter, not murder? If so, the defendant would face a lesser sentence range.

(2) *Passion Killing as Voluntary Manslaughter.* Even if malice aforethought otherwise would be present (because the killing is intentional), the Pennsylvania pattern reduces the grade to voluntary manslaughter for certain killings carried out in the heat of passion. For example, the California statute defines voluntary manslaughter as a killing "upon a sudden quarrel or heat of passion." Cal. Pen. Code § 192.

The underlying theory varies. Some courts reason that malice aforethought is absent in such a case, because the killing was the product of passion rather than reflection, while others treat the additional factor of passion as a kind of defense that coexists with malice but reduces the moral blameworthiness of the killing and therefore reduces the sanction for it.

(3) *Same Facts Can Be Analyzed as Permitting Conviction for Murder or Voluntary Manslaughter.* Often the particular facts of the homicide give the trier of fact the possibility of finding first or second degree murder or voluntary manslaughter, depending on how certain facts are analyzed. For example, V gets drunk and hits D in the face at a bar. D gets angry, rushes home, gets his knife, returns to the bar and stabs V to death. There is an argument that the crime is first degree murder under the Pennsylvania model if D is seen as using the time away from the bar to deliberate and premeditate. Second degree murder is also possible if the jury finds an intent to kill but no deliberation because of D's anger. Finally, the trier of fact could conclude the crime was voluntary manslaughter because committed in the heat of passion.

(4) *Voluntary Manslaughter as a Defense; Burden of Proof.* Careful analysis may lead to the conclusion that most killings that are voluntary manslaughter are also easily categorized as murder because done intentionally. Many jurisdictions face this theoretical dilemma by specifically providing that voluntary manslaughter is a killing that otherwise would be murder except committed in the heat of passion, which reduces the crime level to voluntary manslaughter. *See, e.g.,* Indiana Code 35–42-1–3 (killing under "sudden heat" is mitigating factor reducing what would otherwise be murder to voluntary manslaughter).

If a defendant wants a voluntary manslaughter verdict rather than one for murder, some jurisdictions place the burden *on the defendant* to *prove* heat of passion and the other elements of voluntary manslaughter. Other jurisdictions require the *prosecution* to *disprove* the elements of voluntary manslaughter once some evidence of it is introduced by the evidence.

(5) *Elements of Voluntary Manslaughter.* To reach a verdict of voluntary manslaughter, the jury must find the following factors:

(a) *Adequate Cause or Reasonable Provocation.* For voluntary manslaughter, the killing must have been induced by some event that caused the killer to have the "heat of passion." Often this cause is some type of provocation. But any provocation will not suffice, as the next case indicates. The cause or provocation for the killing must be an adequate one. A typical statute, for example, might mention "sudden quarrel" or "heat of passion" as factors. Often, jurisdictions use a reasonableness test in making this determination. As *Avery*, the case which follows, indicates, the "heat of passion" is not confined to anger; any extreme emotion, such as fear, jealousy, or desperation, will do, as long as the defendant satisfies the elements of the test.

(i) *Common Law Categories of Provocation.* Originally the partial defense of provocation, which reduced a murder to voluntary manslaughter, was only available in certain fixed categories of cases. The defendant had to be in one of these situations in order to qualify for voluntary manslaughter. The recognized categories of provocation that formerly reduced murder to voluntary manslaughter at common law were:

- Mutual combat;

- Serious assault and battery;

- Injury to the defendant's relative or a third party;

- Resisting an illegal arrest;

- Imperfect self-defense—an overreaction to an assault such that self-defense is unavailable because of the excessive response; and

- Discovering one's spouse in an act of intercourse with another. In almost all the small number of states which still retain these fixed categories, finding one's spouse in the act of intercourse with another allows the defendant, providing the evidence meets the test above, to claim voluntary manslaughter instead of murder.

(ii) *Most States Today Reject Limited Categories of Provocation.* Today most states recognize some form of a heat of passion crime, still characterized as voluntary manslaughter in many locales, but they reject the limitation on categories of provocation. Virtually any event that would provoke a reasonable person is deemed adequate. A few jurisdictions continue to mention a few categories that do or do not constitute legal provocation for voluntary manslaughter. *See, e.g.*, Minn. Stat. §609.20 (crying of a child does not constitute provocation).

(iii) *Imperfect Self Defense.* Sometimes people respond to attacks with excessive force, or they misapprehend the need to use force in response to what is inaccurately perceived as an immediate threat of physical injury. For example, A slaps B, and B responds by stabbing A to death. As discussed in Chapter 6, B cannot succeed with a self-defense (sometimes called "perfect self-defense") argument, because B responded with unreasonable force. But in recognition that B was provoked by A's slap, the doctrine of "imperfect self-defense" permits B to be convicted of voluntary manslaughter rather than murder. *See, e.g., State v. Qualls,* 298 P.3d 311 (Kan. 2013) (during barroom fight defendant thought victim was reaching for a gun and then shot victim 9 times; court should have given imperfect self-defense instruction because defendant could have had honest, unreasonable belief in need to use deadly force).

(b) *Provocation Must Induce Passion.* Voluntary manslaughter requires that the provocation must cause or induce the passion.

(c) *Provocation That Would Cause a Reasonable Person to Lose "Cool Reflection."* The severity of mental disturbance usually must be such that it would interfere with "cool reflection," that is, make a reasonable person lose control. In other words, the standard is an objective one, based upon the reasonable, or ordinary, person. (It is also a subjective one, in that the defendant must lose control, but this aspect of the requirement is usually easier to supply.)

Note that the issue is not whether a reasonable person would have killed the victim. (Arguably, no reasonable person would, because voluntary manslaughter is a serious crime.) Instead, the test is whether the reasonable person's ability to reflect "coolly" or exercise self-control would have been sufficiently reduced that he or she would have lost control. Some courts base their analysis not on a hypothetical "objective" reasonable person, but rather on a reasonable or average person with relevant characteristics in common with this defendant.

In a classic case, *Maher v. People,* 1862 Mich. LEXIS 37 (Mich. May 21, 1862), the trial court excluded evidence showing that the victim had had sexual intercourse with the defendant's wife about a half hour before the shooting.

The appellate court reversed the conviction, holding that this evidence could support voluntary manslaughter and was improperly excluded. The adequacy of cause was to be tested by what might make "ordinary" people, "of fair average disposition," liable to "act rashly." As for the "sudden passion" element, the question of cooling time was a matter of degree.

Consider too, for example, the case of Sirhan Sirhan, who was convicted of murder for killing Senator Robert Kennedy, a major candidate for President of the United States. Sirhan claimed he was provoked to do so because Kennedy refused to support the Palestinian cause. As a child, Sirhan observed the condition of Palestinians in refugee camps. Under the case law above, could Sirhan argue provocation or "adequate cause" to reduce the gravity of his crime? Would Sirhan have a better chance of prevailing under the Model Penal Code (which is considered in note 3 following the *Avery* case, below)?

(d) *Timing: Suddenness versus Cooling Time.* A killing that would have been voluntary manslaughter if committed on the spot may be murder if committed at a later time. By definition, voluntary manslaughter requires that the killer be in the "heat of passion" when the killing occurs. The passage of time sufficient for cooling of passion works against manslaughter because the killer may no longer have been acting in the "heat of passion." Courts differ in deciding about the length of time necessary for cooling off to occur.

A related issue is the "boiling water," "stewing," or "brooding" situation when someone is provoked, thinks about it for a few days, gets angrier and angrier over time, then explodes and kills the provocateur. The government will argue a willful, deliberate first degree murder because of length of time between the killing and the provocation was sufficient cooling time, while the defense will argue that the passage of time increased rather than decreased the "heat of passion."

(6) *Last Straw.* Most jurisdictions do not allow the provocation defense on a "last straw" basis, where the killing was induced by the last in a series of provocative events occurring over time but the last event by itself would not have been sufficient provocation on its own. But as *Avery*, the case which follows, notes, past events may be relevant to show the reasonableness of the passion to which the defendant was provoked.

(7) *The Victim.* Must the defendant have killed the provoker to get the benefit of the partial defense? What if the angered defendant kills someone else on purpose or by accident?

(a) *Must Kill Provoker.* Some jurisdictions insist that the victim be someone who was involved in creating the passion. Sometimes this issue is explained as if the victim were at least partially responsible, having provided some provocation that triggered that killing. Thus, if D is provoked, becomes furious, and goes on a killing spree shooting children in a school or shoppers in a mall, in most jurisdictions the crime would likely be murder rather than voluntary manslaughter since the victims did not provoke the killer.

(b) *Accidental Killing of Others Also Covered.* On the other hand, a minority of jurisdictions specifically recognize that a provoked person could try to shoot the provoking person but miss and accidentally kill someone else. On the theory that the carelessness does not take away from the reduced moral blameworthiness of the provoked person, these states permit a conviction for voluntary manslaughter for the accidental death of the innocent person. E.g., Ill. Rev. Stat. 720 5/9/2. However, the intentional death of third persons is not reduced to voluntary manslaughter.

(8) *When Must a Trial Judge Submit a Voluntary Manslaughter Instruction?* Generally, the trial judge is required to submit a jury instruction if any reasonable juror could conclude that the facts support the theory presented by the party requesting the instruction. Often, the facts are contested. The prosecution may present one evidentiary picture, the defense another. The judge cannot resolve this question if the trial is before a jury. Instead, the judge must submit instructions on voluntary manslaughter (as well as instructions on murder) if the possibility is raised by the evidence. Read the next case and consider what kinds of facts are required to merit a voluntary manslaughter instruction.

State v. Avery

120 S.W.3d 196 (Mo. 2003) (en banc)

Laura Denvir Stith, Judge.

Defendant Jamie Avery was convicted of second-degree murder and armed criminal action under [Missouri] section 565.021 and section 571.015. The judge sentenced her to two consecutive terms of thirty years imprisonment. On appeal, Ms. Avery claims that the trial court erred in refusing to instruct the jury on... voluntary manslaughter. This Court agrees. Although Ms. Avery testified at trial that the shooting was an accident, the State introduced evidence of prior statements by her to the police and to her boyfriend that supported submission of the theories that the shooting was intentional but... that it arose out of sudden passion based on adequate cause. Accordingly, the judgment of the trial court is reversed, and the cause is remanded for a new trial.

I. Factual Background

[Ms. Avery lived with her boyfriend, John Hamilton, but at the same time had a sexual relationship with the deceased, Bruce Paris. Mr. Paris's relationship with another girlfriend caused Ms. Avery to make verbal threats against Mr. Paris. Ms. Avery eventually told Mr. Paris she did not intend to see him again, but she changed her mind and saw him, including bringing him to Mr. Hamilton's home. After Mr. Hamilton telephoned, Ms. Avery testified she repeatedly asked Mr. Paris to leave. According to her, he refused. Her further story was that she obtained Mr. Hamilton's revolver and displayed it, and Mr. Paris left.

[The homicide resulted, according to Ms. Avery's testimony, when Mr. Paris returned much later, but after she had accidentally left the door open. Her statements varied as to whether the gun went off by accident during a struggle over it or whether she had "shot an intruder." Other aspects of her testimony are given in connection with the court's discussion of voluntary manslaughter, as follows:]

V. Voluntary Manslaughter

Ms. Avery alleges that the trial court erred in refusing to submit an instruction on voluntary manslaughter because the evidence produced at trial was sufficient to [raise the issue of] sudden passion arising from adequate cause.

Voluntary manslaughter is a lesser-included offense of second-degree murder. [That is, its elements are entirely included within the murder charge.] Instruction on a lesser-included offense is required if the evidence produced at trial, by fact or inference, provides a basis both for the acquittal of the greater offense and the conviction of the lesser offense. When in doubt, courts should instruct on the lesser-included offense, leaving it for the jury to decide of which offense, if any, the defendant is guilty.

A person commits voluntary manslaughter if she "causes the death of another person under circumstances that would constitute murder in the second degree . . . except that [s]he caused the death *under the influence of sudden passion arising from adequate cause.*" Sec. 565.023.1(1) (emphasis added). Ms. Avery had the burden of injecting this issue through evidence showing sudden passion and adequate cause for it. Secs. 565.023.2; 556.051. Upon such a showing, she was entitled to an instruction on voluntary manslaughter[, which the prosecution then had the burden to disprove, beyond a reasonable doubt].

The State says that the events Ms. Avery points to cannot meet this standard, for they all occurred some time before the actual shooting, giving Ms. Avery time to cool down. And, as the State notes, "sudden passion" is "passion directly caused by and arising out of provocation by the victim or another acting with the victim, which passion arises at the time of the offense and is not solely the result of former provocation." Sec. 565.002(7). This may include terror, "but it must be so extreme that for the moment, the action is being directed by passion, not reason." *State v. Fears*, 803 S.W.2d 605, 609 (Mo. banc 1991). This means that sudden passion is not established if there was ample time for that passion to cool.

Moreover, the State argues, even if this evidence caused Ms. Avery to experience sudden passion, she cannot prove adequate cause for such passion under the law because Mr. Paris only uttered a few profane words, and words alone are insufficient to show adequate cause. *Fears*, 803 S.W.2d at 609. "Adequate cause" is "cause that would reasonably produce a degree of passion in a person of ordinary temperament sufficient to substantially impair an ordinary person's capacity for self-control." Sec. 565.002(1).

The State is correct that much of Ms. Avery's factual support comes from events occurring well before the shooting. But, while the statute and relevant cases are clear that prior provocation can never be the sole cause of sudden passion, they do not state that such evidence is irrelevant. Such evidence may be relevant to show why, when combined with other evidence of events occurring immediately before the incident, the precipitating incident was adequate to show sudden passion. *See, e.g., State v. Battle*, 32 S.W.3d 193, 197 (Mo.App. E.D. 2000). . . . Similarly, while words alone are insufficient to show adequate provocation, little more is required—a mere tweaking of the nose has been found sufficient.

Applying these principles here, while evidence of Ms. Avery's past relationship with Mr. Paris and his past conduct toward her is not sufficient in itself to support a claim of sudden passion or adequate cause, it is relevant to show why she feared Mr. Paris and why his conduct immediately before the event caused her such terror. Ms. Avery produced evidence that Mr. Paris made harassing telephone calls to her and her boyfriend in the weeks before the shooting. The evening of the shooting, he grabbed her breast without permission and covered her mouth with his hand in a way that caused her difficulty breathing. She had to bite him to get him to let go. When, earlier in the evening, she told him to leave, he refused to do so until she retrieved her revolver. Then, when walking her dog, she heard a sound but could see no one. She became particularly frightened because it was dark out and she had once been gang-raped in the dark. She ran back inside, pulled out the gun, and pointed it at the door. She knew Mr. Paris had been drinking and smoking marijuana.

When Mr. Paris appeared in the doorway, she said, "he looked mad" and threatened to beat her if she did not drop the revolver. She claimed that when he said this, and then walked quickly toward her and tried to grab the gun, she was "scared to death" and shot him. Immediately afterward, she ran to her bedroom and locked the door because she feared that Mr. Paris would retrieve the revolver and come after her. While in the bedroom, Ms. Avery called Mr. Hamilton. He testified that when Ms. Avery called him, she was "pretty hysterical." She told Mr. Hamilton that she was "scared" and that Mr. Paris was going to hurt her. Finally, one of Ms. Avery's hairs, with the root attached, was found in Mr. Paris' hand.

This evidence was minimally sufficient to inject the issue of sudden passion based on adequate cause. Because Ms. Avery satisfied her statutory burden of injecting the voluntary manslaughter issue through this evidence, she was entitled to a jury instruction on voluntary manslaughter. While the State introduced contrary evidence, the jury as fact finder was entitled to consider all of the evidence and make its own credibility determination. [In fact, the State introduced substantial evidence, summarized elsewhere in the opinion, showing that Ms. Avery's version of these alleged events was not credible, and that the incident instead was unprovoked, intentional murder. Nevertheless, the defendant's version, whether credible or not, raised the issue of sudden passion.] The trial court's refusal to instruct the jury on voluntary manslaughter was reversible error. [Reversed and remanded for a new trial.]

Notes and Questions

(1) *Hot-Blooded Defendants.* Voluntary manslaughter means that the homicide becomes less blameworthy than murder when passion is involved. Why should the

law become more lenient for defendants who kill in the heat of passion (shouldn't we expect people to control their tempers)? Is there an argument that passion is an *aggravating* factor rather than a mitigating one?

(2) *Battered Wife or Spouse Syndrome.* In a later chapter, which sets out the elements of the complete defense of self-defense, we consider whether courts should include evidence and instructions about the state of mind called "Battered Wife/ Battered Spouse Syndrome." Should this evidence also be included in voluntary manslaughter cases involving repeated threats or trauma from a spouse or other intimate? Why or why not, in your view?

(3) *The MPC Approach: Extreme Emotional Distress.* Model Penal Code § 210.3 takes a different approach to manslaughter. First, the MPC has only one category of manslaughter and does not use the term "voluntary manslaughter." MPC manslaughter can be committed in either of two ways: (1) by a reckless killing [discussed later] or (2) by "a homicide. . . . committed under the influence of *extreme mental or emotional disturbance* for which there is reasonable explanation or excuse. The reasonableness of such explanation or excuse shall be determined from the viewpoint of a person in the actor's situation under the circumstances as he believes them to be." How objective or subjective is the MPC's "extreme mental or emotional disturbance" approach, and how would its differences influence the result in Ms. Avery's case, above? (The MPC provision is discussed in greater detail below.)

(4) *The Outer Boundaries of "Adequate Cause" for Voluntary Manslaughter: "Panic" Based on a Sexual Advance without Coercive Contact.* Consider the following case, which comes to the opposite result from *Avery,* above, and which shows the outer boundaries of "adequate cause."

PEOPLE v. PAGE, 737 N.E.2d 264 (Ill. 2000). The defendant was convicted of the murder of John Goodman . . . [and sentenced to death]. He sought to have the trial judge instruct the jury on voluntary manslaughter on the ground that Goodman had allegedly made a same-sex sexual advance toward him. The trial judge refused and disallowed jury argument on the issue. The Illinois Supreme Court agreed that voluntary manslaughter was not raised by the evidence:

> Defendant cites . . . cases which he contends "discuss what could be termed the 'homosexual panic' [theory of voluntary manslaughter]." While these cases likewise involve fact scenarios where the victims made homosexual advances toward the defendants, the defendants' theories of voluntary manslaughter were based on the unreasonable belief in the need for self-defense, not on serious provocation, which is the theory advanced by defendant in this case.

These kinds of cases are controversial. Some commentators believe that voluntary manslaughter should be raised by such circumstances. The argument is that voluntary manslaughter is not exoneration, but is intended to cover unreasonable conduct created by passion, and that it is a serious felony itself. Most of the cases do involve physical contact or the apparent threat of it. What amount of physical contact or apprehension of it should be required to raise voluntary manslaughter in these cases — or should "a mere sexual advance" be enough (and if so, should a heterosexual advance likewise be enough)?

Problem 2B (Intentional Homicide Levels): Voluntary Manslaughter as a Jury Possibility in Commonwealth v. Carroll, Above

(1) *Could Mr. Carroll Have Argued Provocation, Passion, and Voluntary Manslaughter?* We considered *Commonwealth v. Carroll* in an earlier section, above. Imagine that the trial is before a jury. Recall that in *Carroll* the defendant shot his wife. She exhibited serious psychological disturbance, and yet the defendant's psychological expert said that he was dependent upon her. His career as a government employee probably would be over if he did not relocate, but during an argument, his wife said that she would leave if he did move. He estimated that about five minutes intervened between the argument and the killing. Could Carroll's lawyer reasonably have argued that the judge should submit a voluntary manslaughter charge to the jury? What counter-arguments would you expect the prosecutor to present?

(2) *The Burden of Proof.* If you did not think of the burden of proof in considering the defense argument, you may have missed one of your best theories. As noted above, in many jurisdictions, when voluntary manslaughter is raised, the prosecution must not only prove the killing beyond a reasonable doubt, but also must negate voluntary manslaughter beyond a reasonable doubt. How does the burden of proof affect this Problem? Would your answer change if heat of passion were an affirmative defense which the defendant must prove in order to reduce the crime to voluntary manslaughter?

(3) *Changing the Facts.* Consider how the following factors might alter the arguments (and the outcome): (a) a greater or lesser intervening time (imagine that the killing in *Carroll* occurred within seconds, or that it occurred after two days of brooding by the defendant); (b) a killing of someone other than the defendant's wife (imagine that Carroll instead shot his commanding officer, the one who proposed the move, shortly after arguing with his wife); or (c) greater or lesser disagreement (imagine that the defendant' wife had attempted calmly to persuade him not to move, or that she verbally abused him at length with four-letter words).

[D] Depraved-Heart Murder: Malice Aforethought in Unintentional Killings

Notes on the "Abandoned and Malignant Heart" Theory

(1) *Unintentional or "Accidental" Murder?* Although we generally think of murder as limited to intentional killings, it is not so confined under the Pennsylvania

approach. While malice aforethought is satisfied by an intentional killing, malice can also be "implied" if the defendant unintentionally killed the victim but acted with a "depraved heart" (or with an "abandoned and malignant" heart). A depraved-heart killing is second-degree murder under the Pennsylvania model.

(2) *Distinguishing Involuntary Manslaughter (A Lesser Offense).* Under the Pennsylvania model, a careless killing can constitute either second degree murder (for conduct constituting "depraved heart") or involuntary manslaughter, (for reckless or sometimes "criminally negligent" or "grossly negligent" behavior). The difference between the two types of carelessness is degree. "Depraved heart" depends upon a special kind of recklessness: a depraved indifference to life. It can be difficult to make the important distinction between these two crimes.

(3) *Russian Roulette as Depraved Heart Murder: Commonwealth v. Malone*, 47 A.2d 445 (Pa. 1946). This is a classic case in which intent to kill was absent. The killing occurred while the parties were playing Russian roulette. The case arose when the defendant suggested to the decedent (age 13) that they play "Russian Poker." The victim replied: "I don't care; go ahead." The defendant Malone then placed the revolver against the right side of the victim's head and pulled the trigger three times. The third pull resulted in a fatal wound. The victim jumped off the stool and cried: "Oh! Oh! Oh!" and Malone said: "Did I hit you, Billy? Gee, Kid, I'm sorry." The victim died from the wounds two days later.

The defendant testified that the gun chamber he loaded was the first one to the right of the firing chamber and that when he pulled the trigger he did not "expect to have the gun go off." He declared he had no intention of harming the victim, who was his friend and companion. But, the defendant was convicted of second degree murder and appealed.

> Appellant . . . contends that the facts did not justify a conviction for any form of homicide except involuntary manslaughter. This contention we overrule. . . . At common law, the "grand criterion" which "distinguished murder from other killing" was malice on the part of the killer and this malice was not necessarily "malevolent to the deceased particularly" but "any evil design in general; the dictate of a wicked, depraved and malignant heart"; 4 Blackstone 199. Among the examples that Blackstone cites of murder is "coolly discharging a gun among a multitude of people". . . .
>
> . . . When an individual commits an act of gross [recklessness] for which he must reasonably anticipate that death to another is likely to result, he exhibits that "wickedness of disposition, hardness of heart, cruelty, recklessness of consequences, and a mind regardless of social duty" which proved that there was at that time in him "the state or frame of mind termed malice." This court has declared that if a driver "wantonly, recklessly, and in disregard of consequences" hurls "his car against another, or into a crowd" and death results from that act "he ought . . . to face the same consequences that would be meted out to him if he had accomplished death by wantonly

and wickedly firing a gun": *Com. v. Mayberry*, 138 A. 686, 688. . . . [E]ven though [the victim's] death might have been unintended and, therefore, accidental, the evidence showed that the act which caused the victim's death was not accidental. . . .

Notes and Questions

(1) *Implied (or Depraved-Heart) Malice.* Ordinarily an accidental killing is not murder, but the court makes it clear that sometimes an "accident" can be murder. How can a person who kills accidentally act with "malice"? What is the ingredient in *Malone* that convinces the court that defendant's actions were serious enough to justify a conviction for murder?

(2) *What Is the Difference Between "Ordinary" Accidental or Reckless Killings, and Depraved Heart Malice?* Notice that the defendant Malone's version of the facts was that the loaded chamber was "to the right of the firing pin," so that he thought it could not fire, and he "did not 'expect the gun to go off.'" If the jury had credited this explanation, would the crime constitute only a lesser offense, or would it still be second degree murder?

(3) *The Blurry Line Between Depraved-Heart Malice and Involuntary Manslaughter.* When is a defendant's behavior so reckless that it constitutes malice? If the defendant's recklessness is so substantial that it exhibits *extreme indifference to human life*, according to some courts, then it may qualify as depraved heart malice for second-degree murder; if it is not as substantial, the lesser charge of involuntary manslaughter may apply. But it can be hard to distinguish the difference.

For example, the defendant in *United States v. Fleming*, 739 F.2d 945 (4th Cir. 1984), had a blood alcohol level of .315 and drove his car south at speeds between 70 and 100 miles per hour on the George Washington Memorial Parkway in northern Virginia (where the speed limit is at most 45 miles per hour), frequently crossing into the northbound lanes in order to avoid congestion in the southbound lanes. He lost control of the vehicle, crossed into oncoming traffic, and struck another car—which caused the death of the driver of the other car. Affirming a murder conviction under the federal murder statute, 18 U.S.C. § 1111, which requires "malice aforethought," the court stated:

> Malice may be established by evidence of conduct which is "reckless and wanton and a gross deviation from a reasonable standard of care, of such a nature that a jury is warranted in inferring that defendant was aware of a serious risk of death or serious bodily harm." To support a conviction for murder, the government need only have proved that defendant intended to operate his car in the manner in which he did with a heart that was without regard for the life and safety of others. . . .

> The difference between malice, which will support conviction for murder, and gross negligence, which will permit of conviction only for manslaughter, is one of degree rather than kind. . . . In the average drunk driving

homicide, there is no proof that the driver has acted while intoxicated with the purpose of wantonly and intentionally putting the lives of others in danger. . . . In the present case, however, danger did not arise only by defendant's determining to drive while drunk. Rather, in addition to being intoxicated while driving, defendant drove in a manner that could be taken to indicate depraved disregard of human life, *particularly* in light of the fact that *because he was drunk* his reckless behavior was all the more dangerous.

What was it in Fleming's case that led the court to uphold the murder conviction and reject the closely-related offense of involuntary manslaughter, which consists of a "reckless" killing? Is it the dangerousness of the conduct, or Fleming's lengthy persistence in it, or the open flagrantness of it, or the inference that Fleming knew how egregious the risk was?

(4) *How to Explain the Crime to the Jury: Is "Depraved Heart" the Same as "Outrageous Recklessness"?* To some critics, the concept of a "depraved and wicked heart" is a problematic way to define a crime because it gives inadequate guidance to the jury. It is more helpful to instruct the jury as the *Malone* court also defined the crime: "Reckless conduct that results in the death of another is malice." Consider the advantages and disadvantages of both definitions when used before a jury.

(5) *Complaints from Defendants That "Depraved Heart" Instructions Are Arbitrary: Thomas v. State*, 83 P.3d 818 (Nev. 2004). Thomas was sentenced to death for murder after a trial that included a depraved-heart instruction. He argued that such a conviction, on the basis of an instruction that "[m]alice may be implied . . . when all the circumstances of the killing show an abandoned and malignant heart," was "erroneous," because "it uses terms that are archaic, without rational content, and merely pejorative." The court rejected the argument, noting that it had "previously rejected these contentions." But isn't there something to this complaint? Shouldn't murder convictions rest upon more than just an idea of implied malice that turns on interpreting and applying the epithet "depraved"?

Consider whether the next case does a better job with the issues raised in these notes.

People v. Knoller

158 P3d 731 (Cal. 2007)

Kennard, J.

On January 26, 2001, two dogs owned by defendant Marjorie Knoller and her husband, codefendant Robert Noel, attacked and killed Diane Whipple in the hallway of an apartment building in San Francisco. Defendant Knoller was charged with second degree murder and involuntary manslaughter; codefendant Noel, who was not present at the time of the attack on Whipple, was charged with involuntary manslaughter but not murder. Both were also charged with owning a mischievous animal that caused the death of a human being. . . .

[I. Facts and Proceedings]

[Decedent Whipple lived on the sixth floor in the same San Francisco apartment building as defendants Knoller and Noel. Defendants, who were both attorneys, lived and operated their law practice out of their sixth floor, one and one half bedroom apartment, which was down the hallway from Whipple. Defendants brought to their apartment a female Presa Canario named Hera in the spring of 2000. In the fall of that year, defendants brought a male Presa Canario named Bane to their home. The following winter, on January 26, 2001, at about 4:00 p.m., Knoller had taken Bane out of defendants' apartment and was returning to her apartment while Whipple was returning home with groceries. Whipple had unlocked her door, but never made it into her apartment before the Presas attacked her, killing her. What actually occurred was not clear from the record, but the record clearly established that Bane killed Whipple and Hera joined in the attack. The Presas had ripped off all of Whipple's clothing. The hallway carpet was soaked in blood, and streaks of blood covered the walls. Groceries and pieces of Whipple's clothing littered the hallway. Whipple had 77 discrete areas of injury, which covered her body "from head to toe." She died of multiple traumatic injuries and extensive blunt force trauma resulting in a loss of one third of her blood.

[Defendant Knoller denied the dogs had ever given any reason to believe that either posed any danger to any person. But the evidence demonstrated that her testimony was not credible. Literature found in her apartment emphatically described the breed in dangerous terms. The original owner, a friend of the defendants, was a prison inmate and member of the Aryan Brotherhood. He had bred the dogs as "guard dogs" and prevented them from becoming "socialized." The prosecution presented a long list of witnesses who testified to conversations with Knoller about the dogs' dangerousness, events in which the dogs had killed animals, numerous events of aggression toward people by the dogs, and multiple instances of Knoller's and Noel's inability to control them.]

[A] jury convicted defendants on all counts. Both moved for a new trial [The trial court] granted Knoller's motion in part, giving her a new trial on the second degree murder charge, but denying her motion for a new trial on the other two crimes of which she was convicted (involuntary manslaughter and possession of a mischievous animal that causes death).

The Court of Appeal reversed the trial court's order granting Knoller a new trial on the second degree murder charge. . . . [The California Supreme Court then granted Knoller's petition to review her conviction for second-degree murder.] . . .

[W]e reaffirm the test of implied malice we set out in *People v. Phillips* (1966) 64 Cal.2d 574, 414 P.2d 353 and . . . reiterated in many later cases: Malice is implied when the killing is proximately caused by "an act, the natural consequences of which are dangerous to life, which act was deliberately performed by a person who knows that his conduct endangers the life of another and who acts with conscious disregard for life." In short, implied malice requires a defendant's awareness of engaging in conduct that endangers the life of another—no more, and no less.

Measured against that test, it becomes apparent that the Court of Appeal set the bar too low, permitting a conviction of second degree murder, based on a theory of implied malice, if the defendant knew his or her conduct risked causing death or serious bodily injury. But the trial court set the bar too high, ruling that implied malice requires a defendant's awareness that his or her conduct had a high probability of resulting in death. . . . Because the trial court used an incorrect test of implied malice . . . , we conclude that it abused its discretion in granting Knoller a new trial on the second degree murder count. . . .

II. The Elements of Implied Malice

Murder is the unlawful killing of a human being, or a fetus, with malice aforethought. (§ 187, subd. (a).) Malice may be express or implied. (§ 188.) At issue here is the definition of "implied malice."

. . . Second degree murder is the unlawful killing of a human being with malice aforethought but without the additional elements, such as willfulness, premeditation, and deliberation, that would support a conviction of first degree murder. (See §§ 187, subd. (a), 189.) Section 188 provides: "[M]alice may be either express or implied. It is express when there is manifested a deliberate intention to take away the life of a fellow creature. It is implied, when no considerable provocation appears, or when the circumstances attending the killing show an abandoned and malignant heart."

The statutory definition of implied malice, a killing by one with an "abandoned and malignant heart" (§ 188), is far from clear in its meaning. Indeed, an instruction in the statutory language could be misleading, for it "could lead the jury to equate the malignant heart with an evil disposition or a despicable character" instead of focusing on a defendant's awareness of the risk created by his or her behavior. "Two lines of decisions developed, reflecting judicial attempts 'to translate this amorphous anatomical characterization of implied malice into a tangible standard a jury can apply.'" Under both lines of decisions, implied malice requires a defendant's awareness of the risk of death to another.

The earlier of these two lines of decisions . . . originated in Justice Traynor's concurring opinion in *People v. Thomas* (1953) 41 Cal.2d 470, 480, 261 P.2d 1, which stated that malice is implied when "the defendant for a base, antisocial motive and with wanton disregard for human life, does an act that involves a high degree of probability that it will result in death." (We here refer to this as the *Thomas* test.) The later line dates from this court's 1966 decision in *People v. Phillips, supra*: Malice is implied when the killing is proximately caused by "an act, the natural consequences of which are dangerous to life, which act was deliberately performed by a person who knows that his conduct endangers the life of another and who acts with conscious disregard for life." (The *Phillips* test.)

In *People v. Watson* (1981) 30 Cal.3d 290, 300, 637 P.2d 279, we held that these two definitions of implied malice in essence articulated the same standard. Concerned, however, that juries might have difficulty understanding the *Thomas* test's concept of "wanton disregard for human life," we later emphasized that the "better practice in the future is to charge juries solely in the straightforward language of the 'conscious disregard for human life' definition of implied malice," the definition articulated in the Phillips test.

III. The Court of Appeal's Test for Implied Malice

. . . We conclude that a conviction for second degree murder, based on a theory of implied malice, requires proof that a defendant acted with conscious disregard of the danger to human life. In holding that a defendant's conscious disregard of the risk of serious bodily injury suffices to sustain such a conviction, the Court of Appeal erred.

IV. The Trial Court's Grant of a New Trial on the Second Degree Murder Charge

We now turn to the second issue raised by the petition for review—whether the trial court abused its discretion in granting defendant Knoller a new trial on the second degree murder charge. Such an abuse of discretion arises if the trial court based its decision on impermissible factors.

In granting Knoller a new trial, the trial court properly viewed implied malice as requiring a defendant's awareness of the danger that his or her conduct will result in another's death and not merely in serious bodily injury. But the court's ruling was legally flawed in other respects. As we explain below, the trial court based its ruling on an inaccurate definition of implied malice. . . .

Here, the trial court properly instructed the jury in accordance with the *Phillips* test. But when the court evaluated defendant Knoller's new trial motion, it relied on language from the *Thomas* test, and as explained below, its description of that test was inaccurate. The [trial] court stated that a killer acts with implied malice when the killer "*subjectively knows*, based on everything, that the conduct that he or she is about to engage in has a *high probability of death* to another human being" and thus the issue in this case was "whether or not as a *subjective* matter and as a matter of law Ms. Knoller knew that there was a *high probability*" that her conduct would result in someone's death. (Italics added.) But "high probability of death" is the *objective*, not the subjective, component of the *Thomas* test, which asks whether the defendant's act or conduct "involves a high probability that it will result in death." The *subjective* component of the *Thomas* test is whether the defendant acted with "a base, antisocial motive and with wanton disregard for human life." Nor does the *Phillips* test require a defendant's awareness that his or her conduct has a *high probability* of causing death. Rather, it requires only that a defendant acted with a "conscious disregard for human life." . . .

V. Conclusion and Disposition

In sum, the trial court abused its discretion in granting defendant Knoller a new trial on the second degree murder charge. That court erroneously concluded both that Knoller could not be guilty of murder, based on a theory of implied malice, unless she appreciated that her conduct created a high probability of someone's death. . . . It is uncertain whether the trial court would have reached the same result using correct legal standards. Moreover, the Court of Appeal, in reversing the trial court's order, also erred, mistakenly reasoning that implied malice required only a showing that the defendant appreciated the risk of serious bodily injury. Under these circumstances, we conclude that the matter should be returned to the trial court to reconsider its new trial order in light of the views set out in this opinion. [Reversed and remanded.]

Notes and Questions

(1) *"Wanton" Disregard versus "Conscious" Disregard: Are There Really Two Competing Definitions of Implied Malice?* The court points out that some cases imply malice from a "base, antisocial motive . . . with wanton disregard" for life, while others require "conscious disregard for life." Is the law sufficiently clearly defined, if it depends on such terms as "base," "antisocial motive," and "wantonness"? Notice that California courts avoid using these terms in jury instructions. Should judges also avoid basing decisions on these terms, as this court suggests?

(2) *Why Has the Legislature Been Content with the Vague Statutory Language Here, Which Depends Upon Metaphorical Terms Like "Malignant and Abandoned Heart"?* The *Knoller* court criticizes the legislative language, which it calls an "amorphous anatomical metaphor." The language has been in the statute for well over a century, but the legislature has not refined it. The metaphor is so misleading that the court says it should not be told to juries. Thus, the judiciary, the least democratic branch of government, is left not just to interpret the language, but to abandon it and create its own standard — or so one can argue. Has the legislature failed in its duty to define murder? Has it required the courts to go beyond an appropriate judicial role?

(3) *What if the Deceased Actually Consents to Depraved-Heart Treatment by the Defendant? United States v. Williams,* 836 F.3d 1 (D.C. Cir. 2015) (reversing conviction on other grounds). The decedent died as a result of wounds received in a severe beating that was part of an unofficial initiation ritual in the military. When asked whether he wanted to undergo the initiation, the deceased enthusiastically responded, "Hell yeah," and he continued to answer with this phrase throughout. The court held that this consent by the deceased did not prevent the defendant from being convicted of depraved-heart murder. The court held, however, that the consent was evidence to be considered by the jury in deciding whether to find depraved-heart murder. One judge observed that the question whether defendant's actions were murder or (involuntary) manslaughter was a close one.

(4) *The Model Penal Code (and State Laws Based Upon It).* As we shall discuss in the next section of this chapter, the Model Penal Code abolishes the concept of implied malice and defines both murder and manslaughter in terms that arguably are clearer. So do the states that have modeled their laws on the MPC.

(5) *The Distinction in California between Depraved-Heart Murder and Involuntary Manslaughter: It Can Be Defined, but Is It Workable?* The *Knoller* court explains that implied malice for depraved-heart murder requires "subjective" awareness of risk.

Involuntary manslaughter, in California, is different: It does not require actual awareness of risk. Objective gross negligence is enough for the lesser crime of involuntary
manslaughter in California and many other jurisdictions. Thus, the definition seems
clear—in theory. Factually, however, it can be hard to apply. If the defendant drives
with extreme recklessness while intoxicated, for example, it is difficult to say whether
the defendant is subjectively aware of a risk to human life, or is negligent in being
unaware of the risk, under a beyond-a-reasonable-doubt standard. Will it be possible
for jury verdicts based upon this distinction to be consistent?

Notes on Other Kinds of Unintended Malice: Intent to Cause Serious Bodily Injury, Resisting Arrest, and Felony Murder

(1) *Other Kinds of Unintended Malice, in Addition to Depraved Heart Murder:
Serious Bodily Injury, Resisting a Lawful Arrest, and Felony Murder.* The common law
recognized several kinds of implied malice, arising without an intent to kill, in addition to depraved heart malice. If the defendant assaulted the victim *with intent to
cause serious bodily injury*, the common law sometimes implied malice. Some courts
also stated that malice could be inferred if the defendant *resisted a lawful arrest* in
such a way as to kill the arresting officer, even unintentionally. Finally, unintended
killings in the *commission of certain felonies* (the so-called felony murder rule) were
elevated to murder through the device of implied malice. Each of these types of
implied malice is explored below.

(2) *Intent to Cause Serious Bodily Injury.* The common law inferred malice from an
intent to cause serious injury, even if the intention was not to kill. The policy appears
to have been that intending serious injury is culpability enough if death actually
results. Another rationale may also be the recognition that separating out intent to
kill and intent to seriously injure would depreciate many actual murders, without significant gain in crime grading, merely to benefit an accused whose intent was worthy
of severe condemnation anyway *See State v. Jensen*, 236 P.2d 445 (Utah 1951) (large
defendant severely beat small man with fists, after threatening to kill him; murder
could be based either upon intent to kill or "intent to [cause] great bodily harm").

Some jurisdictions have codified this kind of murder in explicit statutes. *E.g.,*
Tex. Penal Code § 19.02(b)(2) (murder includes not only intentional or knowing
killing, but also causing death by "an act clearly dangerous to human life" committed with "intent to cause serious bodily injury"). Other American jurisdictions
refuse to recognize this kind of malice, however, holding that intent to injure cannot suffice for murder; intent to kill is necessary.

(3) *Resisting a Lawful Arrest.* Blackstone wrote that a homicide resulting from
resistance to a lawful arrest was murder on implied malice grounds, even without
an intent to kill. A few American jurisdictions once announced this rule, but none
appears to have retained it today.

(4) *Felony Murder.* Implied malice also arose at common law under some conditions when the defendant killed, even accidentally, while committing a felony. This

category of murder is preserved in most states today, and it is a frequently invoked doctrine. Felony murder is an interesting enough issue to merit its own coverage, and therefore we shall discuss it later in this chapter.

[E] Involuntary Manslaughter and Criminally Negligent Homicide or Recklessness

Notes on Reckless and Negligent Killings

(1) *Involuntary Manslaughter: Recklessness or Its Equivalent.* Under the Pennsylvania approach, unintentional killings less serious than depraved-heart murder can be classified as involuntary manslaughters. This section explores the standards that distinguish involuntary manslaughter and criminally negligent homicide from accidental killings that either are depraved-heart murders or that are not handled by the criminal justice system, but could form the basis for a civil action.

Basically, the cases tend to hold that "recklessness" or its equivalent is the standard for involuntary manslaughter, although some states condition this offense on a mens rea of "criminal negligence" or "gross negligence," perhaps reflecting the early equivalence of the terms "recklessness" and "criminal negligence." The difference between recklessness and criminal negligence depends on proof of an awareness of a risk of causing death.

(2) *Criminally Negligent Homicide: Criminal Negligence.* In addition to involuntary manslaughter, many states define a separate lower level crime of criminally negligent homicide, covering offenses that are criminally "negligent" rather than "reckless." The difference usually depends on the defendant's conscious mental state: recklessness mandates an awareness of an unacceptable risk to human life; negligence involves a lack of awareness in a situation where the defendant "should be aware." Criminal negligence also usually requires greater culpability than civil (tort) negligence: a gross deviation from ordinary conduct. All of these lines are difficult to draw precisely.

(3) *A Classic Example of Involuntary Manslaughter: Commonwealth v. Feinberg,* 253 A.2d 636 (Pa. 1969). Feinberg operated a store in the skid-row section of Philadelphia. One of the products he sold was Sterno, a jelly-like substance composed primarily of methanol and ethanol and designed for cooking. Before September 1963, Sterno contained approximately 3.75% methanol, or wood alcohol, and 71% ethanol, or grain alcohol. Of the two alcohols, methanol is far more toxic if consumed internally. Beginning in September 1963, the Sterno Company began manufacturing a new type of industrial Sterno which was 54% methanol. Between December 21 and December 28, Feinberg sold approximately 400 cans of the new industrial Sterno to individuals that he knew were likely to extract the ethanol and drink it, and he knew that death was likely. Between December 23 and December 30, thirty-one persons died in the skid-row area as a result of methanol poisoning. In many of the cases the source was traced to the new industrial Sterno. Since appellant was the only retail outlet of this type of Sterno in Philadelphia, he

was arrested and convicted on seventeen counts of involuntary manslaughter. The appellate court affirmed:

> [T]o sustain a conviction for [involuntary] manslaughter the Commonwealth must present evidence to prove that the defendant acted in a rash or reckless manner. The conduct of the defendant resulting in the death must be such a departure from the behavior of an ordinary and prudent man as to evidence a disregard of human life or an indifference to the consequences. . . .

> We conclude . . . that the Commonwealth has made out all the elements necessary to warrant a conviction for involuntary manslaughter. First, the record establishes that appellant sold the Sterno with the knowledge that at least some of his customers would extract the alcohol for drinking purposes. . . . Second, appellant was aware, or should have been aware, that the Sterno he was selling was toxic if consumed. The new industrial Sterno was clearly marked as being poisonous. . . . Furthermore, when appellant was informed about the first deaths from methanol poisoning, he told the boy who worked in his shop to tell any police who came around that there was no Sterno in the store. . . .

(4) *In Feinberg's Case, Why Involuntary Manslaughter and Not Second Degree Murder?* The *Feinberg* court finds that the evidence justifies the conclusion that Feinberg acted recklessly. It therefore convicts Feinberg of involuntary manslaughter. But why is Feinberg not guilty of second degree murder, on an implied malice or depraved-heart theory? Can you articulate where the dividing line should be drawn between depraved-heart murder and involuntary manslaughter?

(5) *In Feinberg's Case, Why Involuntary Manslaughter and Not Negligent Homicide?* This distinction can be even more difficult to apply than the division between murder and involuntary manslaughter, especially since some courts use the terms recklessness and gross negligence interchangeably. Is it possible, then, that in a state with both negligent homicide and involuntary manslaughter, Feinberg's crime should be characterized only as negligent homicide? (In some jurisdictions, negligent homicide is not a very serious crime and carries a much lower sentence range.)

And for another example of a case that presents arguments about where these lines should be drawn, consider the following.

Robertson v. Commonwealth
82 S.W.3d 832 (Ky. 2002)

COOPER, JUSTICE.

Michael Partin, a police officer employed by the city of Covington, Kentucky, was killed when he fell through an opening between the roadway and the walkway of the Clay Wade Bailey Bridge and into the Ohio River while in foot pursuit of Appellant Shawnta Robertson. Following a trial by jury in the Kenton Circuit Court, Appellant was convicted of [involuntary] manslaughter in the second degree for wantonly causing Partin's death, KRS 507.040(1), and was sentenced to imprisonment for six years. [We affirm.]

At about 2:00 a.m. on January 4, 1998, Officer Brian Kane of the Kenton County Police Department attempted to arrest Appellant in Covington for possession of marijuana. Appellant broke free of Kane's grasp and began running north on Fourth Street toward the Clay Wade Bailey Bridge which spans the Ohio River between Covington and Cincinnati, Ohio. Kane radioed for assistance and pursued Appellant on foot "at a sprint." When Appellant reached the bridge, he vaulted over the concrete barrier between the roadway and the walkway and began running north on the walkway toward Cincinnati. . . .

Meanwhile, Partin [the deceased] and two other Covington police officers, Steve Sweeney and Cody Stanley, responded to Kane's request for assistance and arrived at the bridge almost simultaneously in three separate vehicles. What was later determined to be Partin's police cruiser proceeded past the point where Appellant was running and stopped. Appellant then also stopped, reversed course, and began running back toward Kane. Kane ordered Appellant to "get down," whereupon, Appellant raised both hands above his head and fell to his knees in apparent submission. . . . Kane thought he saw a shadowy movement or a flash in his peripheral vision. He then heard a voice say that "somebody's off the bridge." . . .

. . . There was a forty-one-inch-wide open space between the concrete barrier and the walkway railing. [It was later determined that Officer Partin had fallen] through the open space into the river ninety-four feet below. His body was recovered four months later.

I. [Manslaughter Evidence Sufficiency]

No one will ever know why Partin fell through the opening between the concrete barrier and the pedestrian walkway. Perhaps, he did not realize the opening was there. Perhaps, he knew it was there and miscalculated his vault. Either way, however, his death resulted from his own volitional act and not from any force employed against him by Appellant. [The Kentucky statutes use the term "wantonly" to cover what usually is called recklessness, and "recklessness" to refer to what most states call "criminal negligence." Here, to avoid confusion, we refer to these concepts as "the Kentucky equivalent of recklessness" and "the Kentucky equivalent of criminal negligence."] Whether Appellant's act of resisting arrest by unlawful flight from apprehension was a legal cause of Partin's death requires application of the provisions of KRS 501.020(3) [definition of the Kentucky equivalent of "recklessness"], KRS 501.020(4) [definition of the Kentucky equivalent of "criminal negligence"], and KRS 501.060 ("causal relationships").

KRS 501.020(3) defines [Kentucky's equivalent of "recklessness"] as follows:

A person acts ["recklessly"] with respect to a result or to a circumstance described by a statute defining an offense *when he is aware of and consciously disregards a substantial and unjustifiable risk* that the result will occur or that the circumstance exists. The risk must be of such nature and degree that disregard thereof constitutes a gross deviation from the standard of conduct that *a reasonable person* would observe in the situation. . . . (Emphasis added.)

KRS 501.020(4) defines [Kentucky's equivalent of "criminal negligence"] as follows:

A person acts [with "criminal negligence"] with respect to a result or to a circumstance described by a statute defining an offense *when he fails to perceive a substantial and unjustifiable risk that the result will occur* or that the circumstance exists. The risk must be of such nature and degree that the failure to perceive it constitutes a gross deviation from the standard of care that *a reasonable person* would observe in the situation. (Emphasis added.)

Thus, [Kentucky's version of "recklessness"] is the awareness of and conscious disregard of a risk that a reasonable person in the same situation would not have disregarded, and [Kentucky's version of "criminal negligence"] is the failure to perceive a risk that a reasonable person in the same situation would have perceived.

KRS 501.060 provides in pertinent part:

(1) Conduct is the cause of a result when it is an antecedent without which the result in question would not have occurred. . . .

(3) [For these "reckless and "criminally negligent" mental states], the [causal] element of the offense . . . is not established if the actual result is *not within the risk of which the actor is aware or, in the case of [criminal negligence], of which he should be aware unless:* . . . (b) The actual result involves the same kind of injury or harm as the probable result and *occurs in a manner which the actor knows or should know is rendered substantially more probable by his conduct.* . . .

Obviously, Appellant's unlawful act of resisting arrest by fleeing from apprehension was a "but for" cause of Partin's fatal attempt to pursue him by vaulting from the roadway of the bridge to the walkway. [T]he issue then becomes primarily one of mens rea. . . .

Thus, the fact that Partin vaulted over the concrete barrier of his own volition does not exonerate Appellant if Partin's act was either foreseen or foreseeable by Appellant as a reasonably probable result of his own unlawful act of resisting arrest by fleeing from apprehension. . . . [I]t is immaterial that it was Partin, as opposed to Kane or one of the other police officers, who fell from the bridge if such was a reasonably foreseeable consequence of the pursuit.

In *Phillips v. Commonwealth*, Ky., 17 S.W.3d 870 (2000), we relied, *inter alia*, on KRS 501.060 in upholding the wanton murder conviction of a defendant who fired shots at an intended victim from inside a vehicle and thereby induced the intended victim to return fire and kill a passenger in the defendant's vehicle. We held that it was reasonably foreseeable that, if shots were fired at another person from inside a vehicle, the other person would return fire in the direction of the vehicle, thus endangering the lives of its other occupants. . . .

Analogous to this set of facts is the case where a person pursued by the police in a high speed motor vehicle chase is held criminally liable for the death of an innocent bystander accidentally struck by a pursuing police vehicle. *E.g., People v. Schmies*, 44 Cal.App.4th 38, 51 Cal.Rptr.2d 185 (1996). [There], the California Court of Appeal directly addressed the effect of the police officers' conduct vis-a-vis the criminal liability of the defendant:

> [T]he negligence or other fault of the officers is not a defense to the charge against defendant.... [T]he "reasonableness" of the officers' conduct, focused upon their point of view and their blameworthiness for the death, is not relevant. *The issue with respect to defendant focuses upon his point of view, that is, whether the harm that occurred was a reasonably foreseeable consequence of his conduct at the time he acted.* Since the officers' conduct was a direct and specific response to defendant's conduct, the claim that their conduct was a superseding cause of the accident can be supported only through a showing that their conduct was so unusual, abnormal, or extraordinary that it could not have been foreseen.
>
> ... The fault or negligence of the officer is not determinative of the defendant's guilt. However, the reasonableness of the officer's response is relevant in determining whether the response was foreseeable by the defendant. The more reasonable the response, the more likely that the defendant should have foreseen it. ...

Here, the conduct that supports Appellant's conviction is not, as the Commonwealth suggests, his own act of vaulting over the concrete barrier. Partin was not present when that act occurred; thus, it was not reasonably foreseeable that he would have vaulted over the barrier in reliance on the fact that Appellant had done so without incident. (That analysis might have been appropriate if Officer Kane had fallen from the bridge when he followed Appellant onto the walkway.) The conduct that supports Appellant's conviction is the continuation of his unlawful flight when he obviously knew that Partin intended to pursue him (as evidenced by the fact that when he saw Partin's vehicle stop, he reversed course and began running in the opposite direction), and that, to do so, Partin would be required to cross the open space between the roadway and the walkway and thereby risk falling to his death.... There was sufficient evidence in this case to present that fact to a jury. [Affirmed.]

Graves, Justice, concurring....

Whether the act of running from an officer when one has been detained, standing alone, if it results in the officer's death, would support a second-degree manslaughter conviction is a question we leave until another day. The act of vaulting the gap between the roadway and the sidewalk is sufficiently wanton to support the jury's verdict in this case. Appellant was aware of the danger of the gap and consciously disregarded it when he jumped. Knowing he was being pursued by at least one officer on foot, Appellant had to assume any pursuing officer would attempt to follow him, also becoming susceptible to the risk. A gap of nearly 4 feet across a drop of 94 feet into moving water cannot be described as anything but a substantial unjustifiable risk. . . .

[The dissenting opinion of Justice Keller is omitted.]

Notes and Questions

(1) *Murder, Involuntary Manslaughter, or Negligent Homicide?: Analyzing The Robertson Case.* The concurring justice points out that Robertson's "wanton [reckless] act" was done with knowledge and disregard of the danger. Doesn't this description make the offense sound like depraved heart murder? On the other hand, maybe Robertson's act was "ordinary" recklessness rather than depraved, so that it was only manslaughter. Or perhaps when Robertson ran away as fast as he could, he was not aware of the risks to a pursuing officer of vaulting the gap. Could his conduct have been merely negligent homicide or even ordinary negligence (and no crime at all)? How can we tell?

(2) *Are Murder, Involuntary Manslaughter, and Negligent Homicide Really a Continuum or Sliding Scale, Rather Than Separate Offenses?* One way to look at these offenses is to see that they shade gradually into each other. The range of human conduct that they encompass is a continuum, from relatively less blameworthy killings to more serious ones, and perhaps the labels simply identify different points on a sliding scale. Perhaps first and second degree murder and voluntary manslaughter, also, are only points on a scale of seriousness. Does this view help to understand the definitions?

(3) *Flaming Discos: What Crime, if Any?* All too frequently, there is a newspaper article regarding a night club fire that results in the death of scores of patrons who cannot escape. (a) Assume that the nightclub owner has been warned of the dangerous conditions but does not take precautions, and a fire breaks out, killing many of his customers. What crime(s) might the owner be guilty of, under what conditions? (b) Alternatively, assume that the nightclub owner has no warning of the dangerous conditions, but a fire breaks out and kills scores of patrons. What crime, if any, might the nightclub owner be guilty of in this situation? Consider the following problem.

STATE v. CARTER, 115 N.E.3d 559 (Mass. App. 2019). Can words alone provide the actus reus of manslaughter? In this strange case, the court said yes. Briefly put, the defendant talked the victim into committing suicide, and the court of appeals upheld a finding of guilt in a bench trial:

> As the victim continued researching suicide methods and sharing his findings with the defendant, the defendant helped plan how, where, and when he would do so, and downplayed his fears about how his suicide would affect his family. She also repeatedly chastised him for his indecision and delay, texting, for example, that he "better not be bull shiting me and saying you're gonna do this and then purposely get caught" and made him "promise" to kill himself. The trial judge found that the defendant's actions . . .

constituted wanton or reckless conduct in serious disregard of the victim's well-being, but that this behavior did not cause his death. This and other evidence, however, informed and instructed the judge about the nature of their relationship and the defendant's understanding of "the feelings that he has exchanged with her—his ambiguities, his fears, his concerns," on the next night.

In the days leading to [the event], the victim continued planning his suicide, including by securing a water pump that he would use to generate carbon monoxide in his closed truck. [On the day of his death,] the victim drove his truck to a local store's parking lot and started the pump. While the pump was operating, filling the truck with carbon monoxide, the defendant and victim were in contact by cell phone. Cell phone records showed that one call of over forty minutes had been placed by the victim to the defendant, and a second call of similar length by the defendant to the victim, during the time when police believe the victim was in his truck committing suicide. There is no contemporaneous record of what the defendant and victim said to each other during those calls[, but there was circumstantial evidence that she continued to urge him to commit suicide until he did, and the trial court convicted the defendant of involuntary manslaughter].

The court of appeals affirmed.

Although we recognize that legal causation in the context of suicide is an incredibly complex inquiry, we conclude that there was sufficient evidence to support a finding of proof of such causation beyond a reasonable doubt in the instant case. The judge could have properly found, based on this evidence, that the vulnerable, confused, mentally ill, eighteen year old victim . . . was badgered back into the gas-infused truck by the defendant, his girlfriend and closest, if not only, confidant in this suicidal planning, the person who had been constantly pressuring him to complete their often discussed plan, fulfill his promise to her, and finally commit suicide. . . . [S]he listened to him choke and die.

Problem 2C (Unintended Homicide Levels): The Thrill-Seeking Skier

(1) *Dangerous Conduct on the Slopes.* Nathan Hall flew off a knoll while skiing and collided with Allen Cobb, who was traversing the slope below. The result was traumatic brain injuries that rapidly killed Cobb. Hall had been drinking, although less than the automatic standard for intoxicated driving. He skied straight down a very steep and bumpy slope, arms to his sides, off balance, thrown from mogul to mogul, at such a high speed that the collision fractured the thickest part of the victim's skull. As an expert skier, he knew how dangerous this conduct was and evidently skied as he did to enhance the thrill. The state has charged Hall with involuntary manslaughter, and the jury has convicted him under instructions requiring a finding that the defendant "consciously disregarded" a "substantial and unjustified

risk" of causing death, constituting a "gross deviation" from ordinary prudence—
in other words, that he acted "recklessly."

(2) *The Meaning of (a) Involuntary Manslaughter; Distinguishing the Crime
from (b) Negligent Homicide, (c) Civil Negligence, or (d) Depraved-Heart Murder.* A
reviewing court must defer to the jury verdict if any reasonable juror could have
reached this decision under a correct application of the law. Given this standard,
consider whether a reviewing court should affirm the conviction for involuntary manslaughter. The defendant, of course, can be expected to argue that his
conduct, at the most, could satisfy only the standard for civil (tort) negligence
(i.e. a deviation (not "gross" deviation) from the standard of a reasonable person),
meaning that he is guilty of no crime at all. As a last resort, the defendant skier
might claim that he is guilty only of the lesser offense of criminally negligent homicide, which requires a gross deviation from ordinary prudence—a higher standard than ordinary negligence—but which allows conviction without awareness
of the risk, without a "conscious disregard," if the defendant "should have been
aware" of the risk.

At some early point in the case, the prosecutor must have faced the question
whether to charge the crime as a depraved-heart second degree murder, involving
not only recklessness but extreme indifference to human life, or whether to charge it
only as involuntary manslaughter. Can you distinguish these crimes, (a) depraved-
heart second-degree murder, (b) involuntary manslaughter, (c) criminally negligent
homicide, and (d) civilly negligent conduct (no crime) in a way that makes sense of
the prosecution of this thrill-seeking skier?

(3) *The Actual Case, which Appears in a More Complete Excerpt in Chapter Three:
People v. Hall*, 999 P.2d 207 (Colo. 2000). The Colorado Supreme Court upheld the
reckless (involuntary) manslaughter charge and remanded for trial. Chapter Three,
which considers mens rea in greater detail, contains a more complete excerpt from
this case, enabling us to study in detail the precise meaning of the term "recklessness." In the meantime, you can see that the hierarchy of offenses forms a kind of
continuum in which the lines blur, and in which it becomes difficult to state with
certainty exactly which offense is proved.

§ 2.04 The Model Penal Code's Homicide Classifications (and Statutes in States Influenced by the MPC)

[A] Homicide under the Model Penal Code

Read MPC §§ 210.1–210.4 [murder, manslaughter, and criminally negligent homi-
cide] in the MPC Appendix.

Notes on Homicide Under the MPC

(1) *No Degrees of Murder under the MPC; Only One Type.* The MPC defines only one crime of murder. It consists of "purposefully" or "knowingly" "causing the death" of "another human being." The MPC rejects some bedrock concepts in the Pennsylvania law by omitting malice, the premeditation-deliberation formula, and the category of second degree murder. Like the more traditional approach, the MPC does impose liability for a category of "accidental" (unintended) murder, committed "recklessly under circumstances manifesting extreme indifference to human life." (This definition corresponds roughly to depraved-heart murder.) Variations in severity of murders are addressed at sentencing.

(2) *Lesser Homicidal Offenses: MPC Manslaughter Includes the Equivalents of Both Voluntary Manslaughter (Passion Killing) and Involuntary Manslaughter (Recklessness).* There also is only one crime of manslaughter under the MPC. It encompasses what would be both voluntary and involuntary manslaughter under the Pennsylvania pattern. First, it covers murder under "extreme mental or emotional disturbance" for which "there is reasonable explanation or excuse." This crime roughly corresponds to the passion-killing definition of voluntary manslaughter under the Pennsylvania pattern, but it is a broader category of killings. Second, manslaughter under the MPC covers "reckless" killings. These "reckless" killings that are merely MPC manslaughter, however, are less culpable than MPC reckless murder, which requires the additional element of "extreme indifference to the value of human life." Manslaughter is a lower-degree felony than murder, with a lower maximum sentence.

(3) *Negligent Homicide under the MPC.* This is still a lesser crime, with a lesser sentence. It is homicide committed with criminal "negligence." Now you should read the MPC provisions.

(4) *Summary of Homicide Under MPC.* Here is a brief outline of homicide under the MPC:

(a) Murder (§ 210.2)

   (i) Intentionally (purposely) or knowingly killing, or

   (ii) Recklessly killing with extreme indifference to the value of life (presumed if engaged in certain serious felonies)

(b) Manslaughter (§ 210.3)

   (i) Recklessly killing, or

   (ii) Killing under influence of extreme mental or emotional disturbance for which there is reasonable explanation or excuse

(c) Negligent Homicide (§ 210.4) — homicide committed with criminal negligence

Notes and Questions

(1) *Why Only One Degree of Murder?: The Vagueness Argument.* By now, one arguable reason for the MPC's policy choice, in creating only one kind of murder,

must be obvious to you. The premeditation-deliberation formula in the Pennsylvania approach leads to seemingly arbitrary decisions as judges apply these terms inconsistently, sometimes using factors that are not in the statutes. And jurors must have even more difficulty when told that "premeditation" is required, but that it can arise "in an instant." Precision in definition is a good thing, provided it targets what is meant to be targeted. Does the MPC avoid a quagmire by having only one degree of murder?

(2) *Why Only One Degree of Murder? The Argument That Some Unpremeditated Homicides Actually Are Worse than Some Premeditated Ones.* But there is more to the MPC's formulation than that. The MPC's drafters decided that the premeditation-deliberation criterion, as the sole determinant of severity, created a false dichotomy. Unexplainable and thoughtless murders were sometimes as morally blameworthy as, or worse than, planned (or premeditated) ones—or so they thought. The MPC drafters' comments give the example of a debtor who, when politely asked to pay an honest debt, instantly grabs a pistol and blows his creditor's brains out. (This homicide might not be premeditated under the Pennsylvania pattern.) Contrast this case to one in which a wife shoots her husband five minutes after an argument (a homicide that a jury might well be permitted to find to be premeditated). The MPC drafters concluded that the premeditation-deliberation pattern might result in backwards results.

Can you answer the drafter's implicit question: Why should the impulsiveness displayed in the first homicide (of the creditor) be considered less blameworthy, and result in a far lesser sentence, than the mental state of the wife in the second killing (of the husband)?

(3) *The Abandonment of "Malice Aforethought."* Under the Pennsylvania pattern, the jury will be told repeatedly that it must find malice aforethought as a requirement for murder. The jury also must be told, however, to ignore the usual meaning of the words "malice" and "aforethought" because they do not mean what they seem to mean. The MPC avoids the term malice, and instead, it defines murder to include "purposeful" and "knowing" killings. Is this language an improvement or does the traditional malice formula have merit in distinguishing the most blameworthy killers?

(4) *Replacing Depraved Heart Murder with "Recklessness" under Conditions of "Extreme Indifference to Human Life."* We have considered depraved-heart murder and asked whether it is wise to make murder depend on this metaphor. Does the MPC formula for unintended murder, depending on "recklessness" under conditions of "extreme indifference to human life," do a better or worse job defining the offense in a way that jurors can apply and that distinguishes the "worst of the worst"?

(5) *"Extreme Mental or Emotional Disturbance" as the Basis of Manslaughter.* Like the Pennsylvania model's creators, the MPC's drafters accepted the concept that some people who kill rashly may be less morally blameworthy and deserve a partial excuse, though not a total acquittal. But instead of the usual passion-killing

formula under the Pennsylvania pattern, the MPC drafters changed the wording and opted for "extreme mental or emotional disturbance" that reasonably "explains or excuses" the homicide. This language arguably expands the traditional voluntary manslaughter conception: the disturbance need not be sudden; no specific provocative act is required; the emotional disturbance doesn't need to have been caused by the deceased; there is no fixed category limitation; words are enough to constitute the emotional disturbance; and there is no cooling off rule.

The most distinctive feature of MPC extreme emotional disturbance is the strongly subjective "person in the actor's situation under the circumstances as he believes them to be" formulation. The MPC Commentary says this doesn't extend to "idiosyncratic moral values." Note too that expert psychiatric evidence is sometimes employed to establish the emotional disturbance, and — perhaps in reaction against the subjective standard — that courts tend to limit the availability of the partial defense by setting a very high hurdle to prove the fact of the emotional disturbance. Is this doctrine a sound one?

(6) *Mental State Definitions.* But even these are not the most significant of the MPC's changes. The drafters carefully (and skillfully, judging from their influence) defined the mental states of "purposefully," "knowingly," "recklessly," and "negligently" — and they limited mens rea elements under the MPC to these four types. The result, they hoped, would be a more functional definition of all crimes, including the homicide offenses.

Read MPC § 2.02 (1)–(2) [defining purposefully, knowingly, recklessly, and negligently] in the MPC Appendix.

Do the MPC definitions of the four types of mens rea result in better definition of the MPC homicidal crimes, and if so, why?

Problem 2D: Applying the MPC to the Cases Earlier in This Chapter

(1) *Reconsider the Intentional Killings in Carroll and Anderson, above, under the MPC.* In the two cases that opened this chapter, Carroll killed his wife in an arguably hastily-formed mental state of intent, and Anderson killed 10-year-old Victoria in a "random, violent, indiscriminate" (but intentional) manner. Under the MPC, both would be guilty of the same offense: murder. Can you explain?

(2) *Reconsider the Intentional Shooting in Avery, which the Defendant Alleged Was Committed under the Influence of Sudden Passion.* In *Avery v. State*, in the voluntary manslaughter section of this chapter, Ms. Avery shot Mr. Paris under circumstances that created fear and resentment, or passion, and the court said the trial judge should have submitted voluntary manslaughter instructions. Under the MPC, would her offense be murder or manslaughter (and if manslaughter, which type)?

(3) *Reconsider the Unintentional Killing in Robertson, Which May Have Involved Indifference, Recklessness, or Negligence.* Robertson was convicted of involuntary manslaughter after he fled, vaulted a dangerous gap, and allegedly caused a pursuing police officer to fall to his death. Under the MPC statutory system considered here, there is no depraved-heart formula, but could Robertson be convicted of murder for "knowingly" causing death? If the jury reasonably doubted whether Robertson "knew" that death was likely, he might still be guilty of reckless manslaughter (as in the actual case) or criminally negligent homicide. Can you explain?

[B] Applying the Model Penal Code's Homicide Provisions
Notes on the MPC's Influence on State Homicide Statutes

(1) *The MPC is an Important Influence on State Criminal Law, Including State Homicide Statutes.* Several states have used the MPC as a basis for drafting their homicide offenses. For example, New Jersey organizes its homicide provisions according to mens rea, and its murder and manslaughter provisions are similar to—but also more detailed than—those of the MPC. *See* N.J. Stat. Ann. § 2C:11–2—11–4. New York uses definitions that are closely related to the MPC's mens rea language, and its homicide provisions display the influence of the MPC. *See* N.Y. Penal Law §§ 15.05, 125.15, 125.20, 125.27.

(2) *But States Also Were Free to Pick and Choose What They Wanted from the MPC.* Some states revised their entire criminal codes in response to the MPC, while many made revisions showing only limited MPC influences, and others ignored the MPC altogether. For example:

(a) *"Intentionally" Rather than "Purposefully."* Many states relied on the MPC's four mens rea categories as well as the link between levels of mens rea and grades of homicide, but they substituted the words "intent" or "intentionally" for "purposefully." See N.Y. Penal Law § 125.27; Or. Rev. Stat. § 163.115(1)(a); Tex. Penal Code § 19.01, 19.02(b)(1).

(b) *"Sudden Passion" Rather than "Extreme Emotional Disturbance."* While a few states chose to adopt the MPC's "extreme mental or emotional disturbance" language, most MPC states retained the traditional provocation or "heat of passion" test. *See, e.g.,* N.J. Stat. § 2C:11–4.

(c) *"Assaultive" Homicide: Intent to Cause Serious Injury.* Unlike the MPC, some jurisdictions retained the common law idea of intent to cause serious injury. *See, e.g.,* N.Y. Penal Law § 125.20(1) (a person who causes death "with intent to cause serious physical injury" is guilty of first degree manslaughter).

(d) *Continuing Evolution.* Finally, even for states that adopted large parts of the MPC, their criminal codes have continued to change over time as the state legislature adds or alters particular statutes, so that the relatively simple offenses derived from the MPC have developed into complex, overlapping, and often confusing modern codes.

(3) *One Degree of Murder—or Two?* Some states have deviated from the MPC by constructing two degrees of murder instead of one. Second degree murder, in these states, has typically been defined by the alternate kind of murder under the MPC: unintentional homicides committed recklessly with "extreme indifference to human life." Other states have only one degree, defined simply as "murder." The following sections of this book will illustrate these differences.

(4) *Elimination of Malice Aforethought, Premeditation, and Deliberation: Instead, "Intent," "Knowledge," "Extreme Indifference," and Similar MPC-Related Terms.* Most importantly, however, you will need to adjust your thinking to consider a system that replaces the traditional system with new terminology. This section involves crimes defined in terms of "intent," "knowledge," "recklessness," "criminal negligence," and other terms. Also, you should be aware that every state places its own interpretations on these terms. Consider the following case.

STATE v. McCOWN, 957 P.2d 401 (Kan. 1998). This case illustrates the change in thinking that the Model Penal Code requires. Defendant was convicted of a version of "intentional" murder under new Kansas statutes, which had been adapted from the MPC. He argued that the jury instructions were erroneous because, like the applicable Kansas homicide statute, they omitted the requirement of malice. The MPC, of course, does not include malice as a requirement, but the defendant argued that it had actually been retained because it was too deeply ingrained in Kansas law to have been tacitly removed by the legislature, even if not mentioned in the statute. "Malice," he asserted, "is so well defined in common law and in Kansas statutory interpretation that legislative silence as to this mental element of malice should not be construed as eliminating malice from the statutory definition of . . . murder."

The court rejected the argument. "Our statute is not silent," said the court. "By express action, the legislature deleted the word 'malicious' from" intentional murder." In fact, the legislative history showed that the legislature, after basing the new definition of murder on the MPC, had explained its deletion of terms such as malice "because they are unnecessary and confusing." The court concluded by saying, "Death of a human being, intent to kill, and causation are the facts that the State is required to prove beyond a reasonable doubt if a person is to be convicted of . . . intentional murder."

[1] MPC Murder and Manslaughter: "Extreme Indifference"
and Negligence

Note on MPC Homicide Laws Using the "Extreme Indifference" Formula

(1) *If Murder Includes "Extreme Indifference," Should There Be One Degree of Murder—or Two?* States vary as to this. One pattern is for state statutes to define first degree murder in terms of "intentional" or "knowing" killings and to define

second-degree murder as killing that involves recklessness with "extreme indiffer-ence to human life." The latter formula, of course, is taken from the MPC, although the MPC does not use it to define second-degree murder because it has only one degree of murder.

Other states follow the MPC more closely, defining only one degree of mur-der but having two or more ways to commit the murder, and some of these states include extreme indifference murder as one method to commit this one degree. The Alaska case below, *Jeffries*, involves two degrees of murder; the Alabama case, *Weems*, involves a pattern that has only one degree.

(2) *How to Distinguish Manslaughter from This Murder Definition.* The distinction between intentional and extreme-indifference murder under the MPC is reasonably well defined by these formulations. However, the distinction between murder and manslaughter becomes blurred, as the next case illustrates. The concept of reck-lessness with "extreme indifference" in murder is different only in degree from the "gross deviation" that defines recklessness, which is the basis of MPC manslaughter.

Jeffries v. State

90 P.3d 185 (Alaska Ct. App. 2004)

This appeal requires us to examine the distinction between two degrees of criminal homicide: manslaughter as defined in AS 11.41.120(a)(1), which requires proof of the defendant's recklessness; and second-degree murder as defined in AS 11.41.110(a)(2), which requires proof of a recklessness so heightened as to constitute "an extreme indifference to the value of human life."

In prior cases, we have upheld second-degree murder convictions for intoxicated drivers who killed other people. But in each of those instances, the defendant drove in ways that were manifestly extremely dangerous (even leaving aside the fact that the defendant's perceptions and reactions were impaired due to intoxication). In the present case, the defendant's physical acts of driving included only one reported lapse: he made a left turn directly in front of an oncoming car.

To prove Jeffries's "extreme indifference to the value of human life", the State relied heavily on evidence that Jeffries had numerous prior convictions for driving while intoxicated, that his license had been revoked for the previous ten years, that he had been drinking all day in violation of the conditions of his probation, and that he had previously refused several times to participate in court-ordered alco-hol treatment programs. On appeal, Jeffries argues that this is an improper way to prove "extreme indifference." He asserts that extreme indifference must be proved solely by the quality of the defendant's conduct during the episode in question.

Jeffries contends that his particular act of careless driving—the dangerous left turn—was not particularly egregious compared to the acts of careless driving that would typically lead to manslaughter convictions. Because Jeffries's physical con-duct involved only a single dangerous left turn, he argues that he should have been convicted only of manslaughter.

[W]e conclude that Jeffries's suggested construction of the second-degree murder statute is too narrow. We have examined court decisions from jurisdictions that (like Alaska) have second-degree murder statutes derived from the Model Penal Code. We have also examined court decisions from jurisdictions that retain a common-law definition of murder—a definition that requires proof of "malice." Both of these groups of jurisdictions have upheld second-degree murder convictions in cases where the government's proof of extreme recklessness rested primarily on an intoxicated driver's persistent recidivism and failures at rehabilitation.

We, too, now hold that "extreme indifference to the value of human life" can be proved in this fashion. . . . We therefore affirm Jeffries's conviction for second degree murder. . . .

Ex Parte Weems

463 So. 2d 170 (Ala. 1984)

FAULKNER, JUSTICE.

We granted certiorari to review the Court of Criminal Appeals' decision affirming petitioner's murder conviction.

On the night of the killing, petitioner, Jared Jerome Weems, had been at a "gambling house" next door to the East North Cafe in Dothan, where he had won about $160.00. While in the house he purchased two cartons of cigarettes. When he left, he encountered a man outside the house who asked him for a pack of cigarettes. When Weems refused, the man slapped him and attempted to cut him with a knife, whereupon Weems fled. Weems had never seen the man before the altercation, but was later told that the man had recently come to Dothan from Florida.

Later that evening Weems returned to the area to retrieve his mother's car, which he had been driving. When he got to the car he discovered that during the course of the evening he had lost the car keys. He surmised that he had probably lost the keys during the altercation with the man from Florida. In an attempt to locate the keys, he decided to go into the East North Cafe to ask if anyone had found them. Fearing the possibility of another encounter with the man from Florida, Weems decided to take into the cafe the gun which his mother kept in the car glove box.

Upon entering the cafe, he surveyed the patrons and determined that the man from Florida was not there. He noticed that a friend of his, Christine Wilson, whom he referred to as "Mama Chris", was at the cafe that night. Weems went over to talk to her. When Weems arrived at the table where Wilson was sitting, he realized that he still had the pistol in his hand. Weems testified that while he was in the process of putting the pistol away, it discharged and hit Ms. Wilson.

Numerous people who were in the cafe at the time of the shooting testified. Their accounts were substantially similar to Weems's and to each other's. . . . [For example, when a witness named] McIntyre heard the shot he looked in that direction and heard Wilson tell Weems, "Mister, you done shot me." McIntyre testified that Weems replied, "Mama Chris, if you are shot let me take you to the hospital." . . .

On appeal, Weems argued that because he did not intend to kill Wilson, his conviction for murder was inappropriate. [In response, the State argued,] "It is uncontradicted that the killing . . . was accidental; nonetheless, ample evidence was produced whereby a jury could easily infer Mr. Weems entered the East North Cafe with a cocked, loaded pistol, intending to shoot someone." . . .

Under Alabama law an accidental killing may support a conviction for murder, manslaughter, or negligent homicide, depending on the circumstances of the case. An accidental death may constitute murder if, "under circumstances manifesting extreme indifference to human life, [the defendant] recklessly engages in conduct which creates a grave risk of death" to the victim and thereby causes the victim's death. Section 13A-6- 2(a)(2); Code 1975. On the other hand, if the defendant's conduct in bringing about the victim's death is simply "reckless," the defendant is guilty of manslaughter. Section 13A-6–3(a)(1). If the death results from "criminal negligence," the defendant is guilty of criminally negligent homicide. Section 13A-6–4(a).

Alabama's homicide statutes were derived from the Model Penal Code. In providing that homicide committed "recklessly under circumstances manifesting extreme indifference to human life" constitutes murder, the drafters of the model code were attempting to define a degree of recklessness "that cannot be fairly distinguished from homicides committed purposely or knowingly." Model Penal Code and Commentaries, § 210.02, Comment, 4 (1980). That standard was designed to encompass the category of murder traditionally referred to as "depraved heart" or "universal malice" killings. . . .

Recklessly causing another's death may give rise to the lesser included offense of manslaughter. A defendant who recklessly causes another's death commits manslaughter if he "consciously disregard[ed] a substantial and unjustifiable risk that his conduct would cause that result." Model Penal Code and Commentaries, § 210.03, Comment 4 (1980). The difference between the circumstances which will support a murder conviction and the degree of risk contemplated by the manslaughter statute is one of degree, not kind. From a comparison of Sections 210.03 and 210.02 of the Model Code, it appears that the degree of recklessness which will support a manslaughter conviction involves a circumstance which is a "gross deviation from the standard of conduct that a law-abiding person would observe in the actor's situation," but is not so high that it cannot be "fairly distinguished from" the mental state required in intentional homicides.

If the homicide is brought about by "criminal negligence," the defendant is guilty of criminally negligent homicide. The essential difference between "recklessness," as that term is used in the murder and manslaughter statutes, and "criminal negligence" is that a reckless defendant is one who has "consciously disregarded" a substantial and unjustifiable risk, whereas a negligent actor needs only to disregard a risk of which he "should have been aware." Model Penal Code and Commentaries § 210.04, Comment 1. In this case there was ample evidence that the defendant consciously disregarded a substantial and unjustifiable risk by carrying the pistol into the cafe. In so doing, Weems committed a "gross deviation" from the standard of conduct which would have been observed by a law-abiding person. . . .

. . . Although Weems was grossly reckless, his disregard for the safety of those around him did not rise to a level of disregard for the value of human life that would be tantamount to proof of an intentional killing. The facts of this case appear to present a clear case of manslaughter. Reversed and remanded.

Notes and Questions

(1) *Unintentional Murder and the Meaning of "Extreme Indifference to the Value of Human Life."* Do you agree with the *Jeffries* court (in the intoxicated driving case) that the defendant exhibited "extreme indifference to the value of human life"? What, if anything, separates Jeffries from the typical drunk driver, or is the point of the case that all drunk drivers are vulnerable to a reckless murder prosecution? Would *Jeffries* come out differently under a "depraved-heart murder" theory?

(2) *Recklessness in Weems.* Does Weems's conduct really show a "conscious disregard of a substantial and unjustifiable risk," or does it show "extreme indifference to the value of human life"?

Changing the facts, what if Assassin was paid to kill Victim, stalked Victim for a month, then killed Victim with a high-powered sniper rifle while Victim jogged. Would Assassin be entitled to a jury charge on reckless manslaughter under the *Weems* logic? In *Howard v. State*, 85 So.3d 1054 (Ala. 2011), the court suggested the answer was "no" because there was no evidence of recklessness by Assassin.

The Model Penal Code Commentaries declare that risk is always "a matter of degree" and that "the motives for risk creation may be infinite in variation." Deciding whether "recklessness is so extreme that it demonstrates [extreme] indifference" to the value of human life "must be left directly to the trier of fact under instructions which make it clear that [a] recklessness that can fairly be [likened] to purpose or knowledge should be treated as murder and that less extreme recklessness should be punished as manslaughter." How helpful are these comments?

(3) *Or, Is Weems Really Guilty Only of Negligent Homicide, Instead? (Or of No Crime at All?).* The court says that Weems's criminal act was "carrying the pistol into the cafe." Was this really a "gross deviation," or the disregard of a "substantial and unjustified risk?" Possibly, the criminal act should have been identified, instead, as the accidental discharge of the pistol. If so, isn't the crime only negligent homicide, and not manslaughter? Or indeed, was the discharge of the pistol only "ordinary negligence," as opposed to criminal negligence (deviation from care of a reasonable person), which requires a "gross deviation" from ordinary care? (In that case, is Weems guilty of any crime at all?)

(4) *The Basic Difficulty: Can We Ever Define Homicides So That They Are Proportionally Graded, but Don't Overlap?* Do you think the real answer, ultimately, is that there is no way to have different homicide levels that grade the crimes proportionally and, at the same time, avoid overlaps and confusion?

(5) *Negligent Homicide Under The MPC: State v. Warden*, 813 P.2d 1146 (Utah 1991). In *Warden*, the court upheld a negligent homicide conviction of a physician for the death of a baby after a home delivery, where the defendant knew the baby had been born prematurely and had symptoms of respiratory distress syndrome but did not inform the family and told them hospitalization was not necessary. The dissent, however, disagreed:

> The Code provisions defining criminal negligence and negligent homicide are taken directly from the Model Penal Code. The commentary to the Model Penal Code states that a primary factor in criminal negligence is the actor's lack of awareness of creation of a risk. . . . The risk created by the inadvertent conduct must be a substantial and unjustifiable risk such that the failure to perceive the risk constitutes a gross deviation from the standard of care that an ordinary person would exercise. . . . Ordinary negligence, which may serve as the basis for damages in a civil action, is "not sufficient to constitute criminal negligence."

The dissent argued that "the criminal law should not be used to punish a physician for a death when he or she makes a decision that turns out to have a fatal consequence, simply because some other physician, acting in more favorable circumstances, would have done differently." Do you agree with this characterization of the case?

[2] Eliminating "Extreme Indifference Murder": Does This Change Make Sense?

Note on State Laws Eliminating "Extreme Indifference" Murder

(1) *Eliminating Extreme Indifference, as Well as Degrees of Murder, to Increase Jury Understanding and Consistency.* By now, you probably have realized that a major criticism of the traditional two-degree, premeditation-deliberation formula for murder is that it is confusing to jurors and creates inconsistency among verdicts and court decisions. Arguably, the MPC improves this situation. But the MPC creates a new problem, because "extreme indifference" murder overlaps the "gross deviation" kind of recklessness that defines manslaughter. The same kind of indeterminacy results, as is shown by the preceding section.

(2) *One Degree of Murder, Defined So That It Is More Readily Distinguishable from Manslaughter: Lay v. State, Below.* The case that follows involves a homicide pattern that eliminates "extreme indifference" altogether. There is only one degree of murder, which does not include extreme indifference. The advantage, arguably, is greater clarity and predictability. But there are critics of this pattern, too. An outrageously reckless homicide, they believe, should qualify as a type of murder, not

as mere manslaughter, and (according to this view) the elimination of extreme-indifference murder leaves a kind of gap. Consider the following case.

Lay v. State

359 S.W.3d 291 (Tex. App. 2012)

Opinion by JUSTICE MOSELEY.

Joshua William Lay did not dispute that he tucked a nine-millimeter pistol into his pocket, pedaled his bicycle to Darryl Dwane Feggett's apartment, and shot Feggett four times, killing him. Rather, he disputed the motives for his actions. A jury convicted Lay of murder and sentenced him to thirty years' imprisonment. On appeal, Lay complains that the evidence was insufficient to establish that he intentionally or knowingly killed Feggett and contends that the trial court erred in refusing to submit instructions to the jury concerning the lesser-included offense of manslaughter. . . . We affirm the judgment of the trial court because we find the evidence sufficient to establish the requisite *mens rea* for murder, [and we] hold the inclusion of [jury instructions about] manslaughter . . . was unwarranted. . . .

[In Texas, there is no first-degree murder and there is no second-degree murder; there is only one degree of murder, as in the MPC. A person commits murder if he or she "intentionally or knowingly causes the death of an individual." The word intentionally is defined in the same way as "purposefully" is defined in the MPC, and the word knowingly is defined in a manner closely similar to the MPC definition.

[Manslaughter is the next homicide crime in this state. A person commits manslaughter if he or she "recklessly" causes the death of an individual. Recklessness, in accordance with the MPC, involves "aware[ness]" of, but "conscious disregard" of, a "substantial and unjustified risk." Together with the lesser crime of criminally negligent homicide, which is not involved in this case, these three offenses make up all of the noncapital homicidal crimes in this state. — Eds.]

I. Sufficient Evidence Established that Lay Intentionally or Knowingly Killed Feggett

. . . Lay contends that the evidence was insufficient to establish the intentional or knowing *mens rea* element of murder. A person acts intentionally, or with intent, with respect to the nature of his conduct or to a result of his conduct when it is his "conscious objective or desire to engage in the conduct or cause the result." Tex. Penal Code Ann. §6.03(a) (West 2011). . . . Intent can be inferred from such circumstantial evidence as the person's acts, words, and conduct because "[o]ne's acts are generally reliable circumstantial evidence of one's intent." . . .

The jury heard that Lay became angry at Feggett. [Witnesses] Davis and Mays both testified that Lay said he was going to kill Feggett. Lay pedaled a bicycle to his home, retrieved a gun, and returned on the bicycle to Feggett's apartment. . . . Smith [a witness] testified the two were just talking when Lay drew his deadly weapon and shot Feggett . . . [W]e find that a rational jury could have found beyond a reasonable doubt that Lay intentionally or knowingly killed Feggett. . . .

II. Trial Court Was Not Required to Submit Manslaughter as a Lesser-Included Offense

Lay argues that the trial court erred in denying his request to include manslaughter in the jury charge as a lesser-included offense. . . . A party is entitled to such a charge when (1) "the offense is a lesser-included offense of the offense charged" in the indictment, and (2) the record includes some evidence to permit a rational jury to find that if the defendant was guilty, he was guilty only of the lesser offense, but not guilty of the greater. . . . Manslaughter is a type of homicide which requires the perpetrator to possess a reckless state of mind which prompts the prohibited act. Tex. Penal Code Ann. § 19.04 (West 2011). A person acts recklessly when he "is aware of, but consciously disregards, a substantial and unjustifiable risk." Tex. Penal Code Ann. § 6.03(c) (West 2011). Manslaughter is a lesser-included offense of murder, [meaning that a charge of murder also charges manslaughter]. Thus, we focus on the second prong of the test.

Lay argues that he did not have the intention to kill Feggett, but that he only "wanted to obtain an apology from" Feggett, and wanted him to "feel what it felt like to be threatened with a deadly weapon."[1] This is the sole evidence that it was not Lay's intention to kill Feggett. "[T]he act of pointing a loaded gun at someone and shooting it toward that person at close range demonstrates an intent to kill." . . . When a deadly weapon per se is used in a deadly manner and death results, there is no need to give a charge of a lesser-included offense. Lay's "denial that he intended to kill the victim does not, of itself, raise the issue of manslaughter." "To raise the issue of manslaughter, there must be evidence of a lack of intent to kill *and* evidence that [the defendant] acted recklessly while ignoring a known risk." . . . [W]e find there was no evidence in the record from which a rational trier of fact could determine that Lay was guilty only of manslaughter. . . . We affirm the trial court's judgment.

Notes and Questions

(1) *What Result in the Drunken Homicide Case Above (Jeffries v. State) if It Were Subject to the Statutes in This Case (Lay v. State): Manslaughter Only?* The one-degree-of-murder pattern in Lay v. State, which is contained in the previous section, does not include "extreme indifference" murder. The system illustrated there

---

1. Lay also argues that the following facts also indicate reckless, rather than intentional or knowing acts: Lay closed his eyes, did not use a high-powered weapon, and was easily identifiable from tattoos and the unique bicycle he rode. He states that "a person who commits a murder might practice using the weapon, use accomplices, shoot witnesses, and have a motorized vehicle available for a quick and inconspicuous escape, or steal one." These facts do not indicate reckless, as opposed to intentional or knowing acts. Rather, they simply emphasize that the murder was not committed by a stealthy criminal.

has murder of the "intentional and knowing" variety. If Jeffries had committed his outrageously reckless, inexcusably drunken crime in Texas, he would be guilty only of manslaughter. Can you explain? (Note that manslaughter in this state carries a maximum sentence of 20 years.)

(2) *What Result in Lay v. State (This Case) if There were Second-Degree "Extreme Indifference" Murder?* The Commentary to the MPC murder statutes says that "extreme indifference" murder is so close to intent that it "cannot be fairly distinguished from [intent.]" Notice that Lay denied an intent to kill; it all happened quickly and thoughtlessly, apparently. If second-degree "extreme indifference" existed, would the trial judge in Lay have been likely to consider submitting second-degree murder to guard against appellate reversal for failing to submit a crime that cannot be fairly distinguished?

(3) *Considering the Homicide Definitions in This State as a System.* Texas has only three noncapital homicide crimes: murder, manslaughter, and criminally negligent homicide. The core definition of each of these crimes is taken from the MPC, but there are variations. One major variation is that there are three different ways to commit murder, only one of which is shown in Lay v. State: the "intentional" or "knowing" kind of murder. There also are an assaultive kind of murder and a version of felony murder (which is treated later in this chapter). Here is a description of noncapital homicides:

(a) *Murder: Tex, Penal Code § 19.02.* Although there is only one degree of murder, there are three ways to commit it:

   (i) *Murder by "Intentionally or Knowingly" Causing Death.* This is the type of murder that is defined in § 19.02(a)(1) and reflected in Lay v. State, above. "Intentionally" means that the defendant "consciously desired" to kill. "Knowingly" means that he was "aware that his conduct was reasonably certain" to cause death.

   (ii) *"Assaultive" Murder.* Texas also defines a crime of murder covering a person who "intends to cause serious bodily injury" and who "commits an act clearly dangerous to human life" that causes death. § 19.02(a)(2). Intent to cause "serious" bodily injury is defined so that only a very serious assault qualifies. It requires an intent to cause the "loss of a bodily member or organ," or protracted loss of use. This is sometimes called "maiming" or "mayhem." For instance, imagine that the defendant beats the victim very severely, intending only to maim, but the defendant overdoes it, and the victim dies. This intent-to-cause-serious-injury definition of murder is not part of the MPC, but it has a long pedigree. Recall that the Pennsylvania model included a species of murder committed by assault that was not intended to kill, only to injure seriously.

(iii) *Certain Murders Connected with Commission of Felonies.* Section 19.02(a)(3) covers certain felony murders. We address felony murder later in this chapter.

(b) *Manslaughter: Tex. Penal Code § 19.04.* This is the other crime considered in Lay v. State, requiring a "reckless" state of mind. A person acts recklessly if he or she is "aware of but consciously disregards" the risk.

(c) *Criminally Negligent Homicide: § 19.05.* For this crime, the defendant need not be aware of anything. Mere inadvertence can be sufficient. But ordinary negligence of the kind that creates civil liability is not enough; instead, following the MPC, the negligence must be a "gross deviation from the standard of care that a reasonable person would exercise." Negligence of an ordinary kind, then, makes one liable for damages in a civil suit, but not for criminal conviction.

(4) *But . . . Texas Doesn't Have Voluntary Manslaughter, So How Does It Treat Passion Killings?* Texas once had a crime of voluntary manslaughter, consisting of an intentional killing motivated by a "sudden passion," but the Texas legislature abolished this crime. Does this mean that passion killings are not recognized? No. Texas replaced the crime of voluntary manslaughter with a system that amounts to the same thing as voluntary manslaughter, under a different name. An intentional killing is murder, even if it is committed under passion circumstances. But if the defendant proves by a preponderance of evidence that the killing was committed under a "sudden passion arising from an adequate cause," the sentence is reduced to a maximum of 20 years.

This statute arguably preserves the basic concept of passion killing under traditional concepts. But it labels the crime as murder. A passion killing is intentional, like other murders; it is not accidental. (Does this characterization of the crime make sense?) The burden of establishing the basis for the sentence reduction is on the defendant, who must convince the jury by a preponderance of the evidence that the killing was motivated by a sudden passion arising from an adequate cause. The defendant is the person who best knows his own motivation, and often the defendant is the only witness to the crime. Does this treatment of the burden of proof make sense?

(5) *Should Lay's Jury Have Had the Option of Finding a Passion Killing, and Should the Jury Have Reduced His Sentence?* The circumstances relevant to the crime of murder in Lay v. State are all in the excerpt of the opinion printed above, but those are not all of the facts. There were other facts giving rise to a possible inference of a passion killing. Specifically, the victim, Feggett, had invited the defendant, Lay, to a cookout, and Lay had given Feggett a hundred-dollar bill for groceries. But "[w]hen Lay went to Feggett's apartment to attend the cookout, he discovered that Feggett had lied—there was no cookout. . . . Feggett (who, unbeknownst to Lay, was a drug addict) refused to return the money, . . . held a knife to Lay's throat, and demanded

that Lay leave." That was when Lay pedaled back to his apartment and retrieved his gun.

Might not these circumstances create a "sudden passion arising from an adequate cause"? If so, Lay's maximum sentence should have been 20 years—but the jury sentenced him to 30 years, instead. Did the jury simply find against the defendant, decide that Lay had not proved that he was acting under a "sudden passion arising from an adequate cause," and therefore properly disregard the 20-year maximum?

[3] Intentional but Mitigated Killings under MPC-Influenced Statutes: Comparing the "Sudden Passion" and "Extreme Emotional Disturbance" Formulas

Notes on Alternative Formulas for Mitigation

(1) *Comparing "Sudden Passion" Homicides to Killings with "Extreme Emotional Disturbance."* As we have already seen, the common law defined the crime of voluntary manslaughter as a means of mitigating the sanction for killings that occurred under the influence of passion. The prototypical example is a case in which a spouse kills an interloper who has just had sexual relations with the other spouse. The common law formulation for voluntary manslaughter required provocation of a kind that would impair the judgment of a reasonable or average person, and it required that the killing occur without much time for reflection, so that it was the product of sudden passion.

More recently, however, the states have adopted several kinds of legislative alterations to the "sudden passion" formula. The biggest departure, probably, is to be found in such states as New York and Oregon, which have adopted the Model Penal Code formula. The MPC defines voluntary manslaughter as a homicide committed under "extreme emotional disturbance." Other states have retained the sudden passion formula, but many have changed or refined it by altering the burden of proof, defining the key terms more carefully, or abolishing voluntary manslaughter as a separate crime and finding another way to express the mitigation concept.

(2) *Retaining the Traditional Mitigation Idea, but Changing It by Placing the Burden of Proof on the Defendant.* Some states, including both sudden-passion states and states that use the emotional disturbance formula, have changed the traditional approach by placing the burden of proof on the defendant. The reason probably is that mitigation should be confined to cases in which the defendant can convincingly justify it, together with a policy recognizing that the defendant is the party with the most complete access to the facts giving rise to the passion or disturbance.

(3) *Changing or Abolishing the Crime of Voluntary Manslaughter while Preserving the Mitigation Principle.* Another idea is to abolish the separate crime of voluntary manslaughter altogether, but to keep the mitigation principle by shortening the sentence, an approach represented in the Texas statute discussed above.

Notes on the Model Penal Code Alternative for Mitigation: "Extreme Mental or Emotional Disturbance"

(1) *Dissatisfaction with the "Sudden Passion" Formula.* The traditional formula limits mitigation to passion that is "sudden." A person who kills immediately after a provocation thus can qualify, but someone who broods about it for a day or so with rising anger before killing perhaps cannot, depending on the jurisdiction, even though it might seem that both reactions are understandable. Furthermore, the traditional formula requires an active provocation that qualifies as "adequate cause." This limit may seem to confine the mitigation principle too severely. Only provocation that would affect average people qualifies. Therefore, the Model Penal Code adopted a different approach.

(2) *The Model Penal Code: "Extreme Mental or Emotional Disturbance" ("EED"), Reflecting "Reasonableness."* The MPC replaces the sudden passion formula with a test of "extreme mental or emotional disturbance ["EED"] for which there is reasonable explanation or excuse." A killing under these circumstances is reduced to manslaughter. There is no time limit or requirement of suddenness; instead, the act may qualify even if it occurs after a long time of brooding. There also is no requirement of a specific kind of provocation. The drafters intended to broaden the availability of the mitigation principle. The principal limit outside of the required disturbance is an element of "reasonableness."

(3) *Dissatisfaction with the MPC's "EED" Formula.* But the EED formula has itself produced dissatisfaction among some critics. The idea of a "disturbed" mind is less precise than the concept of sudden passion, and one can argue that it is too amorphous. Also, a limit of "reasonableness" is likely to produce some results that seem arbitrary, because arguably, no homicide is a "reasonable" response to emotional disturbance. Thus, some states that have modeled their homicide statutes on the MPC have nonetheless retained provocation or sudden passion. You will have to consider the materials that follow and judge for yourself.

People v. Casassa
404 N.E.2d 1310 (N.Y. 1980)

Reaffirmed, People v. Paul
137 A.D.3d 1169 (N.Y. App. 2016)

JASEN, JUDGE.

The significant issue on this appeal is whether the defendant, in a murder prosecution, established the affirmative defense of "extreme emotional disturbance" which would have reduced the crime to manslaughter in the first degree.

On February 28, 1977, Victoria Lo Consolo was brutally murdered. Defendant Victor Casassa and Miss Lo Consolo had been acquainted for some time prior to the latter's tragic death. They met in August, 1976 as a result of their residence in the same apartment complex. Shortly thereafter, defendant asked Miss Lo Consolo to accompany him to a social function and she agreed. The two apparently dated casually on other occasions until November, 1976 when Miss Lo Consolo informed defendant that she was not "falling in love" with him. Defendant claims that Miss Lo Consolo's candid statement of her feelings "devastated him."

Miss Lo Consolo's rejection of defendant's advances also precipitated a bizarre series of actions on the part of defendant which, he asserts, demonstrate the existence of extreme emotional disturbance upon which he predicates his affirmative defense. Defendant, aware that Miss Lo Consolo maintained social relationships with others, broke into the apartment below Miss Lo Consolo's on several occasions to eavesdrop. These eavesdropping sessions allegedly caused him to be under great emotional stress. Thereafter, on one occasion, he broke into Miss Lo Consolo's apartment while she was out. Defendant took nothing, but, instead, observed the apartment, disrobed and lay for a time in Miss Lo Consolo's bed. During this break-in, defendant was armed with a knife which, he later told police, he carried "because he knew that he was either going to hurt Victoria or Victoria was going to cause him to commit suicide."

Defendant's final visit to his victim's apartment occurred on February 28, 1977. Defendant brought several bottles of wine and liquor with him to offer as a gift. Upon Miss Lo Consolo's rejection of this offering, defendant produced a steak knife which he had brought with him, stabbed Miss Lo Consolo several times in the throat, dragged her body to the bathroom and submerged it in a bathtub full of water to "make sure she was dead." . . .

[D]efendant was indicted and charged with murder in the second degree. . . .

. . . The sole issue presented to the trial court was whether the defendant, at the time of the killing, had acted under the influence of "extreme emotional disturbance." (Penal Law, § 125.25, subd. 1, par. (a).) The defense presented only one witness, a psychiatrist, who testified, in essence, that the defendant had become obsessed with Miss Lo Consolo and that the course which their relationship had taken, combined with several personality attributes peculiar to defendant, caused him to be under the influence of extreme emotional disturbance at the time of the killing.

[A government rebuttal witness, a psychiatrist, testified that although the defendant was emotionally disturbed, he was not under the influence of "extreme emotional disturbance"] because his disturbed state was not the product of external factors but rather was "a stress he created from within himself, dealing mostly with a fantasy, a refusal to accept the reality of the situation."

The trial court in resolving this issue noted that the affirmative defense of extreme emotional disturbance may be based upon a series of events, rather than a single precipitating cause. In order to be entitled to the defense, the court held, a defendant must show that his reaction to such events was reasonable. . . . [T]he trial court found defendant guilty of the crime of murder in the second degree. The Appellate Division affirmed.

. . . Defendant asserts that by refusing to apply a wholly subjective standard the trial court misconstrued section 125.25. We cannot agree.

Section 125.25 of the Penal Law provides that it is an affirmative defense to the crime of murder in the second degree where "[t]he defendant acted under the influence of extreme emotional disturbance for which there was a reasonable explanation or excuse." This defense allows a defendant charged with the commission of acts which would otherwise constitute murder to demonstrate the existence of mitigating factors which indicate that, although he is not free from responsibility for his crime, he ought to be punished less severely by reducing the crime upon conviction to manslaughter in the first degree.

In enacting section 125.25, the Legislature adopted the language of the manslaughter provisions of the Model Penal Code. The only substantial distinction between the New York statute and the Model Penal Code is the designation by the Legislature of "extreme emotional disturbance" as an "affirmative defense," thus placing the burden of proof on this issue upon defendant. . . . However, the new formulation is significantly broader in scope than the "heat of passion" doctrine which it replaced.

For example, the "heat of passion" doctrine required that a defendant's action be undertaken as a response to some provocation which prevented him from reflecting upon his actions. (See, e.g., People v. Ferraro, 161 N.Y. 365, 375, 55 N.E. 931.) Moreover, such reaction had to be immediate. The existence of a "cooling off" period completely negated any mitigating effect which the provocation might otherwise have had. In Patterson, however, this court recognized that "(a)n action influenced by an extreme emotional disturbance is not one that is necessarily so spontaneously undertaken. Rather, it may be that a significant mental trauma has affected a defendant's mind for a substantial period of time, simmering in the unknowing subconscious and then inexplicably coming to the fore." . . .

[The thrust of defendant's claim, concerns . . . whether] the standard by which the reasonableness of defendant's emotional reaction is to be tested must be an entirely subjective one. The court rejects this interpretation.] Consideration of the Comments to the Model Penal Code, from which the New York statute was drawn, is instructive. The defense of "extreme emotional disturbance" has two principal components: (1) the particular defendant must have "acted under the influence of extreme emotional disturbance", and (2) there must have been "a reasonable explanation or excuse" for such extreme emotional disturbance, "the reasonableness of which is to be determined from the viewpoint of a person in the defendant's situation under the circumstances as the defendant believed them to be." The first requirement is wholly subjective, i.e., it involves a determination that the particular defendant did in fact act under extreme emotional disturbance. . . .

The second component is more difficult to describe, i.e., whether there was a reasonable explanation or excuse for the emotional disturbance. . . . "The ultimate test . . . is objective; there must be 'reasonable' explanation or excuse for the actor's disturbance." In light of these comments and the necessity of articulating the defense in terms comprehensible to jurors, we conclude that the determination whether there was reasonable explanation or excuse for a particular emotional disturbance should be made by viewing the subjective, internal situation in which the defendant found himself and the external circumstances as he perceived them at the time, however inaccurate that perception may have been, and assessing from that standpoint whether the explanation or excuse for his emotional disturbance was reasonable. . . . We recognize that even such a description of the defense provides no precise guidelines and necessarily leaves room for the exercise of judgmental evaluation by the jury. This, however, appears to have been the intent of the draftsmen. "The purpose was explicitly to give full scope to what amounts to a plea in mitigation based upon a mental or emotional trauma of significant dimensions, with the jury asked to show whatever empathy it can."

By suggesting a standard of evaluation which contains both subjective and objective elements, we believe that the drafters of the code adequately achieved their dual goals of broadening the "heat of passion" doctrine to apply to a wider range of circumstances while retaining some element of objectivity in the process. . . . In the end, we believe that what the Legislature intended in enacting the statute was to allow the finder of fact the discretionary power to mitigate the penalty when presented with a situation which, under the circumstances, appears to them to have caused an understandable weakness in one of their fellows. . . .

We conclude that the trial court, in this case, properly applied the statute. . . . The court obviously made a sincere effort to understand defendant's "situation" and "the circumstances as defendant believed them to be," but concluded that the murder in this case was the result of defendant's malevolence rather than an understandable human response deserving of mercy. We cannot say, as a matter of law, that the court erred in so concluding. Indeed, to do so would subvert the purpose of the statute. . . . [Order affirmed.]

Notes and Questions

(1) *Isn't the Court's "Malevolence" Reasoning Arbitrary?* The court upholds the trial judge's finding that Casassa acted out of "malevolence" rather than "reasonableness." But doesn't this approach contain a contradiction that the court failed to acknowledge? Almost every passion killing is "malevolent." Doesn't the most traditional kind of passion killing, in response to a spouse's sexual escapade, involve anger toward the person killed? And therefore, doesn't it also involve "malevolence"? Thus, the distinction drawn by the court may provide no distinction at all, and it may produce arbitrary results.

In fact, is the idea of a "reasonable explanation or excuse" inconsistent, perhaps, with the idea of a response induced by an "extreme emotional disturbance," at least in practical terms? The court does not clearly disagree, for it says that "reasonable-ness" is "difficult to describe" in this context.

(2) *Is It a Good Thing for the Factfinder to Have "Discretionary Power" When the Discretion Is Restrained Only by Such a Vague Standard?* The court's opinion can be read as allowing the mitigation principle for defendants whom the factfinder sees as having engaged in "understandable human response[s]" while denying mitigation to defendants whom the factfinder does not "understand" as "deserving of mercy." Could the vague legal standard for EED, which the court describes as providing "no precise guidelines," effectively authorize the factfinder to exercise "discretion" that disfavors a defendant whose lifestyle, beliefs, politics, religion, or ethnicity it does not "understand"?

Oregon—which also uses the EED formula—has adopted different wording from New York for jury instructions. *See State v. Ott*, 686 P.2d 1001 (Ore. 1984). There, the court outlined a five-part instruction, which concludes, "Fifth, the jury must determine . . . the defendant's situation in the circumstances which the defendant reasonably believed to exist. The jury must then determine whether an ordinary person in that situation and those circumstances would have experienced extreme emotional disturbance." Does this difference in wording make a difference in meaning?

(3) *In Some States, Characteristics of Defendant Such as Depression Can Justify EED: State v. Craigen,* 439 P.3d 1048 (Ore. App. 2019). This Oregon court held that defendant's depression and brain injury constituted evidence of defendant's situa-tion, and could be considered for purposes of the extreme emotional disturbance (EED) defense.

(4) *Reconsidering the Example of Sirhan Sirhan.* In § 2.04[C], we considered the case of Sirhan Sirhan. The defendant was convicted of the murder of Presidential candidate Robert F. Kennedy. He explained that he acted because he believed that Kennedy had worsened the plight of dispossessed Palestinian refugees. Sirhan prob-ably suffered "extreme emotional disturbance," and it seems "reasonable" to be deeply troubled by the situation of the Palestinian people, especially if one adopts Sirhan's beliefs and perceptions. Would Sirhan qualify for mitigation under an EED statute, then? Should he? And if he does not, even under an EED statute, is the con-clusion based upon Sirhan's beliefs, politics, or ethnicity? In the real case, this issue did not arise, because the jurisdiction in question—California—does not follow EED, but uses the passion formula.

(5) *But Is EED Arguably Better Than the Passion Formula because It Avoids the "Suddenness" Requirement?* Imagine two homicides that are closely similar, except that one involves immediate reflexive action in response to a devastating provoca-tion, whereas the other involves a killing after twenty-four hours of brooding, with rising emotions, over a similarly devastating provocation. Isn't the conduct of both actors equally understandable in human terms? But although the EED formula

would allow mitigation, the sudden passion approach would not. Is the EED formula superior in this respect?

§ 2.05 The Felony Murder Rule

Notes on the History, Function, and Limits of the Felony-Murder Rule

(1) *The Common Law Imputation of Malice to a Death Caused in the Course of Commission of a Felony.* The common law imputed malice to a killing during a felony. Even an accidental death could be murder under this rule. The theory was that the felony (often called the "predicate felony") supplied the ingredient of malice, much as a depraved heart could elevate an unintended killing to murder. The prototypical example is the defendant who shoots a store clerk during a robbery and later testifies that the gun discharged accidentally. The felony murder rule, if applied to this situation, is tantamount to a decision that for purposes of defining murder it does not matter whether the killing was accidental.

(2) *Limiting the Rule: Dangerous Felony, Dangerous Act, Merger, Causation, Etc.* Many jurisdictions limit the scope of this doctrine so that the rule is not applied every time a homicide results from a felony. For example, consider a defendant who has the bad luck of spilling liquid on the floor while reaching to open an unattended cash register. The thief does not intend to harm anyone, but a bystander sees the crime, tries to run away, slips on the liquid, hits his or her head, and dies. For many people, it would seem unfair to hold this defendant guilty of murder, and in fact the limits described below would avoid this anomalous result. The limits include:

(a) *The "Inherently Dangerous Felony" Approach.* Some states (*e.g.,* California) require that the underlying felony be "inherently dangerous." It is the felony's dangerousness in the abstract (often assessed by looking at the statutory elements of the crime rather than the facts of the particular crime) that controls, not any particular act of the defendant in the individual case. This rule requires the courts to look at the elements of each crime and determine which are dangerous enough to elevate a killing to murder. It is not always apparent from the crime elements what felonies are inherently dangerous. For example, is drug dealing an inherently dangerous offense? How about escaping from prison? In the abstract, there are plenty of ways that each of these crimes can be committed without anyone being injured.

(b) *The Dangerous Act Approach.* A very different approach is to require independent proof that this individual defendant performed some act "dangerous to human life" during commission of the felony. This approach does not look to the abstract dangerousness of the felony. Instead, it focuses on the defendant's conduct in the particular case. For example, consider a case where a doctor defrauds a family out of money by pretending to treat a child, but without treating the child, who dies because of the doctor's neglect. Although the underlying felony of fraud is not inherently dangerous in the abstract, this conduct might become felony murder under the "dangerous act" approach.

Notice that either of these "dangerousness" limits (the dangerous felony approach or the dangerous act approach) would prevent the felony murder rule from being applied to our hypothetical thief, above. Theft is not an "inherently dangerous" felony in the abstract, and spilling liquid is not an act normally "dangerous to human life."

(c) *Merger: Lesser Included Crimes Cannot Become Predicate Felonies.* Most states exclude lesser degrees of homicide as predicate felonies, such as voluntary or involuntary manslaughter. Otherwise, every unlawful killing would become a murder. There would be no more manslaughter, because every manslaughter would be automatically elevated to murder, since manslaughter involves an underlying felony (manslaughter) that results in a death. The common law "merger" doctrine prevented lesser homicides from serving as predicate felonies. For related reasons, some jurisdictions do not permit assaults to become the basis of felony murder, and some courts have held that burglary with intent to commit assault also does not suffice. The theory is that the legislature did not intend for these felonies to elevate the resulting homicide to a murder.

(d) *Causation.* The felony murder rule requires proof that the felony or the defendant's conduct "caused" the death. Causation limits the application of the rule. Some states measure causation by applying broad causation of the "but-for" variety. Others limit it by "proximate" causation, requiring that there be a foreseeable link between the conduct and the killing. In fact, reconsider again the case mentioned above of the thief who spills liquid, with the result that someone slips, suffers a head injury, and dies. Not only would the "dangerousness" requirement fail, but proximate causation would also be absent in this case because the death was not foreseeable, meaning that the felony-murder rule would not apply. This result is sensible to most people, and thus causation is an important limit on the doctrine.

(e) *In Furtherance Requirements and Res Gestae.* Courts often hold that the act causing death must have been "in furtherance" of the felony. Thus, the hypothetical thief who spills liquid that causes a person to slip and hit his head may not be murder, because the act was not "in furtherance of" the felony of theft.

As a related concept, some courts have held that the death must take place within the *res gestae* of the felony, that is, the felony and the killing must be "closely connected in point of time, place, and causal relation." Thus for the death to be the basis of a felony murder conviction, it must be *caused* by the felony, as indicated in note (d), above; and the conduct which caused the death, which might *occur* sometime later, must occur during the time-span of the felony, and within the *vicinity* of the felony.

(3) *Should the Felony Murder Rule Be Abolished?* The Model Penal Code purports to abolish felony murder. The MPC's broad definition of murder includes reckless killings committed with extreme indifference to human life, and the drafters decided that it was inappropriate to convict for murder on a lesser mental degree of fault. The MPC does contain a "presumption" of extreme indifference, sufficient for murder, in the case of some violent felonies, but it preserves the question as a jury issue, and the presumption is rebuttable. As we shall see, however, there are arguments both for and against the MPC position, and most states, unlike the MPC, have retained the felony murder rule.

Statutes Governing Felony Murder

Read MPC § 210.02 (1)(b), second sentence, in the MPC Appendix, below ["presuming" recklessness and indifference sufficient to constitute murder if the actor is engaged in any one of seven identified felonies of violence]. (You cannot be directed to the MPC felony murder rule, because the MPC does not contain one. Therefore, consider the following alternatives.)

California Penal Code § 187. Murder is the unlawful killing of a human being, or a fetus, with malice aforethought. [You already have read this provision. Since "malice aforethought" historically included homicides during felonies, this phrase imported into California law the common law felony murder rule, *see People v. Chun*, 203 P.3d 425 (Cal. 2009), which California has limited by judicial decisions requiring an "inherently dangerous felony," as well as by merger and causation restrictions.]

Texas Penal Code § 19.02(b)(3). A person commits [murder] if he: . . . . (3) commits or attempts to commit a felony, other than manslaughter, and in the course of and in furtherance of the commission or attempt, or in immediate flight from the commission or attempt, he commits or attempts to commit an act clearly dangerous to human life that causes the death of an individual. [This provision uses a "dangerous act" requirement, rather than California's "inherently dangerous felony" approach.]

[A] The Felony Murder Rule in Practice: Its Definition and Its Limits

[1] Does the Rule Require an "Inherently Dangerous Felony in the Abstract" — or a "Dangerous Act" by This Individual Defendant?

State v. Anderson
654 N.W.2d 367 (Minn. 2003)

BLATZ, CHIEF JUSTICE.

In this pretrial appeal, appellant Jerrett Lee Anderson challenges the court of appeals' decision reversing the district court's dismissal of the charge of unintentional second-degree felony murder for lack of probable cause. . . . We agree and hold that the predicate offenses of felon in possession of a firearm and possession of a stolen firearm cannot support the charge of unintentional second-degree felony murder.

The facts giving rise to this appeal are not in dispute. On February 26, 2002, Jerrett Lee Anderson arrived at Blake Rogers' residence in Minneapolis and, at about 10:45 p.m., joined Rogers and a friend of Rogers in Rogers' bedroom. While there, Anderson showed them a 12-gauge shotgun, which was missing its rifle stock, and stated that the shotgun had been stolen. Rogers' friend handled the shotgun, and all three noticed that the shotgun was loaded. As the shotgun was returned to Anderson, Rogers was kneeling in front of his stereo system, inserting compact discs. Anderson then pointed the shotgun at Rogers, and it discharged, killing Rogers. Anderson and Rogers' friend fled the residence.

Anderson was charged with second-degree unintentional felony murder and third-degree murder ("depraved mind" killing). The district court dismissed the second-degree felony-murder charge, ruling that felon in possession of a firearm and possession of a stolen firearm are not proper predicate offenses for second-degree felony murder.

The state appealed. . . . In a 2–1 decision, the court of appeals concluded that possession of a loaded, stockless shotgun pointed at the victim was inherently dangerous. Accordingly, the court of appeals held that the district court erred in dismissing the second-degree felony-murder charge. The dissenting judge argued that there is nothing inherently dangerous about the two predicate unlawful firearm possession offenses. Viewing the majority holding as an unwarranted extension of the felony-murder doctrine to "status" offenses, the dissenting judge explained that she "would [have affirmed] the trial court's pretrial order dismissing the unintentional murder in the second-degree (felony-murder) charge on the grounds that the 'status' offenses of unlawful possession of a firearm and possession of a stolen firearm cannot serve as predicate offenses to felony-murder." [Anderson appeals.]

The single issue presented by this case is whether the offenses of felon in possession of a firearm and possession of a stolen firearm are proper predicate offenses for a charge of unintentional second-degree felony murder. . . .

[The two applicable predicate felony statutes make it a felony for a (1) person who has been adjudicated guilty of a crime of violence to possess a firearm and (2) for a person to possess a stolen firearm. It is clear that Anderson has violated both of these felonies. The second-degree felony-murder statute, under which Anderson was charged, covers a person who "causes the death of a human being, without intent to effect the death of any person, while committing or attempting to commit a felony offense" other than a short list of excluded felonies.] This statutory provision does not define what constitutes "a felony offense."

To understand the felony-murder statute, it is helpful to review the historical backdrop surrounding its enactment as well as our case law. To begin, Minnesota's second-degree felony-murder statute codifies the common law felony-murder rule. . . . Viewed in historical context, the common law felony-murder rule, though stated broadly, was limited in scope and consequence because there were few felonies[4] at common law — all were *mala in se*[5] and most were life-endangering — and because all were punishable by death. As a result, application of the felony-murder rule at common law was consistent with the requirement of mens rea because the malice required for murder could be imputed from the wrongful mental attitude for the predicate felony, and "it made little difference whether the felon was hanged for the felony or for the murder."

More recently, because the number of felonies has increased and many comparatively minor offenses are classified as felonies, malice is imputed from crimes that are much less severe than murder. For this reason, many courts have judicially limited the application of the doctrine so that not every felony offense serves as a predicate felony for a felony-murder charge.

In Minnesota, prior to 1981, predicate felonies for felony murder were those felonies "committed upon or affecting the person whose death was caused." This language limited the application of the felony-murder statute so that "a purely property crime would not fall within the clause [as a proper predicate felony]. [Court decisions interpreted the language as requiring courts to "determine whether an offense involved a special danger to human life by examining the offense in the abstract together with the facts of the particular case, including the circumstances in which the felony was committed."]

---

4. The felonies that traditionally supported a felony-murder conviction were: "homicide, mayhem, rape, arson, robbery, burglary, larceny, prison breach, and rescue of a felon." *State v. Aarsvold*, 376 N.W.2d 518, 521 (Minn.App.1985).

5. *Malum in se* means "a wrong in itself[.] * * * An act is said to be *malum in se* when it is inherently and essentially evil, that is, immoral in its nature and injurious in its consequences, without any regard to the fact of its being noticed or punished by the law of the state." *Black's Law Dictionary* 959 (6th ed. 1990). In comparison, *malum prohibitum* means "a thing which is wrong because [it is] prohibited; an act which is not inherently immoral, but becomes so because its commission is expressly forbidden by positive law." *Id.* at 960.

In 1981, the legislature [deleted] the limiting language, "a felony upon or affecting the person whose death was caused." In *State v. Back*, decided after the 1981 amendment was adopted, we held that even a property offense can be used as an underlying felony *when a special danger to human life is present*. 341 N.W.2d 273, 276–77 (Minn.1983). In essence, in interpreting the 1981 statutory amendment, we concluded that the possible universe of predicate offenses was expanded to include property offenses but that the previous limitation-that "a special danger to human life" be present-was not abandoned. . . .

In the instant case, the state argues that Anderson's felon-in-possession and possession of a stolen firearm offenses support a charge of felony murder. In support of its position, the state first contends that under the plain meaning of the second-degree felony-murder statute, any felony, except those expressly excluded by the statute, can serve as a predicate felony.

The plain language of the second-degree felony-murder statute punishes perpetrators of all unintentional deaths caused during the commission of "a felony," with the exception of crimes that are predicates for first-degree murder. . . . Admittedly, under its plain language, except for the three specified exceptions, the statute appears to apply to all other felonies.

However, this interpretation ignores the history of our court's judicial limitation of the felony-murder rule as set forth in precedent. . . . In 1980-before the 1981 amendment-we adopted the "special danger to human life" standard which, in Minnesota, requires consideration of the elements of the underlying felony in the abstract *and* the circumstances under which the felony was committed.

Applying the statute as previously interpreted by us to this record, we conclude that the predicate offenses of felon in possession of a firearm and possession of a stolen firearm are not inherently dangerous. While the use of a firearm can pose significant danger to human life, simple possession-standing alone-does not. In other words, there is nothing about a felon's possession of a firearm, or of a stolen firearm-in the abstract-that in and of itself involves a special danger to human life. As the district court below explained:

> While a felon in possession of a firearm or stolen firearm creates a dangerous situation, there is a material distinction between the level of immanency and probability of the special danger to human life in that situation than in a situation involving the traditional felony predicates. The predicate felony in this case does not require an act of violence in carrying out the crime. Nor can it be persuasively argued that death would be the natural and probable consequence of the Defendant's conduct in carrying out the predicate offense.

Because felon in possession of a firearm and possession of a stolen firearm are not dangerous in the abstract, these predicate felonies fail the special danger to human life standard. Accordingly, we [reverse, holding] that the predicate offenses of felon in possession of a firearm and possession of a stolen firearm cannot support the charge of unintentional second-degree felony murder.

GILBERT, JUSTICE (dissenting).

I respectfully dissent from the majority opinion and would affirm the court of appeals. . . .

The majority acknowledges that the appellant was a felon in possession of a firearm, in fact a stolen firearm. This firearm happened to be a loaded, shortened 12-gauge shotgun. . . . It also appears to be undisputed that the appellant pointed the shotgun at the victim, it discharged, and Rogers was shot in the head.

The majority candidly admits that "under its plain language, except for the three specified exceptions, the statute appears to apply to all other felonies." Accordingly, the majority concedes that the felon in possession statute and felon in possession of stolen goods are predicate acts under Minn.Stat. § 609.19, subd. 2(1) (2002). The majority then holds, "we conclude that the predicate offenses of felon in possession of a firearm and possession of a stolen firearm are not inherently dangerous." I disagree. This case involves exactly the inherently dangerous situation the legislature envisioned.

. . . The majority summarily concludes that "there is nothing about a felon's possession of a firearm, or of a stolen firearm-in the abstract-that in and of itself involves a special danger to human life." First of all, we should not decide this case in the abstract. Second, we must recognize that a felon in possession of a firearm is not one of those "many comparatively minor offenses [that] are classified as felonies" noted by the majority. The legislature has determined that felons and firearms are not a good mix. Likewise, the crime of riot in the second degree is a serious crime of violence, which had been recently committed by appellant. Now, the appellant has not only been adjudicated delinquent, but also acts to possess a stolen gun, which is loaded and had been shortened. Shortly upon entering the house of the victim, this gun, which the appellant was feloniously possessing, was pointed at the victim and used to shoot him in the head. Possession of a loaded gun in these circumstances is indeed the type of felony that is inherently dangerous and represents a special danger to human life. . . .

. . . The majority opinion effectively amends the statute and discounts the legislative process's recognition of the obvious inherent danger of convicted felons possessing firearms. This is precisely the especially dangerous situation that the legislature may have anticipated in expanding the felony-murder statute to include all but a few designated felonies under this statute. The dangerous combination of a felon and an illegally possessed gun made it possible for the most serious of felonies to be committed; that of wrongfully taking an individual's life.

MISSOURI v. CHAMBERS, 524 S.W.2d 826 (Mo. 1980). This decision reaches a result different from that in *Anderson, above,* and holds that the underlying felony need not be inherently dangerous. Instead, the opinion supplies the dangerousness element from the defendant's individual actions in committing the felony. Defendant and his co-felon, after drinking heavily, "busted out" a window in a pickup truck and towed it away on a chain. Defendant drove at a high rate of speed and weaved across the road repeatedly, without lights, and collided with an oncoming car, killing its four occupants. The court reasoned as follows:

> [T]he suggested consideration whether the underlying felony is dangerous or betokens a reckless disregard of life, was satisfied in this case by the evidence showing that the underlying felony of stealing a motor vehicle was accomplished by towing it on a major highway in darkness without lights, weaving from side to side, and after drinking. The collision and resulting deaths attest to the violence and danger in such actions.

The court declined to follow decisions from other jurisdictions, and thus it held that the defendant's act could supply the dangerousness element and that it need not be supplied by an inherently dangerous felony.

Notes and Questions

(1) *Looking at Both the Elements of the Crime and the Facts of the Particular Crime.* The Minnesota Supreme Court in *Anderson* limits the felony murder rule to those that pose a "special danger to human life" by assessing both the elements of the predicate felony in the abstract and the circumstances of the particular crime. In finding that these particular crimes in *Anderson* do not qualify, did the court fault the crime elements or the manner in which the crime occurred? Do you agree that the crime of possession of a weapon by a felon is not a dangerous crime?

Notice that the Texas statute above (Tex. Penal Code § 19.02(a)(3)) contains a more direct statement of this dangerous-act test. In addition to the commission of the underlying felony, the Texas felony-murder rule requires that the defendant actually commit, in the particular case, "an act clearly dangerous to human life." Missouri, in *Chambers,* follows an analogous approach by judicial interpretation. Would a Texas or Missouri court have upheld a felony murder charge in *Anderson,* where defendant pointed a loaded shotgun at the deceased?

(2) *The Narrow Approach: Requiring an Inherently Dangerous Felony in the Abstract.* California and some other states look solely to the dangerousness of the underlying felony "in the abstract," without considering the defendant's conduct in the individual case. Thus, in these jurisdictions possessing a sawed-off shotgun is not "inherently dangerous" because one can possess such a weapon without harming or even endangering anyone. *See People v. Satchell,* 489 P.2d 1361 (Cal. 1971). Even if a person illegally possessed such a weapon and handled it dangerously, felony murder would not apply in California because the crime of possessing a sawed off shotgun is not considered inherently dangerous. Looking at the

difference between the "inherently dangerous felony" approach and the "dangerous act" approach, which one better carries out the policy goals of the felony-murder doctrine?

(3) *Does the Dangerous Act Approach Correlate the Crime with Blameworthiness Better than the Dangerous Felony Concept?* One of the most frequent arguments against the felony murder rule is that it allegedly separates the criminal law from the defendant's individual blameworthiness. The dangerous act approach focuses the crime definition on the defendant's individual act. The inherently dangerous felony approach is less focused on the individual. Does the dangerous act approach better serve the objective of grading the crime according to the defendant's individual blameworthiness?

[2] Merger of Lesser Offenses — or, Is There an "Independent Felonious Purpose"?

Notes on Merger and Related Doctrines

(1) *The Most Basic Meaning of the Merger Doctrine: A Rule against Basing Felony Murder on Lesser Homicides.* We already have seen that the felony-murder rule implicitly requires a felony other than manslaughter. If it were not so, the felony-murder rule would swallow up these lesser homicides, because by definition, manslaughters are felonies in which death results. Since the legislature did not intend for manslaughter and other lesser homicides to be absorbed into murder, the doctrine of merger holds that a felony murder "merges" into the lesser crime.

(2) *Should Merger Prevent Assaultive Crimes from Being Used as the Basis of Felony Murder?:* What about assault, which is the act that really causes many murders? Whether felony murder may be based on an assault is a controversial question that has split the jurisdictions. Some states, such as California, extend the merger doctrine beyond manslaughter, by holding that assault crimes cannot support a felony murder charge. Otherwise a kind of "bootstrapping" would result, because the felony murder rule would effectively preclude the jury from considering the issue of malice aforethought in all cases wherein homicide is committed during a felonious assault — a category which includes the great majority of all homicides. For example, in *People v. Chun*, 203 P.3d 425 (Cal. 2009), the court concluded that the crime at issue (shooting into an occupied vehicle) should merge because it was assaultive in nature. (In other words, the felony of shooting into a vehicle was inherently dangerous, but it was not subject to the felony murder rule because it was assaultive.)

(3) *The Contrary Position: Assaultive Crimes Can Support Felony Murder.* Perhaps the defendant who argues merger, to prevent felony murder from being based on assault, is advancing an unappealing claim. The argument sounds like this: "Yes, I shot the victim (or I ran him over, or I hit him with a pool cue), but I only meant to maim (or injure, or make a paraplegic out of) him. I guess I must have overdone it and killed him, but I shouldn't be guilty of murder." Some states, such as Georgia in

Wyman v. State, 602 S.E.2d 619 (Ga. 2004), reject this reasoning and uphold assault-based felony murders.

(4) *"Independent Felonious Purpose" as a Means of Preventing Merger and Allowing Felony Murder to Be Based on Assaultive Crimes.* Some courts have held that the merger doctrine does not apply to an assaultive crime if the defendant exhibited "a collateral and independent felonious design" that is "separate from the resulting homicide." Does this "independent felonious purpose" theory make sense, or should the courts, instead, either allow or disallow the basing of felony murder on assaultive conduct? Consider the following case.

COMMONWEALTH v. KILBURN, 780 N.E.2d 1237 (Mass. 2003). An unknown gunman shot and killed the victim, Charles Laliberte, after bursting into Laliberte's apartment. Alex Loer was visiting Laliberte and became the only witness to the shooting. First, the gunman brandished the gun and ordered the two men around, and then he took Laliberte into a bedroom and shot him in the back of the head. This defendant (Kilburn) was not present during the shooting, but later he was linked to a conspiracy to punish or discipline Laliberte. In fact, Kilburn confessed to this crime, but he added that the gunman "had just gone there to 'do'" Laliberte, and Laliberte "should never have died."

Kilburn was convicted under the felony-murder rule for a homicide resulting from an armed assault. He argued that the merger doctrine should prevent his murder conviction, since the armed-assault predicate felony had also caused the victim's death. The Massachusetts Supreme Judicial Court rejected this merger argument by finding an "independent" felonious purpose:

> The defendant asks us to overturn his felony-murder conviction because the necessary predicate felony, armed assault in a dwelling, merged with the murder itself. The defendant's claim is complicated by the fact that the evidence presented to the jury indicates that the gunman (and hence the defendant, who is liable as a joint venturer) committed not one, but two separate armed assaults on Laliberte. . . .

> The first armed assault on Laliberte occurred immediately after the gunman entered Laliberte's apartment. According to Loer's uncontested testimony, Laliberte opened the door for an individual who immediately brandished a gun and pushed the victim backward, thereby committing an armed assault in a dwelling. At this point, the gunman noticed Loer for the first time and . . . stopped in confusion. At that time the elements of an assault, namely objectively menacing conduct intended to arouse fear or the apprehension of imminent bodily harm, had already been satisfied. After a short interlude, during which the gunman ordered both Loer and the victim about the apartment, the gunman shot the victim in the back of the head, thus violating [the armed assault statute] a second time.

The doctrine of felony-murder provides that "the conduct which constitutes the felony must be 'separate from the acts of personal violence which constitute a *necessary* part of the homicide itself'" (emphasis added). *Commonwealth v. Gunter*, 427 Mass. 259, 272, 692 N.E.2d 515 (1998). . . . While the act of shooting Laliberte (the second assault on the victim) clearly caused the homicide in this case, the gunman's brandishing of a pistol with the intention of arousing fear in Laliberte (the first assault on the victim) did not. Laliberte died of a gunshot wound; he did not die of fright. . . . [W]e conclude that, while the second of the two assaults on Laliberte merged with the murder, the first did not. [Murder conviction upheld.]

Notes and Questions

(1) *An "Independent Felonious Purpose": Was It Really Present Here, in Kilburn's Case?* It would have been easy for another court to have held that the gunman's assault was a single course of conduct, a holding that presumably would have invoked the merger doctrine to prevent Kilburn's felony-murder conviction. Is the Massachusetts court's reasoning persuasive in upholding Kilburn's felony murder conviction on a "two-separate-assaults" theory?

(2) *Causation: Did Kilburn "Cause" the Death of the Victim, Laliberte?* Kilburn was not present during the homicide, and his statement indicates that he did not intend for Laliberte to die. Nevertheless, he was responsible for the assault as a conspirator or accomplice, and the law does not require him to be present or to intend the death of the victim to be guilty of felony murder. The remaining question, however, is, "Did Kilburn 'cause' Laliberte's death for purposes of felony murder?" That issue was not even raised in this appeal, because the answer, almost certainly, is "yes." Consider the following materials.

[3] Causation as a Limit on the Felony-Murder Doctrine
Notes on Varying Treatments of Causation

(1) *"But-for" Causation versus "Proximate Causation."* The most basic kind of causation requirement is so-called "but-for" causation. This sort of requirement is met whenever the death would not have resulted "but for" the defendant's conduct. This approach, which also is referred to as "cause in fact," sets a relatively low proof standard, because whenever death results in fact and would not have resulted without the felony, but-for causation is present. This is illustrated by a bank robbery when the frightened teller suffers a heart attack and dies during the actual robbery.

Many states, therefore, also require "proximate" causation, which places a more substantial restriction on the felony murder doctrine. Proximate causation exists when there is "foreseeability": that is, when the dangerous felony (or dangerous act) results in the victim's death in a manner that is foreseeable, or in other words, in a way that is related to the dangerousness inherent in the felony or act. For example, consider again the anomalous case of the thief who spills liquid that causes the victim to fall, hit his or her head, and die. But-for causation may be present, but proximate causation is not, because the death is not foreseeably related to any "dangerousness" inherent in either the crime of theft or the act of spilling liquid. On the other hand, if the death of a robbery victim results from the violence inherent in this felony or in the defendant's acts, proximate causation may be present.

(2) *Co-Felons, Bystanders, and the "Cone of Violence."* Causation issues become tricky when someone who is not the victim of the underlying felony is killed accidentally. For example, imagine that police officers or the crime victim shoots one of two robbers during a gun battle. The surviving robber then is tried for murder of the co-felon on the theory that the co-felon's death was caused during the commission of the felony of robbery. Alternatively, imagine that a police officer accidentally shoots a bystander or robbery victim while aiming at the robbers, or that one co-felon carelessly shoots another co-felon. These scenarios have produced inconsistent results in different states, with some courts refusing, for example, to elevate a police officer's killing of a co-felon into a murder conviction for the surviving felon.

Courts that refuse to extend felony murder to the deaths of co-felons may rely on the argument that the killing, in a sense, is "innocent," because most such deaths occur from robbery victims' or police officers' use of force in self-defense. But other jurisdictions perceive what might be called a "cone of violence" that emanates from felonies like robbery: an ever-expanding likelihood of death as the felony progresses, extending foreseeability to the killing of co-felons, bystanders, and police officers, so as to justify felony-murder liability.

(3) *Two Approaches to Deaths of Cofelons: "Agency" Theory (Narrower) and Proximate Causation (Broader).* The differing results in these cases often reflect the difference between two prevailing theories: agency and proximate causation. An "agency" approach would hold a defendant liable only for killings committed by his or her co-felon, who is treated as the defendant's agent, and not for a killing of his co-felon by a police officer, who is not the defendant's agent. A proximate causation approach, on the other hand, might hold the defendant liable for the death of the co-felon on the ground that it is a foreseeable result of the cone of violence set in motion by the defendant's participation in the underlying felony. Consider the following case.

State v. Sophophone

19 P.3d 70 (Kan. 2001)

LARSON, J.:

This is Sanexay Sophophone's direct appeal of his felony-murder conviction for the death of his co-felon during flight from an aggravated burglary in which both men participated. [Sophophone and three other individuals broke into a home. The resident reported the break-in to the police. Police officers responded to the call, saw four individuals leaving the back of the house, and ordered them to stop. The individuals, one being Sophophone, started to run away. One officer ran down Sophophone, handcuffed him, and placed him in a police car. Another officer chased one of the suspects later identified as Somphone Sysoumphone (the deceased). Sysoumphone crossed railroad tracks, jumped a fence, and then stopped. The officer approached with his weapon drawn and ordered Sysoumphone to the ground. Sysoumphone was lying face down but raised up and fired at the officer, who returned fire and killed him.]

Sophophone [this defendant, the survivor] was charged with . . . aggravated burglary . . . and felony murder. . . . Sophophone was convicted by a jury of all counts [and sentenced to life imprisonment]. . . . Sophophone's counsel contends (1) *State v. Hoang*, 243 Kan. 40, 755 P.2d 7 (1988), should be overruled insofar as it allows criminal responsibility for a co-felon's death, (2) he cannot be convicted of felony murder of a co-felon caused by a police officer while he was in custody, and (3) there was not sufficient evidence to support his conviction. . . .

The applicable provisions of K.S.A. 21–3401 read as follows: "Murder in the first degree is the killing of a human being committed: . . . (b) in the commission of, attempt to commit, or flight from an inherently dangerous felony as defined in K.S.A. 21–3436 and amendments thereto [which include aggravated burglary.]"

Sophophone does not dispute that aggravated burglary is an inherently dangerous felony which given the right circumstances would support a felony murder charge. His principal argument centers on his being in custody at the time his co-felon was killed by the lawful act of the officer which he contends was a "break in circumstances" sufficient to insulate him from further criminal responsibility.

This "intervening cause" or "break in circumstances" argument has no merit under the facts of this case. We have held in numerous cases that "time, distance, and the causal relationship between the underlying felony and a killing are factors to be considered in determining whether the killing occurs in the commission of the underlying felony and the defendant is therefore subject to the felony-murder rule." Based on the uncontroverted evidence in this case, the killing took place during flight from the aggravated burglary, and it is only because the act which resulted in the killing was a lawful one by a third party that a question of law exists as to whether Sophophone can be convicted of felony murder. . . .

Although there were clearly different facts, we held in *Hoang* that felony murder may include the accidental death of a co-felon during the commission of arson. The decedents had conspired with Hoang to burn down a building housing a Wichita restaurant/club but died when they were trapped inside the building while starting the fire. Hoang was an active participant in the felony and present at the scene, although he remained outside the building while his three accomplices entered the building with containers of gasoline to start the fire.

We held, in a split decision, that the decedents were killed during the perpetration of a felony inherently dangerous to human life and there was nothing in the statute to exclude the killing of co-felons from its application. It must be pointed out that the facts in *Hoang* [, unlike those in this case,] involved the wrongful acts of a co-felon which were directly responsible for the deaths of his co-felons. . . .

In Dressler, *Understanding Criminal Law*, § 31.07[4] Killing by a Non Felon, pp. 471–72 (1987), the question is posed of whether the felony-murder rule should apply when the fatal act is performed by a non-felon. Dressler states:

> This issue has perplexed courts. Two approaches to the question have been considered and applied by the courts. . . .

> [b] The "Agency" Approach

> The majority rule is that the felony-murder doctrine does not apply if the person who directly causes the death is a non-felon. . . . The reasoning of this approach stems from accomplice liability theory. . . . It is not possible to impute the acts of the antagonistic party — [the non-felon or] the police officer — to [a co-felon] on the basis of agency.

> [c] The "Proximate Causation" Approach

> An alternative theory . . . holds that a felon may be held responsible under the felony-murder rule for a killing committed by a non-felon if the felon set in motion the acts which resulted in the victim's death. . . .

In 2 LaFave & Scott, *Substantive Criminal Law*, § 7.5(d), pp. 217–18 (1986), the author opines: "Although it is now generally accepted that there is no felony-murder liability when one of the felons is shot and killed by the victim, a police officer, or a bystander, it is not easy to explain why this is so." The author discusses forseeability and [argues] that it is not correct to say that a felon is never liable when the death is lawful because it is "justifiable" and goes on to state:

> A more plausible explanation, it is submitted, is the feeling that it is not justice (though it may be poetic justice) to hold the felon liable for murder on account of the death, which the felon did not intend, of a co-felon willingly participating in the risky venture. . . . [W]ith unintended killings it would seem proper to take the victim's willing participation into account.

The leading case adopting the agency approach is *Commonwealth v. Redline*, 391 Pa. 486, 495, 137 A.2d 472 (1958), where the underlying principle of the agency theory is described as follows:

> In adjudging a felony-murder, it is to be remembered at all times that the thing which is imputed to a felon for a killing incidental to his felony is malice and not the act of killing. The mere coincidence of homicide and felony is not enough to satisfy the felony-murder doctrine. . . .

The minority of the states whose courts have adopted the proximate cause theory believe their legislatures intended that any person, co-felon, or accomplice who commits an inherently dangerous felony should be held responsible for any death which is a direct and foreseeable consequence of the actions of those committing the felony. These courts apply the civil law concept of proximate cause to felony-murder situations. . . .

It should be mentioned that some courts have been willing to impose felony-murder liability even where the shooting was by a person other than one of the felons in the so-called "shield" situations where it has been reasoned "that a felon's act of using a victim as a shield in compelling a victim to occupy a place or position of danger constitutes a direct lethal act against the victim." *Campbell v. State*, 293 Md. 438, 451 n. 3, 444 A.2d 1034 (1982).

The overriding fact which exists in our case is that neither Sophophone nor any of his accomplices "killed" anyone. The law enforcement officer acted lawfully in committing the act which resulted in the death of the co-felon. This does not fall within the language of K.S.A. 21–3205 since the officer committed no crime. . . .

Of more assistance to us is our long-time rule of statutory interpretation:

> [C]riminal statutes must be strictly construed in favor of the accused. Any reasonable doubt about the meaning is decided in favor of anyone subjected to the criminal statute. The rule of strict construction, however, is subordinate to the rule that judicial interpretation must be reasonable and sensible to effect legislative design and intent. . . .

It does little good to suggest [that] one construction over another [here] would prevent the commission of dangerous felonies or that it would deter those who engage in dangerous felonies from killing purposely, negligently, or accidentally. Actually, innocent parties and victims of crimes appear to be those who are sought to be protected rather than co-felons.

We hold that under the facts of this case where the killing resulted from the lawful acts of a law enforcement officer in attempting to apprehend a co-felon, Sophophone is not criminally responsible for the resulting death of Somphone Sysoumphone, and his felony-murder conviction must be reversed.

ABBOTT, J., dissenting: . . .

[Our Kansas] statute simply does not contain the limitations discussed by the majority. There is nothing in K.S.A. 21–3401 which requires us to adopt the agency approach or that requires Sophophone to be the shooter in this case. The facts in this case, in my opinion, satisfy all of the requirements set forth in K.S.A. 21- 3401(b).

Moreover, there are sound reasons to adopt the proximate cause approach described in the majority opinion. In *State v. Hoang*, 243 Kan. 40, 755 P.2d 7 (1988), this court took such an approach, although never referring to it by name. In *Hoang*, Chief Justice McFarland . . . stated:

> To support a conviction for felony murder, *all that is required is* to prove that a felony was being committed, which felony was inherently dangerous to

human life, and that the homicide which followed *was a direct result of the commission of that felony. In a felony-murder case, evidence of who the trigger-man is is irrelevant and all participants are principals. . . .* (Emphasis added.)

. . . The majority states that the decision in this case is not inconsistent with the ruling in *Hoang*. I disagree. . . .

The following courts have used a proximate cause approach instead of following the agency theory adopted by the majority in this case. Several of the following cases also involve factual situations where the co-felon was killed by a police officer, as is the situation in the present case. *See State v. Lopez*, 173 Ariz. 552, 556, 845 P.2d 478 (App.1993) (affirming felony-murder conviction where police officer shot co-felon while defendant was already under arrest by using the proximate cause approach as set forth by Arizona statute); *State v. Wright*, 379 So.2d 96, 96–97 (Fla.1980) (holding that there was nothing in the Florida felony-murder statute which limited application to "innocent persons killed" by the defendant); *People v. Dekens*, 182 Ill.2d 247, 252, 230 Ill.Dec. 984, 695 N.E.2d 474 (1998) (Illinois follows the proximate cause theory of felony murder). . . . [The dissent cited additional cases from Indiana, Missouri, New Jersey, Rhode Island, and Wisconsin.]

Here, Sophophone set in motion acts which would have resulted in the death or serious injury of a law enforcement officer had it not been for the highly alert law enforcement officer. This set of events could have very easily resulted in the death of a law enforcement officer, and in my opinion this is exactly the type of case the legislature had in mind when it adopted the felony-murder rule. . . .

I would affirm the conviction based upon the statutory language found in K.S.A. 21–3401, the decision in *Hoang*, and the cases cited from other jurisdictions. . . .

Notes and Questions

(1) *Agency or Proximate Causation: Which Approach (if Either) Is Adopted by the Kansas Majority?* The Kansas court denies that it has adopted the proximate causation approach. The dissent implies that the majority instead uses an agency theory, since the dissent pointedly argues that nothing in the Kansas statute "requires . . . the agency approach." But the majority never explicitly states that it is adopting an agency theory. Which approach—agency, proximate causation, or something else—has Kansas in fact adopted?

(2) *A Similar Example with Different Reasoning: State v. Layman*, 42 N.E.3d 972 (Ind. 2015). A group of juveniles broke into a home that they believed was unoccupied, intending to commit theft. But the homeowner was present, and he shot and killed one of them. The lower court convicted two defendants of felony murder on the basis of these facts. The Indiana Supreme Court reversed:

> [T]he record here shows that when the group broke and entered the residence of the homeowner intending to commit a theft—a burglary—not only were they unarmed, but also neither the Appellants nor their cohorts

engaged in any "dangerously violent and threatening conduct." There was simply nothing about the Appellants' conduct or the conduct of their cohorts that was "clearly the mediate or immediate cause" of their friend's death. Thus, while the evidence is sufficient to sustain a conviction for the underlying burglary, it is not sufficient [for murder]. Accordingly, we reverse [the] convictions for felony murder.

(3) *Considering the "Shield" Cases: Do These Decisions Demonstrate a Flaw in the Agency Theory?* As the majority points out, one controversial situation involves a defendant whose co-felon uses an innocent person as a hostage or shield, with the result that an officer (or another victim) shoots and accidentally kills the person used as the shield. Courts typically have been willing to impose felony murder liability in these cases, even on the defendant who did not use the shield. In such a case, is felony murder inconsistent with the agency theory, since an innocent party (an officer, or another victim) is the one that has fired the fatal gunshot? Or is the death the result of the use of a shield by the co-felon, so that felony murder is consistent with agency theory? Consider whether the proximate cause approach provides a better basis for decision in the shield cases.

(4) *What If One Police Officer Accidentally Shoots Another? Upholding Felony Murder: Santana v. Kuhlman,* 232 F. Supp.2d 154 (S.D.N.Y. 2002). In this case, the undercover drug arrest of the defendant produced a chaotic gun battle that resulted in the death of a New York peace officer, who was accidentally shot by another peace officer. The New York Court of Appeals upheld the defendant's conviction under the felony murder doctrine, reasoning that "[t]he language of [the New York statute] evinces the legislature's desire to extend liability broadly to those who commit serious crimes in ways that endanger the lives of others." A federal court denied habeas corpus, noting that the decision complied with New York's "foreseeability" approach.

[B] Criticisms and Justifications of the Felony Murder Doctrine

Commentary to Model Penal Code § 210.2
(Official Draft and Revised Comments 1980)

[The Model Penal Code Commentary says that the MPC rejects the felony-murder rule. It substitutes a presumption of extreme indifference to human life, sufficient for murder, if death results during certain named felonies. The drafters explain their choice thus:]

... Punishment for homicide obtains only when the deed is done with a state of mind that makes it reprehensible as well as unfortunate. Murder is invariably punished as a heinous offense.... Sanctions of such gravity demand justification, and their imposition must be premised on the confluence of conduct and culpability. Thus, under the Model Code, as at common law, murder occurs if a person kills purposely, knowingly, or with extreme recklessness. Lesser culpability yields lesser liability, and a person who inadvertently kills another under circumstances not amounting to negligence is guilty of no crime at all. The felony-murder rule contradicts this scheme. It bases conviction of murder not on any proven culpability with respect to homicide but on liability for another crime. The underlying felony carries its own penalty and the additional punishment for murder is therefore gratuitous. . . .

Principled argument in favor of the felony-murder doctrine is hard to find [as of the date of the MPC, in 1980. This statement is no longer true, as we shall see.] . . .

Question: by creating a "presumption" of extreme indifference sufficient to support second-degree murder, hasn't the MPC created a back-door version of felony murder? If so, perhaps the MPC version is less attractive than other definitions of felony murder, since there is no guidance to the jury in deciding whether to apply the presumption.

Nelson E. Roth & Scott E. Sundby, The Felony-Murder Rule: A Doctrine at Constitutional Crossroads
70 Cornell L. Rev. 446 (1985)

. . . Despite the widespread criticism, the felony-murder rule persists in the vast majority of states. Most states have attempted to limit the rule's potential harshness either by limiting the scope of its operation or by providing affirmative defenses. Such patchwork attempts to mitigate the rule's harshness, however, have been legitimately criticized because "they do not resolve the rule's essential illogic." . . .

A. The Rule's Historical Development . . .

The purpose of the felony-murder rule at common law is . . . vague. It is frequently argued that the rule's purpose was not fully articulated because all felonies at common law were punished by death and, therefore, the rule had little practical impact. Further research has revealed, however, that execution rates varied widely according to the felony. One suggested purpose is that the rule served as a means of more severely punishing incomplete or attempted felonies, which were only misdemeanors at common law, if a killing occurred. . . .

B. Deterrence

The deterrence rationale consists of two different strains. The first approach views the felony-murder rule as a doctrine intended to deter negligent and accidental killings during commission of felonies. . . .

The second view focuses not on the killing, but on the felony itself, and endorses the felony-murder rule as a deterrent to dangerous felonies. . . .

Both of the deterrence justifications are logically flawed. . . . The illogic of the felony-murder rule as a means of deterring killing is apparent when applied to accidental killings occurring during the commission of a felony. Quite simply, how does one deter an unintended act? . . . Moreover, any potential deterrence effect on unintentional killings is further reduced because few felons either will know that the felony-murder rule imposes strict liability for resulting deaths or will believe that harm will result from commission of the felony. . . .

. . . The lack of a deterrent effect because the defendant does not have killing as an objective also highlights the felony-murder rule's potential to punish a defendant who had no subjective culpability. Yet, the punishment of a killing as murder where subjective culpability is lacking clashes with modern definitions of murder. . . .

D. Retribution and General Culpability: A Strict Liability View of the Felony-Murder Rule

. . . An alternative approach is to view the rule as not requiring a separate mens rea element for the homicide, but as justifying conviction for murder simply on the basis that the defendant committed a felony and a killing occurred.

. . . The justifications advanced for this conceptualization are deterrence of the underlying felony and the notion that the felon has exhibited an "evil mind" justifying severe punishment.

. . . [T]he felony-murder rule conceived from an "evil mind" perspective comported with the retribution theory of punishment prevailing at the time of the rule's development, which focused on the resulting harm, not on the actor's mental state, in deciding the appropriate punishment. A convict, therefore, bore responsibility for his felony and for any harmful result arising from the crime regardless of his specific intentions.

Continued reliance on a general culpability theory to justify the felony-murder rule has been described as a rather "primitive rationale" and as "a tribute to the tenacity of legal conceptions rooted in simple moral attitudes." The "evil mind" theory conflicts with the basic premise that "the criminal law is concerned not only with guilt or innocence in the abstract but also with the degree of criminal liability." . . . Indeed, the felony-murder rule . . . results in the rule operating as a strict liability crime. . . .

David Crump & Susan Waite Crump, In Defense of the Felony Murder Doctrine

8 HARV. J.L. & PUB. POL'Y 359 (1985)

Scholars often criticize the felony murder doctrine. . . . Few authors, however, have attempted systematically to articulate policies in favor of felony murder. . . .

I. The Policies Supporting the Felony Murder Rule

A. Rational Classification and Proportional Grading of Offenses: Actus Reus as an Element of Just Desert

Classical theory divides the elements of crimes into two categories: mens rea and actus reus. . . .

Differences in result must be taken into account as part of actus reus if classification and grading are to be rational. For example, murder and attempted murder may require similar mental states (indeed, attempted murder generally requires proof of a higher mental element), but no common law jurisdiction treats the two offenses as one, and certainly none treats attempted murder more severely. The only difference justifying this classification is that death results in one offense but not in the other. Similarly, it is a misdemeanor for a person to operate a motor vehicle while impaired by drugs or alcohol, but if this conduct causes the death of a human being, the offense in some jurisdictions is elevated to the status of homicide. Most jurisdictions treat vehicular homicide more severely than the misdemeanor of alcohol-impaired driving, even though the actions and mental states of the defendant may be equivalent or identical.

. . . [The] grading of offenses so that the entire scheme of defined crimes squares with societal perceptions of proportionality — of "just deserts" — is a fundamental goal of the law of crimes.

The felony murder doctrine serves this goal, just as do the distinctions inherent in the separate offenses of attempted murder and murder, or impaired driving and vehicular homicide. Felony murder reflects a societal judgment that an intentionally committed robbery that causes the death of a human being is qualitatively more serious than an identical robbery that does not. . . . Thus, the felony murder doctrine reflects the conclusion that a robbery that causes death is more closely akin to murder than to robbery. . . .

There is impressive empirical evidence that this classification does indeed reflect widely shared societal attitudes. Recently, the Bureau of Justice Statistics of the United States Department of Justice released a national survey of public evaluations of the seriousness of 204 hypothetical legal events, ranging from the heinous to the trivial. . . . Some . . . felony murders were ranked by the respondents as more serious than other, apparently intentional killings; in particular, unintended rape- or robbery-homicides were graded far more severely than express-malice family killings. . . .

Scholarly criticisms of felony murder have tended to neglect its relationship to proportionality and grading. The criticisms erroneously tend to regard mens rea as the only legitimate determinant of the grade of a homicide resulting from a felony. This reasoning sometimes leads modern writers into the same rigid formalism, divorced from policy, that they rightly reject in historical justifications of the rule. . . .

B. Condemnation: Reaffirming the Sanctity of Human Life . . .

Condemnation . . . embodies the notion of reinforcement of societal norms and values as a guide to the conduct of upright persons, as opposed to less upright ones who presumably require the separate prod of "deterrence." The felony murder rule serves this purpose by distinguishing crimes that cause human deaths, thus reinforcing the reverence for human life. To put the argument differently, characterizing a robbery-homicide solely as a robbery would have the undesirable effect of communicating to the citizenry that the law does not consider a crime that takes a human life to be different from one that does not — a message that would be indistinguishable, in the minds of many, from a devaluation of human life. . . .

C. Deterrence

. . . Deterrence is the policy most often recognized in the cases. Scholars, however, tend to dismiss this rationale, using such arguments as the improbability that felons will know the law, the unlikelihood that a criminal who has formed the intent to commit a felony will refrain from acts likely to cause death, or the assertedly small number of felony-homicides.

. . . There may be more than a grain of truth in the proposition that felons, if considered as a class, evaluate risks and benefits differently than members of other classes in society. The conclusion does not follow, however, that felons cannot be deterred, or that criminals are so different from other citizens that they are impervious to inducements or deterrents that would affect people in general. . . . The felony murder rule is just the sort of simple, commonsense, readily enforceable, and widely known principle that is likely to result in deterrence. . . .

D. Clear and Unambiguous Definition of Offenses and Sentence Consequences

. . . Particularly when the offense is spontaneous, occupies only a brief time span, and is dependent upon mental impulses evidenced only by the defendant's actions, such terms as premeditation, deliberation, malice, or even "intent" leave jurors with [an unpredictable] judgment. Such ambiguity is undesirable because it produces disparity in verdicts, dissatisfaction with the basis of decision, and a perception of discrimination. These disadvantages are reduced by the felony murder doctrine. . . .

E. Optimal Allocation of Criminal Justice Resources

. . . A small minority of cases is tried before juries. The efforts of judges, courtroom time, lawyering on both sides, and support services are all scarce resources. Although we resist thinking of criminal justice in these terms, and few would be willing to put a specific dollar price upon its proper function, the quality of our justice is limited by the scarcity of these resources and by the efficiency with which we allocate them. . . .

One of our choices might be to improve the allocation of criminal justice resources by adopting some version of the felony murder rule. . . . Indeed, no less a tribunal than the California Supreme Court has stated this rationale:

... Once a person perpetrates or attempts to perpetrate one of the enumerated felonies, then in the judgment of the Legislature, he is no longer entitled to such fine judicial calibration, but will be deemed guilty of ... murder. ...

F. Minimization of the Utility of Perjury

... Scholars criticizing the felony murder rule sometimes argue or assume that juries will disbelieve false claims of accident [when defendants lie about their lack of intent or foresight]. The criticism assumes too much. The accident claim need only rise to the level of reasonable doubt to be effective under conventional homicide law. Experienced trial lawyers would not deny the frequent occurrence of erroneous acquittals, given the standard of proof required. Moreover, the incentive to perjury is itself a liability. ... While this concern would not overcome a strong policy to the contrary, ... the policy of avoiding incentives or rewards for perjury [can be] a legitimate rationale supporting felony murder.

II. [The] Scope or Limitation of Felony Murder

[A. Consistency of the Limits of the Felony Murder Rule with Its Purposes]

Analysis of a rule should take account not only of the rule itself, but of its limits as well. The policy underlying the rule should influence legislatures and the judiciary in fashioning exceptions; conversely, the lack of a relationship between the supporting rationale and the limits may be a sign that the doctrine itself is flawed. ...

[In the case of the felony murder rule,] [t]ypical limitation theories include the merger doctrine, causation requirements, doctrines regarding time or purpose relationships to the underlying crime, enumeration of dangerous felonies, inclusion of intentional commission of a dangerous act as an element, and mens rea. [Here, the authors consider each of these limiting doctrines and conclude that each is consistent with the purposes of the rule, because each one, in some way, prevents application of the rule in cases in which it would not be supported by policy.]

[B.] Abolition as a "Logical Conclusion" of Limitation

It has been suggested that the limitations of felony murder are such an expression of dissatisfaction with the rule that outright abolition would be a "logical conclusion." ...

[But] ... [a]ll doctrines in the law require limitation at some point. Murder itself, for example, is restricted by a variety of complex mens rea concepts and by elaborate defenses. ... Most importantly, as we [have demonstrated], the limitations themselves [on felony murder] are rooted in principled arguments that carry out the ultimate policies of felony murder—imperfectly, to be sure, but no more so than is characteristic of the common law development of any legal doctrine. ...

Notes and Questions

(1) *Does the Felony Murder Rule "Contradict" Our System of Proportionality, as the MPC Drafters Argue, or Does It "Serve This Goal," as Proponents Claim?* The MPC

commentary calls the felony murder rule "gratuitous": "The underlying felony carries its own penalty and the additional punishment for murder is therefore gratuitous." But Crump & Crump argue that the rule, instead, positively serves the goal of proportionality: "[I]f one must categorize a robbery causing death as either a robbery or a murder, it is the latter category that is the 'better fit': calling such a crime robbery, and robbery only, would distort its significance in the scheme of crime grading." Which argument is more persuasive?

(2) *Should the Mens Rea Required for Non-Felony Murders Be the Governing Determinant?* The MPC commentary says, "Punishment for homicide obtains only when the deed is done with a [homicidal] state of mind. . . ." This argument implies that a homicidal mens rea should be the sole determinant of classification. But proponents of the felony murder rule give the examples of attempted murder versus murder and drunk driving versus vehicular homicide, for which severity of sentence depends on result, not on mens rea, and they argue that mens rea is not a "unified field theory" of homicide. Which argument is more persuasive?

(3) *Condemnation and Deterrence.* Does the felony murder rule's condemnation of accidental killing in the course of a felony reaffirm the sanctity of life, promote respect for law among the upright citizenry, and express solidarity with survivors of the victim, as its proponents claim? Or are these purposes already served adequately by other homicide doctrines? What about deterrence—is the felony murder rule likely to lead to greater care, or is it unlikely that the range of potential legal penalties affects a felon's conduct during commission of a crime? How well does the Model Penal Code Commentary address these claims? What about Roth & Sundby, or Crump & Crump?

[C] If We're Going to Have a Felony Murder Statute, How Should We Write It?

David Crump, Reconsidering the Felony Murder Rule in Light of Modern Criticisms: Doesn't the Conclusion Depend Upon the Particular Rule at Issue?

32 Harv. J.L. & Pub. Pol'y 1155 (2009)

[This article begins by arguing that the validity of the arguments for and against the felony murder rule depends upon the version of the rule that is at issue. "Good" formulations of the felony murder doctrine can withstand the criticisms better than "bad" formulations. Given that most jurisdictions retain the rule, the following excerpt considers how the rule should be written.]

II.A. Good Felony Murder Definition (Although "Good" Is Always in the Eye of the Beholder)

A good felony murder statute would have several characteristics. First, it would avoid interfering with the policies underlying other kinds of crime grading contained in statutes defining lesser homicides. . . . It also would tie the murder definition to situations involving relatively high degrees of individual blameworthiness. Such a rule would also maximize effectiveness in carrying out utilitarian goals such as deterrence. It would avoid ambiguity. . . . Finally, it would minimize anomalies that result from schemes of crime grading.

As an example, consider the following state statute, which is excerpted here [with t]he most important language set in italics:

> . . . A person commits an offense if he: . . . *commits or attempts to commit a felony*, other than manslaughter, and in the course *and in furtherance of the attempt*, or in immediate flight from the commission or attempt, *he commits or attempts to commit an act clearly dangerous to human life that causes the death* of an individual.[1]

This law is currently in place in at least one state. It is a relatively good statute, . . . although it is subject to some potential criticisms. . . .

First, this statute is a good law because it ties the crime of murder to relatively high degrees of individual blameworthiness. It does not automatically apply if the defendant commits a felony and a death results, as could happen under a crude definition of the crime. In fact, it does not automatically apply even if the felony, in the abstract, is "dangerous." It requires the defendant to undertake two kinds of actions. First, the defendant must be acting in the course of committing a felony. . . . But second, and more importantly, the defendant must himself engage in an act that is "clearly dangerous to human life."

Thus, under this statute, mere accident is not enough. In fact, dangerousness is not necessarily sufficient either, because the act must be one that is not just dangerous in the abstract, but one that is "clearly dangerous to human life." Furthermore, this clearly dangerous act must be the agency that "causes" the death of an individual. In summary, this statute focuses on individual blameworthiness more than other felony murder statutes. . . .

By the same token, the statute is confined to circumstances that are more readily subject to deterrence. . . . Defining murder in this way confines the label of murder to those situations in which the defendant has the most reason to be both able and motivated to avoid liability for the crime.

The statute does not seem likely to require a great deal of interpretation. Its language is transparent enough to guide jury deliberation, and it can be used directly in jury instructions. . . . And the statute seems less prone than other versions

---

1. Tex. Penal Code § 19.02 (b) (c) (2008).

considered below to exonerating more blameworthy individuals while convicting less blameworthy individuals, because it's "clearly dangerous act" requirement is targeted directly at blameworthy conduct.

A critic could certainly find ways to attack this statute. First, the "act clearly dangerous" component seems to require only an objective standard of dangerousness. That is to say, the "clearly dangerousness" requirement seems to require only that a reasonable person be able to perceive the act as clearly dangerous; the subjective mental state of the individual defendant appears to be irrelevant. A meticulous critic might argue that the statute should be written so that the defendant is liable only if he "knows" that the act is clearly dangerous to human life, and perhaps even then, only if he "intends" to commit the act anyway. But then, this meticulous critic would have much greater difficulty with other common kinds of crime definition, such as the widespread use of "depraved heart" murder statutes, which present more significant possibilities of misapplication. . . .

B. Bad Felony Murder Definition (Although "Bad" Is in the Eye of the Beholder Too)

The definition of felony murder in California is plainly unsatisfactory. Indeed, it is so deficient that at least one respected state supreme court justice has called for abolition of the California jurisprudence altogether and has appealed to the legislature to pass something that makes more sense. . . . California's doctrine does not correlate as well as it might with moral blameworthiness, is clumsy in its application to the deterrence purpose, contains a large amount of ambiguity, and results in exonerating some bad actors on dubious grounds while convicting other bad actors who seem no worse.

The principal limitation upon the felony murder rule in California is the "inherently dangerous felony" requirement. This concept differs sharply from the "clearly dangerous act" requirement in the statute discussed above. In California, the relevant question is whether the felony, "in the abstract," is inherently dangerous. This formulation is subject to criticism because it divorces the definition of murder from the individual blameworthiness of the defendant. The defendant personally need not do anything dangerous other than commit the felony. . . .

But that is not all. The California court has had a great deal of trouble deciding just which felonies are "dangerous." For example, does a felon who commits his particular felony by illegal possessing a sawed-off shotgun, and who points the weapon directly at another person, commit murder if the weapon discharges and kills the victim? The issue, in California, boils down to whether a felon in possession of a sawed-off shotgun is "in the abstract inherently dangerous." One might think that the answer from a California court would be, "yes, absolutely!" . . . [But i]nstead, the court reasoned that this particular felony could possibly be committed in ways that were not dangerous. . . . As an even more outlandish example, the court itself offered the possibility that the felon might keep his sawed-off shotgun . . . "as a keepsake or a curio." The trouble with this reasoning is that every felony, at least theoretically, is capable of being committed in "safe" ways. . . . A criminal can rob someone without using a weapon, and an arsonist can search the premises before committing the act of setting a fire. . . . [T]he list of felonies that the California court has found to be "inherently dangerous" looks completely arbitrary when compared to the list that it has found not to be "inherently dangerous":

> Felonies that have been held inherently dangerous to life include shooting at an inhabited dwelling; poisoning with intent to injure; arson of a motor vehicle; grossly negligent discharge of a firearm; manufacturing methamphetamine; kidnapping; and reckless or malicious possession of a destructive device.

> Felonies that have been held *not* inherently dangerous to life include practicing medicine without a license under conditions creating a risk of great bodily harm . . . or death; false imprisonment by violence, menace, fraud, or deceit; possession of a concealable firearm by a convicted felon; possession of a sawed-off shotgun; escape; grand theft; conspiracy to possess methedrine; furnishing phencyclidine; and child endangerment or abuse.

. . . The California rule gives the appearance of a disconnect between moral blameworthiness and crime definition.

The California formulation also seems to miss opportunities for deterrence. If you are a felon in possession of a sawed-off shotgun, for example, the act of pointing it directly at another person might be deterred. [And] the California doctrine exonerates some truly bad actors while convicting other bad actors who may legitimately think that their conduct is less morally blameworthy. This circumstance, although a constant problem in criminal justice, ought to be minimized, because it tends to encourage disrespect for the law.

. . . California would do well to address the problem via legislation, perhaps of the type contained in Part II.A. There are other kinds of murder definitions that also seem inferior to a good felony murder rule. . . . [T]he MPC, for example, defines murder in situations involving neither intent nor knowledge, but only recklessness, and then "presumes" recklessness in situations involving felonies. One can question whether this back-door method of ostensibly abolishing the felony murder rule — despite actually preserving it through a presumption — introduces ambiguity and confusion that outweigh any perceived disadvantages of keeping the felony murder rule, but defining it better. . . .

Notes and Questions

(1) *"Dangerous Felonies" Versus "Dangerous Acts."* This article draws a sharp distinction between judicial restrictions of the felony murder rule based upon "inherently dangerous felonies" and those based on "acts [by defendants] clearly dangerous to human life." It asserts that the latter formulation fits better with concerns such as blameworthiness and deterrence.

Is there a third way? Some states (such as Oregon) have legislatively defined the "dangerous" felonies that can serve as predicates for felony murder. *See* Or. Rev. Stat. 163.115(1)(b). Oregon's legislative list of violent felonies may improve upon the California approach because the vagueness and arbitrariness in identifying "inherently dangerous" felonies by court decrees is gone. But a legislative list of violent felonies cannot satisfy a critic who asserts that the felony murder doctrine divorces liability from blameworthiness. For such a critic, the problem remains that a pure accident, with no particularly dangerous act by the defendant, can result in a conviction for murder. Is the "legislative list" approach to defining dangerous felonies better, or is the "dangerous act" formula better?

(2) *The Model Penal Code: Certain Felonies Create a "Presumption" of Extreme Recklessness Sufficient to Allow Conviction for Murder.* The article argues that the "act clearly dangerous to human life" formulation is better than the MPC's "presumption" of extreme recklessness (and therefore murder) from the fact of the felony. Is this argument persuasive?

Problem 2E (Felony Murder): Sam Seller, Bobbie Buyer, and the Wayward Bullet

Sam Seller had just finished selling several ounces of cocaine to Bobbie Buyer when Sam discovered that Bobbie had shorted Sam by $100 in the payment. Sam immediately pulled out an automatic pistol and sprayed bullets across Bobbie's departing Pontiac Trans-Am. Bobbie, in response to this attack, quickly extracted an automatic pistol too, and directed a fusillade back at Sam.

Bobbie's self-defensive effort was impaired by erratic driving and over-the-shoulder aim, and the bullets ranged far wide of Sam. One of them pierced the aorta of a 65-year-old shopkeeper named Vic Tumm, who was sweeping his fruit stand three blocks away, killing him instantly. The State has arrested Sam Seller and charged Sam under the felony murder rule, even though it was Bobbie Buyer's bullet that killed the victim.

(1) *The "Dangerousness" Requirement.* Did Sam Seller commit an "inherently dangerous felony" (or, in states that require it instead, a "clearly dangerous act") by the delivery of cocaine (or the armed assault on Bobbie Buyer)?

(2) *Merger (and Independent Felonious Purpose).* If the prosecution attempts to base felony murder on Sam's crime of shooting at Bobbie, does the merger doctrine bar this theory? If merger otherwise would prevent Sam from being convicted of felony murder, can the prosecution avoid the bar by invoking the independent felonious purpose doctrine?

(3) *Causation in Sam Seller's Case: Agency, Proximate Cause, Intervening Cause, and the Self-Defensive Origins of Bobbie Buyer's Bullets.* Next, consider causation. But-for causation seems to be present. Is proximate causation also present, or is Bobbie's shooting back at Sam an intervening cause that breaks the chain of causation tying Sam to the victim's death? Consider the result, also, in a jurisdiction that

limits causation by the agency approach. Finally, notice that Bobbie's actions are self-defensive (and therefore arguably non-criminal) insofar as they targeted Sam, and explain how this factor might affect the outcome, if it does.

(4) *Policy Analysis: Criticisms and Justifications of the Felony Murder Rule.* Consider the policy justifications offered by proponents of the felony-murder rule. Would some or all of these policies be advanced by the conviction of Sam Seller for murder in this case? Which of the criticisms of the rule offered by opponents are most persuasive, if any, in the context of this case?

[D] Homicides Analogous to Felony Murder: Unlawful-Act Manslaughter, Vehicular Homicides, and "Resulting-in-Death" Statutes

Notes and Questions

(1) *The Unlawful Act or Misdemeanor Manslaughter Doctrine.* Just as there is a doctrine imputing malice for murder embodied in the felony murder rule, in some traditional jurisdictions a killing "in the commission of an unlawful act, not amounting to a felony" constitutes involuntary manslaughter. For example, if a defendant is speeding and a child darts out into the street and is killed, the defendant may be guilty of involuntary manslaughter without the ordinary analysis of recklessness. The doctrine is sometimes referred to as the "misdemeanor manslaughter" doctrine because it works for misdemeanors the same way as the felony-murder rule works for felonies. What is the rationale behind the unlawful act/misdemeanor manslaughter doctrine?

(2) *Limitations on the Unlawful Act Doctrine.* Because it imposes culpability without a jury finding that the defendant met the standards ordinarily assigned for negligent homicides, some jurisdictions seek to limit application of this rule as they do for the felony murder rule. There are different ways to impose such limits:

(a) *Proximate Cause Limitation.* Some jurisdictions will limit the scope of the unlawful act doctrine by requiring a strong causal connection between the unlawful act and the homicide that results. Thus, the speeding motorist would not be liable for the death of the darting child unless the speed was so excessive that it "caused" the homicide (as a but-for, foreseeable cause, so that the motorist could have stopped if within the speed limit, but could not because of excessive speed).

(b) *"Inherently Bad" or "Malum in Se" Misdemeanors, or "Dangerous" Offenses.* Some jurisdictions limit the scope of the unlawful act doctrine by applying it only in cases involving "inherently bad" misdemeanors. For regulatory offenses that do not pose an inherent risk of harm, the doctrine is not imposed. Would you favor such a limitation?

(3) *Vehicular Homicides as Potential Murders under Traditional Laws.* As you have seen, vehicular homicides sometimes can be treated as either murders

or manslaughters. In what situations should a death caused by an intoxicated driver be considered murder and in what situations would you classify it as involuntary manslaughter? Would it matter to you if the defendant had been charged before with drunk driving or if the defendant was driving with outrageous recklessness?

(4) *"Resulting-in-Death" Statutes.* Some states have special statutes for certain felonies that define more aggravated crimes (or more severe sentences) if death results. For example, some jurisdictions define separate crimes of child abuse and "child abuse resulting in death," with the latter felony carrying an enhanced sentence. The effect is similar to that of the felony murder rule, but tailored to one particular crime. Are these statutes a good idea?

Perhaps the best-known example of this approach is the federal statute covering civil rights violations that result in death. The statute does not define a separate crime as such, but it authorizes life in prison as the maximum sentence if death results from the crime. In the famous case of civil rights workers Schwerner, Goodman, and Chaney, who during the 1960's were abducted and murdered by a combined group of Mississippi law enforcement officers and Klan members, convictions and sentences were obtained under this federal law.

§ 2.06 Review Problems Based on Newspaper Reports

Note on These "Newspaper Cases"

The following three homicide cases all were covered in newspapers in a single week in a recent year. The news reports and case facts have been rewritten here, however, to emphasize the legal issues. These reports will supply you with review material for this entire chapter on homicide, from first degree murder to lesser degrees. As you read them, consider all the statutory patterns you have studied.

[A] Headline: "Mom Gets Second-Degree Murder in Toddler's Dismemberment"

LOS ANGELES—The judge called the crime "so horrific as to leave one speechless." But still, the jury only convicted Rakeisha Scott, 24, of second-degree murder, not first-degree. Scott was arrested with her boyfriend, Randy Foster, after the body of her 3-year-old daughter, Milan Scott Wilson, was discovered in the trunk of his car, encased in concrete. Scott also was convicted of assault on a child causing death, as well as child abuse causing death. After the child died from abuse, Scott and Foster dismembered her body and entombed the pieces in concrete.

At sentencing, Scott tearfully asked for leniency. "I have no sympathy for Ms. Scott," Judge Michael E. Pastor said, as he sentenced her to 25 years to life. "I have tremendous sympathy for Milan and images [of child abuse] that will last a lifetime."

(1) *Why Second-Degree Murder?* If the crime truly was as horrific as it sounds, why do you think the jury convicted Ms. Scott only of second-degree murder, rather than first-degree? See whether you can infer the kinds of factors that Ms. Scott's lawyer might have advanced to obtain this lesser result from the jury.

(2) *What Result under a Murder Statute Based on the MPC?* There would be a single crime of murder under the MPC. What, if any, homicide crime do you think occurred under the MPC? *Is Felony Murder a Possibility?* Imagine that this case arises in another state, and that the prosecution attempts to base conviction on the felony-murder rule because of Scott's *two felonies of assault* on a child and child abuse. Analyze how "dangerousness" requirements (placed on either the felony or the defendant's acts), "merger" or "independent felonious purpose" limits, and causation doctrines might affect the outcome of this true-life case.

[B] Headline: "Involuntary Manslaughter for Dad Who Beat Son's Hockey Coach to Death"

BOSTON — A Massachusetts jury yesterday convicted Thomas Junta, 44, of involuntary manslaughter after he beat his son's hockey coach to death. Jurors afterward pronounced their decision "very difficult, but proper" under the law, as it was given to them by the trial judge. Junta claimed that he acted in self-defense. He testified that the victim, Michael Costin, 40, actually had attacked him. The altercation began when Costin told his players, "Hockey's about hitting." Junta was quoted as saying, "That's [expletive]. It's about having fun." He scuffled with Costin briefly, then left. But about a minute later, witnesses said, Junta returned, "looking to resume the fight." A rink manager told Junta he could not enter, but Junta pushed her against a wall, injuring her arm. Then, said witnesses, he ran to Costin, threw him to the ice, and beat him repeatedly about the head and neck with his fist, rupturing an artery.

Junta, who outweighed Costin by an estimated 100 pounds, ultimately got up and left. Police who responded found Costin lying on the ice, bloodied, not moving, surrounded by children. Junta testified that he threw three "off-balance" punches and did not realize that Costin was hurt.

(1) *Why Involuntary Manslaughter (as Opposed to Murder)?* Prosecutors argued that Junta was guilty of murder. Assuming the usual definition of malice aforethought as including intent, or a depraved heart, or a felony under circumstances qualifying for the felony murder rule, why do you think the jury thought the involuntary manslaughter (reckless killing) verdict was the "correct" one, rather than murder? Do you agree with the jury?

(2) *Defining Murder as Including Death from an Intent to Cause Serious Bodily Injury: What Result?* As we have seen, some jurisdictions provide that an "intent to

cause serious bodily injury," coupled with an "act clearly dangerous to human life," also suffices for murder (sometimes, second degree). Could the jury have returned a murder verdict if instructed this way?

(3) *Voluntary Manslaughter as an Alternative.* Would the defendant have been entitled to an instruction on voluntary manslaughter (are the elements of sudden passion, adequate cause, and timing present)? Would the jury have been likely to find a reasonable doubt about voluntary manslaughter, so as to find that verdict, assuming they otherwise would have considered murder?

(4) *Why Not Criminally Negligent Homicide?* In a case like this one, depending on the precise statutes, it would not be surprising if the judge found it necessary in some states to submit a choice of at least five (5) verdicts to the jury: first-degree murder, second-degree, voluntary manslaughter, involuntary manslaughter, and negligent homicide. Imagine that the jury harbors a reasonable doubt about whether the defendant actually was subjectively "aware" of a "substantial and unjustified risk" of death from the blows he landed. Then, what do you think is the likely verdict?

[C] Headline: "Baby Dies from Ricocheting Bullet"

YONKERS, N.Y.—Amy Guzman was just days short of her second birthday as she sat on her parent's bed, clutching her Winnie-the-Pooh and watching a Pooh movie. Suddenly, the headboard disintegrated, and Amy went limp. She began to bleed into her stuffed Pooh, mortally wounded by a stray bullet fired by a man out of his apartment window at a hardware store sign across the street.

Police believe that the man, Kashawn Jones, 20, was using the sign for target practice. The bullet was a penetrating, pointed and jacketed type, and it ricocheted from the sign, left a half-inch hole in the outside wall of Amy's parents' bedroom, grazed her mother, killed Amy, exploded the mirrored headboard, and kept going.

"Maybe this was an accident, but it feels like murder," said Salim Samarneh, a grocery worker across the street, as the neighbors assembled a sidewalk memorial. "She was the glory of this family," said Amy's mother. "She didn't deserve this." And the police commissioner pronounced the homicide "a senseless, depraved act of stupidity which resulted in the loss of an innocent life." The grand jury charged Kashawn with second-degree murder.

(1) *Why Second-Degree Murder (as Opposed to a Greater or Lesser Homicide)?* Consider whether Jones can be said to have exhibited the requisite malice afore-thought that usually is required for murder in many states, why the charge might properly be second- rather than first-degree, and whether Jones might instead be found guilty in some states of a lesser homicide, such as involuntary manslaughter or criminally negligent homicide.

(2) *Is Felony Murder a Possibility?* Consider whether, in a state with a typical felony murder doctrine, the "dangerousness" element (either in the felony or in the defendant's act) is present, whether the merger doctrine would bar felony murder,

whether an independent felonious purpose could avoid merger here, and whether causation requirements could be satisfied.

§ 2.07 Simulation Exercise: Jury Argument in a Homicide Case

As is indicated above, follow your professor's instructions. Your professor may decide to use some, all, or none of this simulation exercise.

Simulation Exercise No. 2: Jury Argument in State v. Martinez

(1) *The Evidence: Is It Murder—or Is It a Reduced-Liability Passion Killing?* This problem is based on the evidence in Martinez v. State, 16 S.W.3d 845 (Tex. App. 2000). As summarized by the court,

> Joanie Nash invited Dan Cox to a party. Appellant was also at Nash's party. Appellant had been drinking beer, smoking marihuana, and doing cocaine throughout the evening. Appellant and Cox left the party together to go to Cox's apartment to contact Cox's dealer to get cocaine. Appellant returned to the party alone wearing different clothes. Appellant eventually told Nash and his brother that he had killed Cox because Cox had tried to molest him. No one contacted the police that night.
>
> The next day, . . . Cox's body was found seated on the couch in the living room of his apartment. . . . [H]e had been stabbed 24 times in the neck, and his throat had been cut. Cox also had a broken nose, facial abrasions, a stab wound to the chest, and a stab wound to the abdomen.
>
> . . . Appellant gave the police two written statements. In the first statement, appellant claimed he had stabbed Cox in self-defense after Cox made sexual advances toward him. Appellant stated, "all [he] could see was being raped and killed," and he used his knife "to make him stop" after Cox attempted to pull his shorts down. In the second statement, appellant admitted he took $420 out of Cox's wallet and put the wallet and the clothes he had been wearing in a restaurant dumpster. . . .
>
> A crime scene expert testified appellant's account of how he stabbed Cox, as Cox was leaning over him, pulling at his shorts, was inconsistent with the physical evidence at the scene. The pattern of blood splatter and the absence of blood in the area directly behind Cox's head indicated Cox was seated normally on the couch, in the approximate position in which he was found, while he was being stabbed.

The court affirmed Martinez's murder conviction, holding that he was not entitled to a jury instruction on manslaughter:

> Manslaughter requires a finding that appellant recklessly caused the death of Cox. *See* Tex. Penal Code Ann. § 19.04 (Vernon 1994). . . .

On direct examination, appellant testified to the following: . . .

> Defense counsel: Why were you swinging the knife towards Dan Cox?
>
> Appellant: To get him off me.
>
> Defense counsel: Did you have any intent to kill him at that point?
>
> Appellant: No, Sir.

Throughout the direct examination, appellant denied having any specific intent to kill Cox; however, he repeatedly claimed that he acted in self-defense. During cross examination[, however,] appellant testified that he intended to defend himself by hurting Cox.

> Prosecutor: You testified earlier that you had no intent to hurt Mr. Cox. You plunged a knife two, two and half, a half an inch into him, different variations, 24 times. What did you intend to do?
>
> Appellant: To get him off me.
>
> Prosecutor: By hurting him?
>
> Appellant: Yes, ma'am. I guess it's to defend myself.
>
> Prosecutor: But you meant to hurt him?
>
> Appellant: Yes, ma'am.
>
> Prosecutor: Why did you tell your lawyer that you didn't mean to hurt him?
>
> Appellant: I didn't have intent to go over there to hurt him, but at that time, yes.
>
> Prosecutor: . . . When you pulled the knife out, you intended to hurt him, didn't you?
>
> Appellant: Yes, ma'am.

The record does not establish that appellant, if guilty, was guilty only of the lesser included offense of manslaughter. Even though appellant claimed that he stabbed Cox and cut his throat without intending to kill him, his intent to "hurt him" with a knife is intent to cause serious bodily injury. The commission of an act clearly dangerous to human life suffices to support a conviction for murder under section 19.02(b)(2) of the Texas Penal Code and is not an accidental or reckless act. . . . Furthermore, one cannot accidentally or recklessly act in self-defense.

(2) *Preparing Your Assignment.* For this assignment, your job is to argue for or against Martinez's effort to receive a lesser sentence because he claims he killed under sudden heat of passion. Examine West York Penal Code § 19.02(d), below, for an explanation of those conditions under which a defendant may limit the sentence for his crime. Then, identify the evidence that supports your argument as to why Martinez should or should not receive the benefits of that statute. Then prepare a jury argument consistent with the evidence.

(3) *Grades of Homicide.* In most jurisdictions, the court affixes the penalty after the jury decides on the level of homicide, which may be first degree murder, second degree murder, voluntary manslaughter (passion killing), etc. In a few jurisdictions, however, the jury engages in a two-step process. First, it determines whether the defendant is guilty of murder. Second, it decides whether there was sudden passion (the equivalent of voluntary manslaughter), and if so, the offense is still murder, but the potential sentence is reduced.

(4) *Two Versions of Controlling Statutes: (1) Voluntary Manslaughter or (2) Murder-with-Sentence-Reduction.* These two possible statutes follow the two patterns described above. The jury will be instructed in exactly these words. Use the version your Professor tells you to use (or the statute in your state):

Possible West York Statute No. 1: Voluntary Manslaughter upon Murder Conditions if Prosecution Fails to Disprove Sudden Passion. If your Professor so directs, use this version:

> § 19.02(d). During a trial for any degree of murder, the defendant may raise the issue as to whether he or she caused the death under the immediate influence of sudden passion arising from an adequate cause. If the defendant raises the issue, and if the state fails to disprove it beyond a reasonable doubt, the offense is manslaughter, a felony of the second degree [which carries a maximum of 20 years, not the usual murder maximum of life in prison.]

West York Statute No. 2: Murder with Sentence Reduction if Defendant Proves Sudden Passion. If your Professor so directs, use this version:

> § 19.02(d). At the sentencing stage of a trial after a defendant has been convicted of murder, the defendant may raise the issue as to whether he or she caused the death under the immediate influence of sudden passion arising from an adequate cause. If the defendant proves the issue in the affirmative by a preponderance of the evidence, the offense is [reduced to] a felony of the second degree [which carries a maximum of 20 years, not the usual murder maximum of life in prison].

Both versions include the following definitions, all of which will be given to the jury in the judge's instructions:

> "Adequate cause" means cause that would commonly produce a degree of anger, rage, resentment, or terror in a person of ordinary temper, sufficient to render the mind incapable of cool reflection.

> "Sudden passion" means passion directly caused by, and arising out of, provocation by the individual killed or another acting with the person killed. . . .

(5) *Summarizing the Assignment; Advice on Jury Arguments.* Thus, your job, if you are a prosecutor, is to argue *against* this offense-or-sentence reduction, using whichever version of the statute your instructor says; and your job as a defense lawyer is to argue *for* the reduction. Use the evidence in the *Martinez* case, above. You will also need to read and absorb this chapter.

Chapter 3

The Elements of Crimes:
Actus Reus and Mens Rea

*"To constitute a crime against human laws, there must be first a vitious will;
and secondly, an unlawful act consequent upon such vitious will."* — William
Blackstone, 5 Commentaries *21.

*"If there were no intentional walks, the guy would just walk him anyway,
unintentionally intentionally walk him."* — George Brett

§ 3.01 Analyzing the Elements of Crimes

Note on the Significance of Crime Elements

(1) *Specificity in Crime Definition.* The United States Constitution, principles of
legality, and common sense mandate that crimes be stated with some specificity. In
modern times, virtually all crimes are contained in statutes or administrative regulations. Each crime essentially applies to a very small part of human activity, and
each ideally is defined to cover activity that is prohibited while minimizing intrusion into activity that is not disapproved.

(2) *Crime Elements as Means of Achieving Proper Definition.* A statute defining
a crime achieves these purposes by listing *the elements of the offense.* A particular
crime may have as few as three to as many as a dozen elements. An element is a component that, when combined with the other elements, defines the crime. Someone
violates the statute when he or she behaves in a way that is covered by the particular
terms of that criminal law. The charging instrument (such as an indictment) con-
forms to the statute and sets out the elements of the crime, as does a court's charge
to the jury, which tells jurors the laws they are to apply.

For example, a homicide takes place only when there is a death. But the homicide statute will be far more precise than reaching anyone who kills under any circumstances. The statute requires that the victim be a human being rather than an
animal. And it may deal differently with someone who kills on purpose than with
someone who kills accidentally. All of these distinctions are made by language that
should have been carefully chosen to set out the elements of a particular crime.

(3) *The Functions of Elements: Including Some Activities While Excluding Others.*
When a legislature enacts a criminal statute, it uses language that fine-tunes the

reach of the statute, excluding some actions while including others. For example, the statute may punish "bribery of a juror." To be guilty, the defendant must have committed a "bribery," a term most likely defined by statute or case law. In addition, the person bribed must have been a "juror." This is what is included; what is excluded is the innocent activity of giving a gift to a friend who is not a juror.

(4) *Examples: How Elements Work.* Imagine that a legislature has decided to pass a statute defining and punishing a crime called "arson." Most people have a general idea of this crime. But everyone's idea will differ in the details. The elements that the legislature chooses will express policy decisions about the reach of the statute, from extremely broad to very narrow, and they will determine whether the statute works well or poorly. Here are some examples.

> *Example 1:* Assume that the legislature enacts a statute that punishes "anyone who burns a building." This arson law could easily reach a person who accidentally left the stove on and caused a fire, although that result seems outlandish and likely is unintended.

> *Example 2:* Contrast Example 1 with a statute that penalizes: "anyone who burns a building 'owned by someone else.'" Example 2 would not cover the person who burned her own property. It is limited to people who burn other people's property.

> *Example 3:* An even greater contrast is presented by a statute punishing "anyone who 'intentionally' burns a building owned by someone else." This example adds a mental element: the burning must be *intentional*. It would not cover someone who *accidentally* set fire to his or her own property.

> *Example 4:* Note how the arson statute would cover a different category of offenders if it reached "anyone who 'negligently' burns a building owned by someone else."

Note on How the Burden of Proof Affects Elements

(1) *Why the Requirement of Proof Beyond a Reasonable Doubt Should Affect Your Analysis of Crime Elements.* As several chapters in this book indicate, the prosecution has the burden of proving the existence of each element of a crime—not just some elements, but *each* element—beyond a reasonable doubt. This heavy burden is sometimes difficult to meet, especially for the mens rea or mental elements. Thus, the interplay between crime elements and the burden of proof sharply distinguishes criminal law from, say, a common law claim for damages asserted in a civil case. In criminal cases, a likelihood of guilt is not enough, and even a strong likelihood is still not enough; instead, the prosecution (a) must identify and (b) *rigorously establish* each element beyond a reasonable doubt, the highest standard recognized in the law.

(2) *The Need to Identify Each Statutory Element, Plus Other Elements Outside the Statute, Such as the Identity of the Defendant.* More than in most other circumstances, a lawyer in a criminal case needs to break down the applicable statute and number the elements. The identity of the defendant as the person who committed

the crime is always an additional element, usually unexpressed in the criminal statute itself.

Thus, if the state were to charge someone named "Dale Defendant" with arson under the statute in Example 3 above, the prosecutor and defendant each would number the elements thus: (1) the defendant on trial, "Dale Defendant" [the "anyone" in the statute] (2) "intentionally" (3) "burned" (4) "a building" (5) that was "owned by someone else." The government would have to prove each element, including the fact that the defendant in the courtroom is the Dale Defendant who committed the arson.

(3) *Additional Elements Not in the Statute.* Just as the identity of the defendant is an element—though unexpressed—of a crime and must be proven by the government beyond a reasonable doubt, the date and location of the crime must also be established.

(a) *Date of the Crime.* The date a crime occurred is important for several reasons. First, the government must prove this defendant committed the particular crime with which he or she is charged. Thus, in a trial for a bank robbery allegedly committed on July 3, 2014, the government must prove this defendant committed this particular robbery (as opposed to another one at the same bank on July 30, 2014).

Second, the date of a crime is critical because most crimes (excluding some murders and a few other very serious offenses), have *statutes of limitations.* This is a time limit established by the legislature that requires charges be brought within a certain time from the commission of the crime. Usually, the length of time is greater for more serious crimes. *See, e.g.,* Cal. Pen. Code Ann. §§ 799–802 (no limit for crimes punishable by death; 6 year limit if punished 8 years or more; 3 years for most other felonies; and 1 year from most misdemeanors).

(b) *Location of the Crime.* The government must also establish the location of the crime, so that it shows that the court has jurisdiction and the venue is proper. *See United States v. Warren,* 984 F.2d 325 (9th Cir. 1993) (holding trial court erred because it "did not instruct the jury that [the place of the crime] was within the special territorial jurisdiction of the United States as a matter of law, and also failed to instruct the jury that to convict the jury must find beyond a reasonable doubt that the crime was committed [in that location]").

(4) *Acquittal by the Court upon Omission of Any Element.* Imagine that the prosecutor rests in Dale Defendant's arson case without offering evidence that the thing burned was "a building." The defendant will be entitled to a directed verdict or judgment of acquittal because the prosecutor did not prove each element beyond a reasonable doubt.

(5) *The Search for the Weakest Link.* In preparing a case, the defense lawyer will consider which elements the prosecutor will have the hardest time proving. In an arson case, for example, proving the perpetrator's identity is notoriously difficult

in many cases, and so perhaps the defense lawyer will look especially carefully at prosecution evidence that "Dale Defendant" committed the act of burning. Or another element may form the weakest link. (Perhaps what was burned was an animal pen, and the prosecutor, then, may lack proof that the burned object was "a building.")

(6) *Obviously, "Knowing" That the Elements Are Present Is Not the Same as Supplying Proof Beyond Reasonable Doubt of Each One.* It often happens that government officers "know" that a given individual is guilty of a specific crime. This knowledge may be genuine and accurate, based upon information and experience. Still, the proof may fail, because turning "knowledge" into admissible "proof" can be very difficult.

(7) *The Fifth Amendment's Self-Incrimination Guarantee Means the Defendant Cannot be Required to Provide Any Information That Can be Used to Prove an Element.* The Fifth Amendment's self-incrimination guarantee bars the prosecution from requiring the defendant to testify, even about matters known only to the defendant. This means the government may be unable to prove beyond a reasonable doubt some elements, especially the mens rea, because of the absence of proof from sources other than the accused.

(8) *It Is Entirely Possible for a Legislature to Write a Statute That Seems Sensible but That Is of Little Practical Value in Some Situations Because an Essential Element Cannot Be Proved Beyond a Reasonable Doubt.* Sometimes statutes can be written so that real crimes are unprovable. For example, the common law defined burglary in terms that included entry into a building "at night" with intent to commit a felony. This language, "at night," looks innocuous, but it makes many crimes unprovable. Imagine that the defendant is apprehended at 10 p.m. while wearing surgical gloves in a retail building near the cash register. The problem is, these facts provide little evidence that the defendant's entry occurred "at night." Even if we are willing to infer that the defendant "probably" entered at night, we cannot make this finding beyond a reasonable doubt. Modern statutes are written differently.

Note on How Crime Elements Influence the Prosecutor's Charging Decision

(1) *Prosecutorial Discretion and Crime Elements.* The district attorney or other prosecuting authority has discretion to select which, if any, criminal charges to bring against a defendant. Courts rarely second-guess this decision (unless the defendant can establish that the decision was based on some impermissible criterion, such as race or gender). Why do you suppose the courts give this wide deference to the prosecutor?

When a district attorney decides which charges to pursue, one of the key considerations is whether there is sufficient proof to meet the prosecutor's burden to prove each element beyond a reasonable doubt. A rigorous comparison of the elements and evidence is an important part of this analysis, and it precedes the preparation of a charging instrument such as an indictment.

When a prosecutor finds that there may be inadequate proof of one or more elements, one possibility is to seek additional investigation to obtain more evidence. Another is to charge only those crimes that can be proven or, in some cases, to move to dismiss the criminal case entirely because of the lack of admissible evidence.

(2) *The Prosecutor's Ethical Duty, Crime Elements, and Evidentiary Sufficiency.* Ethical considerations also influence the decision about which charges to bring. The prosecutor's ethical responsibilities stem from the rule that the prosecutor is both an advocate and a "minister of justice." American Bar Association, Model Rules of Professional Conduct, Rule 3.8(a), Comment (2004). In selecting charges, this special role means that a prosecutor has a duty to "refrain from prosecuting a charge that the prosecutor knows is not supported by probable cause." Rule 3.8. Note that the standard is what the prosecutor knows. According to the Model Rules, this means that the prosecutor has "actual knowledge of the fact in question." Rule 1.0(f).

§ 3.02 Five Elements of Crimes

Note on the Five Kinds of Crime Elements

Criminal statutes contain as many as five different types of elements. As discussed above, ordinarily each element must be proved by the state beyond a reasonable doubt. Each type of element, listed below, will be covered in greater detail later in this chapter.

(1) *A Voluntary Act as the Core of the Actus Reus.* Actus reus is often characterized as the physical part of a crime. It ordinarily refers to the conduct punished by the applicable criminal law. Thus, a murder statute will require the offender to "kill," an arson law will punish people who "set fire to" a structure, theft may require someone to "take" something, and conspiracy may punish people who "agree" to certain conduct.

The law of actus reus mandates that the defendant's act must also have been *voluntary*. In some situations, actus reus may even reach people who fail to act when they have a duty to do so. In other words, sometimes the actus reus is an omission to act.

Often, "actus reus" has a broader meaning as well. It can refer not just to the act or conduct of the defendant, but to all of the physical elements in the criminal statute. It may also include all required attendant circumstances, results, and causation, as well as conduct.

(2) *Attendant Circumstances.* Many crimes occur only in a specifically described situation. For example, bribery of a juror requires that the person bribed have been a juror (not another official). Attendant circumstances of this kind can increase the

seriousness of conduct that is already criminal. Thus, bribery may be a crime in certain situations, but it is an especially severe one when the person bribed is a juror. Attendant circumstances can also make lawful conduct into criminal conduct. For example, driving a motor vehicle becomes a crime when the driver is "intoxicated," an attendant circumstance.

(3) *Harm or Result.* Many criminal laws require a specific harm to have occurred before the statute applies. In murder there must be a person killed, in arson there must be a burned structure, in perjury there must have been a lie told. Sometimes the harm element, perhaps more accurately called a *result* element, requires only the creation of the *risk* of harm rather than any actual harm. An illustration is the crime of reckless endangerment.

(4) *Causation.* Often a statute requiring a harm also requires that the defendant *cause* that harm. Thus, the element of causation links two elements: the defendant's actus reus and the harm. In a murder prosecution, for example, the state must prove beyond a reasonable doubt that the defendant's acts caused the death of the victim.

(5) *Mens Rea.* Mens rea is often characterized as the *mental* requirement in a criminal law. Modern statutes often use four categories of mens rea: intentionally (or purposefully or willfully), knowingly, recklessly, and with criminal negligence.

(6) *Each Category of Element Is Not Always Present; Blurred Distinctions.* Each of the five types of elements is not necessarily present in every particular criminal law. Some offenses, for example, do not include a specific harm or result, or do not require causation. Good examples are attempted murder and driving while intoxicated, which do not mandate any specific harm but rather focus on conduct thought to imply a risk of harm. Furthermore, although the five categories of elements appear to be discrete, sometimes the elements are combined or blurred. If a statute punishes someone who "obstructs a sidewalk," the word "obstructs" describes both conduct and result.

Problem Set 3A: Crime Elements, from Burglary to Driving While Intoxicated

EXAMPLE 3A1: A TRADITIONAL BURGLARY STATUTE. Assume that a state has enacted a statute adopting the common law definition of burglary: "Burglary is breaking and entering into the dwelling house of another at night with intent to commit a felony therein." Consider the following questions:

(1) *Which Kinds of Elements?* Examine the elements of this statute. Does it require proof of a result or harm? Attendant circumstances? Causation? Conduct? Mens rea?

(2) *Number the Elements.* Separate and number all elements that the prosecution must prove, by writing (1), (2), etc. in this book alongside each. Don't forget the unexpressed elements (you'll have to write these in): defendant identity, date of the offense, and location (jurisdiction). Depending on how you count them, you should find about ten distinct elements.

(3) *Proof of the Elements.* Which element(s) do you think would be most difficult for the prosecution to prove beyond a reasonable doubt? How would the prosecution prove each element?

(4) *Circumstantial and Direct Evidence.* Some evidence is *direct evidence,* which means that the evidence proves a particular issue without requiring any significant inferences. For example, an eyewitness who saw someone break a window and climb through the opening would provide direct evidence of a "breaking" and "entry." Most evidence, however, is *circumstantial evidence,* which means that inferences must be drawn. For example, assume that a witness saw a man lift a rock and turn toward a nearby window, and then the witness heard the sound of a window breaking. This witness could provide circumstantial evidence that the man broke the window.

(5) *The Impact of Policy Choices.* Recall that each element reflects a policy decision by the entity enacting the law. Recall also that each element narrows the reach of the statute. In general, the more elements the government must prove, the fewer people who can be convicted of the offense. In the burglary statute above, has this legislature made a wise policy decision by including each element? Consider the following possible situations. Should the crime of burglary cover one or more of them or include other factors not mentioned in the statute: (a) daytime entry, (b) intent to steal but without consideration of value (*i.e.,* whether the theft would be of felony grade since theft of an item worth little money is usually a misdemeanor), (c) the requirement of a breaking (as opposed to, say, opening a door), and (d) entry into a locked warehouse as opposed to a home.

EXAMPLE 3A2: BEASTS GALORE, BUT NO ONE CAN PROVE THE CRIME. A city once adopted a criminal ordinance similar to the one that follows. The local district attorney declined any prosecutions under it. Can you see why?

> Any person who keeps within the city limits any number of chickens, goats, swine, [here follows a detailed list of additional beasts], and who is not in the business of boarding animals, is guilty of a misdemeanor, punishable by a fine of up to $500.

(1) *Elements.* What are the elements of this ordinance?

(2) *Burden of Proof.* Assume that the prosecution can prove that Georgina Goatman has a home in the city and keeps 27 goats in her back yard. Can the city meet its burden of proof beyond a reasonable doubt, so as to obtain a conviction of Ms. Goatman under this ordinance?

(3) *"Creative" Evidence?* Some enterprising students have suggested that proof of the "not in the business" element could be supplied by obtaining the defendant's federal income tax returns. It might be impracticable to seek those records for the prosecution of a simple violation of a municipal ordinance. More important, how would these records help — or fail to help — the prosecution?

EXAMPLE 3A3: DRIVING WHILE INTOXICATED: A TWO-WHEELED, SIDE-WALK, CIRCUMSTANTIAL CASE. Assume State Statute § 8A-164 is in effect:

(A) A person commits an offense if the person is intoxicated while operating a motor vehicle in a public place.

(B) "Intoxicated" means not having the normal use of mental or physical faculties by reason of the introduction of alcohol, a controlled substance, a drug, a dangerous drug, a combination of two or more of those substances, or any other substance into the body; or having an alcohol concentration of 0.08 or more.

(C) "Motor vehicle" means a device in, on, or by which a person or property is or may be transported or drawn on a highway, except a device used exclusively on stationary rails or tracks.

(D) Proof of a mental state is not required for conviction of this offense.

Consider the following facts. Police officers on a routine patrol observe a person sleeping on the ground beside a battery-operated, electrically powered wheelchair in a public street. There is a sidewalk nearby, but not parallel to the street where the person is found. The sidewalk runs through an empty lot that is private property. Officers rouse the individual, who spontaneously says he "must've took too much of my medicine," and then identifies himself as "Sam Suspect." Suspect is unable to walk and uses a wheelchair. A breath test shows that Suspect has a blood alcohol concentration of 0.04 (which is below the legal limit and not very high). Officers take him into custody and the state charges him with driving while intoxicated under the statutes above.

(1) *Elements.* What are the elements of driving while intoxicated, State Statute § 8A-164? (Some of them need to be stated in the alternative.)

(2) *The Trial of Sam Suspect.* Can the prosecution meet its burden of proving every element beyond a reasonable doubt if Suspect is prosecuted for driving while intoxicated? [The answer is, "possibly yes—but maybe not." Why, as to each element?]

(3) *Is Operating a Zamboni on the Ice While Drunk a Crime? No Drunk Driving Charge for Zamboni Operator,* www.msnbc.com/id/17930215 (April 3, 2007). Zamboni operator John Peragallo was charged with drunken driving after a fellow employee at a sports arena told police the machine was speeding and nearly crashed into the boards. A Zamboni is a tractor-like machine used to scrape and clean the surface of ice at a rink. Peragallo's blood alcohol level was 0.12 percent, well above the .08 percent required for conviction. Peragallo testified he drank some liquor and took two Valium pills before going to work. The trial judge, however, dismissed the case and ruled that the four ton ice rink grooming machines are not motor vehicles because they are not usable on highways and cannot carry passengers. If the above statute were in effect, would you decide the same way as the actual trial judge did?

§ 3.03 Actus Reus: The Requirement of a Voluntary Act (or Omission)

Note on the Two Varieties of Actus Reus: Commissions and Omissions

(1) *Defining the Proscribed Conduct to Avoid Criminalizing Thoughts.* Actus reus, often referred to as the "wrongful act," is a key element in virtually all criminal statutes. On the surface, it describes *conduct* necessary to commit the crime. The requirement of conduct means that criminal liability does not punish just thoughts or a person's physical condition.

(2) *A Voluntary Act or Omission.* But the concept of actus reus is more complicated, ordinarily mandating that the conduct have been the product of a "voluntary act" (or a failure or omission to act when there was a duty to act). We take up omissions later.

Modern criminal laws often specifically include both voluntary acts and omissions to act. The Model Penal Code is an example: "A person is not guilty of an offense unless his liability is based on conduct that includes a voluntary act or the omission to perform an act of which he is physically capable." MPC § 2.01(1).

(3) *Sleepwalkers (If Genuinely Acting Involuntarily) Can Get Away with (What Otherwise Looks Like) Murder.* The Model Penal Code also lists acts that are not voluntary and therefore are not criminal: a reflex or convulsion, a bodily movement during unconsciousness or sleep, conduct under hypnosis, or a bodily movement not a product of the actor's effort or determination, either conscious or habitual.

Problem 3B (Actus Reus): A Frightening Drawing, by a 12-Year-Old

(1) *What Is a "Threat"?: Commonwealth v. Milo M.*, 740 N.E.2d 967 (Mass. 2001). In this case, a twelve-year-old was adjudicated as a delinquent under a criminal statute covering anyone who "has threatened [the actus reus] to commit a crime against the person or property of another...." The child's actus reus constituting the alleged "threat" was a drawing that depicted himself pointing a gun at his teacher. The Massachusetts Supreme Judicial Court held that the drawing was sufficient evidence of a voluntary act constituting a threat.

(2) *Can a Drawing Suffice to Prove a Threat?* The Massachusetts statute does not define the word "threatened." The court pointed out, however, that prior cases had defined this actus reus element as "an expression of intention to inflict a crime on another and the ability to do so in circumstances that would justify apprehension on the part of the threat's recipient." Notice that this definition does not require an actual intent to carry out the threat. The threat itself is enough as long as it is an "expression of intention." Do these interpretations of the statute faithfully carry out its meaning?

(3) *The Policy Underlying the Criminalization of Threats: The Reaction That Is Caused by Threats, Whether or Not They Are "Real."* Thus, the actus reus amounts to

an "expression" combined with "ability" and circumstances that would have justi-fied "apprehension." The legislative policy is to sanction someone who creates the possibility of a reaction (either emotional or preventive) that threats, as a category of utterances, usually cause. Given the court's definition and the underlying policy, can the court's judgment be defended on the ground that the child's actus reus was complete, there having been an "expression," "ability" to act upon it, and justifiable "apprehension"?

[A] The Requirement of a Voluntary Act

> Read MPC § 2.01 (1)–(2) [voluntary act requirement] in the MPC Appendix.

State v. Sowry

803 N.E.2d 867 (Ohio 2004)

GRADY, JUDGE.

Defendant, Stephen Sowry, appeals from his conviction for knowingly convey-ing drugs onto the grounds of a detention facility in violation of R.C. 2921.36(A)(2).... Sowry was arrested by West Milton police on June 30, 2001, on charges of disorderly conduct and resisting arrest. A patdown failed to reveal any weapons or contraband. Sowry was transported to the Miami County Jail by officers. At the jail, Sowry was asked whether he had any drugs on his person. He replied, "No." A more thorough search when he was booked in revealed a baggie of marijuana in his right front pants pocket. [Sowry was convicted of "knowingly conveying" drugs into the jail, was sentenced to prison for one year, and appealed.]

[The statute allegedly violated, R.C. 2921.36(A)(2), states: "No person shall knowingly convey, or attempt to convey, onto the grounds of a detention facility ... [a]ny drug of abuse, as defined in section 3719.011 of the Revised Code."]

It is undisputed that the marijuana that was in Sowry's pants pocket when he was brought to the jail and which police found when he was searched there is a drug of abuse.... Nor is it disputed that the Miami County Jail is a detention facility.... Rather, Sowry argues that ... his conduct cannot render him criminally liable for a violation of R.C. 2921.36(A)(2) on the facts that the state's evidence demonstrates. We agree.

R.C. 2901.21(A) states:

> Except as provided in division (B) [involving strict liability] of this section, a person is not guilty of an offense unless ... (1) The person's liability is based on conduct that includes either a voluntary act, or an omission to perform an act or duty that the person is capable of performing. ...

. . . The "voluntary act" or "omission" requirement . . . codifies the maxim of criminal law that criminal conduct must rest on an act, and the law will not punish for a guilty mind alone. The same applies to an omission to act, where both a duty to act is imposed by law and a capacity to act exists. The requirement in either instance is the "actus reus" necessary to constitute a violation.

The conduct that a prohibited act involves must be voluntary in order for criminal liability to result. A reflexive or convulsive act is not voluntary and thus cannot be the basis of criminal liability. Similarly, acts performed while unconscious or sleepwalking are not voluntary acts. "In short, any act that is not the product of the actor's conscious determination is not a voluntary act." . . .

Exercising the power to control his person which their arrest of Sowry conferred on them, officers conveyed Sowry to and into the jail to facilitate his detention. That his "person" and the possessions on his person were in the jail was therefore not a product of a voluntary act on Sowry's part. Rather, those events were, as to him, wholly involuntary.

The state argues that Sowry acted knowingly because he responded "No" when he was asked at book-in whether he had any drugs, adding: "The Appellant chose not to be honest, and that was to his detriment."

With respect to an actor's conduct, R.C. 2921.36(A)(2) imposes no legal duty to act in the way the state suggests Sowry ought to have acted in order to avoid being the author of his own misfortune. Even if it did, such a duty could not be enforceable when, as here, performing the duty would implicate him in criminal conduct: possession of drugs. Both the Fifth Amendment to the Constitution of the United States and Section 10, Article I of the Ohio Constitution prohibit compulsion of that kind.

At most, Sowry might be charged with knowing that drugs were on his person when officers conveyed him to jail. However, as we said above, the law will not punish for a guilty mind alone. . . . [T]he trial court erred when it denied Sowry's . . . motion for judgment of acquittal.

STATE v. BARNES, 747 S.E.3d 912 (N.C. 2013). This case involved facts analogous to those in *Sowry,* above. The defendant was conveyed to jail while carrying contraband drugs and was convicted of possessing them in that facility. He argued, as in that case, that he had not committed a voluntary act in doing so. The court reached the opposite result from that in *Sowry* and affirmed the conviction. The court reasoned:

> 3. Voluntariness . . . Defendant's position is inconsistent with the result reached in the majority of decisions from other jurisdictions that have addressed the issue of whether a defendant can be convicted of possessing a controlled substance in a confinement facility after having been involuntarily brought into the facility following an arrest. *See State v. Canas,*

597 N.W.2d 488, 496 (Iowa 1999) (upholding the defendant's conviction because "the defendant in [that case] had the option of disclosing the presence of the drugs concealed in his person before he entered the jail and became guilty of the additional offense of introducing controlled substances into a detention facility").

Notes and Questions

(1) *Voluntary Act.* There is no doubt that Sowry brought drugs into the jail, but the court holds he did not commit a crime because he did not commit a voluntary act. Consider the fact that he voluntarily answered "no" to the officer's question about drugs at the jail, which meant that he voluntarily chose a course of conduct that he knew would inevitably convey the drugs into the booking facility. Doesn't this voluntary choice supply the actus reus element that the court finds wanting? The court in *Barnes* thought so. On the other hand, would a "yes" answer have amounted to compelled self-incrimination?

(2) *Reason for the Voluntary Act Requirement.* Why does the criminal law traditionally not punish involuntary acts? The *harm* may be the same whether or not the act is voluntary. Sowry did introduce drugs into a jail, irrespective of whether he did so voluntarily.

(3) *Role of Knowledge.* Imagine a driver who knows that he is subject to seizures rendering him unconscious, but who continues to drive a car. One evening while driving, he has a seizure and passes out, killing four people. If charged with reckless homicide, can he escape responsibility by arguing that he committed no voluntary act (and hence no actus reus) because at the moment of the collision he had blacked out? The leading case answers "no," on the theory that the voluntary act is driving with the knowledge that the defendant suffered from seizures. *People v. Decina,* 138 N.E.2d 799 (N.Y. 1956). Is this reasoning persuasive, and is it distinguishable from Sowry's lie about his drugs, which was voluntarily done despite the involuntary result?

(4) *Case Illustrations. See, e.g., Martin v. State,* 17 So.2d 427 (Ala. Civ. App 1944) (classic case where defendant was arrested in his home and taken by police onto the highway where he committed the crime of being drunk in a public place; appellate court reversed since the defendant did not "voluntarily" appear in a public place); *People v. Martino,* 970 N.E.2d 1236 (Ill. App. Ct. 2012) (defendant committed no voluntary act when he fell onto the victim's arm, breaking it, after police officer used electroshock weapon on him to break up a domestic dispute); *State v. Newman,* 302 P.3d 435 (Or. 2013) (statutory voluntary act requirement applied to strict liability driving under the influence offense; defendant was entitled to "introduce evidence that he suffers from a sleepwalking disorder and was 'sleep driving' at the time he was stopped in his vehicle"); *State v. Deer,* 287 P.3d 539 (Wash. 2012) (defendant charged with rape of a child argued that she was not liable for this strict liability crime because she was asleep during the sexual acts).

[B] Omissions as Actus Reus: The Legal Duty Requirement

Note on Omission as Actus Reus

(1) *An Omission as Actus Reus—and the Underlying Requirement of Legal Duty.* The second kind of actus reus is, in some ways, the opposite of the first. It covers an *omission* or failure to act. But not just any omission is penalized—the failure to act usually must breach a legal *duty to perform that act.* A parent who does not feed an infant, resulting in the infant's death by starvation, is an example. The parent could be responsible for murdering the child because he or she did not perform the *legally imposed* duty of providing food for the baby.

For example, a New Jersey law provides: "Liability for the commission of an offense may not be based on an omission unaccompanied by action unless: (1) The omission is expressly made sufficient by the law defining the offense; or (2) A duty to perform the omitted act is otherwise imposed by law." N.J. Code Crim. J. 2C:2–1(b); *see also* MPC § 2.01(3) (same).

(2) *Capable of Performing Duty.* The concept of actus reus by omission has an obvious and yet rarely explored underlying corollary: the person who breached the duty ordinarily must have been physically able to perform the duty at the time of the omission. Thus, a parent who suffered an unexpected stroke and was in a coma would be excused from criminal liability for a failure to provide food for his or her children during the time he or she was incapable of doing so. *See, e.g.*, Model Penal Code § 2.01 ("perform an act of which he is physically capable").

This principle is illustrated by *People v. Likine*, 823 N.W.2d 50 (Mich. 2012), where the court held that a defense to the crime of failing to pay child support (an omission) is that the person obligated to pay simply could not do so despite good faith efforts to comply with the obligation. If payment was impossible, then the legal violation was involuntary and not subject to criminal liability.

Read MPC § 2.01 (3) [omission as actus reus; legal duty requirement] in the MPC Appendix.

Notes and Questions

(1) *Sources of Legal Duties, in General.* Note that the rule that an omission may constitute an actus reus only when the omission involved the violation of a duty is universally read as mandating that the duty must be imposed *by law*, not by a moral code. *See People v. Beardsley*, 113 N.W. 1128 (Mich. 1907) ("the duty neglected must be a legal duty, and not a mere moral obligation"). The most obvious illustration of a legal duty is the federal statute requiring the filing of various tax documents and punishing the failure to file. *See, e.g.*, 26 U.S.C. § 7203 (misdemeanor for anyone required by law to file a tax return to willfully fail to do so). Other sources of legal

duties for purposes of omission liability are contracts and the common law. The common law recognized four distinct affirmative duties to act. *See* note (5), below.

(2) *Statutes as Sources of Legal Duties.* The legal duty giving rise to criminal responsibility may come from many sources. A statute may impose such a duty. Thus, family law provisions require a mother or father to take care of a child. For example, in *State v. Martinez*, 68 P.3d 606 (Haw. 2003), a two-year-old child died from wounds while in the care of her mother and the mother's boyfriend. Both were convicted of manslaughter for failing to provide necessary medical care for the child, irrespective of who caused the injuries. The mother violated a state statute requiring parents to provide to the best of their abilities reasonably necessary and available medical services. The boyfriend violated a duty that the court inferred from common law (over a vigorous dissent).

(3) *Good Samaritan Statutes: A Duty to Care for Strangers?* As a general rule, American law imposes no general duty of care. This means that in most situations a person is not *legally* obligated to come to another person's aid, even if aid can be rendered easily without endangering the aider and even if well-accepted moral values dictate that the person should provide aid. An Olympic swimmer who sees an infant drowning in one inch of water has no duty to rescue the baby.

There have been many suggestions that statutes should impose a general duty to care for others if doing so can be done without harm to the caregiver. *See, e.g.,* Daniel Yeager, *A Radical Community of Aid: A Rejoinder to Opponents of Affirmative Duties to Help Strangers*, 71 Wash. U. L. L. Q. 1 (1993). A few American jurisdictions have accepted these suggestions. The most heavily publicized is the Vermont provision:

> A person who knows that another is exposed to grave physical harm shall, to the extent that the same can be rendered without danger or peril to himself or without interference with important duties owed to others, give reasonable assistance to the exposed person unless that assistance or care is being provided by others.

Vt. Stat. Ann. Tit.12, § 519. *See also* Minn. Stat. § 604A.01 subd. 1 (requiring reasonable assistance to someone exposed to grave physical harm at an emergency scene). The Wisconsin statute is more limited, imposing a duty on someone who knows a crime is being committed and that a victim is exposed to bodily harm to "summon law enforcement officers or other assistance or shall provide assistance to the victim." Wis. Stat. Ann. 940.34. These statutes ordinarily impose only a minor punishment for their violation. Should other jurisdictions adopt "general duty of care" statutes?

(4) *Contract as the Source of the Required Duty.* A legally imposed duty of care may be created by contract. For example, a caregiver may enter a contract to provide certain services to a comatose person. The failure to adhere to the contract, causing the death of the patient, can constitute a breach of legal duty triggering criminal liability for the death. *See generally* Melvin A. Eisenberg, *The Duty to Rescue in Contract*, 71 Fordham L. Rev. 647 (2002).

(5) *Common Law Duties.* Duties may also come from the common law. Many common law duties arise from relationships, such that a person will have a legal duty to act based on a particular "status." Thus, a parent has a duty, even in the absence of a statute, to care for a child, sometimes a child to care for a parent, a spouse for a spouse, ship captains for their crews, and masters to aid their servants. *See generally Commonwealth v. Twitchell*, 617 N.E.2d 609 (Mass. 1993) (parent has "a common law duty to provide medical services for a child, the breach of which can be the basis in the appropriate circumstances, for the conviction of a parent for involuntary manslaughter").

An important issue, discussed below, is whether this duty of care for a child applies to an unrelated adult, such as the mother's boyfriend, who is living in a "familial relationship" with the mother and the child.

Another common law duty arises when one voluntarily assumes responsibility for care of a person and thereby causes others not to do so, or sequesters a person so that others cannot help the person. Thus, a babysitter may have a duty to care for a child. Property law may also impose a duty on landowners to use reasonable care to protect the safety of people on their premises.

(6) *Knowledge of Duty or Relevant Circumstances.* When a statute or common law rule creates a duty, does the person who has the duty have to know about it before he or she may be held responsible for breaching that duty? What if the defendant did not know that he or she needed to act to protect defendant's child? *See, e.g., People v. Pollock*, 780 N.E.2d 669 (Ill. 2002) (liability based on omission to act requires knowledge of the need for action; defendant mother was not liable for failure to protect her child from abuse when she did not know that her boyfriend was abusing the child).

(7) *A Duty to Prevent or Redress Actions of Third Parties?* Criminal responsibility also may reach the failure to stop actions of third parties. In *People v. Swanson-Birabent*, 114 Cal. App. 4th 733 (Cal. Ct. App. 2004), a mother was convicted of committing a lewd act when she stood over the bed and watched her boyfriend molest her daughter.

State v. Hocter
262 P.3d 1089 (Mont. 2011)

[Defendant was convicted of child endangerment by omission. The child was not her own, but was the daughter of her live-in boyfriend, who was away, and she was taking care of the child. She left the injured and crying little girl in her crib and turned up the music. (The child's injuries were the result of an assault by the defendant herself, precipitated because the child was colicky and would not stop crying, but that was not the charge at issue; instead, the charge was child endangerment, alleged to have been committed by failing to obtain medical care for the child.) The child, named in the opinion as S.B., was left permanently disabled and blind.

[The defendant challenged the conviction on the ground that there was an insufficient showing of a duty on her part to care for the child, S.B., to support the charge of endangerment by omission. The court here rejects this argument and affirms the conviction.]

This Court has recognized that not every failure to take action subjects a person to criminal liability. "For criminal liability to be based upon a failure to act, there must be a duty imposed by the law to act, and the person must be physically capable of performing the act." *State ex rel. Kuntz v. Montana Thirteenth Judicial Dist. Court*, 2000 MT, 995 P.2d 951. In the absence of "a duty that the law imposes," a person cannot be criminally liable for failure to "rescue or summon aid for another person who is at risk or in danger, even though society recognizes that a moral obligation might exist." *Kuntz*. This Court has recited at least six common law exceptions that apply to the general rule: (1) a duty based on a personal relationship, such as parent-child or husband-wife; (2) a duty based on statute; (3) a duty based on contract; (4) a duty based upon voluntary assumption of care; (5) a duty to control the conduct of others; and (6) a duty based on being a landowner. Whether a legal duty to act exists is a question of law for the court. Whether a defendant failed to act pursuant to that duty is a question for the finder of fact. *Kuntz*.

A parent's criminal liability based upon a failure to act in accordance with common law affirmative duties to protect their children is recognized in numerous jurisdictions, including this one. *State v. Powers*, 645 P.2d 1357, 1362–1363 ([Mont.] 1982) (mother convicted of deliberate homicide for causing child's death by her failure to perform duties as a parent); . . . *see also People v. Stanciel*, 606 N.E.2d 1201 (1992) (mother guilty of homicide by sanctioning ongoing abuse of child by boyfriend); *State v. Walden*, 293 S.E.2d 780 (1982) (mother guilty of assault for failure to prevent abuse); *Smith v. State*, 408 N.E.2d 614 (Ind. App. 1980) (mother held criminally responsible for failing to prevent fatal beating of child by her boyfriend).

Numerous jurisdictions have recognized that in addition to biological and adoptive parents and legal guardians, there may be other adults who establish familial relationships with and assume responsibility for the care of a child, thereby creating a legal duty to protect that child from harm. *See e.g. State v. Miranda*, 715 A.2d 680 (1998) (boyfriend who considered himself victim's stepfather had assumed duty of care for the child) convicted of manslaughter). We have recognized a "mutual reliance" duty owed to "two people, though not closely related, [who] live together under one roof." *Kuntz*.

In *Kuntz*, this Court found the idea that persons in a relationship involving cohabitation would not have a legal duty to summon medical aid for one another "untenable." Not extending this duty to the children present in such relationships would constitute an absurd distinction, particularly given that children are dependent upon others for care and intervention when sick or injured. Census information shows that children under the age of five years frequently live in the households of cohabitating adults. Rose M. Kreider & Diana B. Elliott, *America's Families and*

Living Arrangements: 2007, Current Population Reports, P20–561, 17, U.S. Census Bureau, Washington, DC (2009). "To distinguish among children in deciding which ones are entitled to protection based upon whether their adult caregivers have chosen to have their relationships officially recognized hardly advances the public policy of protecting children from abuse." *Miranda,* 715 A.2d at 690.

In this case, Hocter stated that she had been involved in S.B.'s life since her birth, and that she loved S.B. no differently than her own one-month-old daughter who was also in her care. We conclude that Hocter had established a personal relationship akin to that of a parent with S.B., and that she had voluntarily assumed responsibility for the welfare of S.B. As such, there existed a common law duty of protect S.B. from harm, and the breach of this duty was the appropriate basis for a conviction pursuant to [the child endangerment statute]. . . . Affirmed.

Notes and Questions

(1) *Another Court Disagreed with Hocter, After First Agreeing: State v. Miranda,* 878 A.2d 1118 (Conn. 2006). Defendant was the live-in boyfriend of the injured child's mother and considered himself the child's "stepfather." The mother assaulted the child, and the defendant omitted to prevent the assault or obtain care. In the decision cited in *Hocter,* above, the Connecticut court at first upheld the defendant's conviction for assault. But later, in *"Miranda III,"* it reversed itself and held that the live-in boyfriend could not be convicted of omission. The court splintered so that there was no majority opinion, but one of the judges who voted to reverse the conviction reasoned as follows:

> First . . . parents and guardians fall into clearly recognized legal categories, . . . The same cannot be said for . . . the defendant. . . .

> Second, . . . the emerging demographic trend toward nontraditional alternative family arrangements, which we cited as support in *Miranda I,* now strikes me as a counter argument. Precisely because of that trend, and the concomitant difficulty of determining in advance where it will lead, . . . the boundaries of this . . . liability will be too amorphous . . . to fit comfortably within our Penal Code.

> Third, this amorphousness . . . will discourage others, such as volunteers and close friends, from establishing "familial relationships" with the children who are likely to be the most in need of them.

Is this reasoning persuasive, or is the reasoning in the principal case, *Hocter,* better?

(2) *The Importance of Omission and of Duty in Child Abuse Prosecutions.* There usually are only two or three eyewitnesses to severe child abuse: a child of tender years, a parent or parent-substitute, and perhaps a second parent or companion. Often, it is utterly impossible to reconstruct or fix responsibility for the affirmative acts inflicting injury, because in many cases, none of these three people is usable as a witness. Can you explain why? As a result, omission-based theories are particularly important in prosecutions of child abuse.

(3) *Should There Be a Knowledge-of-Duty Requirement?* Today virtually all American jurisdictions require certain sex offenders (and sometimes all or many convicted felons) to register with a state or local government entity, or both. Sometimes the registration results in information and even a photograph on an internet site. Failure to register as required may constitute a crime. In *Lambert v. California*, 355 U.S. 225 (1958), the Supreme Court struck down a conviction under a municipal ordinance requiring convicted felons to register with the L.A. police department.

Cases interpreting these registration laws ordinarily hold that they comply with *Lambert* by imposing criminal liability only if the offender knew of the legal duty to register. *See, e.g., Dailey v. State*, 65 P.3d 891 (Alaska Ct. App. 2003). The defense fails when the court finds that the offender knew or should have known of the obligation to act. *See, e.g., United States v. Hutzell*, 217 F.3d 966 (8th Cir. 2000). We discuss *Lambert* again in Chapter 13.

(4) *The Function of the Duty Requirement.* People omit an infinite variety of actions daily. Furthermore, many omissions to intervene in others' affairs are to be encouraged. For example, society wants individuals to refrain from interfering with parents when the basis is disagreement with parenting styles. This "omission" might result in injury to a child in a given instance, but criminalizing the omission would encourage people to interfere when they should not. Does this explanation justify the restriction suggested in the *Miranda III* opinion?

Problem 3C: A Duty?

Defendant Deborah met victim Victor at a park. They went to a private area of the park and used cocaine for most of the day. At 9 P.M. defendant Deborah drove Victor to his mother's home in a local trailer park. On the way Deborah saw Victor inject himself with heroin which he had brought with him to the park but had not used. At the trailer park, Deborah was unable to wake Victor in order to ascertain his mother's address within the trailer park. She dragged him from her car, still unconscious, and left him on the grass in the trailer park. Victor was breathing and making noises at that time, but was found unconscious several hours later and died shortly thereafter at a hospital from a drug overdose induced by the combination of heroin and cocaine.

(1) Defendant Deborah is charged with criminally negligent homicide for Victor's death. Did she commit an actus reus? Was it a commission or omission?

(2) If her action was an omission, what legal duties would you argue she violated? *See People v. Erb*, 894 N.Y.S.2d 266 (N.Y. App. Div. 2010).

[C] Possession as Actus Reus

Note on Possession as Actus Reus

(1) *Possession: A Unique Kind of Actus Reus.* Many crimes punish *possession* of an item, such as drugs or weapons. But what is the actus reus of possession? Does the

person have to know that he or she possesses the contraband? Imagine that a prankster has placed a small envelope of heroin in someone else's backpack without telling the backpack owner about it. Does the owner commit the actus reus of heroin possession by carrying the contraband?

(2) *Is Possession Really a Knowing Omission, or a "Status," Rather Than an Affirmative Act?* Many statutes anticipate this issue and provide specifically that the "possessor" commits an actus reus only if he or she *knows* about the contraband and does not get rid of it. Thus, New Jersey law, tracking Model Penal Code § 2.01(4), provides: "Possession is an act . . . if the possessor knowingly procured or received the thing possessed or was aware of his control thereof for a sufficient period to have been able to terminate his possession." N.J. Code Crim. J. 2C-2–1(c). Note that this statute creates a duty on the unknowing possessor to terminate possession when the person becomes aware of his or her control over the item.

United States v. Zandi
769 F.2d 229 (4th Cir. 1985)

[This case appears in Chapter 1, above, and should be reconsidered at this point. Mehdi and Hadi Zandi were brothers who sent money to their brother Morteza in Pakistan and who engaged in a cryptic, recorded telephone conversation with him about a "box of presents" to be sent to them. About the same time, they sent $3,000 to him. The return address used by Morteza was false, so was the name of the shipper, and so was the addressee.

[When the brothers learned that the shipment had arrived at their designated postal address in the United States, they went to the airport to pick it up. They paid $5 to obtain an airway bill receipt and carrier's certificate. They were told they would have to pay a surcharge today, in addition to the usual storage fee of $50, so they returned the next day and Mehdi paid the $50. When told that a customs officer would "clear" the package, however, Mehdi abruptly left.

[Suspicious, a customs officer opened the package and found packets of opium. He closed the package. Mehdi was arrested when he came the next day and presented documents to pick up the package, Hadi was arrested while waiting in his car outside, and both were convicted of possessing opium with intent to distribute. On appeal, they each argued that there was insufficient evidence to prove (1) possession of the package as well as (2) knowledge that the package contained opium. The court affirmed in an opinion excerpted more completely in Chapter 1, and excerpted sparingly here:]

. . . Possession . . . may be either actual or constructive. *United States v. Raper*, 676 F.2d 841, 847 (D.C.Cir.1982). Constructive possession exists when the defendant exercises, or has the power to exercise, dominion and control over the item. . . .

United States v. Martorano, 709 F.2d 863 (3d Cir.1983), amply supports the government's characterization of constructive possession. Martorano intended to distribute large quantities of a controlled substance, P-2-P. He devised a plan under which a DEA informant (unbeknownst to Martorano) would rent a van, place the drugs in the van and park the van in a local square. Martorano gave the DEA agent money for the drugs . . . and the DEA agent, in turn, gave Martorano the key to the van. . . . The Third Circuit ruled that Martorano "acquired constructive possession of the P-2-P when he acquired actual possession of the key to the van". . . . The mere fact that government officials prevented him from taking absolute control over the drugs did not detract from his culpability under 21 U.S.C. § 841(a)(1).

Likewise, in the instant case, the appellants acquired constructive possession of the opium when they acquired actual possession of the shipping documents. . . . [AFFIRMED.]

Notes and Questions

(1) *Is Possession an Act, an Omission, a Status, or Something Else?* This question is raised by the notes above. Now that you have considered *Zandi*, how would you answer it?

(2) *"Actual" Possession and "Constructive" Possession.* Consider how the court defines constructive possession. Is this a concept that could ensnare an innocent person if overzealously extended? (The court elsewhere raised this question but dismissed it in the case because there were "more than sufficient indicia of constructive possession.")

(3) *Knowledge: What Was It That the Zandis Had to "Know" for Conviction?* Consider the possibility that the Zandis were "reasonably sure" that the package contained opium, but not "absolutely certain" (in their minds, perhaps, Morteza might have kept the $3,000 and double-crossed them, though this was unlikely). Could these facts support their conviction? What about the definition of knowledge in MPC § 2.02(2)(b)?

[D] Status Crimes and Actus Reus

Note: Can "Just Being Someone" (or Somewhere) Be Actus Reus?

In certain situations the Constitution places limits on a legislature's capacity to define actus reus. One such area involves what have been called *status crimes*. In *Robinson v. California*, below, the Supreme Court held that "being addicted to . . . narcotics" could not be defined as a crime, but in *Powell v. Texas*, below, it decided that being "drunk . . . in a public place" could be a crime. Can you identify the principle(s) that distinguish the two outcomes?

ROBINSON v. CALIFORNIA, 370 U.S. 660 (1962). A California statute made it a crime for a person to "be addicted to the use of narcotics." The Supreme Court, per Justice Stewart, held that the statute was unconstitutional:

The [trial] judge . . . instructed the jury that the appellant could be convicted . . . if the jury agreed . . . that he was of the "status" [of being addicted]. . . .

. . . This statute [as construed to allow this conviction] is not one which punishes a person for the use of narcotics, for their purchase, sale or possession, or for antisocial or disorderly behavior resulting from their administration. . . .

In this Court counsel for the State recognized that narcotic addiction is an illness. . . . We hold that a state law which imprisons a person thus afflicted as a criminal . . . inflicts a cruel and unusual punishment in violation of the Fourteenth Amendment. . . .

Justice Clark dissented: "California has a comprehensive and enlightened program for the control of narcotism based on the overriding policy of prevention and cure. . . . [T]he majority admits that 'a State might establish a program of compulsory treatment for those addicted to narcotics' which 'might require periods of involuntary confinement.'" He added, "Moreover, 'status' offenses have long been known and recognized in the criminal law. A ready example is drunkenness, which plainly is as involuntary after addiction to alcohol as is the taking of drugs."

Is there merit to Justice Clark's argument? Consider public drunkenness, in the next case.

Powell v. Texas

392 U.S. 514 (1968)

Mr. Justice Marshall announced the judgment of the Court and delivered an opinion in which The Chief Justice, Mr. Justice Black, and Mr. Justice Harlan join.

In late December 1966, appellant was arrested and charged with being found in a state of intoxication in a public place, in violation of Vernon's Ann. Texas Penal Code, Art. 477 (1952), which reads as follows: "Whoever shall get drunk or be found in a state of intoxication in any public place, or at any private house except his own, shall be fined not exceeding one hundred dollars." [Appellant was tried, convicted, and fined $20. He appealed to the County Court where his counsel urged that appellant was afflicted with the disease of chronic alcoholism, that his appearance in public while drunk was not of his own volition, and therefore that to punish him criminally for that conduct would be cruel and unusual, in violation of the Eighth and Fourteenth Amendments to the United States Constitution. The court made specific findings, described below, and ruled as a matter of law that chronic alcoholism was not a defense to the charge. Appellant appealed.]

I.

The principal testimony [on the chronic alcoholism issue] was that of Dr. David Wade. He testified . . . that appellant is a "chronic alcoholic," who "by the time he has reached (the state of intoxication) . . . is not able to control his behavior, and (who) . . . has reached this point because he has an uncontrollable compulsion to drink." . . . On cross examination, Dr. Wade admitted that when appellant was sober he knew the difference between right and wrong, and he responded affirmatively to the question whether appellant's act in taking the first drink in any given instance when he was sober was a "voluntary exercise of his will." . . .

Following this abbreviated exposition of the problem before it, the trial court indicated its intention to disallow appellant's claimed defense of "chronic alcoholism." Thereupon defense counsel submitted, and the trial court entered, the following "findings of fact": (1) That chronic alcoholism is a disease which destroys the afflicted person's will power to resist the constant, excessive consumption of alcohol. (2) That a chronic alcoholic does not appear in public by his own volition but under a compulsion symptomatic of the disease of chronic alcoholism. (3) That Leroy Powell, defendant herein, . . . is afflicted with the disease of chronic alcoholism.

Whatever else may be said of them, those are not "findings of fact" in any recognizable, traditional sense in which that term has been used in a court of law; they are the premises of a syllogism transparently designed to bring this case within the scope of this Court's opinion in *Robinson v. California*, 370 U.S. 660 (1962). Nonetheless, the dissent would have us adopt these "findings" [and] use them as the basis for a constitutional holding that "a person may not be punished if the condition essential to constitute the defined crime is part of the pattern of his disease and is occasioned by a compulsion symptomatic of the disease." . . .

II.

Despite the comparatively primitive state of our knowledge on the subject, it cannot be denied that the destructive use of alcoholic beverages is one of our principal social and public health problems. . . . There is as yet no known generally effective method for treating the vast number of alcoholics in our society. . . . Faced with this unpleasant reality, we are unable to assert that the use of the criminal process as a means of dealing with the public aspects of problem drinking can never be defended as rational. . . . This Court has never held that anything in the Constitution requires that penal sanctions be designed solely to achieve therapeutic or rehabilitative effects, and it can hardly be said with assurance that incarceration serves such purposes any better for the general run of criminals than it does for public drunks. . . .

III. . . .

On its face the present case does not fall within [the] holding [in *Robinson v. California*,] since appellant was convicted, not for being a chronic alcoholic, but for being in public while drunk on a particular occasion. The State of Texas thus has not sought to punish a mere status, as California did in *Robinson*; nor has it attempted to regulate appellant's behavior in the privacy of his own home. Rather, it has imposed upon appellant a criminal sanction for public behavior which may create substantial health and safety hazards. . . .

It is suggested in dissent that *Robinson* stands for the "simple" but "subtle" principle that "(c)riminal penalties may not be inflicted upon a person for being in a condition he is powerless to change." [But the] thrust of *Robinson's* interpretation of the Cruel and Unusual Punishment Clause is that criminal penalties may be inflicted only if the accused has committed some act . . . which society has an interest in preventing . . . . It thus does not deal with the question of whether certain conduct cannot constitutionally be punished because it is, in some sense, "involuntary" or "occasioned by a compulsion." . . .

Ultimately, then, the most troubling aspects of this case, were *Robinson* to be extended to meet it, would be the scope and content of what could only be a constitutional doctrine of criminal responsibility. . . . In the first place, nothing in the logic of the dissent would limit its application to chronic alcoholics. If Leroy Powell cannot be convicted of public intoxication, it is difficult to see how a State can convict an individual for murder, if that individual, while exhibiting normal behavior in all other respects, suffers from a "compulsion" to kill, which is an exceedingly strong influence, but "not completely overpowering." . . .

. . . We are unable to conclude, on the state of this record or on the current state of medical knowledge, that chronic alcoholics in general, and Leroy Powell in particular, suffer from such an irresistible compulsion to drink and to get drunk in public that they are utterly unable to control their performance of either or both of these acts. . . . Affirmed.

[The concurring opinions of Justice Black and Justice White are omitted.]

Mr. Justice Fortas, with whom Mr. Justice Douglas, Mr. Justice Brennan, and Mr. Justice Stewart join, dissenting.

. . . In the present case, appellant is charged with a crime composed of two elements—being intoxicated and being found in a public place while in that condition. The crime, so defined, differs from that in *Robinson*. The statute covers more than a mere status. But the essential constitutional defect here is the same as in *Robinson*, for in both cases the particular defendant was accused of being in a condition which he had no capacity to change or avoid. . . . [I would reverse the judgment.]

Notes and Questions

(1) *If Powell's Conviction Were Unconstitutional, What Alternative Would the State Have?* Was the result in Powell's case dictated by the futility of any other holding? If arresting Powell were unconstitutional, the state might still decide that his public drunkenness interfered with activities of others, threatened his safety, or posed public dangers. Instead of sending police officers to arrest him, the state might send public health officers to "quarantine" him, but those individuals would need to be trained as peace officers, and the process would amount to an "arrest." Then, Powell might be confined and "treated," although the "hospital" in which he would find himself would need to have most of the characteristics of a jail. Finally, even after he was pronounced "cured," Powell might (or, probably would) appear drunk again in

the same public place—and could he be arrested then? Does this (somewhat cynical) depiction of reality provide the true reason for this decision?

(2) *Criminalization for Public Drug Intoxication after Robinson?* After *Powell*, could Robinson be convicted for actually being under the influence of drugs in public? (It would seem so, although the Supreme Court has never ruled on the question.) What about for having a certain concentration of heroin, in his blood? If so, does this result undermine or destroy the holding in *Robinson*?

(3) *What is the Holding of Powell?* If you add Justice White's concurrence to the four *Powell* dissenters, would the result have changed if there were sufficient proof that Powell was a homeless alcoholic? If so, how far would the logic go? Could a drug addict be punished for stealing jewelry to sell to pay for drugs?

(4) *View of Alcoholics.* The result in *Powell* may depend on the Justices' view of alcoholics and alcoholism. Would the result have been different had a majority of the Court believed that an alcoholic could not stop drinking?

(5) *Legal Challenges Based on Powell.* There have been very few allegations that a particular offense is a status offense and therefore unconstitutional. Virtually all such challenges have been unsuccessful. Courts usually hold that the defendant stands convicted for an act rather than a status. *See, e.g., Shivers v. State*, 688 S.E.2d 622 (Ga. 2010) (crime of possession of firearm by convicted felon is not status crime because punished action of obtaining and possessing a firearm, not status of being a felon); *United States v. Black*, 116 F.3d 198 (7th Cir. 1997) (upholding conviction of pedophile for possessing and distributing child pornography; even though it was stipulated that the defendant was a pedophile and his possession of child pornography was a pathological symptom of pedophilia, there was no proof his conduct was involuntary or uncontrollable).

A few challenges have succeeded. *See, e.g., State v. Adams*, 91 So.3d 724 (Ala. Crim. App. 2010) (Eighth Amendment bars punishing homeless sex offender for violating law requiring sex offenders to provide a current address).

(6) *Are Habitual Criminal Statutes, Which Enhance Sentences for Repeat Offenders, a Form of "Status" Offense?* A related unsuccessful use of *Robinson* has been to challenge so-called habitual criminal statutes, which impose enhanced sentences (sometimes life imprisonment) for a third (or other repetitive) felony. Courts routinely reject the claim that such laws punish for a status, reasoning that the sentence merely enhances the sentence for the third crime; it does not punish for a status. *See, e.g., Ziebell v. State*, 788 N.E.2d 902 (Ind. Ct. App. 2003).

§ 3.04 Attendant Circumstances as Crime Elements

Notes and Questions

(1) *The Surrounding or "Attendant" Circumstances as Part of a Crime Definition.* Criminal statutes routinely include "attendant circumstances" that, like every

element, the state must prove beyond a reasonable doubt. For example, we have seen that common law burglary required that an entry into a building occur "at night." The "night" restriction, which is an attendant circumstance, may have reflected a policy decision that people need to be protected during the time they are asleep and therefore most vulnerable.

(2) *Narrowing or Expanding the Statutory Reach by Fine-Tuning Attendant Circumstances as Elements.* As a general rule, the more attendant circumstances in a criminal statute, the fewer people who are likely to violate it. For example, assume a statute punishes a person who "subjects an animal to excessive cruelty." Note how the application of this law would change if the legislature amended the statute by adding one circumstance, as follows: "subjects a *domesticated* animal to excessive cruelty." The addition of the word *domesticated* may exclude cruelty to wild animals. Consider the following case, which involves an unusual controversy about a circumstance element.

COMMONWEALTH v. NOEL, 857 A.2d 1283 (Pa. 2004). The defendant was convicted under a statute providing, "A person shall not drive, operate, or be in actual control of the movement of a *vehicle*. . . . [w]hile under the influence of alcohol to a degree which renders the person incapable of safe driving." The issue in the state supreme court concerned the nature of the defendant's "vehicle," which was—a horse.

Could the required circumstances for intoxicated driving be satisfied if a *horse* was the alleged "vehicle"? Actually, the state's case was better than it might have seemed. Another part of the statute provided, "*Every person riding an animal . . . shall be subject to all of the duties* applicable to the driver of a vehicle . . . , except those provisions . . . which by their very nature can have no application." Furthermore, there was no question that intoxicated animal-riders could create the same dangers as intoxicated automobile drivers. Another defendant in this very case was convicted for the same offense because his pickup truck collided with this defendant's companion's horse.

But the Pennsylvania Supreme Court reversed the conviction. It held that there was unconstitutional vagueness in the extension of duties to animal riders with the proviso, "except those provisions . . . which by their very nature can have no application." The court reasoned, "[I]t is entirely unclear which provisions . . . apply 'by their very nature' to persons riding an animal and which do not." Besides, "it is not at all clear . . . that a horse, which unlike a car is not fully controlled by the rider, would allow itself to be 'driven in an unsafe manner'."

A dissenting justice disagreed. "Due process simply requires the statute in question to contain reasonable standards" so that "ordinary people can understand what is prohibited," without "arbitrary and discriminatory enforcement." Furthermore, said the dissenter, "Mr. Ed [the famous talking television horse] would know which sections . . . apply to his rider, and I attribute the equivalent horse sense to the ordinary reasonable person."

§ 3.05 Harm (or Result) as a Crime Element

(1) *Harm or Result as Crime Elements.* Many criminal statutes require the offender to have caused a particular harm or result. For example, the crime of murder requires the defendant to have caused death.

(2) *Defining the Crime by the Level or Severity of Harm: "Assault" versus "Aggravated Assault," Misdemeanor Theft versus Felony Theft.* Sometimes statutes use gradations of harm in the definitions of crimes. Thus, "assault" (sometimes informally called "simple assault") may involve causing (minor) "bodily injury," while "aggravated assault" involves causing "serious bodily injury."

Another illustration is the law of theft. Someone who steals something worth less than $500 may commit misdemeanor theft, while someone who takes something worth, say, $10,000 is guilty of felony theft.

(3) *Crimes Requiring Risk of Harm; Crimes Not Requiring Any Proof of Harm.* Sometimes the criminal statute depends upon a *risk of harm* rather than actual harm itself. For example, the crime of reckless endangerment covers conduct that creates the risk of physical harm. Then, too, there are crimes that do not require any proof of actual harm or specific risk, usually because of regulatory concerns or because the conduct itself is risky. Intoxicated driving crimes are an example.

§ 3.06 Causation as a Crime Element

[A] The Purposes of the Causation Requirement

Note on the Rationales for Causation

(1) *The Purposes of Causation Requirements.* For some crimes, causation is an important limit on the scope of liability. It is the linkage between the defendant's conduct and the harm proscribed by the criminal law.

Although causation is an interesting issue, it seldom is contested in criminal cases. Most of the time, causation is obvious. Frequently contested causation cases involve homicide and other personal injury offenses.

(2) *The Simplest Model of Causation: "But-For," "Cause in Fact," or "Actual" Causation.* So-called "but-for" (or "cause in fact" or "actual") causation requires a link between the harm such that it would not have occurred but for defendant's acts or omission. Sometimes the defendant started a chain of events that eventually led to the result punished by a criminal statute. For example, if the crime is homicide and if the victim died because the defendant shot the victim, even if the victim contracted pneumonia as the immediate cause of death, the defendant might have satisfied the "but-for" facet of causation.

(3) *Concurrent Causes under the But-For Approach.* Sometimes, the result is the product of two causes, each of which is sufficient to cause the harm and to cause

each actor to be criminally responsible for the harm. For example, in *State v. Rivera*, 12 S.W.3d 572 (Tex. App. 2000), Gilbert Rivera shot the victim three times in fatal ways, and Timotheo Rivera stabbed him six times, also potentially fatally. The court held that causation was present for both:

> Timotheo [the stabber] asserts that . . . , particularly in light of the gunshot wounds inflicted by Gilbert, there is no legal basis for [his] conviction. . . . The State points out that the cause of death as explained by the medical examiner was "multiple gunshot and stab wounds." . . . Not all [of Timotheo's stab] wounds were fatal wounds, but several were extremely serious. Among these was a penetration into the peritoneal cavity, another was a long deep wound that circled Vasquez's leg into his thigh muscle, and yet a third wound went into the lower part of the heart sac and continued into the liver. . . . It is not necessary for this court to decide whether there was a chance that proper medical treatment could have saved Vasquez had he not been shot. "A theoretical rescue does not break the causal chain leading from" Timotheo's acts to Vasquez's death.

Each defendant's conduct would have been sufficient to kill the victim. Under the doctrine of *concurrent causation*, each defendant could be prosecuted for murder. *See also State v. Christman*, 249 P.3d 680 (Wash. Ct. App. 2011) (defendant supplied one of three drugs that in combination caused the victim's death; defendant liable for death even though were other concurrent causes; there can be multiple proximate causes).

(4) *In Some Jurisdictions, But-For Causation Is All That Is Required (Although Many Jurisdictions Require More).* In the *Rivera* case, the court's holding was mandated by a statute providing, "A person is criminally responsible if the result would not have occurred but for his conduct, operating either alone or concurrently with another cause, unless the concurrent cause was clearly sufficient to produce the result and the conduct of the actor clearly insufficient." Tex. Penal Code § 6.04. In this jurisdiction, then, but-for causation is enough. But other jurisdictions require more. *See also Burrage v. United States*, 571 U.S. 204, 211 (2014) (holding the phrase "results from" in the federal Controlled Substances Act imposes "a requirement of actual causality" that "requires proof that the harm would not have occurred in the absence of—that is, but for—the defendant's conduct").

(5) *"Proximate" (or "Legal") Causation: the Model Penal Code Approach.* In many states and under the MPC, even if there is but-for causation, liability may not be imposed on that basis alone. More is required. *See* MPC § 2.03. This second facet of causation is often referred to as *proximate* or *legal* causation. Proximate cause deals with whether the defendant *should* be held responsible for a *foreseeable* result that the defendant actually caused. Proximate cause issues often arise when the defendant does an act and another person does a second act contributing to the result. Another variety is when the defendant does an act and then some other event occurs that unexpectedly contributes to the result.

(6) *The Effect of Independent Intervening Cause upon Proximate Causation.* Thus, the issue may arise when there is a second but-for intervening cause. An "independent intervening" cause would be one that is not intended or reasonably foreseeable; it is so independent of the defendant's conduct that it would be unfair to hold the defendant criminally responsible for the result. The independent intervening cause "breaks the chain." *Cf. Johnson v. Alaska*, 224 P.3d 105 (Alaska 2010) (defendants father and mother of child victim were starving child to death when mother dropped child on head, killing the child; mother's act may be independent intervening cause relieving father of liability for certain starvation that had not yet occurred).

In a bizarre case, the defendant was both drunk driving and texting when his car struck a person lying on the road. Since under state law killing while drunk driving was more severe than killing while texting, the defendant argued that his texting, not drunk driving, caused the accident. In other words, the defendant argued that his own act (texting) was an independent intervening act that caused the death. The court rejected the argument and found that the cause was intoxicated driving. *Davis v. Commonwealth*, 703 S.E.2d 259 (Va. Ct. App. 2011).

A "dependent intervening cause" would be one sufficiently related to the defendant's conduct to merit holding the defendant responsible for the harm. Many courts ask whether the second cause was foreseeable or was intended by the defendant. Sometimes the link is obvious. *See, e.g., State v. Wassil*, 658 A.2d 548 (Conn. 1995) (defendant caused death by supplying drugs to victim who died from an overdose; victim was not an independent intervening actor even though victim chose to take the drugs); *United States v. Pineda-Doval*, 614 F.3d 1019 (9th Cir. 2010) (defendant caused death of ten people in crash occurring during police chase when border officials used "spike strip" to stop his vehicle; use of spike strip was foreseeable, not extraordinary).

(7) *Contributory Negligence.* The usual rule is that contributory negligence is not a defense in criminal cases. Some courts explain this result on the theory that ordinary negligence by the "victim" is reasonably foreseeable. However, there are many cases holding that gross negligence is not foreseeable and may constitute an independent intervening cause. In *People v. Feezel*, 783 N.W.2d 67 (Mich. 2010), the homicide victim was drunk and hit by the defendant, also drunk, while the victim was walking in the middle of a dark road on a rainy night. The court held that the victim's own negligence may be a superseding cause of the death if sufficiently careless to be considered gross negligence.

(8) *An Intended or Foreseeable Result Occurring in an Unexpected Manner.* What if a result is intended or foreseeable, and actually occurs, but in a different manner than expected or likely? The leading case is *People v. Kibbe*, 321 N.E. 2d 773 (N.Y. 1974), where a drunk man was robbed and left near the side of a road on a snowy winter night. The victim wandered onto the road and sat down, where he was killed by a speeding truck. The New York Court of Appeals held that both the victim and

the driver were intervening causes, but the defendant was *responsible* because the victim's death was foreseeable, even though the exact manner was not. *See also Blaize v. United States*, 21 A.3d 78 (Wash. Ct. App. 2011) (defendant shot at victim who ran into street to escape and was killed when struck by hit-and-run driver traveling at excessive speed; defendant caused the death); *State v. Dykas*, 925 N.E.2d 685 (Ohio Ct. App. 2010) (defendant hit victim in head; victim killed when fell to ground and head hit sidewalk; defendant was proximate cause of the death which was the direct, natural, and reasonably foreseeable consequence of defendant's action); *McGrath v. State*, 627 S.E.2d 866 (Ga. Ct. App. 2006) (defendant drunk driver X caused multi-car accident on interstate highway; nurse-victim stopped her car to assist and was struck and killed by another drunk driver as she stood next to the first car trying to help driver X; driver X may be the proximate cause of nurse's death, which was reasonable probable consequence of X's drunk driving).

[B] Defining Causation: The Common Law and the MPC

Commonwealth v. McCloskey

835 A.2d 801 (Pa. Super. Court 2003)

Reaffirmed, Commonwealth v. Tierney

2019 WL 2237063 (Pa. Super 2019) (unpublished decision)

BECK, J.

Judith Claire McCloskey was convicted of three counts of involuntary manslaughter after dozens of teenagers attended a beer party in her home and three of them died in an automobile accident after leaving the party. . . . After a thorough review of the facts and law, we affirm. . . .

On April 28, 2001, one of McCloskey's daughters, 17-year-old Kristen, hosted a party in the basement of McCloskey's home. McCloskey's other daughter, 14-year-old Kelly, also invited guests to her home that night. . . .

Two 18-year-old boys, with the help of a 56-year-old man, brought two kegs of beer to McCloskey's home. Kristen charged party guests $5.00, for which each guest received a plastic cup to use for beer. As the evening progressed, there were in excess of 40 people at the party, all of them under age 21. As many as 20 cars were parked around the house. The teenagers drank beer and played drinking games throughout the evening, from approximately 8:00 pm until 11:00 pm. Several party guests observed 19-year-old Christopher Mowad drinking heavily and exhibiting signs of intoxication.

McCloskey knew that a party was planned and, according to witnesses, assisted in getting ice and blankets ready for the kegs. McCloskey was at home for the entire party, but she stayed upstairs. [She knew about the drinking and had been home on prior occasions when she was aware of underage drinking.]

At some point in the evening, Kimberly Byrne (18 years old) and cousins Court-ney Kiefer (17 years old) and Bryan Kiefer (18 years old) left the party and went to a nearby field. . . . Courtney Kiefer called Mowad, who was still at the party. Mowad informed her that the police had arrived and he was leaving. He ran out of McClo-skey's home, avoided the police and drove his Isuzu Rodeo to the field. There, he picked up the three teens. . . .

. . . [L]ater, while driving around, Mowad sideswiped another vehicle and, in an effort to elude the driver, sped away. He lost control of the car and drove off the road. The vehicle flipped over several times before coming to rest on its roof. All four teenagers were ejected. Mowad, Byrne and Bryan Kiefer died as a result of blunt force trauma to their heads, necks and chests. Courtney Kiefer, the only survivor, sustained multiple serious injuries, including head trauma, and required extended hospitalization. Mowad's blood alcohol content was .20%. . . .

Ultimately, McCloskey faced trial for three counts of involuntary manslaughter, and the jury convicted her of the charges. She was sentenced to three consecutive terms of four (4) to eighteen (18) months in prison, for an aggregate term of one to four and one-half years. This appeal followed. . . .

Involuntary manslaughter is defined as follows: "A person is guilty of involun-tary manslaughter when as a direct result of the doing of an unlawful act in a reck-less or grossly negligent manner, or the doing of a lawful act in a reckless or grossly negligent manner, he causes the death of another person. 8 Pa.C.S.A. §2504(a)." Thus, involuntary manslaughter requires 1) a mental state of either recklessness or gross negligence and 2) a causal nexus between the conduct of the accused and the death of the victim. McCloskey insists that both elements are lacking in this case. [The court here held that the evidence of McCloskey's recklessness was sufficient, and it next considered the "causal nexus."]

. . . McCloskey next claims that the Commonwealth failed to prove causation. She argues that Mowad's voluntary act of drinking to excess, his decision to drive, the fact that he was speeding when he lost control of his vehicle and all of the occu-pants' choices to refrain from wearing seatbelts, were their own "tragic decisions," causing their deaths.

"Criminal responsibility is properly assessed against one whose conduct was a direct and substantial factor in producing the death. This is true even though "other factors combined with that conduct to achieve the result." McCloskey aptly sets out in her brief the relevant standard for determining this element of the crime:

> In order to impose criminal liability, causation must be direct and sub-stantial. Defendants should not be exposed to a loss of liberty based on the tort standard which only provides that the event giving rise to the injury is a substantial factor. . . . In other words, was the defendant's conduct so directly and substantially linked to the actual result as to give rise to the imposition of criminal liability, or was the actual result so remote and attenuated that it would be unfair to hold the defendant responsible for it?

In seeking to define the requirement that a criminal defendant's conduct be a direct factor in the death of another, the courts of this Commonwealth have held that "so long as the defendant's conduct started the chain of causation which led to the victim's death, criminal responsibility for the crime of homicide may properly be found." A victim's contributory negligence is not a defense to a criminal charge.

Our review of the facts in this case leads us to conclude that McCloskey's "furnishing" of alcohol to minors, including Mowad, "started the chain of causation" that led to the death of three teens. The record supports the finding that McCloskey knew the party guests, all of whom were under age 21 and some of whom were as young as 14, were drinking beer in her home. She allowed them to do so for several hours without interruption, supervision or comment. The teens came and went throughout the evening in their cars, nearly twenty of which were parked on McCloskey's property at some point.

That teenagers, alcohol and automobiles can be and often is a fatal combination is not a novel concept. . . .

We conclude that the occurrence of a fatal automobile accident following a teenager's unlimited consumption of alcohol at a wholly unsupervised teenage beer party is neither "remote" nor "attenuated." . . . We reiterate, this is not a case where McCloskey simply failed to supervise a teen party in her home at which beer was secretly being served. McCloskey "furnished" the alcohol to the minors under the plain language of the statute. . . . [Conviction affirmed.]

Notes and Questions

(1) *But-For Causation.* Recall that causation ordinarily consists of two facets: "but-for" (or "actual" or "cause in fact") and policy-based. Was but-for causation established here, and should this, alone, be sufficient for liability? If so, consider whether but-for causation is present or should suffice as to the 56-year-old man who helped buy the kegs, the retailer who sold the beer, the wholesaler of the kegs, or the keg manufacturer—and whether there is a recognizable stopping point in this list.

(2) *Policy-Based Causation.* The court found that the policy-based branch of causation was also satisfied. Do you agree? Recall that the driver of the car, Mowad, was an adult for criminal law purposes (19 years old). For a factually similar case that relies on *McCloskey,* see *Santarelli v. State,* 62 So.3d 1211 (Fla. Dist. Ct. App. 2011).

(3) *Causation in Felony-Murder Cases.* As is described more fully in Chapter 2 (on homicide), felony murder has an important causation component, which varies somewhat from typical criminal law causation principles. For example, if two people rob a bank and one of them shoots the teller, both are responsible for the murder in many jurisdictions. But there are limits. Assume, for example, that the teller pulls a gun and shoots robber A. Is robber B liable for the homicide of robber A? Or what if the bank teller accidentally shoots a police officer or bystander? Is either robber liable for the deaths? The answer depends on complex causation issues that vary among the jurisdictions and are discussed in Chapter 2.

> Read MPC § 2.03 [adding requirements beyond but-for causation] in the MPC Appendix.

Notes on Model Penal Code Causation

(1) *But-For and Legal Cause in MPC.* The Model Penal Code retains the but-for approach of the common law and also adds a different, specific kind of "legal" or "proximate" cause approach. Consider the *McCloskey* opinion, above, which applies common law concepts. How would the MPC's provisions about "contemplation" (subsection 2), "awareness" (subsection 3), or "probable consequences" (subsection 4) change the method of analysis?

(2) *Jury Instructions.* Jury instructions on causation under the MPC would probably track the language in sections 2.03(2) or (3). Do you think these provisions give the jury better guidance about causation than the common law concepts in *McCloskey*?

Problem 3D (Causation): "We Were Street Racing When He Died in a Crash, but Does That Make Me Guilty?"

(1) *A Death from Racing on Public Roads.* One Saturday night at the Star Bar Aaron and Tyvester decided to race their trucks. Each went to his truck in the parking lot and drove to a spot on a winding rural road. Aaron counted to three, and both trucks raced off in the same direction on a two lane road. About a mile down the road, Tyvester sped around a curve at 90 m.p.h., lost control of his truck, and crashed into a tree. He died instantly. Aaron is charged with vehicular homicide.

(2) *The Applicable Statutory Provision.* Here is the governing homicide statute. "Vehicular homicide is the reckless killing of another by the operation of an automobile, airplane, motorboat, or other motor vehicle." The statute, however, does not expressly provide standards for the causation element, which is crucial here.

(3) *What Result, under the Common Law, the MPC, or Pure But-For Causation?* Under the common law approach, did Aaron "cause" Tyvester's death so that he could be held criminally responsible for it? Would your analysis change if the jurisdiction had adopted MPC § 2.03, above, or if it used pure but-for causation, as some jurisdictions do?

(4) *Leading Cases: An Old Decision — and Its Reversal.* In an older case that has become a classic, *Commonwealth v. Root*, 170 A.2d 310 (Pa. 1961), the court held that the surviving drag racer was not a "proximate cause" of the deceased drag racer's death; the deceased racer was a "supervening" cause of his own death. The *Root* court reasoned that a "more direct causation connection" is necessary for a *criminal* conviction than for tort law. But a later Pennsylvania statute reversed the outcome of *Root* decision by providing that a person is legally responsible for the conduct of

his or her accomplice. The two drag racers were accomplices. *See Commonwealth v. Jackson*, 744 A.2d 271 (Pa. Super. Ct. 1999). Most modern decisions disagree with the first *Root decision* and hold the surviving racer responsible for the other racer's death. What is the reason for the policy differences between these approaches?

(5) *A Variation.* Returning to the race involving Aaron and Tyvester, what if Tyvester lost control of his car and collided with Victor's car, killing Victor, who was driving home after work and obeying all traffic laws? Obviously Tyvester would be liable for the homicide of Victor. Would Aaron also be deemed to have caused Victor's death under but-for and "proximate cause" standards? *See, e.g., People v. Tims*, 534 N.W.2d 675 (Mich. 1995); Commonwealth v. Carroll, 936 A.2d 1148 (Pa. Super. Ct. 2007) (A and B drag racing; A lost control of his car which struck B's car, which crossed lanes causing crash that killed the driver of an oncoming car; A and B responsible for the death since both were a direct and substantial factor in the homicide).

Causation Review Notes

Analyze whether there is causation under a pure but-for test, proximate cause (focusing on foreseeability), and the MPC standard.

(a) *Bear in the Car.* What if Barbara is a very drunk driver who loses control of her car and crashes into a tree in a rural area. Peter, her passenger, is injured and stuck in the car. Barbara is unconscious. A bear somehow gets into the car and eats Sam. Did Barbara cause Sam's death? *United States v. Main*, 113 F.3d 1046 (9th Cir. 1997) (suggesting hypothetical).

(b) *Child Pornography.* Donald was arrested for possessing child pornography. The film on his computer, *Children Porn Stars*, contained a short film in which a fifteen-year-old girl performed sex acts with an adult man. The girl has now been identified and is suffering severe mental problems as the result of her participation in *Children Porn Stars*, which was her only porn film. Since child porn is a serious crime because of the harm to the children-actors, the district attorney is considering prosecuting Donald for the state crime of "reckless conduct causing physical or mental harm to a minor." Analyze whether Donald "caused" such harm. *See United States v. Johnston*, 2011 U.S. Dist. LEXIS 125008 (Oct. 28, 2011) (seriously considering causation issue).

(c) *Helmet and Headlight.* Margaret, intoxicated with a 0.11 blood alcohol level, was driving home at 1 a.m. from a night on the town when she turned left, striking a motorcycle coming from the opposite direction. Margaret maintains she did not see the cycle. The motorcycle driver, not wearing a helmet and not having a working headlight on the cycle, was killed instantly. Margaret has been charged with reckless homicide. The medical examiner testified that the cyclist would not have died if he had been wearing a helmet. *See State v. Meekins*, 105 P.3d 420 (Wash. Ct. App. 2005).

§ 3.07   Mens Rea Elements in Crimes

[A] Defining the Elements and Distinguishing Their Gradations

Note on the Meaning and Types of Mens Rea Elements

(1) *The "Evil Mind" Requirement and Its Policy Basis.* For centuries, it has been a fundamental principle of criminal law that there should be no liability without an evil mind, often referred to as the mens rea or, less commonly, scienter. According to Professor Sayre, however, the specific meaning of mens rea changed significantly over time and efforts at greater precision became mired in "hopeless disagreement." *See generally* Francis Bowes Sayre, *Mens Rea*, 45 Harv. L. Rev. 974 (1932). But the consistent theoretical underpinning was the fact that mens rea was how criminal law implemented concepts of moral blameworthiness. By the end of the Seventeenth Century, it was widely accepted that an evil intent was a necessary element in a felony. Today most crimes have mens rea elements that the state must prove beyond a reasonable doubt, although there are significant types of strict liability offenses.

(2) *The Varieties of Mens Rea Elements.* When a legislature selects the mens rea for a criminal law, it makes a significant decision about the reach of that statute. Imagine, for example, if there were only one homicide statute, punishing someone who "intentionally" kills another person. This statute would clearly cover the professional killer who stalked and shot the victim, but it would not include the drunk driver who accidentally killed a pedestrian. Of course, the coverage and policy of the homicide statute would change if the legislature amended the law to punish someone who "negligently or intentionally" killed another person.

(3) *Proof beyond Reasonable Doubt; Blurred Definitions.* Since the state must prove each element, including any mens rea element, beyond a reasonable doubt, both prosecution and defense counsel must carefully assess the mens rea for each possible crime. As noted below, sometimes the statute is not clear as to the mens rea required. Furthermore, some statutes provide mental elements without defining what they mean or which of the physical elements they target.

Problem 3E (Mens Rea Introduction): The Clueless Bigamist

(1) *Husband Learns of (What He Thinks Is) His Quickie Divorce.* From the early years of their marriage, Don and Julia Wan experienced ever more serious marital problems. Finally, Julia packed her belongings and drove to her sister's house in another state. Three weeks later, on May 1st, she sent Don the following letter:

> Dear Don:
>
> I have had enough of your selfishness and excuses. When you were away on your last trip I met a man who really cares about me. He wants to marry me and I have accepted. Last week I went to court here and got a divorce. Wish me well in my new life.

(2) *Husband Remarries.* Don was not surprised, and he welcomed his new freedom. Later that month he met Mary Leonard in a singles bar. The two seemed perfectly suited. Don even let Mary read Julia's May 1st letter. On October 1st Don and Mary were married.

(3) *But There Was No Divorce.* A few months later the police arrested both Don and Mary on Julia's complaint. Julia had never really divorced Don. Julia told the police that her May 1st letter was untruthful and was written to "teach Don he couldn't treat me that way." Don is charged with the crime of bigamy, and Mary is charged with the crime of marrying the husband or wife of another. The applicable statutes follow:

> § 22–200 *Bigamy.* Every person having a husband or wife living, who marries any other person, is guilty of bigamy except:

> [The exceptions include absence for five years, divorce, annulment, or declaration that the marriage is void.] Bigamy is punished by imprisonment not exceeding three years.

> § 22–201 *Marrying Husband or Wife of Another.* Every person who knowingly and willfully marries the husband or wife of another, in any case in which such husband or wife would be guilty of Bigamy under § 22–200, is punishable by imprisonment not exceeding one year.

(4) *Identifying the Elusive Mens Rea.* Mary has been charged with violating § 22–201 because she married Don while he was still married to Julia. To what physical elements of this crime does the stated mens rea apply (how many possibilities can you spot)? Can the state prove the necessary mens rea to convict Mary?

Don is charged with bigamy for violating § 22–200. Notice that the bigamy statute lacks the "knowingly and willfully" language of the other statute. Literally, the bigamy statute criminalizes the conduct of double-marriage without requiring any proof of intent, knowledge, recklessness, or negligence. What mens rea, if any, will (or should) a court require if it faithfully interprets this bigamy statute?

Note on "General" and "Specific" Mens Rea

(1) *The Vague and Variable Concepts of "General" and "Specific" Mens Rea.* At one time in perhaps all American jurisdictions (and still in some jurisdictions), there have been two types of mens rea: general and specific. While the concept of general mens rea is not used in many modern jurisdictions and critics routinely argue that it should be abandoned as meaningless, it still exists in some states and in federal criminal law, though the definition is sometimes difficult to ascertain. The problem is even more complex because usually, no statute identifies a crime as having "general criminal intent," yet some courts find it as an unwritten element even though the statute itself contains no hint of a mens rea element.

The confusion this causes, even for experts, led the MPC drafters to do away with the general intent/specific intent distinction completely.

(2) *General Criminal Intent*. The vague and outmoded concept of general criminal intent has a number of variations in those jurisdictions that retain it as part of their criminal law.

(a) *For Many Crimes Like Common Law Assault, or Battery, "General Intent" Is Intent Merely to Perform the Physical Act; Specific Intent Is Intent Not Only to Perform the Act, but Also to Produce the Result*. General mens rea (sometimes called "general criminal intent" or "general intent") is sometimes said to require proof that the defendant intended to perform the physical act proscribed by the statute; the defendant need not have intended the consequences of that act. *See Carter v. United States*, 530 U.S. 255, 269 (2000) (general intent requires "proof of knowledge with respect to the actus reus of the crime"). For example, the federal crime of "assault resulting in serious bodily injury," 18 U.S.C. § 113(a)(6), has been interpreted as a general criminal intent crime requiring proof only of a general intent to commit the acts of assault and not any specific intent to do any bodily harm. *See, e.g., United States v. Ashley*, 255 F.3d 907 (8th Cir. 2001) (defendant who drove recklessly while drunk, causing serious bodily injury, had general criminal intent for assault because he became intoxicated and drove a vehicle with brakes he knew did not work properly); *see also State v. Jenkins*, 291 P.3d 1073 (Kan. Ct. App. 2013) (aggravated battery requires proof of general criminal intent, which means proof that defendant intended to engage in the conduct that violated the statute; thus the government must prove defendant intentionally accelerated his vehicle but need not prove defendant intended to harm the victim).

(b) *Reasonably Foreseeable Result*. Sometimes the courts also require that the prohibited result (perhaps causing serious bodily injury) be reasonably expected to follow from the offender's voluntary act, but not that the result necessarily be intended. *See, e.g., State v. Miller*, 792 So.2d 104 (La. Ct. App. 2001) (for general intent crime of distributing marijuana, the mental element is established when circumstances indicate that the prohibited result — distribution of marijuana — is reasonably expected to follow from the offender's voluntary act of putting a marijuana buyer in contact with a marijuana seller).

(c) *Morally Blameworthy State of Mind*. Older authority distinguishes between "culpability" and "elemental" mens rea in applying the terms general and specific intent. For example, common law rape is often said to be a general intent crime, and in that context "general intent" means committing the actus reus of the offense with some morally blameworthy state of mind as to the victim's lack of consent

(3) *General Criminal Intent Distinguished from Specific Intent*. In modern jurisdictions, the term "specific intent" is ordinarily used to refer to either the mens rea set out in the offense definition or, more narrowly, to a statutory mens rea requiring a purpose to cause the social harm of the offense; such as the "intent to kill." The classic example is common law larceny, which requires that the prosecution prove not only an intentional taking without consent, but also that the accused intended to permanently deprive another of his or her property.

(4) *When Does Any of This Matter?* The difference between general and specific intent makes a difference in the application of defenses such as mistake of fact, mistake of law, voluntary intoxication, and diminished capacity. In addition, although the Model Penal Code abandoned the general intent-specific intent distinction, the federal system does not follow the MPC and still has general intent crimes. Many states also adhere to the common law understandings of mens rea, including this distinction.

(5) *General Intent Is Less Likely to Be Affected by Intoxication.* We will address intoxication in more detail in Chapter Six, but for now it is important to realize that many criminal defendants might plausibly claim that they were unable to "intend" an action because intoxication prevented them from having the presence of mind required to form a clear intention. For example, a person charged with intentional homicide, a specific intent crime, could argue that she is not guilty because at the time of the shooting she was too drunk to intend to kill. Some jurisdictions reject these claims, at least so long as the defendant's intoxication was voluntary. *See* MPC §2.08.

Courts also give far less weight to intoxication for general intent than for specific intent crimes. Thus, intoxication can be a defense when the prosecution must prove a specific purpose, but it is rarely a defense when the mens rea is something like "knowledge." It is even less likely to help defendant if the crime is one of general intent. Does intoxication support the imputation of intention based on an assumption of risk theory?

UNITED STATES v. KIMES, 246 F.3d 800 (6th Cir. 2001). 18 U.S.C. §111 (a)(1) prohibits an assault on a federal officer. (This is the statute that makes shooting a DEA or FBI agent a federal crime.) But the statute does not specify whether it creates a general intent or a specific intent crime. The difference is important, because if the required mens rea is specific intent, the defendant can only be guilty if the defendant knows that the person assaulted is a federal officer, but if the crime is one of general intent, this knowledge is not required.

Here is one particularly dramatic context in which this issue often surfaces. A federal officer, not wearing any sort of uniform, pretends to be the seller or buyer of heroin or cocaine and infiltrates an existing conspiracy. Because of some real or imagined slight or threat, however, the persons who are being investigated end up beating or shooting the undercover officer but are unaware of the victim's law enforcement status. If the crime is one of specific intent, defendants are guilty only of simple assault (rather than assault of a federal officer) since they did not intend to harm a federal official. If it is a general intent offense, however, the offense is that of assaulting a federal officer, a far more serious crime, since knowledge or intent of harming a federal official is not an element the government must prove In the cited case, (which did not involve this precise scenario, although the holding would extend to it), the court reasoned as follows, in holding the crime of assaulting a federal officer to require only general intent:

> [W]e are guided first and foremost by the fact that §111(a)(1) contains no language suggesting that specific intent must be shown. It is plain from an examination of other federal statutes that Congress is fully cognizant of the general intent/specific intent dichotomy. When it intends to create a specific intent crime, Congress explicitly says so. Consideration of the overall purpose of §111(a)(1) also supports the conclusion that the statute sets forth a general intent crime. . . . Categorizing §111(a)(1) as a general intent crime furthers the congressional objective: "If a person acts in a manner which is assaultive toward a federal official, without specifically intending harm or the apprehension of imminent harm, the official still would be impeded in the performance of his official duties."

It may surprise you to learn that this issue of general versus specific intent, which must arise frequently enough so that you would assume that it would be resolved, has caused a split among the federal circuits—although *Kimes* represents the majority view.

Notes on the Wide Variety of Mental Elements

(1) *Countless Ways of Expressing Mens Rea.* Because criminal laws were adopted piecemeal over a long period of time, crimes contain literally countless varieties of mens rea elements. A survey of state and federal crimes found statutes containing the following illustrative mens rea elements: "willfully fails to pay a support obligation"; "purposefully"; "intentionally defaces . . . any religious real property"; "with the intent to destroy an aircraft"; "knowingly delivers or receives"; "knowing it to be false"; "for the purpose of killing any horse"; and "with intent to retaliate."

(2) *Illustration: The Many Facets of "Wilfulness"* Not only do mens rea terms vary, the meanings of those terms often are not fixed. The term "willful" has many meanings and variations. For example,

> The word "willfully" is sometimes said to be "a word of many meanings" whose construction is often dependent on the context in which it appears. Most obviously it differentiates between deliberate and unwitting conduct, but in the criminal law it also typically refers to a culpable state of mind. [A] variety of phrases have been used to describe that concept. As a general matter, when used in the criminal context, a "willful" act is one undertaken with a "bad purpose." In other words, in order to establish a "willful" violation of a statute, "the Government must prove that the defendant acted with knowledge that his conduct was unlawful."

Bryan v. United States, 524 U.S. 184, 191–92 (1998). As if to increase the complexity, the Supreme Court has also interpreted "willfully" to require specific intent when it appears in "highly technical statutes [such as the tax code and currency laws] that presented the danger of ensnaring individuals engaged in apparently innocent conduct." *Id.* at 194. *See also United States v. Fields*, 500 F.3d 1327 (11th Cir. 2007) (holding the federal Child Support Recovery Act, which makes it a crime to "willfully" fail to pay a past-due support obligation for a child residing in another state, requires proof not only that the defendant willfully failed to pay but also that the defendant knew the child was in other state).

(3) *Multiple Mens Rea Elements in a Single Statute.* Sometimes the statute defines a single mens rea element. But another statute may contain more than one mens rea element. Sometimes the combinations are difficult to understand. Illustrations include: "willfully and maliciously sets fire to," "knowingly and fraudulently conceals . . . property," and "corruptly gives" (perhaps both "corruptly" and "gives" require a mental element). Sometimes mens rea elements are difficult to understand because the words do not have an accepted definition. Moreover, elements such as "corruptly" may have no definition at all. Modern penal codes, however, often provide definitions of mens rea elements.

[B] The Model Penal Code Approach

Note on the Model Penal Code: Four (or Five) Defined Mens Rea Elements

(1) *The Creation and Influence of the MPC.* In 1962 the American Law Institute published the Model Penal Code, which was drafted by leading criminal law experts. The Code contains rules defining crimes, defenses, and some procedural matters. Many states have used it as a starting point for modernizing their criminal laws. Today, most modern state criminal codes reflect the Model Penal Code's influence in at least some provisions—and mens rea is one of the most common areas of MPC influence. For example, the MPC's mens rea formulations are used in such states as Alabama, Arizona, Connecticut, Illinois, Kentucky, New York, Oregon, Tennessee, Texas, and Wisconsin.

(2) *The Four MPC Mens Rea Definitions (or Five, if Strict Liability Is Counted).* In recognition of the chaotic state of mens rea among the states, the Model Penal Code greatly simplified the concept by using only four distinct mens rea elements. The MPC allows another possibility, that of no mental requirement at all (strict liability), which can be considered a fifth variation. Each of the four affirmative mental elements is carefully defined in a way that reflects experience with mens rea problems. You should read carefully the Model Penal Code statutes defining these mental elements, because they are building blocks for what is to come.

Model Penal Code § 2.02: Mens Rea

Section 2.02. General Requirements of Culpability

(1) *Minimum Requirements of Culpability.* Except as provided in Section 2.05 [concerning extremely minor crimes or crimes which define their own mental states], a person is not guilty of an offense unless he acted purposely, knowingly,

recklessly, or negligently, as the law may require, with respect to each material element of the offense.

(2) *Kinds of Culpability Defined.*

(a) *Purposely [many states instead use "Intentionally"]*. A person acts purposely with respect to a material element of an offense when:

(i) if the element involves the nature of his conduct or a result thereof, it is his conscious object to engage in conduct of that nature or to cause such a result; and

(ii) if the element involves the attendant circumstances, he is aware of the existence of such circumstances or he believes or hopes that they exist.

(b) *Knowingly.* A person acts knowingly with respect to a material element of an offense when:

(i) if the element involves the nature of his conduct or the attendant circumstances, he is aware that his conduct is of that nature or that such circumstances exist; and

(ii) if the element involves a result of his conduct, he is aware that it is practically certain that his conduct will cause such a result.

(c) *Recklessly.* A person acts recklessly with respect to a material element of an offense when he consciously disregards a substantial and unjustifiable risk that the material element exists or will result from his conduct. The risk must be of such a nature and degree that, considering the nature and purpose of the actor's conduct and the circumstances known to him, its disregard involves a gross deviation from the standard of conduct that a law-abiding person would observe in the actor's situation.

(d) *Negligently.* A person acts negligently with respect to a material element of an offense when he should be aware of a substantial and unjustifiable risk that the material element exists or will result from his conduct. The risk must be of such a nature and degree that the actor's failure to perceive it, considering the nature and purpose of his conduct and the circumstances known to him, involves a gross deviation from the standard of care that a reasonable person would observe in the situation.

(3) *Culpability Required Unless Otherwise Provided.* When the culpability sufficient to establish a material element of an offense is not prescribed by law, such element is established if a person acts purposely, knowingly, or recklessly with respect thereto.

(4) *Prescribed Culpability Requirement Applies to All Material Elements.* When the law defining an offense prescribes the kind of culpability that is sufficient for the commission of an offense, without distinguishing among the material elements thereof, such provision shall apply to all material elements of the offense, unless a contrary purpose plainly appears.

(5) *Substitutes for Negligence, Recklessness and Knowledge.* When the law provides that negligence suffices to establish an element of an offense, such element also is established if a person acts purposely, knowingly or recklessly. When recklessness suffices to establish an element, such element is also established if a person acts purposely or knowingly. When acting knowingly suffices to establish an element, such element also is established if a person acts purposely. . . .

Notes and Questions

(1) *Test Your Understanding.* Read carefully the four mens rea or mental culpability definitions of the Model Penal Code. Recall that many states have adopted these important formulations. The following questions test your understanding.

(a) *Subjective v. Objective Standard.* Which mens rea elements are judged by subjective standards? Which by objective?

(b) *Punishment.* Ordinarily a person who acts intentionally ("purposefully") is punished more severely than one who acts negligently. Why?

(c) *Motive.* What role does a person's motive play in assessing culpability?

(d) *Difficulty of Proof.* Which mental state is the most difficult for the government to prove beyond a reasonable doubt?

(e) *Knowledge Doesn't Have to Be Absolute: "Awareness" or "Awareness of Practical Certainty" Is Enough.* Imagine that defendant gives rat poison to a victim, who dies. The jury cannot tell whether the defendant "intended" the death and is not sure even that the defendant "knew" absolutely that the victim would die. Still, if killing a person "knowingly," as defined in the Model Penal Code, is sufficient for murder, this defendant may be guilty of that offense if he or she thought death was very likely. Can you explain?

(2) *"Downward Inclusiveness": Purpose Includes Knowledge, Etc.* Note that MPC § 2.02(5) adopts the so-called "downward inclusiveness" rule. It establishes a hierarchy of mental states. Proof of the highest (*i.e.*, purposely or intentionally) automatically establishes all the lower states.

(3) *"Default Position": If No Element Stated, Recklessness Suffices.* Model Penal Code § 2.02(3) establishes that if a statute does not include a mental culpability element, then the default position is that the statute nevertheless includes a mens rea that is satisfied by proving purposely, knowingly, or recklessly. In other words, recklessness suffices.

(4) *Comparing the Recklessness and Negligence Standards.* The MPC's definition of recklessness refers to "the standard of conduct" of "a law-abiding person," while its negligence definition refers to "the standard of care" of "a reasonable person." Does this difference make a difference? Apparently, it was unintentional, but many states have changed the language of these provisions to make them consistent and avoid confusion. *See* David Treiman, *Recklessness and the Model Penal Code*, 9 Am. J. Crim. L. 281 (1981).

(5) *The (Limited) MPC Recognition of Strict Liability: Requirements Include "Plain" Negation of Mens Rea Elements.* The drafters of the MPC disfavored strict liability. The default position described above, requiring at least recklessness, eliminated most strict liability offenses. But the drafters allowed the possibility of strict liability. Crimes could impose liability without fault if they were defined by laws outside the Code and if "a legislative purpose to impose absolute liability . . . plainly appears." So, if a legislature wanted to impose strict liability for a new offense after adopting the MPC, what language would it need to add? We return to strict liability in § 3.10.

Problem 3F (Mens Rea Under the MPC): "I Bumped His Car Because I Was Mad"

(1) *The Angry Used-Car Buyer's Reaction.* Samuel Carr called 911 to report an automobile accident in which Victor Victime, owner of the Easy Buy Used Car Emporium, was killed. The police investigation revealed that the rear end of Victime's new Cadillac had been damaged. Paint matching that of Victime's car was found on the front end of Carr's 1994 Chevy. During routine police questioning, Carr made the following legally admissible statement:

> About two months ago my Ford blew the engine and I needed a car to get to work in. The radio said to "Ease by the Easy Buy for the best deal on earth." So I did. For $850 Victime sold me a green 1994 Chevy, which he said was in perfect shape. The car never sounded right, even when I drove it home. Something went wrong with it about every day. I got madder and madder every time I had to get the car fixed. I asked Victime to fix it or give my money back, but he laughed. Said I was a sucker for buying that heap. I had to get even. I decided to wreck his car so he would know what it was like to have a car that don't work. Last night I parked outside his lot. About 10:00 he left in his big Caddy. I followed him up Big Mountain. I began bumping into the rear of his car. I wanted to ruin his rear axle and maybe even bend the frame of his car, and leave him stuck on the mountain. But the last time I rammed into him his wheels went off the road to the right, and his car just fell down the mountain and crashed into that big rock near Salty Brewer's place and caught on fire. I couldn't get down the mountain in time to do no good.
>
> I called the police and made this statement because I want to show that I didn't mean no harm. It was an accident.

(2) *The Controlling Statutes, All Using MPC-Defined Mens Rea Elements.* You are the prosecutor assigned to assess whether Carr should be charged with a criminal offense. You first locate your jurisdiction's homicide statutes. The following (simplified) homicide laws apply, based upon the MPC: (1) first degree murder, which consists of "purposely" causing the death of another; (2) second degree murder, which requires the accused to have killed "knowingly"; (3) manslaughter, killing "recklessly"; and (4) criminally negligent homicide, killing with "criminal negligence." The sentence for first degree murder can be imprisonment in excess of 30 years (or

death); for second degree, up to 30 years; for manslaughter, up to 15 years; for criminally negligent homicide, up to 5 years.

(3) *Your Assignment: Compare the Available Proof (and Any Other Evidence You Might Seek) to These Mental Elements and Crimes.* It is undisputed that Carr caused Victim's death. The punishment he will receive under these homicide statutes will be determined by his culpable mental state. Your jurisdiction has adopted the four Model Penal Code mental elements. Your supervisor (the District Attorney) has asked for your recommendation of the most serious homicide crime that can be proved. Examine the evidence and assess Carr's liability for homicide in the following order: (a) first degree murder, (b) second degree murder, (c) manslaughter, and (d) criminally negligent homicide.

(4) *Should Mens Rea Be the Exclusive Determinant of Severity?* Note that, irrespective of the mens rea, the defendant has killed the victim. Yet the punishment decreases—automatically—as the mens rea goes from purposely to criminal negligence, and it is controlled solely by the mens rea provided in this statutory homicide pattern (which, again, fits no state). Do you agree with this approach? (Notice that most states also use other physical elements to define homicide severity.)

[1] The Higher MPC Mental States: Intent and Knowledge
Note on the Meanings of Intent ("Purpose") and Knowledge

(1) *Intent (or Purpose) as the Actor's "Conscious Object."* The MPC adopts "purpose" as its highest mental element, although many states instead use the older, better-known terminology of "intent" "or "intentionally," which is close to the same thing. See, e.g., Ore. Rev. Stat. § 161.085(7). For a result or harm, the MPC defines this term as meaning that the result is the actor's "conscious object." Imagine that the defendant is indifferent to the consequences—he or she knows that the death of the victim is certain to result—but just doesn't care. This defendant cannot be held to have acted "purposefully" or "intentionally." Can you explain why?

(2) *Intent or Purpose as Shown by "Probable Consequences": An Inference, Not a Standard.* Courts often observe that a person "can be held to intend the probable consequences of the person's actions," or use words to similar effect. For example, if a defendant points a gun at the victim's head and pulls the trigger, a jury could conclude that this conduct establishes an intent to kill since death is a reasonable result of the actions. This statement, however, does not mean that probable consequences are included in the elements of the crime; it just means that intent or purpose can be inferred from the probable consequences of the conduct. Can you explain the difference?

(3) *Knowledge as Sufficient, Instead of Intent?* Most jurisdictions influenced by the MPC do not limit murder to intentional killings; they allow knowledge to suffice. Thus, a "knowing killing" is a serious offense. Can you see why?

(4) *What Does It Take to "Know" Something Under the MPC?* The mens rea of "knowingly" is misleading. Assume a statute punishes someone who "knowingly kills" another person, but it does not say what "knowingly" means. What does

"knowingly" mean in this context? How certain does one have to be to "know" that something exists or will happen? 100%? 90%? 75%? 51%?

(5) *Knowledge as "Practical Certainty"?* The Model Penal Code as we have seen above, adopts the standard of "practically certain" to describe the degree of certainty necessary for a finding of "knowingly" causing a result. Some jurisdictions use other tests, such as "substantial certainty," "reasonably certain," or "high probability." *See, e.g., People v. Weeks*, 971 N.E.2d 533 (Ill. App. Ct. 2012) (240 pound defendant who regularly used a belt to beat 14 year-old paraplegic with serious heart defects is guilty of knowingly killing the victim since she knew her acts created a "strong probability of death or serious bodily injury; pathologist testified there were too many injuries to count).

(6) *Knowledge of Illegality Usually Is Not Required.* Crimes with a "knowing" mens rea virtually never specify that the crime requires knowledge of the existence of the law violated. To make this point clear, a few states have explicit statutory provisions. *See, e.g.*, Wis. Stat. § 939.23 (intent does not require proof of the knowledge of the existence or constitutionality of the applicable criminal law). But there are crimes that require this knowledge of illegality — *e.g.,* some crimes involving interpretation of tax laws.

(7) *Creating a Knowledge Requirement That Is Not in the Statute.* Sometimes a court will "read in" a mens rea requirement even though the relevant statute contains none. Knowledge is one mens rea that some courts have added to an otherwise strict liability statute. In *State v. Ndikum*, 815 N.W.2d 816 (Minn. 2012), for example, the defendant, a lawyer, was charged with possession of a pistol in public. The government proved he had a pistol in his briefcase when he tried to go through courthouse security. The defendant argued his wife put the gun in the briefcase without his knowledge. Even though the statute appeared to be strict liability, the Minnesota Supreme Court read in a requirement that the government prove the defendant knew he had the gun with him.

State v. Campbell

19 N.E.3d 271 (Ind. 2014)

Rucker, Justice.

Defendant was convicted following a jury trial during which the jury was given a supplemental jury instruction on the definition of "intentionally" after deliberations had begun. Some years later, defendant petitioned for post-conviction relief alleging ineffective assistance of trial counsel, in part, for counsel's failure to object to the instruction. . . . [F]inding no error we affirm. . . .

. . . [A] long-simmering contentious relationship between neighbors, arising out of a property easement dispute, resulted in a physical altercation during which Wayne Campbell entered the home of Jean and Alva Kincaid, beating and seriously injuring both. . . . Campbell was found guilty of two counts of attempted murder, burglary resulting in serious bodily injury as a Class A felony, aggravated battery as a Class B felony, and battery as a Class C felony. . . . Among other claims [in his post-conviction petition,] Campbell contended trial counsel rendered ineffective assistance for . . . failing to object to a jury instruction regarding the definition of "intentionally."

. . . About two hours into deliberations the jury . . . asked the bailiff a follow-up question, namely: "they want to know the definition of intent." . . . [The defendant's trial counsel asked that the state's pattern jury charge defining intent be given, and the court did so orally and in writing, as follows:]

> Indiana Code 35–41–2–2, Intentional is defined by statute as follows. A person engages in conduct intentionally if when he engages in the conduct, it is his conscious objectives [sic] to do so. If a person is charged with intentionally causing a result by his conduct, it must have been his conscious objective not only to engage in the conduct, but also to cause the result.

Concerning Campbell's claim that [the instruction] contained an incorrect statement of the law, Campbell specifically refers to the second sentence of the instruction, namely: "If a person is charged with intentionally causing a result by his conduct, it must have been his conscious objective not only to engage in the conduct, but also to cause the result."

[Simply put, Campbell's argument was that the instruction "relieved the state of its burden" of proving intent as to *both* the act *and* the result. His position is that the instruction should have restated the requirement of proof as to *both* issues, independently.]

Here, the second sentence of the contested instruction serves to emphasize [that the state must] prove that an accused had the "conscious objective" to engage in the prohibited conduct but also that he intended to "cause the result" of his conduct. For clarity the sentence might be amended to read "If a person is charged with intentionally causing a result by his conduct, *the State is required to prove* it must have been his conscious objective not only to engage in the conduct but also cause the result." Nonetheless even in its current form the instruction holds the State to this higher burden of proof even though the statute defining intentionally does not do so in express terms. The State does not contend this is an inappropriate burden and we conclude that Pattern Jury Instruction 9.05 represents a correct statement of the law. As such trial counsel in this case did not render ineffective assistance in failing to object to the instruction. [Affirmed.]

ELONIS v. UNITED STATES, 135 S. Ct. 2001 (2015). In this case, the Supreme Court decided that the federal extortion statute, which criminalizes certain threats but does not particularize the required mens rea, requires either *intent* to make a threat or *knowledge* that others would perceive the communication as a threat. The defendant used Facebook to post graphically violent language and imagery concerning his wife, co-workers, a kindergarten class, and state and federal law enforcement. These posts included statements that they were "fictitious" and not about real persons and that Elonis was exercising his First Amendment rights. But many saw his posts as threatening, including his boss, who fired him, and his wife, who obtained a protection order.

The trial court had instructed the jury that an accused must be "negligent" with respect to the threatening nature of the communication. It did so partly because an "intent to extort" was elsewhere required in the statute. The Supreme Court imposed the intent-or-knowledge requirement by reasoning as follows:

> The Court does not regard "mere omission from a criminal enactment of any mention of criminal intent" as dispensing with such a requirement. *Morissette v. United States* [which is excerpted below in this chapter]. . . . The "general rule" is that a guilty mind is "a necessary element in the indictment and proof of every crime." *United States v. Balint* [also below]. In some cases, a general requirement that a defendant act knowingly is sufficient, but where such a requirement "would fail to protect the innocent actor," the statute "would need to be read to require . . . specific intent."

Question: Should the trial court's jury instructions borrow the definitions of intent and knowledge from the MPC, although the federal criminal code is not based on the MPC?

Notes and Questions

(1) *Is the Defendant's Argument in Campbell So Subtle That It Looks Ridiculous?* It seems likely that anyone applying the instruction would realize that the state must prove intent as to both the act and the result. But when convictions are reversed, jury instructions are a frequent basis, and obviously the court in this case took the issue seriously.

(2) *Knowingly, as Opposed to Intentionally: Ramirez-Memije v. State,* 444 S.W.3d 624 (Tex. 2014). Defendant was convicted of fraudulent possession of identifying information. He possessed a credit-card skimmer with personal information, which he received from another person and transferred to yet another person. The crime required knowledge of the nature of the device, and the trial court correctly instructed the jury on the meaning of knowledge in a statute derived from the Model Penal Code: the defendant must be "aware . . . that the circumstances exist." Defendant argued, and the lower court held, that it was error not to also give an instruction requiring a "voluntary act," because he claimed he did not know the nature of the object he possessed.

The court reasoned, "If there was evidence that the skimmer had been slipped into Appellant's bag without his knowledge, then there may be a question of voluntary possession." But since his voluntary receipt of the skimmer was undisputed, the issue, instead, was knowledge. Is this reasoning correct, given that the statute also required "fraudulent" possession? Four justices dissented.

Problem 3G (Mens Rea): Defendant Knew and Intended Something—But What?

(1) *Unknown Marijuana: What Does It Take to "Know" or "Intend" Something?* Defendant, a college student, was arrested with a half ounce of marijuana in her backpack and charged with possession of marijuana. The statute allegedly violated states: "A person commits the crime of possessing marijuana if the person intentionally or knowingly possesses marijuana of an aggregate weight of one half-ounce or more." The defendant claims that she thought two things: (a) that the substance was cloves, not marijuana, and (b) that the total amount in her backpack was one-quarter ounce. But she also has rolling papers, a lighter, and a wad of cash in the backpack. Can either claim avoid conviction under this statute?

(2) *Interpreting the "Knowingly" Requirement.* The two sides in a criminal case might interpret this marijuana statute differently. Consider how the prosecution would want the statute interpreted and how the defense might, and try to imagine what kinds of proof the two sides would offer to prove or disprove that the defendant "knowingly" possessed the marijuana.

[2] Should a Court Create Mens Rea When the Statute Contains None?

UNITED STATES v. LYNCH, 233 F.3d 1139 (9th Cir. 2000). [The defendant went deer hunting on an uninhabited island in southeast Alaska. The island contained an area which included the remains of an Alaskan native village. He saw a human skull partially covered by soil, and he scraped away dirt, lifted the skull, and took it with him. When interviewed by the Forest Service, Lynch admitted, "Oh, man, it's definitely old. There's not a stitch of clothin' or nothin' with it." Carbon dating showed the skull to be about 1400 years old.]

The defendant was convicted under 16 U.S.C. § 470ee(a), a part of the Archeological Resources Protection Act, which makes a crime of "knowingly" removing an "archeological resource" from public land. (Archeological resources include certain items over 100 years old.) He argued that he had not known that he was violating the law or that the object removed was an "archeological resource," and he further argued that this knowledge was an essential element.

The government, in maintaining that knowledge was not required, said that these later-discovered facts were the "risks one assumes when picking up human bones on government land." The Court of Appeals disagreed and held that the government must prove "that a defendant knows or [has] reason to know that he [is] removing an 'archeological resource'":

> The government argues that [the statute's] use of "knowingly" rather than "willfully" reflects legislative intent that the statute not require a knowledge that one's actions are against the law. We agree. . . .

In most cases, [however,] a requirement that a violation be "knowing" means that the defendant must "know the facts that make his conduct illegal." . . . [T]here exists here the potential for harsh penalties to be applied to those who acted in ignorance of a fact that the statute makes an otherwise noncriminal act a crime: a skull may or may not be an archeological resource. . . . [The law] counsels against convicting an unwitting person of a felony when nobody knew until after a lengthy investigation that the object taken was [an archeological resource]. . . .

UNITED STATES v. CARLSON, 2011 WL 13141452 (D. Idaho) (unreported decision). The defendants spray-painted the rock face of a structure and were charged under a statute making it a crime to willfully damage property of the United States. They argued that they did not know that the property was owned by the United States. Prosecutors filed a Motion in Limine in response to defendants' argument (i.e., a motion to exclude any mention of this argument before the jury). The court granted the Motion in Limine and rejected the defense argument:

The statute at issue makes it a crime to willfully injure or commit depredation against any property of the United States. 18 U.S.C. § 1361. . . . [T]he statute does *not* require the defendants acted "knowingly." . . .

The Court acknowledges that "willfully" has many meanings and "its construction [is] often . . . influenced by its context." Defendants seek to have this Court use the term "willfully" to require the defendants to have direct knowledge the property was owned by the United States. A plain reading of the statute does not support this argument. In the express language of the statute the term "willfully" does not modify the ownership of the property requirement, but modifies whether the injury or damage was done willfully, i.e. intentionally and voluntarily.

Notes and Questions

(1) *What Justifies the Difference between Lynch and Carlson?* The statutes in both cases required a "willful" state of mind, and each statute had two main requirements. But in one case, the court implied a mens rea of knowledge to both requirements, while in the other case, the court required knowledge as to only one. Why?

(2) *Under the Lynch Court's Reasoning, What Does "Knowingly" Mean?* The *Lynch* court holds that a knowledge requirement can be satisfied by evidence merely that the defendant "had reason to know" that he was committing the physical elements of the crime. This federal standard is lower than the "practically certain" requirement for knowledge under MPC § 2.02(2)(b). Arguably, however, the lesser standard of "had reason to know" carries out the policy underlying the federal archeological protection statute, because as the court recognized, a person rarely knows the precise nature of an ancient object but may deprive the public of it, and cause collateral damage, by carrying it away. *See United States v. Quarrell,* 310 F.3d 664 (10th Cir.

2002) (articulating this policy). Can you explain the difference between this court's treatment of "knowingly" and the MPC's knowledge definition?

(3) *Knowledge under the MPC.* What result would occur in this "archeological resource" case if the element of "knowingly" in the statute were construed consistently with the MPC, which requires "practical certainty" for knowledge?

[3] The Lesser MPC Mental States: Recklessness and Negligence

Note on Recklessness, Criminal Negligence, and Civil Negligence

(1) *Liability for Results That Are "Accidental," with Neither Intent nor Knowledge.* Recall that the MPC's mental states of recklessness and criminal negligence require a "gross deviation from the standard of conduct" of a law-abiding or reasonable person. This means that the Model Penal Code accepts the concept that the criminal law should not cover conduct that involves ordinary carelessness as opposed to more serious misconduct.

(2) *Distinguishing Between Recklessness and Criminal Negligence.* Under MPC § 2.02(c), recklessness contains objective *and* subjective components. The accused must have been (a) subjectively "aware" of a risk, and in addition, the risk must have been (b) objectively substantial and unjustified. Thus, someone who commits a profoundly foolish act, but who subjectively is clueless about just how risky the act is, is not reckless, because he or she lacks the necessary awareness of the risk.

(3) *Too Drunk to Be Aware.* What if a person commits an extremely careless act but is so drunk that he or she is not aware of the risk undertaken? Does the intoxication mean the actor is not reckless since he or she was not aware of the risk (remember, recklessness under the MPC requires this awareness)? Many jurisdictions, including the MPC, specifically provide that a person who acts in an extremely careless manner while too drunk to be aware of the risk taken, is still "reckless" despite the lack of awareness. MPC § 2.08(2). Can you see how this alters the basic definition of reckless?

(4) *Distinguishing Criminal Negligence from Civil (Tort) Negligence.* Under MPC § 2.02(d), criminal negligence, on the other hand, is objective. The actor fits this standard if she "should" have been aware of the risk, even if she was not. The clueless-but-monumentally-foolish actor, even if not reckless, can be criminally negligent. Thus, recklessness applies only to someone who is actually aware, while criminal negligence includes someone who is not aware but should be.

Both recklessness and criminal negligence involve a deviation from an objective standard which is quite high: "a gross deviation" from the standard of care of a reasonable person. Thus, ordinary negligence, covered by tort law, would not satisfy either standard; the carelessness must be of a higher order for criminal liability under the MPC.

(5) *These Neat Categories Are Not as Clear in Real Cases as This Logic Makes Them Appear.* These differences are definable, in the abstract. But in real life, they tend to blur into a continuum, as the following decision shows. It is a difficult judgment call

to say whether an act is reckless, criminally negligent, civilly negligent, or not negligent at all, because the decision depends upon elusive gradations and factual details.

People v. Hall

999 P.2d 207 (Colo. 2000)

JUSTICE BENDER delivered the Opinion of the Court.

. . . While skiing on Vail mountain, [defendant Nathan] Hall flew off of a knoll and collided with Allen Cobb, who was traversing the slope below Hall. Cobb sustained traumatic brain injuries and died as a result of the collision. The People charged Hall with felony reckless manslaughter. . . . The district court [at a preliminary hearing] determined that in order for Hall's conduct to have been reckless, it must have been "at least more likely than not" that death would result. Because the court found that "skiing too fast for the conditions" is not "likely" to cause another person's death, the court concluded that Hall's conduct did not constitute a "substantial and unjustifiable" risk of death. . . .

. . . We hold that under the particular circumstances of this case, whether Hall committed the crime of reckless manslaughter must be determined by the trier of fact. Viewed in the light most favorable to the prosecution, Hall's conduct — skiing straight down a steep and bumpy slope, [with a blood alcohol level of 0.09], back on his skis, arms out to his sides, off-balance, being thrown from mogul to mogul, out of control for a considerable distance and period of time, and at such a high speed that the force of the impact between his ski and the victim's head fractured the thickest part of the victim's skull — created a substantial and unjustifiable risk of death to another person. A reasonable person could infer that the defendant, a former ski racer trained in skier safety, consciously disregarded that risk. . . . Thus, we reverse the district court's finding. . . .

As Colorado's criminal code defines recklessness, "A person acts recklessly when he consciously disregards a substantial and unjustifiable risk that a result will occur or that circumstance exists." § 18–1–501(8). Thus, in the case of manslaughter, the prosecution must show that the defendant's conduct caused the death of another and that the defendant:

1) consciously disregarded

2) a substantial and

3) unjustifiable risk that he would

4) cause the death of another.

We examine these elements in detail.

Substantial and Unjustifiable Risk [and Gross Deviation] . . .

A risk does not have to be "more likely than not to occur" or "probable" in order to be substantial. A risk may be substantial even if the chance that the harm will occur is well below fifty percent. Some risks may be substantial even if they carry a low degree of probability because the magnitude of the harm is potentially great. For example, if a person holds a revolver with a single bullet in one of the chambers, points the gun at another's head and pulls the trigger, then the risk of death is substantial even though the odds that death will result are no better than one in six. . . . Conversely, a relatively high probability that a very minor harm will occur probably does not involve a "substantial" risk. Thus, in order to determine whether a risk is substantial, the court must consider both the likelihood that harm will occur and the magnitude of potential harm, mindful that a risk may be "substantial" even if the odds of the harm occurring are lower than fifty percent.

Whether a risk is substantial is a matter of fact that will depend on the specific circumstances of each case. . . .

A court cannot generically characterize the actor's conduct (*e.g.*, "driving a truck") in a manner that ignores the specific elements of the conduct that create a risk (*e.g.*, driving a truck with failing brakes on a highway). For example, "installing a heater" carries little risk under normal circumstances. However, the Connecticut Supreme Court held that improperly wiring a 120-volt heater to a 240-volt circuit, failing to use a lock nut to connect the heater to the circuit breaker, and using other faulty installation techniques creates a substantial risk of "catastrophic fire" and death. Thus, to determine whether the conduct created a substantial risk of death, a court must inquire beyond the general nature of the defendant's conduct and consider the specific conduct in which the defendant engaged.

As well as being substantial, a risk must be unjustifiable in order for a person's conduct to be reckless. Whether a risk is justifiable is determined by weighing the nature and purpose of the actor's conduct against the risk created by that conduct. If a person consciously disregards a substantial risk of death but does so in order to advance an interest that justifies such a risk, the conduct is not reckless. For example, if a surgeon performs an operation on a patient that has a seventy-five percent chance of killing the patient, but the patient will certainly die without the operation, then the conduct is justified and thus not reckless even though the risk is substantial.

In addition[, recklessness requires] a risk that constitutes a gross deviation from the standard of care that a reasonable law-abiding person would exercise under the circumstances. Both the Model Penal Code and the New York Code, which the General Assembly followed in drafting the Colorado criminal code, expressly define a "substantial and unjustifiable risk" as one that is a gross deviation from the reasonable standard of care. . . .

Conscious Disregard

In addition to showing that a person created a substantial and unjustifiable risk, the prosecution must demonstrate that the actor "consciously disregarded" the risk in order to prove that she acted recklessly. A person acts with a conscious disregard of the risk created by her conduct when she is aware of the risk and chooses to act despite that risk. In contrast to acting "intentionally" or "knowingly," the actor does not have to intend the result or be "practically certain" that the result will occur, he only needs to be "aware" that the risk exists.

. . . Although recklessness is a less culpable mental state than intentionally or knowingly, it involves a higher level of culpability than criminal negligence. Criminal negligence requires that, "through a gross deviation from the standard of care that a reasonable person would exercise," the actor fails to perceive a substantial and unjustifiable risk that a result will occur or a circumstance exists. An actor is criminally negligent when he should have been aware of the risk but was not, while recklessness requires that the defendant actually be aware of the risk but disregard it. Thus, even if she should be, a person who is not actually aware that her conduct creates a substantial and unjustifiable risk is not acting recklessly.

A court or trier of fact may infer a person's subjective awareness of a risk from the particular facts of a case, including the person's particular knowledge or expertise. For example, a court may infer a person's subjective awareness of the risks created by firing a gun from the facts that the person served an extended tour of duty in the military as a rifleman and machine gunner and was instructed by both the army and his father not to point a gun at another person. A court may infer from a person's extensive training and safety instruction that the person understood the risks of fire and other "catastrophic dangers" created by the "slipshod" installation of a baseboard heater. In addition, . . . a court may infer the actor's subjective awareness of a risk from what a reasonable person would have understood under the circumstances. . . . [However,] although a court can infer what the defendant actually knew based on what a reasonable person would have known in the circumstances, a court must not confuse what a reasonable person would have known in the circumstances with what the defendant actually knew. . . .

Risk of Death

The final element of recklessness requires that the actor consciously disregard a substantial and unjustifiable risk of a particular result, and in the case of manslaughter the actor must risk causing death to another person. The risk can be a risk of death to another generally; the actor does not have to risk death to a specific individual. Because the element of a "substantial and unjustifiable risk" measures the likelihood and magnitude of the risk disregarded by the actor, any risk of death will meet the requirement that the actor, by his conduct, risks death to another. That is, only a slight risk of death to another person is necessary to meet this element. . . .

V. Conclusion

The prosecution provided sufficient evidence at the preliminary hearing to induce a person of reasonable prudence and caution to entertain the belief that

Hall consciously disregarded a substantial and unjustifiable risk that he might collide with and kill another skier. . . . [W]e remand this case to the district court for trial.

Notes and Questions

(1) *Factors.* Does the court suggest that any time a defendant skier performs foolishly and runs into another skier, defendant has acted recklessly? If not, what factors would induce a court or juror to find that the skier was reckless?

(2) *Role of Expertise.* The *Hall* court found that the defendant's expertise as a skier was an indication that he consciously disregarded the risk. But is this true? Isn't it also possible that his expertise led him to believe that there was little risk in his skiing as he did?

(3) *Reasonable Person.* *Hall* indicates that the jury in assessing awareness of the risk may consider what a reasonable person would have understood. Does this make sense, since the test of recklessness is whether this defendant consciously disregarded the risk? Notice that the court adds that perceptibility of the risk to a reasonable person is not the ultimate standard, but is merely evidence from which the subjective, individual knowledge of the actor can be inferred. Presumably, this purely subjective test would negate recklessness for the abjectly clueless individual who did not perceive the risk even though virtually everyone else would have (although the abjectly clueless person still could be criminally negligent).

(4) *The Hall Case Isn't Over with This Opinion: at Trial, Criminal Negligence and Civil Negligence Probably Will Be Options for the Jury.* Recklessness, criminal negligence, and civil negligence all apply to people who are careless. Before the jury, Hall's lawyer can argue that Hall was merely criminally negligent rather than reckless, or merely ordinarily negligent and not criminally liable, or for that matter, not negligent in any sense. What would you guess that the jury will do?

§ 3.08 Transferred Intent, Differing Crimes, and the Ostrich Problem

[A] Transferred Intent

Note on Intent That, by Chance, Produces a Different (Unintended) Crime

(1) *Transferred Intent Generally.* Assume that A, a hired killer, shoots a rifle at B for the purpose of killing B. If A is successful, A will be guilty of intentional homicide. But imagine that A, the killer, is unlucky. Just as A pulled the trigger, B sneezed and the bullet missed B but hit C, who was standing behind B. Is A guilty of the intentional homicide of C? A might argue that she had no intent to kill C.

But American law long ago adopted the concept of *transferred intent*. A's intent to kill B is essentially "transferred" to the real homicide victim, C. Thus, under this doctrine A is guilty of intentionally killing C even though A had no idea C or anyone else was in the vicinity of B. The same result applies if the crime were some variety of aggravated assault and even voluntary manslaughter, when the wrong person is hurt. As another example, some cases apply transferred intent to arson if an unintended structure is burned.

(2) *Transferred Intent by Judicial Decision or by Statute.* Ordinarily the transferred intent rule is applied by judicial decision, but some states incorporate transferred intent in specific statutes. *See, e.g.,* Ala. Code § 13A-6–2 (a person commits murder if with intent to cause of the death of another person he causes the death of that person or of another person); Tex. Pen. Code § 6.04(b) (a person is criminally responsible for causing a result if the only difference between what actually occurred and what he desired, contemplated or risked is that a different offense was committed or a different person or property was harmed).

(3) *Variations of Transferred Intent.* The doctrine of transferred intent has engendered countless appellate decisions. The doctrine generally applies whether the actor intended to kill a certain person or an unspecified individual or group. *See, e.g., People v. Buford,* 2004 Mich. App. LEXIS 2403 (Sept. 16, 2004) (unpublished decision) (defendant argued with girlfriend then poured gasoline throughout stairwell of her apartment and ignited the gasoline; transferred intent applied to both murder and assault with intent to commit murder of others in the building); *State v. Mason,* 109 So.3d 429 (La. Ct. App. 2013) (drive-by shooting from car; defendant intended to shoot one person but accidentally shot and killed another; transferred intent applies).

(4) *Other Transferred Mental States.* The same reasoning underlying the doctrine of transferred intent has convinced some states to extend the "transferred" mental state concept to mens rea elements other than intent. *See, e.g., Commonwealth v. Taylor,* 979 N.E.2d 722 (Mass. 2012) (if defendant premeditates killing of one person but mistakenly kills another person, the doctrine of "transferred premeditation" means defendant is deemed to have premeditated the killing of the actual homicide victim; same for doctrine of "transferred deliberation" when defendant deliberates the killing of one person but accidentally kills another).

[B] The "Ostrich Problem": Deliberate Ignorance as Knowledge

As noted above, many crimes include a mens rea element requiring that the offender have certain knowledge. For example, New York criminal law punishes the use of a credit card that the person "knows to be revoked or cancelled" (N.Y Pen. Law § 165.17). What if a person lacks the requisite "knowledge" because of a deliberate effort to avoid acquiring the information? Can a jury nonetheless find that the person who deliberately avoids acquiring information still acted with sufficient "knowledge" to merit criminal liability under a statute requiring the actor to have specified knowledge?

As an illustration, assume that Ezekiel has been arrested while carrying a small black briefcase containing a large quantity of pure heroin. He claims that a shadowy figure known only as "Big Dog" paid him $1000 cash to deliver the briefcase to a specific address in another city. Big Dog, he alleges, never said what was in the briefcase. Ezekiel maintains that he did not know it contained heroin, though he admits that he did think "something was up, maybe laundered money, pornography, even marijuana." But he says that he told Big Dog, "I don't want to know what is in that briefcase, so don't tell me!" If Ezekiel is charged with heroin possession under a statute that requires the defendant to "knowingly possess" the drug, is he guilty?

Notes on Deliberate Ignorance and the Jewell (or "Ostrich") Instruction

(1) *"Ignorance [through] Conscious Effort" as Satisfying Knowledge Requirements.* Many jurisdictions resolve the "deliberate ignorance" (also known as "willful blindness") issue by relaxing the definition of "knowing" or "knowledge." In *United States v. Jewell*, 532 F.2d 697 (9th Cir. 1975) (en banc), the court approved the so-called "ostrich" instruction, as follows:

> the government can satisfy its burden of proof as to guilty knowledge by proving beyond a reasonable doubt that, although the defendant was not actually aware that there was a controlled substance in the vehicle at the time of her arrest, she nevertheless was aware of a high probability that the vehicle contained a controlled substance, and her ignorance of the presence of a controlled substance was solely and entirely a result of her having made a conscious effort to disregard the nature of that which was in the vehicle, with a conscious purpose to avoid learning the truth.

(2) *Deliberate Ignorance and Federal Criminal Law.* Every federal circuit court of appeals has adopted a version of the *Jewell* or "Ostrich" instruction. *See United States v. Alston-Graves*, 435 F.3d 331, 338 (D.C. Cir. 2006) (summarizing the various approaches taken by federal courts). Many—perhaps most—of the cases in which courts give an Ostrich instruction involve drug crimes. *Jewell* is such a case, as is *Heredia*, the principle case, below. Yet federal courts have approved the instruction in trials for a variety of crimes including bribery; filing a false tax return; distribution of child pornography; conspiracy, wire fraud, travel fraud, and money laundering; improper disposal of hazardous waste; and mortgage fraud.

(3) *Restricting the Ostrich Instruction.* Some state courts do not follow the *Jewell* instruction and many courts use it only sparingly because they worry that it runs the risk of convicting someone who was reckless or even negligent in inquiring about certain facts. *See United States v. Alston-Graves*, 435 F.3d 331, 340–41 (D.C. Cir. 2006). Some courts require proof of deliberate ignorance as a prerequisite to a

Jewell instruction. Does a *Jewell* or Ostrich instruction markedly alter the definition of "knowingly" in a criminal statute, and if so, is it appropriate for a court to do, or should it be done by the legislature?

United States v. Heredia

483 F.3d 913 (9th Cir. 2007) (en banc)

KOZINSKI, Circuit Judge.

We revisit *United States v. Jewell*, 532 F.2d 697 (9th Cir. 1976) (en banc), and the body of case law applying it.

I

Defendant Carmen Heredia was stopped at an inland Border Patrol checkpoint while driving from Nogales to Tucson, Arizona. Heredia was at the wheel and her two children, mother, and one of her aunts were passengers. The border agent at the scene noticed what he described as a "very strong perfume odor" emanating from the car. A second agent searched the trunk and found 349.2 pounds of marijuana surrounded by dryer sheets, apparently used to mask the odor. Heredia was arrested and charged with possessing a controlled substance with intent to distribute under 21 U.S.C. § 841(a)(1).

At trial, Heredia testified that on the day of her arrest she had accompanied her mother on a bus trip from Tucson to Nogales, where her mother had a dentist's appointment. After the appointment, she borrowed her Aunt Belia's car to transport her mother back to Tucson. Heredia told DEA Agent Travis Birney at the time of her arrest that, while still in Nogales, she had noticed a "detergent" smell in the car as she prepared for the trip and asked Belia to explain. Belia told her that she had spilled Downey fabric softener in the car a few days earlier, but Heredia found this explanation incredible.

Heredia admitted on the stand that she suspected there might be drugs in the car, based on the fact that her mother was visibly nervous during the trip and carried a large amount of cash, even though she wasn't working at the time. However, Heredia claimed that her suspicions were not aroused until she had passed the last freeway exit before the checkpoint, by which time it was too dangerous to pull over and investigate.

[Over defendant's objection, the judge gave a deliberate indifference instruction which read as follows:] . . . "You may find that the defendant acted knowingly if you find beyond a reasonable doubt that the defendant was aware of a high probability that drugs were in the vehicle driven by the defendant and deliberately avoided learning the truth. You may not find such knowledge, however, if you find that the defendant actually believed that no drugs were in the vehicle driven by the defendant, or if you find that the defendant was simply careless."

On appeal, defendant asks us to overrule *Jewell* and hold that section 841(a)(1) extends liability only to individuals who act with actual knowledge. Should *Jewell* remain good law, she asks us to reverse her conviction because the instruction given to the jury was defective and because there was an insufficient factual basis for issuing the instruction in the first place.

II

While *Jewell* has spawned a great deal of commentary and a somewhat perplexing body of case law, its core holding was a rather straightforward matter of statutory interpretation:

> "'[K]nowingly' in criminal statutes is not limited to positive knowledge, but includes the state of mind of one who does not possess positive knowledge only because he consciously avoided it."

In other words, when Congress made it a crime to "knowingly ... possess with intent to manufacture, distribute, or dispense, a controlled substance," 21 U.S.C. § 841(a)(1), it meant to punish not only those who know they possess a controlled substance, but also those who don't know because they don't want to know.

Overturning a long-standing precedent is never to be done lightly.... Since *Jewell* was decided in 1976, every regional circuit—with the exception of the D.C. Circuit—has adopted its central holding. Indeed, many colloquially refer to the deliberate ignorance instruction as the "*Jewell* instruction." Congress has amended section 841 many times since *Jewell* was handed down, but not in a way that would cast doubt on our ruling....

That said, there are circumstances when a precedent becomes so unworkable that keeping it on the books actually undermines the values of evenhandedness and predictability that the doctrine of stare decisis aims to advance. Here, we recognize that many of our post-*Jewell* cases have created a vexing thicket of precedent that has been difficult for litigants to follow and for district courts—and ourselves—to apply with consistency. But, rather than overturn *Jewell*, we conclude that the better course is to clear away the underbrush that surrounds it.

III

The parties have pointed out one area where our cases have not been consistent: Whether the jury must be instructed that defendant's motive in deliberately failing to learn the truth was to give himself a defense in case he should be charged with the crime. *Jewell* itself speculated that defendant's motive for failing to learn the truth in that case was to "avoid responsibility in the event of discovery." Yet the opinion did not define motive as a separate prong of the deliberate ignorance instruction.... Heredia argues that the motive prong is necessary to avoid punishing individuals who fail to investigate because circumstances render it unsafe or impractical to do so. She claims that she is within this group, because her suspicions did not arise until she was driving on an open highway where it would have been too dangerous to pull over. She thus claims that she had a motive other than avoiding criminal culpability for failing to discover the contraband concealed in the trunk.

We believe, however, that the second prong of the instruction, the requirement that defendant have deliberately avoided learning the truth, provides sufficient protections for defendants in these situations. A deliberate action is one that is "[i]ntentional; premeditated; fully considered." *Black's Law Dictionary* 459 (8th ed. 2004). A decision influenced by coercion, exigent circumstances or lack of meaningful choice is, perforce, not deliberate. A defendant who fails to investigate for these reasons has not deliberately chosen to avoid learning the truth.

We conclude, therefore, that the two-pronged instruction given at defendant's trial met the requirements of *Jewell*. . . .

IV

Defendant also claims there was insufficient foundation to give the *Jewell* instruction. . . .

A district court should approach the government's request to give a *Jewell* instruction in the same way it deals with any other proposed jury instruction. In general, a party is entitled to an instruction to help it prove its theory of the case, if the instruction is "supported by law and has foundation in the evidence." *Jones v. Williams*, 297 F.3d 930, 934 (9th Cir. 2002).

In deciding whether to give a particular instruction, the district court must view the evidence in the light most favorable to the party requesting it. When a party requests instructions on alternative theories, the district judge must consider the instructions separately and determine if the evidence could support a verdict on either ground. When knowledge is at issue in a criminal case, the court must first determine whether the evidence of defendant's mental state, if viewed in the light most favorable to the government, will support a finding of actual knowledge. If so, the court must instruct the jury on this theory. . . . In deciding whether to give a willful blindness instruction, in addition to an actual knowledge instruction, the district court must determine whether the jury could rationally find willful blindness even though it has rejected the government's evidence of actual knowledge. If so, the court may also give a *Jewell* instruction.

This case well illustrates the point. Taking the evidence in the light most favorable to the government, a reasonable jury could certainly have found that Heredia actually knew about the drugs . . . because she was involved in putting them there.

The analysis in the foregoing paragraph presupposes that the jury believed the government's case in its entirety, and disbelieved all of Heredia's exculpatory statements. While this would have been a rational course for the jury to take, it was not the only one. For example, a rational jury might have bought Heredia's basic claim that she didn't know about the drugs in the trunk, yet disbelieved other aspects of her story. The jury could, for example, have disbelieved Heredia's story about when she first began to suspect she was transporting drugs. . . .

. . . The government has no way of knowing which version of the facts the jury will believe, and it is entitled (like any other litigant) to have the jury instructed in conformity with each of these rational possibilities. That these possibilities are mutually exclusive is of no consequence. A party may present alternative factual theories, and is entitled to instructions supporting all rational inferences the jury might draw from the evidence.

[We do not agree] that the *Jewell* instruction risks lessening the state of mind that a jury must find to something akin to recklessness or negligence. The instruction requires the jury to find beyond a reasonable doubt that defendant "was aware of a high probability" of criminality and "deliberately avoided learning the truth." Indeed, the instruction actually given in this case told the jurors to acquit if they believed defendant was "simply careless." . . .

V

. . . While the particular form of the [*Jewell*] instruction can vary, it must, at a minimum, contain the two prongs of suspicion and deliberate avoidance. The district judge may say more, if he deems it advisable to do so, or deny the instruction altogether. We review such decisions for abuse of discretion. The instruction given at defendant's trial met these requirements, and the district judge did not abuse his discretion in issuing it. AFFIRMED.

KLEINFELD, Circuit Judge, concurring in the result.

[T]he majority errs in concluding that motivation to avoid criminal responsibility need not be an element of a wilful blindness instruction. . . .

The majority converts the statutory element that the possession be "knowing" into something much less — a requirement that the defendant be suspicious and deliberately avoid investigating. The imposition on people who intend no crime of a duty to investigate has no statutory basis. The majority says that its requirement is enough to protect defendants who cannot investigate because of "coercion, exigent circumstances or lack of meaningful choice." . . . The majority seems to mean that if someone can investigate, they must. A criminal duty to investigate the wrongdoing of others to avoid wrongdoing of one's own is a novelty in the criminal law.

. . . Shall someone who thinks his mother is carrying a stash of marijuana in her suitcase be obligated, when he helps her with it, to rummage through her things? Should Heredia have carried tools with her, so that (if her story was true) she could open the trunk for which she had no key? Shall all of us who give a ride to a child's friend search her purse or his backpack?

No "coercion, exigent circumstances, or lack of meaningful choice" prevents FedEx from opening packages before accepting them, or prevents bus companies from going through the luggage of suspicious looking passengers. But these businesses are not "knowingly" transporting drugs in any particular package, even though they know that in a volume business in all likelihood they sometimes must be. . . . The majority opinion apparently makes these businesses felons despite the fact that Congress did not. . . .

. . . A *Jewell* instruction ought to require (1) a belief that drugs are present, (2) avoidance of confirmation of the belief, and (3) wilfulness in that avoidance — that is, choosing not to confirm the belief in order to "be able to deny knowledge if apprehended." The instruction should expressly exclude recklessness, negligence and mistake (the one given only excluded "simpl[e] careless[ness]" and an "actual belie[f] that no drugs were in the vehicle"). Anything less supports convictions of persons whom Congress excluded from statutory coverage with the word "knowingly." People who possess drugs, but do not do so "knowingly," are what we traditionally refer to as "innocent."

. . . I concur instead of dissenting [because] defendant did not object to these deficiencies in the instruction [at trial]. . . .

GRABER, CIRCUIT JUDGE, with whom PREGERSON, THOMAS, and PAEZ, CIRCUIT JUDGES, join, dissenting.

[A]s a matter of statutory construction, I believe that the *Jewell* instruction is not proper because it misconstrues, and misleads the jury about, the mens rea required by 21 U.S.C. § 841(a)(1). Under 21 U.S.C. § 841(a)(1), it is a crime to "knowingly or intentionally . . . manufacture, distribute, or dispense, or possess with intent to manufacture, distribute, or dispense, a controlled substance." (Emphasis added.) The plain text of the statute does not make it a crime to have a high probability of awareness of possession — knowledge or intention is required. The majority recognizes that willful blindness is a mens rea separate and distinct from knowledge. . . .

The majority recognizes that the *Jewell* instruction embodies a substantive decision that those who possess a controlled substance and "don't know because they don't want to know" are just as culpable as those who knowingly or intentionally possess a controlled substance. But Congress never made this substantive decision about levels of culpability — the *Jewell* court did. . . . [T]he majority directly contravenes the principle that "[i]t is the legislature, not the Court, which is to define a crime, and ordain its punishment." . . .

Thus, I would overrule *Jewell* and interpret 21 U.S.C. § 841(a) to require exactly what its text requires — a knowing or intentional mens rea. . . .

Notes and Questions

(1) *Differing Ideas of Mens Rea.* These opinions deal with at least six different mens rea concepts: actual knowledge, deliberate ignorance, recklessness, negligence, carelessness, and mistake. Consider whether these really are distinct concepts, or whether they represent a continuum of different degrees of awareness which fade into each other.

(2) *Is There a Danger That Juries Will Import Recklessness or Negligence Standards into an Ostrich (or Jewell) Instruction?* The majority concludes that the two requirements it approves, (1) that the defendant have actual "awareness" of a "high probability" of the crime and (2) that the defendant "deliberately avoid" learning the truth, are sufficient to prevent a jury finding of knowledge based on mere recklessness or

carelessness. The concurring judge argues, however, that the instruction also should require (3) a "motive" to "be able to deny knowledge if apprehended" and (4) an express negation of "recklessness, negligence, and mistake." Is the concurrence correct, or do the two protections adopted by the majority express the concept sufficiently to distinguish deliberate ignorance from recklessness or negligence?

(3) *Does the Majority's Deliberate Ignorance Instruction Really Create a New "Duty to Investigate"?* The concurring judge implies that if a mother is suspected sometimes to possess contraband, her son cannot help her with her suitcase without taking on a "duty to investigate." Is this concern valid if the son does not have an actual "awareness" of a "high probability" of contraband on this occasion and does not "deliberately avoid" learning the truth? Consider, also, the concurring judge's example involving FedEx, which is aware that in handling millions of packages, it probably will possess some that contain contraband. Can this example be distinguished on the ground that FedEx does not "deliberately avoid" learning of specific packages containing drugs — or that it is not actually aware of a high probability of drugs in any specific package?

(4) *Does the Majority Violate the Principle That Legislatures, Not Courts, Should Create Crimes?* The dissenters argue that the court is legislating. Are they correct? You might compare this decision with *State v. Sandoval* (in Chapter 1) where the court overruled a line of cases, based on one of its own decisions, that had ignored statutory language and substituted a court-made test. *Sandoval* firmly disapproved this approach. But in *Heredia*, the majority points to Congressional acquiescence as a reason for retaining *Jewell*. Is this argument persuasive? In the alternative, can it be argued that the majority simply carries out the proper judicial function of interpreting the statute, by defining the word "knowingly"?

(5) *What Crime Is Committed if the Defendant Acts as an Ostrich with Respect to One Suspected Offense while Committing the Actus Reus of Another, More Serious Offense?* Imagine that Ruthie is given $2,000 to transport a backpack across the border from Canada into the United States. She complies with instructions not to look inside the backpack or ask any questions, but strongly suspects it contains meth since the person who gave it to her is rumored to manufacture that drug and the fee for transporting the backpack is extraordinarily generous. The backpack actually contains heroin. Is Ruthie guilty of knowingly transporting meth? Heroin? Assuming she is charged with the knowing transportation of heroin, should the judge give a *Jewell* instruction?

Problem 3H: The Knowledgeable Judge Learned Foote

During lunch, Federal District Judge Amy Lampert told her colleague, Judge Learned Foote, that "Your friend David Chapman's name came up in connection with a wiretap application." Foote responded, "Don't tell me exactly what role he played in it. I've had my suspicions about him for a long time." That night Judge Foote called Chapman and repeated the conversation he had with Judge Lampert. Chapman denied knowing anything about a wiretap.

Six months later Judge Foote was arrested for illegally disclosing a federal wiretap under a federal statute (18 U.S.C. § 2232) that punishes someone who:

> having knowledge that a Federal . . . officer has . . . applied for authorization . . . to intercept [an] . . . electronic communication, in order to obstruct, impede, or prevent such interception, gives notice. . . . to another person of the possible interception.

(1) *Actual Knowledge?* Based on the above information, do you think the government can prove that Judge Foote had actual knowledge that a wiretap application had been sought? And what is his mens rea with respect to obstructing a wiretap under 18 U.S.C. § 2232?

(2) *Is a Jewell or "Ostrich" Instruction Appropriate?* If there is inadequate information to establish Judge Foote's actual knowledge, is there enough to support a Jewell instruction about deliberate indifference? *See United States v. Aguilar,* 80 F.3d 329 (9th Cir. 1996).

§ 3.09 Strict Liability Crimes

[A] Strict Liability in General

Note on the Rationale and Meaning of Strict Liability

(1) *Crimes Without Mental Elements.* Sometimes a crime is defined that has no express mens rea element. This may mean that the offense is a strict liability crime, which does not require proof of any particular mens rea. As a general rule, strict liability crimes are not the most serious offenses; they often involve health and safety regulations. Some strict liability offenses, however, are quite serious. Perhaps the most frequent one (outside of intoxicated driving) is statutory rape, which punishes sexual intercourse with a person under a certain age. In many jurisdictions, the defendant's knowledge of the age of the child is immaterial. (We address statutory rape more fully in Chapter Five.)

(2) *The Importance of Legislative Intent.* Courts often have inferred mens rea requirements in statutes that do not express them. But most courts recognize strict liability offenses when the legislature intends them. And as the following case illustrates, the legislative history may matter.

City of Bismark v. King
924 N.W.2d 137 (N.D. 2019)

McEvers, Justice.

. . . King was charged with driving under the influence of alcohol or drugs and/or refusal to submit to a chemical test under Bismarck City Ordinance § 12–10–01(1). The relevant portions of the city ordinance use language identical to [the then-applicable state statute]. This Court has previously held driving under the influence of alcohol under [that statute] is a strict liability offense and there is no culpability requirement. A strict liability offense is punishable without regard to intent, knowledge, willfulness, or negligence. *State v. Olson*, 356 N.W.2d 110, 112 (N.D. 1984). Although we have not specifically addressed criminal refusal under [the refusal statute], the legislature did not amend the language of the statute to require . . . culpability when it added the language making refusal a criminal offense. . . . Nothing in the plain language of [the state statute] indicates an intent to alter our decisions that driving under the influence, including refusal, is a strict liability offense. *See also Hearing on H.B. 1302 Before the House Judiciary Comm.*, 63rd N.D. Legis. Sess. (April 16, 2013) (testimony from Senator Kelly Armstrong) (stating "A refusal to submit to chemical testing is a crime just like a DUI. . . . We added it into 39–08-01 and made it a strict liability statute under the DUI statute."). A person is guilty of refusal to submit to a chemical test if he drives or is in actual physical control of a vehicle and he refuses to submit to a chemical test at the direction of a law enforcement officer.

[King appealed on the ground that the trial court had erred by failing to give his requested charge on "confusion" as a reason for his refusal. But] King's alleged confusion as a reason why he refused to submit to testing was not relevant. This Court has recognized limited affirmative defenses to strict liability crimes when public policy supports the defense or the constitutional interests of the accused are concerned. *See State v. Vandermeer*, 2014 ND 46, ¶ 18, 843 N.W.2d 686. However, no such arguments were made in this case.

Because refusal to submit to chemical testing under Bismarck City Ordinance § 12–10-01 is a strict liability offense, King was not entitled to a jury instruction on confusion. The district court did not err by refusing to give King's requested instruction. [Affirmed.]

Notes and Questions

(1) *What Justifies Imposing Strict Liability?* Driving under the influence, as in *King*, above, seems to justify it, because the defendant's intoxication would furnish a basis for acquittal by itself, if a mens rea were required. Arguably, the refusal crime also justifies strict liability. A cynic might say, "Of course, you were confused, Mr. King. You were drunk!"

Should defendants be able to argue that their good faith or absence of blameworthy conduct is a valid defense to a strict liability crime? *See* Laurie L. Levenson, *Good Faith Defenses: Reshaping Strict Liability Crimes*, 78 Cornell L. Rev. 401 (1993). But could that defense make sense in *King, above?*

(2) *What Offenses Should Carry Strict Liability?* Consider the following possibilities: (a) offenses where proof of the accused's mental state is inherently difficult, such as speeding offenses; (b) those in which requiring mens rea would defeat the purpose, because the accused's successful invocation of a mens rea requirement could cause acquittal by itself, such as driving under the influence; or (c) those in

which the presence of liability without fault makes deterrence particularly effective because of ready means of minimizing risks of violation, such as laws punishing polluters.

(3) *Hostility to Strict Liability Crimes: The MPC.* Some commentators and courts are critical of strict liability offenses, considering them inappropriate as a justification to impose punishment since they do not necessarily reach people who are morally culpable. Model Penal Code §2.05 illustrates this hostility by generally disfavoring strict liability for serious offenses except where the legislative purpose "plainly" calls for strict liability. The commentary to §2.05 explains,

> Crime does and should mean condemnation and no court should have to pass that judgment unless it can declare that the defendant's act was culpable. This is too fundamental to be compromised.

But do you agree, after considering driving under the influence? A statute may say something like, "No mental state is required for the offenses in this chapter." But DUI is a serious crime as a misdemeanor and can become a serious felony.

(4) *Finding Mens Rea Elements in What Appear to Be Strict Liability Offenses: The Role of Courts.* In an earlier case in this chapter, *United States v. Lynch,* the court decided that knowledge would be required as an element of the charged crime, even though the statute did not contain any such requirement. Is it proper for a court to impose a mental state, or is it inconsistent with the separation of powers between the judicial and legislative branches?

[B] Strict Liability and "Public Welfare" or Regulatory Crimes

United States v. Balint

258 U.S. 250 (1922)

MR. CHIEF JUSTICE TAFT delivered the opinion of the court.

. . . Defendants in error were indicted for . . . unlawfully selling to another a certain amount of a derivative of opium and a certain amount of a derivative of coca leaves, not in pursuance of any written order on a form issued in blank for that purpose by the Commissioner of Internal Revenue, contrary to the provisions of §2 of the [federal Narcotic Act]. The defendants demurred to the indictment on the ground that it failed to charge that they had sold the inhibited drugs knowing them to be such. The statute does not make such knowledge an element of the offense [even though violations were subject to a maximum penalty of 5 years imprisonment].

. . . It has been objected that punishment of a person for an act in violation of law when ignorant of the facts making it so, is an absence of due process of law. But [we have held] that in the prohibition or punishment of particular acts, the State may in the maintenance of a public policy provide "that he who shall do them shall do them at his peril and will not be heard to plead in defense good faith or ignorance."

Many instances of this are to be found in regulatory measures . . . . [W]here one deals with others and his mere negligence may be dangerous to them, as in selling diseased food or poison, the policy of the law may, in order to stimulate proper care, require the punishment of the negligent person though he be ignorant of the noxious character of what he sells.

. . . [The] manifest purpose [of this law] is to require every person dealing in drugs to ascertain at his peril whether that which he sells comes within the inhibition of the statute, and if he sells the inhibited drug in ignorance of its character, to penalize him. Congress weighed the possible injustice of subjecting an innocent seller to a penalty against the evil of exposing innocent purchasers to danger from the drug, and concluded that the latter was the result preferably to be avoided. . . . We think the demurrer to the indictment should have been overruled. . . .

Notes on Public Welfare Offenses

(1) *Reaffirming Balint: United States v. Dotterweich*, 320 U.S. 277 (1943). Dotterweich was the president and general manager of a company that purchased drugs from manufacturers, repackaged them under its own label, and sold them. Both misbranded and adulterated drugs were shipped by the company. Dotterweich was convicted of "[t]he introduction or delivery for introduction into interstate commerce of any . . . drug . . . that is adulterated or misbranded," in violation of the Food, Drug and Cosmetic Act. Speaking through Justice Frankfurter, the Supreme Court affirmed his conviction:

> The prosecution to which Dotterweich was subjected is based on a now familiar type of legislation whereby penalties serve as effective means of regulation. Such legislation dispenses with the conventional requirement for criminal conduct—awareness of some wrongdoing. In the interest of the larger good it puts the burden of acting at hazard upon a person otherwise innocent but standing in responsible relation to a public danger. *United States v. Balint*. . . .

This time, however, the Court was badly split. Writing for four dissenters, Justice Murphy declared:

> It is a fundamental principle of Anglo-Saxon jurisprudence that guilt is personal and that it ought not lightly to be imputed to a citizen who, like the respondent, has no evil intention or consciousness of wrongdoing. . . . [I]n the absence of clear statutory authorization it is inconsistent with established canons of criminal law to rest liability on an act in which the accused did not participate and of which he had no personal knowledge.

See also United States v. Freed, 401 U.S. 601 (1971) (extending *Balint* to possession of hand grenades, which are an unregistered firearm under federal law; since statute is regulatory, serves public safety, and involves item no less dangerous than *Balint's* narcotics, government need not prove the defendant knew the grenades were unregistered).

(2) *Broad Liability but Growing Dissent. Balint, Dotterweich* and *Freed* suggest broad possibilities for strict liability in federal criminal law, particularly when the offense involves "public welfare." Yet the *Dotterweich* dissent also displayed the beginning of strong concerns about these same possibilities. The dissenters' concerns bore fruit in the next case.

MORISSETTE v. UNITED STATES, 342 U.S. 246 (1952). The defendant admitted that he took spent bomb casings from a government practice bombing range and sold them for scrap. But he claimed that he thought the casings were abandoned because they had been thrown in a pile and rusting. In the lower courts the defendant unsuccessfully argued that he could not be liable for the "knowing conversion" of government property unless he acted with criminal intent. The lower courts held that criminal intent was not an element of this crime. The Supreme Court reversed. Justice Jackson's opinion recognized the validity of "public welfare" offenses but sought to limit their scope.

Echoing Justice Murphy's *Dotterweich* dissent, Justice Jackson stressed that the requirement of "intention" or an "evil mind" is "as universal and persistent in mature systems of law as belief in freedom of the human will and a consequent ability and duty of the normal individual to choose between good and evil." Even more, "As the states codified the common law of crimes, even if their enactments were silent on the subject, their courts assumed that the omission did not signify disapproval of the principle but merely recognized that intent was so inherent in the idea of the offense that it required no statutory affirmation."

At the same time, Justice Jackson recognized that the risks created by the industrial revolution and urbanization led to "increasingly numerous and detailed regulations which heighten the duties of those in control of particular industries . . . that affect public health, safety or welfare."

> The accused [under these laws], if he does not will the violation, usually is in a position to prevent it with no more care than society might reasonably expect and no more exertion than it might reasonably exact from one who assumed his responsibilities. . . . Under such considerations, courts have turned to construing statutes and regulations which make no mention of intent as dispensing with it and holding that the guilty act alone makes out the crime. This has not, however, been without expressions of misgiving. . . .
>
> Stealing, larceny, and its variants and equivalents, were among the earliest offenses known to the law that existed before legislation . . . . State courts of last resort, on whom fall the heaviest burden of interpreting criminal law in this country, have consistently retained the requirement of intent in larceny-type offenses. . . .
>
> [W]here Congress borrows [as in the statute here] terms of art in which are accumulated the legal tradition and meaning of centuries of practice,

it presumably knows and adopts the cluster of ideas that were attached to each borrowed word . . . . .

. . . We hold that mere omission [in this statute] of any mention of intent will not be construed as eliminating that element from the crimes denounced. . . .

Notes and Questions

(1) *A Presumption in Favor of Criminal Common Law?* *Morissette* holds that where Congress uses — or "borrows" — common law terms when writing a criminal statute, the statute should be interpreted in accordance with the common law, unless Congress tells the courts to do otherwise. Is this the proper presumption? If — as *Morissette* asserts — Congress is familiar with legal tradition, then can one argue that it meant to exclude intent as an element if it did not include it?

(2) *The "Presumption in Favor of Scienter."* After *Morissette*, what should a court — or at least a federal court — do when a statute is silent on mens rea? The Supreme Court has provided the following guide:

> The presumption in favor of scienter requires a court to read into a statute only that mens rea which is necessary to separate wrongful conduct from "otherwise innocent conduct." . . . By contrast, some situations may call for implying a specific intent requirement into statutory text . . . [to protect the innocent actor]. [The issue is whether] a general intent requirement suffices to separate wrongful conduct from "otherwise innocent" conduct.

Carter v. United States, 530 U.S. 255, 269 (2000) (federal bank robbery statute did not include requirement of proof of intent to steal). Of course, the presumption can be rebutted and strict liability upheld. *See Dean v. United States*, 556 U.S. 568 (2009) (use of passive voice — in this instance, "if the firearm is discharged" — may indicate Congress did not want to require proof of intent). Consider how this passage from *Carter* applies to the following case.

United States v. X-Citement Video, Inc.
513 U.S. 64 (1994)

CHIEF JUSTICE REHNQUIST delivered the opinion of the Court.

The Protection of Children Against Sexual Exploitation Act of 1977, as amended, prohibits the interstate transportation, shipping, receipt, distribution, or reproduction of visual depictions of minors engaged in sexually explicit conduct. 18 U.S.C. §2252. . . .

Rubin Gottesman owned and operated X-Citement Video, Inc. Undercover police posed as pornography retailers and targeted X-Citement Video for investigation. During the course of the sting operation, the media exposed Traci Lords for her roles in pornographic films while under the age of 18. Police Officer Steven Takeshita expressed an interest in obtaining Traci Lords tapes. Gottesman complied, selling Takeshita 49 videotapes featuring Lords before her 18th birthday. Two months later, Gottesman shipped eight tapes of the underage Traci Lords to Takeshita in Hawaii.

These two transactions formed the basis for a federal indictment [against Gottesman and others] under the child pornography statute. . . . Evidence at trial suggested that Gottesman had full awareness of Lords' underage performances. The District Court convicted respondents of all three counts. On appeal, Gottesman argued, inter alia, that the Act was facially unconstitutional because it lacked a necessary scienter requirement. . . . [The Ninth Circuit agreed and reversed the conviction.]

Title 18 U.S.C. § 2252 (1988 ed. and Supp. V) provides, in relevant part:

. . . Any person who —

. . . knowingly transports or ships in interstate or foreign commerce by any means including by computer or mails, any visual depiction, if —

(A) the producing of such visual depiction involves the use of a minor engaging in sexually explicit conduct; and

(B) such visual depiction is of such conduct . . . shall be punished as provided in subsection (b) of this section.

The critical determination which we must make is whether the term "knowingly" in subsections (1) and (2) modifies the phrase "the use of a minor" in subsections (1)(A) and (2)(A). The most natural grammatical reading, adopted by the Ninth Circuit, suggests that the term "knowingly" modifies only the surrounding verbs: transports, ships, receives, distributes, or reproduces. Under this construction, the word "knowingly" would not modify the elements of the minority of the performers, or the sexually explicit nature of the material, because they are set forth in independent clauses separated by interruptive punctuation. But we do not think this is the end of the matter, both because of anomalies which result from this construction, and because of the respective presumptions that some form of scienter is to be implied in a criminal statute even if not expressed, and that a statute is to be construed where fairly possible so as to avoid substantial constitutional questions.

If the term "knowingly" applies only to the relevant verbs in § 2252 — transporting, shipping, receiving, distributing, and reproducing — we would have to conclude that Congress wished to distinguish between someone who knowingly transported a particular package of film whose contents were unknown to him, and someone who unknowingly transported that package. It would seem odd, to say the least, that Congress distinguished between someone who inadvertently dropped an item into the mail without realizing it, and someone who consciously placed the same item in the mail, but was nonetheless unconcerned about whether the person had any knowledge of the prohibited contents of the package. . . .

Our reluctance to simply follow the most grammatical reading of the statute is heightened by our cases interpreting criminal statutes to include broadly applicable scienter requirements, even where the statute by its terms does not contain them. [The Court noted *Morissette*'s use of] the background presumption of evil intent to conclude that the term "knowingly" also required that the defendant have knowledge of the facts that made the taking a conversion — *i.e.*, that the property belonged to the United States.

Liparota v. United States, 471 U.S. 419 (1985), posed a challenge to a federal statute prohibiting certain actions with respect to food stamps. The statute's use of "knowingly" could be read only to modify "uses, transfers, acquires, alters, or possesses" or it could be read also to modify "in any manner not authorized by [the statute]." Noting that neither interpretation posed constitutional problems, the Court held the scienter requirement applied to both elements by invoking the background principle set forth in *Morissette*. . . .

The same analysis drove the recent conclusion in *Staples v. United States*, 511 U.S. 600 (1994), that to be criminally liable a defendant must know that his weapon possessed automatic firing capability so as to make it a machine-gun as defined by the National Firearms Act. . . . The Court also emphasized the harsh penalties attaching to violations of the statute as a "significant consideration in determining whether the statute should be construed as dispensing with mens rea."

Applying these principles, we think the Ninth Circuit's plain language reading of § 2252 is not so plain. First, § 2252 is not a public welfare offense. Persons do not harbor settled expectations that the contents of magazines and film are generally subject to stringent public regulation. In fact, First Amendment constraints presuppose the opposite view. Rather, the statute is more akin to the common-law offenses against the "state, the person, property, or public morals," [*Morissette*] that presume a scienter requirement in the absence of express contrary intent. Second, *Staples'* concern with harsh penalties looms equally large respecting § 2252: Violations are punishable by up to 10 years in prison as well as substantial fines and forfeiture. . . .

Morissette, reinforced by *Staples*, instructs that the presumption in favor of a scienter requirement should apply to each of the statutory elements that criminalize otherwise innocent conduct. *Staples* held that the features of a gun as technically described by the firearm registration Act was such an element. Its holding rested upon "the nature of the particular device or substance Congress has subjected to regulation and the expectations that individuals may legitimately have in dealing with the regulated items." Age of minority in § 2252 indisputably possesses the same status as an elemental fact because nonobscene, sexually explicit materials involving persons over the age of 17 are protected by the First Amendment. In the light of these decisions, one would reasonably expect to be free from regulation when trafficking in sexually explicit, though not obscene, materials involving adults. Therefore, the age of the performers is the crucial element separating legal innocence from wrongful conduct.

A final canon of statutory construction supports the reading that the term "knowingly" applies to both elements. [Several cases] suggest that a statute completely bereft of a scienter requirement as to the age of the performers would raise serious constitutional doubts. It is therefore incumbent upon us to read the statute to eliminate those doubts so long as such a reading is not plainly contrary to the intent of Congress.

For all of the foregoing reasons, we conclude that the term "knowingly" in § 2252 extends both to the sexually explicit nature of the material and to the age of the performers. . . .

[The concurring opinion of Justice Stevens is omitted.]

JUSTICE SCALIA, with whom JUSTICE THOMAS joins, dissenting. . . .

I would dispose of the present case, as the Ninth Circuit did, by reading the statute as it is written: to provide criminal penalties for the knowing transportation or shipment of a visual depiction in interstate or foreign commerce, . . . if that depiction was (whether the defendant knew it or not) a portrayal of a minor engaging in sexually explicit conduct. I would find the statute, as so interpreted, to be unconstitutional since, by imposing criminal liability upon those not knowingly dealing in pornography, it establishes a severe deterrent, not narrowly tailored to its purposes, upon fully protected First Amendment activities. This conclusion of unconstitutionality is of course no ground for going back to reinterpret the statute, making it say something that it does not say, but that is constitutional. . . .

Notes and Questions

(1) *What Was Congress Thinking, and Do We Care?* Is the majority's treatment of the prior cases convincing, or is Justice Scalia's focus on the plain language of the statute more appropriate? Presumably Congress intended to write a statute that was constitutional. If that is true, then shouldn't the Court interpret the statute in a way that makes it constitutional?

(2) *Rethinking Strict Liability and Public Welfare Offenses.* Should the Supreme Court reject strict liability in regulatory offenses (or elsewhere)? Or should it recognize them, and refrain from injecting a mens rea unless the Congressional intent to include mens rea appears?

Problem 3I: Negligence, Strict Liability, and Environmental Crimes

(1) *The Criminal Provisions of the Clean Water Act.* The Clean Water Act includes a criminal provision which states that anyone who "negligently [violates certain of its provisions] shall be punished by a fine of not less than $2,500 nor more than $25,000 per day of violation, or by imprisonment for not more than 1 year, or by both." 33 U.S.C. § 1319(c)(1)(A). Offenses committed "knowingly" are designated as felonies and are subject to more stringent punishments. *See* 33 U.S.C. § 1319(c)(2). Thus, actions committed negligently are punished by less severe sanctions than those committed knowingly. Among other things, the Clean Water Act prohibits "the discharge of oil . . . into or onto the navigable waters of the United States." 33 U.S.C. § 1321(b)(3).

(2) *A Negligent Violation Causing Environmental Harm.* Assume that a backhoe operator negligently ruptures a pipeline while working on a highway project, causing 3,000 gallons of oil to spill into a navigable river. If the operator or her supervisor is prosecuted under § 1319, do they have a claim that due process requires a mens rea of more than negligence?

(3) *Or Is a Strict Liability Crime Warranted Here instead of Negligence?* Consider whether water pollution is dangerous enough, and avoidable enough, that it should be treated as many other regulatory offenses are—as a strict liability crime?

§ 3.10 Proof Outlines: Checking the Elements During Trial

Note on the Practical Use of Proof Outlines

Recall that, in a criminal case, the prosecution must prove each element of the crime beyond a reasonable doubt and the defense may have to prove certain elements of defenses. Many prosecutors and defense lawyers use proof outlines to make sure that they prove each element or to track whether the other side has proven its elements.

One possible format is a chart with three columns: *Elements, Proof,* and *Done.* The *Elements* column lists each element to be proved. The *Proof* column indicates which witness or evidence will prove that element. The *Done* column simply provides space for counsel to check when the witness has proven the element.

Note that each side may have a proof outline for its own proof obligations as well as for the other side's proof responsibilities. This is a way to monitor carefully whether the other side has met its burden of proof.

A proof outline may prevent a prosecutor from trying an "unmakeable" case. It can also help the prosecutor anticipate defense attacks. For the defense a proof outline may prevent a guilty plea to an unprovable offense and indicate strategies of attack. Finally, a proof outline may prevent inadvertent omissions of required elements, particularly when they seem either obvious or obscure.

Notes and Questions

(1) *Forgetting to Identify the Defendant.* Imagine that the prosecutor rests without ever having asked the complaining witness to identify the defendant. Although this rarely happens, when it does, the defendant may well move for acquittal at the end of the prosecution's case. Perhaps the judge will not allow the prosecution to reopen its proof, or perhaps the jury has retired to deliberate. In either case, the failure to identify the defendant will be fatal to the prosecution's case. A proof outline reduces the likelihood of this prosecutorial error.

(2) *Failure to Prove Venue.* The prosecutor must prove that the crime occurred in the proper jurisdiction and venue. Ordinarily this means that the court must be

located in the same county and state or judicial region where the crime occurred. The prosecution may inadvertently fail to ask the pivotal question, "Did these events happen in [blank] County and State?" Again, an irrational acquittal may result, and a proof outline is the answer.

(3) *Leaving Out a Non-Obvious Element.* Imagine that the rape statute of a particular jurisdiction applies only if the prosecution proves the victim "is not the wife of the defendant." Imagine that the prosecutor proves a forcible rape but does not ask whether the victim was the wife of the defendant at the time of the rape. (Yes, a few outdated rape statutes still make distinctions on whether the defendant and victim are married.) The failure to prove this element may result in the court's granting the defendant's motion for judgment of acquittal, and a proof outline might prevent this outcome.

§ 3.11 Simulation Exercises: Preparing an Indictment and a Court's Charge

Simulation Exercise No. 3: Preparing the Indictment in State v. Howard

(1) *A Problem Involving Preparing an Indictment.* For the basic facts in the case of *State v. Howard*, please go online to https://caplaw.com/sites/cl4/, then click on "Case File No. 2." This is a homicide case. The assignment is to prepare or attack an indictment for murder. To accomplish the assignment, at the end of the chapter, you first should (1) read Case File No. 2 and (2) read the murder statute in your state (or, if your instructor says so, use the Model Penal Code, and assume, also, that this jurisdiction has a felony-murder provision that says murder also exists when an accused "causes the death of an individual while in the course of committing an inherently dangerous felony other than manslaughter").

(2) *How to Do It.* Most states' Codes of Criminal Procedure contain certain formal elements for an indictment. There is an indictment for a different offense (burglary) contained in the previous case file, Case File No. 1, also at https://caplaw. com/sites/cl4/, and you can use that indictment as a form to draft from. (Suggestion: copy it and hand-draft over it.) The Code often requires that the indictment contain all elements required to be proved. You must also include the name of the victim, identify the on-or-about date, and state the manner and means (e.g., from Richard III, "by drowning him in a barrel of wine"). More likely, a real drafter would use a murder form that has been used successfully in other murder cases and is part of the prosecution's digital form file, but you should use the indicated method for this problem.

(3) *Advice.* First, include all statutory elements. Second, although you must meet the requirements, do not overdescribe, because what you allege must be proved. For example, it might be better to describe the means as "a gun" rather than as "a revolver." Can you see why? Third, use multiple counts charging murder multiple

ways, if they are provable; for example, if you charge murder with intent or malice, you probably also will want to charge murder in other ways, such as felony murder. Fourth, you need not specifically charge lower-seriousness offenses such as manslaughter or negligent homicide, because they are implied within the murder charge (they are "lesser included offenses") and will likely be submitted to the jury anyway.

(4) *The Defense Role.* As defense attorney, describe any ways in which you attack the indictment by a motion to dismiss (for not containing all elements). Also, describe any strategic flaws in the indictment that might make the crime harder for the prosecution to prove. So, now, please go online to https://caplaw.com/sites/cl4/, then click on "Case File No. 2."

Simulation Exercise No. 4: *Preparing the Charge in* State v. Howard

(1) *A Problem Involving Preparation of the Court's Charge.* Again, consider the same materials (the murder statute and Case File 2). Please go online to https://caplaw.com/sites/cl4/, then click on "Case File No. 2."

Prepare a rudimentary court's charge, instructing the jury on the elements of murder, only.

(2) *How to Do It.* As a model or form, a court's charge in a robbery case is included at the end of Case File 2. Photocopy the charge there and (legibly) handwrite whatever you think needs to be rewritten or added. (Again, a real document preparer would not do it this way but would consult a proven murder instruction form. Also, this will not be a complete charge, because you are asked to instruct only about murder, and the defendant will have defenses that we have not yet studied.) Now, please go online to https://caplaw.com/sites/cl4/, then click on "Case File No. 2."

Appendix to Chapter 3

The Logic of Statutes: Identifying and Applying Their Elements

[A] Formal Logic: Putting the Elements Together with Facts

The Format for Deductive Logic: The Syllogism

(1) *Syllogism.* A syllogism is a logical statement that contains a first premise, a second premise, and a conclusion (in that order). "All emeralds are green; this object is an emerald; therefore, this object is green." *See* Figure 1 for another example. This is a type of "deductive" logic, meaning that its result is conclusively valid if the premises are true and syllogistic in form. Notice that the premises in this type of syllogism must be absolute rather than probabilistic (for example, the logic would not be valid if the premise were "*some* emeralds are green," as opposed to "all"), and the premises must be true (not, "all emeralds are *red*").

Figure 1

The Syllogism: Deductive Logic

"All trees are plants."	Premise
"All oaks are trees."	Premise
"Therefore, all oaks are plants."	Conclusion

---

(2) *The Simplicity and Universality of the Syllogistic Concept.* The basic concept of the syllogism is so simple that people often assume it can't be that simple. But it is. "All owls are birds; all birds are animals; therefore, all owls are animals." It also is possible to start with a long, complex premise, connected by "ands" and "ors." In that case, each of the controlling factors must be present in the second premise. But the form remains the same.

(3) *Application of a Criminal Statute to Facts Is Fundamentally Syllogistic.* Whenever a lawyer fits a statute to a fact situation, the fitting is done by a syllogism, as in Figure 2.

Figure 2

Syllogistic Application of a Criminal Statute

The controlling statute here says that all cases in which a person enters a building not then open to the public, with intent to commit theft, are burglaries; Sylvester entered a building not then open to the public, with intent to commit theft; therefore, Sylvester committed a burglary.

---

(4) *Fallacy Arising from Defective Premises or Inaccurate Syllogism Form.* The syllogism is a powerful device because it always produces a correct conclusion. But the concept lends itself to fallacy. For example, it is possible to manipulate the syllogistic form: "All fish can swim; John can swim; therefore, John is a fish." This example has

superficial resemblances to deductive logic, but it's really just an unpersuasive analogy. Still, arguments embodying this kind of fallacy can persuade lawyers, judges, and jurors.

Analogy: A Type of Inductive Reasoning

(1) *Inductive Reasoning as Contrasted to Deductive Logic.* "Deductive" logic is a process in which the conclusion follows necessarily from the premises. (We can imagine a parallel universe in which syllogisms do not hold, but short of that, the result of a syllogism is due absolute confidence.) "Induction," on the other hand, refers to any form of reasoning in which the conclusion does not follow as a matter of necessity. Induction is about possibilities, not certainties.

(2) *Analogy.* "Analogy" is inductive reasoning in which one thing is inferred to be similar to another thing in a certain respect, on the basis of similarities in other respects. If the controlling aspect is the same, the inference is that other aspects are the same too. *See* Figure 3.

Figure 3

Analogy: A Type of Inductive Logic

A whale is like mammals because it is warm-blooded, breathes air, and births its young live.	Comparison
Therefore, a whale probably shares other characteristics with mammals.	Conclusion

---

But whereas the syllogistic form produces uniformly valid deductive logic, analogy does not. It is "fuzzier." An analogy is useful only if we pick out the correct aspects of the known subject on which to build the analogy. (A whale *is* a mammal. But the argument that John is a fish, because he is like a fish in that he can swim, is a species of analogy, and it is not a persuasive one.)

Generalization: Another Type of Inductive Reasoning

(1) *Inductive Generalizations.* The term "induction" also applies to generalizations about the whole class of things from which a sample is taken. "Every year that we know of, the average temperature here has been colder during December than in July. Therefore, December again probably will be colder than July." Figure 4 contains another example.

Figure 4

Generalization: A Type of Inductive Logic

The sun arose in the east on day one, and on day two, . . . and on day 1,000.	Repeated Observations
Therefore, the sun likely will arise in the east tomorrow, too.	Conclusion

---

(2) *Life Experiences and Rules of Thumb as Inductive.* Imagine that you are waiting to meet a friend. You tell yourself, "I shouldn't have come early, because Bill is bound to be late." How do you know? By induction. You predict Bill's behavior from past experience.

(3) *How Inductive Reasoning Can Mislead You: The Fallacy of Bertrand Russell's Chicken.* But induction is only generalization from experience, and it is vulnerable to fallacy. Your friend Bill, whom you expect to be late, arrives right on time, and he explains, "I've changed. My New Year's resolution is to be punctual."

Another illustration, attributed to Bertrand Russell, involves the sad story of a chicken who has been fed by a farmer every day of its life, and who confidently runs to greet the farmer; but one day, instead, the farmer wrings the chicken's neck. Russell's blunt conclusion: "It would have been better for the chicken if its inductive inferences had been less crude."

Notes and Questions

(1) *Which Are Syllogisms, Among the Following Examples?* To test your recognition of deductive logic, consider which of the following examples are in the form of proper syllogisms.

(a) All ABX's are farfles; all farfles are Z3's; therefore, all ABX's are Z3's.

(b) No Wookies have feathers; Chewbacca is a Wookie; therefore, Chewbacca does not have feathers.

(c) Every third Thursday of every month, the court holds its motion docket; today is the third Thursday; therefore, the court holds its motion docket today.

(d) Every third Thursday during the past year, the court has held its motion docket; today is a Thursday; therefore, today the court will hold its motion docket.

(e) I reason; therefore, I exist.

The answer is that (a), (b) and (c) are syllogisms. Notice that you don't need to know what an ABX or a farfle or a Wookie is, to be able to have absolute confidence in the conclusion. (You do, however, need to be certain that the premises are true.)

On the other hand, (d) and (e) are not syllogisms. There is a superficial resemblance between the true syllogism in (c), about the third-Thursday docket, and the non-syllogism in (d), about third Thursdays during the last year. But the resemblance is misleading. The premise in (c) is universal ("every" third Thursday), while in (d) it is not (every third Thursday "in the past year"). The statement in (d) is only an induction, a generalization.

(2) *Descartes' "Cogito" Argument: A Syllogism Without the Right Structure?* "Cogito, ergo sum," said René Descartes. "I reason, therefore I exist." This proof of reality is one of the most famous statements in all of philosophy. But is this "cogito argument" really persuasive? Although it purports to be deductive, it is not a syllogism. It lacks a first premise.

Perhaps the first premise in the cogito argument is implicit. It is there, but unspoken. The trouble is, however, that almost any first premise that we might try to articulate will be debatable. Consider the following attempt: "Everything that reasons exists; I reason; therefore I exist."

But this premise is vulnerable. How can we be sure that "everything that reasons exists"? In Charles Dickens's story, *A Christmas Carol* (1843), Ebeneezer Scrooge encounters three spirits, and his reasoning changes his life. Since Ebeneezer Scrooge "reasons," does he exist? No; Scrooge is a fictional character. (Perhaps this example can be attacked precisely because Scrooge is fictional, but the question remains: how can we know that everything that reasons exists?)

In everyday affairs, we often use one-premise reasoning: "This politician is dishonest, and I'm not going to vote for him." "This jacket is too expensive, so I'm not going to buy it." This reasoning is fine, so long as the omitted premise is noncontroversial. But whenever the issue is doubtful, it's worth analyzing the premise. The assumption of its truth may be unwarranted.

(3) *Supporting Descartes' Cogito Argument with Induction.* Perhaps induction supplies the first premise in Descartes' cogito argument. All of our experience points to the conclusion that every person who reasons exists. Does this solve the problem? Not really. Descartes' effort was to discover a proof based on pure reason. Induction makes the "proof" uncertain. (Also, isn't the use of induction, about realms of existence that we do not fully understand, itself unreliable?)

(4) *Mixing Inductive and Deductive Logic.* History has never disclosed an instance of two different individuals with identical fingerprints. As a matter of inductive logic, we therefore infer that all occurrences of an individual's fingerprint demonstrate the presence of that identified individual. On the basis of this *inductively* created first premise, coupled with the second premise that the defendant's fingerprint was found on the murder weapon, we infer syllogistically, as a matter of *deductive* logic, that the defendant touched the murder weapon.

But this series of logical arguments is vulnerable, as are virtually all complex chains. What are the possible sources of error in the inductive inference of the premise that all fingerprints show the presence of the person to whom they belong? What possibilities of error inhere in the other premise, that this particular item of evidence is the defendant's fingerprint?

(5) *The Imperfection (Treachery?) of Language.* Sometimes language obscures the non-syllogistic form of a given inference. And more insidiously, sometimes language camouflages the lack of validity in a proposition. For example, imagine that the controlling statute, which becomes the first premise, says, "A person commits an offense by operating a motor vehicle . . . while under the influence of [an intoxicant]." A defense lawyer studies the evidence in a particular case and constructs a second premise: "My client, the defendant, wasn't really very drunk." The lawyer's conclusion: "Therefore, my client's not guilty." This reasoning likely is fallacious. Why? On the other hand, it may prove persuasive to a jury. Why?

[B] Formal Logic in Legal Reasoning: Rules, Crimes, and "IRAC"

Note on Deduction and Induction in Applying Statutes: "IRAC"

(1) *The Use of Syllogisms in Legal Reasoning: Applying a Rule or a Statute.* A great deal of reasoning about the law is syllogistic. For example, legal principles, statutes, rules, and definitions of crimes or claims, typically are used as major premises in legal reasoning. Thus, in analyzing a criminal homicide under the Model Penal Code, one might set forth (1) a first premise: "the elements of murder under MPC § 210 are present when a person 'causes the death of another human being recklessly under circumstances manifesting extreme indifference to the value of human life'" [we get this from the statute]; (2) a second premise: "This defendant killed a child by driving 100 miles per hour in a school zone and thus recklessly under circumstances manifesting extreme indifference to the value of human life" [we get this from the case evidence]; and (3) a conclusion: "The elements of murder under the MPC are present."

(2) *Fallacy in Legal Reasoning from Deduction.* This kind of logic lends itself to numerous possibilities of fallacy. For example, if the homicide described above were subject to the defense of insanity, it would not be a murder; the first premise really should be that "some" such incidents are murder. Further, the defendant can be convicted only if the second premise is true, and here, the analysis omits such requirements as proof beyond a reasonable doubt. Nevertheless, this deductive system is a basic form of legal reasoning.

(3) *The "IRAC" Method (Issue, Rule, Analysis, Conclusion): Deductive Reasoning.* Law students are taught the "IRAC" method as a means of answering law examination questions: (I), identify the "issue," (R), state the "rule," (A), "apply" the rule to the case facts, and (C), draw a "conclusion." The steps are abbreviated as I-R-A-C. This IRAC method is a deductive methodology, because the "rule" is the first premise in a syllogism, and its "application" to the case facts is the second premise, from which the conclusion follows. Deductive reasoning is important in the law, just as it is in engineering, accounting, or any other field requiring reasoning.

Admittedly, this explanation oversimplifies the art of writing the "A" law school examination. One must spot all of the right issues, and one must exhaustively state all of the correct rules. Then, one must ferret out all relevant facts and apply the rules to them. But the core of legal method is syllogistic.

(4) *This Analysis, of Course, Is Idealized.* It seems likely that judges and juries sometimes decide "holistically." That is to say, they make a judgment based on the "story" of the case as a whole. Then, the judge's opinion may be an after-the-fact justification. But even so, the deductive method described by the IRAC label is important. It aids predictions of outcomes and therefore facilitates compliance with rules. And even though not all judicial decisions are arrived at syllogistically, many surely are.

(5) *Use of Analogy in Legal Reasoning.* Legal reasoning also includes heavy use of analogy. A lawyer may reason, "'Intoxication,' for purposes of the intoxicated-driving statute, has a certain meaning; this separate statute involving an intoxication crime has a similar purpose; therefore, 'intoxication' probably has the same meaning."

(6) *Induction in Legal Reasoning.* Induction in law is used in several ways. Sometimes it is applied to the evidence: we know from experience that the guilty sometimes flee, and so evidence of flight is often admitted before juries considering criminal cases. Sometimes induction helps a judge or lawyer reading a series of cases to infer a rule that is hidden in them. "In all reported cases in this state where the defendant's car has struck another car from behind, the court has upheld a finding of negligence; therefore, perhaps the courts should recognize an inference of negligence when there is a collision from behind." Induction, like analogy, helps to create or recognize new rules of law.

[C] Additional Ways to Look at Crime Elements: Instrumentalism as Opposed to Formalism, Natural Law as Opposed to Positivism

Formalism and Instrumentalism

(1) *"Instrumentalism" or "Functionalism" Is a Basic Jurisprudential Approach, Distinguished from "Literalism" or "Formalism."* Formalism conceives of law as predefined rules to be rigorously applied in accordance with deductive logic. If the definition of a legal concept is clearly set out, the formalist would apply it exactly, undistracted by purposes or consequences. On the other hand, the instrumentalist or functionalist feels less rigorously bound by the formal elements and seeks instead to discern the purposes or values underlying a legal doctrine and to interpret it accordingly.

(2) *An Example from the Supreme Court's Separation-of-Powers Cases.* For example, in *INS v. Chadha*, 462 U.S. 919 (1983), the majority of the Supreme Court used a jurisprudence of formalism when it struck down a law allowing a single House of Congress to reverse an administrative decision. Chief Justice Burger's majority opinion held that this law was inconsistent with *literal clauses* in the Constitution that required the votes of both Houses of Congress to change a law, coupled with presentment to the President for veto. This approach of Chief Justice Burger can be characterized as *literalist* or *formalist.*

Justice White's dissent in the same case used a *functionalist* or *instrumental* approach. Justice White concluded that the *purposes* of the separation of powers were satisfied by the law in question. The law implicitly required that each of the Houses of Congress, as well as the President, concur in striking down the administrative decision, even though not through the traditional bicameral and presentment methodology. And therefore, Justice White's more *instrumental* or *functional* approach would have upheld the law.

Natural Law and Positivism

(1) *Natural Law: Discernible by Reason, Independently of Political Processes.* Natural law is a legacy of Roman law, among other sources. The concept is that people are endowed with rights and subject to duties that transcend any particular legal regime. "[A]ll men are created equal," says the Declaration of Independence, and they are "endowed by their Creator with certain inalienable rights." These words of Thomas Jefferson did not depend upon rights recognized by any sovereign. In other words, they were natural rights. Precisely which rights are "natural" always will be subject to debate, but reason will discern the basic rights — or, so goes the theory.

(2) *Positivism.* Positivism is a contrasting view, in which legal norms proceed not from nature or reason but from a command issued by a duly recognized sovereign. The statement by some people of norms that they accept through reason does not convert their claims into law; that path leads to anarchy, or so a positivist would reason. Instead, an edict by an established king, or a bill passed by Congress and signed by the President, has the better claim to obedience. It has the status of "positive law."

Notes and Questions

(1) *A Murder Statute, Considered by Formalists and Instrumentalists.* Imagine a murder statute that resembles the Model Penal Code. Murder includes "recklessly" causing the death of another person under certain circumstances. In an appeal to the state supreme court, the defendant argues that his act does not constitute murder. Can you contrast the approaches of a formalist and of an instrumentalist?

(2) *Supreme Court Justices Iredell and Chase: Their Debate About Natural Law and Positivism.* In *Calder v. Bull*, 3 U.S. 386 (1798), Justice Chase set out an expansive philosophy: "The people of the United States erected their constitutions . . . to establish justice. . . . An act of the legislature . . . contrary to the . . . social compact, cannot be considered a rightful exercise of legislative authority. . . . It is against all reason and justice for a people to entrust a legislature with such power; and therefore, it cannot be presumed that they have done it."

But Justice Iredell disagreed: "Some speculative jurists have held, that a legislative act against natural justice must, in itself, be void; but I cannot think that any court of justice would possess a power to declare it so. . . . The ideas of natural justice are regulated by no fixed standard. . . . [I]f the legislature pursue the authority delegated to them, their acts are valid[, but] if they transgressed the boundaries of that authority, their acts are invalid. . . ."

What are the difficulties of Chase's natural law position? Perhaps less obviously, what are the defects in Justice Iredell's positivist position (can one properly read a general and sparse Constitution without natural law, if its drafters believed in natural law)?

[D] Going Outside the Text: Other Interpretive Methods

Professor Bobbitt's "Six Modalities" of Interpretive Argument

(1) *Bobbitt's Description of "Six Modalities of Constitutional Argument" (Which Actually Are Applicable to Other Texts, Not Just to the Constitution).* Professor Philip Bobbitt has described six "modalities" of constitutional argument. Philip Bobbitt, *Constitutional Fate* (1982). Actually, Professor Bobbitt's methods are applicable to any interpretive question, not just to constitutional questions. They are adaptable to statutory construction, or to other kinds of legal instruments such as contracts or wills, or to any kind of text.

(2) *Definitions of the Six Modalities.* Professor Bobbitt's six modalities are:

(a) *Textual:* argument that considers the words and language of the text. For example, an interpretation of a murder statute that focuses upon its terms ("recklessly," with "extreme indifference," under the MPC) uses a *textual argument.*

(b) *Historical:* argument that relies upon the intention of the drafters, the events that produced the provision, or similar kinds of appeals to history. ("Originalism," or the reading of the Constitution according to the Founders' understandings, is identified with this modality.) For example, a claim that "recklessness" is not satisfied by mere negligence, because the legislative history shows that the legislators intended a distinction, is a *historical argument.*

(c) *Structural:* argument that infers relationships among the entities set up or recognized by the document and interprets its provisions accordingly. Thus, the Constitution assigns roles to different branches of government, to the states, to the people, etc. An interpretation of the word "recklessness" that creates a high standard for the government to prove, on the ground that the criminal law should involve heavy protections of innocent people from state oppression, might be based on a *structural argument.*

(d) *Doctrinal:* argument that refers to the tradition of received wisdom, usually to the precedential effects of decisions by courts (but not necessarily). For example, an argument that recklessness requires more than negligence, because the state supreme court said so in a particular case, is a *doctrinal argument.*

(e) *Prudential:* argument that depends upon the practical consequences of differing interpretations, or in other words, "policy" argument. An interpretation of the murder statute setting a low standard of recklessness in handling firearms, on the ground that otherwise people would become careless in using guns, relies upon a *prudential argument.*

(f) *Ethical:* argument that relies on moral or ethical grounds. This modality sometimes may seem indistinguishable from prudential argument; there is, however, a difference. Whereas prudential argument emphasizes the consequences of an interpretation in the practical sense, ethical argument emphasizes the rightness-or-wrongness of its moral content. An argument that self-defense should not be murder, on the ground that it simply is immoral to punish an individual for acting to preserve his or her own life, is an *ethical argument.*

Notes and Questions

(1) *Different Modes of Argument as Applied to the Legality of the Death Penalty.* Justice William H. Brennan took an absolutist position on the unconstitutionality of the death penalty. He argued that it is unconstitutional no matter what the circumstances, on the grounds that it constitutes "cruel and unusual punishment" under the words of the Eighth Amendment, is contrary to the principles allegedly found in past Supreme Court decisions, denies the executed individual's humanity, and violates the "right to have rights."

Consider ways in which each of the suggested modes of argument — textual, historical, structural, doctrinal, prudential, and ethical — could be used to support Justice Brennan's view, or, for that matter, the opposing view. (This question isn't about who is right or wrong, but about the categories of argumentation types.)

(2) *Using the "Six Modalities" to Argue about the Meaning of a Murder Statute.* Now, reconsider an example we have looked at earlier, involving a charge of murder under the Model Penal Code provision covering "reckless" killings, against a defendant who drove at 100 miles per hour in a school zone, causing a child's death. The defendant's murder conviction is now under consideration by the state supreme court. How could the prosecution and the defense each use arguments fitting all six of Bobbitt's modalities — textual, historical, structural, doctrinal, prudential, and ethical — to support their respective interpretations of the statute?

[E] Two Problems or Examples: Court Opinions Interpreting Elements in Criminal Statutes

A Problem Involving Elements of the Federal Mail Fraud Statute

(1) *The Federal Mail Fraud Statute.* The federal mail fraud statute is 18 U.S.C. § 1341, and it reads as follows in pertinent part:

> Whoever, having devised or intending to devise *any scheme or artifice to defraud, or for obtaining money or property by means of false or fraudulent pretenses*, representations, or promises, . . . for the purpose of executing such scheme or artifice or attempting so to do, [uses the mails or causes them to be used], shall be fined under this title or imprisoned not more than five years, or both.

The mens rea element is broadly construed, and the statute has been interpreted to cover virtually any kind of fraudulent taking of property that involves the mails. (We discuss this statute in greater detail in Chapters 7 and 13.)

(2) *The Problem: Does the Actus Reus of the Mail Fraud Statute Cover Fraud Involving "Property" That Consists of a Hoped-for Louisiana Gambling License?* Defendant Carl W. Cleveland made a false statement in an application for a Louisiana video

poker license. (He had tax and financial problems and therefore falsely listed only various other members of his family, and not himself, as potential business owners.) After being convicted of mail fraud, Cleveland now claims that however "fraudulent" his intent may have been, the mail fraud statute does not apply to his conduct. What is meant by "any scheme or artifice to defraud, *or* for obtaining . . . property?" And is the license "property"? Consider the following possible arguments: (1) only "property" is covered, but the hoped-for license is "property" within the meaning of the mail fraud statute, or (2) the statute does not require that the victim's "property" be the object of the fraud because it says "*or*" after "any . . . artifice to defraud." Or (3), is it possible that Cleveland is right and must be acquitted?

The Supreme Court's opinion is excerpted below. Consider how the Court uses the interpretive tools in this section (including several of Bobbitt's "six modalities").

Another Problem, Involving Elements of the Federal Computer Fraud and Abuse Act

(1) *The Federal Computer Fraud and Abuse Act.* 18 U.S.C. § 1030(a)(5)(A) prohibits a person from knowingly transmitting a program, information, code, or command that results in "intentionally caus[ing] *damage* . . . to a protected computer." The term "damage" is defined as "any impairment to the integrity or availability of data, a program, a system, or information, that causes loss . . . to one or more *individuals.*"

(2) *Can the Actus Reus under this Statute, Requiring Damage to an "Individual," Consist of Damage Done to a Corporation?* The first statute in U.S.C. is 1 U.S.C. § 1, which is called the "Dictionary Act," and which applies to the entire Code. The Dictionary Act says that the term "person" includes corporations "as well as individuals." The arguable implication is that an "individual," the term used in this statute, cannot refer to a corporation.

Defendant Middleton, a disgruntled former employee, accessed the computers of the corporation that had employed him. He deleted databases, changed passwords, and destroyed the entire billing system. Upon his conviction under the Federal Computer Fraud and Abuse Act, Middleton now argues that he was entitled to a judgment of acquittal because the property he intentionally damaged belonged to a corporation, not an "individual."

The Ninth Circuit's opinion is excerpted below. (In each of these two cases, the court read the statute in a non-obvious way—in one case to acquit, in the other to affirm conviction.)

Cleveland v. United States
531 U.S. 12 (2000)

JUSTICE GINSBURG delivered the opinion of the Court.

[Defendant, on behalf of his company, applied for a gambling license in Louisiana in a way that involved the mails. Because he had tax and financial problems, he falsely identified the owners as not including himself. He was convicted of crimes that included violations of the federal mail fraud statute. In the Supreme Court, he argued that the statute covered only crimes involving the taking of "property," that the license was not "property," and that he therefore should be acquitted. The government argued the license was "property," and also, that taking property was not necessary, because the mail fraud statute covered any device to defraud "or" to take property fraudulently. The Court agreed with the Defendant:]

II

In *McNally v. United States*, 483 U.S. 350 (1987), this Court held that the federal mail fraud statute is "limited in scope to the protection of property rights." *McNally* reversed the mail fraud convictions of two individuals charged with participating in "a self-dealing patronage scheme" that defrauded Kentucky citizens of "the right to have the Commonwealth's affairs conducted honestly." . . . Reviewing the history of § 1341, we concluded that "the original impetus behind the mail fraud statute was to protect the people from schemes to deprive them of their money or property." . . .

III

. . . For the reasons we now set out, we hold that . . . [a gambling] license is not "property" in the government regulator's hands. . . .

To begin with, we think it beyond genuine dispute that whatever interests Louisiana might be said to have in its video poker licenses, the State's core concern is *regulatory.* Louisiana recognizes the importance of "public confidence and trust that gaming activities . . . are conducted honestly and are free from criminal and corruptive elements." La.Rev.Stat. Ann. § 27:306(A)(1) (West Supp. 2000). . . .

Acknowledging Louisiana's regulatory interests, the Government offers two reasons why the State also has a property interest in its video poker licenses. First, the State receives a substantial sum of money in exchange for each license and continues to receive payments from the licensee as long as the license remains in effect. Second, the State has significant control over the issuance, renewal, suspension, and revocation of licenses.

Without doubt, Louisiana has a substantial economic stake in the video poker industry. . . . It is hardly evident, however, why these tolls should make video poker licenses "property" in the hands of the State. The State receives the lion's share of its expected revenue not while the licenses remain in its own hands, but only *after* they have been issued to licensees. Licenses pre-issuance do not generate an ongoing stream of revenue. . . .

Addressing this concern, the Government argues that Cleveland frustrated the State's right to control the issuance, renewal, and revocation of video poker licenses. . . . But . . . these intangible rights of allocation, exclusion, and control amount to no more and no less than Louisiana's sovereign power to regulate. . . .

The Government compares the State's interest in video poker licenses to a patent holder's interest in a patent that she has not yet licensed. Although it is true that both involve the right to exclude, we think the congruence ends there. Louisiana does not conduct gaming operations itself, it does not hold video poker licenses to reserve that prerogative, and it does not "sell" video poker licenses in the ordinary commercial sense. . . .

We reject the Government's theories of property rights not simply because they stray from traditional concepts of property. We resist the Government's reading of § 1341 as well because it invites us to approve a sweeping expansion of federal criminal jurisdiction in the absence of a clear statement by Congress. Equating issuance of licenses or permits with deprivation of property would subject to federal mail fraud prosecution a wide range of conduct traditionally regulated by state and local authorities. We note in this regard that Louisiana's video poker statute typically and unambiguously imposes criminal penalties for making false statements on license applications. As we reiterated last Term, "'unless Congress conveys its purpose clearly, it will not be deemed to have significantly changed the federal-state balance' in the prosecution of crimes." *Jones v. United States*, 529 U.S. 848 (2000). . . .

Moreover, to the extent that the word "property" is ambiguous as placed in § 1341, we have instructed that "ambiguity concerning the ambit of criminal statutes should be resolved in favor of lenity." *Rewis v. United States*, 401 U.S. 808 (1971). . . . In deciding what is "property" under § 1341, we think "it is appropriate, before we choose the harsher alternative, to require that Congress should have spoken in language that is clear and definite."

Finally, . . . the Government contends that § 1341 . . . defines two independent offenses: (1) "any scheme or artifice to defraud" and (2) "any scheme or artifice . . . for obtaining money or property by means of false or fraudulent pretenses, representations, or promises." Because a video poker license is property in the hands of the licensee, the Government says, Cleveland "obtain[ed] . . . property" and thereby committed the second offense even if the license is not property in the hands of the State.

Although we do not here question that video poker licensees may have property interests in their licenses, we nevertheless disagree with the Government's reading of § 1341. In *McNally*, we recognized that "[b]ecause the two phrases identifying the proscribed schemes appear in the disjunctive, it is arguable that they are to be construed independently." But we rejected that construction of the statute, instead concluding that the second phrase simply modifies the first by "ma[king] it unmistakable that the statute reached false promises and misrepresentations as to the future as well as other frauds involving money or property." Indeed, directly contradicting the Government's view, we said that "the mail fraud statute . . . had its origin in the desire to protect individual property rights, and any benefit which the Government derives from the statute must be limited to *the Government's interests as property holder*." . . .

IV

We conclude that § 1341 requires the object of the fraud to be "property" in the victim's hands and that a Louisiana video poker license in the State's hands is not "property" under § 1341. [Conviction reversed.] . . .

United States v. Middleton

231 F.3d 1207 (9th Cir. 2000)

GRABER, CIRCUIT JUDGE:

[The defendant intentionally damaged data in a computer owned by a corporation by which he had been employed. The federal Computer Fraud and Abuse Act criminalizes intentional damage to data owned by "individuals," and defendant was convicted under this Act. He argued that he must be acquitted because the data he damaged was owned by a corporation, not an "individual." Here, the court rejects his argument and upholds the conviction.]

"In interpreting a statute, we look first to the plain language of the statute, construing the provisions of the entire law, including its object and policy, to ascertain the intent of Congress." *United States v. Mohrbacher*, 182 F.3d 1041, 1048 (9th Cir.1999). When a statutory term is undefined, we endeavor to give that term its ordinary meaning. We are instructed to avoid, if possible, an interpretation that would produce "an absurd and unjust result which Congress could not have intended." *Clinton v. City of New York*, 524 U.S. 417 (1998).

According to Defendant, in common usage the term "individuals" excludes corporations. He notes that the "Dictionary Act," 1 U.S.C. § 1, which provides general rules of statutory construction, defines the word "person" to include "corporations, companies, associations, firms, partnerships, societies, and joint stock companies, as well as individuals." That definition, argues Defendant, implies that the word "person" includes "corporations," but that the word "individuals" does not. . . . For several reasons, we are not persuaded.

We examine first the ordinary meaning of "individuals." That word does not necessarily exclude corporations. *Webster's Third New Int'l Dictionary* 1152 (unabridged ed.1993) provides five definitions of the noun "individual," the first being "a single or particular being or *thing or group of* beings or *things.*" . . .

. . . Because "individual" as a general legal term does not exclude corporations, we next consider applicable precedent.

In *Clinton*, the Supreme Court held that Congress intended to include *corporations* within a provision of the Line Item Veto Act that authorized "any *individual* adversely affected" to challenge the Act's constitutionality. The Court examined the purpose of the provision (to allow expedited judicial review of the Line Item Veto Act) and determined that Congress could not have intended that only natural persons be able to demand expedited review. That interpretation, noted the Court, would produce an "absurd and unjust result which Congress could not have intended."

So, too, here. Defendant was convicted of violating § 1030(a)(5)(A), which criminalizes damage to "protected computers." ... It is highly unlikely, in view of Congress' purpose to stop damage to computers used in interstate and foreign commerce and communication, that Congress intended to criminalize damage to such computers only if the damage is to a natural person. Defendant's interpretation would thwart Congress' intent. . . .

On the basis of the statutory text taken in context, the Supreme Court's *Clinton* decision, and the statute's purpose and legislative history, we conclude that 18 U.S.C. § 1030(a)(5) criminalizes computer crime that damages natural persons and corporations alike. [Conviction affirmed.] . . .

Notes and Questions

(1) *Syllogisms and Analogy.* Parts of these courts' reasoning are syllogistic. For example, the Supreme Court's conclusion in Part IV of *Cleveland* is that all instances of mail fraud must involve property, but all of this defendant's conduct involved a license that was not property, and therefore the defendant is not guilty of mail fraud. Can you explain why this reasoning is syllogistic?

The Court also says, "The Government compares the State's interest in video poker licenses to a patent holder's interest in a patent that she has not yet licensed." This reasoning uses analogy. Why? The Court rejects the argument. Why?

(2) *Formalism and Instrumentalism; Natural Law and Positivism.* Both opinions set down legal rules and apply them in formalist fashion. But *Cleveland* also says that "the original impetus behind the mail fraud statute was to protect people from schemes to deprive them of their money or property." The use of this principle seems more instrumentalist or functional. Why?

Both courts look to the legislature as creator of the statutes that govern. This is the reasoning of a positivist. But *Cleveland* also relies on a principle that "ambiguity [in] criminal statutes should be resolved in favor of lenity." There is no legislation by Congress that says so. Do you think this "lenity" reasoning has its origins in natural law?

(3) *Professor Bobbitt's Six Modalities of Interpretive Argument: Textual, Historical, Structural, Doctrinal, Prudential, and Ethical.* Can you identify examples of reasoning set out in these opinions that demonstrate each of Professor Bobbitt's six modalities of interpretive argument? Consider reasoning initiated by either the courts or the parties.

Chapter 4

The Burden of Proof Beyond a Reasonable Doubt

"Better that ten guilty persons escape than that one innocent suffer."—William Blackstone, *Commentaries on the Laws of England* (1769).

"[M]ercy to the guilty is cruelty to the innocent."—Adam Smith, *The Theory of Moral Sentiments* (1759)

§ 4.01 The Constitutional Requirement of Proof Beyond a Reasonable Doubt

Notes on the Criminal Burdens of Proof

(1) *The Difficulty of Understanding How Profoundly the Burden of Proof Affects Criminal Justice.* The phrase "beyond a reasonable doubt" appears often in popular culture. But folk wisdom creates misleading stories in which good triumphs over evil without the inconvenience of providing proof that would meet the legal standard. In fiction, defendants are often presumed guilty on proof that would not suffice in court. The burden of proof is a transforming aspect of the criminal law that influences its shape, affects the definition of crimes, and sometimes leads to odd results.

(2) *Actually, There Are Several Kinds and Varieties of "Burden of Proof."* The term "burden of proof" is often used in many, sometimes confusing, ways. In general terms, there are three concepts involved. You need to understand each of them, because they apply differently to the elements of crimes and to defenses.

First, the "standard of proof" refers to the legal standard that must be satisfied to win the case. In criminal cases, this standard is "beyond a reasonable doubt" for the elements of a crime. The government must prove each element of the crime beyond a reasonable doubt. In other areas of law, other standards of proof apply, such as "preponderance of evidence" (used in civil cases) and "clear and convincing evidence" (used for some cases).

Second, the "burden of production" refers to rules that require a party to offer some evidence (often called a *prima facie* showing) on an issue in order for that issue to be part of the case.

Third, there is the "burden of persuasion." This refers to which party has the responsibility of convincing the trier of fact, such as the jury, that the applicable standard of proof is satisfied. Determining the burdens of production and persuasion is a complex issue for defenses. For crime elements, it is easy: the government has both the burden of production and the burden of persuasion, and the standard of proof is beyond a reasonable doubt.

To illustrate these concepts, consider an ordinary criminal case where D is charged with shoplifting. The state must prove each of the elements of the crime of shoplifting by the high standard of beyond a reasonable doubt. This means the state must convince the jury that each element is present to the high degree of certainty inherent in the beyond a reasonable doubt standard (*i.e.*, meet its burden of persuasion).

For defenses, on the other hand, the burdens may be different since states have much greater discretion in assigning the burdens of production and persuasion and in setting the standard of proof. In general terms, jurisdictions are free to allocate the three concepts as they see fit for defenses. Thus, they may adopt the standard of proof of beyond a reasonable doubt or preponderance of the evidence. The burden of production for defenses is usually on the defendant. The burden of persuasion may be placed on either the accused (to show the elements of a defense are present) or on the government (to show that one or more of the elements of the defense are lacking).

For example, in the shoplifting case above, assume the defendant wants to be acquitted by using the defense of insanity. If the burden of production is on the defendant, D must offer *prima facie* evidence of insanity or that defense is not part of the case. Once the burden of production is satisfied and this defense is "on the table," usually the defendant also has the burden of persuasion for defenses such as insanity, which requires convincing the jury that the elements of the insanity defense are present, perhaps by a preponderance of the evidence. Or the jurisdiction may place the burden on the prosecution to disprove insanity, beyond a reasonable doubt, when the issue is raised by the evidence.

(3) *Serious Ramifications of Requiring Proof Beyond a Reasonable Doubt.* The quotation from Blackstone that begins this chapter reflects a value choice that innocent people should not be convicted even if their acquittal imposes costs on society. Indeed, both the Blackstone quotation and the accompanying quotation from Adam Smith also highlight the dilemma that the burden of proof creates: it protects the innocent but makes it difficult to convict the guilty. Proof beyond a reasonable doubt is not cost-free. It means frequent nonprosecution of factually guilty people because the prosecutor does not believe there is ample proof to convict under this high standard. It makes the achievement of other values, such as equality, personal security, and solicitude for the more vulnerable members of society, more difficult.

[A] Proof Beyond a Reasonable Doubt as a Requirement of Due Process

In re Winship
397 U.S. 358 (1970)

JUSTICE BRENNAN delivered the opinion of the Court.

[New York allowed a finding of juvenile delinquency to be made by the preponderance of the evidence. Juvenile delinquency did not produce the same consequences as adult conviction for crime, nor was it governed by the same formal procedures. However, a finding of delinquency could be based on an act that would be a crime if committed by an adult. The juvenile in this case was a 12-year-old boy alleged to have stolen $112 from a pocketbook. He was found to be a delinquent and was given an initial term of 18 months in "training school," subject to extension. The trial judge acknowledged that the proof of the alleged larceny might not have established guilt beyond a reasonable doubt but pointed out, "Our statute says a preponderance, and a preponderance it is." Here, the Court reverses and holds that proof beyond a reasonable doubt is not merely a matter of state law but is required by the federal Constitution's Due Process Clause.]

The requirement that guilt of a criminal charge be established by proof beyond a reasonable doubt dates at least from our early years as a Nation. . . . It is a prime instrument for reducing the risk of convictions resting on factual error. The standard provides concrete substance for the presumption of innocence — that bedrock "axiomatic and elementary" principle whose "enforcement lies at the foundation of the administration of our criminal law." . . .

Moreover, use of the reasonable-doubt standard is indispensable to command the respect and confidence of the community in applications of the criminal law. It is critical that the moral force of the criminal law not be diluted by a standard of proof that leaves people in doubt whether innocent men are being condemned. . . .

Lest there remain any doubt about the constitutional stature of the reasonable doubt standard, we explicitly hold that the Due Process Clause protects the accused against conviction except upon proof beyond a reasonable doubt of every fact necessary to constitute the crime with which he is charged. . . . [The Court here holds that the "beyond a reasonable doubt" standard applies equally to juvenile proceedings involving charges of violation of a criminal law.]

Finally, we reject the Court of Appeals' suggestion that there is, in any event, only a "tenuous difference" between the reasonable-doubt and preponderance standards. . . . In this very case, the trial judge's ability to distinguish between the two standards enabled him to make a finding of guilt that he conceded he might not have made under the standard of proof beyond a reasonable doubt. . . .

JUSTICE HARLAN, concurring. . . .

First, in a judicial proceeding in which there is a dispute about the facts of some earlier event, the factfinder cannot acquire unassailably accurate knowledge of what happened. Instead, all the factfinder can acquire is a belief of what *probably* happened. . . . Although the phrases "preponderance of the evidence" and "proof beyond a reasonable doubt" are quantitatively imprecise, they do communicate to the finder of fact different notions concerning the degree of confidence he is expected to have in the correctness of his factual conclusions.

A second proposition . . . is that the trier of fact will sometimes . . . be wrong in his factual conclusions. . . . [An error] can result in . . . the conviction of an innocent man. On the other hand, an erroneous factual determination can result in . . . the acquittal of a guilty man. The standard of proof influences the relative frequency of these two types of erroneous outcomes. . . .

In a criminal case, . . . we do not view the social disutility of convicting an innocent man as equivalent to the disutility of acquitting someone who is guilty. . . . I view the requirement of proof beyond a reasonable doubt in a criminal case as bottomed on a fundamental value determination of our society that it is far worse to convict an innocent man than to let a guilty man go free. . . .

[B] Crime "Elements," "Defenses," "Affirmative Defenses," and Appeals: The Scope of the Constitutional "Beyond a Reasonable Doubt" Requirement

Notes and Questions

(1) *Winship Does Not Govern Every Issue That Might Arise in a Criminal Case.* *Winship* holds that the prosecution must prove beyond a reasonable doubt "every fact necessary to constitute the crime." But this holding depends on which facts are necessary to prove the elements of the crime. Some issues are defined as "defenses" or "affirmative defenses," with the result that the defendant—not the prosecution—may bear the burden of producing sufficient evidence to get the issue to the jury, and may even bear the burden of persuading the jury that the defense applies.

(2) *Proof of Each "Element" of the Specific Crime: Mullaney v. Wilbur,* 421 U.S. 684 (1975). Wilbur attacked and killed a man named Hebert in Hebert's hotel room. Wilbur claimed that he had attacked Hebert in a frenzy provoked by Hebert's homosexual advance. He argued that he lacked criminal intent and that "at most the homicide was manslaughter rather than murder, since it occurred in the heat of passion." The Maine trial court instructed the jury that malice aforethought was an "essential and indispensable" element of murder. Over Wilbur's objection, it also stated that if the prosecution proved the homicide was intentional and unlawful, then the jury should also find malice aforethought unless the defendant proved heat of passion by a preponderance of the evidence. Thus, malice aforethought and heat of passion, in Maine, were "two inconsistent things," but it was up to the defendant

to negate the presumption of malice by proving heat of passion. The jury convicted Wilbur of murder, and the Maine Supreme Judicial Court affirmed.

The Supreme Court, through Justice Powell, reversed. It rejected the state's argument that heat of passion "is not a 'fact necessary to constitute the crime of felonious homicide in Maine.'" The Court stressed that *Winship* does not only apply "to those facts which, if not proved, would wholly exonerate the defendant." The critical fact was that "Maine has chosen to distinguish those who kill in the heat of passion from those who kill in the absence of this factor. . . . By drawing this distinction, while refusing to require the prosecution to establish beyond a reasonable doubt the fact upon which it depends [that the killer acted with malice aforethought], Maine denigrates the interests found critical in *Winship*." Observing that "*Winship* is concerned with substance rather than with this kind of formalism," the Court held that the state was required to negate heat of passion beyond a reasonable doubt since to do so, in reality, was necessary to prove the required element of malice. *See also Sandstrom v. Montana*, 442 U.S. 510 (1979) (holding due process prohibits instructing the jury that "the law presumes that a person intends the ordinary consequences of his voluntary acts," because a jury could interpret it as a mandatory presumption that shifted the burden of proof to the defendant).

(3) *A Different Result If the "Element" Is Recharacterized as a "Defense" or an "Affirmative Defense": Patterson v. New York*, 432 U.S. 197 (1977). Patterson saw his estranged wife in a state of semi-undress with another man, whom he promptly killed by shooting him twice in the head. He was charged with second degree murder, which had two elements: "intent to cause the death of another person," and "caus[ing] the death of such person or of a third person." "Malice aforethought" was not an element of the crime, but an accused murderer could raise the "affirmative defense" that he "acted under the influence of extreme emotional disturbance for which there was a reasonable explanation or excuse." Proof of this "affirmative defense" would reduce the crime to manslaughter.

At Patterson's trial, the court instructed the jury that it must find all elements of murder (*i.e.* intentionally causing death) beyond a reasonable doubt — but that Patterson bore the burden of proving the affirmative defense of extreme emotional disturbance, which would reduce the crime to manslaughter. The jury convicted Patterson of murder. On appeal, he argued that "New York's murder statute is functionally equivalent to the one struck down in *Mullaney* and that therefore his conviction should be reversed." The New York Court of Appeals rejected this argument, holding that the New York statute "involved no shifting of the burden to the defendant to disprove any fact essential to the offense charged since the New York affirmative defense of extreme emotional disturbance bears no direct relationship to any element of murder." In Maine, passion rebutted malice; in New York, intent to kill was separate from extreme emotional disturbance, even though an intentional killing "under the influence of extreme emotional disturbance" could be reduced to manslaughter. The United States Supreme Court agreed, in an opinion by Justice White:

The crime of murder is defined by the statute . . . as causing the death of another person with intent to do so. The death, the intent to kill, and causation are the facts that the state is required to prove beyond a reasonable doubt if a person is to be convicted of murder. The statute does provide an affirmative defense . . . which, if proved by a preponderance of the evidence, would reduce the crime to manslaughter, an offence defined in a separate section of the statute. . . .

. . . Long before *Winship*, the universal rule in this country was that the prosecution must prove guilt beyond a reasonable doubt. At the same time, the long-accepted rule was that it was constitutionally permissible to provide that various affirmative defenses were to be proved by the defendant.

. . . [Unlike in *Mullaney*,] nothing was presumed or implied against Patterson; and his conviction is not invalid under any of our prior cases.

Justice Powell, joined by Justices Brennan and Marshall, dissented on the ground that the case should be governed by the principles of *Mullaney*.

(4) *Is the Restriction of Mullaney in Patterson Just a Play on Words? (Isn't Patterson, in Fact, "Functionally Similar"?)* After *Patterson*, couldn't Maine rewrite its statute to reach the same result, but constitutionally, merely by using different words? Specifically, Maine could simply provide that the intent supplies malice, that intent (and therefore malice) is unaffected by heat of passion, and that heat of passion does not disprove malice but instead is separate from the elements of murder. Justice Powell denounced this kind of "formalism" in his *Patterson* dissent. Is *Patterson* inconsistent with *Mullaney*?

Under Justice Powell's view, the statutes in the two cases are "functionally" similar. But what is wrong with focusing on the "formal" differences between the two statutes? That difference—whether they place the burden of disproving elements of the crime on the defendant—has at least symbolic importance as an expression of how each state defines the crime. Does this reasoning help support the different result in *Patterson*?

(5) *The Court Continues to Follow Patterson.* In *Martin v. Ohio*, 480 U.S. 228 (1987), the Court held that a State could classify self-defense as an affirmative defense and require a defendant to bear the burden of proving it by a preponderance of the evidence. Similarly, the Court has held that defendants may be required to prove duress and insanity. *See Dixon v. United States*, 548 U.S. 1 (2006) (duress); *Leland v. Oregon*, 343 U.S. 790 (1952) (insanity). Because of these decisions, virtually all states place on the defendant the burdens of production and persuasion to raise and establish the existence of many defenses, including insanity, duress, and, sometimes, self-defense.

Note on Elements, Defenses, and Affirmative Defenses and the Various Burdens and Standards of Proof for Each

(1) *"Elements," "Defenses," and "Affirmative Defenses."* Section 1.12 of the Model Penal Code divides substantive issues into three types: "elements," "defenses," and

"affirmative defenses." Many states use this taxonomy to differentiate among the burdens and standards of proof that must be satisfied.

(a) *"Elements"* are parts of the definition of the crime. Thus, homicide statutes typically include such elements as: a mens rea often denoted as intent or malice; causing a death; and a victim who is a deceased human being or fetus. Because they are elements, the prosecution must prove them all beyond a reasonable doubt. Failure to prove even one element may be fatal to the case and cause an acquittal.

(b) *"Defenses"* are different under the MPC and many state laws. They must be "raised" by the defendant (i.e., the defendant has the burden of production). Once the defendant satisfies the burden of production by offering minimally sufficient evidence that the defense is present in the case, the prosecution then must disprove the defense beyond a reasonable doubt. New York's Penal Code § 25.00 makes this clear:

> (1) When a "defense," other than an "affirmative defense," defined by statute is raised at trial, the people have the burden of disproving such defense beyond a reasonable doubt.

Self-defense is sometimes classified as a "defense." If there is no evidence of self-defense (only of an unjustified killing), self-defense is not a part of the case since the burden of production has not been satisfied. The jury is not told about it. But, under the New York statute and many other similar state laws, if there is evidence of self-defense that any reasonable juror could believe (*i.e.* if the burden of production is satisfied), even if the judge does not believe it, the judge must instruct the jurors on the law of self-defense and must tell them that the burden is on the prosecution to disprove self-defense beyond a reasonable doubt.

Not all states follow this "burden shifting" approach to defenses. Instead, some states assign both the burden of production and persuasion to the defendant; the state has no burden.

(c) *"Affirmative Defenses"* typically are like the emotional disturbance defense in *Patterson*, above. They depend on facts that are independent of the crime elements and do not disprove the elements. But "affirmative defenses" are different from true "defenses." The difference is that many states place the burden to prove an affirmative defense on the *defendant*. This means the defendant has the burden of persuasion on the affirmative defense. Again, New York Penal Law § 25.00 provides a clear and typical example:

> (2) When a defense declared by statute to be an "affirmative defense" is raised at trial, the defendant has the burden of establishing such defense by a preponderance of the evidence.

See also MPC § 1.12(2)(b) (referring to "any defense which the Code or another statute plainly requires the defendant to prove by a preponderance of the evidence"). Many jurisdictions, for example, treat insanity as an "affirmative" defense that the defendant must prove. *See generally Smith v. United States*, 586 U.S. 106 (2013) (withdrawal from a conspiracy is an affirmative defense because it does not negate any element of conspiracy; therefore defendant must prove the elements of the affirmative defense of withdrawal).

(2) *As a Matter of Policy, What Facts Should Be Treated as "Elements"? As "Defenses"? As "Affirmative Defenses"? Patterson* suggests that a state may be able to change an element into a defense or an affirmative defense, and *Dixon, Martin,* and *Leland* confirm that States have wide latitude in doing so. Within wide constitutional limits, the question is one of policy. Which kinds of facts ought to be up to the prosecution to both raise and prove? Which should be raised, if at all, by the defendant? And which should be not only raised, but also proved, by the defendant?

Many policy factors might enter into such a decision. For example, information exclusively known by the defendant, coupled with inherent difficulty in collecting information through others, might favor designating a particular issue as an "affirmative" defense requiring the defendant to shoulder the burdens of production and persuasion. Other factors might include dependence on facts that are extraneous to the concern of the statutory definition, or a policy to limit the impact of the defensive theory. All of these factors could support the decision of several states to put the burden of proving heat of passion on the defendant. Can you explain?

(3) *Questions: Which Factors Should Be Designated as Defenses, as a Matter of Policy?* Consider each of the following factors that might affect criminal responsibility and decide whether you think they ought to be elements, defenses, or affirmative defenses:

(a) *The mens rea for murder,* such as intent, knowledge, malice, etc.

(b) *Mistake of law* based on an official statement by a competent government officer. Some statutes provide that a citizen who relies on an official statement of law may do so without incurring criminal liability if it turns out the official statement was incorrect. (In *United States v. PICCO*, 411 U.S. 655 (1973), the Supreme Court held that due process prevents conviction of a defendant who reasonably relied on an official but erroneous interpretation of law.)

(c) *Consent or lack of consent* in a rape or sexual assault case in which force or threat used to accomplish the sexual abuse is an independent element and consent is not mentioned in the statute.

Notes on Appellate Review of Trial Factual Decisions

(1) *Standard of Review on Appeal of Factual Decisions.* If a defendant appeals the jury's guilty verdict on the ground that the evidence was insufficient to support a conviction, how should the appellate court decide that issue? There are many possibilities. At least in theory, the appellate court could defer completely to the jury's

verdict, or it could reweigh the evidence and decide on its own whether the proof at trial was sufficient under *Winship*. In *Jackson v. Virginia*, 443 U.S. 307 (1979), the Supreme Court determined that due process requires more than complete deference but less than reweighing:

> [T]he critical inquiry on review of the sufficiency of the evidence . . . must be . . . whether the record evidence could reasonably support a finding of guilt beyond a reasonable doubt. But this inquiry does not require a court to "ask itself whether it believes that the evidence at the trial established guilt beyond a reasonable doubt." Instead, the relevant question is whether, after viewing the evidence in the light most favorable to the prosecution, any rational trier of fact could have found the essential elements of the crime beyond a reasonable doubt. This familiar standard gives full play to the responsibility of the trier of fact fairly to resolve conflicts in the testimony, to weigh the evidence, and to draw reasonable inferences from basic facts to ultimate facts. Once a defendant has been found guilty of the crime charged, the factfinder's role as weigher of the evidence is preserved through a legal conclusion that, upon judicial review, all of the evidence is to be considered in the light most favorable to the prosecution.

Note that some states, as a matter of state law, allow their appellate courts to engage in a more searching review of the evidence. *Jackson* states only what the Constitution requires at a minimum; it does not forbid a state from doing more.

(2) *Jury Nullification: What if the Jury Acquits Against the Weight of the Evidence?* Can the government appeal the erroneous jury verdict? No. Because of the U.S. Constitution's Double Jeopardy Clause, a jury's verdict of acquittal is final—the prosecution cannot appeal. This rule holds even if the jury recognizes that the prosecution provided proof beyond a reasonable doubt yet still refuses to convict, a result often described as "jury nullification." Some commentators defend jury nullification, often by analogy to colonial juries that refused to convict critics of the British government and pre-Civil War juries that acquitted people who violated the Fugitive Slave Act. *See* Clay Conrad, *Jury Nullification: The Evolution of a Doctrine* (1999). Other commentators are more cautious, perhaps remembering the ways in which jury nullification has enabled racism, as when white juries acquitted people who attacked and sometimes killed civil rights workers in the 1960s. Few judges are willing to endorse jury nullification. *See, e.g., United States v. Boone*, 458 F.3d 321, 329 (3d Cir. 2006) ("a juror who refuses to deliberate or who commits jury nullification violates the sworn jury oath and prevents the jury from fulfilling its constitutional role").

Problem 4A: Defining Passion Killings as Murder-with-Sentence-Reduction ("But If You Claim It, You've Got to Prove It")

(1) *A Statute Making Heat of Passion Irrelevant to Guilt for Murder, but Defining a Sentence Reduction.* In Texas, a passion killing is murder and remains so in spite of the passion; voluntary manslaughter does not exist. Heat of passion claims

are relevant only at sentencing, where the defendant can limit the sentence to a twenty year maximum, as opposed to life. (*See* Chapter 2, on homicide.) The jury is instructed to limit the sentence to no more than twenty years if it finds the sudden passion facts by a preponderance of the evidence.

(2) *Can You Explain Why This Statute Is Probably Constitutional (and Explain the Underlying Policy)?* This provision technically is not an affirmative defense because it applies only at sentencing. Under *Patterson*, however, it appears to be constitutional. It might even be valid under *Mullaney v. Wilbur*, depending on how one reads that decision. Can you explain, and can you identify the arguments of policy that might underlie the state's decision to adopt this provision?

§ 4.02 The Meaning of "Proof Beyond a Reasonable Doubt"

Notes on Attempts to Define Reasonable Doubt

(1) *Statutes Requiring Proof Beyond a Reasonable Doubt.* Model Penal Code § 1.12(1) reflects the constitutional mandate and explicitly requires proof beyond a reasonable doubt. Virtually all states have enacted similar statutes. How is this statutory provision useful, since it does provide for anything beyond what the Constitution already requires?

(2) *Should the Trial Judge Try to Define "Reasonable Doubt," or Is It Better Not To?* The next issue is more difficult. What does "proof beyond a reasonable doubt" mean? This question creates controversy in several ways. The lawyers on each side typically use simple explanations or colorful analogies to get across their adversary views of the legal standard, and questions arise about alleged distortions. Also, judges sometimes try to define the meaning of "reasonable doubt" in their instructions to the jury. This effort, however, inevitably nudges the legal standard in one direction or the other. Thus, there are cases holding that the trial court has committed reversible error by the particular jury instruction that was used. Many courts have held, in fact, that it is preferable to give no definition at all. The rationale is that the phrase "reasonable doubt" uses common language that is easily understood, and its meaning will be developed on each side by the lawyers; a judicial definition, conversely, unavoidably will emphasize one side more than the other, with an official statement amounting to distortion.

(3) *Judicial Explanations.* Thus, courts sometimes attempt to define proof beyond a reasonable doubt in jury instructions. Consider whether the following examples are likely to help lay people understand the burden or whether they create confusion:

(a) the required proof is a demonstration to "*a reasonable and moral certainty* that the accused, and no other, committed the offense, if any."

(b) a reasonable doubt is "that doubt which would *cause a person to hesitate* in the course of his or her most important affairs."

(c) a reasonable doubt is one that is "*an abiding doubt*," one that remains and abides "even after the evidence has been thoroughly considered."

Remember, though: some courts refuse to define reasonable doubt at all. Is it better to define reasonable doubt or to let the phrase speak for itself?

(4) *The Constitution Neither Requires, nor Prohibits, the Defining of Reasonable Doubt (It's Up to the States): Victor v. Nebraska*, 511 U.S. 1 (1994). Here, the Supreme Court summarized the constitutional requirement with respect to defining reasonable doubt:

> The beyond a reasonable doubt standard is a requirement of due process, but the Constitution neither prohibits trial courts from defining reasonable doubt nor requires them to do so as a matter of course. Indeed, so long as the court instructs the jury on the necessity that the defendant's guilt be proved beyond a reasonable doubt, the Constitution does not require that any particular form of words be used in advising the jury of the government's burden of proof.

Applying that standard, the Court upheld the following charge given by a trial judge:

> Reasonable doubt is defined as follows: It is *not a mere possible doubt*; because everything relating to human affairs, and *depending on moral evidence*, is open to some possible or imaginary doubt. It is that state of the case which, after the entire comparison and consideration of all the evidence, leaves the minds of the jurors in that condition that they cannot say they feel an abiding conviction, *to a moral certainty*, of the truth of the charge.

With respect to the term "moral certainty," the Court reasoned that this instruction had sufficient additional content to guide the jury (although the Court insisted it did not "condone the phrase"). The Court also rejected an objection to contrasting "reasonable doubt" with "a mere possible doubt." According to the Court, "'reasonable doubt,' at a minimum, is one based upon 'reason.'" Why is it implicitly more acceptable to use phrases differentiating the standard from "proof beyond *all* doubt" or comparing it to doubt "based on 'reason'"?

(5) *But Some Judicial Definitions of Reasonable Doubt Have Been Held Unconstitutional: Cage v. Louisiana*, 498 U.S. 39 (1990) (per curiam). In *Cage*, the jurors were told:

> [A reasonable doubt] is one that is founded upon a real tangible substantial basis and not upon mere caprice and conjecture. *It must be such doubt as would give rise to a grave uncertainty*, raised in your mind by reason of the unsatisfactory character of the evidence or lack thereof. A reasonable doubt is not a mere possible doubt. *It is an actual substantial doubt*. It is a doubt that a reasonable [person] can seriously entertain. What is required is not an absolute or mathematical certainty, but a moral certainty.

The Court held that the highlighted portions of the instruction rendered it unconstitutional:

> It is plain to us that the words "substantial" and "grave," as they are commonly understood, suggest a higher degree of doubt than is required for acquittal under the reasonable doubt standard. . . . [A] reasonable juror could have interpreted the instruction to allow a finding of guilt based on a degree of proof below that required by the Due Process Clause.

Note that the Court has never held that language of this kind is prohibited for use by counsel, who are expected to take adversarial positions during closing argument.

Notes on Adversarial Attempts by Counsel to Define the Proof Burden

(1) *Explanations by Defense Counsel of Proof beyond a Reasonable Doubt: Often, the Defendant's Most Important Strategy Includes Emphasizing This High Standard.* Even if the court does not define reasonable doubt, defense lawyers ordinarily devote a major part of the voir dire and argument to the subject. Emphasizing the burden of proof is frequently one of the defendant's most important strategies. For example:

> *The Civil-Burden Distinction.* "Across the street, in the civil courthouse, they fight about money, and the 'greater weight' of the evidence is enough. But here, this defendant's freedom is at stake, and the burden of proof is on the state to convince you, beyond a reasonable doubt, that he is guilty."

> *The "Touchdown" Analogy.* "In other words, in a civil case, the plaintiff just has to carry the football across the 50-yard line. This is a criminal case, and so the prosecutor has to carry the ball all the way across the goal line and score a touchdown. That's what proof beyond a reasonable doubt means."

Are these useful tactics for the defense with the jury?

(2) *Explanations by the Prosecutor.* The prosecutor also has an interest in defining the burden of proof. Prosecutors often tell juries that they welcome the burden and intend to meet it. They may also tell the jurors that the burden applies only to the elements of the offense and that what is required is proof beyond a "reasonable" doubt, not beyond "all" doubt. The following is an updated excerpt from an outline originally used by state prosecutors for the voir dire in cases involving the unlawful carrying of a handgun.

III. BURDEN OF PROOF

(a) In this case, as in all criminal cases, the burden of proof is on the state to prove the guilt of the accused beyond a reasonable doubt. That does not mean beyond a shadow of a doubt or beyond [all] doubt. Beyond a reasonable doubt means beyond a doubt based on reason.

(b) Reasonable doubt applies only to the elements of the offense. Those elements are:

1. This defendant on or about the _____ day of_____, _____,

2. In this County and State,

3. [Intentionally, knowingly or recklessly],

4. [Carried on [or] about his person a [handgun]].

Those are the only things the State must prove beyond a reasonable doubt. So, explaining reasonable doubt in another manner—to find this defendant not guilty you would have to have a doubt as to one of the elements and you would have to base it on reason. In other words you might say, "I have a doubt that this offense was committed in this County, and here is my reasoning about that doubt."

(c) The State does not have to prove:

1. That the defendant was the owner of the pistol. We are concerned only with possession, not ownership. . . .

2. That the pistol would fire. If the pistol appears on its face to be in firing order, then it is presumed to be in firing order and it is up to the defendant to show otherwise.

3. That the defendant displayed the pistol to anyone.

4. That the pistol was loaded. The pistol does not have to be loaded.

5. That the defendant fired the pistol.

6. That the defendant threatened anyone with the pistol.

7. That the defendant shot or shot at anyone with the pistol.

Those circumstances, while they may aggravate the offense and may be considered for the purpose of punishment, are not elements and need not be proven beyond a reasonable doubt.

[Note: The prosecutor also would deal with the "carry permit" issue, which involves an exception to the definition of the offense. Ordinarily, the permit exception does not apply; usually, the defendant is being prosecuted precisely because he does not have one.] . . .

Are there any parts of this explanation with which you would disagree (for example, must there be "a reason" for a doubt for it to be "reasonable"?). Do you think the jury is likely to emerge with a better understanding of "reasonable doubt" if the prosecution and defense each explain the concept in adversarial ways?

Problem 4B: "Here's What 'Reasonable Doubt' Really Means. . . ."

(1) *Other Formulae for Explaining the Burden of Proof.* Consider the following formulae. Do you have any trouble identifying which ones would be used by the

defense and which by the prosecution? Which are most useful? Are any of them objectionable (and should a court sustain the objection)?

    (a) In totalitarian countries, the individual has to prove he or she is innocent. In the United States, we don't do it that way. The defendant is presumed innocent and can be found guilty only after the prosecutor proves it to you beyond a reasonable doubt.

    (b) You're reasonable people, members of the jury. If you have any doubt, it's going to be a reasonable doubt. [Note that this explanation might be objectionable. Can you see why?]

    (c) Proof beyond a reasonable doubt means proof based on common sense. You don't have to leave your common sense behind when you step into the jury box.

    (d) A tie goes to the runner in baseball. If it's close, the runner's safe. Same thing here. You're not supposed to "guess" somebody into the penitentiary.

    (e) Ladies and gentlemen of the jury, imagine that you are an aircraft mechanic, and you've just inspected a passenger airplane. You have doubts about whether it should fly. Maybe there's a part that has a chance of failing—you're not sure it'll fail, and the odds are it'll be fine—but you have doubts about that part, because it might cause a crash. If you were the mechanic and it was up to you, would you let that airplane fly? Don't you see: that's exactly your job here. The State's prosecution is like that airplane. If there's a part of it that you have a doubt about, you can't let a disaster happen. Here, the disaster isn't the plane crash; it's an innocent person going to jail. But it's the same thing.

(2) *Analyzing the Proper Response of the Law.* What is the proper way for the law to govern these issues: definition by the judge, or no definition by the judge, with the issue to be developed by counsel's explanation? How about not allowing *anyone*—judge or lawyers—to offer a definition or explanation of the meaning of beyond a reasonable doubt? Consider the next case, below.

State v. Walker

80 P.3d 1132 (Kan. 2003)

The opinion of the court was delivered by LUCKERT, J.:

Michael Walker appeals his jury trial convictions of first-degree felony murder and criminal discharge of a firearm at an occupied dwelling. For his role in the drive-by shooting death of a 16-month-old child, the trial court sentenced Walker to life imprisonment and a consecutive term of 61 months' imprisonment. . . .

[We reverse on the ground that the trial judge's] instruction defining "reasonable doubt" was improper. . . .

Walker [and his companions] had gone to 10th and Cleveland "looking for Crips." The Bloods and Crips had been involved in an earlier shootout, and Walker also believed Crips were responsible for shooting at him near Fairmount Park. Walker initially stated there were only two other people in the car, but when confronted with information that three different kinds of bullets had been recovered from the crime scene, he stated there was a fourth person in the car. [The shots that were fired at the target home killed a 16-month-old child, and hence were critical to the murder charge.]

Did the Trial Court Err in Instructing the Jury [about Reasonable Doubt]? . . .

The reasonable doubt instruction arose in response to a question by the jury. The trial court initially gave the jury an instruction regarding the burden of proof, presumption of innocence, and reasonable doubt that was consistent with PIK Crim.3d 52.02 [Kansas's Pattern Jury Instructions]. The jury sent a note requesting a clear definition of reasonable doubt. The State argued that . . . no definition of reasonable doubt should be given. The trial court informed defense counsel that it would give such an instruction if counsel so desired. Defense counsel asked to see the court's proposed definitions. After being provided two possible definitions, defense counsel stated he knew of no reason to object to either instruction and then chose one. The trial court gave the jury the following, lengthy definition of reasonable doubt:

> "You are instructed that a reasonable doubt is just what the words themselves imply—a doubt founded on reason. *It is such a doubt as a juror is able to give a reason for.*
>
> "A 'reasonable doubt' is not a mere possibility, an imaginary doubt, a doubt arising from a whim, mere fancy or a sudden change of mind without any apparent or adequate reason therefore. It cannot be based on groundless conjecture.
>
> "Reasonable doubt is that state of the case which, after a comparison and consideration of all the evidence presented to you, leaves your mind in that condition that you cannot say you have an abiding conviction to a *moral certainty* of the guilt of Mr. Walker. A juror has a reasonable doubt when he does not have an abiding conviction of mind, founded on the evidence or want of evidence, to a *moral certainty* that convinces and directs his understanding and satisfies his reason and judgment that Mr. Walker is guilty as charged.
>
> "Stated another way, if you have a reasonable doubt as to the existence of any of the claims in instruction no. 10 or no. 11, you must find Mr. Walker not guilty. If you have no reasonable doubt as to the existence of any of the claims in instruction no. 10 or no. 11, you must find Mr. Walker guilty." (Emphasis added.)

Walker takes issue with several components of the instruction, including the phrase: "It is such a doubt as a juror is able to give a reason for." A similar phrase was considered by this court in *State v. Banks*, 260 Kan. 918, 927 P.2d 456 (1996), when deciding whether a mistrial should have been granted after the prosecutor made the following statement during closing argument: "Reasonable doubt means if you are going to say these men are not guilty of something, you have to give a reason for it." In finding the statement "improper" we specifically disapproved contrary language in two other cases where the court had previously approved a definition of reasonable doubt as "such a doubt as a juror is able to give a reason for."

The remaining several paragraphs of the instruction are well described by the words of our Court of Appeals in *State v. Acree*, 22 Kan.App.2d 350, 916 P.2d 61 (1996): "Efforts to define reasonable doubt, other than as provided in PIK Crim.3d 52.02, usually lead to a hopeless thicket of redundant phrases and legalese, which tends to obfuscate rather than assist the jury in the discharge of its duty." . . .

This advice applies even where the request for a more expansive definition comes from the jury. . . . It would not have been an abuse of discretion . . . to have replied to the jury using the advice of this court as long ago as 1882: "'[N]o definition or explanation can make any clearer what is meant by the phrase "reasonable doubt" than that which is imparted by the words themselves.'" *State v. Bridges*, 29 Kan. 138, 141 (1882). Reversed and remanded.

Notes and Questions

(1) *The Case Against Defining Reasonable Doubt: Paulson v. State*, 28 S.W.3d 570 (Tex. Crim. App. 2000). Some state supreme courts require their trial judges to define reasonable doubt. But in sharp contrast, other courts prefer that trial judges give no definition at all. In *Paulson*, the trial judge omitted to give a definition, although the then-controlling decisional law required a specific definition. *See Geesa v State*, 820 S.W.2d 154 (Tex. Crim. App. 1991). The *Paulson* court, however, overruled *Geesa* and held that "better practice" was to give no definition at all, and to affirm Paulson's conviction. "It is ill-advised for us to require trial courts to provide the jury with a redundant, confusing, and logically flawed definition when the Constitution does not require it, no [state] statute mandates it, and over a hundred years of . . . precedent discourages it."

A dissenting judge agreed that the *Geesa* instruction might be flawed, but he argued that "it should be rewritten." He added, "Just because the Supreme Court [does not require a definition] is no reason that we should abdicate our responsibility." Does the jury need a definition to better understand "reasonable doubt," or will any definition result in confusion, distortion, or "nudging" in one direction or the other? *See also Blaine v. United States*, 18 A.3d 766 (Wash. 2011) (finding a violation of due process and reversing conviction when trial court gave jury a "standard" instruction on reasonable doubt and then provided a different reasonable doubt instruction that was "[less] heavily weighted to the defense" after four days of deliberation).

(2) *Is It Logical for State Supreme Courts to Require a Definition Explaining Reasonable Doubt as "That Doubt That Would Make a Reasonable Person Hesitate to Act"?* Several courts have required or approved definitions of reasonable doubt as "doubt that would cause a reasonable person to hesitate" or have used words to

similar effect. *E.g., State v. Kuhn,* 85 P.3d 1109 (Idaho Ct. App. 2004); *State v. Webster,* 637 N.W.2d 392 (S.D. 2001). But is this instruction illogical? Most people would "hesitate" before making a criminal finding of guilt, especially in a case likely to result in a very lengthy prison sentence, and therefore the instruction is inconsistent with such a finding no matter how powerful the evidence happens to be. In *Paulson,* above, the court disapproved the following "hesitate" instruction:

> [Reasonable doubt] is the kind of doubt that would make a reasonable person hesitate to act in the most important of his own affairs.

> Proof beyond a reasonable doubt therefore must be proof of such a convincing character that you would be willing to rely and act upon it without hesitation in the most important of your own affairs.

According to the *Paulson* court,

> [The latter] "definition" is not really a definition at all. . . . The [instruction] says that reasonable doubt makes you hesitate to act; therefore, if you hesitate to act, you have a reasonable doubt. . . . That is like saying, "Pneumonia makes you cough; therefore, if you cough, you have pneumonia." This is [a] logical fallacy . . . .

> If a conscientious juror reads [this required] charge and follows it literally, he or she will never convict anyone. . . . The gravity of the decision and the severity of its consequences should make one pause and hesitate before doing even what is clearly and undoubtedly the right thing to do. Judgments that brand men and women as criminals, and take their money, their liberty, or their lives are deadly serious. They are decisions that make us hesitate if we have any human feelings or sensitivity at all. So to convict, a juror must either ignore the definition, refuse to follow it, or stretch it to say something it does not say.

Is this criticism persuasive? If so, why do you think some states have approved the "hesitate" definition (does it work well rhetorically with a jury, even if it does not "work logically")?

(3) *Arguments by Lawyers That Incorporate Similar Definitions Are Given Wider Latitude.* The defense lawyer almost always will emphasize reasonable doubt—and explain it in ways that make the jury more likely to find it. It seems unlikely that this strategy could be restricted very much without detracting from the defendant's right to be heard. Is it therefore unfair to disallow the prosecutor from making counter-arguments? If both counsel are at least minimally competent, the jury probably obtains a better understanding. But there are limits, and some cases disapprove messages from either side that distort excessively.

(4) *The Difference between a "Reasonable Doubt" and an "Actual Innocence" Finding.* By now, it should be obvious that an acquittal based on the government's failure to satisfy the reasonable doubt standard is not the same as a finding that the defendant is factually innocent. The ancient Scottish verdict, in fact, was "not proven,"

rather than "not guilty," which conveys the point: acquittal can be based on a finding that the evidence is ambiguous, proving neither guilt nor innocence. Or, the verdict may be the product of a careful jury that believes the defendant is actually guilty, but the belief is not strong enough to satisfy the high degree of certainty needed for proof beyond a reasonable doubt.

§ 4.03 The Policy Debate on Reasonable Doubt

By requiring the government to prove each element of a crime by the high standard of beyond a reasonable doubt, the criminal justice system has created a structure that makes it difficult—and sometimes impossible—to prove guilt. This means that jurors may acquit some guilty people because of doubts about the strength of the proof. Conversely, in theory at least, it should also mean that truly innocent people are not convicted since proof of their guilt should not meet this high standard. In other words, the standard of proof beyond a reasonable doubt should result in acquittal of the innocent. But at what cost?

[A] The "*n* Guilty People" Approach: To Save One Innocent, How Many Guilty People Should Be Freed?

Alexander Volokh, *n* Guilty Men
146 Univ. of Pennsylvania L. Rev. 173 (1997)

I. The *n* Controversy

"[B]etter that ten guilty persons escape, than that one innocent suffer," said English jurist William Blackstone. The ratio 10:1 has become known as the "Blackstone ratio.". . . .

But why ten? . . .

[Volokh catalogues the "*n* problem" (how many guilty people, *n*, should be released to save one innocent?) in various contexts: by divine revelation (*e.g.*, references in the Bible), in ancient history, in English legal history, and in American Law. For example: "A British editorial recently surmised that the 'bias against punishment' has its roots in 'the most famous of all miscarriages of justice: Christ's crucifixion.' In fact, however, people have been mulling over the innocent-guilty tradeoff at least since the ancient Greeks. Aristotle allegedly wrote that it is a 'serious matter to decide [that a slave] is free; but it is much more serious to condemn a free man as a slave,' and gave the same judgment, also with *n* = 1, about convicting innocents of murder." "In the seventeenth century, Matthew Hale used *n* = 5 for execution, 'for it is better five guilty persons should escape unpunished, than one innocent person should die.' . . . [Volokh analyzes whether the *n* principle is a "maxim" or "folklore." He builds a chart of references to common numbers such as 1, 5, 12, 20, "hundreds," 1,000, and 5,000, which courts or commentators have plugged in as values for *n*. Then, he turns to the opposing view.]

VIII. *n* Skeptics

Jeremy Bentham, founder of utilitarianism, warned against the warm fuzzy feeling that comes from large values of *n*:

> "[W]e must be on our guard against those sentimental exaggerations which tend to give crime impunity. . . . Public applause has been, so to speak, set up to auction. At first it was said to be better to save several guilty men, than to condemn a single innocent man; others . . . fix the number ten; a third made this ten a hundred, and a fourth made it a thousand. All these candidates. . . . have been outstripped by . . . writers who hold that in no case ought an accused person to be condemned, unless evidence amount to mathematical or absolute certainty. According to this maxim, nobody ought to be punished, lest an innocent man be punished." . . .

The British Isles appear to be entering a golden age of *n*-skepticism, thanks, perhaps, to the efforts of the Irish Republican Army. One British writer asks what use *n* = 10 is "if those [ten] guilty men use their freedom to plant a bomb that kills [a hundred] schoolchildren." Another observer blends judicial theory, gastronomy, and *n* = 1000: "[T]hat, no doubt, is an admirable precept; but it does not tell us who precisely benefits from the liberty of the lucky thousand, with their Semtex and their icing sugar-ammonium nitrate confectionery of murder." . . .

[Volokh also tackles one of the central questions—how is *n* related to crime levels?—as follows:]

. . . Whether there really is a relationship between high values of *n* and high crime rates is controversial. "Tough-on-crime" types believe that there is a positive relationship between *n* and c [the crime rate], or that high values of *n*—a high presumption of innocence—lead to high values of c—an increased incidence of crime. Others believe, however, that *n* and c are negatively related—that punishment may be counterproductive, and that low values of *n* can lead to high values of c. We would like to find a mathematical function that relates *n* and c. . . . Unfortunately, we do not know at the outset what form this function will take. . . .

Others take a still different tack. Just convict all the guilty and acquit all the innocent, say letter writers, state supreme courts, Ulysses S. Grant, and the Chinese [Volokh cites sources]. Blackstone's maxim "supposes a dilemma which does not exist[: t]he security of the innocent may be complete, without favouring the impunity of crime," said Jeremy Bentham. To those who accept the fundamental logic of the proposition, however, *n* = 10 still seems to be the most popular choice, even though, as Susan Estrich reminds us, these ten guilty men may not be acquitted because they are "right or macho or manly." . . .

The story is told of a Chinese law professor, who listened as a British lawyer explained that Britons were so enlightened that they believed it was better that ninety-nine guilty men go free than that one innocent man be executed. The Chinese professor thought for a second and asked, "Better for whom?"

Notes and Questions

(1) *Is There a "Correct" or "Acceptable" Value for n, to Be Adopted by Lawmakers Allocating Risk in a Real-World Criminal Justice System?* Could one argue that the *n* problem is a non-problem, at least in some contexts? For example, it may be true that jury instructions should not tell jurors about an "acceptable" value for the number of guilty people who should be acquitted to prevent conviction of one innocent one. But consider the task faced by lawmakers. They can adopt procedures that will make conviction relatively sure (with *n* being small), or nearly impossible (with *n* being very large), or somewhere in between. To design a criminal justice system, don't they necessarily have to put a value on *n*, either expressly or by implication?

(2) *The Probability That Setting n at Ten Will Mean Acquittal of Ten Guilty Members of a Favored Group, Merely Because of People's Prejudices.* Volokh quotes Susan Estrich, who points out that acquittal of guilty rapists should not be explained on the false basis that they are "right or macho or manly," but because our system acquits the guilty disproportionately. But given that we are talking about erroneous acquittal, or in other words about mistakes in recognizing guilty people, isn't it inevitable that acquittals based on the wrong reasons, *i.e.* on prejudices, will materialize? Consider whether the jury trial process will acquit attractive people more readily than unattractive ones, articulate ones more easily than inarticulate ones, *etc.* Also, analyze whether we should expect defense attorneys to emphasize these characteristics ("this is a decent, hardworking man, a husband and father") in a deliberate effort to take advantage of prejudices.

(3) *"Only Better Is Better."* An old saying holds that "Bigger isn't better; faster isn't better; only better is better." In the context of the *n* debate, one might argue, "Raising *n* isn't better; lowering *n* isn't better; only better is better." Thus, Volokh quotes Bentham to the effect that the *n* debate is a false one, because we can have better criminal justice by reliably convicting the guilty and reliably acquitting the innocent. This approach would make it difficult for anyone to adopt a pervasive or instinctive mind-set as either a law-and-order purist or a dogmatic civil libertarian, and it would make everyone think harder about the advantages or disadvantages of any particular criminal justice process. (This is precisely the kind of thinking that is an objective in a Criminal Law course.)

For example, imagine that a legislator must decide to vote for or against a particular law involving joinder of multiple offenses, evidence admissibility, or jury instructions. If "only better is better," the legislator cannot vote either way because of the likelihood that the new law will increase acquittals and help defense lawyers, or that it may increase convictions and help prosecutors. Instead, the legislator must ask: "Will this law increase conviction of the guilty, and will it minimize the risk of convicting innocents?" Consider whether this view has merit.

[B] The Risks and Consequences of Error (in Defining or Applying the Burden)

[1] The Costs of Erroneous Acquittal

Problem 4C: The Nightmarish Case of Zachary Thomas Langley

[adapted from news reports]

(1) *The First Prosecution of Zachary Thomas Langley, for Murder.* Zachary Thomas Langley was arrested for murder. In the county jail, away from drugs, he apparently became remorseful. The evidence showed that he confessed to the murder to an assistant district attorney, although he did not do so on video or audiotape. He also confessed to his heroin supplier.

The murder itself was brutal and cruel. The body of the victim, a young woman who lived in an apartment near Langley, was discovered nude in a pool of blood. The murder occurred during a break-in, apparently at random. The crime scene photographs showed her to have been savagely beaten. Perhaps the most disturbing detail was a broom handle with a wire in its tip that had the victim's blood and flesh on it. The autopsy showed that the broom handle, with the wire, had been inserted into the victim's vagina.

(2) *Langley's Acquittal.* At trial, the principal evidence identifying Langley as the killer consisted of the testimony of the assistant district attorney and Langley's heroin supplier, both of whom recounted that Langley had confessed to them. The court ruled that the testimony about Langley's confessions was admissible. The alleged confessions, according to the witnesses, contained various details, some of which were not general public knowledge at the time. No fingerprints or other evidence were found, however, to link Langley to the crime scene, and he did not testify.

The jury acquitted. After trial, the jurors explained that they doubted the testimony of the assistant district attorney because of his position. They doubted the testimony of Langley's drug supplier because he was a drug dealer and because he had been released from jail shortly after reporting that Langley had confessed (the release may have been motivated by normal bail or evidentiary considerations, but the jury may have suspected otherwise).

(3) *Langley's Next Crime, Made Possible by His Acquittal.* A short time after his release, Langley broke into the residence of another young woman and assaulted her. He broke her jaw and injured her in other ways. This crime, too, was brutal. Langley bound the victim to her bed and set the mattress on fire. The crime scene photographs included close-ups of the blackened, charred hands of the victim and other parts of her body. But this victim survived. Evidence in addition to her eyewitness identification also linked Langley to the crime. Langley pled guilty in exchange for a sentence of 35 years.

Notes and Questions

(1) *The Jury's Acquittal.* Critique the decision of the jury to acquit Langley of murder. Consider how the standard of proof beyond a reasonable doubt should apply. Although it may be difficult to do so from this summary, construct the argument that proof beyond a reasonable doubt may have been present, and that the jurors' decision was erroneous. Then construct the argument to the contrary: that the system worked properly, and that the jury's decision was correct or at least understandable.

(2) *The Costs of Erroneous Acquittal.* It is likely—perhaps even beyond a reasonable doubt—that Langley was guilty of the murder, given his two independent and mutually reinforcing confessions, together with their nonpublic content. Assuming he was, is the acquittal properly labeled an "error" in the system? Assume for a moment that the evidence, as presented, was overwhelming, so that the acquittal could sensibly be called unreasonable or erroneous, and that the jurors who served may have imposed an unusually high threshold of required proof. Consider the total societal cost of erroneous acquittal, if there is such a thing, in the case of a crime such as Langley's, including any interests of the first victim, the second, the survivors of both, nearby residents, citizens generally, and the body politic.

(3) *Should the Harmfulness of the Alleged Conduct Impact the Reasonable Doubt Standard?* The proof standard contains the word "reasonable." In some contexts, "reasonable" refers to a contextual, balancing decision, in which all the facts, risks, and potential costs are to be considered. Should a jury, then, consider how bad the defendant's alleged misconduct is, or how dangerous a defendant might be, in deciding whether there is proof of guilt beyond a "reasonable" doubt? (In other words, is it less "reasonable" to insist on absolute proof when the defendant's alleged act is heinous and there is danger of its repetition?) Or does the burden of proof follow the same standard, irrespective of the gravity of the offense, from misdemeanors to brutal murders?

The harm factor probably does influence the jury's assessment of the burden of proof. Rightly or wrongly, real-world jurors seem to demand more convincing evidence to convict for a highly technical, minor misdemeanor, with no clear harm to identifiable victims, than for a heinous crime such as that charged against Langley. Is this an appropriate reaction?

[2] The Costs of Erroneous Conviction

Preliminary Note on Eyewitness Testimony

In a later section, we will discuss the problem of eyewitness testimony. For now, you should realize that eyewitness testimony is both necessary and risky. It is necessary because prosecution of many if not most crimes of assault, robbery, murder and rape depend upon it. It is risky because it is vulnerable to error in ways that the criminal justice system cannot effectively minimize.

Problem 4D: We're Sorry. . . . A Case of Mistaken Identity

Time Magazine, Oct. 4, 1982, at 45

(1) *The Misidentification of William Jackson—and Its Ultimate Discovery.* It started out like a routine call. Police in Columbus received a tip that a man was loitering outside a north-side town house. When the officers arrived, the intruder was inside with a ski mask and an array of burglary tools. Arrested was an improbable suspect: Dr. Edward Jackson, 38, a prominent local internist. The case became even more improbable after the police searched Jackson's car. There they found a long list of rape victims, leading them to believe that Jackson was the "Granville rapist," suspected of nearly 100 assaults in that affluent neighborhood. Last week, a Franklin County grand jury indicted Jackson on 94 counts, including 36 rapes and 46 burglaries.

But the improbabilities did not end there. It turned out that another man, William Jackson, 31, had been serving a sentence of 14 to 50 years for two of the rapes now attributed to Dr. Jackson. In an apparent case of mistaken identity, two rape victims had picked William Jackson out of a police lineup in 1977. The resemblance between the two men, who are not related, is indeed striking: both are tall, slender blacks with short Afros, sparse beards, mustaches and similar facial features.

William Jackson was released from prison 7 hours after Edward Jackson was indicted. He holds no grudge against the mistaken witnesses—"It ain't their fault"—but he is bitter at the system of justice that put him behind bars. Ohio law provides no compensation for persons falsely convicted unless it can be show that due process was not observed. Says William Jackson, who was stabbed and repeatedly assaulted during his imprisonment: "They took away part of my life, part of my youth. I spent five years down there, and all they said was 'We're sorry.'"

(2) *Protections Against Erroneous Conviction.* In addition to the presumption of innocence and the burden of proof beyond a reasonable doubt, there are other processes that protect against erroneous conviction. At the risk of omitting several, here is a partial list: the prosecutor has a duty, imposed by Supreme Court cases, to furnish evidence to the defense that is inconsistent with guilt; the defense has the right to cross-examine witnesses; the conduct of a lineup or photograph spread presented to witnesses should not be "impermissibly suggestive"; during a post-indictment lineup, the accused has a right to counsel; the jury observes witnesses' testimony and demeanor; witnesses must testify live except in extraordinary circumstances; the judge has power to grant a judgment of acquittal if the evidence is insufficient; and appellate and habeas corpus processes provide additional opportunities for legal arguments against conviction.

(3) *Why Does Erroneous Conviction Occur?* Presumably these processes (and others) were in place during William Jackson's prosecution. Why were these processes inadequate to prevent William Jackson's two erroneous convictions? A recent study of 460 erroneous convictions and "near miss" cases identified the following factors contributing to the inaccurate verdicts: the age and criminal history of the

defendant, punitiveness of the state, discovery violations by the state, forensic error, weak defense and prosecution case, family defense witness, inadvertent misidentification, false confessions, criminal justice official error, and race effects. Gould *et al.,* *Predicting Erroneous Convictions: A Social Science Approach to Miscarriages of Justice* (Dec. 2012). The Innocence Project has found that of 301 wrongful convictions overturned in the United States on the basis of DNA evidence, 75% had mistaken eyewitness identifications. *See* http://www.innocenceproject.org/fix/Eyewitness -Identification.php (April 1, 2013).

(4) *The Frequency of Erroneous Convictions.* A recent study identified 873 people exonerated in the United States from January 1989 through February 2012. "Almost all had been in prison for years; half for at least 10 years; more than 75% for at least five years." More than 44% (203) of the non-homicide exonerations were for rape, even though the authors believe that the number of people wrongfully convicted of robbery exceeds the number wrongfully convicted of rape. Why? DNA evidence "contributed to 84%" of the rape exonerations, "but DNA is hardly ever useful in proving the innocence of robbery defendants." As a result, although the authors admit that "[i]nevitably, a few exonerated defendants are guilty of the crimes for which they were convicted, in whole or in part," their research also convinced them that they have missed "many exonerations" and "most of the underlying false convictions." Samuel Gross & Michael Shaffer, *Exonerations in the United States: 1989–2012: Report by the National Registry of Exonerations* http://www.law.umich .edu/special/exoneration/Documents/exonerations_us_1989_2012_full_report .pdf (June 22, 2012).

Notes and Questions

(1) *The Costs of Wrongful Conviction.* Consider, enumerate, and evaluate the costs of a wrongful conviction for a serious crime—that is, in a case in which the commission of a crime is clear but a factually innocent person, like William Jackson, is arrested, confined, and perhaps convicted. Consider the interests of the convicted or arrested person, the victim, the factually guilty person, possible future victims of similar offenses, survivors or families of each of these persons, citizens in the community, and the body politic. Compare these costs to the costs of erroneous acquittal, which you considered in the previous section.

(2) *Setting the Balance.* Any criminal justice system will have false positives, cases in which innocent people are convicted, as well as false negatives, in which guilty people are set free. What error rate is acceptable on the guilt side? On the innocence side? How many resources should society expend to reduce these error rates?

(3) *The Death Penalty.* One of the arguments against capital punishment is the claim that the chance of executing an innocent person is unacceptably high. In 1999, Anthony Porter was released after a journalism professor and his students demonstrated that he may well have been innocent, yet he had come within two days of execution. More than ten men were released from Illinois's death row after 1987 because of doubts about their guilt. In 2003, Illinois Governor George Ryan

commuted the sentences of every person on Illinois' death row to life in prison. Supporters of capital punishment point to the extensive legal process required before conviction or sentence, as well as extensive appeals and habeas corpus proceedings, and the sheer amount of time—usually many years—between conviction and execution. Furthermore, they argue that a de facto higher burden of proof of guilt arises with most jurors, even those who are "death qualified" to sit in capital cases. Yet these processes were in place in Illinois. Is Illinois unique, or is it likely that other states have had or continue to have comparable problems?

[C] Erroneous Acquittal or Erroneous Conviction?: Ethical Decisions with Real-World Risks

Notes and Questions

(1) *The Ethical Issue: Is Erroneous Conviction Worse than Erroneous Acquittal?* One often hears the argument that erroneous conviction is qualitatively different from erroneous acquittal because it wrongfully imposes the coercive power of the state on an innocent individual, whereas erroneous acquittal permits only the effects of private violence. Supporters of this view regard the force of the body politic as an ethical ingredient that changes the calculus and makes wrongful conviction morally unacceptable, even at the cost of more wrongful acquittals. One common illustration is that of the state run amok: for example, the perversions of criminal justice, not to mention summary detention and execution, that occurred in Nazi Germany when the power of the state was used to murder millions of people who had committed no crime. Yet one can easily object that such an outrageous and inhumane example says little about the day-to-day application of criminal justice. How persuasive is the ethical argument that erroneous conviction is morally unacceptable in a qualitatively different way from erroneous acquittals?

(2) *Standing the Ethical Question on Its Head: Could Erroneous Acquittals Be Equally Unacceptable?* Is the ethical question really so clear? The state largely claims and enforces a monopoly on the use of force to prevent or redress crimes. Citizens are not allowed proactively to protect themselves by force against persons in their midst whom they believe, even reasonably, to be guilty of crimes that they are likely to repeat. Nor may they use force as a deterrent (*i.e.*, to "teach a lesson" to guilty persons and others who might be tempted to commit crimes). Having arrogated this power to itself and deprived individuals of it, does the state have a powerful ethical duty to prevent the murders, rapes, and robberies of innocent people? Given the fact that many criminals commit multiple crimes over time, erroneous acquittals increase the pool of people willing to engage in crime. Perhaps, then, the state's duty to protect us includes a duty to avoid erroneous acquittals, and that duty may come close to the duty to avoid wrongful convictions.

Put differently, erroneous conviction oppresses innocent individuals by *affirmative conduct* on the part of the state. Erroneous acquittal oppresses other innocent individuals by *inaction* on the part of the state. Ethicists who see a parallel might ask whether (1) *nonaction* by a citizenry that imposes harm on innocent people really is morally different from (2) *action* by a citizenry that imposes harm on innocent people, particularly when the citizenry prevents innocent people from protecting themselves.

(3) *A Critical View of State Inaction: Labor Disputes and the Ku Klux Klan.* The ethical problem goes even deeper. Inevitably, a state policy favoring erroneous acquittal results in uneven protection of different classes of people. Favored groups will be disproportionately free of the risks of either erroneous acquittal of people who have wronged them or erroneous conviction when charged with crimes they did not commit, and the costs of unredressed crime will fall upon disfavored classes of people. At times, this tilt has earned history's condemnation, just as preferences for erroneous conviction have. For example, over many decades (and within the memories of your casebook authors), governments of former slave states carried out a policy of inaction toward the Ku Klux Klan and other groups of white citizens who violently oppressed African-Americans. Prosecution decisions, processes, and jury attitudes made erroneous acquittals commonplace in such cases. And this problem has not been confined to the Ku Klux Klan or to Reconstruction States. In other areas of the country, including the north, strikers in the late nineteenth and early twentieth centuries were subjected to private violence by their employers or their agents, sometimes with law enforcement either too overwhelmed or too indifferent to take action. More recently, the same thing has happened to "replacement workers" at the hands of strikers. In those circumstances, is it correct to maintain that erroneous acquittal is really qualitatively different from erroneous conviction — or, indeed, that either is the only critical problem?

[D] Can We Define Crimes to Make Proof of the Guilt-Innocence Distinction Clearer?

Notes on Proof Requirements and Crime Definition

(1) *A Crime May Be Defined So as to Make Proof of Guilt Beyond a Reasonable Doubt Very Difficult.* As Chapter 3 discusses, it is possible to define a crime so that guilt is extremely difficult for the government to prove beyond a reasonable doubt. For example, imagine a crime that punished someone who "while intoxicated operated a vehicle so as to intentionally kill a person." The fact that the accused was drunk may be used by the defense as proof that he or she did not have the intent to kill ("I was too drunk to intend anything").

(2) *Defining Crime with the Burden of Proof in Mind.* This discussion suggests that the drafters of a criminal statute should carefully consider the burden of proof in defining crime elements.

(3) *An Example: Pennsylvania Defines the Crime of Drunk Driving in Terms of Blood Alcohol Content Two Hours After Arrest.* One issue that sometimes arises in drunk driving cases is that blood alcohol changes over time in the human body. It

is possible, for example, for an arrestee to display a forbidden blood alcohol level an hour or more after the event, but not to have been intoxicated at the time he or she was driving. (This occurs if the arrestee drank a large amount in a short time and then drove before the alcohol fully entered the bloodstream.) It is usually difficult—perhaps even impossible—for the prosecution to prove exactly when the defendant drank what quantity. The resulting uncertainty can create reasonable doubt in many drunk driving cases. In response to this possibility, several states have amended their driving under the influence statutes to include a new crime: driving when the driver has a blood alcohol level of 0.08% within two hours after the event of driving. *See, e.g.,* 75 Pa. Consol. Stat. § 3802(a)(2) (2006).

The Pennsylvania Supreme Court upheld this statute against vagueness and overbreadth challenges. The court stressed what we noted above—that § 3802(a)(2) does not simply amend the already-existing drunk driving statutes; it creates a new crime:

> it is now unlawful, not only to drive while under the influence, but also to ingest a substantial amount of alcohol and then operate a motor vehicle before the alcohol is dissipated to below a defined threshold (here, 0.08 percent), regardless of the level of absorption into the bloodstream at the actual moment of driving.

Commonwealth v. Duda, 923 A.2d 1138 (Pa. 2007); *Compare State v. Baker,* 720 A.2d 1139 (Del. 1998) (invalidating a 4-hour law). Does the Pennsylvania statute make it easier for the state to prove guilt beyond a reasonable doubt in proper cases, or does it go too far?

§ 4.04 Particular Kinds of Evidence

Evidence presented at trial is traditionally characterized as either "direct evidence" or "circumstantial evidence." Lawyers often present both types of evidence in a criminal case.

Direct Evidence requires no inferences to be probative. For example, the bank teller who was robbed would present direct evidence at trial of what happened to him. Perhaps he points to the accused and testifies, "The man at the table with the red tie is the man who robbed me." His description of what he experienced at the bank requires no inferences to prove the events he witnessed. He has provided direct evidence of who robbed him and what occurred at the heist.

Circumstantial evidence requires inferences to make it helpful in the case. In the bank robbery example above, a great amount of circumstantial evidence may be presented. For example, a witness could testify to seeing the defendant walk into the bank with a shotgun and could identify the defendant as that person. This is direct evidence that the defendant walked into the bank carrying a shotgun, but it is circumstantial evidence of the more basic question of who robbed the bank. As circumstantial evidence of the identity of the robber, we must make inferences to draw this conclusion. In a criminal case, most—and sometimes all—the evidence is circumstantial.

A common misunderstanding is that a conviction based "only on circumstantial evidence" is somehow unreliable. While this may be true in some situations, in most cases the circumstantial evidence is quite reliable and can provide extremely strong proof of guilt, satisfying the high standard of proof beyond a reasonable doubt. Fingerprints and DNA are circumstantial evidence. On the other hand, as the next case illustrates, sometimes large amounts of circumstantial evidence may be insufficient to convict.

The value of circumstantial evidence is especially high in a legal system, such as ours, that recognizes that the criminal accused is protected by the Fifth Amendment and ordinarily need not testify. In general terms, this important constitutional guarantee means that a criminal accused does not have to answer police questions or testify at trial. In the most general terms, unless the defendant makes voluntary statements, the prosecution must provide proof beyond a reasonable doubt without using statements made by the defendant. Usually this means that proof beyond a reasonable doubt must be supplied solely by circumstantial evidence for key elements of the crime, such as *mens rea* (intent, knowledge, *etc.*). Other key elements such as *actus reus* also must often be proved circumstantially (*e.g.*, identity in a no-eyewitness murder case) since there is no direct evidence, as the next case suggests.

[A] Circumstantial and Scientific Evidence

Stogsdill v. State

552 S.W.2d 481 (Tex. Crim. App. 1977)

Appeal is taken from a conviction for capital murder. Punishment was assessed at death. Appellant contends that the court erred "in holding evidence to be sufficient to sustain conviction, when circumstances amounted [only] to 'strong suspicion' and 'mere probability' of Appellant's participation in the offense charged."

The indictment upon which the prosecution was based charged in pertinent part that appellant "on or about the 14th day of April A.D. 1975" did then and there

> intentionally cause the death of Billy Ed Price by beating him and stabbing him with a lug wrench, and that the said Kenneth Dee Stogsdill was then and there in the course of committing and attempting to commit robbery of the said Billy Ed Price. . . .

The challenge to the sufficiency of the evidence necessarily requires a detailed review of the evidence. The record reflects that Billy Ed Price was last seen alive on the morning of April 14, 1975, by his brother-in-law, Al Furr, when Furr left Price at the Continental Bus Station in Dallas. Furr testified that Price had over a hundred dollars on his person. On the morning of the next day, . . . Jerry Smith and two co-workers were dispatched to an oil lease south of Burkburnett for the purpose of repairing a salt water leak. In traveling to the lease, Smith and his companions crossed a wooden bridge. . . . [They discovered a body] under the bridge. . . . Investigation revealed that the body under the bridge was nude, beaten, stabbed and sexually mutilated. The body was later identified [as that of] Billy Ed Price.

Dr. Donald Fletcher, a pathologist, performed an autopsy. . . . Dr. Fletcher testified as to numerous lacerations and bruises of the body which included a badly beaten head resulting in an egg-shell fracture. Stab-like perforations resulted in two punctures of the heart, tears and puncture of the lungs, pancreas and stomach. A puncture wound in the scrotal area resulted in a penetration of the large and small bowels. The male reproductive organs had been removed by "a very fine, knifelike cut." In response to a question as to the cause of death, Dr. Fletcher stated, ". . . there are several possibilities, but the most likely would be the perforation and tearing of the heart. That would lead to a very rapid death."

Dr. Fletcher's reply to the question of whether the wounds which resulted in death could have been caused by being stabbed with a lug wrench was, "That would be an excellent tool to do what was done." . . . The autopsy revealed a high content of alcohol and barbiturates in the body, leading Dr. Fletcher to conclude, "My opinion is that . . . he (deceased) or any person with that level of drugs in his system, in his blood, untreated would die, without any further injuries."

Dean Bohannon, a former employee of the Vernon Police Department, and his wife were walking along the Pease River in Wilbarger County . . . , when they "spotted a suitcase and some clothing floating in the river." Bohannon was able to recover the items and took them to the Vernon Police Department. The following day, an investigation of this area of the river resulted in the recovery of clothing and a lug wrench.

A few days later, Deputy Sheriff King of Wilbarger County found a social security card with the name Billy Ed Price on it and some photographs under a bridge on a farm to market road about one and a half miles north of the Pease River bridge.

While en route from Chillicothe to Vernon . . . , Wilburn Hendry at a point "approximately seven miles" north of Vernon observed a boot laying just off the shoulder of the road, "and possibly fifty, maybe seventy-five yards further down the road I noticed another one." Hendry retrieved the boots and turned them over to the Wilbarger County Sheriff's Department. Deputy Sheriff Russell, along with Hendry, returned to the location where the boots were found and a search of the area resulted in the recovery of a leather dress glove. [Price's relatives] identified the boots, the glove, and some of the items of clothing found in Wilbarger County as having belonged to the deceased.

William Kump testified that sometime during the harvest season . . . appellant picked him up at about 8:00 p.m. when he was "hitchhiking" a ride to his motel. According to Kump, they rode around for an hour or two until they stopped at a "roadside park place." Kump and appellant stayed at this location until "4:30 or 5:00, maybe a little later" the next morning. Kump stated that prior to the time they left this location appellant told him that "he wanted to cut my dick and balls off with a pocket knife[;] he wanted to make a woman out of me." Appellant took Kump to his motel and asked him not "to tell anybody about anything that happened, what was said there." The record reflects that these events transpired in and around Vernon.

Steven Laney, a transient, testified he met appellant in the Office Lounge in Wichita Falls . . . around "7:30 or 8:00 o'clock" in the evening after he, Laney, had been drinking beer since noon, that he and appellant later went to another bar and, after leaving the second bar, they "bought some beer and went out towards somewhere south of town." They stopped at a roadside park where additional beer was consumed and Laney "blacked out." The only thing Laney remembered after this point was ". . . being struck from around the right-hand to the rear side [in the head] with an object." Later Laney was aware of ". . . crawling to the highway through kind of a swamp-like thing, through about two feet of water." The first time Laney "came to after blacking out" was after he had been struck with an object. In response to the question, "Who struck you?" Laney responded, "Mr. Stogsdill (appellant), I believe." Laney stated that he saw appellant and he had "more or less a mad expression." . . . Prior to the admission of Laney's testimony, a hearing was held outside the presence of the jury on appellant's motion to suppress the testimony of Laney on the basis that same was inadmissible as an extraneous offense. At the conclusion of the hearing, the court found same to be admissible. . . . The court's action in admitting the extraneous offenses gives rise to the only other ground of error advanced by appellant, which we find unnecessary to discuss in light of our disposition of appellant's contention relative to the sufficiency of the evidence.[1]

. . . [T]he prosecution [also] relies on a comparison of casts of tire tracks at the scene [where the body was found] and two tires taken from a pickup truck sold by appellant to Edward Lee Thomas . . . and the comparison of known hair of the deceased and hairs which were picked up with a vacuum cleaner used on the interior of said truck . . . .

Terry Crone, a chemist for the Department of Public Safety in Garland, testified regarding the comparison of the tires and casts made of [tire] tracks at the scene. The report which he identified as having been given by his office to Wichita County authorities appears to fairly summarize his testimony. It reads in pertinent part:

> . . . We have completed our examinations and wish to report that both of the tires exhibit a tread design similar to that shown by one of the plaster casts. However, the plaster casts do not show enough detail to identify either of these tires as having made the impressions from which the cast was taken. . . .

---

1. In a footnote, without expressly deciding the issue, the court strongly suggested that the "extraneous offense" shown by Laney's testimony was excludable under the rules of evidence and should not have been admitted. — Eds.

On redirect examination, Crone was asked, "But you're not saying that one of those tires did not make that impression either, are you?" and the witness answered, "That is correct, it's possible it could have made it." On recross, Crone testified that the cast was made by some tire of the same type of tread, of the same tread design and the same size, but he could not say that the tires in question made it.

Deputy Inglish testified that he took the measurements of the track and wheel base of the pickup appellant sold Thomas and found same to be "almost identical" to the measurements of tracks of an unknown vehicle at the murder scene. . . .

John Hippard, a special agent assigned to the F.B.I. laboratory in Washington, D. C., testified that the nature of his work with the F.B.I. was conducting "microscopic examinations and comparisons of hairs, fibers and related materials." After examining microscopically known hairs from the head of the deceased and two hairs taken from "debris from the pickup," Hippard concluded they were microscopically alike and explained "whenever they are microscopically alike then my conclusion is that they could have come from the same source." Hippard's examination of the lug wrench or tire tool revealed that known body hairs of the deceased were "microscopically like" those on the tire tool, "and accordingly my conclusion would be that they could have come from the same source." In response to a question on cross examination, Hippard stated that . . . ". . . hairs do not possess enough individual microscopic characteristics to be positively identified as originating from a particular person to the exclusion of all others."

Dr. Irving C. Stone, Chief of the Physical Evidence Section at the Institute of Forensic Sciences in Dallas, testified that known body hair taken from the deceased and hair found on the tire tool "could have come" from the same source. With respect to his comparison of known head hairs of the victim and hairs taken from the debris of the pickup, Dr. Stone concluded, "Everything I saw in the one set of hairs were identical in all characteristics to the other set." [He added:]

> It's my experience you cannot positively associate a hair or set of hairs exclusively to a person to the exclusion of all other people in the world, but after you've looked at hairs for a number of years and you have an experience factor, you come to see that it is easy to differentiate. I can say positively that this hair could not have come from somebody but once you've got two hairs that are the same in all observable characteristics and you've concluded that they might have come from the same person, what you're saying in essence is that it's highly unlikely it came from anybody else other than this person, but you're still not saying conclusively, positively, that this hair is that person's. . . .

On cross examination, Dr. Stone agreed that a definite identification of hair cannot be made. . . .

Dr. John Randall, Director of the Nuclear Science Center at Texas A&M University, testified that he made a neutron activation analysis of known head hair samples of the deceased and three hairs Dr. Stone selected from the debris taken from the pickup as having compared extremely well with the known head hairs of the victim. Dr. Randall related that in using this procedure,

> ... we're looking to find the trace minerals that are contained within the hair, and this we do and then we compare the distribution of minerals. ... The object ultimately is to come up with some answer as to do these two hairs come from the same origin, that's the reason of interest for the forensic application.

Dr. Randall stated that he observed sodium, bromide, manganese, copper, aluminum, zinc and gold, and:

> Based on the analysis I found that six of the elements compared favorably for us to say they came from the same source, they compared favorably within the limits of the experiment. One element, the sodium, did not compare. In fact, looking at the ratio, the sample that was identified as the [victim], all of those hairs had an amount of sodium four times greater than that which came from the pickup.

Disregarding the discrepancy in the sodium element, Dr. Randall concluded that the probability of the match of the known head hair and the hairs found in the debris of the truck "is twenty-five thousand to one." Dr. Randall suspected that the known hair from the victim had been contaminated by salt because "I have been informed that the victim's head was immersed in a very salty stream, a stream that discharged salt waste." ...

Appellant did not testify, nor did he offer any evidence in his defense. ...

The rule has long been that a conviction on circumstantial evidence cannot be sustained if the circumstances do not exclude every other reasonable hypothesis except that of the guilt of the accused, and proof amounting to only a strong suspicion or mere probability is insufficient. In a very recent case, *Flores v. State*, 551 S.W.2d 364 (1977), where circumstantial evidence was relied on for conviction, this Court pointed out that it is not necessary, however, that every fact point directly and independently to the defendant's guilt. It is enough if the conclusion is warranted by the combined and cumulative force of all the incriminating circumstances.

In *Flores*, the defendant was charged with capital murder. ... Under evidence more persuasive of the accused's guilt than we find in the instant case, this Court in *Flores* found the evidence insufficient to support the conviction.

As was the case in *Flores*, appellant was not placed in company of the deceased. In *Flores* the defendant was shown to have been in possession of the deceased's car about twenty-four hours after the deceased was last seen alive. About six weeks later defendant was still in possession of the deceased's car, at which time the vehicle bore license plates issued to another car. Clothing and other items belonging to the deceased were found in a suitcase in a car trunk where they had been left by defendant and a companion. Bloodstains were found on the seat of the car and on defendant's shirt. While the stains did not respond to typing procedures, it was determined that the stains were of human blood.

In *Flores*, as in the instant case, there [was] no showing that defendant was at or near the scene of the crime. While the defendant in *Flores* was placed in the victim's car the next day, it was not until almost four months after the crime that head hairs which bore the same characteristics as deceased's were found in a pickup appellant sold about two weeks after Price's murder. While the testimony of Dr. Randall regarding the results of the tests he performed on known head hairs of the deceased and the hairs found in the pickup reflected that the odds were extremely high that the hairs came from the same person, it was undisputed that the vehicle defendant was driving in *Flores* belonged to the victim. In *Flores*, clothing and personal items of the deceased were placed in the defendant's possession. In the instant case, clothing and personal effects of the victim were recovered but appellant was not shown to have ever been in possession of same, nor was he shown to have been at or near the place where such items were recovered. In *Flores*, human bloodstains, though their origin was not shown, were found on the defendant's shirt and in the victim's car he was driving. No such showing is made in the instant case. In *Flores*, the victim's car had license plates affixed to it which were issued to another vehicle when the defendant was discovered driving same six weeks after the crime. In the instant case, there is no showing of such a deceptive circumstance. The results of the comparison of the plaster casts of tire tracks at the scene and two tires taken from the pickup sold by appellant are clearly inconclusive. The same is true of the comparison of track and wheel base measurements made at the scene and those taken of the pickup in question. The record contains evidence which reflects that a lug wrench was probably the murder weapon. Appellant was never placed in possession of same, nor was he shown to have been at or near the place it was discovered. The incident related by William Kump and the extraneous offense where Steven Laney was beaten, which was admitted by the court on the issue of identity, do not prove that appellant committed the crime.

While all of the circumstances shown may very well amount to proof of strong suspicion or a probability that appellant committed the crime charged, the evidence does not exclude all other reasonable hypotheses except appellant's guilt. For the failure of the evidence to meet the required burden of proof, the judgment is reversed and the cause remanded.

Notes and Questions

(1) *The Proper Weight of Circumstantial Evidence: Did the Court Consider It Incorrectly?* Did the court properly consider the weight of the circumstantial evidence in either *Flores* or *Stogsdill*? The court says in *Stogsdill*, for example, that the "incident related by William Kump," *i.e.*, that Stogsdill told him he wanted to "cut my dick and balls off with a pocket knife[;] he wanted to make a woman out of me," does not "prove that appellant committed the crime." In other words, appellant's odd statement, about treatment identical to the murder victim, was not enough, independently, to prove the case beyond a reasonable doubt all by itself.

But did this one piece of evidence have to "prove" the entire case by itself? Elsewhere, the court says, "It is enough if the conclusion is warranted by the combined and cumulative force of all the incriminating circumstances." Would the result have been different if the court had considered Kump's testimony (which, at the very least, puts Stogsdill in an extremely small group of accused murderers) in combination with the scientific evidence about the tire treads (which does the same) and, further, in combination with the hair evidence (which cumulatively does the same)? Remember the opposing principle: the state must "exclude every other reasonable hypothesis except that of the guilt of the accused."

(2) *Did the Court Also Misconstrue the Standard of Review on Appeal, which Resolves Inferences in Favor of the Jury's Verdict?* In a jury-tried case, appellate review of the sufficiency of the evidence recognizes the role of the jury. The standard of review on appeal is whether "any rational trier of fact could have found the essential elements of the crime beyond a reasonable doubt," with the evidence "considered in the light most favorable to the prosecution." *Jackson v. Virginia*, above. In other words, the appellate court will draw inferences in favor of the ways that the jury could permissibly have drawn them in evaluating the evidence as sufficient to convict the accused beyond a reasonable doubt. Thus, the issue in *Stogsdill* was not whether the appellate court, as a fact finder (*i.e.*, if it were the jury), would have concluded that the proof excluded every reasonable hypothesis other than guilt; it was whether a reasonable juror, properly following the law, could have concluded so. Notice that the court never refers to this principle. Couldn't reasonable people find proof beyond a reasonable doubt from the cumulative weight of the evidence? Does application of the proper standard of review therefore undermine the court's conclusion?

(3) *The Fallacy of "Motive, Opportunity, and Means."* The burden of proof typically gets brutalized in fiction, especially on television shows about lawyers. It is an understatement to say that the popular understanding of the burden of proof is confused. In one television lawyer drama, for example, an intrepid attorney could be overheard telling a fellow barrister that the defendant could be convicted with proof that he had "the motive, the opportunity, and the means." Can you explain why proof of those three factors, however catchy they might sound on television, usually will not be sufficient to establish guilt beyond a reasonable doubt?

(4) *Assessing Each Element in Stogsdill: Were There Other Essential Ingredients That Were Missing?* Reconsider the indictment in this case, which is quoted in the second full paragraph of the opinion. It charges that Stogsdill (1) "on or about the 14th day of April A.D. 1975" (2) "intentionally" (3) "cause[d] the death of" (4) "Billy Ed Price"(5) "by beating him and stabbing him with a lug wrench" (6) while robbing him. These elements all were required to be proved beyond a reasonable doubt. Were they all proved?

Compare the elements, and the proof of each, in *Stogsdill*. There apparently is sufficient proof that Billy Ed Price is dead, the autopsy testimony gives sufficient reason for inferring that his killing was intentional, and there is evidence of the date. Is there proof beyond a reasonable doubt, however, that the killing was committed "in the course of" robbery (as was required, under the indictment, to make it a capital murder)?

Next, was the evidence of the manner and means (a "lug wrench") sufficient to prove the use of a lug wrench, beyond a reasonable doubt? That evidence consisted of scientific testimony that a hair on the lug wrench was consistent with Price's, and the pathologist's statement that the wrench would have been "an excellent tool" to cause these wounds. And finally, what about causation, given the testimony that the deceased had a near-life-threatening concentration of barbiturates and alcohol in him? Were all of these required elements proved? Beyond a reasonable doubt?

(5) *Would DNA Evidence Change the Result?* DNA analysis involves comparison of alleles (strands) of DNA (deoxy ribonucleic acid) from an unknown sample to a known sample taken from an identified person. Statistical testimony about DNA produces a result relative to random members of the population. Thus, for example, witnesses might testify (1) to a match of alleles from the defendant's DNA to an unknown sample and (2) that the odds of such a match are "one in one million." This testimony does not mean that the odds are a million to one that the defendant is guilty. Instead, it means only that the odds are a million to one against a random member of the population having alleles that match the unknown sample. In short, DNA evidence is not completely conclusive, but it can justify a high degree of confidence in the conclusion that both samples either did or did not come from the same person.

DNA evidence would therefore almost certainly be more powerful than the scientific analysis available when *Stogsdill* was decided. Would (or should) the availability of new techniques of DNA analysis change the result in *Stogsdill*?

Before you answer "yes," consider carefully what the court actually held in *Stogsdill*—and in *Flores*, which was relied on in *Stogsdill*. In *Flores*, the court held that the defendant's possession of the victim's vehicle (and effort to hide that fact), together with other evidence that the court characterized as "stronger" than that in *Stogsdill*, was not enough to provide proof beyond a reasonable doubt. In *Stogsdill*, the scientific evidence was offered to show something similar: that defendant and victim were in the same vehicle (as well as that a lug wrench found at the scene had the victim's hair on it, but the lug wrench never was connected to the defendant). Arguably, then, DNA analysis would have made no difference in *Stogsdill*, given the court's approach to review of circumstantial evidence. In spite of the reflexive tendency to believe that DNA can resolve everything, under the court's analysis it might not have changed anything.

(6) *Has DNA Evidence Been Oversold?* DNA evidence definitively resolves a relatively small percentage of cases—most famously, certain kinds of cases of people wrongly convicted of rape (or less often, of murder)—and it almost always does so by circumstantial inferences. But it only works when the presence of a person's DNA in a given location creates or eliminates reasonable doubt about guilt. Some people have concluded that elimination of suspects by DNA is more reliable than its use to convict.

But what if jurors expect DNA proof, even in cases it cannot help to solve? Some news reports suggest that this already has happened. One article cited a case in which DNA evidence was available and convincing, but the jurors acquitted—in part, because they had learned from the television show CSI that "debris" from the victim's clothes sometimes could be compared to crime scene soil, and they wondered why that evidence was not also included. "Television's diet of forensic fantasy projects the image that all cases are solvable by highly technical science, and if you offer less than that, it is viewed as reasonable doubt," according to one state's attorney. And the other side is problematic too, as the article points out, with examples of juries that overvalue some forensic evidence. "Too often, . . the science is unproven, the analyses unsound, and the experts unreliable." And so "[p]rosecutors have a name for the phenomenon: 'the CSI effect'." *See The CSI Effect*, U.S. News & World Report, April 25, 2005, at 49–54. *See also Charles v. State*, 997 A.2d 154 (Md. 2010) (holding trial court erred in asking prospective jurors whether "they would be unable to convict the defendant in the absence of 'scientific' evidence").

[B] Eyewitness Testimony

Notes on the Apparent Preference for Eyewitness Identifications Over Circumstantial Evidence

(1) *Why Do We Prefer Eyewitnesses Over Circumstantial Evidence? Daniel Goleman, Studies Point to Flaws in Lineups of Suspects*, N.Y. Times, Jan 17, 1995, at C1. If there had been an eyewitness in the *Stogsdill* murder case, above, the result might have been dramatically different, even if cross-examination had shown reasons to disbelieve the eyewitness. Why? Eyewitness evidence is essential to the proof of most kinds of cases; our system cannot practically do without it; it is familiar; and there is an assumption that jurors can understand and evaluate it. But there are indications that this assumption can be questioned. According to the Innocence Project, the "most common element in all wrongful convictions later overturned by DNA evidence has been eyewitness misidentification." "Mistaken identifications contributed to approximately 75% of the 301 wrongful convictions" overturned on the basis of DNA proof. *See* http://www.innocenceproject.org/fix/Eyewitness-Identification.php. (April 1, 2013).

(2) *The Prototypical Law Enforcement Method: Finding Suspects Who Fit Descriptions and Placing Them in Lineups—but Does This Approach Maximize the Likelihood of Misidentification?* As another cautionary note about eyewitness testimony, consider the manner in which most robberies are solved, as well as some serial rapes or murders. Police officers obtain descriptions of the perpetrator. They hope, through mug books or apprehensions of suspects in other, similar cases, to locate individuals as suspects who "fit" these descriptions. When they do, they place these suspects in photographic spreads or lineups, to be viewed by witnesses who already have given descriptions that the suspects "fit." Consider the possibility that this method maximizes the likelihood of causing a misidentification (but maybe it can't be avoided).

(3) *Expert Witnesses on Eyewitness Identification—and the Reluctance to Allow Their Use.* Why not, then, allow the defendant to present a psychologist as an expert witness who will inform juries about the fallibility of eyewitness identification?

There is a considerable literature on the subject, and psychologists can identify specific risks or factual variables that influence (or do not influence) accuracy. Some courts have allowed their testimony, particularly when it has particular bearing on specific factors in the identification at issue. Other courts have been reluctant to allow routine evidence on this subject. Their concerns include the risk that the expert testimony may be misleading, the existence of a cottage industry of partisan experts hired because they give the "right" answers to each side, and the possibility that indigents may gain a right to be furnished with eyewitness experts at considerable state expense. A generalized problem is the difficulty of limiting the principle to eyewitnesses; in theory, the issue is whether any and every witness's testimony is true or false. This consideration raises the possibility that every witness might be followed by another, a psychologist, who has been paid to provide testimony that the first witness is either untruthful or mistaken. Consider the following decision.

People v. Lerma
19 N.E.3d 95 (Ill. App. 2015)

JUSTICE HARRIS delivered the judgment of the court, with opinion.

A jury convicted defendant, Eduardo Lerma, of [the] first degree murder ... of Jason Gill. The only living eyewitness to the shooting, Lydia Clark, identified defendant. Clark and Jason Gill's father, Bill Johnson, both testified that a critically wounded Gill stated that defendant had shot him. Prior to trial, defendant sought to have an expert witness, ... testify on eyewitness identification. The circuit court denied the motion, finding that because Clark, Gill, and defendant were acquaintances, [expert testimony was to be excluded.] During trial, defendant indicated to the court that he had secured a new expert witness, Dr. Geoffrey Loftus. He renewed his motion and submitted a report describing Dr. Loftus's anticipated testimony, which ... directly addressed the effects of eyewitness identification when the eyewitness and the suspect are acquaintances. The circuit court denied the motion, relying on its reasoning as stated in its [earlier] denial . . . . We hold the circuit court abused its discretion because it did not carefully consider or scrutinize Dr. Loftus's anticipated testimony before denying defendant's motion. . . .

Midway through trial, defendant asked the court to reconsider its ruling on its expert witness. . . . Defense counsel provided a report from Dr. Loftus describing his anticipated testimony. In his report Dr. Loftus stated he reviewed police reports, witness statements and interviews, photo montages, lineup photos, and transcripts from court hearings in developing the report. Dr. Loftus stated he would discuss the general theory of perception and memory and how scientific evidence addressing the following topics related to eyewitness testimony: circumstances where memory fails; effects of low lighting; effects of distance on visual perception; effects of divided attention, including weapons focus; time durations and how people overestimate time durations in stressful or eventful circumstances; effects of cross-racial identification; effects of stress; consequences of a person's face being partially obscured; effects of expectations; consequences of nonindependent identifications;

effects of suggestive postevent information; and the effect of the confidence of an eyewitness. Dr. Loftus stressed that he would not "issue judgments about whether a particular witness's memory and assertions * * * are correct or incorrect." . . .

Additionally, and unlike [the pretrial motion], Dr. Loftus anticipated discussing the implications of an eyewitness being acquainted with the identified person. Specifically, Dr. Loftus stated that "[i]t would seem intuitive to a jury that if a witness identifies a suspect with whom he or she is acquainted, the witness's identification would likely be accurate. However, this is not necessarily true." Dr. Loftus explained that "if circumstances are poor for a witness's ability to perceive a person," and "the situation fosters a witness's expectations that he or she will see a particular acquaintance[,]* * * then the witness will tend to perceive the person as the expected acquaintance even if the person is in fact someone else." He noted those poor circumstances included low lighting; viewing longer distances in the dark; divided attention of the witness, including a focus on a weapon; time duration, with less time leading to less available information, . . . witness's tendency to overestimate time durations; cross-racial identification; stress; and a partially obscured face. Dr. Loftus stated such situations may lead to misidentification because:

> "In such circumstances, the witness's acquaintance with the expected — and hence perceived — person works against accurate identification for two reasons: First, it would be natural and easy for the witness to subsequently pick the acquaintance in an identification procedure * * * (because the witness already knows whom she is seeking in a lineup procedure, she could immediately rule out all the fillers, and zero in on the acquaintance/suspect). Second, the witness could use his or her prior knowledge of the acquaintance's appearance to reconstruct his or her memory of the original events — the crime — such that the in fact poor original memory of the actual criminal is replaced with a stronger and more confidence-evoking memory of the acquaintance* * *."

The State maintained that expert testimony was not needed because Clark knew defendant before the shooting. . . .

The circuit court noted it reviewed Dr. Loftus's report and resume, but denied the motion for reasons "consistent with the reasons [it] set forth in detail when [it] made the ruling on [defendant's] similar motion [before trial]."

Lydia Clark testified at the time of the shooting, she was 17 years old. She also knew defendant as "Lucky," and estimated she had seen him on the porch of the house across the street approximately 10 times prior to the shooting. She did not know his real name and had never spoken with him or been in the same house with him. At approximately 11:20 p.m. on the day of the incident, she and Gill were sitting on the front steps of Gill's house. The streetlights were on. She saw defendant wearing all black with a hooded sweatshirt with the hood down. Defendant pointed a black gun toward her and Gill and shot it two to five times. Gill covered her with his arms. Gill fell and Clark dragged him into the house through the door. She called the police and heard Gill's father, Bill Johnson, come downstairs. Johnson asked Gill who shot him and Gill stated "'Lucky shot me.'" Gill's voice sounded "[l]ike he was gasping for air." She told the two police officers who first responded to the scene what had happened. That next morning, at 1:25 a.m., she went to the police station, where she was shown six photographs of Hispanic males, one of which was defendant. She identified defendant from the photographs as the shooter. . . . [S]he identified defendant [in person] at the police station.

On cross-examination, Clark testified that although she had seen defendant, she "did not know him." She admitted that she testified before the grand jury, . . . several days after the shooting, that she had only seen defendant once or twice before the shooting. She also admitted that . . . . she told Detective Hughes that she had known defendant for a couple of months. She testified she had never had a conversation with defendant prior to the shooting. She denied that she told Detective Hughes shortly after the shooting that defendant's hood on his sweatshirt was up at the time of the shooting. She agreed that when the shooter approached she saw the gun; she felt fear and wanted to get out of the way. The gun was already in the shooter's hand. Gill's house did not have a front porch light. The shooter came from across the street in front of an abandoned house. She testified that there were no lights on in the yard of the abandoned house. Clark testified that she told the officers that responded to the shooting that defendant shot Gill and that defendant had been in a feud with Gill's family. When she identified defendant at the police station in the holding cell, he was alone.

Bill Johnson, Gill's father, testified consistently with Clark's testimony concerning Gill's statement that "Lucky" had shot him. . . .

Chicago police officer John Layne testified he responded to the scene of the shooting and found Clark "in shock." He testified that "All [Clark] could say basically to us was Lucky shot him. He just walked up and shot him." She later told Officer Layne that "Lucky," who was Hispanic, aged 23 to 28, and lived on the block, shot Gill.

Detective Thomas Benoit of the Chicago police testified he assembled a photo array, which included defendant and five others, to show to Lydia Clark. When shown the photo array, Clark identified defendant as the shooter. On cross-examination, Detective Benoit testified the photos of the people in the array other than defendant were generated from a computer.

Detective Halloran testified that on May 5, 2008, in the early morning, Lydia Clark told him that "Lucky" shot Gill. Detective Halloran did a "show-up" identification procedure whereby defendant stood alone in a room. Clark, looking through a window, identified defendant as the shooter. He explained he did a "show up" identification procedure as opposed to a lineup because Clark knew the shooter beforehand. . . .

Taurhern Gill, the victim's brother, testified . . . that defendant had been hanging around the block that day. . . .

The circuit court sentenced defendant to 45 years' imprisonment.

Analysis

. . . According to defendant, the circuit court relied on a common misconception of eyewitness testimony, *i.e.,* that such identification by a prior acquaintance is reliable, which his expert witness's report directly disputed. . . . [T]he State argues the circuit court conducted a meaningful inquiry before denying the motion. The State maintains any error made by the circuit court here was harmless because defense counsel managed to elicit any relevant point that his proposed expert witness would have covered by way of cross-examination and closing argument.

. . . "In Illinois, generally, an individual will be permitted to testify as an expert if his experience and qualifications afford him knowledge which is not common to lay persons and where such testimony will aid the trier of fact in reaching its conclusion." *People v. Enis,* 564 N.E.2d 1155 (1990). . . . [T]he necessity and relevance of the expert testimony should be carefully considered in light of the facts of the case. *Id.* . . . [W]e review the trial court's decision to admit evidence, including expert witness testimony, for an abuse of that discretion.

The trial court here ruled [pretrial] that [expert] testimony was not needed principally because Clark and Gill knew defendant before the shooting. The court found that "it is a fact that persons who are less likely to misidentify someone they have met or know or seen before than a stranger." . . . Dr. Loftus's report, unlike [the pretrial motion], directly addressed the implications of an eyewitness being acquainted with the identified person. The trial court, . . . denied defendant's renewed motion to call Dr. Loftus for reasons consistent with its prior ruling. Both our supreme court and this court have stressed that expert testimony should be carefully considered and scrutinized in light of the facts of the case. . . . It is clear that the trial court here, in relying on its prior reasoning, did not carefully consider or scrutinize Dr. Loftus's report where the report directly contradicted the court's prior finding that it is common knowledge that an eyewitness is less likely to misidentify an acquaintance.

We find this court's decision in *People v. Allen,* to be instructive here. In *Allen,* this court held that the trial court abused its discretion when it failed to scrutinize, weigh, or consider, relevant proposed testimony from the report of an expert on eyewitness identification. *People v. Allen,* 875 N.E.2d 1221 (2007). This court explained:

> "No careful scrutiny took place in this case. Relevance of the different parts of [the] proposed testimony was not seriously considered. Nor their weight.
> * * * The balancing test requires a weighing of 'probative value against its prejudicial effect.' [Citation.] The test cannot be accomplished without an inquiry into the probative value of the proposed testimony and its relevance to the issues in the case. It is then that the inquiry shifts to the risk of unfair prejudice. . . ."

In the case at bar, we cannot say that any meaningful inquiry took place where the circuit court denied Dr. Loftus' proposed testimony based on the same reasoning it applied to the pretrial motion], even though Dr. Loftus' report directly contradicted that reasoning. As in *Allen,* the trial court's failure here to carefully scrutinize Dr. Loftus' anticipated testimony, as stated in his report, constituted an abuse of discretion.

We also find it difficult to accord the customary degree of deference to the trial court's discretion in this case because the trial court, in relying on its prior ruling explained itself with little more than a series of conclusions based on its personal belief. The trial court found "everybody knows" that eyewitnesses are less likely to misidentify an acquaintance, describing it as "a function of human nature." As discussed above, Dr. Loftus directly contradicted these statements in his report, stating such sentiments are "not necessarily true," especially when various circumstance were present, many of which were present in the case at bar. The circuit court further feared such testimony would "generate * * * a referendum on the efficacy of identification testimony generally" and that the expert could voice his opinion on the credibility of witnesses. Dr. Loftus also addressed these fears in his report, stating that when testifying, he does not "issue judgments about whether a particular witness's memory and assertions in the case at hand are correct or incorrect." He further noted that "any testimony on my part . . . implies only that the eyewitness evidence should be viewed with appropriate caution." . . .

We acknowledge that courts in Illinois and around the country have recognized that scientific studies have shown significant errors in eyewitness identifications and that the public have misconceptions of eyewitness identification. The advent of DNA testing, particularly in postconviction reviews, has shown a significant percentage of conviction reversals involve eyewitness identifications that turn out to be false [Reversed and remanded.]

PEOPLE v. CALIZ, 2017 WL 2061428 (Cal. App. 2017) (unpublished opinion). This case shows a more common treatment of eyewitness experts — by exclusion:

> [T]he probative value of an eyewitness expert's testimony in this case was minimal. Caliz argues "[t]estimony from an eyewitness identification expert was critical for the defense to explain to the jury how various psychological factors affected the accuracy of Mr. Wade's identification . . ." including the significance of the fact that "the shooter was visible for less than five seconds," during which time "multiple gunshots were fired, undoubtedly drawing attention to the gun used in the shooting." However, "[t]he jury did not need edification on the obvious fact that an unprovoked gang attack is a stressful event or that the passage of time frequently affects one's memory." . . . As the trial court stated, "I think having an eyewitness ID expert would be totally confusing to the jury because it would cause them to believe that . . . this is all about whether you can and cannot determine what happened in a five second burst of fire, which I think everybody naturally recognizes" . . . . [Conviction affirmed.]

Notes and Questions

(1) *What's Wrong with Eyewitness Testimony? United States v. Smithers*, 212 F.3d 206 (6th Cir. 2000), gave the following description of problems with eyewitness testimony:

> A plethora of recent studies show that the accuracy of an eyewitness identification depends on how the event is observed, retained and recalled. *See generally* Roger V. Handberg, *Expert Testimony on Eyewitness Identification: A New Pair of Glasses for the Jury*, 32 Am. Crim. L. Rev. 1013, 1018–22 (1995). Memory and perception may be affected by factors such as:
>
> > (1) the retention interval, which concerns the rate at which a person's memory declines over time; (2) the assimilation factor, which concerns a witness's incorporation of information gained subsequent to an event into his or her memory of that event; and (3) the confidence-accuracy relationship, which concerns the correlation between a witness's confidence in his or her memory and the accuracy of that memory. Other relevant factors include: (4) stress; (5) the violence of the situation; (6) the selectivity of perception; (7) expectancy; (8) the effect of repeated viewings; (9) and the cross-racial aspects of identification, that is where the eyewitness and the actor in the situation are of different racial groups. . . .
>
> [I]gnorance [of these factors] can lead to devastating results. One study has estimated that half of all wrongful convictions result from false identifications. *See* Elizabeth F. Loftus, *Ten Years in the Life of an Expert Witness*, 10 Law & Hum. Behav. 241, 243 (1986). . . . A principal cause of such convictions is 'the fact that, in general, juries are unduly receptive to identification evidence and are not sufficiently aware of its dangers.'"

(2) *Questioning the Science underlying Eyewitness Experts.* The dissenting judge responded to the majority's arguments in *Smithers* with the following discussion of social science evidence:

> The difficulty arises in treating psychological theories as if they were as demonstrably reliable as the laws of physics. . . . [Social scientists] typically base their opinions on studies of small groups of people under laboratory conditions; those studies are then interpreted and extrapolated to predict the likelihood that another person under similar but noncontrolled conditions will manifest similar behavior. Each step of this analysis . . . is influenced by the personal opinion of the individual expert. . . . The studies are virtually always based on college students or other readily available test subjects in a controlled environment (which are the most easily measurable), not individuals involved in real world incidents such as actual robbery victims. *See, e.g.,* Brian L. Cutler and Steven D. Penrod, *Assessing the Accuracy of Eye-Witness Identifications*, in *Handbook of Psychology in Legal Contexts* 193 (R. Bull and D. Carson ed. 1995). . . .

> No psychological study will ever bear directly on the specific persons making an eyewitness identification in court. . . . Expert testimony on eyewitness identifications can also be unduly prejudicial when it is phrased so as to comment directly on the credibility of the eyewitness. . . .

Who gets the better of this argument?

(3) *Will the Admission of Expert Testimony about Eyewitness Identification Create a Battle of the Experts?* If courts permit defense expert testimony about the unreliability of eyewitness identification, isn't it likely that prosecutors will produce their own experts to testify that eyewitness identification is valuable and that the circumstances in the case at trial support its accuracy? If so, how will juries decide between the competing claims of experts? Can jury instructions help, or should courts simply exclude all eyewitness experts?

In addition to the *Smithers* and *Caliz* courts, many state and federal courts have taken account of studies such as those cited in note 1 and have reexamined their reliance on eyewitness testimony. *See State v. Guilbert*, 49 A.3d 705, 720 n.8 (Conn. 2012) (citing numerous cases); *see also Young v. Conway* 698 F.3d 69 (2d Cir. 2012); *State v. Lawson*, 291 P.3d 673 (Or. 2012).

§ 4.05 Other Burdens of Proof

[A] Sentencing: Complex Proof Requirements, to be Dealt with in a Later Chapter

Notes on Proof Burdens at Sentencing

(1) *Discretionary or Advisory Sentencing Involves Different Proof Considerations.* There are some questions for which it is arguably inappropriate to demand proof beyond a reasonable doubt. For example, once proof of guilt has been established beyond a reasonable doubt, the question of sentencing arises. Sentencing, unlike the guilt decision, involves conflicting goals, diffuse and open-ended factors, and an indefinite array of potentially relevant kinds of evidence. Requiring that every potentially influential consideration be proved beyond a reasonable doubt might distort the result, at least when discretion within broad ranges is involved. And, in fact, trial courts sometimes are able to find sentencing facts under a preponderance of the evidence standard.

(2) *The Beyond-a-Reasonable-Doubt Standard Applies to Significant Fact Finding at Sentencing.* Modern approaches to sentencing sometimes involve fixed sentence enhancements that result from defined fact findings. Recent Supreme Court decisions have required findings of this kind to be made beyond a reasonable doubt, with the defendant having the right to a jury determination. Assume that the jurisdiction has enacted a hate crime law authorizing an additional ten year sentence if the crime was "motivated by racial, ethnic, religious, or gender hatred." Under the

Supreme Court precedents, ordinarily the jury must decide beyond a reasonable doubt whether the assault was motivated by hatred.

[B] Other Examples of Lower Burdens of Proof

Notes on Preponderance and Lesser Standards

While proof beyond a reasonable doubt is required for the elements of a crime and a few other matters, in some criminal procedural settings a lesser standard of proof is used. Here are a few illustrations.

(1) *Probation and Parole Revocation.* Criminal courts generally do not impose a reasonable doubt standard for probation or parole revocation; the preponderance standard usually applies.

(2) *Discretion with No Burden of Proof: Bail, Evidence, Etc.* The decision whether to admit a piece of evidence sometimes is governed by a preponderance standard. Other evidence decisions involve balancing without an explicit proof standard. The bail decision, in some jurisdictions, involves merely an unquantified balancing of competing considerations and does not subject most of them, or the balancing process, to any explicit proof burden.

(3) *Probable Cause and Reasonable Suspicion.* "Probable cause" refers to an amount of evidence that would warrant a reasonable belief that a crime has been committed by the accused. The probable cause standard applies to "screening" processes, including certain searches or arrests. Since these are investigatory processes, perhaps it makes sense to apply a lesser standard than proof beyond a reasonable doubt. The grand jury usually is said to be governed by a probable cause standard when it indicts, and so is a magistrate at a preliminary hearing who binds over the accused for trial. For some kinds of searches, an even lower standard applies: "reasonable suspicion" (for border searches or weapons patdowns).

[C] Corroboration Requirements

California Penal Code § 1111 Corroboration of Testimony of Accomplice

A conviction cannot be had upon the testimony of an accomplice unless it be corroborated by such other evidence as shall tend to connect the defendant with the commission of the offense; and the corroboration is not sufficient if it merely shows the commission of the offense or the circumstances thereof. An accomplice is hereby defined as one who is liable to prosecution for the identical offense charged against the defendant. . . .

Notes and Questions

(1) *Special Rules on Accomplice Witnesses.* Not all jurisdictions have statutes or evidentiary rules that limit or forbid the use of uncorroborated accomplice testimony.

For example, there is no corroboration requirement under federal law for accomplice testimony. Is it wise to have such a statute?

(2) *The Problem with Absolute Corroboration Requirements: Unprovable Crimes, Some of Them Serious.* Imagine a prosecution for the crime of "compelling prostitution," which often involves violence. The victim of the offense has testified about the defendant's violence against her, her resulting acts of prostitution in compliance with his commands, and her having turned over all the money to the defendant. The state rests without any corroborating witness who can link the defendant to the crime, because the conduct took place in private—even though there is convincing physical evidence that the victim was treated violently by someone. The defense attorney moves for a directed verdict of acquittal. How does the California statute address this situation?

(3) *Corroboration Requirements for Sexual Assault and Related Offenses.* Historically, the testimony of sexual assault victims has largely been discredited by courts and juries. Uncorroborated testimony about force and lack of consent at best was portrayed as a "he said-she said" issue that almost by definition translated into reasonable doubt. At worst, the uncorroborated testimony of a victim was treated as unreliable, suspect, and insufficient to establish a conviction. Most jurisdictions have passed statutes to address these problems. One such example is the following statute:

> The credibility of a complainant of an offense under this chapter [sexual offenses] shall be determined by the same standard as is the credibility of a complainant of any other crime. The testimony of a complainant need not be corroborated in prosecutions under this chapter. No instructions shall be given cautioning the jury to view the complainant's testimony in any other way than that in which all complainants' testimony is viewed.

18 Pa. Consol St. § 3106 (1995).

(4) *Corroboration and Eyewitness Testimony.* Recall the importance of eyewitness testimony to criminal prosecutions—and also the fact that erroneous eyewitness testimony is the leading cause of wrongful convictions. Despite this problem, courts and legislatures are unlikely to ban eyewitness testimony, and as we have seen the admission of expert testimony on the issue of reliability is controversial. One commentator suggests that the best solution for the inadequacy of eyewitness testimony is "a corroboration rule in cases in which eyewitness identification testimony is offered. . . . Normally, . . . it would preclude a conviction that was based solely on the eyewitness identification testimony." Sandra Guerra Thompson, *Beyond a Reasonable Doubt? Reconsidering Uncorroborated Eyewitness Identification Testimony*, 41 U.C. Davis L. Rev. 1487, 1541 (2008).

But what about the problems noted above with corroboration requirements for sexual assault crimes? Remember that concerns about eyewitness testimony primarily involve its use to prove identity—was this defendant the person who committed the crime?—and not the other details of the crime. Thompson suggests an "obvious exception to the rule should allow for convictions based solely on eyewitness testimony in cases in which the victim knows the culprit through a relationship existing prior to the date of the crime." Do these qualifications suffice for the specific issue of sexual assault? Is requiring corroboration of eyewitness testimony a good idea in general?

§ 4.06 Review Problems Based on Newspaper Reports

Note on These "Newspaper Cases"

The following cases all were reported in newspapers. The reports have been rewritten here, however, to emphasize the legal issues, without changing the underlying facts. These reports will provide you with review material from which to look back at Chapter 3, on crime elements, as well as the present Chapter on proof beyond a reasonable doubt.

[A] Headline: Eight-Year-Old Charged with Negligent Homicide after Stabbing Four-Year-Old

NEW YORK—An eight-year old boy was charged with negligent homicide yesterday for stabbing a four-year-old neighbor to death. His nine-year-old brother was charged with assault in the same incident. The two children, both treated as juveniles, were among the youngest ever charged in connection with a homicidal crime in America. The boys were released into the custody of their uncle after being interviewed by law enforcement officers.

Police department spokespersons said that the eight-year-old stabbed four year-old Emanuel Barima in the neck, cutting his jugular vein. "From what we understand, it was one smack to the neck area," Deputy Police Chief Joseph Reznick added. "It all happened so fast, they may not have realized they actually caused the death." The two boys had bullied four-year-old Emanuel for over a year, he said. The weapon may have been either a pen or a set of house keys, and forensic experts were doing tests to determine whether either of these implements was used. Law enforcement officials considered intentional murder and heat-of passion voluntary manslaughter as potential offenses before exercising discretion to present charges for negligent homicide and assault.

Prosecutors differ over the precise standard they apply in exercising their discretion, but virtually all would agree that it is inappropriate to charge an offense for which proof beyond a reasonable doubt of all elements is not a practical possibility. How might this consideration have influenced law enforcement officers in this case, in deciding to pursue negligent homicide rather than murder or manslaughter? (Their discretion may also have been influenced by the age of the respondents, but for now, consider the elements and proof burden.)

[B] Headline: Government Unlikely to Convict Top Enron Executive Ken Lay, Experts Say

WASHINGTON—Ken Lay was the Chief Executive Officer of Enron when it began to undergo the manipulations that produced the then-largest financial collapse in American history, as well as dozens of indictments. But legal analysts said that if Lay himself were to be indicted, he probably could not be convicted.

Law professor Geraldine Szott Moohr explained that mail fraud or wire fraud, which are two common federal offenses in white collar cases, the government would be required to prove that Lay acted with intent to defraud, Szott Moohr said. "It would be hard to prove a criminal case. Intent to deceive is a very hard standard to meet."

In addition, Lay has two other advantages, according to legal experts. First, he would be an excellent witness in his own defense. Second, as an executive of a large corporation, he routinely relied upon the advice of others, including lawyers and accountants. "It will be the hardest thing for the government to get around the fact that businessmen every day rely on what lawyers and accountants tell them," said Chuck Meadows, a well-known white-collar defense lawyer from Dallas. "I would be very surprised if Ken Lay were convicted of any act involving securities at Enron."

Meadows added, "I don't think it's credible to say, 'I'm the chairman, and I didn't know about these major financial transactions.' But he can say, 'I don't know about the exact accounting methods of Arthur Andersen.'" Also, Lay could explain, "I had all these professionals, and I paid them millions of dollars. And whatever they told us to do, we did," Meadows said.

(1) *Offense Elements and the Burden of Proof.* Can you explain why, taking into account both Lay's likely persuasiveness as a witness and his potential advice-of-others defensive theory, it would be "hard to prove" beyond a reasonable doubt that he acted with intent to deceive or defraud, as an element of mail fraud?

(2) *The "Watkins Memorandum," Potential Cooperating Witnesses, and Their Effects.* Some of the commentators who believed that Lay was unlikely to be convicted also mentioned, however, that a document called "the Watkins Memorandum" would be a "real hurdle" (as Szott Moohr put it) for Lay. In that Memorandum, an Enron accountant named Sherron Watkins explained how certain of Enron's transactions that were claimed to "hedge" against losses were not hedges at all because they obligated the company to make up those very losses, and she referred to one document as a "smoking gun" that showed that the accounting was false. Watkins said that she had met with Lay to discuss her Memorandum. However, her evaluation of Lay's response was, "He was concerned." On the other hand, looking at the Memorandum from another view, could it actually favor Lay, in the end, given the proof burden and intent requirement? Another possibility was that other indicted Enron executives, such as Chief Financial Officer Andrew Fastow, who pled guilty and began to assist prosecutors, might testify to conversations in which

Lay allegedly was informed about, or showed that he was familiar with, the illegality of some transactions. How might Lay's defenders attack this evidence so that it also might prove insufficient to supply proof beyond a reasonable doubt?

(3) *But Lay Did Get Convicted—What Happened?* Despite the concerns of the experts, Lay was convicted. How could they have been so wrong? The answer lies in the possibility, mentioned above, of testimony from other indicted Enron executives. In fact, numerous former Enron officers testified for the government, and they were able to supply convincing information about Lay's knowledge. Note that Lay died after he was convicted but before he could appeal, and for that reason his conviction was ultimately vacated.

§ 4.07 Simulation Exercises: Voir Dire and Motion for Acquittal

Simulation Exercise No. 5: Defense Voir Dire Outline in a Murder Case

(1) *A Problem Involving Preparing a Voir Dire Outline.* Read the outline of the prosecutor's voir dire examination in this chapter, above, and prepare a counterpart voir dire outline for the defense in a murder case. You should emphasize the presumption of innocence, reasonable doubt, elements of any defenses, the defendant's right not to testify, and any possible prejudgments the jury might have about crimes, criminal investigators, any circumstances of this alleged offense, the defendant, or you as his attorney. Also, be sure to personalize the defendant.

(2) *Using the Howard Case as a Model.* Consider the *Howard* case as a reference. Please go online to https://caplaw.com/sites/cl4/, then click on "Case File No. 2." Assume that the defendant will raise defenses involving self-defense (the deceased made threatening gestures). Make your outline general, however, so that it could be used in any murder case. You will find the prosecution voir dire useful, but remember which side you are on and revise accordingly.

Simulation Exercise No. 6: Motion for Judgment of Acquittal in a Burglary Case

(1) *A Problem about Document Preparation and Advocacy for a Motion for Judgment of Acquittal.* Federal Rule of Criminal Procedure 29 provides for a motion for judgment of acquittal to be made at the conclusion of the prosecutor's case or at the close of evidence. The standard is the same as a directed verdict: at least one element is supported by legally insufficient evidence, so that no reasonable jury could convict while properly following the law and evidence.

(2) *Applying This Concept to the Burglary Charge in State v. Bates (in a Federal Case).* Using the facts of *State v. Bates*, prepare a written motion, titled "Defendant Bates's Rule 29 Motion for Judgment of Acquittal." For facts and documents in the

Bates case, please go online to https://caplaw.com/sites/cl4/, then click on "Case File No. 1." Your motion should state the legal standard for judgment of acquittal, identify the relevant facts, and explain the deficiency of proof. Assume the case is tried in a federal court under a definition of burglary identical to that in the Model Penal Code, and that the prosecution has just rested. Also, be prepared to give an argument to the judge for either side.

Chapter 5

Assault, Sexual Assault, and Related Offenses

"Rape . . . is an accusation easily to be made and hard to be proved, and harder to be defended by the party accused, tho never so innocent." — Sir Matthew Hale, Lord Chief Justice of England, *Pleas of the Crown* 635 (1680)

"If inaccuracy or indifference to consent is 'the best that this man can do' because he lacks the capacity to act reasonably, then it might well be unjust and ineffective to punish him for it. But such men will be rare. . . . More common is the case of the man who could have done better but did not; could have paid attention, but did not; heard her refusal or saw her tears, but decided to ignore them. . . . By holding out the prospect of punishment for negligence, the Model Penal Code commentators point out, the law provides an additional motive to men to 'take care before acting. . . .' The injury of sexual violation is sufficiently great, the need to provide that additional incentive pressing enough, to justify negligence liability for rape as for killing." — Susan Estrich, *Real Rape* (1988).

§ 5.01 Assault

Notes: Introduction to Assault

(1) *Crimes Against the Person When No One is Killed: Assault and Related Crimes.* If D kills V, the crime may well be some form of homicide, such as murder. But this chapter deals with another set of criminal laws: assault and related crimes that may involve physical harm but not death. In general terms, the chapter starts with crimes traditionally characterized as assault (or in some states, assault and battery) and concludes with various sexual assault laws, such as rape and statutory rape.

(2) *Traditionally, Assault-Type Crimes Were the Separate Offenses of Assault and Battery.* Historically, the basic crimes involving non-fatal actual or threatened physical harm were assault and battery. A "battery" occurred when the actor intentionally inflicted physical harm or at least an "offensive touching" on the victim. The crime of "assault" embraced two different activities: causing the fear of physical harm or attempting a battery. Thus, battery required physical contact between defendant and victim, while assault did not.

(3) *Misdemeanors and Felonies.* Often both an assault and battery were misdemeanors (sometimes called "simple" or "misdemeanor" assault or battery). However,

both crimes were often elevated to a felony if the victim suffered serious harm, a very dangerous weapon was used, or the victim was in a category meriting special protection, such as a young child, elderly person, or law enforcement officer.

(4) *Modern Expansions.* The traditional assault and battery crimes (or just assault, covering both) have survived in every jurisdiction, usually in an expanded and more nuanced form. However, the terminology and definition of assault vary widely from state to state, with some jurisdictions defining a separate crime of battery but many merely including it in an assault provision. The range of assault-type conduct subject to criminal punishment today, then, includes

- *battery*, sometimes, which involves injurious or offensive touching;
- *simple or basic assault*, which may (or may not) include both attempted battery assaults and conduct that is intended to frighten victims;
- *aggravated assaults*, enhanced by factors such as an especially blameworthy mens rea, for example an intent to kill; the use of a weapon; or the occupation or qualities of the victim, for example being a law enforcement or corrections officer or being very young or old; and
- *other offenses*, involving conduct ranging from *threats* or *reckless conduct* (*e.g.*, pointing a firearm toward someone) to *child endangerment*. These offenses cover gaps caused by mens rea requirements or physical elements of assault, so that they otherwise might not be crimes.

Again, jurisdictions vary. Many do not distinguish between "assaults" and "batteries," but treat these labels as immaterial. Others distinguish carefully. Most jurisdictions define more serious assaults as well as simple assault, but the concepts they use to make these distinctions are diverse.

(5) *Some Significant Issues in Assault Law.* Some jurisdictions criminalize only attempted battery assaults. (Can you see why this approach would lead to some odd results? Example: pointing a gun at another person would not be an assault, even though the act frightened the victim severely, because there was no "attempted battery.") Further, assault sometimes is a specific intent crime, so the quantity and kind of evidence that will establish the mens rea for different kinds of assault is often an important issue in assault cases.

[A] Traditional Assault

State v. Billings

4 Wash. App.2d 1014 (Wash App. 2018)

BJORGEN, J.

. . . Jury Instructions and Elements of the Offense

The superior [*i.e.*, trial] court instructed the jury that, in order to convict Billings of second degree assault, it had to find that he had "assaulted Angela Frank with a deadly weapon." It then instructed the jury on three different types of assault as follows:

> [1] An assault is an intentional touching or striking or cutting of another person that is harmful or offensive, regardless of whether any physical injury is done to the person. A touching or striking or cutting is offensive if the touching or striking or cutting would offend an ordinary person who is not unduly sensitive.

> [2] An assault is also an act done with intent to inflict bodily injury upon another, tending but failing to accomplish it and accompanied with the apparent present ability to inflict the bodily injury if not prevented. It is not necessary that bodily injury be inflicted.

> [3] An assault is also an act done with the intent to create in another apprehension and fear of bodily injury, and which in fact creates in another a reasonable apprehension and imminent fear of bodily injury even though the actor did not actually intend to inflict bodily injury. The superior court provided the following transferred intent instruction: "If a person acts with intent to assault another, but the act harms a third person, the actor is also deemed to have acted with intent to assault the third person." Finally, in response to a jury question, the court correctly clarified that transferred intent applies to all three types of assault.

Under these instructions, in order to find an assault of Frank, the jury had to find that (1) Billings performed an act with specific intent to inflict bodily injury on Frank (attempted battery [assault], or (2) even though Billings did not actually intend to inflict bodily injury on Frank, Billings performed an act with specific intent to cause bodily injury to or reasonable apprehension of bodily injury on the part of Soden [attempted bodily injury or fear assault], and (3) Frank had a reasonable apprehension and imminent fear of bodily injury [fear in fact assault].

. . . Evidence Sufficient [for] Second Degree Assault with a Deadly Weapon

The record viewed in the light most favorable to the State contains sufficient evidence to prove that Billings intended to assault Soden with a machete and, in the process, created a reasonable apprehension and imminent fear of bodily injury on Frank's part. The record shows that Billings approached Soden's vehicle from the passenger side and carried a machete with a two foot blade. Soden was seated in the driver's seat and Frank was in the passenger seat. Billings slashed at Soden with the machete while Frank was in the car and lacerated Soden's wrist to the bone. Frank testified had the machete not hit Soden's wrist, it would have struck her in the leg. She testified the situation scared her, and she was afraid Billings might slash her "with the machete or do something worse."

Billings acted with specific intent to inflict bodily injury on Soden. However, because the act caused Frank reasonable apprehension and imminent fear of bodily injury, Billings is also deemed to have acted with intent to assault Frank.

Accordingly, we hold that the record contains sufficient evidence to permit a rational trier of fact to find Billings guilty of second degree assault with a deadly weapon on count II. [Affirmed.]

Notes and Questions

(1) *Why "Fear in Fact" Assault, Instead of "Actual Injury" Assault, in Billings?* The case appears to support either. But is it possible that either or the two methods of proof would support the same crime of "second degree assault with a deadly weapon," and the appellate court considered the method that was easier to analyze?

(2) *Legislative Choices in Drafting Assault Statutes.* Jurisdictions across the U.S. use widely differing formulations for criminalizing assault. Thus, you need to search various areas of a criminal code to determine what kinds of assaults are criminalized. Furthermore, you will also need to look at offenses that might be labeled "menacing" or "threatening."

(3) *Some Models for Criminalizing Assault, from Precise Definition to Common Law Evolution.* In Ohio's very comprehensive Code, assaults include both batteries and assaults of the attempted battery kind, and different provisions criminalize simple assault, felony assault, and different categories of aggravated assault. Assaults of the "reasonable apprehension of battery" kind are treated as different kinds and degrees of "menacing." *See* Ohio Revised Code 2903.08–2908.37.

By contrast, in Virginia there is no definition in the statute of what "assault" means, so lawyers must turn to common law definitions, as is often the case in that state. In still other states, there is specific legislative prohibition only of the "reasonable apprehension" or intent-to-frighten kind of assault, which may not be labeled assault at all, and attempted battery assaults are prosecuted under attempt statutes. These are just some of the possible statutory formulations for criminalizing assault.

The attempted battery formulation is arguably not a good way to define assault. An attempt is a separately defined crime, and it has elements that are not suited to the assault situation. Consider the next note, in which what looks like an assault turns out not to be one—because of attempt doctrine.

(4) *An Inadequate Definition of Assault May Prevent Law Enforcement from Addressing Real Incidents of Violence—State v. Boutin*, 346 A.2d 531 (Vt. 1975). After a scuffle with his victim, Boutin advanced toward the victim with a bottle raised over his head, from about ten feet away, in obvious preparation to hit the victim with it. Two constables (who became the state's principal witnesses at trial) intervened to end the incident. The state charged Boutin with assault, but the Vermont Supreme Court ordered his acquittal because the Vermont statute provided that a person was guilty of simple assault only if he "attempts to cause or purposely, knowingly, or recklessly causes bodily injury to another." Boutin had not caused any actual injury, and he was not physically close enough to complete a criminal "attempt" to injure. And Vermont had no intent-to-frighten assault provision. How

would the result in *Boutin* change if Vermont had an intent-to-frighten provision? Would the addition increase public safety in such conditions?

(5) *What Is a Deadly Weapon, and Why Does It Matter?* The usual definition includes virtually any object, provided it is used in a manner likely to cause death or serious bodily injury. The author of this book who resides in Oregon reports having seen cases in which steel-toed boots, feet, scalding water, and a concrete floor were deadly weapons, but a hand was not. The author who resides in Texas recalls cases in which a car, a coat hanger, and "a salt shaker and her [the defendant's] feet" became deadly weapons — because of the way they were used. A finding that the defendant used a deadly weapon matters, because it may support a higher grade of assaultive offense with a greater sentence.

[B] Gradations of Assault and Assault-Related Crimes

Read Model Penal Code § 211.1(1) (Assault); § 211.1(2) (Aggravated Assault); as well as § 211.2 (Recklessly Endangering Another Person); § 211.3 (Terroristic Threats) (and consider them in the context of § 210.0 (Definitions)), in the MPC Appendix.

Notes on Interpreting Assault Provisions

(1) *Consider State v. Boutin Under These MPC Provisions.* In *State v. Boutin*, above, two constables arrived on the scene and saw defendant Boutin walking toward another man with a bottle raised over his head, and the other man backing away. Boutin was convicted under a Vermont statute that said, "A person is guilty of simple assault if he . . . attempts to cause or purposely, knowingly, or recklessly causes bodily injury to another." But because the evidence showed no bodily injury and was insufficient to prove a criminal attempt, the court ordered Boutin's acquittal.

Now, consider how this case would be dealt with under the MPC sections above. Those definitions are simpler and cover intent, knowledge, or recklessness (depending on the circumstances) in causing injury or fear. Is Boutin provably guilty beyond a reasonable doubt of any offenses defined in the MPC? Consider whether the MPC is more congruent with policy than the statute in *Boutin*.

(2) *How Close to Successful Perpetration Must the Attempted Battery Be?* In the case of attempted battery assaults, a special issue in attempt law arises: when does a perpetrator cross the line between mere preparation, which is insufficient to constitute attempt, and criminal perpetration? The *Boutin* court held that, "To constitute an attempt to commit a crime, the act must be of such a character as to advance the conduct of the actor beyond the sphere of mere intent. It must reach far enough towards the accomplishment of the desired result to amount to the commencement of the consummation. Here the holding of a bottle in one hand ten feet from the

intended victim does not make it likely to end in the consummation of the crime intended." Do you agree with this logic?

(3) *Criminalizing "Reckless" Assaults. See* MPC 211.2 for an example of a provision criminalizing an assault where the specific intent to injure need not be proven. Recklessness is enough. Is it appropriate to criminalize injury that cannot be proven to have been intentional?

(4) *Other, Related Offenses.* Note that the MPC defines a number of what might be called assault-related offenses. Some conduct that should be criminalized does not fit precisely within the definition of assault, and therefore the MPC defines crimes of "reckless endangerment" and "terroristic threats," among others. It also defines "aggravated assault," which includes more serious assaults with enhanced sentences. Consider the following problem.

Problem 5A (Assaultive Offenses): "Is It a Crime, and If So, Which One?"

(1) *Hypothetical Cases, Using These MPC Provisions.* Consider the following hypothetical problems and evaluate whether they constitute any crime, and if so, of what grade, under the MPC provisions assigned above.

(a) *Just a Simple Assault?* The defendant unjustifiably beats a victim with his fists, causing serious bleeding and bruising. Do you agree that this should be classed as nothing more serious than a simple assault? If not, how would you change the MPC to achieve the result that you think is appropriate?

(b) *Now, Is This Aggravated Assault?* The same defendant also knocks out one of the victim's teeth.

(c) *Negligent Injury to a Child: Not an Assault?* A parent clumsily drops an infant on the floor, causing severe brain injury. The parent has a blood alcohol level of 0.16, twice that defined as intoxication for driving in many jurisdictions, and is holding a bottle of gin in one hand. [Note: Under § 211.1, assault requires at least "recklessness." Imagine that this parent is subjectively unaware of the risk because of intoxication or that, for other reasons, the jury rejects recklessness and finds the parent only negligent; then, is this defendant guilty of any crime? Many jurisdictions define a crime of child endangerment, which requires only negligence *and the creation of risk of harm to a child.* Can you explain why this additional crime might be needed?]

(d) *Reckless Endangerment (or Assault)?* The defendant points a pistol at a location a few inches over the victim's head, but does not discharge the pistol.

(e) *Simple or Aggravated Assault?* The defendant discharges a pistol which or she he believes contains live ammunition, intending to injure the victim, but the pistol contains blank ammunition.

(f) *Terroristic Threat.* The defendant, at an airport security checkpoint, jokes that "I've got nothing in these suitcases except a couple of bombs." (*See also* 18 USC § 35 (the federal "Bomb Hoax Act").)

(2) *Statutory Words That Lead to Surprising Results.* Reconsider the MPC definition of serious bodily injury. Notice that an assault can seem very serious, involving what seems to be a serious injury, but still not qualify for "aggravated assault" classification because the injury does not amount to "serious bodily injury" under the strict MPC definition. Should it be revised?

Problem 5B: Can Leaving a Firearm in the Wrong Place Become an Assault?

(1) *A Child Finds a Firearm, Takes It, and Causes Injury: State v. Bauer,* 295 P.3d 1227 (Wash. Ct. App. 2013). Bauer, an adult, left a loaded .45 pistol on a dresser. His girlfriend's young son took the firearm to school and kept it in his backpack. But he handled the backpack so that the gun discharged and injured another child. The State of Washington charged Bauer with third-degree assault, which is defined so that criminal negligence suffices for conviction if an injury results.

(2) *Can These Circumstances Prove an Assault by Bauer?* The criminal negligence standard under the Washington statute, said the court, could support conviction, because criminal negligence in turn was defined as failure to be aware of a substantial risk of harm, with the lack of awareness being a "gross deviation" from ordinary care. But unfortunately, leaving a firearm on a dresser, though careless, is behavior that some ordinary people do engage in; Bauer presumably would argue that if what he did was negligence, it was simple negligence and not a gross deviation. Should a jury decide that Bauer's conduct was a criminally negligent assault?

(3) *Higher Degrees of Mens Rea: What Result?* Some definitions of assault require recklessness, and some require intent or knowledge (especially for aggravated levels of assault). Thus, the Model Penal Code requires extreme recklessness for aggravated assault causing serious bodily injury, and it requires purpose (*i.e.,* intent) or knowledge for aggravated assault committed by use of a deadly weapon. What would happen if Bauer were charged under an assault statute that required extreme recklessness, or a statute that required purpose, or knowledge?

[C] Specific versus General Intent in Enhanced Assault Statutes

United States v. Kimes

(In Chapter 3, Section 3.07[A] above)

An excerpt from this case appears in Chapter 3, above, and you should reconsider it at this point. 18 U.S.C. § 111 (a)(1) prohibits an assault on a federal officer. But the statute does not specify whether it creates a general intent (that the defendant intended to perform the physical act proscribed by the statute; the defendant need not have intended the consequences of that act), or specific intent crime (for which the government has to prove beyond a reasonable doubt that the alleged assailant knew that his victim was a federal officer). The difference is important, because if the offense is one of general intent, then the defendant can be guilty even without knowing that the victim is a federal officer and without specifically intending to hurt him, whereas if the offense requires specific intent, the defendant cannot be guilty unless he knows that the victim is a federal officer and intends to injure. One dramatic context arises when a federal officer works under cover to infiltrate a heroin or cocaine conspiracy. Because of some real or imagined slight, the other coconspirators assault the officer, not knowing that he is a federal officer.

The Supreme Court earlier had held that the crime required only general intent. In other words, the defendant must intend to assault a person, but the defendant does not need to know that the person assaulted is a federal officer. *United States v. Feola*, 420 U.S. 671 (1975). At the same time, the Supreme Court pointed out that knowledge of the victim's status could still matter in some cases, because "there may be circumstances in which ignorance of the official status of the person assaulted negates the very existence of *mens rea*" (*i.e.*, it negates the existence of an assault). The Court gave the example of a federal officer who fails to identify himself, so that the defendant believes he is being attacked, has the right to self-defense, and does not commit an assault at all.

The Court's reference is obviously to the intent to assault, not to knowledge that the victim is a federal officer. But some lower courts have confused the issue. For example, in United States v. Caruana, 652 F.2d 220 (1st Cir. 1981), which surprisingly does not cite *Feola*, the court used the term "specific intent," but knowledge of the officer's official status was not in issue there, because it was obvious. The specific intent that the court mentioned must have referred only to the intent to assault. *See generally United States v. Ettinger*, 344 F.3d 1149 (11th Cir. 2003) (pointing out that majority of circuits, following *Feola*, hold that the crime requires only general intent; distinguishing cases like *Caruana*). Question: Why does the specific-intent-versus-general-intent issue cause so much confusion?

Notes and Questions

(1) *Is It Sound Policy to Create a Requirement of Specific Intent for Aggravated Types of Assault, and to Find Only Simple Assault if Specific Intent is Absent?: Maher v. People*, 10 Mich. 212 (1862). Maher shot his victim in the head in an attempt to kill him. Understandably, the jury convicted him of the crime of "assault with intent to murder." But the Michigan Supreme Court reversed because Maher may have acted in the heat of passion. If so, said the court, a successful killing would have been voluntary manslaughter, not murder; the specific intent "to murder" would have been absent. Therefore, Maher would have been guilty only of simple assault. Should an assault with intent to kill, with a firearm, become a mere simple assault under these circumstances, or a relatively minor misdemeanor?

(2) *The "Assault-with-(Specific)-Intent-To" Formula—and Alternatives.* Is it a good idea to create a proliferation of "assault-with-specific-intent-to" crimes? These offenses depend on precise readings of subjective factors, and they leave odd gaps (as in *Maher*).

(3) *The MPC Approach to Aggravated Assault: Objective Definition.* The MPC approach does not require specific intent to constitute an assault or an aggravated assault when there is an actual, serious bodily injury. Under MPC § 211.1, knowledge or recklessness is sufficient, and negligence can suffice for assault where there is an actual injury and a deadly weapon is used. For aggravated assault there must be proof beyond a reasonable doubt of "serious bodily injury" (a specifically defined, objective standard), or an attempt to cause it. However, if defendant uses a deadly weapon, the prosecution need show only mere "bodily injury" to establish aggravated assault.

The effect of the MPC is that "aggravated" assault is not tested by "intent to kill," "intent to rob," or similarly fine gradations of mens rea, but rather by objective factors: serious bodily injury (which is objectively defined) or use of a deadly weapon. Do these approaches make sense?

[D] Offensive Assault and Battery, without Threat of Injury — and Consent as Negating the Crime

Notes and Questions

(1) *Offensive Touching without Actual Injury as Assault or Battery: The Model Penal Code and Other Approaches.* Model Penal Code § 211.1 criminalizes conduct causing physical injury as assault, using the formula "causes bodily injury," but it does not criminalize offensive touching. Many other jurisdictions do. *See United States v. Bayes*, 210 F.3d 64 (1st Cir. 2000), for an example of an offensive touching (of a flight attendant's buttocks) constituting battery. In jurisdictions that criminalize offensive touching as battery, spitting can constitute the actus reus. *See e.g. United States v. Masel*, 563 F.2d 322 (7th Cir. 1977). Consider whether the Model Penal Code is wrong in failing to provide a provision for offensive touching. Shouldn't spitting on another person be a crime?

(2) *How Much Force Is Required for Battery or Assault?: A Laser Pointer Is Enough — Adams v. Commonwealth*, 534 S.E.2d 347 (Va. Ct. App. 2000). The force required for battery may be direct or indirect, through an object or a force. In *Adams*, a twelfth-grade student shone a laser pointer in a police officer's eyes. While surrendering the pointer, the defendant said, "It can't hurt you." But the officer testified that he had felt a "stinging sensation," and the defendant testified that he "saw [the officer] flinch" when he was "hit" by the laser. The jury convicted the defendant both of assault and of battery, with the latter crime being defined as "the actual infliction of corporal hurt on another (*e.g.*, the least touching of another's person, wilfully or in anger, whether by the party's own hand, or by some means set in motion by him)." The court of appeals rejected the defendant's arguments (1) that he had caused no "corporal hurt" and (2) that he had not been proved to have the requisite "wilfulness" or intent to injure, and it affirmed this laser-pointer conviction. Does this analysis make sense? (Note that assault and battery of a police officer under the law applicable to Adams called for a mandatory 6-month prison sentence.)

(3) *What if the "Victim" Consents?—From Football to Injurious Sadomasochism.* In some circumstances, consent is a defense to assault or battery. Thus, consent prevents a football player from being guilty of assault each time he tackles an opposing runner or a doctor from being guilty of assault each time she performs surgery. The Model Penal Code explains this as "negativing an element of the offense" or precluding the harm or evil sought to be prevented by the law defining the offense. Model Penal Code § 2.11.

The consent defense has its limits. Other than in the medical context, consent does not permit the infliction of serious injury. Moreover, the harm must be within the scope of the consent. For example, a football player consents to being blocked by an opposing player but does not consent to being stabbed by that player. Model Penal Code § 2.11(2)(b) explains this by noting that the conduct and injury must be "reasonable foreseeable hazards of joint participation in a lawful athletic contest . . . or other concerted activity not forbidden by law."

While consent is a traditional defense in assault-type cases, the controversial case of *R. v. Brown* [1994] 1 A.C. 212, rejected it as against public policy in an unusual context. *Brown* involved charges against a group of men who privately engaged in consensual sadomasochistic sexual activity. The House of Lords held that while the prosecutor usually was required to prove lack of consent to obtain an assault conviction, consent was irrelevant in this case because "such encounters are injurious to the participants and unpredictably dangerous," and it was "in the public interest that society should be protected from the possibility and danger of the proselytization and corruption of young men by such cult violence."

On the other hand, consent furnished a defense in *Guarro v. United States*, 237 F.2d 578 (D.C. Cir. 1956), where the court found the consent of a plain clothes policeman apparently working a movie theater with a view to arresting patrons for making homosexual advances to him was a defense to a battery of the offensive sexual touching kind. Defendant approached the undercover officer in the lobby of a theater and engaged the officer in conversation about the movie, then reached down and "touched the officer's "private parts." The court reasoned that "[g]enerally where there is consent, there is no assault." For discussion of these issues, see Vera Bergelson, *The Right to Be Hurt: Testing the Boundaries of Consent*, 75 George Washington L. Rev. 165 (2007).

§ 5.02 Beyond Assault: Stalking and Harassment — and Legislative Attempts to Address Them

While the crime of assault reaches conduct inducing fear of physical harm, there are many subtle forms of fear-causing actions that may be too inconclusive or ambiguous to merit an assault conviction. We have all heard of people who make repeated efforts to bother others. For example, a rejected suitor may make hundreds of hang-up phone calls to the person who rejected him or may follow the person by foot or automobile, causing considerable inconvenience at the least and even fear of physical harm, including death. The problem with criminalizing such conduct is that it often involves ordinarily legal activities. The stalker has a right to walk the streets or use the phone. On the other hand, at some point the stalker's rights must be curtailed to protect the victim. Jurisdictions today have enacted crimes called "stalking" or "harassment" to deal with these situations.

Notes on Anti-Stalking Statutes

(1) *Stalking Statutes: There Is No Common Law Antecedent.* Stalking statutes are a legislative response to a late twentieth century social phenomenon. The common law did not criminalize it, but now it is covered by legislation in every state and by 18 U.S.C. § 2261A. A model anti-stalking act was drafted in 1993, but it has not been adopted uniformly or in full. Some victims' advocates have also argued that it should be revised to reflect current understandings of stalking behavior. *See* National Center for Victims of Crime, *The Model Stalking Code, Revisited: Responding to the New Realities of Stalking* (2007).

(2) *Cyber-Stalking.* The phenomenon of "cyber-stalking" has led some legislatures to amend their anti-stalking provisions to cover this conduct.

(3) *Constitutional Challenges Based on Vagueness and Overbreadth.* Anti-stalking provisions sometimes encounter legality challenges on the basis of alleged vagueness or overbreadth, although most statutes have been written so that the challenges have been unsuccessful, as was the case with challenges to the District of Columbia's first stalking statute. *See United States v. Smith*, 685 A.2d 380 (D.C. 1996). (Chapter 13 provides a more extended discussion of constitutional challenges.)

Nonetheless, D.C. repealed its earlier stalking statute and replaced it with an entirely new version. *See* D.C. Code §§ 22–3131–3135. The central provision is the following:

§ 22–3133. Stalking

(a) It is unlawful for a person to purposefully engage in a course of conduct directed at a specific individual:

(1) With the intent to cause that individual to:

(A) Fear for his or her safety or the safety of another person;

(B) Feel seriously alarmed, disturbed, or frightened; or

(C) Suffer emotional distress;

(2) That the person knows would cause that individual reasonably to:

(A) Fear for his or her safety or the safety of another person;

(B) Feel seriously alarmed, disturbed, or frightened; or

(C) Suffer emotional distress; or

(3) That the person should have known would cause a reasonable person in the individual's circumstances to:

(A) Fear for his or her safety or the safety of another person;

(B) Feel seriously alarmed, disturbed, or frightened; or

(C) Suffer emotional distress.

(b) This section does not apply to constitutionally protected activity.

(c) Where a single act is of a continuing nature, each 24-hour period constitutes a separate occasion.

(d) The conduct on each of the occasions need not be the same as it is on the others.

Does this more recent statute improve on the earlier version? Why or why not?

(4) *Repeated Conduct Plus a Threat: Commonwealth v. Cullen*, 947 N.E.2d 1147 (Mass. Ct. App. 2011). Many jurisdictions have addressed concerns about their stalking statutes by requiring a threat in addition to repeated contact. But what is a "threat"? In this case, repeated reference to the "Latin Kings," a violent gang, was held "sufficiently explicit," together with a message saying, "look over your shoulders 4 life," to prove a threat. Should it be necessary to prove a threat?

(5) *But the Need to Survive Constitutional Challenges Arguably Means That Statutes Must Be Drawn So That They Do Not Adequately Protect Victims.* Surviving vagueness challenges necessarily means limited scope in the statutory definition, and this, in turn, may mean a failure to address real harm to victims. Stalking is difficult to address.

(6) *Is Stalking a Precursor to Murder?: State v. Morquecho*, 54 A.3d 609 (Conn. App. Ct. 2012). In a disturbing number of cases, stalking is followed by homicide. In this case, the defendant was convicted of both crimes. Isn't one of the goals of an anti-stalking statute to prevent more serious crimes? Consider the following problem.

Problem 5C (Stalking): "I Just Know He's Going to Kill Me"

(1) *The Frightening Library Patron and the Strange Student Who Features Real People as Victims in Violent Stories.* A distraught employee of a public library consults security officers to report that a patron, who "looks weird," shows up regularly and stands behind a column to stare at her. On one occasion, she says, she encountered him by accident face to face, and he "looked angry" while making a vague reference to her that was not exactly a threat but that suggested violence to her. "I just know that he's going to follow me and kill me." Or: A student who customarily wears a black trenchcoat and Nazi gear, similar to those worn by notorious perpetrators of highly-publicized school violence, circulates a fictional "story" that features himself torturing and killing an instructor (or another student).

(2) *Real Harm, but the Law Probably Does Not Address It.* These examples are adapted from real cases. They scare individuals out of their wits, frighten them into changing their lives, and cause real harm. But, are they covered by either version of the District of Columbia stalking statute above?

§ 5.03 Beyond Assault: Domestic Violence Legislation

Notes on Special Law Enforcement Provisions in Domestic Violence Cases

(1) *Domestic Violence and Assault.* When a spouse or lover or parent or child strikes another member of the "family," it is very likely that an assault or battery occurs. Nevertheless, because many people regard existing assault and battery laws as inadequate to prevent and punish domestic violence, American jurisdictions have adopted specialized laws addressing the problem.

(2) *A Historical Note from Long Ago: The "Rule of Thumb": Henry A. Kelly, The Rule of Thumb and the Folklaw of the Husband's Stick*, 44 J. Legal Educ. 341 (1994). Some scholars suggest that early authority allowed husbands a right of physical "chastisement" of their wives, although others dispute the existence of such an historical rule. This doctrine is referred to as the "rule of thumb," that is, that it entitled a husband to use a stick no thicker than his thumb to "discipline" his wife.

(3) *Moving Domestic Violence into the "Public Sphere": Elizabeth M. Schneider, Battered Women: Feminist Lawmaking and the Struggle for Equality* (2000). Assaults and other criminal violence within the context of family, romantic, or intimate relationships historically have been underprosecuted, and many would claim that they still are. The reasons vary. For example, law enforcement officers often complain (correctly, in some instances) about the reluctance of domestic violence witnesses to approve criminal complaints or to testify, and theorists point to the law's reluctance to regulate the "private sphere" of the home. Professor Schneider's work offers a history of feminist-driven law reform (for example, by providing civil protection orders and the range of responses under the Federal Violence Against Women Act).

(4) *The Enormous Volume of Domestic Violence.* The Department of Justice's Bureau of Justice Statistics reports in its National Crime Victimization Survey for 2011 that, out of an estimated 5,805,430 crimes of violence committed that year, 851,340 (or nearly 15%) involved "intimate partners" (defined as "current or former spouses, boyfriends, or girlfriends"), and another 502,000 (or nearly 9%) involved other "family members." The total was 1,353,340 violent crimes, more than 23% of the total. See Crime Victimization, 2011 (Oct. 2012).

(5) *An Example of the Law's Response: The New Jersey Prevention of Domestic Violence Act.* Many jurisdictions address domestic violence with special legislation, even when the acts in question already are criminal offenses. The policy behind such legislation is articulated in the New Jersey Prevention of Domestic Violence Act, as follows:

> ... The Legislature ... finds and declares that even though many of the existing criminal statutes are applicable to acts of domestic violence, previous societal attitudes concerning domestic violence have affected the response of our law enforcement and judicial systems, resulting in these

acts receiving different treatment from similar crimes when they occur in a domestic context. . . .

It is the intent of the Legislature to stress that the primary duty of a law enforcement officer when responding to a domestic violence call is to enforce the laws allegedly violated and to protect the victim. . . . It is further intended that the official response to domestic violence shall communicate the attitude that violent behavior will not be excused or tolerated, and shall make clear the fact that the [law] will be enforced without regard to the fact that the violence grows out of a domestic situation.

(6) *Depriving Peace Officers of Discretion by Imposing Mandatory Duties of Arrest and Seizure: A Partial Remedy?* One partial solution is to require—not merely to authorize, but to require—mandatory arrests of perpetrators of domestic violence. But this statement begs the question: under what circumstances? As you read the New Jersey statute (which is excerpted below), try to pinpoint when this duty arises. Also, you should take note of how different this mandatory duty is from the normal discretion afforded to law enforcement officers (which many would defend as necessary for sound criminal justice administration).

(7) *Prosecutions That Override the Preferences of Unwilling Victims: Another Partial Remedy?* Another idea adopted by some district attorneys is to prosecute as a matter of policy even if the victim seeks dismissal—or even if the victim refuses to testify. Historically, large percentages of domestic victims have filed "affidavits of nonprosecution" or similar documents, saying that the alleged events did not occur as reported, that the defendants' conduct was subject to a defense ("I hit him first"), or simply that the victims wished not to prosecute. The frequency of dismissals meant that officers were reluctant to arrest, and prosecutors were unwilling to charge whenever they perceived an uncooperative victim. The filing of large volumes of unprosecutable offenses is detrimental to the criminal justice system, and perhaps this was the reason. But nonprosecution had disadvantages. It sent the message that the crime was tolerable, left survivors unprotected, and created automatic credibility gaps for repeat victims. It also probably encouraged perpetrators to negotiate with victims at an emotional level, to use dependency of victims as a bargaining chip, or even to make tacit or express threats to harm the victim unless the victim refused to pursue prosecution.

(8) *Compelled Victim Testimony and Victimless Prosecution.* Prosecution in spite of the victim's wishes may tend to counteract these disadvantages. Therefore, some district attorneys have adopted this approach as a matter of policy. They prosecute by subpoena of victims even if the victims plead for dismissal. Sometimes, they apply this policy even if the victim recants or cannot be forced to testify—by undertaking "victimless prosecutions" that use evidence from 911 calls, physical evidence, children, bystanders, or other circumstances. In *State v. Mizenko*, 127 P.3d 458 (Mont. 2006), the court interpreted evidence law so as to facilitate victimless prosecution (and affirmed a conviction for "Partner or Family Member Assault").

(9) *Changes in Evidence Rules: The Example of Spousal Privileges.* Prosecutions with unwilling victims historically were very difficult, because evidence rules privileged spouses to refuse to testify. Some jurisdictions have changed this privilege to make exceptions for domestic violence. Therefore, after the New Jersey statute that follows, we have included materials describing one particular prosecution that overrode the desires (and the claims of privilege not to testify) of an unwilling victim.

[A] Mandatory Arrest in Domestic Violence Cases

The New Jersey Prevention of Domestic Violence Act

N. J. Stat. Ann. Ch. 25

2C:25–19. Definitions. [The statute designates nineteen existing offenses as "domestic violence," ranging from homicide to lewdness. It also defines who is protected.]

2C:25–20. Training course and curriculum; domestic crisis teams. [This provision requires every law enforcement officer to attend a training course developed by the Division of Criminal Justice, with specified subjects related to domestic violence. It also requires training for judges.]

2C:25–21. Arrest; criminal complaint; seizure of weapons [imposing mandatory arrest and weapon seizure].

a. When a person claims to be a victim of domestic violence, and where a law enforcement officer responding to the incident finds probable cause to believe that domestic violence has occurred, the law enforcement officer shall arrest the person who is alleged to be the person who subjected the victim to domestic violence and shall sign a criminal complaint if:

(1) The victim exhibits signs of injury caused by an act of domestic violence; [or]

(2) A warrant is in effect; [or]

(3) There is probable cause to believe that the person has violated [a domestic relations order], and there is probable cause to believe that the person has been served with the order alleged to have been violated. If the victim does not have a copy of a purported order, the officer may verify the existence of an order with the appropriate law enforcement agency; or

(4) There is probable cause to believe that a weapon as defined [by law] has been involved in the commission of an act of domestic violence. . . .

2C:25–22. Immunity from civil liability. [This section immunizes from civil liability officers who act in good faith under this law.]

Notes and Questions

(1) *Mandatory Arrest: The Policy Arguments for and Against.* Consider the policies that can be argued to support mandatory arrest, under New Jersey's statute, outlined above. On the other side of the issue, is it possible that unjust arrests will result, or that there might be other negative policy implications?

(2) *Even if the "Victim" as Well as the "Perpetrator" Denies That the Offense Occurred (as Frequently Happens), the Duty of Mandatory Arrest Still Exists: Wildoner v. Borough of Ramsey,* 744 A.2d 1146 (N.J. 2000). In this case, a New Jersey police officer responding to a domestic violence call was told by both the husband (the alleged perpetrator) and the wife (the alleged victim) that the alleged crime had not occurred at all. (This state of affairs occurs frequently.) The other available information included the officer's observation of a knife on the floor, a red mark on the wife's arm, and a seventy-year-old neighbor's report of loud and abusive language by the husband, featuring a threat to "throw knives." Could these circumstances trigger the statute's mandatory duty of arrest?

Yes, said the court. Nothing indicated that the neighbor's complaint was motivated by anything but concern for the wife's safety, but by inference, both husband and wife had motives to fabricate. The officer should "consider" the wife's denial, but the "totality of the circumstances" furnished probable cause here, and probable cause, in turn, is what creates the mandatory duty. A principal purpose of the arrest, said the court, was to remove the alleged perpetrator and allow the parties time to cool off. Is this result sound policy, or is it undue interference with the freedom of a citizen, who almost certainly cannot be convicted?

(3) *What about Violence Flowing from a Dating Relationship?: D.C. v. F.R.,* 670 A.2d 51 (N.J. App. Div. 1996). Imagine an estranged boyfriend or girlfriend who has never shared a residence with the victim, but who commits an act of domestic violence after their relationship no longer exists. Is this act covered by the statute? Yes, said the court, citing the definition section, which includes "a dating relationship."

(4) *It Can Be Hard to Draw the Line as to Appropriate Application of These Statutes: Kamen v. Egan,* 730 A.2d 873 (NJ Super. Ct. App. Div. 1999). In this case, a daughter committed a single act of trespass by entering her father's home without his permission to visit her children who resided there, on a day that was not a court-ordered visitation day. Trespass is not one of the designated domestic violence offenses, but it was argued that the New Jersey Act applied because the daughter's conduct threatened the commission of domestic violence. The court held the Act inapplicable.

(5) *Can a Police Department Defeat This Law Simply by Not enforcing It?: Town of Castle Rock v. Gonzales,* 545 U.S. 748 (2005). The answer seems to be yes. Here, a woman had obtained a restraining order as part of her divorce proceedings. Her husband took their children in violation of the order. She repeatedly notified the police

of the violation. A statute made police enforcement of such orders mandatory, but as a matter of policy, this department took no action until the husband showed up at the police department and opened fire—at which point they shot and killed him and then discovered in his truck the bodies of their three children whom he had already murdered. The woman filed a civil rights suit, claiming that the police violated her due process rights by failing to follow the mandatory language. The Supreme Court held that no civil rights liability arose in this "horrible" situation.

[B] Rejecting Victims' Nonprosecution Requests in Domestic Violence Cases

Problem 5D (Domestic Violence): The Trial of Warren Moon for Allegedly Assaulting Felicia Moon—A Report of a Prosecution Featuring an Unwilling Witness

[Based upon newspaper reports beginning July 19, 1995]

(1) *The Initial Evidence Supporting the Prosecution of Warren Moon: Felicia Moon's Complaint.* On July 18, 1995, Felicia Moon, married to Minnesota Vikings quarterback Warren Moon, gave a statement to police in which she charged her husband with having struck and choked her until she "saw black and could not breathe." She feared for her life, she said, and she apparently fled in her car with her husband pursuing her at speeds up to 100 mph. Police photographs showed injuries to her face, including scratches and abrasions. Her son, Jeffrey, also made an emergency telephone call describing the alleged assault. Under these facts, the state where the couple resided charged Warren Moon with Class A misdemeanor assault and subpoenaed both Felicia and Jeffrey.

(2) *But Then, Felicia Moon Resisted the Prosecution She Had Initiated.* Several months after the event, however, Felicia Moon filed a motion to quash the subpoenas. She declared that she was not a battered woman but was "an independent, strong-minded, college-educated woman who wants the State to stay out of her bedroom." She alleged that her family was singled out because of celebrity status: "Leave me, my privacy and the sanctity of my marriage alone." She denied any coercion or intimidation by her husband. Forcing her son Jeffrey to testify would "damage his fragile emotional health" because he was "extremely devoted to his father." Finally, Felicia stated that she would invoke the Fifth Amendment and refuse to testify anyway, unless granted "full immunity." *See* Patti Muck, *Felicia Moon Wants Subpoenas Dropped*, Hous. Chronicle, §A, at 1, col. 1 (1996).

(3) *But if Granted Immunity, Felicia Moon Had No Privilege Not to Testify.* Article 38.10 of the state's Code of Criminal Procedure deliberately removed any privilege of a spouse not to testify in a domestic violence case:

> *Exceptions to the Spousal Adverse Testimony Privilege.* The privilege of a person's spouse not to be called as a witness for the state does not apply in any proceeding in which the person is charged with a crime committed

against the person's spouse, a minor child, or a member of the household of either spouse.

Questions:

(1) "Victimless" Prosecution. What chance is there of successful prosecution of Warren without Felicia's testimony?

(2) Testimonial Privilege. Are there sound policies underlying the privilege of a spouse not to testify involuntarily, and if so, are there overriding policies for abolishing it here?

(3) Official Discretion. A District Attorney has wide discretion over initiation of prosecutions or subpoenas. In fact, in this case the District Attorney predicted that he would not call the son, Jeffrey, as a witness. Should the District Attorney exercise discretion to withdraw the subpoenas or decline prosecution here? [Picture a press conference at which a public official justifies such a decision by reference to the college-educated or celebrity status of the participants; consider also whether a fair uniform policy for discretionary dismissal could be devised and applied here.]

(4) Reasons for Reluctance to Testify. What are all of the reasons that might make a victim of domestic violence resist a prosecution after initiating it?

(5) The Self-Incrimination Claim. What is the likely effect of Felicia Moon's self-incrimination claim? In the case, the state gave her immunity and compelled her to testify. Her husband was acquitted by the jury.

(6) Assessing Victim-Resisted Prosecutions. Can the District Attorney justify his policy, here, of prosecuting in spite of the victim's objections?

§ 5.04 Sexual Assault or Rape

[A] The Nature of Sexual Offenses

Notes on the Nature of Sexual Offenses

(1) *Crime of Violence or Crime Violating a Person's Autonomy?* What kind of crime is rape? A wide variety of crimes fall under the category of "sexual offenses." These offenses range from violent sexual attacks to prohibited sexual encounters between adults and minors. The law regarding sexual offenses has changed dramatically over the years. Yet, it still continues to be one of the most challenging areas of criminal law. There is even disagreement as to the very nature of rape. Some view it as a crime of violence, fundamentally the same as any other type of assault. Others see an additional dimension, so that it is also a crime against the survivor's sexual autonomy. *See* Catharine A. MacKinnon, *Feminism Unmodified* 86–87 (1987).

(2) *Challenges in Prosecuting Rape Crimes.* By all accounts, rape is one of the most underreported of all crimes. According to a 2012 report by the U.S. Department of

Justice's Bureau of Justice Statistics, fewer than half of rapes or sexual assaults are reported to the police. *See* Crime Victimization, 2011 (Oct. 2012) (55% reported in 2002, 49% in 2010, and 27% in 2011). Why is this?

(3) *Cultural Miscues.* Sex is a very difficult issue for many people to discuss. Thus, the law regarding sexual assaults must deal with the reality that people do not always clearly communicate their willingness or unwillingness to engage in sexual activity. When there are miscues about the willingness to engage in sexual conduct and the victim does not believe he or she is consenting, but the defendant does, how should the law respond?

[B] The Elements of Sexual Assault

Notes on the Elements of Sexual Assault

(1) *The Definition of Rape.* Many people would define rape as "sex without consent." Yet the law of sexual assault is more complicated than that. Because it is not always clear whether there has been consent, and there was traditionally a fear that men would be falsely accused of the crime, the law of rape has conventionally involved four factors.

(a) *Force.* Traditional definitions of sexual assault require force (or a substitute for it, such as threat or fraud). With evidence of force, courts could ensure that the defendant clearly realized the victim was not consenting to the sexual activity.

(b) *Resistance.* It should come as no surprise that, today, most jurisdictions do not require resistance. But historically, most jurisdictions required resistance to ensure that it was clear the sex was non-consensual. Of course, such a requirement not only makes it more difficult to prove rape, but may not reflect how rape victims actually act. Rather than resist, some victims may simply freeze in the situation. Also, does requiring resistance put victims at greater physical risk?

(c) *Nonconsent.* Perhaps the most obvious element of rape is that the victim does not consent, but mens rea requirements sometimes make this issue confusing. What does that mean? First, it is clear that the victim must not subjectively want to engage in the sexual conduct. Second, in some jurisdictions, there must be some objective manifestation of nonconsent which puts the defendant on notice that the sex is without consent. Third, there is the question whether the defendant must actually realize the victim did not consent or whether it is enough that the defendant should have realized the sex was not consensual. This latter aspect is also addressed in the mens rea requirements for the crime.

(d) *Should Force, or Compulsion, be Enough, Rather than a Requirement that the Defendant "Knows" that the Victim Has Not Consented?* Some modern statutes remove the requirements of a mens rea about consent if the defendant uses force or compulsion. Texas Penal Code § 222.011 defines sexual assault and provides, "A sexual assault . . . is without the consent of the other person if: (1) the actor compels the other person to submit or participate by the use of physical force, violence, or coercion." Thus, if the defendant performs a defined sexual act and uses compulsion of another person, the act is a crime without any requirement that the defendant knows about nonconsent. (Some other types of sexual assaults do require knowledge.)

(e) *Different Mens Rea Requirements.* Jurisdictions vary widely in the degree of mental fault necessary for rape. Some require that the defendant actually know that his victim has not consented. Others only require that the defendant act with "recklessness." Yet others require only "negligence," so that a person is guilty of rape, even if he honestly believes the victim is consenting, but turns out to be wrong and a reasonable person would have realized the victim did not consent. And as is indicated above, some do not require any mens rea about consent if there is compulsion.

(2) *The Traditional Definition of Rape.* The traditional definition of rape set forth by Blackstone was "carnal knowledge of a woman forcibly and against her will." In interpreting this definition, jurisdictions often added that a woman must resist in order to show that the sex was really against her will.

(3) *Should Mistake be a Defense?* Inherent in selecting a definition for rape is the question whether a defendant's mistake should be a defense to the crime. Why should it matter whether the defendant knew the victim did not consent if, in fact, the victim did not consent? Is a defendant negligent or reckless (as is required in some states) if he mistakenly believes a victim has consented? Should it matter whether his mistake is reasonable, or is it enough that he honestly (even if unreasonably) believes the victim has consented?

(4) *Different Crimes for Different Mental States?* As we explore in this chapter the different approaches to rape, consider whether there should be different crimes, with different punishments, depending on whether the defendant knowingly, recklessly or negligently acted without the victim's consent.

(5) *Law Reform: The Special Importance of Statutes Defining Sexual Assault.* There are ongoing efforts to reform the law of rape. The plethora of statutes used by states for sexual offenses reflects this reform movement.

> In the 1950s, the Model Penal Code "abolished the requirement that existed in many states requiring the victim to offer the 'utmost' (or at least 'reasonable') resistance and refocused the crime from the nonconsent of the woman to the conduct of the defendant." The 1970s saw the second wave of reform, prompted by feminist analysis of sexual assault law. Many jurisdictions introduced rape-shield laws [protecting a rape victim's sexual past from disclosure in the rape trial], modified or removed the marital rape exemption [which provided a defense if the victim was the defendant's spouse], [made] rape statutes gender neutral, and made additional alterations in the substantive requirements of force and nonconsent to facilitate convictions.

Penelope Pether, *Critical Discourse Analysis, Rape Law, and the Jury Instruction Simplification Project*, 24 So. Ill. U. L.J. 53, 64 (1991). And today, in some jurisdictions, force or compulsion removes the need for proof of knowledge about nonconsent, as is indicated above. Indeed, the American Law Institute is currently attempting to revise the MPC provisions on sexual assault, which are now badly outdated, despite their reformist origins.

(6) *A Note on Terminology: Should the Crime be Called "Sexual Assault" or "Rape"?* Statutes, cases, and books now use different terms to describe the same or similar offenses. For example, the term "sexual assault" is frequently used now to describe crimes that used to be called "rape." Perhaps "sexual assault" is preferable to a survivor, even if the harsher term, "rape," describes the offensiveness of the crime.

Notes on Problems with Traditional Definitions of the Offense

(1) *The Traditional Definition of Rape.* The traditional definition of rape was "the carnal knowledge of a woman forcibly and against her will." The overlap in requiring both "force" and an act "against her will" masked a basic difficulty in understanding sexual assault law that persists today: How can the act be done with "force" but not be "against her will"? It also concealed the requirement of "utmost resistance" by the survivor that was long a required element of rape. And the traditional definition hid the requirement of mens rea: the defendant's degree of mental culpability in failing to respond to the fact of nonconsent.

(2) *A Problematic Definition: The Force/Nonconsent Paradox.* The traditional requirement of both force and nonconsent means that intercourse accompanied by conduct that many people would construe as the exercise of force may be interpreted by a court, nevertheless, to be consensual. Likewise, clearly nonconsensual sex may not be criminalized because there is inadequate evidence of force, although some would argue that force is implicit in nonconsensual sex. This paradox means that while "very forced" sex, perpetrated with sufficient violence to result in serious bodily injury or death, is relatively likely to result in a conviction, intercourse accompanied or achieved by lesser degrees of force is less likely to be successfully prosecuted, unless the survivor physically resists the perpetrator sufficiently vigorously for him to use extreme force to achieve intercourse.

(3) *A Problematic Definition Involving Mens Rea: Force Combined with Nonconsent May Not Be Enough, Either, Without Adequate Proof of Intent, Knowledge, Recklessness or Criminal Negligence, Depending on the Jurisdiction.* While some states make forcible compulsion enough without proof of nonconsent, many jurisdictions at least in theory require mens rea on the defendant's part as well as force and nonconsent. When mens rea is in issue, this requirement may mean that even if he used force that overcomes nonconsent, the defendant cannot be found guilty unless the prosecution proves intent, knowledge, recklessness or negligence, depending on the statute, as to nonconsent.

(4) *A Problematic Definition Involving Actus Reus: The Overlap of the Force, Nonconsent, and Resistance Requirements.* Additionally, the persistence of the force and resistance requirements may mean that saying "no" may not be enough. Verbal

resistance may not meet the test for resistance on the one hand, and where there is an allegation that the sex was consensual, clear verbal nonconsent may be held to be consistent with unforced sex on the other. While some courts have required no more than contextually "reasonable" resistance, others have held that a survivor must resist "the attack in every way possible," continuing "such resistance until . . . overcome by force, insensible through fright, or cease[s] resistance from exhaustion, fear of death or great bodily harm," *King v. State*, 357 S.W.2d 42, 45 (Tenn. 1962).

[C] Mens Rea for Rape or Sexual Assault under Modern Statutes

[1] *Abolishing Mens Rea as to Nonconsent if There Is Force*

Uniform Code of Military Justice

Art. 120 Rape and sexual assault generally

(a) **Rape.**—Any person subject to this chapter who commits a sexual act upon another person by—

(1) using unlawful force against that other person;

(2) using force causing or likely to cause death or grievous bodily harm to any person;

(3) threatening or placing that other person in fear that any person will be subjected to death, grievous bodily harm, or kidnapping;

(4) first rendering that other person unconscious; or

(5) administering to that other person by force or threat of force, or without the knowledge or consent of that person, a drug, intoxicant, or other similar substance and thereby substantially impairing the ability of that other person to appraise or control conduct;

is guilty of rape and shall be punished as a court-martial may direct . . . .

. . . .

(g) **Definitions.**—In this section:

. . . .

(4) **Force.**—The term "force" means—

(A) the use of a weapon;

(B) the use of such physical strength or violence as is sufficient to overcome, restrain, or injure a person; or

(C) inflicting physical harm sufficient to coerce or compel submission by the victim. . . .

(7) Consent.—

(A) The term "consent" means a freely given agreement to the conduct at issue by a competent person. An expression of lack of consent through words or conduct means there is no consent. Lack of verbal or physical resistance does not constitute consent. Submission resulting from the use of force, threat of force, or placing another person in fear also does not constitute consent. A current or previous dating or social or sexual relationship by itself or the manner of dress of the person involved with the accused in the conduct at issue does not constitute consent. [Following provisions define situations of nonconsent.] . . .

[Other sections of the article define lesser crimes called "sexual assault," "aggravated sexual contact," and "abusive sexual contact."]

Note on the Structure of the Statute

(1) *Rape Does Not Require Knowledge of Nonconsent under Article 120.* Four of the five means of committing rape do not require lack of consent. Under provision (a) (1)-(3), for example, certain kinds of force or threats are sufficient, without other proof of mens rea except the intent to commit the act.

(2) *Lesser but Related Offenses.* Notice that the statute defines several other crimes that are less serious than rape. (Those definitions are not set out here. If the jury finds reasonable doubt about rape, it can convict on a lesser crime.) Is this a good idea?

(3) *What Is the Effect of This Statute?* If there are certain kinds of force, the government does not need to prove anything about the survivor's nonconsent or the defendant's knowledge of it. The government also does not need to prove recklessness or even negligence if there is this kind of force. And this feature of the law supports convictions that would be impossible under some other laws. Consider the following case.

United States v. Coble

U.S. Navy-Marine Corps Court of Criminal Appeals.
2017 WL 712787 (unpublished opinion)

HUTCHISON, JUDGE:

[This is a sexual assault case in the U.S. Coast Guard ranks. Ensign H ("ENS H") alleges she is a survivor of an assault by the defendant (appellant here). Defendant/appellant alleges his encounter with her was voluntary (although at times he alleged it didn't happen). This military court uses initials instead of names for witnesses.]

I. Background

. . . United States Coast Guard Ensign (ENS) H, a trainee pilot, reported to flight training at NAS Whiting Field, Florida. She met the appellant, an instructor pilot, while conducting her aircraft egress training. After learning that ENS H had served with a friend of his who was also a Coast Guard pilot, the appellant requested and was granted permission to serve as the "on-wing" instructor pilot for ENS H. While serving as the "on-wing," the appellant and ENS H had sexually charged conversations that eventually escalated into phone sex and flirtatious behavior. While on a detachment to New Mexico, . . . the appellant accompanied ENS H on her last training flight, replacing another instructor. During the flight, ENS H and the appellant had another sexually charged conversation, and after landing, ENS H told the appellant they were "never having sex," to which the appellant replied, "I know."

After both returned to their separate (but nearby) hotel billeting, the appellant, ENS H, and three other instructors went to dinner, where ENS H and the appellant consumed alcohol. Afterwards, the group returned to the lobby of the instructors' hotel and continued to drink. While seated next to ENS H, the appellant surreptitiously placed his room key on the table adjacent to where ENS H was seated. The appellant then, trying to conceal his invitation from the other instructors, texted ENS H and encouraged her to join him in his room. ENS H took the room key but responded to the text and declined the appellant's request. Instead, ENS H returned to her room and changed into "underwear, sweatpants and a sports bra." Shortly after ENS H departed, and while the appellant remained in the lobby of his hotel, he was informed by a hotel employee that there was an incoming telephone call for him on the hotel's phone. The appellant testified that the phone call came from ENS H; the employee that answered the phone testified that the caller identified herself as the appellant's wife, but noticed that the Caller ID indicated the call came from ENS H's hotel. ENS H testified that she did not remember making any call. After the appellant received the phone call he went directly to ENS H's room.

The appellant knocked on ENS H's door and kissed her when she opened it. She kissed him back, then, "realized what was going on, and . . . pushed him off," saying "we can't do this." Though "hazy," ENS H then recalls the appellant being on top of her, holding her wrists down, and "squeezing them tightly," while "trying to insert his penis into [her] vagina"; while she said, "[n]o," the appellant persisted and started "laughing," saying "I didn't know how strong you were," and "[y]ou're such a tease." Finally, ENS H "laid there, and . . . let him put his penis inside [her]" because she "couldn't fight him back anymore." The next morning, ENS H made restricted reports of sexual assault to a Sexual Assault Response Coordinator and the squadron flight surgeon and went on emergency leave.

[Soon after,] ENS H made a pretext phone call to the appellant which was recorded by Naval Criminal Investigative Service (NCIS). During the call the appellant acknowledged that ENS H told him "no" and "stop" and was squirming, but reiterated that he thought she was being "playful." The appellant asserted that at no time did he force ENS H, reminding her that "when you would say like, '[s]top,' I was like, '[h]ey if you want me to go, just—just tell me.'" When ENS H asked the appellant why he pushed himself on her and why he held her wrists after "[she] kept saying '[n]o' and to 'think about [their] careers, think about [their] families,'" the appellant responded:

[ENS H], my story is not going to change . . . [I]t was a playful thing and I did say, "[h]ey if you want me to go, tell me," but you never once said . . . "[o]kay, I want you to leave."

Finally, when asked by ENS H why he did not stop that night, the appellant answered, "I was under the impression that it was—that we were joking around and that it was like that you didn't want to, but you wanted to, and that's the impression I was on . . . ."

Two days after the pretext telephone call, NCIS interviewed the appellant. He denied going to her hotel room and having sex with ENS H. The appellant repeated those denials even after the NCIS agent advised him that lying to an NCIS agent was a crime.

At trial, over defense objection the appellant's Commanding Officer (CO) at the time of the allegations, testified as a government rebuttal witness that in his opinion, the appellant's "character for truthfulness" was "[b]elow [his] expectations." . . .

II. Discussion

[The court considered and rejected defendant's claims that inadmissible evidence was received and that the prosecution's final argument was improper. In the course of that analysis, the court evaluated the strength of the evidence of guilt.]

. . . *Strength of the government's case.* The government's case, although primarily based upon the testimony of ENS H, was reasonably strong when taken as a whole. ENS H reported the assault the same day it occurred and testified credibly and consistently. The appellant, on the other hand, initially corroborated many of the details surrounding the sexual assault during the pretext phone call, then wholly denied any sexual encounter when interrogated.

. . . [T]he government's case was strong relative to the defense case. ENS H . . . testified . . . credibly to the appellant's actions of holding her wrists and having sexual intercourse with her after she said "no." The appellant's defense that the sex was consensual [and his credibility were] undermined by his denial to the NCIS agent that he had sex with ENS H, as well as by the recorded, pretext phone call with ENS H in which the appellant failed to deny most of the details later raised by ENS H at trial. . . . [T]he appellant acceded to most of the complaining witness' testimony regarding the conduct at issue: the appellant acknowledged ENS H had resisted him, that she was "squir[ming]—you know, like messing around" while he had sex with her, notwithstanding his unreasonable assumption she was "playing. . . ."

III. Conclusion

The findings and sentence [of three years' confinement] are affirmed.

Notes and Questions

(1) *Is This Really a "Strong" Case?* The appellate court, in pronouncing the case "strong," did not decide that the proof was "beyond a reasonable doubt." An actual jury, following a charge about reasonable doubt, might convict—or might not.

(2) *Force of Certain Kinds Is Enough under Article 120, But Should It Be?* Article 120 certainly makes the *Coble* evidence appear stronger, because it does not require awareness of nonconsent if there are certain kinds of force. Does this feature make sense? On the one hand, many jurisdictions impose a requirement of a mental state about nonconsent. On the other hand, if the sexual act is accomplished by force, a jury could conclude that the defendant acted against the survivor's consent.

(3) *Force Is Enough in Several States.* Several states provide, as does the Military Code, that a defendant who has compelled sexual activity by force is guilty even if he did not know and could not have reasonably known that the victim did not consent to the sexual act. *See, e.g.,* Tex. Penal Code § 22.011 (compulsion by force is sufficient in Texas); *see also, e.g., State v. Reed,* 479 A.2d 1291 (Me. 1984); *Commonwealth v. Lopez,* 745 N.E.2d 961 (Mass. 2001) (rape by force does not require knowledge of nonconsent). *Lopez* makes the point that "this is not to say . . . that . . . rape [is] a strict liability crime," because it requires intent to use force. *See, also, e.g.,* 18 Pa. C.S. § 3121 (2008); Kit Kinports, *Rape and Force: The Forgotten Mens Rea,* 4 Buff. Crim. L. Rev. 755 (2001) (questioning this standard in cases of acquaintance rape).

(4) *What Result in Coble if Negligence, Recklessness, or Knowledge Were Required?* As we will see in the next section, some states require the defendant to be reckless about nonconsent. That is, he must be actually aware of the risk that she was not consenting. A jury might see the defendant in *Coble* as clueless rather than aware, or have a reasonable doubt about that issue—and greater doubt as to whether he had knowledge. What result in this case if, after conviction, the defendant were to appeal under a statute requiring recklessness? Or knowledge?

(5) *Inconsistency.* Results in rape prosecutions are difficult to predict. Under a statute like article 120, above, they will produce inconsistencies. Consider the following case.

UNITED STATES v. WHISENHUNT, 2019 WL 2368568 (Army Ct. Crim. App. 2019) (unreported decision). Defendant and the assault survivor were part of an assignment that had them sleeping in sleeping bags in the open, closely surrounded by other members of their squad so that sleeping bags were touching. The survivor had a "crackly" blanket around her. The sexual act happened after the defendant slipped out of his bag and into hers. She testified that she had awakened during the encounter but "froze" in a fetal position. This court had the duty to undertake its own review of the evidence: an approach very different from the usual appellate approach, which asks only whether the jury could have had sufficient proof. The court, after this review, held that the evidence was insufficient to support the defendant's conviction for sexual assault because the survivor must have consented, so that the act was not perpetrated by force. The court thus reversed the conviction:

> ... [T]o be convinced of appellant's guilt, we would have to conclude beyond a reasonable doubt that the sexual acts could plausibly occur (and would not be discovered) without active cooperation from both parties. Given different circumstances, this might not be a stretch. But in the unique circumstances here—which include a bivy cover, a noise-producing space blanket, and numerous squad mates in very close proximity—it is hard to conclude beyond a reasonable doubt that appellant could complete the charged offenses without cooperation . . . .

[2] Alternatives of Recklessness and Negligence about Consent
Notes and Questions on Mens Rea and Consent

(1) *Mental States Required for Sexual Assault.* There are multiple levels of mens rea required for sexual assault. First, the defendant must have the intent to do the sexual assault itself. Second, where required by the statute, the defendant must intend to use force, the threat of force, or deception in accomplishing the sexual assault. Third, in some states, there is the additional question of whether the defendant must realize the victim has not consented. Here, difficult questions rise.

(2) At common law, many courts considered rape to be a general intent crime. Thus, if a defendant used force to have sex, and the rape survivor did not consent and resisted, the defendant could not claim that he did not realize the survivor had not consented. Of course, given the requirements that force be used and that the surivor resist, it was highly unlikely that a defendant would be successful with such a claim anyway. However, some courts disagreed. What if the defendant honestly believed that the survivor wanted the defendant to use force during sex? Should mens rea focus on whether the victim had the intent to consent or whether the defendant was aware the victim was not consenting?

(3) *Two Arguments about Mens Rea.* The quotes at the beginning of this chapter reflect radically different views regarding rape and the issue of defendant's awareness that the survivor did not consent. For those who believe, as did Sir Matthew Hale, Lord Chief Justice of England, that rape is an "accusation easily made and hard to be proved," it is important that the prosecution prove that the defendant actually knew that she did not consent. Therefore, if the defendant made an honest, but even unreasonable mistake as to consent, the defendant should not be convicted. However, as reflected in Professor Estrich's quote, many others believe that defendant's behavior should not be excused simply because the defendant was too clueless or self-absorbed to realize that the survivor did not consent, and especially in the acquaintance rape scenario, defendants should be held responsible under a negligence standard, because it will make them try harder to assess the victim's wishes.

Note: Knowledge, Recklessness, and Negligence

(1) *Four Different Approaches to Mens Rea about Consent.* One approach, as we have seen, is to require no proof of a mental state of the defendant about consent if the defendant used force to compel the act. The rationale is that force supplies an implied kind of mens rea. A second approach, placing a higher burden on the state, is to require negligence. The clueless rapist is guilty if he should have been aware that the survivor wasn't consenting, even if he wasn't actually aware. A third approach is to require recklessness: defendant must have been aware of a substantial and unjustified risk but consciously disregarded it. The fourth approach is to require actual knowledge.

(2) *Knowing Mens Rea.* If the law requires proof that the defendant knowingly (with substantial certainty) engaged in non-consensual sex, then the defendant cannot be convicted so long as the defendant can convince the jury that there is a reasonable doubt whether he honestly believed the rape survivor had consented. The problem with this standard is that the defendant can point to aspects of the survivor's behavior and claim that he was unaware that she was not consenting. For example, if she allows the defendant to remove her clothes because she is too afraid to protest, the defendant can claim that he did not realize that she was not consenting.

(3) *Reckless Mens Rea.* If the mens rea standard is recklessness, prosecutors must prove that the defendant was on notice that the survivor did not wish to have sex, but they do not have to prove that the defendant was reasonably certain she did not want to have sex. *See, e.g., Reynolds v. State,* 664 P.2d 621, 623 (Alaska Ct. App. 1983), below. This approach makes it slightly easier for the prosecution to prove its case, but it still does not cover some situations when the defendant misreads the victim's words and conduct and believes she has consented.

(4) *Negligent Mens Rea.* Another approach is to hold the defendant responsible for rape if he was negligent: he should have been aware that the survivor was not consenting. *See, e.g., People v. Dancy,* 102 Cal. Ct. App. 4th 21 (2002). In such cases, there is no consent, but the defendant misinterprets the survivor's words and conduct, and believes that she has consented—even though he should have realized she did not. Under traditional (and many modern) approaches, this kind of encounter is not a crime. But is this standard too low?

(5) *The Model Penal Code Approach: Recklessness, but Otherwise Traditional.* MPC § 213.1 defines "Rape" and "Gross Sexual Imposition." Because the MPC dates from 1962, it contains traditional elements of rape that many states have abolished. (As noted above, the American Law Institute is revising Chapter 213 to reflect the many changes in this area of law over the past 50 years.) The current version of the MPC also does not set forth an express mens rea requirement for rape. Under the MPC, if a mens rea is not listed, the default requirement is recklessness. *See* MPC § 2.02(3). For rape, therefore, the prosecution would have to prove that the defendant was subjectively aware that there was a substantial and unjustifiable risk that the victim had not consented.

Reynolds v. State

664 P.2d 621 (Alaska Ct. App. 1983)

SINGLETON, JUDGE.

[This case featured a constitutional challenge to Alaska's sexual assault statute as vague and overbroad. The defendant, an acquaintance of the rape survivor, offered to take her home but instead took her to his apartment. Her evidence was that he forced her to enter the apartment, locked the door and pocketed the key, had intercourse with her, and prevented her from leaving until morning. She also testified that she verbally objected, but never physically resisted, because she was afraid of the defendant (and had seen a handgun on a chair in the apartment).]

[On these facts, the Alaska Court of Appeals affirmed the defendant's conviction for first-degree sexual assault. It rejected his argument that the statutory mens rea of "reckless" disregard of nonconsent was too ambiguous. It also rejected defendant's argument that the statute was unconstitutionally vague or overbroad. The court noted that the legislature had relaxed the statutory requirements for the offense. First, the requirement of resistance had been abolished. Intercourse "without consent" meant that the survivor, "with or without resisting, is coerced by the use of force against a person or property, or by the express or implied threat of imminent death, imminent physical injury, or imminent kidnapping." Second, force was defined to include "any bodily impact, restraint, or confinement," or "threat" thereof, and third, physical injury included any "physical pain or impairment of physical condition." These changes, the court opined, "enhanced the risk of conviction in ambiguous circumstances" and were the basis of the defendant's constitutional challenge.]

. . . To counteract this risk of conviction in ambiguous circumstances, some courts, notably the Supreme Court of California, have held that the defendant is entitled to an instruction on reasonable mistake of fact. *See People v. Mayberry*, 542 P.2d 1337 (Cal.1975). . . .

Under *People v. Mayberry*, when a defendant argues "consent" as a defense, the state must prove that he intentionally engaged in intercourse and was at least negligent regarding the rape victim's lack of consent. [Thus, the effect of the decisions is that California requires negligence for rape.] . . .

. . . [The Alaska] legislature has substantially enhanced the risk of conviction in ambiguous circumstances by eliminating the requirement that the state prove "resistance" and by substantially broadening the definitions of "force" and "physical injury." We are satisfied, however, that the legislature counteracted this risk through its treatment of *mens rea*. It did this by shifting the focus of the jury's attention from the victim's resistance or actions to the defendant's understanding of the totality of the circumstances. Lack of consent is a "surrounding circumstance" which under the Revised Code, requires a complementary mental state as well as conduct to constitute a crime. *See Neitzel v. State*, 655 P.2d 325, 329 (Alaska App.1982). No specific mental state is mentioned in AS 11.41.410(a)(1) governing the surrounding circumstance of "consent." Therefore, the state must prove that the defendant acted "recklessly" regarding his putative victim's lack of consent [because Alaska, following the MPC, requires recklessness if no mens rea is in a statute]. This requirement serves to protect the defendant against conviction for first-degree sexual assault where the circumstances regarding consent are ambiguous at the time he has intercourse with the complaining witness. While the legislature has substantially reduced the state's burden of proof regarding the *actus reus* of the offense, it has at the same time made it easier for the defendant to argue the defense of mistake of fact. The Alaska rule is more favorable to Reynolds than the rule of *People v. Mayberry*. This follows from the distinction the code draws between negligence and recklessness. The senate committee suggested:

> When a statute in the code provides that a person must recklessly cause a result or disregard a circumstance, criminal liability will result if the defendant "is aware of and consciously disregards a substantial and unjustifiable risk that the result will occur or that the circumstance exists." The test for recklessness is a subjective one—the defendant must actually be aware of the risk. On the other hand, if criminal negligence is the applicable culpable mental state, the defendant will be criminally liable if he "fails to perceive a substantial and unjustifiable risk that the result will occur or that the circumstance exists." The test for criminal negligence is an objective one—the defendant's culpability stems from his failure to perceive the risk.

In order to prove a violation of AS 11.41.410(a)(1), the state must prove that the defendant knowingly engaged in sexual intercourse and recklessly disregarded his victim's lack of consent. Construed in this way, the statute does not punish harmless conduct and is neither vague nor overbroad. We therefore reject Reynolds' constitutional attack on AS 11.41.410. . . .

Notes and Questions

(1) *What Effect Does the Mens Rea Requirement of Recklessness Have?* The court in *Reynolds* applied the recklessness standard. However, consider whether the result of the case would have been different if the applicable mens rea standard were knowingly or negligently.

(2) *California's Negligence Standard.* As noted in the decision, a defendant in California is guilty of rape if he intentionally engaged in intercourse and was at least negligent regarding the survivor's consent. This negligence standard is also reflected in California's mistaken consent defense, as set forth in *People v. Mayberry*. If a defendant claims that he honestly believed the survivor consented, he only has a defense if his mistaken belief is reasonable. How does this mistake defense reflect the negligence standard, and how is it different from the recklessness standard adopted by the Alaska court? Consider the *Jones* case below.

STATE v. JONES, 804 N.W.2d 409 (S.D. 2011). This case illustrates the use of a negligence standard about consent. "Defendant was convicted of raping a twenty-three-year-old woman called E.B. who testified that she was too intoxicated to have consented. He appeals asserting that although [the South Dakota statute] does not explicitly include a knowledge element, the circuit court erred when it failed to instruct the jury that the State must prove that he knew that the woman's intoxicated condition made her unable to consent." The court rejected this argument:

> Because mere silence by the Legislature on whether knowledge is a necessary element of an offense will not always negate a knowledge requirement, especially for crimes with potentially severe punishments, we conclude that the Legislature intended that a rape conviction under SDCL 22–22-1(4) requires proof that the defendant knew or reasonably should have known that the victim's intoxicated condition rendered her incapable of consenting.

Two justices dissented. One dissenter reasoned that the statute did not require proof of any mental element and that the court should not invent one by requiring proof that the defendant "should have known." The other dissenter wrote,

> Human experience reflects that the degree of impairment resulting from mental disability and alcohol consumption falls along a broad continuum . . . . Thus, this is the type of case in which ". . . the state may in the maintenance of a public policy provide 'that he who shall do [certain acts] shall do them at his peril and will not be heard to plead in defense good faith or ignorance.'" . . .

[3] *Knowledge of Nonconsent as a Requirement for Rape*
Note on Incapacity as Nonconsent

Incapacity Can Prove Nonconsent but May Require Knowledge. Many States define nonconsent as including incapacitation or similar conditions that make consent impractical, such as being unaware of the act or being mentally deficient. But these types of nonconsent are different from rape by force, because the use of force implies that the actor knows he is applying force. How does incapacity differ? Two people may drink alcohol excessively, with one incapacitated and the other not blameworthy because he is unaware that the rape survivor is incapable of consent—or so some jurisdictions seem to have reasoned. Consider the following case, which involves drugs rather than alcohol.

Davis v. State
581 S.W.3d 885 (Tex. App. 2019)

DAVID J. SCHENCK, JUSTICE

A jury found appellant Christopher Allen Davis guilty of sexual assault. . . . He . . . contends that the evidence is insufficient to support the jury's verdict. We affirm.

Background

... K.R. and her friend D.R. drove together to a house ... where appellant lived with his roommate, Chris Norton, and Norton's girlfriend, H.L. Evidence established that people often went to the house to "hang out" and "get high." That morning, K.R., D.R., Norton, and appellant all smoked methamphetamine. All except appellant consumed a half-cap of gamma-hydroxybutyric acid (GHB), which apparently gives an enhanced but short high to its users. When the effects of the GHB were wearing off, appellant prepared and offered the women wine coolers. Shortly thereafter, K.R. found it almost impossible to walk, and she blacked out. She awoke later that morning, in her car, which had been abandoned and parked in a warehouse area. D.R. was unconscious in the back seat of the car. At trial K.R. described having only flashes of memory that involved both men having sex with her. ...

Discussion

A person commits sexual assault if he intentionally or knowingly causes the penetration of the sexual organ of another person by any means, without that person's consent. [Penal Code] § 22.100(a)(1). The penal code defines "consent" as "assent in fact, whether express or apparent." *Id.* § 1.07(a)(11). The statute disjunctively lists eleven manners of proving that a sexual assault was without consent. *Id.* § 22.011(b). The trial court's charge included five of the eleven:

> . . .
>
> [The first two methods include force or threats, even without a mens rea.] ...
>
> [or] the other person has not consented and the actor knows the other person is unconscious or physically unable to resist;
>
> [or] the other person has not consented and the actor knows the other person is unaware that the sexual assault is occurring; or
>
> the actor has intentionally impaired the other person's power to appraise or control the other person's conduct by administering any substance without the other person's knowledge.

Id. § 22.011(b)(1)–(3), (5)–(6). The State has the burden to prove the sexual act at issue was not consensual. *Moon v. State*, 607 S.W.2d 569, 570 (Tex. Crim. App. 1980) ("Lack of consent to the sexual intercourse in a rape case is an essential element of the State's case."). ...

Appellant argues the State failed to carry its burden on the element of consent. He contends that the jury "speculated and guessed" about the consent issue. We disagree. ...

Justin Schwane, the toxicology lab supervisor at SWIFS, testified that K.R.'s urine sample taken at Parkland [Hospital] contained a high level of GHB. A test is deemed positive at a level of 10; K.R.'s sample was measured at 60, both when it was initially tested and when re-tested for confirmation. When questioned, Schwane testified that he would expect GHB to be gone from a subject's body after eight to ten hours, but he stated that the greater the dose of GHB, the longer the detection window.

Dr. Stacey Hail, who is board certified in emergency room medicine and medical toxicology, testified that GHB is a well-known date rape drug. It acts very quickly, it causes amnesia, and it is difficult to detect in biological specimens. Accordingly, if the GHB was detected in urine twelve to sixteen hours after it was taken, it was probably a large dose. She testified that a person who tested at K.R.'s level would not have been capable of giving consent to sex. She stated that such a person would be unconscious during most of the encounter, could wake up momentarily, open her eyes, and see what was happening, but would be physically unable to resist. Hail's testimony comports with K.R.'s description of momentary, or flash, memories of appellant (and Norton) attacking her.

As to the source of the large dose of GHB, Norton testified that—although he did not see appellant put GHB in the wine cooler he made for K.R.—he saw appellant put a straw in the drink and knew what appellant was doing: GHB is heavier than water and settles to the bottom of drinks, so sipping with a straw allows all the GHB to be consumed quickly. Norton agreed that appellant "could pretty much do whatever he wanted" to K.R. because he gave her that GHB.

. . . Appellant argues that the State offered no evidence that he knew K.R. was unconscious, unable to resist, or unaware that he was having sex with her. What an actor knew or intended may be inferred from circumstantial evidence, including his acts, words, and conduct. *Guevara v. State*, 152 S.W.3d 45, 50 (Tex. Crim. App. 2004). The jury could have inferred from the testimony of these witnesses that appellant administered a large dose of GHB to K.R., without her knowledge, precisely so he could have sex with her when she could not resist. Norton testified that he saw K.R. "passed out" on the living room floor. He also testified that he and appellant had to carry K.R. to her car later that morning. K.R.'s unconscious status was apparent to Norton; the jury could certainly have inferred that it was apparent to appellant as well. . . .

[A] rational jury could have found beyond a reasonable doubt that appellant intentionally impaired K.R.'s ability to control her conduct by administering a large dose of GHB to her without her knowledge, *see* § 22.011(b)(5), and then—without her consent—had sex with her while he knew she was unconscious and physically unable to resist, *See id.* § 22.011(b)(3), and while he knew she was unaware the assault was occurring, *See id.* § 22.011(b)4). [Affirmed.]

Notes and Questions

(1) *Requirements about Consent and Knowledge Often Cause Confusion.* Make sure you understand the structure of the statute here and its effects, which are similar to statutes in some other jurisdictions. Lack of consent is required. But must the defendant know that the survivor is not consenting? Under some conditions, such

as when the defendant uses force or threats, he does not need to know of noncon-sent in some jurisdictions to be guilty of rape. Under other conditions, the stat-ute provides a knowledge-of-her-condition requirement, such as nonconsent from incapacity.

(2) *Does the Difference in Treatment Make Sense?* One possible justification is that there are differing degrees of incapacity, and the defendant might underestimate the actual drunkenness of another person. But is this a justification for a high mens rea, such as knowledge, which means reasonable certainty? Perhaps the standard should be lower, such as negligence, to deter the clueless rapist.

Problem 5E (Sexual Assault): An Example of the Complexity of Sexual Assault Law

(1) *The Facts Underlying the Charge.* These facts are drawn from the opinion in *People v. Bowen*, 609 N.E.2d 346 (Ill. App. Ct. 1993): While there are a number of significant differences in their accounts of what happened next, both the survivor and the defendant testified that he knocked on her bedroom door and entered, ask-ing if she wanted to join others who had gone up on the apartment building's roof. Both agreed that he penetrated her digitally and with his penis. And both agreed that she said "no" several times. There were, however, ways in which their accounts differed. The defendant claimed that they initially talked and kissed, while the sur-vivor stated that she asked him to leave and tried to go back to sleep and was startled when he instead got on her bed and straddled her. The defendant testified that he thought that when she said "no" she really meant "[s]low down. You're going too fast. Take your time." While the defendant testified that he eventually "rolled over" and off the victim after she had said no several times, she testified in addition to repeatedly saying no, she also had pushed him away repeatedly after he straddled and then penetrated her. The victim additionally testified that "she did not scream because she could not believe what was happening, thought she could control the situation, and was scared."

The doctor who examined her at the hospital at around 6 a.m. that morning testified that "he did not observe any signs of [physical] trauma, *i.e.*, cuts, bruises, bleeding in the pelvic area, but testified this lack of physical evidence was not incon-sistent with her claim of being sexually assaulted"; that "he found no evidence of a struggle, nor did he find any bruises or red marks on her body indicating she had been held down"; and that the survivor's "demeanor [w]as atypical of a sexual assault victim because she was not emotionally distraught."

(2) *The Applicable Statute.* Criminal sexual assault under the then applicable Illi-nois Code imposed criminal responsibility on a defendant who "committ[ed] an act of sexual penetration by the use of force or threat of force." "Force or threat of force" was defined as "the use of force or violence, or the threat of force or violence, including but not limited to . . . : (1) when the accused threatens to use force or vio-lence on the victim or on any other person, and the victim under the circumstances

reasonably believed that the accused had the ability to execute that threat; or (2) when the accused has overcome the victim by use of superior strength or size, physical restraint or physical confinement." The Code further provided that consent is a defense to any charge "where force or threat of force is an element of the offense." "Consent" was defined as "freely given agreement to the act of sexual penetration or sexual conduct in question," and the Code additionally provided that "[l]ack of verbal or physical resistance or submission by the victim resulting from the use of force or threat of force by the accused shall not constitute consent."

(3) *The Defendant's Argument.* The defendant in *Bowen* argued that he had consensual sex with the victim. If his claim was honest, can you explain why he raised it in his defense?

(4) *What Is Needed to Prove Criminal Sexual Assault?* What evidence might have enabled the prosecutor in this case to prove criminal sexual assault beyond reasonable doubt, and what—in evidence or in cultural context—might have enabled the defense to raise a reasonable doubt about any of the elements of the offense? A partial answer lies in the paradox of sexual assault law, which is characterized by multiple, overlapping doctrines: resistance, mens rea, (non)consent, and force. [Note: The trial court convicted the defendant of sexual assault, and the court of appeals affirmed, but the case prompted the judges to engage in extensive analyses of force and nonconsent.]

[D] Attitudes and Controversies about Rape

Notes on Cultural Contexts

(1) *Assumptions About Gender Roles and Sexuality Affect the Law of Rape.* Even when there is evidence that substantial force was used to achieve intercourse, influential cultural stories about gender and sexuality may lead to differing outcomes where, although the evidence of force is more or less identical, one rape is viewed as a "stranger rape," or what the legal scholar and rape survivor, Professor Susan Estrich, calls "real rape," and the other is perpetrated by an acquaintance of the survivor. The same is true where a survivor is perceived to be chaste or respectable on the one hand, or "responsible" for the rape on the other.

Research done on the attitudes of college students showed that they believed that a woman who was divorced, facing drug charges, and worked as a topless dancer had much more responsibility for her rape than did a married social worker, when all other aspects of the rape scenario, which involved a forcible stranger rape, were identical, and that the rapist of the "respectable" survivor should be punished much more harshly than the rapist of the dancer. This study also showed a gendered difference in comprehending the survivor's responsibility for her rape: male students focused on the topless dancer's character, and women on her behavior of walking alone at night. Another study showed that jurors' scores on a "rape empathy" scale, which measured whether they thought the perpetrator or survivor was more responsible for the rape, significantly impacted whether they would convict or acquit in another hypothetical stranger rape scenario.

Cultural attitudes that many claims of rape are false, that stereotypically unchaste women "ask for it," and that innocent men are frequently falsely accused of rape echo Sir Matthew Hale's (in)famous claim that rape "is an accusation easily to be made and hard to be proved, and harder to be defended by the party accused, tho never so innocent," 1 M. Hale, *Pleas of the Crown* 635 (1680), which appears at the beginning of this chapter. Many contemporary scholars would argue that "[i]n a rape case it is the victim, not the defendant, who is on trial." Cassia C. Spohn, *The Rape Reform Movement: The Traditional Common Law and Rape Law Reforms*, 39 Jurimetrics 119 (1999).

The effect of such cultural beliefs is not confined to influencing the ways that judges define the law and judges and jurors apply the law to the evidence, and the ways that prosecuting and defending lawyers shape their cases and their rhetoric. It leads to policing practices that major studies around the world have concluded result in rape "attrition," or low rates of reporting rape, and arresting, prosecuting, and convicting accused rapists. Professor LaFave additionally argues that the attitude reflected by Hale "accounts not only for the narrow and curious fashion in which the crime of rape came to be defined, but also for the array of procedural and evidentiary rules that are both unique to and inimical to rape prosecutions." Wayne R. LaFave, *Criminal Law* 893 (6th ed. 2017). In many states, efforts have been made to reduce these.

(2) *Sexual Assault and Racism.* Some scholars argue that it is impossible to understand the law of sexual assault without understanding its historical interconnections with racism, including the disproportionately high prosecution and the severe punishment of black men for alleged rapes of white women, especially under Jim Crow laws. Other notorious examples include the "Scottsboro case" and the inapplicability of rape law to nonconsensual sex with enslaved African-American women, including under "slave-breeding" economies after the importation of slaves ceased to be legal. *See, e.g.,* Pamela D. Bridgewater, *Un/Re/Discovering Slave Breeding in Thirteenth Amendment Jurisprudence*, 7 Wash. & Lee Race & Ethnic Ancestry L.J. 11 (2001); Dorothy E. Roberts, *Rape, Violence, and Women's Autonomy*, 69 Chi-Kent. L. Rev. 359 (1993).

(3) *Some Statistics on Sexual Assault.* In a 1997 report, *Sex Offenses and Offenders: Analysis of Data on Rape and Sexual Assault*, the Department of Justice's Bureau of Justice Statistics provided the following information:

- 91% of sexual assault survivors are female and almost 99% of alleged offenders (when there is a single offender) are male;

- while the incidence of sexual assaults nationally dropped by 14% between 1992 (84 forcible rapes per 100,000 women in the population) and 1995, it rose significantly in cities outside metropolitan areas and in rural counties in the same period;

- 7 out of 10 sexual assault survivors report taking self-protective action, with just over half reporting that doing so helped them and 1 in 5 reporting that it either made the situation worse or both helped and worsened the situation;

- 3 out of 4 sexual assaults involve an offender who is a family member, intimate, or acquaintance of the victim;

- roughly two thirds of sexual assaults occur between 6 p.m. and 6 a.m., and 6 out of 10 occur in the victim's home or that of a friend, relative or neighbor; and

- per capita rates of sexual assault are highest among people aged 16–19, low-income residents, and urban residents, but race does not impact one's statistical likelihood of being the victim of a sexual assault.

More recent statistics remain remarkably similar. For example, in 2010, the Bureau of Justice Statistics reported 169,370 sexual assaults of females (82,100 by acquaintances, 41,950 by strangers, 3,390 unknown) and 15,020 of males (11,730 by acquaintances, 1,220 by strangers, 2,070 unknown). Ronet Bachman *Measuring Rape and Sexual Assault: Successive Approximations to Consensus* 9 (National Academy of Sciences 2012).

[E] The Historic Requirement of Resistance

Note on Resistance as an Element of Sexual Assault

(1) *Nonconsent: The Relic of "Utmost Resistance"* — *People v. Dohring*, 59 N.Y. 374 (1874). In this (very old) case, New York's highest court held that the nonconsent element of rape required "utmost resistance" by a woman, to "the extent of her ability." The court reasoned, "If a woman . . . does not resist to the extent of her ability . . . , must it not be that she is not entirely reluctant?" The court also approved jury instructions that "she must resist until exhausted or overpowered, for a jury to find that it is against her will."

(2) *The Modern Approach.* Contemporary statutes often do not specify resistance as such to define basic rape. They focus instead on force, consent, and (sometimes) mens rea about consent. But the consent element is one of the underlying issues that created the *Dohring* case, and in old cases, some courts have "read in" a requirement of resistance even where it is apparently absent from the statute.

(3) *Criticism of Advice Against Resistance.* Should the rape survivor resist? Or avoid resisting to avoid further injury? In the article excerpt that follows, Michelle Anderson critiques judicial attitudes from both directions. She argues that courts sometimes idealize resistance so that reasonable conduct by a survivor may prevent conviction for what should be called sexual assault. But she also criticizes

courts that advise against resistance in the sense of conduct that might provoke the attacker. Anderson believes that this advice is misguided.

Michelle Anderson, *Reviving Resistance in Rape Law*
1998 U. Ill. L. Rev. 953, 956–61

[The author begins with analysis of a case in which resistance was an issue. She argues, "Both the majority and the dissent were wrong," with the implication that courts generally have treated this issue in erroneous ways.]. . . .

. . . First, courts have judged a woman's actual resistance against an ideal standard. If a woman did not resist a sexual attack in a way that met that standard, she was not raped. Second, courts have increasingly discouraged resistance as an imprudent strategy for women who face rapists. Both of these seemingly contradictory perspectives on resistance are legally counterproductive and, ultimately, dangerous to women. . . .

For women to do what they were taught to do as girls — to remain passive in the face of a rapist — all but ensures rape completion. Contrary to popular belief, passivity does not protect women from being raped or from suffering serious physical injuries beyond the scope of the rape itself. The argument that fighting back against a rapist increases a woman's risk of serious bodily injury or death finds little to no support in the studies on the relationship between resistance and injury. . . . Resistance can thus deter rape both specifically and generally.

In addition to helping to deter rape, active resistance may decrease the psychological damage a woman experiences from sexual attack, even if the rape is completed. Women who fight back blame themselves less for having been raped. They are less depressed and less suicidal afterward, and ultimately, they recover from the trauma of rape more quickly. . . .

[Anderson adds, "The solution is that resistance cannot be necessary to obtain a conviction, but it should be sufficient. A woman's verbal and physical resistance should each be sufficient to prove nonconsent and force in a rape prosecution. It is time to reject the assumption that women cannot and should not resist sexual assault. It is time for the law to value women's verbal and physical resistance without penalizing those women who, for any number of reasons, do not resist." Thus, resistance is to be encouraged, but the required element should be nonconsent, demonstrable by verbal or physical evidence.]

Notes and Questions

(1) As a policy matter, do you think there should be a resistance requirement, in addition to force, nonconsent, and the act of intercourse, to establish rape?

(2) *Anderson's Position on the Law and Advice to Women.* Notice that Anderson, while endorsing resistance in some cases, argues that it should not be a requirement

for rape conviction. In general, she argues that resistance decreases rape, reduces psychological damage, and does not increase injuries. Do you agree with her on the law or on her advice about resistance? Consider a person who is confronted by a criminal with a knife who threatens serious injury if there is resistance and who appears to mean it.

[F] The Actus Reus of Sexual Assault: What Is Enough to Prove Force or Threats?

Notes and Questions

(1) *Actus Reus: Force, Threats, Fraud.* Traditional definitions of rape require particularized kinds of force, threat, or fraud.

(2) *Force or Threats of Force: What Kind and How Much?* Sometimes this element is clearly made out: the defendant carries out the act by using a weapon or by inflicting injury. But the case becomes more difficult under the traditional definition if the force is less explicit, or where force is apparently used but the defendant testifies that the intercourse was consensual. In some cases a surprisingly difficult problem arises under the traditional definition if the defendant has a weapon nearby early in the encounter but sets it aside well before the completion of the act. The defendant's version then is that "she may have been fearful at first, but she consented at the time," and jurors sometimes find reasonable doubt about force in such cases, even though the act in fact may have been assaultive.

(3) *Implied Force and Acquaintance Rape.* The most difficult practical problem for the legal system in adequately responding to the social harm of rape is created in an acquaintance rape situation, when the defendant's conduct contains only implied force and the survivor submits from fear of assault that never becomes explicit. By far the highest number of rapes fall into this category, as opposed to the stranger rape paradigm. What should be the law's response to such a case?

COMMONWEALTH v. BERKOWITZ, 641 A.2d 1161 (Pa. 1994). This case shows the influence of historical attitudes toward rape. The defendant was the roommate of a friend whom the rape survivor had gone to visit. The friend was not there, but the defendant asked her to stay. The court found insufficient the following facts, among others:

> Appellee then moved to the floor beside her, lifted up her shirt and bra and massaged her breasts. He then unfastened his pants and unsuccessfully attempted to put his penis in her mouth. They both stood up, and he locked the door [but it still could be opened from inside]. He returned to push her onto the bed, and removed her undergarments from one leg. He then penetrated her vagina with his penis. After withdrawing and ejaculating on her

stomach, he stated, "Wow, I guess we just got carried away," to which she responded, "No, we didn't get carried away, you got carried away."

[The survivor testified that she said "no" throughout the encounter, so that there was no controversy as to sufficiency of evidence to show nonconsent.]

[The Pennsylvania rape statute, 18 Pa. C.S. § 3121, required proof of "forcible compulsion that would prevent resistance by a person of reasonable resolution."]

... In regard to the critical issue of forcible compulsion, the complainant's testimony is devoid of any statement which clearly or adequately describes the use of force or the threat of force against her. She agreed that Appellee's hands were not restraining her in any manner during the actual penetration, and that the weight of his body on top of her was the only force applied. She testified that at no time did Appellee verbally threaten her. [The court also stated, that saying "no is not relevant to the use of force."] [Conviction reversed.]

The court did, however, uphold Berkowitz's conviction for indecent assault, which was a misdemeanor.

Notes and Questions

(1) *Assessing Berkowitz: How Much Force?* Do you agree that "no" is not "relevant to the issue of force"? Is there any other evidence in this case that a jury could have found established the "force" required by the Pennsylvania rape statute ("forcible compulsion that would prevent resistance by a person of reasonable resolution")?

(2) *She Didn't Consent, but That Wasn't the Issue in Berkowitz.* The evidence showed clearly that she said "no." The evidence was sufficient to show nonconsent. The issue was the extent of the force, and Pennsylvania then required more force than the evidence showed. But there are other ways of considering force. The next case considers "domination" as force.

Commonwealth v. Gonzalez

109 A.3d 711 (Pa. Super. 2015)

Opinion By JENKINS, J.:

David Gonzalez met K.M., a cerebral palsy patient, on a Christian dating website.... [A]fter dating for several months, they had sexual intercourse. K.M. claimed that Gonzalez raped her; Gonzalez claimed that she consented to intercourse. The jury believed K.M. and found Gonzalez guilty of rape, aggravated indecent assault and sexual assault.... For the reasons articulated below, we affirm....

[The defendant challenges the sufficiency of the evidence to show the element of force required by the Pennsylvania statute for rape. The court describes the encounter at issue between Gonzalez and K.M.]

... They sat down on the couch and began watching [a] movie. The victim testified that she started kissing [Gonzalez] and they both began touching and rubbing one another's genitals over their clothes. This lasted for about half an hour. Eventually, the victim noticed that [Gonzalez] was erect. Next, the victim testified that [Gonzalez] asked her if she wanted to go to the bedroom, to which she agreed. The victim assumed that we would continue doing what we were doing in the living room in the bedroom "... [b]ecause ... [Gonzalez] knew that I didn't want to have sex before I was married." Before they moved, the victim testified that [Gonzalez] took her phone out of a pouch connected to her jeans and placed it on a TV tray in the living room. The victim then got her crutches, got off the couch, and walked to [Gonzalez]'s bedroom. ...

The victim testified that [Gonzalez] "took my crutches [and] put them out of reach." ... The victim lay down by herself. When asked "is there any way you could have gotten up from that point?" She responded "no."

The victim testified that [Gonzalez] then removed her jeans and underwear, and lay on top of her. The victim did not say anything while [Gonzalez] took off her pants and underwear, but when he lay on top of her, she said "no, don't." When he lay on top of her, her legs were flat, straight, and unopened because "I can't open my legs by myself."

Next, the victim testified that [Gonzalez] got on his knees and forced her legs apart "with his hands and put them on his shoulders. And he had his hands cuffed around my ankles." She testified that "[h]e put my ankles around his shoulders." "He bent [her knees] because they were up on his shoulders." She then felt his penis inside her, and she "kept saying ow." [Gonzalez] told the victim she "had to be quiet." The victim testified that at some point [Gonzalez] took her legs off his shoulders and put his finger in her vagina. He then put her legs back on his shoulders and penetrated her again with his penis. The victim was asked if she tried at all to kick off [Gonzalez] during the penetration. She responded, "I couldn't move my legs. My legs don't move like that." When asked if she tried to push him off, she said, "[n]o ... because he's too big. And I was scared."

... At some point, [Gonzalez] suddenly stopped, and the encounter ended. There was blood on the mattress and blood on the victim's underwear after she put them back on. The victim testified that after she got dressed, [Gonzalez] said to her, "I'm sorry. I have a weakness." ...

Alternatively, [Gonzalez] testified that the encounter was consensual. ...

Gonzalez' first argument on appeal is a challenge to the sufficiency of the evidence. We first consider the evidence of rape. The Crimes Code defines rape in pertinent part as follows: "A person commits a felony of the first degree when the person engages in sexual intercourse with a complainant ... by forcible compulsion." 18 Pa.C.S. § 3121(a)(1). The Crimes Code defines "forcible compulsion" in relevant part as "compulsion by use of physical, intellectual, moral, emotional or psychological force, either express or implied." 18 Pa.C.S. § 3101. This Court has observed "forcible compulsion" as the exercise of sheer physical force or violence and has also come to mean an act of using superior force, physical, moral, psychological or intellectual to compel a person to do a thing against that person's volition and/or will. *Commonwealth v. Ables*, 590 A.2d 334, 337 (1991). A determination of forcible compulsion rests on the totality of the circumstances, including but not limited to this list of factors:

> the respective ages of the victim and the accused, the respective mental and physical conditions of the victim and the accused, the atmosphere and physical setting in which the incident was alleged to have taken place, the extent to which the accused may have been in a position of authority, *domination* or custodial control over the victim, and whether the victim was under duress.

Commonwealth v. Rhodes, 510 A.2d 1217, 1226 (1986) (emphasis added). It is not mandatory to show that the victim resisted the assault in order to prove forcible compulsion. *Id.* . . .

The distinction between forcible compulsion and lack of consent is important to remember. . . . "Forcible compulsion" means "something more" than mere lack of consent. *Commonwealth v. Smolko*, 666 A.2d 672, 676 (1995). "Where there is a lack of consent, but no showing of either physical force, a threat of physical force, or psychological coercion, the 'forcible compulsion' requirement . . . is not met." *Id.* . . .

We agree with the trial court's astute analysis by construing the evidence in the light most favorable to the Commonwealth. K.M.'s testimony establishes that she told Gonzalez that she did not want premarital intercourse. Gonzalez . . . maneuvered her into a position in which she was powerless to resist his advances. He took her to his apartment, where she had never been before. He placed her cell phone out of reach in a living room tray, and . . . he placed her crutches out of reach. Without her phone or crutches, she could not escape from the bed or contact an outside agency for help. He then disrobed her and lay on top of her. She uttered "no, don't," but instead of stopping, he forced her legs apart and cuffed them on his shoulders— movements she was incapable of performing herself due to her cerebral palsy. He then penetrated her with his penis and told her to be quiet when she repeatedly called out "ow". K.M.'s lack of consent ("no, don't"), combined with Gonzalez's use of domination and physical force, provide sufficient evidence of forcible compulsion to justify his conviction for rape. . . . [Conviction affirmed.]

Notes and Questions

(1) *Berkowitz and Gonzalez: Is the Treatment of Force and Compulsion Consistent?* Gonzalez's actual use of force, which the court found sufficient, seems lesser than that used by Berkowitz, which the court found insufficient. Are the two decisions consistent? The *Gonzalez* court introduced the concept of "domination," which may

be easier to find than "compulsion by force," and perhaps this explanation of force lowered the force requirement.

(2) *Remember, Force Is Distinct from Lack of Consent, Which May Not Be Enough.* This jurisdiction and some others require two distinct elements for rape: (1) compulsion by force and (2) lack of consent. If this is what is required, lack of consent is not enough. Submission from fear is not enough for rape. Saying "no" is not enough without force, in such a jurisdiction.

(3) *California Focused on "Fear" to Uphold a Rape Conviction: People v. Iniguez,* 872 P.2d 1183 (Cal. 1994). This decision found sufficient evidence of force by looking to the fact that the survivor submitted because of fear:

> At the time of the crime in this case, section 261, subdivision (2), provided, "Rape is an act of sexual intercourse accomplished with a person not the spouse of the perpetrator, under any of the following circumstances: . . . (2) Where it is accomplished against a person's will by means of force, violence, or fear of immediate and unlawful bodily injury on the person or another." The deletion of the resistance language from section 261 by the 1980 amendments thus effected a change in the purpose of evidence of fear of immediate and unlawful injury. Prior to 1980, evidence of fear was directly linked to resistance; the prosecution was required to demonstrate that a person's resistance had been overcome by force, or that a person was prevented from resisting by threats of great and immediate bodily harm. As a result of the amendments, evidence of fear is now directly linked to the overbearing of a victim's will; the prosecution is required to demonstrate that the act of sexual intercourse was accomplished against the person's will by means of force, violence, or fear of immediate and unlawful bodily injury.

The statute includes acts "accomplished . . . by . . . fear of unlawful bodily injury." But this rape definition seems to depend not on the defendant's actions, but on the survivor's subjective mental state. Does it remove the requirement that the defendant used force?

(4) *Acquaintance or Date Rape with Only Implied Force.* A difficult problem arises in an acquaintance rape situation when the defendant's conduct contains only implied force and the survivor submits from fear of assault that never becomes explicit. Large numbers of rapes fall into this category, as opposed to the stranger rape paradigm. What should be the law's response?

(5) *The Confusing Interplay between Force and Consent: Who Has the Burden of Proof?: State v. W.R. Jr.,* 336 P3d 1134 (Wash. 2014). Here, the trial court instructed the jury that if there was force, the defendant must prove consent as an affirmative defense. The Washington Supreme Court, however, overruled prior cases and held that consent was not an affirmative defense; instead, it was a rebuttal to the proof of force, and therefore it concerned an element of the crime. And as we saw in Chapter 4, the state must prove all elements of the crime beyond a reasonable doubt:

. . . [W]hen a defense necessarily negates an element of an offense, it is *not* a true affirmative defense and the legislature may not allocate to the defendant the burden of proving the defense. . . . *Mullaney v. Wilbur,* 421 U.S. 684, 699, 704 (1975). In such a case, the legislature can require the defendant only to present sufficient evidence to create a reasonable doubt as to his or her guilt. [Reversed.]

Does consent really "negate" force, or are consent and force separate concepts?

Note on Abolishing the Force Requirement

(1) *Abolishing the Force Requirement: In the Interest of M.T.S.,*609 A.2d 1266 (N.J. 1992). In this case, the New Jersey Supreme Court considered an amended statute that removed any separate force requirement, allowing rape to be based only on lack of consent. The case involved a degree of force that might not have been sufficient in Pennsylvania after *Berkowitz.* But sufficient evidence showed a lack of consent, and the court therefore upheld the conviction:

> . . . We conclude, therefore, that any act of sexual penetration engaged in by the defendant without the affirmative and freely-given permission of the victim to the specific act of penetration constitutes the offense of sexual assault. Therefore, physical force in excess of that inherent in the act of sexual penetration is not required for such penetration to be unlawful. The definition of "physical force" is satisfied . . . if the defendant applies any amount of force against another person in the absence of what a reasonable person would believe to be affirmative and freely-given permission to the act of sexual penetration.

(2) *Some Other Jurisdictions Also Criminalize Nonconsensual Sex without Requiring Force.* Vermont's basic sexual assault statute requires only lack of consent (although the state can also prove the crime by showing threats or coercion). Aggravated sexual assault requires deadly force or infliction of serious bodily injury. *See* 13 V.S.A. §3252. In Florida, the second degree felony of sexual battery requires no force beyond penetration, and the first degree felony of sexual battery requires that the defendant be physically helpless to resist, which the courts have defined to mean "no opportunity to communicate her unwillingness." *State v. Sedia,* 614 So. 2d 533 (Fla. App. 1993). California courts have suggested that nothing in the force requirement requires substantially more force than "the physical force inherent in an act of consensual sexual intercourse" and need only show force was "of a degree sufficient to support a finding that the act . . . was against the will of the [victim]." *People v. Griffin,* 94 P.3d 1089 (Cal. 2004).

(3) *Withdrawn Consent: People v. John Z.,* 60 P.3d 183 (Cal. 2003). In this case, the court held that initially consensual intercourse that persisted after the survivor "expresse[d] an objection and attempt[ed] to stop the act" was forcible rape. Other courts have focused on initial consent and held that intercourse that forcibly persisted after withdrawal of consent was not rape.

(4) *Fraud and Other Circumstances.* A less frequent category of sexual assault results if the defendant uses fraud, trickery, or abuse of a situation. Some of the cases involve doctors who perform sexual acts on patients while telling them what is happening is a vaginal examination. Others involve impersonators who pretend to be the victim's spouse or boyfriend in circumstances where the survivor cannot see the perpetrator clearly or is groggy from sleep. Others involve actors who assault survivors who do not know of the act (*e.g.*, the victim is drunk and unconscious), and still others involve abuse of quasi-fiduciary relationships, such as those involving teachers or clergy. Some modern statutes specifically cover these cases.

[G] Lesser Crimes Than Rape: "Indecent Assault" and Like Offenses

(1) *Pennsylvania's Response to Berkowitz.* In the wake of *Berkowitz*, above, the Pennsylvania Legislature enacted a separate "sexual assault" provision, 18 Pa. Cons. Stat. § 3124.1 (1995), which criminalized "engag[ing] in sexual intercourse or deviate sexual intercourse with a complainant without the complainant's consent." This was a separate offense from the forcible rape statute involved in *Berkowitz*. Remember, also, that in *Berkowitz*, the court upheld a conviction for another lesser crime, called "indecent assault."

(2) *The Uniform Code of Military Justice: Several Lesser Offenses, in Addition to Rape.* Recall, from an earlier section, the Military Code. It defines rape and several lesser offenses, including those called "sexual assault," "aggravated sexual contact," and "abusive sexual contact." The last offense, for example, is defined as follows in U.C.M.J. art. 120(d):

> **Abusive sexual contact.**—Any person subject to this chapter who commits or causes sexual contact upon or by another person, if to do so would violate subsection (b) (sexual assault) had the sexual contact been a sexual act, is guilty of abusive sexual contact. . . .

(3) *Is It a Good Idea to Create Lesser Alternatives to Rape?* On the one hand, lesser crimes may tempt a trier of fact to reach a compromise verdict of lesser guilt in the case of a person who is actually not guilty. On the other hand, lesser crimes mitigate the problems created by overly technical definitions of rape by allowing a conviction if lesser conduct fits a lesser statute.

[H] Evidentiary Issues in Sexual Assault Cases

[1] Historical Constraints on Survivor Credibility: Corroboration and Outcry Requirements

> Read MPC § 213.6 (4)–(5) [no prosecution in the absence of "prompt complaint" or outcry; no conviction on "uncorroborated testimony of alleged victim"] in the MPC Appendix.

Notes and Questions

(1) *The Meaning of These Requirements—How do Evidentiary Requirements Add to the Elements of Sexual Assault Case?* Notice that the MPC, by requiring a prompt outcry and corroboration of the survivor's claims, essentially adds more elements to the crime of sexual assault. If an attacker successfully completes the offense in private with no witnesses other than the survivor, and if there is no detectable physical evidence, there is no crime. If the survivor delays reporting to the police for three months because she is afraid, shaken, or ashamed, the crime likewise cannot be proved. A robbery, burglary, or theft case would be perfectly capable of prosecution under these circumstances, but not sexual assault. What were the historical policy considerations that drove these laws?

(2) *Abolition of Outcry and Corroboration Requirements in Most Jurisdictions.* Remember, the MPC is over 50 years old (and is undergoing revision on these topics). It reflects attitudes that had crystallized before that time. Most jurisdictions have abolished these requirements.

(3) *Although False Claims of Sexual Assault Exist, They Are in the Minority.* There is significant scholarly and journalistic debate about how often a person falsely claims rape. *See, e.g.,* Dick Haws, *The Elusive Numbers on False Rape*, Columbia Journalism Review (Nov./Dec 1997) (noting that claims as to the percentage of false rape allegations vary between 2% and 25%). FBI statistics "consistently" put the number of "unfounded" rape accusations at 8%, but "'unfounded' is not synonymous with false" because it may reflect a conclusion by authorities that the alleged crime is unprosecutable. *See False Accusation of Rape*, http://en.wikipedia.org/wiki/false_accusation_of_rape (last visited April 22, 2013).

Beliefs about rape and survivor credibility affect whether rape is investigated, made the subject of criminal charges, and prosecuted, and some studies of jury behavior indicate that jurors' pre-existing beliefs about rape and masculine and feminine sexuality impact their decisions. *See, e.g.,* Lynda Olsen-Fulero & Solomon M. Fulero, *Commonsense Rape Judgments: An Empathy-Complexity Theory of Rape Juror Story Making*, 3 Psychol. Pub. Pol. & L. 402 (1997). Trial and appellate judges occasionally express views about these issues in making decisions on jury instructions, on guilt, and at sentencing in rape cases. *See, e.g., Rusk v. State*, 406 A.2d 624 (Md. Ct. Spec. App. 1979) (Wilner, J. dissenting) (opining that the majority of the Court of Special Appeals had "perpetuated and given new life to myths about the crime of rape that have no place in our law today").

(4) *A Major Reversal in the Law: Liberal Admissibility of Other Sexual Misconduct against the Defendant, but a "Shield" for the Survivor.* Historically, in a rape trial even if the defendant had made repeated or serial sexual attacks against other survivors, those offenses usually were inadmissible, while the survivor's sexual reputation and acts were broadly admissible. But there has been a remarkable change in these laws: a full reversal. Today, evidence rules freely admit incidents of past sexual misconduct against the accused (although such evidence is not similarly admissible in robbery, murder or drug cases), and most states and Congress have adopted "rape shield" statutes that exclude most evidence of the survivor's sexual history. The shield laws are designed to avoid "putting the survivor on trial" by defense counsel who seek to introduce the survivor's past sexual history to suggest that she consented to sexual relations with the accused. The possibility that their sexual history would be part of the trial discouraged many survivors from pressing charges and introduced information that was likely irrelevant but would color the jury's assessment of the survivor's credibility. *See* Richard I. Haddad, *Shield or Sieve? People v. Bryant and the Rape Shield Law in High-Profile Cases*, 39 Colum. J.L. & Soc. Probs. 185 (Winter 2005).

[2] Modern Statutes Protecting Sexual Assault Survivors
The Colorado "Rape Shield" Statute
Colo. Crim. Code § 18–3-407

(1) Evidence of specific instances of the victim's or a witness' prior or subsequent sexual conduct, opinion evidence of the victim's or a witness' sexual conduct, and reputation evidence of the victim's or a witness' sexual conduct shall be presumed to be irrelevant except:

> (a) Evidence of the victim or witness' prior or subsequent sexual conduct with the actor;

> (b) Evidence of specific instances of sexual activity showing the source of origin of semen, pregnancy, disease, or any similar evidence of sexual intercourse, offered for the purpose of showing that the act or acts charged were or were not committed by the defendant.

[Section (2) sets up a procedure for pretrial determination of defense claims of exceptions that allegedly allow the prohibited evidence. Section (3) authorizes protective orders against disclosure of information about a survivor or witness.]

Problem 5F (Sexual Assault): "I No Longer Want to Prosecute" — The Kobe Bryant Case

Adapted from Associated Press reports Sept. 2, 2004

(1) *The Facts Underlying the Charge against Kobe Bryant.* Kobe Bryant was a star with the NBA's Los Angeles Lakers. At a resort hotel near Vail, Colorado, a female employee gave him a tour of the premises and escorted him to his room. Only Bryant and the woman have personal knowledge of what happened next. Promptly afterward, however, she reported that Bryant had raped her. Witnesses described her immediate behavior in a manner consistent with rape trauma, and she had injuries that reinforced the claim. But Bryant, while admitting to the act of intercourse and issuing a public apology to his wife for infidelity, asserted that the woman had consented. He was able to afford well-funded counsel, who set out to discover evidence to bolster his defense.

(2) *The Prosecutors' Confidence in Their Case—and Its Ultimate Dismissal.* Months later, the alleged victim no longer wished to participate, and the trial judge dismissed after a motion by the prosecution. A series of rulings had made some of the victim's other sexual activity admissible in evidence, courthouse mistakes had led to the public release of her name and medical history, discovery initiated by the defense had been relentless and intrusive, and media attention to her remained intense. The dismissal "is not based upon a lack of belief in the victim," the District Attorney announced. "She is an extremely credible and extremely brave young woman. Our belief in her has not wavered." (The victim did, however, continue her civil suit against Bryant.)

(3) *Kobe Bryant's Apology.* Bryant then offered an unusual and public apology. "I want to apologize to her for my behavior that night. . . . I can only imagine the pain she has had to endure." He went on to say, "Although I truly believe this encounter between us was consensual, I recognize now that she did not and does not view this incident the same way I did. After months of reviewing discovery, . . . *I now understand how she feels that she did not consent to this encounter*" (emphasis added). Members of the public might well ask why it isn't rape, if the defendant himself admits that the victim "feels that she did not consent." As we have seen however, this area of law is affected by multiple, overlapping doctrines about force, mens rea, resistance, and nonconsent. Can you explain how the elements of sexual assault might excuse Bryant, even if the victim subjectively did not consent?

(4) *Does Sexual Assault Law Still Discourage Witnesses from Proceeding?* The law of sexual assault has undergone pervasive change in both substance and process. In many jurisdictions, at least in theory, the substantive law places more realistic expectations on the conduct of the survivor at the time of the attack and makes the defendant liable on lesser mens rea. Additionally, evidence is more freely admissible against the defendant, while evidence attacking the survivor is less readily admissible, again in theory. Why, then, with such strong support from the District

Attorney, did the survivor in the Kobe Bryant case determine that it was not in her interest to continue?

[I] More Serious Degrees of the Offense: "Aggravated" Sexual Assault

Maryland Criminal Code § 3–303 ("Rape in the First Degree")

[Most jurisdictions make sexual assault with aggravating circumstances a more serious class of felony than basic forcible rape, or they make it subject to higher penalties. Examples of typical aggravating circumstances can be found in § 3–303 of the Maryland Criminal Code, which provides as follows:]

§ 3–303. Rape in the first degree

(a) . . . A person may not:

(1) [commit the crime of "ordinary" rape, and also:]

(2) (i) employ or display a dangerous weapon, or a physical object that the victim reasonably believes is a dangerous weapon;

(ii) suffocate, strangle, disfigure, or inflict serious physical injury on the victim or another in the course of committing the crime;

(iii) threaten, or place the victim in fear, that the victim, or an individual known to the victim, imminently will be subject to death, suffocation, strangulation, disfigurement, serious physical injury, or kidnapping;

(iv) commit the crime while aided and abetted by another; or

(v) commit the crime in connection with a burglary in the first, second, or third degree. . . .

(d) (1) Penalty. . . . . . [A] person who violates subsection (a) of this section is guilty of the felony of rape in the first degree and on conviction is subject to imprisonment not exceeding life.

———————

Another section allows for life without possibility of parole if other aggravating factors are present.

In contrast, rape without aggravating circumstances ("ordinary" rape) is a second degree felony carrying a maximum sentence of 20 years in Maryland.

Notes and Questions

(1) *The Aggravating Circumstances in Maryland and Their Effect.* In summary, Maryland defines first degree rape to include crimes involving (1) dangerous weapons, (2) "serious physical injury," (3) "threats" of serious physical injury, (4)

multiple perpetrators, or (5) burglaries. These factors enhance the sentence maximum from 20 years to life.

(2) *Will This Statute Do What the Drafters Intend, by Sentencing Rapists More Severely if They Hurt Their Victims?* The most common aggravating circumstances under this Maryland statute probably will apply to defendants who "(ii) inflict . . . serious physical injury" or "(iii) threaten . . . serious physical injury." A rapist who also physically injures the survivor deserves an enhanced sentence. But this statute's literal wording may not achieve the purpose. It may mean that many physical injury cases will stay as "ordinary" rapes, as if the injury had not been inflicted. Why?

Here is why. Maryland defines most enhanced rapes in terms of "serious physical injury," and then it defines "serious physical injury" as injury causing either (1) a "substantial risk of death" or (2) "protracted . . . disfigurement [or] . . . loss [or impairment] of the function of a bodily member or organ." Unless the survivor is disfigured or has a bodily organ impaired for a "protracted" period, the rape is not aggravated; it is only "ordinary" rape. Therefore, if a rapist beats a survivor severely, leaving blood and bruises all over the body, the literal words of the statute may mean the crime will remain only "ordinary" rape, however undesirable that result may seem — arguably because of clumsy drafting. Can you explain why? Consider the case that follows, which closely parallels results under the Maryland statute above.

RUCKER v. STATE, 599 S.W.2d 581 (Tex. 1979). Rucker apparently chose his victim at random and hid in her car while she was inside a post office. After she drove out of the parking lot, he grabbed her face. The opinion describes what happened next:

> . . . The complainant struggled to get free, but the appellant crawled into the front seat and began to hit the complainant's face and chest with his fist. The complainant was dazed by the blows, which caused her nose and mouth to bleed. She obeyed the appellant's instructions to turn left and to stop after driving about half a block, but she refused to back her car into a gravel, side road. The appellant continued to hit the complainant's face and chest. He pulled the complainant out of the passenger side of the car and, holding her by the arm, walked down the gravel road a few feet before pushing her down into some weeds by the side of the road. The appellant took off one of the complainant's shoes. The complainant struggled to get up. The appellant grabbed her again, and they walked further down the road, where the appellant again pushed the complainant down in the weeds. . . . She struggled and kicked her feet, trying to get up. The appellant pulled off the complainant's pants and undergarments. . . . The complainant suffered scratches and pain from lying on the weeds and gravel. The appellant then forcibly had sexual intercourse with the complainant. During this act,

the appellant asked the complainant . . . whether she was "enjoying it." The appellant [committed various other degrading and assaultive acts]. The appellant . . . told her to run as far and as fast as she could, or he would shoot her; the complainant ran. There was no evidence that the appellant had a gun or any other weapon. [A few minutes later, the appellant again struck the complainant and stole her car.]

The jury convicted Rucker of "aggravated rape" and assessed his sentence at life imprisonment. Unfortunately, however, the governing statute defined aggravated rape in terms similar to the Maryland statute above. The relevant provisions required a "threat" of "serious bodily injury." Serious bodily injury, in turn, required "protracted" loss of use of a "bodily member or organ": language functionally identical to Maryland's. "The only medical treatment given complainant was some 'pain medicine.'" The court therefore reversed:

> The only verbal threat was that the complainant would be shot if she did not run. This threat was made after the rape was completed; it did not "compel submission to the rape" as is required by [the statute] for the element of aggravation. The jury's verdict on the element of aggravation can be upheld only if an implied threat of death or serious bodily injury was communicated by the appellant's acts and conduct. . . .
>
> . . . Although the evidence was sufficient to prove simple rape, it was not sufficient to prove the element of aggravation. [Reversed.]

One judge dissented, citing a case in which a similar conviction was upheld although the only evidence of a threat was that the defendant had struck the complainant "several times in the face." He added, "Logic compels us to conclude that if a rapist repeatedly strikes his victim while insisting that she have intercourse, then should she refuse, . . . he will escalate the force. . . ."

Notes and Questions

(1) *The Rucker Court Reached the Same Result on Rehearing.* The *Rucker* decision produced a firestorm of criticism. On rehearing, the court maintained the same result. *See also Mayes v. State*, 440 A.2d 1093 (Md. App. 1982) (interpreting the Maryland statute, above, and reaching the same result as *Rucker* on similar facts).

(2) *The Legislature Quickly Changed the Statute.* In response to *Rucker*, the state legislature amended the statute at issue, so that the crime now is aggravated if the defendant "*by acts or words* places the victim in fear that . . . serious bodily injury will be imminently inflicted." Tex. Penal Code § 22.021 (aggravated sexual assault). It appears that this amendment achieved the desired result, with courts deferring more to jury findings of threats and expressly looking to the "totality of the circumstances," *See* Contreras *v. State*, 838 S.W.2d 594 (Tex. App. 1992). But notice how difficult statutory definition can be. Lapses and omissions can lurk in the language, unnoticed.

[J] Defining Sexual Assault as Occurring If There Is No Evidence of "Affirmative Consent"

Notes and Questions

(1) *Requiring Affirmative Consent as a Condition of Avoiding Rape: KC Johnson et al., Will the ABA Reject Due Process?* Wall St. J., Aug. 12, 2019, at A21. The American Bar Association Criminal Justice Section has suggested that the law should require affirmative "assent" by both parties in advance of any "specific act" of sex. And assent is expressed by "words and actions in the context of all the circumstances." State laws in California, Connecticut and New York require educational institutions to follow this approach, and some universities have adopted it on their own. *See id.*

(2) *What Justifies This Approach?* Advocates of the proposal say that "current research" discloses a phenomenon called "frozen fright," which they say makes "a person confronted by an unexpectedly aggressive partner or stranger succumb[] to panic" and "become paralyzed by anxiety or fears." *Id.* There also is the argument that an affirmative consent requirement would make consent cases clearer, although the totality-of-the-circumstances approach may make that unlikely.

(3) *What It Means: The Burden of Proof Is Shifted to the Accused to Prove Affirmative Consent.* The Journal cites the case of Corey Mock, a student at the University of Tennessee, who was found guilty of sexual assault after evidence that he believed that the accuser had consented. His claim to this effect was uncontradicted, but Mr. Mock "failed to prove that he had obtained 'affirmative consent.'" He sued the school and won. The judge concluded that affirmative consent "is flawed and unworkable." *Id.* The National Association of Criminal Defense Attorneys has opposed this "radical change in the law" that "assumes guilt in the absence of any evidence of consent" and argues that it violates the Due Process Clauses. *Id.* Who has the better of this debate? For academic discussions of affirmative consent, see Mary Graw Leary, *Affirmatively Replacing Rape Culture with Consent Culture*, 49 Tex. Tech. L. Rev. 1 (2016), and Jonathan Witmer-Rich, *Unpacking Affirmative Consent: Not as Great as You Hope, Not as Bad as You Fear*, 49 Tex. Tech. L. Rev. 57 (2016).

§ 5.05 "Statutory Rape" — Sexual Assault Upon a Child

Notes on Strict Liability for This Offense

(1) *Strict Liability with Respect to the Child's Age.* A majority of states make statutory rape (typically of a person under seventeen years of age) a strict liability offense with respect to the child's age. This principle results in some prosecutions in which the intercourse is undisputedly consensual and the child is nearly the age of consent,

with the defendant reasonably believing her to be of lawful age. In an occasional case, a defendant even may have taken special precautions to verify ages that were told him, but was convicted anyway when the child's statements have been proved false (and also, in the hardest cases, her fake identification card exposed). These are the cases that test the viability of strict liability.

(2) *Reasonable Mistake of Fact Sometimes Is a Defense (Meaning That Awareness Is Not a Crime Element, but the Defendant May Be Able to Avoid Liability by Shouldering the Burden)*. Legislatures and courts in a few jurisdictions permit mistake of fact defenses, usually where the defendant can establish an honest and reasonable mistake of fact as to the young person's age. In most jurisdictions, however, the courts do not recognize mistake even as a defense. They reason that the offense is intended by the legislature to be a strict liability crime.

(3) *Other Defenses and Limits: Variations in Statutory Rape Provisions*. Consensual sexual intercourse with a "minor" may or may not be a criminal offense, and may have a differentially severe penalty, depending on the age of the young person and the difference in age between the young person and the accused. Some states, like the Model Penal Code, make the promiscuity of the young person a defense. A few jurisdictions restrict the offense to sexual relations with female minors, and some do not criminalize consensual sex between young people who are close in age.

(4) *Policy Rationales for and Problems with Statutory Rape: Strict Liability for a Mentally Limited Defendant*. In *State v. Garnett*, 632 A.2d 797 (Md. 1993), a 20-year-old man with an IQ of 52, was convicted of second degree rape of a 13 year old girl (an acquaintance) under the statutory rape provision of the Maryland Code. Relying on contextual statutory interpretation and legislative history, and over two strong dissents, the majority of the Court of Appeals held that the offense was a strict liability offense even while conceding that "it is uncertain to what extent [Garnett's] intellectual and social retardation may have impaired his ability to comprehend imperatives of sexual morality [that justify strict liability statutory rape on the theory that the accused 'deserves punishment for having . . . violated moral teachings that prohibit sex outside marriage']."

(5) *The Contrary View (That a Mens Rea Requirement Should Be Inferred): People v. Hernandez*, 393 P.2d 673 (Cal. 1964), the California Supreme Court held that, absent a legislative directive to the contrary, a lack of criminal intent was a defense to a charge of statutory rape. It reversed the trial court's refusal to permit the defendant to present evidence of his reasonable belief that the complaining witness had reached the age of consent. The court also expressed the opinion that "the sexually experienced 15-year-old may be far more acutely aware of the implications of sexual intercourse than her sheltered cousin who is beyond the age of consent."

Commonwealth v. Hacker

15 A.3d 333 (Pa. 2011)

Justice EAKIN.

Appellee's then-13-year-old nephew, CG, and his 12-year-old female friend, NA, regularly visited her apartment. One night, playing a game of "truth or dare," appellee dared NA to perform oral sex on CG; when NA refused, appellee threatened to inform NA's mother that she had misbehaved. Appellee then took NA by the hand, walked her across the bedroom, and sat her down next to CG. NA then performed oral sex on CG.

A jury convicted appellee of solicitation to commit the rape of a child . . . . In post-trial motions, appellee argued she could not be convicted of solicitation because the Commonwealth failed to prove she knew NA was under the age of 13. The trial court, noting mistake of age is not a defense to the underlying crime, found the Commonwealth need not prove appellee knew NA was under the age of 13.

The Superior Court reversed appellee's solicitation conviction. The court reasoned that § 3121(c) [rape of a child] was a strict liability offense, but § 902(a) [solicitation of a crime] was a specific intent crime, such that appellee must have had a specific intent relative to all the elements of § 3121(c) [which criminalizes rape of a child]. The court acknowledged the legislative purpose of protecting children, but found it was constrained by the statutory language. Accordingly, the court concluded "without evidence that [appellee] knew N.A. was under thirteen, a jury could not conclude [appellee] intended to promote or facilitate the rape of someone under thirteen." As there was insufficient evidence appellee knew NA was under 13 years of age, the court reversed the solicitation conviction . . . .

The Commonwealth, noting that proof the actual perpetrator knew his victim's age is unnecessary, argues such proof [in a solicitation case]is therefore irrelevant . . . . The Commonwealth claims "intent," as used in § 902(a) [solicitation], merely modifies the requirement of the defendant's "promoting or facilitating" [of the crime]"; thus, it need only prove the solicitor intended to promote or facilitate acts which comprise a crime, not that the solicitor had knowledge those acts would comprise a crime . . . . The Commonwealth contends the General Assembly would have phrased the solicitation [statute differently] had it intended solicitation to include the intent to commit all the material elements of the underlying offense.

Appellee contrasts solicitation with § 3121(c) [defining rape of a child], which she contends "is not a specific intent crime. The only intent required is the intent to engage in sexual intercourse." She contends solicitation is a specific intent offense, requiring the Commonwealth to prove she believed NA was under the age of 13. Appellee alleges the Commonwealth's position would untenably render solicitation's *actus rea* and *mens rea* indistinguishable. . . .

We hold the Superior [*i.e.*, appellate] Court erred in stating § 3121(c) [rape of a child] was a strict liability offense. There are two main elements contained in the definition of rape of a child: (1) engaging in sexual intercourse, (2) with a person under the age of 13. 18 Pa.C.S. § 3121(c). As to the first element, no one argues a conviction may be had without some level of *mens rea*; one must intend to have (or cause) sexual intercourse. However, the General Assembly has expressly barred any mistake of age defense. Therefore, while § 3121(c) requires some *mens rea* for the sexual intercourse element, *mens rea* is immaterial to the age element of § 3121(c). The statute is, at most, an "impure strict liability [crime where] culpability is required with respect to at least one material element but is not required as to others." *Commonwealth v. Samuels*, 778 A.2d 638, 642 n. 3 (2001) (Saylor, J., concurring).

The purpose of the solicitation statute is to hold accountable those who would command, encourage, or request the commission of crimes by others. Clearly, without appellee's commands, encouragements and requests, there would never have been a crime against NA. The statute requires proof of such encouragement, but with the intent to accomplish the *acts* which comprise the crime, not necessarily with intent specific to all the *elements* of that crime, much less those crimes with elements for which scienter is irrelevant. Appellee intentionally encouraged the specific conduct which comprised this crime. The encouragement was with the intent of facilitating or promoting commission of that conduct. That is sufficient to satisfy the requirements of the solicitation statute.

When a statute includes a level of culpability, that level of culpability "shall apply to all the material elements of the offense, unless a contrary purpose plainly appears." 18 Pa.C.S. 302(d). The General Assembly has expressed a contrary purpose here. It has rendered a defendant's belief regarding a complainant's age irrelevant. *See* 18 Pa.C.S. § 3102 (limiting mistake of age defense). It is well-settled that the General Assembly has an interest in "recogniz[ing] that older, more mature individuals are in a position that would allow them to take advantage of the immaturity and poor judgment of very young minors." *Commonwealth v. Albert*, 758 A.2d 1149, 1154 (2000).

Given this interest, and that a defendant's belief regarding a complainant's age is immaterial [for rape of a child], a contrary purpose plainly appears [against requiring knowedge of age under the solicitation statute]. It is difficult to believe the legislature intended to require extra proof for an inchoate crime but excuse it for the underlying offense. As the General Assembly has expressly disapproved mistake of age defenses, and as the solicitation statute does not require proof of all elements of the underlying crime, we find a solicitor may not escape liability for the rape of a child merely by proffering ignorance as to the victim's age. [Reversed and conviction reinstated.]

JUSTICE SAYLOR, dissenting:

... The majority ... pronounces that a solicitor need not necessarily have intent specific to all elements of a crime. However, criminal solicitation expressly requires the "intent of promoting or facilitating [a crime's] commission," and a crime is nothing more or less than the sum total of its elements.

I acknowledge the deplorable factual circumstances presented here. Nevertheless, it remains my considered perspective that the criminal law should be enforced as it is written and according to conventional interpretive principles, consistently applied. To do otherwise, in my estimation, yields uncertainty and increased litigation and, thus, risks doing more harm than good. . . .

§ 5.06 Review Problems Based on Newspaper Reports

Note on These "Newspaper" Cases

The following cases all were recently covered in newspapers. The reports have been rewritten here, however, to emphasize the legal issues, although a newspaper style has been retained, as have the case facts. The reports will supply you with review material concerning some of the issues raised in this chapter about both assaultive and sexually assaultive offenses.

[A] Headline: "Too Many Items in the Express Checkout Leads to Assault"

LOWELL, Mass. — Karen Morgan, 38, hit a fellow grocery shopper with her hand and foot. Police charged her with "assault and battery with a dangerous weapon": her foot.

The victim, whose name was not disclosed, was a 51-year-old woman who said that the altercation stemmed from her having accidentally brought thirteen items into the express lane, which allowed only twelve or fewer items. The resulting dispute apparently enraged Ms. Morgan to such a degree that her conduct followed.

(1) *Is This Alleged Offense an Aggravated Assault, or Is It Merely a Simple One?* The use of "a foot" as a deadly or dangerous weapon is unlikely, but not impossible under the law. For example, as you have seen in this chapter, the MPC defines "deadly weapon" to include a firearm or, in addition, any material or substance "which in the manner it is used. . . . is known to be capable of producing death or serious bodily injury." Serious bodily injury, in turn, means "protracted loss or impairment" of a "bodily member or organ" or "serious, permanent disfigurement." Is a foot such a "weapon," and if so, under what circumstances? (If the charge is accurate, the defendant must have acted very forcefully indeed.)

(2) *What If Injury in Fact Results, in the Form of Bruising and Bleeding?* Even if an assault of this alleged kind causes serious bleeding and bruising, and even though "serious bodily injury" may provide an alternative way, in addition to use of

a deadly or dangerous weapon, in which an assault can become aggravated, the definition of serious bodily injury makes this pathway for aggravated assault unlikely here. Why? (Perhaps it could be made out by "serious, permanent disfigurement," which is another way of finding such an injury, but not unless disfigurement actually resulted.)

(3) *What if the Key Contacts and Injuries Were Unintentional?* Sometimes, in situations of this kind, accused persons may testify that given contacts between a foot or fist and the other persons were unintended: "I didn't mean to kick him/her, but in the confusion, with both of us thrashing around on the ground, it's possible that contact resulted." Even if this version of events is true, and even if the contact is unintended, an assault or battery may have taken place; the MPC, for example, provides that assault can be committed recklessly (or if done with a deadly weapon, negligently). Can you explain why, in light of these mental state requirements, an unintentional contact could suffice for assault?

[B] Headline: "Former Teacher Sentenced in Sexual Assault of Student"

HOUSTON—An ex-teacher got a 78-year sentence Friday for sexual activities with two students who were thirteen and fourteen years old. The judge also delivered a ringing condemnation of the defendant.

"You're a bigger threat to our culture and our students than Osama bin Laden and his cave dwellers," said District Judge Ted Poe to the defendant, Lonnie Ray Andrews, who committed some of the acts on his desk. "The arrogance to have sexual relations with a student in a classroom is beyond belief." The judge imposed the maximum sentence of 20 years on each of three sexual assault of a child counts, and 18 years on an indecency with a child count, and ordered the sentences to be served consecutively. The defendant had sexual intercourse with the older girl six times. His crime with the younger one involved sexual activity committed when he put his hand into her pants.

(1) *Sexual Assault of a Child.* Obviously, the prosecution had a lighter burden in charging the intercourse-related crimes as sexual assaults of a child rather than as sexual assaults. Why? Consider the proof elements that would have applied if the sexual assaults had been committed instead by force, as well as the proof elements that substituted for them in light of the age of the students.

(2) *Sexual Assault of an Adult under Similar Circumstances?* In some jurisdictions, however, the crime would be made out even if the students were adults, and even if the victims ostensibly consented, because of the relationship between the parties, irrespective of the age of the students. Can you explain the kind of statutory provision that would cause this result?

(3) *Aggravated Sexual Assault?* The judge evidently considered the circumstances of the crimes egregious. Yet they did not qualify as aggravated (or first-degree,

in some jurisdictions) sexual assaults, and the judge probably imposed consecutive sentences as an alternative means of making the result fit the crimes. Can you explain why, even if they were particularly blameworthy, these offenses did not qualify for "aggravated" treatment, with enhanced sentences, but were only "ordinary" sexual assaults with lesser (though still substantial) sentences?

Chapter 6

General Defenses to Crimes

"The better part of valour is discretion; in the which better part I have saved my life." — Shakespeare, *Henry IV*, Part One V: 4

"Every puny whipster gets my sword." — Shakespeare, *Othello* V: 2

§ 6.01 Introduction to Defenses

(1) *Sources of Defenses: Mainly Statutes Today with Some Common Law Additions.* At one time, defenses were common law doctrines. Courts, not legislatures, defined them. Today, defenses are primarily statutory. Modern criminal codes list and define defenses, including former common law defenses such as self-defense and insanity. Many new codes also specifically repeal common law defenses, so that defenses are limited to those enumerated in the criminal code. In other jurisdictions, the common law "fills in the gaps" of statutes by adding defenses not mentioned in statutes and by adding definitions to defenses that are only partially defined by statutes. *See, e.g.,* N.J. Code Crim. Just. § 2C:2–5 (retaining common law defenses not covered by statute but not when it "plainly appears" the legislature intended to exclude the defense). Note, however, that in the federal system, defenses still derive primarily from the common law.

(2) *Overlapping Defenses.* Several criminal defenses may be available in a single case, depending on the policy interests implicated by the allegedly criminal activity. Assume, for example, that a burglar breaks into a house and threatens to kill people inside. If the occupants resist the burglar with deadly force, they could defend against a homicide charge by asserting self-defense, defense of others, defense of property, and crime prevention.

(3) *The Dilemma that Underlies Criminal Defenses — and Their Limits.* The two quotations from Shakespeare that open this chapter emphasize the problem of defenses in general, and particularly self-defense. There is tension between allowing citizens to protect themselves, on the one hand, and punishing those who unnecessarily kill or injure fellow human beings, on the other. The law would depreciate the value of human life if it allowed a person to use his "sword" on "[e]very puny whipster." As Shakespeare's other character said, "Discretion is the better part of valour," and all of the defenses in this chapter are limited by principles that force the actor to use discretion.

Note on Defensive Theories and the Burden of Proof: "Failure of Proof" Defenses, Rebuttals, True Defenses, and Affirmative Defenses

(1) *Three Different Kinds of Defensive Theories: "Failure of Proof" Defenses, Defenses, and Affirmative Defenses.* There are many kinds of "defenses" in criminal cases, and they fall into several categories. The terminology is confusing and inconsistent. In the most general terms, there are two broad categories of defenses: failure of proof defenses (the defendant rebuts an element of the crime) and true defenses. In many jurisdictions, "true defenses" are often further divided into "defenses" and "affirmative defenses." The main difference may be that the defendant, not the state, must prove "affirmative defenses."

(2) *True Defenses v. Failure of Proof Defenses.* Is a particular defensive theory a true "defense," or does it merely attack the prosecution's proof? The distinction is important and subtle. A true defense adds another element to the case, one that the defendant must raise and usually offer evidence to establish, whereas a failure-of-proof defense does not add an element; it merely asserts that the government cannot prove its case. Indeed, one could argue that a failure-of-proof defense isn't really a defense; it simply rebuts the government's proof on an element of the crime.

For example, self-defense is categorized as a "true defense" to prosecution for a crime of violence such as assault or murder. The accused must raise the defense by offering some supporting evidence. By contrast, a defendant facing charges of intentional murder may testify that "I had no intent to kill" or introduce evidence that "someone else killed the victim." The attempt to counter prosecution proof is a failure of proof defense, not a true defense.

(3) *Rebuttals.* A "rebuttal" is similar to a failure-of-proof defense and sometimes is described in the same terms. A rebuttal involves evidence presented by the defense that inferentially contradicts an element of the crime. A defense of alibi is an illustration of rebuttal evidence.

(4) *Procedural Requirements.* Sometimes, a defendant who wants to offer proof to contradict prosecution evidence must take certain procedural steps. With alibi, for example, the defendant may have to give pretrial notice to the prosecution, so that the government can investigate the alibi.

(5) *Confusion of These Terms in Informal Speech.* People often refer to claims such as alibi as "defenses." But true "defenses" and "affirmative defenses" are different from failure-of-proof defenses, because they place burdens on the defendant.

(6) *Standard of Proof, Burden of Proof, Burden of Going Forward, and Burden of Persuasion.* The prosecution has the burden of proving each element of a crime beyond a reasonable doubt. Yet the broad use of the term "burden of proof" actually combines three distinct ideas (standard of proof, burden of production, and burden of persuasion).

(a) *Standard of Proof.* The standard of proof refers to the degree of certainty that the law requires before a jury may make a particular finding. In a criminal case, the standard of proof for the elements of a crime is beyond a reasonable doubt.

For defenses, however, the rules vary. States may set the standard of proof as they see fit. For example, a state may require proof of a defense beyond a reasonable doubt (a very high standard), by clear and convincing evidence (a high standard), or by a preponderance of the evidence (the same standard as in civil cases). *See, e.g.,* N.H. Rev. Stat. Ann. § 628.2 (defendant has burden of proving insanity defense by clear and convincing evidence).

(b) *Burden of Production.* Commentators distinguish between (1) burden of production and (2) burden of persuasion. The *burden of production* (sometimes referred to as the burden of going forward) refers to which side must present sufficient evidence to raise an issue. Without this modicum of proof (sometimes called a *prima facie* case), the issue cannot go to the jury.

For the elements of a crime, the government has the burden of production. By contrast, the defense has the burden of producing some proof of the existence of a defense. For example, a defendant who wants to raise an insanity defense must introduce some proof of insanity. If not, the issue of insanity is not raised and the jury will not receive a jury charge on the issue.

(c) *Burden of Persuasion.* The *burden of persuasion* refers to which side must sustain the relevant standard of proof. The prosecution has the burden of persuasion for each element of a crime. But for true defenses, a jurisdiction is free to allocate the burden of persuasion as it sees fit. For example, the burden of persuasion on the insanity defense often is placed on the defendant, who must not only raise the issue (satisfy the burden of production) but also convince the jury (burden of persuasion) by the applicable standard (such as preponderance of the evidence).

(7) *The New York Statute, Below: Defenses and Affirmative Defenses.* To fine tune the relevant burdens of production and persuasion and the standard of proof, several states divide true defenses into two categories: "defenses," where the defendant must raise the defense (burden of production) but the government must persuade the jury beyond a reasonable doubt that the defense does not apply, and "affirmative defenses," which instead require the defendant not only to offer some evidence (burden of production), but also to persuade the jury (burden of persuasion). New York's statute is fairly typical in making this distinction. Other sections of New York law indicate whether a particular issue is a "defense" (*e.g.,* self-defense, defense of third persons, crime prevention) or an "affirmative defense" (*e.g.,* duress, entrapment, renunciation, insanity).

New York Penal Law § 25.00: "Defenses" and "Affirmative Defenses"

(1) When a "defense," other than an "affirmative defense" defined by statute, is raised at a trial, the people have the burden of disproving such defense beyond a reasonable doubt.

(2) When a defense declared by statute to be an "affirmative defense" is raised at a trial, the defendant has the burden of establishing such defense by a preponderance of the evidence.

Read MPC § 1.12 (2), (4) (defenses and affirmative defenses) in the MPC Appendix.

Note on "True" Defenses and "Affirmative" Defenses

(1) *"Defenses" in New York: Defendants First Must "Raise" Them by Evidence, and Only Then Must the Prosecution Disprove Them.* In many states, including New York, "defenses" are different from failure-of-proof exculpatory theories. The defendant, not the prosecution, must inject the defense (burden of production) into the case. This is the meaning of N.Y. Penal Law § 25.00(1), above, which requires the defendant to offer enough evidence to "raise" the defense before it can be part of the case at all.

The burden of production on the defendant is real, but it is not very difficult to satisfy. The defendant must provide some evidence but need not prove the defense. In states that follow this pattern, a defendant injects a defense into the case (establishes a prima facie case) if he provides enough evidence for a reasonable juror to find that the defense creates a reasonable doubt. The defendant has met the burden of production, and the true defense is "raised."

(2) *What Happens Once a True Defense Has Been "Raised"?* Under the New York provision, once the defendant "raises" a "defense" with this minimal amount of evidence, the burden shifts to the prosecution to disprove the "defense" beyond a reasonable doubt. *See* above. If the defendant raises a defense (*i.e.*, meets the burden of production), the trial judge must instruct the jury about it even if the judge does not believe the defense. If a defendant fails to raise a defense (*i.e.*, fails to meet the burden of production), the judge will not instruct the jury about it.

(3) *"Affirmative" Defenses in New York: The Defendant Must Not Only Raise Them, but Also Prove Them by the Preponderance of the Evidence.* An "affirmative defense" in New York and many other states requires the defendant to satisfy the burden of production and also persuade the jury that the defense is proven by the preponderance of the evidence. *See* above. The jury will receive an instruction that it may acquit because of the affirmative defense, but only if the defendant has convinced the jury by the greater weight (preponderance) of the evidence.

Notes and Questions

(1) *The Differing Treatment of Self-Defense (a "Defense") and Insanity (an Affirmative Defense") under Some Statutory Systems.* In many jurisdictions, self-defense is a "defense," while insanity is an "affirmative defense." In the following cases, assume that the offense is murder and that the New York statute controls. What difference would result from this distinction between the types of defenses?

(a) *Evidence of Murder Only.* The prosecution has offered sufficient evidence to prove a murder. The defense rests without offering any evidence, but the defendant requests that the judge charge the jury to acquit if there is a reasonable doubt about self-defense. Self-defense is a true defense and a "defense" under the New York statute. The judge should not charge the jury on self-defense, at all. Why?

(b) *Weak Evidence of Self-Defense.* Same as (a), except the defendant testifies that the deceased made a "hip-pocket motion, as if to draw a weapon." The judge believes this testimony is not credible. But still, the judge must give the self-defense charge. Why?

(c) *Weak Evidence of Insanity.* Instead of self-defense, assume the defendant calls a psychologist to testify that the defendant suffered from clinical depression that "could have precipitated" the homicide. But the expert is thoroughly impeached on cross-examination, and a credible prosecution expert testifies against insanity. Recall that insanity is an affirmative defense. The judge now must give a jury charge on insanity, but the jury probably should not acquit. Why? (Has the burden of persuasion been met?)

(2) *Reasons for a Legislature to Distinguish Affirmative Defenses from Defenses.* Why do you think some state legislatures might decide to define self-defense as a "defense" but insanity as an "affirmative defense"? Consider the nature of the two defenses and the public desirability of accepting each.

Note on Defenses of Justification or Excuse

(1) *The Distinction between Defenses of Justification and Defenses of Excuse.* The common law and many other codes provide a separate and more fundamental distinction, between "justification" defenses and "excuse" defenses.

A defendant who raises a *justification* defense admits she committed the elements of the offense but denies doing anything morally wrong. Indeed, the defendant may claim that she has done something right. For example, self-defense is classified as a "justification" because it is based on a societal decision that using reasonable force to defend oneself is not wrong and, in addition, protects law-abiding people.

By contrast, a defendant who raises an *excuse* defense admits he committed the elements of the offense and did wrong but also asserts he is not criminally responsible for these actions. The conduct is not justified, but it is excused because the defendant's decisionmaking ability was impaired so that he is not morally blameworthy.

(2) *Why Does It Matter?* Ordinarily, the classification of a defense as a justification or excuse has little practical significance. The Model Penal Code even suggests that "any possible value of attempting such a line would be outweighed by the cost of complicating the [definitions]." MPC, art. 3, Introduction. Yet the theoretical difference between justification and excuse may determine legislative differences in treatment. For example, the law may be more generous in recognizing a justification (self-defense) than an excuse (insanity).

§ 6.02 Failure-of-Proof Defensive Theories and Rebuttals: The Example of the "Alibi Defense"

Note on Alibi and Notice-of-Alibi Requirements

(1) *The First Element of Every Crime.* The first element of every crime is that this defendant committed it. An effort to raise a reasonable doubt about any element, including whether the defendant is really the perpetrator, is not a true "defense." In our terms, it is a failure-of-proof defense. Likewise, so is an attack on the prosecution's proof, such as an alibi, that introduces a contradictory theory or rebuttal. People often refer to alibi as a "defense," however, and alibi does have characteristics that distinguish it from other kinds of failure-of-proof theories.

(2) *Pretrial Notice as a Requirement before the Defendant May Present Alibi Witnesses.* One characteristic of alibi that makes it resemble a true defense (although it is not one) is that the defendant usually raises it with her own evidence, just as in the case of true defenses. For example, if a robbery occurred in Chicago and the defendant claims she was in San Francisco at the time, the defense may offer witnesses who saw the defendant in San Francisco.

"Alibi" comes from Latin syllables meaning "another place." The concept seems clear, but the cases raise difficult issues. For example, if the prosecution does not know the defendant will offer the alibi and has no idea who the alibi witnesses will be or where they might claim the defendant was, the prosecution cannot investigate the alibi. For this reason, many jurisdictions require a defendant to give pretrial notice to the prosecution before offering an alibi. Using the illustration above, a notice requirement will allow the prosecution to investigate whether the defendant was actually in San Francisco.

State v. Deffebaugh

89 P.3d 582 (Kan. 2004)

Reaffirmed in State v. Greene

329 P.2d 450 (Kan. 2014)

The opinion of the court was delivered by GERNON, J.:

Charles R. Deffebaugh, Jr., appeals his conviction for one count of selling cocaine. Deffebaugh's conviction resulted from a controlled purchase of two rocks of cocaine by a police informant who was cooperating with the Coffeyville police to avoid prosecution for a DUI.... [The informant, provided the officers with a description of the man named "Jimmie" who had taken her money and given her two rocks of cocaine, and she also picked the defendant from a photo lineup as one of the four men at the controlled sale.]

Within 24 hours of the controlled purchase, Detective Robson obtained a search warrant for the house associated with the controlled purchase. When the warrant was executed, the police found Deffebaugh and 10 other black males in the house, along with cash, cocaine, and guns. Deffebaugh claimed ownership of some of the money found on the floor, including one of the marked bills from the controlled purchase.

At trial, Deffebaugh called [a witness named] Shobe to testify that Shobe was present at the controlled purchase but Deffebaugh was not there. The State objected to Shobe's testimony, claiming that Deffebaugh [had]failed to give notice of an alibi defense [as required by state criminal procedure]. The trial court [agreed with the State and] prohibited Shobe from testifying that Shobe was present at the controlled purchase but that Deffebaugh was not there. . . .

The State argues that the trial court correctly prohibited Shobe from testifying regarding Deffebaugh's presence at the drug sale. The State contends that Shobe's testimony falls squarely under K.S.A. 22–3218, which requires a defendant to provide notice before offering . . . an alibi. . . .

K.S.A. 22–3218 provides in pertinent part:

> (1) In the trial of any criminal action where . . . the defendant *proposes to offer evidence to the effect that he was at some other place* at the time of the crime charged, he shall give notice in writing of that fact to the prosecuting attorney except that no such notice shall be required to allow testimony as to alibi, by the defendant himself, in his own defense. *The notice shall state where defendant contends he was at the time of the crime, and shall have endorsed thereon the names of witnesses he proposes to use in support of such contention.* . . .

> (4) Unless the defendant gives the notice as above provided he shall not be permitted to offer evidence to the effect that he was at some other place at the time of the crime charged. . . . (Emphasis added.)

Although the defense does not generally have to disclose the names of defense witnesses prior to trial, the disclosure of alibi witnesses is an exception to that rule. The purpose of K.S.A. 22–3218 is to protect the State from last minute, easily fabricated defenses. The notice requirement allows the State to investigate and call rebuttal witnesses if necessary.

Kansas case law has not addressed the question of what is an alibi subject to the notice provisions of K.S.A. 22–3218. Dicta in prior Kansas cases has established two definitions for "alibi" . . . . In *State v. Pham*, 675 P.2d 848 (1984), this court distinguished an alibi defense from a general denial by noting that "[a]n alibi places the defendant at the relevant time in a different place than the scene involved and so removed therefrom as to render it impossible for the accused to be the guilty party."

Dicta in other Kansas cases [provide] a broader definition for alibi [and the cases also note that an alibi jury instruction] is not necessary for the alibi defense because it "is not an affirmative defense, as is entrapment or insanity; it consists only of evidence showing that the defendant was not present at the time or place of the crime." *State v. Peters*, 656 P.2d 768 (1983) (concluding that courts need not instruct on alibi as an affirmative defense). . . .

K.S.A. 22–3218 is ambiguous. In the first sentence, the statute defines alibi as "evidence to the effect that [the accused] was at some other place at the time of the crime charged." By using the phrase "to the effect that," the legislature does not limit alibi evidence to direct testimony but includes evidence that raises an inference that the accused was at some other place. The State is relying on this inference as the basis for its argument that Shobe's proposed testimony is alibi evidence. Even though there is no direct evidence of where Deffebaugh was at the time of the drug sale, Shobe's testimony that Deffebaugh was not there [implies] that Deffebaugh was at some other place.

The State's argument, however, overlooks the language in the second sentence of the statute, which provides that "[t]he notice shall state where defendant contends he was at the time of the crime, and shall have endorsed thereon the names of witnesses he proposes to use in support of such contention." K.S.A. 22–3218. This sentence appears to limit alibi evidence to direct evidence that the defendant was at another specific place. Otherwise, the defendant cannot state where he contends he was in the notice.

[We hold] that Shobe was not an alibi witness under K.S.A. 22–3218 because Shobe could not testify regarding Deffebaugh's specific whereabouts at the time of the drug sale. . . .

. . . In this case, the State knew it had the burden of proving that Deffebaugh was present when the drug sale occurred. . . . The State had an opportunity to interview Shobe when he was arrested with Deffebaugh. . . . These facts do not support the conclusion that Shobe's testimony as an eyewitness was a surprise to the State or that the State needed time to investigate Shobe's statement. Consequently, there is no reason to exclude Shobe's eyewitness testimony simply because he would have testified that Deffebaugh was not there.

. . . K.S.A. 22–3218 does not require a defendant to provide notice when he or she intends to introduce eyewitness testimony regarding his or her presence at the scene of the crime. . . . [Conviction reversed.]

Notes and Questions

(1) *Is the Court Wrong in Deffebaugh about the Prosecution's Need for This Information About the Witness?* The Kansas court reasons that the prosecution did not need notice of the witness's identity in this particular case because Shobe was arrested with Deffebaugh, and it uses this conclusion to support its result. But could the court be wrong? The prosecution may have been justified in believing that there would be no "presence elsewhere" evidence, given the absence of notice and the wording of the Kansas statute. And thus, the prosecution had no reason to investigate what it argued was Deffenbaugh's alibi.

In the next case that arises in Kansas, the witness who testifies, "the defendant wasn't there," may be someone the prosecution cannot identify or investigate before trial. Arguably, this possibility is even stronger if the "elsewhere" testimony is a recent falsification. For example, a defendant who can cajole (or coerce) perjurious testimony may be able to obtain a witness who falsely says that "the defendant wasn't there." The policy favoring notice is at its strongest in this situation. Did the court undervalue this possibility?

(2) *What Is an Alibi?* Different jurisdictions provide different answers. For example, in *State v. Tutson*, 899 A.2d 598 (Conn. 2006), the court considered whether evidence that a particular vehicle was in a specific distant location should be considered an alibi for purposes of the notice requirement. The state argued that notice was necessary because testimony about the location of the car allowed an inference about the location of the defendant. The court agreed. In *United States v. Llinas*, 373 F.3d 26 (1st Cir. 2004), the court held there was no "alibi." It decided that documents were not "witnesses," and therefore employment records dealing with the defendant's presence at work were not covered by the notice-of-alibi requirement. But didn't the prosecution have as great a need for pretrial investigation as in cases with persons as alibi witnesses? (Actually, there must have been a live "alibi" witness to authenticate the documents!) *But see United States v. Ford*, 683 F.3d 761 (7th Cir. 2012) (witness who testified it would have been psychologically impossible for the defendant to have committed the bank robbery was an alibi witness).

(3) *The Defense Lawyer's Dilemma: What to Do with Alibi Witnesses Who Transparently Are Not Credible.* An alibi need not be fully persuasive to cause an acquittal; it need only create a reasonable doubt. This conclusion, paradoxically, leads to a dilemma for the defense lawyer: whether to present alibi witnesses who are not completely credible. If the jury hears alibi testimony that it concludes is false, it might be more likely to convict. But if the defense lawyer declines to call alibi witnesses because they are not credible, the defendant is deprived of a potential defense.

The defense lawyer with a weak alibi witness thus faces a no-win situation, with a very real danger of being labeled "ineffective" for either strategy. *Compare Clinkscale v. Carter*, 375 F.3d 430 (6th Cir. 2004) (concurring judge invited defendant to file another habeas corpus petition asserting trial counsel was ineffective for presenting an alibi that the jury was unlikely to credit), *with Jacobs v. State*, 880 So.2d 548 (Fla. 2004) (granting hearing to determine whether counsel was ineffective for failing to present alibi witness). Public accusations of ineffectiveness are acutely damaging to defense lawyers, and the risk of being found ineffective could lead to decisions that are contrary to rational defense strategies about presenting alibis.

(4) *Should the Prosecution Be Required, Reciprocally, to Give the Defense Notice of "Anti-Alibi" Testimony?* Federal Rule of Criminal Procedure 12.1(b) establishes a two-way notice process for alibis. Once the defendant provides notice of alibi, the Government must notify the defense if it intends to call rebuttal witnesses, and it must also identify them.

(5) *A Jury Instruction on Alibi.* Many states authorize an instruction that tells the jury to acquit if the alibi witnesses create a reasonable doubt. Strictly speaking, this instruction is unnecessary because it is implicit in the state's burden to prove

the defendant's commission of the crime beyond a reasonable doubt—although defense counsel might favor such an instruction.

Some states allow a jury instruction that could weaken the defense's alibi proof:

> An alibi is easy to prove and hard to disprove, and testimony offered to prove this defense should be subjected, like all other evidence in the case, to rigid scrutiny for the reason that witnesses, even when truthful, may be honestly mistaken of, or forgetful of times and places.

State v. Peters, 656 P.2d 768 (Kan. 1983). Is this jury instruction appropriate, or does it tip the scales too much against the defendant?

Note on Frequency of "True" Defenses

(1) *What Little Is Known: Some Surprises.* Little is known about the actual use of defenses in criminal cases, but the available information suggests that formal defenses are seldom used at trial, that some defenses are virtually never used, and that defenses play only a minor role in the nonjudicial resolution of criminal cases. *See* Neil P. Cohen, Michael G. Johnson & Tracy B. Henley, *The Prevalence and Use of Criminal Defenses: A Preliminary Study*, 60 Tennessee L. Rev. 957, 981 (1993) (survey of judges, prosecutors, and defense lawyers about cases they handled in last 12 months).

(2) *Self-Defense Is the Most Common.* The study cited above showed that self-defense is by far the most common trial defense, at issue in 1.9% of trials (the study excluded alibi, which is not a "true defense"). Other defenses arise far less frequently: intoxication (0.7%), insanity (0.7%), defense of property (0.4%), defense of others (0.2%), duress (0.2%), entrapment (0.2%), necessity (0.2%), diminished responsibility (0.1%), and crime prevention (0%).

(3) *Non-Trial Use of Defenses.* The *possible use* of a defense had an impact in approximately 7% of cases, meaning that it affected the outcome of the case by, for example, affecting a plea agreement or leading to a dismissal. Again, self-defense had the greatest impact (2.5% of cases), followed by intoxication (1%), diminished responsibility (0.7%), entrapment (0.6%), insanity (0.6%), duress (0.3%), defense of third persons (0.3%), defense of property (0.3%), necessity (0.2%), and crime prevention (0.1%).

§6.03 Justification ("I Had a Right to Do It") as a Basis for True Defenses

[A] Self-Defense: A "True" Defense of Justification When Its Elements Are "Raised" by the Defendant

(1) *Why Does the Law Recognize Self-Defense?* Self-defense is based on the widely-shared idea that people ought to be permitted to defend themselves when attacked. An additional argument is that the urge to preserve or defend oneself is so embedded

in human nature that the legal system likely could not prevent it even if there was some reason to do so.

(2) *General Definition.* In general terms, self-defense is both a true defense and a justification. It allows a person to use reasonable force to defend against the imminent use of unlawful force by another person. Thus, in those situations when the defense applies, it permits a person to inflict (or threaten) an appropriate amount of physical harm on another person without incurring criminal liability for the injury. In virtually all American jurisdictions, however, the defense is limited to instances in which a reasonable person would react as the defendant did.

(3) *For What Crimes Is Self-Defense Available?* While most self-defense cases arise in the homicide or attempted homicide context, the defense also can be invoked when non-deadly force is used, and it is an available defense to other crimes, at least those of the "assaultive" type. A few jurisdictions bar the use of self-defense if the defendant is charged with a crime of recklessness or negligence. *See, e.g.,* Ala. Code § 13A-3–21. Thus, if a person is attacked with deadly force and negligently or recklessly shoots wildly in response and kills a bystander, the amount of force may have been reasonable, but self-defense may not be available if the defendant is charged with a homicide crime involving reckless or negligent conduct.

[1] Overview of Self-Defense Doctrine

Note on the Elements and Limits of Self-Defense

(1) *Elements of Self-Defense.* Most jurisdictions employ a common definition of self-defense.

(a) *Belief in the Need to Use Force Must Be "Reasonable."* A key element of self-defense is that the defendant must act under a *reasonable* belief that self-defense is necessary. For example, assume that an aggressor points a gun at the defendant and threatens to shoot the defendant on the spot. Even if the aggressor's gun is only a toy, the accused may be justified in using self-defense if the toy gun looked so authentic that self-defense was reasonable.

(b) *Reasonable Belief that the Attack is Imminent.* Another key element is that the actor does not have to wait until he or she is attacked, but the actor must have a reasonable belief that the actual or threatened harm is "imminent." A vague threat of future violence likely will not create a justification. Likewise, verbal provocation alone ("mere words") usually will not support a claim of self-defense. *See, e.g.,* Ariz. Rev. Stat. Ann. § 13–404 (self-defense not authorized in response to "verbal provocation alone").

(c) *Only a Reasonable Amount of Defensive Force.* Just as the person asserting self-defense must have a reasonable belief in the need to use force immediately, the amount of force must be reasonable under the circumstances. Excessive force is not justified. For example, if the attacker slaps the defendant in the face, this non-deadly force, though unlawful, would not justify the defendant in pulling a pistol and killing the aggressor. The amount of force is unreasonable under the circumstances.

(d) *Force Threatened or Used Against Person Asserting Self-defense Must Be Unlawful.* The defense of self-defense only permits a response to *unlawful* force. If the person who is the initial aggressor is using lawful force—such as a police officer using legal force to arrest the defendant—then the person being arrested may not resist and then assert self-defense.

(e) *Actual Belief: Sometimes a Forgotten Element.* Self-defense requires the actor to entertain reasonable *beliefs* about the need to use force and the amount of force used to repel the aggression. What gets forgotten is that the actor must also have an *honest or actual belief* that he or she is being attacked and that this amount of force is needed to protect against the attack. Thus, a person who knew that deadly force was not needed in the situation, even if a reasonable person would believe it was, may not assert self-defense after shooting the attacker.

(2) *Deadly Force: More Restricted.* In many jurisdictions, deadly force may only be used to prevent the risk of imminent death or serious bodily injury, as opposed to less harmful injuries. But some states also allow deadly force if the actor reasonably believes that the other person was engaged in specified serious crimes. *See, e.g.,* Ala. Code § 13A-3–23.

(3) *First Aggressor and Escalation.* The law of self-defense generally denies the initial aggressor the benefit of the defense, which reaches only those who respond to actual or imminent "unlawful" force; not to those who first use unlawful force. If X attacks Y and Y attacks back in lawful self-defense, X usually does not have the right of self-defense against Y's self-defense (although there are exceptions, such as X's withdrawal or excessive force by Y).

(4) *"Imperfect" Self-Defense Claims.* Many jurisdictions offer an incomplete defense, called *imperfect self-defense*, resulting in a verdict of manslaughter (usually called "voluntary" manslaughter) rather than murder, where the defendant's belief that he or she was under immediate attack is honest but unreasonable, or where the defendant used excessive force in self-defense. In essence, this incomplete defense shows sudden passion and reduces the severity of the crime but does not relieve all criminal liability for the use of force.

Note on Deadly Force, the Retreat Rule, and the Stand-Your-Ground Alternative

(1) *The Retreat Rule versus Stand-Your-Ground.* While one is never required to retreat before using non-deadly force against an aggressor, many jurisdictions require a person to retreat before using *deadly force* in self-defense, if it is safe to retreat. This rule, called the *retreat* rule, differs from the common law, which did not require retreat. The common law approach was sometimes called the "true man rule," on the theory that a "true man" would not retreat, but instead would stand his ground even if it meant the use of deadly force. Thus, the retreat rule emphasizes nonviolence and the value of life. Some jurisdictions still do not require retreat; the no-retreat doctrine is often called "stand your ground."

(2) *Rejecting the Retreat Rule: Florida's Stand Your Ground Rule.* In recent years, some states have rejected the retreat rule. Florida extends self-defense to include a person's "right to stand his or her ground and meet force with force, including deadly force," if he or she reasonably believes it is necessary to do so, "to prevent imminent death or great bodily harm to himself or herself or another." *See* Fla. Stat. § 776.013(3). *See also* Oh. Rev. Code § 2901.09; *State v. Sandoval*, 156 P.3d 60 (Or. 2007) (holding the Oregon code does not require retreat).

(3) *Arguments for and Against.* The Florida bill's sponsor, State Rep. Dennis Baxley, declared that following the retreat requirement is "a good way to get shot in the back." Baxley added that after his bill, "criminals will think twice," and Governor Jeb Bush called it "a good, common sense, anti-crime" measure. Opponents pointed out that no one has to retreat if getting shot in the back is a possibility; retreat is required only when it is safe. They also argued that retreat issues rarely involve attacks by violent strangers. Most self-defense cases raising a duty to retreat involve escalating violence between people who know each other. The stand-your-ground amendment, they claimed, would encourage people to escalate the violence rather than discontinue it. Which position is persuasive?

(4) *Much Ado About Nothing?* If the defendant ordinarily must retreat before using deadly force unless retreat would be unsafe, will there be many cases where the defendant should have retreated but did not do so? Because of the imminent harm requirement of self-defense, it must be rare that the defendant would be entitled to use deadly force but could retreat safely. In other words, it may be that the actual result under the retreat rule and Florida's stand-your-ground will be the same. Consider the following problem.

Problem 6A (Self-Defense): Who Was the Aggressor; Who Was Entitled to Stand His Ground?

(compiled from news accounts)

(1) Trayvon Martin, a 17-year-old African American male, was walking toward the home of his father's fiancé in a gated community in Sanford, Florida. He was not armed. George Zimmerman, a resident of the gated community and its neighborhood watch coordinator, was in his car when he noticed Martin. He called the Sanford police department and made the following statements: "Hey, we've had some break-ins in my neighborhood, and there's a real suspicious guy. . . . This guy looks like he's up to no good, or he's on drugs or something. It's raining and he's just walking around, looking about." The conversation continued, and Zimmerman stated that Martin had noticed him, was looking at him, and was running away. The dispatcher told Zimmerman that he did not need to follow Martin and that he should stay "near the mailboxes" to meet up with a police officer who was on his way.

Instead, Zimmerman, who was armed with a semi-automatic pistol, got out of his car and followed Martin. Zimmerman later claimed that Martin appeared "out of nowhere" and attacked him, while other witness reports suggest that Zimmerman confronted Martin. A scuffle ensued, during which Zimmerman sustained a bloody nose and other contusions. Zimmerman testified that Martin was bashing his head against concrete. But he was able to draw his gun, and he shot Martin once in the chest. Police arrived soon after and took Zimmerman into custody. Martin died at the scene.

Zimmerman was detained, questioned, and initially released without being charged, because the Sanford police initially accepted his claim of self-defense. After intense public scrutiny, including allegations that race played a role in the decision not to charge Zimmerman, a Special Prosecutor was appointed, and Zimmerman was charged with second degree murder.

(2) How does the law of self-defense interact with these events, including initial aggressor issues, reasonableness, and deadly force? How does Florida's stand your ground law impact your answer? (Perhaps not at all; maybe retreat was not possible or safe.)

(3) The jury acquitted Zimmerman of second degree murder. Is this result consistent with the purposes of self-defense doctrine?

Illinois Criminal Code § 7.1: Self-Defense
720 Ill. Comp. Stat. 5/7–1

§ 7–1 *Use of Force in Defense of Person.* A person is justified in the use of force against another when and to the extent that he reasonably believes that such conduct is necessary to defend himself or another against such other's imminent use of unlawful force. However, he is justified in the use of force which is intended or likely to cause death or great bodily harm only if he believes that such force is necessary to prevent imminent death or great bodily harm to himself or another, or the commission of a forcible felony.

New York Penal Law § 35.15: Justification; Use of Physical Force in Defense of a Person

1. A person may, subject to the provisions of subdivision two, use physical force upon another person when and to the extent he or she reasonably believes such to be necessary to defend himself, herself or a third person from what he or she reasonably believes to be the use or imminent use of unlawful physical force by such other person, unless:

(a) The latter's conduct was provoked by the actor with intent to cause physical injury to another person; or

(b) The actor was the initial aggressor; except that in such case the use of [defensive] physical force is nevertheless justifiable if the actor has withdrawn from the encounter and effectively communicated such withdrawal to such other person but the latter persists in continuing the incident by the use or threatened imminent use of unlawful physical force; or

(c) The physical force involved is the product of a combat by agreement not specifically authorized by law.

2. A person may not use deadly physical force upon another person under circumstances specified in subdivision one unless:

(a) The actor reasonably believes that such other person is using or about to use deadly physical force. Even in such case, however, the actor may not use deadly physical force if he or she knows that with complete personal safety, to oneself and others he or she may avoid the necessity of so doing by retreating; except that the actor is under no duty to retreat if he or she is:

(i) in his or her dwelling and not the initial aggressor; or

(ii) a police officer or peace officer or a person assisting a police officer or a peace officer at the latter's direction, acting pursuant to section 35.30; or

(b) He or she reasonably believes that such other person is committing or attempting to commit a kidnapping, forcible rape, forcible criminal sexual act or robbery; or

(c) He or she reasonably believes that such other person is committing or attempting to commit a burglary, and the circumstances are such that the use of deadly physical force is authorized by subdivision three of section 35.20.

[2] Decisional Law Applying the Self-Defense Statutes

People v. Goetz
497 N.E.2d 41 (N.Y. 1986)

Reaffirmed, People v. Valentin
74 N.E.3d 632 (N.Y. 2017)

CHIEF JUDGE WACHTLER. . . .

[This New York case made major national and international news. It was given the title of "The Subway Vigilante Case," although the label might not be accurate.]

A Grand Jury has indicted defendant on attempted murder, assault, and other charges for having shot and wounded four youths on a New York City subway train after one or two of the youths approached him and asked for $5. The lower courts, concluding that the prosecutor's charge to the Grand Jury on the defense of justification was erroneous, have dismissed the attempted murder, assault and weapons possession charges. We now reverse and reinstate all counts of the indictment.

I . . .

On Saturday afternoon, December 22, 1984, Troy Canty, Darryl Cabey, James Ramseur, and Barry Allen boarded an IRT express subway train in The Bronx and headed south toward lower Manhattan. The four youths rode together in the rear portion of the seventh car of the train. Two of the four, Ramseur and Cabey, had screwdrivers inside their coats, which they said were to be used to break into the coin boxes of video machines.

Defendant Bernhard Goetz boarded this subway train at 14th Street in Manhattan and sat down on a bench towards the rear section of the same car occupied by the four youths. Goetz was carrying an unlicensed .38 caliber pistol loaded with five rounds of ammunition in a waistband holster. The train left the 14th Street station and headed towards Chambers Street.

It appears from the evidence before the Grand Jury that Canty approached Goetz, possibly with Allen beside him, and stated "give me five dollars." Neither Canty nor any of the other youths displayed a weapon. Goetz responded by standing up, pulling out his handgun and firing four shots in rapid succession. The first shot hit Canty in the chest; the second struck Allen in the back; the third went through Ramseur's arm and into his left side; the fourth was fired at Cabey, who apparently was then standing in the corner of the car, but missed, deflecting instead off of a wall of the conductor's cab. After Goetz briefly surveyed the scene around him, he fired another shot at Cabey, who then was sitting on the end bench of the car. The bullet entered the rear of Cabey's side and severed his spinal cord.

. . . Goetz told the conductor that the four youths had tried to rob him.

[G]oetz . . . jumped onto the tracks and fled. . . . Ramseur and Canty, initially listed in critical condition, have fully recovered. Cabey remains paralyzed, and has suffered some degree of brain damage.

[Nine days later, Goetz surrendered to police in New Hampshire and identified himself as the gunman being sought for the subway shootings in New York. He also stated that he had first purchased a gun in 1981 after he had been injured in a mugging.] Goetz also revealed that twice between 1981 and 1984 he had successfully warded off assailants simply by displaying the pistol.

According to Goetz's statement, the first contact he had with the four youths came when Canty, sitting or lying on the bench across from him, asked "how are you," to which he replied "fine." Shortly thereafter, Canty, followed by one of the other youths, walked over to the defendant and stood to his left, while the other two youths remained to his right, in the corner of the subway car. Canty then said "give me five dollars." Goetz stated that he knew from the smile on Canty's face that they wanted to "play with me." Although he was certain that none of the youths had a gun, he had a fear, based on prior experiences, of being "maimed."

Goetz then established "a pattern of fire," deciding specifically to fire from left to right. His stated intention at that point was to "murder [the four youths], to hurt them, to make them suffer as much as possible." When Canty again requested money, Goetz stood up, drew his weapon, and began firing, aiming for the center of the body of each of the four. Goetz recalled that the first two he shot "tried to run through the crowd [but] they had nowhere to run." Goetz then turned to his right to "go after the other two." One of these two "tried to run through the wall of the train, but . . . he had nowhere to go." The other youth (Cabey) "tried pretending that he wasn't with [the others]" by standing still, holding on to one of the subway hand straps, and not looking at Goetz. Goetz nonetheless fired his fourth shot at him. He then ran back to the first two youths to make sure they had been "taken care of." . . . Goetz noticed that the youth who had been standing still was now sitting on a bench and seemed unhurt. As Goetz told the police, "I said '[y]ou seem to be all right, here's another'," and he then fired the shot which severed Cabey's spinal cord. Goetz added that "if I was a little more under self-control . . . I would have put the barrel against his forehead and fired." He also admitted that "if I had had more [bullets], I would have shot them again, and again, and again."

II . . .

[A] Grand Jury filed a 10-count indictment, containing four charges of attempted murder, four charges of assault in the first degree, one charge of reckless endangerment in the first degree, and one charge of criminal possession of a weapon in the second degree [possession of loaded firearm with intent to use it unlawfully against another]. . . . Goetz moved to dismiss the charges . . . alleging, among other things, . . . that the prosecutor's instructions to that Grand Jury on the defense of justification were erroneous and prejudicial to the defendant so as to render its proceedings defective. . . .

[The trial court] dismissed all counts, other than the reckless endangerment charge, with leave to resubmit these charges to a [new] Grand Jury. . . . It held . . . that the prosecutor, in a supplemental charge to the grand jury elaborating upon the justification defense, had erroneously introduced an objective element into this defense by instructing the grand jurors to consider whether Goetz's conduct was that of a "reasonable man in [Goetz's] situation." The court, citing prior decisions . . . , concluded that the statutory test for whether the use of deadly force is justified to protect a person should be wholly subjective, focusing entirely on the defendant's state of mind when he used such force. . . .

[The intermediate appellate court agreed that the law considered by the Grand Jurors, given them by the prosecutor, was erroneous. Specifically, in the intermediate appellate court, two of the five judges held that only Goetz's "subjective" state of mind was determinative, and a third concurred on the ground that the prosecutor's instruction did not focus sufficiently on Goetz's "background and learning." Two justices dissented, arguing that objective reasonableness was also required.]

[W]e agree with the dissenters that neither the prosecutor's charge to the Grand Jury on justification nor the information which came to light while the motion to dismiss was pending required dismissal of any of the charges in the . . . indictment.

III

. . . Penal Law 35.15 (1) sets forth the general principles governing all [self-defensive] uses of force: "[a] person may . . . use physical force upon another person when and to the extent he *reasonably believes* such to be necessary to defend himself or a third person from what he *reasonably believes* to be the use or imminent use of unlawful physical force by such other person."

Section 35.15(2) sets forth further limitations on these general principles with respect to the use of "deadly physical force": "A person may not use deadly physical force upon another person under circumstances specified in subdivision one unless (a) He *reasonably believes* that such other person is using or about to use deadly physical force . . . or (b) He *reasonably believes* that such other person is committing or attempting to commit a kidnapping, forcible rape, forcible sodomy or robbery" (emphasis added).[4] . . .

When the prosecutor had completed his charge, one of the grand jurors asked for clarification of the term "reasonably believes." The prosecutor responded by instructing the grand jurors that they were to consider the circumstances of the incident and determine "whether the defendant's conduct was that of a reasonable man in the defendant's situation." It is this response by the prosecutor—and specifically his use of "a reasonable man"—which is the basis for the dismissal of the charges by the lower courts. As expressed repeatedly in the Appellate Division's plurality opinion, because section 35.15 uses the term "*he* reasonably believes," the appropriate test, according to that court, is whether a defendant's beliefs and reactions were "reasonable *to him.*" Under that reading of the statute, a jury which believed a defendant's testimony that he felt that his own actions were warranted and were reasonable would have to acquit him, regardless of what anyone else in defendant's situation might have concluded. Such an interpretation defies the ordinary meaning and significance of the term "reasonably" in a statute, and misconstrues the clear intent of the Legislature, in enacting section 35.15, to retain an objective element as part of any provision authorizing the use of deadly physical force. . . .

[The current New York Penal Law was influenced by the Model Penal Code. But it differs from the MPC, and one of those differences is important here.] [U]nder Model Penal Code § 3.04(2)(b), a defendant charged with murder (or attempted murder) need only show that he [subjectively] "believe[d] that [the use of deadly force] was necessary . . ." to prevail on a self-defense claim. If the defendant's belief was wrong, and was recklessly, or negligently formed, however, he may be convicted of the type of homicide charge requiring only a reckless or negligent belief, as the case may be [but may not be convicted of intentional homicide].

The drafters of the Model Penal Code recognized that the wholly subjective test set forth in section 3.04 differed from the existing law in most States by its omission of any requirement of reasonableness. . . .

New York did not follow the Model Penal Code's [language]. The drafters of the new Penal Law, crucially, inserted the word "reasonably" before "believes."

---

4. Section 35.15(2) (a) further provides, however, that even under these circumstances a person ordinarily must retreat "if he knows that he can with complete safety as to himself and others avoid the necessity of [using deadly physical force] by retreating."

We cannot lightly impute to the Legislature an intent to fundamentally alter the principles of justification to allow the perpetrator of a serious crime to go free simply because that person believed his actions were reasonable and necessary to prevent some perceived harm. To completely exonerate such an individual, no matter how aberrational or bizarre his thought patterns, would allow citizens to set their own standards for the permissible use of force. . . . We can only conclude that the Legislature retained a reasonableness requirement to avoid giving a license for such actions.

Goetz also argues that the introduction of an objective element will preclude a jury from considering factors such as the prior experiences of a given actor and thus, require it to make a determination of "reasonableness" without regard to the actual circumstances of a particular incident. This argument, however, falsely presupposes that an objective standard means that the background and other relevant characteristics of a particular actor must be ignored. To the contrary, we have frequently noted that a determination of reasonableness must be based on the "circumstances" facing a defendant or his "situation." . . . Furthermore, the defendant's circumstances encompass any prior experiences he had which could provide a reasonable basis for a belief that another person's intentions were to injure or rob him or that the use of deadly force was necessary under the circumstances.

Accordingly, a jury should be instructed to consider this type of evidence in weighing the defendant's actions. . . .

The prosecutor's instruction to the . . . Grand Jury that it had to determine whether, under the circumstances, Goetz's conduct was that of a reasonable man in his situation was thus essentially an accurate charge. It is true that the prosecutor did not elaborate on the meaning of "circumstances" or "situation" and inform the grand jurors that they could consider, for example, the prior experiences Goetz related in his statement to the police. We have held, however, that a Grand Jury need not be instructed on the law with the same degree of precision as the petit [trial] jury. . . .

[T]he Grand Jury has indicted Goetz. It will now be for the petit jury to decide whether the prosecutor can prove beyond a reasonable doubt that Goetz's reactions were unreasonable and therefore excessive. . . . [Order reversed, so that the indictment is reinstated.]

Notes and Questions

(1) *The Result and Contexts of Goetz's Trial.* The jury that heard Goetz's case acquitted him of attempted murder, assault, and endangerment. It convicted him only of the weapons violation, and he served eight months in jail. Three of the young men whom Goetz shot subsequently brought a civil suit against him. Goetz won two of the suits but lost a multi-million dollar judgment (presumably uncollectible) to Cabey, the person who was paralyzed. The young men who allegedly assailed Goetz were black, and Goetz was white; both the legal and racial issues in the case became points of contention and occurred at a time of a perceived "law and order"

crisis in New York. Do these considerations mean that the reasoning and result in *Goetz* might be different, as a practical matter, in different contexts? (Might he be convicted today, with respect to the sitting victim, Cabey?)

(2) *Subjective Belief, Objective Reasonableness, and the Circumstances or Standpoint of the Defendant.* The *Goetz* court makes clear that self-defense contains a subjective element: a subjective, or honest, "belief" in the threat that faces the self-defender. It adds that self-defense also contains an objective element: "objective reasonableness," judged from the standpoint of an ordinary or reasonable person. The defendant's honest and reasonable belief relates to both the unlawfulness and the imminence of the harm, as well as the necessity and proportionality of his response.

But the court also holds that reasonableness must be considered in light of the "circumstances" or "situation" of the defendant. These terms, the court emphasizes, include not only what happens in the immediate encounter but also the defendant's knowledge, his past experiences, and the "attributes" of all the parties. This qualification arguably modifies the "objective reasonableness" standard by a focus on perceptions, qualities, and experiences unique to the defendant.

Does the circumstances-of-the-defendant proviso convert the objective standard, de facto, into a subjective one? The answer might vary from state to state. In Georgia, the defendant in a self-defense case may offer relevant expert testimony concerning his or her mental condition at the time of the offense, including facts about family history that form the basis for the expert's testimony. *See* Ga. Code Ann. § 16–3-21(d). But a Texas court refused to allow an expert to testify about the defendant's training as a Marine, stating: "How a trained Marine instinctively reacts to a perceived threat is not relevant to the issue of whether an ordinary and prudent [person], viewing the circumstances from [defendant's] viewpoint, would have formed a reasonable belief that deadly force was immediately necessary to protect himself." *Echavarria v. State*, 362 S.W.3d 148, 154 (Tex. App. 2011). Which is the better approach?

(3) *Race and Reasonableness?* Professor Jody Armour suggests that Goetz tried to present himself as a "reasonable racist."

> The Reasonable Racist asserts that, even if his belief that blacks are "prone to violence" stems from pure prejudice, he should be excused for considering the victim's race before using force because most similarly situated Americans would have done so as well. . . . Few would want to agree with the Reasonable Racist's assertion that every white person in America harbors racial animus as he does; nonetheless, it is unrealistic to dispute the depressing conclusion that, for many Americans, crime has a black face.

Armour suggests that the problem with such a claim is the "primary assumption that the sole objective of criminal law is to punish those who deviate from statistically defined norms":

> [E]ven if the "typical" American believes that blacks' "propensity" toward violence justifies a quicker and more forceful response when a suspected assailant is black, this fact is legally significant only if the law defines

reasonable beliefs as typical beliefs. The reasonableness inquiry, however, extends beyond typicality to consider the social interests implicated in a given situation. Hence not all "typical" beliefs are per se reasonable.

... If we accept that racial discrimination violates contemporary social morality, then an actor's failure to overcome his racism for the sake of another's health, safety, and personal dignity is blameworthy and thus unreasonable, independent of whether or not it is "typical."

Jody Armour, *Race Ipsa Loquitur: Of Reasonable Racists, Intelligent Bayesians, and Involuntary Negrophobes*, 46 Stanford L. Rev. 781, 787–90 (1994). Is Amour correct, even if a defendant knows that black defendants appear disproportionately in crime statistics (*i.e.*, is this consideration illegitimate)?

(4) *Reasonable Beliefs about Necessity, Proportionality, and Imminence.* Many self-defense cases turn on the issue of reasonable belief in the imminence of the unlawful threat of harm facing the defender. Notice, however, that the reasonableness requirement also attaches to the "extent" of force used. The reasonable belief, then, must justify the amount of force that the defendant uses. Can Goetz's shooting of Cabey (who separated himself from the others, and whom Goetz returned to shoot again) be justified in these terms?

(5) *Deadly Force: A Special Case of Necessity and Proportionality.* A separate provision in the New York Statute further limits the availability of deadly force. The actor must reasonably believe that another "is about to use deadly force [or commit a violent felony]." This reflects the common law position, which holds that one may not successfully plead self-defense if one uses deadly force in response to a non-deadly threat. Imagine the case of a defendant who fears a serious beating, although not one with deadly force, from a much larger assailant, so that the defendant can only repel the assault by using a firearm (deadly force). Must the defendant, then, submit? Consider whether the *Goetz* case conformed to this pattern.

(6) *New Yorkers Agree: "It's Hard to Imagine" the Goetz Case Happening Today.* At the time of the *Goetz* case, there were roughly 15,000 felonies a year in the New York subway system. In 2004, there were only 2,760 felonies. Killings in the subway peaked in 1990 at 26; in 2004, there were zero. "Could [the *Goetz* case] happen now?" asked Ron Kuby, who represented Cabey. "Inconceivable. Inconceivable that the attack would take place. Inconceivable that the attacker would be hailed as a hero." Former Chief of Detectives Richard Nicastro said, "It's hard to imagine it happening again. What it showed was the fear most people had in traveling about." *See 20 Years after Goetz, N.Y. a Changed City*, USA Today, Dec. 16, 2004.

Problem 6B (Self-Defense): "Massachusetts Jury Rejects Hockey Dad's Claim of Innocence"

(1) *A Dubious Claim of Self-Defense, Rejected by the Jury.* Thomas Junta beat his son's hockey coach to death. He claimed to have acted in self-defense. (Another report of this case, which is taken from newspaper reports, appears at the end of the

Homicide chapter, above.) He testified that the victim, Michael Costin, 40, actually had attacked him. The altercation began when Costin told his players, "Hockey's about hitting." Junta was quoted as saying, "That's [expletive]. It's about having fun." He scuffled with Costin briefly, then left. But about a minute later, witnesses said, Junta returned, "looking to resume the fight." A rink manager told Junta that he could not enter, but Junta pushed her against a wall, injuring her arm. Then, said witnesses, he ran to Costin, threw him to the ice, and beat him repeatedly about the head and neck with his fists, rupturing an artery. Junta, who outweighed Costin by an estimated 100 pounds, ultimately got up and left. Police who responded found Costin lying on the ice, bloodied, not moving, surrounded by children. Junta testified that Costin attacked him first, and that he threw three "off-balance" punches and did not realize that Costin was hurt. A Massachusetts jury rejected Junta's self-defense claim and convicted him of voluntary manslaughter. Why did the jury reject self-defense (maybe for multiple reasons)?

(2) *Could the Judge Properly Have Refused Even to Submit a Self-Defense Instruction?* Self-defense is a "true" defense, which must be submitted to the jury if it is "raised" by the evidence. The trial judge probably had no choice but to submit the instruction here, even if he thought Junta's claim of self-defense was perjurious and outlandish. Can you explain why?

(3) *"Imperfect" Self-Defense and Voluntary Manslaughter.* Junta and his counsel probably knew that the self-defense theory was weak. Nevertheless, they may have concluded, even if the jury rejected the defense, that presentation of the claimed defense might help them to avoid a murder conviction and persuade the jury to opt for a lesser offense. Can you explain?

[3] The Self-Defense Requirements as Affected by Cultural and Psychological Factors: Claims of Battered Woman Syndrome

Notes and Questions

(1) *Who Is the "Reasonable Person" and What Is a Threat of Deadly Force? "Battered Woman Syndrome."* Most jurisdictions allow evidence of some subjective elements in connection with determining who the "reasonable person" is. Imagine the case of a woman whose husband has regularly assaulted her. One night he comes home drunk, assaults her again, then falls asleep on the couch. Hours later the wife, extremely distressed over the husband's repeated violent abuse and her own helplessness, gets a knife from the kitchen and kills her sleeping husband. A traditional application of self-defense would deny the wife the defense since the sleeping husband did not pose a reasonable threat of immediate physical harm.

But in the case of spouses who kill abusive intimates, a special kind of evidence— expert evidence of what is called "Battered Woman Syndrome" ("BWS")—may be admitted in some jurisdictions to address issues about the reasonableness of the defendant's belief in the necessity of self-defense. *See, e.g,* Wyo. Stat. Ann. §6–1-203 (in domestic violence case involving self-defense, defendant may introduce expert testimony that she suffered from BWS to establish requisite belief of imminent danger or serious harm).

(2) *Is It Appropriate to Make BWS a Special Case?* An argument can be made against recognizing the relevance of BWS, to the effect that the objective standard of reasonableness should not vary across persons. Also, some observers are skeptical of self-defense claims in cases of sleeping or otherwise helpless spouses or of the use of highly disproportionate force. They would say, "Get a divorce."

But proponents of BWS evidence respond that these perceptions emerge from common (but contested) cultural messages, including those which hold that the appropriate response to domestic abuse is for the abused party to leave the relationship, or which perceive inconsistencies between the act of killing and claims of victimhood. Also, the "reasonable person" test is said by some critics to be gendered, that is, to reflect a tacit bias, which actually causes the standard to be based on the response of a reasonable *man* to a perceived threat, rather than a reasonable *person*.

This view sees the battered woman as reasonably experiencing perceptions that create a special situation. For example, the characteristics of BWS and its sufferers are typically said to include "battering cycles," "learned helplessness," "escalation" of abuse, and "hyper-vigilance." Do these arguments justify modification of the self-defense standards?

(3) *The Ongoing Debate.* Although the clear tendency has been to allow BWS evidence, there is extensive debate on the desirability of admitting it in cases where the "defensive" killing occurs outside of a direct and immediate confrontation. Disputes also exist about the validity of the research that supports BWS. In addition, some feminists oppose BWS because they view it as a symptom of law's need to pathologize women's experiences and only to credit them through the testimony of "experts" who are sometimes said to use a "masculine discourse."

(4) *Unsatisfactory Issues, Part I: The Evidence in BWS Homicide Cases Usually Comes Mainly from the Defendant Alone, and In Some Cases, It May Be Exaggerated or Even Perjurious.* In many homicide cases, the only witness to the claimed acts underlying BWS is the defendant. This factor raises concerns about false or distorted depictions of the deceased, who by definition cannot correct the record. No one doubts that there are BWS cases, but the difficulty lies in telling which ones are genuine and which ones are not. (The case that follows is a compelling example of BWS evidence, but not all cases are as credible.) *See* Ky. Rev. Stat. Ann. § 503.050 (in self-defense case, permitting evidence of prior acts of domestic violence by the person against whom the defendant used force).

(5) *Unsatisfactory Issues, Part II: Should the Standard for Self-Defense Be Changed to Accommodate Unreasonable Killing by One Class of Persons?* Many classes of people who kill can legitimately claim to suffer cognitive or affective impairment. For most of these individuals, the law still demands "objective reasonableness." The usual accommodation created by the law is a reduction of a homicide charged as murder to the lesser grade of voluntary manslaughter. But the BWS defendant, as

the following case demonstrates, may argue that in this one kind of case, the very standard for self-defense should be changed, to eliminate the requirement of objective reasonableness. Should it be?

State v. Edwards

60 S.W.3d 602 (Mo. Ct. App. 2001)

ELLIS, JUDGE. . . .

. . . Larna Edwards shot her husband, Bill Edwards, four times with a 38 caliber handgun. [The jury acquitted her of murder but rejected her defense of self-defense and convicted her of voluntary manslaughter, for which she was sentenced to five years imprisonment. The court here reverses.]

[On appeal, Mrs. Edwards argues that in light of Mo. Stat. Ann. § 563.033, which admits evidence about "battered spouse syndrome," the trial court's instructions on self-defense were inadequate. [T]he instructions did not explicitly address the special case of the battered spouse, and Mrs. Edwards's appeal argues that in this special case, this was error. The jury did, however, hear extensive evidence about battered spouse syndrome. The jury also heard the testimony of Mrs. Edwards.] The following is a summary of [Mrs. Edwards's] evidence. . . .

Mrs. Edwards dropped out of school to elope with Mr. Edwards . . . when she was sixteen years old. . . . [Mrs. Edwards was 61 when she killed Mr. Edwards. The evidence purported to show that] Mr. Edwards began verbally and physically abusing Mrs. Edwards from the first day of their marriage, often hitting her with his fist, the back of his hand, or pieces of furniture. Mr. Edwards would also kick her and pull out some of her hair. When Mrs. Edwards was pregnant with their fourth child, Mr. Edwards struck her in the stomach, causing a miscarriage. He frequently threatened to kill Mrs. Edwards and their children, and he told her that he would track her down and kill her if she tried to run away.

Mr. Edwards also frequently struck the children with his fists or a belt, held them by the hair and/or kicked them. On one occasion, Mr. Edwards kicked their oldest son down a flight of stairs. In 1966, when their daughter Jackie was approximately thirteen years old, Mr. Edwards held a gun to her . . . head, forced her to have sexual intercourse with him repeatedly and threatened to kill her if she did not comply or told anyone. . . . Mrs. Edwards left Mr. Edwards two different times, but on both occasions she . . . returned home after Mr. Edwards promised that the beatings would not happen again.[3] However, after she returned, this "honeymoon" period would only last two or three days. . . .

---

3. Mrs. Edwards also stated that she returned because Mr. Edwards controlled all of the family's finances and she had no money of her own on which to live. . . . Mrs. Edwards testified that she had stolen money from the store to buy her medication because Mr. Edwards would not give her money for it.

Co-workers, customers [of businesses run by the Edwardses,] family members and acquaintances testified at trial that they often saw Mrs. Edwards with bruises on her face and arms and black eyes, and an employee . . . testified that he witnessed Mr. Edwards screaming and swearing at Mrs. Edwards. . . . [So did the Caldwell County Sheriff, who testified at trial but had filed no reports.]

[The killing of Mr. Edwards took place when] Mr. and Mrs. Edwards . . . began to argue about the purchase [of a truck on their return from contracting to purchase it.] The argument continued after they got home. During that argument, Mr. Edwards pushed Mrs. Edwards and struck her with a hard object. Mrs. Edwards then went to bed, but remained awake all night for fear Mr. Edwards would kill her in her sleep. . . .

The following morning at about 6:15 a.m., Mr. Edwards struck Mrs. Edwards, knocking off her glasses and causing her wristwatch to stop. . . . Once they arrived at work, Mr. Edwards continued the argument about the truck. During that argument, Mr. Edwards severely struck Mrs. Edwards' arm, apparently with a length of lead pipe, as she raised . . . her arm to protect her face. At that point, Mrs. Edwards thought her arm might be broken. Mrs. Edwards testified at trial that this blow was the most painful she had ever experienced. She stated that from the look in Mr. Edwards' eyes and her past experience with him, she was certain that he was going to try to kill her. Mrs. Edwards testified, "I knew one of us was not going to walk out of that store." . . .

After Mr. Edwards hit her, Mrs. Edwards picked up a .38 caliber handgun that was kept under the front counter in the store for security. When Mr. Edwards started to swear at her, Mrs. Edwards shot him four times from a distance of about five feet, striking him in the head, upper arm, and back. Mr. Edwards died from those wounds.

[The trial court gave the jury the standard instruction on self-defense. The jury rejected the defense and found Mrs. Edwards guilty of voluntary manslaughter.]

. . . The Missouri Legislature [recently] enacted § 563.033, which allows evidence . . . of battered spouse syndrome to be submitted into evidence on the issue of self-defense. . . . Over the last twenty or so years, battered spouse syndrome has gained substantial . . . scientific acceptance and has been recognized in numerous jurisdictions. . . . The syndrome . . . manifests itself in a collection of symptoms including a highly fearful state, isolation, withdrawal, and a heightened sensitivity to situations that precede violence or an increase in violence. . . . Victims exhibit a "learned helplessness" in which repeated trauma causes the victims to learn that they have no control and cannot escape, and therefore, they stop trying to escape from the situation, even when an opportunity to do so is present. . . .

While evidence of the battered spouse syndrome is not in and of itself a defense to a murder charge, its function is to aid the jury in determining whether a defendant's fear and claim of self-defense are reasonable. . . . The battering relationship is otherwise beyond the understanding of the average juror. . . . Indeed, a juror may otherwise conclude by "common sense" that if the abuse were so bad the woman would have left the relationship. . . .

Mrs. Edwards argues [that] the pattern instruction submitted by the trial court failed to provide the jury with a mechanism for applying the battered spouse syndrome provisions of § 563.033. She contends that [it] improperly applied the "reasonable person" standard without reference to battered woman syndrome. . . .

. . . [I]t is not completely accurate to say that the conduct should be evaluated as a reasonable battered woman would have perceived it. This language seems to be something of an oxymoron. . . . A battered woman is a terror-stricken person whose mental state is distorted. Thus, a more accurate statement of the law is that, if the jury believes the defendant was suffering from battered spouse syndrome, it must weigh the evidence in light of how an otherwise reasonable person who is suffering from battered spouse syndrome would have perceived and reacted in view of the prolonged history of physical abuse.

. . . As a result, applying the foregoing principles, it is readily apparent that the [standard instruction] failed to properly instruct the jury. . . . The instruction did not allow the jury to consider previous acts of violence or threats . . . . Furthermore, "reasonable belief" for purposes of the instruction was defined as "a belief based on reasonable grounds, that is, grounds which could lead a reasonable person in the same situation to the same belief." . . . Thus, the instruction precluded the jury from making a determination as to whether Mrs. Edwards was suffering from battered spouse syndrome and, if so, whether she had a reasonable belief that she was in imminent danger based on what an otherwise reasonable and prudent person who is suffering from battered spouse syndrome would think. [Reversed and remanded.]

HENDRIX v. STATE, 369 S.W.3d 93 (Mo. App. 2012). A court in the same state cited *Edwards,* above, in holding that counsel was not incompetent in failing to develop certain medical evidence of defendant's "degenerative joint disease" to support his self-defense claim. The defendant had fired several shots in his neighbors' direction and threatened to "kill them all" during an argument about ownership of a truck frame. One neighbor was walking toward him. The court upheld the conviction:

. . . [According to] *State v. Edwards,* 60 S.W.3d 602, 612 (Mo.App. W.D. 2001)[, self-defense] is available "when and to the extent [the person] reasonably believes such force to be necessary to defend . . . from what [the person] reasonably believes to be the . . . imminent use of unlawful force . . . ." . . . [R]easonableness . . . is determined from an objective test ". . . based on [an] ordinary reasonable and prudent person . . . ."

Hendrix's medical records . . . would have merely established that he suffered from degenerative joint disease . . . . [A] defendant's "proclivities or propensities are irrelevant" to the issue of whether the defendant acted as a "reasonable person."

But if battered woman syndrome is relevant to the reasonableness of self-defense, why is degenerative joint disease "irrelevant" to the defendant's reasonableness in using force?

Notes and Questions

(1) *Did the Court in Edwards Abandon the Objective Reasonableness Standard and Adopt a Standard Based on Emotional Factors Creating Subjective Unreasonableness?* The *Edwards* court flatly states that expecting a person suffering BWS to act reasonably creates "an oxymoron," and instead the court produces a separate construct: the "reasonable person affected by BWS," whom the court describes as mentally distorted, and therefore *not* reasonable. The reasonableness factor is supposed to check the effect of self-defense as a license for irrational killings. Does it cease to perform that function under the test created by the Missouri court?

(2) *Should a Subjective Test Be Used to Reflect "Emotional Disturbance" (But Isn't That the Function of Voluntary Manslaughter?)* BWS sufferers are not the only persons influenced by psychological factors that might make them less capable of reasonable conduct. The court in *Hendrix*, above, confronted a case in which a disabled person with leg braces might have perceived conditions differently, but the court considered that evidence irrelevant. And consider these possibilities: (a) a person afflicted with clinical depression kills under unreasonable conditions but claims the right to a specially drafted self-defense instruction on the ground that depression distorted his or her mental state, just as her alleged condition did to that of Mrs. Edwards. (b) An Army veteran suffering post-traumatic stress disorder claims the same right. (c) A diagnosed alcoholic suffering from this medical condition who killed while intoxicated seeks the same (in which event, the standard no longer is objective).

The jury that heard Mrs. Edwards's case received extensive evidence about BWS, and it was told to view the issues from Mrs. Edwards's sole vantage point, as she saw them. Was the court correct, here, in deciding that her case was not properly presented?

[B] Defense of a Third Person

> Read MPC § 3.05(1) [belief in necessity for force to defend a third person is sufficient even if mistaken] in the MPC Appendix.

Notes and Questions

(1) *Overview.* Just as the criminal law permits people to defend themselves, it also authorizes one person to defend another. Like self-defense, the defense of third persons is a justification rather than an excuse.

(2) *Three Approaches: Reasonable Belief, Honest Belief (MPC), and Stand-in-the-Shoes.* American law has developed three approaches to defense of third persons.

(a) *Reasonable Belief Rule.* The prevailing rule is that, similarly to self-defense, a person may assert the defense of third persons if he or she used a reasonable amount of force to respond to what reasonably appeared to be the use or threat of unlawful force against another person. *See, e.g.,* Ore. Rev. Stat. § 161.209. This objective test protects the rescuer even if he or she is mistaken, so long as the mistake was reasonable under the circumstances.

For example, "defender" sees A using force against B and intervenes with force against A to protect B. Unbeknownst to the defender, A is an undercover police officer lawfully arresting B. (Or, B actually has attacked A, who is lawfully exercising his own right of self-defense.) Many states allow defense of a third party if the defender's belief was reasonable.

(b) *Subjective or Honest Belief Rule.* A small minority of American jurisdictions adopt the MPC's subjective approach, allowing the defender to assert defense of third parties if the defender honestly (and even unreasonably) believes the intervention is necessary. *See, e.g.,* Neb. Rev. Stat. § 28–1410; *see also* Model Penal Code § 3.05.

(c) *Stand-in-the-Shoes Rule.* The third rule is the older common law "alter ego" rule, which narrowly limited the right to defend a third person. The defendant in *People v. Young,* 183 N.E.2d 319 (N.Y. 1962), for example, came to the aid of an individual who was being assaulted by two men. The two "assailants," however, were peace officers, and the person whom Young aided was actually resisting arrest. The court held that Young had no greater right to defend the arrestee than the arrestee had for himself. Because the arrestee had no right to resist the lawful arrest, Young's defense was invalid. This is the "step into the shoes" or "alter ego" approach. The defender steps into the shoes of the person defended, with no greater right to use force than that person, even if the defender's conduct is reasonable.

State v. Mayo
113 A.3d 250 (N.H. 2015)

Lynn, J.

The defendant, Josiah Mayo, appeals his convictions ... of first degree assault with a deadly weapon and reckless second degree assault. He argues that the Superior Court erred by ... failing to instruct the jury that his use of force in defense of his cousin was justified if he reasonably believed that his cousin was not the initial aggressor or provoker. ... We reverse and remand.

I

The jury could have found the following facts. ... [T]he defendant and his cousin, Daniel Mayo, were in Portsmouth at The Page, a restaurant and bar. They left at around 12:30 a.m. and went their separate ways, with plans to meet later at another area restaurant. The victim [Green] and his friends Kevin Donahue, Robert Yitts, Jacob Losik, William Ryan Paris, and Charles "Costa" McCreed were also at The Page that night. The victim, Zachary Green, had consumed three alcoholic beverages earlier in the day but did not drink any more that evening because he was the designated driver. Most of the victim's friends had consumed alcohol . . . , some to the point of intoxication.

Shortly before closing time at 1:00 a.m. . . . , the bouncers at The Page began moving patrons outside into . . . the Vaughan Mall (Mall), an area that often became very crowded with people leaving other area establishments. The defendant testified that at around 1:00 a.m. he was walking through the Mall. The victim [Green] and his friends were leaving The Page around the same time, and also ended up in the Mall.

Various witnesses testified about what next occurred. Donahue testified that "small scuffles started to break out," during which he was hit in the head and kicked . . . . Donahue testified that he saw Paris get punched in the side of the head and Losik get knocked to the ground.

Paris testified that "a black gentleman . . . was upset" with one of his friends: the man was yelling and "seemed like he was trying to make a move like he was going to go fight them or something like that." Paris tried to de-escalate the situation by standing in front of the man and stating that no one wanted any trouble. In response, the man told Paris to "get out of his face and things of that sort" . . . and the man's hand came into contact with Paris. Then, according to Paris, the man stated, "don't f'ing touch me," and punched Paris in the face. The victim [Green] then came over to Paris and held his hands up, saying "whoa, whoa, whoa," at which point another man kicked the victim in the face. . . .

The victim [Green] testified that, upon leaving The Page, he started to walk through the Mall toward the parking lot . . . . At some point the victim noticed Yitts and two men "looking funky at one another," as in "not happy." The victim "immediately tried to get [Yitts] to go walk away." He told Yitts that they were not going to fight . . . . The victim then turned back around and "scolded" the two men for acting immature, telling them "to grow up and we're not fighting." He testified that the next thing he remembered was waking up in the hospital.

The defendant testified that as he was walking through the Mall, he heard the word "n. . . . r." When he turned around, he noticed [that] . . . "something happened, and people just kind of converged on [his cousin]," "limbs were flying," and his cousin was "physically assaulted." He testified that hearing people yell racial slurs and seeing the group of individuals converge on his cousin made him believe that his "cousin was in danger at that time." . . . [T]he defendant noticed the victim [Green] approaching from his right "fairly quickly" . . . and assumed that he was going after his cousin. The defendant responded by kicking the victim.

The witnesses agreed that the defendant kicked the victim once in the face. As a result of the kick, the victim was immediately rendered unconscious and fell, hitting his head on the pavement. The victim was transported to the hospital, where he was diagnosed with a concussion, a skull fracture, and an inter-cranial hemorrhage. The defendant was subsequently arrested and charged . . . . At trial, the defendant claimed that he acted in defense of his cousin. After a four-day trial, the defendant was convicted on both charges. . . .

II

The defendant . . . contends that the trial court erred by failing to instruct the jury that his use of force in defense of his cousin was justified if he reasonably believed that his cousin was not the initial aggressor . . . .

The trial court instructed the jury as follows:

> The defendant is not justified in using force if he or [a] third person was the initial aggressor, unless after such aggression he and the other person withdraw from the encounter and effectively communicate to the assailant their intent to do so, but the assailant notwithstanding continues the use [of] or threaten[s] unlawful force.

The defendant does not have the right to use force to defend another if he or the person he was defending provoked the use of force. . . .

The defendant asserts that this instruction was erroneous because it required the defendant to be factually correct that his cousin was not the initial aggressor or provoker in order for his use of force to be justified, which he argues is an incorrect statement of the law. He contends that the trial court should have instructed the jury that he was justified in using force if he had an honest and reasonable belief that his cousin was not the initial aggressor or provoker. The defendant argues that, under the court's instruction, if the jury believed that his cousin was the initial aggressor or provoker, it would have been required to conclude that his actions were not justified without considering either his subjective state of mind or the reasonableness thereof . . . .

The State responds that such "reasonable belief" language regarding the third person's status as the initial aggressor or provoker is inconsistent with the plain language of the defense-of-others statute . . . and the common law "alter-ego rule," under which the defendant "steps into the shoes" of the third person (here, his cousin) with regard to whether the use of force is justifiable. The State further argues that the legislature considered the Model Penal Code (MPC) . . . but that its failure to adopt the MPC's exact language left the alter-ego rule intact. . . .

RSA 627:4 sets forth the circumstances under which a person is justified in using physical force in defense of a person. It states, in pertinent part:

> I. A person is justified in using non-deadly force upon another person in order to defend himself *or a third person* from what he reasonably believes to be the imminent use of unlawful, non-deadly force by such other person, and he may use a degree of such force which he reasonably believes to be

necessary for such purpose. However, such force is not justifiable if . . . [the defendant provoked the use of force or was the first aggressor]. . . . .

II. A person is justified in using deadly force upon another person when he reasonably believes that such other person: (a) Is about to use unlawful, deadly force against the actor *or a third person* . . . .

III. A person is not justified in using deadly force on another to defend himself or herself *or a third person* from deadly force by the other if he or she knows that he or she *and the third person* can, with complete safety:

(a) Retreat from the encounter, except that he or she is not required to retreat if he or she is within his or her dwelling, its curtilage, or anywhere he or she has a right to be, and was not the initial aggressor. . . .

RSA 627:4 (emphasis added).

Paragraph I states that "a person"—here, the defendant—is justified in defending himself or a third person from what he reasonably believes to be the imminent use of unlawful, non-deadly force by another person. The statute contains an additional requirement: the degree of force he uses must be that which "he reasonably believes to be necessary for such purpose." This paragraph makes clear, by its use of the phrase "or a third person," that the basic reasonableness requirements regarding imminent, unlawful force and the degree of force necessary apply to both the defendant's acts taken in his own defense, as well as those taken in defense of a third person.

Then, in sub-paragraphs I(a), I(b), and III(a), the statute imposes several limitations on when a person's defensive use of force is justified. These limitations specifically apply only to the person who actually takes the putatively defensive action. The phrase "or a third person," which appears in paragraphs I and III, is not included in the limitations language contained in sub-paragraphs I(a), I(b), or III(a). The trial court's instructions, on the other hand, informed the jury that if it found that the defendant *or the third person* (his cousin) was in fact the initial aggressor or provoker, then the defendant's actions in defense of his cousin were not justified.

The court's addition of the phrase "or the third person" into the limitations on the defensive use of force is not supported by a plain reading of the statute. . . . [H]ere, . . . the general requirements of paragraphs I, II and III mention the actor "or a third person," whereas the limitations applicable to an initial aggressor or provoker found in sub-paragraphs I(a), I(b), and III(a) mention only the actor. Under a plain reading, then, these limitations apply only to the conduct of the actor, not to the conduct of the third person.

. . . The omission of third persons from the provisions that limit an actor's ability to use defensive force makes sense because each limitation involves conduct squarely within the actor's personal knowledge: whether he was the initial aggressor, or whether he provoked the use of force. By adding the phrase "or the third person" to the jury instructions, the trial court precluded the defendant from relying on the [third person] defense if his cousin was in fact the initial aggressor or provoker, regardless of whether the defendant knew or reasonably should have known this to be true. . . . [T]he trial court essentially imported the common law "alter-ego rule" into the statute. That rule [meant that] . . . a defendant "stepped into the shoes" of the third person he was defending, and his actions would be justifiable only if he was actually correct that the person he defended could have acted in self-defense . . . .

III

The defendant next argues that the trial court erred in finding . . . sufficient evidence to prove that his shod foot met the . . . definition of a deadly weapon. . . . [H]e was wearing ordinary sneakers and . . . delivered only a single kick . . . . We are not persuaded. . . .

RSA 625:11, V (2007) defines "deadly weapon" as "any firearm, knife or other substance or thing which, in the manner it is used, intended to be used, or threatened to be used, is known to be capable of producing death or serious bodily injury." . . . In this case, there was sufficient evidence . . . that the defendant's shod foot constituted a deadly weapon. . . . *Reversed and remanded.*

Notes and Questions

(1) *The Result under "Step into the Shoes" versus the Result under Reasonable Belief.* Sometimes, different results follow under the alter ego rules, as compared to the results under reasonable belief. The prosecution certainly believed there would be a different result under the step-into-the-shoes approach in *Mayo,* above. Can you explain why?

But step-into-the-shoes probably doesn't create a different result in most cases, because usually the true facts are apparent to the defender. In *State v. Cook,* 515 S.E.2d 127 (W. Va. 1999), the state supreme court of appeals observed that West Virginia followed the older rule: "One simply steps into the shoes of the victim and is able to do only as much as the victim himself would lawfully be permitted to do." Still, the court held as a matter of law that the defendant had the right of defense of another under the circumstances of that case and ordered him acquitted.

(2) *What Policies Support the "Reasonable Belief" Standard, and What Arguments Support the "Step into the Shoes" Approach?* Some advocates have suggested that the step into the shoes approach reflects a desirable policy against the escalation of violence. Proponents of the reasonableness approach, by contrast, argue that it encourages citizens to help each other and counteracts the "I don't want to get involved" syndrome that is prevalent in some places. They also suggest that the reasonableness approach provides sufficient incentives for people to figure out what is going on before contributing unthinkingly to widening a brawl. (But did that concept work well in the *Mayo* case?)

The clear modern trend is toward reasonable belief. But consider the policy underlying the alter ego approach. Is there some merit to it as well?

[C] Defense of Property (and of Habitation)

Read MPC § 3.06(1), (3)(a), (3)(d), (5) [use of force to protect property; limits; use of deadly force; devices] in the MPC Appendix.

Note on Defense of Property

(1) *The Interests in Conflict.* The defense of property defense rests on the intuition that people should be able to use some force to protect their property. For most people, the same intuition treats defense of property as less important than personal self-defense. Reflecting these intuitions, the law places more restrictions on the use of force to protect property than on force to protect humans from unlawful physical attack.

(2) *The Limits of Lawful Force to Protect Property: Sometimes, Unfortunate Results.* Imagine that Amanda is suddenly surprised by a purse-snatcher. Can she lawfully pursue the thief and snatch the purse back? Yes. But what if Amanda's entire life savings are in the purse and she cannot catch the thief—can she shoot the fleeing thief? Probably not. The question for defense of property is where to draw the line between the use of slight force and the use of deadly force.

(3) *Life Matters More than Property: No Deadly Force Just to Protect Property.* The general rule is that a person may use reasonable *nondeadly* force to protect property. But severe limits exist on the use of deadly force for this purpose. The commentaries to the MPC, explaining the prevailing view, observe that "the preservation of life has such moral and ethical standing in our culture and society, that the deliberate sacrifice of life merely for the protection of property ought not to be sanctioned by law." MPC § 3.06, comments at 72. But the Commentaries add that, although this general principle is easy to state, "drafting [the law] proved complex." The result: "The general principle is that moderate but not deadly force may be used to defend property in certain instances." Wisconsin's statute is a good example of this approach:

> A person is privileged to threaten or intentionally use [non-deadly] force against another for the purpose of preventing or terminating what the person reasonably believes to be an unlawful interference with the person's property. Only such degree of force or threat thereof may intentionally be used as the actor reasonably believes is necessary to prevent or terminate the interference. . . .

Wis. Stat. § 939.49.

(4) *Extent of Nondeadly Force.* The use of non-deadly force to protect property includes force necessary to terminate the trespass or unlawful interference with property as well as the force needed to recover the property. The prevailing view is that the extent of even non-deadly force must be reasonable. For example, if a thief grabs a briefcase from a person walking to work, the victim may use reasonable

force to prevent the briefcase from being taken and may chase the thief and use reasonable force to recover the stolen property.

(5) *Exceptions: Deadly Force Sometimes Permitted to Protect a Dwelling or Prevent Certain Property Crimes.* Although they recognize the general rule against the use of deadly force to protect property, the MPC and a majority of states provide an exception in two situations: (1) in response to an attempt to dispossess the defender of his or her dwelling, and (2) in response to an attempt to commit certain felonies that involve violence against the defender. Many states provide an even broader exception. Consider Colorado's "make-my-day" statute:

> any occupant of a dwelling is justified in using any degree of physical force, including deadly physical force, against another person when that other person has made an unlawful entry into the dwelling, and when the occupant has a reasonable belief that such other person has committed a crime in the dwelling in addition to the uninvited entry, or is committing or intends to commit a crime against a person or property in addition to the uninvited entry, and when the occupant reasonably believes that such other person might use any physical force, no matter how slight, against any occupant.

Colo. Rev. Stat. § 18–1-704.5(2); *see also* N.Y. Penal Law § 35.20, 30.25 (allowing deadly force to prevent certain felonies, including arson and burglary, even if they do not involve violence against a person, although larceny or destruction of property cannot justify deadly force).

Reconsider the dilemma faced by Amanda in note 2. These exceptions do not seem to allow deadly force to prevent the theft of her life savings. Should they?

(6) *Non-Human Devices for Protection of Property.* Next, consider the owner of an automobile-parts yard who protects it against fence-climbers with a large, vicious dog capable of causing serious injury. The dog is clearly visible, and a sign advertises the dog's prowess in inflicting deadly force. Or, imagine a property owner who installs a trap gun, together with a warning sign, to deter intruders. If injury results in either case to a would-be thief, is the owner liable? The MPC approach (and that of many states) is to deny a defense for the use of a device that inflicts deadly force and to hold the owner criminally liable for assault or murder.

People v. Ceballos

526 P.2d 241 (Cal. 1974)

[Ceballos set up a trap gun in the garage that was part of his dwelling, because he had been the victim of prior burglaries. Two boys attempted a burglary of the garage while no one was at home, and one boy, named Stephen, was injured when the trap gun mechanically discharged. The jury convicted defendant of assault with a deadly weapon.

[The defendant argued on appeal that Cal. Civil Code § 50 empowered him to use necessary force "to protect from wrongful injury [his] person or property." Reading this provision in light of the common law rule that deadly force ordinarily cannot be used solely to protect property, the court rejected this argument. The court also held that the erection of a deadly device that discharges in the absence of the actor is different from the actor's own use of force while the actor is present.]

Defendant contends that had he been present he would have been justified in shooting Stephen since Stephen was attempting to commit burglary, that under [case law] defendant had a right to do indirectly what he could have done directly, and that therefore any attempt by him to commit a violent injury upon Stephen was not "unlawful" and hence not an assault. The People argue that as a matter of law a trap gun constitutes excessive force, and that in any event the circumstances were not in fact such as to warrant the use of deadly force. . . .

In the United States, courts have concluded that a person may be held criminally liable under statutes proscribing homicides and shooting with intent to injure, or civilly liable, if he sets upon his premises a deadly mechanical device and that device kills or injures another. However, an exception to the rule that there may be criminal and civil liability for death or injuries caused by such a device [sometimes] has been recognized where the intrusion is, in fact, such that the person, were he present, would be justified in taking the life or inflicting the bodily harm with his own hands. . . .

Allowing persons, at their own risk, to employ deadly mechanical devices imperils the lives of children, firemen and policemen acting within the scope of their employment, and others. Where the actor is present, there is always the possibility he will realize that deadly force is not necessary, but deadly mechanical devices are without mercy or discretion. . . .

It seems clear that the use of such devices should not be encouraged. . . . [S]etting forth an exception to liability for death or injuries inflicted by such devices "is inappropriate in penal law for it is obvious that it does not prescribe a workable standard of conduct; liability depends upon fortuitous results." We therefore decline to adopt that rule in criminal cases. . . .

Defendant also argues that had he been present he would have been justified in shooting Stephen under subdivision 4 of Penal Code section 197, which provides, "Homicide is . . . justifiable . . . (4) When necessarily committed in *attempting*, by lawful ways and means, *to apprehend* any person for any felony committed. . . ." (Italics added.) The argument cannot be upheld. . . . Here no showing was made that defendant's intent in shooting was to apprehend a felon. Rather it appears . . . that his intent was to prevent a burglary, to protect his property, and to avoid the possibility that a thief might get into defendant's house and injure him upon his return. . . .

. . . We conclude that as a matter of law the exception to the rule of liability for injuries inflicted by a deadly mechanical device does not apply under the circumstances here appearing. [Conviction affirmed.]

Notes and Questions

(1) *Defense of Others at Common Law and in Statutes.* The excerpts from *Ceballos* focus on common law principles. At the time of the case, California statutory law provided that homicide is "justifiable . . . [w]hen committed in defense of habitation, property, or person, against one who manifestly intends of endeavors, by violence of surprise, to commit a felony." The *Ceballos* court also observed that "[s]ince a homicide is justifiable under the circumstances specified in section 197, a fortiori an attempt to commit a violent injury upon another under those circumstances is justified." Yet, when Ceballos sought to rely on that provision, because he was seeking to defend his property against someone committing a felony, the court responded that "a literal reading of that section is undesirable," and it chose instead to read (and limit) the defense of others provision in light of the common law.

The court departed from the language of the statute and construed it against the defendant. The court expressed concern about the potential disproportion between the felony and the defensive force. But was it appropriate for the court to interpret the statute to maintain an overall balance of goals, or is that the legislature's job?

(2) *A Change in Law, But Any Change in Result?* The California legislature changed the defense of property law in 1984, ten years after *Ceballos*, to create a presumption that a person had a reasonable fear of imminent serious injury or death if deadly force was used against a person who the actor knew or had reason to believe had unlawfully and forcibly entered his or her residence. Cal. Penal Code § 198.5. *See also* Fla. Stat. ch. 776.013(1) (creating a virtually identical presumption). How would Ceballos have fared under this version of the law?

(3) *State Statutes Permitting Devices to Protect Property.* A few states specifically authorize the use of devices to protect property, but limit them to devices not designed to cause death or serious bodily harm. The use of such devices must be reasonable in the circumstances as the actor believes them to be, and their existence must be made known to probable intruders [*e.g.*, by a sign]. *See, e.g.*, Neb. Rev. Stat. § 28–1411(8).

[D] Law Enforcement — Effecting Arrest and Preventing Escape

> Read MPC § 3.07(1)–(2) [force to affect arrest; deadly force] in the MPC Appendix.

Note on the Authority to Make an Arrest

(1) *Law Enforcement Personnel.* Law enforcement personnel may make arrests based on probable cause (a reasonable belief that the arrestee has committed a

criminal offense). While an arrest warrant, issued by judicial personnel, is the preferred grant of authority for law enforcement officials to make an arrest, warrantless arrests are permitted in some circumstances, such as when the arrestee commits a felony or misdemeanor in the officer's presence. Some jurisdictions permit a warrantless arrest for a misdemeanor committed outside the officer's presence in cases such as domestic violence or drunk driving, where immediate action is needed.

(2) *Private Persons.* A private person may participate in an arrest in two ways: when aiding a law enforcement officer and when making an independent "citizen's arrest." A citizen's arrest is more limited than that of a law enforcement officer. See the note below. *See also* Ore. Rev. Stat. § 133.225 (setting limits).

Note on the Law Enforcement Defense

(1) *A Lawful Arrest Likely Fits the Elements of Assault, but the Law Enforcement Defense Usually Exonerates the Actor.* Arrests involve force, but the law allows law enforcement officers to make proper arrests without incurring criminal liability for their use of reasonable force. In general terms, this is often referred to as a *law enforcement defense.*

(2) *Private Persons and the Law Enforcement Defense.* A private person making a "citizen's arrest" may also rely on the law enforcement defense, but the scope is more restricted than when she acts to assist an officer. The citizen may face strict liability (*i.e.*, be guilty of assault) if she is wrong and the crime was not in fact committed. Some jurisdictions restrict the use of force by a private person to felony arrests. *See, e.g.,* Ala. Code § 13–3-27. The citizen may also face resistance from the person being arrested. *See People v. Chirico*, 272 P.3d 1170 (Colo. Ct. App. 2012) ("the right to self-defense necessarily applies in circumstances . . . in which a person reasonably believes that force used or threatened to be used by a private citizen is not in furtherance of effecting what the private citizen may claim to be a lawful citizen's arrest").

(3) *Amount of Force: Reasonable, Nondeadly, and Deadly.*

(a) *Nondeadly Force.* The general rule is that a law enforcement officer or private citizen (whether assisting law enforcement or making a citizen's arrest) may use *reasonable nondeadly force* to effectuate an arrest, including the nondeadly force needed to overcome resistance. *See, e.g.,* 720 Ill. Comp. Stat. 5/7–5 (law enforcement officer or citizen assisting officer need not retreat or desist from effort to make lawful arrest because of resistance to arrest). Sometimes this authority extends to threatening (but not using) deadly force. *See, e.g.,* Alas. Stat. § 11.81.370.

(b) *Deadly Force.* The common law permitted the use of deadly force for the arrest of a fleeing felon, at least when capital punishment applied to the underlying felony (as it usually did when most felonies were capital). MPC § 3.07 and many states modify this rule to allow deadly force where the underlying felony involved a use or threat of deadly force or where delayed apprehension will create a "substantial risk" that the felon will cause death or serious bodily harm. Usually, a person making a citizen's arrest has no privilege to use deadly force but may be able to invoke self-defense and defense of third parties, including the deadly force sometimes permitted by those defenses. *See, e.g.,* Ore. Rev. Stat. § 161.255.

(4) *Constitutional Limits on Police Use of Force.* In *Tennessee v. Garner,* 471 U.S. 1 (1985), a peace officer used deadly force to stop a fleeing nonviolent, 15-year-old boy who was suspected of having been involved in a burglary. The officer saw a person run from the scene, ordered the person to stop and identified himself as a police officer, then shot the fleeing person who was climbing a fence to escape. The suspect, a 15-year-old unarmed boy who had a purse taken from the burglary, died. The parents sued the police officer for violating their son's constitutional rights.

The United States Supreme Court concluded that a police officer who killed a fleeing suspect had made a "seizure" for purposes of the Fourth Amendment; that the seizure was unlawful if it was "unreasonable"; and that authorization to kill a fleeing suspect without regard to whether the suspect posed a risk of injury to anyone was "per se unreasonable" and therefore violated the victim's Fourth Amendment rights. In effect, *Garner* constitutionalized limits on the use of deadly force by law enforcement officers roughly similar to those imposed by the MPC, at least for purposes of civil rights liability.

(5) *High Speed Chases by Police Officers: Scott v. Harris,* 550 U.S. 372 (2007). Harris fled from the police after committing a traffic offense. After a high speed chase, Officer Scott used his police cruiser to push Harris' car off the road. The resulting crash left Harris a quadriplegic, and he sued for damages. The Court denied that *Garner* had created a special rule for the use of deadly force and stated, "Whether or not Scott's actions constituted 'deadly force,' all that matters is whether Scott's actions were reasonable." The Court went on to hold that "[a] police officer's attempt to terminate a dangerous high-speed car chase that threatens the lives of innocent bystanders does not violate the Fourth Amendment, even when it places the fleeing motorist at risk of serious injury or death."

(6) *The Cases on Civil Liability Do Not Determine the Outcome of Criminal Prosecutions of Officers.* What would have happened if the peace officer in *Garner* or *Scott* had been prosecuted criminally? Those decisions do not provide an answer. But such prosecutions are rare. In addition, a state may, and often does, permit a defense to criminal liability in cases that would support an award of civil damages. The answer depends on the specifics of state criminal statutes.

Note on the Crime Prevention Defense and Other Applicable Defenses

(1) *Crime Prevention.* Other law enforcement defenses exist, such as crime prevention. Both private persons and law enforcement personnel may use force to prevent crimes. Deadly force usually may only be used to prevent felonies, not

misdemeanors, and most jurisdictions confine the right to use deadly force to cases of serious felonies. *See, e.g.,* Ariz. Rev. Stat. Ann. § 13–411 (physical force, including deadly force, permissible to person who reasonably believes force immediately necessary to prevent certain arsons, burglaries, kidnapping, homicides, and sexual offenses; retreat not necessary; is presumption of reasonableness); Iowa Code § 704.7 (reasonable force to prevent perpetration of forcible felony).

(2) *Other Defenses May Also Apply.* It is only in cases where there is no threat to person or property that the law enforcement defense becomes determinative. Not infrequently, other criminal defenses may also apply in the context of an arrest by police or citizens. In these cases, the other defense may be broader than the law enforcement defense, providing the actor with protection denied by the law enforcement defense.

(a) *Defense of Property.* The right to use reasonable nondeadly force to protect property may overlap with a law enforcement defense if the arrest is being made to stop an actor from invading, stealing, or harming property. The arresting officer may use one or even both of these defenses to justify the use of force against the actor.

(b) *Self-Defense and Defense of Others During an Arrest.* If the arrestee resists arrest in a way that endangers the arresting officer (or someone else), the officer may be able to rely on self-defense or defense of another, as would any citizen.

Problem 6C (Various Defenses): "I Caught Him Stealing My Stereo, and He Seemed Violent"

(1) *The Killing of a Car Burglar.* Asleep in his apartment, John Owner heard his car alarm sound. He armed himself with a pistol and went to investigate. In the darkness, he saw a scruffy, bearded man holding something near his car and realized that the object was his car stereo equipment. The man had broken a window with a tire iron, which he was also holding. In a shaky voice, Owner ordered the man (who later was identified as Carl Crooker), to "stop right there and come with me," intending to turn him over to the apartment security guard.

Instead, the man later identified as Crooker "lunged" at him and swung the tire iron, then ran to the other side of the car. "He had a real wild look in his eyes," Owner says. "I didn't know whether he was going to run away with my stereo or come at me again." Over the hood of his car, from ten feet away, Owner shot Crooker twice, and one of the bullets proved to be fatal.

The district attorney's office is considering whether to seek an indictment for voluntary manslaughter against Owner, and Owner has hired an attorney to persuade the prosecutor not to do so. Owner can assert several kinds of defenses, but each of them is subject to difficulties.

(2) *Analyzing Defense of Property and Law Enforcement Defenses.* Will Owner be able to "raise" defense of property with sufficient evidence to require a jury instruction? If so, given the elements of that defense, is it likely that a jury will have a

reasonable doubt about it? Consider, also, the same questions about the law enforcement defense (the justification that Owner might offer by way of apprehending a thief).

(3) *Self-Defense, Defense of Property, and Law Enforcement Together.* Cases that involve defenses of property or law enforcement also often present self-defense issues as well. How likely is it that Owner can "raise" self-defense? Or succeed with it?

[E] Resisting an Unlawful Arrest or the Use of Excessive Force

---

Read MPC § 3.04(2)(a)(i) [no defense for resisting unlawful arrest] in the MPC Appendix.

Note on the Use of Force to Resist Arrest

(1) *Resisting Arrest: No Right to Use Force to Resist Lawful Arrest Involving Appropriate Force by Person Who Should be Known to be a Police Officer.* Related to but separate from the defense of law enforcement is the question of what to do when a suspect resists arrest. The general rule is that the arrestee has no privilege to resist arrest if the arrest is lawful and the officer is using the permissible amount of force. A person who resists arrest may be convicted of assault or battery or a separate crime called resisting arrest.

Often, this rule applies only when the person being arrested knows or reasonably should know that the person effectuating the arrest is a peace officer. *See, e.g.,* Ala. Code § 13A-3–28. The situation is more difficult when a person resists a citizen's arrest. *See People v. Chirico*, 272 P.3d 1170 (Colo. Ct. App. 2012) (noted above; defendant who does not realize that force is in furtherance of a citizen's arrest has the right to defend against that force).

(2) *Unlawful Arrest.* Even if a court later determines that the arrest was unlawful (perhaps because it was not supported by probable cause), the MPC and many jurisdictions still prohibit resistance. *See, e.g.,* Ariz. Rev. Stat. Ann § 13–404 (may not resist lawful or unlawful arrest by someone arrestee should know is police officer unless was excessive force). Some jurisdictions even specify that it does not matter whether the arrestee believes the arrest is unlawful and it turns out to be so. *See, e.g.,* 720 Ill. Comp. Stat. § 5/7–7. The theory is that police officers should be protected from injury, that resistance is often futile because other officers will support the arrest, that the law therefore protects citizens, and that determination of the lawfulness of the arrest should be done in court.

(3) *Excessive Force.* While there may be no defense simply because the arrest was unlawful, some jurisdictions do allow the arrested person to use self-defense if the

arrest is effectuated with unlawful force. The case excerpted below explores these issues.

PEOPLE v. CURTIS, 450 P.2d 33 (Cal. 1969). In this case, a uniformed California police officer received a prowler report and a description. He stopped Curtis, who generally fit the description, and attempted to arrest him. Curtis resisted, and a violent struggle ensued, during which both men were injured. Curtis was acquitted of burglary but convicted of felony battery on a peace officer engaged in lawful duties. The arrest was later found unlawful for lack of probable cause. A California statute, Penal Code §834a, provided that "it is the duty of [an arrested person] to refrain from using force or any weapon to resist such arrest."

On the basis of this statute, the court rendered a complex holding: (1) Curtis's resistance to the arrest was not privileged even if the arrest was unlawful; (2) still, if the arrest was unlawful, Curtis could not be convicted of battery upon a police officer engaged in "lawful" activities, but only of simple battery; and (3) the right to self-defense remained valid if the force used by the officer was unreasonable. The court remanded for retrial:

> While defendant's rights are no doubt violated when he is arrested and detained . . . without probable cause, we conclude [that] removing the right to resist does not contribute to or effectuate this deprivation of liberty. In a day when police are armed with lethal and chemical weapons, and possess scientific communication and detection devices readily available for use, it has become highly unlikely that a suspect, using *reasonable* force, can escape from or effectively deter an arrest, whether lawful or unlawful. . . . Indeed, self-help not infrequently causes far graver consequences for both the officer and the suspect than does the unlawful arrest itself. Accordingly, the state, in deleting the right to resist, . . . has merely required a person to submit peacefully to the inevitable and to pursue his available remedies through the orderly judicial process. . . .
>
> [We] confirm that a resisting defendant commits a public offense; but if the arrest is ultimately determined factually to be unlawful, the defendant can be validly convicted only of simple assault or battery. . . .
>
> Defendant contends that his arrest was not only lacking in probable cause and thus unlawful, but also was accomplished with excessive force and hence he was justified in employing counterforce in self-defense. . . .
>
> . . . Liberty can be restored through legal processes, but life and limb cannot be repaired in a courtroom. Therefore any rationale. . . for outlawing resistance to unlawful arrests and resolving the dispute in the courts has no determinative application to the right to resist excessive force.

[F] Public Duty: Conduct of Government Functions Authorized by Law

Read MPC § 3.03(1) [public duty defense] and 2.10 [military orders defense] in the MPC Appendix.

Notes and Questions

(1) *The Need for a Public Duty Defense.* What if a police officer exceeds the lawful speed limit while pursuing a felon, or a sheriff executes an eviction order and physically removes a person from an apartment, or an executioner carries out a death warrant and injects the person with lethal drugs pursuant to state law? These acts, though proper, fit the definitions of crimes. Therefore, the "public duty" defense provides that a public employee performing his or her job is protected from criminal liability. The defense is broadly available to public officials. *See, e.g.,* N.D. Cent. Code § 12.1–05-01 (conduct engaged in by public servant in the course of official duties is justified when required or authorized by law); Haw. Stat. § 703–303(3) (public duty defense extended to actor who believes his or her conduct is required or authorized to assist public officer in the performance of the officer's duties; defense applies even if officer exceeds his or her legal authority).

(2) *Invalid Exercise of the Authority: Should Reasonableness and Good Faith Be Required?* Jurisdictions divide on the extent to which the public duty defense is available if the authority under which it is carried out is invalidly exercised, such as when the court order authorizing the action is void for want of jurisdiction.

Some states take a subjective approach that permits the public servant to act on his or her actual understanding. *See, e.g.,* Haw. Stat. § 703–303 (public duty applies when actor "believes" the conduct is authorized by court of competent jurisdiction). Other states use an objective test, asking whether the actor "reasonably believes" that the conduct was lawful and authorized. *See, e.g.,* Alas. Stat. § 11.81.420 (person reasonably believes the conduct is lawful).

(3) *Conduct During War: Following Orders or Perceived Duty.* Would this public duty defense apply to a member of the military or to a police officer who invokes the "Nuremberg defense" (the defense of following orders given by a superior)? Note that the defense failed at the Nuremberg trials of Nazi officials, and it has not fared well in other contexts. *See* MPC § 2.10; *Calley v. Callaway,* 519 F.2d 184 (5th Cir. 1975) (denying defense in case of the My Lai massacre of unarmed Vietnamese civilians, when conduct and orders were transparently unlawful); *People v. Lesslie,* 24 P.3d 22 (Colo. Ct. App. 2000) (deputy sheriff's defense of reliance upon superior's order to place wiretap rejected where such an order obviously would have been unsupported by law).

[G] Defense Based on Relationships: Parents, Teachers, and Others

(1) *Use of Reasonable Force for Safety and Other Purposes.* Recognizing the need for people to use force in some circumstances to protect people and maintain order and discipline, the law permits a limited defense for the use of such force. For example, a person may use reasonable force to stop a suicide, maintain order on a school bus or in a prison or mental institution, or aid someone in an emergency situation. Although technically qualifying as an assault, the use of force in these situations is protected by a "relationship" defense.

(2) *Reasonable Force for Discipline or Other Appropriate Purposes.* Whether parents, teachers, and others in similar capacities should be allowed to use force as a disciplinary tool is an unresolved social issue. The general rule is that a parent and others in a caretaking role may use reasonable force when reasonably necessary to maintain discipline. A minority view rejects the "reasonableness" standard and adopts a more subjective one. *See, e.g.,* Model Penal Code § 3.08 (teachers and similarly situated people may use force to maintain discipline in school if the teacher "believes" the force is necessary for that purpose); *cf.* Haw. Rev. Stat. § 703–309 (prison official may use force the actor "believes" is "necessary" to enforce institutional rules). Does the subjective standard allow too much discretion, or is such discretion appropriate for people who must make quick decisions affecting lives and safety?

[H] Necessity — The "Choice of Evils"

Consider the case of the mountain hiker who is caught in a sudden snowstorm and believes she will die unless she finds shelter and food. She breaks into a remote cabin and stays for several days — until the storm is over — eating the canned food stored in a cupboard. Can the hiker be convicted of criminal trespass or theft for entering the cabin without permission and eating the food?

In cases involving extreme circumstances, the *necessity* or *choice of evils* defense allows people to escape criminal liability because the choice they made was the socially preferred one, even though it violated the criminal law. The next case explores the limits of this defense.

> Read MPC § 3.02(1) [choice of evils defense] in the MPC Appendix.

Commonwealth v. Leno

616 N.E.2d 453 (Mass. 1993)

[Massachusetts prohibited distribution of hypodermic needles without a prescription. In defiance of the applicable statutes, under which they were convicted,

Leno and others operated a needle exchange program that provided clean needles to drug users, in an effort to reduce the spread of AIDS. The trial judge refused Leno's requested jury instruction on the defense of necessity. The Massachusetts Supreme Judicial Court affirmed:]

[T]he application of the defense [of necessity] is limited to the following circumstances: (1) the defendant is faced with a clear and imminent danger, not one which is debatable or speculative; (2) the defendant can reasonably expect that his [or her] action will be effective as the direct cause of abating the danger; (3) there is [no] legal alternative which will be effective in abating the danger; and (4) the Legislature has not acted to preclude the defense by a clear and deliberate choice regarding the values at issue. . . .

The prevention of possible future harm does not excuse a current systematic violation of the law in anticipation of the eventual over-all benefit to the public. . . . The defendants did not show that the danger they sought to avoid was clear and imminent, rather than debatable or speculative. . . . That some States prohibit the distribution of hypodermic needles without a prescription, and others do not, merely indicates that the best course to take to address the long-term hazard of the spread of AIDS remains a matter of debate. . . .

Citizens who disagree with the Legislature's determination of policy are not without remedies. "[T]he popular initiative is coextensive with the Legislature's law-making power. . . ." *Paisner v. Attorney Gen.*, 458 N.E.2d 734 (1983). *See also* Mass. Const. Pt. I, art. 19 (the right of people to petition the Legislature). Thus, the defendants did not meet the requirement that there be no legal alternative to abate the danger. [Affirmed.]

Notes and Questions

(1) *The Necessity Defense in General.* The defense of necessity is a catchall defense that brings in an indefinite variety of values that may override the policies underlying defined crimes. Thus, its application inevitably involves a tension between competing policies, and it is generally extremely fact-sensitive.

(2) *A Case to Compare with Leno: The Exoneration of an Intoxicated Driver.* Compare *Leno* with the New Jersey court's decision to reverse a DWI conviction in *State v. Romano*, 809 A.2d 158 (N.J. Super. Ct. App. Div. 2002). Romano was attacked in a restaurant by three men, who beat, kicked, and bloodied him. When he escaped to the relative safety of his car, his "attackers jumped onto the hood of his car, shook and kicked the car and screamed 'come out here, we're going to get you, you're dead after this, you'll see what's going to happen.'" Lacking a cellphone or any means of calling for help, seriously injured, and fearing for his life, the defendant, who proved to be legally intoxicated, drove off:

[D]efendant had no other reasonable alternatives available to him. . . .
In addition, the gravity of the harm defendant faced in this case was . . .

significantly higher than the harm faced by the defendants in [cases that have denied the necessity defense.] . . .

. . . Here, the "facts [are] so bizarre and remote from the public policy underlying the law that even a court as committed as this one to the strict enforcement of the drunk-driving statutes can pause to make certain that no injustice has been done." To not apply the defense of necessity in these circumstances is to allow an injustice.

The *Romano* court analogized to three other cases applying the necessity defense to intoxicated driving: *People v. Pena*, 149 Cal. App. 3d Supp. 14 (Cal. App. Dep't Super. Ct.1983) (applying necessity defense to DWI conviction of man who drove his car to follow a deputy sheriff who, allegedly for her protection, had searched and driven off with defendant's girlfriend, who was clad in a "see-through nightgown"); *State v. Knowles*, 495 A.2d 335 (Me. 1985) (allowing necessity instruction in case of DWI defendant who claimed to have been beaten and apparently needed to drive to escape); *State v. Shotton*, 458 A.2d 1105 (Vt. 1983) (applying necessity defense to prosecution against intoxicated woman who drove herself to hospital after assault by her husband). *See also Greenwood v. State*, 237 P.3d 1018 (Alaska 2010) (reversing DUI conviction of woman fleeing former boyfriend).

(3) *Limitations on the Necessity Defense.* The defense of necessity contains several restrictions that limit its availability.

(a) *Balancing Evils. Leno* sets out a typical four-part test for the defense of necessity, but the availability of the defense is usually qualified in two additional ways. First, the defendant's unlawful act must cause a lesser harm or "evil" than the harm the defendant seeks to avoid in committing it. A typical standard is:

> [The commission of a crime is necessary as an emergency measure] to avoid an imminent public or private injury . . . which is of such gravity, that, according to ordinary standards of intelligence and morality, the desirability and urgency of avoiding such injury clearly outweigh the desirability of avoiding the injury sought to be prevented by the statute defining the offense in issue.

N.Y. Penal Law § 35.05; *see also Romano*, above; *United States v. Aguilar*, 883 F.2d 662, 693 (9th Cir. 1989) (defense to smuggling and hiding illegal immigrants seeking asylum in U.S.).

(b) *Defendant Not at Fault in Causing Exposure to Risk.* Second, the defense is often limited or unavailable if the defendant was at fault in causing the situation that produced the claim of necessity. *See* MPC § 3.02 (2).

(c) *Especially Clear Necessity.* Many jurisdictions impose further limits. For example, some states require that the necessity of violating the statute be especially clear, and they measure this clarity by a reasonable person standard. In effect, these states require that the necessity be unmistakably evident to any reasonable person, not just to the actor.

(d) *Affirmative Defense.* Another limiting device is to make necessity an affirmative defense, requiring the defendant to persuade the jury about it. Is this an appropriate burden?

(e) *The Legislature Has Made the Choice of Evils.* The *Leno* court also limited the defense to situations in which "the Legislature has not acted to preclude the defense by a clear and deliberate choice regarding the values at issue." What does this mean? After all, the defendant is on trial for violating a criminal law passed by the legislature—is any other choice of values necessary? *See also United States v. Oakland Cannabis Buyers' Cooperative,* 532 U.S. 483 (2001) (rejecting necessity defense to federal charges of manufacturing and distributing marijuana because the federal Controlled Substances Act indicated that Congress had made a controlling choice of values, specifically "that marijuana has no medical benefits worthy of an exception (outside the confines of a Government-approved research project)").

(f) *Necessity is Usually Not a Defense to Homicide Cases.* The usual rule is to deny the necessity defense in homicide cases. *See Regina v. Dudley & Stephens,* 14 Q.B. 273 (U.K. 1884) (rejecting the argument that "to save your own life you may lawfully take the life of another, when that other is [not] threatening yours," when, days after a shipwreck, the defendants, at sea in a lifeboat and convinced that they would starve otherwise, killed the weakest of their number and subsisted by eating his body until their rescue). *See also, e.g.,* Ky. Rev. Stat. § 503.030 (necessity defense unavailable for intentional homicide).

The commentaries to the Model Penal Code articulate a different view: the necessity defense should apply to homicide if there is a "net saving of lives." MPC § 3.02, comment 3. Thus, it could be used when taking three lives would save four. Does the MPC provide a better rule? Is it so easy to weigh and compare lives?

A third approach allows necessity as a partial defense to homicide, lowering the crime to a less severe grade. *See, e.g.,* Wis. Stat. § 939.47 (killing by necessity lowered from first degree intentional homicide to second degree intentional homicide). Is a killing in a situation triggering the necessity defense less morally culpable than one not precipitated by the external force?

(4) *Two Kinds of Recurring (but Usually Unsuccessful) Necessity Cases.* There are two kinds of cases in which the necessity defense appears to recur, although it is not often successful.

(a) *Political Protestors.* Political protesters sometimes seek to justify disobedience to law, such as trespass or property destruction, as a means of expressing values they argue are more important than the criminal laws they violate. The availability of other outlets of communication and the restrictions on the necessity defense usually limit its usefulness for civil disobedience defendants. The *Leno* case, essentially, falls into this category. *See also United States v. DeChristopher,* 695 F.3d 1082 (10th Cir. 2012) (rejecting necessity defense for interfering with gas lease auction by making highest bid on leases, as protest against gas drilling; other options were available). Not only do defendants usually lose necessity claims like these; sometimes they know in advance that they will lose. What then is the point of raising the defense in such cases?

(b) *Prison Escape.* Courts have sometimes recognized a necessity defense in prison escape cases in which the defendants have claimed the necessity of avoiding assault or rape, but states often limit the defense by imposing conditions that escapees usually cannot meet. *See, e.g.*, Haw. Rev. Stat. § 703–302(3) (necessity unavailable to escaping prisoner unless no force was used against prison personnel, there was no time to resort to the courts to remedy the actual or threatened harm, complaint to authorities was impossible or would be futile, and the actor promptly reports to proper authorities when attaining position of safety).

In *People v. Lovercamp*, 43 Cal. App. 3d 823 (Cal. Ct. App. 1974), a prisoner claimed her escape was necessary because she repeatedly had been accosted by other inmates who demanded that she either submit to sexual acts or fight. She testified that complaints to prison authorities produced no protection. The court of appeals reversed her conviction and remanded for consideration of a limited defense of necessity that required proof of (1) a specific threat of immediate future death, forcible sexual attack, or substantial bodily injury; (2) lack of time for, or futility of, complaints to authorities; (3) lack of time or opportunity for resort to the courts; (4) no use of force or violence in the escape; and (5) an immediate reporting to authorities by the prisoner once safety is reached.

(5) *Necessity That Grows Out of Major Disasters, Such as Hurricane Katrina in New Orleans.* Hurricane Katrina swamped most of New Orleans with flood water after breaking the city's levees. Three days later, the Memorial Medical Center sat in 10 feet of putrid flood waters, with no electrical power and no means of evacuating four terminal patients, ages 62 to 90. Two nurses and a doctor provided the patients with higher than usual therapeutic doses of morphine and Versaid, a sedative, and all four died. The physician later explained that "there were some patients there who were critically ill who, regardless of the storm, had the orders of do not resuscitate. In other words, if they died, to allow them to die naturally and to not use heroic methods to resuscitate them." Nevertheless, said the doctor, "we did everything in our power to give the best treatment that we could to the patients in the hospital to make them comfortable." Although the doctor and nurses were arrested and initially charged with second degree murder, a grand jury refused to return an indictment and the charges were expunged.

Less serious acts were pervasive in New Orleans. A man walked down Canal Street with a pallet of food on his head. His wife insisted they were not stealing from the nearby supermarket: "It's about survival right now. We've got to feed our children." To what extent does the necessity defense apply to these various cases of ostensible homicide and theft? For discussion in the context of theft, see Stuart P. Green, *Looting, Law, and Lawlessness*, 81 Tul. L. Rev. 1129 (2007).

§ 6.04 Excuse ("I Had No Right but I'm Not Responsible")

[A] Duress or Compulsion

Note on the Duress Defense

(1) *Duress and Necessity: Both Are Lesser-Evil Defenses.* Defendants sometimes raise the necessity and duress defenses at the same time. Both defenses involve the choice of evils. The traditional distinction between the two is that the dilemma underlying (1) *necessity* arises from nature, or from chance, so that the defendant chooses the lesser of two evils that are presented without any human purpose to create the defendant's choice, whereas (2) *duress* (sometimes called *coercion*) arises from a human agency in the form of another person's threat that if the defendant does not commit the crime, the other individual will carry out the threat. While modern statutes tend to preserve this distinction, some cases and commentators treat duress as a specialized form of necessity or collapse the distinctions between the two defenses.

Under the prevailing approach, necessity usually is characterized as a justification: "I did the right thing, by choosing the lesser of two evils." Duress, on the other hand, is an excuse: "I did something wrong, but I'm not responsible because I was forced to do it."

(2) *General Application.* A duress defense arises when a person commits a criminal act because of another person's threats of physical harm if the crime is not committed. For example, X holds a gun to Y's head and says she will shoot Y unless Y stabs Victim. If Y stabs Victim under the circumstances Y may have a successful duress defense if charged with a crime.

(3) *Limits on the Duress Defense.* There are many limits on the duress defense.

(a) *Threat of Immediate Physical Harm.* Duress generally applies only when the crime is committed because of the threat of immediate physical harm. Future harm is generally insufficient. Sometimes the threat must be of serious harm. *See, e.g.,*Wash. Rev. Code § 9A.16.060 (immediate death or immediate grievous bodily injury); Minn. Stat. § 609.08 (immediate death). Other provisions require less harmful physical threats. *See, e.g.,* Conn. Gen. Stat. § 53a-14 (imminent use of physical force); Haw. Rev. Stat. § 702–231 (unlawful force).

(b) *Harm to Actor or Third Person.* The prevailing view is that the threat may be directed at the actor or someone else. *See, e.g.,* Wis. Stat. § 939.46 (harm to the actor or another). A minority view allows the defense only for threats directed at the person who is pressured to commit the crime. *See, e.g.,* 720 Ill. Comp. Stat. 5/7–11.

(c) *Overcoming the Will of a Person of Reasonable Firmness.* Out of concern that a broad duress defense would excuse too much criminal activity, the law limits the duress defense by establishing an objective test: the threat must be sufficient to overcome the will of a person of reasonable firmness. *See, e.g.,* N.Y. Penal Law

§ 40.00 (person of reasonable firmness in his situation would have been unable to resist); Ore. Rev. Stat. § 161.270 (threat of such nature or degree to overcome earnest resistance). Thus, a vague threat that "you'll be fired" is probably not enough compulsion to excuse a kidnapping or robbery, but a specific and credible threat that "I'll kill you and all of your family" likely will excuse a theft.

(d) *Recklessly Placing Oneself in Position to be Subject to Duress.* MPC § 2.09(2) and many state codes disallow the duress defense for defendants who "recklessly" [or, sometimes, intentionally or negligently] placed themselves "in a position in which it was probable that [they] would be subjected to duress." Consider the following case.

Read MPC § 2.09(1)–(2) [duress] in the MPC Appendix.

United States v. Contento-Pachon
723 F.2d 691 (9th Cir. 1984)

BOOCHEVER, CIRCUIT JUDGE.

This case presents an appeal from a conviction for unlawful possession with intent to distribute a narcotic controlled substance in violation of 21 U.S.C. § 841(a)(1) (1976). At trial, the defendant attempted to offer evidence of duress and necessity defenses. The district court excluded this evidence on the ground that it was insufficient to support the defenses. We reverse because there was sufficient evidence of duress to present a triable issue of fact.

I. Facts

The defendant-appellant, Juan Manuel Contento-Pachon, is a native of Bogota, Colombia and was employed there as a taxicab driver. He asserts that one of his passengers, Jorge . . . proposed that Contento-Pachon swallow cocaine-filled balloons and transport them to the United States. Contento-Pachon agreed to consider the proposition. He was told not to mention the proposition to anyone, otherwise he would "get into serious trouble." Contento-Pachon testified that he did not contact the police because he believes that the Bogota police are corrupt and that they are paid off by drug traffickers

Approximately one week later, Contento-Pachon told Jorge that he would not carry the cocaine. In response, Jorge mentioned facts about Contento-Pachon's personal life, including private details which Contento-Pachon had never mentioned to Jorge. Jorge told Contento-Pachon that his failure to cooperate would result in the death of his wife and three-year-old child. . . .

[Later] Contento-Pachon swallowed 129 balloons of cocaine. He was informed that he would be watched at all times during the trip, and that if he failed to follow Jorge's instruction he and his family would be killed. . . .

After leaving Bogota, Contento-Pachon's plane landed in Panama. Contento-Pachon asserts that he did not notify the authorities there because he felt that the Panamanian police were as corrupt as those in Bogota. Also, he felt that any such action on his part would place his family in jeopardy.

When he arrived at the customs inspection point in Los Angeles, Contento-Pachon consented to have his stomach x-rayed. The x-rays revealed a foreign substance which was later determined to be cocaine.

At Contento-Pachon's trial, the government moved to exclude the defenses of duress and necessity. The motion was granted. We reverse.

A. Duress

There are three elements of the duress defense: (1) an immediate threat of death or serious bodily injury, (2) a well-grounded fear that the threat will be carried out, and (3) no reasonable opportunity to escape the threatened harm. Sometimes a fourth element is required: the defendant must submit to proper authorities after attaining a position of safety. . . .

The trial court found Contento-Pachon's offer of proof insufficient to support a duress defense because he failed to offer proof of two elements: immediacy and inescapability. . . .

Immediacy: The element of immediacy requires that there be some evidence that the threat of injury was present, immediate, or impending. "[A] veiled threat of future unspecified harm" will not satisfy this requirement. The district court found that the initial threats were not immediate because "they were conditioned on defendant's failure to cooperate in the future and did not place defendant and his family in immediate danger."

Evidence presented on this issue indicated that the defendant was dealing with a man who was deeply involved in the exportation of illegal substances. Large sums of money were at stake and, consequently, Contento-Pachon had reason to believe that Jorge would carry out his threats. Jorge had gone to the trouble to discover that Contento-Pachon was married, that he had a child, the names of his wife and child, and the location of his residence. These were not vague threats of possible future harm. . . .

Escapability: The defendant must show that he had no reasonable opportunity to escape. The district court found that because Contento-Pachon was not physically restrained prior to the time he swallowed the balloons, he could have sought help from the police or fled. Contento-Pachon explained that he did not report the threats because he feared that the police were corrupt. The trier of fact should decide whether one in Contento-Pachon's position might believe that some of the Bogota police were paid informants for drug traffickers and that reporting the matter to the police did not represent a reasonable opportunity of escape.

If he chose not to go to the police, Contento-Pachon's alternative was to flee. . . . To flee, Contento-Pachon, along with his wife and three-year-old child, would have been forced to pack his possessions, leave his job, and travel to a place beyond the reaches of the drug traffickers. A juror might find that this was not a reasonable avenue of escape. . . .

Surrender to Authorities: As noted above, the duress defense is composed of at least three elements. The government argues that the defense also requires that a defendant offer evidence that he intended to turn himself in to the authorities upon reaching a position of safety. Although it has not been expressly limited, this fourth element seems to be required only in prison escape cases. Under other circumstances, the defense has been defined to include only three elements. . . .

B. Necessity

The defense of necessity is available when a person is faced with a choice of two evils and must then decide whether to commit a crime or an alternative act that constitutes a greater evil. Contento-Pachon has attempted to justify his violation of 21 U.S.C. § 841(a)(1) by showing that the alternative, the death of his family, was a greater evil.

Traditionally, in order for the necessity defense to apply, the coercion must have had its source in the physical forces of nature. The duress defense was applicable when the defendant's acts were coerced by a human force. . . .

Contento-Pachon's acts were allegedly coerced by human, not physical forces. In addition, he did not act to promote the general welfare. Therefore, the necessity defense was not available to him. . . .

II. Conclusion

. . . Because the trier of fact should have been allowed to consider the credibility of the proffered evidence [of duress], we reverse. The district court correctly excluded Contento-Pachon's necessity defense. REVERSED and REMANDED.

Coyle, District Judge (dissenting in part and concurring in part): . . .

In cases where the defendant's duress has been raised, the courts have indicated that the element of immediacy is of crucial importance. The trial court found that the threats made against the defendant and his family lacked the requisite element of immediacy. This finding is adequately supported by the record. The defendant was outside the presence of the drug dealers on numerous occasions for varying lengths of time. There is no evidence that his family was ever directly threatened or even had knowledge of the threats allegedly directed against the defendant.

[Moreover,] [t]he record supports the trial court's findings that the defendant and his family could have sought assistance from the authorities or have fled. Cases considering the defense of duress have established that where there was a reasonable legal alternative to violating the law, a chance to refuse to do the criminal act and also to avoid the threatened danger, the defense will fail. . . .

UNITED STATES v. MAYORQUIN-ROMERO, 2019 WL 1167984 (W.D. Ohio 2019). The defendant was charged with illegal entry into the United States. His offer of proof in support of a duress defense was that members of the notorious MS-13 gang in Honduras threatened to kill him because his tattoo resembled that of a rival gang. Citing *Contento-Pachon,* above, the court held that his evidence was insufficient to raise the defense:

> The third element [of duress] requires a showing that Defendant had no reasonable, legal alternative to illegally entering the United States. Defendant's testimony establishes just the opposite, that he had other reasonable, legal alternatives. Defendant testified that he felt safer in the United States than in Guatemala and Mexico, but he did not identify any imminent and impending threat to his safety in those countries. . . . In addition, fully crediting Defendant's testimony, the threat to his safety stemmed from his tattoo, not his membership in any gang. Based on the placement of Defendant's tattoo, . . . it would have been possible to keep his tattoo hidden indefinitely in Guatemala or Mexico, thus eliminating the risk of misinterpretation by MS-13 or another gang until he could have it removed or altered.

> Defendant also had an opportunity to seek asylum in the United States before illegally entering the country. He testified that he was in Reynosa, Mexico for approximately eight months before his most recent entry into the United States. During that time, Defendant could have applied for admission [but did not].

> The fifth element of the prima facie case requires Defendant to present evidence that he did not maintain the illegal conduct any longer than "absolutely necessary." Defendant was in the United States for three months before his arrest. He did not seek asylum . . . . [Presentation of defense denied.]

Notes and Questions

(1) *The Federal Common Law Duress Defense. Contento-Pachon* describes the federal common law duress defense. Instead of the simple MPC standard, the federal duress defense requires (1) an "immediate threat" (immediacy), of (2) "death or serious bodily injury" (severity), with (3) a "well-grounded fear" (objectively justified), and (4) "no reasonable opportunity to escape" (unavailability of escape), as well as, sometimes, (5) "submission to proper authorities" when safety is attained (prompt surrender). Does the court properly apply these duress factors to Contento-Pachon's circumstances?

(2) *Is It Duress—or Is It Necessity? The Intoxicated Driving Cases as Examples of the Confusion between These Defenses.* Reconsider the notes that introduced duress, as well as the notes in the preceding section, involving necessity defenses asserted in intoxicated driving cases. Those cases involve intoxicated defendants who, after being attacked and unlawfully beaten, drive their automobiles to other locations, where they are arrested for driving while intoxicated. But are these really "necessity" cases, or are they, instead, "duress" cases? The two defenses blend into each other, yet necessity is a justification, and duress is an excuse.

(3) *Should Duress Excuse Homicidal Crimes?* Many jurisdictions exclude homicide crimes such as murder from being excused by duress. *See State v. Toscano*, 378 A.2d 755 (N.J. 1977); Wash. Rev. Code § 9A.16.060 (duress inapplicable to murder, manslaughter, or murder by abuse); 720 Ill. Comp. Stat. 5/7–11 (duress inapplicable to offense punishable by death); *see also* Iowa Code § 704.10 (duress inapplicable for intentional or reckless physical injury to another person). The MPC, by contrast, rejects this limit (as it does with necessity). *See* MPC § 2.09, comment 3.

In *People v. Anderson*, 50 P.3d 368 (Cal. 2002), the defendant was convicted of first degree murder for killing a woman suspected of molesting two girls, one of whom was the daughter of his accomplice. He argued that the father threatened to harm him if he did not participate in killing the woman. The Court rejected Anderson's duress claim and held that duress cannot be a defense to murder and cannot reduce murder to manslaughter. The court explained,

> At common law, the general rule was, and still is today, what Blackstone stated: duress is no defense to killing an innocent person. . . . The basic rationale behind allowing the defense of duress for other crimes "is that . . . it is better that the defendant, faced with a choice of evils, choose to do the lesser evil (violate the criminal law) in order to avoid the greater evil threatened by the other person." This rationale, however, "is strained when a defendant is confronted with taking the life of an innocent third person in the face of a threat on his own life. . . . When the defendant commits murder under duress, the resulting harm—*i.e.* the death of an innocent person—is at least as great as the threatened harm—*i.e.* the death of the defendant." We might add that, when confronted with an apparent kill-an-innocent-person-or-be-killed situation, a person can always choose to resist. As a practical matter, death will rarely, if ever, inevitably result from a choice not to kill. The law should require people to choose to resist rather than kill an innocent person.

In dissent, Justice Kennard argued that California law should make duress "unavailable as to capital murder but available as to noncapital murder":

> the Model Penal Code allows the defense of duress to be asserted against *all* criminal charges, including murder. . . .
>
> . . . [T]he weight of scholarly commentary [also] favors the Model Penal Code's definition of duress and its abolition of the common law murder exception to the duress defense. . . .
>
> . . . I do not here suggest that the Legislature should adopt the Model Penal Code approach, under which duress is available as a defense to any crime, including capital murder. I suggest only that a construction of [the statute] under which duress is a defense to noncapital murder, but not to capital murder, represents a moderate, middle-of-the road approach . . . .
>
> The majority's discussion appears to assume that murder necessarily involves a *choice* to take an innocent life. Second degree murder, however,

does not require an intent to kill. A person who engages in a provocative act or who drives with great recklessness may be convicted of second degree murder under an implied malice theory. Yet, under the majority's construction, [California law] does not allow a duress defense even in situations of unintentional implied malice killings.

Still, Justice Kennard agreed that on the facts of the case, Anderson would not be able to raise duress even if duress were available as a defense to non-capital murder. Who is right?

Problem 6D (Necessity; Duress): "I'm in Terrible Pain and I Need It Now"

(1) *The Wife Who Steals Demerol for Her Husband.* Bill Vaughan, a physician licensed in the State of Maryland, was severely burned while on a ski vacation in Colorado. His wife Brenda stayed with him in the hospital. Two days after the accident, Bill complained repeatedly of excruciating pain. Brenda attempted to find a nurse or aide but was unable to find anyone who could come promptly. As the minutes dragged by and stretched into an hour, Bill wept and screamed. Finally, he said "If you don't give me something, I'm going to do something drastic." Following instructions from her husband, who knew where to look, what to take, and how to administer it, Brenda broke into a locked cabinet and procured Demerol, and again with his instructions, administered it to him. The grand jury, though sympathetic, felt that it had no choice but to indict Brenda for theft and for possession and delivery of a controlled substance.

(2) *Does Brenda Have a Defense of Either Necessity or Duress?* Consider the elements of necessity, and then of duress, and decide whether or not Brenda might be able to succeed with either defense.

[B] Entrapment

Note on the Entrapment Defense

(1) *The Defense of Government Instigation.* How should courts respond when an overzealous government official "manufactures" a crime by overcoming the resistance of an "otherwise innocent" individual by "inducement" or "instigation"? The entrapment defense is rare, but it addresses this problem.

(2) *Theoretical Basis: Government Should Not Create Crime.* The basis for the entrapment defense is that the government should not convert innocent citizens into criminals. "Entrapment" captures both the idea that the government's conduct in such a situation is improper and the intuition that a person who was persuaded to commit crime is not as morally reprehensible as someone who committed crime without inducement. Note, however, that the defendant in an entrapment case usually is factually guilty of the offense. He or she actually sold the drugs or stole the item with the necessary mens rea. Therefore, the defense is limited.

(3) *Elements of Entrapment.* Entrapment has several elements, which may differ sharply among jurisdictions.

(a) *Action by Government Agent.* Entrapment requires action by a government agent or a person working in cooperation with the government.

(b) *Inducement or Persuasion.* The government agent must somehow induce or persuade the citizen to commit the crime. The inducement could be provided by money, sexual favors, or some other benefit. Sometimes the action must be done for the purpose of instituting criminal activity. *See, e.g.,* Conn. Gen. Stat. § 53a-15.

(c) *Two Approaches to Assessing the Government Activity.* The law of entrapment reflects two competing approaches. The first focuses on the criminal inclination of the accused (the subjective approach), while the second focuses on the extent of government misbehavior (the objective or MPC approach).

> (i) *The MPC's "Objective" Standard, Focusing on the Existence of "Risk" That the Offense Might Result from Improper Government Inducement.* MPC § 2.13, representing a minority view known as the "objective" or "government misconduct" approach, allows an entrapment defense when the government uses methods that "create a substantial risk" that persons who "are not ready to commit the offense" might be induced to commit it. This objective approach allows even a "predisposed" defendant to use the defense if the government went too far in creating a "risk" that people without predisposition might be persuaded. *See People v. Barraza,* 591 P.2d 947 (Cal. 1979) (adopting objective defense, potentially exonerating even predisposed persons, if official persuasion was "likely to induce a normally law-abiding person" to violate the law).

> (ii) *The Subjective Approach Requiring an Otherwise Innocent Actor, as Opposed to a Predisposed Actor.* The subjective approach is the prevailing view of entrapment in the federal courts. The key inquiry is whether (1) the government "instigated" the offense by persuading an "otherwise innocent" person to commit it, or whether (2) the defendant was "predisposed" to commit it and merely responded to the opportunity afforded by the government. This is a "subjective" test, because it focuses upon the particular, individual defendant's mental state and depends upon predisposition.

> For example, the defendant in *United States v. Poehlman,* 217 F.3d 692 (9th Cir. 2000), was convicted of crossing state lines to commit sexual offenses with minors. The Court of Appeals, however, over a forceful dissent, held that persuasion by a law enforcement officer posing as the "mother" of the two intended "victims," had instigated and overcome the will of the defendant, who was not "predisposed" to commit the offense. The evidence thus entitled the defendant to a defense of entrapment.

(4) *The Dilemma: Distinguishing "Affording an Opportunity" from Entrapment.* Some offenses are difficult to detect without government initiatives or "stings." For

example, the work of undercover officers who purchase drugs makes possible the prosecution of many contraband offenses, and the efforts of federal agents to infiltrate and supply materials to groups who may be planning acts of violence makes possible many terrorism prosecutions. The subjective and objective approaches agree that these examples of "affording an opportunity" are not entrapment. *See, e.g.*, N.Y. Penal Law § 50.05 (conduct merely affording an opportunity to commit an offense is not entrapment); Ore. Rev. Stat. § 161.270 (same). But the difficulty arises in drawing the line.

(5) *Variations: Supplying an Essential or Important Ingredient; Outrageous Governmental Misconduct.* Some commentators would extend the entrapment defense to any situation in which the government becomes "an active participant" in the crime by "supplying a [necessary] ingredient." Also, some proponents of the subjective (predisposition) approach have suggested that truly "outrageous" governmental misconduct may furnish a separate but related defense, applicable even to predisposed defendants. Consider the case that follows, which raises all four of these approaches (subjective, objective, ingredient, and outrageousness).

Read MPC § 2.13(1) [entrapment, defined by an objective standard] in the MPC Appendix.

United States v. Russell

411 U.S. 423 (1973)

Mr. Justice Rehnquist delivered the opinion of the Court. . . .

There is little dispute concerning the essential facts in this case. . . . Joe Shapiro, an undercover agent for the Federal Bureau of Narcotics and Dangerous Drugs, went to respondent's home . . . where he met with respondent and his two codefendants, John and Patrick Connolly. Shapiro's assignment was to locate a laboratory where it was believed that methamphetamine was being manufactured illicitly. He then made an offer to supply the defendants with the chemical phenyl-2-propanone, an essential ingredient in the manufacture of methamphetamine, in return for one-half of the drug produced. This offer was made on the condition that Agent Shapiro be shown a sample of the drug . . . and the laboratory where it was being produced.

During the conversation, Patrick Connolly revealed that he had been making the drug since May [of that year] and since then had produced three pounds of it. John Connolly gave the agent a bag containing a quantity of methamphetamine that he represented as being from "the last batch that we made." . . . At the [laboratory], Shapiro observed an empty bottle bearing the chemical label phenyl-2-propanone. [Shapiro was given a bag of meth, observed its manufacture, supplied propanone, and bought meth. Propanone was found at Connolly's house.]

There was testimony at the trial of respondent and Patrick Connolly that phenyl-2-propanone was generally difficult to obtain. At the request of the Bureau of Narcotics and Dangerous Drugs, some chemical supply firms had voluntarily ceased selling the chemical. . . . [T]he jury found the respondent guilty on all counts charged. On appeal, the respondent conceded that the jury could have found him predisposed to commit the offenses, but argued that on the facts presented there was entrapment as a matter of law. The Court of Appeals agreed, [expanding] . . . the traditional notion of entrapment, which focuses on the predisposition of the defendant, to mandate dismissal of a criminal prosecution whenever the court determines that there has been "an intolerable degree of governmental participation in the criminal enterprise." In this case the court decided that the conduct of the agent in supplying a scarce ingredient essential for the manufacture of a controlled substance established that defense.

This new defense was held to rest on either of two alternative theories. One theory [would find] entrapment, regardless of predisposition, whenever the government supplies contraband to the defendants. The second theory, a nonentrapment rationale, [asks whether] a government investigator was so enmeshed in the criminal activity that the prosecution of the defendants was held to be repugnant to the American criminal justice system. . . . In any event, [the court below] held that "[b]oth theories are premised on fundamental concepts of due process and evince the reluctance of the judiciary to countenance 'overzealous law enforcement.'"

This Court first recognized and applied the entrapment defense in *Sorrells v. United States*, 287 U.S. 435 (1932). In *Sorrells*, a federal prohibition agent visited the defendant while posing as a tourist and engaged him in conversation about their common war experiences. After gaining the defendant's confidence, the agent asked for some liquor, was twice refused, but upon asking a third time the defendant finally capitulated, and was subsequently prosecuted for violating the National Prohibition Act.

Mr. Chief Justice Hughes, speaking for the Court, held that as a matter of statutory construction the defense of entrapment should have been available to the defendant. Under the theory propounded by the Chief Justice, the entrapment defense prohibits law enforcement officers from instigating a criminal act by persons "otherwise innocent in order to lure them to its commission and to punish them." Thus, the thrust of the entrapment defense was held to focus on the intent or predisposition of the defendant to commit the crime. "[I]f the defendant seeks acquittal by reason of entrapment he cannot complain of an appropriate and searching inquiry into his own conduct and predisposition as bearing upon that issue." . . .

In . . . *Sherman v. United States*, [356 U.S. 369 (1958), the Court affirmed] the theory underlying *Sorrells*. [The Court] held that "[t]o determine whether entrapment has been established, a line must be drawn between the trap for the unwary innocent and the trap for the unwary criminal." . . .

In the instant case, respondent asks us to reconsider the theory of the entrapment defense as it is set forth in the majority opinions in *Sorrells* and *Sherman*.

His principal contention is that the defense should rest on constitutional grounds. He argues that the level of Shapiro's involvement in the manufacture of the methamphetamine was so high that a criminal prosecution for the drug's manufacture violates the fundamental principles of due process. . . . But he would have the Court go further in deterring undesirable official conduct by requiring that any prosecution be barred absolutely because of the police involvement in criminal activity. . . .

Respondent would [have] the Court adopt a rigid constitutional rule that would preclude any prosecution when it is shown that the criminal conduct would not have been possible had not an undercover agent "supplied an indispensable means to the commission of the crime that could not have been obtained otherwise, through legal or illegal channels." Even if we were to surmount the difficulties attending the notion that due process of law can be embodied in fixed rules, . . . the rule he proposes would not appear to be of significant benefit to him. For, on the record presented, it appears that he cannot fit within the terms of the very rule he proposes. . . .

While we may some day be presented with a situation in which the conduct of law enforcement agents is so outrageous that due process principles would absolutely bar the government from invoking judicial processes to obtain a conviction, *cf. Rochin v. California*, 342 U.S. 165 (1952), the instant case is distinctly not of that breed. Shapiro's contribution of propanone to the criminal enterprise already in process was scarcely objectionable. The chemical is by itself a harmless substance and its possession is legal. . . .

[The infiltration of drug rings] is a recognized and permissible means of investigation; if that be so, then the supply of some item of value that the drug ring requires must, as a general rule, also be permissible. For an agent will not be taken into the confidence of the illegal entrepreneurs unless he has something of value to offer them. Law enforcement tactics such as this can hardly be said to violate "fundamental fairness" or "shocking to the universal sense of justice." . . .

Nor does it seem particularly desirable for the law to grant complete immunity from prosecution to one who himself planned to commit a crime, and then committed it, simply because government undercover agents subjected him to inducements which might have seduced a hypothetical individual who was not so predisposed. . . .

Several decisions [have attempted to bar prosecutions for] "overzealous law enforcement." But the defense of entrapment enunciated in those opinions was not intended to give the federal judiciary a "chancellor's foot" veto over law enforcement practices of which it did not approve. The execution of the federal laws under our Constitution is confided primarily to the Executive Branch of the Government, subject to applicable constitutional and statutory limitations and to judicially fashioned rules to enforce those limitations. We think that the decision of the Court of Appeals in this case quite unnecessarily introduces an unmanageably subjective standard which is contrary to the holdings of this Court in *Sorrells* and *Sherman*.

Those cases establish that entrapment is a relatively limited defense. It is rooted, not in any authority of the Judicial Branch to dismiss prosecutions for what it feels to have been "overzealous law enforcement," but instead in the notion that Congress could not have intended criminal punishment for a defendant who has committed all the elements of a proscribed offense but was induced to commit them by the Government. . . . [Reversed.]

MR. JUSTICE DOUGLAS, with whom MR. JUSTICE BRENNAN concurs, dissenting. . . .

In my view, the fact that the chemical ingredient supplied by the federal agent might have been obtained from other sources is quite irrelevant. Supplying the chemical ingredient used in the manufacture of this batch of "speed" made the United States an active participant in the unlawful activity. . . .

MR. JUSTICE STEWART, with whom MR. JUSTICE BRENNAN and MR. JUSTICE MARSHALL join, dissenting. . . .

In *Sorrells v. United States, supra,* and *Sherman v. United States, supra,* the Court took what might be called a "subjective" approach to the defense of entrapment. In that view, the defense is predicated on an unexpressed intent of Congress to exclude from its criminal statutes the prosecution and conviction of persons, "otherwise innocent," who have been lured to the commission of the prohibited act through the Government's instigation. The key phrase in this formulation is "otherwise innocent," for the entrapment defense is available under this approach only to those who would not have committed the crime but for the Government's inducements. Thus, the subjective approach focuses on the conduct and propensities of the particular defendant in each individual case. . . . And, in the absence of a conclusive showing one way or the other, the question of the defendant's "predisposition" to the crime is a question of fact for the jury. The Court today adheres to this approach.

The concurring opinion of Mr. Justice Roberts, joined by Justices Brandeis and Stone, in the *Sorrells* case, and that of Mr. Justice Frankfurter, joined by Justices Douglas, Harlan, and Brennan, in the *Sherman* case, took a different view of the entrapment defense. In their concept, the defense [rests] on the belief that "the methods employed on behalf of the Government to bring about conviction cannot be countenanced." Thus, the focus of this approach is not on the propensities and predisposition of a specific defendant, but on "whether the police conduct revealed in the particular case falls below standards, to which common feelings respond, for the proper use of governmental power." . . .

In my view, this objective approach to entrapment advanced by the Roberts opinion in *Sorrells* and the Frankfurter opinion in *Sherman* is the only one truly consistent with the underlying rationale of the defense. . . . I find it impossible to believe that the purpose of the defense is to effectuate some unexpressed congressional intent to exclude from its criminal statutes persons who committed a prohibited act, but would not have done so except for the Government's inducements. . . .

The purpose of the entrapment defense, then, cannot be to protect persons who are "otherwise innocent." Rather, it must be to prohibit unlawful governmental activity in instigating crime. As Mr. Justice Brandeis stated in *Casey v. United States*, "This prosecution should be stopped, not because some right of Casey's has been denied, but in order to protect the government. To protect it from illegal conduct of its officers. To preserve the purity of its courts." If that is so, then whether the particular defendant was "predisposed" or "otherwise innocent" is irrelevant; and the important question becomes whether the Government's conduct in inducing the crime was beyond judicial toleration.

Moreover, a test that makes the entrapment defense depend on whether the defendant had the requisite predisposition permits the introduction into evidence of all kinds of hearsay, suspicion, and rumor—all of which would be inadmissible in any other context—in order to prove the defendant's predisposition. It allows the prosecution, in offering such proof, to rely on the defendant's bad reputation or past criminal activities, including even rumored activities of which the prosecution may have insufficient evidence to obtain an indictment, and to present the agent's suspicions as to why they chose to tempt this defendant. . . .

Notes and Questions

(1) *The Subjective Test (Predisposition) versus the Objective Test (Government Misconduct).* The *Russell* opinions discuss the arguments for and against the objective and subjective approaches to entrapment. The majority of states and the federal courts use the subjective test, whereas most scholars favor the objective test. Which test is better?

(2) *"Affording an Opportunity": Is It Really Separable from "Instigation or Creation"?* The *Russell* dissenters agree that "affording an opportunity" for commission of a crime is not entrapment. As noted above, many state statutes specifically adopt this rule. Arguably, a line can be drawn between "affording an opportunity" and "instigating or creating," at least in some cases. But the distinction may often blur in real-world situations.

Imagine that the police department responds to a series of auto-parts thefts by setting up a "sting" operation in which officers pretend to act as "fences" or receivers of stolen property. Housed in a large, attractive garage, the undercover officers send out word that they will buy high-demand items. Arguably, the government has merely "supplied an opportunity" in such a case. But doesn't it also "supply an ingredient" of the offense, namely, a buyer? And doesn't its conduct create a "risk" that its conduct may persuade some people who otherwise would not be "ready" to commit the offense? Consider whether "offering an opportunity" can really be distinguished from "creating the offense."

(3) *One Reason the Entrapment Defense Is a Last Resort: It Opens up the Trial to Otherwise Excluded (and Very Damaging) Evidence.* As Justice Stewart points out, the defendant's reliance on the subjective defense of entrapment means that the defendant's predisposition unavoidably becomes the determinative issue. Predisposition, by definition, concerns states of mind before the elements of the crime

occurred. Therefore, the rules of evidence broaden to enable the prosecution to offer evidence of defendant's prior crimes and reputation, evidence that is otherwise inadmissible.

For example, imagine that the defendant is your client, who has a long "rap sheet" of arrests and convictions for drug offenses and who is accused of selling drugs. If you raise an entrapment claim, the government may establish predisposition by offering testimony about your client's other offenses, as well as character witnesses who will describe your client as a "known peddler of narcotics." Arguably, if predisposition is the issue, this evidence is highly relevant. It may deter you, however, from using the defense out of concern that the jury will use the "predisposition" proof in deciding whether your client committed the drug sales at issue in the case. Does this concern, as Justice Stewart argues, mean that the objective test should be preferred, or is it merely the fair consequence of defendant's raising of a (subjectively oriented) defense that ought to be limited?

(4) *Defendant Often Has the Burden of Persuading the Jury.* MPC § 2.13(2) and many state statutes provide that to obtain an entrapment acquittal, the defendant must not only raise the defense but must also prove it by the preponderance of the evidence. Is this extra proof burden for entrapment under the MPC justified? (Some other jurisdictions do not impose the burden of persuasion on the defendant in entrapment cases. *See Jacobson v. United States*, 503 U.S. 540 (1992) (prosecution bears burden of disproving entrapment in federal cases).)

Problem 6E (Entrapment): "Is It Proper for the Police to Catch Car Thieves That Way?"

(1) *A Law Enforcement Campaign Against Car Thieves.* Assume local police have set up a sting operation that involves parking high-theft cars—those frequently the target of thefts—on the street, with doors unlocked and keys in the ignition. If a thief attempts to drive it, however, the car will stop, automatically lock all doors, and emit a signal that will summon nearby officers.

(2) *Is This "Steal-Me-Car" Sting a Form of Entrapment, under the Objective, Subjective, Ingredient, or Outrageousness Approaches?* The federal courts and many states use a subjective version of entrapment, in which a person who is "predisposed" cannot have the benefit of the defense. How should this law enforcement tactic be analyzed under the subjective standard? The objective approach asks whether the government's persuasion is strong enough to induce persons not inclined to commit the offense to commit it. Would the steal-a-car tactic persuade ordinary people to commit theft? Still another approach is to find entrapment if the state supplies an ingredient necessary for the offense. A final approach is to define entrapment as including outrageous conduct by the government. What result would follow under these approaches?

(3) *More Inducement?* If you are not certain whether the "steal-me car" is entrapment by itself, what if an undercover officer was also nearby to point out the car to

suspected thieves, and to say things like, "someone should just drive off with that," or "you could make lots of money off of that car"?

[C] Insanity (and Incompetency)

Introductory Note on Insanity and Incompetency

(1) *Incompetence to Stand Trial.* A defendant's mental condition plays a different role, unlike that with mens rea, with respect to capacity to stand trial or participate in other proceedings. In general terms, a person who is mentally incompetent cannot be tried, sentenced, or executed. Among the rationales for this rule is the precept that it would be unfair to subject a mentally incompetent person to a proceeding in which the person's mental infirmity prevents meaningful participation. Thus, incompetency does not furnish a defense, but it prevents a trial until and unless the defendant's competency is restored.

(2) *The Defense of Insanity.* The insanity defense is an excuse that can prevent conviction. Based on the notion that someone who commits a crime while insane is not morally responsible for the offense and should not be punished for it, Anglo-American law has long provided an insanity defense that bars criminal liability for those few people who can meet the applicable standard.

(3) *Congruencies and Inconsistencies.* Since mental state affects so many aspects of the criminal justice system, multiple mental health issues may arise in the same case. For example, a defendant with serious mental problems, facing trial for intentional homicide, may claim incompetency to stand trial, diminished capacity (in some states), and insanity. Because the test for each issue is different, the defendant could be found to be competent to stand trial and also found not to be insane, yet he or she could be sufficiently mentally ill to succeed with a diminished capacity defense to intentional homicide in some jurisdictions.

Note on the Rationales for the Insanity Defense

(1) *Moral Responsibility.* One argument for having an insanity defense is that a person who commits a crime while insane is not morally responsible for the offense. The insane person lacks the ability to act responsibly and thus does not deserve punishment.

Sometimes the moral rationale for the insanity defense is expressed in terms of free will. A person whose crime was the product of insanity lacked free will or even "rationality," and should not be punished for something he or she could not help. As the following quotation suggests, this view takes the position that the defendant could not have the mens rea or guilty mind that is essential to criminal responsibility:

> The concept of mens rea, guilty mind, is based on the assumption that a person has a capacity to control his behavior and to choose between alternative courses of conduct. This assumption, though not unquestioned by

theologians, philosophers and scientists, is necessary to the maintenance and administration of social controls. . . . [T]he fact that a defendant was mentally diseased is not determinative of criminal responsibility in and of itself but is significant only insofar as it indicates the extent to which the particular defendant lacked normal powers of control and choice at the time he committed the criminal conduct with which he is charged. . . .

United States v. Currens, 290 F.2d 751, 773 (3d Cir. 1961).

(2) *Ineffective Punishment.* One could also argue that the criminally insane should not be held accountable for their criminal activity because punishing them would be ineffective. For example, incarcerating a person whose crime stemmed from a serious mental condition would not serve the goal of deterrence (deterring this offender so he or she will not reoffend in the future) if such a person cannot be deterred. Similarly, the goal of retribution (an eye for an eye) holds that a person who commits a crime deserves punishment for violating the criminal law—but a person who is legally insane arguably does not deserve punishment because the crime was not based on the offender's free will.

Another punishment rationale, incapacitation, presents a difficult argument. Incarceration is appropriate to remove the offender from a position where he or she may reoffend. Supporters of the insanity defense, however, suggest that the mental health system, including involuntary civil commitment, is a more appropriate way of crime prevention since it will both incapacitate the offender (locked up in a secure mental hospital) and provide useful treatment (such as medication or psychotherapy).

Note on the Four Major Tests of Insanity

(1) *Four Tests of Insanity.* American law provides four tests of insanity. A criminal accused who seeks an acquittal on the basis of insanity must identify the test in the jurisdiction and meet the applicable burden of proof.

(a) *The "Cognitive," "Right-Wrong," or "M'Naghten" Test: A Traditional, Relatively Narrow Approach.* The traditional approach, taken from an English decision called *M'Naghten's Case*, limits insanity acquittals to situations in which the defendant either does not understand what he or she is doing or does not know that the action is wrong. Thus, a homicide defendant is entitled to acquittal if he or she suffers from psychotic delusions leading to the perception that the victim is a giant green worm that is about to attack the defendant, but not if depression or personality disorders contribute to the crime by interfering with the defendant's affective (emotional) processes. The *M'Naghten* approach limits insanity to "cognitive" or "moral" incapacity—that is, conditions that affect conscious reasoning or knowledge.

(b) *Adding an "Irresistible Impulse" Element to M'Naghten.* Some authorities have broadened the cognitive test by adding an excuse for conduct induced by an "irresistible impulse." This approach exonerates not only actors who meet the *M'Naghten* cognitive test, but also those whose affective processes are "irresistible."

(c) *The "Durham" Test, or the "Product-of-a-Mental-Disease-or-Defect" Approach.* During the 1960s, the D.C. Circuit expressed dissatisfaction with the narrowness of the *M'Naghten* test and devised a different approach that allowed acquittal if the offense was the "product of a mental disease or defect." This approach broadened the insanity defense to such an extent that nearly all jurisdictions ultimately rejected it. Was alcoholism or drug dependency a "mental defect" that could excuse an offense? If a defendant suffered from "compulsive gambling syndrome" and committed a robbery to continue gambling, was the defendant entitled to acquittal?

(d) *The MPC Approach: A Lack of "Substantial Capacity" to "Appreciate" Wrongfulness or to "Conform."* MPC §4.01 differs sharply from all of these formulations. It provides a defense to a defendant who, as a result of a mental disease or defect, "lacks substantial capacity" to "appreciate" the wrongfulness of the criminal conduct or to "conform his conduct" to the requirements of the law. This formulation avoids some of the ambiguities of the *Durham* "product test," yet it is considerably broader than the *M'Naghten* cognitive approach. It does not require a complete interference with knowledge-based processes, because lacking "substantial" capacity is enough. The word "appreciate" broadens the defense, because it contrasts to "knowledge" in *M'Naghten*. And a lack of "substantial capacity . . . to conform" to the law is an alternative excuse, based on affective or emotional compulsion.

(2) *The Ultimate Dilemma: Determinism and Responsibility.* Each test seeks a balance between (1) acquitting those who are less capable of exercising responsibility, and (2) retaining individual responsibility for crimes. Critics of broad definitions of insanity tend to describe them as "determinism": erroneously viewing criminal actors as unable to respond to the law, when in fact these actors are sufficiently (if not ideally) responsible to be able to follow the law. These critics prefer the *M'Naghten* standard (or even abolition of the defense). Critics of narrow insanity provisions, by contrast, argue that they impose criminal liability upon those who cannot fairly be expected to exercise responsibility. These critics prefer the MPC approach (or even the *Durham* test).

(3) *Procedural Aspects of the Insanity Defense.* Jurisdictions differ sharply about the nature of the insanity defense, as well as about procedural issues such as burdens, notice, and verdicts.

(a) *Presumption of Sanity.* The general rule is that a defendant is presumed sane. A defendant who wants to raise an insanity defense must meet the burden of production—*i.e.* must offer some evidence that he or she is insane.

(b) *Affirmative Defense.* Many American jurisdictions classify insanity as an affirmative defense, requiring the defendant both to raise the issue (meet the burden of production) and convince the trier of fact that the defense exists (burden of persuasion). A minority approach is the burden-shifting view. The defendant has the burden of production to offer some evidence (a prima facie case) of insanity, and the burden then shifts to the government to disprove insanity.

(c) *Burden and Standard of Proof.* Jurisdictions differ on the standard of proof needed to establish an insanity defense, but the burden of persuasion usually rests on the defendant. *See, e.g.,* Ala. Code § 13A-3–1 (defendant must prove insanity defense by preponderance of evidence); 720 Ill. Comp. Stat. § 5/6–2 (defendant must prove insanity by clear and convincing evidence). In *Leland v. Oregon*, 343 U.S. 790 (1952), the United States Supreme Court upheld a state law (no longer in effect) that required the defendant to prove the defense beyond a reasonable doubt — a burden that sharply limits a defense that is rarely successful in most jurisdictions.

(d) *Pretrial Notice of Intent to Raise Insanity Defense.* Many jurisdictions require the defendant to give the prosecution pretrial notice of intent to raise an insanity defense or to use expert testimony on insanity or diminished responsibility. Notice gives the prosecution an opportunity to respond to defendant's mental health proof and to present its own proof. Such rules also give the government the opportunity to have the defendant examined before trial.

(e) *Possible Verdicts When Insanity is Issue.* Traditionally, there are three possible verdicts when insanity is an issue in a case: Guilty, Not Guilty, or Not Guilty by Reason of Insanity (NGRI). The NGRI verdict is a not guilty verdict (*i.e.* an acquittal), but it subjects the defendant to post-verdict assessment by mental health authorities and the possibility of civil commitment. Some jurisdictions have added a fourth option: Guilty But Mentally Ill (GBMI). This is a guilty verdict that subjects the defendant to criminal punishment but directs that the sentence first be served in a location providing mental health services.

(4) *Empirical Data about the Insanity Defense.* According to a study in one state, defendants raise the insanity defense in only about 1% of felony cases, and it is successful only about one-quarter of the time. About 95% of people found not guilty by reason of insanity serve a relatively long period of time in a mental hospital, often significantly longer than the prison sentences of people convicted of similar crimes but who did not claim insanity. Such people ordinarily have long histories of mental illness and are clearly not faking their serious mental problems. *See generally* Marc Rosen, *Insanity Denied: Abolition of the Insanity Defense in Kansas*, 8 Kan. J. L. & Pub. Pol'y 253 (1999).

[1] The M'Naghten *Test: Knowing Right from Wrong*

M'NAGHTEN'S CASE, 8 Eng. Rep. 718 (House of Lords 1843). In this famous case, the House of Lords laid out a test for insanity that has been followed in England and in most American jurisdictions until modern times:

> the jurors ought to be told in all cases that every man is to presumed to be sane, and to possess a sufficient degree of reason to be responsible for his crimes, until the contrary be proved to their satisfaction; and that, to establish a defence on the ground of insanity, it must be clearly proved that,

at the time of the committing of the act, the party accused was labouring under such a defect of reason, from disease of the mind, as not to know the nature and quality of the act he was doing, or, if he did know it, that he did not know he was doing what was wrong.

[2] Reaction to M'Naghten: *The Irresistible Impulse or Control Test*

Many experts criticized *M'Naghten* for not including those offenders who are fully aware of their actions and know right from wrong (therefore sane under *M'Naghten*) but who cannot control their behavior and thus—according to these experts—are not criminally responsible. These criticisms led some American jurisdictions to add the so-called irresistible impulse test, so that both *M'Naghten* and irresistible impulse provided tests of criminal insanity.

PARSONS v. STATE, 2 So. 854 (Ala. 1887). In this case, the court provided one of the first American formulations of the irresistible impulse approach. The defendant is not "legally responsible if the following conditions occur":

(i) if by reason of the duress of such mental disease, he had so far lost the power to choose between the right and wrong, and to avoid doing the act in question, as that his free agency was at the time destroyed; (ii) and if, at the same time, the alleged crime was so connected with such mental disease, in the relation of cause and effect, as to have been the product of it solely.

The focus of the irresistible impulse test, in short, is not about knowledge or understanding—as with *M'Naghten*—but rather about volition. The fact-finder must ask whether the defendant has the ability to control his or her actions. For that reason, it is often called the "control" test.

[3] Reaction to M'Naghten: *The Durham or*
Product-of-a-Disease-or-Defect Test

M'Naghten, with or without the irresistible impulse option, was also criticized for being too restricted and not including people with serious mental illnesses who should be excused from criminal responsibility but who do not fit into the rigid cognitive categories of *M'Naghten* and irresistible impulse. These experts wanted a much broader definition of insanity that reached those people who committed crimes simply because of their mental condition, regardless of cognitive or control limitations. In 1954, the D.C. Circuit in *Durham* adopted another test that was much more expansive than *M'Naghten* or irresistible impulse.

DURHAM v. UNITED STATES, 214 F.2d 862 (D.C. Circuit 1954). Durham, who had a "long history" of imprisonment and psychiatric hospitalization, was convicted of housebreaking. Among other diagnoses, he was described as a "psychopathic personality." The defense psychiatrist testified that Durham was "of unsound mind" at the time of the offense, but also said that "if the question of . . . right and wrong were propounded to him, he could give a right answer." The expert later said that he was unable to form an opinion on the right-wrong issue. The trial judge concluded that there was no evidence to support an insanity defense. The Court of Appeals, through Judge Bazelon, held that the testimony did contain "some" evidence of insanity, and it remanded because the trial judge had not "weighed 'the whole evidence.'"

More importantly, Judge Bazelon criticized and rejected the *M'Naghten* rule: "By its misleading emphasis on the cognitive, the right-wrong test requires court and jury to rely upon what is, scientifically speaking, inadequate, and most often, invalid and irrelevant testimony in determining criminal responsibility." Judge Bazelon added that insanity should not "rest on any particular symptom," such as knowledge of right and wrong. The court also held that addition of the so-called "irresistible impulse" test did not adequately expand the defense. "The term 'irresistible impulse' . . . carries the misleading implication that 'diseased mental condition(s)' produce only sudden, momentary or spontaneous inclinations to commit unlawful acts." A proper insanity defense, Judge Bazelon wrote, would recognize "mental illness characterized by brooding and reflection."

The court then proceeded to "invoke our inherent power" to "adopt[] a new test." Specifically, the new rule "is simply that an accused is not criminally responsible if his unlawful act was the *product of a mental disease or defect*" (italics added). Judge Bazelon explained:

> [U]nder the rule now announced, any instruction should in some way convey to the jury the sense and substance of the following: If you the jury believe beyond a reasonable doubt that the accused was not suffering from a diseased or defective mental condition at the time he committed the criminal act charged, you may find him guilty. If you believe he was suffering from a diseased or defective mental condition when he committed the act, but believe beyond a reasonable doubt that the act was not the product of such mental abnormality, you may find him guilty. Unless you believe beyond a reasonable doubt either that he was not suffering from a diseased or defective mental condition, or that the act was not the product of such abnormality, you must find the accused not guilty by reason of insanity. . . .

> The legal and moral traditions of the western world require that those who, of their own free will and with evil intent (sometimes called mens rea), commit acts which violate the law, shall be criminally responsible for those acts. Our traditions also require that where such acts . . . are the product of a mental disease or defect . . . , moral blame shall not attach, and hence there will not be criminal responsibility.

Notes and Questions on M'Naghten, *Irresistible Impulse,* and Durham

(1) *The M'Naghten (Right-Wrong) Rule, Irresistible Impulse, and the Durham (Product of a Mental Disease or Defect) Test.* As noted above, the *M'Naghten* test focuses on cognitive ability to distinguish right from wrong. Adding an "irresistible impulse" test to *M'Naghten* allows acquittal of some defendants who know the difference between right and wrong, if their mental problems amount to irresistible compulsion. The *Durham* test asks a different question: whether the defendant's action is the product of a mental disease or defect. Judge Bazelon concludes that this last approach will enable the jury to consider more relevant, more scientific evidence, in a way that is more consistent with blameworthiness. But will it?

(2) *What Is a Mental Disease or Defect? Does It Include Alcohol or Drug Abuse? Compulsive Gambling? An Antisocial Personality?* The three tests of insanity seem to require that the offender suffer from a mental disease or defect, but none of them defines mental disease or defect, even though the term is critical to each. What psychological conditions qualify?

In the opinions of some mental health professionals who may be permitted to testify as expert witnesses, compulsion to gamble or to abuse alcohol or drugs can be the basis of "mental disease or defect." Because the *Durham* terminology acquits if the action is the "product" of these ingredients, perhaps a compulsive gambler or drug user in a court recognizing the *Durham* test can offer an insanity defense to the crime of gambling, drug possession, or even stealing to obtain money to purchase drugs. Is this the meaning of *Durham* (and if not, how does Judge Bazelon's reasoning avoid this result)?

In fact, a frequent diagnosis of Durham himself was that he was "psychopathic." This terminology, from the American Psychological Association's *Diagnostic and Statistical Manual of Mental Disorders*, was revised to "antisocial personality" in the 1994 fourth edition (DSM-IV) and DSM-V. Antisocial personalities are narcissistic, hedonistic, grossly selfish, irresponsible, and impulsive, with interests that concentrate on satisfaction of immediate desires. They often are intelligent and superficially charming, and they are not subject to delusions, hallucinations or neuroses, but they are chronically untruthful, offering rationalizations or blaming others for their behavior. Although a "history of . . . offenses" is not alone indicative, DSM-IV, in one diagnostic criterion, described the antisocial personality in terms of "lack of remorse as indicated by being indifferent to, or rationalizing having hurt, mistreated, or stolen from another." Thus, the psychopathic condition that Durham allegedly exhibited might be called a recognized "mental disease or defect." Should it be the basis of an insanity acquittal?[*]

---

* The American Psychiatric Association released a new and controversial version of the DSM — the DSM-V — in May 2013 — Eds.

(3) *The "Product" Terminology in Durham: What Does It Mean?* Judge Bazelon's *Durham* test acquits if the crime is the "product" of a mental disease or defect. What does the "product" terminology mean? Perhaps it means that mental disease played "some part" in the actions of the accused. Or maybe it means that the actions would not have occurred "but for" the disease. Possibly it means that the actor was "pushed over the edge" by effects of a disease, after unsuccessfully wrestling with them and then deciding to commit the offense. Imagine that an expert testifies, "The accused was suffering from clinical depression and simply did not care about the crime or the harm it caused." Would, or should, this testimony be sufficient to require acquittal on the theory that the accused's conduct was the "product" of depression?

[4] *The Model Penal Code: "Substantial Capacity" to "Appreciate" Wrongfulness or "Conform" Conduct*

Criticisms of all three tests (*M'Naghten*, Irresistible Impulse, and *Durham*) led the American Law Institute to make an extensive study of the insanity defense. The result was Model Penal Code §4.01, which provides, "A person is not responsible for criminal conduct if at the time of such conduct as a result of mental disease or defect he lacks substantial capacity either (1) to appreciate the wrongfulness of his conduct or (2) to conform his conduct to the requirements of the law." This standard is variously referred to as the "MPC test," the "ALI test," or the "substantial capacity" test.

Does the MPC approach provide an acceptable middle course between *M'Naghten* and *Durham*? Consider the following case, which concludes that it does.

United States v. Freeman

357 F.2d 606 (2d Cir. 1966)

KAUFMAN, CIRCUIT JUDGE:

After a trial before Judge Tenney without a jury, Charles Freeman was found guilty [of selling narcotics. His] principal allegation at trial was that, at the time of the alleged sale of narcotics, he did not possess sufficient capacity and will to be held responsible for the criminality of his acts. In rejecting this contention, the District Court understandably relied upon the familiar *M'Naghten* Rules. . . . Since he could not find that Freeman's condition satisfied the rigid requirements of this test, Judge Tenney had no alternative but to hold the defendant guilty as charged. . . .

. . . Freeman's expert witness at trial was Dr. Herman Denber. . . . The Doctor noted that Freeman's body had become accustomed to the consumption of large amounts of heroin over a fourteen-year period, and that the defendant was in the habit of drinking one or two bottles of wine daily to increase the potency of the narcotics. In addition, he observed, Freeman regularly imbibed six to nine "shots" of whiskey each day.

Describing his examination in some detail, Dr. Denber testified that Freeman displayed no depth or variation in his emotional reactions, spoke in a flat monotone and paused for excessively long periods before responding to questions. Dr. Denber also noted that as a result of taking impure narcotics for so long a time, Freeman suffered from frequent episodes of toxic psychosis leading to a clouding of the sensorium (inability to know what one is doing or where one is) as well as delusions, hallucinations, epileptic convulsions and, at times, amnesia. The witness testified, moreover, that Freeman had suffered "knock-outs" on three occasions while engaging in prize fighting, and that these had led to a general vagueness about details. Finally, Dr. Denber observed that Freeman had experienced "innumerable brain traumata" which produced such organic and structural changes as destroyed brain tissue.

Restricted to stating a conclusory opinion within the confines of *M'Naghten*, Dr. Denber initially averred that Freeman was incapable of knowing right from wrong, even under a strict interpretation of that limited test. However, upon amplifying this conclusion, the defense expert acknowledged that Freeman had an awareness of what he was doing on the nights of June 24 and August 1 in the sense that he possessed cognition that he was selling heroin. The Doctor also added . . . . "[I]t is my feeling about him, in particular, that as far as the social implications or the nature or meaning of what this meant to him at that moment, he was not aware of it."

To respond to Dr. Denber's testimony, the government called on psychiatrist Dr. Robert S. Carson, [who] testified that Freeman was able to distinguish between right and wrong within the meaning of the *M'Naghten* test despite his heavy use of narcotics and alcohol. . . . Dr. Carson pointed to the fact that on the evening of August 1, 1963, Freeman had been sufficiently fearful of being apprehended that he had suggested that the transfer of narcotics take place in the privacy of the men's room of Marvin's Bar. . . .

[As had *Durham*, the court critiques *M'Naghten* and finds it deficient for focusing exclusively on cognitive effects. It says that irresistible impulse is "too narrow" on the ground, among others, that psychiatrists question whether any literally "irresistible" impulses actually exist. It then critiques the *Durham* test:]

The advantages of *Durham* were apparent and its arrival was widely hailed. The new test entirely eliminated the "right-wrong" dichotomy, and hence interred the overriding emphasis on the cognitive element of the personality which had for so long plagued *M'Naghten*. . . .

Finally, . . . too often, the unrealistic dogma of *M'Naghten* had compelled expert witnesses to "stretch" its requirements to "hard cases"; sympathetic to the plight of a defendant who was not, in fairness, responsible for his conduct, psychiatrists had found it necessary to testify that the accused did not know his act was "wrong" even when the defendant's words belied this conclusion. . . .

In the aftermath of *Durham*, however, many students of the law recognized that the new rule . . . also possessed serious deficiencies. It has been suggested, for example, that *Durham*'s insistence that an offense be the "product" of a mental disease or defect raised near-impossible problems of causation . . . .

The most significant criticism of *Durham*, however, is that it fails to give the fact-finder any standard by which to measure the competency of the accused. As a result, psychiatrists when testifying that a defendant suffered from a "mental disease or defect" in effect usurped the jury's function. This problem was strikingly illustrated in 1957, when a staff conference at Washington's St. Elizabeth's Hospital reversed its previous determination and reclassified "psychopathic personality" as a "mental disease." Because this single hospital provides most of the psychiatric witnesses in the District of Columbia courts, juries were abruptly informed that certain defendants who had previously been considered responsible were now to be acquitted.

[The D.C. Circuit abandoned the *Durham* test in favor of the MPC, and in this part of the opinion the Second Circuit also adopts the MPC. — Eds.]

[MPC] Section 4.01 provides that "A person is not responsible for criminal conduct if at the time of such conduct as a result of mental disease or defect he lacks substantial capacity either to appreciate the wrongfulness of his conduct to the requirements of law." [We] believe this test to be the soundest yet formulated and we accordingly adopt it as the standard of criminal responsibility in the Courts of this Circuit.

[T]he Model Penal Code formulation views the mind as a unified entity and recognizes that mental disease or defect may impair its functioning in numerous ways. The rule, moreover, reflects awareness that from the perspective of psychiatry absolutes are ephemeral and gradations are inevitable. By employing the telling word "substantial" to modify "incapacity," the rule emphasizes that "any" incapacity is not sufficient to justify avoidance of criminal responsibility but that "total" incapacity is also unnecessary. The choice of the word "appreciate," rather than "know" in the first branch of the test also is significant; mere intellectual awareness that conduct is wrongful, when divorced from appreciation or understanding of the moral or legal import of behavior, can have little significance.

While permitting the utilization of meaningful psychiatric testimony, the American Law Institute formulation, we believe, is free of many of the defects which accompanied *Durham*. Although it eschews rigid classification, the Section is couched in sufficiently precise terms to provide the jury with a workable standard when the judge charges in terms comprehensible to laymen. . . .

We do not delude ourselves in the belief that the American Law Institute test is perfect. Perfection is unattainable when we are dealing with a fluid and evolving science. . . .

And lest our opinion be misunderstood or distorted, some additional discussion is in order. First, we wish to make it absolutely clear that mere recidivism or narcotics addiction will not of themselves justify acquittal under the American Law Institute standards which we adopt today. . . .

Secondly, ... some mention should be made of the treatment to be afforded individuals found to lack criminal responsibility under the test we adopt. There is no question but that the security of the community must be the paramount interest.... It would be obviously intolerable if those suffering from a mental disease or defect of such a nature as to relieve them from criminal responsibility were to be set free to continue to pose a threat to life and property.

... Accordingly, we suggest that those adjudged criminally irresponsible promptly be turned over to state officials for commitment pursuant to state procedures.... [REVERSED.]

STATE v. ANDERSON, 851 N.W.2d 760 (Wis. 2014). Anderson stabbed two people, killing one of them, and walked with a knife toward a police officer, asking to be killed. The officer tased him. At trial, Anderson pleaded insanity, explaining that he had taken prescription medicine for attention deficit disorder, which made him "edgy," and had also drunk alcohol. He presented a mental health expert who testified that Anderson had suffered a temporary mental defect at the time of the homicide that made him unable to control himself or conform his conduct to the requirements of the law. The state presented contrary expert testimony.

Wisconsin followed a definition of insanity similar to that in the MPC. "[T]he defendant may establish an insanity defense by demonstrating that he lacked substantial capacity either to (1) appreciate the wrongfulness of his conduct, or (2) conform his conduct to the requirements of the law." The court of appeals reversed Anderson's conviction on the ground that the trial court's instructions deprived him of this defense. The state supreme court held that Anderson's evidence did not raise any defense:

> We have never held that consumption of prescription medication can give rise to a mental defect that would sustain an insanity defense. We decline to craft a new affirmative defense that would incorporate elements of the involuntary intoxication and insanity defenses simply because Anderson cannot meet the requirements of the involuntary intoxication defense statute.

Is this decision a correct application of the MPC "substantial capacity to appreciate wrongfulness" test? What result under the *Durham* "product" test? Does Anderson seem less likely to meet the *M'Naghten* cognitive test (even if irresistible impulse is added)?

Notes and Questions

(1) *Do Such Terms as "Substantial Capacity" and "Appreciate" Really Make the MPC Approach "Sufficiently Precise"?* The *Freeman* court says that the terminology of the MPC is "sufficiently precise" to provide a workable standard for the jury. Is the MPC test more precise than the *Durham* "product" test? Is it as precise as the

M'Naghten test? As you consider these questions, remember that the MPC retains the term "mental disease or defect" without defining it.

(2) *The Ingredient of Substantial Capacity to Conform.* Aside from the issue of workable precision, what about a defendant who appreciates the criminality of the act, but who commits it anyway because of inner compulsion? Again, consider a person who has committed a crime during major depression and who simply did not care very much whether the act was criminal. Is there ground for arguing that this state of mind should not suffice for insanity-based acquittal, and that exoneration should be reserved for persons who are delusional?

(3) *Exclusion of Psychopathic or Antisocial Personality.* As noted above, there is a mental diagnosis of antisocial or psychopathic personality, characterized by repeated criminal activity and other symptoms. On the theory that persistent crime should not result in an insanity acquittal, the MPC and many other jurisdictions have enacted statutes that exclude conditions such as these from qualifying as "mental diseases." *See* MPC § 4.01(2) (mental disease does "not include an abnormality manifested only by repeated criminal or otherwise antisocial activity").

(4) *The Rise and Fall of the MPC Test.* By 1980, the MPC test was the rule in the majority of states and federal circuits. Then, in 1981, John Hinckley shot President Ronald Reagan. Under D.C. law, the prosecution had the burden of proving Hinckley's sanity under the MPC test, beyond a reasonable doubt. National outrage followed when Hinckley was acquitted on insanity grounds. The tide of broadening insanity rapidly reversed.

Problem 6F (Insanity): "Mom Who Stoned Sons to Death Seeks Insanity Acquittal"

(1) *The Acts Committed by Deanna Laney.* 39-year-old housewife Deanna Laney led her sons to a rock garden and killed two of them by crushing their skulls with heavy stones. According to testimony, Laney believed God had commanded it, and she believed that she and Andrea Yates (another mother who was serving a life sentence for drowning her five children) were chosen by God to witness the imminent end of the world. Her only defense was insanity.

In opposition, District Attorney Matt Bingham pointed to efforts by Laney to keep her husband from finding out about the killings, because she feared he would intervene, as evidence that she knew her actions were wrong. He also pointed to other aspects of her conduct that showed the same thing. He likened Laney to a foreign terrorist who straps a suicide bomb to his body because he believes an attack on an enemy is God's will and can get him into heaven. "Does that exempt him from man's law? Is he [the terrorist] insane?" Bingham asked. He added, "Sanity is not a medical term. It is a legal term and should be decided by a legal body." Laney, like Yates, followed the killing by dialing 911 and announcing that she had just "killed my boys." (Why did she immediately call 911 if all she had done was to carry out a delusionally perceived religious duty?)

Two defense psychiatrists, one prosecution expert, and a court-appointed psychiatrist all testified that Laney suffered from a serious mental defect that prevented her from knowing that her conduct was wrong. Defense counsel reminded the jury that, under state law, it was his burden to prove the insanity defense by the preponderance of the evidence, but he displayed a feather during his final argument and argued that if the evidence favoring the defense of insanity was heavier by just a feather's weight, the jury must acquit. (The jury did acquit Ms. Laney.)

(2) *Analyzing the Insanity Defense under the M'Naghten, Irresistible Impulse, Durham, and Model Penal Code Approaches.* The governing law in Laney's case used the *M'Naghten,* or right-wrong test. Analyze how the elements of this test would apply to the evidence. Also consider the evidence under irresistible impulse, the *Durham* product-of-a-mental-defect, and the Model Penal Code appreciate-the-wrongfulness-or-substantial-capacity-to-conform approaches.

[5] *Modern Approaches That Narrow or Abolish the Insanity Defense*
Notes and Questions

As we noted above, many states and the federal government narrowed and restricted the insanity defense in a variety of ways after the insanity-based acquittal of John Hinckley.

(1) *Abolishing the Insanity Defense: Idaho Code § 18–207.* Idaho's criminal law abolishes insanity as a defense. Section 18–207 flatly provides, "Mental condition shall not be a defense to any charge of criminal conduct." If the defendant requires treatment, the statute directs the court to commit the defendant; but conclusion of the treatment does not affect the sentence, which still must be served. Kansas, Montana, and Nevada passed similar legislation. Utah also abolished the insanity defense but allows the jury to return a verdict of Guilty But Mentally Ill (discussed below).

In *Finger v. State,* 27 P.3d 66 (Nev. 2001), the Supreme Court of Nevada held that state's abolition statute unconstitutional, and the legislature returned to the *M'Naghten* test. The Idaho Supreme Court recently upheld that state's repeal of the insanity defense in *State v. Delling,* 267 P.3d 709 (Idaho 2012). As of this writing, the Supreme Court has before it a case that may require it to decide whether abolishing the insanity defense violates the United States Constitution.

(2) *Restricting the Kind of Mental Difficulties That Qualify for the Insanity Defense.* Recall that MPC § 4.01 and many states provide that a defect defined merely by repeated crimes cannot satisfy the insanity defense as a matter of law. Other mental issues have also been excluded from coverage under the insanity defense. *See, e.g.,* Cal. Penal Code § 29.8 (insanity defense may not rely "solely on personality or adjustment disorder, seizure disorder, or addiction to or abuse of intoxicating substances"); Conn. Gen. Stat. § 53a-13 (insanity defense may not rely on voluntary ingestion of intoxicating substance, antisocial conduct, or compulsive gambling).

(3) *Adding Another Possible Verdict: Guilty but Mentally Ill (GBMI)*. Recall that a jury presented with an insanity defense often will have three verdicts available: (1) Guilty, (2) Not Guilty, or (3) Not Guilty by Reason of Insanity (NGRI)—but that some states have added the fourth option of Guilty But Mentally Ill (GBMI).

GBMI addresses a concern that there were too many insanity acquittals. The belief was that juries, faced with weak evidence that a defendant was mentally ill, would find the defendant not guilty by reason of insanity (rather than guilty) simply to avoid putting the mentally ill defendant in prison where he or she would receive no meaningful mental health treatment and may be exploited by other inmates.

A GBMI verdict is a guilty verdict and subjects the defendant to the same period of liberty deprivation as if the verdict had been simply "guilty." The difference is that a defendant found GBMI is sent first to a mental institution or forensic ward of a prison rather than to the general prison population. Once mental health officials think treatment has adequately succeeded, the defendant is transferred to a jail or prison to serve the remaining part of the sentence. Thus, a defendant found GBMI and given a 15-year sentence, may serve the first five years in a mental hospital and the last ten in a prison.

[6] *Commitment, Release, and Other Dispositions upon Incompetence or Insanity*

Notes on Commitment of Insanity Acquittees

(1) *Commitment upon Insanity Acquittal*. What happens after an insanity acquittal? The general rule is that a person found not guilty by reason of insanity is automatically committed to a mental facility for a limited period of time to undergo a mental evaluation. After the evaluation by mental health professionals, the acquittee may face civil commitment proceedings, which could involve a judicial decision that the person is committed to a mental hospital.

But the defendant acquitted through insanity is *acquitted*. This person is not guilty of any crime and cannot be held under any sentence. The usual assumption after a heinous act is that an insane actor will be committed forever. But that may not be true at all.

If the court finds the person to be dangerous to self or others, the acquittee is committed to a mental institution and held there until the mental health experts deem her no longer a threat to herself or others. Sometimes the commitment decision for an insanity acquittee may be based on a lower standard of proof (such as preponderance of evidence) than required for others facing civil commitment. Although civil commitment laws often do not contain a limit on the duration of the commitment, due process standards, discussed below, require states to release someone detained in this way who is no longer mentally ill, even if the person's criminal record shows a potential danger to the public. This approach may mean that the confinement is shorter or longer than jurors might expect. (But see the note below on "Sexually Violent Predator" statutes.)

(2) *Due Process Limits: Defendant May Be Held Either for a Longer, or Much Shorter, Time Than Might Be Provided upon Conviction: Jones v. United States, below.* Because a person found not guilty by reason of insanity may be civilly committed for a short or a long period of time, the result may be that he or she spends either much less or much more time in a restricted prison-like facility (albeit in a different place with different access to treatment) than if convicted. To prevent excessively lengthy commitments (and to comply with due process, since the person is innocent), statutes or judicial decisions in some jurisdictions limit the maximum amount of time a successful acquittee may spend civilly committed without a new determination of dangerousness. *See, e.g. State v. Hawkins*, 720 N.E.2d 521(Ohio 1999); *In the Matter of D.S.*, 818 A.2d 368 (N.J. Super. Ct. App. Div. 2002).

In the *Jones* case, below, the Supreme Court noted that because insanity acquittees are not guilty of a crime, they cannot be held indefinitely once the reason for their civil commitment has ended. After the defendant "has regained his sanity or is no longer a danger to himself or society," civil commitment must end.

JONES v. UNITED STATES, 463 U.S. 354 (1983). In this case, an insanity acquittee was civilly committed to a mental institution for a longer period than the maximum sentence for his alleged crime of shoplifting. The Supreme Court, through Justice Powell, allowed the commitment, holding that an insanity acquittee may be held for the period necessary to regain sanity or no longer pose a danger to self or society. As noted above, this period could be shorter, or longer, than an appropriate criminal sentence for the underlying conduct.

> In light of the congressional purposes underlying commitment of insanity acquittees, we think petitioner clearly errs in contending that an acquittee's hypothetical maximum sentence [for the crime] provides the constitutional limit for his commitment. . . .

> Different considerations underlie [civil] commitment of an insanity acquittee. As he was not convicted, he may not be punished. His confinement rests on his continuing illness and dangerousness. Thus, under the District of Columbia statute, no matter how serious the act committed by the acquittee, he may be released within 50 days of his acquittal if he has recovered. In contrast, one who committed a less serious act may be confined for a longer period if he remains ill and dangerous. There simply is no necessary correlation between severity of the offense and length of time necessary for recovery. The length of the acquittee's hypothetical criminal sentence therefore is irrelevant to the purposes of his [civil] commitment.

> We hold that when a criminal defendant establishes by a preponderance of the evidence that he is not guilty of a crime by reason of insanity, the Constitution permits the Government, on the basis of the insanity judgment, to confine him to a mental institution until such time as he has regained his sanity or is no longer a danger to himself or society. . . .

Justice Brennan and two other Justices dissented, arguing that an insanity acquittal, by itself, should not provide "a constitutionally adequate basis for involuntary, indefinite commitment to psychiatric hospitalization." Justice Stevens also dissented.

State statutes provide a variety of approached to the commitment process, although, of course, they all must comply with the *Jones* decision. For example, Chapter 46C of the Texas Code of Criminal Procedure provides an extensive array of procedures for dealing with defendants found not guilty by reason of insanity. Consider what the practical effects of an insanity acquittal are under the following provisions (which are only a small part of an extensive statutory scheme).

Texas Code of Criminal Procedure Chapter 46C

Art. 46C.157. Determination Regarding Dangerous Conduct of Acquitted Person

If a defendant is found not guilty by reason of insanity, the court immediately shall determine whether the offense of which the person was acquitted involved conduct that:

(1) caused serious bodily injury to another person;

(2) placed another person in imminent danger of serious bodily injury; or

(3) consisted of a threat of serious bodily injury to another person through the use of a deadly weapon.

Art. 46C.158. Continuing Jurisdiction of Dangerous Acquitted Person

If the court finds that the offense of which the person was acquitted involved conduct that caused serious bodily injury to another person, placed another person in imminent danger of serious bodily injury, or consisted of a threat of serious bodily injury to another person through the use of a deadly weapon, the court retains jurisdiction over the acquitted person until either:

(1) the court discharges the person and terminates its jurisdiction under Article 46C.268; or

(2) the cumulative total period of institutionalization and outpatient or community-based treatment and supervision under the court's jurisdiction equals the maximum term provided by law for the offense of which the person was acquitted by reason of insanity and the court's jurisdiction is automatically terminated under Article 46C.269.

[*Note*: Although the Court's jurisdiction over a potentially dangerous insanity acquittee automatically terminates, Texas Code of Criminal Procedure art. 46C.269(d) provides that "This subchapter does not affect whether a person may be ordered to receive care or treatment under Subtitle C or D, Title 7, Health and Safety Code." The following section, which addresses further proceedings for non-dangerous insanity acquittees, also provides more information about the Health and Safety Code proceedings.]

Art. 46C.201. Disposition: Nondangerous Conduct

(a) If the court determines that the offense of which the person was acquitted did not involve conduct that caused serious bodily injury to another person, placed another person in imminent danger of serious bodily injury, or consisted of a threat of serious bodily injury to another person through the use of a deadly weapon, the court shall determine whether there is evidence to support a finding that the person is a person with a mental illness or with mental retardation.

(b) If the court determines that there is evidence to support a finding of mental illness or mental retardation, the court shall enter an order transferring the person to the appropriate court for civil commitment proceedings to determine whether the person should receive court-ordered mental health services under Subtitle C, Title 7, Health and Safety Code, or be committed to a residential care facility to receive mental retardation services under Subtitle D, Title 7, Health and Safety Code. The court may also order the person:

(1) detained in jail or any other suitable place pending the prompt initiation and prosecution of appropriate civil proceedings by the attorney representing the state or other person designated by the court; or

(2) placed in the care of a responsible person on satisfactory security being given for the acquitted person's proper care and protection.

Notes and Questions

(1) *The Government's Inevitable Reversal upon Insanity Acquittal: A Sudden Acceptance of the Defendant's Insanity, Particularly in Brutal Cases.* Notice the effect of these constitutional and statutory principles in the unusual cases in which insanity acquittal follows a brutal crime. (The more inhumane the crime, ironically, the better the defendant's chance of acquittal may be.) The prosecution, which unsuccessfully fought against the insanity defense during the trial, now must embrace and indeed advocate the defendant's mental illness in order to have the accused civilly committed and prevented from harming the public. This change of position looks unseemly, but it may be necessary to protect the public.

(2) *Will Commitment Really Protect the "Security of the Community" as a "Paramount Concern"?* To put the matter in concrete terms, imagine that the defendant has been accused of a bizarre and brutal murder, has pled insanity and, aided by the incomprehensibility of the act, has been acquitted. Under state law, the defendant is automatically committed to a state mental hospital for evaluation. After being treated with drugs, the committed individual now—only a few weeks after trial—seeks release from the hospital. He has some helpful evidence.

The superintendent of the facility in which he is held reports that the acquittee has been very amenable to drug therapy, "has recovered," and "no longer meets the criteria for involuntary commitment." The superintendent has limited beds, just as any hospital does, and needs the beds for other people. The district attorney who prosecuted the case, however, fears that the acquittee poses a serious public danger, because (among other reasons) he is unlikely to follow a treatment regime outside of the supervised commitment or to take his drugs, which involve unpleasant side effects. What can or should the district attorney do? (The usual answer is, argue that the person's insanity still persists, so as to keep him committed—even though the district attorney may have vigorously argued at the criminal trial that the defendant was not insane.)

(3) *"Temporary" Insanity as a Misnomer: Isn't All Insanity Really "Temporary" (and Is This a Reason Why Some States Have Abolished the Insanity Defense)?* People often ask, "What happens if the defendant is acquitted by reason of 'temporary' insanity?", as if "temporary" insanity were different from "regular" insanity. The *Jones* case (and statutes written to comply with *Jones*, such as the Texas one, above) assume that all insanity may be temporary, and the acquittee may recover sufficiently to be released into the community. And this concern, in turn, has led to skepticism in some states about civil commitment as a remedy, and may also underlie their abolition of the insanity defense. Can you explain?

(4) *The Defense Attorney's Dilemma.* The prosecutor is not the only one who faces a tactical and ethical dilemma. Imagine a defense attorney for an accused who faces a moderately serious assault charge but who shows signs of psychosis, paranoid ideation, and impaired reality testing. Defense counsel knows that defendants convicted of this offense ordinarily receive sentences of probation and fines, or short incarceration. Civil commitment, however, may be indefinite. Does the defender, here, have a duty to seek (or not to seek) insanity acquittal—a duty either to the defendant, or as an officer of the court?

Note on Sexually Violent Predator Laws

(1) *The Rise of Sexual Predator Laws.* Some jurisdictions have decided that people who commit certain violent sex crimes likely suffer from a mental disorder that puts them at high risk of reoffending, with the result that it may be necessary for them to be confined for longer than the period authorized for the crime itself. Normal civil commitment laws will not serve this goal because the accused can be released at any time once the reason for commitment has ended, and in sexual predator cases it may be difficult for the government to prove the necessary mental disease required for continued civil commitment. These jurisdictions have enacted "sexual predator" laws that permit long-term commitment in secure mental health-type facilities. The sexual predator laws permit the court to order the person to be confined upon a finding that it is likely he or she will engage in sexual violence unless incapacitated. The person may be kept in the institution until a finding that he or she no longer poses a threat, and the defendant may have the burden of proof on this amorphous issue.

The underlying theory is that a person with an extensive record of sexual offenses suffers from a mental condition (characterized by such terms as a personality disorder or mental abnormality) that makes reoffending very likely. Whether there is empirical evidence to support this assertion is a matter of some debate. Proponents of these laws assert that the public can only be protected if the "sexual predator" is housed in a secure facility.

(2) *Due Process and Indefinite Commitment.* In *Kansas v. Hendricks*, 521 U.S. 346 (1997), the United States Supreme Court upheld the Kansas Sexually Violent Predator Act, which authorized commitment of sexually violent persons for periods longer than criminal sentences corresponding to their crimes, even in the absence of mental defect. The Court, through Justice Thomas, extended *Jones v. United States*, above, and held that the Kansas Act's definition of "mental abnormality" was a basis for commitment consistent with the Due Process Clause. Furthermore, since the Act did not establish "criminal" proceedings, but only civil commitment for treatment, it did not violate either the Double Jeopardy or Ex Post Facto Clauses.

Later, in *Kansas v. Crane*, 534 U.S. 407 (2002), the Court clarified the Due Process requirements for sexual predator commitments. For example, the Court held that the Constitution required the State to prove some degree of lack of control on the part of the committee over his sexual conduct, but it did not require "total or complete lack of control," because most people, even the most dangerous ones, have *some* ability to guide their conduct. The Court did hold, however, that indicia of criminal stigma or punishment were improper. Are these standards appropriate? *See generally* Eric S. Janus, *Failure to Protect: America's Sexual Predator Laws and the Rise of the Preventive State* (2006).

(3) *The Federal Sexually Violent Predator Statute.* Federal law allows a district judge to prevent the release of a federal prisoner by ordering civil commitment. The Department of Justice must prove by clear and convincing evidence that the prisoner has previously "engaged or attempted to engage in sexually violent conduct or child molestation," currently "suffers from a serious mental illness, abnormality, or disorder," and, finally, "as a result of" that mental illness, abnormality, or disorder is "sexually dangerous to others" because "he would have serious difficulty in refraining from sexually violent conduct or child molestation if released." 18 U.S.C. §§ 4247(a), 4248. The Supreme Court upheld this scheme against a Commerce Clause challenge in *United States v. Comstock*, 560 U.S. 126 (2010), but it has not addressed any potential equal protection or due process challenges to the statute. Should Congress have required the government to prove dangerousness beyond a reasonable doubt instead of by clear and convincing evidence? Does due process require the higher standard?

Note on Incompetence to Stand Trial and Participate in Other Legal Proceedings

(1) *Incompetency Is Different from Insanity.* While insanity refers to the defendant's mental status at the time of the crime, "incompetency" deals with the status at the time of trial or other legal proceeding. In general terms, a defendant who is incompetent may not be tried, sentenced, or executed. The reason is that a fair trial is less likely if the defendant is unable to assist in the defense.

(2) *Test of Incompetency for Most Proceedings.* The general standard is that a person is incompetent if unable to understand the proceedings and assist in the defense. *See, e.g., Dusky v. United States,* 362 U.S. 402 (1960) (defendant must have present ability to consult with defense counsel with a reasonable degree of rational understanding and a rational as well as factual understanding of the proceedings against him).

(3) *Test of Incompetency to Be Executed.* American law also bars execution of a prisoner who is insane. The relevant standard is whether the mental illness prevents the prisoner from comprehending the reasons for the penalty or its implication. *See Panetti v. Quarterman,* 551 U.S. 930 (2007); *Ford v. Wainwright,* 477 U.S. 399 (1986).

(4) *Procedure.* A defendant's incompetency may be raised at any time by any party, or by the judge. The court will often order the defendant to be examined by a mental health professional. Due process allows the defendant to be required to prove lack of competency by the preponderance of evidence (although not to a higher standard).

(5) *Result of a Successful Competency Challenge.* If a defendant or some other party challenges a defendant's competence to stand trial and the court so holds, the trial or other proceeding is suspended or even cancelled. Ordinarily, the defendant will be sent to a mental facility for further evaluation and treatment and will remain there until he or she regains competence.

Because it is possible that the defendant could never regain competence, there is a theoretical possibility the defendant could essentially be given a life sentence in a mental hospital. However, there are constitutional limits on the duration of institutionalization if the defendant cannot be restored to competency: the nature and duration of commitment should bear some reasonable relation to the purpose for commitment. If there is no real probability of restoration of competence, the defendant must be civilly committed under separate standards or released.

(6) *Forcible Medication.* A related issue is the constitutionality of forcible medication in order to make a defendant competent to stand trial. In *Sell v. United States,* 539 U.S. 166 (2003), the Court held that defendants could be forcibly medicated to restore them to competency under proper conditions, but that they could not be medicated indefinitely if there was no hope of their restoration to sanity.

[D] Intoxication and Diminished Capacity

The intoxication and diminished capacity defenses are closely related. Both are "failure of proof" defenses that provide a partial defense to criminal liability in some jurisdictions because the defendant's condition negates or affects an element of a crime. Thus, a defendant may argue that he or she was too drunk to intend to kill or too mentally ill to form the intent to kill. As you can imagine, both defenses are heavily criticized and sometimes severely limited in scope.

Note on the Intoxication Defense

(1) *Two Types of Intoxication: Voluntary and Involuntary.* A person's intoxication from drugs or alcohol may provide a defense to criminal charges. The precise nature of the defense depends on whether the intoxication was voluntary or involuntary.

Voluntary intoxication occurs when the person knowingly ingests a substance with a least a general knowledge that the substance may cause intoxication. Sometimes this is called "self intoxication."

Involuntary intoxication involves ingesting (or voluntarily allowing others to introduce into the person's body) a substance without knowing what the substance is (for example, a sugar cube that the person does not know is laced with a hallucinogenic drug) or what its likely effect will be (for example, if the person has a unique reaction to the substance), or ingesting a substance without free will (such as ingesting the drug because of trickery or force). Some definitions add an objective alternative. *See, e.g.,* Wyo. Stat. Ann. §6–1-202 (voluntary intoxication includes substances which the defendant knows or ought to know has a tendency to cause intoxication).

(2) *Jurisdictions Differ as to Whether Both Types of Intoxication Can Negate the Mental State for the Offense (or Prevent Its Proof).* Consider a defendant charged with attempted murder. The defendant cannot be convicted unless the prosecution proves a specific intent to kill, but imagine that the defendant was so heavily intoxicated at the time of the alleged offense that it is quite doubtful he or she could have such an intent. Should the defendant be acquitted on this ground?

The most common basis for intoxication as a defense is as a failure of proof defense, where it negates the mental element of an offense, such as intent or knowledge, or perhaps premeditation and/or deliberation. In some jurisdictions, both voluntary and involuntary intoxication can support the defense that the defendant was unable to form the necessary mens rea. In the above hypothetical, the defendant whose intoxication made it unlikely that he or she had the intent to kill could be acquitted of intentional homicide because the government might not be able to prove mens rea beyond a reasonable doubt. *See, e.g.,* Minn. Stat. §609.075 (fact of intoxication may be considered in determining the defendant's intent or state of mind).

Some other states, however, hold that voluntary intoxication is not a defense (and cannot reduce the grade of the offense).

(3) *Involuntary Intoxication — an Insanity-like Defense.* In some states, if involuntary intoxication causes a person's mental processes to be impaired to a degree similar to the impairment produced by legal insanity, the defendant may have a viable defense that has the same effect as an insanity defense, although it technically is not an insanity defense. *See, e.g.,* 720 Ill. Comp. Stat. §5/6–3 (person not criminally responsible if involuntary intoxicated or drugged condition deprives the person of substantial capacity to appreciate the criminality of the conduct or to

conform conduct to requirements of the law); Wis. Stat. § 939.42(1) (involuntary intoxication is a defense if it makes actor incapable of distinguishing between right and wrong for the alleged criminal act).

(4) *Laws Providing That Voluntary Intoxication "Is Not a Defense": Do They Mean That Intoxication Cannot Negate a Required Mental State?* Some jurisdictions provide that intoxication "is not a defense." *See* Tex. Penal Code § 8.04 (stating "[v]oluntary intoxication does not constitute a defense to the commission of a crime" but adding, "Evidence of temporary insanity caused by intoxication may be introduced . . . in mitigation" of the sentence"). Such a statute appears to do much more than negate a "defense"; in effect, it seems to mean that intoxication cannot negate intent (or that intoxication supplies or substitutes for the required mens rea). *See Baker v. State*, 625 S.W.2d 840 (Tex. App. 1981) ("evidence of voluntary intoxication does not negate the elements of intent or knowledge"); *Juhasz v. State*, 827 S.W.2d 397, 406 (Tex. App. 1992) ("Voluntary intoxication is not a defense to a crime. . . . [It cannot] negate the element of intent."). What does it mean for a statute to provide that intoxication furnishes no "defense" in such a case? Can someone be convicted of a crime requiring proof of intentional conduct when he or she was simply too drunk to intend anything?

(5) *Constitutionality of Excluding Evidence of Intoxication Offered by the Defendant to Rebut Mens Rea*: *Montana v. Egelhoff*, 518 U.S. 37 (1996). Here, the Supreme Court split three ways on this issue, thus illustrating the difficulties of intoxication issues. Egelhoff killed two people while in a heavy state of intoxication. He was charged with "deliberate homicide," defined as killing purposely or knowingly. He argued that he lacked mens rea. A Montana statute provided that intoxication may not be taken into consideration "in determining the existence of a mental state which is an element of the offense," and the trial court therefore excluded Egelhoff's evidence of intoxication.

Justice Scalia, for the Court, concluded that the Due Process Clause did not bar Montana from excluding evidence of intoxication. Montana had argued that a jury might be excessively influenced toward discounting mens rea by intoxication evidence. Justice Scalia deferred to this argument on the ground that states, not federal courts, are responsible for defining state crimes and defenses. Justice Ginsberg reached the same result by concluding that Montana's statute was equivalent to redefinition of the crime of murder. In other words, according to Justice Ginsberg, the Montana statute meant that an intoxicated killing was murder, because the Montana statute effectively made intoxication a substitute for the required mental state.

The dissenting justices argued that Montana had defined murder by reference to a specified mens rea that could be negated by intoxication. Denial of the opportunity to offer this evidence, which could have demonstrated Egelhoff's innocence of murder, therefore violated the Due Process Clause, in the dissenters' view. Who has the best of this argument?

Note on the Diminished Capacity Defense

(1) *Mental Difficulties Less Than Insanity.* A defendant who is legally sane may still suffer from an impairment that results from mental illness or intoxication and that affects his behavior, but that does not rise to the level of satisfying the applicable test of insanity. Many commentators have concluded that some kind of defense or claim should be available to the defendant in these circumstances. Often it is referred to as diminished capacity or diminished responsibility. But there is considerable disagreement about exactly what diminished capacity is and how to address it. *See State v. Balderama*, 88 P.3d 845 (N.M. 2004) ("the term 'diminished capacity,' although a term of art, is somewhat misleading and has resulted in considerable confusion").

(2) *Definition of "Diminished Capacity"?* Black's Law Dictionary defines diminished capacity as "[a]n impaired mental condition—short of insanity—that is caused by intoxication, trauma, or disease and that prevents a person from having the mental state necessary to be held responsible for a crime." When it applies, diminished capacity is usually a partial defense. For example, a defendant charged with a premeditated killing may argue that his mental condition was such that he was not capable of premeditating and thus could only be guilty of second degree murder, not first degree murder.

(3) *Two Varieties of Diminished Capacity Defense: Incapacity v. Lack of Mens Rea.* A person's impaired mental condition may be a diminished capacity defense in two ways.

(a) *Incapable of Forming Particular Mens Rea Element.* One approach treats diminished capacity as a junior version of insanity that renders the accused incapable of forming a particular mens rea. *See People v. Henderson*, 386 P.2d 677 (Cal. 1963) (holding defendant who was not legally insane could present evidence of mental illness "that prevented his acting with a malice aforethought or with premeditation and deliberation" to avoid first degree murder).

Few jurisdictions adhere to this view today. In California, for example, the legislature rejected the doctrine developed by the courts. *See* Cal. Penal Code § 25(a) ("The defense of diminished capacity is hereby abolished.... [E]vidence concerning an accused person's intoxication, trauma, mental illness, disease, or defect shall not be admissable to show or negate ... [a] mental state required for the commission of the crime charged.").

(b) *Negating or Creating Reasonable Doubt About Mens Rea.* Most jurisdictions that allow evidence of diminished capacity do so only on the question whether the defendant had the required mens rea for the crime. As the Missouri Court of Appeals explained,

> The diminished-capacity doctrine recognizes that [a non-insane defendant's] mental capacity may have been diminished by intoxication, trauma, or mental disease so that he did not possess the specific mental state or

intent essential to the particular offense charged. A defendant claiming diminished capacity concedes his responsibility for the act but claims that, in light of his abnormal mental condition, he is less culpable.

State v. Thompson, 695 S.W.2d 154, 157–58 (Mo. Ct. App. 1985). *See also* Cal. Penal Code § 28 ("Evidence of mental disease, mental defect, or mental disorder is admissible solely on the issue of whether or not the accused actually formed a required specific intent, premeditated, deliberated, or harbored malice aforethought, when a specific intent crime is charged.").

(4) *Rejecting Diminished Capacity.* Some jurisdictions have rejected diminished capacity altogether, so that evidence of a defendant's mental illness is relevant to the insanity defense but not to mens rea. *See Chestnut v. State*, 538 So. 2d 820 (Fla. 1989); *State v. Wilcox*, 436 N.E.2d 523 (Ohio 1982); *State v. Bouwman*, 328 N.W.2d 703 (Minn. 1982).

(5) *Confusion and Arguably Dysfunctional Results.* Is diminished capacity a true defense that must be raised by the defendant? A rebuttal? A failure of proof defense? The authorities are confusing on these questions. Also, diminished capacity may produce results that seem dysfunctional. An intoxicated person may have a way to escape liability through diminished capacity when a sober person would not, a result that many lawmakers would oppose.

UNITED STATES v. ETTINGER, 344 F.3d 1149 (11th Cir. 2003). Ettinger was in pretrial detention on charges that he imported and possessed cocaine with intent to distribute. While being taken to the visiting room in the detention center, he attacked a federal corrections officer. He was then charged with violating 18 U.S.C. § 111, which criminalizes assaults upon federal officials who are engaged in performing their official duties. The district court rejected Ettinger's offer of evidence of mental defect to show diminished capacity. The court of appeals agreed and affirmed, but it also discussed when evidence of diminished capacity would be admissible:

> Ettinger argues that the district court erred in ruling that an offense charged under 18 U.S.C. § 111(a) and (b) is a general intent crime that precluded his claimed defense of diminished capacity. Ettinger contends that § 111 is a "specific intent" statute and that he can raise a "diminished capacity defense."
>
> A defendant can attempt to introduce psychiatric evidence to negate specific intent when such is an element of the offense charged. *See United States v. Cameron*, 907 F.2d 1051, 1063 (11th Cir. 1990). Admitting psychiatric evidence to negate mens rea does not constitute a defense, but only negates an element of the offense....
>
> *Cameron* is a perfect example of a "specific intent" crime and the use of a "diminished capacity defense" to negate the specific intent element of the

crime. Cameron was charged with participating in a conspiracy to distribute "crack" cocaine in violation of 21 U.S.C. § 841(a)(1). Section 841(a)(1) makes it unlawful for a person knowingly and intentionally to possess with intent to distribute a controlled substance. The statute on its face sets forth the specific intent, "with intent to distribute." [Therefore, Cameron could offer evidence of diminished capacity if it could demonstrate his inability to form that intent.] Section 111, under which Ettinger is charged, does not contain specific intent language. . . .

Notes and Questions

(1) *Only for Specific Intent Crimes?* The *Ettinger* decision suggests that evidence of diminished capacity is usually relevant only for crimes that require proof of specific intent. *See People v. Wright*, 111 P.3d 973 (Cal. 2005) (Brown, J., concurring) (observing that abolition of diminished capacity defense does not prevent defendant from claiming lack of the required mens rea due to diminished capacity). Can you explain why courts or legislators might not want to allow diminished capacity evidence to negate general intent?

(2) *Expert Testimony and Pretrial Notice.* The person asserting a diminished capacity defense may want to offer mental health expert testimony on his or her condition. Some states permit this; others do not. Often the defendant must provide the prosecution with advance notice of an intent to use expert testimony on diminished capacity. This is similar to the procedure for insanity.

[E] Mistake and Ignorance as Defenses

[1] The MPC Approach: Mistake Can Negate a Required Element of the Crime (but Is Not a General Defense)

Read MPC § 2.04(1)–(2) [mistake as negating crime element] in the MPC Appendix.

Note in Mistake Negating Mens Rea

(1) *A Defense in Limited Circumstances.* A person accused of a crime may have been mistaken or ignorant about a matter and assert that the lack of accurate knowledge is a defense to the criminal charges. In a few circumstances, this argument will be successful.

(2) *"Mistake of Fact" versus "Mistake of Law."* Some jurisdictions, for some purposes, distinguish mistakes of fact from mistakes of law.

A *mistake of law* occurs when the defendant is mistaken about a legal principle or the legal effect of a situation or status. For example, the accused may believe that it is legal to sell liquor on Sunday though the law is actually to the contrary. Or a driver may erroneously believe the speed limit is 70 m.p.h. when it is really 55 m.p.h. These mistakes usually are not defenses.

Mistake of fact occurs when the error is about some fact in the case. For example, if defendant thinks a person for whom she bought an alcoholic beverage was 21 years old when in fact the person was only 20 years old, the defendant has made a mistake of fact about the person's age.

(3) *General Rule: Mistake or Ignorance is a "Defense" if It Negates Mens Rea.* MPC § 2.04, followed in many jurisdictions, provides that ignorance or mistake can exonerate only if it "negatives [the mental state] required to establish a material element" of the crime or if the "state of mind established by such ignorance or mistake constitutes a defense." *See, e.g.,* Wis. Stat. § 439.43 (honest error of fact or law, other than about the criminal law, is a defense if it negatives the existence of a state of mind essential to the crime). This kind of mistake claim is really a failure of proof theory, not a general "defense."

People v. Russell

144 Cal. App. 4th 1415 (Cal. Ct. App. 2006)

Reaffirmed, People v. Molano

443 P.3d 856 (Cal. 2019)

McADAMS, J.

Defendant Philip Russell was convicted by jury of one count of receiving a stolen motor vehicle, a felony. . . .

Facts

I. Prosecution Case

[On Sunday, March 6, 2005, Doug Foster pushed his 1982 Yamaha motorcycle to a nearby repair shop, but the shop was closed until the following Tuesday.] Foster parked the motorcycle next to a fenced area near the repair shop; trash bins were located inside the fenced area. Foster did not leave the keys with the motorcycle; however he did not lock the forks to the motorcycle. . . .

When Foster called the repair shop the following Tuesday about his motorcycle, the person he spoke to said, "What motorcycle?" Foster reported the motorcycle missing to the police either on Tuesday, March 8, 2005, or the following day. . . .

On March 30, 2005, San Jose police officers Lisa Gannon and Ellen Ciaburro responded to a complaint about a homeless encampment near [the repair shop]. [While there, they saw Foster's motorcycle.] The officers did a license plate check and discovered the motorcycle had been reported stolen. . . .

As Officer Ciaburro exited the fenced area, defendant rode up on a bicycle. . . .

Defendant told Officer Ciaburro he found the motorcycle around 4:00 a.m. on March 7, 2005, in a commercial parking lot near Parkmoor and Meridian. He said he contacted an employee in a nearby shop, who told him a man had left the motorcycle there. Defendant told the officer he did not have the keys to the motorcycle and had walked it back to his camp. He "punched the ignition," which is the same as hot-wiring a car, to get it running. Officer Ciaburro searched defendant and found a traffic citation dated March 14, 2005, for a traffic violation involving the motorcycle. The citation listed Foster as the registered owner of the motorcycle.

II. Defense Case . . .

Defendant testified. In March 2005, he was homeless. He lived in the tent near Parkmoor Avenue and Race Street and operated a mobile bicycle repair business, repairing bicycles at his clients' homes or offices.

Defendant got up early on March 7, 2005, to recycle. At about 4:00 a.m., he saw the motorcycle sitting next to the dumpsters behind [the shop] and thought it was abandoned. The following factors led defendant to conclude the motorcycle was abandoned: (1) the front right turn signal was covered with packing tape; (2) there was rust on the mirror, the post to the mirror, the exhaust pipes, and fenders; (3) there were cobwebs and leaves in the front wheel; (4) the aluminum cast blocks on the motor were severely tarnished; (5) the motorcycle was located next to the trash area; (6) the registration tags had expired 22 months before; and (7) the forks on the motorcycle were not locked. Defendant frequented the area and knew the repair shop's policy was to bring all the motorcycles that were being repaired inside the shop at night. Defendant testified he assumed someone left the motorcycle there for the repair shop to use for parts or that the owner had told the repair shop not to do the work because it was going to cost more than the motorcycle was worth. The motorcycle had been left in neutral, so defendant wheeled it to his camp. . . .

During the week that followed, defendant took the battery out of the motorcycle and had the repair shop recharge it, replaced the spark plugs, changed the oil, drained and flushed the fuel tank, and tuned up the motorcycle.

On March 14, 2005, at about 5:30 a.m., defendant was riding the motorcycle with a friend on the back when he was pulled over by Officer Kate Reyes for a traffic violation. He told the officer he found the motorcycle behind [the repair shop] and had just gotten it running the night before. He told the officer he had "punched the ignition" to start the motorcycle. The officer ran the vehicle identification number (VIN) on the motorcycle and told defendant the motorcycle had not been reported stolen. Defendant told the officer he intended to fix the motorcycle and register it in his own name. The officer wrote up a traffic citation. Defendant asked her to put the name of the registered owner on the ticket. The officer let defendant keep the motorcycle as long as he promised to walk it and not ride it.

At 1:00 p.m. that same day, defendant went to Foster's apartment at the address listed on the citation. He wanted to register the motorcycle in his name and hoped Foster would sign the motorcycle over to him. [The apartment manager] told him Foster had not lived there for 18 months [and that he] did not know Foster's new address. . . .

Defendant told the jury he had prior convictions for grand theft and robbery in 2001.

On cross-examination, defendant admitted that he knew the place where he found the motorcycle was a repair shop and that people take motorcycles there to be fixed. He agreed the motorcycle was intact when he found it. . . . He did not contact the Department of Motor Vehicles (DMV), the phone company, or the police for help in finding Foster. He did not ask anyone in the repair shop about the motorcycle when he got the battery recharged. . . .

Discussion . . .

To sustain a conviction for receiving stolen property, the prosecution must prove: (1) the property was stolen; (2) the defendant knew the property was stolen (hereafter the knowledge element); and, (3) the defendant had possession of the stolen property.

Although receiving stolen property has been characterized as a general intent crime, the second element of the offense is knowledge that the property was stolen, which is a specific mental state. . . . The defendant therefore should have an opportunity to request instructions regarding the lack of requisite knowledge.

At common law, an honest and reasonable belief in the existence of circumstances, which, if true, would make the act with which the person is charged an innocent act, was a good defense. A person who commits an act or makes an omission under a mistake of fact which disproves his or her criminal intent, is excluded from the class of persons who are capable of committing crimes. . . .

[The court discussed an earlier theft case, *People v. Navarro*, 99 Cal. App. 3d Supp. 1 (Cal. App. Dep't Super. Ct. 1979), in which the court had held that, under California law, an unreasonable but good faith mistake of fact is also an excuse. The *Navarro* court explained: "It is true that if the jury thought the defendant's belief to be unreasonable, it might infer that he did not in good faith hold such belief. If, however, it concluded that defendant in good faith believed he had the right to take the [property], even though such belief was unreasonable as measured by the objective standard of a hypothetical reasonable man, defendant was entitled to an acquittal since the specific intent required to be proved as an element of the offense had not been established."]

. . . [D]efendant presented substantial evidence from which the jury could have inferred that he had a good faith belief that the motorcycle was abandoned. First, defendant testified repeatedly that he thought the motorcycle was abandoned.

Second, the condition and location of the motorcycle supported an inference that it had been abandoned. . . .

Third, defendant's conduct could lead the jury to conclude that he had a good faith belief the motorcycle had been abandoned. . . . When he was stopped by Officer Reyes, he told her he had found the motorcycle "abandoned," he had punched the ignition to get it running, and intended to register it in his own name. Officer Reyes told him the motorcycle had *not* been reported stolen. After he learned the identity of the registered owner, he went to Foster's apartment, hoping to persuade Foster to sign the motorcycle over to him. He told the apartment manager he had found the motorcycle "abandoned." He did not sell the motorcycle, remove its license plate, or try to disguise it. Instead, he invested time and money to fix it up. He left the motorcycle parked in an open lot near his tent in broad daylight and told the police officer it belonged to him. He told Officer Ciaburro he thought the motorcycle was "abandoned" and that he had "punched the ignition." After Officer Ciaburro told him the motorcycle had been reported stolen, he did not attempt to flee. He was friendly, cooperative, and eager to talk to the officer about the motorcycle. . . .

For these reasons, we conclude there was substantial evidence that supported instructing the jury on . . . mistake-of-fact . . . and that the trial court erred when it failed to instruct the jury on these defenses.

. . . Since the defenses at issue negate one of the elements of the offense, defendant needed only to raise a reasonable doubt regarding the existence of that element. The jury was not instructed that a good faith belief that the motorcycle had been abandoned or a mistake-of-fact on the question of whether the motorcycle had been abandoned would negate the knowledge element of the offense. These instructions would have clarified the knowledge element by ensuring that the jury understood that a good faith belief, even an unreasonable good faith belief, would negate one of the elements of the offense. . . .

We disagree with the Attorney General's assertion that the evidence supporting a finding that defendant knew the motorcycle was stolen was so overwhelming that a rational jury could not reach a contrary result. The evidence that defendant believed the motorcycle had been abandoned was relatively strong. . . . In addition, defendant's testimony regarding his actions and mental state was corroborated by independent witnesses. . . . [Reversed.]

PEOPLE v. MOLANO, 443 P.3d 856 (Cal. 2019). The defendant committed two strangulation rape-murders, was convicted, and was sentenced to death. He cited *People v. Russell*, above, to support an argument that even if he was unreasonable in forming a mistaken belief that the women had consented, he should be able to use the defense of "*unreasonable* mistake of fact." The court cited *Russell* with approval, but it (understandably!) declined to reverse. The court relied on a harmless error approach and held that it was not reversible error for the trial court to refuse such a defense to Molano, because his acts of strangling required lengthy force and could not reflect a "mistake."

Notice that in *Russell*, the mistake of fact did not have to be reasonable to furnish a defense, because it was directly connected to the mens rea, whether reasonable or not. Intent to deprive the owner of value did not exist in *Russell* if the defendant honestly but unreasonably thought that the property was abandoned. In *Molano*, the relationship between "unreasonable mistake of fact" and mens rea for rape and murder was different. (Or was it? But this metaphysical question may seem beside the point in such a case.)

Notes and Questions

(1) *Who Should Win on Remand?* The court concludes there was substantial evidence to support Russell's claim of mistake and that it is "reasonably probable" that a properly instructed jury would acquit him. Do you agree that he will be acquitted?

(2) *Failure of Proof or True Defense—and What to Tell the Jury?* According to the *Russell* court, mistake of fact is a defense that requires a special jury instruction. Yet the court also recognizes that Russell's mistake claim works by negating mens rea. The notes preceding *Russell* ask whether it is necessary to have special provisions about mistake of fact, precisely because it is essentially a failure of proof claim. Do those arguments mean that a special jury instruction on mistake of fact should, or should not, be given?

(3) *Mistake of Law as Negating Required Mental Elements.* A mistake of law may also negate a required element. For example, imagine a defendant who walks away from a public place with another person's overcoat. She knows that this overcoat is not the one she brought (and therefore has no mistake of fact argument), but she believes (perhaps from her upbringing in another country) that any member of the community can lawfully appropriate any overcoat that fits. This is a serious misunderstanding of American law and perhaps it is an objectively "unreasonable" belief; but it negates intent to deprive the owner of the property, which is a required element of theft. Thus, this mistake of law (if that is what it is) might also exonerate the defendant—not as a "defense," but as a failure of proof.

(4) *Cases in Which Mistake Claims Successfully Negated Mens Rea. See, e.g., State v. Nozie,* 207 P.3d 1119 (N.M. 2009) (defendant was charged with aggravated battery of police officer, which required proof that defendant knew the victim was a police officer; court holds that there should have been a jury charge on mistake since defendant claimed he thought the victim was a private security guard rather than a police officer); *State v. Armstrong,* 122 P.3d 321 (Idaho 2005) (in drug possession case, mistake of fact defense available to counter element that defendant knowingly possessed the drug; the defense covers ignorance of presence of substance and mistake about nature of substance); *People v. Garcia,* 23 P.3d 590 (Cal. 2001) (sex offender required to register must have actual knowledge of duty to register; ignorance of requirement is defense).

(5) *Harmful Effects of Offering Mistake Defense.* While a mistake defense may be appealing, defense counsel must consider the wisdom of tendering it, because it may have a negative impact on other aspects of the defense.

(a) *A Mistake Defense May Be Inconsistent with Other Defenses.* A decision to pursue a mistake defense may render other possible defenses not feasible because it requires the defendant to admit that he or she did the criminal act but maintain that the required mens rea was absent because of a mistake. For example, in *Sheppard v.*

State, 678 S.E.2d 509 (Ga. Ct. App. 2009), the defendant in a kidnapping and assault case foolishly — and unsuccessfully — argued both that (1) he did not commit the act, and (2) that he committed it by mistake.

(b) *A Mistake Defense May Open the Door to Harmful Evidence.* A common evidence rule allows the government to disprove lack of mistake by offering evidence of previous similar events. *See, e.g.*, Fed. R. Evid. 404(b). For example, if a defendant maintains she did not know that a substance purchased on the street was cocaine, the government may be able to prove a previous purchase of cocaine from that same street dealer.

[2] Reasonable Mistake of Fact as a "True" Defense

Notes on Factual Mistakes That Do Not Negate Mens Rea — But That Still May Provide a Defense

(1) *Differentiating Factual Mistakes That Do, or Do Not, Negate Mens Rea.* Many factual mistakes have no effect on mens rea. Imagine defendant kills John Jones in an act of revenge for getting the defendant fired from his job and is charged with intentional murder. But the defendant is mistaken; it was John Smith, not John Jones, who got him fired. This mistake of fact is genuine, but it has nothing to do with the defendant's guilt for killing his intended victim. If, however, the defendant is mistaken in a way that destroys mens rea (he believes that he is safely shooting only at a target, but he hits John Jones, who is carelessly standing behind the target), the mistake may prevent criminal liability for an intentional homicide.

(2) *Reasonable Mistake of Fact That Does Not Negate Any Required Mens Rea.* Sometimes, the law does not require proof of any mens rea with respect to certain acts that the prosecution must prove beyond a reasonable doubt. But a defendant may commit those acts only because of an honest and perhaps even reasonable mistake about them.

An example is the statutory rape defendant who has consensual intercourse with an underage person (a child just under seventeen) but who reasonably believes the child is older. Statutory rape in many jurisdictions does not require proof of any mens rea about the child's age, and ignorance of age thus does not negate the crime since it does not negate a mental element. But if the defendant is mistaken about the child's age and has acted reasonably — perhaps by asking about age and attempting reasonably to verify it — a few jurisdictions hold out the possibility of a mistake defense. In such a case, does the defendant's mistake substantially reduce or even eliminate moral culpability for his actions? Consider the following case.

Perez v. State

803 P.2d 249 (N.M. 1990)

FRANCHINI, JUSTICE.

... Loretta, the child in this case, was out for the weekend with her girlfriend, Missy. The girls went to the home of Billy McGinnis, Missy's boyfriend. Defendant

[Perez] was a friend of Billy and was introduced to Loretta. Defendant had sex with Loretta that evening; there is no question that the sex was consensual. Missy testified that defendant asked Loretta her age and Loretta said she was seventeen. Evidently, defendant also was told by someone else that Loretta was seventeen. In fact, Loretta was fifteen. Defendant was twenty years old.

Defendant was charged with criminal sexual penetration under Section 30–9-11(D), which prohibits sexual penetration of a child thirteen to sixteen years of age if the perpetrator is at least eighteen years of age and at least four years older than the child. The trial court found that the defendant in good faith believed that Loretta was seventeen, but the court nevertheless found defendant guilty. . . .

Defendant argues. . . . that his reasonable mistake of fact about the victim's age is a defense which the court should have considered, and that the court erred in refusing to consider the defense, believing that Section 30–9-11(D) imposes strict liability. . . . The court of appeals affirmed defendant's conviction, holding that knowledge of the victim's age is not an element of the offense. . . .

The fact that knowledge of a child's age is not an essential element of the crime does not dispose of defendant's argument that mistake of fact may be raised as a defense. It simply means that the state does not have to prove defendant knew the victim was under the age of sixteen. Whether or not mistake of fact may be raised as a defense depends on whether the legislature intended the crime to be a strict liability offense [for which mistake of fact is excluded as a defense]. . . .

. . . We have recognized that the legislature may enact a statute which makes illegal certain acts without regard to the defendant's evil intentions, consciousness of wrongdoing, or honest beliefs. The rationale for a strict liability statute is that the public interest in the matter is so compelling, or the potential for harm is so great, the interest of the public must override the interest of the individual.

At one time, mistake of age as a defense was legislatively controlled. One statute specifically stated, "[r]ape of a child is committed when a male has sexual intercourse with a female who is under the age of thirteen [13] years, regardless of the male's knowledge of or mistaken belief about her age." NMSA 1953, § 40A-9–4 (repealed 1975). At the same time, the statutory rape statute provided that "[a] reasonable belief on the part of the male at the time of the alleged crime that the female was sixteen [16] years of age or older is a defense to criminal liability for statutory rape." See NMSA 1953, § 40A-9–3 (repealed, 1975). . . .

Our present statutory scheme, like the former statutes, retains the distinction between cases of criminal sexual penetration involving victims under thirteen and those thirteen to sixteen years. Where the victim is under thirteen years of age, consensual sexual activity is prohibited and is a first degree felony. Where, however, the child is thirteen to sixteen years of age, there must be an additional factor for the act to be a crime. [This statute, for example, specifies not only the age of the child but also requires that] "the perpetrator [be] at least eighteen years of age and . . . at least four years older than the child."

As amended, these statutes clearly reflect the legislature's intention that defendants charged with criminal sexual penetration shall be treated differently depending on the age of the victim. . . . While a child under the age of thirteen requires the protection of strict liability, the same is not true of victims thirteen to sixteen years of age. We recognize the increased maturity and independence of today's teenagers and, while we do not hold that knowledge of the victim's age is an element of the offense, we do hold that under the facts of this case the defendant should have been allowed to present his defense of mistake of fact. [Reversed and Remanded.]

Notes and Questions

(1) *Most Decisions Reject Reasonable Mistake as a Defense to Statutory Rape.* Most cases hold, contrary to the opinion above, that reasonable mistake of fact is not a defense to statutory rape and other sex-related offenses. *See, e.g., Denhart v. State,* 987 So. 2d 1257 (Fla. Dist. Ct. App. 2008) (sexual performance by a child), as well as the materials on statutory rape in Chapter Five. This result has been justified on the ground that the act of fornication is inherently wrong and the defendant should not be acquitted merely because he "thought he was committing a different kind of wrong from that which in fact he was committing." *White v. State,* 185 N.E. 64 (Ohio Ct. App. 1933). Does that explanation still hold true?

In fact, the decision in *Perez* may no longer be the law of New Mexico. The United States Court of Appeals for the Armed Forces recently summarized the state of the law in this area:

> Absent the affirmative creation of either an actual mens rea requirement with respect to the age of the child or a mistake of fact defense even where proof of mens rea is not otherwise required by the appropriate policy-making body, an age-based mistake of fact defense has been found by only four courts. *[People v.] Hernandez,* 393 P.2d [673 (Cal. 1969)]; *Perez v. State,* 803 P.2d 249 (N.M. 1990); *State v. Elton,* 680 P.2d 727 (Utah 1984); *State v. Guest,* 583 P.2d 836 (Alaska 1978). But *Perez, Elton,* and *Guest* have been superseded by statute, leaving California as the only jurisdiction currently operating under a judicially created mistake of fact defense. *See* Alaska Stat. § 11.41.445(b) (2007); N.M. Stat. Ann. § 30–9-11 (West 2007); Utah Code Ann. § 76–2-304.5 (2007).

United States v. Wilson, 66 M.J. 39, 43 (C.A.A.F. 2008).

(2) *Distinguishing This Mistake Defense from a Failure of Proof Defense.* The defense in *Perez* makes the defendant's mistake as to the victim's age a "true defense" because it requires the defendant to offer proof about an issue (reasonable mistaken belief about the victim's age). This is different from a failure-of-proof defense when the defendant's mistake negates a mental element.

(3) *When the Defense of Reasonable Mistake of Fact Is Recognized, the Burden of Raising This Defense Usually Is on the Defendant.* As a "true" defense, reasonable

mistake of fact usually places the burden of production on the defendant. Once the defendant meets this burden, often the burden of persuasion shifts to the prosecution to disprove reasonable mistake of fact. For example, Tex. Penal Code § 8.02 provides that mistake of fact is a "defense," and § 2.03 provides that a defense, such as mistake of fact, "is not submitted to the jury unless evidence is admitted supporting the defense." But once that happens, the burden shifts to the prosecution to disprove it beyond a reasonable doubt. Why do you think this particular combination of burdens applies?

[3] Mistake (or Ignorance) of Law: Sometimes a Defense

Read MPC § 2.04(3)–(4) [mistake of law based on nonpublication or erroneous official statement] in the MPC Appendix.

Notes on the Ignorance of Law Defense

(1) *General Rule: "Ignorance of the Law Is No Excuse."* Most people are familiar with this maxim, which originated in the Latin phrase, "Ignorantia juris neminem excusat." This principle receives support from a number of reasons. For example, allowing an ignorance defense could have the undesirable effect of encouraging people not to examine the law. Such a broad defense would also create anomalous differences in treatment of those who knew of the prohibition and those who suspected that it existed but strategically avoided finding out. It could also burden prosecutions with difficult subjective fact issues. How could a prosecutor disprove a defendant's statement that she did not know that the conduct was illegal? Finally, because most crimes involve conduct that is generally accepted as wrong, it makes sense to exclude lack of knowledge as a defense, at least most of the time.

(2) *Exception: When Knowledge of the Law Is a Required Element of the Crime.* A small number of crimes include an element that requires the accused to have acted with certain knowledge of the law. Ignorance of the law may be a defense to these crimes. *See, e.g., United States v. Whaley*, 577 F.3d 254 (5th Cir. 2009) (sex offender charged with failure to register as required by law; "When a law requires someone to undertake an affirmative act to avoid criminal punishment, some knowledge or notice of the law is required"); *United States v. Awad*, 551 F.3d 930 (9th Cir. 2008) (for Medicare fraud, government must prove defendant acted "willfully" which requires proof that defendant had knowledge that his conduct was unlawful).

A good illustration is the crime of tax evasion, which includes a mens rea of "willfulness," which has been defined as "a voluntary intentional violation of a known duty." In *Cheek v. United States*, 498 U.S. 192 (1991), the defendant was an America Airlines pilot charged with tax evasion, who claimed he did not believe he had to pay income tax. The trial court instructed the jury that "an objectively reasonable good-faith misunderstanding of the law would negate willfulness." The jury convicted Cheek on all counts.

The Supreme Court held it was error for the trial judge to instruct the jury that an "objectively reasonable" belief was required to negate "willfulness." Even an unreasonable ignorance of the law, honestly held, would negate the required mens rea of violating a *known* legal duty. The defendant's ignorance of tax law, if true, meant that he acted on the basis of an "innocent" mistake. The Court noted, "Of course, the more unreasonable the asserted beliefs . . . , the more likely the jury will consider them to be nothing more than" willfulness.

But there was an additional twist. Cheek based his belief on the legal argument that the Internal Revenue Code was unconstitutional. The Supreme Court held that a claim of unconstitutionality was of a different character from a claim of ignorance of a known duty. The tax statute permitted a defense for someone who was not aware of a duty, but not for someone who was aware of the duty but thought it was unconstitutional. Does this distinction make sense? (The case was remanded for retrial, and a jury convicted Cheek on all counts.)

(3) *Reasonableness of Mistaken Impression May or May Not Be Required.* When knowledge is a mens rea element, it ordinarily refers to actual knowledge. If the defendant lacked knowledge because of negligence or even recklessness, he or she still lacked the mens rea for the crime.

A few jurisdictions have added a requirement that the defendant must act "reasonably," with the result that unreasonable ignorance will not support a defendant's argument that he lacked the knowledge that was an element of the crime. The "reasonableness" requirement may be extended to any mistake negating a mens rea element. *See, e.g.*, Tex. Pen. Code § 8.02(a); *State v. Godbolt*, 950 So. 2d 727 (La. Ct. App. 2006) (reasonable mistake or ignorance of fact is a defense that can preclude the presence of a mens rea element). As the *Cheek* tax evasion case indicates, the requirement of reasonableness is ordinarily considered inconsistent with the subjective requirement of the "knowledge" element.

Note on Reliance Defenses

(1) *The General Problem of Reliance.* A different kind of exception arises when the accused committed all elements of the crime (including the mens rea) but did so because the law was unpublished and unknown, or in reasonable reliance on an authoritative interpretation by a government officer whose duty includes clarifying the law. *See* MPC § 2.04(3). Some cases refer to this defense as "entrapment by estoppel" (although strictly speaking it is not entrapment), and some simply (and correctly) perceive it as a kind of due process defense.

(2) *The Reasonableness Requirement.* The various statutes and doctrine in this area ordinarily require that the reliance on a statute or person be *reasonable*. This is an objective standard that looks at all the facts in the situation.

Note on Inadequate Publication of Law

(1) *The Rare Problem of Constitutionally Inadequate Publication.* A person is entitled to rely on statutes and rules, but what if those items are not readily available for the public? Many statutes, reflecting the due process requirement of fair warning, provide a very narrow defense to a criminal charge based on inaccessible laws. For example, MPC § 2.04(3) permits a defense if the defendant believed his or her conduct was legal and the statute or other enactment defining the crime that was not published or otherwise reasonably made available.

(2) *How Accessible Must Laws Be?* Courts do not require much publicity in order to uphold a statute. "Generally a legislature need do nothing more than enact and publish the law, and afford the citizenry a reasonable opportunity to familiarize itself with its terms and to comply." *Texaco v. Short*, 454 U.S. 516, 531–532 (1982).

(3) *Reasonable Diligence.* A defendant who relies on inadequate publication may have to establish that he or she could not have acquired knowledge of the applicable law by the exercise of due diligence. *See* 720 Ill. Comp. Stat. 5/4–8. This puts the onus on the citizen to be aggressive in acquiring knowledge about the law.

Note on the Defense of Reliance on a Statute

(1) *The Best Way to Learn the Law?* In a legal system where so much law is contained in statutes, criminal law has long recognized that a person may be entitled to rely on statutes. A person who does so, even if the statute is deemed to have been erroneously published or improperly passed by the legislature, has a defense to a crime committed while complying with the statute. *See* MPC § 2.04(3) (defense to a criminal charge if actor reasonably relies on official statement of the law, later determined to be invalid or erroneous, contained in a statute or other enactment).

(2) *But What Does It Mean to Comply with a Statute?* The defendant in *People v. Marrero*, 507 N.E.2d 1068 (N.Y. 1987), was a federal corrections officer who carried a handgun into a social club without a license. He claimed to have relied on a New York statute that created an exception from the license for "any penal correctional official." The court ruled that Marrero's interpretation was erroneous — the statute only applied to state officials; he was a federal officer.

When Marrero claimed that the reasonableness of his interpretation should make a difference, the court responded that "the 'official statement' mistake of law defense [is] a statutory protection against prosecution based on reliance on a statute that did in fact authorize certain conduct," regardless of reasonableness. The court explained that "the idea was simultaneously to encourage the public to read and rely on official statements of the law, not to have individuals conveniently and personally question the validity and interpretation of the law and act on that basis." Thus, the court upheld the conviction.

The dissenters objected that the majority's approach "leads to an anomaly: only a defendant who is not mistaken about the law when he acts has a mistake of law defense. In other words, a defendant can assert a defense . . . only when his reading of the statute is correct—not mistaken." The majority insisted that a meaningful, if narrow, defense remained: "mistake of law is a viable exemption in those instances where an individual demonstrates an effort to learn what the law is, relies on the validity of that law and, later, it is determined that there was a mistake in the law itself." Does the majority or dissent get the better of the argument? For discussion of the case, see Dan M. Kahan, *Ignorance of Law is an Excuse—But Only for the Virtuous*, 96 Mich. L. Rev. 127 (1997).

Note on the Defense of Reliance on Official Interpretations of the Law

In recognition of basic fairness, and consistent with the requirements of due process, a limited "reliance" defense exists when people base their actions on misinformation given by public officials. *See United States v. Pennsylvania Industrial Chemical Corp.*, 411 U.S. 655, 674 (1973). But the Supreme Court has never given a clear definition of the due process component of the defense, and other courts as well as legislatures have adopted a variety of approaches. The reliance defense thus combines due process, statutory law, and common law. *See* John T. Parry, *Culpability, Mistake, and Official Interpretations of Law*, 25 Am. J. Crim. L. 1 (1997).

Miller v. Commonwealth

492 S.E.2d 482 (Va. App. 1997)

ANNUNZIATA, JUDGE.

Martin M. Miller was convicted for knowingly and intentionally possessing a firearm after having been previously convicted of a felony, in violation of Code § 18.2–308.2. Raising an issue of first impression in the Commonwealth, Miller argues that his conviction was obtained in violation of his right to due process of law. We agree, reverse his conviction and dismiss the charge against him.

I . . .

Miller, a convicted felon, knew he was prohibited from possessing a firearm. Knowing the prohibition extended to his hunting activities, Miller, a lifetime hunter, sold his hunting guns following his conviction. He continued to hunt with a bow and arrows until his bow was stolen. Wanting to pursue his sport, Miller sought to determine whether he, as a convicted felon, could possess a muzzle-loading rifle. Miller knew that Virginia law distinguished muzzle-loading rifles from other guns. Specifically, he knew that Virginia did not require a criminal background check to be performed on individuals seeking to purchase muzzle-loading rifles. He also knew that Virginia defined different hunting seasons for and issued different licenses to hunters using muzzle-loading rifles.

Miller testified that he "talked to everyone who [he] thought might know the answer." He spoke with his probation officer, who told him he could have a muzzle-loading rifle. He also inquired of the Federal Bureau of Alcohol, Tobacco and Firearms (ATF) and the Virginia Department of Game and Inland Fisheries (VDGIF), and representatives from each, who knew Miller was a convicted felon, told him he could have a muzzle loader.... Relying on the interpretation provided by the government officials contacted, Miller purchased a muzzle loader and obtained a license to hunt with it. In short, Miller, a convicted felon, knowingly and intentionally possessed a muzzle-loading rifle.

Miller argued at trial that his "good faith reliance" on the advice he received regarding the propriety of his possession of the muzzle loader, regardless of the accuracy of that advice, precludes his conviction.... The trial court believed Miller's testimony concerning the content of the information he received but concluded that the sources of Miller's information were not sufficient to preclude his conviction on due process grounds.

II

Reflecting the axiom that everyone is "presumed to know the law," the common law rule that "ignorance of the law is no excuse" admitted of few exceptions. The common law position was based on the fact that most common law crimes were *malum in* se [*i.e.,* "evil in themselves"]. Seen as "inherently and essentially evil ... without any regard to the fact of [their] being noticed or punished by the law of the state," *Black's Law Dictionary* 959 (6th ed.1990), ignorance of the prohibition of such crimes was simply untenable.

The rationale underlying the rule is less compelling for crimes that are *malum prohibitum, viz.,* acts that are "wrong because prohibited," not by virtue of their inherent character. Yet, the proposition that ignorance of the law is no excuse generally maintains with respect to crimes *malum prohibitum,* largely for pragmatic purposes....

Nonetheless, "[w]ith 'the increasing complexity of law, the multiplication of crimes *mala prohibita,* and a more exact definition of fundamental principles of criminal liability,' certain exceptions to the general rule have emerged." ...

The exception at issue addresses the legal consequences of a violation of the criminal law by an individual who takes measures to learn what conduct the government has proscribed, but is misadvised by the government itself. A number of states have adopted statutes bearing on the subject, but Virginia has not. Miller, thus constrained to rely on constitutional principles for his defense, contends that his prosecution and conviction for possessing a firearm violates his right to due process of law.

The defense Miller advances grew from a trilogy of United States Supreme Court cases, *Raley v. Ohio,* 360 U.S. 423 (1959); *Cox v. Louisiana,* 379 U.S. 559 (1965); [and] *United States v. Pennsylvania Chem. Corp.,* 411 U.S. 655 (1973) (*PICCO*)....

The defendant corporation in *PICCO* was convicted for discharging industrial refuse into a river, in violation of § 13 of the Rivers and Harbors Act of 1899. In its regulations promulgated under the Act, the Army Corps of Engineers had consistently construed § 13 as limited to discharges that affected navigation. PIC-CO's discharge was such that it would not affect navigation. Relying on *Raley* and *Cox*, the Court reversed the conviction, finding

> [t]here can be no question that PICCO had a right to look to the Corps of Engineers' regulations for guidance. The Corps is the responsible administrative agency under the 1899 Act, and "the rulings, interpretations and opinions of the [responsible agency] . . . , constitute a body of experience and informed judgment to which . . . litigants may properly resort for guidance." . . .

The Court remanded the case for a determination of whether PICCO's reliance was reasonable. The defense derived from the *Raley, Cox, PICCO* trilogy applies where a defendant has reasonably relied upon affirmative assurances that certain conduct is lawful, when those assurances are given by a public officer or body charged by law with responsibility for defining permissible conduct with respect to the offense at issue. The defense is a due process defense, grounded in "traditional notions of fairness inherent in our system of criminal justice." . . .

The due process argument is, in essence, "that the criminal statute under which the defendant is being prosecuted cannot constitutionally be applied to the defendant without violating due process of law, where government officials have misled the defendant into believing that his conduct was not prohibited."

The ultimate due process inquiry is whether a defendant's conviction, for reasonably and in good faith doing that which he was told he could do, is fundamentally unfair in light of the content of the information he received and its source. The cases addressing the defense demonstrate that the defendant must establish, as a threshold matter, the legal sufficiency of the content and source of the information received. The application of the defense then requires a factual determination whether the defendant's reliance upon the information received was reasonable and in good faith. The defendant bears the burden of establishing the affirmative defense.

With respect to content, the defense is available only where the information upon which the defendant has relied is an affirmative assurance that the conduct giving rise to the conviction is lawful. . . .

As to the source of the information, it must be established that the information was received from a "government official." *See . . . United States v. Indelicato,* 887 F.Supp. 23, 25 (D.Mass.1995), *modified in part on other grounds,* 97 F.3d 627 (1st Cir.1996) (private attorney not government official). . . .

However, a government official's status as "state actor" has not alone been sufficient to invoke the defense in cases recognizing its availability. . . . [The defense is] implicated only when the source of the information is a public officer or body charged by law with responsibility for defining permissible conduct with respect to the offense at issue. . . .

III

In the present case, the trial court found that Miller's probation officer and representatives from ATF and VDGIF told Miller that he could possess a muzzle-loading rifle. . . .

We hold that Miller's case fails as a matter of law with respect to the ATF agent and the VDGIF agent. Neither of those agents was charged by law with responsibility for defining permissible conduct under Code § 18.2–308.2. The ATF agent, although arguably charged with such responsibility under federal firearms laws, has no such duty with respect to Virginia law. . . . Likewise, the Commonwealth of Virginia has not charged the VDGIF with the duty of defining permissible conduct under Code § 18.2–308.2. The VDGIF exists to provide public, informational and educational services related to Title 29.1, which concerns Game, Inland Fisheries and Boating. . . .

By contrast, however, Miller's probation officer was charged by the Commonwealth with responsibility for defining Miller's permissible conduct with respect to Code § 18.2–308.2. The legislature granted the probation officer supervisory responsibility for Miller's conduct and treatment during the course of his probation, *see* Code § 53.1–145, including the responsibility for arresting him for a violation of his probation. . . . It follows that a probation officer . . . is, *a fortiori*, charged by law with defining a probationer's permissible or impermissible conduct. . . . For these reasons, we hold that the trial court erroneously concluded that Miller's probation officer was not a source legally sufficient to invoke the Due Process Clause as a bar to his prosecution and conviction.

It remains only to be determined whether, based on the totality of the circumstances, Miller's reliance on the advice of his probation officer was reasonable and in good faith. Upon review of the uncontradicted evidence in this case, we find, as a matter of law, that it was. [Reversed and prosecution ordered dismissed.]

Notes and Questions

(1) *Reliance on Negligent Officials?* Does *Miller* permit a poorly informed state official to dictate what is and is not a crime? Even if that is true, does the *Miller* outcome correctly assess moral responsibility?

(2) *Human Sources of Information Covered by Reliance Defense.* The reliance defense permits a person to rely on bad information in certain, limited contexts.

(a) *Judicial Opinions.* People may rely on judicial opinions for authoritative statements of the law. But what about opinions that are overruled by a higher court after the defendant has relied on the lower court ruling? And can a defendant legitimately rely on a lower court opinion that conflicts with other lower court opinions?

United States v. Albertini, 830 F.2d 985 (9th Cir. 1987), involved a nuclear arms protester who was convicted of activities on a military base, but who successfully appealed on the ground that his conduct was protected by the First Amendment. He then resumed his activities, relying on that appellate opinion which led him to believe that his protests were legal — and he was prosecuted again for the same activities. The United States Supreme Court then reversed the original Court of Appeals decision and held his original conduct was *not* protected by the First Amendment.

Reviewing the second conviction, the Ninth Circuit held that the Due Process Clause allowed the defendant to rely on its original Court of Appeals opinion permitting his political activities. The court reasoned that the reliance-on-official-interpretations defense encompasses reliance on a judicial opinion that is later overruled: "It would be an act of 'intolerable injustice' to hold criminally liable a person who had engaged in certain conduct in reasonable reliance upon a judicial opinion instructing that such conduct is legal." The court also made clear that the period of reasonable reliance ended when the Supreme Court overturned the Ninth Circuit.

But the Ninth Circuit later ruled in *United States v. Qualls*, 172 F.3d 1136 (9th Cir. 1999) (en banc), that reliance is no defense if the later decision was "foreseeable," and foreseeability always exists if there are conflicting decisions among the Courts of Appeals. Is it sensible to require a person to scan appellate decisions, possibly from across the country, before being able to rely on the one directly applicable to his or her conduct?

(b) *Official Statement of Law by Person with Actual Authority to Make Such Statement.* The most obvious source of misinformation, represented by the *Miller*, is a statement about the law from a public official entrusted with providing such information. Consistent with the constitutional requirement of due process of law, MPC § 2.04(3) and many similar state provisions authorize a "reliance" defense when a person, believing conduct is not criminal, acts "in reasonable reliance upon an official statement of the law," later determined to be erroneous, "contained in an official interpretation of the public officer or body charged by law with responsibility" for interpreting, administering, or enforcing the law defined in the offense.

Courts often have to decide whether the person who gave the mistaken legal information actually had the authority to provide that information. *Compare State v. Cote*, 945 A.2d 412 (Conn. 2008) (building inspector, who mistakenly told defendant a particular hazardous waste disposal method was permissible, was not authorized to interpret environmental laws), *with State v. Minor*, 174 P.3d 1162 (Wash. 2008) (en banc) (judge failed to provide defendant with required information about nonaccess to firearms). In *United States v. Tallmadge*, 829 F.2d 767, 773–75 (9th Cir. 1987), the court held that a federally-licensed firearms dealer was a federal agent for purpose of gathering and dispensing information about the purchase of firearms and that the defendant was entitled to rely on the dealer's interpretation of the law. How would this case be decided under *Miller*? If the result would be different, which result is more appropriate?

(c) *Statement by Public Official with Apparent Authority.* Some courts allow the reliance defense when a person relies on the advice of an official who has "apparent authority" to interpret the law, as opposed to only actual authority. Which is the better rule, particularly in light of "traditional notions of fairness"?

(d) *Private Legal Counsel.* It is widely accepted that the reliance defense does not extend to reliance on the advice of a private lawyer. But should this be so? Note that advice of counsel may be relevant in cases like *Cheek*, above, in which the crime requires proof that the defendant knew he or she was violating the law. In such a case, a defendant may testify that advice of counsel helped form the good faith but erroneous belief that he or she was not violating the law.

(e) *Private Citizens.* The general rule, endorsed in *Miller*, is that a defendant may not rely on the legal judgments of private citizens to support a mistake-of-law reliance defense. The reason is that the public is held to a higher standard than reliance on the statements of people who have no authority to provide a defense to criminal activity. In addition, the due process aspect of the defense applies only to state actors, not to private citizens.

(3) *Oral Interpretations?* Some "reliance" statutes also require that the interpretation be in writing. Thus, Miller would have complied with most of the elements of the defense under that statute as well—but not if the advice given him by his probation officer had been oral. Why do you think a state might decide to limit the defense to "written" interpretations? Does this requirement go too far, particularly in light of the due process aspects of the defense?

[4] Ignorance of the Law and the Due Process (Fair Warning) Defense

A constitutional mistake-of-law defense falls outside the "failure of proof" category. It is based on the fair warning facet of due process. This defense is very rare, but it can apply to certain kinds of crimes in which the defendant naturally is unaware even that the law might exist because "circumstances which might move one to inquire [about the law] are completely lacking." We also address this issue in Chapter 13.

(1) *Lambert v. California*, 355 U.S. 225 (1957). This case involved a prosecution for failure to register as a convicted felon in accordance with a Los Angeles ordinance requiring registration for felons in the city for more than five days. The defendant, who had lived in Los Angeles for seven years, claimed that she did not know of her obligation under this law. The United States Supreme Court held that under the circumstances, due process was violated by the criminal prosecution. The Court reasoned that for passive conduct (such as presence in a city without registering) when there are no "circumstances which might move one to inquire as to the necessity of registration," due process bars a criminal conviction because of a lack of "notice" that is engrained "in our concept of due process."

(2) *Lambert Has Been Narrowly Applied. Lambert* has been construed narrowly by courts hesitant to expand a constitutional defense based on ignorance of the law. Accordingly, later decisions generally apply it only to passive conduct (*i.e.* failure to take do something required by statute) when the accused had no reason to inquire about the duty established by statute. *See, e.g., United States v. Gould, 568* F.3d 459 (4th Cir. 2009) (disallowing *Lambert* defense for failure to register as a sex offender

under federal law; defendant had received notice of duty to register under state law which was sufficient notice of a duty to register under federal law); *People v. Garcia*, 23 P.3d 590 (Cal. 2001) (*Lambert* does not bar conviction for failure to register as sex offender because defendant had knowledge of the requirement).

[F] Age Affecting Criminal Responsibility: Juvenile Law
Note on the Infancy Defense

(1) *Policy Basis.* The justice system both historically and currently recognizes that children have mental capacities that differ markedly from adults. Accordingly, in many areas of criminal law there are different rules for juveniles. Part of the rationale is that some aspects of a child's mind and ethical system are not fully developed until the child approaches adulthood. Moreover, the child, particularly when young, is immature and may be a very different person than he or she will be later in life.

(2) *Capacity to Commit a Crime: The Common Law Rule of Sevens.* The common law long put juveniles in a special category, assuming that early in life the child simply did not have the mental capacity to commit a crime. The rule that evolved classified children in three groups. Children under the age of seven were conclusively presumed incapable of committing a crime. Children from seven to thirteen were presumed capable of committing a crime, but the presumption was rebuttable and was stronger as the child approached age thirteen. It could be rebutted by government proof that the child could distinguish between good and evil or could tell that the criminal activity was wrong in a moral sense. Children fourteen to twenty-one (the age of adulthood) were presumed to be the same as adults, capable of criminal responsibility.

(3) *The Rise of Juvenile Courts.* Since 1899, American jurisdictions have created juvenile courts charged with the responsibility of dealing with criminal behavior by juveniles (as well as other issues, such as dependency and neglect of minors). The underlying theory, expressed in *Winship* below, is that juvenile courts are designed to rehabilitate rather than punish children who do acts that would be considered criminal if committed by adults. Accordingly, for most criminal activity by children (sometimes called acts of "delinquency" rather than crimes), juvenile courts have jurisdiction and deal with the child and often the child's family and school.

State law provides age limits for juvenile jurisdiction. Often the juvenile court has jurisdiction for most criminal-type activities of children under age eighteen, though for more serious crimes sometimes that age is lower, such as fifteen. Children older than the cut-off age are processed as adults in the ordinary criminal courts rather than in juvenile court.

In addition, it is common for a jurisdiction to have a procedure to *transfer* children from juvenile to adult court. Ordinarily this procedure is for older children alleged to have committed serious crimes. *See, e.g.*, N.H. Rev. Stat. Ann. §628.1

(authorizing transfer to adult court of case involving child 13 or older alleged to have committed one of a long list of serious crimes such as homicide, some assaults, kidnapping, and sexual assault).

(4) *The Modern Infancy Defense.* Today statutes deal with the criminal responsibility of juveniles. Some still provide an age below which a child is not criminally responsible and often use categories that show vestiges of the common law approach. *See, e.g.,* Cal. Penal Code § 26 (all persons presumed capable of committing crimes except for children under age 14 in the absence of clear proof that at the time of the crime they knew its wrongfulness); 720 Ill. Comp. Stat. § 5/6–1 (no conviction for crime unless at least 13 years old at time of time); Nev. Rev. Stat. § 194.010 (persons not liable for punishment include children under age 8; children 8–14 years old in absence of proof that at time of crime they knew its wrongfulness).

In re Winship
(in Chapter 4, Section 4.01[A], on Burden of Proof)

This case appears in Chapter 4, on Burden of Proof. The Court's opinion illustrates both the similarities and the differences between adult and juvenile proceedings. In the juvenile courts, age is a defense to criminal responsibility, proceedings are more informal, and dispositions are more focused upon rehabilitation. But involuntary restraint also is a possibility, and the Supreme Court therefore has required certain procedures that are characteristic of adult trials as a condition of due process.

§ 6.05 Review Problems Based on Newspaper Reports

Note on These "Newspaper" Cases

The following cases all were covered in newspapers in a recent year. The reports have been rewritten to emphasize the legal issues, although a newspaper style has been retained, as have the case facts. The reports will supply you with review material concerning the more common defenses contained in this chapter, such as self-defense, defense of property, law enforcement, and insanity.

[A] Headline: "Citizen Shoots and Kills Alleged Thief"

DALLAS — Steve Ford went outside with a semiautomatic rifle at 6 a.m., after his mother heard noise and awakened him. He noticed that his driveway gate had been opened, and he saw his flatbed truck moving toward him.

"He said he fired three or four shots at the ground as warning shots," said Sgt. Ross Salverino of the Police Department's homicide division. "The truck [had] to stop because the wind blew the gate shut, but it [started] to back up, and . . . he said he feared the driver was going to run him over."

Neighbors reported that Ford had experienced two other attempted thefts of the same vehicle by individuals who had attempted to take it from his driveway. After firing warning shots at the ground, he then fired "one or two more" shots at the truck while it still was on his property, said police. One shot struck the driver, who is as yet unidentified. Though wounded, he continued backing the vehicle and drove through the area until he veered into a field filled with rainwater. He died at the scene.

The state criminal law at issue provides that a person is justified in using deadly force in defense of property "to prevent the other who is fleeing immediately after committing burglary, robbery, aggravated robbery, or theft during the nighttime from escaping with the property," provided other conditions for the use of force in defense of property are met. Also, state law recognizes the defenses of self-defense and law enforcement.

Mr. Ford was arrested but promptly released. He was not charged with any offense.

(1) *Self-Defense.* Is it likely that, under these conditions, that Mr. Ford could succeed with a defense of self-defense if he had used non-deadly force? Or, with the deadly force that he actually used? Remember that most jurisdictions (including this one) require the jury to consider reasonableness objectively, but from the point of view of the accused in the circumstances.

(2) *Defense of Property; Law Enforcement (Arrest).* Is it likely under the applicable law that Mr. Ford could raise (or succeed with) the justification of defense of property? What about a law enforcement defense?

[B] "Psychiatrist Testifies That Mother Who Drowned Her Children Did Not Know Right from Wrong"

HOUSTON—Testifying for the defense, a psychiatrist yesterday told the jury that Andrea Pia Yates, who drowned all of her five children in a bathtub, was so seriously mentally ill that she did not know that her actions were wrong.

Dr. George Ringholz is a physician who also has a doctorate in psychology and heads the neuropsychology service at Baylor College of Medicine. "The type and severity of the psychosis [were such that] she did not know that her actions were wrong," he explained.

Prosecutor Joe Owmby challenged this conclusion by inviting Ringholz to examine more than ten different factors, each of which, he implied, showed instead that Yates did fully understand the wrongfulness of her actions. For example, he asked Ringholz to consider Yates's decision to wait until no other adult was at home so that the killings could not be prevented. He asked about Yates's admitted belief that killing would be sinful and the worst of the Seven Deadly Sins. Then, he proceeded sequentially to note that Yates promptly called 911 after the killings and asked for the police to come, that she admittedly knew that she would be arrested and put in jail, her question to a detective after her arrest in which she inquired when her trial would be held, and other conduct by the defendant surrounding the crime and indicating an awareness of wrongfulness. In every instance, Dr. Ringholz replied, "That's not a factor."

Yates has given notice of intent to present a defense of insanity. State law provides that this defense exists only if the actor, "as a result of severe mental disease or defect, did not know that his conduct was wrong." Insanity is an "affirmative defense," meaning that the burden is not on the prosecution, but on the defendant, to establish the elements of the defense by a preponderance of the evidence.

Earlier, Dr. Melissa Ferguson told the jury that Yates suffered from "major depressive disorder with psychotic features" and should be tested for schizophrenia. Dr. Ringholz diagnosed schizophrenia in Yates and, on the basis of a set of tests, testified that depression alone could not account for her symptoms. Another defense witness, Dr. Eileen Starbranch, said that when she had treated Yates three years earlier, she also had diagnosed depression with psychotic features as well as possible long-term schizophrenia. According to Starbranch, who has practiced more than 25 years, Yates "would probably rank among the five sickest people" she has ever examined.

Prosecutors concede that Yates is mentally ill. They contend, however, that she understood that her conduct was wrong. In addition to their arguments founded on the conduct and statements of the defendant, which they maintain are evidence of sanity, the prosecutors will present expert witnesses who will testify, contrary to the defense witnesses, that Yates knew and fully understood the wrongfulness of drowning her children. The children ranged from seven-year-old Noah, who put up a fight for his life, to six-month-old Mary.

(1) *Analyzing the Yates Case under a Statute Based on the M'Naghten Test; The Jury's Verdict of Guilty.* The statute applicable to Yates was based on the M'Naghten test. In addition, state law required Yates to prove the insanity defense by a preponderance of the evidence; the prosecution carried its burden by proving the killings and showing that they were intentionally or knowingly done. The jury convicted Yates of capital murder, but it rejected the death penalty, meaning that Yates received a sentence of life in prison. Can you explain how the applicable law operated on the evidence to cause the jury to return its verdict of guilty and to reject the defense of insanity? Yates subsequently successfully appealed her conviction on evidentiary grounds.

(2) *Reconsidering the Yates Evidence against the Irresistible Impulse Approach, the Durham Product-of-a-Mental-Disease-or-Defect Rule, and the MPC Lacks-Substantial-Capacity-to-Appreciate-or-Conform Standard.* Each of the other approaches to insanity that we have considered in this chapter provides a broader defense than the M'Naghten test. How would each of the other approaches affect the jury's verdict in Ms. Yates's case? In addition, some jurisdictions require the prosecution to negate insanity by proof beyond a reasonable doubt, instead of requiring the defendant to prove it by the preponderance. What sort of difference might this principle make?

(3) *Disposition upon a Finding of Insanity, the Limited Sphere of Commitment as a Remedy, and the Approach of Some States in Abolishing the Insanity Defense.* Many people who supported Yates in her efforts to establish an insanity defense probably justified their position by the belief that any person who had engaged in her actions would be certain to undergo long-term involuntary confinement by way of commitment for insanity. This assumption is inaccurate, at least insofar as it predicts this outcome as a matter of certainty (although Yates remained confined despite her successful appeal). Can you explain why, and describe the conditions under which it might be conceivable for a person acquitted by reason of insanity to be released within a relatively short time? Some states have acted to abolish the defense of insanity, as we have seen in this chapter, and dissatisfaction with commitment as a remedy might be one consideration that those jurisdictions would consider as part of their policy. Can you explain why?

(4) *Andrea Yates's Retrial: Acquittal by Reason of Insanity.* Yates was retried in 2006. This time, the jury acquitted her on evidence very similar to that in her first trial and with jury instructions that were virtually identical. What kind of factors do you think could have led to such a difference in result?

§ 6.06 Simulation Exercises: Preparing a Court's Charge on Defenses in a Homicide Case, Trial, and Post-Trial

Simulation Exercise No. 7 (Document Preparation): State v. Howard

Drafting the Court's Charge: Defenses. Reconsider the case of *State v. Howard* (in the Chapter 3 Simulation Exercises), as well as the online materials about the case. Please go online to https://caplaw.com/sites/cl4/, then click on "Case File No. 2." Your assignment: prepare the parts of the court's charge that deal with self-defense, to be inserted in the charge on murder elements previously drafted (assigned earlier, in the homicide chapter).

For the substantive law, use the New York statutes contained in the section on self-defense in this chapter, above. (Or, use the law of the state where you are located, if your professor directs.) Use the robbery charge contained in the *Howard* Appendix as a model of the format. Prepare only the self-defense instructions. Note: Most of your language should come directly from the New York statutes, unchanged.

Simulation Exercise No. 8 (Trial Advocacy): State v. Howard

A Mock Trial. Using the relevant online materials (including Rules and Advice), conduct a mock trial of the same case (*Howard*). Please go online to https://caplaw. com/sites/cl4/, then click on "Case File No. 2." Students will perform voir dire, opening statement, evidence presentation, trial motions, charge objections, and jury arguments as assigned. Other students will serve as witnesses and jurors. Be sure to read the online instructions for methodology (all students).

Simulation Exercise No. 9 (Document Preparation): State v. Howard

Preparing Post-Trial Motions. Prepare a post-trial motion for judgment of acquittal in the same case (*Howard*), and for a new trial, as assigned. Again, please go online to https://caplaw.com/sites/cl4/, then click on "Case File No. 2."

Chapter 7

Theft and Related Property Crimes

"[S]ince by the verdict the jury determined that [the defendant] did fraudu-lently appropriate the property, it is immaterial whether or not they agreed as to the technical pigeonhole into which the theft fell."—People v. Woods, 233 P.2d 897 (Cal. 1951)

"The life of the [common] law has not been logic: it has been experience."— Justice Oliver W. Holmes, *The Common Law*

§ 7.01 The Historical Treatment of Theft: Formalism Over Policy

Notes on Four Offenses: Larceny, Larceny by Trick, Theft by False Pretenses, and Embezzlement

(1) *The Influence of History.* The law of theft has traveled far since its common law beginnings. The modern trend is away from technical, complex crimes to gen-eral, simplified offenses. But modern provisions make sense only if one understands their history. Moreover, many theft laws maintain some or all of the traditional distinctions.

(2) *Property Law as the Source of Rules That Fit Uncomfortably in the Law of Crimes.* The traditional law of theft relied heavily on definitions from property law. *Larceny*, the "original" theft offense, reached thefts that occurred when the thief wrongfully carried away or *"asported"* property from the possession of the victim. The thief did not commit larceny if he or she legitimately borrowed or held prop-erty, so that the initial possession was *rightful*, but then decided to keep it.

(3) *Dysfunctional Formalism?* The common law, above all, was a set of formal rules. The law of larceny is the core of what we think of today as theft. But the influence of property law meant that larceny was defined by artificial elements. The quotation from Justice Holmes, above, is especially applicable to the common law of larceny. Its shape was the product of history and experience, not logic.

Still, the genius of the common law was its adaptability. What it did, specifically, in theft law was to (1) enlarge the defined offenses to fit some additional criminal situations and (2) prompt legislatures to create distinct new crimes to cover differ-ent types of harm not covered well or at all in existing theft law.

(4) *Four Kinds of Offenses: Larceny, Larceny by Trick, False Pretenses, and Embezzlement.* An example of this adaptability is the extension of (a) "straight" larceny (the taking and carrying away of property) to cover a different situation called (b) "larceny by trick." There also was another crime called (c) "theft by false pretenses" that differed from larceny by trick. Then, too, there was (d) "embezzlement." Actually, false pretenses and embezzlement were created by statute, and so they are not common law offenses; and yet they were influenced by the common law, because they filled gaps left by the limits of larceny. There were other theft-related crimes, too. Each had formal elements, and the prosecution was required to charge the right one (which sometimes called for guesswork).

[A] Larceny: Property of Another, Caption, Asportation from Possession, Intent to Deprive, Permanence, Etc.

[1] *"Straight" Larceny: A Trespassory Taking*

Notes on the Formal Requirements for Larceny

(1) *The Formal Elements of (Straight) Larceny: A Trespassory Taking.* Larceny had a disconcertingly large number of highly formal elements. First, there had to be a taking, or "caption." The defendant had to seize and possess the item. Second, "asportation" was required. Asportation means carrying away; the defendant had to remove the item. It was impossible, for example, to commit larceny of real estate. Caption and asportation were related to a third requirement: a "trespassory" taking, usually by force or stealth; if the owner consented to the other's possession, there was no larceny, even if induced by fraud. Fourth, the item had to be "property," and fifth, it had to be "of another." Services were not covered, and so if the "thief" had someone repair a vehicle with no intention to pay for the service, larceny was not available.

Common law larceny also had a complex mens rea requirement. It had to include both the element of (sixth) intentional "deprivation" from the possessor, and (seventh) the intent to deprive had to be "permanent." Unauthorized borrowing, for example, was not larceny.

(2) *The Trouble with Common Law Theft: Formalism Separated from Policy.* These distinctions provided notice to defendants, protected innocent conduct, and often coincided with policy. Also, at one time larceny was a capital offense, and the courts sometimes created formal distinctions to avoid the death penalty. But sometimes, the technical distinctions produced results divorced from any reasonable objective. The effort to categorize real world situations so as to charge the right crime sometimes resembled a shell game, in which the state had to guess which offense to charge. The facts often remained ambiguous, so that charging the right crime could become a guessing game — even when it was clear that *some* crime must have been committed.

(3) *Contrasting the Modern Approach: The Model Penal Code's Consolidation and Redefinition.* As we shall see later, the Model Penal Code consolidates these various offenses into one. The quotation, above, from the California Supreme Court shows

the result: a single crime of theft, instead of the patchwork crimes of history. But the traditional law of theft is influential, and we shall consider its "pigeonholes" next.

(4) The technical distinctions among the theft crimes were taken seriously. If the proof at trial showed that the defendant actually had committed embezzlement or false pretenses, the defendant could not be convicted of larceny even if larceny was the only crime with which the defendant was charged. Sometimes this dysfunction appears in modern cases. *See, e.g., Bruhn v. Commonwealth*, 559 S.E.2d 880 (Va. Ct. App. 2002) (defendant indicted for larceny could not be convicted if the proof showed he was instead guilty of embezzlement).

(5) *An Example of High Formalism in Larceny: The Requirement of Carrying Away or "Asportation."* Here is one example (among many) that shows how technical the common law of theft could be. Larceny requires that the stolen property be *carried away*. *"Asportation,"* as the carrying-away element is called, is satisfied by even a slight movement, but there has to be some movement, even if the distance is short.

The classic—though frequently debated—case of insufficient asportation involves the theft of a wheelbarrow lying upside down on the ground. If the thief picks up the barrow and puts it back on the ground in an upright position, ready to be wheeled away, there is authority for the proposition that the wheelbarrow has not been carried away (and there is no larceny). For a contemporary variation, see *State v. Johnson*, 558 N.W.2d 375 (Wis. 1997), in which the defendant brandished a gun, ordered the occupant of a car to get out, then got in the car himself and unsuccessfully tried to start it. He was arrested later. Held, no asportation—and therefore no larceny—because the car never moved. And consider the following case.

People v. Meyer
17 P. 431 (Cal. 1888)

SHARPSTEIN, J.

The defendant was [convicted of larceny on an allegation that he feloniously] carried away one overcoat, of the value of twenty dollars, the personal property of Harris Joseph and Lewis Joseph. On the trial, Lewis Joseph testified as follows:

> I had, as usual, placed and buttoned an overcoat upon a dummy which stood on the sidewalk outside of my store. I was inside [and] heard the chain of the dummy rattle, and on coming outside found defendant with said coat unbuttoned from the dummy and under his arm, . . . and about two feet therefrom . . . , and the accused was . . . walking off with said coat when grabbed by me, he being prevented from taking it away because said coat was chained to the dummy . . . , and the dummy was tied to the building by a string.

This was the only evidence introduced to prove the charge of larceny. . . .

"Larceny," as defined in the Penal Code of this state, "is the felonious stealing, taking, carrying, leading, or driving away the personal property of another." This is substantially the common-law definition, under which it was held that it must be shown that the goods were severed from the possession or custody of the owner, and in the possession of the thief, though it be but for a moment. Thus where goods were tied by a string, the other end of which was fastened to the counter, and the thief took the goods and carried them towards the door as far as the string would permit, and was then stopped, this was held not to be a severance from the owner's possession, and consequently no felony. (3 Greenl. Ev., sec. 155.) . . .

"In the language of the old definition of larceny," says Bishop, "the goods taken must be *carried away*. . . . The doctrine is, that any removal, however slight, . . . is sufficient; while nothing short of this will do." (2 Bishop's Crim. Law, sec. 794.) . . .

In *State v. Jones*, 65 N. C. 395, the court says: "There must be an asportation of the article alleged to be stolen to complete the crime of larceny. The question as to what constitutes a sufficient asportation has given rise to many nice distinctions. . . ." Judgment and order reversed.

Notes and Questions

(1) *Which Element Really Is Missing in Meyer (Is It Carrying Away or "Asportation," as the Court Seems to Suggest, or Is It Really Taking, or "Caption")?* The cases sometimes treat "caption," or possession by the thief, as a separate element from "asportation," or carrying the item away. As the court points out, any movement, however slight, is enough. But here, arguably, although the facts do show that the defendant moved the property (asportation), perhaps he did not reduce it to his possession (caption). The court refers to the "carry[ing] away" element and cites a case about "asportation," but is the missing element really asportation, or is it, instead, caption?

(2) *Is This Any Way to Define a Crime?* The conduct of Mr. Meyer should be a crime, or at least many people might think so. But it is not larceny. Even if it is covered by some other crime, a problem remains: guesswork will be required to determine which one. What is the solution?

Notes on the Other Elements of Larceny: More Formal Requirements

Remember: Larceny Is a (1) Trespassory (2) Taking (Caption) and (3) Carrying off (Asportation) of the (4) Personal Property (5) of Another, with Intent to (6) Deprive (7) Permanently. The key to larceny is that it is a crime against *possession*. Larceny had seven elements, each with its own specific legal meaning: (1) trespassory (2) taking and (3) carrying away of the (4) personal property (5) of another with intent to (6) deprive the possessor of the property (7) permanently. Another key to understanding is to remember that at the time courts were developing these elements, the penalty for larceny was death. To avoid that result, courts created fine distinctions. *See generally* George P. Fletcher, *Metamorphosis of Larceny*, 89 Harv. L. Rev. 469 (1976).

(1) *A "Trespassory" Taking Was Required.* This meant that the taking must be without the consent of the person in possession. If the thief obtained possession

consensually but by fraud, there originally was no larceny (although the law later extended the crime to cover "larceny by trick," as we shall see). For example, if the thief asked to inspect the owner's horse and then rode away with the intention to keep the horse, originally there was no larceny.

(2) *Caption, or Taking, and "Asportation," or Carrying Away.* Caption meant that the thief had to take possession. Then, asportation is the element that the court discusses in the case above, in which Mr. Meyer pulled a coat off a dummy, intending to steal it—but was not guilty of larceny because a chain prevented the act of asportation, or carrying it away.

(3) *Personal Property.* Larceny covers only the theft of personal property, as distinguished from realty. Ordinarily this rule presents no problem since items that people steal are virtually all personal property and subject to larceny. But some items have attributes of both personal and real property, such as newly cut timber. Theft law has had to categorize these items. Moreover, for historical reasons too arcane for elaboration, some items could not be the object of a larceny.

(a) *Stealing Animals: Sometimes Larceny—but Sometimes Not.* Animals of a "base nature" could not be the object of larceny, including pigs, chickens, horses, cows, and even dogs. Other animals were not as "base" and were covered by larceny, including cats and, shockingly, foxes. Wild animals were also excluded from larceny since they belonged to no one.

(b) *Items Once Attached to Land.* Real property could not be the subject of larceny. A tree was real property but often was deemed personal property once cut down. Some jurisdictions acted to include specific kinds of real property. An interesting illustration is *People v. Dillon*, 668 P.2d 697 (Cal. 1983), where the court had to decide whether the theft of growing marijuana was larceny. Refusing to follow traditional distinctions between growing and severed crops, the court held that standing marijuana was subject to larceny.

(c) *Documents Might Be Valuable—but Sometimes They "Merged" with the Underlying Property.* Many decisions held that documents evidencing title merged with the property and, by themselves, could not be the object of larceny. For example, a deed to land merged with it and was not covered by larceny law. Some modern authorities have held the same is true for the theft of a credit card, which has no value by itself. Similarly, larceny was held not to cover the theft of negotiable bills, notes, and checks. As you can imagine, statutes were passed to make these items subject to larceny or an equivalent offense. *See, e.g.* Mass. Gen. Law. Ann. 266 § 30 ("property" includes, among other items, money, bank notes, promissory notes, and realty documents).

(d) *Theft of Services: Not Larceny?* Services were not "property." Larceny usually would not cover the diversion of power lines or leaving a restaurant without paying the bill. States handled the issue in two ways. Some created a specific crime of *"theft of services."* Others defined "property" to include services. *See, e.g.*, Vern. Ann. Mo. Stat. § 570.030 (crime of stealing includes services).

(e) *Electronic Impulses? Trade Secrets? Information?* Many other items have raised similar issues. *See, e.g., Lund v. Commonwealth*, 232 S.E.2d 745 (Va. 1977) (defendant devised a scheme to get free computer time fraudulently from a university computer system; held, computer processing time is not "property" covered by larceny); *In re Vericker*, 446 F.2d 244 (2d Cir. 1971) (stolen F.B.I. records have no commercial value and are not "goods, wares, or merchandise" subject to a statute punishing the interstate transfer of stolen items). Some courts simplify the matter by viewing "property" as describing items of value, irrespective of their form. These decisions hold that "property" covers such items as maps, trade secrets, bootleg music discs, and electronic documents. Increasingly, legislatures have enacted specific statutes to address these issues.

(4) *Property of "Another": The Importance of Possession and the Fiction of the "Special Owner."* Taking abandoned property is not larceny, since no one possesses it. On the other hand, the crime is larceny as long as someone had possession. For example, someone who rents a car has possession, even if not ownership. If a thief steals the rented car, the thief has committed larceny from the renter. The person in rightful possession sometimes is referred to as the "special owner." Today, the most common context in which this issue arises is robbery: an accused points a gun at a store clerk and takes money. The indictment, in some states, may allege that the money was "owned" by the clerk, because the clerk is the one who has possession.

(5) *With Intent to Deprive the Owner of the Property—Permanently.* The mens rea of larceny is, in essence, the intent to steal the property. But the thief must intend to deprive the owner of it *permanently* (or at least for a substantial enough time to deprive the owner of a significant portion of its economic value). For example, if a person intends to steal a block of ice and keep it in the sun until it melts, then returns the melted water to the owner, the necessary intent for larceny exists, since he or she kept the property long enough to deprive the owner of the value of the ice block. But if an actor hotwires a car to joyride and abandons it across town, there is no larceny. *See People v. Brown*, 38 P. 518 (Cal. 1894) (joyriding is not larceny).

(6) *Mistake (Even if Unreasonable) Can Negate the Mens Rea of Intent to Deprive.* Also, although we often say that ignorance of law is no excuse, ignorance of law is indeed an excuse in this area. If the accused sincerely believes that she is not "depriving" the true owner (perhaps because she thinks that she is the owner, or that there is no owner), there is no larceny. Thus, if Jane sees a $50 bill lying on a table and thinks it is abandoned, she does not commit larceny by taking it.

Problem 7A (Larceny): "Laptop Theft"—Or, "Is That a Crime?"

(1) *A Trespassory Taking from the Victim's Backpack.* Seth, a law student, carries his books and laptop inside a backpack. Melinda, another law student, comes up behind Seth, reaches in the backpack, takes Seth's laptop, and runs away, planning to sell the laptop on Ebay to get money for a drug purchase. Is this act larceny? (Probably yes. Go over the elements: trespassory, caption, asportation, personal property, of another, with intent to deprive, permanently.)

(2) *Theft in Progress—but the Thief Doesn't Get the Booty.* Changing the facts, assume that Seth senses that someone is fiddling with his backpack and turns around just as Melinda lifts the laptop from the backpack. The laptop falls back into the backpack and Melinda runs away. Larceny? (Maybe not; arguably, no asportation, even though there is a trespassory caption.)

(3) *The Alleged Thief Thinks, "It's Mine"—or, "I'll Borrow It."* Changing the facts, imagine that Melinda believes that Seth stole her laptop and hid it in his backpack. She sneaks up behind him and takes the laptop from the backpack. The laptop she takes is the same brand as her own, and she thinks it is hers, but it actually belongs to Seth. Larceny? (Maybe not.)

[2] *Extending Larceny: "Larceny by Trick"*

Notes on Larceny by Trick

(1) *Shouldn't Fraudulent Takings of Possession Be Larceny, Too?* Larceny at early common law required a "trespassory" taking, usually by force or stealth. Takings by fraud, deception, or trick were not covered. Ultimately, the common law adapted to include this situation—in typical fashion, almost like biological evolution.

(2) *The Birth of Larceny by Trick: Pear's Case.* Pear stole a horse, but not by trespass. He obtained possession fraudulently. The case that resulted created a new kind of larceny.

THE KING v. PEAR, 1 Leach 212, 168 Eng. Rep. 208 (House of Lords 1779). The charge against Pear involved the larceny of a horse. Pear obtained possession of the horse from the true owner by fraud, intending to steal it, but without the usual kind of trespassory taking involving asportation and caption. Specifically, he pretended to inspect and ride it, but instead he rode away with it. He then converted the horse to his own use. Although this kind of conduct originally was not larceny because it lacked the element of a trespassory taking of possession (the owner consented to Pear's test ride), the Lords held that Pear's act was "larceny by trick," in which the element of fraudulent obtaining of possession became the equivalent of the asportation and caption that would underlie a trespassory taking.

Notes and Questions

(1) *The Crime of Larceny by Trick Is Merely Larceny, and It Is Charged as Such.* Notice that Pear was charged with larceny, even though that crime technically did not fit. The charge was, in a sense, fictitious. Before that time, "larceny" meant a trespassory taking, and Pear might have understood the indictment as charging him with something he did not do. By referring to larceny, the charging instrument said in effect that he took the property by stealth or force, although he did not. The Lords upheld his conviction by holding that his deception substituted for trespass.

(2) *Modern Proceedings Sometimes Retain This Fiction.* Some states authorize conviction for larceny by trick when the charging instrument alleges "straight" larceny. In some cases, defendants have objected on the ground that the proof varies from the indictment, so that the accused claims to have believed he or she was charged with one crime, but convicted of a different one. If the charging instrument flatly says that the crime was committed under one statute covering an "unlawful [trespassory] taking," whereas the proof shows another statutory crime involving theft by "deception," does the defendant have a legitimate complaint about the confusion?

Problem 7B (Larceny): "You're Charged with Theft by 'Deception,' but I'm Convicting You of Theft by 'Unlawful Taking'"

(1) *The Facts: State v. Jonusas,* 694 N.W.2d 651 (Neb. 2005). The court described the facts in this case as follows.

> Michael Young and his wife became interested in purchasing a bar and grill in Elkhorn, Nebraska. [Vytas A.] Jonusas, who worked for Pinnacle Business Brokerage, acted as the broker for the deal between the Youngs and the owner of the bar and grill. . . .

> [T]he purchase price was to be $70,000. The Youngs wrote Pinnacle [checks for $50,000] and agreed to sign a note on the remaining $20,000. The Youngs' payment of $50,000 was to be held in escrow by Pinnacle because the agreement was contingent upon the Youngs obtaining a liquor license. It was agreed that the $50,000 would be returned in the event that their application was not approved.

> . . . It then came to light that the Youngs had previous convictions for driving while under the influence. . . . The Youngs never received a liquor license.

> . . . Michael Young requested the return of the $50,000. Jonusas ignored this request. . . . [Later,] Jonusas revealed that he had invested the money and lost it all. . . . Jonusas was charged by information with theft by deception [analogous to larceny by trick] pursuant to [Neb. Rev. Stat.] § 28–512. . . .

The district court found Jonusas guilty, stating: "[T]he court just found you guilty . . . under § 28–511, Subsection 1, which is theft by unlawful conduct." But, although the court stated that § 28–511(1) governs "theft by unlawful conduct," the statute actually governs "theft by unlawful taking or disposition," which is a different kind of theft than that charged and which is analogous to "trespassory larceny."

(2) *Can the Defendant Be Convicted of One Kind of Theft When the Evidence Shows a Different Kind?* According to the appellate court, "Jonusas claims the district court erred in [convicting him of a crime that the evidence showed he did not commit]. Jonusas was charged with theft by deception [and the proof showed this offense], but . . . the court [instead] found Jonusas guilty of violating § 28–511(1), theft by unlawful [trespassory] taking or disposition. The issue presented is whether

a defendant may be charged with theft by one manner and . . . convicted of theft by another manner."

(3) *What Is the Correct Answer?* What historic crime would have been committed here (is there evidence of either "straight" larceny or larceny by trick)? Should the judge's finding of the wrong crime, a crime that the evidence clearly shows was not committed, be reversible error?

[In the real case, the Nebraska Supreme Court affirmed by citing a Nebraska statute, based on the Model Penal Code, providing: "An accusation of theft may be supported by evidence that it was committed in any manner that would be theft under [§§] 28–509 to 28–518, notwithstanding the specification of a different manner in the indictment or information." How does this statute affect the issue?]

[B] Theft by False Pretenses (and Its Elusive Distinction from Larceny): Taking "Title," Not Merely "Possession"

Notes on Distinguishing the Statutory Crime of Theft by False Pretenses from Larceny by Trick

(1) *Theft by False Pretenses: Obtaining "Title," Not Merely "Possession."* What if the defendant actually obtains the title to the property (not just possession) by using fraud? Then, the crime is not larceny. It is a distinct offense, created by statute, called "theft by false pretenses."

(2) *Mistake, "Puffery," or Opinion Can Negate the Crime.* For false pretenses, the facts must actually be untrue (as opposed to the thief mistakenly thinking they are untrue). Also, the misrepresentation must cover statements about past or current facts; it cannot state only a belief, opinion, or prediction of the future. Thus, the crime would not cover the statement, "I think this antique rug will be worth $10,000 in five years, so it is a deal at $1,000." It also would not cover "mere puffing," meaning promotion by laudatory opinion or commercial exaggeration: "It's a high quality rug at an amazingly low price." But it could cover, "This rug is no longer being made [a lie] and is being sold elsewhere for $5,000 [another lie]." Early common law treated this kind of fraudulent acquisition of title as purely civil, but an English statute later made it a crime.

(3) *The Will O' the Wisp Distinction between Theft by False Pretenses and Larceny by Trick: An Elusive Formalism?* Larceny by trick consists of obtaining of *possession* by fraud. The separate crime of theft by false pretenses, on the other hand, is committed when the thief's intent is to obtain not mere possession, but *title* to the property, by false pretenses. Imagine that the thief in *King v. Pear* fraudulently gets the owner to sign a bill of sale to the horse. That might be theft by false pretenses.

You might ask what difference this strange distinction should make. And probably, the answer is, it should not make any difference at all. But historically, sometimes it made all the difference in the world. And it even makes a difference, sometimes, in more recent cases.

People v. Phebus

323 N.W.2d 423 (Mich. Ct. App. 1982)

ALLEN, JUDGE.

Which criminal offense, larceny [by trick] or obtaining property by false pretenses, is committed when a shopper switches a price tag on merchandise he proposes to buy so that a lower price appears on the merchandise?

Defendant was charged [erroneously] with larceny . . . , M.C.L. § 750.360; M.S.A. § 28.592. At the preliminary examination, a store detective for Meijer's Thrifty Acres testified that she had observed defendant remove a price tag marked $1.88 from an unfinished decorator shelf and place it on a finished decorator shelf, which had been marked $6.53. . . . Defendant and his wife went through the check-out area and paid the marked price of $1.88 for the finished shelf usually priced $6.53. While defendant was loading his car . . . he was stopped by the store detectives. . . .

Defendant was bound over for trial on the charged offense [of larceny]. [But] the . . . Circuit Court quashed the information, finding that the elements of false pretenses, but not those of larceny, were made out at the preliminary examination. The prosecution has appealed. . . .

Although the elements of the two crimes are quite distinct, the determination of whether a certain course of action should be punished under one statute or the other is often not easily made. The Michigan Supreme Court noted recently in *People v. Long*, 294 N.W.2d 197 (1980):

> There is, to be sure, a narrow margin between a case of larceny [by trick] and one where the property has been obtained by false pretenses. . . . In the former case, where, by fraud, conspiracy, or artifice, the possession is obtained with a felonious design, and the title still remains in the owner, larceny is established; while in the latter, where title, as well as possession is absolutely parted with, the crime is false pretenses. It will be observed that the intention of the owner to part with [only possession of] his property[, not title,] is the gist and essence of the offense of larceny. . . .

. . . [W]e conclude that here, where defendant attempted to secure both title and possession of the shelf, the applicable crime is false pretenses. . . . Affirmed [larceny charge quashed].

Note on Ownership, Title, Possession and Bailment: Property Concepts that Controlled Historical Theft Law

(1) *Why It Matters.* The crimes that we are studying depend heavily on technical property concepts. Did the thief, by fraud, obtain "title"? Or merely "possession"? If title, "theft by false pretenses" is the crime; if mere possession, it's "larceny."

(2) *Ownership and "Title."* A person *owns* property if he or she has a legal right to dispose of it. A good illustration is your wallet. You may sell, give away, burn, bury, or do just about anything you want to do with your wallet. A person who

owns property has title to it. Title is simply a legal conclusion that someone owns the property.

(3) *Distinguishing "Possession" from "Title."* As noted above, ownership is separate from possession. Although often an owner has both such interests, that is not necessarily the case. For example, you may own your car but rent it to a friend. The renter has possession. These arcane distinctions are important because, first, the crime of larceny involves taking property *from someone else's possession.* If the thief already has possession of property owned by someone else, *then decides to keep the property,* the thief, for historical reasons, may not have committed larceny. And second, the thief who obtains title rather than possession has not committed larceny, historically, but theft by false pretenses.

(4) *"Larceny by Bailee": Bailment Is a Contractual Transfer of Possession for a Limited Purpose, Necessitating Creation of Yet Another Crime.* A bailment is a legal relationship in which a "bailor" transfers possession and physical control of property to a "bailee" for a particular purpose. Bailment is created by express or implied contract. The bailee gets possession but, of course, not title. A typical example occurs at a parking lot. The parking lot owner is a bailee and the driver who parks in the lot is a bailor. Another illustration occurs if you take your clothes to the cleaners. The cleaner is the bailee and the person who leaves clothing is the bailor. A bailee lawfully gets possession, so if he or she later decides to steal the item, the crime is not larceny. But it is not larceny by trick, either, or theft by false pretenses, since no deception was used to obtain possession. The common law handled this dilemma by expanding larceny to cover the subcategory of larceny called "*larceny by bailee.*"

(5) *Forgery and Bad Checks.* If someone forges another's name on a document, including a check, and thereby obtains goods or money, the crime is widely considered to be false pretenses. The legal issue is more complex if the person signs his or her own name to a check, then cashes it, but knows that the account does not have sufficient funds. What theft crime did the person commit? While some decisions held that the crime was larceny, and a greater number found it to be false pretenses, many jurisdictions have enacted separate crimes covering bad checks, for clarity.

[C] Embezzlement

Notes on the Statutory Offense of Embezzlement

(1) *The Limits of Larceny in an Era of White Collar Crime.* A strict application of the elements of larceny excluded much white collar crime. Often there was no trespassory taking, because the possessor of the property consented to the transfer of possession to the thief. The thief often was a trusted associate who betrayed the trust—but who committed no larceny.

(2) *Embezzlement: Rightful Possession, Wrongful Conversion.* Embezzlement is a statutory (not common law) crime that was created to fill in a gap in larceny law,

which did not cover a theft by someone who initially, with a "clean mind," obtained possession of property, then converted it to his or her own use. It reached thieves in positions of trust, such as employees and agents, who acquired possession of property rightfully, then converted the property. Though the property was stolen, the crime was not larceny, because the taking was not *trespassory*. Nor was possession obtained by trick or bailment.

(3) *Flexibility in Judging the Requirements: Often, the "Clean Mind" Was a Fiction.* The rule that the embezzler had to acquire the property with a clean mind was honored more in the breach. Courts instead looked at whether the person acquired it in a position of trust and then converted it (irrespective of whether the taking was with a clean mind). If so, the crime was embezzlement.

Problem 7C: Larceny or Embezzlement?

(1) *Debt Collection—But an Employee Pockets the Money.* Imagine a defendant who has been indicted for embezzlement and larceny for the same act. He worked for a debt collection company. A man came into the office and paid $75 on a debt the company was collecting for another business. What crime if the defendant took the money from the debtor and pocketed it immediately: Embezzlement? Larceny? (Probably embezzlement.) *See State v. Matthews*, 226 S.W. 203 (Tenn. 1920) (holding that the crime can be embezzlement from the company, but not larceny).

(2) *Putting It in the Drawer, Then Taking and Pocketing It.* Now, assume that the defendant took the money from the debtor, put it in the agency's cash register, then took the money from the register. Larceny? Embezzlement? Consider the following case.

Commonwealth v. Ryan

30 N.E. 364 (Mass. 1892)

HOLMES, J.

This is a complaint for embezzlement of money. The defendant was employed by one Sullivan to sell liquor for him in his store. Sullivan sent two detectives to the store, with marked money of Sullivan's, to make a feigned purchase from the defendant. The defendant dropped the money into the money-drawer of a cash-register, . . . but he did not register this sale, as was customary, and afterwards—it would seem within a minute or two—he took the money from the drawer. The question presented is whether . . . as a matter of law . . . the defendant was not guilty of embezzlement, but was guilty of larceny, if of anything. The defendant [argues] . . . that, after the money was put into the drawer it was in Sullivan's possession, and therefore the removal of it was a trespass and larceny [but not embezzlement]. . . .

. . . [I]t is not larceny for a servant to convert property delivered to him by a third person for his master, provided he does so before the goods have reached their destination, . . . (*Com. v. King*, 9 Cush. 284;) while, on the other hand, if the property is delivered to the servant by his master, the conversion is larceny, (*Com. v. Berry*, 99 Mass. 428; *Com. v. Davis*, 104 Mass. 548.)

This distinction is not very satisfactory, but it is due to historical accidents in the development of the criminal law, coupled, perhaps, with an unwillingness on the part of the judges to enlarge the limits of a capital offense. . . .

. . . An obvious case [of larceny] was when the property was finally deposited in the place of deposit provided by the master, and subject to his control, although there was some nice discussion as to what constituted such a place. *Reg. v. Reed*, Dears. Cr. Cas. 257. No doubt a final deposit of money in the till of a shop would have the effect. But it is plain that the mere physical presence of the money there for a moment is not conclusive while the servant is on the spot, and has not lost his power over it, as, for instance, if the servant drops it, and instantly picks it up again. . . .

It follows from what we have said that the defendant's . . . position cannot be maintained, and that the judge was right in charging the jury that, if the defendant, before he placed the money in the drawer, intended to appropriate it, and with that intent simply put it in the drawer for his own convenience in keeping it for himself, that would not make his appropriation of it just afterwards larceny. The distinction may be arbitrary, but, as it does not affect the defendant otherwise than by giving him an opportunity, whichever offense he was convicted of, to contend that he should have been convicted of the other, we have the less uneasiness in applying it. . . . [Conviction affirmed.]

Notes and Questions

(1) *How's That Again?: The Elusive Distinction between Larceny and Embezzlement—An Appropriation by the Employee During Rightful Possession by the Employee Is Embezzlement, but a Wrongful Taking After the Property Has Been Delivered to the Employer Is Larceny.* If Ryan had stolen money that was firmly at rest in the employer's possession, such as taking it after delivery to a sealed cashbox, the crime would have been larceny. If he had pocketed the money immediately without putting it into the drawer or box, the crime would have been embezzlement.

As things happened, however, Ryan uncooperatively engaged in neither of these clear-cut crimes. Instead, he committed an "in-between" act. If he had left the money in the cash drawer and walked away, to return and take it later, that act might be larceny, but his recapture of money that remained in his own immediate reach, is near enough to embezzlement to be labeled as such. Or so the court holds.

(2) *Sister Crimes: Embezzlement, Fraudulent Breach of Trust, Fraudulent Conversion.* Embezzlement under some statutes may require that the perpetrator occupy a stated position, such as employee. Recognizing that people may acquire possession of property in other situations as well, many jurisdictions have enacted statutes expanding embezzlement to any situation where someone acquires possession in any position of trust. These broad statutes have created crimes named fraudulent breach of trust, fraudulent conversion, etc. But does this make sense?

[D] The Federal Approach to White Collar Theft: Building on the Historical Offenses to Define Mail Fraud, Bank Fraud, and Related Offenses

Notes on Mail Fraud and Federal Bank Crimes

(1) *"White Collar Crime": What Is It?—Conceptions Differ, but Most Cases Arise Under a Few Statutes.* Conceptions of "white collar crime" differ. The phrase is not directed at a specific offense, but rather connotes crimes by offenders who are more capable than "street" criminals. This concept helps to explain why the pigeonholes of the historic crimes are ill-suited to dealing with white collar offenses. To counteract the problem of ambiguity in the historical definitions, the federal criminal code includes statutes that are broader, and just a few of these can cover a wide spectrum of white collar offenses.

(2) *The Federal Mail and Wire Fraud Statutes.* These statutes are broad enough to cover almost all of the historic forms of theft, or at least broad enough to encompass crimes broader than those covered by larceny. This result is partially accomplished by the mail fraud statute, which is worded to include anyone who obtains property by any "scheme or device to defraud [or] by means of false or fraudulent pretenses, representations or promises." 18 U.S.C. § 1341. The statute has been interpreted to reach larceny and beyond. As with most federal offenses, the mail fraud provision contains a jurisdictional element, requiring a use of the mail or other instrumentalities of interstate commerce. "Wire fraud" under 18 U.S.C. § 1343 similarly criminalizes a broad spectrum of theft committed electronically. Offenses often fit both statutes.

(3) *Stealing That Involves a Bank: The Federal Bank Theft-or-Robbery Statute.* The federal statute covering thefts from (or using) banks is commonly known as the federal "Bank Robbery Statute" for historical reasons, and it does cover robbery (*i.e.*, stealing by force), but it also covers larceny. The statute applies to anyone who "takes and carries away, with intent to steal or purloin, any property or money" from a bank or other covered institution. The reference to taking and carrying away makes the statute sound as though it is limited to straight larceny, but the additional language that mentions "intent to steal or purloin" is more inclusive. The case that follows shows that it covers more than larceny.

[1] The Bank Theft Act

Bell v. United States

462 U.S. 356 (1983)

JUSTICE POWELL delivered the opinion of the Court.

The issue presented is whether 18 U.S.C. § 2113(b), a provision of the Federal Bank Robbery Act, proscribes the crime of obtaining money under false pretenses.

I

On October 13, 1978, a Cincinnati man wrote a check for $10,000 drawn on a Cincinnati bank. He endorsed the check for deposit to his account at Dade Federal Savings & Loan of Miami and mailed the check to an agent there. The agent never received the check. On October 17, petitioner Nelson Bell opened an account at a Dade Federal branch and deposited $50—the minimum amount necessary for new accounts. He used his own name, but gave a false address, birth date, and social security number. Later that day, at another branch, he deposited the Cincinnati man's $10,000 check into this new account. The endorsement had been altered to show Bell's account number. . . . [Several days later,] Bell closed the account and was paid the total balance [including interest] in cash.

Bell was [convicted of] violating 18 U.S.C. §2113(b). The statute provides, in relevant part:

> Whoever takes and carries away, with intent to steal or purloin, any prop-erty or money or any other thing of value exceeding $100 belonging to, or in the care, custody, control, management, or possession of any bank, credit union, or any savings and loan association, shall be fined not more than $5,000 or imprisoned not more than ten years, or both. . . .

[The Court of Appeals] affirmed the conviction. In so doing, it concluded that the statute embraces all felonious takings—including obtaining money under false pretenses. The court thus rejected Bell's argument that §2113(b) is limited to common-law larceny. . . .

II

In the 13th century, larceny was limited to trespassory taking: a thief committed larceny only if he feloniously "took and carried away" another's personal property *from his possession*. The goal was more to prevent breaches of the peace than losses of property, and violence was more likely when property was taken from the own-er's actual possession.

As the common law developed, protection of property also became an impor-tant goal. The definition of larceny accordingly was expanded by judicial interpreta-tion to include cases where the owner merely was deemed to be in possession. [The Court here cited cases extending larceny to cover larceny by trick and by bailee.]

By the late 18th century, courts were less willing to expand common-law defini-tions. Thus when a bank clerk retained money given to him by a customer rather than depositing it in the bank, he was not guilty of larceny, for the bank had not been in possession of the money. *King v. Bazeley*, 2 Leach 835, 168 Eng.Rep. 517 (Cr. Cas.Res.1799). Statutory crimes such as embezzlement and obtaining property by false pretenses therefore were created to fill this gap.

The theoretical distinction between false pretenses and larceny by trick may be stated simply. If a thief, through his trickery, acquired *title* to the property from the owner, he has obtained property by false pretenses; but if he merely acquired *possession* from the owner, he has committed larceny by trick. In this case the parties agree that Bell is guilty of obtaining money by false pretenses. When the teller at Dade Federal handed him $10,080 in cash, Bell acquired title to the money. The only dispute is whether 18 U.S.C. §2113(b) proscribes the crime of false pretenses, or whether the statute is instead limited to common-law larceny.

III

A

Bell's argument in favor of the narrower reading of §2113(b) relies principally on the statute's use of the traditional common-law language "takes and carries away." . . . In §2113(b), however, Congress has not adopted the elements of larceny in common-law terms. . . . [But] "taking and carrying away," although not a necessary element of the crime, is entirely consistent with false pretenses.

Two other aspects of §2113(b) show an intention to go beyond the common-law definition of larceny. First, common-law larceny was limited to thefts of tangible personal property. . . . Section 2113(b) is thus broader than common-law larceny, for it covers "any property or money or any other thing of value exceeding $100." Second, . . . common-law larceny required a theft from the possession of the owner. . . . Section 2113(b), however, goes well beyond even this expanded definition. It applies when the property "belong[s] to," or is "in the care, custody, control, management, or possession of," a covered institution.

In sum, the statutory language does not suggest that it covers only common-law larceny. Although §2113(b) does not apply to a case of false pretenses in which there is not a taking and carrying away, it proscribes Bell's conduct here. . . .

B

The legislative history of §2113(b) also suggests that Congress intended the statute to reach Bell's conduct. As originally enacted in 1934, the Federal Bank Robbery Act governed only robbery—a crime requiring a forcible taking. Congress apparently was concerned with "'gangsters who operate habitually from one State to another in robbing banks.'"

By 1937 the concern was broader, for the limited nature of the original Act "'ha[d] led to some incongruous results.'" H.R. Rep. No. 732, 75th Cong., 1st Sess., 1 (1937). It was possible for a thief to steal a large amount from a bank "'without displaying any force or violence and without putting any one in fear,'" and he would not violate any federal law. Congress amended the Act to fill this gap, adding language now found at §§2113(a) and (b). Although the term "larceny" appears in the legislative reports, the congressional purpose plainly was to protect banks from those who wished to steal banks' assets—even if they used no force in doing so.

. . . We cannot believe that Congress wished to limit the scope of the amended Act's coverage . . . on the basis of an arcane and artificial distinction more suited to the social conditions of 18th century England than the needs of 20th century America. . . . [Conviction affirmed.]

JUSTICE STEVENS, dissenting.

[Justice Stevens noted that criminal statutes should be narrowly construed unless it is clear Congress intended them to cover particular situations, then turned to the history of larceny.] The history of the bank robbery and bank larceny legislation enacted in 1934 and 1937 persuades me that Congress did not intend federal law to encompass the conduct of obtaining funds from a bank with its consent, albeit under false pretenses. . . . Congress [initially] responded to local requests for federal assistance by enacting a statute that prohibited robbery of federal banks, but rejected the section initially passed by the Senate that made larceny by false pretenses a federal offense. . . .

Three years later the bank robbery statute was amended . . . . The Attorney General specifically described the anomaly created by the statute's failure to cover larceny by stealth, theft of money from a bank without violence but also clearly without the bank's consent. It is fair to infer that Congress viewed the amendment as a limited change [covering only larceny without the bank's consent]. [I dissent.]

UNITED STATES v. DAVIS, 742 Fed. Appx. 435 (11th Cir. 2018). Davis was a Brinks employee and had custody of funds supplied by a bank for replenishing ATM's. He placed money from his armored car into a bag, which he put into his wife's car when she came to pick him up. When he told her what was in the bag, she "freaked out" and told him to get it out of the car. Davis threw the bag out of the window into a parking lot. He returned later, but he did not find the money.

Without analyzing what common law crime might have been committed, the court of appeals affirmed Davis's conviction. (Perhaps the crime would have been embezzlement? Or larceny by trick? Or theft by bailee?) The bank theft statute was broad enough to cover whichever common law offense was at issue.

Notes and Questions

(1) *Even with Expanded Statutes, the Historical Distinctions Are Influential.* Note how theft law's historical distinctions are still relevant in some contexts (see the note below). Do you agree that the Bank Theft Act was meant to include theft by false pretenses?

(2) *Does the Bank Robbery Statute Reach Other White Collar Variations?* Bell closed the account and was paid in cash. If he had not closed the account and all but a negligible amount of the money sent electronically to his account in the Cayman Islands instead of taking it with him in cash, would he then have committed this federal offense? Notice that the Court suggests that a "taking and carrying away" is still required, as it was for historical larceny.

[2] Mail Fraud: Does It Cover Property? "Honest Services?"

CLEVELAND v. UNITED STATES, 531 U.S. 12 (2000). Mail fraud is usually limited to thefts of "property." Cleveland was convicted of mail fraud after using deception to obtain a gambling license from the State of Louisiana. The Government argued that the license was property. The Supreme Court disagreed and reversed the conviction:

> We reject the Government's theories of property rights not simply because they stray from traditional concepts of property. We resist the Government's reading of [the mail fraud statute] as well because it invites us to make a sweeping expansion of federal criminal jurisdiction in the absence of a clear statement by Congress. [The theory would infringe upon] a wide range of conduct traditionally regulated by the states. . . .

SKILLING v. UNITED STATES, 561 U.S. 358 (2010). In just a few years after its founding, Enron Corporation became the seventh-largest revenue-grossing company in America. But then, its stock plummeted suddenly, and the corporation collapsed into bankruptcy, causing huge losses to investors. Skilling was Enron's CEO at relevant times, and eventually, the Federal Government charged him with mail fraud under what was called the "honest services" theory. This claim asserts that a business agent has acted in some manner inconsistent with the interests of the business represented, and in favor of undisclosed personal interests, so as to deprive the business of "honest services." The Government's theory was that Skilling (and others) had engaged in a scheme to deceive investors about Enron's true performance by manipulating public reports and making false and misleading statements, in order to maintain the value of securities that he held. The jury convicted Skilling of this alleged crime.

The questions for the Supreme Court were whether honest-services fraud was, indeed, a crime covered by the mail fraud statute, and if so, whether it included Skilling's conduct. The Court pointed out that earlier, in *McNally v. United States*, 483 U.S. 350, 360 (1987), the Supreme Court had called a complete halt to the use of the honest-services theory. The mail fraud statute was "limited in scope to the protection of property rights." The Supreme Court added, "If Congress wants to go further, it must speak more clearly." So, Congress promptly did exactly that. The very next year, Congress passed 18 U.S.C § 1346, which provides, "For the purposes of th[e] chapter [of the U.S. Code that prohibits, inter alia, mail fraud, § 1341, and wire fraud, § 1343], the term 'scheme or artifice to defraud' includes a scheme or artifice to deprive another of the intangible right of honest services." With these words, Congress revived the doctrine of honest-services fraud—in some form, as yet unclear.

So: how far did the statute reach? The Supreme Court interpreted this new law as covering the conduct that had been covered by the pre-*McNally* lower court decisions. The statute was intended to return the mail fraud jurisprudence to the status it had occupied before the Supreme Court abolished it. This reasoning, the Court concluded per justice Ginsburg, meant that the honest-services theory extended only to conduct involving bribery or kickbacks. And this, in turn, meant that Skilling had not committed the crime of honest-services fraud. The Court's reasoning included the following:

> Satisfied that Congress, by enacting § 1346, "meant to reinstate the body of pre-*McNally* honest-services law," we have surveyed that case law. . . . While the honest-services cases preceding *McNally* dominantly and consistently applied the fraud statute to bribery and kickback schemes—schemes that were the basis of most honest-services prosecutions—there was considerable disarray over the statute's application to conduct outside that core category. . . . In view of [its] history, there is no doubt that Congress intended § 1346 to reach *at least* bribes and kickbacks. Reading the statute to proscribe a wider range of offensive conduct, we acknowledge, would raise the due process concerns underlying the vagueness doctrine. To preserve the statute without transgressing constitutional limitations, we now hold that § 1346 criminalizes *only* the bribe-and-kickback core of the pre-*McNally* case law. . . . [Honest-services conviction vacated.]

Justice Scalia, joined by Justices Thomas and Kennedy, dissented in part; he would have held the entire honest-services statute unconstitutionally vague on its face.

§ 7.02 Which Historic Theft Offense Applies?: An Elusive Determination

Problem 7D: Theft—But Which Historic Offense? *"I'll Collect a Pool of Money for Shared Baseball Tickets"*

So far, we have concentrated on the historic offenses one at a time. But that approach understates the problem. "Thefts" sometimes are committed in ways that do not fall neatly into one of the traditional patterns. Then, historically, the prosecution faced the dilemma (or trilemma) of specifying which offense was at issue, with the knowledge that the defendant could not be convicted unless the right crime was charged. This problem requires you to face that dilemma. It is based upon a real case, although the case was decided under a modern statute.

A Chart of Traditional Theft Crimes

How Acquired	Acquired Possession	Acquired Title
Stealth	Larceny	n/a
Deceit	Larceny by Trick	False Pretenses
Threats	Extortion	n/a
Rightfully, Then Convert	Embezzlement Fraudulent Conversion Fraudulent Breach of Trust Larceny by Bailee	Shopping [If you rightfully acquired title, there is no crime.]

(1) *People v. Rishel*, 50 P.3d 938 (Colo. 2002). This was an attorney disciplinary proceeding that resulted in the disbarment of John B. Rishel on a finding that he committed "an act . . . which violates the criminal laws of this State." The hearing board implicitly found Rishel guilty of theft. But this problem calls for you to answer the question: "Which historic theft-related offense is involved? Larceny, Larceny by Trick, False Pretenses, or Embezzlement?"

The following comes from the opinion: "[Rishel collected money from] a group of individuals who pooled funds to purchase Rockies baseball team season tickets for division among the group. . . . Rishel informed them [of] their share of the cost [in each relevant instance, on the order of $1,000] and asked them to pay immediately by cashier's check rather than the personal check they had used in the past. . . . Rishel cashed the check[s]. . . . [Some of the group later] contacted the Rockies' ticket office and learned that the tickets had not been purchased. . . . [Rishel did not respond to repeated efforts to contact him by telephone, mail, and attorney demand letter. Finally], Rishel filed for personal bankruptcy protection. He listed [unpaid group members] as unsecured, nonpriority creditors. . . . [H]e had no funds in his checking account, and claimed only twenty dollars as cash on hand."

(2) *Rishel's Arguments (and Potential Arguments): "You Didn't Prove the Crime You Charged."* Rishel argued that "he did not form the intent to permanently deprive" the group members of their funds. If the fragmented crimes of larceny [or larceny by trick], theft by false pretext, and embezzlement were the governing law, Rishel might have had another argument: namely, that whichever theft-related offense the State had charged, it had charged the wrong crime. Thus, if Colorado had charged larceny, he could have claimed that the offense was either theft by false pretext or embezzlement; if theft by false pretext, either larceny or embezzlement; if embezzlement, either larceny or theft by false pretext. (As the cases above demonstrate, these kinds of arguments sometimes have succeeded.)

(3) *Which Historic Offense Would You Charge, if You Were Counsel for the State (and What Would You Argue if You Represented the Defendant, to Show that the "Wrong Offense" Was Charged)?* Imagine that you are the district attorney in a state with old-fashioned theft law, and you must handle Rishel's case by deciding whether it shows larceny, larceny by trick, theft by false pretenses, or embezzlement. How would you charge him?

(4) *The Disciplinary Board's Actual Decision: Rishel's Disbarment Could Be Based upon Colorado's Unitary Offense of "Theft," and Further Specification of the Offense as Larceny, False Pretenses, or Embezzlement Was Unnecessary.* The disciplinary board quoted the applicable Colorado law defining a new, unitary offense of "theft": "A person commits theft when he knowingly obtains or exercises control over anything of value of another without authorization, or by threat or deception, and knowingly uses, conceals, or abandons the thing of value in such manner as to deprive the other person permanently of its use or benefit." The board went on to say, "To constitute theft . . . , '[c]ontrol of the property need not be unauthorized from the outset.' . . . 'It is sufficient [for purposes of this statute] that the intended use of such

thing be inconsistent with the owner's use or benefit.'" As for Rishel's argument that he never intended to permanently deprive the group members of their funds, "[T]he crime of theft may be committed [under the Colorado statute] when the offender . . . even though not intending to deprive the other person permanently of the . . . property, nonetheless knowingly uses the property in such manner as to deprive the other person permanently of the . . . property."

Notice that this Colorado law departs sharply from the historical distinctions. This problem, nevertheless, calls upon you to apply those distinctions. And here is another question: Why do you suppose that Colorado changed its law to create its unitary definition of theft?

§ 7.03 Modern Consolidated Theft Laws

Read MPC § 223.1–223.8 [consolidated theft statute] in the MPC Appendix.

Notes on Consolidated Theft Statutes

(1) *The Need for Consolidation.* It should be obvious that the historical law of theft was complicated, involved needless distinctions, and was in need of modernization. Common sense tells us that proven thefts should be punished. It also suggests that many technical distinctions should not be devices for manipulation by people who intentionally steal other people's property.

(2) *The Model Penal Code Approach.* The Model Penal Code accepted this challenge and recommended the adoption of what is now called a "consolidated theft statute," substituting a single unified offense of "theft" for the formerly separate crimes of larceny, larceny by trick, larceny by bailee, embezzlement, false pretenses, receiving stolen property, and similar other offenses. This consolidated approach, now adopted in a clear majority of jurisdictions, markedly simplifies theft law. It creates a generic crime, generally called "theft," though occasionally other names are used, such as "larceny" (Conn. Gen. Stat. Ann. § 53a-119) or "stealing" (Vern. Ann. Mo. Stat. § 570.030).

Problem 7E (Theft Consolidation): The Colorado Consolidated Theft Statute

(1) *Examining a Consolidated Theft Statute: What's Changed?* Consider the following modern consolidated theft statute:

Colorado Statute 18–4–401. Theft.

(1) A person commits theft when he knowingly obtains or exercises control over anything of value of another without authorization, or by threat or deception, and:

(a) Intends to deprive the other person permanently of the use or benefit of the thing of value; or

(b) Knowingly uses, conceals, or abandons the thing of value in such manner as to deprive the other person permanently of its use or benefit; or

(c) Uses, conceals, or abandons the thing of value intending that such use, concealment, or abandonment will deprive the other person permanently of its use and benefit; or

(d) Demands any consideration to which he is not legally entitled as a condition of restoring the thing of value to the other person.

(2) *Did They Cover Everything*? The Colorado consolidated theft statute, typical of modern provisions in most jurisdictions, is designed to replace the traditional theft crimes. Review the elements of these crimes. Does this consolidated statute cover larceny? Embezzlement? False pretenses? Receiving stolen property?

Problem 7F (Theft Consolidation): Switching Price Tags

(1) *Switcheroo.* Defendant took the $2.99 price tag from a box of nails and placed it on top of the $4.99 price tag for a box twice as large. A store detective saw the switch and Defendant was arrested when he left the store after paying $2.99 for the larger box.

(2) *What Crime(s)? (a)* What, if any, traditional theft offense did Defendant commit? *(b)* Is this conduct covered by the Colorado consolidated theft crime?

Notes on the Effects of Historical Offenses After Consolidation

(1) *Consolidations That Continue to Use the Distinct Historical Offenses: The Massachusetts Example.* The Colorado statute above, which is based on the MPC, redefines theft completely. But that is not the only way to consolidate. The Massachusetts statutes, for example, keep the three historical offenses as distinct definitions. Larceny, false pretenses, and embezzlement remain similar to their historical patterns. What Massachusetts has done to bring its law of theft into the modern era, however, is to change the method of charging the offense: by a unitary indictment, alleging only that the defendant "stole" the property in question. This allegation supports proof of any of the three offenses. *See Commonwealth v. Mills,* 764 N.E.2d 854 (Mass. 2002).

(2) *But This Consolidation Method Means That Jury Instructions and Analysis of the Facts Must Conform to the Traditional Crimes.* But because Massachusetts continues to rely on larceny, false pretenses, and embezzlement, the courts must use these definitions to consider evidence sufficiency. And jury instructions must conform to the type of theft that is shown by the evidence. The game of guessing which shell conceals the pea must still be played. Thus, the court in *Mills* held that the defendant's conviction for larceny did not fit the evidence and that he would need to be retried under instructions covering theft by false pretenses.

(3) *Comparing Colorado's Consolidation to Consolidation in Massachusetts.* Colorado, as we have seen, not only consolidates the forms of theft but also defines a unitary crime that uses new terminology. This approach means that in Colorado, unlike Massachusetts, the courts do not need to consult multiple theft crimes in analyzing sufficiency or instructing juries. After you have read the case that follows, you should be able to decide: which consolidation approach is better, that of Massachusetts, or that of Colorado?

Simon v. State

349 P.3d 191 (Alaska 2015)

MANNHEIMER, Judge.

The earliest, most classic definition of theft is laying hold of property that you know belongs to someone else and carrying it away without permission, with the intent to permanently deprive the owner of the property. The present case requires us to examine how this general notion of theft applies to modern retail stores—stores where customers are allowed to take merchandise from the shelves or display cases, and walk around the store with these items, until they ultimately pay for the items at a checkout station.

The State contends that if a person intends to take the property without paying for it, then the crime of theft occurs at the moment the person removes an article of merchandise from a shelf or display case within the store. The defendant, for his part, contends that the crime of theft is not complete until the person physically leaves the store.

For the reasons explained in this opinion, we conclude that the true answer lies in between the parties' positions: In the context of a retail store where customers are allowed to take possession of merchandise while they shop, the crime of theft is complete when a person, acting with the intent to deprive the store of the merchandise, performs an act that exceeds, or is otherwise inconsistent with, the scope of physical possession granted to customers by the store owner. . . .

Underlying facts

The defendant, Harold Evan Simon, went into a Walmart store in Anchorage. Like many other retail merchants, Walmart allows its customers to exert control over its merchandise before making a purchase: customers are allowed to [carry items as] they walk through the store, before going . . . to pay for these items.

While Simon was walking through the Walmart store, he took a jacket from a sales rack, put it on, and continued to wear it as he walked through the store. Simon also took a backpack and started carrying it around. At some point, Simon placed several DVDs in the backpack. Simon also picked up a couple of food items. Finally, Simon went to the row of cash registers. He paid for the food items—but he did not pay for the jacket, the backpack, or the DVDs hidden in the backpack.

Simon then left the cash register area and headed for the store exit. Before Simon reached the exit, a Walmart employee approached him and detained him. Simon handed the backpack to the employee, and then he removed the DVDs from the backpack. Simon told the Walmart employee, "There you go; there's your stuff. I'm sorry; I was going to sell it." A short time later, the police arrived, and they noticed that Simon's jacket was also unpaid-for. (It still had the Walmart tags on it.)

Based on this incident, and because of Simon's prior convictions for theft, Simon was indicted for second-degree theft under AS 11.46.130(a)(6) (*i.e.*, theft of property worth $50 or more by someone with two or more prior convictions for theft within the previous five years). Simon ultimately stipulated that he had the requisite prior convictions, so the only issue litigated at Simon's trial was whether he stole property worth $50 or more. . . .

[The trial court's instructions to the jury contained the following:] "The issue for you to decide is whether the State proved, beyond a reasonable doubt, that Mr. Simon intended to take the items from Walmart without paying for them, *without regard to any particular area where he was confronted* by [the Walmart employee]." . . . (emphasis added by editors).

[T]he judge's instruction was potentially flawed . . . —because, depending on how the phrase "exert control over property of another" is defined in the context of a retail store, Simon's location at the time he was apprehended might possibly be the factor that distinguished a completed act of theft from an attempted theft. . . .

Why we conclude that . . . Alaska's definition of theft requires proof that the defendant did something with the merchandise that was . . . inconsistent with the possession authorized by the store

The general definition of the crime of theft is contained in AS 11.46.100(1). Under this definition, theft occurs if a person "obtains the property of another", acting with the intent "to deprive another of property or to appropriate property of another to oneself or a third person" . . . .

For purposes of the issue raised in Simon's case, the key portion of this definition is the word "obtains". This word is defined in AS 11.46.990(12); the relevant portion of that definition is: "to exert control over property of another". [It is intended to generally cover conduct that fell under multiple crimes at common law.]

In situations where the accused thief had no right at all to exert control over the other person's property, this definition expresses our traditional notion of theft. It describes what most of us think of when we hear the word "theft"—situations where a thief picks up someone else's property and makes off with it. . . .

[But here, the possession of the property within the store and before checkout was consented to and authorized by the owner. The court describes some of the common law theft-related offenses covered above in this chapter, as well as the need for consolidation and the Model Penal Code response. The court notes that the applicable Alaska statute, which was drawn from the Oregon theft statute, generally follows the Model Penal Code, but it omits the words "unauthorized" and "unlawful," which the MPC defines in terms of a taking "without the effective consent of the owner." Without this "unauthorized" concept, the statute could cover possession that should be perfectly lawful.]

[W]hen the drafters of the Alaska theft statutes composed our [statute] (based on the Oregon statute), the Oregon courts had already construed their statute to require proof of an *unauthorized* exertion of control (even though the statute did not explicitly mention this requirement). . . .

[The court adopts the requirement that the theft be "unauthorized" for the reasons above and also because that interpretation is consistent with the common law and is in line with the laws of every other state.]

Application of this law to Simon's case

We have just held that the *actus reus* of theft requires proof, not just that the defendant exerted control over someone else's property, but that this exertion of control was unauthorized. Thus, the instruction that the trial judge gave to Simon's jury was technically wrong. Depending on the facts of a particular case, it might make a difference where a shoplifter is apprehended — because there might be cases where defendants could plausibly argue that they had not yet taken the merchandise anywhere that was inconsistent with the scope of their implicit authority as customers. . . .

Turning to the facts of Simon's case, we conclude that any technical flaw in the [instruction] to the jury was harmless beyond a reasonable doubt. . . .

[U]nder any version of the evidence, Simon had already gone through the checkout line — where he paid for a couple of food items while, at the same time, either hiding or disguising the jacket, the backpack, and the DVDs he had taken — and he was headed toward the exit when he was apprehended.

Even viewed in the light most favorable to the defense, Simon's conduct constituted the *actus reus* of theft. His conduct was inconsistent with the scope of possession granted to customers — regardless of whether Simon had reached the outer door, or even the entrance to the vestibule, when he was stopped. . . . [Conviction affirmed.]

Notes and Questions

(1) *Even if the Case Was Tried under an Erroneous Theory of Theft, It Can Be Upheld in Some Jurisdictions if It Fits Another Theory of Theft.* The defendant in *State v. DeGennaro*, 46 A.3d 1147 (Me. 2012), received a check for construction work, but he kept the funds and did not perform the work. He was charged under the state's consolidated theft statute. The trial court found that he "never intended" to pay subcontractors or do the work, and following the state's theory of the case, found the defendant guilty of "theft by unauthorized taking or transfer." On appeal, the defendant pointed out that he received the check with the authority of the payor, not

in any "unauthorized" way. The court of appeals agreed, but it affirmed the conviction anyway, holding that the defendant was guilty of theft by deception, since he had received the check on a false promise to do what he did not do. Under the consolidated theft statute, it was no longer necessary to pick out the correct theory of theft in the trial court.

(2) *But Some Jurisdictions Still Splinter Theft into Multiple Crimes, and This Kind of Crime Definition Still Causes Irrational Results.* In *Commonwealth v. Foster*, 33 A.3d 632 (Pa. Super. Ct. 2011), the defendant was tried for "theft from a motor vehicle." The state proved that he stole a grille from an automobile. The jury found him guilty, but the court upheld a judgment of acquittal. The crime requires a theft of "moveable property" from a vehicle, reasoned the court, and the grille was not "moveable" with respect to the vehicle. Furthermore, the crime requires a theft "from" the vehicle, and this was a theft "of" a part of the vehicle. In a footnote, the court listed fully fourteen (14) different species of theft, in addition to the "general charge of theft," which the court suggested should have been used in this case.

§ 7.04 Receiving Stolen Property:
The Historical Crime (and Modern Consolidation)

Notes on the Historically Separate Crime of Receiving

(1) *Historically, a Separate Crime.* Assume a burglar breaks into a home and steals antique jewelry. While the thief may enjoy wearing the stolen items, more likely he or she will seek to turn the jewelry into cash. Someone who buys the stolen property, colloquially called a fence, may be guilty of the crime of "receiving stolen property." This crime covers a defendant who receives (or conceals) property that was stolen by someone else, and who knew that the property was stolen and who had the intent to deprive the owner of that property.

(2) *Proof Difficulties Created by the Pigeonhole of a Distinct Crime of Receiving.* The word "stolen" in this crime can be troublesome, since actually there is no such historical crime. Courts had to decide which theft crime qualified as "stolen." Property taken by larceny was always considered to be "stolen," and often robbery (discussed elsewhere) was included, but property obtained by embezzlement or false pretenses was often deemed not to have been "stolen" for this purpose.

(3) *A Bigger Proof Problem: Was It "Larceny," or Was It "Receiving"?* And there was a greater problem. Historically, it was necessary to prove beyond a reasonable doubt either that the crime was "larceny" (the defendant stole it) or that it was "receiving" (the defendant did not steal it but received it directly or indirectly from the thief). It could not be both. But what if a theft occurred without any direct witnesses, and the property quickly turned up in the possession of the defendant under circumstances such that the defendant obviously either stole it personally or knew it to be stolen?

It is clear that one crime or the other has been committed, but the proof leaves the question unanswered: which crime?

This is a common situation. Sometimes, proof of the distinct crime was available (*e.g.*, the thief testified). But often it was not. That meant that even if guilt was clear, it was unprovable. And eliminating receivers is unusually important, because their crime is what supports burglary and theft.

Notes on Modern Crimes of Receiving Stolen Property

(1) *Consolidation of the Crimes of Larceny and Receiving.* Perhaps the most significant change in modern statutes is that they often consolidate receiving stolen property, as well as larceny, false pretenses, and embezzlement, into a single offense. This consolidation removes the need to prove whether the possessor of recently stolen property stole it personally or received it.

(2) *Addition of "Concealing."* A number of statutes added the words "or concealing" as an alternative to "receiving." This extended the crime to the person who received the property with a clean mind, then concealed the property after learning it had been stolen and deciding to deprive the owner of it.

(3) *Police Stings: Will They Be Impossible as a Means of Catching Receivers?* Imagine an undercover operation in which an officer, posing as a burglar, goes to a pawn shop reputed to buy stolen merchandise. Assume that the undercover officer sells a watch worth $200 to the pawn broker for $15, after telling the pawn broker that "I got the watch in a heist last week." In truth, the new watch has been loaned to the police by a local jewelry store. Is the pawn broker guilty of receiving stolen property? If not, how should the police conduct such sting operations?

Some decisions have held that the pawn broker cannot be guilty, here, because the underlying crime of larceny is not present (the property was not stolen but consensually borrowed, so the defendant never received "stolen property"). In fact, even if law enforcement officers intercept a theft and use that very stolen property to conduct a sting, some courts have held that the property no longer is "stolen" because it was sold to the receiver by officers having lawful possession. Modern statutes often change this rule.

(4) *Modern Statutes.* Many of these problems and others have been addressed by modern statutes that reflect the importance of receivers in motivating burglaries and thefts. These statutes may include some or all of the following features:

(a) *Knowledge.* Proof of knowledge that the property is stolen (a frequent failure-of-proof defense) still is required to be found beyond a reasonable doubt. BUT. . . .

(b) *Corroboration.* Many jurisdictions that require corroboration of accomplice testimony to prove guilt for most crimes have removed the corroboration requirement for receiving. The thief's testimony can be sufficient.

(c) *Similar Transactions.* Usually, rules of evidence exclude proof of separate crimes of the same general kind, but some modern statutes make these separate crimes broadly admissible in receiving cases, irrespective of the usual rules. Thus, the state may be permitted to show the defendant also possessed other stolen property.

(d) *Recordkeeping.* In many statutes, recordkeeping requirements are imposed on pawn shops or second-hand dealers, and the absence of records creates the presumption of knowledge.

(e) *Stings by Law Enforcement.* Some statutes provide that even if the property isn't stolen, the offense is complete if the receiver believes a law enforcement officer who says that it is. And some statutes expressly authorize the use of deception and severely limit the usual entrapment defense.

Is it appropriate to single out this offense, receiving, for all of these special rules that facilitate convictions of receivers?

(5) *"Unexplained Possession of Recently Stolen Property" as Supporting an Inference of Knowledge.* In *Uyamadu v. State*, 359 S.W.3d 753 (Tex. App. 2011), the court made clear that proof of *mens rea* "almost invariably depends upon circumstantial evidence" in a theft-by-receiving case. In particular, many jurisdictions quote the common-law principle that unexplained possession of recently stolen property is itself evidence from which "the factfinder may draw an inference of guilt." The privilege against self-incrimination probably means that "unexplained" here really means "improbable" or "unexplainable," and usually, there is other evidence of the defendant's state of mind, as there was in the *Uyamadu* case. Should the fact that the defendant possesses property of a kind that it is extremely improbable that he or she would possess (hundreds of thousands of dollars' worth of unusual merchandise, or a rare Picasso painting), coupled with the fact that it was stolen last week, be sufficient for conviction?

§ 7.05 Mens Rea: Defendants Who (Unreasonably) Believe That Taking Is Not Wrongful

MORISSETTE v. UNITED STATES, 342 U.S. 246 (1952). Morissette entered a practice bombing range owned by the United States, in spite of a sign that said "Danger—Keep Out." He hunted but did not obtain a deer. Seeking to meet his expenses, he carried away and sold (for $84) three tons of spent casings from simulated bombs, which were lying in heaps and rusting. He was convicted under a federal statute, 18 U.S.C. § 641, covering "whoever embezzles, steals, purloins, or knowingly converts" property of the United States. The statute did not contain any mens rea requirement.

Morissette's defense was that he had "no intention of stealing" but thought that the property was "abandoned, unwanted, and considered of no value." The trial judge, however, instructed the jury that the crime was complete if Morissette acted without permission, even if he believed the property was abandoned. The jury convicted Morissette. The Supreme Court, through Justice Jackson, here reverses. The federal statute does not enact a strict liability crime. Instead, it incorporates, by implication, the mens rea of the common law offense of larceny:

> Neither this Court nor, so far as we are aware, any other has undertaken to delineate a precise line ... for distinguishing between crimes that require a mental element and crimes that do not. ... The conclusion reached in the *Balint* and *Behrman* cases [which applied strict liability to regulatory and drug offenses] has our approval. ... [But] [a] quite different question here is whether we will expand the doctrine of crimes without intent to include those charged here. ...

> Congress ... omitted any express prescription of criminal intent from the enactment before us in the light of an unbroken course of judicial decision ... holding intent inherent in this class of offense, even when not expressed in a statute. ...

> Had the statute applied to conversions without qualification, it would have made crimes of all unwitting, inadvertent and unintended conversions. [Instead, it expressly requires "knowing" conversion.] ... [I]t is not apparent how Morissette could have knowingly or intentionally converted property that he did not know could be converted, as would be the case if it was in fact abandoned or if he truly believed it to be abandoned. ...

> ... Had the jury convicted on proper instructions it would be the end of the matter. ... [But alternatively, jurors who were instructed that intent was required] might have concluded that the heaps of spent casings left in the hinterland to rust away presented an appearance of unwanted and abandoned junk, and that lack of any conscious deprivation of property ... was indicated ... Had they done so, that too would have been the end of the matter. [Reversed.]

Notes and Questions

(1) *Even an Unreasonable Belief Requires Acquittal for Larceny.* Larceny is defined so that sometimes a subjective mistake, however unreasonable, requires acquittal if it is sincerely believed, because the mistake is inconsistent with the mens rea of "intent to deprive."

(2) *Sometimes, Even a Misapprehension of the Law, such as a Mistake about Who Has Title, Can Negate Theft.* Imagine that the defendant legally has lost title to a certain piece of property to someone else, perhaps through a government-forced sale or judicial decision. But the defendant misunderstands the law, sincerely thinks she still is the "true owner," and takes back the property. There is an argument that this act is not theft, because there is no intent to deprive the true owner of the property. The mens rea of intent to deprive the true owner cannot exist if the alleged "thief" sincerely considers himself or herself the true owner.

Problem 7G (Theft Mens Rea): Variations on the "I Didn't Know It Belonged to Someone Else" Defense

Consider the following episodes and analyze whether they actually describe larcenous conduct:

(1) *The jury disbelieves Morissette* and decides, beyond a reasonable doubt, that he was not in fact mistaken and knew the property was not abandoned. The conviction is valid. Why?

(2) *The jury concludes that Morissette was grossly negligent* and, indeed, was incredibly foolish in believing the property was abandoned. But the jury believes (or has a reasonable doubt about whether) he so believed. (Not larceny. Why?)

(3) *Morrissette enters a modern grocery store* and sees, next to the other goods offered for sale, a commodity that is fat-free and advertises this fact by large letters saying "FREE" (meaning "free of fat," not "free to take"). He places the commodity inside his jacket and takes it without paying. Upon being apprehended, he protests, "But . . . but . . . I thought it was '*free*'!"

(4) *Morrissette thinks the theft statute makes it legal to take anything labeled "free,"* *even if the owner does not mean to give it away for free.* Now, imagine that Morrisette testifies that he knew perfectly well that "FREE" meant fat-free, not free to take. He knew that the item belonged to someone else and that the owner did not mean to authorize anyone to take it without paying. "But my understanding of theft law is that if it says free, no matter what the owner means by that word, anyone can take it, and it's not stealing." Does this amateur-lawyer reasoning exonerate him?

Problem 7H (Theft Mens Rea): "The Bank Made a Mistake. Do I Get to Keep the Money?"

(1) *A Problem: What if Your Bank Makes a Million-Dollar Error in Posting Your Account Balance (Do You Get to Keep the Money)?: United States v. Rogers*, 289 F.2d 433 (4th Cir. 1961). There have been several cases in which the defendant has requested that a bank provide the defendant's account balance and in which the bank, through clerical error, has provided the customer access to a much larger sum of money. Imagine a defendant whose account contains a balance of $41.06, but to whom the bank erroneously reports instead an amount a million dollars larger: $1,000,041.06. (Usually, the defendant in these circumstances leaves the bank shell-shocked, returns several times to check the balance, finally asks for small bills, puts the money in a satchel, and disappears. As the prosecutor argued to the jury in one such case, the defendant enters the bank "with a heart full of larceny" and leaves "with a sack full of money.")

(2) *Does This Conduct Amount to Bank Larceny?* The applicable provision of the federal bank larceny statute (see above) has been interpreted to cover common law larceny and other historical offenses. Can the defendant be convicted of larceny in these circumstances? In the case cited above, Rogers's removal of the money from the bank was held to be bank larceny. Is this holding correct as to mens rea?

§ 7.06 Gap Fillers: Criminal Conduct Not Covered by Some Modern Theft Statutes

> Read MPC § 223.7, 223.9 [theft of service, unauthorized use of vehicles] in the MPC Appendix.

Notes on Theft of Service and Related Crimes

(1) *Theft of Service.* Even after consolidation, modern statutes still do not reach all conduct that ought to be criminalized. In § 7.01 of this chapter, we noted *State v. Lund*, where Lund "stole" computer services. The Virginia Supreme Court acquitted him of larceny, because it decided that what he misappropriated (computer processing) was not "property." This principle has prompted the enactment of theft-of-service laws and other kinds of laws covering intangibles. Consider the MPC provision cited above and evaluate whether it would cover Lund's conduct.

(2) *Joyriding and "Unauthorized Use of a Vehicle"* In *People v. Brown*, also in § 7.01, the court held that Brown's taking of a bicycle could not fit any common-law theft crime if he intended only to take, ride, and abandon it. Consider this case in light of the similar taking of automobiles today. Would the MPC provision cited above, covering unauthorized use of vehicles (§ 223.9), cover this conduct?

Notes on Other Theft-Related Offenses, from Forgery to Deceptive Business Practices

(1) *Forgery, Simulation, Credit, Check, Business, and Computer Crimes.* Consider the coverage of the crimes defined by modern consolidated theft statutes, such as Colorado's, and their application to the following cases:

(a) *Forgery and Related Crimes.* (1) A defendant prepares a "check" on a form that appears to be that of a wealthy individual, signs that person's name, and gives it to another person as a sample of how well the defendant can imitate commercial paper. (2) Another defendant prints phony $100 bills resembling United States currency and passes them at a retail store.

(b) *Credit Offenses and Checks.* (1) A teenager buys a dozen CDs at a store with a parent's credit card by falsely representing that the parent who owns the card has authorized the teenager to use it (in fact, the teenager did not ask permission). (2) A defendant uses a check drawn on insufficient funds to buy a watch and fails to respond to numerous notices sent by the merchant.

(c) *Business Practices.* (1) A business person carelessly sells a pizza with infectious bacteria. (2) A business person pays $1,000 to an employee of another firm for the promise of awarding a lucrative contract.

Many of these acts would not be covered by any of this historic theft-related crimes.

(2) *Reconsidering Lund v. Commonwealth: Computer Crime.* We already have considered whether Lund's unauthorized use of computer time might fit a theft-of-service statute. If not, might it fit a statute defining computer crimes? Consider the section below.

§ 7.07 Modern Specialized Areas

[A] Computer Crimes

The universal presence of computers has made computer crimes, including related thefts, a serious issue. Every jurisdiction and the federal government have enacted statutes punishing vast arrays of computer crimes.

United States v. Thomas

877 F.3d 591 (5th Cir. 2017)

Gregg Costa, Circuit Judge:

Michael Thomas worked as the Information Technology Operations Manager for ClickMotive, LP, a software and webpage hosting company. . . . [He] embarked on a weekend campaign of electronic sabotage. He deleted over 600 files, disabled backup operations, eliminated employees from a group email a client used to contact the company, diverted executives' emails to his personal account, and set a "time bomb" that would result in employees being unable to remotely access the company's network after Thomas submitted his resignation. Once ClickMotive discovered what Thomas did, it incurred over $130,000 in costs to fix these problems.

A jury found Thomas guilty of "knowingly caus[ing] the transmission of a program, information, code, or command, and as a result of such conduct, intentionally caus[ing] damage without authorization, to a protected computer." 18 U.S.C. § 1030(a)(5)(A). Thomas challenges the "without authorization" requirement of this provision of the Computer Fraud and Abuse Act. He contends that because his IT job gave him full access to the system and required him to "damage" the system—for example, at times his duties included deleting certain files—his conduct did not lack authorization. . . . [Thomas also argues that the Act is so vague that he lacked notice of his potential crimes.] But we conclude that Thomas's conduct falls squarely within the ordinary meaning of the statute and affirm his conviction. . . .

Thomas was not happy when his friend in the IT department was fired. It was not just a matter of loyalty to his former colleague; a smaller IT staff meant more work for Thomas. So Thomas, to use his word, "tinkered" with the company's system. . . .

At trial, company employees and outside IT experts testified that none of the problems ClickMotive experienced as a result of Thomas's actions would be attributable to a normal system malfunction. They further stated that Thomas's actions were not consistent with normal troubleshooting and maintenance or consistent with mistakes made by a novice. . . .

Employees explained, however, that there were policies prohibiting interfering with ClickMotive's normal course of business and the destruction of its assets . . . . Thomas's own Employment Agreement specified he was bound by policies that were reasonably necessary to protect ClickMotive's legitimate interests . . . .

The jury instructions included the statutory definition of "damage," which is "any impairment to the integrity or availability of data, a program, a system, or information." . . . After the jury returned a guilty verdict, the district court sentenced Thomas . . . to time served (which was the four months since he had been detained . . .) . . . , and ordered restitution of $131,391.21. . . .

II. . . .

Because Thomas's argument that he was authorized to damage a computer seems nonsensical at first glance, it is helpful at the outset to explain the steps he takes to get there. He first points out that his job duties included "routinely deleting data, removing programs, and taking systems offline for diagnosis and maintenance." . . . Thomas says this conduct damaged the computer within the meaning of the Computer Fraud and Abuse Act because damage is defined to just mean "any impairment to the integrity or availability of data, a program, a system, or information," 18 U.S.C. § 1030(e)(8); there is no requirement of harm. And the damage he caused by engaging in these routine tasks was not "without authorization" because it was part of his job. So far, so good. Next comes the critical leap: Thomas argues that because he was authorized to damage the computer when engaging in these routine tasks, *any* damage he caused while an employee was not "without authorization." Thus he cannot be prosecuted under section 1030(a)(5)(A). This argument is far reaching. If Thomas is correct, then the damage statute would not reach any employee who intentionally damaged a computer system as long as any part of that employee's job included deleting files or taking systems offline.

Thomas's support for reading the statute to cover only individuals who "had no rights, limited or otherwise [to] impair" a system comes from cases addressing the separate "access" provisions of section 1030. *See, e.g., LVRC Holdings LLC v. Brekka,* 581 F.3d 1127, 1133 (9th Cir. 2009) ("[A] person who uses a computer 'without authorization' has no rights, limited or otherwise, to access the computer in question) . . . . But there are important differences between the "access" and "damage" crimes that make it inappropriate to import access case law into the damage statute. . . .

Section 1030(a)(5)(A) is the only independent "damage" provision, meaning it does not also require a lack of authorization to access the computer. . . . It prohibits "intentionally caus[ing] damage without authorization." . . . [T]he plain meaning of the damage provision is that it makes it a crime to intentionally impair a computer system without permission. And notably, it applies to particular acts causing damage that lacked authorization. . . . Nothing in the statutory text says it does not apply to intentional acts of damage that lacked permission if the employee was allowed to engage at other times in other acts that impaired the system.

Crimes involving unauthorized *access* are more numerous in the Computer Fraud and Abuse Act. *See, e.g.*, 18 U.S.C. § 1030(a)(1), (2), (3). Some of these provisions distinguish between "intentionally access[ing] a computer without authorization," and "exceed[ing] authorized access." ... To give meaning to the separate provisions, courts have interpreted "access without authorization" as targeting outsiders who access victim systems, while "exceeds authorized access" is applied to "insiders," such as employees of a victim company. *See* [*United States v.*] *Valle*, 807 F.3d at 524 [((2d Cir. 2015))] (citing *United States v. Nosal*, 676 F.3d 854, 858 (9th Cir. 2012) (en banc)). It is this attempt to police that statutory line— between those who have no permission to access a system and those who have some permission to access but exceed it—that led to the language Thomas invokes about a "no authorization" case being limited to a person with "no right[], limited or otherwise, to *access* the computer in question." This ensures that "access without authorization" applies to outsiders....

None of these concerns translates to the damage statute. "Without authorization" modifies damage rather than access. *Id.* at 1661 (explaining that the federal damage statute uses "without authorization" in "a very different way" from how it is used in the access statutes).... Because section 1030(a)(5)(A) is the one subsection of the damage statute that also applies to insiders, it would make no sense to import a limitation from the access statutes that is aimed at excluding insider liability....

Nor is there a significant threat that liability under the damage statute would extend to largely innocuous conduct.... Applying the damage statute to employees like Thomas... does not extend the law beyond what Congress intended. The Senate Report on the 1996 amendments to the Computer Fraud and Abuse Act stated that section 1030(a)(5)(A) "protect[s] computers and computer systems... from damage both by outsiders, who gain access to a computer without authorization, and by insiders, who intentionally damage a computer." S. Rep. No. 104–357, at 9 (1996). It characterized these dual threats as "outside hackers" and "malicious insiders." By providing immunity from the damage statute to any "malicious insider" who was permitted to cause "damage" in some situations as part of his job duties, Thomas's interpretation would substantially curtail the statute's intended reach....

We conclude that Section 1030(a)(5)(A) prohibits intentionally damaging a computer system when there was no permission to engage in that particular act of damage....

III.

What we have just said about the straightforward application of the damage statute to Thomas's conduct also dooms his claim that the law is unconstitutionally vague. That is because even if a statute might be vague when applied to some situations, "a defendant whose conduct is clearly prohibited cannot be the one making that challenge." . . .

[In addition to scholarly writing that includes this very situation as an example of violation of the Act, Thomas's own statements] undermine[] the contention that Thomas lacked notice that his conduct was criminal. . . . [B]efore the FBI had contacted Thomas, he told the friend whose firing had set this in motion that "he thought he might have broken the law." Which law, the friend inquired? Thomas's response: "the Computer Fraud and Abuse Act." [Conviction affirmed.]

Notes and Questions

(1) *"Access" Crimes and "Damage" Crimes.* The crime of accessing a computer (entering electronically to see contents) requires that the access be "without authorization." The crime of damaging a computer is different: It applies even if the access (and some acts of damage) are authorized, if the particular act of damage is "without authorization."

(2) *"Damage" Is a Term of Art, and Damage Can Be Innocuous.* A second confusing aspect of the law is that "damage" just means making changes. An IT employee has authorization to make some changes, which are technically acts of "damage." The crime of damaging is committed when the damage is inflicted "without authorization."

(3) *"Access" Crimes Are So Broadly Defined That They Become Too Broad if Taken Literally: United States v. Valle, 807 F.3d 508 (2d Cir. 2015).* Valle was a police officer who used department computers during work for personal business, and his personal business was strange: Valle was interested in sexual fetishes, and he participated in chat rooms that depicted and discussed sexual murder, torture and mutilation. The Government argued that his conviction should be affirmed because his accessing of the computer for this purpose was "without authorization." The court disagreed and reversed Valle's conviction:

> . . . [C]ommon usage of "authorization" suggests that one "accesses a computer without authorization" if he accesses a computer without permission to do so at all. *See, e.g., LVRC Holdings LLC v. Brekka,* 581 F.3d 1127, 1133 (9th Cir.2009). . . .
>
> Whatever the apparent merits of imposing criminal liability may seem to be *in this case,* we must construe the statute knowing that our interpretation of "exceeds authorized access" will govern many other situations. *See* 18 U.S.C. § 1030(e)(6). . . . [We] are obligated to "construe criminal statutes narrowly so that Congress will not unintentionally turn ordinary citizens into criminals." While the Government might promise that it would not prosecute an individual for checking Facebook at work, . . . [a] court should not uphold a highly problematic interpretation of a statute merely because the Government promises to use it responsibly. . . .

[B] Identity Theft

Notes on Identity Theft

(1) *The Kinds of Identity Theft.* Identity theft occurs when people use various techniques to obtain detailed personal information about others, then use that information to assume that person's identity. Perhaps the identity theft is designed to obtain property by charging a purchase to someone else's credit account by representing that the thief is the account holder. Another reason is to escape apprehension by assuming another's identity. If identity theft is used to obtain property, the crime could be larceny (perhaps through larceny by trick) or false pretenses, but if no property is actually taken the traditional theft crimes may be inapposite.

(2) *Statutes Addressing the Problem.* Many jurisdictions address this problem by enacting identity theft crimes. These offenses punish a defendant who, without permission, uses information about another person (such as telephone number, name, address, driver's license, or social security number) for the purpose of representing that the other person's information is the defendant's own information. The statutes also prohibit the defendant from allowing another person to use the defendant's information to commit fraud. *See, e.g.,* Ohio Rev. Code § 2913.49. These modern provisions create a host of technical issues about coverage. *See, e.g., Lee v. Superior Court,* 989 P.2d 1277 (Cal. 2000) (identity theft includes using the identity of someone who is dead).

(3) *Identity Theft under Federal Law.* Crimes that include appropriating the identity of another person can sometimes be addressed as mail or wire fraud under federal law (see above). But those crimes do not always reach harmful conduct, including some kinds of identity theft. The Federal False Identity Crime Control Act, 18 U.S.C. § 1028, therefore covers various misuses of "means of identification." In *United States v. Agarwal,* 314 Fed. Appx. 473 (3d Cir. Nov. 20, 2008), for example, the defendant "paid an undercover FBI agent $150.00 for a counterfeit Carnegie Mellon University student identification card, with which he had hoped to gain access to various campus facilities." One issue was whether the offense was connected to interstate commerce (the court held, yes). Notice that this crime would not be addressed by most statutes covering theft of property (or perhaps even theft of services), but the court affirmed Agarwal's conviction.

United States v. Gandy

926 F.3d 248 (6th Cir. 2019)

RONALD LEE GILMAN, Circuit Judge.

Anthony Gandy, his brother Christopher Gandy, their sister Sharon Gandy-Micheau, and Sharon's husband Durand Micheau sought tax refunds for 21 separate fictitious trusts that they created. The defendants' scheme was to submit fictitious tax returns to the Internal Revenue Service (IRS) for the purpose of claiming refunds for nonexistent excess withholding. They were successful in obtaining refund checks based upon many of these returns, receiving over $360,000 in ill-gotten money [and making more than $1 million in claims]. The defendants were convicted of several crimes, including . . . aggravated identity theft. [Aggravated identity theft is simply identity theft coupled with one of certain specified felonies.] . . .

Anthony and Sharon . . . challenge their convictions [for] aggravated identity theft, in violation of 18 U.S.C. § 1028A(a)(1). They argue that the record is devoid of evidence proving that they knew that they were using the names and personal identifying information of real people. . . .

A conviction for aggravated identity theft under 18 U.S.C. § 1028A(a)(1) requires proof of the following elements: (1) the defendant committed a specified predicate felony; (2) the defendant knowingly transferred, possessed, or used a means of identification of another person without lawful authority; (3) the defendant knew that the means of identification belonged to another person; and (4) the transfer, possession, or use was during and in relation to the predicate felony offense. Section 1028A(a)(1) also provides for a mandatory minimum sentence of two years' imprisonment, to be served consecutively with sentences imposed for convictions on other counts. . . .

The predicate felonies in the present case are mail fraud and conspiracy to commit mail fraud, both of which are enumerated as predicate felonies under § 1028A(c). . . . But Anthony and Sharon argue that there is no evidence in the record proving the third element of aggravated identity theft — that they knew that they were using the names and personal identifying information of real people. . . .

[W]e conclude that [there is sufficient] evidence demonstrating that Anthony and Sharon knew that they were using the names and personal identifying information of real people. This evidence includes the two notebooks found in Sharon's house that had personal identifying information of identity-theft victims. She also had some of these victims' original identification documents. And her trash contained documents and other items demonstrating that she and her husband were using these stolen identities in the fraudulent-tax-refund scheme. In total, law-enforcement officers recovered information in Sharon's house relating to almost 100 different identity-theft victims. [Evidence against Anthony was analogous.] . . . [Affirmed.]

§ 7.08 Review Problems Based on Newspaper Reports

Note on These "Newspaper Cases"

These are descriptions of cases involving theft-related issues, taken from recent newspaper reports. As before, the reports have been rewritten to emphasize the legal questions that they raise, but the facts are preserved as reported. And as before, these cases should help you to review the coverage of this chapter.

[A] Headline: Auditors Say the Port Authority's "Fun Fund" Broke No Laws

HOUSTON—The Port Authority of Houston spent almost $40,000 of its "promotional and development fund" on retreats at expensive resorts, employee picnics, and even jewelry for Port Commissioners. But state auditors say that officials who spent these funds did not break any laws.

The officials called the money they spent "the fun fund." They used $5,670 for a retreat at a country club in Austin, $9,000 for a hotel meeting, $22,000 for picnics, and $2,540 for Port-insignia cuff links and earrings for the Commissioners. Auditors also noted several other expenditures that they would have questioned if made by other agencies, such as $19,000 for luncheons in New York, $12,000 for coaster sets given as gifts, $32,000 for golf fees, and $43,000 for a reception.

"This may be legal, but it's probably improper," said State Representative Rick Noriega, D-Houston, who was one of the legislators who had called for the audit. "Here you've got a public entity that receives taxpayer dollars, and this just cries out for more accountability." Noriega said that he might offer legislation to require the Port Authority to conform to the same purchasing limits as those applicable to state agencies generally. But Jim Edmonds, Chair of the Port Authority, said that he could not see anything troublesome about the audit: "I didn't think they would find anything material, and they didn't." He added that he would oppose any legislation restricting the Port Authority's spending.

(1) *A Case of No Mens Rea, No Actus Reus, or Both?* Can you explain why the officials involved in these expenditures were not guilty of any theft-related crime, even if the expenditures could be labeled "improper"? Consider, among other issues, the mission of the Port Authority, which includes promoting the use of the Port by others, as well as the possibility that any alleged "impropriety" was ambiguous.

(2) *Would the Case Be Different if a Commissioner Had Induced Managers of the "Fun Fund" to Buy Other Jewelry, Worth $10,000, Chosen by That Commissioner, for the Commissioner's Own Use?* If so, how is such a case distinguishable from that in which the fund was used to buy "cuff links and earrings" (with Port Authority insignia) for Commissioners? If there is no viable distinction, how could the insignia-jewelry purchases be considered lawful?

[B] Headline: Hundreds of Rotting Corpses Lead to Multiple Charges against Crematory Operator

LAFAYETTE, GA.—Brent Ray Marsh found a way to steal from hundreds of families whose loved ones he was paid to cremate. His scheme was simple. He simply discarded the corpses but kept the money and sent ashes of various different origins to his victims.

So far, 339 decaying bodies have been found on the crematory grounds. Law enforcement officers have begun to drain a lake nearby, because last month, a skull and torso were found there. Yesterday, the State of Georgia filed 56 additional charges against Marsh, bringing the total number of theft-by-deception charges against him to 174. Identifications of bodies and communications with deceived victims are incomplete, and therefore it has not been possible to charge Marsh in all possible cases. Marsh stacked the bodies in sheds and vaults, in holes, and in piles on the ground.

(1) *What Crimes Might Be at Issue, if the Historical Law of Theft Governed Marsh's Conduct?* Actually, statutes in Georgia define several separate theft crimes, including: (a) "theft by taking," which generally corresponds to straight larceny; (b) "theft by deception," which seems to correspond to both larceny by trick and theft by false pretenses; and (c) "theft by conversion," which roughly corresponds to embezzlement because it covers actors who rightfully obtain possession (although this crime in Georgia is broader than historical embezzlement). This Georgia system appears to reduce but not avoid the guesswork necessary in some common-law cases, and "theft by deception" is probably the appropriate crime here. But consider the historical theft crimes. If Marsh had committed his acts in a jurisdiction that required choosing among larceny, larceny by trick, theft by false pretenses, or embezzlement, which crime should be charged? Might it make a difference whether Marsh obtained the victims' money before or after deciding not to perform the services for which he was paid?

(2) *If the Conduct Were Subject to a Consolidated Theft Law Adapted from the Model Penal Code, What Differences Would There Be in the Application of the Law to Marsh's Case?* Consider the application of the law in a state (such as Massachusetts or Colorado) that has adopted a modified version of the Model Penal Code's theft provisions.

[C] Headline: Court Orders Ex-Employee Not to Withdraw Funds Mistakenly Deposited in Her Account

HOUSTON—A Verizon Wireless manager testified yesterday that she told Tonya Young the exact amount of her severance package before Young was laid off. "It was fully explained to her how much she was to receive: $10,014.49," Connie Jackson told State District Judge Sherry Radack. But in an accounting error, Verizon sent a check with misplaced commas and a decimal point in the wrong place. The amount of the check, before taxes, was $1,001,449. "Taxes" reduced it to $709,471.38, which was $701,860.13 more than Young should have been paid.

By the time Verizon discovered the error and took action, Young had already spent more than $130,000 of the money, which she said she had used "to pay bills." Verizon sued Young, alleging that she "continue[d] to aggressively seek to make" transfers out of her bank accounts, into which she had deposited the money, and that Young said she did not plan to return any of the funds. Before her layoff, Young made $39,500 a year as a customer service clerk. Judge Radack issued an injunction ordering Young not to withdraw or transfer any further funds.

(1) *What Historical Offense, if Any, Might Cover Ms. Young's Conduct?* Consider whether Ms. Young's conduct would amount to larceny, theft by false pretenses, or embezzlement.

(2) *What Result Would You Expect Under a Theft Consolidation Statute Adapted from the Model Penal Code?* The MPC consolidates theft crimes and redefines them. Is it possible that Young's conduct would be theft under a statute adapted from the MPC?

Chapter 8

Property Crimes That Threaten Personal Security: Robbery, Extortion, and Burglary

"[Robbery] is the overcoming of resistance without the voluntary cooperation of the subject whose resistance is repressed: this is the test." — *State v. Snyder,* 172 P. 364 (Nev. 1918)

"He's a businessman. I'll make him an offer he can't refuse." — Don Vito Corleone, in Mario Puzo, *The Godfather* (1969)

§ 8.01 Robbery

[A] The Traditional Definition of Robbery (And Its Odd Results)

Notes on Robbery as a "Theft-Plus" Crime

(1) *Robbery as a Crime of "Theft Plus Violence."* We have seen that larceny, embezzlement, and false pretenses all involve theft by taking or deceit, but none requires the use of force or threats of force. But physical harm makes theft more serious, and the law therefore recognizes the offense of "robbery." The traditional robbery definition was the use or threat of force to take property from the person or presence of the victim with the intent to deprive permanently. *See, e.g.,* Kan. Stat. § 21–5420 ("robbery is knowingly taking property from the person or presence of another by force or by threat of bodily harm to any person").

(2) *"From the Person or Presence of Another."* Robbery traditionally required a theft from the person or presence of another. The term "presence" was not taken literally. As long as the item was taken in close physical proximity to the robbery victim, the "presence" requirement was satisfied. For example, if a victim was tied up in one room of a two room office, and the thief went into the second room and took cash from a drawer, case law would find the theft occurred from the victim's presence even though the victim never saw the thief take the money. But does it make sense to limit the definition of robbery to takings of property from the physical person or presence of the defendant, or should it be sufficient that the perpetrator

used violence to take property from the victim? (The Model Penal Code removes any such requirement by providing only that the force must have been used "in the course of committing a theft.")

(3) *Aggravated Robbery.* American jurisdictions have created another version of the crime called *aggravated robbery,* which occurs when the defendant uses deadly force or, in some jurisdictions, inflicts serious bodily injury.

(4) *Historically, Robbery Had Technical Elements.* At common law, formal elements sometimes defeated the policy of punishing serious violence. Consider the following case.

State v. Holmes
295 S.W. 71 (Mo. 1927)

[Holmes answered an advertisement offering diamonds for sale at the seller's home. He asked to examine the diamonds. While holding them in his hand, he drew a pistol, forced the seller (Mrs. Newell) into her basement, and locked the door. The court here reverses Holmes's conviction for robbery because the force was not used to *take* the property, as common-law robbery required, but only to *keep* it after the defendant had already acquired possession.]

[T]he taking . . . must be accomplished by violence to the person who theretofore had the property in his possession, or must be accomplished by putting such person in fear of immediate injury to his person. . . . [A]ppellant was actually holding the diamonds before he drew the revolver, [and thus] he had accomplished [the taking] before he put [Mrs. Newell] in fear. . . .

[T]he court should have instructed the jury that it might convict of [grand larceny] and should have directed an acquittal of the crime of robbery.

Notes and Questions

(1) *Assessing Holmes.* If the offense includes not merely theft but also the thrusting of a firearm in the victim's face, most people would regard the crime as more blameworthy than a nonviolent theft. Accordingly, perhaps it should not make a difference whether the firearm is used to take the property or to keep it after taking it. Is the result in *Holmes* sensible? (Modern formulations find a robbery when force is used to "maintain control" as well as "obtain" it.)

(2) *Theft as an Afterthought to Assault.* Consider a defendant who violently assaults a victim from a non-economic motive, such as anger, and then, seeing a wallet protruding, takes the victim's wallet as an afterthought. As *Holmes* suggests, this conduct was not robbery at common law, because the force was not used for the purpose of obtaining property. Is this result consistent with policy? (Modern laws cover crimes "in the course of" theft.)

(3) *Carjacking: Is There a Need for a Separate Crime, or Is the Crime Appropriately Defined as Robbery?* Just as "joyriding" is a larceny spinoff crime involving only a

temporary taking of a vehicle, the crime of "carjacking" is car theft involving the use or threat of violence. *See, e.g.,* 18 U.S.C. §2119. The intent may be satisfied even if it is conditional—the thief would have caused death or serious bodily injury if the driver did not surrender the vehicle. *See, e.g., Holloway v. United States,* 526 U.S. 1 (1999) (interpreting federal carjacking statute). Some carjackings are robberies. But a new crime was needed, because robbery doesn't always apply. Consider the following problem.

Problem 8A: "Is It Robbery?"

(1) *Is Carjacking Robbery . . . Or Not? Moorer v. United States,* 868 A.2d 137 (D.C. 2005). Willie Moorer approached Steven Trowell while Moorer was apparently high on drugs or alcohol and repeatedly asked for a cigarette. Trowell, talking to another man, attempted to ignore Moorer. Then, Moorer announced that he was "going to drive [Trowell's] car." He pulled out a gun and held it at his waist. Trowell three times "told Moorer he wasn't" going to drive the car. Moorer then pointed the gun at the center of Trowell's forehead and said that he was "going to show [Trowell] how much of a bitch ass [expletive]" Trowell was. Trowell surrendered the car, and Moorer "flop[ped] in . . . [and] slammed it in gear." There was a passenger, Ms. Davis, in the front seat, whom Moorer told he had "to go kill somebody" and asked if she wanted to "come along." She said no, and he let her out. Trowell's car was found, later, a short distance away, abandoned by Moorer. At trial, Moorer testified that he intended only to "go around the block and come back" so as to "mess with" Trowell, and denied using "any force at all" (although the latter testimony must have seemed incredible to the jury).

(2) *Do We Need a Separate Crime of Carjacking?* The appellate court, in affirming Moorer's conviction, considered why the distinct crime of carjacking exists. One reason may be that many jurisdictions define robbery by following the Model Penal Code, requiring force or threat while the defendant is "in the course of committing theft." If Moorer's intention was to "go around the block and come back" or to abandon the vehicle a short distance away, he had no intent to permanently deprive the owner and he could not be acting "in the course of committing theft." Since robbery may not apply, it makes sense to define the new crime of carjacking. Can you explain?

(3) *Shouldn't It Be a Crime to Take a Car at Gunpoint Even if the Defendant Doesn't Drive It Away?* As the D.C. court also held, carjacking is defined so that "it can be committed by putting a gun to the head of the person in possession and ordering the person out of the car." Thus, movement or "asportation of the vehicle is not required for carjacking." But since asportation is required for theft, and again, a "course of committing theft" is required in many jurisdictions for robbery, robbery might not cover a carjacking where the car is not moved at all. Can you explain?

[B] Contemporary Prohibitions of Robbery

> Read MPC § 222.1(1) [defining robbery to include force used "in the course of committing theft," which includes force during "an attempt to commit theft or in flight after the attempt or commission"] in the MPC Appendix.

Notes and Questions

(1) *Applying the MPC to a Robbery Case Such as Holmes, in Which the Force Is Used After the Taking, Only to Maintain Control of the Property.* Under the MPC and many state codes, the scope of robbery has been increased by extending it to situations where force is used before, during, or after the actual taking of property. Thus, the MPC robbery provision covers the use of force "in the course of committing a theft." MPC § 222.1(1); *see also* Tex. Penal Code § 29.01 (defining "in the course of" committing a theft as conduct occurring in an attempt to commit, during the commission, or in immediate flight after the attempt or commission of theft). Under the MPC, Holmes would be guilty of robbery even though he used force only after the taking. Can you explain?

(2) *A Non-Economic Assault, Followed by a Taking: Is the MPC Ambiguous Here?* Also, reconsider the accused robber in subsection A, note 2, above, who committed a non-economic assault and then took property as an afterthought. Does the MPC address this offense?

(3) *A Non-Aggravated Assault Combined with Theft: Is the MPC Definition of Robbery Inadequate?* The MPC robbery provision applies only if the defendant commits or threatens serious bodily injury (or threatens a serious felony such as rape or murder). "Serious bodily injury" is an objective, high standard, usually satisfied only by a "substantial risk of death" or "prolonged loss or impairment of the function of any bodily member or organ." MPC § 210.0. Imagine a defendant who "merely" beats a victim in order to take his or her property. Can you explain why this crime may not be robbery under the MPC? Many state robbery statutes require far less force than the MPC. *See, e.g.,* Minn. Stat. § 609.24 (uses or threatens the "imminent use of force"); N.Y. Pen. Law § 160.00 ("uses or threatens the immediate use of physical force").

(4) *Robbery Is Involved in the Majority of Death-Penalty Sentences, Usually with a Broad Definition: Bunch v. Commonwealth, 304 S.E.2d 271 (Va. 1983).* Capital murder is defined in a "murder-plus" manner: that is, murder combined with specified aggravating factors. One common kind of capital murder is murder during the commission of robbery. In fact, one might say that this is "the" prototype of capital murder, because about 2/3 of death sentences come from robbery-murders. Most of these death penalty cases use a broader, modern definition of robbery, not the narrower common law formula.

In *Bunch v. Commonwealth*, for example, the defendant killed the victim in her residence by hanging and shooting her. He then took her Rolex watch and expensive jewelry. The court defined robbery as a "common law offense": "the taking . . . of the personal property of another, from his person or in his presence, . . . by violence or intimidation." The court added that the violence "must precede or be concomitant with the taking." Understandably, Bunch argued that (1) there was no showing that he had taken the victim's property from her person or presence (as opposed to taking them from other parts of the residence), and (2) that there was no evidence of any linkage between the killing of the victim and the theft, especially since "at least one if not two hours elapsed between the shooting of [the victim] and the taking of the . . . property." The Virginia Supreme Court nevertheless affirmed Bunch's death sentence and rejected these arguments, stating that "the important considerations are that robbery was the motive for the killing and that Bunch had the intent to rob when he killed Thomas."

People v. Space

103 N.E.3d 1019 (Ill. App. 2019)

JUSTICE ROCHFORD delivered the judgment of the court, with opinion.

[The Illinois court here was called upon to review a conviction for felony murder. The questions presented included issues of causation, among others. In the course of that analysis, the court considered cases involving robbery that featured thefts after an assault or killing. Specifically, in *People v. Griffith*, 777 N.E.2d 459 (2002), and *People v. Stout*, 460 N.E.2d 1205 (Ill. 1984), Illinois courts upheld convictions for felony murder based on so-called "afterthought" robbery:]

The defendant in *Griffith* was living in the victim's apartment. Following an argument after the victim left the apartment, the defendant pried open the victim's safe in an attempt to take his cash but found no money. The victim then returned to the apartment. The defendant, fearing the victim would hurt him or call the police when he discovered that he had pried open the safe, beat and stabbed the victim. The defendant then took the victim's wallet. The defendant later made statements that he had killed the victim for the money. At trial, however, the defendant testified that he took the wallet as an "afterthought." The defendant was found guilty of felony murder and armed robbery. This court affirmed the defendant's convictions, finding:

> "The afterthought defense does not work. [The defendant] was able to take the money because he had rendered [the victim] helpless. The jury did not have to find [the defendant] formed the criminal intent to commit armed robbery before committing the murder. [*People v. Pitsonbarger*, 568 N.E.2d 783 (Ill. 1990)] ('it is sufficient that the State proved the elements of the crime and the accompanying felonies were part of the same criminal episode'). . . ."

A similar result was reached in *Stout*. There, the defendant and the codefendant argued with and then beat the victim because the victim refused to give the defendant a drink. During the beating, the defendant took the victim's watch. The defendant, on appeal, argued that he took the watch as an "afterthought." The appellate court affirmed the defendant's felony murder conviction based on the robbery, stating:

> "In any event, no Illinois case has stated that the fact that robbery is an afterthought of acts of beating prevents the operation of the felony murder rule. The rule is broad in scope. Responsibility attaches to an accused 'for those deaths which occur during a [forcible] felony and which are the foreseeable consequence of his initial criminal acts.' . . .".

As such, there was no requirement that the defendants in *Griffith* and *Stout* formed the intent to commit the robbery before they began to act in order for the State to establish a valid predicate felony. Rather, the robberies — the predicate felonies — began and were accomplished by the conduct that resulted in the victims' deaths. Accordingly, . . . a conviction for felony murder was appropriate.

[But the court still reversed this felony murder conviction. In a complex opinion, the court based its holding on causation and merger doctrines that are not relevant to the robbery issues here.]

STATE v. LOPEZ, 900 A.2d 779 (N.J. 2009). In several states, a theft done afterward does not support robbery. In *Lopez*, the New Jersey Supreme Court held that "afterthought robbery" does not exist in that state. The holding is an interpretation of the state's robbery statute, and specifically, what is meant by "course of committing theft":

> Our current statute, *N.J.S.A.* 2C:15–1(a), provides:

> . . . A person is guilty of robbery if, in the course of committing a theft, he: [injures, uses force on, or threatens another in certain ways; and]

> An act shall be deemed to be included in the phrase "in the course of committing a theft" if it occurs in an attempt to commit theft or in immediate flight after the attempt or commission. . . .

[T]he sequence of events is critical; the intention to steal must precede or be coterminous with the use of force. That is why a person who has stolen goods and thereafter uses violence in flight is guilty of robbery — the intention to commit the theft generated the violence. That model simply does not work where a violent fracas occurs for reasons other than theft, and the perpetrator later happens to take property from the victim. In the former example, the theft is the reason for the violence and a robbery has occurred. In the latter, the violence and the theft are unconnected, and the perpetrator is guilty of assault and theft but not of robbery.

Notes and Questions

(1) *Is an Afterthought Theft "Part of the Same Episode," or Are the "Theft and Violence Unconnected?"* Illinois follows the first approach, New Jersey the latter, with similar statutory language. As a matter of best definition, isn't the taking of property accomplished afterward by violence as serious as that resulting from a prior intention to take the property?

(2) *Reinforcement of the Modern View of Robbery as a Violent Crime, Not Primarily a Property Crime: Holder v. State*, 736 S.E.2d 449 (Ga. Ct. App. 2012). This incident was frightening:

> Four masked assailants entered the residence; they wore bandanas over their faces. Gillespie was made to sit down on a chair in the living room; his head was duct-taped and his hands were taped together. A gun was held to his neck at all times. An assailant armed with a gun forced Brown out of the bedroom where she had been sleeping and to the living room, where he began taping Brown's face. Two armed assailants moved Patterson from a bedroom to the living room; they duct-taped his hands, feet, and head. The assailants moved Johnson from the bedroom to the living room, where they duct-taped her hands, legs, and eyes.

One of the crimes at issue on appeal was a robbery in which the assailants "took Brown's purse and money but later returned them to her." The court said, defendant "Holder contends that the evidence was insufficient to support the conviction for armed robbery of Brown because one of the assailants returned to Brown her purse and money. We disagree." The court cited and interpreted the applicable robbery statute: "A person commits the offense of armed robbery when, with intent to commit theft, he takes property of another from the person or the immediate presence of another by use of an offensive weapon. . . . [T]he slightest change of location whereby the complete dominion of the property is transferred from the true owner to the trespasser is sufficient asportation to meet the statutory criterion." The court added, "It is not required that the property taken be permanently appropriated." The court further explained,

> In *Bramblett v. State*, the defendant kidnapped the victim and told her to drive her car to an automatic teller machine and to withdraw money for him. Nothing in the opinion suggests that the defendant ever actually touched the money . . . because the robbery was foiled when the defendant left the vehicle for a short time and the victim drove away with her money. This court held that [the defendant's actions] constituted a taking. Here, Brown's purse was taken forcibly, by use of a gun, while she was immobilized . . . .

(3) *Robbery as a Predicate for Capital Murder and the Death Penalty: Pope v. Netherland*, 113 F.3d 1384 (4th Cir. 1987). Questions about robbery appear often in

death penalty cases. In *Pope,* the court upheld Virginia's interpretation of common law robbery to include taking and concealment of the property before the murder, as not so "novel" as to violate due process. Because robbery was an aggravating offense, the court also upheld Pope's conviction for capital murder.

§ 8.02 Extortion and Related Offenses

Read Model Penal Code § 223.4 [theft by extortion] in the MPC Appendix, below.

Notes on the Definition of Extortion

(1) *A Threat to Injure Property or Reputation, Combined with an Intent to Extort Property of Another.* In many jurisdictions, the crime of extortion (called "blackmail" in the popular media) combines two elements: (a) an intent to obtain the property of another by means of (b) a threat to injure the property or reputation of another. Note that an intent to injure a person is *not* included in traditional extortion, though it is in the Model Penal Code and many states. The federal extortion statute, 18 U.S.C. § 875(d), includes these two elements and also adds the requirement of a communication in interstate commerce. "Pay me protection money or I'll blow up your building" is an extortionate communication, and so is "Pay me $10,000 or I'll tell the newspapers you had an extramarital affair."

(2) *The Overlap (and the Distinction) between Robbery and Extortion.* Depending on the robbery and extortion statutes, the facts may fit either or both offenses. But the distinction between robbery and extortion is that the core of traditional robbery is threatened or actual force against the person, while extortion typically is a threat against property or reputation in order to obtain something (usually property).

(3) *An Implicit (and Complex) Requirement: The Extortionate Threat Must Be "Wrongful."* But there is a complication in defining extortion. Legitimate threats are a part of life, and sometimes they can be a proper means of producing action by a person who does not want to do what should be done. "Pay me what you owe, or I will sue" is a threat, made to obtain another's property; but normally we do not think of it as extortion. And here is a subtler example. A contractor defrauded by a public figure states that he or she will "go to the newspapers" and ruin the public figure's reputation by exposing the fraud, unless the public figure "makes it right." Isn't publicity a lawful tool to induce reluctant people to do what they should? As you read the following case, consider where the line should be drawn between legitimate and wrongful threats.

United States v. Jackson

180 F.3d 55 (2d Cir. 1999)

KEARSE, CIRCUIT JUDGE:

Defendants Autumn Jackson [and] Jose Medina . . . were convicted of threatening to injure another person's reputation with the intent to extort money, in violation of 18 U.S.C. §§ 875(d). . . .

I. Background

The present prosecution arises out of defendants' attempts to obtain up to $40 million from William H. ("Bill") Cosby, Jr., a well-known actor and entertainer, by threatening to cause tabloid newspapers to publish Jackson's claim to be Cosby's daughter out-of-wedlock. . . .

A. Jackson's Relationship With Cosby

In the early 1970s, Cosby had a brief extramarital affair with Jackson's mother, Shawn Thompson. After Jackson was born in 1974, Thompson told Cosby that he was the father. Cosby disputed that assertion, and according to Jackson's birth certificate, her father was one Gerald Jackson. . . .

For more than 20 years after Jackson's birth, Cosby provided Thompson with substantial sums of money, provided her with a car, and paid for her admission to substance-abuse treatment programs. Thompson repeatedly telephoned him saying that she needed money, and in the course of the conversations she would usually reiterate her claim that Cosby was Jackson's father and state that she did not want to embarrass Cosby's wife. [Cosby gave Thompson] a total of more than over $100,000, typically having traveler's checks or cashier's checks issued in the name of an employee rather than his own name. . . .

[Cosby also offered to pay for the education of Jackson and Thompson's other children.] Cosby thereafter also created a trust to pay for Jackson's college tuition and [college expenses.] While Jackson was in school, Cosby spoke with her by telephone approximately 15 times to encourage her to pursue her education, telling her that although he was not her father, he "loved her very, very much" and would be a "father figure" for her. In these conversations, she addressed him as "Mr. Cosby."

[The trustee stopped payments in April 1995 upon discovering] that Jackson had dropped out of college. . . . From the spring of 1995 until December 1996, Jackson had no contact with Cosby or any of his attorneys.

B. The Events of December 1996 and early January 1997

[In December 1996, Jackson began making contact with Cosby or his representatives, calling herself "Autumn Cosby" and stating that she would "go to [a] tabloid" and provide a public story that would represent that she was Cosby's daughter, say that he had left her "out in the cold," and generally embarrass Cosby, CBS, and Cosby's livelihood, unless Cosby supported her financially.] Cosby and his representatives repeatedly refused, denied paternity, and told Jackson that her actions amounted to "extortion". . . .

[Thereafter, the defendants collaborated to "intensify the pressure." They sent letters to various politicians, Cosby sponsors such as Eastman Kodak and Phillip Morris, and various other entities and individuals, as well as Cosby and his representatives. When these efforts did not produce results, they sent more letters, accompanied by a contract with a tabloid, *The Globe*. Jackson had obtained the agreement of a *Globe* principal to sell her story for $25,000. . . . At one point, John P. Schmitt, Cosby's lawyer, returned one of Jackson's calls and the following conversation was recorded, with law enforcement assistance:] . . .

SCHMITT: [Clears throat] How, how much money are you asking for, Autumn?

JACKSON: I'm wanting to settle, once and finally.

SCHMITT: What, what are you asking for?

JACKSON: I'm asking for 40 million, to settle it completely [pause].

SCHMITT: And if our answer to that is no?

JACKSON: Well, like I said, I have offers, and I will go through with those offers.

SCHMITT: And those offers are to sell your story to the Globe? [Pause]. . . .

JACKSON: Them, as well as any others. [Pause].

SCHMITT: Well, I'm, I'm sure you know the answer to that is no, Autumn. Thank you very much.

Jackson asked to have her "father" call her; Schmitt responded that Jackson's father was "Mr. Jackson," and that she should "not expect a call from Mr. Cosby." . . .

II. Discussion

On appeal, Jackson and Medina contend principally that the district court gave an erroneous jury charge on the elements of extortion as prohibited by §875(d) because it omitted any instruction that, in order to convict, the jury must find that the threat to injure Cosby's reputation was "wrongful." . . .

Section 875(d), the extortion statute under which Jackson and Medina were convicted, provides as follows:

(d) Whoever, with intent to extort from any person . . . any money or other thing of value, transmits in interstate or foreign commerce any communication containing any threat to injure the property or reputation of the addressee or of another . . . shall be fined under this title or imprisoned not more than two years, or both.

18 U.S.C. §875(d). This statute does not define the terms "extort" or "intent to extort." At trial, Jackson asked the court to instruct the jury that

[t]o act with intent to "extort" means to act with the intent to obtain money or something of value from someone else, with that person's consent, but caused or induced by the *wrongful* use of fear [emphasis added],

and to explain that

> [t]he term "wrongful" in this regard means that the government must prove beyond a reasonable doubt, first, that the defendant had no lawful claim or right to the money or property he or she sought or attempted to obtain, and, second, that the defendant knew that he or she had no lawful claim or right to the money or property he or she sought or attempted to obtain. . . .

The court informed the parties that it would not give these requested instructions, stating its view that "threatening someone's reputation for money or a thing of value is inherently wrongful." Consistent with that view, after instructing the jury that a §875(d) offense has four elements, to wit, (1) an interstate communication, (2) containing a threat to reputation, (3) with intent to communicate such a threat, (4) with intent to extort, the court described the "intent to extort" element as follows, without mentioning any ingredient of wrongfulness:

> [The fourth element is intent to extort.] In this connection, to extort means to obtain money or a thing of value from another by use of threats to reputation. . . .

> [I]t is not a defense that the alleged threats to another's reputation are based on true facts. In other words, it is irrelevant whether Bill Cosby in fact is the father of Autumn Jackson. Rather, you must determine whether the defendant you are considering communicated a threat to injure Bill Cosby's reputation, and whether that defendant did so with intent to extort money from Bill Cosby. In addition, . . . it makes no difference whether the defendant was actually owed any money by Bill Cosby or thought he or she was. That is because the law does not permit someone to obtain money or a thing of value by threatening to injure another person's reputation.

. . . [T]he court did not use the words "unlawful" or "wrongful" or any equivalent term in its instructions as to the scope of §875(d).

The government contends that §875(d) contains no "wrongfulness" requirement, and that even if such a requirement is inferred, threats to injure another person's reputation are inherently wrongful. . . . Such an inference would be consistent with the established principle that, when a threat is made to injure the reputation of another, the truth of the damaging allegations underlying the threat is not a defense to a charge of extortion under §875(d). . . .

[But we] are troubled that §875(d) should be interpreted to contain no element of wrongfulness, for plainly not all threats to engage in speech that will have the effect of damaging another person's reputation, even if a forbearance from speaking is conditioned on the payment of money, are wrongful. For example, the purchaser of an allegedly defective product may threaten to complain to a consumer protection agency or to bring suit in a public forum if the manufacturer does not make good on its warranty. Or she may threaten to enlist the aid of a television "on-the-side-of-the-consumer" program. Or a private club may threaten to post a list of the club members who have not yet paid their dues. We doubt that Congress intended §875(d) to criminalize acts such as these. . . .

. . . We conclude that not all threats to reputation are within the scope of §875(d), that the objective of the party employing fear of economic loss or damage to reputation will have a bearing on the lawfulness of its use, and that it is material whether the defendant had a claim of right to the money demanded.

We do, however, view as inherently wrongful the type of threat to reputation that has no nexus to a claim of right. There are significant differences between, on the one hand, threatened disclosures of such matters as consumer complaints and nonpayment of dues, as to which the threatener has a plausible claim of right, and, on the other hand, threatened disclosures of such matters as sexual indiscretions that have no nexus with any plausible claim of right. . . . In the former category of threats, the disclosures themselves — not only the threats — have the potential for causing payment of the money demanded; in the latter category, it is only the threat that has that potential, and actual disclosure would frustrate the prospect of payment. . . .

. . . We conclude that where a threat of harm to a person's reputation seeks money or property to which the threatener does not have, and cannot reasonably believe she has, a claim of right, or where the threat has no nexus to a plausible claim of right, the threat is inherently wrongful and its transmission in interstate commerce is prohibited by §875(d). Within this framework, we conclude that the district court's instruction to the jury on the meaning of "extort" as that term is used in §875(d) was erroneous. . . . [Reversed and remanded.] [But: the next note shows that the outcome changed.]

Notes and Questions

(1) *But There's a Twist: The Court Reversed Itself on Rehearing and Reinstated the Convictions, after Considering the Standard of Review for Improper Jury Instructions.* The day after the Second Circuit decided *Jackson*, the Supreme Court decided *Neder v. United States*, 527 U.S. 1 (1999), in which it held that jury instructions were harmless error unless they had "a natural tendency to influence, or [were] capable of influencing," the outcome. On a petition for rehearing of *Jackson*, the Second Circuit interpreted *Neder* as mandating that a reviewing court begin by asking, in light of the evidence at trial, whether correction of a mistaken instruction "could rationally lead to a finding favoring the defendant."

Applying this standard, the Second Circuit noted that there was "no plausible" basis for a juror to believe that the $40 million demand was predicated on any "claim of right." Accordingly, the court reversed itself and reinstated the convictions. *United States v. Jackson*, 196 F.3d 383 (2d Cir. 1999). Do you agree with the ultimate result in the case?

In 2018, a Pennsylvania jury found Cosby guilty of sexual assault arising out of a 2004 incident. He was sentenced to 3–10 years in prison.

(2) *The Combination of Threats and a Plausible Legal Claim.* Consider the result if Jackson had linked her tabloid-related threats to a claim for lawful support from Cosby (or rather, since Jackson was an adult, a claim for unpaid childhood support). Although $40 million seems large for such a claim, assume Jackson believed it was reasonable or it was simply part of her negotiating strategy. Under these facts, would the court's initial reasoning make sense? If so, perhaps one can camouflage extortion by offhand reference to an impossible lawsuit.

(3) *Threats to Invoke the Criminal Process.* Would the answer change if the threat was to assert a criminal complaint, as opposed to a civil one? Compensation and settlement of claims are a less central aim of the criminal process, but they are not an inconceivable result (a criminal court may order restitution). As another possibility, imagine that a defendant's representative contacts the victim and offers total or partial restitution in exchange for an affidavit of nonprosecution (requesting that the District Attorney withhold charging the defendant). Is defendant's demand for the affidavit extortionate (or, if the victim negotiates, has she committed extortion by making a demand for more compensation than is offered)? As you will learn in your professional responsibility class, using the threat of criminal process to collect a civil debt is a disciplinary offense in most jurisdictions. But should it be?

§ 8.03 Burglary and Criminal Trespass

Read MPC § 221.1(1) [burglary] in the MPC Appendix.

Notes on the Definition of Burglary

(1) *Burglary at Common Law: A Cramped Formulation That Depended Upon "Arcane Distinctions."* In Chapter 3, we discussed the common law definition of burglary. The common law required a "breaking and entering" (not an entry through an opening), of a "dwelling" (not a commercial building), at "nighttime" (daytime "burglaries" were not burglaries), with intent to commit a felony (if the defendant intended only to steal "something," perhaps of less-than-felony value, so that the object offense might be only a misdemeanor, there would be no burglary).

(2) *Most Statutes Depart from This Definition: The Example of the Model Penal Code.* Consider the case that follows, which shows how the common law has been modified by modern approaches. In general terms, modern burglary covers entering or remaining in a building with the intent to commit a crime. The MPC, for example, requires only an "entry" (dispensing with the requirement of a "breaking"), and it eliminates the "dwelling," "nighttime," and "felony" requirements (a purpose to commit any "crime" will do).

(3) *Aggravated Forms of Burglary.* Many jurisdictions follow the policy of increasing the punishment for burglary if specified circumstances exist making the crime more morally blameworthy. This occurs either by adding a crime called "aggravated burglary" or increasing the sentence for standard burglary in certain situations. Common aggravators are the commission of a violent act during the burglary, being armed with a dangerous weapon, the presence of people during the burglary, or entry into a "habitation" (a home).

Quarles v. United States
139 S. Ct. 187 (2019)

JUSTICE KAVANAUGH delivered the opinion of the Court.

[Defendant pled guilty to being a felon in possession of a firearm and was sentenced to a 204-month prison term under the Armed Career Criminal Act, [18 U.S.C. § 924(e) (ACCA)], based in part on a prior Michigan conviction for third-degree home invasion. ACCA required a 15-year minimum sentence. He claimed, however, that the Michigan conviction for third-degree home invasion did not qualify, even though ACCA defines "violent felony" to include "burglary," and the generic statutory term "burglary" means "unlawful or unprivileged entry into, *or remaining in*, a building or structure, with intent to commit a crime," *Taylor v. United States*, 495 U.S. 575, 599 (1990) (emphasis added).

[Quarles argued that Michigan's third-degree home invasion statute—which applies when a person "breaks and enters a dwelling or enters a dwelling without permission and, *at any time* while he or she is entering, *present in*, or exiting the dwelling, commits a misdemeanor"—swept too broadly. Specifically, he claimed, it encompassed situations where the defendant forms the intent to commit a crime *at any time* while unlawfully remaining in a dwelling, while generic remaining-in burglary occurs only when the defendant has the intent to commit a crime *at the exact moment* when he or she *first* unlawfully remains in a building or structure. Therefore, his crime was not "burglary," as ACCA requires. The Court here rejects the argument.]

At common law, burglary was confined to unlawful breaking and entering a dwelling at night with the intent to commit a felony. See, *e.g.*, 4 W. Blackstone, Commentaries on the Laws of England 224 (1769). But by the time Congress passed and President Reagan signed the current version of § 924(e) in 1986, state burglary statutes had long since departed from the common-law formulation. *See Taylor.* In addition to casting off relics like the requirement that there be a breaking, or that the unlawful entry occur at night, a majority of States by 1986 prohibited unlawfully "remaining in" a building or structure with intent to commit a crime. Those remaining-in statutes closed a loophole in some States' laws by extending burglary to cover situations where a person enters a structure lawfully but stays unlawfully—for example, by remaining in a store after closing time without permission to do so.

In ... *Taylor* ... , this Court interpreted the term "burglary" in § 924(e) [ACCA] in accord with the more expansive understanding of burglary that had become common by 1986 .... The Court concluded that generic burglary under § 924(e) means "unlawful or unprivileged entry into, *or remaining in*, a building or structure, with intent to commit a crime." *Id.*, at 599 (emphasis added). A defendant's prior conviction under a state statute qualifies as a predicate burglary under § 924(e) if the state statute — regardless of its "exact definition or label" — "substantially corresponds" to or is narrower than the generic definition of burglary. *Id.*

In this case, we must determine the scope of generic remaining-in burglary under *Taylor* — in particular, the timing of the intent requirement. Quarles argues that remaining-in burglary occurs only when the defendant has the intent to commit a crime *at the exact moment* when he or she *first* unlawfully remains in a building or structure.... According to the Government, remaining-in burglary occurs when the defendant forms the intent to commit a crime *at any time* while unlawfully present in a building or structure. We agree with the Government.

... In ordinary usage, "remaining in" refers to a continuous activity. This Court has followed that ordinary meaning in analogous legal contexts. For example, when interpreting a federal criminal statute punishing any "'alien crewman who willfully remains in the United States in excess of the number of days allowed,'" the Court stated that "the crucial word 'remains' permits no connotation other than continuing presence." [*United States v.*] *Cores*, 356 U.S. at 408 [(1958)]. [In t]he law of trespass ... , the term "remain" refers to "a continuing trespass for the entire time during which the actor wrongfully remains." Restatement (Second) of Torts § 158, Comment m, p. 280 (1965). ...

Because the *actus reus* is a continuous event, the *mens rea* matches the *actus reus* so long as the burglar forms the intent to commit a crime at any time while unlawfully present in the building or structure.

Quarles insists, however, that to constitute a burglary under § 924(e), the intent to commit a crime must be contemporaneous with unlawful entry or remaining. ... But the defendant's intent *is* contemporaneous with the unlawful remaining so long as the defendant forms the intent at any time while unlawfully remaining. ... For burglary predicated on unlawful *remaining*, the defendant must have the intent to commit a crime at the time of remaining, which is any time during which the defendant unlawfully remains.

That conclusion is supported by the States' laws as of 1986 when Congress enacted § 924(e). As of 1986, a majority of States proscribed remaining-in burglary. ... [A]ll of the state appellate courts that had definitively addressed this issue as of 1986 had interpreted remaining-in burglary to occur when the defendant forms the intent to commit a crime at any time while unlawfully present in the building or structure. [The Court here cites a number of state decisions.] ...

For the Court's purposes here, the Michigan statute substantially corresponds to or is narrower than generic burglary [and is sufficient to trigger ACCA].

UNITED STATES v. STITT, 139 S. Ct. 399 (2018). This opinion reviews two consolidated cases and is another challenge to sentencing under ACCA. The defendants questioned prior convictions that were, again, for burglary, this time under state statutes that prohibited burglary of a structure or vehicle that had been adapted or was customarily used for overnight accommodation. In both cases, the courts of appeals reversed. Here, the Supreme Court reverses the reversals and upholds sentencing under the ACCA:

> The relevant language of the Tennessee and Arkansas statutes falls within the scope of generic burglary's definition as set forth in *Taylor* (which is cited in the case above.). For one thing, we made clear in *Taylor* that Congress intended the definition of "burglary" to reflect "the generic sense in which the term [was] used in the criminal codes of most States" at the time the Act was passed. In 1986, a majority of state burglary statutes covered vehicles adapted or customarily used for lodging—either explicitly or by defining "building" or "structure" to include those vehicles. [The Court cites a number of state statutes.]
>
> For another thing, Congress, as we said in *Taylor,* viewed burglary as an inherently dangerous crime because burglary "creates the possibility of a violent confrontation between the offender and an occupant, caretaker, or some other person who comes to investigate." . . . An offender who breaks into a mobile home, an RV, a camping tent, a vehicle, or another structure that is adapted for or customarily used for lodging runs a similar or greater risk of violent confrontation. [Reversal of ACCA sentences reversed.]

Notes and Questions

(1) *Applying the Elements of Common Law Burglary.* Does the common law definition of burglary apply to an entry achieved by picking a lock? What about breaking and entering a warehouse? Is breaking and entering at night worse than in the daytime? (Does your answer depend upon whether burglary is limited to dwellings?) Finally, should the specificity of what the thief intends to steal in terms of value make a difference to whether the crime is burglary?

(2) *Statutory Definitions.* Modern burglary statutes broaden and depart from the common law, as well as from the "generic" or MPC approach. Imagine that a person breaks into a building without any intent to steal but then commits a theft while inside, because a valuable object catches her eye. (This hypothetical may seem far-fetched, but in fact, many situations resemble it, because if the prosecution has the burden of proving that the intent to steal coincided with the entry, this element often cannot be proved if all that is known is that the defendant broke in and committed a theft—and often, this is all that is known.) Many jurisdictions, therefore, have amended the definition to include entry plus actual theft, regardless of the timing of the intent to steal. *E.g.,* Tex. Penal Code § 30.02. The MPC does not cover these issues. Should it?

(3) *What is a Building? People v. Gibbons*, 273 P. 32 (Cal. 1928). Gibbons took aluminum from a storage bin that was completely open on one side and faced a fenced yard. The court held there was no burglary because there had been no entry of a building. But in *People v. Franco*, 79 Cal. App. 682 (Cal. Ct. App. 1926). Franco broke into a shoe store showcase in an open staircase that led from the sidewalk to the entrance to the store, but which was not accessible from inside the store. The court held the showcase was "under the roof" of the shoe store and was part of it, so that there had been an entry of a building. Both cases interpreted California Penal Code § 459, which provides: "Every person who enters any house, room, apartment, tenement, shop, warehouse, store, mill, barn, stable, outhouse or other building . . . with intent to commit grand or petit larceny or any felony is guilty of burglary." Are the results in *Gibbons* and *Franco* consistent?

(4) *What is Meant by Entering a Building? People v. Davis*, 958 P.2d 1083 (Cal. 1998). Davis presented a forged check to a teller at a check-cashing business by placing it in a chute at a walk-up window. He was convicted of burglary on the theory he had "entered" a building under California Penal Code § 459. In reversing, the California Supreme Court stressed the need for "reasonable limits as to what constitutes an entry" under the statute. Because Davis presented no safety danger and did not breach any "possessory interest" in the building, he had not committed an entry and was not guilty of burglary. The court also discussed an earlier lower court decision, *People v. Ravenscroft*, 198 Cal. App. 3d 639 (Cal. Ct. App. 1988). Ravenscroft had stolen his companion's ATM card. He inserted the card into two ATMs, punched in her PIN, and withdrew funds from her account. The court of appeals held that "the insertion of a fraudulently obtained ATM card effectuates an entry into the bank's ATM for larceny just as surely as does a crowbar when applied to a vent." The *Davis* court expressly rejected the reasoning and result of *Ravenscroft*. Which case provides the best interpretation of the statute?

Hornbook law is that the "least degree" of intrusion suffices for a burglary. *See* 4 Blackstone, *Commentaries* *227. If Davis had reached into the chute with his hand, would he be guilty of burglary?

(5) *What is a Dwelling, Habitation, or Occupied Structure?* Modern statutes often define burglary of a habitation, dwelling, or occupied structure as aggravated burglary. These provisions raise many fact-specific questions. Is it burglary of an occupied structure to break into a temporarily unoccupied home (occupants are away for the weekend), a vacant house being renovated for resale, or a garage? Some statutes provide definitions. *See, e.g.,* Ga. Stat. § 16–7-1 ("dwelling" means any structure or portion of a structure "designed or intended for occupancy for residential use").

(6) *Criminal Trespass.* Consider the case of a teenager who, as a prank, enters a recently constructed but not yet occupied locked building just to look around, or who breaks in just for the thrill of gaining access to a prohibited space. There is no burglary because the intent to commit an object crime is absent. Should this entry be a crime of some sort, perhaps a lesser included crime of burglary? Many

jurisdictions have answered yes and created a crime called "criminal trespass," usually categorized as a misdemeanor. In general terms, a criminal trespass occurs when a person knowingly enters or remains on property or in a structure with the knowledge that he or she does not have the proper consent to do so. Consider the following Model Penal Code definition of "criminal trespass" and evaluate how it would apply to the hypothetical teenage prankster. Why do you think property owners routinely post "No Trespassing" signs?

Read MPC § 221.2(1) and (3) [criminal trespass and defenses] in the MPC Appendix.

Problem 8B: "Is It Burglary?"

(1) *Does Pouring Motor Oil Over the Roof and Sides of a Building Constitute Burglary?: United States v. Eichman*, 756 F. Supp. 143 (S.D.N.Y. 1991). As a protest to American policy in the Persian Gulf, defendants used a ladder to climb to the roof of an Armed Forces Recruiting Station at Times Square, poured motor oil over the surface of the roof and down the sides, lowered the American flag that flew over the building, and set it on fire. During motion hearings, the Government explained that it could have charged attempted arson, but it charged the defendants with burglary, even though that crime carried a lower penalty than attempted arson, because burglary "better fit the defendants' conduct." The prosecution requested a pretrial ruling by the court on the elements of burglary in this fact situation, directed specifically at whether a burglary defendant must enter by personally intruding within the roof or walls, whether extended objects or substances could accomplish the entry, and whether more than slight entry was required.

(2) *Controlling Authority: People v. King*, 463 N.E.2d 601 (N.Y. 1984). New York law applied (because federal law "borrows" state law for general crimes in federal enclaves). The *King* case, in which the defendant cut a small hole in a security gate in front of an open vestibule leading into the entry door of a jewelry store. Even though the hole was too small for the defendant to pass through with his entire body, the court upheld a conviction for attempted burglary on the ground that "entry" covered anyone who "intrudes within a building, however slightly." Even though the vestibule was an open area, there was "entry" of a building, because the defendant had penetrated "an area of or related to [the] building."

(3) *Is There an "Entry" into a "Building" Here, and of What Significance Is the Policy of Protecting the "Security" of the Building and Its Occupants?* How should the court define burglary for the jury in these circumstances? The defense supported a view in which "some breaking of the planes created by the threshold and the four walls," or "penetra[tion of] the exterior," was required. Can entry be accomplished by the defendant's presence on the roof, since that was "an area . . . related to [the] building to which the public has been . . . denied access"? If not, the motor oil undoubtedly "penetrated," however "slightly," into cracks in the roof or into its substance; is

this penetration sufficient? Also, the court noted that the "predominant" policy for creating the crime of burglary is "to protect the security of [buildings], and the person within [a building]." Here, the defendant's conduct created significant security issues, even if they did not "break the plane" of the roof. (The court agreed with the defense and ruled that the jurors would be instructed that they could not convict unless a defendant "actually entered within the four walls or beneath the roof.")

(4) *Trespass.* Is this crime, instead, merely a criminal trespass?

Problem 8C: Can a Person Burgle His Own Home?

(1) *Entry by an Owner Prohibited by a Court Order.* Bob and Nancy have been married for six years. They jointly own a home. But Nancy has become frightened that Bob might hurt her. She files for divorce and obtains a protection order that prohibits Bob from contacting her or from entering their home. Yet one night, two weeks later, Bob uses his key to enter their home, where he confronts Nancy and threatens her. She calls the police, who quickly arrest Bob.

(2) *Is It Burglary?* Bob has violated the protection order. And he may be criminally liable for some kind of assault. Some courts have said he's also guilty of burglary. Is this conclusion justified, given that some statutes require entry "without the consent of the owner"? (The MPC requires entry into the dwelling of another for the more severe crime.) *See* Jeannie Suk, *Criminal Law Comes Home*, 116 Yale L.J. 2, 22–42 (2006) (collecting and discussing cases).

Chapter 9

Sentencing: Theory and Practice

"[S]ome . . . say . . . it is unjust to punish anyone for the sake of example to others; that punishment is just, only when intended for the good of the sufferer himself. Others maintain the extreme reverse, contending that to punish persons . . . for their own benefit, is despotism and injustice, . . . but they may justly be punished to prevent evil to others. . . . [Others] affirm[] that it is unjust to punish at all; for the criminal did not make his own character. . . . All these opinions are extremely plausible. . . ."—John Stuart Mill, *Utilitarianism* (1863)

"But what kind and what amount of punishment is it that public justice makes its principle and measure? None other than the principle of equality (in the position of the needle on the scale of justice), to incline no more to one side than to the other. . . . [A]ll other principles are fluctuating and unsuited for a sentence of pure and strict justice because extraneous considerations are mixed into them."—Immanuel Kant, *The Metaphysics of Morals* (1797)

§ 9.01 An Introductory Problem on the Goals of Sentencing: Two Similar Cases, Different Outcomes

Problem 9A: Comparing Two Sentences (Bergman and Olis)

(1) *Two Analogous Cases, with Very Different Sentences.* In the two cases that follow, compare the facts surrounding the crimes, the defendants, and the sentences. Try to explain whether and why the sentence in either case seems inappropriate (or why either seems correct).

(2) *Analyzing How Sentences Should Be Determined.* What factors should the law take into account in measuring a sentence? Should the decision be left to judicial discretion, or controlled by legislation, or some of both?

United States v. Bergman

416 F. Supp. 496 (S.D.N.Y. 1976)

FRANKEL, DISTRICT JUDGE.

Defendant appeared until the last couple of years to be a man of unimpeachably high character, attainments, and distinction. A doctor of divinity and an ordained rabbi, he has been acclaimed by people around the world for his works of public philanthropy, private charity, and leadership in educational enterprises. . . . In addition to his good works, defendant has managed to amass considerable wealth in the ownership and operation of nursing homes, in real estate ventures, and in a course of substantial investments.

Beginning about two years ago, investigations of nursing homes in this area, including questions of fraudulent claims for Medicaid funds, drew to a focus upon this defendant among several others. The results that concern us were the present indictment and . . . elaborate plea negotiations[, which led to two guilty pleas by Bergman].

. . . [T]he plea on Count One (carrying a maximum of five years in prison and a $10,000 fine) confesses defendant's knowing and willful participation in a scheme to defraud the United States in various ways, including the presentation of wrongfully padded claims for payments under the Medicaid program to defendant's nursing homes. Count Three, for which the guilty plea carries a theoretical maximum of three more years in prison and another $5,000 fine, involves the filing of a partnership return which was false and fraudulent. . . .

The conspiracy to defraud, as defendant has admitted it, is by no means the worst of its kind. . . . At the same time, the sentence . . . is imposed for two federal felonies including . . . a knowing and purposeful conspiracy to mislead and defraud the Federal Government.

[The court sentenced Bergman "to a term of four months in prison." Later in this chapter, we shall consider Judge Frankel's justification of this sentence; for now, compare Bergman's four month sentence to the 24-year sentence in the case that follows.]

United States v. Olis

Adapted from Simon Romero, *Ex-Executive of Dynergy Is Sentenced to 24 Years*, New York Times, March 26, 2004, at C2

A federal judge yesterday sentenced a former midlevel executive at Dynergy Inc. to more than 24 years in prison for his role in a conspiracy to disguise the company's financial difficulties. Olis assisted in listing loan proceeds as cash, thereby making the company's balance sheet look impressive by disguising debt. The company's overvalued stock led to massive stockholder losses (possibly exceeding $500 million). The company paid $468 million to settle a class action by investors. . . .

Born in South Korea to a Korean mother and an American soldier who abandoned them, Jamie Olis, now 38, rose from poverty to become a tax-planning executive at Dynergy. The company engaged in natural gas trading and other businesses. Several friends and family members appeared in court to support Olis, and many cried or suppressed anger at the sentence. "He's a decent person," said Rita Recio, a co-worker of Mr. Olis's wife. "Where are the higher-ups in all of this? Where's the former C.E.O.?" Even the lead prosecutor described Olis as a "tragic figure." Olis risked a lengthy sentence after choosing to go to trial rather than reach a plea agreement with prosecutors. Two other Dynergy executives—Mr. Olis's former boss, Gene S. Foster, and Helen C. Sharkey—pleaded guilty and were expected to receive sentences of less than five years.

Judge Sim Lake said that he had considered Olis's background but also noted that many investors in Dynergy had lost their retirement savings. He also stressed that he had little discretion to impose a lesser sentence because he was bound by sentencing guidelines that reflected congressional concern that business crimes were not being punished severely enough.

Question: Given that these two crimes (and these two defendants) do not exhibit obvious differences that would explain such different sentences (four months in one and 24 years in the other), what differences in sentencing philosophy might have produced these results?

Note: Olis's sentence ultimately was reduced to six years. We explain the reasons later in this chapter.

§ 9.02 The Philosophical Bases of Sentencing

[A] "Utilitarianism" and "Kantianism": Two Ethical Philosophies That Influence Sentencing

Notes on "Consequentialism" (Good Results) Versus "Deontology" (Right or Justice)

(1) *A Brief Detour into Ethical Philosophy.* There are two historically influential branches of ethical philosophy: "Consequentialism," of which the traditional model is called (1) "Utilitarianism"—a philosophy that tests rightness by good results; and "Deontology," represented by (2) "Kantianism"—which tests rightness by intrinsic justice. There are other ethical philosophies, but these two have exerted the greatest influence on criminal law. You will need some understanding of these philosophies before you can fully examine sentencing.

(2) *Distinguishing Consequentialism from Deontology.* "Consequentialism" is the ethics of producing good results. A consequentialist may compare costs and benefits to decide what actions are right and wrong. In this view, murder is illegal because it destroys the social fabric, invites retaliation, and causes others to live in fear. In other words, murder is bad because of its results.

"Deontology," on the other hand, refuses to quantify benefits and costs. Instead, it emphasizes justice, or rightness or wrongness. Murder is illegal because it is wrong. It subordinates one human being, the victim, to the satisfaction of the needs of another, the murderer. In summary, consequentialist philosophies emphasize "the good" (or good results), while deontological ethics emphasizes what is intrinsically right, or "justice."

Notes on Utilitarianism and Kantianism

(1) *Utilitarianism: Bentham and Mill's Consequentialist Philosophies.* Jeremy Bentham and John Stuart Mill are identified with "Utilitarianism." In the most basic form of Utilitarianism, the good, or pleasurable satisfaction, is the highest value. Bentham expressed his essential principle succinctly: "It is the greatest happiness of the greatest number that is the measure of right and wrong" (or, "the greatest good for the greatest number").

(2) *The Consequentialist and Aggregative Nature of Utilitarianism.* Utilitarian philosophy therefore was a branch of consequentialism, *i.e.,* philosophy that depends upon results. Government intervention was valid only if it resulted in greater happiness, not because of its "rightness." Utilitarians also looked to "aggregate" effects: Disadvantages felt by some people were not to be judged by whether they were intrinsically right or wrong but rather by whether they led to greater aggregate good. It was moral, then, for a social rule to disadvantage some people, so long as it increased the happiness of others enough to enhance the sum of happiness. Some forms of utilitarianism are therefore vulnerable to the charge that they disadvantage minorities.

(3) *The Contrasting Deontological Philosophy of Kant: The Categorical Imperative.* In contrast, Immanuel Kant developed a deontological philosophy. He concluded that every individual must act in ways that could be imitated by everyone, as "universal laws." For example, if you accept a rule against falsehood, you cannot exempt yourself, and you cannot make exceptions for lies that might be beneficial (as a Utilitarian might). Kant called such a universal rule a "categorical imperative": a rule that should be rigorously adhered to without variation and regardless of consequences.

(4) *Kant's Anti-Objectification Principle: All Humans Are Valuable Ends in Themselves, Never to Be Treated Only as Means to Others' Ends.* Another categorical imperative was that every actor must treat each person as individually valuable, and not merely as an object to be used only as a means to ends preferred by others. Kant also derived principles that required the keeping of promises no matter what the cost, and the telling of the truth regardless of consequences. One could not "objectify" another person by lying or breaking promises — not ever.

Notes on the Limits of Both Philosophies

(1) *The Trouble with Utilitarianism, Part One: Capital Punishment for Intoxicated Drivers?* Utilitarian reasoning supports results that we would reject today. For instance, a single-minded Utilitarian might favor the death penalty for intoxicated driving, if persuaded that the execution of the first unfortunate convict would likely reduce traffic fatalities. Can you explain? On the other hand, Kantian deontology would oppose this result. Why? (Some Utilitarians have addressed this problem by proposing proportional condemnation, as we shall see.)

(2) *The Trouble with Utilitarianism, Part Two: Vulnerable Minorities and Confiscation.* The Americans with Disabilities Act (ADA) imposes costs on the non-disabled majority so that disabled persons can be better off. What would Utilitarianism make of the ADA (might it support a repeal)? Since one of Kant's categorical imperatives involved helping others, his deontology probably supports the ADA more easily. Or, imagine that an entrepreneur has built a valuable theme park. The population wants to confiscate the park so that everyone can use it without paying. What would Utilitarianism say? What would Kant say?

(3) *The Trouble with Kant, Part One: Conflicting Categorical Imperatives.* But there are also problems with Kant's deontology. For example, imagine that you have entered into a contract (a promise, which categorically must be performed). But your performance is prohibited by a later-passed law (compliance with which also is a categorical imperative). You have to obey the law and also keep the promise, but you can't do both. Does Kant point to an answer? Utilitarianism?

(4) *The Trouble with Kant, Part Two: Inflexibility Disallows Balancing, Even When Losses Overwhelm Gains.* Imagine that a terrorist is pursuing your neighbor, who is hiding in her closet. You would like to save her life by telling the terrorist, falsely, that your neighbor is at another location across town. What would be Kant's evaluation of this lie? What about Bentham's or Mill's? Or, imagine that a CEO signed a contract years ago that, because of bad luck, will bankrupt the firm and abolish thousands of jobs, while providing only minimal benefit to the other party. If the CEO seeks to withhold performance, what would Kant say? Or Utilitarians?

Problem 9B (Sentencing Philosophy): "Please Commute My Death Sentence, Governor, so That I Can Become an Organ Donor"

(1) *A Clemency Petition That Raised an Odd Ethical Dilemma.* Gregory Johnson brutally murdered 82-year-old Ruby Hutslar while committing a burglary in her home. From Indiana's death row, Johnson filed a clemency petition asking for a stay, or an outright commutation, so that he could donate a segment of his liver to his sister. Johnson claimed to be a close tissue match to his sister. Lethal injection would make Johnson's liver unsuitable, but doctors told Johnson's lawyers that it might be possible to perform a split-liver or segmented transplant if Johnson's execution was postponed. (Actually, Johnson's petition was not as unusual as you might expect. Delaware had previously granted a stay so a condemned man could donate a kidney to his mother, but Florida had denied a similar petition.)

(2) *Contrasting the Utilitarian and Kantian Approaches to Sentencing.* A Utilitarian would be more likely than a Kantian to favor Johnson's petition. Why? (In fact, Kant gives the eerily relevant example of convicts volunteering for "medical experiments" in exchange for lighter sentences—and he ridicules the idea. In the real case, Indiana Governor Mitch Daniels denied Johnson's petition, but the decision may have been based partly upon doubts about Johnson's suitability as a donor.)

[B] Utilitarian and Kantian Approaches to Sentencing: Deterrence, Incapacitation, Rehabilitation, and Retributive Justice

> Read MPC § 1.02(1) & (2) [purposes] in the MPC Appendix.

Notes on Four Goals of Sentencing

(1) *Identifying the Goals of Sentencing.* Different writers have phrased the objectives of sentencing in different ways, but some commentators have distilled them down to four basic factors. How does Model Penal Code § 1.02 address (or fail to address) each of these goals?

(a) *Deterrence*—to create incentives that will motivate would-be offenders not to engage in crime;

(b) *Incapacitation*—to restrain dangerous or repeat offenders so that they cannot commit crimes even if they are not deterred;

(c) *Rehabilitation*—to reform the offender and channel the offender into lawful pursuits;

(d) *Retribution or Justice*—to impose a sentence that corresponds to the offender's just deserts.

(2) *The Difference between Utilitarian Sentencing Goals (Deterrence, Incapacitation, and Rehabilitation) and the Kantian Ideal (Retributive Justice).* Utilitarians want all sentences to serve broad purposes that maximize human happiness. Deterrence, incapacitation, and rehabilitation are Utilitarian goals. A Kantian, however, would resist sentencing that is based on serving broad societal purposes such as deterrence (because those purposes would objectify the accused), and instead, would measure the sentence by the defendant's individual blameworthiness. Retributive justice, therefore, is the Kantian or deontological ideal.

(3) *But the Problem Is: These Goals Often Conflict.* As W.S. Gilbert (of Gilbert & Sullivan) wrote in *The Mikado*, the idea is to apply these policies to reach an appropriate result: "My object all sublime/ I shall achieve in time/ To make the punishment fit the crime." Unfortunately, sentencing goals frequently point in different directions. The quotation from Mill that begins this chapter highlights the reason. Deterrence, reform, retributive justice, and incapacitation are all "plausible" factors. Mill did not include retribution because he was a Utilitarian, but adding retribution to the list—as the quotation from Kant should indicate—heightens the tension.

(4) *Most Sentences Pursue Multiple Goals Even if Those Goals Conflict.* The various goals of sentencing may conflict, yet many people wish to pursue more than one of the traditional goals at the same time. Also remember that the mix of goals may

change over time. MPC § 1.02(2), for example—which was published in 1962—focused on two sentencing goals: deterrence and rehabilitation. The 2017 revision of the MPC's sentencing provisions takes a very different tone while still pursuing multiple goals:

(2) The general purposes of [sentencing] are: . . .

(i) to render sentences in all cases within a range of severity proportionate to the gravity of offenses, the harms done to crime victims, and the blameworthiness of offenders; [and]

(ii) when reasonably feasible, to achieve offender rehabilitation, general deterrence, incapacitation of dangerous offenders, restitution to crime victims, preservation of families, and reintegration of offenders into the law-abiding community, provided these goals are pursued within the boundaries of proportionality in subsection (a)(i); . . .

Thus, the primary purpose of sentencing under the new version is retributive justice. Why do you think the American Law Institute made such a dramatic revision?

Problem 9C (Sentencing Philosophy): What Would a Utilitarian Say—or a Kantian?

(1) *Very Long Sentences to "Stop This Kind of Crime."* Imagine that a state legislature enacts a twenty-year minimum sentence for certain white collar crimes after a string of corporate frauds has devastated pensioners. The sponsor says he wants to "stop this kind of crime [deterrence]" and "get these pin-striped con artists off the streets [incapacitation]." "I don't care about trying to teach them to become law abiding citizens [rehabilitation]." But opponents argue that the enactment "is going to result in crushing penalties for small fry who don't deserve them [retributive justice]." What would a Utilitarian say about these arguments? A Kantian?

(2) *Habitual or Three-Strikes Laws.* Many States require enhanced minimum sentences for repeat offenders. How would a Utilitarian or a Kantian justify these laws—or argue against them?

§ 9.03 The Four Classical Sentencing Factors: Deterrence, Incapacitation, Rehabilitation, and Retributive Justice

[A] Deterrence: The Historical Focus of Utilitarianism

Notes on the Beginnings of Modern Sentencing: Beccaria's View

(1) *Punishment Before the Enlightenment.* Modern sentencing philosophy has its roots in the eighteenth century, during the period of European history commonly called "the Enlightenment." Before that time, criminal punishment is generally understood to have revolved around execution or the infliction of pain on

convicted defendants, with some use of confinement as well. Dignitary offenses against authorities were subject to severe punishment.

(2) *The Beginnings of Modern Sentencing Philosophy: Beccaria's Theory of Deterrence.* Enlightenment thinking saw these punishments as barbaric. Cesare Beccaria argued that wise legislators would allow sentences with "only this end in view, the greatest happiness of the greatest number." Beccaria argued both that deterrence was the overriding goal of sentencing and that it represented a humane alternative to existing practices. He also argued that "Crimes are more effectually prevented by the certainty, than the severity of punishment."

Cesare Beccaria, On Crimes and Punishments
(1764) (David Young trans. 1986)

XII. *Purpose of Punishments. . . .* [T]he purpose of punishments is not to torment and afflict a sentient being or to undo a crime which has already been committed. . . . The purpose of punishment, then, is nothing other than to dissuade the criminal from doing fresh harm to his compatriots and to keep other people from doing the same. Therefore, punishments and the method of inflicting them should be chosen that, mindful of the proportion between crime and punishment, will make the most effective . . . impression on men's minds and inflict the least torment on the body of the criminal.

Notes and Questions

(1) *Is Beccaria's Insistence on Deterrence, as the Sole Basis of Sentencing, Too Narrow?: The Deontological Critique.* Deontological philosophers such as Immanuel Kant criticized Beccaria on the ground that his theories omitted considerations of justice. If a particular class of defendants (say, educated offenders) could be deterred by short sentences, Beccaria's philosophy might depreciate the blameworthiness of their crimes. On the other hand, if life without parole could deter major societal harm, such as deaths resulting from intoxicated driving, would Beccaria's philosophy call for life without parole for intoxicated driving?

(2) *Doesn't Criminal Law Need a Connection to Moral Blameworthiness?* Other philosophers pointed out that Beccaria separated the criminal sanction from its moral anchors. Do Beccaria's critics have a point? (Beccaria did advocate "proportionality," but he meant proportionality to societal harm, not necessarily to blameworthiness.)

Notes on Deterrence in Utilitarian Theory

(1) *Background to Utilitarianism: Bentham and Mill.* During the late 1700s and early 1800s, Jeremy Bentham developed an influential philosophy of "hedonistic Utilitarianism." Building in part on the work of Beccaria, Bentham argued (as is reported above) that "It is the greatest happiness of the greatest number that is the measure of right and wrong." *Fragment on Government* (1776). John Stuart Mill,

a student of Bentham, modified the theory in the 1800s to argue that aggregate good is best served by respecting personal autonomy unless it results in harm to others (and he insisted that moral offense does not count as harm). *On Liberty*, ch. 4 (1859). Thus, government intervention is valid to a Utilitarian only if it results in greater happiness, not because of its intrinsic "rightness."

(2) *Deterrence Theory and Criminal Punishment.* Bentham's writings evidence a concern that punishment be carefully calibrated—that is, proportional to the crime—so as to deter further crime and maximize resources rather than to express the desire of a community for retributive justice. He also concluded that people will respond to a system of proportional punishment.

Jeremy Bentham, The Principles of Morals and Legislation
(1789)

Ch. XXVII. It may be of use . . . to recapitulate the several circumstances, which [establish] the proportion betwixt punishments and offenses. . . . These seem to be as follows:

I. *On the part of the offence*:

1. The profit of the offense;

2. The mischief of the offense;

3. The profit and mischief of other greater or lesser offences, of different sorts, which the offender may have to choose out of;

4. The profit and mischief of other offenses, of the same sort, which the same offender may probably have been guilty of already.

II. *On the part of the punishment:*

5. The magnitude of the punishment: composed of its intensity and duration;

6. The deficiency of the punishment in point of certainty;

7. The deficiency of the punishment in point of proximity;

8. The quality of the punishment;

9. The accidental advantage in point of quality of a punishment, not strictly needed in point of quantity;

10. The use of a punishment of a particular quality, in the character of a moral lesson.

III. *On the part of the offender:*

11. The responsibility of the class of persons in a way to offend;

12. The sensibility of each particular offender;

13. The particular merits or useful qualities of any particular offender, in case of a punishment which might deprive the community of the benefit of them;

14. The multitude of offenders on any particular occasion. . . .

Notes and Questions: Conceptions of Deterrence

(1) *Specific and General Deterrence.* Most contemporary theorists recognize two kinds of deterrence: specific and general. Specific deterrence "means that the punished offender will be deterred from future offenses," while general deterrence means that "others will thereby be influenced not to commit the same crime." George P. Fletcher, *Rethinking Criminal Law* 414 (1978). If we punish to make an offender learn a lesson, that is specific deterrence. If we make the offender an example, that is general deterrence.

(2) *Deterrence and Proportionality.* Deterrence theories usually seek a form of proportionality—that is, to grade the amount of punishment to fit the crime. But to a pure Utilitarian, the "fit" for purposes of deterrence is not about moral justice; rather, it is about achieving the most deterrence for the least cost.

(3) *Deterrence and Economic Analysis: Richard Posner, An Economic Theory of the Criminal Law*, 85 Colum. L. Rev. 1193 (1985). Judge Posner developed a distinct Utilitarian approach to sentencing. The key feature is an intense focus on economic costs and benefits and the relationship between criminal activity and market efficiency. For example, Posner notes that some criminal acts are "wealth-maximizing." He suggests the need for calibration between the amount and the certainty of punishment:

> Once the expected punishment cost for the crime has been set, it becomes necessary to choose a combination of probability and severity of punishment that will bring that cost home to the would-be offender. Let us begin with fines. An expected punishment cost of $1000 can be imposed by combining a fine of $1000 with a probability of apprehension and conviction of one, a fine of $10,000 with a probability of .1, a fine of one million dollars with a probability of .001, etc.

Posner applies the same analysis to imprisonment and concludes that optimal deterrence is more likely to result from large punishments than from certainty of punishment. Others disagree and insist that increasing certainty is more effective. *See* John M. Darley, *On the Unlikely Prospect of Reducing Crime Rates by Increasing the Severity of Prison Sentences*, 13 J. L. & Pol'y 189 (2005).

(4) *Criticisms of Deterrence Theory: The Measurement Problem—Dan M. Kahan, The Secret Ambition of Deterrence*, 113 Harvard L. Rev. 413, 426–27 (1999). How do we assign the proper weights to the various costs and benefits (or pains and pleasures), and how do we compare them to each other? If we can't measure the relative harm of each act, we cannot determine how much punishment is appropriate for either one. As Kahan observes, "Deterrence, in short, presupposes a consequentialist theory of value. Yet nothing intrinsic to the deterrence theory supplies one."

Other critics argue that crime rates do not respond to the incentives created by deterrence-based punishment. *See* Christopher Slobogin, *The Civilization of the Criminal Law*, 58 Vand. L. Rev. 121, 140 (2005). If that is true, should courts reject deterrence altogether, or should they simply recognize that the incentives created by punishment work within a much larger context? Consider the following analysis.

David Crump, *Deterrence*

49 St. Mary's L. Rev. 317 (2018)

. . . The Economic or Market Model of Deterrence . . .

[The "economic theory" of deterrence is a simplistic model that imagines the potential criminal as making choices the way a consumer does in a market.] . . . If there is a high probability of detection, apprehension, conviction and sentence, together with a severe expected punishment, the deterrent against the commission of a particular crime is greater . . . or so goes the theory. . . .

At least one judge has put three of the factors underlying deterrence into . . . [an] equation, or rather an inequality, while realizing it cannot be treated as having mathematical exactitude. . . . :

$$C \times S > R$$

where C is the probability of punishment, S is its severity, and R is the reward expected from the crime. . . . If the product on the left side of the inequality exceeds the reward, deterrence operates to suppress the crime [according to the economic or market model].

[The] "market model" . . . builds on the assumption that offenders, as members of the human race, respond to incentives . . . . [T]his has been the justification for applying economic analysis to all illegal activities, from speeding and tax evasion to murder . . . . At least in the economic literature, there has been little controversy concerning this approach. . . .

In any event, the version of the mathematical inequality above omits the factor of delay [or D,] . . . [w]hich . . . theoretically should be represented as a divisor of the $C \times S$ product: . . .

$$[(C \times S) / D] > R$$

. . . If this relationship holds, the strength of the deterrent is proportional to the certainty of punishment, multiplied by the severity of the expected punishment, divided by the length of the delay before its imposition. [If the result is greater than R, deterrence results . . . .]

[But] [s]cholars of economics base their diagrams, equations, and laws on several assumptions . . . . The most basic of these assumptions is that actors making economic decisions fit a mold called "homo economicus," the economic person . . . . Homo economicus is always . . . informed [about all considerations, which here include C, S, D, and R. But it is unlikely that they have information about these legal details]. . . .

In fact, people's perceptions about the crimes of robbery and murder may not be based on . . . the law at all. . . . [One] survey showed that participants [instead] imagined the law to be consistent with their [own personal] moral inclinations. In other words, a person thinking about a particular harmful course of action is likely to consider it lawful or unlawful according to whether the person believes it is wrong enough to be criminal, rather than according to . . . the law. Presumably, the individual also imagines an estimated sentence [in a similar way]. . . . The possible conclusion . . . is that sentencing "for deterrence" is likely to be inferior to sentencing for just-deserts distribution. . . .

In summary, there are defects in a theory of rational choice that assumes accurate perception. . . . [C]ommentators have advanced the theory that sentences based on individual criminal laws do not deter, and instead, it is the criminal justice system as a whole that deters. This model . . . might be called "systemic" deterrence . . . .

. . . What Is Systemic Deterrence, and How Does It Work?

The theory of deterrence that comes first to mind is likely the market or economic model. In *Gregg v. Georgia*, [excerpted below,] the case that upheld modern death penalty statutes, the Supreme Court accepted this market model . . . . [The Court concluded that capital punishment might force an offender to face a "cold calculus" of risk and reward.] . . .

But in general, this is probably not the way that deterrence works. Instead, the more likely mechanism is that an offender is affected by what can be called "systemic" deterrence. The research suggests that deterrence from manipulation of precise sentence ranges . . . is marginal at best for most offenses. But the consensus is that deterrence does result from the criminal justice system. The conclusion might be stated as: sentences for particular crimes do not deter, but the criminal justice system as a whole deters.

Sometimes courts have taken surprisingly narrow views of systemic deterrence. For example, in *United States v. Edwards*, [595 F.3d 1004 (9th Cir. 2010)], the court affirmed a sentence of probation and restitution for what it described as a "serious" white collar offense, where the defendant had been previously convicted of a similar crime and was described by another judge in another case as a "big time thief." The district court [in considering deterrence] concluded that only people residing in the defendant's "community" were likely to know of his sentence. A dissenting judge criticized the majority's "unnecessarily restrictive view of general deterrence." In fact, both the majority and dissent confined their analysis to the particularized economic model, and neither considered systemic deterrence.

How does systemic deterrence work? The experiments and studies do not tell us, so the mechanism is a matter of conjecture. Perhaps the first step is that persons contemplating crime are solidly aware of the criminal justice system as a general concept, in that they surely know that police officers arrest offenders and that courts convict them, with the result that they serve sentences. . . . The second step is that, not knowing the exact sentence for the intended crime, the subject . . . must guess at it. Third, since research shows that people generally picture the criminal justice system as conforming to their own images of what the collective moral code should be, the offender installs this conception into the factor representing the severity of the probable sentence that would result from conviction. Fourth, the potential offender arrives at a probability of conviction according to a similarly formed estimate of certainty. And finally, he or she must decide whether the reward expected from the crime is worth the risk.

This scenario is highly theoretical, because the research does not disclose the stepwise mechanism of the deterrence process. . . . For example, it may be that the potential criminal imagines a guesstimated risk of a potential sentence all in a single idea. In any event, it is usually the system, not the precise sentence likelihood for the particular crime, that does the work of deterrence. . . .

Notes and Questions

(1) *If Systematic Deterrence Is a Valid Model, Then Sentences for One Crime Can Deter Other, Unrelated Crimes.* The consequences of systemic deterrence might be far-reaching. If a jurisdiction is known for serious sentences for serious crimes, the potential offender "installs" his or her impression of the collective morality, and serious sentences for one kind of crime can deter other, unrelated crimes:

> Given the nature of systemic deterrence, maybe sentences for robbery can deter other crimes such as burglary. Maybe sentences for robbery can even exert some minimizing effect on crimes of distant character, such as driving while intoxicated. If the estimates of potential sentences arrived at by potential criminals are indeed products of the criminal justice system as a whole, rather than of particular statutes or practices, there is no reason to conclude that deterrence cannot result across the range of crimes from punishments of a given crime.

Deterrence, 49 St. Mary's L. Rev. at 354.

(2) *Systemic Deterrence as the Mechanism for the "Broken Windows" Theory.* The "broken windows" theory was popularized by criminologist James Q. Wilson and used to significant effect in the past in New York. *See id.* at 356. The theory is that vigorous enforcement of minor crimes deters major crimes. Thus, pursuit of crimes such as graffiti, aggressive panhandling, and vandalism (broken windows) creates an impression that leads to systemic deterrence. Stamping out these crimes also deters robbery and assault.

(3) *Experimental Support for Broken Windows Theory (and for Systemic Deterrence)?* Researchers in the Netherlands placed five-Euro bills in mailboxes so that they protruded, inviting theft. They surrounded them with three different environments: one with graffiti-covered walls, one with litter covering the ground, and one clean. The graffiti- and litter-filled environments produced significantly more thefts

of five-Euro bills than the clean environment. *See* Kees Keizer et al., *The Spreading of Disorder*, 322 Science 1681 (2008). Does this remarkable experiment support the broken windows theory? If so, does it also support systemic deterrence?

[B] Incapacitation

James Q. Wilson, Selective Incapacitation

in *Principled Sentencing* 148–49 (Andrew von Hirsch
and Andrew Ashworth eds. 1992)

When criminals are deprived of their liberty, as by imprisonment . . . , their ability to commit offenses against citizens is ended. We say these persons have been "incapacitated," and we try to estimate the amount by which crime is reduced by this incapacitation.

Incapacitation cannot be the sole purpose of the criminal justice system; if it were, we would put everybody who has committed one or two offenses in prison until they were too old to commit another. . . . Justice, humanity, and proportionality, among other goals, must also be served. . . .

But there is one great advantage to incapacitation as a crime control strategy — namely, it does not require us to make any assumptions about human nature. By contrast, deterrence works only if people take into account the costs and benefits of alternative courses of action and choose that which confers the largest net benefit (or the smallest net cost). . . . [I]t is difficult to be certain by how much such considerations affect their behavior and what change, if any, in crime rates will result. . . .

Incapacitation, on the other hand, works by definition: its effects result from the physical restraint placed upon the offender and not from his subjective state. . . .

All the evidence we have implies that, for crime-reduction purposes, the most rational way to use the incapacitative powers of our prisons would be to do so selectively. Instead of longer sentences for everyone, or for persons who have prior records, or for persons whose present crime is especially grave, longer sentences would be given primarily to those who, when free, commit the most crimes.

Notes on Incapacitation

(1) *Incapacitation as Resignation?* As Wilson suggests, incapacitation surely works as a method of preventing recidivist crimes. An example is the wave of "three strikes and you're out laws" that provide a severe minimum sentence upon conviction for a third felony. Yet incapacitation can also be seen as akin to throwing up one's hands: there is a lot of crime, we don't know what to do, so we'll just lock up all the criminals. Still, from a consequentialist point of view — and incapacitation is plainly consequentialist — the goal is to get results, and incapacitation holds out the possibility of concrete results.

(2) *The Problem of False Positives: Andrew von Hirsch, Prediction and False Positives, in Principled Sentencing* 120–122 (Andrew von Hirsch & Andrew Ashworth eds. 1992). Or does it? Incapacitation may make people feel more secure because they believe the criminals most likely to keep committing crimes are safely behind bars. But what if we pick the wrong people for extended incarceration? We may not be as safe as we feel, and some people in jail will suffer unjustly. Perhaps, for example, the person who commits three felonies and is incarcerated may never have committed another one. And the problems may go deeper, as von Hirsch says:

> [A]ny system of preventive incarceration conceals erroneous confinements, while revealing erroneous releases. The individual who is wrongly identified as dangerous is confined, and thus has little or no opportunity to demonstrate that he would not have committed [another] crime had he been released. The individual who is wrongly identified as nondangerous remains at large, so it comes to public attention if he later commits a crime. Thus, once a preventive system is established, it creates the illusion of generating only one kind of evidence: evidence of erroneous release, that prompts decision makers to expand the categories of persons who are preventively confined. . . .

In other words, incapacitation may fail on consequentialist grounds. How should a proponent of incapacitation respond to von Hirsch's argument?

(3) *Selective Incapacitation: "Career Criminals."* In certain crime categories, disproportionate numbers of offenses are committed by just a few "career" offenders. This is among the reasons that Wilson argues for "selective" incapacitation. Many prosecutors' offices have attempted to identify these "career" offenders, concentrate resources on them, and seek lengthy sentences that will incapacitate them. Three-strikes laws, which enhance penalties on second and third convictions, reflect the same idea. Do these policies, as applied, answer von Hirsch's concerns?

(4) *Can a Shorter Sentence (Say, of Five Years) "Incapacitate"?* James Q. Wilson argues that systematic imposition of sentences of at least five years to all armed robbers would incapacitate, even if not as effectively as longer sentences. The result would be to prevent the robberies that otherwise might be committed by a rolling five-year period for multiple robbers, thus reducing recidivist robberies by a five-year proportion on average. Is this "incapacitation"?

[C] Rehabilitation

Notes on Rehabilitation

(1) *Reform of the Offender as a Utilitarian Goal.* One way to increase the likelihood that criminals do not continue engaging in criminal activity is to "rehabilitate" them by providing education, job-training, counseling, or therapy, or so says the theory.

(2) *The Historical Quest for the "Rehabilitative Ideal": Reform as the Dominant, or Even the Exclusive, Goal.* In the mid-twentieth century, rehabilitation appeared to be the dominant theory of punishment. In 1962, the Model Penal Code embraced

rehabilitation as a dominant goal. A few years later, Karl Menninger famously claimed that the overriding goal of punishment should be to provide appropriate therapy and that the majority of offenders could be "cured." *The Crime of Punishment* (1968). Punishment had failed, Menninger announced, and a scientific approach would not "waste" so much money, but would instead use a "civilized" program of psychotherapy. Soon, however, criticisms from a variety of perspectives left advocates of rehabilitation scrambling to retain a role in correctional policy. The new version of MPC § 1.02(2), discussed above, indicates that the challenge to rehabilitation continues.

Francis A. Allen, The Decline of the Rehabilitative Ideal
2–5 (1981)

One might begin by saying that the rehabilitative ideal is the notion that a primary purpose of penal treatment is to effect changes in the characters, attitudes, and behaviors of convicted offenders . . . .

[T]he nature of the rehabilitative ideal is profoundly affected by whether rehabilitation is seen as the exclusive justification of penal sanctions . . . , as a dominant purpose, or only as a part of a penal strategy that may sometimes require rehabilitative objectives to give way to other important social interests. Clearly, too, the content of the rehabilitative ideal is significantly affected by the means employed and assumed to be effective in achieving rehabilitation. A remarkable range of rehabilitative techniques has been espoused in the United States. . . . Obviously, the meanings and impact of the rehabilitative ideal are quite different depending on whether the appropriate means are thought to be the promotion of literacy, the provision of vocational education, programs of psychotherapy, brainwashing, or the surgical removal of brain tissue. . . .

Notes on the Decline and Persistence of Rehabilitation

(1) *Criticism of Rehabilitation: "Nothing Works."* The most basic and persistent criticism of rehabilitation has been best captured, albeit crudely, by the slogan "nothing works." A series of studies over the past thirty years indicates that rehabilitation is difficult, or perhaps impossible to achieve, for many offenders. For overviews of the "nothing works" assertion and other practical objections, see Richard C. Boldt, *Rehabilitative Punishment and the Drug Treatment Court Movement*, 76 Wash. U. L. Q. 1206, 1223–29 (1998), and Michael Vitiello, *Reconsidering Rehabilitation*, 65 Tul. L. Rev. 1011, 1032–38 (1991).

(2) *Criticism of the "Paternalism" Inherent in the Rehabilitative Ideal: Michael Moore, Law and Psychiatry: Rethinking the Relationship* 234–35 (1984). Other critics have attacked the "paternalistic" aspects of rehabilitation that justify treatment for the good of the convicted criminal. Consider whether you agree with Michael Moore, who has suggested three reasons why "[t]his paternalistic type of rehabilitative theory has no proper part to play in any theory of punishment":

> First, such a paternalistic reform theory allocates scarce societal resources away from other, more deserving groups that want them (such as retarded

and autistic children or the poor), to a group that hardly can be said to deserve such favored status and, moreover, does not want such "benefits." . . . Second, . . . [c]riminals are not in the standard classes in society for which paternalistic state intervention is appropriate, such as the severely disordered, the young, or others whose capacity for rational choice is diminished. . . . Third, such recasting of punishment in terms of "treatment" for the good of the criminal makes possible a kind of moral blindness that is dangerous in itself. . . . [It] makes it easy to inflict treatments and sentences that need bear no relation to the desert of the offender.

(3) *The "Medical Model" and the Indeterminate Sentence: David Crump, Determinate Sentencing*, 68 Kentucky. L.J. 1, 29–31 (1979). The quest for the rehabilitative ideal led to the ascendancy of the "indeterminate sentence." The judge would sentence the offender to a broad indeterminate range, perhaps five years to life. This approach essentially substituted the parole board as the "real" sentencing entity. The board would release the defendant when he or she was "cured." And this concept, in turn, was closely related to the "medical model" of crime:

> [T]he "medical model" regards criminal acts as analogous to "symptoms" of a "disease" that correctional "experts" may "treat" and "cure." . . . [It] reached its ultimate expression in the indeterminate sentence, in which the court sentenced the convict to a broad range of years so that the parole board could evaluate his ["medical"] treatment and readiness for release.

> There were a number of difficulties. . . . [W]ithout consideration of moral blameworthiness, rational grading of sentences and equal justice were lost . . . . At the same time, [the] assumption that the disease of crime could be treated and cured was too facile; worse yet, this scientific terminology gave an impression of accuracy that was unrealistic, and it probably led to the unnecessary incarceration of persons diagnosed as dangerous when in fact they were not (as well as to the premature release of others mistakenly considered harmless). Furthermore, the medical model implied no logical limits on the power of government to tamper with the personalities of individuals within its care. . . . In some states, wardens have placed greater blame for prison violence upon dissatisfaction with the indeterminate sentence than upon food, overcrowding or conditions of incarceration.

> The . . . rehabilitative ideal . . . thus came under attack from both ends of the political spectrum. Those who emphasized crime control argued that it was not working, and those concerned with prisoners' rights protested that it was unfair.

(4) *Rehabilitating Rehabilitation.* Defenders, however, have argued "that some offenders are amenable to rehabilitation and that social scientists can identify those offenders by use of objective criteria." Michael Vitiello, *Reconsidering Rehabilitation*, 65 Tul. L. Rev. 1011, 1037 (1991). In response to the claim that rehabilitation is dehumanizing, some defenders have emphasized its "humane" foundations, associating

it with a "useful and moral goal" that contrasts with retributive moralism and incapacitation. Francis T. Cullen & Karen E. Gilbert, *Reaffirming Rehabilitation* (1982).

(5) *Variations; Facilitative and Noncoercive Rehabilitation: Norval Morris, The Future of Imprisonment* 27 (1974). Commentators have also pointed out that rehabilitative approaches are not monolithic. One can distinguish broadly between facilitative rehabilitation, in which prisoners choose to participate in programs (and release from prison is not conditioned on it), and coercive rehabilitation, in which prisoners are forced to participate in programs.

(6) *Coming Full Circle: Perhaps Rehabilitation Is Still Dominant, Although in a Different Way from the Historical "Ideal."* Although rehabilitation is not the "ideal" that it once was, it continues to have an important place in sentencing. Inmates often complete high school coursework and obtain GED's, and some take college-level courses. Job training is often available. The use of parole and probation, as well as specialized courts for juveniles and drug offenders, also reflect rehabilitative goals. In fact, the number of probationers and parolees in the United States typically has been much more than the prison population. Their sentences are consistent with rehabilitation.

Kevin R. Reitz *et al.*, Model Penal Code: Sentencing—Workable Limits on Mass Incarceraton
48 Crime and Justice 255 (2019)

. . . The new *Model Penal Code: Sentencing* (MPCS) won final approval from the American Law Institute in 2017. . . . It . . . replaces about half of the old code—the half concerning sentencing and corrections. . . .

[MPCS] approaches sentencing from a human, rather than a doctrinal, perspective. That is, it concerns itself with all the ways people convicted of crimes experience punishment. . . .

This essay highlights a number of the MPCS's major proposals to introduce rational limits on sentences in individual cases as well as system-wide controls over aggregate sentencing severity. . . .

In addition, the MPCS addresses sentencing law and policy at the individual-case level and gives close attention to the distinctive principles at work for each sanction type. For example, it greatly restricts the utilitarian purposes that may be used to justify incarceration sentences. It would abolish all mandatory imprisonment laws . . . . In community supervision, the MPCS counsels in favor of smaller probation and parole populations, with more resources devoted to clients with the greatest needs. The MPCS advocates shorter supervision terms, the parsimonious use of conditions, and defined incentives that allow clients to earn early termination. It further takes the view that many people currently on probation do not need supervision at all . . . . As a law-reform priority, diversion from probation is a significant goal under the MPCS, as well as diversion from prison. On the expanding panoply of financial sanctions imposed on criminal offenders . . . , the MPCS recommends drastic cutbacks. . . . In the domain of collateral consequences of conviction—although these are usually classified as "civil" measures—the MPCS gives courts the power to exempt defendants from the mandatory effects of such sanctions. It also empowers courts to grant "certificates of rehabilitation" . . . , which would clear away nearly all collateral sanctions. . . .

[In a footnote, the authors add:] The MPCS rejects rehabilitation by itself as a justificatory goal of incarceration, although it requires prisons and jails to provide reasonable opportunities to those incarcerated to participate in rehabilitative activities . . . . And, as just explained, it disapproves the consideration of general deterrence by sentencing judges as a reason to incarcerate or to lengthen a term of stay.

Notes and Questions

(1) *Recognition of All Major Principles of Sentencing, Maybe Including Rehabilitation?* The former Model Penal Code was arguably objectionable because of its dominant emphasis on rehabilitation. The new Sentencing Code expressly says that rehabilitation is not a goal of incarceration "by itself." Is this an improvement?

(2) *"Limiting Mass Incarceration": Does the Code Properly Consider the Costs?* The authors of this article do not assess the costs associated with their stated goal of limiting mass incarceration. Isn't there a risk that crime will increase as a result of reduced imprisonment (especially without a focus on rehabilitation)? From the other direction, might one respond that, even if the MPCS (improbably) cuts the prison population in half, to something under 1 million, we will still have a system of "mass incarceration"?

(3) *In Focusing on the "Experience" of the Offender, Does the MPCS Depreciate the "Experience" of Crime Victims and the Public?* The authors characterize the Code as "concerning itself with all the ways people convicted of crimes experience punishment." They call this approach a "human" perspective. What about the humans who are victims of murder, robbery, rape, and burglary? And what about the enormous costs all humans in the public must bear to minimize exposure to crime?

(4) *Less Use of Probation, with "Parsimonious" Conditions and Less Reporting?* Historically, probationary sentences have been considered rehabilitative. But the new Code calls for less of it (for those the authors refer to as "clients," rather than probationers, who receive "more resources"). Does this proposal make sense?

[D] Retributive Justice

[1] *The Kantian Ideal of Retribution: An Unvaryingly Equal Jus Talionis ("An Eye for an Eye")*

Notes on Retribution in Deontological Theory

(1) *Kant and Deontological Theory.* As we have seen, Kant contended that every individual has a duty to act in ways that can be imitated as "universal laws," which he

called "categorical imperatives." And as we have also seen, one categorical imperative was that every action must treat each person as individually valuable, and not as an object. *Groundwork of the Metaphysics of Morals* 39 (1785) (Mary Gregor trans. 1997).

(2) *Retributive Justice: Blameworthiness Is the Measure.* These ideas also allowed Kant to develop a rigorously retributive philosophy of sentencing. Punishment is matched to the crime and the offender. The offender gets just what he or she deserves, no more and no less. A strictly retributive theory of punishment prohibits punishing someone severely as an example to others. If the authorities catch a burglar during a period of frequent and unsolved burglaries, a retributive approach to punishment would reject a lengthy sentence based solely on general deterrence, because aggravating the sentence would treat the defendant as a means, not an end. In this sense, retribution is humanitarian. It emphasizes proportionality, consistency, and uniformity, and it limits the sentence so that it does not exceed the offender's blameworthiness.

(3) *Kant's Reliance on the "Jus Talionis": Retaliation in Kind.* Kant here adopts the principle of "jus talionis," which can be roughly translated as "the justice of the claw." Jus talionis refers to punishment in kind: "an eye for an eye, a tooth for a tooth." Kant recognizes that this principle is impossible to carry out literally in most cases, but it is from the jus talionis that he borrows his measure of strictly equal sentencing, in proportion to blameworthiness.

Immanuel Kant, The Metaphysics of Morals

105–06 (1797) (Mary Gregor trans. 1991)

. . . Punishment by a court . . . can never be inflicted merely as a means to promote some other good for the criminal himself or for civil society. It must always be inflicted upon him only because he has committed a crime. For a human being can never be treated merely as a means to the purposes of another . . . . He must previously have been found punishable before any thought can be given to drawing from his punishment something of use for himself or his fellow citizens. The law of punishment is a categorical imperative. . . .

But what kind and what amount of punishment is it that public justice makes its principle and measure? None other than the principle of equality. [Here, Kant suggests that this "principle of equality" means that the same harm done *by* the convict should be done *to* him; a thief should lose his possessions, and a murderer should be put to death.] [O]nly the *law of retribution* (*ius talionis*)—it being understood, of course, that this is applied by a court (not by your private judgment)—can specify definitely the quality and the quantity of punishment . . . . Whoever steals makes the property of everyone else insecure and therefore deprives himself (by the principle of retribution) of security in any possible property. [The law should treat him as though he] has nothing and can also acquire nothing. . . . But since the state will not provide for him free of charge, he must [perform] any kind of work it pleases (in convict or prison labor) . . . .

If, however, he has committed murder he must die. Here there is no substitute that will satisfy justice. There is no . . . likeness between the crime and the retribution unless death is judicially carried out upon the wrongdoer. . . . Even if a civil society were to be dissolved by the consent of all its members (*e.g.*, if a people inhabiting an island decided to separate and disperse throughout the world), the last murderer remaining in prison would first have to be executed, so that each has done to him what his deeds deserve and blood guilt does not cling to the people for not having insisted upon this punishment; for otherwise the people can be regarded as collaborators in this public violation of justice.

Notes and Questions on Retribution

(1) *Is Kant's Reference to the Jus Talionis Simply a Metaphor for Proportionality, or Something Else?* John Salmond contended that Kant's reference to the jus talionis is "metaphorical and symbolic," rather than literal. *Jurisprudence* 118 (Glanville L. Williams 10th ed. 1947). Morris Cohen saw the same reference as an argument for proportionality: "But if the old form of the *lex talionis*, an eye for an eye or a tooth for a tooth, sounds too barbaric today, may we not . . . put it thus: Everyone is to be punished alike in proportion to the gravity of his offense or to the extent to which he had made others suffer?" *Reason and Law* 53 (1961).

(2) *The Position of the "Retributivist in Distribution": Proportionality, Uniformity, and Blameworthiness as Overlays That Modify Utilitarian Sentencing.* The "retributivist in distribution" believes that purposeless suffering is unjust even when inflicted on convicted criminals and, therefore, disagrees with Kant about disconnecting sentencing from deterrence, incapacitation, and rehabilitation. But the retributivist-in-distribution also agrees with Kant and adopts the Kantian ideal of proportionality to blameworthiness as a limit on the "distribution" of sentences, or their relative lengths. Thus, the retributivist-in-distribution uses Kantian proportionality as a restriction on Utilitarianism, to prevent excessive or disparate sentences. Purely Utilitarian sentencing, without Kantian proportionality based on blameworthiness, could not achieve uniformity, consistency, and proportionality. Do you agree?

(3) *Contemporary Formulations of Retribution: Andrew von Hirsch, Proportionate Punishments* in *Principled Sentencing* 197 (Andrew von Hirsch and Andrew Ashworth eds. 1992). Consistently with these views, von Hirsch describes retribution as "commensurate deserts." This principle

> ensures that offenders are not treated as more (or less) blameworthy than is warranted by the character of the offense. . . . A criminal penalty is not merely unpleasant (so are taxes and conscription): it also connotes that the offender acted wrongfully and is reprehensible for having done so . . . That being the case, it should be inflicted only to the degree that it is deserved.

(4) *Is Retribution Really "Revenge"—or Is It "Justice"?* Kant's supporters often avoid the label of "retributivism" and use a more appealing word: "justice." Meanwhile,

Kant's opponents call it "revenge." But are the two terms merely positive and negative descriptions of the same idea?

(5) *James Fitzjames Stephen's View: "Hatred of [Criminal] Conduct" Is "Health[y]," Even if Some People "Call It Revenge [or] Resentment."* James Fitzjames Stephen saw retribution as an expression of society's "hatred" of criminality, a hatred that was "health[y]." Consider these words from chapter 4 of his attack on utilitarianism, *Liberty, Equality, Fraternity* (1873):

> [Crimes are] subjected to punishment not only because they are danger-
> ous to society, . . . but also for satisfying the feeling of hatred—call it
> revenge, resentment, or what you will—which the contemplation of such
> conduct incites in healthily constituted minds. . . . [C]riminal law is . . .
> an emphatic assertion of the principle that the feeling of hatred and the
> desire of vengeance above-mentioned are important elements of human
> nature which ought in such cases to be satisfied in a regular public and legal
> manner.

Stephen does not suggest hatred of the criminal as an *individual*, but rather of the criminal *act:* "hatred of the conduct." His view is that society benefits from revulsion against criminal conduct. Still, he sees "desire for vengeance" as [an] "important element [] of human nature." Is Stephen's philosophy one of revenge, or of justice, or both?

(6) *Stephen's Apparent Justification of Retribution as Preventing Private Violence or Vigilantism in a "Regular Public and Legal Manner" (and the Supreme Court's Adoption of This Argument).* Stephen's reference to expressing "hatred" for criminal conduct raises the spectre of vigilantism that might emerge if society were to fail to produce justice. It is preferable for a state to exercise this function in a "regular pubic and legal manner" so that it can avoid excess; but if individuals lose confidence in the state, they will take the law into their own hands (or so the argument goes). Is there anything to this proposition? In *Gregg v. Georgia*, which appears later in this chapter, the Supreme Court agreed, concluding that without retributive justice, "there are sown the seeds of . . . vigilante justice and lynch law."

(7) *Michael Moore's Different View: The Moral Worth of Retribution, in Responsibility, Character, and the Emotions* 217 (Ferdinand Schoeman ed. 1987). In an effort to "rescue" retributivism from Stephen, Michael Moore suggests the need to "recognize the dangers retributive punishment presents for the expression of resentment, sadism, and so on." The response, he argues, is not to reject retributivism, but rather "to design our punishment institutions to minimize the opportunity for such feelings to be expressed. There is no contradiction in attempting to make a retributive punishment humane . . . ."

Is Moore's version of retribution preferable to that of Stephen—and is it even possible? Consider whether Moore engages in the Fallacy of Definition, in favoring "retribution" but disfavoring what he refers to as "resentment."

[2] The Utilitarian Analogue to Retributivism: "Condemnation" That "Act[s] on Upright People"

Notes on the Synthesis of Utilitarian and Kantian Ideals: Is It Possible?

(1) *A Synthesis of Consequentialism and Deontology: The Kantian Who Defers to Utilitarianism and the Rule-Oriented Utilitarian.* In this section, we shall see that Utilitarians often reach conclusions that resemble those of Kantians. Few people are exclusively consequentialists or deontologists. The deontologist, for example, cannot claim to use purely moral principles to derive all of the answers to economic questions, even if they benefit some people more than others. Thus, even Kantians may have to defer to Utilitarianism sometimes. Likewise, the Utilitarian cannot pretend that every decision can be based upon individualized determination of costs and risks, as opposed to rules or norms. Hence, there is the "rule-based Utilitarian." Moreover, the consequentialist cannot persuasively defend a regime that imposes crushing burdens on random individuals to achieve general goals.

(2) *The Synthesis: Perhaps Deontology and Consequentialism Are Merely Different Ways of Seeing the Same Things?* It is possible to argue that Utilitarianism is really a disguised form of Kantianism. Justice is beneficial even to the Utilitarian, because it avoids hidden costs such as public rebellion against unfair punishments. (Perhaps it is equally possible to view some kinds of deontology as disguised forms of consequentialism: reckless risks to other lives are wrong because of the consequences.)

(3) *When Should You Use Consequentialism — and When Deontology?: Heidi M. Hurd, The Deontology of Negligence,* 76 B.U. L. Rev. 249, 251–52 (1996). The trouble with this "synthesis" is that sometimes Utilitarian and Kantian views still point to different solutions. Then, which approach is superior? Professor Hurd argues, "[T]he principal payoff of deontological maxims is their ability to define and patrol the borders of consequential justification." In other words, the law should follow Utilitarian considerations in most applications, but it should impose Deontological limits in extreme (or borderline) cases. Do you agree?

(4) *"Condemnation": A Utilitarian Analogue to Kantian Retribution.* It stands to reason, then, that Utilitarians ultimately would come to recognize certain values analogous to those articulated by Kant. Utilitarian sentencing that produced overly harsh results, as in the example of capital punishment for intoxicated drivers, would engender disrespect for law. And therefore, pushing deterrence to the limits of its logic cannot maximize happiness. In one of the epigrams that introduced this chapter, John Stuart Mill explains that his Utilitarian philosophy involves pluralistic values that conflict among themselves. Compromise is necessary. To be accepted, punishments need to reflect blameworthiness. In this, Utilitarianism sounds remarkably like Kantian retribution, with the main difference being that the Kantian view was based on moral rightness, whereas the Utilitarian view derived instead from the consequences: the utility of public acceptance. The Utilitarian goal

sometimes is referred to by the word "condemnation," a word that makes it sound more functional and purposive than retribution.

(5) *Durkheim's View: Punishment as Condemnation and Reinforcement, "Above all, Designed to Act on Upright People."* Perhaps the goal of punishment is the preservation of social cohesion, the common conscience, and community solidarity. It does this, ironically, by fulfilling the same "passion" as revenge does, but in a more controlled way. This control, according to Durkheim, is the only difference between vengeance and social cohesion. To put it another way, a society that failed to achieve justice would ultimately fall apart. Condemnation, then, is not an effort to correct the criminal. Instead, it is a reinforcement of faith in the law. Durkheim thus is able to state his thesis "without paradox": Condemnation "is designed to act upon upright people."

Emile Durkheim, The Division of Labor in Society

85–87, 96, 108 (4th ed. 1911) (George Simpson trans. 1933)

[P]unishment consists of a passionate reaction. . . . [But] [i]t is an error to believe that vengeance is [only] useless cruelty. . . .

Although [punishment] proceeds . . . from movements which are passionate . . ., it does play a useful role. [But] this role is not where we ordinarily look for it. It does not serve, or else only serves quite secondarily, in correcting the culpable or in intimidating possible followers [through deterrence]. From this point of view, its efficacy is justly doubtful and, in any case, mediocre. [Instead,] [i]ts true function is to maintain social cohesion intact, while maintaining all its vitality in the common conscience. . . . [That common conscience] would necessarily lose its energy, if an emotional reaction of the community did not come to compensate its loss, and it would result in a breakdown of social solidarity. It is necessary, then, that [the common conscience] be affirmed forcibly . . . by an authentic act which can consist only in suffering inflicted upon the agent.

[T]his suffering is not a gratuitous cruelty. It is the sign which witnesses that collective sentiments are always collective. . . . We can thus say, without paradox, that punishment is above all designed to act upon upright people . . . since it serves to heal the wounds made upon collective sentiments.

Notes and Questions

(1) *Punishment Operates Most Directly on the Convicted Individual—and So, How Can Durkheim Say That It Is "Designed to Act upon Upright People"?* To understand the idea of condemnation as reinforcement, you must understand why Durkheim says that it acts, above all, "upon upright people." How does he support this argument?

(2) *Revisiting the Distinction between "Revenge" and "Justice"—and the Views of James Fitzjames Stephen and Michael Moore.* According to Durkheim, revenge and punishment for societal preservation are the same thing. Vengeance is not "useless,"

because it is protective of community. The only way to "express the unanimous aversion" of the community to a criminal act is to impose "suffering inflicted on the agent." And so, perhaps one can argue that there is indeed a difference between revenge and justice, but it is only that revenge inflicts suffering that is poorly understood and controlled, whereas justice is better directed at its purpose to inflict suffering. Is Durkheim's treatment of this subject persuasive?

§ 9.04 Traditional Punishment Theory in Practice

United States v. Bergman

416 F. Supp. 496 (S.D.N.Y. 1976)

FRANKEL, DISTRICT JUDGE.

[Defendant is being sentenced for Medicaid-related fraud involving nursing homes. Judge Frankel's description of the facts appears at the beginning of this chapter. The excerpt that follows provides the court's explanation of why a sentence of four months in prison is an appropriate punishment.]

The court agrees that this defendant should not be sent to prison for "rehabilitation." . . . [T]his court shares the growing understanding that no one should ever be sent to prison for rehabilitation. . . . Imprisonment is punishment. . . . If someone must be imprisoned for other, valid reasons we should seek to make rehabilitative resources available to him or her. But the goal of rehabilitation cannot fairly serve in itself as grounds for the sentence to confinement.

Equally clearly, this defendant should not be confined to incapacitate him. He is not dangerous. It is most improbable that he will commit similar, or any, offenses in the future. . . .

Contrary to counsel's submissions, however, two sentencing considerations demand a prison sentence in this case:

> First, the aim of general deterrence, the effort to discourage similar wrongdoing by others. . . .

> Second, the related . . . concern that any lesser penalty would, in the words of the Model Penal Code, § 7.01(1)(c), "depreciate the seriousness of the defendant's crime."

Resisting the first of these propositions, defense counsel invoke Immanuel Kant's axiom that "one man ought never to be dealt with merely as a means subservient to the purposes of another." . . . As for Dr. Kant, it may well be that defense counsel mistake his meaning in the present context. [A] criminal punished in the interest of general deterrence is not being employed "merely as a means. . . ." Reading Kant to mean that every man must be deemed more than the instrument of others, and must "always be treated as an end in himself," the humane principle is not offended here. Each of us is served by the enforcement of the law, not least a person like the defendant in this case, whose wealth and privileges, so long enjoyed, are so much founded upon law. More broadly, we are driven regularly in our ultimate interests as members of the community to use ourselves and each other, in war and in peace, for social ends. One who has transgressed against the criminal laws is certainly among the more fitting candidates for a role of this nature. . . .

But the whole business, defendant argues further, is guesswork; we are by no means certain that deterrence "works." The position is somewhat overstated; there is, in fact, some reasonably "scientific" evidence for the efficacy of criminal sanctions as deterrents, at least as against some kinds of crimes. . . . The shared wisdom of generations teaches meaningfully, if somewhat amorphously, that the Utilitarians have a point; we do, indeed, lapse often into rationality and act to seek pleasure and avoid pain. . . .

The idea of avoiding depreciation of the seriousness of the offense implicates two or three thoughts, not always perfectly clear or universally agreed upon, beyond the idea of deterrence. It should be proclaimed by the court's judgment that the offenses are grave, not minor or purely technical. Some attention must be paid to the demand for equal justice; it will not do to leave the penalty of imprisonment a dead letter as against "privileged" violators while it is employed regularly, and with vigor, against others. There probably is in these conceptions an element of retributiveness, as counsel urge. And retribution, so denominated, is in some disfavor as a reason for punishment. It remains a factor, however. . . . It may become more palatable, and probably more humanely understood, under the rubric of "deserts" or "just deserts." . . .

Resisting prison above all else, defense counsel included in their thorough memorandum on sentencing two proposals for what they call . . . a "preferable" form of "behavioral sanction." One is a plan for Dr. Bergman to create and run a program of Jewish vocational and religious high school training. The other is for him to take charge of a "Committee on Holocaust Studies" . . . .

[B]oth of the carefully formulated "sanctions" in the memorandum involve work of an honorific nature, not unlike that done in other projects to which the defendant has devoted himself in the past. It is difficult to conceive of them as "punishments" at all. . . .

In cases like this one, the decision of greatest moment is whether to imprison or not. . . .

The criminal behavior, as has been noted, is blatant in character and unmitigated by any suggestion of necessitous circumstance or other pressures difficult to resist. . . . [I]t calls for more than a token sentence.

On the other side are factors that take longer to enumerate. Defendant's illustrious public life and works are in his favor, though diminished, of course, by what this case discloses. . . . Defendant is 64 years old and in imperfect health, though by no means so ill . . . that he could be expected to suffer inordinately more than many others of advanced years . . . .

How, then, should the particular sentence [be] adjudged in this case? . . . [I]t verges on cruelty to think of confinement for a term of years. We sit, to be sure, in a nation where prison sentences of extravagant length are more common than they are almost anywhere else. By that light, the term imposed today is not notably long. For this sentencing court, however, . . . it is a stern sentence. For people like Dr. Bergman, who might be disposed to engage in similar wrongdoing, it should be sufficiently frightening to serve the major end of general deterrence. For all but the profoundly vengeful, it should not depreciate the seriousness of his offenses. [The court sentenced Bergman to four months in prison.]

Notes and Questions

(1) *Did the Court Properly Consider and Apply the Various Goals of Sentencing?* The goals of sentencing inevitably collide in some cases, with some factors counseling a lesser sentence and some a greater. Is the judge's analysis persuasive in evaluating how the purposes of deterrence, retribution, rehabilitation, and incapacitation should affect the sentence? (For example, consider whether a sentence in the range of several years might provide a greater deterrent.)

(2) *Is Our Sentencing System "Characterized by Disparity?* Elsewhere, Judge Frankel was critical of a sentencing system whose "lack of meaningful criteria . . . leave[s] sentencing judges far too much at large." A judge sitting in the courtroom next door could have sentenced Bergman to two years, or four, or more. Yet a third judge could have sentenced Bergman to probation without imprisonment. Does good sentencing policy demand guidelines that channel judges' discretion? Judge Frankel thought so. *See* Marvin E. Frankel, *Criminal Sentences: Law Without Order* (1973). We take up this topic later in this chapter.

Problem 9D: Justifying and Opposing the Olis Sentence (A Return to Problem 9A, at the Beginning of This Chapter)

(1) *A Sentence of Twenty-Four Years for Conduct Analogous to That Underlying Bergman's Four Months.* Reconsider the story at the beginning of this chapter that describes the twenty-four (24) year sentence given to Jamie Olis. How could that sentence be justified or opposed in light of the four major goals of punishment?

(2) *What Method and Length Is Appropriate?* Bergman's four months resulted from a system of unguided discretion, while Olis's twenty-four years was the product of federal sentencing guidelines (which then were mandatory but now are advisory only). What method is best: guidelines, discretion, or a combination? And what would be an appropriate sentence for Olis (and, by implication, for Bergman)?

Note on the Revision of Olis's Sentence

(1) *The Court of Appeals Reversed, the Sentencing Guidelines Became Discretionary Rather Than Mandatory, and Olis Received a Much Shorter Sentence.* The court of appeals decided that the district court had used the wrong measure of the monetary

loss caused by Olis, which was an important determinant of his sentence under the guidelines. "Because the District Court's approach to the loss calculation did not take into account the impact of extrinsic factors on Dynegy's stock price decline, Olis is entitled to resentencing. . . ." Meanwhile, the Supreme Court had decided *United States v. Booker*, which appears later in this chapter, and which required the guidelines to be treated as discretionary rather than mandatory. In other words, the guidelines still were relevant as guidelines, but they did not absolutely determine the sentence.

(2) *Olis's Ultimate Sentence: Six Years.* Judge Sim Lake recalculated the monetary loss, and this time, the result was a guideline sentence between 12½ and 15½ years. However, Judge Lake exercised his discretion to sentence Olis to six years in prison, observing, "A lengthy sentence is not needed to deter Mr. Olis from future criminal conduct." [A]fter five years and three months in prison, a halfway house, and home confinement, Olis was freed.

§ 9.05 Variations on Sentencing Philosophies: The Expressive and Restorative Alternatives

[A] The Expressive Theory of Punishment

Joel Feinberg, The Expressive Function of Punishment

in *Doing and Deserving* 98–116 (1970)

Symbolic public condemnation . . . may help or hinder deterrence, reform, and rehabilitation — the evidence is not clear. On the other hand, there are other functions of punishment, often lost sight of in the preoccupation with deterrence and reform, that presuppose the expressive function and would be difficult or impossible without it.

Authoritative disavowal. Consider the standard international practice of demanding that a nation whose agent has unlawfully violated the complaining nation's rights should punish the offending agent. For example, suppose that an airplane of nation A fires on an airplane of nation B . . . over international waters. Very likely high authorities in nation B will send a note of protest to . . . nation A demanding . . . that the transgressive pilot be punished. Punishing the pilot is an emphatic, dramatic, and well-understood way of . . . *disavowing* his act. It tells the world . . . that his government does not condone that sort of thing. . . .

Symbolic nonacquiescence: "Speaking in the name of the people." The symbolic function of punishment also explains why even those sophisticated persons who abjure resentment of criminals . . . are likely to demand that certain kinds of conduct be punished when or if the law lets them go by. In the state of Texas, [at one time,] so-called paramour killings were regarded by the law as not merely mitigated, but completely justifiable. Many humanitarians . . . will feel quite spontaneously that a great injustice is done when such killings are left unpunished. . . . [E]ffective public denunciation and, through it, symbolic nonacquiescence in the crime seem virtually to require punishment. . . .

Vindication of the law. Sometimes the state goes on record through its statutes, in a way that might well please a conscientious citizen in whose name it speaks, but then . . . gives rise to doubts that the law really means what it says. It is murder in Mississippi, as elsewhere, for a white man intentionally to kill a Negro; but if grand juries refuse to issue indictments or if trial juries refuse to convict . . . then it is in a purely formal and empty sense indeed that killings of Negroes by whites are illegal in Mississippi. . . . A statute honored mainly in the breach begins to lose its character as law, unless, as we say, it is *vindicated.* . . .

Absolution of others. When something scandalous has occurred and it is clear that the wrongdoer must be one of a small number of suspects, then the state, by punishing one of these parties, thereby relieves the others of suspicion. . . . Moreover, quite often the absolution of an accuser hangs as much in the balance at a criminal trial as the inculpation of the accused. [Consider a case in which a woman testifies to a sexual assault, but the defendant responds with a defense of consent and also besmirches her character.] If the jury finds him guilty of rape, . . . her reputation as well as his rides on the outcome. . . .

[Thus, the] condemnatory aspect of punishment . . . is precisely the element . . . that makes possible . . . such symbolic functions as disavowal, nonacquiescence, vindication, and absolution.

Notes on Expressive Theories of Punishment

(1) *Punishment as an Assessment of Value: Jean Hampton, The Retributive Idea*, in Jeffrie Murphy & Jean Hampton, *Forgiveness and Mercy* 141–42 (1988). By comparing the relative punishments handed down for similar acts, some theorists claim to find an expression of how much society values the victim of the crime:

> [H]ow society reacts to one's victimization can be seen by one as an indication of how valuable society takes one to be. . . . If society allows the wrongdoer to suffer no painful consequences . . . , he (and others) may conclude that the ones against whom he transgressed are not valuable enough for society to construct a significant protective barrier. . . . So another idea behind victims' insistence [on punishment] is that society shouldn't allow the wrongdoers . . . to conclude . . . that they were right to believe the victims lacked value. . . .

(2) *The Argument in Favor of "Shaming" as a Sanction: Dan M. Kahan, What Do Alternative Sanctions Mean?*, 63 U. Chicago L. Rev. 591 (1996). Kahan suggests the value of punishments that "shame" criminals—such as newspaper advertisements with names and pictures of people convicted of driving under the influence of alcohol—because they allow inexpensive expression of moral condemnation while also providing strong deterrence.

(3) *Opposition to Shaming as a Sanction.* Others have questioned the use of expressive theories of punishment to support shaming sanctions. Toni Massaro contends that "public shaming by a criminal court judge will be, at most, a retributive spectacle that is devoid of other positive community-expressive or community-reinforcing content and which will not significantly deter crime. . . ." Toni M. Massaro, *Shame, Culture, and American Criminal Law*, 89 Mich. L. Rev. 1880, 1884 (1991). *See also* James Q. Whitman, *What is Wrong with Inflicting Shame Sanctions?*, 107 Yale L.J. 1055 (1998) (expressing similar concerns).

Problem 9E (Expressive Sanctions): "Please Shame My Client by Requiring Her to Carry a Sign"

(1) *Many Shame Sanctions Are "Creative Sentencing," Proposed Not by the Prosecution, but by the Defendant as an Alternative to Incarceration (Does This Make a Difference?).* Imagine that you represent a defendant who has been convicted of embezzling $20,000 from her employer. You realize that the judge is likely to sentence your client to two to three years in state prison. You scramble to find alternatives. You propose restitution, of course (in small amounts per month); you add probation terms that are onerous, plus hundreds of hours of community service; and reluctantly, your client authorizes you also to suggest a period of confinement in the county jail, to be served on weekends. But all of this does not seem to be enough to persuade the judge. More creatively, as the deal-closer, you suggest a condition of probation requiring your client to carry a sign saying, "I stole $20,000 from my employer" up and down Main Street for a week.

(2) *Is This Sentence, Using Shaming, Good Advocacy or Good Policy?* The prosecutor still opposes this alternative sentence, for reasons of deterrence and retribution, but the judge now is not so sure about sending your client to prison. By "playing the shaming card," you may have saved your client from incarceration. Does this scenario change your idea of shaming sanctions?

[B] Restorative Justice

Erik Luna, Introduction: The Utah Restorative Justice Conference

2003 Utah L. Rev. 1, 3–4

[R]estorative justice generally can be described as an approach to criminal sanctioning that includes all stakeholders in a particular offense in a process of group decisionmaking on how to handle the effects of the crime and its significance for the future. . . . [A]ffected individuals, family members, and supporters are considered central to crime control and appropriate resolutions. . . . [They meet with the offender.]

A primary objective of restorativism is making amends for the offending, particularly the harm caused to the victim, rather than inflicting pain upon the offender. Accountability is demonstrated by recognizing the wrongfulness of one's conduct, expressing remorse for the resulting injury, and taking steps to repair any damage. . . .

. . . Various programs from around the world seem to square with this understanding of restorative justice[, including] . . . victim-offender mediation throughout North America and Europe—all aimed at gathering stakeholders together to fashion appropriate resolutions for crime by means of mediated dialogue.

Notes and Questions

(1) *Restorative Justice as Substantive Ideal: John Braithwaite, A Future Where Punishment Is Marginalized: Realistic or Utopian?*, 46 UCLA L. Rev. 1727 (1999). To some extent, the restorative justice movement is an idealistic response to crime. According to its leading proponent, Braithwaite, "Punishment adds to the amount of hurt in the world, but justice has more meaning if it is about healing rather than hurting." Braithwaite adds, "But restorative justice will often fail, and when it does, deterrence and incapacitation may be needed as back-up strategies."

(2) *Criticisms of Restorative Justice: Richard Delgado, Goodbye to Hammurabi: Analyzing the Atavistic Appeal of Restorative Justice*, 52 Stanford L. Rev. 751 (2000). Critics of restorative justice suggest that it will lead to inconsistent results as different groups of stakeholders come up with wildly disparate "sentences" for near-identical crimes. Also, they raise a number of other concerns, ranging from coercion of defendants and aggrandizement of state power to coercion of victims into forgiving before they are ready.

§ 9.06 The Law of Sentencing: How Legal Rules Implement the Underlying Philosophies

Notes on Legal Rules in Sentencing

(1) *The Law of Sentencing: Ranges, Discretion, Guidelines, Limits, and Options.* We now turn to a different subject. In the preceding sections of this chapter, we have considered the philosophy of sentencing. But that is not all there is to it. Legislatures and courts have produced legal principles that exert more definite influences on sentences. For example, legislatures impose sentencing ranges. The trial judge often retains significant discretion—but sometimes it is confined narrowly. Constitutional limits restrict the legislature's and court's ability to impose sentences, and options such as incarceration, probation, and fines are set by law.

(2) *James Q. Wilson's View: Sentencing Usually Is the "Real" Issue.* To paraphrase criminologist James Q. Wilson, "Most of the time, in most of our busiest courts, the real issue concerns sentencing, and not guilt or innocence." Wilson's statement seems startling. But sentencing *is* prominent, because most criminal convictions result from guilty pleas, not full trials.

Notes on the Methods of American Sentencing

(1) *The American Tradition of Broad Sentencing Discretion.* One of the historical features of the American sentencing system has been broad discretion. Typically, statutes have provided judges with options and furnished little guidance in selecting among them.

(2) *The Role of Settlement or Plea Bargaining.* Although sentencing laws assign the function almost exclusively to judges, in reality many sentences are imposed without actual determination by judges. Over ninety percent of persons charged with crimes plead guilty. Routinely, a bargain sets the sentence the defendant will receive (or the crimes of which the defendant will be convicted). The court ordinarily accepts the agreement, making the prosecutor, defense attorney, and defendant the most important decisionmakers.

(3) *Fixed vs. Indeterminate Sentences.* Sentences can be "fixed" or "indeterminate." A fixed sentence is one for a set amount of time, such as two years in prison. An indeterminate sentence is one where the release date is not established at sentencing. An example is a sentence of three to five years in prison. The parole board or another agency will determine the date of release.

(4) *Concurrent vs. Consecutive Sentences.* If an offender is convicted of more than one crime, the sentencing judge will determine whether the sentences will be served concurrently or consecutively. A "concurrent sentence" is one that is served at the same time as another sentence. A "consecutive sentence" is one that is served after completion of another sentence. Statutes or case law may provide factors to guide the court in making this determination.

§ 9.07 Constitutional Limits on Sentence Lengths

Notes on Cruel and Unusual Punishment and "Disproportion"

(1) *Non-Capital Cases: Severity of Sentence.* The Cruel and Unusual Punishment Clause sometimes is used to argue that a particular sentence is so disproportionate that it is unconstitutional. But these claims are rarely successful. It is not clear to what extent the Eighth Amendment even requires that sentences be proportionate to offenses.

(2) *The Supreme Court's Changing Views about How (or Whether) the Eighth Amendment Affects Alleged Disproportionate Sentences: Rummel, Solem and Harmelin.* Although the Supreme Court has discussed the disproportionality issue in a series of cases, there is no agreement on the standards governing it. In *Rummel v. Estelle*, 445 U.S. 263 (1980), the Court held that the Cruel and Unusual Punishment Clause did not prohibit life imprisonment for a three-time felony offender. But then, in *Solem v. Helm*, 463 U.S. 277 (1983), the Court appeared to change course, because it held that the Eighth Amendment was violated by a sentence of life without parole

for a recidivist who had been convicted of many crimes. Next, in *Harmelin v. Michigan*, 501 U.S. 957 (1991), in which the defendant was convicted of possession of 672 grams of cocaine and was given a sentence of life without possibility of parole (which was mandatory in that State), the Court seemed to change course again. It refused to follow *Solem* and upheld the sentence.

(3) *Ewing v. California: The Three-Strikes Case.* The Court faced the issue again in the following case and upheld a three-strikes law. Notice how the Court is fractured.

Ewing v. California
538 U.S. 11 (2003)

Reaffirmed, Kernan v. Cuero
138 S. Ct. 4199 (2017)

Justice O'Connor announced the judgment of the Court and delivered an opinion in which the Chief Justice and Justice Kennedy join.

In this case, we decide whether the Eighth Amendment prohibits the State of California from sentencing a repeat felon to a prison term of 25 years to life under the State's "Three Strikes and You're Out" law.

I . . .

California's three strikes law reflects a shift in the State's sentencing policies toward incapacitating and deterring repeat offenders who threaten the public safety. The law was designed "to ensure longer prison sentences and greater punishment for those who . . . have been previously convicted of serious and/or violent felony offenses." Cal.Penal Code Ann. § 667(b) (West 1999).

. . . [Under this law, if] the defendant has one prior "serious" or "violent" felony conviction, he must be sentenced to "twice the term otherwise provided. . . ." If the defendant has two or more prior "serious" or "violent" felony convictions, he must receive "an indeterminate term of life imprisonment." Defendants sentenced to life under the three strikes law become eligible for parole on a date [that is subject to calculations but cannot be less than 25 years.] . . .

[California courts do have discretion to treat some prior felonies as misdemeanors or to vacate counts alleging prior felonies. But the discretion is limited.]

[Ewing stole three golf clubs, priced at $399 each (for a total of roughly $1200), from a golf pro shop. At the time, he was on parole from a 9-year prison term. He had an extensive criminal record, including thefts, robbery, battery, burglaries, drug crimes, and other offenses, committed over a lengthy period.]

[For stealing the golf clubs, Ewing was]convicted of one count of felony grand theft of personal property in excess of $400. . . . [T]he trial court . . . found that Ewing had been convicted previously of four serious or violent felonies for the three burglaries and the robbery. [Ewing was sentenced under the three strikes law to 25 years to life. The court of appeals rejected Ewing's claim that his sentence was grossly disproportionate, reasoning that enhanced sentences serve the "legitimate goal" of deterring and incapacitating repeat offenders.] . . .

II

The Eighth Amendment, which forbids cruel and unusual punishments, contains a "narrow proportionality principle" that "applies to noncapital sentences." *Harmelin v. Michigan,* 501 U.S. 957 (1991) (Kennedy, J., concurring . . .). We have . . . addressed the proportionality principle as applied to terms of years in a series of cases beginning with *Rummel v. Estelle,* 445 U.S. 263 (1980) [and including *Solem v. Helm,* 463 U.S. 277 (1983), both of which are discussed in the notes above]. . . .

Eight years after *Solem,* we grappled with the proportionality issue again in *Harmelin v. Michigan,* 501 U.S. 957 (1991). *Harmelin* was not a recidivism case, but rather involved a first-time offender convicted of possessing 672 grams of cocaine. He was sentenced to life in prison without possibility of parole. A majority of the Court rejected Harmelin's claim that his sentence was so grossly disproportionate that it violated the Eighth Amendment. The Court, however, could not agree on why his proportionality argument failed. [For example, Justice Scalia argued that the Eighth Amendment does not incorporate principles of proportionality.]

[The plurality decides to adopt an approach described by Justice Kennedy in a concurring opinion in *Harmelin.* There, Justice Kennedy began by recognizing four factors:] "the primacy of the legislature, the variety of legitimate penological schemes, the nature of our federal system, and the requirement that proportionality review be guided by objective factors"—that inform the final one: "The Eighth Amendment does not require strict proportionality between crime and sentence. Rather, it forbids only extreme sentences that are 'grossly disproportionate' to the crime."

The proportionality principles . . . in Justice Kennedy's *Harmelin* concurrence guide our application of the Eighth Amendment in the new context that we are called upon to consider.

. . . Our traditional deference to legislative policy choices [means] that the Constitution "does not mandate adoption of any one penological theory." A sentence can have a variety of justifications, such as incapacitation, deterrence, retribution, or rehabilitation. . . .

III

Against this backdrop, we consider Ewing's claim that his three strikes sentence of 25 years to life is unconstitutionally disproportionate to his offense of "shoplifting three golf clubs." We first address the gravity of the offense compared to the harshness of the penalty. At the threshold, we note that Ewing incorrectly frames the issue. The gravity of his offense was not merely "shoplifting three golf clubs." Rather, Ewing was convicted of felony grand theft for stealing nearly $1,200 worth of merchandise after previously having been convicted of at least two "violent" or "serious" felonies. Even standing alone, Ewing's theft should not be taken lightly. . . .

In weighing the gravity of Ewing's offense, we must place on the scales not only his current felony, but also his long history of felony recidivism. . . . [His sentence] reflects a rational legislative judgment, entitled to deference, that offenders who have committed serious or violent felonies and who continue to commit felonies must be incapacitated. . . . Ewing's is not "the rare case in which a threshold comparison of the crime committed and the sentence imposed leads to an inference of gross disproportionality." . . . [Affirmed.]

[Justices Scalia and Thomas concurred in separate opinions, both concluding that the Eighth Amendment contained no proportionality principle at all.]

[Justice Stevens' dissenting opinion is omitted.]

JUSTICE BREYER, with whom JUSTICE STEVENS, JUSTICE SOUTER, and JUSTICE GINSBURG join, dissenting. . . .

. . . I believe that the case before us is a "rare" case — one in which a court can say with reasonable confidence that the punishment is "grossly disproportionate" to the crime. [The dissenters proceeded to apply the analysis suggested by Justice Kennedy and used by the plurality.] . . .

Three kinds of sentence-related characteristics define the relevant comparative spectrum: (a) the length of the prison term in real time . . . ; (b) the sentence-triggering criminal conduct . . . ; and (c) the offender's criminal history. . . .

Now consider the present case. The third factor, *offender characteristics*—*i.e.*, prior record—does not differ significantly here from that in *Solem*[, where the sentence was held unconstitutional]. Ewing's prior record consists of four prior felony convictions (involving three burglaries, one with a knife) contrasted with Helm's six prior felony convictions (including three burglaries, though none with weapons). The second factor, *offense behavior*, is worse than that in *Solem*, but only to a degree. It would be difficult to say that the actual behavior itself here (shoplifting) differs significantly from that at issue in *Solem* (passing a bad check) or in *Rummel* (obtaining money through false pretenses). . . .

. . . Ewing's sentence, unlike Rummel's (but like Helm's sentence in *Solem*), is long enough to consume the productive remainder of almost any offender's life. (It means that Ewing himself, seriously ill when sentenced at age 38, will likely die in prison.) . . .

. . . [These] circumstances make clear that Ewing's "gross disproportionality" argument is a strong one. . . .

Believing Ewing's argument . . . sufficient to pass the threshold, I turn to the comparative analysis. First, how would other jurisdictions (or California at other times, *i.e.*, without the three strikes penalty) punish the *same offense conduct*?

Second, upon what other conduct would other jurisdictions (or California) impose the *same prison term*? . . . [The dissenters conclude that neither California before its three-strikes law nor any other jurisdiction would have sentenced Ewing to so long a term of years.]

[Finally, the dissenters conclude that Ewing's sentence fails to serve any legitimate objective:] I see [no] way in which [this treatment] of Ewing's conduct (as a "triggering crime") would further a significant criminal justice objective. One might argue that those who commit several *property* crimes should receive long terms of imprisonment in order to "incapacitate" them. . . . But that is not the object of this particular three strikes statute. Rather, as the plurality says, California seeks "to reduce *serious* and *violent* crime." . . .

[I]n terms of "deterrence," Ewing's 25-year term amounts to overkill. And "rehabilitation" is obviously beside the point. The upshot is that, in my view, the State cannot find in its three strikes law a special criminal justice need sufficient to rescue a sentence that other relevant considerations indicate is unconstitutional. . . .

Notes and Questions

(1) *Grossly Disproportionate to What?* Justice O'Connor attempts to compare the gravity of the offense to the harshness of the penalty. In assessing the gravity of the offense, Justice O'Connor characterizes the offense as theft by someone already convicted of several felonies—not just his last theft. Is this an accurate depiction of Ewing's crime?

(2) *State Constitutional Provisions.* Although the federal Cruel and Unusual Punishment Clause is not likely to lead to appellate reversal of lengthy sentences, occasionally a state constitution's equivalent provision will support a successful challenge. *See, e.g., People v. Bullock*, 485 N.W.2d 866 (Mich. 1992) (mandatory life-without-parole sentence for possessing 650 grams of cocaine mixture violated state cruel and unusual punishment guarantee); *State v. Barker*, 410 S.E.2d 712 (W. Va. 1991) (life sentence for repeat offender, with no history of crimes involving personal violence, violated state cruel and unusual punishment clause). *See also Humphrey v. Wilson*, 652 S.E.2d 501 (Ga. 2007) (holding 10-year sentence for consensual sexual act between 17-year-old male defendant and 15-year-old female disproportionate under both state and federal constitutions).

§ 9.08 Sentencing Options

Note on the Range of Sentence Types

Judges often must decide between very different kinds of sentences. Should the defendant serve a short prison term? Or a long one? Should the sentence be limited to a fine only? Is the defendant a sound candidate for release on probation, and if so, is a probationary sentence lawful? This section deals with these kinds of issues.

[A] Probation, Diversion, and Monetary Sanctions

[1] Probation

Notes on Suspended Sentences, Community Corrections, and Conditions of Probation

(1) *Rehabilitation as a Still-Dominant Goal; Probation as the Most Frequent Sentence.* Probation is a common sentence, perhaps the most common. In the past, probationers and parolees may have outnumbered prisoners by five or six to one, although the proportion is less today. Probation allows for rehabilitation, which these numbers indicate is still an important penal goal. Also, incarceration is an expensive, scarce resource that cannot be used for every case. Probation commonly is used even for serious crimes such as burglary, especially when the defendant has no prior record.

(2) *Is Probation Just a "Slap on the Wrist"?: Community Corrections Terminology.* Public distrust of probation is so profound in some quarters that legislators have renamed it "community corrections." In some cases probation may be an inadequate sentence (*e.g.*, for murder or armed robbery), but a convicted burglar whose conditions include many hours of community service at menial labor, periodic drug testing, reporting requirements, maintaining employment, large financial assessments, restitution, and perhaps incarceration on weekends, undergoes a real deprivation of freedom, and probably does not consider the sentence a "slap on the wrist." But crime victims sometimes disagree. Would you consider probation an appropriate sentence for someone who invades your apartment, breaks the door, steals your electronics, and makes you insecure enough that you want to move to another city?

(3) *Eligibility Restrictions: What about Murder or Aggravated Sexual Assault?* Many jurisdictions limit probation eligibility. For example, probation may be illegal for offenses such as murder, aggravated sexual assault, or deadly-weapon crimes. Probation might not adequately deter, incapacitate, or do retributive justice.

(4) *Probation Conditions: Their Range and Number.* A probationer ordinarily is obligated to adhere to a list of *probation conditions.* Often courts use standard lists, sometimes adding or subtracting conditions for the particular offender. Common conditions include: (1) violate no criminal law, (2) hold a job, (3) support dependents, (4) report to a probation officer (and, sometimes, a mental health professional), (5) not consume (sometimes, to excess) alcohol, (6) remain in a specified geographical area unless given written permission, (7) report changes of circumstances to the probation officer, (8) not associate with convicted felons, (9) avoid contact with specific persons or groups, and (10) avoid certain locations such as bars or casinos.

(5) *"Split Confinement" or "Shock Probation."* Split confinement combines incarceration and probation. The offender serves a short prison or jail term, then is released on probation, sometimes without knowing in advance (hence the term

"shock probation"). This innovation gives the offender an unpleasant experience without long-term removal from family and job. Will this "taste of incarceration" help rehabilitate or deter offenders?

(6) *Limits on Conditions.* Although courts have wide discretion to impose probation conditions, their authority has limits. Some conditions have been struck down as unreasonable, as violating probation statutes, or as unconstitutional. *See, e.g., People v. Brandao*, 210 Cal. App. 4th 568 (Cal. Ct. App. 2012) (invalidating probation condition barring contact with gang members; violated First Amendment and not justified because no evidence of defendant's current or past gang ties); *Jackson v. State*, 968 N.E.2d 328 (Ind. Ct. App. 2012) (invalidating probation term requiring community service because condition exceeded punishment agreed to in plea bargain); *United States v. Evans*, 155 F.3d 245 (3d Cir. 1998) (court cannot order reimbursement of defense counsel's fees as condition of probation); *People v. Pointer*, 151 Cal. App. 3d 1128 (Cal. Ct. App. 1984) (striking probation condition that offender have no children while on probation). *But see State v. Oakley*, 629 N.W.2d 200 (Wis. 2001) (defendant's "ongoing victimization of his nine children and extraordinarily troubling record" was "compelling justification" for upholding condition that probationer have no more children). In general, trial judges have wide discretion, and sentences requiring probationers to carry shaming signs, clean out stables, and avoid certain public locations have been upheld—usually. Consider the following problems.

Problem 9F (Probation Conditions): "Warning: A Violent Felon Lives Here!"

(1) *A Warning Sign as a Condition of Probation for Aggravated Battery: People v. Meyer*, 680 N.E.2d 315 (Ill. 1997). Meyer was convicted of an aggravated battery that caused severe injuries. He had committed similar offenses recently against a creditor who sought to collect for his bad checks and against one of his customers. The trial judge placed Meyer on probation for 30 months with standard conditions, plus requirements of over $9,000 restitution, a $7,500 fine, psychiatric treatment, and one year's home confinement. In addition, the court attempted to "protect society" by requiring Meyer to post a sign of a specified size at each entrance to his home, reading, "Warning! A Violent Felon Lives Here. Enter at Your Own Risk!" Ultimately, however, the Illinois Supreme Court struck down this sign condition as "unreasonable," as incompatible with the Illinois probation statute (which did not expressly recognize shaming sanctions), and as likely to have unintended consequences (including stigmatizing Meyer's relatives occupying the same residence).

(2) *Might (or Should) Another Court Uphold This Sign Condition?* Public identification of sex offenders is common today. It is possible that another state supreme court might uphold the kind of condition at issue in *Meyer*. Can you identify the reasoning that such a court might use?

(3) *Would a Condition Requiring a Defendant to Carry a Sandwich-Board Sign for a Specified Period Be More Likely to be Upheld?* Imagine that instead of a sign affixed

to a residence, a judge were to order a probationer to carry a sandwich-board sign announcing his conviction. *See* Problem 9E, above. Would this condition be more likely to be upheld, at least in some states, since it would be temporary and non-stigmatizing to others? *Cf. Lindsay v. State*, 606 So.2d 652 (Fla. Dist. Ct. App. 1992) (upholding condition requiring defendant to place mug shot and conviction information in a newspaper advertisement).

(4) *What if, Instead, the Defendant Proposes a Warning-Sign Condition as a Means to Avoid Imprisonment?* In some cases, shaming conditions result from defendants' own creative-sentencing proposals, aimed at avoiding imprisonment. Does it matter if the *defendant* proposes the condition?

Notes on Probation Revocation

(1) *The Probation Revocation Hearing: Gagnon v. Scarpelli*, 411 U.S. 778 (1973). If the offender violates a condition of release, the court may *revoke probation*, sending the offender to prison. But probationers enjoy a "conditional liberty" which cannot be taken away without due process. The defendant is entitled to a hearing and has a right to counsel and to present evidence. *See generally* Neil P. Cohen, *The Law of Probation and Parole* (2d ed. 1999). But because of the "conditional" nature of the probationer's liberty interest, there is no federal constitutional right to grand jury review, a jury trial, or proof beyond a reasonable doubt. Instead, the prosecutor files a simple "Motion to Revoke," the hearing is held before the judge alone, and many states impose only a preponderance-of-the-evidence requirement.

(2) *When Probation is Revoked, the Court May Have Multiple Options.* The court may modify the release conditions rather than incarcerate the offender. For example, if the offender acquires a drinking problem, the court may add a probation condition that the offender attend Alcoholics Anonymous. For some violations, however, such as a new criminal conviction, the legislature may require that the probationer be incarcerated if probation is revoked.

Problem 9G (Probation Revocation): "Stay Away from Kids"

(1) Melanie Watts was convicted of unlawful touching of a minor, a charge resulting from "fondling" a three-year-old boy at a day care center where she worked as an assistant. At her sentencing, the judge placed her on probation for five years, requiring, among other conditions, that she not be within twenty-five feet of a child under age six. Is this a good condition?

(2) *What Reasons Support Preponderance Standards and Use of Hearsay?* Imagine a probationer who seems to have violated a condition such as avoiding six-year-olds. If the evidence is equivocal, should probation be revoked upon a preponderance-of-evidence standard? Consider whether a trial judge, who cannot provide jury trials for the court's backlog of unadjudicated criminal cases, would ever want to use probation if revocation required the same kind of trial as that required for serious criminal cases. Is this a sound argument for using a preponderance standard instead of reasonable doubt?

[2] Fines

Notes on Laws and Purposes Underlying Fines

(1) *Statutory Provisions for Fines.* Every jurisdiction authorizes its courts to impose fines as criminal sanctions, ordinarily in addition to other sanctions such as incarceration. The typical pattern is that a dollar amount (such as $10,000) is authorized as the maximum.

(2) *Purposes of Fines.* Fines may serve as both general and special deterrents and provide retributive justice in many cases. As pressures on government finances increase, fines become ever more attractive as a source of public funds. (Is this use of the criminal justice system appropriate?) But fines may discriminate against the poor and favor the wealthy. Or, the opposite may be true: A fine may be designed to exhaust all of a wealthy defendant's net worth (as is often the objective in serious cases), while a less wealthy defendant pays no fine, *e.g., United States v. Blarek*, in Chapter 1. Are fines unfair in either direction?

(3) *Should Fines be Required in "All Cases"?: The Federal Approach.* The Federal Sentencing Guidelines provide, "The court shall impose a fine in all cases, except where the defendant establishes that he is unable to pay and not likely to become able to pay any fine." What lies behind this federal mandate for fines? The Guidelines also provide an advisory schedule of fines, keyed to the severity of offense levels.

(4) *What if the Defendant Is Unable to Pay?* What should be done then? A historical solution was to have the indigent "lay out" the fine by spending time in jail at a certain number of dollars per day. A more modern solution, required by Supreme Court decisions, is to set up a schedule of installment payments, with incarceration only on willful nonpayment. And some jurisdictions stay the fines and fees altogether if the defendant is indigent. Consider the following.

PEOPLE v. DUENAS, 30 Cal. App. 5th 1157 (2019). "Velia Dueñas, an indigent and homeless mother of young children, pleaded no contest to driving with a suspended license." She had committed this crime repeatedly, and she spent 51 days in prison across four cases. The trial court placed her on probation, imposed $220 in fees and fines, and ordered that if an outstanding debt remained at the end of probation, the amount would "go to collections." "Dueñas contends that imposing the fees and fine without considering her ability to pay violates state and federal constitutional guarantees." The appellate court agreed:

> Dueñas argues that laws imposing fines and fees on people too poor to pay punish the poor for their poverty. These statutes, she asserts, are fundamentally unfair . . . . We conclude that due process of law requires the trial court to conduct an ability to pay hearing . . . before it imposes court facilities and court operations assessments . . . . We also hold that . . . the execution of any restitution fine . . . must be stayed unless and until the trial court holds an ability to pay hearing and concludes that the defendant has the present ability to pay the restitution fine.

But doesn't this holding mean that California has no ability to impose any sanction—neither incarceration or monetary penalties—even though this defendant committed many crimes and cost the state many scores of thousands of dollars in costs for proceedings? Consider whether an installment payment order might be more appropriate. Note, as well, that a different California appeals court disagreed with the *Duenas* court, calling its reasoning "inconsistent with the purposes and operation of probation" and stating that reform of the fines and restitution system was a matter for the legislature, not the courts. *People v. Hicks*, 40 Cal. App. 5d 320 (Cal. App. 2019). The California Supreme Court recently decided to review this issue. *See People v. Kopp*, 451 P.3d 776 (Cal. 2019).

[3] Restitution

Notes on Purposes and Standards for Restitution

(1) *The Nature of Restitution. Restitution* is compensation to the victim for the harm caused. Most jurisdictions authorize or require it. The Federal Sentencing Guidelines, for example, provide that the court "shall" order restitution if there is an identifiable victim, "for the full amount of the victim's loss." A burglar may be sentenced to repay the value of the items taken (*e.g.*, $750) plus the cost of replacing a damaged door (*e.g.*, $200). Restitution may also be ordered for such losses as wages, medical costs, and even pain and suffering, although victims seeking consequential damages, such as loss of profits, usually must resort to civil remedies.

(2) *The Hearing to Determine the Amount of Restitution.* The amount of restitution should be set only after a hearing in which the accused has had an opportunity to contest the value of the losses. The procedure becomes more complicated if there are multiple offenders, particularly if some have not been apprehended or have no resources. If two people destroy a car, is it appropriate to hold each responsible for the entire loss if one thief is unable to pay for any of it?

[4] Diversion

Notes on Diversion: A Kind of "Shelf Probation"

(1) *Diversion Programs.* Another option is *diversion*, which removes the offender from the criminal justice system. Diversion can occur at various stages of the process and can be either informal or very structured. An example of the former is the decision of police officer or prosecutor to refrain from initiating charges if the offender is not apprehended again in the next year. A structured diversion statute imposes formal criteria. Sometimes, under formal programs, diversion is ordered only if the offender undertakes probation-like conditions, such as paying court costs or restitution or performing community service. Diversion sometimes is called "shelf probation," because the prosecutor sets the file aside, "on the shelf."

(2) *Purposes of Diversion.* Diversion is consistent with rehabilitation. But diversion has a downside: a reduction in retribution, deterrence, or incapacitation. More basically, is diversion fair to victims? Consider the following case.

STATE v. CURRY, 988 S.W.2d 153 (Tenn. 1999). Curry was an assistant clerk for the City of McKenzie, Tennessee, until her superiors discovered that she had embezzled more than $27,000 over a two-year period. She applied for pretrial diversion. The applicable statute permitted diversion only if the prosecutor consented. The district attorney denied her application and explained, "This was a calculated criminal scheme that took planning and thought. It manifests a criminal intent for a long period of time. . . . We cannot believe that it would be in the best interests of . . . justice to overlook a criminal scheme of this proportion and grant pretrial diversion." But because diversion was a formal program governed by statute in Tennessee, Curry argued that the prosecutor's grounds were inconsistent with the statutory criteria for diversion, which required the prosecutor to "focus on the defendant's amenability to correction." The trial court held that the denial of diversion to Curry was an abuse of the prosecutor's discretion, and the state Supreme Court agreed:

> The State argues . . . that the seriousness of the offense itself may justify a denial of diversion. A review of the case law reveals, however, that the circumstances of the offense and the need for deterrence may alone justify a denial of diversion, *but only if all of the other relevant factors [about the defendant's potential for correction] have been considered as well* (emphasis in original). . . .

One justice dissented, on the ground that the majority had failed to respect the discretion of the prosecutor in a case involving an "extremely serious crime" that was not isolated but "complicated, calculated, and deliberate," as well as lengthy in time. Should diversion programs provide room for the kind of discretion the prosecutor attempted to exercise here?

[5] Community Service

Notes on Purposes and Uses

(1) *The Option for Community Service.* Many jurisdictions have added this sentencing option. The offender is ordered to spend a set number of hours, say one hundred, working at no pay for a public or charitable purpose. Examples include picking up trash in a park, working in a hospital emergency room, or speaking to school groups about the dangers of drugs.

(2) *Advantages and Disadvantages.* Consider whether, in addition to providing the public with labor, community service could help rehabilitate offenders or provide deterrence. But community service is not without disadvantages. Could unions or public employee organizations reasonably object to a community service program? Who is liable if an offender commits a violent crime on a co-worker or a passerby? Who pays if the defendant incurs a serious injury?

BANKS v. STATE, 262 So. 3d 876 (Fla. App. 2019). This opinion is effectively a warning to trial judges not to give a defendant any choice about conditions of probation, including the choice to perform community service rather than paying court costs:

> We . . . cannot affirm revocation [of her probation] due to Banks' failure to perform community service because the probation order did not obligate her to do so [but instead it required her to pay court costs *or* perform community service]. . . . Banks was required to pay court costs ("You *will* pay . . . court costs") and permitted to perform community service hours (you "*may* perform" community service "in lieu of court costs"). This . . . condition provided Banks with an alternative to paying costs if she wished, but she did not. [T]he requirement to pay costs remained in place, and Banks cannot have her probation revoked for failing to pay costs unless the court finds that she has the ability to pay.

Does this decision make sense?

[B] Incarceration

Notes on the Use and Frequency of Incarceration

(1) *The Prison Population—and the Theoretical Use of Incarceration as a Last Resort.* Many jurisdictions (and the American Bar Association) recommend that incarceration be ordered only when it is absolutely necessary. Are you convinced, however, that incarceration should be a "last resort" for a serious felony? Actual practice is different. According to the U.S. Department of Justice's Bureau of Justice Statistics, the number of people in federal or state prison, or in local jails, peaked at 1,615,500 in 2009 and was 1,489,363 as of the end of 2017. Another 874,800 people were on parole (not including probation). Women made up 7% of the incarcerated population, while African Americans were 33.1%, whites were 30.3%, and Hispanics were 23.4%. Noncitizens were 7.6% of the prison population.

At the end of 2017, another 3,673,100 people were on probation, more than twice the number incarcerated. What goals of sentencing are carried out by incarceration as opposed to probation?

(2) *Impact on African-Americans, Hispanics, and Women: Marc Mauer, Race to Incarcerate* 118–126 (1999). Incarceration falls especially heavily on African-Americans and Hispanics. According to Mauer's study, while African-Americans constitute about 13% of the population, they comprise about half of all prison inmates (more recent statistics, noted above, put the number at about one-third), and an African-American has a seven times greater chance of being incarcerated than does a white person. In addition, new sentencing practices have led to sharp increases in the incarceration of women, who critics argue suffer greater penalties (for example, they often have custody of children). Do these data mean that incarceration is being used unfairly? *See* Michelle Alexander, *The New Jim Crow: Mass Incarceration in the Age of Colorblindness* (2010) (arguing incarceration of black men perpetuates a racial caste system).

(3) *Parole and Actual Release Date.* Often a *parole board*, a group of three or more executive branch officials, will decide the actual release date. The precise time to be served is the product of a number of laws permitting reductions in sentence for good behavior and other achievements (*e.g.*, obtaining a G.E.D.). Upon release, the offender must satisfy a list of probation-like requirements, such as holding a job, and must be in contact with a parole officer on a regular basis. Some jurisdictions, however, have abolished parole (*e.g.*, the federal).

COMMONWEALTH v. BOYLE, 440 P.3d 720 (Utah 2019). This case illustrates a court's choice of prison over probation. Boyle argued that the trial judge had abused his discretion in sentencing him to prison. The appellate court disagreed. The court began with the principle that "the decision whether to grant probation is within the complete discretion of the trial court":

> Specifically, Boyle asserts that the court failed to consider factors that favored probation. The record does not support his contention. During sentencing, the State acknowledged that Boyle's criminal history matrix scored him in the probation category. But [the Probation Department] nevertheless recommended prison, considering Boyle's criminal history, which included four previous assaults (three as a juvenile and one as an adult), his ongoing substance abuse . . . , and the seriousness of Victim's injuries [whom Boyle had stabbed four times and severed a neck artery]. . . . [Taking into consideration Boyle's history of "assaultive behavior" and the seriousness of Victim's injuries, the trial court concluded that Boyle posed too great a risk to be put "back out in the community."]

[C] Semi-Incarceration

Notes on Home and Halfway-House Confinement as Alternatives

(1) *Prison Space as a Limited Resource.* Incarceration in America is expensive, and often prisons and jails are filled to capacity. Moreover, incarceration can separate an offender from family and job, reducing the likelihood of rehabilitation. These are punishments that involve deprivations of liberty, although not to the same extent as incarceration.

(2) *Home Confinement.* A recent trend is toward *home arrest* or *house confinement*, although it is more often used for pretrial detainees than convicted criminals. The offender, usually a non-violent person with a minimal criminal history, is required to remain at home for a certain period or during certain hours each day. For example, an offender might be required to be at home during all hours not at work. To ensure that the offender does not leave, a device can be placed in the offender's home that picks up a signal from a plastic anklet. Split sentences, involving periods of actual incarceration followed by home confinement, are another alternative.

(3) *Halfway Houses.* Another alternative is an order that the offender reside in a *halfway house*, a residential facility where offenders live when not at work or participating in another program. Offenders' behavior is monitored by staff, and offenders may be required to take part in group or individual therapy sessions. A halfway house may be an attractive option for offenders who need structure, but who have jobs or other responsibilities. Also, many jurisdictions use halfway houses as way stations between prison and release. Does a halfway house adequately protect the public, serve retributive goals, or provide deterrence?

[D] Civil Remedies: Forfeiture and Administrative Penalties

Notes on Civil Alternatives to the Criminal Sanction

(1) *Forfeiture: Sometimes Penal; Sometimes Not.* Forfeiture ordinarily involves a process through which the government takes property, such as crime proceeds, or a gun, car, or building used to commit a crime, or bought with crime proceeds. Civil forfeiture is subject only to civil processes, with a lesser proof burden. Although it obviously hurts owners who lose their property, forfeiture generally is classified as a non-criminal remedy. It usually is motivated at least in part by non-penal purposes: depriving the offender of the fruits of the offense or removing implements of crime so that offenders cannot use them again. But some kinds of forfeiture are penal in nature. An example is forfeiture under the Racketeer-Influenced, Corrupt Organizations (RICO) statute, which is broad, reaching not only criminal fruits and implements but also other property. That kind of forfeiture is covered in the RICO section, later in this book.

(2) *Civil Penalties: Hudson v. United States,* 522 U.S. 93 (1997). In this case, the Office of the Comptroller of the Currency had imposed monetary penalties and occupational debarments on Hudson and others who arranged loans in violation of OCC regulations. Later, a federal grand jury indicted these defendants for banking violations made up of essentially the same conduct. The defendants moved to dismiss under the Double Jeopardy Clause. The Supreme Court denied dismissal and reasoned that these monetary assessments and occupational prohibitions were not so "punitive" as to make them criminal in nature. Does this reasoning make sense?

(3) *Constitutional Limits on Fines and Forfeitures: Timbs v. Indiana,* 139 S. Ct. 682 (2019). In this case, the U.S. Supreme Court held that the Excessive Fines Clause, in the Eighth Amendment, applies to the states as well as to the federal government. Timbs pled guilty to a drug offense, and prosecutors sought forfeiture of his Land Rover because he had used it to transport heroin. The trial court denied forfeiture, because Timbs had recently paid $42,000 for the vehicle, which was more than four times the maximum fine that could be assessed against him. The Indiana Supreme Court reversed the trial court's ruling, but the U.S. Supreme Court reversed the state court. After ruling that the Excessive Fines Clause applies to state criminal proceedings, the Court sent the case back to the Indiana courts.

§ 9.09 The Sentencing Hearing

Notes on Sources of Information at Sentencing

(1) *Information for Sentencing.* Unless the court follows a plea bargain that specifies the sentence, the court will need additional information about the defendant and the offense. Courts obtain information from a number of sources.

(2) *The Presentence Investigation (PSI) and Presentence Report (PSR) by a Probation Officer.* Often the court will have a *presentence report* prepared by a probation officer. The PSR will include such information as the defendant's family situation, educational and work history, physical and mental condition, and financial status. *See* Fed. R. Crim. P. 32(d). It may also include information about the impact of the crime on the victim and others. In some jurisdictions, the PSR explains and computes a Guideline Sentence or provides sentencing recommendations.

The Federal Rules of Criminal Procedure require the probation officer to disclose the PSR to the defense and the government before the sentencing hearing. If the parties object to facts in the report, the rules provide procedures and deadlines for resolving the dispute. Fed. R. Crim. P. 32.

(3) *Information from Lawyers and Victims.* Another source is the lawyers, who may file affidavits or similar factual documents. Each also may file a memorandum or brief. In many jurisdictions, the victim also is asked or permitted to provide the court with information about the impact of the crime or recommendations for sentencing. The victim's information may be included in the presentence report, in a separate document, or through live testimony.

Notes on the Sentencing Hearing

(1) *The Sentencing Hearing before the Judge.* The *sentencing hearing* is an adversary proceeding in which both the prosecution and defense are permitted to provide the court with information. In all except capital cases, the sentencing hearing is ordinarily conducted by the judge without the use of a jury, although a jury may have to decide certain fact issues, particularly in light of the Sixth Amendment cases discussed in § 9.14. The sentencing hearing may be held immediately after a trial or guilty plea or several weeks or even months later.

(2) *Sentencing Hearings before Juries: Fact Findings, Elections for Jury Sentencing, and Capital Cases.* The participation of juries in sentencing hearings is more common today than ever, for three reasons. First, as we shall see below, the Supreme Court has held that if a fact finding increases a sentence by a determinate amount, the defendant has a right to have a jury make the fact finding. In *Ewing v. California* (the three-strikes case, above), findings about Ewing's prior convictions were made by the jury. Similarly, a jury that has found a defendant guilty may next be required to find, for sentencing purposes, whether the victim was "especially vulnerable" in an assault case, or the "amount of loss" in a theft case.

Second, some states give the defendant a right to have the jury assess the sentence, instead of the judge. In these jurisdictions, defendants usually will elect jury sentencing unless they have reason to believe that judges will assess lesser sentences. Can you see why?

Third, the Supreme Court has held that there is a right to jury sentencing in capital cases. This issue, too, is dealt with later in this chapter.

(3) *Facts Determining the Sentence.* Although procedures differ among the jurisdictions, ordinarily the sentencing hearing is less formal than the trial. The rules of evidence may be inapplicable or only applied to some kinds of information. For example, some written reports may be admissible at a sentencing hearing though they would be inadmissible at trial. The defendant also is accorded the right of "allocution," or an opportunity personally to address the judge. If the defense offers a plan for a probationary sentence, a useful witness would be a person who has promised to employ the defendant. The prosecution's evidence may include the victim, who will describe the impact of the crime, as well as witnesses to other crimes, character witnesses, and evidence proving the defendant's criminal record.

§ 9.10 Parole and Clemency: Executive Reductions of Sentences

Notes on the Existence, Determination, and Revocation of Parole

(1) *Many Factors Determine the Duration of Sentence: Various Credits.* The sentencing judge determines the sentence that the offender *could* serve, but in many jurisdictions, the judge has little control over the *actual* sentence. Correctional authorities are usually authorized to grant credit for good behavior or participation in rehabilitative programs. Sometimes prison crowding results in sentence reductions through release provisions.

(2) *Parole Release: The Majority Approach.* Parole is an executive branch process. A parole board or commission, usually comprised of three or more people, is authorized to make an individual determination of the time each offender (at least the more serious offenders) will spend in prison and the time on parole after release. Ordinarily, the decision is made after a *parole hearing.* The board reviews the offense (perhaps including the views of the victim, the prosecuting lawyer, and the sentencing judge), the offender's prison record, the recommendations of prison officials, and other relevant data. If the offender is paroled, he or she usually will report to a parole officer, subject to conditions similar to probation conditions.

(3) *The Minority Approach: No Parole, But Sometimes, Supervised Release.* A minority of American jurisdictions, including the federal government, have abolished parole. The usual practice is to allow slight, nondiscretionary reduction of the

sentence (on the order of fifteen percent) for proper behavior, and to add *supervised release*. At the time of sentencing, the offender is given both a prison term and a specific period of supervised release. *See* 18 U.S.C. § 3583. A person on supervised release, like a parolee, is subject to conditions. The primary difference from parole is that the judge (not the parole board) determines the duration of supervised release. *See generally* Neil P. Cohen, *The Law of Probation and Parole* (2d ed. 1999).

(4) *Revocation of Parole.* Violation of a parole condition can result in revocation proceedings and reincarceration of the parolee. At the revocation hearing, the offender's rights are far less comprehensive than at trial. *See, e.g., Pennsylvania Bd. of Probation v. Scott*, 524 U.S. 357 (1998) (parole boards need not exclude evidence obtained in violation of the Fourth Amendment).

McDERMOTT v. McDONALD, 24 P.3d 200 (Mont. 2001). Petitioner Michael McDermott was serving a thirty-year sentence for assault and bail jumping. The Montana Board of Pardons and Parole denied his application for parole, based in part on his failure to participate in a sex offender program (SOP). He petitioned for habeas corpus, alleging that the Board had violated the Due Process Clause. The Montana court first considered whether McDermott even had a "liberty interest" in discretionary parole sufficient to invoke the Due Process Clause at all. "As a general rule, inmates have no liberty interest in parole. *Greenholtz v. Inmates of the Nebraska Penal and Correctional Complex* (1979), 442 U.S. 1, 7." But the Montana court had recognized "an exception . . . for inmates who committed their offenses prior to 1989," because before that year, Montana's parole eligibility statute stated "the board *shall* release [a prisoner] on parole . . . when . . . the prisoner can be released without detriment . . . (emphasis in opinion)." This language, "*shall* release," gave McDermott a sufficient liberty interest to invoke the Due Process Clause.

But "[t]he requirements of due process are flexible," said the court. "The United States Supreme Court has held that due process is satisfied when the prisoner seeking parole is . . . provided with an opportunity to be heard and a written statement explaining why he was denied parole." Under this standard, the Montana court denied habeas corpus to McDermott:

> As a complement to its broad discretion to grant, deny, or condition parole, the Board is authorized to consider factors that may not be considered by the district court at trial and sentencing. For instance, parole authorities . . . may consider evidence of offenses which were charged in dismissed counts. . . .

> [T]he Board's statutory authority is broad enough to permit its consideration of McDermott's dismissed incest counts, the results of his initial needs assessment showing severe sexual problems, and his refusal to participate in [a particular prison program], when determining whether to grant him an early release on parole.

Notes on Executive Clemency

(1) *Executive Sentencing Review: Clemency and Pardons.* Another area of executive authority is clemency. The nomenclature and procedures vary among the jurisdictions and may include such terms as pardon, commutation, reprieve, and remission. In general, federal or state constitutional provisions authorize the President or Governor to reduce all or part of a sentence, to delay implementation, or to absolve the offender from all guilt.

Executive clemency has been relied on to correct injustices (such as when new evidence shows that a prisoner is actually innocent), to spare judicial resources (death sentences may be commuted to life imprisonment), or to recognize unique circumstances (a life prisoner with terminal cancer may be given clemency to spend the last weeks of life at home).

(2) *Conditions on Clemency.* Sometimes a grant of executive clemency is conditional. For example, a governor may commute a sentence on the condition that the released offender commit no more felonies, support dependents, and refrain from involvement in certain businesses. Violation of such a condition can lead to revocation.

OHIO ADULT PAROLE AUTHORITY v. WOODARD, 523 U.S. 272 (1998). Woodard had been sentenced to death for aggravated murder committed in the course of carjacking. His sentence was affirmed on appeal. While simultaneously petitioning for habeas corpus, he sought clemency. Ohio law required the Parole Authority to conduct an investigation, during which the inmate could request an interview. Counsel was not allowed at that interview. Woodard sued and argued that the interview procedure violated the Due Process Clause.

The district court denied relief, but the court of appeals reversed and agreed with Woodard. It held that the interview presented Woodard with a "Hobson's choice": remaining silent in accordance with his Fifth Amendment right or participating in the clemency process without his lawyer. The Supreme Court reversed the reversal and denied relief to Woodard. Chief Justice Rehnquist's plurality opinion said:

> Clemency proceedings are not part of the trial—or even of the adjudicatory process. . . . And they are usually discretionary, unlike the more structured and limited scope of judicial proceedings. [C]lemency has not traditionally "been the business of courts." . . .
>
> . . . Procedures mandated under the Due Process Clause should be consistent with the nature of the governmental power being invoked. Here, the executive's clemency authority would cease to be a matter of grace . . . if it were constrained by the sort of procedural requirements that respondent urges. Respondent is already under a sentence of death, determined to have been lawfully imposed. If clemency is granted, he obtains a benefit; if it is denied, he is no worse off than he was before.

§ 9.11 Discretionary and Determinate Models of Sentencing

[A] Discretionary Sentencing, Confined Only by Broad Ranges

WILLIAMS v. NEW YORK, 337 U.S. 241 (1949). A New York statute empowered a judge to consider wide ranges of sentences with unguided discretion and to "seek any information that [would] aid the court in determining the proper [sentence]." The judge could consider information obtained outside the courtroom and weigh it in an unspecified manner. Williams argued that his trial judge's consideration of a Presentence Report violated the Due Process Clause. The court, through Justice Douglas, disagreed:

> In determining whether a defendant shall receive a one-year minimum or a twenty-year maximum sentence, we do not think the Federal Constitution restricts the view of the sentencing judge to the information received in open court. . . . [I]t is conceded that no federal constitutional objection would have been possible if the judge here had sentenced appellant . . . because appellant's trial manner impressed the judge that appellant was a bad risk for society, or if the judge had sentenced him . . . [after] giving no reason at all.

Notes and Questions

(1) *Is Discretion Necessary because of the Multidimensional Aspect of Sentencing?* This Court reasons that sentencing requires different processes from determining guilt or innocence. The question whether the defendant "killed" another person is one-dimensional, and so is the question whether he acted "intentionally"; but the question whether the defendant "can be rehabilitated" or "needs incapacitation" is qualitatively different and must be balanced against other inquiries. Does this consideration require the absence of guidance by law when a judge chooses "a one-year minimum," or "a twenty-year maximum," using pure discretion?

(2) *What Kinds of "Abuses" Might Result from Purely Discretionary Sentencing?* At another point in his opinion, Justice Douglas concedes that sentencing discretion is "susceptible of abuse." Broad judicial discretion may mean that sentences depend more on idiosyncratic beliefs of judges than on actual differences among cases. Thus, proportionality among sentences for different crimes may disappear, and disparities among sentences for similar crimes may increase. And finally, citizens may feel that there is no control over sentences from either "Maximum John" or "Cut-'em-Loose Bruce" (nicknames for real judges in two different jurisdictions), which they perceive as excessive or inadequate. Do these concerns justify constraints on sentencing discretion?

(3) *How Much Discretion?: "Necessary" Discretion, but "Confined, Structured, and Checked"—the View of Kenneth Culp Davis, Discretionary Justice* 216 (1969). Davis says that his "broad framework" is expressed in this one sentence: "The vast quantities of unnecessary discretionary power that have grown up in our system should be cut back, and the discretionary power that is found to be necessary should be properly confined, structured, and checked." What do you think Davis means by "confining, structuring, and checking" discretionary power?

[B] Determinate or Guideline Sentencing: Confining Discretion

David Crump, *Determinate Sentencing: The Promises and Perils of Sentence Guidelines*
68 Ky. L.J. 1, 3–10 (1979)

[This article appeared during the early days of determinate sentencing, but this excerpt provides a concise introduction to the subject.—Eds.]

[T]he potential advantages of determinate sentencing in producing consistent results are so readily apparent that its widespread legislative adoption in the near future seems a real possibility.

[Yet some commentators] argue that the benefits of determinate sentencing are offset by the problems it may create . . . . The major change in philosophy that definite sentencing reflects will, they accurately observe, result in challenges to some of our most deeply felt values. Finally, they cite the . . . complexity and cost of some determinate systems . . . as serious drawbacks. . . .

Many who hear the phrase "determinate sentencing" mistakenly assume that it describes a system in which all penalties are mandatory and fixed. In fact, no sentencing system is either perfectly mandatory or perfectly discretionary. Even those jurisdictions that provide great discretion to sentencing judges put outer limits on the range, and even jurisdictions with relatively rigid sentencing do not provide across-the-board mandatory sentences. Various terms such as "fixed," "presumptive," "guideline" or "flat-time" sentencing . . . have no universal meaning. . . . What "determinate sentencing" really describes is a system in which discretion deemed excessive has been removed or controlled . . . but in which that discretion deemed necessary remains. . . .

The most determinate sort of sentencing is mandatory sentencing. In this pattern, the determination of certain facts leads inexorably to a prescribed sentence, which cannot be avoided except perhaps by proof of other facts in mitigation or aggravation. The primary drawback of mandatory sentencing is that the varieties of offenses and offenders are infinite; hence, it produces some ill-fitting sentences and leads to judicial "fudging." . . .

[Some] sentencing, however, is at the opposite pole from the mandatory model, because [some] jurisdictions vest virtually uncontrolled discretion in sentencing judges. . . .

Between these two extremes there is a range of alternatives offering varying control over discretion. In presumptive sentencing systems, for example, a fixed sentence is postulated for a given situation, but the judge has discretion to depart from it . . . . Such a system gives the promise of consistent results without requiring that individual differences be ignored . . . . Guidelines that do not bind the sentencing entity but that merely inform its discretion are a variation on the presumptive model. Similar results may be obtained by narrowing the range of sentence options — by making sentence ranges of three to five years, for example, rather than of one to ten . . . . Each of these controlled-discretion systems may be extended by the specification of factors adding to, or subtracting from, the sentence . . . — a system that might be called the "base-plus-enhancement" model.

. . . Each of the different approaches — mandatory, presumptive, guideline, base-plus-enhancement and discretionary — could be incorporated into a single system. . . .

Notes and Questions

(1) *"Quasi-Mandatory" Sentencing: The Three-Strikes Law in Ewing v. California as an Example.* The California Statute at issue in *Ewing v. California*, above, illustrates quasi-mandatory sentencing. A triggering felony, combined with specified prior convictions, requires an automatic 25-year-to-life sentence, which would be mandatory — except that California provides for sentencing judges to vacate allegations of prior convictions and to reduce some triggering felonies to misdemeanors. Is this a system in which discretion has been reduced to the amount "necessary," and in which remaining discretion has been "confined, structured, and checked"?

(2) *Base-Plus-Enhancement Sentencing: The Hate-Crime Statute in Apprendi v. New Jersey*, 530 U.S. 466 (2000). The base-plus-enhancement model is illustrated by a New Jersey "hate-crime law," which authorized an extended term of imprisonment for certain felonies motivated by "a purpose to intimidate . . . because of race" or other invidious discriminants. In other words, the statute specified a "base" sentence range for each offense, but added a potential "enhancement." This New Jersey statute was the subject of the Supreme Court's decision in *Apprendi v. New Jersey*, which is discussed later in this chapter.

(3) *Constitutional Difficulties.* Determinative sentencing has given rise to substantial constitutional claims. The Supreme Court has invalidated aspects of state determinate sentencing schemes — such as judicially-based findings for hate-crime laws — and it has overturned mandatory application of the Federal Sentencing Guidelines. We shall consider the cases below.

(4) *The Federal Sentencing Guidelines: No Longer Mandatory, but Still Important.* The next section of this book will examine the Federal Sentencing Guidelines. For almost twenty years, these Guidelines were mandatory in federal cases. As we shall see later in this chapter, however, the Supreme Court has ruled that the fact-finding

procedure under the Guidelines is unconstitutional. The practical result is that the Guidelines are no longer mandatory, but they persist as advisory guidelines that district courts must continue to consult and which provide presumptively valid sentences.

§9.12 The Federal Sentencing Guidelines

Notes on Guidelines in General

(1) *Guidelines: Who Drafts Them?* In virtually all jurisdictions that use them, sentencing guidelines are the product of a group called a *sentencing commission*, comprised of representatives of various constituencies. Commissioners may include judges, prosecutors, law enforcement officers, defenders, academics, legislators, and members of the public.

(2) *The General Structure of Guidelines: Presumptive Sentences.* Most sentencing guidelines involve *presumptive sentences*, or sentences that should be imposed in typical cases. Courts usually are given discretion to depart from them. To determine a presumptive sentence, one may have to consult a grid or matrix that combines two or more variables. The usual matrix combines offense severity and offender characteristics. Each crime receives a base number. For example, robbery may be a "Class Five" offense. Each offender is also placed in a category, usually based on prior convictions. For example, an offender with two prior felony convictions could be in "Category Two."

Then, the guideline sentence may be determined by consulting the grid to find the cell at the intersection of the offense classification and offender category. The cell for a Class Five offense and Category Two offender may indicate a sentence of (perhaps) 6 to 9 years. The judge then decides the actual sentence within this 6-to-9 year range. Guidelines also may influence whether a non-custodial sentence such as probation should be assessed.

Notes on the Federal Sentencing Guidelines

(1) *Pre-Guidelines Federal Sentencing.* Prior to the Federal Sentencing Guidelines, federal judges had great discretion in assigning sentences, and the United States Parole Board determined the prisoner's release date. This structure was criticized on the bases that it (1) relied on a rehabilitative model that had proved unsuccessful, (2) facilitated sentencing disparity, and (3) produced a lack of certainty (and "honesty") about when offenders would be released.

(2) *Development of the Federal Sentencing Guidelines: Mistretta v. United States,* 488 U.S. 361 (1989). Congress rejected the traditional sentencing system in 1984 when it passed legislation that created the seven-member United States Sentencing Commission and charged it with drafting mandatory guidelines. Congress

abolished the Parole Commission and established a determinate system in which the offender usually served most of the sentence. In *Mistretta*, the United States Supreme Court upheld the Federal Guidelines against a constitutional challenge based on unlawful delegation of sentencing authority and alleged violation of the separation of powers.

(3) *How the Federal Guidelines Work: The "Offense Level," the "Criminal History Category," and the "Sentencing Table."* The Guideline Sentence depends upon two numbers: the *offense level* and the *criminal history category*. These numbers are determined by adding and subtracting points for various factors. Then, the Guideline Sentence can be determined by consulting the "Sentencing Table" reproduced on the following page. The offense level is the vertical scale and the criminal history category is the horizontal. It should be repeated that recent Supreme Court decisions make the Federal Sentencing Guidelines *advisory*. Federal trial courts need not follow them. It is important to understand the Guidelines, however, because federal judges continue to rely on them.

(4) *Using the Sentencing Table.* The sentencing table is reproduced below. Remember, the offense level score is read down the left-hand side, vertically, and the defendant's criminal history category is read across the top, horizontally. The cell where the defendant's offense level and criminal history category intersect gives the Guideline Sentence. For example, for a defendant whose offense level is 38 (a relatively serious crime) and whose criminal history category is IV (a relatively extensive record of convictions), the Guideline Sentence ranges from 324 months to 405 months (or 27 years to $33^3/_4$ years). Any sentence within this range is a Guideline Sentence. For a defendant whose offense level is 6 and whose criminal history category is I, the Guideline Sentence ranges from zero to six months (and normally would allow for probation).

Notes on Steps in Computing a Guideline Sentence

(1) *Finding the "Base Offense Level": The First Step toward Finding the Offense Level.* To use the Sentencing Table, you must calculate the Offense Level. The first step is to find what is called the "Base Offense Level" for the crime of conviction. For example, assume that Dan Defendant has been convicted of burglary of a post office, in violation of 18 U.S.C. § 2115. The proper Guideline for "burglary" is § 2B2.1, which appears below. The Base Offense Level for this crime is 12. Can you see where that Base Offense Level appears in this Guideline?

(2) *Next, All Other "Relevant Conduct" in the Crime Must Be Considered and the Base Offense Level Increased or Decreased Accordingly.* The Guidelines attempt to sentence the offender for the *actual* conduct committed, not just for the crime of conviction. Let us add these facts: our burglar, Dan Defendant, carried a pistol, and he did $5,000 worth of damage. These facts are aspects of Dan's "Relevant Conduct." The Guidelines take them into account, with what are called "Specific Offense Characteristics," and these "Characteristics" will guide our next step.

Sentencing Table

(in U.S. Sentencing Commission, *Guidelines Manual* 396 (Nov. 2012))

SENTENCING TABLE
(in months of imprisonment)

	Offense Level	Criminal History Category (Criminal History Points)					
		I (0 or 1)	II (2 or 3)	III (4, 5, 6)	IV (7, 8, 9)	V (10, 11, 12)	VI (13 or more)
Zone A	1	0-6	0-6	0-6	0-6	0-6	0-6
	2	0-6	0-6	0-6	0-6	0-6	1-7
	3	0-6	0-6	0-6	0-6	2-8	3-9
	4	0-6	0-6	0-6	2-8	4-10	6-12
	5	0-6	0-6	1-7	4-10	6-12	9-15
	6	0-6	1-7	2-8	6-12	9-15	12-18
	7	0-6	2-8	4-10	8-14	12-18	15-21
	8	0-6	4-10	6-12	10-16	15-21	18-24
Zone B	9	4-10	6-12	8-14	12-18	18-24	21-27
Zone C	10	6-12	8-14	10-16	15-21	21-27	24-30
	11	8-14	10-16	12-18	18-24	24-30	27-33
	12	10-16	12-18	15-21	21-27	27-33	30-37
	13	12-18	15-21	18-24	24-30	30-37	33-41
	14	15-21	18-24	21-27	27-33	33-41	37-46
	15	18-24	21-27	24-30	30-37	37-46	41-51
	16	21-27	24-30	27-33	33-41	41-51	46-57
	17	24-30	27-33	30-37	37-46	46-57	51-63
	18	27-33	30-37	33-41	41-51	51-63	57-71
	19	30-37	33-41	37-46	46-57	57-71	63-78
	20	33-41	37-46	41-51	51-63	63-78	70-87
	21	37-46	41-51	46-57	57-71	70-87	77-96
	22	41-51	46-57	51-63	63-78	77-96	84-105
	23	46-57	51-63	57-71	70-87	84-105	92-115
	24	51-63	57-71	63-78	77-96	92-115	100-125
	25	57-71	63-78	70-87	84-105	100-125	110-137
	26	63-78	70-87	78-97	92-115	110-137	120-150
Zone D	27	70-87	78-97	87-108	100-125	120-150	130-162
	28	78-97	87-108	97-121	110-137	130-162	140-175
	29	87-108	97-121	108-135	121-151	140-175	151-188
	30	97-121	108-135	121-151	135-168	151-188	168-210
	31	108-135	121-151	135-168	151-188	168-210	188-235
	32	121-151	135-168	151-188	168-210	188-235	210-262
	33	135-168	151-188	168-210	188-235	210-262	235-293
	34	151-188	168-210	188-235	210-262	235-293	262-327
	35	168-210	188-235	210-262	235-293	262-327	292-365
	36	188-235	210-262	235-293	262-327	292-365	324-405
	37	210-262	235-293	262-327	292-365	324-405	360-life
	38	235-293	262-327	292-365	324-405	360-life	360-life
	39	262-327	292-365	324-405	360-life	360-life	360-life
	40	292-365	324-405	360-life	360-life	360-life	360-life
	41	324-405	360-life	360-life	360-life	360-life	360-life
	42	360-life	360-life	360-life	360-life	360-life	360-life
	43	life	life	life	life	life	life

(3) *Specific Offense Characteristics.* The next step, then, is to consult the Guideline to find whatever "Specific Offense Characteristics" reflect this "Relevant Conduct" by adding points to the Base Offense Level. In the case of the post-office burglary, since the burglar, Dan, possessed a firearm and caused a loss of $5,000, the Specific

Offense Characteristics provision in §2B2.1 says that the Base Offense Level is to be increased by a total of three points for these "characteristics," and therefore, the level now is increased from 12 to 15. Can you explain all of this by referring to the burglary Guidelines?

(4) *Next: "Adjustments" to the Base Offense Level.* The next step is to make "Adjustments" to the Base Offense Level. Chapter Three of the Guidelines contains five factors that permit the court to add or subtract points from the Base Offense Level. For example, there are "Victim-Related Adjustments." If the victim is "unusually vulnerable," the base offense level is increased by two levels. Other adjustments relate to the offender's "Role in the Offense" (for example, was he, on the one hand, an "organizer" or, on the other hand, a "minor participant"), "Obstruction of Justice" during the case, "Multiple Counts" (more than one conviction), and "Acceptance of Responsibility." For example, a defendant convicted of three burglaries ("Multiple Counts"), or who committed perjury ("Obstruction of Justice"), would merit "Adjustments" for these factors. *See* Guidelines, Chapter Three—Adjustments. (The relevant provisions of the Guidelines appear in Appendix D.)

To use the example of the post office burglary, let us assume that Dan Defendant faces only one burglary count and did not obstruct justice. Instead, he "clearly accepted responsibility" for the crime, timely notified the Government of his intention to plead guilty—and did so. These factors call for an Adjustment for "Acceptance of Responsibility"—a two point reduction for acceptance, and one more for timely notification and plea. Dan gets 3 points subtracted from the Offense Level of 15. And now, we have his final Adjusted Offense Level: 15 minus 3, or 12.

An Excerpt from the Federal Guidelines: Burglary

(in U.S. Sentencing Commission, *Guidelines* (2015)

§2B2.1 Burglary of a Residence or a Structure Other than a Residence

(a) Base Offense Level

(1) 17, if a residence; or

(2) 12, if a structure other than a residence.

(b) Specific Offense Characteristics

(1) If the offense involved more than minimal planning, increase by 2 levels.

(2) If the loss exceeded $2,500, increase the offense level as follows:

Loss (Apply the Greatest)	Increase in Level
(A) $5,000 or less	No Increase
(B) More than $5,000	add 1
(C) More than $20,000	add 2
(D) More than $95,000	add 3

(E) More than $500,000	add 4
(F) More than $1,500,000	add 5
(G) More than $3,000,000	add 6
(H) More than $5,000,000	add 7
(I) more than $9,500,000	add 8

(3) If a firearm, destructive or controlled substance was taken, or if the taking of such item was an object of the offense, increase by 1 level.

(4) If a dangerous weapon (including a firearm) was possessed, increase by 2 levels.

(5) *Criminal History.* After determining this Offense Level of 12, the next step is to calculate the defendant's "Criminal History Category." For example, an offender receives three points for each prior sentence of imprisonment exceeding thirteen months. Guidelines §4A1.1. There are other criminal history Guidelines, including severe enhancements if the offender is a "career offender" (with two prior convictions for violent or drug crimes, if the current offense is a violent felony or a drug crime). Guidelines §4B1.1.

Imagine that Dan Defendant, the post office burglar, has one prior burglary conviction for which he served two years, seven years ago. His Criminal History will earn a score of 3 (3 points for each incarceration of over 13 months). We now have point totals for both the "Offense Level" and the "Criminal History Category," which are the factors that control the Sentencing Table.

(6) *The Sentencing Table: Using the Offense Level and Criminal History Category to Find the Guideline Sentence.* We now are ready to consult the Sentencing Table. We scan down the left side to find 12, which is Dan's Offense Level, and we scan across from left to right to find 3 points, and we see that this total puts Dan in "Criminal History Category II." The intersection of the row for Offense Level 12 and the column for Criminal History Category II (3 points) says "12–18," meaning that a prison term between twelve and eighteen months (or, between one year and one-and-one-half years) is the advisory Guideline Sentence.

(7) *Presumptively Valid, but Not Mandatory.* This potential sentence range of 12 to 18 months is presumptively valid, but it is not mandatory. The judge has discretion to sentence for any length of time from 12 months to 18 months, but the judge is not bound by this range and has discretion, also, to impose a longer or shorter term.

(8) *Probation; Mandatory Maximums and Minimums.* The Guidelines also advise the judge whether to use probation (that's what the zigzag lines on the Sentencing Table are for). As you probably have guessed, the Guidelines do not advocate probation for our recidivist burglar, Dan Defendant. And finally, the judge must

not assess a sentence below the minimum or above the maximum provided by the statute governing the crime. Guidelines § 5G1.1.

Notes and Questions

(1) *"Real Offense Sentencing": United States v. Watts*, 519 U.S. 148 (1997). The Guidelines attempt to produce what is called "real offense" sentencing. The drafters tried to reflect the defendant's actual conduct in committing the crime. Accordingly, the guidelines permit the court to use "Relevant Conduct" in determining the defendant's Offense Level by consulting "Specific Offense Characteristics" and "Adjustments." Relevant conduct includes the defendant's acts and, also, all reasonably foreseeable acts of others involved in the crime. Real offense sentencing is an ambitious undertaking, and this aspect of the Federal Guidelines is controversial. For example, the Supreme Court in *Watts* held that a sentencing court may consider even conduct of which a jury has acquitted a defendant if it is part of the "Relevant Conduct."

(2) *An Example of Real Offense Sentencing: Taking into Account Not Only the Drugs That Defendant Possessed in This One Offense of Conviction, but Also All Other Quantities Related to It, Whether in This Case or Not: United States v. Crawford*, 991 F.2d 1328 (7th Cir. 1993). In *Crawford*, the defendant entered a plea of guilty to the crime of possession with intent to distribute marijuana. The Guidelines specify drug quantities as part of the Specific Offense Characteristics. The judge therefore considered both the 875 pounds of marijuana that the defendant admitted he "offloaded" in this case, and also, an additional 736 pounds of marijuana that was never delivered (it was described as "under negotiation" between an accomplice and a police informant). The appellate court affirmed the increased sentence because the defendant had participated in negotiations for the additional 736 pounds.

In other words, the "Relevant Conduct" approach permitted the sentencing court to rely upon facts (*i.e.*, the additional marijuana) for which the defendant was not convicted. Of course, the judge in a discretionary system also could (and probably would) enhance the sentence for such a factor, and so, the Guidelines arguably do not do anything new by factoring in the Relevant Conduct.

(3) *The Federal Guidelines Have Been Heavily Criticized.* As one would expect from such a complex, significant change in sentencing procedure, the Federal Sentencing Guidelines have engendered a tremendous amount of analysis and criticism. For example, sentence categories are criticized as contributing to prison crowding and decreasing the prospect of rehabilitation.

(4) *Defending the Guidelines: Justice Stephen Breyer, Federal Sentencing Guidelines Revisited (interview)*, 14 Criminal Justice 28, 35 (Spring 1999). Justice Breyer, who was a member of the Sentencing Commission, defends the Guidelines:

> Despite the criticism of the guidelines, and even recognizing the bias that may arise from my own participation in the creation of the guidelines, I remain cautiously optimistic about their future. They have opened up the

"black box" of sentencing. They have begun to lead broader segments of the legal community to focus upon the question of punishment. They have helped to diminish disparity in sentencing. And most importantly, they have begun to put in place a system for sentencing research that, in principle, can transmit to sentencing policymakers the results of judicial sentencing experience in the field. For all these reasons, I would not recommend a return to preguidelines practice.

For another response to criticisms of the guidelines, see Frank O. Bowman III, *The Quality of Mercy Must Be Restrained, and Other Lessons in Learning to Love the Federal Sentencing Guidelines*, 1996 Wis. L. Rev. 679.

§ 9.13 Interpreting the Sentencing Guidelines

Notes on Interpretive Issues Raised by the Guidelines

(1) *The Kinds of Interpretive Issues Raised by the Guidelines.* What is meant by "minor" participation? How does the judge measure a "loss" to a victim? Words and phrases like these, throughout the Guidelines, create difficulties. The Guidelines contain "Commentary" and "Application Notes," but interpretive questions remain frequent.

(2) *Do Interpretive Difficulties Prevent the Guidelines from Producing Consistent or Fair Sentences?* In some cases, the answer is yes. In the case that follows, different interpretations of the word "intended" (as in "intended loss") make a six-fold difference in sentence length. In the case after that, reinterpretation of the term "minor participation" results in roughly doubling the sentence. It will be up to you to decide whether these difficulties overshadow the benefits of the Guidelines.

United States v. Geevers
226 F.3d 186 (3d Cir. 2000)

Reaffirmed, United States v. Diallo
710 F.3d 147 (3d Cir. 2013)

BECKER, Chief Judge:

[Geevers pleaded guilty to one count of bank fraud. The offense, described as a "check-kiting" scheme, involved the use of worthless checks to inflate accounts in various banks, from which Geevers intended to withdraw the proceeds. The applicable Guideline was § 2F1.1, "Fraud and Deceit," which provided a Base Offense Level of 6. But the Guideline also contained Specific Offense Characteristics that increased the Offense Level according to the amount of loss, and another Guideline, § 2X1.1, provided that "if an *intended* loss that the defendant was attempting to inflict can be determined, this figure will be used if it is greater than the actual loss (emphasis added)." The trial judge therefore measured the loss as the amount Geevers "intended" to take, which the judge determined by the total amount of worthless checks Geevers deposited as part of his scheme. The amount was over $1.5 million, and Specific Offense Characteristics for this amount of loss provided for an 11-point enhancement over the 6-point Base Offense Level. Thus, Geevers received a sentence of 33 months (2 2/3 years), instead of the relatively short sentence he sought.]

[Geevers argued that "no reasonable check writer would think that he could get away with withdrawing the full face amount of the checks." Therefore, he said, the face amount of the deposited checks "cannot be the figure" representing the intended loss. The court of appeals rejected this argument, however, and upheld Geevers's sentence:]

. . . While we agree that Geevers may not have reasonably expected to extract the full face value of his fraudulent checks from the banks, it does not necessarily follow that he did not intend to extract every cent possible. Furthermore, the commentary to §2F1.1 makes clear that losses "need not be determined with precision." . . .

. . . It is clear that a district court errs when it simply equates potential loss with intended loss without deeper analysis. In *United States v. Kopp*, 951 F.2d 521 (3d Cir.1991), . . . we stated that "[t]he fraud guideline thus has never endorsed sentencing based on the worst-case scenario *potential* loss. . . ." [And] [i]n *United States v. Yeaman*, 194 F.3d 442, 460 (3d Cir.1999), we applied *Kopp* to explain that "[i]ntended loss refers to the defendant's subjective expectation, not to the risk of loss to which he may have exposed his victims." . . .

Though *Kopp* and *Yeaman* appear to aid Geevers's cause, the argument that intended loss is not per se equivalent to potential loss only takes him so far. . . . The District Court must determine Geevers's subjective intention, and it can draw inferences from the nature of the crime that he sought to perpetrate. . . .

It seems likely that a defendant in Geevers's position does not expect to obtain the full amount of his fraudulent checks. Common sense suggests that a check kite will always be incomplete, and that a kiter will either abscond or be discovered before exhausting the kite. But expectation is not synonymous with intent when a criminal does not know what he may expect to obtain, but intends to take what he can. We believe that a sentencing court may plausibly conclude that a defendant like Geevers would likely have taken the full amount of the deposited checks if that were possible. [Affirmed.]

United States v. Carpenter

252 F.3d 230 (2d Cir. 2001)

Reaffirmed, United States v. Tang Yuk

885 F.3d 57 2d Cir. 2018)

Meskill, Circuit Judge,

[Donald Carpenter was recruited by Marty Wise, a salesman at a gun store, into a conspiracy to steal firearms from a dealer in violation of 18 U.S.C. §924(m). The district judge determined that Carpenter was less culpable than Wise, decided that

Carpenter therefore was a "minor" participant in the Wise-Carpenter conspiracy, and granted Carpenter a 3-point downward adjustment under § 3B1.2. But the court of appeals vacated the sentence, and ordered resentencing—without the 3-point adjustment—because it determined as a matter of law that Carpenter's participation was not "minor."]

[A] "minor role" adjustment applies to "any participant who is less culpable than most other participants, but whose role could not be described as minimal." The Guidelines further provide that a ["minor role"] adjustment is appropriate if the defendant is "substantially less culpable than the *average participant* (emphasis in opinion)." . . .

Our review of the totality of the district court's statements indicate that its decision to grant Carpenter a three-level mitigating role adjustment was based "*solely* upon the relative culpability of [Carpenter] and his co-conspirator[ ]." Under our well-settled precedent, a finding that Carpenter was less culpable than Wise, his co-conspirator, is an impermissible basis . . . for granting a downward [adjustment] under section 3B1.2 [because such a finding did not make him minor compared to the "average" gun-theft conspirator]. . . .

Notes and Questions

(1) *What Difference Do These Interpretations Make?* In *Geevers*, the Guideline Sentence would have been only 0-to-6 months, but the addition of the 11-point enhancement (and another one) produced roughly a six-fold increase: a Guideline Sentence of 30-to-37 months. In *Carpenter*, the Guideline Sentence roughly doubled, from 10-to-12 months to 18-to-24 months. Varying interpretations of seemingly clear language make enormous differences.

(2) *Are Concerns About Applying the Guidelines Alleviated Now That They Are Merely Advisory, Rather Than Mandatory?* Geevers's and Carpenter's sentences resulted during a time when the Guidelines were mandatory. As a result of the Supreme Court's decision in *Booker*, below, the Guidelines now are merely advisory. Does this fact reduce the concern raised by interpretive differences? The tempting answer is yes. But "advisory" guidelines still are intended to be used to determine real sentences, and judges still follow them. A sixfold increase (or decrease) thus could be based upon mistaken interpretations of phrases such as "intended loss."

§ 9.14 The Constitutional Invalidation of Mandatory Judicial Guidelines

Notes on Factfinding Under the Guidelines

(1) *The Preponderance-of-the-Evidence Standard.* Originally, the Federal Sentencing Guidelines required the judge to use a preponderance of the evidence standard in making fact findings. One frequently stated reason was that sentencing criteria

were multifaceted. Critics argued that this preponderance standard was inappropriate for mandatory guidelines.

(2) *Requiring Jury Findings Beyond a Reasonable Doubt for Enhancements that Increase the Maximum Penalty.* In *Apprendi v. New Jersey*, 530 U.S. 466 (2000), a New Jersey statute provided that possession of a firearm for an unlawful purpose was punishable by imprisonment for between 5 and 10 years. Apprendi pleaded guilty to this offense. A separate statute, described as a hate crime law, provided for an "extended term" of imprisonment if the trial judge found, by a preponderance of the evidence, that "[t]he defendant . . . acted with a purpose to intimidate . . . because of race" or certain other invidious discriminants. The extended term authorized by the hate crime law for Apprendi was imprisonment for between 10 and 20 years.

The evidence about Apprendi's motive was equivocal. But the trial judge found "by the preponderance of the evidence" that Apprendi's crime was racially motivated. This finding enabled the judge to exceed the 10-year maximum, and the judge sentenced Apprendi instead to 12 years. The Supreme Court reversed, over the dissents of four Justices:

> [T]rial by jury has been understood to require that *"the truth of every accusation . . .* should afterwards be confirmed by the unanimous suffrage of twelve of [the defendant's] equals and neighbours. . . ."* 4 W. Blackstone, *Commentaries on the Laws of England* 343 (1769). . . . Equally well founded is the companion right to have the jury verdict based on proof beyond a reasonable doubt. . . .

> [We hold that,] [o]ther than the fact of a prior conviction, any fact that increases the penalty for a crime beyond the prescribed statutory maximum must be submitted to a jury, and proved beyond a reasonable doubt. . . .

Justice O'Connor's dissent in *Apprendi* predicted that the decision would cause significant changes in sentencing practice. Then, in *Blakey v. Washington*, 542 U.S 296 (2004), the Supreme Court struck down a sentence imposed under state guidelines that provided enhancements without jury findings. *Blakey* did not decide the constitutionality of the Federal Sentencing Guidelines. But the handwriting was on the wall.

(3) *Invalidating the Federal Sentencing Guidelines.* Soon after *Blakely*, the Court confronted the question whether the Federal Sentencing Guidelines were also unconstitutional. In light of *Apprendi* and *Blakely*, the Court's answer was no surprise.

UNITED STATES v. BOOKER, 543 U.S. 220 (2005). A jury found Booker guilty of possessing 92.5 grams of crack cocaine with intent to distribute. The Guidelines prescribed a sentence of 210–262 months for Booker's criminal history and the quantity of drugs found by the jury. But the judge "concluded by a preponderance of the evidence that Booker had possessed an additional 566 grams of crack and that he was guilty of obstructing justice. Those findings mandated that the judge select a sentence between 360 months and life imprisonment; the judge imposed a sentence at the low end of the range . . . a 30-year sentence."

In an opinion by Justice Stevens, a five justice majority of the Supreme Court ruled that the sentence was unconstitutional, relying on *Blakely*:

> In [*Blakely*], we dealt with a determinate sentencing scheme similar to the Federal Sentencing Guidelines. . . . The application of Washington's sentencing scheme violated the defendant's [Sixth Amendment] right to have the jury find the existence of "'any particular fact'" that the law makes essential to his punishment. . . .
>
> As the dissenting opinions in *Blakely* recognized, there is no distinction of constitutional significance between the Federal Sentencing Guidelines and the Washington procedures at issue in that case. . . . This conclusion rests on the premise, common to both systems, that the relevant sentencing rules are mandatory and impose binding requirements on all sentencing judges.
>
> If the Guidelines as currently written could be read as merely advisory provisions that recommended, rather than required, the selection of particular sentences in response to differing sets of facts, their use would not implicate the Sixth Amendment. We have never doubted the authority of a judge to exercise broad discretion in imposing a sentence within a statutory range. . . .
>
> The Guidelines as written, however, are not advisory; they are mandatory and binding on all judges. . . .

Thus, the Guidelines were unconstitutional. But what followed from that holding? A different five justice majority of the Court answered that question in an opinion by Justice Breyer:

> We answer the question of remedy by finding the provision of the federal sentencing statute that makes the Guidelines mandatory incompatible with today's constitutional holding. We conclude that this provision must be severed and excised. . . . So modified, the Federal Sentencing Act makes the Guidelines effectively advisory. . . .

Notes on the Guidelines After *Booker*

(1) *"Advisory" Guidelines.* The practical result of this decision, as the Court explains, is that the Guidelines now are "advisory," rather than mandatory. But sentencing judges must "take [them] into account" and explain nonconforming sentences. The Probation Department will compute Guideline Sentences as part of every presentence report (PSR). And courts of appeals can reverse sentences that are "unreasonable," using the Guidelines as benchmarks.

(2) *Does All of This Mean That after Booker, the Guidelines Really Are "Quasi-Mandatory," Rather Than Advisory?* The result of *Booker*, obviously, is not a pure-discretion system. Instead, it is a hybrid. Is the new "advisory" system better?

(3) *Using the Federal Sentencing Guidelines after Booker.* The Supreme Court has issued several decisions to clarify the impact of *Booker.* In *Kimbrough v. United States*, 552 U.S. 85 (2007), the Court emphasized the advisory nature of the guidelines and emphasized the statutory factors that district courts must consider when sentencing a criminal defendant:

> [18 U.S.C. §3553(a)], as modified by *Booker*, contains an overarching provision instructing district courts to "impose a sentence sufficient, but not greater than necessary" to accomplish the goals of sentencing . . . . "In sum, while the statute still requires a court to give respectful consideration to the Guidelines, *Booker* 'permits the court to tailor the sentence in light of other statutory concerns as well.'"

In *Rita v. United States*, 551 U.S. 338 (2007), and *Gall v. United States*, 552 U.S. 38 (2007), the Court clarified the federal sentencing process at trial and on appeal—specifically including the role and relevance of the Guidelines. The following passage from *Gall* summarizes the holdings of the two cases:

> [A] district court should begin all sentencing proceedings by correctly calculating the applicable Guidelines range. . . . In so doing, [the judge] may not presume that the Guidelines range is reasonable. He must make an individualized assessment based on the facts presented. If he decides that an outside-Guidelines sentence is warranted, he must consider the extent of the deviation and ensure that the justification is sufficiently compelling to support the degree of the variance. . . . After settling on the appropriate sentence, he must adequately explain the chosen sentence to allow for meaningful appellate review and to promote the perception of fair sentencing.
>
> Regardless of whether the sentence imposed is inside or outside the Guidelines range, the appellate court must review the sentence under an abuse-of-discretion standard. . . . If the sentence is within the Guidelines range, the appellate court may, but is not required to, apply a presumption of reasonableness. But if the sentence is outside the Guidelines range, the court may not apply a presumption of unreasonableness. It may consider the extent of the deviation, but must give due deference to the district court's decision. . . .

On the one hand, this process seems designed to ensure some uniformity among sentences. Yet the abuse of discretion standard clearly shifts power away from appellate courts and back to district courts.

(4) *Actual Practice in the Federal Courts: Far More Sentences Below Than Above the Guidelines, But Most Sentences Still Fall Within the Guidelines Range.* Since *Booker*, sentences below the relevant Guidelines range, where the government does not support the lower sentence, have increased, from 6.3% shortly before *Booker* to 17.4% in 2011. Government-sponsored sentences below the range account for another 26.3%. Only 1.8% of sentences are above the relevant range. That leaves 54.5% of

sentences within the Guidelines range. U.S. Sentencing Commission, *2011 Annual Report* 3536 (2011); *see also* Stephanos Bibas & Susan Klein, *The Sixth Amendment and Criminal Sentencing*, 30 Cardozo L. Rev. 775, 789–90 (2008).

(5) The Model Penal Code's new sentencing provisions strongly endorse state sentencing commissions and sentencing guidelines, subject to the constitutional constraints outlined above. *See* American Law Institute, *Model Penal Code: Sentencing* arts. 8&9 (2017). Do you agree? Recognizing that every system is imperfect, which do you believe presents the fewest disadvantages: mandatory guidelines, quasi-mandatory guidelines, suggested-or-merely-advisory guidelines, or pure discretion?

§ 9.15 The Death Penalty: Justifying, Opposing, or Limiting Its Imposition

Notes on the Constitutionality of the Death Penalty

(1) *The Past: Open, Discretionary Death Penalty Sentencing.* In the early twentieth century, the death penalty was imposed in many states for serious homicides as well as, less frequently, for other crimes. Throughout the twentieth century, however, reformers sought limits on or abolition of the death penalty. Then, in *Furman v. Georgia*, 408 U.S. 238 (1972), the Supreme Court declared the traditional death penalty unconstitutional because the jury was given no guidance about when to impose it.

(2) *Jury Guidance under Modern Capital Statutes.* Four years later, the "modern era" of capital punishment began when the Supreme Court upheld Georgia's more limited death penalty statute in *Gregg v. Georgia*, 428 U.S. 153 (1976). After *Gregg*, states began to carry out executions slowly at first, later in numbers approaching those of the early twentieth century, and still more recently, in lesser numbers.

[A] The Constitutionality of the Death Penalty: The Basic Cases

FURMAN v. GEORGIA, 408 U.S. 238 (1972). In a brief per curiam opinion, the Supreme Court struck down the death penalty as then administered. Each justice filed a separate concurring or dissenting opinion. Justices Brennan and Marshall would have held that the death penalty itself is a cruel and unusual punishment in violation of the Eighth Amendment. Three other justices reasoned that the death penalty was unconstitutional as applied because state statutes allowed juries to assess death penalties in their unstructured discretion. Four justices dissented. In response, states revised their statutes.

Gregg v. Georgia

428 U.S. 153 (1976)

JUSTICE STEWART, JUSTICE POWELL, AND JUSTICE STEVENS announced the judgment of the Court and filed an opinion delivered by JUSTICE STEWART. . . .

[Gregg and another man, while hitchhiking, were picked up by two other men. The four halted at a ditch for a rest stop. Gregg told his companion that he planned to rob the two men. He took his pistol, positioned himself on the car to steady his aim, and shot the two without warning as they came up the embankment. Then, at close range, he fired a shot into the head of each. He robbed them of valuables and drove away. Two days later, he was arrested in the same car.]

[The "new" Georgia death penalty, enacted after *Furman*, did not apply to most murders. It only applied if one of certain defined "aggravating circumstances" were present.]

[The jury convicted Gregg of two counts of murder. The judge instructed the jury on the applicable "aggravating circumstances" under Georgia's death penalty statute: (1) murder during armed robbery, (2) murder for the purpose of "receiving money," and (3) murder that was "wantonly vile, horrible and inhumane" so that it involved "depravity of mind." The jury positively found the first two aggravating circumstances beyond a reasonable doubt (although it declined to find the third, "wanton vileness"), and it returned verdicts of death on each murder count. In the Supreme Court, Gregg argued that the death penalty in general, as well as Georgia's statute in particular, was unconstitutional in all cases. The Court here affirms the death sentence.]

[Precedent establishes] that the Eighth Amendment has not been regarded as a static concept. As Chief Justice Warren said, . . . "[t]he Amendment must draw its meaning from the evolving standards of decency that mark the progress of a maturing society." Thus, an assessment of contemporary values concerning the infliction of a challenged sanction is relevant to the application of the Eighth Amendment. . . .

[H]istory and precedent strongly support a negative answer to [the] question [whether the death penalty is per se unconstitutional]. It is apparent from the text of the Constitution itself that the existence of capital punishment was accepted by the Framers. . . . Despite the continuing debate, . . . there is now evidence that a large proportion of American society continues to regard it as an appropriate and necessary criminal sanction. . . . The legislatures of at least 35 states have enacted new statutes that provide for the death penalty for at least some crimes that result in the death of another person. . . .

The death penalty is said to serve two principal social purposes: retribution and deterrence of capital crimes by prospective offenders. . . .

In part, capital punishment is an expression of society's moral outrage at particularly offensive conduct. This function may be unappealing to many, but it is essential in an ordered society that asks its citizens to rely on legal processes rather than self-help to vindicate their wrongs.

"The instinct for retribution is part of the nature of man, and channeling that instinct in the administration of criminal justice serves an important purpose in promoting the stability of a society governed by law. When people begin to believe that organized society is unwilling or unable to impose upon criminal offenders the punishment they 'deserve,' then there are sown the seeds of anarchy, of self-help, vigilante justice, and lynch law." *Furman v. Georgia*, 408 U.S., at 308 (Stewart, J., concurring).

. . . Indeed, the decision that capital punishment may be the appropriate sanction in extreme cases is an expression of the community's belief that certain crimes are themselves so grievous an affront to humanity that the only adequate response may be the penalty of death. . . .

As for the deterrence purpose, [s]tatistical attempts to evaluate the worth of the death penalty as a deterrent to crimes by potential offenders have occasioned a great deal of debate. The results simply have been inconclusive. . . .

Although some of the studies suggest that the death penalty may not function as a significantly greater deterrent than lesser penalties, there is no convincing empirical evidence either supporting or refuting this view. We may nevertheless assume safely that there are murderers, such as those who act in passion, for whom the threat of death has little or no deterrent effect. But for many others, the death penalty undoubtedly is a significant deterrent. There are carefully contemplated murders, such as murder for hire, where the possible penalty of death may well enter into the cold calculus that precedes the decision to act. And there are some categories of murder, such as murder by a life prisoner, where other sanctions may not be adequate. . . .

We hold that the death penalty is not a form of punishment that may never be imposed, regardless of the circumstances of the offense, regardless of the character of the offender, and regardless of the procedure followed in reaching the decision to impose it.

[Justice White, joined by Chief Justice Burger and Justice Rehnquist, filed a concurring opinion, as did Justice Blackmun. Justices Brennan and Marshall dissented and reiterated their view that the death penalty is unconstitutional no matter how it is applied.]

Notes and Questions

(1) *Gregg's Companion Cases: Upholding Florida's and Texas's Laws.* In *Proffit v. Florida*, 428 U.S. 242 (1976), and *Jurek v. Texas*, 428 U.S. 262 (1976), the Court upheld statutes that, while different from Georgia's, similarly limited the death penalty to aggravated cases of murder, allowed consideration of mitigating evidence, and guided jury findings.

(2) *But "Mandatory" Capital Sentencing Is Unconstitutional.* By contrast, the Court invalidated two statutes that had attempted to solve the problem of unguided jury discretion by removing all discretion and mandating death sentences in certain

aggravated cases of murder. *Woodson v. North Carolina*, 428 U.S. 280 (1976); *Roberts v. Louisiana*, 428 U.S. 325 (1976).

(3) *Retribution and the Death Penalty.* The *Gregg* Court focused on the two most familiar justifications for punishment—deterrence and retribution—and found that neither theory undermined the death penalty. Retributive approaches arguably provide the easiest way to justify the death penalty. If the goal is to reset the moral balance in the manner urged by Kant, then putting a killer to death is a just punishment. Similarly, if murder is among the worst of crimes, then the death penalty is an expression of society's revulsion and of the value of the life taken.

But retribution also turns on ideas of moral justice. Some moral theorists consider human life to be sacred, and others speak of an inherent right to life. For these theorists, murder is a great moral wrong, but imposing the death penalty compounds the harm by adding another death to the list. Some retributivists also argue that the death penalty creates moral harm because it coarsens society and delays the conclusion of cases for victims' families. Finally, many retributivists worry about the inevitability and immorality of executing the innocent. Thus, it is unlikely that there will ever be a consensus retributivist position on the death penalty. How, then, should the courts assess retributivist rationales: Should they simply defer to the legislature's assessment?

(4) *General Deterrence and the Death Penalty.* The question for deterrence theorists is the extent to which a less costly penalty, such as life without the possibility of parole, would achieve general deterrence. One might think that the imposition of such a severe penalty would lead some potential killers to reconsider. Justice Stewart's opinion in *Gregg* takes some level of deterrence for granted. Yet empirical studies have come to differing conclusions, and the more recent studies seem to undermine deterrence claims. Some studies even claim that the death penalty could encourage homicide by "brutalizing" society through the spectacle of state-sponsored killing.

Deterrence theorists who support the death penalty can respond in several ways. First, they can argue that the death penalty achieves some level of deterrence by inculcating useful values about respecting human life. Further, they can attack the studies that find no deterrence as flawed. For example, it may impossible to account for all of the social pressures that help produce homicides, yet if those pressures are increasing and producing more killings, then the death penalty would be a meaningful deterrent even if it only slowed the rate of increase. Similarly, they could plausibly claim that the death penalty would be a more effective deterrent if it were imposed more swiftly and certainly rather than after years of protracted litigation. How should courts and legislatures respond to the deterrence debate?

(5) *Other Rationales: How Do Incapacitation Theories Apply?* The Supreme Court did not consider incapacitation as a rationale for punishment in *Gregg*. But should it have? If an overriding goal of punishment is to keep criminals away from the law-abiding population, then doesn't life imprisonment serve that goal and make capital punishment unnecessary?

Many states have created the sentence of "life without possibility of parole." But some murderers have killed again while in prison, have escaped and committed crimes, or have been released and killed again. As we shall see, Texas actually limits its death penalty to cases in which incapacitation is a factor, by requiring a jury finding that there is a "probability" of "future violence" by the defendant. Do these situations suggest a purpose for the death penalty?

(6) *Other Rationales: What About Rehabilitation?* The death penalty obviously discounts rehabilitation. Assume, however, that some convicted murderers can be rehabilitated. Should the death penalty be confined to cases in which the prospect of rehabilitation is remote? Even if we can reliably identify offenders who are good prospects for rehabilitation, are there some crimes that nevertheless merit the ultimate penalty?

[B] Capital Sentencing Statutes: Defining Death-Penalty Eligibility after *Gregg*

Notes on Death Penalty Statutes

(1) *The Structure of Modern Death Penalty Statutes: Narrowing Death Eligibility.* As a result of *Furman, Gregg,* and a host of other cases, modern death penalty statutes are complex. In general terms, death penalty statutes contain four parts: (1) the definition of homicides for which the death penalty is authorized, (2) a list of aggravating circumstances that indicate the death penalty may be imposed, (3) a list of mitigating circumstances that justify not imposing the death penalty, and (4) a set of procedures for capital cases.

Not all murders are "death eligible." The "aggravating circumstances" include such factors as the identity of the victim (*e.g.,* a police officer), whether more than one person was killed, whether the offender was committing another crime (*e.g.,* robbery), and the manner in which the killings were carried out. States use a variety of terms to describe aggravating factors related to the manner of the killing. *See, e.g., Walton v. Arizona,* 497 U.S. 639 (1990) (upholding "especially heinous, cruel, or depraved" as an aggravating factor).

(2) *Statutory Criteria for Decision.* The procedure for imposing the death penalty is also complicated. The defendant is first tried for murder, and the jury will be asked to determine whether the crime is the kind of murder that is eligible for the death penalty. *See Hurst v. Florida,* 136 S. Ct. 616 (2016) (invalidating Florida death penalty statute under which the judge, not the jury, made the final determination of aggravating factors). If the jury so determines, the jury next decides between death and life imprisonment (sometimes the choice is between death and life without possibility of parole).

(3) *The Texas Statutory Scheme.* Since the *Gregg* decision in 1976, Texas has executed more people than any other state. (California has more people awaiting execution but has executed only a few.) As a result, Texas's statutes have been subjected

to (and amended because of) intense judicial scrutiny, including numerous cases before the Supreme Court.

Texas Penal Code § 19.03: Capital Murder
(Defining Murders That Are Death-Eligible)

(a) A person commits [the] offense [of capital murder] if the person commits murder . . . and:

(1) the person murders a peace officer or fireman who is acting in the lawful discharge of an official duty and who the person knows is a peace officer or fireman;

(2) the person intentionally commits the murder in the course of committing or attempting to commit kidnapping, burglary, robbery, aggravated sexual assault, arson, obstruction or retaliation, or terroristic threat [of certain types],

(3) the person commits the murder for remuneration or the promise of remuneration or employs another to commit the murder for remuneration or the promise of remuneration;

(4) the person commits the murder while escaping or attempting to escape from a penal institution;

(5) the person, while incarcerated in a penal institution, murders another: (A) who is employed in the operation of the penal institution; or (B) with the intent to establish, maintain, or participate in a combination or in the profits of a combination;

(6) the person: (A) while incarcerated for an offense under this section or Section 19.02, murders another; or (B) while serving a sentence of life imprisonment or a term of 99 years for [certain aggravated violent offenses,] murders another;

(7) the person murders more than one person: (A) during the same criminal transaction; or (B) during different criminal transactions but the murders are committed pursuant to the same scheme or course of conduct;

(8) the person murders an individual under ten years of age; or

(9) the person murders another person in retaliation for or on account of the service or status of the other person as a judge or justice of [a court].

(b) An offense under this section is a capital felony [for which the sentence must be either death or life imprisonment].

Texas Code Crim. Proc. Art. 37.071: Procedure in Capital Cases
(Defining Procedure and Jury Findings in Capital Cases)

Sec. 2 (a) . . . [O]n a finding that the defendant is guilty of a capital offense, the court shall conduct a separate sentencing proceeding to determine whether the defendant shall be sentenced to death or life imprisonment without parole. . . . In the proceeding, evidence may be presented by the state and the defendant or the defendant's counsel as to any matter that the court deems relevant to sentence, including evidence of the defendant's background or character or the circumstances of the offense that mitigates against the imposition of the death penalty. . . .

(b) On conclusion of the presentation of the evidence [in the sentencing hearing], the court shall submit the following issues to the jury:

(1) whether there is a probability that the defendant would commit criminal acts of violence that would constitute a continuing threat to society; and

(2) in cases in which the jury charge at the guilt or innocence stage permitted the jury to find the defendant guilty as a party under Sections 7.01 and 7.02, Penal Code [on accomplice liability], whether the defendant actually caused the death of the deceased or did not actually cause the death of the deceased but intended to kill the deceased or another or anticipated that a human life would be taken.

(c) The state must prove each issue submitted under Subsection (b) of this article beyond a reasonable doubt, and the jury shall return a special verdict of "yes" or "no" on each issue submitted under Subsection (b) of this Article.

(d) The court shall charge the jury that: . . . it may not answer any issue submitted under Subsection (b) of this article "yes" unless it agrees unanimously and it may not answer any issue "no" unless 10 or more jurors agree. . . .

(e)(1) The court shall instruct the jury that if the jury returns an affirmative finding to each issue submitted under Subsection (b) of this article, it shall answer the following issue:

Whether, taking into consideration all of the evidence, including the circumstances of the offense, the defendant's character and background, and the personal moral culpability of the defendant, there is a sufficient mitigating circumstance or circumstances to warrant that a sentence of life imprisonment without parole rather than a death sentence be imposed. . . .

(2) The court shall [inform the jury that life without the possibility of parole means what it says—that the defendant would be] ineligible for release . . . on parole.

(f) The court shall charge the jury that in answering the issue submitted under Subsection (e) of this article, the jury:

(1) shall answer the issue "yes" or "no";

(2) may not answer the issue "no" unless it agrees unanimously and may not answer the issue "yes" unless 10 or more jurors agree; [and] . . .

(4) shall consider mitigating evidence to be evidence that a juror might regard as reducing the defendant's moral blameworthiness.

(g) If the jury returns an affirmative finding on each issue submitted under Subsection (b) and a negative finding on an issue submitted under Subsection (e)(1), the court shall sentence the defendant to death. [Otherwise,] the court shall sentence the defendant to confinement in the Texas Department of Criminal Justice for life without parole. . . .

(h) The judgment of conviction and sentence of death shall be subject to automatic review by the Court of Criminal Appeals. . . .

Problem 9H: Results of the Texas Death Penalty Statute

(1) *Answering the Texas Questions: Three Possible Cases.* Imagine the following jury answers in response to the three questions in sections (b) and (e) of Art. 37.071. Explain what result would follow under each of the following three sets of responses, and explain the sentencing philosophy that arguably is carried out:

(a) Case One: Question (1), "Yes"; (2), "Yes"; (3), "No."

(b) Case Two: (1), "Yes"; (2), "No."

(c) Case Three: (1), "Yes"; (2), "Yes"; (3), unanswered (hung jury).

(Note that question (1) asks whether there is a probability of future violent acts constituting a continuing threat; question (2), whether the defendant personally caused the death or, if not, intended or anticipated death; and question (3), whether sufficient mitigation warrants a life sentence instead.)

(2) *Burdens of Proof and Relevant Factors.* Notice that the jury must answer "No" to the first two questions unless it finds proof beyond a reasonable doubt. For question (3), however, which inquires whether the mitigating evidence suffices to warrant a life sentence, there is no burden of proof. Should the question be rewritten to require proof beyond a reasonable doubt that the aggravating evidence outweighs the mitigating evidence? The courts have tended to hold that proof beyond a reasonable doubt requirements do not apply to the weighing process, at least in the absence of statutory requirements. Their reasons: that the "weighing" of two variables is not a "fact finding" of the kind that triggers a constitutional requirement of proof beyond reasonable doubt, and that the weighing of multiple incommensurate factors is a "judgmental" decision that is not logically suited to this kind of proof. *See Nunnery v. State,* 263 P.3d 235 (Nev. 2011) (citing other cases).

(3) *The Broad Evidence Standard.* Evidence at the sentencing hearing may be presented "on any matter the court deems relevant to sentence." Notice that this provision allows evidence, from either side, that might not be admissible in a noncapital case. Why? The Supreme Court decisions require a degree of accuracy beyond that of noncapital cases, and therefore, the jury should have all relevant evidence. Question: If we allow broader admissibility of evidence against capital defendants, why not against non-capital defendants?

(4) *What Evidence Is "Deemed Relevant"?* Imagine that the defendant offers the following kinds of evidence, and consider whether each is admissible under the Texas statute. (Similar evidence has been offered, and sometimes received, in actual Texas cases.) (1) statistical evidence purporting to demonstrate that the death

penalty does not deter murder. (2) a photograph of an electric chair (no longer used in this jurisdiction). (3) pictures of the defendant's six sisters. (4) expert testimony purporting to show that some other crimes for which the death penalty was not assessed were more brutal than this defendant's. (5) testimony by the defendant's eight-year-old daughter about her need for "my daddy." (6) testimony about the defendant's abusive childhood. (7) hearsay evidence, inadmissible on guilt or innocence, indicating that defendant's role in the offense was relatively minor. And consider the following case about prosecution evidence.

PAYNE v. TENNESSEE, 501 U.S. 808 (1991). Should jurors hear from victims and survivors before determining a death sentence? More specifically, should they consider the harm done to survivors by the crime? In *Booth v. Maryland*, 482 U.S. 496 (1987), the Supreme Court said no. The only relevant question was the "blameworthiness" inherent in the "decision to kill," and later-resulting harm was irrelevant and unconstitutional. In *Payne*, however, the Court determined that *Booth* was "unworkable," overruled it in an opinion by Chief Justice Rehnquist, and held that evidence of impact of the crime was not barred by the Eighth Amendment:

> *Booth* and [a related case] [*South Carolina v.*] *Gathers*, 490 U.S. 805 (1989), were based on two premises: that evidence relating to a particular victim or to the harm that a capital defendant causes a victim's family do not in general reflect on the defendant's "blameworthiness," and that only evidence relating to "blameworthiness" is relevant to the capital sentencing decision. However, the assessment of harm caused by the defendant as a result of the crime charged has understandably been an important concern of the criminal law, both in determining the elements of the offense and in determining the appropriate punishment. . . . "If a bank robber aims his gun at a guard, pulls the trigger, and kills his target, he may be put to death. If the gun unexpectedly misfires, he may not. His moral guilt in both cases is identical, but his responsibility in the former is greater." *Booth*, 482 U.S. at 519 (Scalia, J., dissenting). . . .

Three justices dissented. Justice Marshall's opinion charged that the decision rested on "[p]ower, not reason." Do you agree with the Court's conclusion—is testimony about the impact of the crime a valid basis upon which to distinguish sentences of life or death?

Notes and Questions

(1) *Other Statutory Approaches.* The Texas statutes determine which murders are death-eligible at the guilt phase of the trial. Other States, such as Georgia, save that decision for the penalty phase, but most of the aggravating factors and required findings are analogous. The difference is in the stages at which the jury makes these decisions. Also, the Texas statute directs the jury to answer three specific questions, which include a focus on the defendant's "future dangerousness." Other states

ask the jury to engage in a more general weighing of aggravating and mitigating evidence.

(2) *The Federal Death Penalty Act, 18 U.S.C. §§ 3591–3598: Defining the Aggravating Factors.* The Federal Death Penalty Act provides a long list of aggravating factors that will make a homicide eligible for the death penalty.

18 U.S.C. § 3592(c): The Federal Death Penalty Act

[The Act allows the possibility of the death penalty when]:

(1) *Death during commission of another crime.* The death, or injury resulting in death, occurred during the commission or attempted commission of, or during the immediate flight from the commission of [a long series of specific federal crimes of violence].

(2) *Previous conviction of violent felony [federal or state] involving firearm. . . .*

(3) *Previous conviction of offense [state or federal] for which a sentence of death or life imprisonment was authorized. . . .*

(4) *Previous conviction of other serious offenses.* The defendant has previously been convicted of 2 or more Federal or State offenses, punishable by a term of imprisonment of more than 1 year, committed on different occasions, involving the infliction of, or attempted infliction of, serious bodily injury or death upon another person.

(5) *Grave risk of death to additional persons.* The defendant, in the commission of the offense, or in escaping apprehension for the violation of the offense, knowingly created a grave risk of death to one or more persons in addition to the victim of the offense.

(6) *Heinous, cruel, or depraved manner of committing offense.* The defendant committed the offense in an especially heinous, cruel, or depraved manner in that it involved torture or serious physical abuse to the victim.

(7) *Procurement of offense by payment.* The defendant procured the commission of the offense by payment, or promise of payment, of anything of pecuniary value.

(8) *Pecuniary gain.* The defendant committed the offense as consideration for the receipt, or in the expectation of the receipt, of anything of pecuniary value.

(9) *Substantial planning and premeditation.* The defendant committed the offense after substantial planning and premeditation to cause the death of a person or commit an act of terrorism.

(10) *Conviction for two felony drug offenses.* The defendant has previously been convicted of 2 or more State or Federal offenses punishable by a term of imprisonment of more than one year, committed on different occasions, involving the distribution of a controlled substance.

(11) *Vulnerability of victim.* The victim was particularly vulnerable due to old age, youth, or infirmity.

(12) *Conviction for serious Federal drug offenses* . . . for which a sentence of 5 or more years may be imposed or had previously been convicted of engaging in a continuing criminal enterprise.

(13) *Continuing criminal enterprise involving drug sales to minors.* . . .

(14) *High public officials.* The defendant committed the offense against [the President, Vice-President, "a chief of state, . . . of a foreign nation," certain foreign officials, a judge, law enforcement officers, or prison employees killed while performing or because of their official duties or status].

(15) *Prior conviction of sexual assault or child molestation.* . . .

(16) *Multiple killings or attempted killings.* The defendant intentionally killed or attempted to kill more than one person in a single criminal episode. . . .

In addition, "The jury, or if there is no jury, the court, may consider whether any other aggravating factor for which notice has been given exists," and the government may also present evidence about "the effect of the offense on the victim and the victim's family." With respect to mitigating evidence, a federal jury may consider an unlimited range of factors.

(3) *Proof Requirements and the Balancing Process for the Federal Death Penalty.* The government must prove the existence of aggravating factors beyond a reasonable doubt, while the defense must prove mitigating factors by a preponderance of the evidence. The jury "shall consider whether all the aggravating factor or factors found to exist sufficiently outweigh all the mitigating factor or factors found to exist to justify a sentence of death." Is this general balancing requirement better or worse than the Texas process, which requires answers to two guided questions before balancing and then asks whether mitigating factors outweigh aggravating ones?

[C] The Continuing Debate over Capital Punishment

Notes on Proportionality and Process in the Administration of the Death Penalty

(1) *Proportionality and the Death Penalty: Accomplice Killings and Felony Murder.* Supreme Court case law requires sentences to be proportionate to the crime, on the theory that lack of proportionality makes a death sentence "cruel and unusual" in violation of the Eighth Amendment. In practice, the death penalty is reserved for aggravated forms of murder. But some persons convicted of murder were convicted as accomplices, whether or not they personally killed anyone. For example, should the getaway car driver be eligible for the death penalty? What about perpetrators of serious crimes other than murder, such as repeated rape of a child or torture that does not cause death?

The Supreme Court has permitted states to impose the death penalty on persons guilty of felony-murder, even if an accomplice carried out the killing, so long as they were "major participants" in the underlying felony and acted with "reckless indifference to human life." *Tison v. Arizona*, 481 U.S. 137 (1987); *compare Enmund v. Florida*, 458 U.S. 782 (1982) (holding death penalty is excessive punishment for felony murder if defendant did not kill, attempt to kill, or intend to kill, and also stating death penalty would be excessive for armed robbery).

(2) *Proportionality and Nonhomicidal Crimes (Including Crimes Against the State)*. Whether the Constitution permits imposition of the death penalty where there has been no taking of a human life remains an open question. The Court struck down a death sentence for the rape of an adult woman on the ground that it was "grossly disproportionate and excessive." *Coker v. Georgia*, 433 U.S. 584 (1977). Then, the Court held by a 5–4 vote that states may not impose the death penalty for the rape of a child. *Kennedy v. Louisiana*, 554 U.S. 407 (2008). Louisiana argued that the number of states that had authorized or proposed capital punishment for the rape of a child had increased in recent years, so that there was no consensus against it, but the majority rejected this argument. The Court also made the following statement:

> Our concern here is limited to crimes against individual persons. We do not address, for example, crimes defining and punishing treason, espionage, terrorism, and drug kingpin activity, which are offenses against the State . . . .

Kennedy thus appears to have held that the death penalty cannot be imposed for non-homicide crimes against individuals—but that the same rule may not apply to "offenses against the State." The federal government sought the death penalty in a 2003 espionage case, but a jury rejected it. Should the death penalty be available in such cases?

(3) *Proportionality: Insane or Incompetent Persons*. In addition to deciding which crimes can be punished with death, the Supreme Court has decided several cases about particular classes of offenders. For example, the Court has held that the Constitution forbids execution of the insane or mentally incompetent. *Ford v. Wainwright*, 477 U.S. 399 (1986). Speaking for a plurality, Justice Marshall said that the category of mentally incompetent includes "one whose mental illness prevents him from comprehending the reasons for the penalty and its implications."

(4) *A Concrete Case of Executing a Potential Incompetent*. Consider the case of John Brewer, who beat his pregnant girlfriend to death. Brewer pled guilty and informed the jury at his sentencing hearing that he deserved execution. The jury agreed, and Brewer sought to waive all appeals. Because review of death sentences is mandatory in Arizona, the state supreme court nonetheless reviewed the sentence and affirmed. Brewer then refused to petition for a federal writ of habeas corpus. He explained that he wanted to be executed because a god known as Dantain had told him that he and his victim would be reincarnated on the planet Terracia. Two

state-appointed experts testified that Brewer was competent, although one of them apparently had second thoughts, while a third expert testified that Brewer was not competent. Brewer's waiver of further proceedings resulted in his execution. *See Brewer v. Lewis*, 989 F.2d 1021 (9th Cir. 1993). But was he competent under *Ford?*

(5) *Proportionality: The Mentally Retarded or Juveniles.* The Court has also struggled with execution of juveniles and the mentally retarded (which is the term the Supreme Court uses). At first, it upheld death sentences. But in *Atkins v. Virginia*, 536 U.S. 304 (2002), it ruled by a 6–3 vote that the Eighth Amendment forbids executing mentally retarded persons. Three years later, in *Roper v. Simmons*, 543 U.S. 551 (2005), the Court ruled 5–4 that the Eighth Amendment forbids imposing the death penalty on offenders who were under the age of 18 at the time of the crime. The Court decided that juveniles and the mentally retarded are less culpable than the average capital murderer.

(6) *Arguments of Opponents about Fairness and Accuracy.* Much debate about the death penalty focuses on process. Although people sentenced to death receive a great deal of process relative to other criminal defendants, questions remain. Concerns about the accuracy of decisions in capital cases suggest a problem with accuracy in criminal cases generally, but the irreversibility of execution arguably makes the problem more pressing.

Opponents of the death penalty point out the enormous amount of discretion inherent in the criminal justice system, from decisions by police, to prosecutorial charging decisions, to the discretion of trial judges, to the jury, all the way to executive clemency. This discretion, they contend, permits inconsistency and bias. They also argue that attorneys for defendants in capital cases sometimes are inadequate.

Opponents also highlight the risk that innocents will be convicted of capital murder, sentenced to death, and ultimately executed. Even among murderers, some may be wrongly sentenced to death because their actions were not sufficiently aggravated, so that they are "innocent of the death penalty." Before he left office in 2003, Illinois Governor George Ryan commuted all of his state's death sentences to life imprisonment after doubts arose about the convictions and sentences of 13 people — some of whom had already been executed.

(7) *The Response of Death Penalty Supporters to These Arguments.* Supporters of the death penalty respond that discretion is both inherent in and necessary to any functioning criminal justice system, and that discretion advances just results far more often than it enables biased results. With respect to the qualifications of defense counsel, some support or at least concede some need for improved qualifications. On the issue of accuracy, supporters of the death penalty take different approaches. Some cast doubt on the validity of studies suggesting high rates of error (studies often conducted, they point out, by death penalty opponents). Others support reforms that could improve accuracy. Still others suggest that some errors are inevitable in any real world system.

(8) *Arguments about Racial Discrimination: McCleskey v. Kemp, 481 U.S. 279 (1987).* Consider the possibility that the death penalty is imposed in a racially discriminatory manner. In *McCleskey*, the Court was presented with evidence that the killers of white victims in Georgia were significantly more likely to be sentenced to death than the killers of other victims and that black defendants were more likely to receive a death sentence than any other category of defendant. The Court ruled 5–4 that the Equal Protection Clause requires proof of *intentional* discrimination, so that racial disparities in imposition of the death penalty would not alone support a claim. Because McCleskey could provide no evidence of system-wide intentional discrimination, nor any evidence of intentional discrimination in his case, the Court affirmed his sentence.

(9) *Abolition Movements.* The debate over the death penalty generates different results in different jurisdictions. A majority of states and the federal government continue to sentence defendants to death, although not all of those jurisdictions actively carry out death sentences. Illinois (2011), Connecticut (2012), and Maryland (2013) recently abolished the death penalty through legislative action.

§ 9.16 Can Long Juvenile Sentences Be Cruel and Unusual?

Note: Juvenile Sentences and Capital Punishment

(1) *Non-Homicidal Life-without-Parole Sentences for Juveniles: Held Unconstitutional in Graham v. Florida,* 560 U.S. 48 (2010). At 16, Graham was placed on probation for burglary. He continued to commit additional crimes. The trial court eventually sentenced him to life in prison for the burglary. Because Florida had abolished parole, the sentence amounted to life without parole. The Supreme Court, per Justice Kennedy, held that the sentence was unconstitutional. The Court decided that its death penalty jurisprudence should be the basis of analysis, including considerations of "evolving standards of decency." The Court noted that the majority of states permitted nonhomicidal LWOP (life without parole) sentences for juveniles, but concluded that because there were relatively few such sentences nationwide (123, in 11 states), this kind of sentence was actually "rare." And "because juveniles have lessened culpability, they are less deserving of the most severe punishments." Finally, it stated that this kind of sentencing has been rejected in other countries.

(2) *Is This Reasoning Persuasive? Justices Thomas, Scalia and Alito Dissented.* "Until today, the Court has based its categorical proportionality rulings on the notion that the Constitution gives special protection to capital defendants because the death penalty is a uniquely severe punishment. . . . Today's decision eviscerates that distinction. 'Death is different' no longer." Furthermore, "[n]o plausible claim of a consensus against this sentencing practice can be made. . . . Not only is there

no consensus against this penalty, there is a clear legislative consensus *in favor* of its availability."

(3) *The Court Has Extended This Holding to Mandatory Life without Parole for Juveniles Convicted of Homicidal Crimes: Miller v. Alabama*, 132 S. Ct. 2455 (2012). At age 14, Miller murdered another juvenile by setting a fire and causing smoke inhalation and beating him repeatedly with a baseball bat while robbing him. Miller told the victim, "I'm God. I'm here to take your life." He was certified for trial as an adult, convicted of murder, and sentenced to life in prison without parole because Alabama law made that sentence mandatory for murder in the course of arson. In a 5-to-4 opinion by Justice Kagan, the Court cited *Graham* in holding that juvenile life sentences were "analogous to capital punishment." The Court did not hold that life without parole was unconstitutional itself for juvenile homicides; only mandatory sentences were affected. Chief Justice Roberts and Justices Thomas, Scalia, and Alito dissented.

§ 9.17 Review Problems Based on Newspaper Cases

Note on These Newspaper Cases

The following cases involving sentencing decisions were reported recently in newspapers. They have been rewritten here to emphasize the legal issues, although the facts remain as they were reported. As you read about these cases, consider how the sentencing decision was made in each, whether it carries out the four basic purposes of the criminal sanction, and how it might have been affected by laws in other sentencing systems.

[A] Headline: "Dad Who Beat Hockey Coach to Death Sentenced to 6 to 10 Years"

CAMBRIDGE, Mass.—Thomas Junta beat Michael Costin to death with his fists after disagreeing with Costin about his way of coaching hockey. At his trial, Junta, who outweighed Costin by roughly a hundred pounds, claimed self-defense, but witnesses testified that Junta was the aggressor. A rink manager had told Junta that he could not enter the ice, but he pushed her aside, ran to Costin, threw him to the ice, and beat him repeatedly about the head and neck, rupturing an artery. Police found Costin bleeding, unconscious, and surrounded by children. The State charged Junta with murder, but the jury convicted him of voluntary manslaughter instead.

Yesterday, Judge Charles Grabau followed prosecutors' recommendation and sentenced Junta to 6 to 10 years in prison. But he called the recommendation "most generous" and said that he had considered imposing a higher sentence. The maximum was 20 years.

The dead man's 13-year-old son, who was one of those children present, asked the judge to "teach [Junta] a lesson." In a firm voice, the boy added, "Let the world know that a person can't do what he did to my family. No matter how much of a sentence that you give to Thomas Junta, my dad got more." Junta himself did not call character witnesses. In a subdued tone, he read a prepared statement that included the words, "I'd just like to apologize to both families and thank my family for their support for me." He looked down while Costin's family members described the incident and its impact upon them. Constin's 14-year-old son also testified and said, "I can still remember being hysterical trying to wake him up as the blood streamed down his face." The trial judge recalled the testimony of a police officer at the trial, reporting that soon after the event, Junta had said, "I got the better of him. I got in a lot more shots." The judge also took into account an earlier incident when Junta's wife obtained a restraining order after accusing him of beating her in front of their children.

(1) *Sentencing Factors: Deterrence, Incapacitation, Rehabilitation, and Retributive Justice.* Can you identify evidence in this report that bears upon each of the traditional sentencing factors and analyze which ones might have influenced the judge?

(2) *Presentence Investigation.* The newspaper report did not mention whether the judge consulted a presentence report prepared by the probation department, but it is likely that he did. Would this report have contained information going beyond factors like deterrence and retribution, which sometimes are determinable from the crime itself, and bearing on more difficult issues, such as the defendant's susceptibility to rehabilitation and need for incapacitation?

(3) *How Would the Result Change if Determinate Sentencing or Guidelines Were in Effect?* The Federal Sentencing Guidelines would produce a remarkably similar sentence here, of roughly 5 to 6 years. Judge Grabau's decision in Massachusetts was reached under a broad-discretion system. Does this comparison demonstrate that the two systems are likely to produce similar sentences? Consider, however, whether the Guideline Sentence in a federal case similar to Junta's would be increased by other factors. Would Costin be a "vulnerable victim," a factor that would call for upward adjustment? Unlike the defendant in the Problem case, Junta did not plead guilty but was convicted as the result of a trial. Thus, he would not receive the downward adjustment that the defendant in the Problem received. Furthermore, the trial judge evidently considered Junta's trial testimony untrue, and this factor might call for an adjustment for obstruction in the form of perjury. Can you explain these adjustments?

(4) *Parole: How Long Is the "Real" Sentence?* Junta's lawyer explained that he would be required to serve at least four years before becoming eligible for parole. The federal system has abolished parole and substituted a slight reduction in sentence applied without discretion. Which system is better?

[B] Headline: "Parole Near for Mom Who Killed Baby, Returned to Prom"

CLINTON, N.J.—Melissa Drexler is expected to be freed on Monday from the Edna Mahan Correctional Facility. Now 23, she has served just over three years for killing her 6-pound, 6-ounce baby boy. The circumstances of the killing received national attention because Drexler gave birth in a restroom at her high school prom, threw the child into a trash can, and returned to dancing. She had hidden her pregnancy from her parents and from the father.

Drexler had been charged with murder but pleaded guilty to aggravated manslaughter. She was sentenced to 15 years but was eligible for parole at this time. If the killing had occurred just a few days later, Drexler would not have been so lucky. Three days after she killed her son, the State's "No Early Release Act" went into effect, requiring inmates to serve at least 85% of their sentences (similarly to the federal system). Drexler then would have faced a minimum of 12½ years. The prosecutor's office had objected to Drexler's parole "because we oppose early parole on principle," said Monmouth County Prosecutor John Kaye. "But the likelihood of her constituting a threat to the public is minimal." He added, "She did her time." Drexler's lawyer asked, "Would it have done society any better to have her do 10 years?" At some point, he said, "it becomes pure retaliation by the State."

(1) *Are Deterrence, Incapacitation, and Rehabilitation Inadequate Reasons for a Longer Sentence in This Case?* The statements of the prosecutor and defense lawyer indicated that they believed that the usual Utilitarian purposes of sentencing would not have been served by longer confinement for Drexler. Is this true?

(2) *"At Some Point It Becomes Pure Retaliation by the State"—but Is There an Argument That This Is Exactly the Justification for a More Substantial Sentence?* The defense lawyer evidently meant to suggest that "retaliation" was not a legitimate consideration and should not have influenced Drexler's sentence at all. Most commentators, however, seem to agree that retributive justice is a necessary consideration in a sound sentencing system. In Drexler's case, perhaps it can be conceded that three years is long enough to deter anyone who is deterrable from a crime of this kind; that incapacitation is not needed because the defendant is not a "threat to the public" (as the prosecutor said); and that a sentence of more than three years is unlikely to enhance any rehabilitative effects of the sanction. Why, then, did New Jersey change its law to require future convicts in Drexler's position to serve approximately four times as many years as she did? Consider whether this case presents a situation in which retributive justice would be the principal justification for a substantial sentence. Or, to put the same question in Utilitarian terms, consider whether Emile Durkheim is right in calling for a sentence that adequately "condemns" the crime, so that the sentence "is designed to act upon upright people," who will then not lose respect for the law.

[C] Headline: "Actress Gets Three Years' Probation for Misdemeanor Vehicular Manslaughter"

HOLLYWOOD—Actress Rebecca Gayheart, 29, who starred in [the original version of] "Beverly Hills, 90210," pleaded no contest yesterday to vehicular manslaughter and was sentenced to three years' probation and a fine. As a special, additional condition of probation, she was required to perform community service by producing a safe-driving video. Gayheart has no prior criminal record.

In California, this particular offense of vehicular manslaughter is applicable to grossly negligent driving that causes a death when the driver is not intoxicated. Gayheart's driving resulted in killing a nine-year-old boy, whose parents have sued Gayheart in civil court for medical, hospital, funeral, and other expenses, as well as loss of the child's companionship and future earnings.

(1) *Probation Conditions: Should There Be at Least Some Deprivation of Liberty for a Homicidal Offense, However Brief?* Recall the kinds of conditions that courts usually impose on probationers, and consider why the judge imposed the additional condition of production of a safe-driving video. Is it possible that defense counsel suggested or concurred in this condition to avoid a more serious sanction? (Community service involves a kind of deprivation of liberty, although not of a severity similar to incarceration; perhaps the order for community service in this case served that function.) Consider, also, whether probation in a case of this kind merits the public criticism that it often receives, as an inadequate "slap on the wrist."

(2) *How Do Deterrence, Incapacitation, Rehabilitation, and Retributive Justice Affect This Sentencing Decision?* There probably is not a need to incapacitate Ms. Gayheart, she probably is familiar with the norms of society and does not need rehabilitation at least in the educative sense, deterrence arguably is served by the civil suit, and retributive justice (while a factor) probably does not demand a severe sentence. Recall, however, that mere civil negligence is not enough to make out most crimes; instead, Ms. Gayheart was convicted of voluntary manslaughter which involved gross negligence under the applicable state statute. Does this consideration indicate that the purposes of sentencing would indeed be served by some deprivation of liberty for the defendant in this case?

(3) *Imagining a Similar Case, but One Caused by Intoxicated Driving.* If a defendant were to cause a similar vehicular homicide, but commit the offense while intoxicated, many people would consider the crime to be more serious, and likewise, many states, including California, would place a different label on it. And many people (as well as many states) would impose more serious sentences for intoxicated manslaughter. Do deterrence and rehabilitation require different analysis in the intoxicated-manslaughter situation? Does incapacitation enter into the calculus in a different way? And does retributive justice demand a more severe penalty? Consider why, in terms of

the four classical punishment factors, an intoxicated manslaughter seems to require a more serious sentence than one caused by non-intoxicated grossly negligent driving — and try to figure out what a reasonable sentence would be for someone who commits this offense, and who, like Gayheart, has no criminal record, but who, unlike Gayheart, is intoxicated at the time of the offense.

§ 9.18 Simulation Exercises: Sentencing Hearings and Sentencing Advocacy

Simulation Exercise No. 10 (Advocacy): Contested Sentencing Hearing in State v. Lipman

(1) *The Sentencing of One Defendant in a Two-Person Robbery-Rape.* Consider the materials in Case File No. 3 online (*State v. Lipman*). Please go online to https:// caplaw.com/sites/cl4/, then click on "Case File No. 3." Then, (1) Represent the State or (2) represent Lipman in his sentencing hearing. Assume that plea negotiations have resulted in an agreement that there will be a guilty plea to one count of robbery and a dismissal of the rape indictment, although the entire episode can be considered, and the judge will determine the defendant's sentence.

(2) *A Contested Sentencing Hearing on a Plea of Guilty.* Conduct a sentencing hearing at which the parties have made this agreement but cannot agree on a sentence. Both the prosecutor and the defense attorney are free to oppose or advocate any sentence. Assume that the parties agree that the evidence will consist of the victim's statement and the defendant's statement contained in the appendix (both stipulated admissible). Represent (1) the State or (2) the defendant in giving an argument about sentence.

Simulation Exercise No. 11 (Document Preparation): United States v. Smith

(1) *A Problem Involving Disputes about a PSR and Sentencing Options.* Consider the online materials in the case of *United States v. Smith.* Please go online to https:// caplaw.com/sites/cl4/, then click on "Case File No. 4." Then, (1) Prepare a document disputing relevant aspects of the PSR (presentence report). Consider, in particular, the Federal Sentencing Guidelines that are excerpted in this Chapter and the discussion of PSR. (2) Also, in the same document, point to factors that would produce the most desirable reasonable sentence, but one that you can advance honestly, and advocate it. (3) Prepare an affidavit for your client to sign using what he has told you (see below).

(2) *Possible Points of Dispute.* Notice that the PSR places the "intended loss attributable" at $64,712, so that there is a "five (5) level increase." Your client says, "We never thought we'd get anything like that amount." Carefully read the PSR and determine whether a dispute of this five-level increase might reduce it. Further, the PSR says

that Smith "is deemed a manager and the offense involved five or more participants," for an increase of three (3) levels. "Manager" is not specifically defined, and the cases vary as to indications of "management." (In a real case, you might research and cite cases, but here, use "common-sense" arguments.) Your client says, "I didn't manage anything. I just did what the big man told me. Whatever I gave to the runners, I got from him. In fact, I was so bad as a manager that I cashed a check at my own bank, where they knew me. I had no clue how to do it." Also, consider whether any other factor should be disputed or added. As to sentence alternatives, consider (1) decisions about selection within the guideline range, (2) alternatives to incarceration, etc.

Simulation Exercise No. 12 (Figuring a Guideline Sentence): "Bubba Shot the Jukebox Last Night"

(1) *A Sentencing Problem Based on Mark Chesnutt's Ballad, "Bubba Shot the Juke-box Last Night."* This sentencing problem is based on a piece of popular culture. A best-selling country ballad sung by Mark Chesnutt features a gentleman named "Bubba," whom listeners meet while he is drinking at the local bar. Bubba isn't feeling good anyway, and the jukebox isn't helping because "the song, it sure was a sad one." Suddenly, Bubba has had enough. He walks to his pickup, retrieves one of his firearms, and fires it into the offending jukebox. Chesnutt's song reaches its climax when the sheriff says,

> "Now reckless discharge of a gun,
> That's what the officers are claimin'"
> Bubba hollered out, "Reckless! Hell!
> I hit just where I was aimin'."

The following facts are not part of the song, but assume them. The Federal Guidelines apply, because the bar is within a federal enclave (land owned by the United States). The applicable Guidelines are in Appendix D. The jukebox was worth $20,000, but now it is a total loss. Further, because he later becomes remorseful, Bubba promptly lets the government know that he intends to plead guilty to "malicious destruction of property," and the government files "a downward adjustment motion." Bubba has one previous conviction for theft, for which he served three years and was released seven years ago.

(2) *What Are the Steps in Figuring a Guideline Sentence for This Crime?* Explain how a federal court would go about figuring the sentence for this crime. In other words, describe how each of the following factors would be used: 1. The "Base Offense Level"; 2. The "Relevant Conduct"; 3. Any "Specific Offense Characteristics"; 4. Adjustment for "Acceptance of Responsibility"; 5. The "Criminal History Category"; and 6. The "Sentencing Table".

(3) *Explaining the Calculation.* Here is a possible calculation. (It is based on the Guidelines that are reproduced online under "Federal Guidelines.")

- To find the Guidelines, please go online to https://caplaw.com/sites/cl4/, then click on "Federal Guidelines." The Base Level for destruction of property is 6;

the Level increases to 10, because the Relevant Conduct and Specific Offense Characteristics depend on the amount of loss (and for a loss of over $10,000, the increase is 4 points); but then, the Specific Offense Characteristics increase the score further, to 14 (because of the use of a firearm); and the defendant earns a 3-point downward Adjustment for acceptance of responsibility.

- Thus, the final (adjusted) Offense Level is 14 minus 3, or 11.

- The defendant's Criminal History score is 3 (that is what the Guidelines specify for a prior sentence of two years).

- The Sentencing Table (inside Chapter 9) gives the Guideline Sentence as 10–16 months for this Offense Level (11) and Criminal History Category (3 points). There does not seem to be any obvious ground for a departure, but the court might consider Probation under other applicable Guidelines.

Can you explain all of this?

Simulation Exercise No. 13 (Figuring a Guideline Sentence): "Bubba Shot the Owner of the Bar Last Night, Too"

(1) *Applying the Guidelines (Excerpted Below) to a More Serious Crime: Bubba Also Shoots and Kills the Jukebox Owner.* Now, imagine that after shooting the jukebox, Bubba also shot and killed the owner of the bar after the owner expressed outrage at Bubba's destruction of his property. It was a sadly typical, thoughtless crime, committed after Bubba had been drinking.

Now, use the Guidelines to determine the advisory sentence that a federal court might consider. Please go online again to https://caplaw.com/sites/cl4/, then click on "Federal Guidelines." Assume that the offense of conviction is voluntary manslaughter (this defendant probably lacks "adequate cause," but assume that voluntary manslaughter is what the jury has found). Assume the same criminal record and acceptance of responsibility as in the preceding problem. (Note that there could not be any multiple-count adjustment for the property destruction, because the Guidelines tell you to "[d]isregard any [conviction] that is 9 or more levels less serious" than the main conviction.) Now, use the Guidelines below and the Sentencing Table above to figure the advisory sentence.

(2) *How Should the Judge Decide What Sentence in the Sentencing Table Range Is Appropriate?* Using the Guidelines available in this book, you should produce an Offense Level of 26, a Criminal History score of 3, and an advisory sentence of 70 to 87 months (or 5 5/6 to 7 1/4 years). How should a judge decide whether the best guideline is 70 months, or 87 months, or something in between?

Simulation Exercise No. 14 (Advocacy): Capital Murder Sentencing Hearing in State v. Smith

A Capital Murder Sentencing Hearing. Consider the materials online relating to *State v. Smith.* Please go online to https://caplaw.com/sites/cl4/, then click on "Case File No. 5." Represent (1) the State or (2) the defendant in deciding upon and describing the items of evidence you might consider presenting, describing how you would go about questioning the relevant witnesses, and describing how you would oppose or limit the other side's evidence. For the defendant, you should go beyond the circumstances outlined and freely consider any useful mitigating evidence of any kind that you might seek.

Chapter 10

Preparatory Crimes

"The attempt and not the deed confounds us." — Shakespeare, *Macbeth II: 2*

"There is nothing either good or bad, but thinking makes it so." — Shakespeare, *Hamlet II: 2*

§ 10.01 Introduction to Preparatory Crimes

Notes on Preparatory (or Inchoate) Offenses

(1) *Overview.* Assume that A, the owner of a decrepit warehouse, decides to burn down the building in order to collect insurance. A calls B and asks for help, offering 25% of the insurance proceeds. B accepts and then photographs the outside of the building in order to assist in the planning. A and B are arrested when B tells others about the scam. Note that the two were arrested before going very far in the process. Has A or B (or both) committed a crime?

(2) *Attempt, Solicitation, and Conspiracy.* Even though no actual harm has resulted, both A and B might be guilty of several preparatory (sometimes called "inchoate") offenses. This chapter concerns the three primary inchoate crimes: attempt, solicitation, and conspiracy. An "attempt" is complete when the actor, with intent, has taken significant steps toward commission of the "target crime." A "solicitation" occurs when the defendant tries to get another person to engage in criminal activity, as A has done with B. "Conspiracy" is present when the other person agrees to be part of the scheme with "intent to promote" it, and, in some jurisdictions, when one of the conspirators commits an "overt act." Here, A and B may both be guilty of conspiracy to commit arson and conspiracy to commit insurance fraud.

(3) *If Target Crime Committed: Multiple Convictions?* The general rule is that if the defendant committed the target crime, he or she may not be convicted of both the target crime (arson) and attempt to commit that crime. However, some jurisdictions permit conviction of both the target crime and conspiracy. *Compare* Alas. Stat. § 11.31.140 (forbidding conviction of attempt or solicitation and target crime but allowing conviction of conspiracy and target crime), *with* Ore. Rev. Stat. § 161.485 (forbidding conviction of target offense and any inchoate offense).

(4) *Punishment for Inchoate Crimes.* The punishment for an inchoate crime represents a statement about its relative seriousness. Is an attempt, solicitation, or conspiracy as serious as the completed crime?

(a) *Attempt.* The usual rule is that an attempt to commit a target crime is punished slightly less severely than the punishment authorized for the target crime. The theory is that the harm is lesser than for the target crime. But some jurisdictions punish an attempt in the same way as the target crime. *See, e.g.,* Conn. Gen. Stat. §53a-51 (attempt and conspiracy are same grade as target crime).

(b) *Solicitation.* Solicitation is often viewed as the least serious of the three inchoate crimes because it involves the least risk of harm. Recall that a solicitation often occurs at the very preliminary stages of the criminal course of conduct. *See also* Tex. Penal Code Ann. §15.01–15.03 (except for most serious crimes, attempt, solicitation and conspiracy all punished one level below target crime). If the person who was solicited attempts or completes the crime, then the offense of solicitation merges with the attempt crime or target offense.

(c) *Conspiracy.* Conspiracy often is deemed more serious than solicitation because it involves group agreement, while a solicitation is merely an attempt to enlist group participation. Accordingly, conspiracy is ordinarily punished less severely than the target crime, but more harshly than solicitation.

§ 10.02 Attempt Crimes

Notes on Attempt Statutes

The Elements of Criminal Attempt. The elements of attempt usually include both a mens rea and an actus reus. As you read the following statutes, try to identify both:

Cal. Penal Code §21(a). "An attempt to commit a crime consists of two elements: a specific intent to commit the crime, and a direct but ineffectual act done toward its commission."

Tex. Penal Code §15.01(a). "A person commits an offense if, with specific intent to commit an offense, he does an act amounting to more than mere preparation that tends but fails to effect the commission of the offense intended."

Read Model Penal Code §5.01(1)(c) and (2) [general attempt provision] in the MPC Appendix.

[A] The Elements of Attempt

Notes on the Elements of Attempt

(1) *The Mens Rea of Attempt: Specific Intent (Usually).* The mens rea of attempt is widely accepted as specific intent. Thus, while the crime of murder may require

only that a defendant kill with malice, which often can be supplied by an extremely reckless, knowing, or intentional state of mind, a defendant usually is not guilty of attempted murder without the specific purpose to kill. Why do you think attempted murder requires purpose to kill when murder can be committed with a lesser mens rea?

(2) *Special Mens Rea Problems: Object Crimes That Do Not Include Intent, by Definition.* Given the specific intent requirement, is it possible for a defendant to "attempt" an involuntary manslaughter, which is often defined as a reckless or even criminally negligent killing (how can a person have the specific intent to commit an unintentional crime)? Not surprisingly, many jurisdictions have held that it is impossible to attempt a crime defined by recklessness. Other jurisdictions avoid the specific intent requirement by providing that an actor needs to exhibit only the degree of culpability that is required for the object offense. *See also* Model Penal Code §§ 5.01(1)(a)–(b) (attempt exists "if, acting with the kind of culpability otherwise required for commission of the crime," he or she purposely engages in specified conduct).

(3) *What Is the Actus Reus of Attempt—and What Purpose Does It Serve?* The state statutes above are vague about the act component, with California saying only that it must be "direct" (what does that mean?) and Texas defining it only by saying what is insufficient ("more than mere preparation"). Perhaps the reason is to avoid criminalizing mere thoughts, or "thoughtcrime." Or maybe the actus reus is a means of minimizing mistaken convictions for attempt.

(4) *A Variety of Possible Tests for the Actus Reus of Attempt: The "Dangerous Proximity," "More than Mere Preparation," and "Substantial Step" Approaches.* In contrast to the wide acceptance of specific intent as the mens rea of attempt, the law has proposed differing tests for the actus reus. Each test is designed to determine that the defendant has gone far enough to show a real attempt. For example, the common law "dangerous proximity" test asks whether the act comes close to completion of the object crime. Typically, the standard is not met unless the defendant is dangerously close to succeeding. On the other hand, MPC § 5.01, cited above, asks whether the defendant has taken a "substantial step" that is "strongly corroborative" of an intent to commit the crime. It shifts the focus from what remains to be done, to what the actor has already done. Thus, if the actor's actions corroborate an intent to commit the crime, the defendant may not need to be dangerously close to completing the crime. Then, there is the possible rule that the defendant must have done "more than mere preparation,"

(5) *Historically, There Have Been Many Other Actus Reus Tests.* The Commentary to the MPC's attempt provisions catalogues a number of different formulations for the actus reus. Each is designed to determine when the defendant has crossed the line from mere beginnings to actual attempt. In addition to the ones above, the various actus reus tests include: "physical proximity" (the actor is close in physical distance to the object); "indispensable element" (the actor has acquired control of everything required for the object crime); "probable desistance" (the actor has done

enough to show that he probably wasn't going to stop); and others. Consider the following problem, about a case in which the actus reus was found insufficient.

Problem 10A (Attempt): "They Were About Ten Feet Apart When the Constables Stopped Him"

(1) *Reconsidering State v. Boutin, Noted in § 5.01[A] Following State v. Billings.* The state statute at issue in *State v. Boutin* defined assault in terms of an "attempt to . . . inflict injury." The facts were as follows: After a scuffle, the defendant picked up a bottle, held it over his head, and advanced toward the victim, who had picked up a rock and was backing away. The two men were about ten feet apart when interrupted by constables. The court reversed Boutin's conviction, holding that there was no attempt.

(2) *Evaluating the Actus Reus for Attempt.* What result would you expect in *Boutin* under a substantial step test for attempt? What result under other actus reus tests for attempt, such as dangerous proximity, more than mere preparation, or probable desistance?

[B] Attempt and Abandonment

Notes: Attempt and Renunciation (or Abandonment)

(1) *The Renunciation/Abandonment Defense.* At early common law, once a defendant met the legal requirements for attempt, the defendant was guilty, regardless of any change of mind. However, modern laws generally recognize a renunciation (abandonment) defense.

(2) *Limits on the Renunciation Defense.* The renunciation defense is not intended for situations where the defendant sees a danger of getting caught or is waiting for a better opportunity to commit the crime. Accordingly, the abandonment must be voluntary and must avoid harm. Consider the following case and problem.

Reid v. State

404 S.E.2d 101 (Ga. App. 2019)

RICKMAN, Judge.

Following a bench trial, Richard Allen Reid was convicted on one count of criminal attempt to commit child molestation and [other crimes]. On appeal, Reid contends that the evidence was insufficient to support his conviction for criminal attempt to commit child molestation . . . . For the following reasons, we affirm. . . .

[T]he evidence showed that . . . an investigator with the Effingham County Sheriff's Office placed an ad on Craig's List stating that he was a female and was "home alone bored." Reid responded to the ad, "I am very much interested in hanging out. I'm a lot of fun to be around but will let you be the judge of that if you're interested.

Hit me up and let's see what kind of fun we can get into." When the investigator replied that she was 15-years-old, Reid stated, "[o]h wow, but you're only 15 though."

The investigator sent a photograph purporting to be a photograph of the 15-year-old girl, but it was actually a photograph of a female deputy at the sheriff's office, and Reid sent a photograph of himself. After communicating through Craig's List, Reid and the investigator, posing as the 15-year-old girl, began exchanging text messages. The investigator testified that Reid "constantly ask[ed] for nude photos of the child" and stated that he was a "horny old man." Reid sent text messages to the investigator stating that the child was a "very attractive young lady" and that he was "really a lot older than [her]," Reid asked the investigator what kind of "fun" she liked and he replied, "I lik all kinds and mayb even new stuff." Reid responded, "[d]on't tease me girl[.]" Reid expressed concern . . . about being discovered by law enforcement and told [the "child"] to "get rid of" all of their conversations so that a parent did not discover them.

Reid and the investigator arranged to meet at a gas station. Prior to their meeting, Reid requested more revealing photos that showed more skin so that he would have something to look forward to. The investigator testified that Reid stated, "[w]e can still play and get all worked up and be ready to have fun when I do make it up there" and that he wanted to "see [her] naked before I see you Friday, that'd also prove that you're serious." Reid confirmed that the investigator would be alone when he met with the child after work and stated that he was "pretty excited" about meeting with her. After they met, Reid planned to go back to the child's house.

Once Reid indicated that he was close to the arranged meeting location, the investigator began surveillance. The investigator observed a male in a Jeep pull into a parking space toward the end of the parking lot. The male sat in his vehicle for several minutes without exiting before backing up and attempting to leave the location. Thereafter, the investigator conducted a traffic stop and identified the male as Reid. The investigator testified that Reid initially stated that "he was just simply riding around" but then admitted "that he was coming to meet a female that he knew was underage."

. . . Following a bench trial, Reid was convicted on all counts. . . . Reid contends that the evidence was insufficient to support his conviction for criminal attempt to commit child molestation. Specifically, Reid argues that he never took a substantial step towards committing child molestation or, alternatively, that he abandoned any attempt to commit to child molestation. We disagree.

"A person commits the offense of criminal attempt when, with intent to commit a specific crime, he performs any act which constitutes a substantial step toward the commission of that crime." OCGA § 16–4–1. To establish that Reid attempted to commit child molestation, the State was required to prove that he took a substantial step toward doing "any immoral or indecent act to or in the presence of or with any child under the age of 16 years with the intent to arouse or satisfy the sexual desires of either the child or the person." OCGA § 16–6-4 (a) (1). . . .

Here, Reid communicated with someone he believed to be a 15-year-old girl. Reid asked the alleged child repeatedly for nude photographs, told her that he was a horny and dirty old man, and asked her not to "tease" him when she told him that she would like to try new things. Prior to Reid's arranged meeting with the alleged child, he told her they could "play and get all worked up and be ready to have fun" before meeting, that he wanted to see her naked to prove that she was serious, and that he was "pretty excited" about meeting her. This was enough evidence for the trial court to determine that, with the intent toward doing an immoral or indecent act with a 15-year-old girl, Reid took a substantial step toward committing child molestation by arranging to meet the child, and traveling to the meeting place. See *Schlesselman* [*v. State*], 773 S.E.2d 413 (Ga. App. 2015) (affirming defendant's conviction for attempted child molestation where the defendant arranged to pay for a night of "companionship" with a 14-year-old girl and drove to the meeting location) . . . .

Alternatively, Reid argues that he abandoned any criminal purpose when he left the arranged meeting place without exiting his vehicle. "When a person's conduct would otherwise constitute an attempt to commit a crime under Code Section 16–4-1, it is [a] . . . defense that he abandoned his effort to commit the crime or in any other manner prevented its commission under circumstances manifesting a voluntary and complete renunciation of his criminal purpose." OCGA § 16–4-5 (a). ". . . [T]he State has the burden of disproving that defense beyond a reasonable doubt."

. . . The evidence established that, prior to the arranged meeting, Reid expressed concern that he would be discovered by law enforcement or the child's parents, and that Reid was under law enforcement surveillance the entire time he was at the gas station. After Reid was apprehended, he never explained to the investigator why he left the gas station or expressed a change of heart. "It was for the [factfinder] to determine whether the State met any burden to disprove [a] . . . defense of abandonment—a determination which the [factfinder] made in the State's favor." Accordingly, we find that the trial court's determination that the State met any burden to disprove the affirmative defense of abandonment was supported by the evidence. . . . [Affirmed.]

MᴄFᴀᴅᴅᴇɴ, Presiding Judge, concurring in part and dissenting in part.

. . . This is a classic case of abandonment. Reid drove to the scene of a planned crime, hesitated, then drove away. That's really all we know. . . .

[T]he state had the burden of disproving [abandonment] beyond a reasonable doubt. . . .

The state could have met that burden by proving that Reid's departure "result[ed] from, (1) [a] belief that circumstances exist[ed] which increase[d] the probability of detection or apprehension . . . ; or (2) [a] decision to postpone the criminal conduct until another time." OCGA § 16–4-5 (b).

But the state offered no evidence to show Reid's frame of mind when he decided to leave without meeting the girl with whom he thought he had been communicating—other than the departure itself. . . . [T]here is no evidence that Reid realized that he was under law enforcement surveillance when he left. The fact that Reid did not explain his reason for leaving, either to the investigator at the time or to the court at trial, cannot be said to supply that deficiency—Reid was under no obligation to explain.

. . . Reid had seemed concerned with being caught. But that is not enough. Abandonment inspired by the general deterrent effect of the criminal law is still abandonment. . . . See generally Comment 8 to Model Penal Code § 5.01, Part I Commentaries, vol. 2, at 356–357 ("A 'voluntary' abandonment occurs when there is a change in the actor's purpose that is not influenced by outside circumstances. . . . A reappraisal by the actor of the criminal sanctions applicable to his contemplated conduct would presumably be . . . voluntary . . . as long as the actor's fear of the law is not related to a particular threat of apprehension or detection."). . . . [This judge would reverse.]

Notes and Questions

(1) *The "Substantial Step" Test of the Model Penal Code and Its Influence.* Many jurisdictions have adopted the MPC "substantial step" approach, as does the court in this case. For example, Texas gives meaning to its "more than mere preparation" requirement, in the statute reproduced above, by also using substantial step.

(2) *Comparing Various Tests of Attempt with the Facts of This Case: Dangerous Proximity, Probable Desistance, More than Mere Preparation, Etc.* Consider the other tests for attempt. The defendant has probably come far enough to satisfy a dangerous proximity test with his communications and travel, although that test might be more difficult than substantial step. Perhaps his communications and travel amount to more than mere preparation, although that test is more ambiguous. It is arguable that the defendant did not cross the line of dangerous proximity, because he never got close to confronting the (imaginary) child. Is this analysis correct?

(3) *Abandonment: If Defendant Fears the Law, Is the Renunciation Still Abandonment?* At common law, there was no renunciation or abandonment defense to attempt. Modern criminal codes, however, generally recognize this defense. *See* MPC § 5.01(4). In *Reid*, the majority finds no abandonment because the defendant was afraid of being apprehended and did not express any change of heart when confronted by a police officer at the scene—and thus he did not voluntarily renounce his criminal purpose. Notice the subtle distinction shown by the dissenting judge: it's still voluntary if the abandonment results from a general fear of the law, as opposed to a specific reason for fear of apprehension. Is this correct?

(4) *Resistance or Injury as Negating Voluntary Abandonment.* Imagine that the defendant encounters resistance to a violent crime. Alternatively, he fears that he may be committing a more serious crime than he intends because of injuries he has

inflicted. But then again, imagine that the circumstances suggest that he may have abandoned the crime out of remorse. Do these possibilities prove an attempt and destroy any abandonment defense? Consider this problem:

Problem 10B (Renunciation): "I Refrained from Completing a Sexual Assault Because of Her Injuries"

(1) *The Accused's Attempt and His Abandonment Defense in State v. Mahoney*, 870 P.2d 65 (Mont. 1994). Mahoney broke into a store, repeatedly stabbed the clerk, and exposed his penis to rape her. But "[w]hen he saw a large amount of blood from her wounds, he stopped his actions, went around the checkout counter and called the Billings police, reporting that he had cut a clerk and that an ambulance was needed. . . . [W]hen the police arrived at the scene, Mahoney was cooperative, . . . and he provided a factual account of the incident."

(2) *Was the Actus Reus Sufficient for an Attempt Here?* The defendant exposed himself and presumably communicated his intention. Was this conduct sufficient to prove a "substantial step" toward sexual assault? Was it "more than mere preparation"?

(3) *Was the Renunciation of Sexual Assault "Voluntary" and "Complete"?* A Montana statute provided that a "voluntary and complete renunciation" was a defense to attempt. The court held, however, that Mahoney had not sufficiently raised this defense. "Mahoney did not abandon his criminal conduct until he met with unanticipated difficulties and unexpected resistance." Therefore, "Mahoney's conduct is not a manifestation of voluntary and complete renunciation" The court upheld the conviction for attempted sexual assault. Do you agree with this reasoning?

[C] Impossibility: When Does It Negate Attempt?

Notes and Questions

(1) *The Never-Never-Land Idea of "Impossibility."* Assume that the defendant has met both the actus reus and mens rea requirements for attempt. In fact, assume that the defendant has done all that is humanly possible to commit the crime, but is unable to do so because he or she has misconceived the facts (or the law), which make the object crime impossible to commit. For example, imagine that the defendant intends to commit murder and he shoots at what he thinks is his victim — only to discover that the "victim" is a dummy. Or, the defendant smuggles a drug into the United States, one that he or she believes is illegal to import; but later, she learns that its importation was not illegal after all. Is the defendant still guilty of attempt?

(2) *Impossibility as a Confusing Concept.* Many students find impossibility a confusing and unsatisfying concept. It depends upon "what ifs" that sometimes do not correspond to reality. Further, impossibility arises in different situations, but those situations often seem indistinguishable.

(3) *Four Variations: True Legal Impossibility, False (or Hybrid) Legal Impossibility, Factual Impossibility, and Inherent Impossibility.* Impossibility appears in each of the following guises (at least):

(a) *"True" Legal Impossibility.* This variation occurs when the object that the actor has attempted to accomplish is not a crime at all even if completed and even though the actor *believed* that it was a crime. For example, imagine that the defendant goes to elaborate lengths to smuggle a particular drug through customs, believing that its importation is illegal. But unbeknownst to the actor, importing this drug is not illegal at all. The actor has the specific intent to import illegally, and has performed a substantial step; but even if the facts were as the actor sees them, there could be no completed object crime. This sort of "true" legal impossibility usually negates the crime of attempt.

(b) *Factual Impossibility.* In this variation, the defendant misperceives the facts, but if the facts were as the defendant believes them to be, the defendant could accomplish the object crime. For example, the defendant shoots bullets into the head of a dummy, believing it to be the intended human victim. The defendant could be guilty of murder if the facts were as the defendant believes. This is "factual" impossibility, and it is not a defense to attempt.

(c) *"False" or "Hybrid" Legal Impossibility: Factual Impossibility Disguised as Legal Impossibility.* In a case like the "attempted murder" of a dummy, the (clever but erroneous) defender may argue, "It is impossible, as a matter of law, for shooting a dummy to be murder. Therefore, the object crime is *legally* impossible, and there cannot be any conviction for attempt." This reasoning sometimes is referred to as "false" or "hybrid" legal impossibility because it tries to sidestep the reality that, if the facts were as the defendant *believed* them to be (if the intended human victim had been the one that the defendant shot), the object crime of murder could have been completed. But . . . sometimes courts have accepted this defensive argument.

(d) *Inherent Impossibility.* The examples that often illustrate "inherent" impossibility include the clueless or crazy defendant who attempts to kill a victim by exploding what the defendant knows is talcum powder. Or, a defendant attempts to kill by sticking pins in a voodoo doll. The impossibility, here, arguably is of the factual variety and theoretically should not prevent conviction for attempt, but the defendant's incompetence is so apparent, and makes the attempt so harmless, that it is labeled "inherently" impossible and is deemed not an attempt.

(4) *The Fluid Nature of These Categories (or, the Impossibility of Defining Impossibility).* Return to the hypothetical importer who attempts to smuggle a drug illegally (but who fails to commit a crime because the importation is not illegal). We have used this case as an example of true legal impossibility, which would negate the crime of attempt. But is it really? Or is it a case of factual impossibility?

Imagine that this defendant's confusion has come about because this drug is a whatchamacallit, which is legal but is easily mistaken for another group of drugs, thingamabobs, which cannot lawfully be imported. If the defendant thinks the whatchamacallit is a (criminally illegal) thingamabob, the case looks like factual impossibility. Or, perhaps, the defendant has made a factual error in reading the list of prohibited imports, misinterpreting the word "thingamabobs" for "whatchama-callits." Is this factual impossibility? Or legal? (We do not suggest trying to solve this mystery; the point is that it is confusing.)

(5) *The Model Penal Code Approach.* The drafters of the Model Penal Code tried to eliminate the defense of impossibility in almost all situations. The MPC provides that the attempt is a crime if the objective would be a crime "if the attendant circumstances were as [the actor] believes them to be." This formulation eliminates factual and "false legal" impossibility. The key is that it focuses on *what the defendant believed* about the facts. There is an attempt if there would have been a crime if the "circumstances *were as [the actor] believed them to be.*"

> Read Model Penal Code § 5.01(a) [eliminating most impossibility] in the MPC Appendix.

People v. Thousand

631 N.W.2d 694 (Mich. 2001)

Young, J.

[This is another attempted child molestation resulting from a police undercover sting, analogous to *Reid v. State, above.* A deputy sheriff entered a chat room posing as a female child, "Bekka," and was approached by defendant, who called himself "Mr. Auto-Mag." Defendant later described himself as a twenty-three year old man named Chris Thousand, and "Bekka" said she was a fourteen year old girl. "Defendant made repeated lewd invitations to Bekka to engage in various sexual acts." He sent her a picture of his genitalia. After several discussions of places to meet, they agreed to meet at a McDonalds. She asked him to bring her a present and said she liked white teddy bears. Defendant arrived there and was arrested. "Two white teddy bears were recovered from defendant's vehicle."

[Defendant was charged with attempted distribution of obscene material to a minor (and other offenses). He filed a motion to quash the indictment on the ground that the object crime was impossible, and therefore there could be no attempt. The object crime required a child, and there was no child. The trial court granted the motion. The Michigan Supreme Court here disagrees with that decision, rejects the impossibility defense, and remands for trial.]

The doctrine of "impossibility" . . . represents the conceptual dilemma that arises when, because of the defendant's mistake of fact or law, his actions could not possibly have resulted in the commission of the substantive crime underlying an attempt charge. Classic illustrations of . . . impossibility include: (1) the defendant is prosecuted for attempted larceny after he tries to "pick" the victim's empty pocket; (2) the defendant is prosecuted for attempted rape after . . . [being] unsuccessful because he is impotent; (3) the defendant is prosecuted for attempting to receive stolen property where the property he received was not, in fact, stolen; and (4) the defendant is prosecuted for attempting to hunt deer out of season after he shoots at a stuffed decoy deer. In each of these examples, despite evidence of the defendant's criminal intent, he cannot be prosecuted for the *completed* offense . . . . The question . . . becomes whether the defendant can be prosecuted for the *attempted* offense, and the answer is dependent upon whether he may raise the defense of "impossibility."

"Factual impossibility," which has apparently never been recognized in any American jurisdiction as a defense to a charge of attempt, "exists when [the defendant's] intended end constitutes a crime but she fails to consummate it because of a factual circumstance unknown to her or beyond her control." An example of a "factual impossibility" scenario is where the defendant is prosecuted for attempted murder after pointing an unloaded gun at someone and pulling the trigger, where the defendant believed the gun was loaded.

The category of "legal impossibility" is further divided into two subcategories: "pure" legal impossibility and "hybrid" [or "false"] legal impossibility. Although it is generally undisputed that "pure" legal impossibility will bar an attempt conviction, the concept of "hybrid legal impossibility" has proven problematic. . . . "*Pure legal impossibility* exists if the criminal law does not prohibit D's conduct or the result that she has sought to achieve." In other words, the concept of pure legal impossibility applies when an actor engages in conduct that he believes is criminal, but is not actually prohibited by law. . . . As an example, consider . . . a man who believes that the legal age of consent is sixteen years old, and who believes that a girl with whom he had consensual sexual intercourse is fifteen years old. If the law actually fixed the age of consent at fifteen, this man would not be guilty of attempted statutory rape, despite his mistaken belief that the law prohibited his conduct. [This is "true" or "pure" legal impossibility.] . . .

It is notable that "the great majority of jurisdictions have now recognized that legal and factual impossibility are 'logically indistinguishable' . . . and have abolished impossibility as a defense." *United States v. Hsu*, 155 F.3d 189, 199 (C.A.3, 1998). For example, several states have adopted statutory provisions similar to Model Penal Code §5.01(1), which provides: "A person is guilty of an attempt to commit a crime if, acting with the kind of culpability otherwise required for commission of the crime, he: (a) purposely engages in conduct which would constitute the crime if the attendant circumstances were as he believes them to be. . . ." [Remanded for trial.]

Marilyn J. Kelly, J. [dissenting with respect to the remand for trial].

. . . Because "legal impossibility" is a viable defense, I would affirm the . . . dismissal of [the charge for] attempted distribution of obscene material to a minor. . . .

Even if "legal impossibility" were not part of Michigan's common law, I would disagree with the majority's interpretation of the attempt statute. . . .

Examination of the language of the [Michigan] attempt statute leads to a reasonable inference that the Legislature did not intend to punish conduct that a mistake of legal fact renders unprohibited. The attempt statute makes illegal an ". . . attempt to *commit an offense prohibited by law.* . . ." It does not make illegal an action not prohibited by law. Hence, one may conclude, the impossibility of completing the underlying crime can provide a defense to attempt. . . .

Notes and Questions

(1) *Factual Impossibility, or Legal?* The court elsewhere cited the classic case of *People v. Jaffe*, 78 N.E. 169 (N.Y. 1906), in which the defendants successfully used impossibility as a defense to the crime of attempted receiving of stolen property. They believed the property was stolen, but in fact it was offered to them consensually by law enforcement officers, as part of a "sting." The New York high court described the case as one of "legal impossibility." But is it? Or is it, instead, a case of false or hybrid legal impossibility that really is factual impossibility (and therefore, a criminal attempt)?

If the facts had been as the defendants believed them to be, and the property actually had been taken by stealth from the true owner, the defendants would have been guilty of the target crime, that is, of receiving stolen property. This analysis would characterize the case as one of factual impossibility. The court in *Thousand* adopts this reasoning. But the dissenting judge disagrees because (among other reasons) the Michigan statute depends on an attempt to commit "an offense prohibited by law" and does not contain language focusing on facts as defendant "believed them to be." Who is right?

(2) *Does the Michigan Court Really Intend to Abolish "True" Legal Impossibility (or Only "False" or "Hybrid" Legal Impossibility)?* The Michigan court suggests that the state has never adopted a defense of "impossibility" of any kind. Perhaps by this, the court means to abolish only factual impossibility and "false" or "hybrid" legal impossibility (the kind that really amounts to factual impossibility). But what about "true" legal impossibility? The court gives the example of a defendant who believes he is committing a crime with a minor, because he believes the cutoff age is 16, when actually the law says that it is 15. Committing the acts with a 15-year-old would not be an attempt crime, says the court. Does the court, then, preserve a defense of "true" legal impossibility?

(3) *"Inherent" Impossibility: The Model Penal Code Approach.* MPC § 5.05(2) also provides that when "particular conduct charged to constitute a criminal attempt . . . is so inherently unlikely to result or culminate in the commission of a crime that neither such conduct nor the actor presents a public danger . . . , the Court shall exercise its power . . . to enter judgment and impose sentence for a crime of lower grade or degree or, in extreme cases, may dismiss the prosecution." Does the Model Penal Code, in essence, recognize a defense of "inherent" impossibility when the attempt is so ineffectual that little danger is posed by the defendant's conduct? Consider the following problem.

Problem 10C (Attempt and Impossibility):
"I Hope You Die, You Pig"

(1) *An HIV-Related Assault: But Is It Attempted Murder?* Gregory Smith, who was HIV-positive, was convicted of attempted murder for biting a corrections officer with intent to kill him. The court's recitation of the facts is replete with descriptions of defendant's repeated threats to kill in this manner, repeated snapping at or attempting to bite various individuals, attempts to spit in their eyes, and other conduct. The incident at issue occurred when defendant claimed to have injured his back (although two doctors' diagnosis was that he was malingering) and was taken to the hospital with a back board and shackles. After snapping his teeth and threatening various individuals, he was returned to jail. The correctional officers described the result:

> "Gregory just kept on saying if I get my — if I get my mouth on you I'm going to bite you, I'm going to give you AIDS, Waddington, he says if I see you out on the street I'm going to come get you, I'm going to kill you, I'm going to go after your family, just basically threatening us that he's going to give us this virus or HIV positive blood that he has he's going to transfer to us."

> After Officer Polk arrived with a patrol car, Waddington and Snow dragged defendant out of the hospital. He tried to break loose and hit Snow with the handcuffs. In the ensuing tussle, all three fell into the street. By that point in the struggle, the officers' rubber gloves had come off. Snow said that he "saw as Gregory pulled his teeth off Al's hands, Officer Waddington, there were several puncture wounds". . . .

> During the ride back to the jail, defendant continued his harangue; he spit in Waddington's face saying, "I hope you die, you pig, Waddington." According to Waddington, defendant "said something to Snow about if he gets a chance he's going to bite him, give him AIDS and he says you, Waddington, he goes and he spit on the back of my neck, he said now die, you pig, die from what I have." Defendant then leaned over and "tried to bite Snow on the side of the face." . . .

(2) *Specific Intent.* Defendant testified that he believed that the HIV virus could be spread in only three ways: "sexually, blood transfusion, or using needles." He swore that he believed transmission by biting was "impossible." If this testimony had created a reasonable doubt, what effect would it have on the jury's verdict in a jurisdiction requiring specific intent for attempt?

(3) *Actus Reus.* Under the "substantial step" test, the defendant's commission of the actus reus seems obvious. So, too, under several other formulations of the test. But under some tests, such as "probable desistance," the actus reus is unclear. Can you explain (is it "probable" that defendant would have "desisted" before actually killing anyone)?

(4) *Factual and Legal Impossibility.* The statute at issue provided, among other ways to commit attempt, that an attempt existed "where the actor has done all that he

believes necessary to cause the particular result which is an element of the crime." But expert witnesses testified that there was only a "theoretical possibility" of transmitting HIV by saliva, and the court pointed out that there were "no 'documented cases'" (although there were reports). The officer tested negative for HIV. Is this a case of factual impossibility (criminal attempt) or of legal impossibility (possibly, no attempt)?

(5) *Inherent Impossibility.* The defendant also argued that any possibility of his transmitting HIV and killing the officer by AIDS was so far-fetched that it should not support a criminal attempt. Is the theory of inherent impossibility valid here?

(6) *The Actual Result: Affirmance—State v. Smith*, 621 A.2d 493 (N.J. App. 1993). The court held that a "theoretical" possibility of death was a "possibility" that could support attempt. It also rejected Smith's legal, factual, and inherent impossibility argument. Consider whether its reasoning is persuasive:

> Defendant invokes . . . the commentary to the Model Penal Code as authority for his [inherent impossibility] theory . . . . Defendant equates his biting Waddington with a "voodoo incantation" which is medically incapable of causing death . . . .
>
> There was no proof at trial that biting could not possibly transmit HIV. Rather, the evidence was equivocal, with even defendant's expert conceding that there was at least a "remote" possibility of transmission. In any event, the objective likelihood of transmission is irrelevant to liability under *N.J.S.A.* 2C:5–1(a)(2). It is sufficient that defendant believed his attack would infect Waddington. Such a belief would not necessarily be "absurd" in the same way that a belief in the efficacy of a voodoo curse is unfounded. . . .

§ 10.03 Solicitation of Crime

Read MPC § 5.02(1) [criminal solicitation] in the MPC Appendix.

Notes and Questions

(1) *Overview.* Solicitation is a common law crime, now routinely included in statutes, that ordinarily reaches early stages of a criminal activity. Imagine that X wants a certain politician to be killed. X calls Y and asks, implores, orders, pays, or threatens Y to undertake the homicide. Solicitation is the crime that reaches X's conduct.

(2) *Rationales.* Arguments in favor of having the crime of solicitation include the fact that it reaches those who try to tempt others into criminal activity, thereby limiting the general public's exposure to such people and their temptations. More importantly, by allowing the police to intervene at an early stage of a crime, it may prevent commission of the target crime.

(3) *Elements of Solicitation.* Solicitation is a crime in every state. The various statutes have similar elements that often resemble those in the Model Penal Code.

(a) *Mens Rea.* Solicitation is a specific intent crime. MPC § 5.02 states the prevailing standard: the solicitor must act "with the purpose of promoting or facilitating" the commission of a crime.

(b) *Actus Reus.* The applicable statutes use a wide range of verbs to describe the necessary efforts to have the other person join in commission of the crime. MPC § 5.02(1), followed in many states, covers a person who "commands, encourages or requests another person to engage" in specific criminal conduct. Note that solicitation punishes the *effort* to get someone to join in criminal activity. Those efforts need not be successful, and the crime solicited need never occur. A rejected solicitation is still a criminal solicitation.

(4) *Unsuccessful Efforts to Communicate.* The focus of solicitation is on the solicitor's efforts to engage another person in the commission of a crime. But what if the attempts to communicate are unsuccessful? MPC § 5.02(2) specifically provides that a solicitation occurs whether or not the effort to enlist the other person was actually communicated. This result is consistent with the view that the crime of solicitation is designed to deal with the solicitor, who is dangerous whether or not the solicitation is successful. Some jurisdictions disagree with this view and require that the communication actually be received. *See, e.g., State v. Andujar,* 899 A.2d 1209 (R.I. 2006) (solicitation must actually be received; defendant wrote a letter asking intended recipient to commit murder but letter was never received or read).

(5) *Relation to Attempt and Conspiracy.* Solicitation, like attempt and conspiracy, is an inchoate crime. But it differs from both in significant ways.

(a) *Solicitation and Attempt.* The mens rea for solicitation is the same as the standard for attempt—the defendant must have the purpose (specific intent) to have a crime committed. But the actus reus for solicitation is much less than the requirement for attempt. Attempt usually requires a "substantial step" or other act "beyond mere preparation," but solicitation does not.

(b) *Solicitation and Conspiracy.* Solicitation has been called an "attempted conspiracy." It represents a solicitor's efforts to form a conspiracy by enlisting at least one other person to join the criminal enterprise. Thus, if the solicitation is successful, a conspiracy may be created. Because the solicitation is essentially attempted conspiracy, the defendant cannot be convicted of both solicitation and conspiracy when the solicitation leads to the conspiracy.

(6) *Renunciation and Impossibility as Defenses to Solicitation.* Recall that many statutes, including the Model Penal Code, make renunciation a defense to attempt. The same statutes also extend this defense to solicitation (and conspiracy). *See, e.g.,* Model Penal Code § 5.02(3) (affirmative defense that after a solicitation, the solicitor persuades the solicitee not to commit the crime or otherwise prevents its commission under circumstances manifesting a complete and voluntary renunciation

of criminal purpose). Additionally, "true" legal impossibility can be a defense (but not "factual" impossibility or "false legal" impossibility).

(7) *An Example of a Defense of "True Legal" Impossibility: People v. Thousand.* This case is excerpted in the section on attempt, above. The defendant was also charged with solicitation as well as attempt. The "solicitation" allegedly consisted of his solicitation of the imaginary fourteen-year-old Bekka, which certainly occurred, but Bekka's conduct could not possibly have been a crime under the law. Solicitation, as a crime, involves soliciting another person to commit a crime. But the child, in a child molestation case, does not commit a crime, as the court reasoned (over a vigorous dissent):

> Our solicitation statute provides . . . , "[A] person who solicits another person to commit a felony, or who solicits another person to do or omit to do an act which if completed would constitute a felony, is [guilty of solicitation]." . . .

> What is lacking here is defendant's request to another person to commit a crime. "Bekka," the fourteen-year-old online persona of Detective Liczbinski, was not asked to commit a crime. . . . While it would be a crime for defendant to engage in sexual intercourse with a fourteen-year-old girl, a fourteen-year-old girl is not committing a criminal offense [then] . . . .

(8) *Corroboration Requirements, as in the Case That Follows.* Many jurisdictions impose corroboration requirements. These requirements, along with the intent-to-promote element, help prevent innocent conduct from becoming criminal. (Imagine that a spectator at a football game yells "Kill 'em!" to his team.) Some jurisdictions require not only that the existence of the solicitation be corroborated, but also that the solicitor's intent to complete the object crime be corroborated, too. In such a jurisdiction, a solicitation can be preserved on videotape and still not support conviction if there is no separate evidence corroborating the actor's intent to complete the object crime. In the case that follows, the controlling statute requires "strong" corroboration of both the act and the intent.

Ganesan v. State

45 S.W.3d 197 (Tex. App. 2001)

KIDD, J.

A jury convicted appellant Apparajan Ganesan on two counts of solicitation to commit murder. The jury found that appellant [Ganesan] solicited Reda Sue Prier to kill Sudha Vallabhaneni, appellant's wife, and Amy Wright, the lawyer representing Vallabhaneni in her divorce action. . . . We will affirm the conviction on one count, but reverse . . . on the other. . . .

. . . The two counts of the indictment alleged that appellant, with the requisite intent, requested Prier "to engage in specific conduct, to wit: to kill [the complainants]" under circumstances that "would have made Reda Sue Prier a party to the commission of murder." It is undisputed that appellant did not ask Prier to kill either Vallabhaneni [the wife] or Wright [the lawyer]. Instead, Prier testified that appellant repeatedly asked her to find someone to kill them. Appellant contends that Prier's testimony does not reflect a criminal solicitation, but merely a noncriminal "solicitation of solicitation." . . . [The court rejects this argument.]

Appellant . . . also contends that Prier's testimony was not adequately corroborated. A person may not be convicted of criminal solicitation on the uncorroborated testimony of the person allegedly solicited and [also may not be convicted] "unless the solicitation is made under circumstances strongly corroborative of both the solicitation itself and the actor's intent that the other person act on the solicitation." Tex. Penal Code Ann. § 15.03(b) (West 1994). . . . [The applicable test of the corroboration is that] we must eliminate Prier's testimony from consideration and determine whether there is other evidence tending to connect appellant to the crime. The corroboration must go to both the solicitation and the alleged intent, but need not be sufficient in itself to establish guilt. . . .

[Vallabhaneni, defendant's wife, filed for divorce.] The record reflects that appellant believed that his wife's actions were damaging his ability to market the computer chip [he had designed]. During a telephone conversation with Vallabhaneni in January 1997, which she tape recorded on Wright's advice, appellant said that her divorce action was "making sure that this product will die." Appellant went on, "Let me tell you this. I don't care what you do. If this product dies, one of us will be dead, yeah, I promise you that." Vallabhaneni replied, "What do you mean, you'll kill me?" Appellant answered, "I will kill myself or I'll kill you or I'll kill both of us or you will kill yourself. That much I can tell you. If . . . this product dies, one of us will die. I know that. Because I won't be able to live with the shame. Maybe you will be able to live with it."

. . . [A]ppellant's belief that his wife's litigation threatened to derail a potentially lucrative business opportunity was evidence of motive that tends to support Prier's testimony that appellant solicited the murders of his wife and her attorney. While evidence of motive is insufficient in itself to corroborate an accomplice, it may be considered with other evidence to connect the accused with the crime.

Appellant's statement that "one of us will be dead" if the chip design did not succeed adds some additional support to the existence of the solicitation of Vallabhaneni's murder. In his brief, appellant dismisses his remarks during the telephone conversation as nothing more than hyperbole, and notes that the conversation took place twenty months before the alleged solicitation. But viewing the evidence in the light most favorable to the jury's verdict, as we must, we cannot disregard the threat implicit in appellant's statement.

Appellant was arrested in May 1997 for violating a protective order obtained by Vallabhaneni. While in the Travis County Jail, he met James Hammonds, who was awaiting his release on bail following an arrest for theft. Hammonds testified that appellant told him "about how his wife and the system and the judge had destroyed his life and his business and how he was losing everything." According to Hammonds, appellant asked, "Do you know of anyone, or can you take care of my wife for me?" When Hammonds replied, "Excuse me?" appellant said, "You know what I mean." Hammonds said that this "really scared me" and that he thought he was "being set up by the cops." Hammonds refused to give appellant his address but gave appellant a telephone number where he could be reached, not expecting appellant to call.

A few weeks later, however, appellant called Hammonds and asked if he "remember[ed] the conversation in the cell that we had." Appellant added, "I need to talk to you about this again. We need to talk about this." . . . After giving the matter further consideration, Hammonds contacted the police and reported what appellant had said. Subsequently, under the supervision of a Texas Ranger, Hammonds . . . called appellant while being recorded. When Hammonds attempted to talk about their previous conversations, appellant "started back-peddling. He started trying to get out of the conversation. He didn't want to talk about that." The call ended and the police did not pursue the matter to Hammonds's knowledge.

That appellant solicited Hammonds to kill his wife, albeit sixteen months before the alleged solicitation of Prier, tends to corroborate Prier's testimony both as to the solicitation itself and appellant's intent that Prier act on the solicitation. But Hammonds's testimony corroborates Prier only with respect to the solicitation of Vallabhaneni's murder. It does not tend to connect appellant to the alleged solicitation of Wright's murder.

Prier testified that during the months appellant was asking her to arrange the murders, he instructed her to go to a post office near the Arboretum shopping center and watch who came and went. She also testified that appellant told her to watch an office on Lake Austin Boulevard, which he identified as Wright's husband's law office. The State contends this testimony was corroborated by Vallabhaneni's testimony that she received her mail at the Arboretum post office and by Wright's testimony that her husband's law office was in a building on Lake Austin Boulevard. Standing alone, however, this alleged corroborative evidence does not connect appellant to the criminal solicitations. Vallabhaneni's and Wright's testimony is meaningless except by reference to Prier's testimony. Such "bootstrapping" . . . cannot be used to corroborate a solicitee.

The State also contends that Prier's testimony was corroborated by appellant's bankruptcy attorney. This witness testified that in November 1998, following appellant's arrest for the instant offense and at appellant's direction, he retrieved over $100,000 in cash from appellant's house. [But the defendant's possession of money is unremarkable and is not tied to the case.]

. . . We conclude that the evidence of motive, the veiled threat during the telephone conversation, and the earlier solicitation of Hammonds adequately corroborates Prier's testimony both as to appellant's solicitation of Vallabhaneni's murder and appellant's intent that Prier act on the solicitation. We find, however, insufficient corroboration for Prier's testimony regarding appellant's solicitation of Wright's murder. [Conviction affirmed as to solicited murder of wife but reversed as to lawyer.]

Notes and Questions

(1) *Why a Corroboration Requirement?* A number of states, like Texas, require corroboration as an element of solicitation. But these same jurisdictions do not require corroboration for most other crimes. Why would a jurisdiction conclude that corroboration is appropriate for solicitation?

(2) *Isn't the Solicitation of Murder of the Lawyer Corroborated Too?* The *Ganesan* court holds that there is sufficient corroboration of Ganesan's intent and acts involving the death of his wife but not of his wife's lawyer. But isn't the corroborated solicitation to kill the wife also adequate corroboration of the plan to kill the lawyer?

(3) *But Here's What's Bad about the Strong Double Corroboration Requirement: Law Enforcement May Not Be Able to Prevent a Contract Murder.* Imagine that you are a police officer who has learned of a potential criminal who is trying to hire a murderer to kill his wife. You manage to set up a sting in which the potential criminal actually solicits an undercover officer, on videotape. Should you arrest the actor? No. You don't have enough evidence. You can't yet corroborate his intent to complete the crime. Next, the actor withdraws money from his bank, presumably to pay the pretend hit man. But *Ganesan*, above, tells you this still isn't enough(!), because possessing money is unremarkable. So, you keep waiting and listening. Meanwhile, there is the possibility that the actor may hire someone else and get the murder done while you are sitting around doing nothing.

What can law enforcement officers do about this dilemma? In fact, the scenario is the beginning of a novel by one of the authors: David Crump, *Murder in Sugar Land* (2016) (but you'll have to get it from Amazon or another platform to find out the rest).

§ 10.04 Conspiracy

[A] The Rationale and Elements of Conspiracy

Read Model Penal Code § 5.03(1) & (5) [conspiracy definition; overt act requirement] in the MPC Appendix.

---

(1) *The Rationale for Defining Conspiracy as a Distinct Crime.* Conspiring with others to commit a crime is a separate offense from actually committing the object crime. Even if the conspiracy is unsuccessful, its members may still be guilty of the preparatory offense of conspiracy. And if the object crime does occur, in some

jurisdictions the actors may be guilty of *both* a conspiracy to commit the object crime and commission of the object crime.

There are a number of rationales for defining conspiracy as a crime. Most reflect the possibility that when groups of people cooperate and act together in order to commit a crime, they are more dangerous than solo actors. They can cause harm on a larger scale. A related explanation is that conspiracy is deliberate; it involves planning. Thus, the attacks of 9/11 on the World Trade Center, with hijacked passenger aircraft as weapons, were possible only because a large number of criminal actors worked together in a conspiracy. The criminal conduct may be considered more egregious because of their deliberation and planning.

Additionally, members of a group may provide one another with mutual support that increases the likelihood that they will accomplish their criminal purpose. And a person who enters a conspiracy may be considered more dangerous than someone who is merely thinking about a crime. The conspirator has actually taken steps toward carrying out the object crime and may be more of a public threat than the less aggressive person who simply dreams of committing an offense.

Another rationale for conspiracy is more practical. Conspiracies are more amenable than most other offenses to law enforcement techniques, such as infiltration or interception of communications, making it feasible to actually intervene in the early stages of a conspiracy. The possibility of government intervention, as well as possible cooperation by conspirators-turned-informants, may destabilize the conspiratorial relationship, making it less able to achieve its criminal goals.

(2) *Elements of a Conspiracy: Overview.* In general terms, a conspiracy is an agreement of two or more people, each having the intent to agree and the intent to promote the object of the conspiracy, to commit a criminal act. Sometimes an "overt act" (in addition to the agreement itself) toward completion of the target or object crime is also required.

There are several elements, summarized below and then discussed in greater detail in subsequent sections of this chapter.

(a) *Plurality requirement.* For the crime of conspiracy, the "plurality" rule means that ordinarily two or more conspirators are required. "It takes two to tango."

(b) *Agreement.* Second, there must be an "agreement" between the parties. The agreement need not be express; it can arise by implication or be shown by consciously parallel conduct. If only one person "agrees," perhaps erroneously thinking that the other person(s) also agrees, this element is technically lacking. As discussed below, however, some jurisdictions and the MPC allow a conspiracy to exist with only a "unilateral" agreement.

(c) *Intent to Agree.* Third, a conspirator must have intent to enter into the agreement.

(d) *Intent to Promote Object of Conspiracy.* Fourth, there must be intent to promote the object of the conspiracy. The intent to agree and the "intent to promote" the object are closely related and are not always distinguished (or distinguishable) in the cases. Usually, some of the same evidence that supports intent to promote also supplies intent to agree (as well as proof of the agreement).

(e) *Overt Act.* The common law did not include this requirement, and some statutes dispense with it. But most jurisdictions require proof that an overt act occurred. Only one overt act by one of the conspirators is required; the other conspirators are guilty even if they did nothing except agree. The overt act need not be criminal in itself. It can be an act that otherwise would be innocent.

Note on the Unlawful Objective of the Agreement

Conspiracy is not a free-floating, independent crime. It must consist of a "conspiracy to do something"—usually, to commit an object crime. Thus, an actor is not guilty of "conspiracy," but rather "conspiracy to commit first degree murder" or "conspiracy to commit embezzlement."

Conspiracy statutes reflect this requirement by insisting that there be an agreement to commit a "crime" or "criminal offense," terms which include misdemeanors. On the other hand, some locales limit conspiracy to more serious crimes, such as a "felony," "serious felony offense," "aggravated misdemeanor or felony," or crimes specifically listed.

[B] The Plurality Requirement

(1) *Requirement of a Plurality: Bilateral Approach.* Traditionally, conspiracy has required at least two "guilty" conspirators—also known as the "bilateral" approach to conspiracy. The trier of fact must find that two individuals actually entered a conspiracy with one another. For example, if X thinks she is entering a conspiracy with Y, who is really an undercover police agent, there is no conspiracy under the bilateral approach because there is only one conspirator; Y, the agent, lacks the mens rea to be a conspirator.

Case law has dealt with the bilateral approach in many fact-specific situations. One issue is how separate the two parties must be. For example, one internal division of a corporation probably cannot conspire with another division.

(2) *The MPC's "Unilateral" Approach: With the Defendant Erroneously Believing That There Is Another Conspirator.* MPC § 5.03(1) departs from the traditional bilateral rule and adopts a "unilateral" approach that defines a conspiracy in terms of a person who "agrees with" another person to commit a crime. Under this view, the "other person" may be someone, such as an undercover police officer, who is pretending to agree. The first person has committed a conspiracy under the MPC even though there is actually only one conspirator.

The rationale for the unilateral approach reflects the MPC's focus on the culpability of each actor rather than that of other actors. Liability is measured subjectively, according to how the actor perceives the world. If the actor *believes* he or she is in a conspiracy with someone else to commit a crime, under the MPC the actor is deemed sufficiently dangerous to merit criminal conviction, irrespective of whether there is, in fact, an agreement.

STATE v. PACHECO, 882 P.2d 183 (Wash. 1967). Pacheco bragged to Dillon about his illegal activities, including contract murders ("hits"). Dillon discovered that Pacheco was a deputy sheriff and, evidently disgusted, contacted the FBI and agreed to inform on Pacheco. Dillon pretended to have been cheated in a drug transaction and sought help from Pacheco, who agreed to kill the drug buyer for $10,000. After further activities, the local police arrested Pacheco (who defended, of course, by claiming that instead of being guilty of the case built against him, he was following police procedures to "build a case against" Dillon). The jury convicted Pacheco of conspiracy with the police informant, Dillon.

The state supreme court reversed the conviction. It held that state law had retained the traditional common law "bilateral approach to conspiracy." Therefore, "a government agent feigning agreement with the defendant does not constitute a conspiracy . . . because no genuine agreement is reached." The language of the Washington conspiracy statute was ambiguous, and the State argued that it had adopted the MPC approach, which requires only "unilateral" agreement. Under the MPC, a conspiracy with an undercover officer *could* be a crime, said the *Pacheco* court, because only the mens rea of the accused is determinative under a unilateral approach. The court justified its rejection of the MPC unilateral approach not only by statutory language and precedent, but also by suggesting that unilateral conspiracy did not punish criminal activity but "merely criminal intentions" and that it had "potential for abuse" because government officers could "create the offense."

A dissenting justice argued that the Washington statute "explicitly envisages so-called unilateral conspiracies" of the kind at issue. He criticized the majority for freeing "an aspiring hit man, [who] planned a murder for money" and who "took a substantial step toward that objective." Although sharing the majority's "concern for abuse of unilateral conspiracy," the dissenter argued that if there really were abuse, the defendant could claim an entrapment defense.

Notes and Questions

(1) *Bilateral or Unilateral?* As noted above, some American jurisdictions follow the traditional bilateral approach to conspiracy. But there are strong arguments in favor of the unilateral view. Does the *Pacheco* conspiracy convince you that the unilateral approach is better?

(2) *Degree of Risk in Pacheco.* Pacheco thought he had been hired by a "criminal" who, in fact, was a police informant and who never intended to participate in a homicide. Conspiracy reaches those who pose a risk of committing the object crime. Does Pacheco qualify as someone posing a risk of a homicide?

(3) *Other Conspirator Not Convicted, Incompetent, etc.* While the general rule is that a conspiracy requires two conspirators, it does not require that two people actually be convicted of the conspiracy. Rather, the jury must find that beyond a reasonable doubt there were two conspirators. Thus, if A and B enter a conspiracy but B dies or escapes or is never apprehended, A may still be found guilty as long as the jury finds that the missing person conspired with A. *See, e.g.,* Wash. Rev. Code § 9A.28.040. Statutes reach this result in both bilateral and unilateral jurisdictions.

(4) *Other Conspirators' Identities Unknown.* Sometimes people enter a conspiracy with a particular person but others, whose names are unknown, are also involved in it. The applicable rule is that a person who is in a conspiracy and knows (some jurisdictions add: "or has reasonable cause to believe") others are in it as well but does not know their identities is nevertheless in a conspiracy with the unknown participants. *See, e.g.,* Ore. Rev. Stat. § 161.455.

[C] The Agreement

Notes on the Agreement Requirement

(1) *Formal or Informal.* An agreement in conspiracy law includes any formal agreement such as those covered in the contracts course, but it also embraces far more subtle "understandings." *See generally* Neal Kumar Katyal, *Conspiracy Theory,* 112 Yale L.J. 1307 (2003). The agreement may be tacit or express and may be formed by words or actions. Prosecutors routinely prove it by circumstantial evidence. As one court explained, "the conduct and words of co-conspirators are generally shrouded in silence, furtiveness, and secrecy." *State v. Samuels,* 914 A.2d 1250, 1255 (N.J. 2007). Thus, "it is not necessary to establish that the defendant and his coconspirators signed papers, shook hands, or uttered the words 'we have an agreement.'" *State v. Ortiz,* 911 A.2d 1055 (Conn. 2006).

(2) *Does Conspiracy, Then, Make a State of Mind into a Crime?* Some critics have challenged the notion that the agreement is an appropriate guide for criminality, as it is with conspiracy. One scholar observed: "conspiracy doctrine comes closest to making a state of mind [*i.e.* the agreement] the occasion for preventive action against those who threaten society but who have come nowhere near carrying out the threat. No effort is made to find the point at which criminal intent is transformed into the beginnings of action. Instead, the mystique of numbers, of combination, becomes the measure of danger." Abraham Goldstein, *Conspiracy to Defraud the United States,* 68 Yale L.J. 405 (1959). Do you agree with traditional conspiracy law that using the formation of an "agreement" is a sensible way to assess whether the criminal justice system should intervene?

United States v. Daniel [and Alabi]

933 F.3d 370 (5th Cir. 2019)

Jerry E. Smith, Circuit Judge:

Folarin Alabi, Justice Daniel, and Letrishia Andrews were convicted of crimes related to their involvement in a marriage-fraud conspiracy. They appeal, raising issues regarding their convictions and sentences. [The conspiracy issues, however, relate principally to Alabi.] We affirm. . . .

Co-conspirators recruited U.S. citizens to marry Nigerian nationals so that the Nigerians could obtain legal immigration status. [Marriage to an American citizen is a pathway to legal status, but some of these marriages are shams.] . . .

[Citizenship and Immigration Service] Officers . . . reviewed the files for Daniel and others and determined that their marriages to U.S. citizens were fraudulent. The investigation [was extensive]. . . .

All . . . defendants were . . . charged with [and convicted of] conspiracy to commit marriage fraud in violation of 8 U.S.C. § 1325(c) and 18 U.S.C. § 371, [as well as substantive counts]. . . .

Alabi asserts that "[t]he evidence was insufficient to prove that [he] knowingly entered the conspiracy to commit immigration fraud . . . ." He maintains that neither the testimony of Anisha Gable, another co-conspirator [who cooperated with the Government], nor the immigration agents' testimony, including the evidence of red flags indicative of marriage fraud that were present in Daniel's marriage, supported that Alabi intended to join the conspiracy or knew of Daniel's and Andrews's intent to evade the immigration laws by marrying. Alabi attacks Gable's testimony as uncorroborated and circumstantial and therefore insufficient to support the inference that he had the requisite knowledge and intent to join the conspiracy. . . .

Alabi repeatedly mentions his view that absent evidence he received money to introduce a U.S. citizen to a Nigerian for marriage purposes, the requisite intent is not shown. Alabi further maintains that "[t]he indicators of fraud discovered by investigators . . . were false statement and altered documents that were submitted after the marriage," but "there was no evidence that [he] had any involvement or knowledge" of those documents when the marriage was entered into. He urges that "there was no evidence that [he] was involved with submitting documents connected to any of the marriages in this case or that [he] instructed or directed others about how to submit these documents that were determined to be indicative of fraud." Consequently, "[t]he evidence was . . . insufficient to support an inference that Alabi knew about the conspiracy and intentionally joined the conspiracy." . . .

"To prove a conspiracy under 18 U.S.C. § 371, the government ha[s] to prove (1) an agreement between two or more persons to pursue an unlawful objective; (2) the defendant's knowledge of the unlawful objective and voluntary agreement to join the conspiracy; and (3) an overt act by one or more of the members of the conspiracy in furtherance of the objective of the conspiracy." *United States v. Ongaga,*

820 F.3d 152, 157 (5th Cir. 2016) (citation omitted). "An agreement may be inferred from concert of action, voluntary participation may be inferred from a collocation of circumstances, and knowledge may be inferred from surrounding circumstances." *United States v. Bieganowski*, 313 F.3d 264, 277 (5th Cir. 2002). . . .

Title 8 U.S.C. § 1325(c) states that "[a]ny individual who knowingly enters into a marriage for the purpose of evading any provision of the immigration laws shall be imprisoned for not more than 5 years, or fined not more than $250,000, or both." To prove marriage fraud, the government must show "only that the defendant (1) knowingly entered into a marriage (2) for the purpose of evading any provision of the immigration laws." *Ongaga*, 820 F.3d at 160. . . .

The evidence was sufficient to support the verdict that Alabi knowingly entered the conspiracy to commit . . . marriage fraud. . . . Gable, referring to herself and Alabi as "the arrangers," testified that she and Alabi had arranged about ten to fifteen marriages between U.S. citizens and Nigerian nationals. Gable met Alabi when he and a third party visited Gable's house to appraise her for a sham marriage . . . , sometime after which they began working together. Alabi was the person who taught Gable how the marriage scheme worked, instructing her how to answer potential questions immigration officials might ask . . . , where to obtain documents, and how to find a judge for the marriages.

Alabi would find the Nigerians, and Gable would recruit the U.S. citizens to marry them. Gable would assist the sham couples in their fraud, showing them where to get a marriage license in the courthouse, taking pictures of the wedding, and obtaining copies of the marriage certificate. Alabi paid Gable to take pictures of the weddings as documentation to be submitted as part of the immigration process. Shakietha Joseph, a U.S. citizen who had previously pleaded guilty of committing marriage fraud by marrying a Nigerian national through the same conspiracy at issue here, corroborated that Alabi was active in the marriage-fraud conspiracy and arranged fraudulent marriages.

. . . [A] rational trier of fact could have found, beyond a reasonable doubt, the essential elements of conspiracy to commit marriage fraud . . . . Alabi nevertheless contends that it is insufficient to support his conviction. Each of his challenges fails.

First, contrary to Alabi's contention, because "all of the elements of marriage fraud are satisfied when the defendant enters into the marriage," he did not have to be involved with or know about the fraudulent documents that the sham couples submitted to immigration officials.

Second, neither Gable nor any other witness had to testify directly that Alabi knew the sham couples intended to evade the immigration laws. The jury was entitled to rely on circumstantial evidence.

Third, Alabi's attempt to undermine Gable's credibility on appeal is unavailing. This court "ha[s] repeatedly stated that the jury is the final arbiter of the credibility of [witnesses] . . . . The jury convicted Alabi after hearing Gable's testimony and thus made its credibility determination. [Affirmed.]

Notes and Questions

(1) *Wrong Result, According to Alabi?* Alabi points out that there is no evidence that he received any money. Could there be a reasonable inference of his agreement to the conspiracy if he didn't? He also points out that there is no evidence that he knew about false documents that showed the marriage of Daniel was fraudulent. But all details of the conspiracy do not have to be proved, and circumstantial evidence of agreement is sufficient. Was there enough here?

(2) *If Daniel Was Only Part of One Fraudulent Marriage, Did She "Agree" to the Whole Conspiracy?* The opinion is unclear about Daniel's activities, but imagine that Daniel participated in only one sham marriage. Even so, she can be guilty of conspiracy, because she agreed with others such as Gable and Alabi to accomplish this result.

(3) *What if Daniel Had "Conspired" Only with Her Pretended Spouse?* Marriage fraud can only be committed by two people. Can the two people who are a necessary minimum for the crime be guilty of "conspiring" to commit it? An ancient doctrine called Wharton's Rule says that there is no conspiracy when a crime requires multiple participants and only those participants are involved. But the participants can be guilty of conspiring with others (as Daniel was, with Gable and Alabi). Wharton's Rule is considered below, in § 10.05.

[D] The Mens Rea of Conspiracy: Agreement and Promotion

Note on the Intent to Agree

A conspiracy requires an "agreement." Because the act of agreeing requires an intent to agree, this mens rea is an important, though often unspoken, element. The concept of "intent to agree" should not be taken literally since it actually requires no positive thoughts of "I join the burglary team." Rather, it requires a person to have some kind of vague sense that he or she is in this criminal enterprise with others, perhaps whose identities and even number are unknown. The intent to agree is proved when the agreement is proved.

Notes on the Intent to Promote

(1) *Intent to Promote.* A separate mens rea is the intent to promote the object of the conspiracy. MPC § 5.03(1) requires "the purpose of promoting or facilitating" the commission of the object crime. Another version of this mens rea element is the "intent that a crime be committed" and an agreement "for the purpose of committing" the object crime. Wis. Stat. Ann. § 939.31.

(2) *The Falcone Case: Intent to Promote Ordinarily Requires More Than "Knowledge" of Illegality or Even Intent to Facilitate.* The "intent to promote" requirement for conspiracy is subtle and complicated, especially when a person knows that he or she is assisting another in the commission of a crime. Knowledge alone is insufficient;

there must be an intent to promote the crime. For example, a merchant who sells an ingredient to a drug ring is not usually a member of the conspiracy, even if the seller has knowledge of the illegal purpose. The Supreme Court's decision in *United States v. Falcone*, 311 U.S. 205 (1940), expresses this idea, by holding that a person who sold sugar to a known moonshiner was not a "co-conspirator" with the moonshiner. Something more than sale in the marketplace is required, even when the criminal purpose is known.

(3) *The (Contrasting) Direct Sales Case: Finding Intent to Promote.* But courts have not been clear in defining this "something more." Repeated transactions, inordinate profits, assistance in concealment—these factors may or may not be enough. In *Direct Sales Co. v. United States*, 319 U.S. 703 (1943), the Court distinguished *Falcone* and upheld the conspiracy conviction of a pharmaceutical manufacturer that sold inordinate amounts of morphine to a rogue physician. The Court noted that the items were "restricted" and harmful. The facts were enough to show "a stake in," "participation in," or "intent to promote" a conspiracy to distribute morphine.

(4) *Drawing the Line: Two Closely Similar Cases, Both Involving Indictments for Conspiracy to Commit Prostitution, but with Different Outcomes: People v. Lauria,* 251 Cal. App.2d 471 (1967), *and People v. Roy,* 251 Cal. App.2d 459 (1967). Lauria was indicted for a prostitution conspiracy. Numerous "call girls" had used his telephone answering service with his knowledge of their "business purposes." Nevertheless, the California court acquitted Lauria. First, the court declared that *Falcone* and *Direct Sales*

> provide a framework for the criminal liability of a supplier of lawful goods or services put to unlawful use. Both the element of knowledge of the illegal use . . . and the element of intent to further that use must be present in order to make the supplier a participant in a criminal conspiracy. . . .

Lauria had knowledge, but not intent:

> Inflated charges, the sale of goods with no legitimate use, [and] sales in inflated amounts, each may provide [evidence] from which the intent of the seller to participate in the criminal enterprise may be inferred. . . . Yet there are cases in which it cannot reasonably be said that the supplier has a stake in the venture . . . , but in which he has been held liable as a participant on the basis of knowledge alone. . . . The duty to take positive action to dissociate oneself . . . is far stronger . . . for felonies than it is for misdemeanors or petty offenses. . . . With respect to misdemeanors, we conclude that positive knowledge of the supplier that his products or services are being used for criminal purposes does not, without more, establish an intent of the supplier to participate in the misdemeanor. With respect to felonies, . . . we leave the matter open.

But the same court reached the opposite result from *Lauria* in the companion case, *People v. Roy.* Teresa Roy's case was very similar to Lauria's, except that she also advised one prostitute of precautions she should take and introduced her to another prostitute for the purpose of arranging business. The court affirmed Roy's conviction. Did these additional actions by Ms. Roy show that there was "intent to promote" rather than mere "knowledge"?

(5) *Can Intent to Promote the Object of the Conspiracy Be Distinguished Persuasively from Mere Knowledge, by an Assessment of the "Seriousness" of the Object (Is This Reasoning Sound)?* In *Lauria*, the court suggests that mere knowledge can suffice if the object crime is "serious." For example, a seller of gasoline may be guilty of conspiracy, the court said, if the seller knows that the object is "to make Molotov cocktails for terroristic use." Is this reasoning sound?

United States v. Lawrence
970 F.2d 283 (7th Cir. 1992)

EASTERBROOK, CIRCUIT JUDGE.

[The defendant, Thomas Lawrence, was convicted of conspiracy to manufacture and distribute methamphetamine. The evidence showed that he had come to an arrangement to provide manufacturing space to a group that the court describes as the "Nietupski ring" in exchange for $1,000, after learning what the "ring" planned to do and adapting the space to their purpose.] Nancy Nietupski, a grandmother in her early 60s, ran a methamphetamine ring through her extended family. She started [while] working with her nephew William Zahm. . . . [Later,] [w]hile sister Violet Blankenship supplied a base of operations, nephew Robert Blankenship helped distribute the drug and collect debts.

. . . "Cooking" methamphetamine is messy, and there is a risk of explosion when volatile chemicals such as acetone reach high temperatures. Nietupski and Zahm moved their laboratory frequently, to reduce the risk of detection. In February 1989 Zahm leased from Thomas Lawrence a house trailer in which to set up shop for a day. Nietupski told Lawrence what Zahm planned to make and offered $1,000 or one ounce of methamphetamine; Lawrence preferred the cash and took $100 as a down payment. He covered the floor of the trailer with plastic for protection. Zahm postponed the operation when he could not find a heating control. A few days later Lawrence got cold feet, telling Marvin Bland (one of Nietupski's assistants) that he wanted the chemicals and equipment removed. Bland complied.

[After drug authorities infiltrated the ring, Zahm implicated Lawrence, who was convicted of conspiracy to manufacture and distribute meth.] Lawrence has [appealed, arguing that the evidence is insufficient to support his conviction as a member of the conspiracy. The court here agrees with him and reverses his conviction]. . . .

Conspiracy is an agreement to violate the law. Unless Lawrence willingly joined the Nietupski venture, he did not commit the crime of conspiracy. What evidence was there that Lawrence . . . joined? Nietupski and Zahm told Lawrence what they planned to do in his trailer; Zahm and Lawrence sampled some of the product scraped off the apparatus; for $1,000 he furnished the space, covered the floor with plastic, supplied refreshments, and let Zahm take a shower to wash some acid off his legs. If providing assistance to a criminal organization were the same thing as conspiracy, then Lawrence would be guilty. Yet there is a difference between supplying goods to a syndicate and joining it, just as there is a difference between selling goods and being an employee of the buyer. Cargill sells malt and barley to Anheuser Busch, knowing that they will be made into beer, without being part of Busch; by parallel reasoning, someone who sells sugar to a bootlegger knowing the use that will be made of that staple is not thereby a conspirator, *United States v. Falcone*, 311 U.S. 205 (1940) . . . .

Falcone illustrates the doctrine that "mere" sellers and buyers are not automatically conspirators. If it were otherwise, companies that sold cellular phones to teen-age punks who have no use for them other than to set up drug deals would be in trouble, and many legitimate businesses would be required to monitor their customers' activities. *Cf. People v. Lauria*, 251 Cal.App.2d 471 (1967) (answering service furnished to prostitute). Yet this does not get us very far, for no rule says that a supplier *cannot* join a conspiracy through which the product is put to an unlawful end. *Direct Sales Co. v. United States*, 319 U.S. 703 (1943), makes that point in holding that the jury may infer that a pharmaceutical house selling huge quantities of morphine to a physician over a seven-year span conspired with the physician to distribute the drug illegally.

Where does the "mere" sale end, the conspiracy begin? One may draw a line, as *Falcone* and *Direct Sales* did, between knowledge of other persons' crimes and intent to join them, but this restates the elements of the offense without telling us when an inference of intent to join is permissible. . . . Stating polar cases is easy, but locating the line of demarcation is hard. . . .

When writing for the court of appeals in *Falcone*, 109 F.2d 579 (2d Cir.1940), Learned Hand concluded that a supplier joins a venture only if his fortunes rise or fall with the venture's, so that he gains by its success. . . . [W]e adopted his approach in *United States v. Pino-Perez*, 870 F.2d 1230, 1235 (7th Cir.1989) (in banc). On this view the sale of a staple commodity such as sugar or telephone service does not enlist the seller in the criminal venture; in a competitive market . . . , the buyer could turn to other sources. . . .

. . . Trailers do not rent for $1,000 per week—not in legitimate markets, anyway. By charging a premium price, Lawrence seemingly threw in his lot with the Nietupski operation and may be convicted under Judge Hand's approach. Yet the price cannot be the end of things. What does the $1,000 represent: a piece of the action, or only a premium for the risks? Lawrence bore two [risks]. One was that the chemicals would damage his trailer. Although he took precautions by spreading plastic on the floor, an explosion would have spattered chemicals on the walls and ceiling. Lawrence would have charged for taking this risk even if the manufacture of methamphetamine were entirely legal. The other risk was the hazard of criminal liability, a cost of doing business. One who covers his own costs and no more does not share in the venture's success. Using a price calculated by reference to the risk of criminal conviction as support *for* that conviction would be circular. Reduce the risk of conviction, and you reduce the price. Either way, the price responds to the legal system rather than to the potential profits of the Nietupski gang and does not establish a desire to promote its success. Repeat business, as in *Direct Sales*, might show such a desire, but Lawrence did not carry through with the initial transaction and never realized even the $1,000.

... [C]ases from this court speak reverentially of Judge Hand but actually ask a different, and more functional, question. It is whether the imposition of liability on transactions of the class depicted by the case would deter crime without adding unduly to the costs of legitimate transactions.... "[A] stationer who sells an address book to a woman whom he knows to be a prostitute is not an aider and abettor. He can hardly be said to be seeking by his action to make her venture succeed, since the transaction has very little to do with that success and his livelihood will not be affected appreciably by whether her venture succeeds or fails. And ... punishing him would not reduce the amount of prostitution — the prostitute, at an infinitesimal cost in added inconvenience, would simply shop for address books among stationers who did not know her trade." Treating the stationer as [a conspirator] would, however, raise the costs of legitimate business ....

If the product is itself contraband — for example, the methamphetamine Nietupski bought in California early on — the analysis differs but the result is the same: an isolated sale is not the same thing as enlisting in the venture. A sale of methamphetamine is a substantive crime. Because the substance is illegal, the seller knows that the buyer will put the drug to an illegal use, yet this does not make the sale a second, inchoate offense.... [A] long course of sales may permit a finding of conspiracy ..., for such conduct is both more dangerous (it is harder to ferret out crime when the criminals have a closed circle of suppliers) and more likely that the vendor's welfare is bound up with that of the organization to which he sells. So too with "fronting" of drugs, a credit arrangement in which the parties to the sale share the profits.

Sometimes a single transaction extends over a substantial period and is the equivalent of enduring supply.... Periodic payments of rent link the landlord with the criminal enterprise. Because a lessor almost inevitably knows his tenant's business, the imposition of a criminal penalty is likely to deter but not to raise the costs of legitimate transactions. A bookie needs a wire room; if the law deters landlords from providing space for these operations, it will substantially cut down on crime.

... [Here,] Lawrence negotiated for one payment, not a stream of rentals. ...

Some states have statutes forbidding "criminal facilitation," an apt description of Lawrence's acts. *E.g.,* N.Y. Penal Code § 115.05. Lawrence agreed to facilitate the manufacture of methamphetamine, but the United States Code lacks a facilitation statute. It does forbid aiding and abetting substantive offenses.... Yet the prosecutor did not charge Lawrence with assisting this offense .... Instead the prosecutor not only selected the conspiracy component of § 846 but also lumped Lawrence with a single, overarching conspiracy, the entire Nietupski venture. Neither joining nor abetting this whole conspiracy is an appropriate description of Lawrence's fling.

In charging Lawrence with joining the Nietupski conspiracy, the prosecutor sought to hold him responsible for that organization's entire activities.... *Pinkerton v. United States*, 328 U.S. 640 (1946).... Thus ... Thomas Lawrence, who obtained $100 by opening his trailer to a single failed "cook," received [the same sentence as received by one of the conspirators who had been involved in manufacturing and selling throughout the entire conspiracy] — ten years in prison without possibility of parole.

... If the United States Code contained a facilitation statute along the lines of New York's, Lawrence would receive a sentence proportioned to his own iniquity rather than that of Nietupski and her henchmen.... But it does not ....

Lawrence knew what Zahm wanted to do in the trailer, but there is a gulf between knowledge and conspiracy. There is no evidence that Lawrence recognized, let alone that he joined and promoted, the full scope of the Nietupski organization's activities. He may have joined, or abetted, a more limited agreement to manufacture a quantity of methamphetamine, but he was not charged with that offense.... [Conviction reversed.]

Notes and Questions

(1) *Why Isn't the "Inflated Charge" (Rent) in Lawrence Enough, Especially in Light of His Other Acts?* *Lauria* expressly held that one way of proving intent to participate is by evidence of "inflated charges." Why does Lawrence's "inflated charge" of $1,000 for one day's use of a trailer not qualify under this test, especially in light of his preparation of the space with plastic sheeting, sampling of the product, acceptance of $100 as a down payment, and other acts? The court even says that Lawrence joined "a more limited agreement to manufacture a quantity of methamphetamine." Isn't that a description of a conspiracy?

(2) *Did Lawrence's Withdrawal from the Conspiracy Influence the Court to Decide as It Did?* Obviously, Lawrence's "cold feet," as well as his directions to the conspirators to remove their equipment and chemicals, are sympathetic facts. But the hornbook law is that conspiracy is complete upon the existence of its elements. In theory, if the court meant to consider Lawrence's withdrawal as supporting his exoneration, it should not have relied on an absence of sufficient intent to promote the conspiracy; instead, it should have looked to the defense of "renunciation," a recognized defense with defined elements. The renunciation defense is a different question, which we shall consider further below.

Notes on Facilitation as Separate Crime

(1) *"Facilitation" as a Crime.* Should Lawrence's knowing contribution of an essential factor for the crime, itself be a crime, even if he did not actually "join" the conspiracy? Many jurisdictions have enacted a separate crime called *facilitation* to

deal with people who provide items they know will be used in the commission of a crime. The New York provision (N.Y. Pen. Law § 115.05) is typical:

> A person is guilty of criminal facilitation in the second degree when, believing it probable that he is rendering aid to a person who intends to commit a class A felony, he engages in conduct which provides such person with means or opportunity for the commission thereof and which in fact aids such person to commit such class A felony.

(2) *Lawrence in New York.* If meth distribution were a Class A felony, would Lawrence be guilty under the New York facilitation statute, as the *Lawrence* decision suggests?

[E] The Overt Act Requirement

(1) *Requirement of an Overt Act in Addition to the Agreement?* Some conspiracy statutes, following the common law, make conspiracy a completed crime upon formation of the agreement. No more conduct is needed. Many others, however, require an *overt act* in addition to the agreement for at least some crimes. In an overt act jurisdiction, a phone call where the two parties agree to steal a car is not sufficient for conspiracy to commit auto larceny. *See, e.g.,* Utah. Code Ann. § 766-4-201 (overt act required for conspiracy to commit most crimes, but no overt act needed for capital felony or felonies against the person, arson, burglary or robbery).

(2) *Rationale for Overt Act Requirement.* But why isn't the agreement itself sufficient? In many ways, the agreement itself is an act. The rationale for requiring an overt act is a concern that people, posing no real public threat, could be convicted if the only necessary proof was a conversation. Perhaps they said something ambiguous in the conversation or were not serious or were misunderstood. Requiring an act in addition to the agreement means that there is at least some evidence that the conspiracy was more than idle talk.

(3) *What Kind of Act is Needed?* The usual rule is that an overt act may be an innocuous one as long as it leads toward commission of the object crime. It need not be a significant act or one that would satisfy the higher requirements for attempt.

(4) *Overt Act: By Whom?* The clear rule is that when an overt act is necessary, it must be made by at least one conspirator. Once one conspirator has done this, the conspiracy has occurred even if no other conspirator has done anything toward the object crime. This rule has been questioned in one context: when the only overt act was completed by an undercover agent who has infiltrated the conspiracy. Some statutes specifically provide that the overt act may not be made by a law enforcement officer acting in an official capacity. *See, e.g.,* Vt. Stat. Ann. tit. 13, § 1401(b).

(5) *Reconsidering Pacheco, Above: Was There a Sufficient Overt Act?* In *Pacheco*, the defendant agreed to the killing, set the price, armed himself, and went to the lobby of the motel where the victim was staying. However, he left without killing the victim, and indeed without trying to contact him, and at that point, he was

arrested. Notice that traditionally, conspiracy does not require that the overt act be independently criminal. Were the alleged overt acts in *Pacheco* sufficient to meet this traditional test?

[F] Number of Conspiracies

Conspiring about Two Object Crimes. If A and B conspire to kidnap a child, they may be convicted of conspiracy to kidnap. But what if their scheme involves kidnapping two children. Is this still one conspiracy or have they committed two crimes of conspiracy to kidnap? The answer is important since it is at least theoretically possible that they could receive separate, consecutive sentences for the two offenses.

Only One Conspiracy? The general rule is that an agreement to commit more than one offense is still only one conspiracy. Some jurisdictions expand this to say there is only one conspiracy if several crimes are pursued during a continuous conspiratorial relationship. *See, e.g.,* Ohio Rev. Code Ann. § 2923.01. This means that if A and B agree to rob The First State Bank, complete that heist, then decide to rob the Second Trust Bank, they have only committed one conspiracy despite the multiple criminal objectives.

§ 10.05 Conspiracy Defenses and Limits

[A] Parties to the Conspiracy (And How Big Is It)?

(1) *The Rule: Knowledge of Others.* In order to determine who is in a conspiracy with whom, we need to look inside the head of each conspirator. According to MPC § 5.03(2), a person who is personally guilty of being a conspirator (person A) is in a conspiracy with particular other people (B and C) if knowing that a person with whom he or she conspires to commit a crime (D) has also conspired with one or more others (B and C) to commit the same crime. The exact identity of the others (B and C) need not be known. Thus, A, B, C, and D may all be in a conspiracy together. Note that this subjective approach may mean that people involved in a large scheme may actually conspire with different people.

For example, if D is in a conspiracy with E to commit bank loan fraud and D knows that E is working with "someone" (F) in the bank who will approve the misleading loan applications in exchange for $1000, then D and E are in a three person conspiracy which includes the unknown bank employee (F). D is in a conspiracy with someone whose identity D does not know.

(2) *Structure of Conspiracies: Chains and Wheels.* For purposes of analyzing who is in a conspiracy with whom, sometimes it is helpful to conceptualize the structure of the conspiracy. In general terms, conspiracies often resemble one of two models: "chain link" or "spoke-wheel."

(a) *Chain Link Conspiracies.* A chain link conspiracy involves people who are in a "line" and deal directly with the people in front and back of them in the line. For example, assume A grows marijuana, sells it to wholesaler B who sells it to distributor C who provides it to D, a street seller. The question is whether A is in a conspiracy with C and D, or only with B, who is A's only contact.

(b) *Spoke-Wheel Conspiracies.* A spoke-wheel conspiracy occurs when one person (the center or hub) deals with other conspirators (the spokes) but they do not deal with one another. This would occur if A grows marijuana and sells it to users B, C, and D. The issue is with whom each person is a co-conspirator. This could be one large conspiracy with four conspirators: A, B, C, and D. On the other hand, it could be three small ones: A-B, A-C, and A-D.

(3) *A Classic Illustration of the Wheel Conspiracy: Kotteakos v. United States,* 328 U.S. 750 (1946). This case involved a conspiracy to obtain federal housing loans by false statements. One man, Brown, assisted a number of people in using false applications to apply for loans. The government charged Brown and thirty-one other persons of being in a large conspiracy to get the loan money. The Supreme Court rejected the argument, holding that it was a wheel conspiracy with Brown at the center. The large conspiracy did not exist, because each person dealt only with Brown. Thus, there were many small conspiracies between Brown and each loan applicant. The result in *Kotteakos* would have changed, however, had there been proof that the loan applicants had all met together and knew they were participating in a larger crime than their own application.

(4) *Illustrating the Chain Link Conspiracy: United States v. Peoni,* 100 F.2d 401 (2d Cir. 1938). Peoni sold counterfeit bills to Regno who sold them to Dorsey who was arrested trying to pass them. All three knew the bills were counterfeit. Peoni was charged with conspiracy with Dorsey to possess the fake bills. Judge Learned Hand's opinion held that Peoni could not be convicted since he was not in a conspiracy with Dorsey, only Regno. Peoni knew someone beside Regno "might get them, but a conspiracy also imports a concert of purpose." Judge Hand observed that Peoni "had no concern with the bills after Regno paid for them." Peoni's "connection with the business ended when he got his money from Regno."

(5) *Wharton's Rule Sometimes Means That There Is No Conspiracy When the Definition of a Crime Already Requires Multiple Participants.* Some criminal statutes define a crime in such a way that the object offense already requires two people. If only two people (the minimum number required under the statue) engage in the prohibited conduct, may they also be convicted of conspiracy to violate that statute? For example, delivery of a controlled substance requires the participation of two people (the person delivering the drug and the person receiving it). Would it be overkill to convict the buyer and seller not only of delivery, but also of "conspiracy"?

"Wharton's Rule," named after the commentator who proposed it, holds there can be no conspiracy between the necessary parties in such a case because the legislature in enacting the crime requiring multiple participants did not intend for anyone to also be guilty of conspiracy. But Wharton's Rule is merely an interpretive presumption that implements the intent of the legislature. The legislature may choose to authorize conviction for both the object offense and the conspiracy. In *Iannelli v. United States*, 420 U.S. 770 (1975), for example, the Court held that the defendants could properly be convicted both of the object crime, which required "five or more persons" to conduct an illegal gambling operation, *and also* of conspiracy—because Congress intended this redundancy.

[B] Duration of a Conspiracy and Withdrawal from It

(1) *Why Duration is Important—and Complicated.* The duration or time period during which a conspiracy is in existence is important because the statute of limitations begins to run once the conspiracy is over. It may also begin to run for an individual once that person leaves the conspiracy. And, once the conspiracy is over, procedures applicable only to conspiracies no longer apply. But determining when a conspiracy begins and ends is more complicated than it might appear, because the conspiracy may have been created by communications over days or even weeks. A related problem is that people may join and leave the conspiracy over time.

(2) *When Conspiracy Is Over: Obtaining Criminal Objectives and Other End Points.* Conspiracy is a *continuing crime* that exists from the time of agreement until it is over (thus, the statute of limitations does not run during that period). To some extent, the agreement may control when the conspiracy starts and ends. For example, is escape part of the conspiracy, or does the conspiracy end once the bank is robbed or the victim is killed? Ordinarily it continues until the participants receive the expected benefits. If the agreement includes concealing the crime, escape, or any other method of avoiding apprehension, then the conspiracy continues until those goals are met. North Dakota, for example, defines a conspiracy's objectives to include "escape from the scene of the crime, distribution of booty, and measures, other than silence, for concealing the crime or obstructing justice in relation to it." N.D. Cent. Code § 12.1–06-04.

(3) *Withdrawal (aka Abandonment): The End for an Individual Conspirator.* If one person withdraws from the conspiracy, the conspiracy may be over for that person in most locales, but it may continue with the remaining conspirators. Similarly, the statute of limitations begins to run for that person, even if the actual conspiracy continues without the person. *See Smith v. United States*, 556 U.S. 106 (2013).

SMITH v. UNITED STATES, 586 U.S. 106 (2013). Withdrawal is important in statute-of-limitations cases, because if the statute of limitations runs after the defendant has withdrawn, the defendant has a complete defense. Smith was convicted of a huge conspiracy to deliver heroin and cocaine that included many crimes, including 31 murders. He pointed out that he was in prison during the conspiracy and that his alleged withdrawal, then, caused the statute to run as to him. "Withdrawal," the trial court told the jury, "must be unequivocal." Over objection, the court also said that "[o]nce the government has proven that a defendant was a member of a conspiracy, the burden is on the defendant to prove withdrawal . . . by a preponderance of the evidence." The jury then convicted Smith of the conspiracy crimes. The Supreme Court, per Justice Scalia, upheld these instructions:

> Allocating to a defendant the burden of proving withdrawal does not violate the Due Process Clause. While the Government must prove beyond a reasonable doubt "every fact necessary to constitute the crime with which [the defendant] is charged," "[p]roof of the nonexistence of all affirmative defenses has never been constitutionally required," *Patterson v. New York*, 432 U.S. 197, 210 (1977). . . .

> Withdrawal does not negate an element of the conspiracy crimes charged here . . . . Far from contradicting an element . . . , withdrawal presupposes that the defendant committed the offense. . . .

> Of course, Congress may choose to assign the Government the burden of proving the nonexistence of withdrawal . . . . It did not do so here. "[T]he common-law rule was that affirmative defenses . . . were matters for the defendant to prove." Because Congress did not address . . . the burden of proof for withdrawal, we presume that Congress intended to preserve the common-law rule. . . .

[C] Renunciation as a Defense to Conspiracy

> Read Model Penal Code § 5.03(6) [renunciation] in the MPC Appendix.

Notes and Questions

(1) *Renunciation as a Defense to Conspiracy.* Modern statutes often allow a *renunciation* defense to conspiracy (as well as to attempt and solicitation). But this defense applies only if the defendant actually prevents the success of the conspiracy by stopping the object crime from occurring. Additionally, as with attempt and solicitation, the defendant must completely and voluntarily renounce the conspiracy. Renunciation, therefore, must be contrasted with mere abandonment of or withdrawal from a conspiracy.

(2) *Renunciation and Withdrawal (Discussed Above) Are Very Different Concepts.* Renunciation and withdrawal are easily confused but differ in important ways. While withdrawal is forward-looking in that it prevents liability for future consequences of the conspiracy, it does not provide a defense for past liabilities. Thus, if a conspirator withdraws from a conspiracy, he or she is still liable for the conspiracy. Renunciation, on the other hand, is a defense to the conspiracy itself.

(3) *Reconsidering the Lawrence Case, Above, in Which the Defendant Withdrew from His Agreement to Furnish Space for Manufacturing Methamphetamine: Should Lawrence Have Succeeded with a Renunciation Defense?* In *Lawrence,* above, the court held that the defendant's acts of agreeing to inflated rent, sampling the product, preparing the laboratory floor, and receiving $100 as a down payment were insufficient to prove intent to promote the object of the conspiracy. This result, however, is debatable. Imagine a different court that is willing to affirm the conviction on these facts, and consider whether Lawrence, then, might have successfully asserted a defense of renunciation. Lawrence got cold feet, and he told the conspirators to remove their equipment, which they did. He prevented that plan from being carried out. (The group promptly switched to working with other people in what the court called a "new" conspiracy. Does this fact destroy the renunciation defense?)

[D] Impossibility and Conspiracy: No Defense?

What If the Object Is "Impossible"? At some point the object crime of a conspiracy may become impossible to accomplish. For example, unbeknownst to conspirators, the bank they agreed to rob burned down several days before the scheduled heist. Is the conspiracy over, or does it evaporate, since the object crime cannot be committed?

Not a Defense. The general rule is that impossibility is no defense to conspiracy. The underlying theory is that the danger of group activity does not disappear merely because the object of the conspiracy cannot be achieved. For example, the Supreme Court considered a case where government agents seized drugs before delivery and the defendant argued that he could not be convicted of drug conspiracy because he joined the conspiracy after the drugs were taken by government agents. The Court rejected this "impossibility" defense because the "essence" of the conspiracy—the agreement to commit the crime—remained. "[T]he government's defeat of the conspiracy's objective will not necessarily and automatically terminate the conspiracy." *United States v. Recio,* 537 U.S. 270, 275 (2003).

§ 10.06 Putting the Conspiracy Rules Together

Problem 10D (Conspiracy): "Yes, We All Were Part of a Planned Network for Heroin Distribution—But None of Us Is Guilty of Conspiracy!"

(1) *A Foiled Plan for Distributing Heroin: Alpha, Betty, Gammy, and Delta's Unsuccessful Collaboration.* Alpha, Betty, Gammy, and Delta all have been involved, in different ways, in forming and carrying forward a plan to distribute heroin. The issue, however, is whether this plan amounts to a criminal conspiracy that is provable against any one of these actors.

(2) Imagine that the first actor, named Alpha, visits a car rental agency, where Alpha tells Betty (the rental agent), "I need to rent a vehicle, preferably a large van

with lots of hidden spaces, so that Gammy and I can transport my merchandise to Capital City to open a new and profitable business." Alpha is somewhat of a braggart, and she also lets it slip to Betty that the business plan is for Alpha to relocate, together with Gammy, to Capital City to distribute several pounds of highly pure heroin that Alpha has acquired, of which Delta is a potential buyer. Betty congratulates Alpha on this venture and begins filling out the rental papers, but then stops because Alpha promises to come back to get the vehicle when the travelers are ready for their journey.

Unfortunately, Alpha has been the object of intense police scrutiny and a warrant has been issued authorizing the state anti-drug task force to record the car-rental conversation between Alpha and Betty. In fact, unbeknownst to Alpha, Gammy is a federal law enforcement officer who has infiltrated Alpha's group. Gammy already has recorded conversations among herself, Alpha, and Delta, in which all three have expressed agreement to a plan in which Alpha and Gammy will make the move to Capital City to set up a network to distribute Alpha's heroin, and Delta, who lives in Capital City, will buy some of it. Before the date for travel, however, Delta discovers that her daughter is ill, and she [Delta] withdraws from the plan to buy heroin. Alpha responds, "Okay, I'll just bring Gammy with me, and you can buy from us later."

At this point, state anti-drug task force agents appear on the scene and arrest Alpha, Betty and Delta. The prosecution now has a great deal of evidence that shows a plan to violate laws against heroin possession and distribution—but can it actually prove a conspiracy against anyone?

(3) *Consider the Elements of Conspiracy: Agreement, Intent, Promotion, Overt Act, and Plurality, as Well as the Defense of Renunciation.*

(a) *First*, there probably is enough evidence of an agreement, of some kind, by some of the defendants (but perhaps not agreement to a conspiracy, because of the other elements).

(b) *Second*, as to intent to agree, is there sufficient intent, on Betty's [the rental agent's] part?

(c) If so, *third*, consider the promotion issue. Has Betty (the car rental agent), by knowing of the plan and beginning the process of renting the car, obtained enough of a stake in the alleged conspiracy to have participated in or joined it with "intent to promote"?

(d) *Fourth*, does Delta have a defense of renunciation?

(e) *Fifth*, plurality is another issue, with two parts.

First: Alpha will argue that the bilateral theory of conspiracy should apply, and therefore she cannot have conspired with Gammy (the government agent). And if both Betty and Delta are exonerated, Alpha also must be exonerated—since there is no one left for Alpha to have conspired with! (The prosecution will prefer to have the court adopt the unilateral theory instead; why?)

Second: Also, in connection with the plurality requirement, Delta argues that all she was going to do was to buy heroin, in an unspecified quantity, from Alpha. The crime of distributing or purchasing heroin is one that depends by definition on the involvement of more than one person, and therefore Delta argues that it is "bootstrapping," inconsistent with Wharton's Rule, and a violation of the plurality principle, for Delta to be held to have "conspired" with Alpha. Is she right?

(f) *Sixth and finally:* If that is not enough, consider the overt act requirement. Everyone argues that the overt act requirement is not fulfilled by Alpha's merely appearing and conversing with Betty at the car rental agency. Is this argument persuasive?

§ 10.07 Procedural Differences When a Conspiracy Exists

(1) *The Law of Conspiracy Also Contains Other Consequences, and These May Create Significant Advantages for the Prosecution That Are Not Available in Other Kinds of Cases.* A conspiracy case is different from other cases not just in the substantive law, but in the way it is tried and in the results it may produce. Details of criminal procedure are beyond the scope of this book, but we shall attempt to sketch a few of those other consequences. None of these differences is illogical in itself, even though some are controversial; all of them derive from the very nature of conspiracy itself. But most of the differences favor the prosecution, and they have influenced the development of the substantive law to such an extent that one cannot understand conspiracy law without absorbing their impact. Here are some examples:

(a) *Venue: An Opportunity for Forum Shopping?* A large conspiracy, such as the one depicted in *Lawrence v. United States,* above, involves acts that occur in multiple counties or multiple states. Venue statutes typically permit prosecution in any county or jurisdiction where any act in furtherance of the conspiracy was committed by any conspirator. The prosecution may choose a venue that provides the government with relatively favorable law, a speedy docket, or judges or jurors who are more inclined its way.

(b) *Joinder of Multiple Coconspirators in a Single Case.* The prosecution has greater ability in conspiracy cases to join multiple defendants in a single trial. This principle results not only in judicial economy, but also in wider admissibility of evidence.

(c) *The Statute of Limitations.* A theft may be completed in a few seconds, and the statute of limitations starts running immediately. But the statute of limitations for a conspiracy ordinarily begins to run when the conspiracy is over. Thus, if a conspiracy lasts for ten years, the statute of limitations begins to run ten years after the conspiracy began.

(d) *Evidence: Co-Conspirator's Statements During and in Furtherance of the Conspiracy Are Not Excluded by the Hearsay Rule.* Sometimes the government wants to introduce evidence of a statement by one conspirator in order to prove the existence or activities of the conspiracy. This statement may be hearsay. The rules of evidence, however, include a so-called co-conspirator's hearsay exception that allows evidence about these kinds of communications. It should be added that this particular rule, although it depends on the existence of a conspiracy, does not require that conspiracy be among the crimes charged in the indictment. Even if conspiracy is not among the charges, if a conspiracy is proved, co-conspirators' statements during and in furtherance of the conspiracy are admissible and are exempted from the hearsay rule.

(2) *Should the Concerns Raised by These Differences Persuade a Court to Limit the Definition of Conspiracy?* In some cases, courts have taken these differences into account as reasons for limiting the substantive law of conspiracy. Consider *Lawrence v. United States*, the principal case above. The court noted that if Lawrence were guilty of conspiracy, he would be liable for all foreseeable completed crimes as well, and under the then-existing sentencing regime, this rule meant that he would be sentenced to a far longer term: one that was similar to sentences for managers and leaders of the conspiracy (since he would be liable for all of their foreseeable crimes). In part for this reason, the court decided that the law should be interpreted to exonerate Lawrence from conspiracy liability. Is it appropriate for a court, in this manner, to "bend" the substantive definition of conspiracy to avoid the consequences of guilt — or should it instead apply the substantive law as it exists, and find guilt or innocence without regard to the consequences?

Chapter 11

Complicity: Multiple-Party Completed Crimes

"Tell me what company you keep, and I'll tell you what you are."—Miguel de Cervantes, *Don Quixote* Pt. II, Ch.23

"In for a penny, in for a pound."—Proverb

§ 11.01 The Scope of Liability in Conspiracies: The *Pinkerton* Doctrine

Notes on the Relationship Between Conspiracy and Accomplice Liability

(1) *Conspiracy Is a Bridge Between the Last Chapter and This One.* Conspiracy belongs in the preceding chapter because it is a preparatory offense. But it also creates vicarious liability for completed crimes. You are a "party" or accomplice to certain completed crimes that your co-conspirators commit. This liability is in addition to your liability for the conspiracy.

(2) *An Example.* If A steals a car and takes it to B who removes and sells valuable parts from the stolen car, A and B may be in a *conspiracy* to commit auto theft. B may also be guilty of auto theft as an *accomplice* if the government can prove B's involvement in the theft itself, such as by helping A. In sum, if A and B each assisted in the theft, both are guilty of (a) conspiracy to commit auto theft as well as (b) the crime of automobile theft for being accomplices to that theft (by aiding and abetting each other).

(3) *The "Pinkerton Rule."* But there is a second way to make A and B liable for the substantive crime of theft. It's called the *Pinkerton* rule. Every conspirator is guilty of all "reasonably foreseeable" crimes committed by other conspirators during and in furtherance of the conspiracy. Thus, if a robbery conspiracy is furthered by a completed bank robbery, a shooting of a teller, a kidnapping, and a later "switch-car" theft, the getaway driver may be guilty of all of these crimes as a member of the conspiracy if they were "reasonably foreseeable," even if the driver was not physically involved in any of them, and even if the driver did not personally think about them. The rule creates a great breadth of potential criminal liability, and it applies in federal courts and in a number of states. Here is the *Pinkerton* decision, which sets out the rule.

Pinkerton v. United States

328 U.S. 640 (1946)

Mr. Justice Douglas delivered the opinion of the Court.

Walter and Daniel Pinkerton are brothers who live a short distance from each other on Daniel's farm. They were indicted for violations of the Internal Revenue Code. The indictment contained ten substantive counts and one conspiracy count. The jury found Walter guilty on nine of the substantive counts and on the conspiracy count. It found Daniel guilty on six of the substantive counts and on the conspiracy count. . . .

A single conspiracy was charged and proved. . . . Each of the substantive offenses found was committed pursuant to the conspiracy. Petitioners therefore contend that the substantive counts became merged in the conspiracy count, and that only a single sentence not exceeding the maximum two-year penalty provided by the conspiracy statute could be imposed. . . .

[We cannot] accept the proposition that the substantive offenses were merged in the conspiracy. . . . It has been long and consistently recognized by the Court that the commission of the substantive offense and a conspiracy to commit it are separate and distinct offenses. . . .

A conspiracy is a partnership in crime. It has . . . implications, distinct from the completion of the unlawful project. . . . Moreover, it is not material that overt acts charged in the conspiracy counts were also charged and proved as substantive offenses. . . . As stated in *Sneed v. United States*, [298 F. 911, 912, 913 (5th Cir. 1924)], "If the overt act be the offense which was the object of the conspiracy, and is also punished, there is not a double punishment of it."

. . . There is, however, no evidence to show that Daniel participated directly in the commission of the substantive offenses on which his conviction has been sustained, although there was evidence to show that these substantive offenses were in fact committed by Walter in furtherance of the unlawful agreement or conspiracy existing between the brothers. The question was submitted to the jury on the theory that each petitioner could be found guilty of the substantive offenses, if it was found [that] petitioners were parties to an unlawful conspiracy and the substantive offenses charged were in fact committed in furtherance of it. . . .

. . . There is here no evidence of the affirmative action on the part of Daniel which is necessary to establish his withdrawal from it. *Hyde v. United States*, 225 U.S. 347, 369. As stated in that case, "having joined in an unlawful scheme, having constituted agents for its performance, . . . until he does some act to disavow or defeat the purpose he is in no situation to claim the delay of the law. As the offense has not been terminated or accomplished, he is still offending. And we think, consciously offending . . . ." And so long as the partnership in crime continues, the partners act for each other in carrying it forward. . . . The rule which holds responsible one who counsels, procures, or commands another to commit a crime is founded on the same principle. . . .

A different case would arise if the substantive offense committed by one of the conspirators was not in fact done in furtherance of the conspiracy, did not fall within the scope of the unlawful project, or was merely a part of the ramifications of the plan which could not be reasonably foreseen . . . . But as we read this record, that is not this case. [Affirmed.]

MR. JUSTICE RUTLEDGE, dissenting in part.

The judgment concerning Daniel Pinkerton should be reversed. In my opinion it is without precedent here and is a dangerous precedent to establish.

[D]aniel in fact was in the penitentiary, under sentence for other crimes, when some of Walter's crimes were done. . . .

The court's theory seems to be that Daniel and Walter became general partners in crime by virtue of their agreement and because of that agreement without more on his part Daniel became criminally responsible as a principal for everything Walter did thereafter . . . of the general sort the agreement contemplated . . . . [T]he result is a vicarious criminal responsibility as broad as, or broader than, the vicarious civil liability of a partner for acts done by a co-partner . . . .

Such analogies from private commercial law and the law of torts are dangerous, in my judgment . . . . The effect of Daniel's conviction in this case . . . is either to attribute to him Walter's guilt or to punish him twice for the same offense, namely, agreeing with Walter to engage in crime. . . .

Notes and Questions

(1) *Applying the Pinkerton Doctrine: "In for a Penny, in for a Pound."* The *Pinkerton* rule is a broad imputation, to all conspirators, of liability for any substantive crime committed by any conspirator, with or without the participation or even knowledge of the other conspirators, if committed during and in furtherance of the conspiracy and reasonably foreseeable. The *Pinkerton* rule is a principle of rough justice. It resembles the quotation from Cervantes that begins this chapter: you are judged according to the reasonably foreseeable crimes committed by the "company you keep," at least if you have passed the threshold of entering into a conspiracy. The other quotation captures the *Pinkerton* rule even better: "In for a penny, in for a pound!" Not surprisingly, then, the rule has been the subject of criticism. Even federal courts, which apply the doctrine, have expressed due process concerns about the doctrine's potential reach. *See, e.g., United States v. Lawrence*, in the previous chapter; *United States v. Alvarez*, 755 F.2d 830 (11th Cir. 1985). Professor Neal Katyal, on the other hand, has defended the "functional benefits" of *Pinkerton* liability. *See* Neal Kumar Katyal, *Conspiracy Theory*, 112 Yale L.J. 1307 (2003).

(2) *The Model Penal Code Approach: Rejecting Pinkerton and Its "Agency" Basis.* The reasoning underlying *Pinkerton* is the law of partnership. But Justice Rutledge rejects the idea that conspirators are each other's "agents" and argues against "analogies from private commercial law." The Model Penal Code and many States also reject the *Pinkerton* rule.

(3) *The In-Furtherance Requirement.* Justice Douglas distinguishes the situation in *Pinkerton* from a case in which a conspirator commits a crime that is not "in furtherance" of the conspiracy, one that "could not be reasonably foreseen." If one conspirator does something unexpected as a separate initiative—if one member of a band of embezzlers shoots someone, for example—the others may not be liable. Do these requirements place reasonable limits on *Pinkerton*, or is it still too broad?

(4) *Separate Conspiracies, or One? Wheel, Spoke, Wheel-and-Spoke, and Chain Conspiracies.* The cases show different conspiratorial patterns. A "wheel" conspiracy consists of individuals who all conspire with each other. A "spoke" arrangement is different: a single central figure deals with several coconspirators in different conspiracies, but they do not conspire with each other. A "wheel-and-spoke" arrangement features the same central figure but also exhibits agreement among the other individuals (the spokes), who act toward a common purpose in a single conspiracy. Another arrangement is the "chain" or "chain-link" pattern. Here one person (W) deals with a second person (X) who, in turn, deals with a third person (Y) who then works with a fourth person (Z). Perhaps W imports contraband and wholesales it to X, who retails it to Y, who then resells it to Z.

The difference, for *Pinkerton* purposes, can be significant. If you are in a wheel-and-spoke conspiracy, you may be liable for the crimes of many co-conspirators. In a chain conspiracy, on the other hand, if you conspire only with one other person, there are fewer possibilities for *Pinkerton* liability.

Problem 11A (Pinkerton *Liability*): "How Many Offenses Would Lauria Have Committed, If He Had Joined the Conspiracy?"

(1) *A Problem Based on* People v. Lauria, *in the Preceding Chapter.* In *People v. Lauria, supra*, the court considered whether the defendant, Lauria, became guilty of a conspiracy to promote prostitution by furnishing telephone answering services knowingly to prostitutes. For this problem, assume that Lauria is provably guilty of the conspiracy crime and as an accomplice to prostitution (assume, for example, that he charged an increased fee to prostitutes and provided them with assistance in obtaining customers). Of all of the offenses committed by others with whom Lauria would have conspired, how many substantive crimes, aside from conspiracy, could then be imputed to Lauria?

(2) *The "Reasonable Foreseeability" and "in Furtherance" Requirements.* Next, imagine that one of Lauria's coconspirators assaults a customer for the purpose of robbing him. Further, assume that Lauria, like the rest of us, knows that robberies by prostitutes happen periodically, even though he doesn't want them to. Would Lauria be guilty of assault under *Pinkerton*? (Consider the "reasonable foreseeability" and "in furtherance" requirements.)

(3) *The Extent of the Conspiracy:* Assuming all the prostitutes were part of the conspiracy, now consider each prostitute's liability. Is each one liable for every criminal act of prostitution committed by every other one? In *Anderson v. Superior*

Court, 78 Cal. App. 2d 22 (Cal. App. 1947), the court held that a defendant who referred patients to an abortionist was liable to conviction for large numbers of illegal abortions performed on women she did not know and who had been referred to the abortionist by others.

(4) Pinkerton *and the "Natural and Probable Consequences" Doctrine of Accomplice Liability Compared. Pinkerton* extends liability for foreseeable crimes committed by other conspirators. As noted below, in some states, accomplice liability takes a similar approach by making accomplices responsible for crimes that are the "natural and probable consequences" of the crime they commit as accomplices. A key difference is that the former requires proof of a conspiracy while the latter does not. However, in many situations accomplices are also conspirators and both *Pinkerton* and natural-and-probable-consequences may make them liable for unintended results of their criminal acts.

(5) *Withdrawal—Or Continuing Conspiracy?* Applying the *Pinkerton* doctrine, Lauria might continue to be liable for substantive crimes even if he were to retire from the telephone answering business (just as Daniel Pinkerton's liability continued after he was jailed). Can you explain why?

§ 11.02 Complicity: Multiple-Person Liability Without the Need to Prove a Conspiracy

[A] Accomplices under the Common Law: Principals and Accessories

Notes and Questions

(1) *Introduction.* We turn now to multiple-party crimes independent of any conspiracy liability. The doctrine of accomplice liability, or complicity, means that a person can become derivatively liable for the crime of another, provided they have the appropriate mens rea and commit one of the required criminal acts. *See* Sanford H. Kadish, *Complicity, Cause and Blame: A Study in the Interpretation of Doctrine*, 73 Cal. L. Rev. 323, 336–7 (1985). The two principal modern justifications for accomplice liability are by analogy to civil agency law (you consent to be bound by the actions of another) or the doctrine of "forfeited personal identity" (if you aid in a crime you forfeit your right to be treated as an individual). The accomplice is not charged with a separate offense called "complicity" or "aiding and abetting"; rather, he or she is charged with the crime committed by the parties. *See, e.g.,* California Penal Code, § 31; South Carolina Code § 16–1-40.

(2) *Common Law: Principals, First and Second Degree; Accessories, Before and After.* Assume that A hires B and C to kill a rival drug kingpin. B drives the getaway car to the victim's house. C enters the house, shoots the victim, and escapes in B's car. B and C are chased by the police and go to the house of D (C's friend) who is told about the crime and hides B and C in the basement. Assume further that C,

the shooter, is guilty of first degree murder. What is the liability of A (who hired the others), B (who drove the getaway car but was not present when the victim was shot), and D (who hid B and C to avoid apprehension). Are they all also guilty of first degree murder, or something less serious?

The common law used *four categories* to distinguish these actors: principals of the first and second degree and accessories before and after the fact. Here is a brief description of each:

(a) *"Principals in the first degree"* actually committed the offenses (*e.g.,* C who personally killed the victim). This person is responsible for his or her own conduct and may be directly prosecuted for it.

(b) *"Principals in the second degree"* aided and abetted and were present (either actually or "constructively") at the scene (*e.g.,* B, the driver of the getaway car). Sometimes people in this category are called "aiders and abettors." They assist.

(c) *"Accessories before the fact"* aided and abetted beforehand, often being the brains behind the crime (*e.g.,* A, the mastermind who conceived the homicide and hired killer C and driver B but was not present during the crime). Often the accessory before the fact is characterized by such verbs as solicits, procures, induces, causes advises, counsels, encourages, hires, or compels.

(d) *"Accessories after the fact,"* like D, know that the offender committed a crime and provide aid after the offense was complete.

(3) *The Distinctions Mattered.* At common law, there was a great focus on technical precision, because the historical English practice of imposing the death penalty for many felonies led to highly complex procedural rules in relation to accomplice liability. The right kind of complicity had to be guessed at and charged, and there were many procedural differences.

(4) *The Trouble with Principals and Accessories: These Artificial Distinctions Were Difficult to Apply and Only Tangentially Related to Blameworthiness.* Imagine a getaway-car driver. Is this actor a principal in the first or second degree, or only an accessory before or after the fact? Or, consider the instigator or mastermind who plans and directs but never goes near the crime scene. Is this person merely an accessory before the fact and not a principal? It may be difficult to compartmentalize these co-participants in some cases. Also, the designated crimes may not fall at appropriate points on a scale of blameworthiness.

(5) *Modern Approaches: One Category, Usually, for Complicity.* Modern criminal laws are far less rigid than the common law. The basis for them is the conclusion that principals of the first and second degree as well as accessories before the fact should be treated the same and the traditional distinctions between them serve no useful purpose. Accordingly, today's criminal statutes usually simplify the process and combine them into one category, variously called "parties," "principals,"

"accomplices," "accessories," or simply people who are "legally accountable." Thus A, B, and C would all be co-parties to the crime and guilty of murder.

(6) *Post-Crime Aid Is Different, Even Under Modern Statutes.* While modern jurisdictions combine the traditional categories of complicity, the law still treats accessories after the fact in a different way, as discussed below. Because these actors entered the crime after it was completed, their involvement is considered a variety of obstruction of justice rather than part of the crime itself. Thus, the punishment is often much less.

(7) *Modern "Aiding and Abetting" in the Federal System.* The modern approach is illustrated in the next case where federal law combines the three categories into a single generic category.

[B] Aiding and Abetting under Modern Statutes

Rosemond v. United States

572 U.S. 651 (2014)

JUSTICE KAGAN delivered the opinion of the Court.

[Defendant Rosemond participated in a drug sale that went bad. Someone, either he or one of his confederates, fired a firearm. The Government charged Rosemond with violating 18 U.S.C. § 924(c) either by using or carrying a firearm in connection with a drug trafficking crime, or, in the alternative, aiding and abetting that offense under 18 U.S.C. § 2. The trial judge instructed the jury that Rosemond was guilty of aiding and abetting the offense if he (1) "knew his cohort used a firearm in the drug trafficking crime" and (2) "knowingly and actively participated in the drug trafficking crime." The judge rejected the defendant's proposed instruction that the jury must find that he acted intentionally "to facilitate or encourage" the use of a firearm, as opposed to merely aiding the predicate drug offense. The jury convicted Rosemond, but the Supreme Court here reverses.]

II.

The federal aiding and abetting statute, 18 U.S.C. § 2, states that a person who furthers — more specifically, who "aids, abets, counsels, commands, induces or procures" — the commission of a federal offense "is punishable as a principal." That provision derives from . . . common-law standards for accomplice liability.

We have previously held that under § 2 "those who provide knowing aid to persons committing federal crimes, with the intent to facilitate the crime, are themselves committing a crime." Both parties here embrace that formulation, and agree as well that it has two components. As at common law, a person is liable under § 2 for aiding and abetting a crime if (and only if) he (1) takes an affirmative act in furtherance of that offense, (2) with the intent of facilitating the offense's commission. . . .

The questions that the parties dispute, and we here address, concern how those two requirements — affirmative act and intent — apply in a prosecution for aiding and abetting a §924(c) offense. Those questions arise from the compound nature of that provision. Recall that §924(c) forbids "us[ing] or carr[ying] a firearm" when engaged in a "crime of violence or drug trafficking crime." The prosecutor must show the use or carriage of a gun; so too he must prove the commission of a predicate (violent or drug trafficking) offense. . . . For purposes of ascertaining aiding and abetting liability, we therefore must consider: When does a person act to further this double-barreled crime? And when does he intend to facilitate its commission? . . .

A . . .

[A]s he tells it, [Rosemond] took no action with respect to any firearm. He . . . did not carry a gun to the scene; he did not use a gun during the subsequent events constituting this criminal misadventure. His acts thus advanced . . . one element (the drug element) of a two-element crime. Is that enough to satisfy the conduct requirement of this aiding and abetting charge, or must Rosemond, as he claims, have taken some act to assist the commission of the other (firearm) component . . . ?

The common law imposed aiding and abetting liability on a person . . . who facilitated any part—even though not every part—of a criminal venture. As a leading treatise, published around the time of §2's enactment, put the point: Accomplice liability attached upon proof of "*[a]ny* participation in a general felonious plan" carried out by confederates. . . . Or in the words of another standard reference: If a person was "present abetting . . . *any* act necessary, . . ." he could be charged as a principal—even "though [that act was] *not the whole thing necessary.*" . . .

That principle continues to govern aiding and abetting law under §2: As almost every court of appeals has held, "[a] defendant can be convicted as an aider and abettor without proof that he participated in each and every element of the offense." In proscribing aiding and abetting, Congress used language that "comprehends all assistance rendered by words, acts, encouragement, support, or presence"—even if that aid relates to only one (or some) of a crime's phases or elements. So, for example, in upholding convictions for abetting a tax evasion scheme, this Court found "irrelevant" the defendants' "non-participation" in filing a false return; we thought they had amply facilitated the illegal scheme by helping a confederate conceal his assets.

Under that established approach, Rosemond's participation in the drug deal here satisfies the affirmative-act requirement for aiding and abetting a §924(c) violation. . . . Rosemond therefore could assist in §924(c)'s violation by facilitating either the drug transaction or the firearm use (or of course both).

Rosemond argues, to the contrary, that the requisite act here "must be directed at the use of the firearm," because that element is §924(c)'s most essential feature. . . ." But Rosemond can provide no authority for demanding that an affirmative act go toward an element considered peculiarly significant; rather, as just noted, courts have never thought relevant the importance of the aid rendered. . . .

Rosemond's related argument that our approach would conflate two distinct offenses—allowing a conviction for abetting a §924(c) violation whenever the prosecution shows that the defendant abetted the underlying drug trafficking crime—fares no better. That is because an aiding and abetting conviction requires not just an act facilitating one or another element, but also a state of mind extending to the entire crime. Aiding and abetting law's intent component—to which we now turn—thus preserves the distinction between assisting the predicate drug trafficking crime and assisting the broader §924(c) offense.

B . . .

As previously explained, a person aids and abets a crime when (in addition to taking the requisite act) he intends to facilitate that offense's commission. An intent to advance some different or lesser offense is not, or at least not usually, sufficient: Instead, the intent must go to the . . . entire crime charged—so here, to the full scope (predicate crime plus gun use) of §924(c). *See* Model Penal Code §2.067 And the canonical formulation of that needed state of mind . . . is Judge Learned Hand's: To aid and abet a crime, a defendant must not just "in some sort associate himself with the venture," but also "participate in it as in something that he wishes to bring about" and "seek by his action to make it succeed." *Nye & Nissen v. United States*, 336 U.S. 613, 619 (1949) . . .

We have previously found that intent requirement satisfied when a person actively participates in a criminal venture with full knowledge of the circumstances constituting the charged offense. In *Pereira* [*v. United States*, 347 U.S. 1 (1954)], . . . we found the requisite intent for aiding and abetting because the defendant took part in a fraud "know[ing]" that his confederate would take care of the mailing. 347 U.S., at 12. Likewise, in *Bozza v. United States*, 330 U.S. 160, 165 (1947), we upheld a conviction for aiding and abetting the evasion of liquor taxes because the defendant helped operate a clandestine distillery "know[ing]" the business was set up "to violate Government revenue laws." . . .

The same principle holds here: An active participant in a drug transaction has the intent needed to aid and abet a §924(c) violation when he knows that one of his confederates will carry a gun. In such a case, the accomplice has decided to join in the criminal venture, and share in its benefits, with full awareness of its scope—that the plan calls not just for a drug sale, but for an armed one. In so doing, he has chosen (like the abettors in *Pereira* and *Bozza* or the driver in an armed robbery) to align himself with the illegal scheme in its entirety—including its use of a firearm. . . . He may not have brought the gun to the drug deal himself, but . . . he intended the commission of a §924(c) offense—*i.e.*, an armed drug sale.

For all that to be true, though, the §924(c) defendant's knowledge of a firearm must be advance knowledge—or otherwise said, knowledge that enables him to make the relevant legal (and indeed, moral) choice. When an accomplice knows beforehand of a confederate's design to carry a gun, he can attempt to alter that plan or, if unsuccessful, withdraw from the enterprise . . . . But when an accomplice knows nothing of a gun until it appears at the scene, . . . he may at that late point have no realistic opportunity to quit the crime. And when that is so, the defendant has not shown the requisite intent to assist a crime involving a gun.

Both parties here find something to dislike in our view of this issue. Rosemond argues that a participant in a drug deal intends to assist a §924(c) violation only if he affirmatively desires one of his confederates to use a gun. . . . [A]ccording to Rosemond, the instructions must also permit the jury to draw the . . . conclusion . . . that although the defendant participated in a drug deal knowing a gun would be involved, he did not specifically want its carriage or use. . . .

We think not. What matters for purposes of gauging intent, and so what jury instructions should convey, is that the defendant has chosen, with full knowledge, to participate in the illegal scheme — not that, if all had been left to him, he would have planned the identical crime. Consider a variant of Rosemond's example: The driver of a getaway car wants to help rob a convenience store (and argues passionately for that plan), but eventually accedes when his confederates decide instead to hold up a national bank. Whatever his original misgivings, he has the requisite intent to aid and abet *bank* robbery; . . . he put aside those doubts and knowingly took part in that more dangerous crime. . . .

A final, metaphorical way of making the point: By virtue of §924(c), using a firearm at a drug deal ups the ante. A would-be accomplice might decide to play at those perilous stakes. Or he might grasp that the better course is to fold his hand. What he should not expect is the capacity to hedge his bets, joining in a dangerous criminal scheme but evading its penalties by leaving use of the gun to someone else. . . .

The Government, for its part, thinks we take too strict a view of when a defendant charged with abetting a §924(c) violation must acquire that knowledge. . . . [T]he Government recognizes that the accused accomplice must have "foreknowledge" of a gun's presence. But the Government views that standard as met whenever the accomplice, having learned of the firearm, continues any act of assisting the drug transaction. According to the Government, the jury should convict such a defendant even if he became aware of the gun only after he [has passed the point when he could realistically] opt[] out of the crime.

But that approach, we think, would diminish too far the requirement that a defendant in a §924(c) prosecution must intend to further an *armed* drug deal. Assume, for example, that an accomplice agrees to participate in a drug sale on the express condition that no one brings a gun . . . . But just as the parties are making the trade, the accomplice notices that one of his confederates has a (poorly) concealed firearm in his jacket. The Government would convict the accomplice of aiding and abetting a §924(c) offense if he assists in completing the deal without incident, rather than running away . . . . But behaving as the Government suggests might increase the risk of gun violence . . . .

III

Under these principles, the District Court erred in instructing the jury, because it did not explain that Rosemond needed advance knowledge of a firearm's presence. Recall that the court stated that Rosemond was guilty of aiding and abetting if

"(1) [he] knew his cohort used a firearm in the drug trafficking crime, and (2) [he] knowingly and actively participated in the drug trafficking crime." . . .

In telling the jury to consider merely whether Rosemond "knew his cohort used a firearm," the court did not direct the jury to determine *when* Rosemond obtained the requisite knowledge. So, for example, the jury could have convicted even if Rosemond first learned of the gun when it was fired, and he took no further action to advance the crime. [Vacated and remanded to consider other issues.]

Notes and Questions

(1) *The Act Requirement: Isn't the Court Necessarily Right That an Act as to Only Part of the Crime Is Enough?* Consider whether Rosemond's argument, that the act component must address the whole crime (or its biggest component), makes any sense at all. For example, Louise commits part of a robbery by pointing a gun at the victim, while Thelma contributes the theft part of robbery by taking money from the cash register. It would be strange to argue that Thelma is exonerated of robbery because her act did not complete the whole crime (or the violent part). But isn't that Rosemond's argument about actus reus (which the Court rejects)?

(2) *The Intent Requirement: Is Rosemont Right in Arguing That "Intent" Must Mean More Than Knowledge?* The Model Penal Code defines intent (or purpose) as a "conscious desire or objective." Is there an argument that Rosemond is right, that the requisite intent is more than knowledge, and that (as he says), it requires "affirmative desire" for gun use? (But the Court has serious reasons for rejecting the argument.)

(3) *But Maybe the Government Is Right: Isn't Congress Unlikely to Have Intended the Precise Timing of Knowledge That the Court Requires?* The Court considers scenarios and strategic considerations in offenders' minds that there is no way to attribute to Congress. Is it more likely that Congress meant to hold offenders liable whenever they acquired knowledge, if they didn't withdraw? Maybe Congress was less sympathetic than the Court, which deals offenders a leisurely chance to "fold" if the "ante" increases!

[C] The Actus Reus of Accomplice Liability

(1) *The Actus Reus of Accomplice Liability — How Much Aid, and of What Kind?* To be an aider and abettor to another's crime, the actor must somehow assist or attempt to assist in that crime. The actus reus for accomplice liability includes both aiding (physical help) or abetting (psychological help) part or all of the actus of the primary crime, as the following case suggests.

(2) *Omissions to Act.* The actus reus of complicity can be satisfied by omission if the accomplice has a legal duty to act, providing the accomplice has the required mens rea. For example, in *State v. Williquette*, 370 N.W.2d 282 (Wisc. 1985), a mother knew her husband was abusing their children but did not act to stop the

abuse. She was chargeable on a complicity theory for child abuse because of her legal duty to protect her children.

(3) *Rhetoric of Encouragement: When Is It Enough?* Imagine that Alpha says, in anger, "I hate that guy and I'd like to see somebody kill him." If a listener, Betty, were to respond to Alpha's words by doing just that, would Alpha be guilty of murder? She has encouraged and, therefore, by a stretch of the concept, "aided and abetted" Betty's crime. But the ramifications of this theory are cautionary. Careless commentators often accuse politicians of both parties of encouraging violence "by their rhetoric"; surely that inference does not justify much confidence. But there is encouragement, and then there is direct, serious, and excessive encouragement. And courts have taken notice of the difference.

PEOPLE v. MOORE, 679 N.W.2d 41 (Mich. 2004). The defendants were convicted of a crime referred to as "felony-firearm" under an aiding and abetting theory. (Felony-firearm was the crime of possessing a firearm during the commission of a felony.) The Michigan aiding and abetting statute made a person who "procures, counsels, aids, or abets" a crime liable "as if he had directly committed such offense." Moore's conduct consisted of taunting DeJuan Boylston as a means of persuading him to shoot the victim, Jacky Hamilton. The court here upholds the conviction:

> In this case, defendant Moore procured, counseled, aided, or abetted the possession of a firearm during the commission of a felony—the murder of Jacky Hamilton. Although Moore did not "obtain or retain" the gun that killed the victim, nor did he pull the trigger, his words and actions incited Boylston to use the firearm that was in his possession to do exactly that. Moore provoked Boylston to shoot at the victims by attempting to grab the gun away from him and by telling him to "give me the gun; I'll do it." When Boylston first refused to shoot and turned to walk away . . . , Moore attacked his sense of masculinity and threatened to dissociate himself from Boylston . . . . In so provoking and inciting a hesitant Boylston to use the gun that he was carrying, Moore necessarily induced Boylston to [commit the crime]. Thus, applying the general aiding and abetting standard . . . , we hold that there was sufficient evidence in the record to establish that defendant performed acts or gave encouragement that assisted in the commission of the felony-firearm violation. Accordingly, we affirm Moore's . . . conviction.

Notes and Questions

(1) *Statutory Interpretation and Fair Warning.* The *Moore* court overruled a precedent that was more than twenty years old, stating that it was inconsistent with the language of the statute. That decision, *People v. Johnson*, 303 N.W.2d 442 (Mich. 1981), adopted a narrow reading of aiding and abetting, so that one could not aid

and abet a possessory offense. The *Moore* court reasoned simply: *Johnson* was inconsistent with the aiding and abetting statute, which broadly covered one who "procures, counsels, aids or abets" a crime, and the statute did not exclude aiding and abetting possessory offenses. Do you agree that the older decision was inconsistent with the statute?

Regardless of the correct interpretation of the statute, the defendants in *Moore* could argue that they were entitled to rely on the law that existed at the time they acted. A federal court granted the habeas corpus petition of Moore's co-defendant Harris, holding that the Michigan Supreme Court's overruling of the earlier case was unforeseeable, in violation of due process. *Harris v. Booker*, 738 F. Supp. 2d 734 (E.D. Mich. 2010). Note, though, that this decision does not affect the law of Michigan as stated in *Moore*.

(2) *What Other Conduct Satisfies the Actus Requirement for Accomplice Liability?* As to physical aiding and abetting, Professor La Fave details the many ways that an accomplice may aid the commission of the crime. He or she may "furnish guns, money, supplies, or instrumentalities," "act as a lookout or man the getaway car," "signal the approach of the victim, send the victim to the actor, prevent a warning from reaching the victim, prevent escape by the victim," or remove the victim or witnesses from the area of the crime. The accomplice can act directly or through another person, and—in contrast to a conspiracy—the principal need not even know of the assistance at all.

As to psychological aiding and abetting, LaFave notes that an accomplice can induce a person to commit a crime "through threats or promises, by words or gestures of encouragement, or by providing others with a plan." Even more, a person is an accomplice if he or she is present with the required mens rea "at the scene of the crime ready to give some aid if needed." Wayne R. La Fave, *Criminal Law* 709–11 (6th ed. 2017).

(3) *Limits of Liability.* Encouragement is a particularly contested form of conduct in accomplice liability decisions. Courts have consistently held that more than mere presence is required, although persons are frequently held liable on the basis of much less involvement in the primary party's crime than was the case in *Moore*. For example, in *People v. Campbell*, 25 Cal. App. 4th 402 (Cal. App. 1994), the court affirmed the conviction of Campbell's accomplice, Smith, on the charge of attempted robbery of Timothy Branch, holding that the trial court had not erred in instructing the jury on an aiding and abetting theory, based on these facts:

> Timothy Branch and his girlfriend Deborah Sester sat on a fence in front of an apartment complex. [Campbell and Smith walked past and then returned.] When Campbell and Smith were in front of them, Branch heard Campbell say something like "this is a robbery, break yourself." Branch understood [that] to mean empty your pockets. . . . [Branch responded,] "What do you mean? You don't know me and I don't know you and there ain't no future in this meeting."

Campbell responded by pointing a handgun an inch from Branch's head. . . . Branch swatted the gun away . . . . He then ran off, zigzagging . . . . Campbell held on to the gun, used a nearby mailbox to steady his arm, aimed at the fleeing Branch, and fired several times. . . . The second [shot] hit Branch . . . . Thereafter, Campbell started chasing Branch, firing as he ran. . . .

[Smith, the other party, was convicted of aiding and abetting Campbell's act of robbery. He claimed that the evidence was insufficient.] We disagree . . . .

Smith correctly points out that in general neither presence at the scene of a crime nor knowledge of, but failure to prevent it, is sufficient to establish aiding and abetting its commission. However, "[a]mong the factors which may be considered in making the determination of aiding and abetting are: presence at the scene of the crime, companionship, and conduct before and after the offense."

Here, virtually all of these factors are present. Smith did not independently happen by . . . . He had walked by Branch and Sester with Campbell and thus was aware of their isolation and vulnerability . . . . Smith then decided with Campbell to return to them. Together they approached Branch and Sester, stopping closely in front of them. Their concerted action reasonably implies a common purpose, which Campbell immediately revealed when he told Branch this was a robbery and then enforced this purpose with a firearm. During this time, Smith remained in position in front of Sester. Since there is no evidence he was surprised by Campbell's conduct or afraid to interfere with it, the jury could reasonably conclude that Smith assumed his position in front of Branch and Sester to intimidate and block them, divert suspicion, and watch out for others who might approach. Such conduct is a textbook example of aiding and abetting. Thus, the evidence, in our view, reasonably indicates that Smith played an affirmative supportive role in the attempted robbery and was not simply an innocent, passive, and unwitting bystander.

Furthermore, after Campbell left to chase after Branch, Smith forcibly prevented Sester from leaving and asked what *she* had, that is, he attempted to rob her. . . .

Problem 11B (Aiding and Abetting): "Here's a Map That Will Take You to a Place Where You Can Buy Drugs"

(1) *How Much Aid, and How Far Must It Go?* In *State v. Gladstone*, 78 (Wash. 1970) the court took a narrow view of aiding and abetting. An undercover officer testified that he tried to complete a drug buy from Gladstone. Gladstone said he did not have enough marijuana to sell but directed the officer to an individual named Kent and drew a map to Kent's residence. The officer purchased marijuana from

Kent. The state then prosecuted Gladstone for aiding and abetting the sale by Kent. The Washington Supreme Court held that Gladstone's actions were insufficient to constitute aiding and abetting,

> There being no evidence whatever that the defendant ever communicated to Kent the idea that he would in any way aid him in the sale of any marijuana, or said anything to Kent to encourage or induce him or direct him to do so, or counseled Kent in the sale of marijuana, or did anything more than describe Kent to another person as an individual who might sell some marijuana, . . . there was no proof of an aiding and abetting, and the conviction should, therefore, be reversed as a matter of law.

One Justice dissented, reasoning that "the majority has stepped into the jury box." Washington law, he added, "does not require the presence at the scene of" an aider and abettor. Nor did it require a "community of intent." It required only an intent by Gladstone to promote the offense completed by Kent and an action that would "instigate, induce, procure or encourage" the primary crime.

(2) *Should Prior Planning, Communication, or an Economic Stake in the Crime Be Required, as the Gladstone Majority Seemed to Think (or Are Those Elements Relevant, Instead, Only for the Separate Theory of Conspiracy)?* The majority in *Gladstone* appears to have confused aiding and abetting with conspiracy. But aiding and abetting, unlike conspiracy, does not require an agreement, and does not require that the accomplice participate in the target crime.

For example, if two people act on the spur of the moment to kill a third person and each intentionally advances the design although they never expressly communicate, traditional concepts of aiding and abetting would still make each liable for murder. Shouldn't the court instead have focused on whether Gladstone aided and abetted the offense with the requisite mens rea (even if Kent did not know of Gladstone's participation until the undercover officer visited him)?

(3) *The Mens Rea of Aiding and Abetting: Again the Gladstone Court Took a Narrow View.* The *Gladstone* majority also held that mens rea was a "fatal gap" in the prosecution's case, because the officer did not testify to "any prior conduct, arrangements, or communications between Gladstone and Kent . . . ." Is this reasoning sound (what other "design" did Gladstone have in drawing the map)? The *Gladstone* result may not seem troublesome since the crime was only marijuana delivery. But consider whether the *Gladstone* analysis would hold up in a more serious case—*e.g.*, a contract murder, where an aider-and-abetter draws a map showing how to find the hit man.

[D] The Mens Rea of Accomplice Liability

(1) *Introduction.* As *Moore* illustrates, Michigan law specifies that the mens rea for accomplice liability exists where "the defendant intended the commission of the crime or had knowledge that the principal intended its commission at the time

that [the defendant] gave aid and encouragement." Traditionally, the mens rea for accomplice liability required two kinds of intent:

(a) the intent to assist the principal offender, and

(b) the intent that the principal offender commit the offense.

Thus, contemporary Michigan law has a broader basis for liability than the common law position, extending liability to cases where the accomplice merely *knows* that the primary party will commit the crime, *if the accomplice also has the purpose to assist him*. A major issue is whether a criminally culpable mens rea should exist where the accomplice gives *knowing* assistance to the principal or should only exist where there is *a purpose or intent to facilitate* the commission of the primary offense. Most but by no means all jurisdictions require proof of purpose. Sometimes this mens rea is formulated as "intent that the offense be committed." N.D. Cent. Code § 12.1–03-01. The question then arises, what evidence could impute purpose, and specifically whether we can sometimes infer purpose from what looks like knowledge?

(2) *The MPC and Complicity Mens Rea.* For *result* offenses, such as homicide, the mens rea for attempt under the MPC is the mens rea required for the primary crime. Thus, under the MPC (and in the majority of U.S. jurisdictions) a defendant has complicity liability for voluntary or involuntary manslaughter if he or she has the mens rea required to be guilty of that crime *provided that he or she also has the intent to assist the principal offender in the conduct that forms the basis of the offense.* For example, one does not have to intend the death of a person in order to be liable if, as a passenger in a vehicle you encourage the driver to speed, with the result that he kills a pedestrian.

(3) *Natural and Probable Consequences Doctrine.* In most jurisdictions, accomplice liability exists not just for the primary crime but for any other crime that was a "natural and probable consequence" of the primary crime in which the defendant intentionally assisted. But MPC § 2.06(4) has no "natural and probable consequences" doctrine.

For example, assume A and B are paid to severely beat up X. A inflicts the beating while B serves as a lookout. X dies from the beating. Neither A nor B intended for X to die, but under *Pinkerton*, both could be responsible for murder or manslaughter because the death was foreseeable and the beating was in furtherance of the conspiracy. They may also be liable for the homicide as accomplices to the beating, because X's death is the natural and probable consequence of the beating.

Problem 11C (Pinkerton *and Aiding and Abetting*): "Yes, I Found Out That Someone Else Brought Along an M-16, But I Wasn't Involved in That!"

(1) *A Case of Insufficient Aiding and Abetting: United States v. Luciano-Mosquera*, 63 F.3d 1142 (1st Cir. 1995). This case involved a major drug delivery to a Puerto Rican beach that was interrupted by law enforcement officers, who found an M-16

rifle under a jeep where two of the drug conspirators were hiding. The court reversed the convictions of two defendants, including one of the men under the jeep, but affirmed the convictions of three others for aiding and abetting the carrying of a firearm in the commission of a drug trafficking offense. The court was doubtful about whether the man under the jeep "knew about" the firearm, because it was dark and the rifle was on the other side, near the other defendant (whose conviction was affirmed). Even if he did know about it, there was insufficient evidence that he did anything to "facilitate" its carrying.

(2) *The Elusive Mens Rea (to Promote the Entire Offense).* Can you explain why the court reversed the conviction of the man under the jeep, if he was involved in the drug trafficking offense itself?

[E] Persons Who Are "Legally Accountable": The Model Penal Code

Read Model Penal Code §§ 2.06(1)–(3) [accomplices] in the MPC Appendix.

Notes on Multiple-Party Liability Under the MPC

(1) *"Soliciting" or "Aiding" under the Model Penal Code.* MPC § 2.06 provides that a party is liable for a completed crime of another if the party "solicits," or "aids," or "agrees or attempts to aid" the other person, while acting with the "purpose of promoting or facilitating the commission" of the offense. Note how this combines the traditional categories of principal in the first and second degree and accessory before the fact and makes them all responsible for the crime committed by the person who was solicited or aided. The MPC obviously meant to eliminate the pigeonholes of the common law; and thus, the MPC employs broad new terms: "soliciting" and "aiding."

(2) *The Defendant Does Not Have to Succeed in Helping the Other Actor, to Be Guilty of the Crime.* Notice that under the MPC encouraging someone else to commit a crime ("soliciting") creates liability even if no other aid is given. Thus, a telephone call may be sufficient to satisfy this element. And "agreeing" or "attempting" to aid is enough even if the aid is ineffectual. The defendant, in other words, does not have to provide actual help, or "cause" the crime at all. Imagine that A, B and C agree to kill the victim. A says to C, "shoot him [the victim]," and C does. Meanwhile, B attempts to help C kill the victim, but B's gun jams. A (the "solicitor") and B (the "attempted aider") are as guilty as C if they intended to "promote or facilitate" the crime.

(3) *Are "Solicitors" and "Attempted Aiders" under the MPC Similar to "Aiders and Abettors" under Federal Law?* At least superficially, the MPC "soliciting-or-aiding" concept seems to be similar to federal "aiding and abetting," but the MPC

terminology sounds less archaic. Perhaps it connotes a breadth that will avoid some technical interpretations?

Rivera v. State

12 S.W.3d 572 (Tex. App. 2000)

PHIL HARDBERGER, CHIEF JUSTICE.

In this San Antonio backyard drama, a barbecue ended in murder. Vasquez went to the home of his friend, Abel Rivera, to watch the Tyson-Holyfield fight. By night's end, Vasquez was in the morgue. This unexpected conclusion to the evening was effectuated by two of Rivera's brothers, Timotheo and Gilbert, who alternatively stabbed and shot Vasquez until he died. Timotheo did the stabbing: six times. Gilbert did the shooting: three times. While there was evidence that Vasquez, the victim, had a bad disposition, he was not armed with a knife or a gun, or anything more dangerous than a can of beer.

Timotheo was convicted and sentenced to life imprisonment. . . . Timotheo asserts that the evidence is . . . insufficient to prove beyond a reasonable doubt that he murdered Vasquez. . . .

[The trial court instructed the jury that Timotheo was guilty if either (1) he killed the victim himself or (2) he "acted as a party" together with Gilbert to complete the killing. This instruction was a modified version of MPC §2.06(3)(a). Specifically, the court told the jury, "A person is criminally responsible for an offense committed by the conduct of another if, acting with intent to promote or assist the commission of the offense, he solicits, encourages, directs, aids, or attempts to aid the other person to commit the offense." The instruction did not require any prior arrangement or communication with Gilbert, because merely "aiding" Gilbert (or "attempting" to aid him) was enough to make Timotheo a party; and likewise, it did not require that Timotheo's conduct would be enough to kill by itself, because one objective of the MPC is to make people liable who merely "attempt" to aid. The appellate court upheld this instruction.]

[With respect to the sufficiency of the evidence, the court was terse:] The evidence is . . . sufficient to show that Timotheo and his brother acted together, each contributing his part to assault and kill Vasquez, which was their common purpose. . . .

Notes and Questions

(1) *Actus Reus for Conviction under the MPC: Distinguishing the* Gladstone *Majority's Analysis Above, which Seems to Require Prearrangement for Aiding and Abetting.* The *Gladstone* case, discussed in Problem 11B, above, held that drawing a map to a drug seller's location was insufficient aiding and abetting because there was no communication between the map drawer and the seller. The *Gladstone* court thus emphasized the issue of prearrangement and economic unity. Neither was proved in *Rivera*, but the court still held that Timotheo could be a party. Are

the facts in *Rivera* different from those in *Gladstone*, or is the law different (probably, the law)?

(2) *Mens Rea: Is Mutual Intention Required?* From all that appears, Timotheo acted in an effort to kill the victim himself and not merely to help Gilbert. Nevertheless, in *Rivera*, where the MPC pattern governs, the court looks to Timotheo's intent to promote a purpose also engaged in by Gilbert even if there was no prearranged plan. In contrast, the *Gladstone* majority focused instead on intention to follow a plan with Kent and decided that the absence of this element left a fatal "gap" in aiding and abetting. Is this difference, in the law of mens rea, the difference between *Gladstone* and *Rivera*?

Notes on the Use of an Innocent Agent and the Intentional Omission to Perform a Legal Duty

(1) *Three Ways to Become a Party to a Crime: The MPC Approach.* The Model Penal Code (in addition to incorporating other statutes that create multiple-party crimes) sets out three different ways to prove vicarious liability (*i.e.* criminal liability for the conduct of someone else). The first is the obvious: an affirmative act, done with intent to solicit or aid another responsible actor, as in *Rivera*, above. This is by far the most frequently applicable provision. An illustration is a person who talks another into shooting a politician or who provides information about the politician's security arrangements in order to facilitate the killing. The MPC would make the person liable for the homicide.

(2) *A Second Pathway: Use of an "Innocent Agent."* The second avenue to liability for another's acts is to use an "innocent or irresponsible" person. MPC § 2.06(2) (a). This could occur if an adult instructs a child, or mentally disabled or intoxicated person, or innocent post office employee, to take a package to a particular address. The package contains a bomb that explodes and kills several people. The actor giving the bomb to be delivered would be responsible for the deaths by the use of an "innocent agent." In essence, the acts of the innocent agent are deemed to be those of the actor who caused them to occur. Note that the innocent or irresponsible person would not likely be guilty of any crime since he or she was unaware of the nature of the criminal act or was not responsible under the criminal law. Thus, the person originating the crime would be criminally responsible, but the one who actually performed the crime would not.

(3) *The Third Pathway: Failure to Perform a Legal Duty.* The third involves a failure to act: not performing a "legal duty," with the intent to promote or facilitate the crime. An illustration would be a police sergeant who is paid to alter a patrol schedule so that a robbery can occur, undetected. Under the MPC, the officer is guilty of the robbery. *See* MPC § 2.06(3)(iii) (failure to make a "proper effort" to perform a "legal duty to prevent" the offense). Would the police officer's potential liability change if she looked the other way solely because she was too frightened to confront the robbers? No, because the cited provision requires a "purpose of promoting or facilitating the offense."

Notes on Defenses to Accomplice Liability

In some jurisdictions, a person is not responsible as an accomplice even though he or she encouraged or aided the commission of a crime, either because the person is a victim of the crime or because he or she renounces the criminal attempt.

(1) *Victims Cannot Be Accomplices to Crimes Committed Against Them.* In rare and sometimes bizarre situations, a victim of a crime may technically qualify as an accomplice to that crime. For example, if an underage person encourages an adult to have sexual relations with her, the adult may be guilty of statutory rape. But statutes in many jurisdictions specifically exempt victims from being accomplices even though all the elements of accomplice liability are satisfied. *See, e.g.,* Mont. Code Ann. §45–2-302. The rationale for this exemption is that the legislature did not intend for the victim to be criminally responsible for his or her own victimization even if she "aided or abetted it."

(2) *Renunciation.* When you studied the law of attempt, you noted that many modern jurisdictions provide a defense to that crime (as well as to conspiracy and solicitation) if the offender has a change of mind, voluntarily abandons the crime, and stops the ultimate crime from occurring. Some jurisdictions extend the renunciation defense to accomplices, providing them with a defense to accomplice liability if they abandon the intended crime and prevent its commission. *See, e.g.,* Wash. Rev. Code § 9A.08.020 (no liability if aider-and-abetter terminates complicity and either gives timely warning to law enforcement authorities or otherwise makes a good faith effort to prevent the commission of the crime by others).

§ 11.03 Post-Crime Liability

Read Model Penal Code §§ 242.3; 242.5 [hindering and compounding] in the MPC Appendix, below.

Notes and Questions

(1) *Accessory After the Fact as Variety of Obstruction of Justice.* The traditional category of *accessory after the fact* was a variety of obstruction of justice and reached those actors who did not participate in the felony but purposely helped the felon escape arrest, punishment, or trial. An accessory after the fact faced a different, ordinarily lesser, sentence than the primary felon.

(a) *Modern Jurisdictions Retain Accessory After Fact, which May Be Called "Hindering."* Modern jurisdictions have maintained this crime, though some change the name. MPC § 242.3 refers to this as the crime of "hindering." Hindering under the

MPC is post-crime liability. Imagine a defendant who (a) allows a relative who is a fugitive to stay in the defendant's residence, (b) refuses to speak to police officers, and later, (c) falsely says, "I haven't seen [the fugitive]."

(b) *What Conduct is Required?* State statutes often characterize the actus reus for this crime as "harboring," "aiding," or "concealing." Obviously, some positive act is needed, such as hiding the defendant, lying to authorities about the defendant's whereabouts, or providing a car to facilitate the escape. A few statutes contain extensive lists of the forbidden acts. *See, e.g.,* Ala. Stat. § 13A-10–42 (hindering; harboring, concealing, warning, etc.).

(c) *What Is the Mens Rea?* State accessory after the fact (or hindering) statutes routinely include two mental elements. First, the accessory must know that the person has committed a crime (sometimes a felony). Second, he or she must render assistance (the actus reus) for the purpose of assisting (the mens rea) the offender avoid apprehension. *See, e.g.,* Cal Pen. Code § 32 (intent to avoid or escape arrest, trial, conviction, or punishment).

(d) *Exceptions: Relatives.* Some legislatures or courts maintain that a close relative, such as a parent or child, should not be liable as an accessory after the fact or hinderer. They reason that imposing criminal liability would be ineffective and routinely ignored. They also contend that the criminal justice system should encourage offenders to confide in their close relatives about past crimes so that the relatives can encourage them to surrender. For example, some jurisdictions exclude from liability the spouse of the person whose apprehension is thwarted. Some statutes extend this exception to broad categories of relatives. *See, e.g.,* R.I. Stat. § 11–1-4 (exempting husband, wife, parent, grandparent, child, grandchild, brother, or sister).

(2) *"Withholding Evidence," "Misprision of Felony," or Nonreporting: Not a General Crime.* TV detectives sometimes get witnesses to talk by threatening them with the "crime" of withholding evidence, but there is no such general crime. In early England, "misprision of felony," which consisted of deliberate nonreporting of a known felony, was a common law crime. But this crime has been practically obsolete in America for more than a century. Still, there are some object crimes for which nonreporting is made a crime. For example, failure to report child abuse is a crime in many states, at least for people in certain situations (such as teachers, physicians, and social workers). In addition, there are a few statutes which penalize the failure to report a serious felony. *See, e.g.,* Tex. Penal. Code § 38.171 (misdemeanor not to immediately report a known felony involving serious bodily injury or death if the person could do so without placing herself in danger).

(3) *"Compounding": Receiving the Fruits of Crime.* Compounding under MPC § 242.5 and similar state provisions is a separate offense that consists of accepting pecuniary benefits in exchange for not reporting crime information. Some states extend this to concealing the crime, not prosecuting for it, or not giving evidence about it. Consider a defendant who is charged with compounding after telling

another person, "I won't squeal on you to the police if you use the proceeds from that robbery you committed to pay that promissory note you owe me."

(a) *Reasonable Compensation Exception.* The MPC and some states recognize that the crime of compounding should not be extended to cover legitimate demands for restitution in exchange for a promise not to pursue criminal charges. For example, what if a bookkeeper is caught after embezzling $150 from an employer? The employer agrees that if the $150 is repaid and the employer leaves the job, the employer will not report the incident to the police. Viewing this as serving the public purpose of encouraging reasonable non-judicial resolutions, MPC § 242.5 provides a defense to compounding if the benefit exchanged for nonreporting is reasonable restitution for the crime. Had the employer demanded $15,000 to not report the $150 embezzlement, the restitution exception would not apply, and the employer could be liable for compounding.

(b) *Minor Crimes Exception.* Some jurisdictions extend the crime of compounding only to more serious crimes. *See, e.g.,* Fla. Stat. § 843.14 (any crime punishable by death or incarceration in prison).

§ 11.04 Corporate or Organizational Liability

Read Model Penal Code §§ 2.07(1)(c); (5) [reckless toleration; diligence] in the MPC Appendix, below.

Notes and Questions

(1) *Why Make Organizations Criminally Responsible?* The common law regarded an organization such as a corporation as a nonentity for purposes of the criminal law. A corporation could not commit a crime. Organizational liability is relatively recent. Arguably, holding the entity liable is unnecessary since it acts through individuals who can be held criminally liable.

The counterargument supporting corporate liability, however, includes the idea that if the crime is divided into small parts among numerous individuals, their responsibility may be diluted in a way that depreciates its seriousness, or there may be no one individual who has committed enough parts of the crime to be convicted. Furthermore, crime committed for the benefit of the corporation should be punished as such, both as a matter of justice and of deterrence. The entity, which may have made money from the illegal actions of its employees, may be held liable to pay a substantial fine, one that is beyond the resources of any individual. The possibility of a large fine may also make owners, such as stockholders, more likely to insist on internal controls. Finally, corporate liability may discourage an organization that might otherwise prey upon employees who might be persuaded by entity culture to commit crimes.

(2) *Matching the Liability to Organizational Responsibility: "Reckless Toleration."* These considerations only apply, however, to crimes for which the organization is somehow responsible. Imagine, for example, that a janitor angrily assaults a patron who litters the floor. The civil law may hold the organization responsible in damages, but we may be reluctant to hold the organization criminally liable for an isolated crime committed by a low-ranking employee.

But our attitude might change if a department manager tells janitors to "do whatever you have to do to stop littering, including physically confronting customers." Consider the effect of the MPC, which requires "reckless toleration" by a high managerial agent.

(3) *What Sentence for a Guilty Corporation?* If a corporation is found guilty of committing a crime, what sentence is appropriate? The most frequent sanction is a fine, sometimes quite large. Another possibility is to put the corporation on probation, subject to conditions that can include community service. Corporations may also be required to pay restitution. Sometimes these sentences are found improper if the payments are unrelated to the offense. *See, e.g., United States v. Blue Mountain Bottling Co. of Walla Walla*, 929 F.2d 526 (9th Cir. 1991) (district court lacked authority to order a corporation convicted of soft drink price fixing to make payment to local substance abuse programs).

Problem 11D (Corporate Liability): Defensive Strategies Involving Diligence— Will the "Director of Environmental Compliance" Become a "Throwdown Prisoner"?

(1) *Defenses to Corporate Liability.* Diligent efforts to avoid corporate crime furnish a defense in some States. Thus, MPC § 2.07(5), cited above, creates a "due diligence" defense. Sometimes, so do laws that allow deflection of responsibility onto designated individuals.

(2) *Is This Promotion Really Just an Invitation to Become a "Throwdown Prisoner," So That Your Corporation Can Have a Defense?* Consider the due diligence defense in light of MPC § 207(6), cited below. Imagine that the president of the corporation by which you are employed comes to you and says, "Congratulations! The Board of Directors has voted to create a new position called 'Director of Environmental Compliance' and to name you to that post." The corporation's action may be commendable, and you may get a large salary increase. In light of this statute, however, is there any concern of which you should be wary?

Read Model Penal Code § 2.07(6) [individuals; designated officer liability] in the MPC Appendix below.

§ 11.05 The RICO Statute: Liability for "Racketeer-Influenced, Corrupt Organizations"

[A] The Elements of RICO

Notes on "Enterprises" and "Patterns" Under Rico

(1) *The RICO Statute.* In 1970, Congress passed the "Racketeer-Influenced, Corrupt Organizations" ("RICO") statute, reproduced in part below, as a response to organized crime, which used illicit organizations of its own creation and also manipulated ostensibly legal organizations that it either created or influenced. After several years of neglect, prosecutors and civil litigants realized the potential uses of RICO—although its later applications produced urgent demands for greater limits on it. The Act creates liability for a "person" who engages in a "pattern of racketeering activity" in connection with the activities of an "enterprise."

(2) *The Breadth of the RICO Statute: "Enterprises" and "Patterns of Racketeering Activity."* The phrase, "pattern of racketeering activity," includes any "pattern" of "at least two" predicate crimes within ten years. The predicate crimes range from murder to gambling to mail fraud. An "enterprise" includes not only any business entity but any (informal) "group of individuals." RICO provides criminal penalties, but it does not stop there; it also allows for civil suits, which sometimes permit triple damages. And RICO provides for forfeiture of any property or interest "acquired or maintained in violation."

(3) *Broad, Vague, and Powerful: RICO as the "Tyrannosaurus Rex" of the Law.* It is ironic that prosecutors did not see the potential of RICO at first. RICO is like our conception today of Tyrannosaurus Rex: broad, vague, and powerful. This is what its drafters intended: a flexible but devastating weapon against organized crime. The trouble is, this objective is expressed in language that is hard to contain, and only a fraction of its attempted uses involve what we usually think of as organized crime. A "pattern" of crimes—what does that mean? A Fortune 500 company could have a division somewhere that produces repeated illegal acts in a way unknown to management. Is this a "pattern"? If so, it probably is a pattern "of racketeering" even though the company is legitimate, because that phrase is defined broadly.

Since the Act creates civil liability as well as criminal, and since it provides for treble damages, it sometimes can be used in garden-variety litigation about over-billing or breaches of warranty. The forfeiture provision, alone, is an extensive remedy that can reach buildings, homes, vehicles, aircraft, and of course, large amounts of money. The breadth of RICO carries out the legislative intent, but the challenge is, can it be limited to what was intended?

18 U.S.C. § 1961–62 (Racketeer-Influenced, Corrupt Organizations)

§ 1961. Definitions. As used in this chapter—

(1) "racketeering activity" means

(A) any act or threat involving murder, kidnapping, gambling, arson, robbery, bribery, extortion, dealing in obscene matter, or dealing in a controlled substance or listed chemical . . . , which is chargeable under State law and punishable by imprisonment for more than one year;

(B) any act which is indictable under any of the following provisions of title 18, United States Code: Section 201 (bribery), section 224 (sports bribery), sections 471, 472, and 473 (counterfeiting), section 659 (theft from interstate shipment) if the act indictable under section 659 is felonious, section 664 (embezzlement from pension and welfare funds) . . . . [Here, the Act includes many other kinds of gambling, obstruction, property, administrative, and personal crimes that can be "racketeering activity," including mail fraud.]

(2) "person" includes any individual or entity capable of holding a legal or beneficial interest in property;

(3) "enterprise" includes any individual, partnership, corporation, association, or other legal entity, and any union or group of individuals associated in fact although not a legal entity;

(4) "pattern of racketeering activity" requires at least two acts of racketeering activity, one of which occurred after the effective date of this chapter and the last of which occurred within ten years (excluding any period of imprisonment) after the commission of a prior act of racketeering activity . . . .

§ 1962. Prohibited activities.

(a) It shall be unlawful for any person who has received any income derived, directly or indirectly, from a pattern of racketeering activity or through collection of an unlawful debt in which such person has participated as a principal . . . to use or invest, directly or indirectly, any part of such income, or the proceeds of such income, in acquisition of any interest in, or the establishment or operation of, any enterprise which is engaged in, or the activities of which affect, interstate or foreign commerce. . . .

(b) It shall be unlawful for any person through a pattern of racketeering activity or through collection of an unlawful debt to acquire or maintain, directly or indirectly, any interest in or control of any enterprise which is engaged in, or the activities of which affect, interstate or foreign commerce.

(c) It shall be unlawful for any person employed by or associated with any enterprise engaged in, or the activities of which affect, interstate or foreign commerce, to conduct or participate, directly or indirectly, in the conduct of such enterprise's affairs through a pattern of racketeering activity or collection of unlawful debt.

(d) It shall be unlawful for any person to conspire to violate any of the provisions of subsection (a), (b), or (c) of this section.

[Other sections of the Act allow severe criminal penalties and forfeitures. Furthermore, the Act creates a private civil remedy that can be the basis of suit by any person "injured" by a "pattern of racketeering activity." Such suits have proliferated because of special damage provisions. In some instances, suits based upon what appeared to be ordinary traffic accidents have included RICO claims that alleged interstate patterns of recordkeeping, maintenance, or the like, which were said to violate federal laws that triggered RICO.]

Sedima, S.P.R.L. v. Imrex Company, Inc.

473 U.S. 479 (1985)

JUSTICE WHITE delivered the opinion of the Court.

The Racketeer Influenced and Corrupt Organizations Act (RICO), 18 U.S.C. §§ 1961–1968, provides a private civil action to recover treble damages for injury "by reason of a violation of" its substantive provisions. 18 U.S.C. § 1964(c). The initial dormancy of this provision and its recent greatly increased utilization are now familiar history. In response to what it perceived to be misuse of civil RICO by private plaintiffs, the court below construed [RICO] to permit private actions only against defendants who had been convicted on criminal charges, and only where there had occurred a "racketeering injury." While we understand the court's concern over the consequences of an unbridled reading of the statute, we reject both of its holdings.

I

RICO takes aim at "racketeering activity," which it defines as any act "chargeable" under several generically described state criminal laws, any act "indictable" under numerous specific federal criminal provisions, including mail and wire fraud, and any "offense" involving bankruptcy or securities fraud or drug-related activities that is "punishable" under federal law. § 1961(1). Section 1962, entitled "Prohibited Activities," outlaws the use of income derived from a "pattern of racketeering activity" to acquire an interest in or establish an enterprise engaged in or affecting interstate commerce; the acquisition or maintenance of any interest in an enterprise "through" a pattern of racketeering activity; conducting or participating in the conduct of an enterprise through a pattern of racketeering activity; and conspiring to violate any of these provisions.

Congress provided criminal penalties of imprisonment, fines, and forfeiture for violation of these provisions. § 1963. In addition, it set out a far-reaching civil enforcement scheme, § 1964, including the following provision for private suits: "Any person injured in his business or property by reason of a violation . . . may sue therefor . . . and shall recover threefold the damages he sustains and the cost of the suit, including a reasonable attorney's fee." . . .

. . . [P]etitioner Sedima, a Belgian corporation, entered into a joint venture with respondent Imrex Co. to provide electronic components to a Belgian firm. . . . The agreement called for Sedima and Imrex to split the net proceeds. Imrex filled roughly $8 million in orders placed with it through Sedima. Sedima became convinced, however, that Imrex was presenting inflated bills, cheating Sedima out of a portion of its proceeds by collecting for nonexistent expenses.

. . . Sedima [therefore] filed this action. . . . The complaint set out common law claims of unjust enrichment, conversion, and breach of contract, fiduciary duty, and a constructive trust. In addition, it asserted RICO claims under § 1964(c) against Imrex and two of its officers. Two counts alleged violations of § 1962(c), based on predicate acts of mail and wire fraud. A third count alleged a conspiracy to violate § 1962(c). Claiming injury of at least $175,000, the amount of the alleged overbilling, Sedima sought treble damages and attorney's fees. . . .

[The District Court] dismissed the RICO counts for failure to state a claim. . . . A divided panel of the Court of Appeals for the Second Circuit affirmed. . . . [I]t held that Sedima's complaint was defective in two ways. First, it failed to allege [a "racketeering"] injury "by reason of a violation of section 1962." In the court's view, this language [reflected] Congress' intent to compensate victims of "certain specific kinds of organized criminality," not to provide additional remedies for already compensable injuries. Analogizing to the Clayton Act, which had been the model for § 1964(c), the court concluded that just as an antitrust plaintiff must allege an "antitrust injury," so a RICO plaintiff must allege a "racketeering injury"—an injury "different in kind from that occurring as a result of the predicate acts themselves, or not simply caused by the predicate acts, but also caused by an activity which RICO was designed to deter." Sedima had failed to allege such an injury.

The Court of Appeals also found the complaint defective for not alleging that the defendants had already been criminally convicted of the predicate acts of mail and wire fraud, or of a RICO violation. This element of the civil cause of action was inferred from § 1964(c)'s reference to a "violation" of § 1962, the court also observing that its prior-conviction requirement would avoid serious constitutional difficulties, the danger of unfair stigmatization, and problems regarding the standard by which the predicate acts were to be proved. . . .

III

The language of RICO gives no obvious indication that a civil action can proceed only after a criminal conviction. The word "conviction" does not appear in any relevant portion of the statute. To the contrary, the predicate acts involve conduct that is "chargeable" or "indictable,' and "offense[s]" that are "punishable," under various criminal statutes. . . . Indeed, if either § 1961 or § 1962 did contain such a requirement, a prior conviction would also be a prerequisite, nonsensically, for a criminal prosecution. . . .

The legislative history also undercuts the reading of the court below. . . . The only specific reference in the legislative history to prior convictions of which we are aware is an objection that the treble-damages provision is too broad precisely because "there need *not* be a conviction under any of these laws for it to be racketeering.". . . .

Finally, we note that a prior-conviction requirement would be inconsistent with Congress' underlying policy concerns. Such a rule would severely handicap potential plaintiffs. A guilty party may escape conviction for any number of reasons — not least among them the possibility that the Government itself may choose to pursue only civil remedies. Private attorney general provisions such as § 1964(c) are in part designed to fill prosecutorial gaps. . . . [A]ccordingly, the fact that Imrex and the individual defendants have not been convicted under RICO or the federal mail and wire fraud statutes does not bar Sedima's action.

IV

In considering the Court of Appeals' second prerequisite for a private civil RICO action — "injury . . . caused by an activity which RICO was designed to deter" — we are somewhat hampered by the vagueness of that concept. . . . [But] [w]e need not pinpoint the Second Circuit's precise holding, for we perceive no distinct "racketeering injury" requirement. . . . A reading of the statute belies any such requirement. Section 1964(c) authorizes a private suit by "[a]ny person injured in his business or property by reason of a violation of § 1962." Section 1962 in turn makes it unlawful for "any person" — not just mobsters — to use money derived from a pattern of racketeering activity to [commit the predicate acts]. . . .

A violation of § 1962(c), the section on which Sedima relies, requires (1) conduct (2) of an enterprise (3) through a pattern[14] (4) of racketeering activity.. . . . [T]he statute requires no more than this. . . .

Underlying the Court of Appeals' holding was its distress at the "extraordinary, if not outrageous," uses to which civil RICO has been put. Instead of being used against mobsters and organized criminals, it has become a tool for everyday fraud cases brought against "respected and legitimate enterprises." . . . It is true that private civil actions under the statute are being brought almost solely against such defendants, rather than against the archetypal, intimidating mobster. Yet this

---

14. [The Court explores the meaning of a "pattern of racketeering activity" in this footnote. It suggests that "continuity plus relationship" may be the test.] As the Senate Report explained: "The target of [RICO] is thus not sporadic activity. The infiltration of legitimate business normally requires more than one 'racketeering activity' and the threat of continuing activity to be effective. It is this factor of *continuity plus relationship* which combines to produce a pattern." . . . Significantly, in defining "pattern" in a later provision of the same bill, Congress was more enlightening: "[C]riminal conduct forms a pattern if it embraces criminal acts that have the same or similar purposes, results, participants, victims, or methods of commission, or otherwise are interrelated by distinguishing characteristics and are not isolated events." This language may be useful in interpreting other sections of the Act.

defect — if defect it is — is inherent in the statute as written, and its correction must lie with Congress. . . .

V

Sedima may maintain this action if the defendants conducted the enterprise through a pattern of racketeering activity. . . . The judgment below is accordingly reversed, and the case is remanded for further proceedings consistent with this opinion.

JUSTICE POWELL, dissenting. . . .

The language of this complex statute is susceptible of being read consistently with [Congress's] intent. For example, the requirement in the statute of proof of a "pattern" of racketeering activity may be interpreted narrowly. Section 1961(5), defining "pattern of racketeering activity," states that such a pattern "requires at least two acts of racketeering activity." . . . The definition of "pattern" may thus logically be interpreted as meaning that the presence of the predicate acts is only the beginning: something more is required for a "pattern" to be proved. . . .

The legislative history bears out this interpretation of "pattern." Senator McClellan, a leading sponsor of the bill, stated that "proof of two acts of racketeering activity, without more, does not establish a pattern." Likewise, the Senate Report considered the "concept of 'pattern' [to be] essential to the operation of the statute." It stated that the bill was not aimed at sporadic activity, but that the "infiltration of legitimate business normally requires more than one 'racketeering activity' *and* the threat of continuing activity to be effective. It is this factor of continuity *plus* relationship which combines to produce a pattern." . . .

. . . Only a small fraction of the scores of civil RICO cases now being brought implicate organized crime in any way. Typically, these suits are being brought . . . against legitimate businesses seeking treble damages in ordinary fraud and contract cases. There is nothing comparable in those cases to the restraint . . . exercised by Government prosecutorial discretion. [I]t defies rational belief . . . that Congress intended this far-reaching result. Accordingly, I dissent.

Notes and Questions

(1) *Could Sedima and Its Responsible Officers Be Held Criminally Liable under RICO?* Imagine, for the moment, a case in which allegations such as those in Imrex's complaint are true and can be proved beyond a reasonable doubt. Can the defendants (the corporate defendant as well as responsible individuals) be found criminally guilty under RICO (which provides enhanced penalties) as well as for those predicate acts of mail and wire fraud which constitute "racketeering activity" under RICO?

(2) *What Is a "Pattern" of Racketeering Activity? The "Continuity Plus Relationship" Dictum in Footnote 14 of* Sedima. Although the RICO statute requires "at least two" predicate crimes, it seems clear that commission of only two covered crimes that are unrelated (*e.g.*, gambling and obscenity) is not what was contemplated,

because a "pattern" is required. In its often-quoted footnote 14, the *Sedima* court suggested that "continuity plus relationship" was an appropriate test. The predicate acts must be continuing and related. But this idea just defines the word "pattern," without suggesting any functional limit. What, then, is enough? Do the predicate crimes need to be close together in time? Or is it enough for them to exhibit a common scheme? The cases do not provide a definitive answer. Perhaps a "pattern" just means whatever the ordinary mind would characterize as a pattern, one that a jury reasonably can recognize as such.

(3) *What Is an Enterprise? United States v. Turkette*, 452 U.S. 576 (1981). In some instances, the statute converts what look like garden-variety conspiracies into RICO violations. Turkette and 12 others were charged in a nine-count indictment with participating in an enterprise that consisted of "a group of individuals associated in fact for the purpose of trafficking in narcotics and other dangerous drugs, committing arsons, using the United States mails to defraud insurance companies, bribing and attempting to bribe local police officers, and attempting to corruptly influence the outcome of state court proceedings. . . ." The other eight counts charged the predicate offenses as substantive crimes. "The common thread to all these crimes was [Turkette's] alleged leadership of this alleged organization. . . ."

The defendants argued that the RICO statute contemplated a "legitimate" enterprise, one separately established for some non-criminal purpose, as opposed to an ad hoc "group" of criminals. The Court of Appeals agreed and reversed the convictions. The Supreme Court disagreed and, emphasizing the broadly remedial purpose of RICO, reinstated the convictions: "Neither the language nor structure of RICO limits its application to legitimate 'enterprises.' . . . On the contrary, insulating the wholly criminal enterprise from prosecution under RICO is the more incongruous position." *See also National Organization of Women v. Scheidler*, 510 U.S. 249 (1994) (group that committed crimes to impede abortion clinic access was a RICO "enterprise").

(4) *Does RICO Reach Out Internationally?* The answer is, yes, sometimes it does. RICO can create liability from events overseas, as the next case shows. It also shows that sovereign European countries that have their own laws to prevent illegal activities are attracted to the use of this powerful statute.

RJR NABISCO v. EUROPEAN COMMUNITY, 136 S. Ct. 2090 (2016). This civil case again shows the breadth of RICO. The plaintiffs were the European Community and 26 of its member countries. They filed suit under RICO, alleging that defendants, RJR Nabisco and related entities, participated in a global money-laundering scheme in association with various organized crime groups. Allegedly, drug traffickers smuggled narcotics into Europe and sold them for euros that—through transactions involving black-market money brokers, cigarette importers, and wholesalers—were used to pay for large shipments of RJR cigarettes into Europe. The complaint alleged that RJR violated RICO by numerous predicate acts of money laundering, material support to foreign terrorist organizations, mail fraud, wire fraud, and other violations.

The District Court granted RJ's motion to dismiss on the ground that RICO did not apply outside U.S. territory or to foreign enterprises. The Second Circuit reinstated the claims, concluding that RICO applies extraterritorially to the same extent as the predicate acts of racketeering, and that certain predicates in this case expressly apply extraterritorially. The court held further that RICO's civil action does not require a domestic injury, but permits recovery for a foreign injury. The Supreme Court, per Justice Alito, here affirmed in part, reversed in part, and remanded:

> RICO defines racketeering activity to include a number of predicates that plainly apply to at least some foreign conduct. These predicates include the prohibition against engaging in monetary transactions in criminally derived property, which expressly applies, when "the defendant is a United States person," to offenses that "tak[e] place outside the United States." 18 U.S.C. § 1957(d)(2). Other examples include the prohibitions against the assassination of Government officials, § 351(i) . . . and the prohibition against hostage taking, which applies to conduct that "occurred outside the United States" if either the hostage or the offender is a U.S. national, if the offender is found in the United States, or if the hostage taking is done to compel action by the U.S. Government, § 1203(b). At least one predicate — the prohibition against "kill[ing] a national of the United States, while such national is outside the United States" — applies *only* to conduct occurring outside the United States. § 2332(a). . . .

> Congress's incorporation of these (and other) extraterritorial predicates into RICO gives a clear, affirmative indication that § 1962 applies to foreign racketeering activity — but only to the extent that the predicates alleged in a particular case themselves apply extraterritorially. . . .

Some of the statutes defining predicate acts alleged by the European Community did apply extraterritorially, and the Court upheld the RICO claims as to those, but the Court reversed as to those statutes that did not by their terms apply extraterritorially. Justices Ginsburg, Breyer, and Kagan dissented in part.

[B] Forfeiture under RICO

Notes on RICO Forfeiture as a Punitive Sanction

(1) *Forfeiture Usually Is Characterized as a Civil Remedy, but under RICO, It Is Punitive and Is Part of the Criminal Sentence.* RICO forfeiture is a criminal sanction, according to the cases. As the cases below demonstrate, it reaches farther than merely disgorging profits or instrumentalities. RICO forfeiture must be proved to a jury under criminal procedures.

(2) *An Example of the Breadth and Power of RICO Forfeiture: United States v. DeFries*, 129 F.3d 1293 (D.C. Cir. 1997). DeFries and others were charged with RICO

violations involving union election tampering, corruption, and exercising control of the union for their personal benefit. The court of appeals held that "but for the elections, [which were] tainted by appellants' racketeering activities, they would not have received their [official positions and] their salaries." Therefore, RICO authorized forfeiture of their jobs, their salaries, and their severance pay. The defendants argued that this salary forfeiture should be reduced by the amount of taxes that they had paid on their salaries, because that amount had been "already forfeited." The court rejected this argument, however, and ordered forfeiture of the defendants' entire pre-tax salaries, because "the punitive purpose of the forfeiture provision should not be subverted by a rule that could obscure the purpose with technical tax calculations." Also, consider the following case, which orders the forfeiture of an ostensibly "nonforfeitable" pension annuity.

UNITED STATES v. INFELISE, 159 F.3d 300 (7th Cir. 1998). Until he was convicted of racketeering and sentenced to 63 years in prison, Rocco Infelise was the boss of the "Ferriola Street Crew." Its business included collecting protection money from bookmakers, houses of prostitution, and pornographic bookstores; illegal gambling; and "making juice loans." It also included bribery and murder. The jury, which convicted Infelise of RICO and other violations, also entered a verdict of forfeiture of his interest in his primary residence in River Forest, Illinois, and $3 million from his racketeering activity. The government sought to collect the $3 million through the substitute assets provision found at 18 U.S.C. § 1963(m) and appealed from an order of the district court refusing to forfeit Infelise's "nonforfeitable" annuity.

Section 1963(a) provides for the forfeiture of, among other things, any interest the defendant has in property acquired through racketeering activity or with the proceeds. Section 1963(m), the substitute assets provision, allows the government to take other property of the defendant when the illegally obtained property cannot be located. The government here sought to forfeit Infelise's annuity under this provision. The annuity was governed by the provisions of 26 U.S.C. § 408(b), which Infelise argued immunize it from criminal forfeiture. That section provides that "[t]he entire interest of the owner is nonforfeitable." But the court held that Infelise's argument was "too literal" and ordered Infelise's annuity forfeited anyway:

> We consider not only the bare meaning of the word ["nonforfeitable"] but also its placement and purpose in the statutory scheme. . . . [The statute] was enacted as part of the Employee Retirement Income Security Act ["ERISA"]. . . . The purpose of the statute was to protect the interests of beneficiaries of pension plans. . . . The termination of plans [by employers] was found to deprive employees of anticipated benefits. . . .
>
> . . . Notably, the definition specifically states that the benefit is nonforfeitable "against the plan."

... [T]he word "nonforfeitable" as used in [ERISA] refers to a requirement that an individual retirement annuity must be vested in the owner. That means that ... Infelise's annuity is vested. But [ERISA] says nothing at all about whether the government, as part of a criminal proceeding, can obtain forfeiture of the account owned by a defendant, especially as the provisions of [RICO forfeiture] are to be liberally construed. [Forfeiture ordered.]

§ 11.06 Review Problems Based on Newspaper Reports

Note on These "Newspaper Cases"

The following cases all were covered in recent newspaper stories that involved issues related to preparatory crimes and complicity. The descriptions contained here reflect the actual facts and evidence, but they have been rewritten to clarify and emphasize the legal issues. As in other chapters, these reports should enable you to review the major concepts covered here (in this instance, for the last two chapters).

[A] Headline: Air Passenger Attacked Cockpit; Wanted to "Destroy Everything": Attempt?

MIAMI—Pablo Moriera Mosca, 29, kicked in an airline cockpit door and tried to wrestle his way through until crew members stopped him with the blunt end of an axe. Later, after being taken into custody, Moriera said that he had "wanted to destroy everything."

Moriera, a bank employee from Uruguay, had boarded a United Airlines flight bound for Buenos Aires with 179 passengers. A few hours into the trip, passengers said, he began shouting that he wanted to talk to the pilot, and he ran to the front of the aircraft. Officials said that he did not appear to be intoxicated, was not armed, and did not seem to be a terrorist. Upon the arrival of the aircraft in Argentina, officials investigated whether he was mentally impaired or using drugs. "His brother said he often becomes upset when there is turbulence, and passengers told us he had been drinking a lot on the plane," said Argentine Air Force Officer Jorge Reta. But "he told me he had one whiskey." Moriera was returned to Miami yesterday, where U.S. Attorney Guy Lewis, when asked whether Moriera was mentally unhinged, said, "I'm comfortable with his medical condition."

United had reinforced its cockpit after the Sept. 11, 2001 attacks on the World Trade Center. Airline officials said that these reinforced doors were the reason that Moriera was unable to gain access to the cockpit. Only two months earlier, in an unrelated incident, British Subject Richard Reid, an alleged Al Qaeda-trained terrorist, had lit a match on board a trans-Atlantic flight and tried to use it to trigger a bomb hidden in his shoes, but he was prevented from doing so by passengers.

Attempted Murder: Are the Actus Reus ("More than Mere Preparation") and Mens Rea Provable? Obviously, Moriera did not actually succeed in entering the cockpit and was firmly prevented from his expressed goal of "destroy[ing] everything." Assume that Moriera is charged with attempted murder. Did he commit the actus reus for attempt? Consider whether he committed an act amounting to more than mere preparation under the "substantial step" test, the "physical proximity" test, or the "probable desistance" test. Also, consider whether Moriera's mental state, as affected by his evident panic, possible intoxication, and expressed desire to "talk to the pilot," was sufficient to amount to specific intent to commit murder.

[B] Headline: Three Students Arrested in Plot to "Kill as Many as Possible": Conspiracy?

NEW BEDFORD, Mass.—Three high school students planned to imitate the Columbine massacre by "killing as many as possible" of their classmates. But a janitor found a letter explaining the plan, which was reminiscent of the mass killings carried out by two students at Columbine High School in Colorado several years ago. After a month long investigation, police arrested the three students, one adult and two juveniles, at their homes yesterday.

Officers executing a search warrant at the boys' homes found shotgun shells, knives, a flare gun, pictures depicting violence, and a loose-leaf binder with instructions on making bombs. The letter detailed plans to set off explosions at the school on an upcoming Monday, then to shoot people as they fled from the building. After that, the three had agreed to kill themselves.

Conspiracy to Commit Murder? Consider whether the elements of conspiracy to commit murder are provable against these arrested subjects. Are the elements of plurality, agreement, intent to agree, intent to promote, and overt act all present? (Also, consider whether this episode shows why conspiracy should be a crime, even if it is prevented far short of its goal.)

[C] Headline: Protesters Demand Cardinal's Resignation for Enabling Child-Molesting Priest: Complicity? Conspiracy? Entity Liability? RICO?

BOSTON—Protesters carried signs and sang hymns yesterday outside the home of Cardinal Bernard Law, who is accused of repeatedly transferring a pedophile priest to unsuspecting new parishes after knowing that the priest had molested children at each location.

One protester, Steven Lynch, 42, said he had been molested by a priest when he was 9. "A father does not trick or deceive his sons and daughters," Lynch told the crowd, with tears running down his face. "A father does not fill his children with shame, fear, guilt or darkness." Other demonstrators carried signs that said, "Law Breaks Law—Resign" and "Jesus Wept."

Law has admitted that he knew of the offenses committed by Father John Gehogan, 66, when he transferred the now-defrocked priest over and over again, always without advising the new congregation. More than 130 adults have accused Gehogan of molesting them as children. The now-defrocked priest has been convicted of the sexual abuse of a ten-year-old boy and awaits sentencing. He also faces other criminal trials and more than 80 civil suits, which also include the Church Diocese as a defendant. The Diocese already has settled a number of suits for more than $10 million.

Father Gehogan was assigned to six different churches over a 30-year period. Church documents produced in the civil lawsuits showed that church officials became aware that Gehogan was a pedophile soon after he was ordained in 1962.

They continued to settle lawsuits quietly and to transfer Gehogan in spite of frequent complaints and in spite of periods in which Gehogan obtained treatment in mental health facilities.

(1) *Aiding and Abetting (or Soliciting, Aiding, or Attempting to Aid).* Is it possible that a prosecutor might conclude that Cardinal Law or others, under these facts, could be charged with aiding and abetting Gehogan's completed crimes of sexual abuse (or with soliciting, aiding, or attempting to aid those crimes under a statute based on the Model Penal Code)? Notice that the federal aiding-and-abetting requirements include both knowledge and facilitation, and the MPC requires "intent to promote or facilitate."

(2) Pinkerton *Liability: Is There Any Argument for Imposing It on Cardinal Law? Pinkerton* liability requires a conspiracy. Is it possible that a prosecutor could conceive of theories by which this kind of vicarious liability could be asserted against Cardinal Law or others? Remember that the agreement element can be inferred from consciously parallel conduct and does not require an express agreement. Furthermore, some cases indicate that the intent to participate, although it requires more than knowledge, can be inferred from a lengthy course of dealings, especially if the crime is a "serious" one. If a conspiracy can possibly be inferred, it would appear that the "reasonable foreseeability," in-furtherance, and duration requirements would be met. Can you explain?

(3) *Corporate or Enterprise Liability.* Is it possible that a prosecutor might consider the Diocese itself criminally liable for Gehogan's offenses? Remember that for this kind of liability, the entity must be responsible for the crimes (for example, the MPC requires that a high managerial officer has "recklessly tolerated" them).

(4) *Potential RICO Liability.* Is it possible that a federal prosecutor might generate a theory by which Gehogan, Law, and others are liable under RICO, which requires (1) participation in (2) an enterprise through (3) a pattern of (4) predicate crimes defined as racketeering activity? The enterprise would be the Diocese, which might seem unlikely to be covered—until one remembers that "legitimate" organizations are potential RICO organizations too.

Chapter 12

Other Crimes: Contraband and Terrorism

"The illicit manufacture of drugs is not a sporadic, isolated criminal incident, but a continuing, though illegal, business enterprise. [Nevertheless,] . . . the gathering of evidence . . . frequently proves to be an all but impossible task."—Justice William H. Rehnquist, in *United States v. Russell*, 411 U.S. 423 (1973).

"Does the reversal by the majority amount to a holding that, where one is in possession of [a residence] and contraband is found therein and other people are present, no one may be found to be responsible for its possession?"—*Williams v. State*, 498 S.W.2d 340 (Tex. Crim. App. 1973) (Douglas, J., dissenting).

§ 12.01 Statutes Covering Controlled Substances

Notes on Controlled Substances Crimes

(1) *Kinds of Drug Offenses: Possession, Intent to Distribute, Delivery, Manufacturing, Etc.* Controlled substances statutes typically criminalize wide ranges of unauthorized dealing with illicit drugs, of ascending seriousness, from possession, through possession with intent to distribute, delivery, distribution, and manufacturing. They usually also create crimes involving "precursors" needed for manufacture. Furthermore, there may be situationally defined offenses (delivery to a minor, for example), as well as attempt, solicitation, and conspiracy offenses (because a general preparatory crimes statute may not fit well with possession or distribution crimes). And there will be a registration system for lawful dispensation.

(2) *The Structure of a Typical Controlled Substances Act.* Typical controlled substances statutes begin with detailed definitions sections that specify what is meant by such terms as "deliver" or "manufacture." (Is a noncommercial gift covered? What about growing or harvesting?) Next, there will be "schedules" of controlled substances grouped according to differing abuse potentials, coverage of yet-unknown "analogue" drugs, and provisions for adding new substances quickly to these schedules. Finally, crimes, penalties, forfeiture, and enforcement powers will be defined, in a way that is related to the schedules.

(3) *Penalty Regimes in Controlled Substances Statutes.* Typically, controlled substances statutes impose increasing penalties for more serious conduct (illegal

distribution attracts a higher penalty than simple possession). But they also provide higher penalties for more "dangerous" drugs (those in "Schedule I," the high-abuse substances) and for larger amounts of drugs.

(4) *The Uniform Controlled Substances Act; State and Federal Regimes of Regulation.* Both the federal government and the States regulate controlled substances, the former in 21 U.S.C. §§ 801–971. Many state statutes are based on the Uniform Controlled Substances Act, promulgated by the National Conference of Commissioners on Uniform State Laws in 1994 and designed to promote coordination of federal and state regulation. *See, e.g.,* Nev. Rev. Stat. § 453.011 et seq. The Act follows the organization described above. Here are excerpts:

Excerpts from the Uniform Controlled Substances Act
National Conference of Commissioners on Uniform State Laws (1994)

Article 1: Definitions

Section 101. Definitions.

As used in this [Act]: . . .

(3) . . . "controlled substance analog" means a substance the chemical structure of which is substantially similar to the chemical structure of a controlled substance listed in or added to Schedule I or II. . . .

(4) "deliver," unless the context otherwise requires, means to transfer a substance, actually or constructively, from one person to another. . . .

(7) "distribute" means to deliver . . . a controlled substance [other than by a registrant such as a physician].

(13) "manufacture" means to produce, prepare, propagate, compound, convert, or process a controlled substance, directly or indirectly, by extraction from substances of natural origin, chemical synthesis, or a combination of extraction and chemical synthesis, and includes packaging or repackaging of the substance or labeling or relabeling of its container. . . .

(21) "production," unless the context otherwise requires, includes the manufacturing of a controlled substance and the planting, cultivating, growing, or harvesting of a plant from which a controlled substance is derived.

Article 2: Standards and Schedules

Section 201. Authority to Control.

. . . The [appropriate person or agency] shall administer this [Act] and may add substances to or delete or reschedule substances listed in [schedules]. . . .

Section 204. Schedule I.

Unless specifically excepted by state or federal law or state or federal regulation or more specifically included in another schedule, the following controlled substances are listed in Schedule I. [Note that we have excerpted only a few samples — Eds.]

(1) any of the following synthetic opiates, including any isomers, esters, ethers, salts, and salts of isomers, esters, and ethers of them that are theoretically possible within the specific chemical designation: (i) acetyl-alpha-methylfentanyl (N-[1-(1- methyl-2-phenethyl)-4-piperidinyl]-N-phenylacetamide); (ii) acetylmethadol . . . ;

(2) any of the following opium derivatives, including any salts, isomers, and salts of isomers of them that are theoretically possible within the specific chemical designation: (xi) heroin; . . . (xv) morphine [compounds of specified types] . . . ;

(3) material, compound, mixture, or preparation containing any quantity of the following hallucinogenic substances . . . : (xvii) lysergic acid diethylamide; (xviii) marijuana; (xix) mescaline; . . . (xxi) peyote; . . .

Section 206. Schedule II.

. . . [T]he following controlled substances are listed in Schedule II:

(1) any of the following substances, however manufactured: (i) Opium and opium derivative; . . . including: (A) raw opium; (B) opium extracts; . . . codeine; . . . (iv) Coca leaves and any salt, compound, derivative, or preparation of coca leaves, including cocaine and ecgonine and their . . . derivatives; . . .

(2) any of the following synthetic opiates, . . . (xv) methadone; . . .

(3) material, compound, mixture, or preparation containing any quantity of the following substances, their salts, isomers, or salts of isomers, having a stimulant effect on the central nervous system: (i) amphetamine; (ii) methamphetamine; . . .

(6) material, compound, mixture, or preparation containing any quantity of the following substances: (i) Immediate precursor to amphetamine and methamphetamine: phenylacetone (other names: phenyl-2-propanone; P2P; benzyl methyl ketone; methyl benzyl ketone); (ii) Immediate precursors to phencyclidine (PCP). . . .

Section 208. Schedule III.

(a) . . . the following controlled substances are listed in Schedule III: . . .

(2) a material, compound, mixture, or preparation containing any quantity of the following substances having a depressant effect on the central nervous system: . . . (C) pentobarbital; . . .

(4) a material, compound, mixture, or preparation containing . . . (i) not more than 1.8 grams of codeine per 100 milliliters or not more than 90 milligrams per dosage unit, with an equal or greater quantity of an isoquinoline alkaloid of opium; . . .

Section 210. Schedule IV.

. . . [T]he following controlled substances are listed in Schedule IV: . . . (xiv) diazepam; . . .

Section 212. Schedule V.

. . . [T]he following controlled substances are listed in Schedule V: . . . (2) a compound, mixture, or preparation containing any of the following . . . (i) not more than 200 milligrams of codeine per 100 milliliters or per 100 grams; . . .

Section 214. Controlled Substance Analog Treated as Schedule I Substance.

A controlled substance analog, to the extent intended for human consumption, must be treated, for the purposes of this [Act], as a substance included in Schedule I. Within [] days after the initiation of prosecution with respect to a controlled substance analog by indictment or information, the [prosecuting attorney] shall notify the [appropriate person or agency] of information relevant to emergency scheduling as provided for in Section 201(g). After final determination that the controlled substance analog should not be scheduled, no prosecution relating to that substance as a controlled substance analog may be commenced or continued.

Article 3: Regulation of Manufacture, Distribution, and Dispensing of Controlled Substances

Section 302. Registration Requirements.

(a) A person who . . . proposes to engage in the manufacture, distribution, or dispensing of a controlled substance within this State, shall obtain annually a registration issued by the [appropriate person or agency]. . . .

(b) A person registered . . . may possess, manufacture, distribute, dispense, or conduct research with those substances to the extent authorized by the registration and in conformity with this [article].

Section 308. Prescriptions. . . .

(c) Except when dispensed directly by a practitioner, other than a pharmacy, to an ultimate user, a substance included in Schedule II may not be dispensed without the written prescription of a practitioner. . . .

Article 4: Offenses and Penalties

Section 401. Prohibited Acts A; Penalties.

(a) Except as authorized by this [Act], a person may not knowingly or intentionally manufacture, distribute, or deliver a controlled substance, or possess a controlled substance with intent to manufacture, distribute, or deliver, a controlled substance. . . .

(c) A person is guilty of a crime and upon conviction may be imprisoned for not more than [], fined not more than [], or both, for a violation of subsection (a) in the case of a controlled substance included in Schedule I or II. . . .

(d) A person is guilty of a crime and upon conviction may be imprisoned for not more than [], fined not more than [], or both, for a violation of subsection (a) in the case of a controlled substance included in Schedule III.

(e) A person is guilty of a crime and upon conviction may be imprisoned for not more than [], fined not more than [], or both, for a violation of subsection (a) in the case of a controlled substance included in Schedule IV or V.

(f) A person is guilty of a crime and upon conviction may be imprisoned for not more than [], fined not more than [], or both, for a violation of subsection (a) in the case of marijuana. . . .

Section 402. Prohibited Acts B; Penalties.

(a) A person who is subject to [Article] 3 may not distribute or dispense a controlled substance in violation of Section 308.

Section 405. Imitation Controlled Substances Prohibited; Penalty.

(a) A person may not knowingly or intentionally deliver, or possess with intent to deliver, a noncontrolled substance representing it to be a controlled substance. . . .

Section 406. Possession as Prohibited Act; Penalties.

(a) An individual may not knowingly or intentionally possess a controlled substance unless the substance was obtained directly from, or pursuant to, a valid prescription or order of a practitioner while acting in the course of the practitioner's professional practice, or was otherwise authorized by this [Act].

(b) An individual who violates subsection (a) with respect to a substance included in Schedule I or II, except for less than [29] grams of marijuana, is guilty of a [felony] and upon conviction may be imprisoned for not more than [], fined not more than [], or both. (c) An individual who violates subsection (a) with respect to a substance included in Schedule III, IV, or V is guilty of a[felony] [misdemeanor] and upon conviction may be imprisoned for not more than [], fined not more than [], or both. (d) An individual who violates subsection (a) with respect to less than [29] grams of marijuana is guilty of a[misdemeanor] and upon conviction may be imprisoned for not more than [], fined not more than [], or both. . . .

Section 419. Criminal Forfeiture.

(a) In addition to other penalties provided by this [article], a person convicted for conduct that subjects property to forfeiture under Section 503 forfeits property related to the offense forfeitable under [Article] 5.

Notes and Questions

(1) *Registration, Reports, Etc.* Other parts of the Uniform Controlled Substances Act cover registration procedures, record-keeping, and reporting by persons who may legally deal with controlled substances, such as doctors and pharmacists.

(2) *How Do Prosecutors Establish Intent to Distribute in the Absence of Direct Evidence?* Prosecutors typically rely on circumstantial evidence in establishing intent

to distribute. Possession of a large amount of a controlled substance is evidence of intent to distribute. Other factors courts consider in establishing intent to distribute or possession for personal use include the way contraband is packaged and whether it is found in the vicinity of paraphernalia typically used for distribution (*e.g.* weighing machines, baggies) or use (*e.g.* "crack pipes" or "roach clips").

(3) *Forfeiture.* Many jurisdictions provide for forfeiture of broadly defined proceeds of drug crimes or of property used or intended to "facilitate" drug crimes. *See, e.g.*, Uniform Controlled Substances Act (1994), Art. 5 (Forfeiture). These powers are typically sweeping and invest the government with a great deal of the discretion that characterizes the prosecutorial process.

(4) *"Delivery," "Distribution" and Like Terms: What Do They Mean?* Legislatures and courts typically define "distribution" or "delivery" of controlled substances broadly, to cover conduct such as gifts or loans, in addition to sales. But the definitions may still require interpretation. Consider the following problems.

Problem 12A (Controlled Substances Crimes): "What Quantity, of What Substance, and What Did the Defendant Do with It?"

(1) *Possessory Offenses.* Under the Uniform Controlled Substances Act, how is the sentence range determined for (a) possession of a small amount of heroin and (b) possession of enough heroin of sufficient purity to make thousands of doses at the street level?

(2) *Distribution.* Under the Uniform Act, how would crimes and sentences be determined for a person who (a) gives a packet containing a personal-usage amount of heroin to another person or (b) hands such a packet to another person so that she can "look at it"?

(3) *Manufacturing.* How would the Act define crimes and sentences for someone who (a) synthesizes heroin or (b) grows marijuana?

Problem 12B (Controlled Substances Crimes): "I'm Not Guilty of 'Distribution' or 'Delivery,' Because I Told Her She Could Only Look at It!"

(1) *Morris v. Commonwealth*, 1999 Va. App. LEXIS 629 (Va. App.) (unpublished decision). In this case, the Court considered Morris' conviction for "knowingly or intentionally distributing" Rohypnol "to any person under eighteen years of age who is at least three years his junior." Candace Pruitt, a minor, went to a friend's apartment with Roger Erickson. On their arrival, Pruitt saw two guests use marijuana and another with Rohypnol ("roofies"). Later, Defendant Morris arrived at the apartment and Pruitt sat next to him, asking him "what a roofie was and what it did to you." Morris "told her that roofies make you feel like you are intoxicated on alcohol." He then "produced a Rohypnol pill and handed it to Pruitt so she could look at it." Erickson took the pill from Pruitt and swallowed it.

(2) *Is Morris Guilty of "Distribution" of a Controlled Substance to a Minor?* Consider Morris's conduct under the Uniform Act, above. Under its definition, is Morris guilty of "distribution" to Pruitt, a minor, if he truly intended only to let Pruitt "look at" the "roofie"? [In the real case, the Virginia court affirmed Morris's conviction for distribution to a minor by interpreting the term "distribute" broadly. The Virginia Code provides that distributing includes "delivery" and that "deliver" means "the actual, constructive, or attempted transfer of any controlled substance." Furthermore, in *Wood v. Commonwealth*, 197 S.E.2d 200 (Va. 1973), the Virginia Supreme Court had found a legislative intent to give the term "the broadest possible meaning" and to "proscribe not only the illegal sale, barter, exchange or gift of controlled drugs but also any delivery or transfer, actual or constructive, of possession or title."]

Notes on Contraband That Is Not Really Contraband: Imitations, Counterfeits, and Precursors

(1) *Imitation or Counterfeit Controlled Substances: Precursors.* Controlled Substances statutes also typically regulate the manufacturing, possession, and distribution of "imitations" or "counterfeits," *e.g.,* Uniform Controlled Substances Act §§ 404, 405, and of "precursors," or substances that can be used to make controlled substances, *e.g.,* Uniform Controlled Substances Act §§ 101(2) & (11). Precursor regulation or prohibition can be an especially effective way to reduce controlled substance crimes. Can you see why?

(2) *"Imitation" Controlled Substances, Represented as Real.* The Uniform Act defines "imitations" in such a way as to criminalize the conduct of a person who sells what is represented to the buyer as a controlled substance, when it is not one (it is powdered sugar, which becomes an "imitation" because of a representation that it is heroin). Can you see why this crime is needed? "Counterfeits," incidentally, are different from imitations; they include real controlled substances that are falsely trademarked, such as, for example, pills marked as "Valium" (a registered mark) that contain actual diazepam (the generic name) but that were made by someone other than the authorized manufacturer.

(3) *The Effectiveness of Precursor Restrictions.* Concerns about methamphetamine and the proliferation of "meth labs" (which pose fire and environmental hazards) led many states to regulate over-the-counter cold and allergy medications containing pseudoephedrine and related chemicals, because they are precursors of methamphetamine. Also, major national store chains, including Rite-Aid and Wal-Mart, voluntarily took steps to restrict sales of cold medicine. In 2006 the federal government's Combat Methamphetamine Epidemic Act limited the daily amount of these precursors that consumers can purchase, mandated keeping them behind store counters in locked cabinets, and required purchasers to show identification and sign logbooks. Does it seem silly to govern *cold medicine* by regulations backed up by criminal penalties? (Perhaps not. Drug enforcement officers in Oklahoma

reported that new laws, treating cold medicine containing pseudoephedrine with tight restrictions, had an almost miraculous effect. They (initially) pronounced themselves amazed but pleased when meth labs virtually disappeared overnight. The Federal law had an equally dramatic effect.)

(4) *Precursor Reports.* Some states have adopted detailed provisions regulating reports in lawful dealing with precursors. To varying degrees, this approach may reduce the availability of illegal substances just as the Oklahoma and federal laws mentioned in the note above did.

Problem 12C (Controlled Substances Crimes):
"It's Only Sugar, and This Was a Buy-Burn"

(1) *The Buy-Burn Scenario.* Officer Lauren Norder has worked for months to set up an undercover buy of heroin from a group known as The Beagle Boys. She ultimately made three controlled buys, all recorded and videotaped, using marked money that later was recovered from the pockets of one of the Beagle Boys. But the laboratory report has come back negative. "Sorry, officers," says the chemist. "It's powdered sugar." Lauren Norder, having risked her life to make this major collar, now realizes that she is the victim of a buy-burn. "They told me it was 'real quality smack.' And that it was 50% pure 'horse.' Those Beagle Boys used a whole bunch of slang terms meaning heroin, and now it's only sugar!"

(2) *Is There a Crime Here, Involving "Imitation" Substances?* Consider the sections in the Uniform Controlled Substances Act that cover distribution of "imitation" substances.

(3) *Is the Uniform Act Well Drafted?* Imagine that a grand jury indicts various members of the Beagle gang for distributing "imitation" heroin. But the Beagles are crafty. All of them testify, in substance, as follows: "We never told her it was heroin. We said we'd sell her some 'smack,' meaning sugar, and that's what we delivered, but we never used the word 'heroin.'" Some courts, interpreting statutes written like the Uniform Act, hold that slang representations using ambiguous words, such as "smack" or "horse," are not sufficient to constitute "representations" that the item is heroin. How should such a statute be drafted?

§ 12.02 Proof of Possession Beyond a Reasonable Doubt

Notes on Proof of Constructive Possession

(1) *The Typical Drug Possession Arrest — and the Separate, More Difficult Issue of Proving Possession Beyond a Reasonable Doubt.* What happens when a law enforcement officer discovers a controlled substance in a car in which the defendant is a passenger or an apartment in which the defendant is a tenant or guest? Does it

matter if there are other people there? Courts' interpretive approaches to proof of possession beyond reasonable doubt vary, and the cases such as these may not be as simple as they look—as the following decision suggests.

(2) *The Elements of Possession.* Because of the circumstances in which controlled substances are unlawfully sold and used, circumstantial evidence is often used to establish elements of possession offenses, and the courts make and apply law about the inferences that may properly be drawn. Also, courts often must rely on evidence of constructive possession.

Possession may be either exclusive or joint. In some jurisdictions, conviction depends on discovery of a sufficient quantity of a drug (a "usable amount" or alternatively "measurable amount"); in others, any amount of a drug, even a trace, is enough.

(3) *Constructive Possession; Joint Possession; Quantities.* To establish constructive possession, the prosecution must prove both that the defendant had "dominion and control" over the drugs and that the defendant knew of their presence and character. Facts that may give rise to inferences establishing constructive possession beyond reasonable doubt include whether the defendant is the owner of a vehicle (or the owner or lessee of a residence) in which drugs are found; whether others are present in the car or residence; whether the drugs are found near property identifiable as the defendant's; and how long (and how close in time to the discovery of the drugs) the defendant was in their vicinity.

Thomas v. State

269 So. 3d 681 (Fla. (Fla. App. 2019)

BADALMENTI, Judge.

[Thomas was convicted of possession of controlled substances on evidence described below.] Thomas maintains, the State presented insufficient evidence to sustain his convictions.

It is undisputed that Thomas was not found in actual possession of illegal drugs or drug paraphernalia. To convict him, the State therefore had to prove that he constructively possessed the illegal drugs. To convict . . . of constructive possession, the State was required to prove beyond a reasonable doubt (1) that Thomas had knowledge of the contraband and (2) that he had the ability to exercise dominion and control over it. *See Santiago v. State,* 991 So. 2d 439, 441 (Fla. 2d DCA 2008). In the milieu of constructive possession, knowledge of and the ability to exercise dominion and control over illegal contraband may not be inferred from the defendant's proximity to it and must be shown by independent proof. . . .

Here, the undisputed evidence demonstrates illegal drugs were discovered in a location that was accessible to many individuals who either resided in the home or who had access to the home. Thomas's mother testified that she resided in the house with her six children, all of whom had access to the house and each of the four bedrooms within the house. She further testified that her nieces and her sons' girlfriends also had access to the house. While the State offered evidence that Thomas occupied the bedroom containing the illegal drugs, the evidence also established that women's clothing and "possibly" shoes were discovered in the bedroom. Under such circumstances, it is settled that we may not infer Thomas's knowledge of the contraband's presence and ability to exercise dominion and control over it. . . .

In *Santiago,* under similar facts, this court held that the State's evidence failed to prove that the defendant constructively possessed illegal drugs. There, the police searched a house that was occupied by the defendant and five other people. The defendant was present in the bedroom containing illegal drugs when the officers executed the search warrant. The drugs were found "in the pocket of what was described as likely men's jean shorts," in an opaque pink tube underneath the bed, and in football shoulder pads located in the open bedroom closet. In the same room, the police also found an identification card bearing the defendant's name and a retail store receipt issued to the defendant and bearing the same address as the residence where the search warrant was executed. The defendant's name was etched on a mirror in the room. However, the police also found a motor vehicle title registered to another individual and an identification card under the name of a third individual. In reversing the defendant's conviction for trafficking in heroin, the *Santiago* court explained that the evidence "demonstrates only that [the defendant] was one of three people who may have occupied the bedroom where drugs were concealed."

Here, like *Santiago,* the police searched a house that was occupied by the defendant and at least two other people. Also like *Santiago,* many items in the room supported the State's theory that Thomas constructively possessed the drugs found in the dresser drawer: namely, [a] prescription pill bottle with his name on it, a court document relating to him, CDs with his picture on it, empty shoe boxes displaying the same shoe size he was wearing when arrested, and a picture collage displaying photographs of him and a woman. However, critically, like *Santiago,* the evidence — women's clothing and "possibly" shoes — tied at least one other person to the room. The testimony of Thomas's mother also tied several individuals to the house and the bedroom containing the drug contraband. [Conviction reversed.]

Notes and Questions

(1) *Did the Court Confuse "Possession" with" Exclusive" Possession, which Is Not Required?* Possession may be joint, *i.e.,* shared by two or more people. And joint possession is still possession. Exclusive possession is not required, although the court here seems to require it. All that is required is proof of defendant's (1) knowledge of the contraband and (2) dominion and control over it. Didn't the evidence, which included defendant's actual presence in the room, testimony that it was his room,

and numerous items that obviously were his, enable a reasonable juror to have the requisite proof of joint possession that included the defendant?

(2) *Proof of Possession in a Home Is Difficult for the Prosecution.* There are many decisions analogous to *Thomas. E.g., State v. Webb,* 648 N.W.2d 72 (Iowa 2002) (reversing conviction on similar facts).

(3) *New York's Joint-Possession Presumption: Is This a Good Solution?* A New York Statute provides that, with certain exceptions, the presence of a firearm in an automobile creates a presumption of its illegal possession by all persons then occupying the vehicle. Could (or should) adoption of a similar presumption about contraband in a home enable the jury to consider a case such as that of Thomas's alleged possession in the case above?

(4) *The Supreme Court's Upholding of the New York Joint-Possession Presumption: County Court of Ulster County v. Allen,* 442 U.S. 140 (1979). In this case, the Supreme Court upheld the New York approach (the presumption of possession) against a constitutional attack under the Due Process Clause. The Court emphasized that a criminal presumption cannot be mandatory; it must require the jury to find guilt beyond a reasonable doubt in the individual case. Otherwise, it would violate the right to a jury trial as well as the Due Process Clause. In the case of a firearm in a car with multiple occupants, said the Court, "the presumption of possession is entirely rational."

Problem 12D (Proof of Possession): "Sure I Knew, but It Was My Wife's, and I Didn't Put It There"

(1) *A Problem Involving Knowingly Remaining in the Proximity of Contraband, Adapted from People v. Ireland,* 348 N.E.2d 277 (Ill. App. Ct. 1976). Imagine that wife, before marriage, owned a residence in which evidence shows that she stored and regularly sold large quantities of contraband drugs. Assume that the evidence shows that the quantity maintained by wife was such that no person inhabiting the residence could avoid knowing that the contraband was present. There were drugs in stacks in every part of the home. Husband marries wife and comes to live in her residence. Months later, peace officers enter the residence with a valid search warrant. They find and arrest husband in a room in which masses of contraband are openly visible. Husband confesses that he knew the contraband was there, but plaintively says, "But I didn't put any of it there!" Wife, who arrives later, says, "I didn't put it there. I haven't been involved with drugs since I got married."

(2) *Is Knowledge and Willing Proximity Enough?* If a jury convicts the husband, can his conviction stand? (What "act" has he provably done?) Consider whether anyone can ever be convicted of a possessory crime based on a search, if the answer is no. [In *People v. Ireland,* the court held out the prospect that husband could be convicted but required strict instructions, confining the jury's inferences of husband's possession and requiring not only knowledge, but also control of the contraband by

the husband.] How would the New York approach (the presumption of joint possession) affect this case?

§ 12.03 Why Criminalize the Use of Illicit Drugs?

Note on Statistics About Illicit Drug Usage
(compiled from various government and government-sponsored reports)

(1) *What Proportion of the Population Uses Drugs?* 41.7% of Americans admit
using an illicit drug at least once in their lifetimes (2003). Almost 9% of Americans
over age 11 used illicit drugs in the past month, including 6.6% who used marijuana
(2009).

(2) *How Young Does It Start?* According to a 2012 study, 49% of high school
seniors admitted using an illicit drug at least once in their lifetimes.

(3) *The Correctional Implications of the Criminalization of Recreational Drug
Usage.* In 2011 there were almost 200,000 sentenced prisoners under federal jurisdiction; 95,000 were serving time for drug offenses while only 15,000 for violent
offenses. In the states, of about 1.4 million prisoners, 237,000 were serving time for
drug offenses, compared to 725,000 for violent crimes. In 2004, about 18% of state
and federal prisoners said they committed their current offense to obtain money
for drugs. According to a 2010 report, someone is arrested for a drug offense in the
United States *every nineteen seconds.*

(4) *Illicit Drug Usage and Other Crimes.* People arrested for alleged crimes of any
type have very high levels of positive illicit drug tests. A 2011 study reported that a
majority of adult males arrested for various crimes tested positive for illegal drugs.
The rate was as high as 81%.

(5) *What Does It Cost?* In 2006, Americans spent $38 billion dollars on cocaine, $34
billion on marijuana, $11 billion on heroin and $18 billion on methamphetamine.
Law enforcement, court system, and corrections costs of criminalizing illicit drug
use are enormous. Federal spending in 2011 alone was about $25 billion. Indirect
economic costs of illicit drug use include heath care and worker productivity costs.

Note on Legalization of Marijuana

In recent years, many states have "legalized" medical or recreational cultivation,
possession, and/or use of marijuana. But these actions are valid only as state law.
Remember that federal law also criminalizes the use of controlled substances such
as marijuana. Under the federal Constitution's Supremacy Clause, the federal statute displaces and preempts conflicting state law. Thus, a state's decision to decriminalize marijuana, by itself, cannot prevent federal prosecutors in those states from
filing charges—although legalization does put pressure on federal officials to consider the federalism implications of any decision to prosecute, particularly when a
significant number of states have taken similar steps.

§ 12.04 Race, Gender, and Drug Crimes

Notes on Arguments About Discrimination

(1) *Crack Cocaine Penalties That Are Much Greater than for Comparable Amounts of Powder: Is the Difference Racially Discriminatory?* Initially, federal law and the Federal Sentencing Guidelines imposed dramatically different penalties on offenses involving crack cocaine and powder cocaine—with far harsher sentences for crack cocaine offenses. Some commentators argued that this disparity—and the related charging discretion of federal prosecutors—was racially discriminatory. *See, e.g.,* Angela J. Davis, *Prosecution and Race: The Power and Privilege of Discretion*, 67 Fordham L. Rev. 13 (1998). Supporters of the sentencing differential contended that "crack is more addictive than powder cocaine; it accounts for more emergency room visits; it is most popular among juveniles; it has a greater likelihood of being associated with violence; and crack dealers have more extensive criminal records than other drug dealers and tend to use young people to distribute the drug at a greater rate." *Disapproval of Sentencing Guideline Amendments*, H. Rep. 104–272, 104th Cong., 1st Sess. 3 (Sept. 29, 1995). Notwithstanding these claims, the U.S. Sentencing Commission took action in 2007 and 2008 to reduce the disparity between powder cocaine and crack cocaine sentences. The Fair Sentencing Act of 2010 took further steps, and so did federal legislation in 2019.

(2) *Other Alleged Racial Effects of "The War on Drugs."* In *New Voices on the War on Drugs: Collateral Damage in the War on Drugs*, 47 Vill. L. Rev. 839 (2002), Graham Boyd suggests other racial effects of the criminalization of illicit drug use:

> Whites and Blacks use drugs at almost exactly the same rates. Because there are five times as many Whites as Blacks in the United States, it follows that the overwhelming majority of drug users are white. Nevertheless, African-Americans are admitted to state prison at a rate that is 13.4 times greater than Whites, a disparity driven largely by the gross racial targeting of drug laws. In some states, . . . Blacks make up 90% of drug prisoners and are up to fifty-seven times more likely than Whites to be incarcerated for drug crimes.

Critics of this view might respond that Boyd's statistics are selective, and his argument is overstated. Even if that is true, do his claims suggest that something is wrong with drug enforcement polices? *See also* Tracey L. Meares, *Place and Crime*, 73 Chicago-Kent L. Rev. 669 (1998).

§ 12.05 Weapons as Contraband

Notes on Other Contraband: Weapons and Related Items

(1) *When Else Can Possessing Something Be a Crime?* While the focus of the previous sections is on controlled substances, jurisdictions often criminalize the possession of other things considered dangerous, including firearms, explosives, and silencers. Flat prohibition of possession applies to some kinds of firearms. For example, Virginia

criminalizes the possession of the "Striker 12, commonly called a 'streetsweeper,' or any semi-automatic folding stock shotgun of like kind with a spring tension magazine drum capable of holding twelve shotgun shells." Va. Code § 18.2–308.8.

(2) *Firearms That Are Lawful to Possess in Some Places or Circumstances.* The Second Amendment and cultural and political factors place limitations on criminalizing the possession of firearms. Still, many jurisdictions limit the circumstances, including locations, in which some or all firearms may be carried or used, or they require their registration. They often provide especially heavy penalties for possession of particular firearms such as machine guns or short-barrel shotguns. Additionally, possession of firearms by certain groups, including convicted felons, aliens, and persons subject to protective orders, may be criminalized.

§ 12.06 Terrorism and Criminal Justice

[A] Anti-Terrorism Laws: The Statutory Framework

[1] *Defining Terrorism*

Why Is the Definition of Terrorism Difficult, and Why Does It Matter?

(1) *"One Person's Terrorist Is Another Person's Freedom Fighter."* Many people in pre-revolutionary America cheered the Boston Tea Party, in which colonials boarded a vessel and dumped its cargo as a protest against British taxes. In Britain the event may have been seen as an early equivalent of what we now recognize as terrorism. In various parts of the world, political violence against civilian populations is seen by some elements as the best alternative for social change.

(2) *An Official Definition: Motive to "Intimidate" or "Coerce."* In 18 U.S.C. § 2331, the motivation for "international terrorism" is referred to as an apparent intention "to intimidate or coerce a civilian population; to influence the policy of a government by intimidation or coercion; or to affect the conduct of a government by mass destruction, assassination, or kidnapping." Sometimes, terrorism is defined by the combination of motivation with a list of offenses, as in § 2332b. Because administrative agencies must take certain kinds of action, including identification of "terrorist organizations," there is another definition in the Federal Register, at 28 C.F.R. § 0.85(l), governing the duties of the Attorney General: "Terrorism includes the unlawful use of force and violence against persons or property to intimidate or coerce a government, the civilian population, or any segment thereof, in furtherance of political or social objectives."

What if a foreign national kills an American in another country because he or she hates the victim (and all or part of the hatred seems to be based on anti-American animus)? Literally, the language defining terrorism does not seem to fit. Consider the following problem.

Problem 12E (Terrorism Crimes): "I Hate Americans and I'm Going to Kill You"

(1) *The Achille Lauro Incident.* In the not-too-distant past, four heavily armed Palestinians hijacked the Italian cruise ship Achille Lauro, which had more than 400 passengers and crew, in the Mediterranean Ocean. They demanded that Israel free fifty Palestinian prisoners. During their two-day occupation of the ship, the Palestinians shot and killed a disabled 69-year-old American tourist Leon Klinghoffer, and threw his body overboard with his wheelchair. The hijackers surrendered in exchange for an assurance of safe passage, and an Egyptian aircraft took off to fly them to freedom. U.S. Navy F-14 fighters intercepted it and forced it to land in Sicily. Italian authorities took them into custody.

(2) *Under the Technical Definitions in the Laws Above, Did the Killing of Klinghoffer Qualify as an Act of "Terrorism"?* The hijacking itself seems to qualify, because there was "a purpose to coerce a government [Israel] to do something [release prisoners]." But was the murder of the disabled American, Klinghoffer, also an act of terrorism? It was not done to "intimidate or coerce" Israel or America (although that may have been the motive for the original hijacking), but it certainly reflected animus against Americans. Is hatred of Americans coupled with crimes against them, in the absence of a purpose to "coerce or intimidate," sufficient to be labeled "terrorism" under the definitions above?

[2] Anti-Terrorism Statutes

Notes on the Major Enactments Defining Crimes

(1) *The Omnibus Diplomatic Security and Terrorism Act of 1986.* Fifteen years before 9/11, concerns about terrorism were expressed in this Act primarily in legislation about multi-national cooperation, processes for apprehending terrorists, and security for diplomatic missions. But the Act also created a new crime, covering assaults, homicidal attempts or conspiracies, or homicides, committed against American citizens abroad. The murder provision, for example, provides, "whoever kills a national of the United States, while such national is outside the United States, shall . . . if the killing is murder . . . , as defined under this Title, be punished by death or imprisonment for any term of years or for life, or both."

Prosecution under this provision is restricted to cases in which the attorney general certifies to a judgment that "such offense was intended to coerce, intimidate or retaliate against a government or a civilian population." This provision creates the terrorism link. Notice, however, that terrorism is not a part of the crime definition. Instead, it is expressed only in required findings by the Attorney General. Can you explain why the law is set up this way?

(2) *The Anti-Terrorism and Effective Death Penalty Act of 1996.* Probably the most important anti-terrorism provision in this Act, in terms of new crimes, is 18 U.S.C. § 2339B, which prohibits "providing material support or resources to designated

foreign terrorist organizations." The State Department is responsible for making the designation pursuant to regulation.

(3) *The USA PATRIOT Act.* The popular name of this statute is probably our longest legislative acronym. It stands for "Uniting and Strengthening America by Providing Appropriate Tools Required to Intercept and Obstruct Terrorism." For the most part, the PATRIOT Act covers law enforcement tools, such as surveillance and wiretapping. But it also creates offenses of "domestic terrorism" and "international money laundering."

(4) *The Homeland Security Act of 2002.* This enactment brought about a long-sought-after reorganization of parts of more than a dozen departments into the "Department of Homeland Security."

(5) *The Intelligence Reform and Terrorism Prevention Act of 2004.* This statute brought about another sweeping reorganization of the federal government, creating the new position of Director of National Intelligence, facilitating information transfer, and consolidating functions of various intelligence groups. It also provided additional procedural and law enforcement tools. Finally, of interest to us here, it refined the definitions of some existing terrorism crimes to make their coverage fit legislative intent and withstand constitutional challenges.

(6) *Other Enactments: The Classified Information Procedures Act of 1980; the Foreign Intelligence Surveillance Act of 1998.* These statutes dealt with procedural matters. For example, defendants in terrorism cases often seek discovery of classified information. Therefore, the Classified Information enactment requires the court to examine the relevance of requested information prior to discovery and to provide substitute information when possible, as well as providing other remedies. *See, e.g., United States v. Rezaq,* 134 F.3d 1121 (D.C. Cir. 1998) (substitute discovery); *United States v. Bin Laden,* 58 F. Supp. 2d 113 (S.D.N.Y. 1999) (security clearance for counsel as a remedy).

(7) *Related Statutes: The Detainee Treatment Act of 2005; the Military Commissions Acts of 2006 and 2009.* These statutes address the confinement, treatment, and prosecution before military courts of people detained on suspicion of involvement in terrorist activities.

[3] *Prohibitions upon "Material Support" to Designated "Terrorist Organizations"*

Notes on "Material Support" to "Terrorist Organizations"

(1) *Prosecuting People for Terrorist Activity.* Many actions identified as "terrorist" are also straightforward crimes, such as homicide, kidnapping, or conspiracy. But federal law reaches beyond these traditional offenses. The materials that follow provide an overview of one of the most significant crimes directed exclusively at terrorist activity.

(2) *Section 2339B.* Enacted in 1996 and amended several times since, 18 U.S.C. § 2339B makes it a crime to provide "material support or resources to a foreign terrorist organization." To commit this offense, "a person must have knowledge" of the character of the organization, as defined. The State Department has the authority to identify "terrorist organizations." Section 2339A defines "material support" to include "any property, tangible or intangible, or service," and it provides numerous specific examples, including "personnel."

(3) *Due Process and the Designation of Terrorist Organizations.* In *People's Mojahedin Organization of Iran v. Dept. of State*, 182 F.3d 17 (D.C. Cir. 1999), the court upheld the designation concept against a variety of constitutional and statutory attacks. Two years later, however, the same court held that State Department designations, which previously had been done unilaterally without notice or opportunity to be heard, must comply with the Due Process Clause when the organization has a sufficient presence in the United States to qualify for due process protections. *National Council of Resistance v. Dep't of State*, 251 F.3d 192 (D.C. Cir. 2001).

(4) *The Offense Defined by § 2339B.* What is "material support"? Does it include actions on the battlefield? What else? Consider the cases that follow.

United States v. Lindh

212 F. Supp. 2d 541 (E.D. Va. 2002)

[Lindh was an American citizen who was charged in a ten-count indictment with crimes arising from his alleged participation in armed combat against United States armed forces in Afghanistan. The indictment alleged that Lindh, who had obtained training in Pakistan by Harakat-al-Mujahideen ("HUM"), "a [designated] terrorist group dedicated to an extremist view of Islam," traveled to Afghanistan "for the purpose of taking up arms with" the Taliban government of Afghanistan. He then received "extensive military training at an al Qaeda training camp," including "training in ... weapons, orienteering, navigation, explosives, and battlefield combat," and he learned the use of "shoulder weapons, pistols and rocket-propelled grenades, and the construction of Molotov cocktails." Lindh had sworn allegiance to the "holy war" or "jihad" and declined to carry out operations inside the United States. He preferred instead to go to battle against the United States and its allies.

[Lindh was furnished with an AKM rifle, "with a barrel suitable for long-range shooting," and traveled with a group of approximately 150 non-Afghan fighters to Northeastern Afghanistan under the command of an Iraqi citizen who also had joined the same cause. Eventually, Lindh's group were detained by the United States. While in detention, Taliban detainees, joined by Lindh, attacked CIA agents and killed one of them, and Lindh, who was wounded in that incident, retreated with his group to the basement of the prison, where they were recaptured. Lindh was charged in the United States with various crimes, including conspiracy to murder United States nationals in violation of section 2332(b), discussed above, as well as providing "material support and resources" to Al Qaeda, a designated "terrorist organization," in violation of section 2339B.

[Lindh moved to dismiss the 2339B indictment on various grounds, including overbreadth and vagueness. The court here rejects these arguments:]

Lindh also argues that Section 2339B [is] facially unconstitutionally overbroad, as Section 2339B's prohibition of providing "personnel" penalizes mere association . . . . This argument is meritless. As an initial matter, to prevail on a facial challenge to a statute or regulation, it is not enough for a party to show merely "some" overbreadth. Rather, "the overbreadth of a statute must not only be real, but substantial as well." *Broadrick v. Oklahoma*, 413 U.S. 601, 615 (1973). . . . [T]he term "personnel" entails more than mere presence. Indeed, a person can circulate a pamphlet or give a speech in support of an organization without also working within the organization's body of "personnel." "Personnel" refers to individuals who function as employees or quasi-employees . . . . [T]here is no danger, let alone a substantial one, that Section 2339B will be applied to infringe upon legitimate rights of association. . . .

Lindh also argues that Section 2339B [is] unconstitutionally vague. The vagueness doctrine, which protects both free speech and due process values, is "concerned with clarity"; it "requires that a penal statute define the criminal offense with sufficient definiteness that ordinary people can understand what conduct is prohibited and in a manner that does not encourage arbitrary and discriminatory enforcement." *Kolender v. Lawson*, 461 U.S. 352, 357 (1983). Of course, the Constitution does not impose "impossible standards of clarity" on Congress or the regulatory agencies. . . .

As already noted, the plain meaning of "personnel" is such that it requires, in the context of Section 2339B, an employment or employment-like relationship between the persons in question and the terrorist organization. . . . Thus, the term "personnel" in Section 2339B gives fair notice to the public of what is prohibited and the provision is therefore not unconstitutionally vague. . . . [Motions to Dismiss denied.]

[Note: Lindh eventually pleaded guilty to terrorism charges involving weapons and received a sentence of 20 years imprisonment. — Eds.]

Problem 12F (Terrorism Offenses): "I Didn't Provide 'Personnel' or 'Training'; I Just Showed Them How to Kill Americans with Improvised Car Bombs"

(1) *Training and Expert Advice to Designated or Acting Terrorist Organizations: Is It Covered?* Anti-terrorism crime definition is a new art, and it is hard to do perfectly. The earlier versions of 2339B covered providing material support in the form of "personnel" to a designated or active terrorist organization, but it did not define "personnel." It also covered the providing of "training," again undefined. Imagine that a longtime bomb expert visits a terrorist training camp for a day and provides expert advice on how to improvise and deploy car bombs so that they can effectively be used against off-duty United States military personnel—or the civilian

population of a country allied with the United States. Has this bomb expert provided "personnel"? Or "training"?

(2) *Are the Terms "Personnel" and "Training" Vague?* In *Humanitarian Law Project v. Reno*, 205 F.3d 1130 (9th Cir. 2000), the Ninth Circuit decided that 18 U.S.C. § 2339B's prohibition on providing "personnel" to a designated terrorist organization was unconstitutionally vague because it "blur[red] the line" between providing advocacy of the cause, which would free up organization members to do other things, and actual terrorist actions. The court refused to construe "personnel" narrowly on the ground that to do so would "rewrite the law." And the court added that "'training' fares no better," because it is "easy to imagine protected expression that falls within the bounds of this term." The conclusion follows that this court would not have permitted "personnel" or "training" to cover the bomb expert referred to above. *Lindh* arguably was an easier case, involving battlefield capture.

(3) *Amendment of § 2339B.* In the Intelligence Reform and Terrorism Prevention Act of 2004, Congress defined "personnel" to include "1 or more individuals who may be or include oneself," defined "training" as "instruction or teaching designed to impart a specific skill, as opposed to general knowledge," and added "expert advice or assistance" to material support, meaning "advice or assistance derived from scientific, technical or other specialized knowledge." It also clarified the mental state required by the statute: the defendant "must have knowledge that the organization is a designated terrorist organization." The Supreme Court rejected vagueness and First Amendment objections and upheld the amended version of § 2339B in *Holder v. Humanitarian Law Project*, 130 S. Ct. 2705 (2010).

(4) *Civil Suits Based on Claims of Material Support to Terrorism: Republic of Sudan v. Harrison,* 139 S. Ct. 1048 (2019), *and Rubin v. Islamic Republic of Iran,* 138 S. Ct. 816 (2018). Although these cases did not interpret the terrorism statutes, both included claims against foreign governments based on their provision of material support to terrorism, and the Court cited the term with apparent approval.

[B] Executive Authority

Notes on the President's Authority Under the Constitution

(1) *The Commander-in-Chief Provision.* The Constitution makes the President the "Commander-in-Chief" of American armed forces. This provision is the primary source of whatever presidential powers exist to compose military tribunals, as well as to deal with battlefield capture. The President also is given certain diplomatic and foreign affairs powers (*e.g.*, sending and receiving ambassadors).

The limit of Presidential authority is unclear. The constitutional language is general, and the cases have been few, comparatively speaking. Presidents have tended to take an expansive view of their power, to include the authority to do such things as "targeted killings," prohibit or authorize assassination by agents of the United States abroad, and "extraordinary rendition" (the capturing of wanted fugitives in other countries for delivery to the United States or, more commonly, to other nations for interrogation or trial). Likewise, they have claimed the power to detain and interrogate suspected suspects and to bring them to trial before military tribunals.

(2) *Military Tribunals: Ex Parte Quirin*, 317 U.S. 1 (1942). Presidents have claimed broad authority to use military tribunals to try persons for violations of the laws of war and other war-related offenses. In *Quirin*, the court upheld this power on grounds of Congressional authorization, and for that reason it did not explore the limits of the President's authority. The extent of Presidential power derived from the Commander-in-Chief Clause remains unclear and controversial. *See also* note 3 following *Hamdi v. Rumsfeld*, below.

(3) *Assassination: Prohibitions in the Past — but an Unclear Policy Today.* President Ford signed an Executive Order prohibiting "political assassination" by employees of the United States. President Reagan signed an Executive Order that was broader, prohibiting any kind of "assassination" (not just "political" assassination), and disallowing even "indirect participation." After the 9/11 attacks, the Bush Administration interpreted these policies to allow "self-defense" by the United States (an interpretation that apparently would mean that assassinations were authorized if "defensive") and adopted a policy allowing American agents to attack Al Qaeda operatives worldwide, although for various logistical reasons no such attacks were carried out. *See* Siobhan Gorman, *CIA Had Secret Al Qaeda Plan*, Wall Street Journal, July 13, 2009, A1.

The Obama Administration has dramatically increased the use of drone missiles to kill people it claims are members of al Qaeda or associated groups. Because such persons arguably fall within the scope of the post-9/11 Authorization to Use Military Force (AUMF), the act of identifying them as targets and killing them with drones is (again, arguably) a lawful use of military force and not an assassination. The use of drones to kill people who are not affiliated with al Qaeda, however, arguably falls outside the AUMF and is not lawful.

(4) *Detention and Interrogation: "Pressure"? "Torture"?* The federal government seeks to detain suspected terrorists for multiple reasons. One reason is prosecution, but another is interrogation. The Bush administration approved the use of interrogation methods that caused pain, fear, and disorientation, and in some instances these methods probably amounted to torture. The justification for these methods was that the people subjected to them might have had — and in some cases did have — information about the organization of a terrorist group, or about possible future attacks. Yet federal law bans the use of tactics that rise to the level of torture. *See, e.g.,* 18 U.S.C. § 2340 (criminalizing torture committed outside the U.S. by U.S. nationals or by persons later found in the United States). If an interrogator is prosecuted for torture or some other form of ill-treatment, should a defense such as necessity be available? *See* John T. Parry & Welsh S. White, *Interrogating Suspected Terrorists: Should Torture Be an Option?*, 63 U. Pitt. L. Rev. 743 (2002) (insisting torture must remain illegal but suggesting the necessity defense could be available in rare cases).

(5) *Detention of Prisoners of War or "Enemy Combatants": Is Due Process Required?*
Again, Presidents have claimed broad powers to detain both lawful combatants, who
become Prisoners of War subject to the Geneva Conventions, as well as unlawful or
illegal combatants (as to whom the Bush administration claimed the Geneva Conventions did not apply). In response to the 9/11 attacks, Congress passed an Authorization to Use Military Force that arguably expanded whatever inherent authority
the President possessed. Federal courts subsequently recognized the administration's authority to detain "unlawful enemy combatants." But this authority still has
limits. Consider the following decision.

HAMDI v. RUMSFELD, 542 U.S. 507 (2004). Hamdi, like Lindh, above, was
captured by the Northern Alliance while allegedly fighting for the Taliban and
engaging "in armed conflict against the United States." The government contended
that Hamdi, although an American citizen, was an illegal "enemy combatant" who
could be detained indefinitely. The Court first upheld the authority to detain persons "legitimately determined to be enemy combatants" for "the duration of hos-
tilities." The Court did not address the precise limits of Presidential power because
it found that the Authorization to Use Military Force (AUMF) in Afghanistan provided congressional authorization. The Court then addressed the question, what
procedures are required under the Due Process Clause? Hamdi called for a habeas
corpus hearing not dependent on hearsay, whereas the government argued that
any more process than a unilateral hearsay declaration would be both unworkable
and "constitutionally intolerable." The government pointed out, for example, that
access to an attorney could easily destroy the kind of relationship of trust between
detainee and captor that would lead most naturally to successful interrogation.
The Court rejected the arguments of both sides and announced an intermediate
holding:

> We therefore hold that a citizen-detainee seeking to challenge his clas-
> sification as an enemy combatant must receive notice of the factual basis
> for his classification, and a fair opportunity to rebut the Government's fac-
> tual assertions before a neutral decisionmaker. . . . These essential constitu-
> tional promises may not be eroded.

> At the same time, the exigencies of the circumstances may demand that,
> aside from these core elements, enemy combatant proceedings may be tai-
> lored to alleviate their uncommon potential to burden the Executive at a
> time of ongoing military conflict. Hearsay, for example, may need to be
> accepted as the most reliable available evidence from the Government in
> such a proceeding. Likewise, the Constitution would not be offended by
> a presumption in favor of the Government's evidence, so long as that pre-
> sumption remained a rebuttable one and fair opportunity for rebuttal were
> provided. Thus, once the Government puts forth credible evidence that the
> habeas petitioner meets the enemy-combatant criteria, the onus could shift

to the petitioner to rebut that evidence with more persuasive evidence that he falls outside the criteria . . . .

We think it unlikely that this basic process will have the dire impact on the central functions of warmaking that the Government forecasts. The parties agree that initial captures on the battlefield need not receive the process we have discussed here; that process is due only when the determination is made to *continue* to hold those who have been seized. . . .

Notes and Questions

(1) *Dissents from Different Directions.* Justices Souter and Ginsburg dissented in part in an opinion that would have held Hamdi's detention illegal without describing Due Process procedures. Justices Scalia and Stevens argued that trial for treason in a federal court was appropriate, but they dissented on the ground that the Court "has proceeded to meet the current emergency in a manner the Constitution does not envision." Justice Thomas dissented on the ground that "[t]his detention falls squarely within the Federal Government's war powers, and we lack the expertise and capacity to second-guess that decision." He would have denied Hamdi's habeas petition without a remand.

(2) *Creating a Process in Response to* Hamdi. In response to *Hamdi* and its companion case, *Rasul v. Bush*, 542 U.S. 466 (2004), the Bush administration created a process for reviewing the detentions of citizens and aliens detained at Guantanamo Bay. This process led to the release of a few detainees, and the transfer of many more to other countries. In the Detainee Treatment Act of 2005, Congress created a structure for reviewing these decisions. Responding to the Bush administration's use of coercive interrogation methods, the Act also declared that all interrogations must conform to the U.S. Army Field Manual and that no person in U.S. custody, "regardless of nationality or physical location, shall be subject to cruel, inhuman, or degrading treatment or punishment."

(3) *Military Commissions; Counsel.* The *Hamdi* Court also suggested the "possibility" that its requirements could be met by a "properly constituted military tribunal." But it rejected a standard that would allow the decision to be made solely on "some evidence" and held that Hamdi "unquestionably" had the "right to access to counsel in connection with the proceedings on remand."

In *Hamdan v. Rumsfeld*, 548 U.S. 557 (2006), the Supreme Court held that the President did not have inherent authority to establish military commissions and that legislation was necessary. In response, Congress passed the Military Commissions Act of 2006 to create a statutory basis for military trials of suspected terrorists. The Supreme Court ruled that a portion of the Act was unconstitutional because it suspended the right to petition for habeas corpus, *see Boumediene v. Bush*, 553 U.S. 723 (2008), but did not disturb the rest of the Act. Later, the Obama and Trump administrations have gone forward with military commission prosecutions under the more recent Military Commissions Act of 2009 and revised regulations (which, among other things, forbid the use of evidence obtained by coercion).

Chapter 13

The Legality and Justification of Criminal Laws

"Human law is law only by virtue of its accordance with right reason. . . . In so far as it deviates from right reason it is called an unjust law; and in such a case it is no law at all, but rather an assertion of violence." — Thomas Aquinas, *Summa Theologiae*

"Not only may vast numbers be coerced by laws which they do not regard as morally binding, but it is not even true that those who do accept the system voluntarily, must conceive of themselves as morally bound to do so, though the system will be most stable when they do so. . . . There is indeed no reason why those who accept the authority of the system should not examine their conscience and decide that, morally, they ought not to accept it, yet for a variety of reasons continue to do so." — H.L.A. Hart, *The Concept of Law* (1961)

§ 13.01 The Legality Principle and Its Limits

(1) *Nulla Poena Sine Lege and Other Latin Maxims.* Criminal law has long been concerned that governments should inform their people about the content of the law. This principle not only permits law-abiding citizens to avoid committing crimes, but it also constrains government by providing limits within which it must operate in acting against citizens. The concept that criminal laws (including permissible sentences) should be reasonably specific has been referred to as a part of the principle of "legality." The traditional Latin version is *nulla poena sine lege*, no punishment without law.

(2) *This Concept Applies to Both Statutes and Common Law.* As the following materials suggest, the principle of legality applies to the definition of crimes and sentences, irrespective of whether the source is statute or common law. It has a constitutional dimension as well since it is included, to some extent, in the Due Process guarantees of the Fifth and Fourteenth Amendments.

[A] Crime Definition, Retroactivity, and the Principle of Fair Warning

United States v. Lanier

520 U.S. 259 (1997)

JUSTICE SOUTER delivered the opinion of the Court.

[Lanier was convicted under 18 U.S.C. § 242 of criminally violating the constitutional rights of five women by assaulting them sexually while he served as a state judge. Section 242 is the basic statute criminalizing conduct that deprives persons of their federal civil rights under color of state law. The question was not whether Lanier's conduct might be illegal under some statute somewhere; instead, the issue was whether there was a right, specifically enough defined, to be free of sexual misconduct, that was protected in the Constitution. Or, more to the point, the issue was whether the statute or Constitution, neither of which expressly covers freedom from sexual misconduct, was clear enough in creating the right the women claimed. The right might be protected somewhere in the law, but was it somewhere in the Constitution, and if so, was it sufficiently well defined for criminal prosecution?

[The trial judge had instructed the jury that the Government had to prove as an element of the offense that Lanier had deprived the victims of their Fourteenth Amendment due process right to liberty, and that that right included the right to be free from sexually motivated assaults. But the en banc Sixth Circuit set aside the convictions for lack of any notice to the public that § 242 covers sexual assault crimes. The Sixth Circuit held that § 242 criminal liability may be imposed only if the constitutional right at issue is first identified in a decision of the Supreme Court, and only when the right has been held to apply in a factual situation "fundamentally similar" to the one at bar.

[The Supreme Court held that the Sixth Circuit had employed the wrong standard for deciding whether criminal liability under § 242 applies to particular conduct. Section 242's general language prohibiting "the deprivation of any rights . . . secured . . . by the Constitution" does not describe the conduct it forbids, but incorporates constitutional law by reference. And yet, before criminal liability may be imposed for violation of any penal law, procedural due process also requires "fair warning . . . of what the law intends." The Court also stated that the Fifth Amendment's Due Process Clause provides the substantive standards that govern sex discrimination by federal officials.]

The right to due process enforced by § 242 and said to have been violated by Lanier presents . . . the irony that a prosecution to enforce one application of its spacious protection of liberty can threaten the accused with deprivation of another [due process right]: what Justice Holmes spoke of as "fair warning . . . in language that the common world will understand, of what the law intends to do if a certain line is passed. To make the warning fair, so far as possible the line should be clear." *McBoyle v. United States,* 283 U.S. 25, 27, 51 (1931). "'The . . . principle is that no [person] shall be held criminally responsible for conduct which he could not reasonably understand to be proscribed.'" . . .

There are three related manifestations of the fair warning requirement. First, the vagueness doctrine bars enforcement of "a statute which either forbids or requires the doing of an act in terms so vague that [people] of common intelligence must necessarily guess at its meaning and differ as to its application." . . . Second, as a sort of "junior version of the vagueness doctrine," the canon of strict construction of criminal statutes, or rule of lenity, ensures fair warning by so resolving ambiguity in a criminal statute as to apply it only to conduct clearly covered. . . . Third, although clarity at the requisite level may be supplied by judicial gloss on an otherwise uncertain statute, due process bars courts from applying a novel construction of a criminal statute to conduct that neither the statute nor any prior judicial decision has fairly disclosed to be within its scope. . . . The touchstone is whether the statute, either standing alone or as construed, made it reasonably clear at the relevant time that the defendant's conduct was criminal. . . .

The Sixth Circuit, in this case, added two glosses to the made-specific standard of fair warning. In its view, a generally phrased constitutional right has been made specific [enough] . . . [only] if a prior decision of this Court has declared the right, and then only when this Court has applied its ruling in a case with facts "fundamentally similar" to the case being prosecuted. None of the considerations advanced in this case, however, persuade us that either a decision of this Court or the extreme level of factual specificity envisioned by the Court of Appeals is necessary in every instance to give fair warning. . . .

In the civil sphere, we have [required] . . . that defendants "reasonably can anticipate when their conduct may give rise to liability," by attaching liability only if "[t]he contours of the right [violated are] sufficiently clear that a reasonable official would understand that what he is doing violates that right." So conceived, the object of the [civil] standard is not different from that of "fair warning" as it relates to law "made specific" for the purpose of validly applying § 242. The fact that one has a civil and the other a criminal law role is of no significance; both serve the same objective, and in effect the "clearly established" test is simply [an] adaptation of the fair warning standard . . . . To require something clearer than "clearly established" would, then, call for something beyond "fair warning." . . .

In sum, as with civil liability, all that can usefully be said about criminal liability under § 242 is that it may be imposed for deprivation of a constitutional right if, but only if, "in the light of pre-existing law the unlawfulness [under the Constitution is] apparent." Where it is, the constitutional requirement of fair warning is satisfied.

[Vacated and remanded for application of the proper standard.]

Notes and Questions

(1) *What Does Lanier Mean about Instructions at Trial?* At the next trial under the civil rights statute, should the trial court just lift the Supreme Court's statement and

tell the jury: "[You may find the defendant guilty] if, but only if, in the light of pre-existing law, the unlawfulness [of the defendant's conduct was] apparent"? If that is enough, perhaps the court of appeals in *Lanier* should affirm the trial judge, whose instruction seems similar to that instruction.

(2) *The Constitution as a Collection of "Grandiloquent Generalities."* It has been said that the Constitution consists of "grandiloquent generalities." Virtually every clause creates extensive debate. That being so, can the Constitution ever supply meaning that is sufficiently specific that "unlawfulness is apparent"? If not, the civil rights statute would support no criminal prosecutions at all, but that conclusion hardly seems supportable!

(3) *Legality and Homicide Offenses: Commonwealth v. Booth*, 766 A.2d 843 (Pa. 2001). In this case, the Pennsylvania Supreme Court considered "whether the Commonwealth may rely upon the death of an unborn child as the predicate for the crime of homicide by vehicle [75 Pa. C.S. §3735(a)] while driving under the influence." The Court rejected the application of the statute to unborn children. It observed that there were no common law crimes in Pennsylvania and that penal statutes were to be strictly construed to resolve ambiguities in favor of the defendant. The Court then noted that the traditional rule of interpretation was to read "person" as meaning someone who was born alive. *See also State v. Jardine*, 61 P.3d 514 (Haw. Ct. App. 2002) (holding statutory defense for use of force to protect another "person" does not apply to use of force to protect a fetus); *Keeler v. Superior Court of Amador County*, 470 P.2d 617 (Cal. 1970) (holding California prohibition on killing a "human being" did not apply to the killing of a fetus because the common law definition of "human being" only included those who were "born alive").

(4) *Can the Courts Expand the Reach of Crimes When the Policy for Doing So Is Obvious?* Decisions like *Booth* seem to suggest that common-law evolution means reading crimes ever more narrowly and that courts should not expand the reach of criminal laws, although legislation can do so. *Lanier*, by contrast, suggests a slightly more flexible standard. And, in fact, courts sometimes do use common law interpretation to expand crimes. When? One instance when many courts will expand the scope of crimes arises when the policy is clear and the defendant neither lacked notice nor relied on any rule of exoneration. Consider the following case. Is Tennessee's expansion of the scope of its murder statute consistent with decisions such as *Booth* and *Lanier*?

ROGERS v. TENNESSEE, 532 U.S. 451 (2001). Murder under the common law was limited by an exception called the "year-and-a-day rule." If the victim did not die within a year plus one day after the defendant's act, the defendant could not be convicted of murder. In this case, Rogers's victim did not die until 15 months after Rogers stabbed him. Rogers argued that the year-and-a-day rule precluded his conviction for murder. The Tennessee Supreme Court recognized that the year-and-a-day rule existed in Tennessee, was incorporated into the State's common law, and governed the State's murder statute. It held, however, that the rule no longer had any support in policy and should be abolished.

The Tennessee Supreme Court noted that the year-and-a-day rule had made sense when medicine was primitive, because a long period between injury and death suggested a break in causation, but advances in medicine now meant that delayed deaths were common but still traceable to causes more than a year old. Further, a person in Rogers's position could scarcely lack notice that his conduct was likely to be punishable as murder, and he had no right to rely on the year and a day rule, because the victim's survival was fortuitous. The Tennessee court also held that its decision did not violate the Due Process Clause by reason of its retroactive application to Rogers.

The United States Supreme Court, in an opinion by Justice O'Connor, affirmed the conviction. The Court emphasized that medical advances had rendered the rule obsolete, it had been legislatively or judicially abolished nearly everywhere, and it had "only the most tenuous foothold" in Tennessee:

> [A] judicial alteration of a common law doctrine of criminal law violates the principle of fair warning, and hence must not be given retroactive effect, only where it is "unexpected and indefensible by reference to the law which had been expressed prior to the conduct at issue". . . .

> [This extension of the law also did not violate the Ex Post Facto Clause, which expressly applies only to legislatures. To hold otherwise would show] too little regard for the important institutional and contextual differences between legislating, on the one hand, and common law decisionmaking, on the other. . . .

Four justices dissented. Justice Scalia's dissenting opinion argued that the majority had departed from the Framer's conception of common law judging, which he said did not allow a court retroactively to abolish a required crime element while acknowledging its existence in the existing law. *See also Metrish v. Lancaster*, 569 U.S. 351 (2013) (no due process violation when, in its first opinion on the issue, state supreme court rejects longstanding lower court interpretation of statute and applies the new interpretation retroactively).

[B] The Persistence of the Common Law

Notes on Common Law Crime

(1) *Common Law Crimes.* Recall that at one time most crimes were common law crimes, which means they were created by courts rather than legislatures. Many states have statutes or court decisions declaring that common law crimes no longer exist. *See, e.g., State v. Palendrano*, 293 A.2d 747 (N.J. Super. Ct. 1972) (holding common law crime of being a "common scold" to have been subsumed within legislative definitions of disorderly conduct). At the federal level, common law crimes have long been forbidden. *See United States v. Hudson and Goodwin*, 11 U.S. 32 (1812). Nonetheless, the common law and common law reasoning continue to be a critical part of the criminal law.

(2) *Incomplete Statutory Definitions.* In some states, today, the criminal code sets punishments but does not define crimes. Virginia, for example, has no statutory definition of robbery. *See* Va. Code Ann. § 18.2–58. Massachusetts has no statutory definition of manslaughter. *See* Mass. Gen. Laws 265 § 13. Thus, although recognition of these crimes depends upon statutes, the definition of the crimes depends upon the common law. As a result, courts—not the legislature—play the central role in defining crimes in these states. Other states have enacted statutes that list the elements of crimes but do not define all of the terms that they use, with the result that courts look to traditional common law definitions.

For example, in *Smith v. United States,* 586 U.S. 106 (2013), discussed in the conspiracy section of Chapter 10, the Court had to decide who had the burden of proving withdrawal from a conspiracy. The statute provided no answer. The Court therefore said, "[T]he common-law rule was that affirmative defenses . . . were matters for the defendant to prove." Because "Congress did not address . . . the burden of proof for withdrawal, we presume that Congress intended to preserve the common-law rule. . . ."

(3) *Interpretation: The Examples of Federal Fraud-Based Statutes and Their Expansion.* Sometimes, especially for poorly-drafted or open-ended statutes, interpretation comes very close to creating new crimes. For example, the federal criminal fraud statutes provide for judicial crime creation in response to incomplete and open-ended statutes. The mail and wire fraud statutes (18 U.S.C. §§ 1341 & 1343) prohibit "devis[ing] or intending to devise any scheme or artifice to defraud, or for obtaining money or property by means of false or fraudulent pretenses." In an early decision, the Supreme Court ruled that this language "includes everything designed to defraud by representations as to the past or present, or suggestions and promises as to the future." *Durland v. United States,* 161 U.S. 306, 313–14 (1896). According to one commentator, federal courts have used the expansive language of the mail and wire fraud statute to create new crimes:

> The [mail and wire fraud] statutes have been applied to scores of distinct forms of misconduct—from business and consumer fraud, to securities and commodities fraud, to blackmail, to lottery schemes, to public corruption, to misappropriation of confidential information (both private and governmental). Had courts been unwilling to treat "fraud" as a generative concept, each of these applications would have required the enactment of a separate criminal statute. . . . [A]ll of these doctrines . . . must be understood to be the product of federal common-lawmaking.

Dan M. Kahan, *Lenity and Federal Common Law Crimes,* 1994 Supreme Court Rev. 345, 375–76; *but see Cleveland v. United States,* 531 U.S. 12 (2000) (holding a gambling license is not property for purpose of the federal fraud statutes). Is the Supreme Court's treatment of these statutes troubling?

(4) *"Reception" Statutes or "Saving Clauses": Common Law Crimes as "Gap Fillers."* A handful of states have enacted "reception statutes" or "saving clauses" that

recognize the persistence of common law crimes. For example, a Michigan statute, discussed in the next case, provides, "Any person who shall commit any indictable offense at the common law, for the punishment of which no provision is expressly made by any statute of this state, shall be guilty of a felony, punishable by imprisonment in the state prison not more than 5 years or by a fine of not more than $10,000.00, or both in the discretion of the court." Mich. Comp. Laws § 750.505; *see also* Fla. Stat. § 775.02 ("Punishment of common-law offenses"). Prosecutions under statutes such as this are rare, but here is an example.

People v. Kevorkian
527 N.W.2d 714 (Mich. 1994)

CAVANAGH, C.J., and BRICKLEY and GRIFFIN, JJ.

[Defendant Jack Kevorkian helped several terminally ill people commit suicide. He was indicted for murder, but the trial court quashed some of the indictments. The prosecutor appealed.]

The crime of murder has been classified and categorized by the Legislature, but the definition of murder has been left to the common law. *People v. Aaron*, 409 Mich. 672; 299 N.W.2d 304 (1980); *People v. Scott*, 6 Mich. 287 (1859). . . . Under the common-law definition, "murder is where a person of sound memory and discretion unlawfully kills any reasonable creature in being, in peace of the state, with malice prepense or aforethought, either express or implied." . . . Early decisions indicate that a murder conviction may be based on merely providing the means by which another commits suicide. However, few jurisdictions, if any, have retained the early common-law view that assisting in a suicide is murder. The modern statutory scheme in the majority of states treats assisted suicide as a separate crime, with penalties less onerous than those for murder. . . .

. . . [T]his Court has modified the common law when it perceives a need to tailor culpability to fit the crime more precisely than is achieved through application of existing interpretations of the common law. . . . [W]e perceive such a need here. . . . Only where there is probable cause to believe that death was the direct and natural result of a defendant's act can the defendant be properly bound over on a charge of murder. Where a defendant merely is involved in the events leading up to the death, such as providing the means, the proper charge is assisting in a suicide.

However, even absent a statute that specifically proscribes assisted suicide, prosecution and punishment for assisting in a suicide would not be precluded. Rather, such conduct may be prosecuted as a separate common-law offense under the saving clause of MCL § 750.505. . . . Our reinterpretation of the common law does not enlarge the scope of criminal liability for assisted suicide, but rather reduces liability [from murder to assisting in suicide] where a defendant merely is involved in the events leading up to the suicide, such as providing the means. Therefore, there is no violation of the prohibition on ex post facto laws. . . .

BOYLE, J. (concurring in part and dissenting in part).

[The majority] finds that one who has only participated in a suicide but has not done the final act causing death may be prosecuted under the saving clause. The statute is applicable only when two conditions obtain: the conduct is not otherwise punishable by statute and the conduct was indictable at common law. . . . Culpability for persons assisting in suicide at common law was based on participation as parties to the crime of suicide. The saving clause furnishes no basis for the Court's creation of a new crime. The usurpation of legislative authority in the lead opinion's approach is evident if one considers the reach of its rationale. . . . Contrary to the lead opinion's conclusion, the saving clause is not a delegation of legislative authority to this Court to create new crimes.

Notes and Questions

(1) *Judicial Crime Creation?* The majority creates a new common law crime of assisted suicide, different from common law murder, to cover Kevorkian's conduct, even though that conduct occurred before anyone in Michigan ever recognized the crime of assisted suicide. The court points to the Michigan "reception statute" or "saving clause," which preserves some room for common law. Is the result in *Kevorkian* justifiable (is this an appropriate role for courts)?

(2) *Wrongful Conduct.* Some theorists distinguish between inherently wrongful conduct (sometimes called *malum in se*) and conduct that is wrong only because it is illegal (sometimes called *malum prohibitum*). For example, rape is a *malum in se* crime while failing to file a tax return is *malum prohibitum*. Is it more appropriate for a court to recognize conduct as criminal if that conduct is appropriately described as "inherently wrongful"? If so, is it clear that assisting in a suicide is inherently wrongful (does the fact that conduct was indictable at common law mean that it is inherently wrongful)?

(3) *Assisted Suicide Statutes.* As *Kevorkian* notes, several states have specific prohibitions on assisted suicide. Would your assessment of the case change if you knew the Michigan legislature had passed an assisted suicide statute that applied to some of Kevorkian's conduct but was passed too late to cover all of it (under ex post facto principles, see § 13.03(A), below)?

§ 13.02 The Rule of Lenity and the Problem of Overbreadth

[A] The Rule of Lenity

Note on Favoring "Lenity" in Cases of Ambiguity

(1) *The Basic Idea of Lenity.* The rule of lenity holds that where all else is equal, courts should resolve ambiguities in criminal statutes in favor of defendants and against the prosecution. As the Supreme Court has put it, "When there are two

rational readings of a criminal statute, one harsher than the other, we are to choose the harsher only when Congress has spoken in clear and definite language." *McNally v. United States*, 483 U.S. 350, 359–360 (1987); *see also United States v. Lanier, supra*; *Cleveland v. United States*, 531 U.S. 12 (2000) ("we have instructed that 'ambiguity concerning the ambit of criminal statutes should be resolved in favor of lenity'").

One rationale for the rule of lenity is that the government is responsible for enacting a statute and should be the party to suffer if there is a lack of clarity. A closely related theory is that citizens are entitled to clarity in criminal statutes and should receive the benefit of doubt when the laws fail to provide adequate precision. *See Liparota v. United States*, 471 U.S. 419, 427 (1985) ("Application of the rule of lenity ensures that criminal statutes will provide fair warning and strikes the appropriate balance [among] the legislature, the prosecution, and the court.").

As the *Lanier* Court observed, the rule of lenity has an obvious connection to the vagueness doctrine, which we take up in § 13.03[B][2].

(2) *Limits on the Rule of Lenity.* Although the rule of lenity is frequently invoked, it has only sporadic effectiveness as a limit on criminal statutes. Consider some of the U.S. Supreme Court's justifications for not applying the rule in particular cases:

"'[T]he touchstone of the rule of lenity is statutory ambiguity.' [The statute at issue] is not a model of the careful drafter's art. But neither is it 'grievous[ly] ambigu[ous].'" *United States v. Hayes*, 555 U.S. 415, 429 (2009).

"Lenity applies only when the equipoise of competing reasons cannot otherwise be resolved." *Johnson v. United States*, 529 U.S. 694, 713 n.13 (2000).

"Absent ambiguity, the rule of lenity is not applicable to guide statutory interpretation." *United States v. Johnson*, 529 U.S. 53, 59 (2000).

In short, although the rule of lenity can be a powerful tool in a few kinds of cases, it does not provide an across-the-board principle of leniency.

(3) *Statutory Versions — or Rejections — of the Rule of Lenity.* Criminal codes typically provide courts with guidance in interpreting state statutes. Some statutes adopt the rule of lenity. *See, e.g.*, Fla. Stat. Ann. § 775.021 (criminal statutes "shall be strictly construed; when the language is susceptible of differing constructions, it shall be construed most favorably to the accused"). Others reject it, preferring what has been called the "fair meaning" approach. *See, e.g.*, Ariz. Rev. Stat. § 13–104 ("The general rule that a penal statute is to be strictly construed does not apply" to Arizona statutory crimes, "but the provisions . . . must be construed according to the fair meaning of their terms to promote justice and effect the objects of the law"). The Model Penal Code also includes a "fair import" provision. *See* MPC § 1.02(3).

A rather bizarre version, the product of a political compromise between prosecutors and criminal defense lawyers, appears to adopt *both* approaches. Tenn. Code Ann. § 39–11-104 (criminal statutes "shall be construed according to the fair import of their terms [i.e. rejecting the rule of lenity], including reference to judicial decisions and common law interpretations [which include the rule of lenity], to promote justice, and effect the objectives of the criminal code").

[B] Judicial Review When Lenity Cannot Prevent a Statute from Infringing on Constitutionally Protected Conduct

Note on Constitutional Limits on Criminal Laws

(1) *Constitutions are the Ultimate Limit on the Content of Criminal Laws.* It is obvious that neither state or federal legislatures, nor a court, may create a criminal law that violates the United States Constitution. Often state constitutions also place similar limits on criminal laws. For example, the Supreme Court would waste little time invalidating a state or federal statute that barred citizens "from entering a house of worship for any reason." The First Amendment's religious freedom guarantee would prohibit this absurd statute.

(2) *Great Variety of Constitutional Limits.* There are many constitutional guarantees that limit criminal sanctions. Though an in-depth discussion is beyond the scope of this course (and may be covered in your constitutional law course), a few of these limits are noted below.

LAWRENCE v. TEXAS, 539 U.S. 558, 578 (2003). Texas Penal Code § 21.06 provided, "A person commits an offense if he engages in deviate sexual intercourse with another individual of the same sex." A separate statute defined "deviate sexual intercourse" to include anal and oral sex. When police and prosecutors enforced the statute, traditional common law reasoning and interpretive principles, as well as the rule of lenity, were of little help to the defendants. The statute clearly prohibited certain sexual activity between people of the same sex.

When the meaning of a criminal statute is clear, the rule of lenity cannot mitigate its impact. Therefore, the defendants claimed that the statute was unconstitutional because it violated the Fourteenth Amendment's prohibition on taking "life, liberty, or property" without "due process of law." The Supreme Court agreed:

> The case . . . involve[s] two adults who, with full and mutual consent from each other, engaged in sexual practices common to a homosexual lifestyle. The petitioners are entitled to respect for their private lives. . . . Their right to liberty under the Due Process Clause gives them the full right to engage in their conduct without intervention of the government. . . . The Texas statute furthers no legitimate state interest which can justify its intrusion into the personal and private life of the individual.

Notes and Questions

(1) *Unconstitutionality of This Kind, for Lack of a "Legitimate State Interest," Is Rare.* As you may learn in your constitutional law class, criminal statutes are rarely

declared unconstitutional in this way. Consider the *Lawrence* Court's reasoning. How often will a criminal statute fail to advance a "legitimate state interest"? Even if judges disapprove of a statute that is justified primarily by publicly accepted principles of morality with little or no harm to others, it is far from clear that they should declare it illegitimate. *See* § 13.04 of this chapter, below (exploring the limits of the relationship between law and morality).

(2) *Substantive Due Process.* Traditional constitutional law has classified statutes that are invalidated for lack of a legitimate state interest as violating "substantive due process." While courts today are understandably hesitant to second-guess a legislature's assessment that a statute does serve a proper purpose, on occasion, as *Lawrence* illustrates, substantive due process is used successfully to challenge a statute that a court believes has little relationship to the public interest.

(3) *First Amendment.* The First Amendment places significant limits on laws making certain conduct criminal. Laws that reach conduct that is protected by the First Amendment are often said to suffer from "overbreadth." *See, e.g., Lewis v. City of New Orleans,* 415 U.S. 130 (1974) (invalidating ordinance punishing "opprobrious" language to police officer; law is overbroad in banning speech protected by First Amendment); *R.A.V. v. City of St. Paul,* 505 U.S. 377 (1992) (invalidating ordinance that punished the display of a symbol that a person should know "arouses anger, alarm or resentment in others on the basis of race, color, creed, religion or gender"; government generally cannot punish speech on basis of content).

(4) *The Related, but Different, Issues of Notice and Vagueness.* As discussed in the next section, on "notice," the possibility is somewhat more likely that a statute will suffer from a constitutional defect that is different from, but related to, retroactivity and the rule of lenity. These latter principles deal with crime definition, while notice deals with the problem of expecting the defendant to know that the definition applies and what it means.

§ 13.03 Notice and Vagueness: The Due Process Right to "Fair Warning"

[A] The Meaning of Notice

Notes on the Multiple Policies Expressed by the Notice Requirement

(1) *A Shorthand Expression for Several Related Ideas.* The requirement of "notice" is a shorthand expression for a number of different policies, several of which we have already begun to discuss. Briefly stated, these policies include the following.

(2) *Avoiding Ex Post Facto Problems, or Retroactive Statutes.* Society ought to define punishable conduct in advance, through legislation, rather than deciding to condemn it after the fact. Article I of the Constitution provides that neither the

states nor the federal government may enact *ex post facto* laws. An ex post facto law, in general, is a legislative enactment that criminalizes past conduct (or increases its punishment). *See Calder v. Bull*, 3 U.S. 386 (1790).

(3) *The Due Process Implications of Novel Judicial Interpretations.* As we have seen, the Ex Post Facto Clause applies to legislation, but the Due Process Clause limits novel judicial acts (in other words, it restricts retroactive applications of judicial interpretations). The Supreme Court, in *Bouie v. City of Columbia*, 378 U.S. 347 (1964), held that the application to a defendant of a novel or unforeseeable judicial interpretation of the criminal law violates due process. Although the *Bouie* doctrine provides an important check on judicial expansion of criminal statutes, it rarely will be useful to defendants who have engaged in conduct that a court thinks is obviously wrong. The Court stressed that the interpretation at issue must be "unexpected and indefensible by reference to the law which had been expressed prior to the conduct in issue." *See Rogers v. Tennessee, supra*, 532 U.S. 451 (2001) (holding the *Bouie* doctrine does not prevent judicial abolition of the common law rule that a person's conduct can be murder only if the victim dies within "a year and a day").

(4) *Sufficient Clarity of Definition: The Vagueness Problem.* Yet another notice-related concern is that the crime definition should be relatively clear as opposed to unnecessarily vague (although the imperfection of language and the concern for adequate coverage of harmful conduct limit this objective). *See* subsection [B][2], below, on vagueness.

(5) *Deference to Legislative Definition.* A court should hesitate to fill a perceived gap in a statute, because it should defer to democratic will as expressed by the legislature rather than exercise judicial power that is insulated from democratic influence. *See United States v. Lanier*, 520 U.S. 259, 265 n.5 (1997). At the same time, however, the court also has a duty to interpret the statute to achieve the legislative intent, and this duty may require closing the "gap."

(6) *Even-Handed Enforcement: Clear Crime Definition as a Restriction upon Arbitrary or Discriminatory Law Enforcement.* Also, crime definition should be adequate to prevent government officers from enforcing laws arbitrarily against some chosen individuals, and it should give at least minimal assurance that it applies equally to all persons. In fact, this kind of "notice" problem often is described as more important than individual notice. Usually, individuals can adopt safe-harbor methods of avoiding violating vague laws, but lack of notice to law officers, judges, and juries means that they are without guidance in exercising their power. Subsection [B][2] of this chapter, on vagueness, discusses this issue as well.

(7) *"Notice" as Referring to the Rule of Lenity.* As discussed in § 13.02[A], courts will often resolve reasonable ambiguities in criminal statutes in favor of defendants. Although technically distinguishable from the problem of notice (because the defendant theoretically has notice of a plausible meaning of a criminal law), courts sometimes describe the issue of crime definition as one of notice. In *United States v. Lanier*, 520 U.S. 259, 266 (1997), excerpted *supra*, for example, the Court listed the

rule of lenity as one of "three relevant manifestations of the fair warning requirement" and "a sort of 'junior varsity version of the vagueness doctrine.'"

[B] Constitutional Aspects of Notice

[1] The "Pure Notice" Problem: When the Law is Clear, but the Defendant Is Unlikely to Know It Exists

LAMBERT v. CALIFORNIA, 355 U.S. 225 (1957). A municipal ordinance in Los
Angeles required anyone previously convicted of a felony to register with the Chief
of Police within five days of arriving in the city. Lambert, who was convicted of violating this ordinance, claimed not to have known of the duty to register and argued
that her conviction violated the notice requirement of the Due Process Clause. The
Supreme Court, per Justice Douglas, agreed. In a five-to-four decision it reversed
her conviction:

> The rule that "ignorance of the law will not excuse" is deep in our
> law. . . . On the other hand, due process places some limits on its exercise.
> Engrained in our concept of due process is the requirement of notice. . . .
>
> Registration laws are common and their range is wide. Many such laws
> are akin to licensing statutes in that they pertain to the regulation of busi-
> ness activities. But the present ordinance is entirely different. Violation of
> its provisions is unaccompanied by any activity whatever, mere presence in
> the city being the test. Moreover, circumstances which might move one to
> inquire as to the necessity of registration are completely lacking. . . .
>
> . . . Where a person did not know of the duty to register and where there
> was no proof of the probability of such knowledge, he may not be convicted
> consistently with due process. . . . REVERSED.

Notes and Questions

(1) *Lambert Is Unusual, and Lack of Notice of a Criminal Law That Is Violated Is
Rarely an Excuse: United States v. Wilson*, 159 F.3d 280 (7th Cir. 1998); *United States
v. Miller*, 646 F.3d 1128 (8th Cir. 2011). A little-publicized but widely applicable federal statute, 18 U.S.C. § 922(g)(9), provides that it is illegal for any person convicted
of a crime of domestic violence (including a misdemeanor), or subject to a domestic relations restraining order, to possess a firearm. In *Wilson*, Judge Posner argued
in dissent that § 922(g)(9) was "obscure" and that it trapped firearms owners who
had no reason to guess that their "apparently innocent conduct" of continuing to
possess guns that they already owned was a federal crime. But the *Wilson* majority
disagreed, and so have other courts. In *Miller*, for example, the court reasoned that
the dangerous propensities of persons convicted of domestic abuse and the heavily
regulated nature of domestic violence defendants were "common knowledge," and

therefore, a person so convicted or restrained could not reasonably expect to be free of firearms regulation. In summary, *Lambert* is unusual.

(2) *Distinguishing the "Notice" Problem in Lambert from the "Vagueness" Problem (Below).* The notice problem in *Lambert* is different from the problem of vagueness, which is the subject of the next section. In *Lambert*, the law at issue was not ambiguous, but the Court decided that notice of its existence could not be imputed to the defendant. The vagueness cases involve a subtly different type of "notice": ambiguities that force a reasonable person to "guess at the meaning" of a statute, even after having notice of its text.

[2] *The Vagueness Problem: Notice of the Existence of the Law, but with Terms So Ambiguous that Readers Must "Guess" at Its Meaning*

Lanzetta v. New Jersey

306 U.S. 451 (1939)

Mr. Justice Butler delivered the opinion of the Court.

By this appeal we are called on to decide whether, by reason of vagueness and uncertainty, a recent [criminal] enactment of New Jersey is repugnant to the due process clause of the Fourteenth Amendment. It is as follows: "Any person not engaged in any lawful occupation, known to be a member of any gang consisting of two or more persons, who has been convicted at least three times of being a disorderly person, or who has been convicted of any crime, in this or in any other State, is declared to be a gangster." . . .

The phrase "consisting of two or more persons" is all that purports to define "gang." The meanings of that word indicated in dictionaries and in historical and sociological writings are numerous and varied. [In a different case, the New Jersey Court of Errors and Appeals dealt with "gang" as follows:] "Public policy ordains that a combination designed to wage war upon society shall be dispersed and its members rendered incapable of harm. This is the objective . . . and it is therefore a valid exercise of the legislative power. . . . The evident aim of this provision was to render penal the association of criminals for the pursuit of criminal enterprises; that is the gist of the legislative expression. . . . If society cannot impose such taint of illegality upon the confederation of convicted criminals, who have no lawful occupation, under circumstances denoting . . . the pursuit of criminal objectives, it is helpless against one of the most menacing forms of evil activity. . . ."

The descriptions and illustrations used by the court to indicate the meaning of "gang" are not sufficient to constitute definition, inclusive or exclusive. [I]t does not purport to give any interpretation generally applicable. The state court did not find, and we cannot, that "gang" has ever been limited in meaning to a group having purpose to commit any particular offense or class of crimes, or that it has not quite frequently been used in reference to groups of two or more persons not to be suspected of criminality or of anything that is unlawful. . . .

The lack of certainty of the challenged provision is not limited to the word "gang" or to its dependent "gangster." Without resolving the serious doubts arising from the generality of the language, we assume that the clause "any person not engaged in any lawful occupation" is sufficient to identify a class to which must belong all capable of becoming gangsters within the terms of the provision. The enactment employs the expression, "known to be a member." It is ambiguous. There immediately arises the doubt whether actual or putative association is meant. If actual membership is required, that status must be established as a fact, and the word "known" would be without significance. If reputed membership is enough, there is uncertainty whether that reputation must be general or extend only to some persons. And the statute fails to indicate what constitutes membership or how one may join a "gang." . . . [Statute invalidated.]

City of Chicago v. Morales
527 U.S. 41 (1999)

JUSTICE STEVENS announced the judgment of the Court and delivered the opinion of the Court with respect to Parts I, II, and V, and an opinion with respect to Parts III, IV, and VI, in which Justice Souter and Justice Ginsburg join.

In 1992, the Chicago City Council enacted the Gang Congregation Ordinance, which prohibits "criminal street gang members" from "loitering" with one another or with other persons in any public place. . . . Commission of the offense involves four predicates. First, [a] police officer must reasonably believe that at least one of the two or more persons present in a "public place" is a "criminal street gang member." Second, the persons must be "loitering," which the ordinance defines as "remaining in any one place with no apparent purpose." Third, the officer must then order "all" of the persons to disperse and remove themselves "from the area." Fourth, a person must disobey the officer's order. If any person, whether a gang member or not, disobeys the officer's order, that person is guilty of violating the ordinance.

Two months after the ordinance was adopted, the Chicago Police Department promulgated General Order 92–4 to provide guidelines to govern its enforcement. That order purported to establish limitations on the enforcement discretion of police officers "to ensure that the anti-gang loitering ordinance is not enforced in an arbitrary or discriminatory way." . . .

Vagueness may invalidate a criminal law for either of two independent reasons. First, [1] it may fail to provide the kind of notice that will enable ordinary people to understand what conduct it prohibits; second, [2] it may authorize and even encourage arbitrary and discriminatory enforcement. *See Kolender v. Lawson*, 461 U.S. [352,] 357 [(1983)]. Accordingly, we first consider whether the ordinance provides fair notice to the citizen and then discuss its potential for arbitrary enforcement.

IV

[T]he term "loiter" may have a common and accepted meaning, but the definition of that term in this ordinance — "to remain in any one place with no apparent purpose"—does not. It is difficult to imagine how any citizen of the city of Chicago standing in a public place with a group of people would know if he or she had an "apparent purpose." . . . The city's principal response to this concern about adequate notice is that loiterers are not subject to sanction until after they have failed to comply with an officer's order to disperse. . . . We find this response unpersuasive for at least two reasons.

First, the purpose of the fair notice requirement is to enable the ordinary citizen to conform his or her conduct to the law. "No one may be required at peril of life, liberty or property to speculate as to the meaning of penal statutes." *Lanzetta v. New Jersey*, 306 U.S. 451, 453 (1939). Although it is true that a loiterer is not subject to criminal sanctions unless he or she disobeys a dispersal order, the loitering is the conduct that the ordinance is designed to prohibit. If the loitering is in fact harmless and innocent, the dispersal order itself is an unjustified impairment of liberty. . . . Because an officer may issue an order only after prohibited conduct has already occurred, it cannot provide the kind of advance notice that will protect the putative loiterer from being ordered to disperse. Such an order cannot retroactively give adequate warning of the boundary between the permissible and the impermissible applications of the law.

Second, the terms of the dispersal order compound the inadequacy of the notice afforded by the ordinance. It provides that the officer "shall order all such persons to disperse and remove themselves from the area." This vague phrasing raises a host of questions. After such an order issues, how long must the loiterers remain apart? How far must they move? . . . [The plurality also faulted the phrase "from the area" for being too "elastic."]

Lack of clarity in the description of the loiterer's duty to obey a dispersal order might not render the ordinance unconstitutionally vague if the definition of the forbidden conduct were clear, but it does buttress our conclusion that the entire ordinance fails to give the ordinary citizen adequate notice of what is forbidden . . . . This ordinance is therefore vague . . . .

V

The broad sweep of the ordinance also violates "'the requirement that a legislature establish minimal guidelines to govern law enforcement.'" *Kolender v. Lawson*, 461 U.S. at 358. . . . In any public place in the city of Chicago, persons who stand or sit in the company of a gang member may be ordered to disperse unless their purpose is apparent. The mandatory language in the enactment directs the police to issue an order without first making any inquiry about their possible purposes. . . .

Recognizing that the ordinance does reach a substantial amount of innocent conduct, we turn, then, to its language to determine if it "necessarily entrusts lawmaking to the moment-to-moment judgment of the policeman on his beat." *Kolender v. Lawson*, 461 U.S. at 359. . . . As the Illinois Supreme Court interprets [the ordinance,] it "provides absolute discretion to police officers to determine what activities constitute loitering." . . .

It is true, as the city argues, that the requirement that the officer reasonably believe that a group of loiterers contains a gang member does place a limit on the authority to order dispersal. That limitation would no doubt be sufficient if the ordinance only applied to loitering that had an apparently harmful purpose or effect, or possibly if it only applied to loitering by persons reasonably believed to be criminal gang members. But this ordinance . . . applies to everyone in the city who may remain in one place with one suspected gang member as long as their purpose is not apparent. . . . Friends, relatives, teachers, counselors, or even total strangers might unwittingly engage in forbidden loitering if they happen to engage in idle conversation with a gang member. . . .

[T]he Illinois Supreme Court refused to accept the general order issued by the police department as a sufficient limitation on the "vast amount of discretion" granted to the police in its enforcement. We agree. That the police have adopted internal rules limiting their enforcement to certain designated areas in the city would not provide a defense to a loiterer who might be arrested elsewhere. . . . [Ordinance invalidated.]

JUSTICE SCALIA, dissenting.

What counts [in evaluating vagueness in the sense of lack of notice] is not what the Ordinance is "designed to prohibit," but what it actually subjects to criminal penalty. [T]hat consists of nothing but the refusal to obey a dispersal order, as to which there is no doubt of adequate notice of the prohibited conduct. The plurality's suggestion that even the dispersal order itself is unconstitutionally vague, because it does not specify how far to disperse (!), scarcely requires a response. [See] *Boos v. Barry*, 485 U.S. 312, 331 (1988) (rejecting overbreadth/and vagueness challenge to a law allowing police officers to order congregations near foreign embassies to disperse); *Cox v. Louisiana*, 379 U.S. 536, 551 (1965) (rejecting vagueness challenge to the dispersal-order prong of a breach-of-the-peace statute).

[As for "the second aspect" of vagueness], which requires sufficient specificity to prevent arbitrary and discriminatory law enforcement[, t]he criteria for issuance of a dispersal order under the Chicago Ordinance could hardly be clearer. First, the law requires police officers to "reasonably believe" that one of the group to which the order is issued is a "criminal street gang member." This resembles a probable-cause standard . . . . Under the Order, officers must have probable cause to believe that an individual is a member of a criminal street gang, to be substantiated by the officer's "experience and knowledge of the alleged offenders" and by "specific, documented and reliable information" such as reliable witness testimony or an individual's admission of gang membership or display of distinctive colors, tattoos, signs, or other markings. . . .

[Furthermore,] the Ordinance requires that the group be "remaining in one place with no apparent purpose." [The] assertion that this applies to "any person standing in a public place" is a distortion. . . . There may be some ambiguity at the margin, but "remaining in one place" requires more than a temporary stop, and is clear in most of its applications. . . . As for the phrase "with no apparent purpose". . . . Chicago police officers enforcing the Ordinance are not looking for people with no apparent purpose (who are regrettably in oversupply); they are looking for people who "remain in any one place with no apparent purpose"—that is, who remain there without any apparent reason for remaining there. That is not difficult to perceive. . . .

JUSTICE THOMAS, with whom THE CHIEF JUSTICE, and JUSTICE SCALIA join, dissenting.

In order to perform their peace-keeping responsibilities satisfactorily, the police inevitably must exercise discretion. Indeed, by empowering them to act as peace officers, the law assumes that the police will exercise that discretion responsibly and with sound judgment. That is not to say that the law should not provide objective guidelines for the police, but simply that it cannot rigidly constrain their every action. By directing a police officer not to issue a dispersal order unless he "observes a person whom he reasonably believes to be a criminal street gang member loitering in any public place," Chicago's ordinance strikes an appropriate balance between those two extremes. . . .

The plurality's conclusion that the ordinance "fails to give the ordinary citizen adequate notice of what is forbidden and what is permitted," is similarly untenable. There is nothing "vague" about an order to disperse. While "we can never expect mathematical certainty from our language," *Grayned v. City of Rockford*, 408 U.S. 104, 110 (1972), it is safe to assume that the vast majority of people who are ordered by the police to "disperse and remove themselves from the area" will have little difficulty understanding how to comply. . . .

Notes and Questions

(1) *Vagueness in Lanzetta and Morales.* Should the Court's reasoning in these cases be applicable to other fluid concepts that are historical anchors of the law—terms such as "depraved heart malice" in the law of murder? Like the New Jersey statute in *Lanzetta*, this phrase has "numerous and varied" meanings. Like the Chicago ordinance in *Morales*, it is not clear what "standard of conduct" is specified.

(2) *Questions about Lanzetta.* Is the Court correct that the New Jersey "gangster" statute is fatally vague? The statute requires a finding of (1) no lawful occupation, (2) known membership in a "gang," and (3) prior conviction of a crime or of being a disorderly person. How many people are likely to fit such a definition? There is little risk that prosecutors will go after individuals who have never been convicted of anything, or after people who have steady jobs. Although the statute is not a model of clarity, don't you have at least some sense of the circumstances in which it would be applied?

(3) *Questions about Morales.* The same questions apply to *Morales*. Is the statute really so vague? Do you think police would arrest people chatting on a park bench just because one of them was a known gang member? But perhaps the answer is not so clear. Maybe the Court believed that an open-ended statute is more likely to be

applied to hassle specific people, or in lower-income communities against young unemployed individuals. If your prediction about how the police will enforce the statute requires consideration of factors such as these, then perhaps the problem is that the statute creates too much discretion in its enforcement.

(4) *Vagueness and "Residual Clauses": Johnson v. United States*, 135 S. Ct. 2551 (2015). The federal Armed Career Criminal Act, 18 U.S.C. § 924(e)(2)(B), imposes a prison term of 15 years to life on a person who engages in certain prohibited conduct and who also has three or more earlier convictions for a "violent felony." The Act defines "violent felony" to include certain specific crimes but also has a catch-all "residual clause" that includes any crime that, as a general matter, "otherwise involves conduct that presents a serious potential risk of physical injury to another." In a 5–4 decision, the Supreme Court held that the residual clause is unconstitutionally vague. The Court explained that the task of determining the violence risk associated with a specific crime, assessed in general and not with reference to particular cases, was too difficult: "the indeterminacy of the wide-ranging inquiry required by the residual clause both denies fair notice to defendants and invites arbitrary enforcement by judges." *See also United States v. Davis*, 139 S. Ct. 2319 (2019) (applying *Johnson* to invalidate a similar residual clause in a different federal sentencing enhancement statute, 18 U.S.C. § 924(c)(3)(B)).

(5) *The Rule of Lenity Can Be a Kind of "Tie-Breaker" in Vagueness Disputes: Skilling v. United States*, 561 U.S. 358 (2010). Skilling was convicted of wire fraud for withholding his "honest services" as an officer of his company, Enron Corporation, which eventually collapsed. The government's theory of the crime was that Skilling had acted in dishonest ways to keep the price of the company's stock artificially high, at a level that benefited him personally, without disclosing what he was doing. The theory was novel, in part because the doctrine of "honest services fraud" had a complicated history.

The Supreme Court reversed the conviction. The Court's primary reason was a lack of sufficiently clear definition to provide notice of the criminality of the conduct at issue. The Court held that honest-services fraud related to bribery or kickbacks was sufficiently clearly included, because Congress intended to follow the earlier court-of-appeals decisions, and they covered this conduct unmistakably. But the support in those cases for the government's theory against Skilling was much more ambiguous. The rule of lenity, then, functioned as a kind of tie-breaker. The Court cited "the familiar principle that 'ambiguity concerning the ambit of criminal statutes should be resolved in favor of lenity.'"

(6) *Assessing the Purposes of the Vagueness Doctrine: Kolender v. Lawson*, 461 U.S. 352 (1983). In *Kolender*, a California statute provided that persons who loiter or wander must provide "credible and reliable" identification when requested by a police officer. The Supreme Court, through Justice O'Connor, struck down the statute as vague. The Court reinforced the purposes emphasized in *Lanzetta* and *Morales*: (1) providing notice so that people can arrange their conduct to avoid unlawful acts and (2) preventing arbitrary and discriminatory enforcement of the criminal laws.

The Court also noted a third purpose: (3) minimizing intrusions into freedom of speech and expression. Then, the Court made this nonobvious point: the most important objective is guidance to law enforcement, more so than guidance to individual citizens. The Court explained that in the absence of guidelines, "a criminal statute may permit a standardless sweep that allows policemen, prosecutors and juries to pursue their personal predilections." Is this, in fact, the more important aspect of the vagueness doctrine?

(7) *The Limits of Vagueness: United States Civil Service Commission v. National Ass'n of Letter Carriers*, 413 U.S. 548 (1973). The Hatch Act prohibits federal employees from taking "active parts" in political "management" or "campaigns." In this case, the Supreme Court, through Justice White, admitted that the terms contained some vagueness, but still, it upheld the statute. First, the enactment had to be read in light of the "limitations in the English language with respect to being both specific and manageably brief." Second, the vagueness standard assumes a "person exercising ordinary common sense" who is sincerely trying to "understand and comply," not a game-player "intent on finding fault at any cost." Do you think *Letter Carriers* is consistent with *Lanzetta* and *Morales*?

[C] Matters of Degree in Crime Definition: How Much Vagueness Is Tolerable?

Notes on Some Difficult Problems of Ambiguity

(1) *Ambiguity and Bad Judgment: Nash v. United States*, 229 U.S. 373 (1913). The defendant was convicted of criminal violations of the antitrust laws. He contended that the undefined statutory prohibitions on contracts "in restraint of trade" and "monopolization" were unconstitutionally vague. Writing for the Court, Justice Holmes disagreed:

> [T]he law is full of instances where a [person's] fate depends on his estimating rightly, that is, as the jury subsequently estimates it, some matter of degree. If his judgment is wrong, not only may he incur a fine or a short imprisonment, as here; he may incur the penalty of death. "An act causing death may be murder, manslaughter, or misadventure, according to the degree of danger attending it" by common experience in the circumstances known to the actor. "The very meaning of the fiction of implied malice in such cases at common law was, that a [person] might have to answer with his life for consequences which he neither intended nor foresaw." "The criterion in such cases is to examine whether common social duty would, under the circumstances, have suggested a more circumspect conduct." . . . We are of opinion that there is no constitutional difficulty in the way of enforcing the criminal part of the act.

"Restraint of trade" and "monopolization" are not self-defining terms with clear and obvious limits. Arguably, then, they are similar to the gang statutes struck down in *Lanzetta* and *Morales*. Why did the antitrust criminal law survive when laws in those cases did not?

(2) *Ambiguity Without Vagueness: McBoyle v. United States*, 283 U.S. 25 (1931). The National Motor Vehicle Theft Act prohibited the interstate transportation of "any . . . self-propelled vehicle not designed for running on rails." The statute was not vague because it clearly applied, at least, to stolen cars and trucks, but McBoyle stole an airplane and when charged with this crime, he claimed the statute did not apply to him. Speaking again through Justice Holmes, the Court agreed. Holmes admitted it was "etymologically . . . possible" to construe "motor vehicle" to include "a conveyance working on land, water, or air." Nonetheless, the Court adopted a narrower reading:

> Although it is not likely that a criminal will carefully consider the text of the law before he murders or steals, it is reasonable that fair warning should be given to the world, in language that the common world will understand, of what the law intends to do if a certain line is passed. When a rule of conduct is laid down in words that evoke in the common mind only the picture of vehicles moving on land, the statute should not be extended to aircraft simply because it may seem to us that a similar policy applies, or upon speculation that, if the legislature had thought of it, very likely broader words would have been used.

If the principle of fair warning has any relationship to actual notice, then it ought to be crucial that any person who steals an airplane surely knows that her conduct is illegal. For that matter, isn't the airplane thief more likely to have notice that her conduct is illegal than the person who "restrains trade"?

(3) *"Common Sense," Wrongfulness, and the Risk of Harm*. Remember the distinction between *malum prohibitum* (bad because prohibited) and *malum in se* (bad because wrong in itself). Would you agree that McBoyle's conduct was intrinsically wrong, while Nash's antitrust activity is harder to categorize? Yet both types of conduct caused harm. Was *McBoyle* (which held that stealing an airplane was not covered by a statute that applied to "self-propelled vehicles") therefore wrongly decided? The "common sense" reading of "motor vehicle," there, likely did not include airplanes. *See United States. v. Reid*, 206 F. Supp. 2d 132 (D. Mass. 2002) (following *McBoyle* to hold an aircraft is not a "vehicle" for purposes of federal criminal law and dismissing one count of the indictment against the "shoe bomber," Richard Reid).

Problem 13A (Notice and Vagueness): The Challenge of Criminalizing "Harassment," Even If It Causes Real Harm

(1) *Stalking That Results in Harrassment, but Without Specific Threats*. Harassment by stalking occurs in jurisdictions throughout the country. The prototypical scenario involves an ex-boyfriend who repeatedly follows the victim at a close distance, accosts and surprises her, repeatedly attempts to engage her in conversation, makes personal and embarrassing revelations, contacts the victim's friends and

co-workers, drives his car behind hers, waits by her home and place of employment, and attempts to enter private places where she is located, perhaps by misrepresentations. Sometimes the duration is brief; sometimes it lasts indefinitely. This conduct may embarrass, annoy, and harass the victim, make her choose to limit her travel, activities and acquaintances, put her in reasonable fear for her personal safety, and require special security. There is no question that it can be harmful, even if it does not involve physical fear or threats.

Several states have criminalized acts that combine stalking with other definable conduct, such as explicit threats. This kind of definition arguably avoids problems of vagueness. The problem is, however, this approach does not deal with a wide range of obviously harmful conduct. The gist of the harm lies in the stalker's repeated contacts, which often will not include express threats. Indeed, a stalker readily can succeed in severely frightening a victim without resort to explicit threats. Can you explain why it is challenging to draft a proposed statute that criminalizes "stalking without threats," so that it covers other kinds of harassment?

(2) *An Example: The Invalidation of Washington's Criminal Harassment Statute in State v. Williams*, 26 P.3d 890 (Wash. 2001) (en banc). The State of Washington adopted a criminal stalking statute, Wash. Rev. Code § 9A46.020, that applied not only when the accused threatened physical injury, but also when he offered "maliciously to do any other act which is intended to harm the person threatened . . . with respect to his or her physical *or mental health* or safety. . . . [emphasis added]." The issue centered on the phrase "mental health." The court decided that this term was both vague ("because each person's perception of . . . the mental health of another will differ based upon . . . subjective impressions") and overbroad (because many actions or statements that might disturb sensitive people, and thereby affect their "mental health," are expressive, and therefore they are protected by the freedom of speech and cannot be criminalized). Applying the principle of severability, it struck the word "mental" from the statute. Is the reasoning in *Williams* persuasive—and, if so, is the statute's remaining reference to "physical health or safety" vulnerable to similar objections? Can you see how similar holdings by courts would make it difficult to enact any sort of statute that would be effective against "stalking without threats"?

§ 13.04 Harm, Morality, and Crime: What Conduct Should Be Criminalized?

Notes on Criminalization: Justifying the Law

(1) *Beyond the Constitutional and Legal Issues: "Is It Wise to Criminalize?"* So far, we have explored a number of legal limits on criminal laws. Many of these restrictions have constitutional bases and prohibit legislatures from making conduct criminal. But that is not all there is to it. Lawmakers also must ask themselves,

"Even if we don't like a particular kind of conduct, and even if we can lawfully criminalize it, is it *wise and right* to make it a crime?"

(2) *Broader Considerations: The Proper Role of Government and the Justification of Criminal Laws.* In other words, there are also broader issues in the discussion of what should be made criminal. These focus on the proper role that government should play in regulating the lives of its citizens, but they deal with fundamental philosophical issues unrelated—directly at least—to the Constitution. For example, assuming that the Constitution permits a state to make prostitution or the medical use of marijuana a crime, should a jurisdiction exercise its power to do so? Theories underlying the question, "What should be made criminal?", have a long history of debate among lawmakers. This important question is addressed in the following materials.

[A] Crimes against "Common Decency" or against the "Tone of Society"

City of Erie v. Pap's A.M. dba "Kandyland"

529 U.S. 277 (2000)

JUSTICE O'CONNOR announced the judgment of the Court [and delivered an opinion within a fractured Court with concurring Justices supporting the judgment.]

The city of Erie, Pennsylvania, enacted an ordinance banning public nudity. Respondent Pap's A.M. (hereinafter Pap's), which operated a nude dancing establishment in Erie, challenged the constitutionality of the ordinance and sought a permanent injunction against its enforcement. The Pennsylvania Supreme Court, although noting that this Court in *Barnes v. Glen Theatre, Inc.,* 501 U.S. 560 (1991), had upheld an Indiana ordinance that was "strikingly similar" to Erie's, found that the public nudity sections of the ordinance violated respondent's right to freedom of expression under the United States Constitution.... We hold that Erie's ordinance is a content-neutral regulation that satisfies [the First Amendment].... Accordingly, we reverse the decision of the Pennsylvania Supreme Court and [uphold the ordinance]....

[The Court's First Amendment analysis required it to decide whether the ordinance furthered a legitimate state interest. With the following reasoning, the Court decides that it does, because the ordinance reduces "secondary effects" of public nudity.]

As to ... whether the regulation furthers the government interest—it is evident that, since crime and other public health and safety problems are caused by the presence of nude dancing establishments like Kandyland, a ban on such nude dancing would further Erie's interest in preventing such secondary effects. To be sure, requiring dancers to wear pasties and G-strings may not greatly reduce these secondary effects, but [First Amendment jurisprudence] requires only that the regulation further the interest in combating such effects. Even though the dissent questions the wisdom of Erie's chosen remedy, the "'city must be allowed a reasonable opportunity to experiment with solutions to admittedly serious problems'" . . . .

Even if we had not already rejected the view that a ban on public nudity is necessarily related to the suppression of the erotic message of nude dancing, we would do so now because the premise of such a view is flawed. The State's interest in preventing harmful secondary effects is not related to the suppression of expression. In trying to control the secondary effects of nude dancing, the ordinance seeks to deter crime and the other deleterious effects caused by . . . such an establishment in the neighborhood. . . .

[The concurring opinions of Justices Scalia and Souter are omitted.]

Justice STEVENS, with whom Justice GINSBURG joins, dissenting.

Far more important than the question whether nude dancing is entitled to the protection of the First Amendment are the dramatic changes in legal doctrine that the Court endorses today. Until now, the "secondary effects" of commercial enterprises featuring indecent entertainment have justified only the regulation of their location. [T]he Court has now held that such effects may justify the total suppression of protected speech. . . .

In what can most delicately be characterized as an enormous understatement, the plurality concedes that "requiring dancers to wear pasties and G-strings may not greatly reduce these secondary effects." To believe that the mandatory addition of pasties and a G-string will have any kind of noticeable impact on secondary effects requires nothing short of a titanic surrender to the implausible. . . .

Notes and Questions

(1) *Is This Decision Based on the "Wisdom" of the Questioned Law?* The plurality characterizes Justice Stevens's dissent as attacking the "wisdom" of the ordinance here. Is that what he is doing, and if so, is reasoning about "wisdom" appropriate?

(2) *Does the Questioned Law Really Enforce "Morals" through the Criminal Sanction?* Whether the criminal law can or should express moral disapproval in the absence of other harm is a longstanding issue (addressed in a later section). Perhaps that is why the City of Erie put its arguments in terms of secondary effects like crime and health. But was the ordinance really about morality rather than secondary effects?

(3) *The Scope of Decency and Morals Legislation.* In *Paris Adult Theatre v. Slaton*, 413 U.S. 49 (1973), the Court suggested that regulation of public morality and decency is pervasive:

The state statute books are replete with constitutionally unchallenged laws against prostitution, suicide, voluntary self-mutilation, brutalizing "bare fist" prize fights, and duels, although these crimes may only directly involve "consenting adults." Statutes making bigamy a crime surely cut into an individual's freedom to associate, but few today seriously claim such statutes violate the First Amendment or any other constitutional provision. Consider also the language of this Court in [cases upholding restrictions on adultery, fornication, "white slavery," billiard halls, and gambling, as well as state statutes against "bearbaiting, cock-fighting, and other brutalizing animal 'sports.'"] The main reason [these "sports" were] abolished was because it was felt that they debased and brutalized the citizenry who flocked to witness such spectacles.

Does the existence of statutes such as these prove that criminal law simply reflects the moral judgments of a majority? Regardless of whether or not it does as a descriptive matter, the question remains, whether or to what extent it should.

(4) *The "Tone of Society": Is It a Legitimate Governmental Interest?* In *Paris Adult Theatre*, the Court also suggested that government has an interest in "the tone of society," and that this interest supported its regulation of adult book and film stores. Is the tone of society an interest different from the enforcement of morals?

[B] Harm and the Criminalization of Morals: Is "Immorality" a Sufficient Justification for Prohibition?

Notes and Questions

(1) *Is Some "Harm" to Others Necessary for Legitimacy in the Criminal Law?* The Court in *Paris Adult Theatre*, discussed *supra*, quoted former Chief Justice Warren for the proposition that the government may act to preserve a "decent" society. This concept, if extended to its limits, might appear to justify the prohibition of otherwise harmless acts engaged in by a substantial minority because the majority considers them indecent. The proper basis in such cases for criminal legislation is an issue that philosophers have debated for millennia.

(2) *But Often "Harm" Exists, Even if Not to Identifiable Persons: Is It Arguable That Crimes Sometimes Described as "Victimless" Are Not Really Victimless?* Consider, first, the definition of "harm." Some conduct easily qualifies as harmful (such as murder or sexual assault, as well as many takings of property), because the victims are identifiable individuals. What, then, about so-called "victimless crimes" such as drug use or prostitution?

One response is to assert that prostitution and drug use are not "victimless"; they merely do not impact single, identifiable victims. They do, however, have harmful effects on communities, individuals, and families: an argument similar to the one adopted by the Court in *City of Erie* and *Paris Adult Theatre*. A group of merchants may find their community suddenly less attractive to customers because of the congregation of prostitutes or topless bars, and schools or places of worship may have similar (or even worse) experiences. Or, one could argue that the defendants are the victims, and that society may properly act paternalistically to override certain forms of behavior (in other words, becoming a prostitute may be a more complicated process than the term "free choice" would suggest). Beyond disputing their empirical claims, a common response to these arguments is the objection that criminalization (and not the underlying conduct) is the primary source of harm because it drives the conduct underground and thereby fosters and enhances its harmful effects. But this argument assumes that the conduct can be "contained" by non-criminal means, that is, confined so that it does not unduly affect anyone in the community.

(3) *"Quasi-Zoning" as a Solution: The "Combat Zone" Approach.* Perhaps one approach is to limit prostitution and pornography to one area of town. In that way, merchants along Fifth Avenue, Post Oak Boulevard, or Rodeo Drive are not perceptibly harmed. Boston's onetime "Combat Zone" seemed to embody this proposal for some adult entertainments. There were several problems, however. Other kinds of crimes flourished in the Combat Zone, because the "tone of the community" made it difficult to prevent them there. People who lived or worked nearby experienced spillover effects. And it was impossible to limit these activities to the Combat Zone because "free agent" capitalists, although they established their trade in the Combat Zone, saw profit in exporting them to all areas of the city. Finally, it was impractical, of course, to "contain" the Zone by fencing out minors, sexual predators, and others.

Notes on the Hart-Devlin Debate (and Contemporary Views)

(1) *The "Tone of the Community" Versus Ideals of Liberty: H.L.A. Hart, Law, Liberty, and Morality* 46–47 (1963). What about the claim—similar to the *Paris Adult Theatre* Court's concern for "the tone of society"—that the community itself is harmed by such activity regardless of whether additional harms exist? This kind of argument gets to the heart of the tension between ideals of liberty and ideals of public order. As we shall see, some writers have contended that this concern provides a sufficient justification for criminal regulation of morality. Against these claims, H.L.A. Hart suggested that, while criminal law legitimately may extend "protection from shock or offense to feelings caused by . . . public display," nevertheless, "a right to be protected from the distress which is inseparable from the bare knowledge that others are acting in ways you think wrong, cannot be acknowledged by anyone who recognizes individual liberty as a value."

Do you agree with Hart's argument, and if so, will it always be possible to separate "bare knowledge" from "public display"? Consider the example of an individual who does no other harm to his neighbors than discreetly to conduct cock fights in his basement for his own private amusement (or who tortures and kills animals in other ways, but never with any "public display"). Can the law prohibit this conduct on the ground that, although it does not "harm" any identifiable individual other than by the "bare knowledge" that animal torture is going on next door, it is immoral or "wrong"?

(2) *Debating the Relationship Between Law and Morality: The Argument That Morality Is a Necessary Condition for Criminalization, but That Morality Is Not Alone Sufficient: Herbert Packer, The Limits of the Criminal Sanction 262, 264 (1968).* This discussion of harm leads into the question of the relationship between criminal law and morality. Most commentators seem to agree that criminal law must have *some* relation to moral norms, at least in the sense that the existence of shared moral revulsion at a given harm-causing act makes it more readily subject to prohibitions that the citizenry will follow. The real question is whether the connection can go deeper, with the law enforcing moral positions that do not involve harm to persons other than through moral offensiveness itself. For Herbert Packer, as for Hart (see above), the answer was "no." Morality was a useful and perhaps necessary tool of the criminal law, but nothing more:

> [O]nly conduct generally considered "immoral" should be treated as criminal.... If the criminal sanction is used to deal with morally neutral behavior, law enforcement officials are likely to be at least subconsciously defensive about their work, and the public will find the criminal law a confusing guide....
>
> If the immorality of conduct is a generally necessary condition for invocation of the criminal sanction, is it a generally sufficient one?... The usual lines of attack on this argument are, first, that there is no easy way to determine what should count as immoral and, second, that other considerations (primarily of enforceability) should also be taken into account in determining whether immoral conduct should be made criminal.

To the extent you think criminal law should enforce moral norms, what is your assessment of Packer's argument? Consider whether Packer's reasoning would prevent the state from criminalizing the kind of animal torture, without public display, referred to in an earlier note.

(3) *The Contrary Argument, That Crimes May Be Defined to Enforce the Public Morality: Lord Devlin's View—Patrick Devlin, The Enforcement of Morals 9–11* (1965). By contrast, British Judge Patrick Devlin provided a sustained defense of the use of criminal law to preserve and promote morality:

> The institution of marriage is a good example for my purpose.... Marriage is part of the structure of our society and it is also the basis of a moral code which condemns fornication and adultery. The institution of marriage would be gravely threatened if individual judgments were permitted about the morality of adultery; on these points there must be a public morality. But public morality is not to be confined to those moral principles which support institutions such as marriage. People do not think of monogamy [merely] as something which has to be supported because our society has chosen to organize itself upon it; [instead,] they think of [monogamy] as something that is good in itself and offering a good way of life and that it is for that reason that our society has adopted it.... [S]ociety means a community of

ideas; without shared ideas on politics, morals, and ethics no society can exist. . . . A common morality is part of the bondage. The bondage is part of the price of society; and mankind, which needs society, must pay its price.

> . . . [I]f society has the right to make a judgment and has made it on the basis that a recognized morality is as necessary to society as, say, a recognized government, then society may use the law to preserve morality in the same way as it uses it to safeguard anything else that is essential to its existence.

Is Devlin right that "no society can exist" in the absence of a common moral code? Put differently, if there is to be a common moral code, must it be complete, or is it sufficient to limit the criminal enforcement of it to conduct that nearly all would agree is harmful?

(4) *Responses to Devlin: Kelsen's View — Hans Kelsen, Pure Theory of Law* 68 (1967). Kelsen's argument was that there were many moralities, not just the one common morality that Devlin perceived:

> It . . . cannot be emphasized enough . . . that not only one moral order exists, but many different and even conflicting ones; that a positive legal order may on the whole conform with the moral views of a certain group of the population, yet may conflict with the moral views of another group; and that . . . the judgment of what is morally good or evil . . . is subject to continuous change, as is the law . . . .

But does Kelsen's argument prove too much, because it might support a total disconnection between law and morals, on grounds of moral diversity?

(5) *The Hart-Devlin Debate in Contemporary Thought — James Allan, Revisiting the Hart-Devlin Debate: At the Periphery and by the Numbers,* 54 San Diego L. Rev, 423 (2017), Allan adopts the following evaluation of the debate, taken from Peter Cane, *Taking Law Seriously: Starting Points of the Hart/Devlin Debate,* 10 J. Ethics 21, 22 (2006):

> 1. It is a mistake to base what the limits of the law ought to be on some . . . Hartian . . . or any other theorist's . . . harm principle, with their attendant worked out elaborations of that harm principle, plus some needed ancillary distinctions. Just do a straight out consequentialist analysis. "[T]he limits of the law are better fixed by open-endedly assessing reasons for and against legal regulation than by [appeal to the more limited harm principle and its elaborations]."
>
> 2. This debate, and the question of legal moralism generally, should not be limited to the criminal law. Regulation by the civil law or private law, most obviously by tort law, but contract law too, covers much the same ground. Bankruptcy can be worse for some than imprisonment . . . . Why should we determine the limits of law by reference to the perspective of the

minority of people who obey it only because of its coercive capacity, rather than the perspective of those who view law as a legitimate source of standards of behavior? . . .

3. The relationship between law and morality is not, or at least need not be, as competitive as it is conceived to be in the Hart-Devlin debate.

Allan adds that he believes Devlin was "the overall, big picture winner of this contest, but . . . on some of the finer philosophical points, he was outscored by Hart."

Problem 13B (Crime, Harm, and Morals): "Don't Legalize Prostitution and Destroy Our Community!"

(1) *A Proposed Statute to Legalize and Regulate Prostitution.* You are an aide to state legislator Lucy Goodhart, from the town of Glenhaven, who has filed a bill that would repeal the state's laws against prostitution—and would substitute a licensing and regulatory system that would purport to address health, safety, overreaching, fraud, and violence with respect to both customers and prostitutes. In the preamble to the proposed statute, Goodhart's words describe prostitution as a "victimless crime," the harmful effects of which "are produced directly by fruitless attempts to enforce laws against it," and which "can be successfully regulated, with all costs of regulation defrayed by licensing fees."

A group of homeowners and businesspeople, including many of Goodhart's supporters, have formed the "Glenhaven Protective Corporation" and have visited you and Goodhart to complain that prostitution is "immoral," "destroys families," "can't by its nature be contained away from our youth, or regulated," and results in "neighborhood blight." As one of them put the matter, "Don't make prostitution legal, because it'll destroy our community!" In fact, it is undisputed that one notorious house of prostitution in Glenhaven has negatively affected the nearby homes and businesses, and constituents say that "only our constant complaints to the police have kept it from coming back." But Goodhart has responded to these visitors with conviction: "Only by licensing and regulating prostitution can we keep it from continuing to hurt the community."

(2) *Your Assignment: Collect, Describe, and Rank All of the Arguments about Legalizing or Prohibiting Prostitution, Pro and Con, for This Legislator—Neutrally, in the Manner of an "Honest Broker."* Goodhart is shaken by the vehemence of the Glenhaven Protective Corporation. Goodhart is courageous, wants to "do what is right and wise," and plans not to run for re-election, but she wonders whether it would be a good idea to "show some deference to my constituents, because after all, they have their convictions too, and prostitution has been treated as a criminal offense just about everywhere for as long as anyone can remember." Your assignment, then, is to collect, describe, and rank all of the arguments, pro and con, as if you were going to write a memorandum about them to Goodhart—except that the assignment will involve class discussion rather than a written document.

[C] Constitutional Limits on the Criminalization of Morals

Notes

(1) *Constitutional Limits on the Crime-Morality Overlap—The Example of Contraception: Poe v. Ullman*, 367 U.S. 497 (1961). In this case, the Supreme Court refused to decide whether a Connecticut statute that criminalized the use of contraceptives by married couples was constitutional. In a dissenting opinion, Justice Harlan argued the statute was unconstitutional despite Connecticut's claim to be promoting good morals:

> [Society] has traditionally concerned itself with the moral soundness of its people. . . . Certainly, Connecticut's judgment is no more demonstrably correct or incorrect than are the varieties of judgment, expressed in law, on marriage and divorce, on adult consensual homosexuality, abortion, and sterilization, or euthanasia and suicide. . . .
>
> . . . [But] the State [here] is asserting the right to enforce its moral judgment by intruding upon the most intimate details of the marital relation with the full power of the criminal law. Potentially, this could allow the deployment of all the incidental machinery of the criminal law, arrests, searches and seizures; inevitably, it must mean at the very least the lodging of criminal charges, a public trial, and testimony as to the *corpus delicti*. . . .

Four years later, in *Griswold v. Connecticut*, 381 U.S. 479 (1965), the Court struck down the Connecticut contraception statute as an unconstitutional interference with marital privacy.

(2) *Sodomy Statutes: Bowers v. Hardwick*, 478 U.S. 186 (1986), *overruled by Lawrence v. Texas*, 539 U.S. 558 (2003). Another example involves sodomy statutes. In *Bowers*, the Supreme Court upheld Georgia's criminal prohibition on sodomy. The plaintiff argued that the statute was irrational because it rested on a moral judgment. Writing for the Court, Justice White rejected that claim:

> [R]espondent asserts that there must be a rational basis for the law and that there is none in this case other than the presumed belief of a majority of the electorate in Georgia that homosexual sodomy is immoral and unacceptable. This is said to be an inadequate rationale to support the law. The law, however, is constantly based on notions of morality, and if all laws representing moral choices are to be invalidated under the Due Process Clause, the courts will be very busy indeed. . . .

In a concurring opinion, Chief Justice Burger suggested that "[t]o hold that the act of homosexual sodomy is somehow protected as a fundamental right would be to cast aside millennia of moral teaching."

Seventeen years later, however, the Court overruled *Bowers* in *Lawrence*, above, which addressed Texas's prohibition on same-sex sodomy. The majority recognized that condemnation of homosexual activity, "[f]or many persons," derives from "profound and deep convictions accepted as ethical and moral principles to which they aspire . . . ." But "[t]he issue is whether the majority may use the power of the State to enforce these views on the whole society through operation of the criminal code." Because the conduct at issue was a form of consensual, private, sexual intimacy between adults (and because most states no longer punished such conduct), the Court declared the statute unconstitutional as a violation of the right of privacy.

[D] The Failure to Criminalize: Questions of Equality, Harm, and Morals

Notes and Questions: What Isn't a Crime

(1) *What Isn't Covered by the Criminal Law: Creative Arguments.* Some conduct may "seem" criminal—or one might think it "ought" to be criminal—but no defined offense appears to cover it. In such cases, police and prosecutors struggle over what to do. Sometimes, they do not bring charges, although they might ask the relevant legislative body to address the situation. Often, however, they come up with creative interpretations of existing statutes, which courts may or may not accept. (For example, federal prosecutors made the claim that the federal fraud statutes criminalized dishonest applications for state licenses, an argument that the Supreme Court rejected in *Cleveland v. United States*, 531 U.S. 12 (2000) (holding a gambling license is not property for purpose of the federal fraud statutes).)

(2) *Noncrimes.* Imagine the following situations, all of which are based upon real occurrences. Are these actions morally wrong? Are they crimes, or should they be?

(a) *Impersonation without Theft.* An individual goes about town impersonating a local celebrity who is a private citizen, setting up meetings with other people, making telephone calls in the celebrity's name, etc., all without any apparent effort to appropriate property or to commit theft. The ostensible motive is to have fun impersonating the other individual, but the actions cause harm to real people and require a police response, which results in no arrest.

(b) *The Magic-Marker Doctor.* A physician uses a non-permanent magic marker to draw "smiley faces" on the genitalia of patients under anesthesia.

(c) *The Bad-Samaritan Doctor.* Upon seeing a person convulsing with a heart attack, a physician crosses to the other side of the street and walks by; furthermore, although he possesses a mobile telephone and is familiar with 911 emergency services, he does not pause to call for assistance. (This example is analogous to many noncriminal situations involving refusals to aid others in distress in America. Similar behavior is a crime in many civil law countries and some states.)

(3) *Can the Existence of Noncrimes Make Defined Crimes Less Legitimate?* In a few settings, the creation of criminal sanctions for defined crimes, when closely similar situations are not criminalized, has raised issues of legitimacy. In *Skinner v. Oklahoma*, 316 U.S. 535 (1942), the Court struck down, on equal protection grounds,

a statute providing for three-times convicted habitual criminals to be sterilized. Larceny convicts were covered, but embezzlers were not, and this noncoverage was what the Court found to be an equal protection violation. This kind of reasoning must be used sparingly, however—perhaps only in egregious cases. Broad application might create more problems than it would solve. Can you see why?

Chapter 14

Perspectives: Non-Criminal Methods, Victims' Interests, Plea Agreements, and Lawyer Competencies

"A philosopher of imposing stature doesn't think in a vacuum."—Alfred North Whitehead

"We must not make a scare crow of the law . . . , and let it keep one shape."— William Shakespeare, *Measure for Measure, Act II, Scene 1*

"Historically, this country has overlooked, even ignored, victims who, as a result, have suffered further victimization by the criminal process. [Persons accused of crime] have several individuals whose role it is to protect their rights, but there does not appear to be one clear-cut shining knight for victims like the role the defense attorney plays for the accused."—Arthur L. Rizer III, *Prosecutors: The "Other" Defenders of the Constitution*, 38 *The Prosecutor* 37, 39 (August 2004)

§ 14.01 Non-Criminal Means of Crime Reduction

[A] Why Seek Alternatives to Criminal Law Enforcement?

Notes on Crime Reduction by Civil Means

(1) *Criminal Justice Is Only One Method.* When people think of ways to reduce crime, often the immediate reaction is "catch the criminals and give them long sentences." And it is true, of course, that criminal sanctions are *one* of the means of reducing crime.

(2) *Why Seek Alternatives? Resources, Impact, and Prevention.* This chapter takes a broader view. It looks at a number of means, other than criminal sanctions, that American law uses in an attempt to reduce the incidence of crime. Criminal justice is a heavy, resource-intensive endeavor, and to put it bluntly, it is too expensive to use as the only means. Furthermore, it is the method with maximum harmful impact upon defendants and their dependents. And criminal justice operates *after*

the fact, after the harm has been caused to victims and society. Other means may prevent the harm with fewer resources and less adverse impact.

Because of the scope of the issue and the fact that it ranges far from the traditional approach in American criminal law classes, this chapter is merely an introduction to a topic that deserves attention. One result should be that, if there is a non-criminal alternative that can reduce crime equally, you begin thinking about the wisdom of enforcing a given criminal sanction.

[B] Non-Criminal Resolution of Criminal Cases

Notes on Discretionary or Formal Diversion

(1) *Resolution of Criminal Charges by Discretionary or Formalized Diversion.* It is not infrequent that crimes are "resolved" without resort to the criminal justice system, or at least without resort to a formal finding of guilt. Every police department and court system has developed informal—and sometimes formal—methods of dealing with criminal activity without invoking the full measure of the criminal process. A good illustration is an effort by a patrol police officer who is called to deal with a disturbance at a bar. The officer may separate the potential combatants and send them home. This use of discretion may resolve the matter.

(2) *Judicial Deference to Executive Discretion—and Limits.* There are few limits on the exercise of this discretion. Courts are reluctant to intervene because of concerns about separation of powers and a floodgate of lawsuits challenging decisions that may not be documented. *See, e.g., Inmates of Attica Correctional Facility v. Rockefeller*, 477 F.2d 375 (2d Cir. 1973) (prosecutor not required to proceed in "good faith" to investigate possible crimes committed against inmates at Attica Prison during riot that killed 32 inmates).

The few limits on this prosecutorial discretion ordinarily require proof that the government official used an unjustifiable standard such as race or gender. *See, e.g., Oyler v. Boles*, 368 U.S. 448 (1962) (no equal protection violation in selection of people charged with being habitual criminals; no proof that selection was deliberately based on an unjustifiable standard such as race, religion, or other arbitrary classification). Another avenue to attack this discretion is to establish that some other constitutional right was violated. *See, e.g., Wayte v. United States*, 470 U.S. 598 (1985) (no first amendment violation in prosecuting only some men who failed to register for the draft).

(3) *Mediation and Diversion as Formal Programs.* Some courts, prosecutors, and police departments may also have more formal processes, such as mediation programs, that attempt to resolve disputes without resort to the criminal justice system. In other situations, the prosecutor's office may invoke "diversion" as an alternative means of nonprosecution, based on an agreement for restitution (if called for), treatment, or other conditions (which usually include a probation-like period of

committing no further offenses). *See, e.g.*, Stephanos Bibas & Richard Bierschbach, *Integrating Remorse and Apology into Criminal Procedure*, 114 Yale L.J. 85 (2004). Often, private citizens volunteer to mediate such disputes. Sometimes, this process can provide greater catharsis for the victim than the criminal process, through confrontation of the offender, expression of grievances, and restitution.

[C] Decriminalization

Notes on Selective Repeal of Criminal Laws

(1) *Decriminalization Proposals.* It is obvious that one way to reduce crime is to "decriminalize" some conduct so that its commission is not a crime. One popular book suggested decriminalizing public intoxication, drug possession and purchase, gambling, abortion, and any sexual activities among consenting adults as a way of reducing both crime and the fear of crime. The authors reasoned that the criminal justice system should focus on the protection of people and property and not cover crimes affecting only private morality or social welfare. Norval Morris & Gordon Hawkins, *The Honest Politician's Guide to Crime Control* (1969). Today, some people would add white collar crimes, such as insider trading, that arguably can be addressed instead by private markets or civil suits.

Actually, decriminalization may reduce "crime" but may or may not reduce the actual incidence of harm. Indeed, it could increase the harm. An example is public intoxication. Some jurisdictions have decriminalized this behavior, markedly reducing their "crime statistics" and jail population. They treat is as a social welfare or health issue, not a criminal justice matter unless the person also commits a more serious offense, such as assault or drunk driving. Will this approach decrease the actual harm caused by public intoxication?

(2) *Partial Deregulation.* A similar suggestion is to decriminalize various drug offenses, such as possession of a small quantity of marijuana. In recent years, several states have decriminalized marijuana offenses. Opponents argue that this solution would encourage greater use of marijuana, making it readily available to minors. Some also argue that it would ease access to more serious drugs by making the use of drugs more socially acceptable. Is a sensible compromise to decriminalize the consumption of marijuana but to continue to punish the production and trafficking of it?

(3) *Regulatory Issues That Remain.* And there is another, very significant problem with decriminalization. Most of the crimes that one might think of as candidates for decriminalization cause actual harm, even if not to identifiable victims. Prostitution, for example, causes intangible damage to landowners nearby, and the harm may be serious enough to affect businesses and the quality of life in an entire neighborhood. Prostitution also breeds other kinds of crime, from fraud or robbery to exploitation and violence upon prostitutes.

Licensing and regulation are partial solutions, but they tend to be unworkable unless backed up by frequent use of the criminal sanction, which leaves criminal

law still very much involved and partly defeats the purpose. What should the ultimate conclusion be?

[D] Forfeiture as a Civil Remedy (But Is It, Really?)

Notes on Forfeiture as a Non-Criminal, Non-Punitive Device

(1) *Forfeiture of Criminal Instrumentalities.* Another non-criminal option is a *forfeiture* of property. The typical pattern is a statute that permits a court to order
forfeiture of property in two contexts. First, a court may be authorized to order
the forfeiture of property used in the commission of a particular offense, such as
a drug violation. In some locales, a car, boat, house, or money used in illegal drug
activities can be ordered to be forfeited to the government. Second, forfeiture may
be aimed at fruits purchased with gains from crime. These forfeiture provisions are
often classified as civil rather than criminal. Do you agree with this classification?

(2) *Justifying (and Questioning) the Civil Nature of Forfeiture.* If you remain skeptical about this kind of forfeiture as a civil remedy, consider the following hypothetical.
The government has seized a helicopter filled with heroin that has just been imported
into the United States. Evidence shows that the helicopter has been used repeatedly
by different shadowy groups for similar heroin runs. Conviction of the pilots in past
cases has not deterred its use. The helicopter has been recently sold several times
among foreign nationals known to be involved in drug trades. The government
wants to have the helicopter forfeited. This forfeiture, to be sure, will be "punitive" in
a sense. But doesn't the government also have a legitimate purpose that is noncriminal: a *preventive* purpose of keeping the helicopter from use in the drug trade?

(3) *Forfeiture of Fruits of Crime.* The second approach reaches the proceeds of illegal activity. A statute may authorize the forfeiture of property obtained by money
earned in certain crimes. A good example is the so-called RICO (Racketeer Influenced and Corrupt Organizations Act) law which, in general terms, bars a person
receiving income from a pattern of racketeering activity or unlawful debt collection to use or invest such income in an enterprise affecting interstate commerce. 18
U.S.C. § 1962. Among the authorized remedies is the forfeiture of "any interest in;
security of; claim against; or property or contractual right of any kind affording a
source of influence over; any enterprise which the person has established, operated,
controlled, conducted, or participated in the conduct of, in violation of" the RICO
statute. 18 U.S.C. § 1963. It also reaches "any property constituting, or derived from,
any proceeds which the person obtained, directly or indirectly, from racketeering
activity or unlawful debt collection in violation of RICO."

Some forfeitures can be very large in amount. *See FCC v. Fox Television Stations,
Inc.*, 132 S. Ct. 2307 (2012) (reversing forfeitures amounting to $27,500 against each
of 44 television stations, on due process grounds).

(4) *Forfeitures Can Present Significant Constitutional Issues.* As is noted in the next
case, the Supreme Court has held that civil forfeitures in general do not constitute

punishment and therefore do not offend the double jeopardy clause. Such forfeitures are viewed as actions against the property rather than actions against the owner.

UNITED STATES v. URSERY, 518 U.S. 267 (1996). Michigan police found marijuana growing near Ursery's house and marijuana remnants and a grow light within the house. The United States instituted civil forfeiture proceedings against the house, alleging that the property was subject to forfeiture under 21 U.S.C. § 881(a)(7), because it had been used for several years to facilitate the unlawful processing and distribution of a controlled substance. Ursery ultimately paid the United States $13,250 to settle the forfeiture claim in full. Shortly before the settlement was consummated, Ursery was indicted and convicted for manufacturing marijuana and sentenced to 63 months in prison. The Court of Appeals reversed the conviction, finding that the double jeopardy clause was violated because he had already been punished by the civil forfeiture proceeding and could not be punished again.

The Supreme Court reversed and reinstated the conviction, holding that civil forfeitures generally are not "punishment" for purposes of the Double Jeopardy Clause. Therefore, the civil forfeiture did not bar the subsequent criminal conviction. Was the forfeiture "not penal"?

Notes and Questions

(1) *Limits of Forfeiture: The Factual Issue of Punitive Versus Civil Purpose.* If forfeitures are civil in nature and may occur at the same time as a criminal conviction, what are the limits on the extent or amount of a forfeiture? In *United States v. Bajakajian*, 524 U.S. 321 (1998), the Supreme Court applied the Eighth Amendment's excessive fine clause to strike down a forfeiture. The case involved a man who was apprehended leaving the United States with $357,144 in his luggage, in violation of a federal statute requiring reporting of currency in excess of $100,000 taken out of the country. A lower court authorized forfeiture of the $357,144 in accordance with federal law. But the Supreme Court held that the forfeiture violated the excessive fines clause of the Eighth Amendment to the Constitution because the forfeiture was punitive rather than remedial and bore no relationship to the injury suffered by the government.

(2) *Evading Forfeiture.* Forfeitures create a number of unique procedural difficulties. Many stem from the fact that property subject to forfeiture can be transferred to others or may be owned at least in part by several people. Also, the presence of property in the vicinity of a respondent may not be enough to establish his control of it.

(3) *Interests of Third Persons.* There are also provisions to protect the interests of non-criminals who own an interest in property subject to forfeiture. For example, what if a lender holds a security interest in an automobile that is forfeited—or it is owned by an innocent rental company? *See, e.g.,* 18 U.S.C. § 1963 (containing protections for some kinds of innocent interest-holders).

[E] Other Civil Sanctions and Civil Restitution

Note on Regulatory Fines and Civil Restitution

Sometimes the state collects monetary penalties, which are the equivalent of fines, but are not criminal sanctions. They do not carry the same stigma as criminal sanctions, and often they require only the lower civil standard of proof by a preponderance of the evidence.

Securities law violations are a frequent example, and so are consumer law violations. You may read in the newspaper that a well-known securities dealer has settled a matter by paying a penalty, often with the denial of any admission of actual liability. As a means of deterring infrequent violations by actors who usually are law-abiding, these measures may be adequate, may obtain more satisfaction for victims, and may do so at much lesser expense through civil means.

[F] Licensing and Registration

Notes on Controlling Access to Implements of Crime

(1) *Licensing.* Another non-criminal method of crime reduction is the use of licensing and similar laws to deny certain people access to situations or items that could facilitate their commission of a crime. One illustration is laws requiring licenses to possess handguns. Often such a license is granted only after the applicant has demonstrated the absence of a criminal record, plus education and training that are intended to restrain use.

Another common illustration is the denial or revocation of a driver's license to people convicted of intoxicated driving. The theory is that at least some of the defendants will not drive during the period of suspension and will therefore not reoffend during that time. A less well known example is licensing that controls the possession and use of hazardous substances and precursors, including those for controlled drugs.

(2) *But the Criminal Justice System Is Still Necessary.* These laws work only if there is rigorous enforcement of criminal sanctions for unlicensed actors. Still, licensing laws reduce the volume and seriousness of prosecution of the crimes that otherwise might result.

[G] Premises Redesign and Safety Measures

Notes on Physical Changes in the Environment
That Reduce Crime, from Architecture to Technology

(1) *Physical Surroundings as Affecting Crime.* Crime also may be reduced by measures that have virtually nothing to do with the legal system. One illustration is measures that use technology and changes in the physical environment to reduce crime. For example, sometimes crime can be reduced by making an area more

visible to passersby. Shrubs can be trimmed, and lighting can be improved. Some universities, for example, have reduced person-on-person crime simply by ensuring wide lines of sight across their campuses. Convenience stores have reduced crime by stationing their cashiers up front, installing floor-to-ceiling glass so that passersby can see clearly, and lighting their interiors well.

(2) *Controlling Access.* A related measure is to close streets for some or all of the time to prevent access to certain areas. In a high crime area, for example, all entrances to the area except one or two can be closed late at night and police can have a presence at the entrances.

(3) *Public Areas.* Another illustration of the environmental safety approach is a project to reduce crime in public bathrooms in a transportation hub. To deal with drug and prostitution offenses occurring in the restrooms, the facilities were redesigned for the purpose of reducing such offenses. To increase visibility, the restrooms were located nearer to retailers, corner mirrors were installed, attendants were added, lighting was improved, and nooks were eliminated. Research showed a considerable reduction in criminal activity after these renovations. Moreover, there was little evidence that the crime that would have occurred in the restrooms was simply "displaced" to other locations. Martha J. Smith & Ronald V. Clarke, *Crime and Public Transport*, 27 Criminal Justice 169, 209 (2000).

Similar results may be produced by architectural modifications in banks, convenience stores, warehouses, homes, and other buildings. Can you suggest how to improve safety in buildings with which you are familiar?

(4) *The Costs of These Kinds of Modifications to Reduce Crime.* These changes are not cost-free. They may reduce convenience, business, and economic viability. For example, imagine that a convenience store locks the door at, say, 10:00 p.m. each night, after a study shows an increase in the incidence of robberies after that hour. A customer must ring a bell and be admitted by a clerk. While these changes could eliminate some crimes, they probably would increase the time a customer would need to shop, deter some customers, and provide opportunities for discrimination.

[H] Police Presence; Community Policing; the "Broken Windows" Theory

Notes on Police Methods Intended to Prevent Crime, Rather Than Redressing It

(1) *Federal Initiatives Regarding Specific Theories of Police Strategy.* Recent federal initiatives have targeted major increases in the number of police officers available to states and localities. Federal spending usually specifies the use of the funds narrowly. For example, "community policing" with "beat cops," who walk or patrol certain neighborhoods, regularly has been preferred as the object of federal funds. Other police expenditures, including money for new technology, communications equipment, undercover operations, organized crime prosecution, and

assault-homicide investigation also have been funded in recent years. Do you think increasing expenditures for police personnel will reduce crime? If so, do you think community policing is the best answer?

Opponents of this approach point out that this year's preferred method, *e.g.* community policing, may not reduce serious crime in a given neighborhood. A community that is overrun with drug-related crimes, for example, may find that beat cops are less effective than undercover officers, and suburban areas with high rates of burglary and robbery may prefer radio patrol by officers in vehicles. Federal funding tends to distort resources in situations such as these.

(2) *Quality-of-Life Enforcement: Reducing Serious Crime by Rigorously Eliminating Minor Crimes or Neighborhood Blight That Signals Fraying of the Social Fabric.* Another approach has been dubbed the "broken windows" theory or "quality of life" enforcement. Criminologist James Q. Wilson is credited with first having articulated this theory. James Q. Wilson & George L. Kelling, *Broken Windows: The Police and Neighborhood Safety*, Atlantic Monthly, Mar. 1982, at 29. The underlying concept is that the amount of crime is correlated with the disintegration of social institutions. By enforcing even petty offenses, police may prevent crime in general, including more serious offenses. For example, if vandals break a window in an abandoned building, the solution is to repair the window immediately and to vigorously pursue the offenders. Pursuing this rather minor offense, plus others, helps stop the fraying of the social fabric and, according to the theory, contributes to a lessening of more serious crime.

(3) *The Broken Windows Theory: See Jon Brooks, Oakland Hires Proponent of Broken Windows Theory as Police Consultant*, News Fix, Dec. 27, 2012. Mayor Rudolph Giuliani tried this approach in New York City and credited it with a significant reduction in crime, although some research disagrees with this conclusion. *See, e.g.,* Bernard E. Harcourt, *Illusion of Order: The False Promise of Broken Windows Policing* (2001). The reduction in per capita violent crime in New York under Giuliani was dramatic by all accounts, significantly greater than reductions in other major cities. But the specific role of broken windows policing is difficult to quantify. In any event, the broken windows theory still has many adherents, as the article cited at the beginning of this note shows.

[I] Private Security Personnel

Notes on Private Firms as an Alternative to Police

(1) *The Uses of Private Security.* Today private security personnel are routinely found in malls, restaurants, bars, nightclubs, and subdivisions. The United States military also uses private guards. Some apartment complexes provide subsidized or free living accommodations for police officers so that law enforcement officers are physically present much of the time. The complex is especially pleased if the tenant-officer is allowed to bring home a police cruiser that is visible in the area. An

extreme example is the report that some apartment owners are hiring private security firms to oust drug dealers and other troublemakers from the building, allegedly because the police will not do so. *See* B.A. Glesner, *Landlords as Cops: Torts, Nuisance, and Forfeiture Standards Imposing Liability on Landlords for Crime on the Premises*, 42 Case Western Res. L. Rev. 679 (1992).

(2) *Incentives and Costs.* As is noted in the next section, sometimes these precautions are encouraged by private lawsuits against landowners who do not maintain safe premises. Insurance companies may also insist on precautions as a condition of insuring particular premises. The use of private security officers may breed lawsuits, however, when the "private cops" harm someone. *See, e.g.*, Myriam Gilles, *Private Parties as Defendants in Civil Rights Litigation*, 26 Cardozo L. Rev. 1 (2004) (discussing civil rights actions against private security officers).

(3) *Should Crime Reduction That Benefits the Public at Large Become a Private Expense?* This is a controversial question. Economists who see crime reduction generally as a public benefit may see disadvantages to a regime that relies on private security to lower the incidence of crime. So-called "free riders," who reside or have businesses near a facility with excellent private security, may benefit without contributing to the cost. Ultimately, this situation may disintegrate into a "tragedy of the commons," in which everyone would benefit from crime reduction, but everyone counts on someone else to supply it, so that ultimately no one does.

[J] Preventive Detention and Civil Commitment

Notes on Crime Reduction by Confinement Without Criminal Conviction

(1) *Incapacitation or Prevention as a Goal of the Criminal Sanction.* The typical vehicle for confining someone who has committed a crime is to convict the person of the offense and sentence him or her to a period of incarceration. As is discussed in our coverage of sentencing, one reason for doing this is to prevent the offender from committing another crime. The American legal system also uses other means, however, to incapacitate allegedly dangerous people.

(2) *Preventive Detention: Bail Denial and Confinement for Public Safety.* The usual reason for pretrial confinement is to ensure appearance. But another, less frequently articulated purpose is preventive detention: a person awaiting trial for an alleged crime may be detained in some circumstances because of concerns that he or she will commit another crime if released on bail. While at one time the constitutionality of preventive detention was questionable, the United States Supreme Court approved it as a consideration in bail decisions in *United States v. Salerno*, 481 U.S. 739 (1987). The Court upheld provisions in the Federal Bail Reform Act of 1984 that authorized a court to detain a person until trial if the government proves by clear and convincing evidence that no other procedure could "reasonably assure the safety of any other person and the community." 18 U.S.C. § 3142(f).

(3) *Civil Commitment for Insanity.* For many years American law has authorized the government to confine mentally ill people in mental hospitals, even against their will. Ordinarily this confinement follows a judicial determination that the person is dangerous to himself or herself or to others. In the latter case, it is designed to prevent the patient from committing a crime in the future. (Another example, discussed in the Chapter Three, is confinement of persons found drunk in public.)

This involuntary confinement is viewed as regulatory rather than punitive. The Due Process Clause guarantees various procedural rights but does not bar civil confinement even though the patient may not have violated any criminal law. *See, e.g., Addington v. Texas*, 441 U.S. 418 (1979) (Texas civil commitment law does not violate due process). There are, however, serious difficulties with this kind of confinement, not only from a civil libertarian but also from a law enforcement standpoint, in that the laws may require release even though safety is not assured. These matters are dealt with in greater depth in Chapter Six, on defenses.

(4) *Civil Confinement under Sexual Predator Laws as a Preventive Measure.* Following the example of confinement upon insanity, some jurisdictions have enacted "sexual predator" laws that apply civil commitment to people convicted of (or sometimes simply charged with) one or more sex crimes and who are considered likely to reoffend. The Kansas Sexually Violent Predator Act, for example, authorizes the civil commitment of people who, due to "mental abnormality" or "personality disorder," are "likely to engage in repeat acts of sexual violence if not treated." Kans. Stat. Ann. §59-29a01 (1994). Often these provisions operate to block the release from confinement of offenders who have completed sentences for sex offenses.

The offender may be kept in confinement even if it lasts longer than any potential or actual sentence for an underlying crime. The United States Supreme Court has upheld the constitutionality of these provisions in a case involving a repeat child sex offender. *Kansas v. Hendricks*, 521 U.S. 346 (1997) (sexual predator law does not violate substantive due process); *United States v. Comstock*, 560 U.S. 126 (2010) (upholding Congress's power to authorize civil confinement of prisoners as "sexually dangerous persons" after their service of prison terms).

[K] Crime-Reducing Decisions by Potential Victims; Education

Notes on Citizens' Own Efforts to Avoid Situations of Likely Criminal Harm

(1) *Reducing Situational Crime by Reducing Criminal Opportunities.* Sometimes crime happens to particular people because they place themselves in positions that make them particularly vulnerable. Someone who walks alone through a high crime area runs a greater risk of becoming a crime victim than someone who does not. The same is true for people who exhibit cash while paying bar bills or who

drink too much in social situations and agree to the company of strangers. While this observation is not designed to suggest that the victim is the primary person at fault (or even at fault at all), it is true that some crimes can be reduced in this way.

(2) *The Limits of This Method: Ultimately, an Incursion upon Freedom.* This kind of crime reduction, however, may have early limits. Avoidance of high crime areas (many of which are residential) may be impossible, and curtailing activities, or scheduling them only when escorts or groups are available, results in a significant loss of freedom. The ultimate extension of this strategy is permanent self-confinement in a fortress-like home. This approach involves a significant tradeoff with other values.

[L] Social and Economic Changes

Notes on Values, Education, and Economics as Affecting Crime

(1) *The Economy, Families, and Social Institutions.* While the efforts described earlier in this chapter deal with common ways of affecting the incidence of crime, there are other possibilities that work indirectly — but that work nevertheless. Since some crime is affected by the state of the economy, an improving economy will lead to a reduction of some crime. Prosecutors observe a sharp increase in shoplifting, for example, when economic growth slows and unemployment increases.

(2) *Education, Treatment, and . . . Midnight Basketball?* Similarly, many people contend that increases in public spending on education, drug treatment, counseling, and even "midnight basketball" would reduce the incidence of crime.

§ 14.02 The Interests of Crime Victims and Survivors

[A] The Victim's Rights Movement

Notes on the Law's Changing Treatment of Crime Victims

(1) *The Historical Conception: The State Had a Legal Interest in the Crime, but the Victim Did Not.* The victim of crime is often characterized as the forgotten person in the criminal justice system, though in recent years this situation has improved. At one time, a crime was considered an offense against the state, not the victim. Accordingly, the victim was involved in the process but was not treated as the prosecutor's client (the government was) or even as someone who had significant interests in the criminal case.

The victim's remedy was simple: bring a civil case against the defendant, which was theoretically possible since virtually all crimes against victims are also torts. Practically, of course, the civil process was of little value. The defendant usually would be judgment proof.

(2) *A Changing Perception: Rights for Victims and Survivors?* In recent decades, however, the public, courts, and legislatures have changed their approaches. Today, in most jurisdictions, there are laws that recognize the victim's interests in the criminal case and that attempt to meet some of the victim's needs. Some call this trend the Victim's Rights Movement.

Victims' advocates may see this section as containing material in which they are intensely interested. Committed civil libertarians or future defense lawyers may hold the opposite view, seeing many of the concepts here as infringing on protections of the accused; but in any event, these opponents of the Victim's Rights Movement need to know about it so that they can understand the impact it may have upon crime definition. Ultimately, the question is, where should the line be drawn among the interests of the accused, the state, and the victim? Consider the following case.

Gansz v. People
888 P.2d 256 (Colo. 1995)

Justice Erickson delivered the Opinion of the Court.

[The Jefferson County District Attorney charged Bradley John Herron with the second-degree assault of Sarah Jane Gansz. After reviewing the case before trial, the district attorney filed a motion to dismiss the case, asserting that the charges could not be proven beyond a reasonable doubt.

[In most jurisdictions, including Colorado, the prosecutor cannot unilaterally dismiss. The prosecutor makes a motion to dismiss, which the trial judge may either grant or deny. Denial is rare, but the option is there for the judge. Usually it reflects a judge's strongly different assessment of the evidence in a very serious case—and willingness to appoint a special prosecutor.

[The trial judge in this case dismissed the charge without a hearing, which is the usual disposition of prosecutors' motions to dismiss. After receiving a letter from Gansz objecting to the dismissal, however, the trial judge vacated the dismissal and ordered a hearing. At the hearing, the trial judge ruled that Gansz lacked standing to proceed. . . . During the hearing, the deputy district attorney stated that the prosecution sought to dismiss the case because Gansz was not a credible witness. The trial judge therefore granted the motion to dismiss. The court of appeals also held that Gansz lacked standing to pursue an appeal. Now, in the state supreme court, Gansz claims that article II, section 16a of the Colorado Constitution, as implemented by the Colorado General Assembly, grants her legal standing to appeal the trial court's dismissal.] . . .

Article II, section 16a [of the Colorado Constitution] provides:

> Rights of crime victims. Any person who is a victim of a criminal act, or such person's designee, legal guardian, or surviving immediate family members if such person is deceased, shall have the *right to be heard* when relevant, informed, and present at all *critical stages* of the criminal justice

process. *All terminology, including the term "critical stages," shall be defined by the General Assembly.* [Emphasis added.]

[We hold, however, that] Section 16a of the Colorado Constitution does not confer legal standing upon an alleged crime victim to appeal an order granting the district attorney's motion to dismiss a criminal charge. . . .

The Colorado Constitution establishes the office of district attorney and vests in the office the right to file an information on behalf of the People of the State of Colorado and the discretion to determine the charges that will be filed. The decision to charge "is the heart of the prosecution function. The broad discretion given to a prosecutor in deciding whether to bring charges . . . requires that the greatest effort be made to see that this power is used fairly and uniformly." . . .

To implement Article II, section 16a, the General Assembly [has] defined "critical stage" to include numerous stages within the criminal process, including the "disposition of the complaint or charges" and "any appellate review or appellate decision." § 24–4.1–302(2)(f),(I), 10A C.R.S. (1994 Supp.).

[Colorado law actually provides many kinds of victim's rights. For example, a] crime victim has the right to be present for and informed of all critical stages of the criminal justice process. § 24–4.1–302.5(1)(c), 10A C.R.S. (1994 Supp.). A victim's "right to be heard" is limited, however, to "any court proceeding which involves a bond reduction or modification, the acceptance of a negotiated plea agreement, or the sentencing of any person accused or convicted of a crime" against the victim. § 24–4.1–302.5(1)(d), 10A C.R.S. (1994 Supp.).

Article II, section 16a of the Colorado Constitution authorizes the General Assembly to define "[a]ll terminology." The enactment of section 24–4.1–302.5(1) (d) reflects a legislative determination as to when a victim's input would be relevant, and, therefore, when a right to be heard would be appropriate. There is no statutory right to be heard at a hearing on a district attorney's motion to dismiss criminal charges. [Rather than granting a right to be heard, t]he legislation grants crime victims the "right to confer with the prosecution after any crime against the victim has been charged, prior to any disposition of the case . . . and the right to be informed of the final disposition of the case. . . ." § 24–4.1–302.5(1)(e), 10A C.R.S. (1994 Supp.). "[T]he district attorney shall consult, where practicable, with the victim regarding any decisions concerning the case, including decisions concerning . . . dismissal, or other disposition." § 24–4.1–303(4), 10A C.R.S. (1994 Supp.).

Article II, section 16a of the Colorado Constitution does not grant an alleged crime victim standing or the right to contest a district attorney's decision to dismiss criminal charges or the right to appellate review of the order dismissing the charges. . . . [Affirmed.]

PEOPLE v. CHAVEZ, 368 P.3d 943 (Colo. 2016). Court-ordered discovery from victims is a sore point in the victim's rights area. Chavez was charged with sexual assault, allegedly committed in the victim's home while Chavez was a guest of another occupant. He filed a motion requesting court-ordered access to the victim's home and bedroom—the crime scene. He alleged that he needed access "in order to be able to investigate and photograph the property for his defense." Chavez cited Colorado Rule of Criminal Procedure 16(I)(d) and argued that, under that rule, the court had "discretionary power" to order the disclosure of "relevant material and information." The trial court ordered the victim to allow access to Chavez. The state supreme court, citing *Gansz*, above, here reversed:

> [A] trial court lacks authority to order defense access to a third party's private home that is not in the possession or control of the government. Similarly, the trial court here lacked authority to grant Chavez access to the alleged victim's home. Given our decision in [*People in the Interest of*] *E.G.*, 2016 CO 19, 368 P.3d 946, the trial court's order, issued in reliance on the court of appeals' now-overruled opinion, cannot stand. We therefore [reverse]

The discovery order in this case was highly intrusive, but not voluminous. Other discovery orders have created onerous burdens for victims. These orders differ among jurisdictions and among courts. See the notes, below.

Notes and Questions

(1) *Whose Interests?* Whose interests are involved in the issues in the *Gansz* case? The [alleged] victim's? Justice system's? Defendant's? District attorney's? Do you think the court (and the Colorado statute) adequately considered each of these interests?

(2) *Why Not Standing?* Article II, § 16 is designed to give crime victims certain rights. Does *Gansz* hold that the alleged victim *never* has standing to assert such rights at trial and on appeal (shouldn't the alleged victim *always* have standing to assert his or her rights to ensure that these rights are actually recognized)? Note that Gansz would have at least some of the rights she seeks if, instead, the controversy were about a bond, a plea bargain, or a sentence. Why in those cases, but not dismissal, where there is only the right to be consulted?

On the other hand, consider whether affording these rights to an alleged victim would likely extend the pendency of some unmeritorious criminal charges against innocent citizens for years after the state officer empowered to prosecute has decided that the alleged victim's complaint is not credible. Is this an instance in which awarding a right to one party is likely to result in oppression of another party (as well as waste of public resources)?

(3) *Successful Assertion of Victim's and Survivor's Rights against Onerous Discovery: N.G. v. Superior Court*, 291 P.3d 328 (Alaska Ct. App. 2012). Although the courts have continued to limit the participation of victims and survivors in criminal prosecutions to conform to statutes and constitutions, both appellate and trial courts

honor actual rights of victims. For example, in the *N.G.* case, the state supreme court held that a trial judge had violated the victim's rights when it ordered her to identify all of her health care providers from the past 20 years and to sign a release allowing production of her psychiatry records. Victim privacy has become a more widely respected value. And consider the Kobe Bryant case, Problem 5F in Chapter 5. There, extensive court-ordered discovery was among the motivations for a rape survivor to request dismissal of the charges, although the prosecutors found her credible.

[B] Crime Victim Compensation: Damages, Restitution, and Publicly Funded Reparations

One critical issue for crime victims is to be compensated for their losses. Some recent laws have eased the victim's efforts to obtain compensation for losses. The defendant is an obvious and appropriate source of compensation for the crime victim, but not the only one.

[1] From the Defendant

Notes on Damage Suits and on Restitutionary Sentencing

(1) *Civil Suits against Perpetrators: Collateral Estoppel and Other Devices.* As is noted above, civil suits against the victim are technically viable but are often cumbersome, expensive, and fruitless. A clear majority of American jurisdictions now have statutes or case law that make such suits easier, by applying the doctrine of collateral estoppel. Once a defendant is found guilty of a crime, the victim may use collateral estoppel in a subsequent civil case to establish facts that were already proven in the criminal case. *See generally* Center for Law and Justice, *In Favor of "Trina's Law": A Proposal to Allow Crime Victims in Ohio to Use the Criminal Convictions of the Perpetrators as Collateral Estoppel in Subsequent Civil Cases*, 32 Cap. U. L. Rev. 351 (2003). Some jurisdictions have reached this result by common law adjudication.

(2) *Restitution as a Remedy at Sentencing: State v. Cosgaya-Alvarez*, 291 P.3d 939 (Wash. Ct. App. 2013). Another approach is the use of restitution, which requires the defendant to compensate the victim for the victim's loss. Every jurisdiction now authorizes (and some require) orders for the payment of restitution as part of its sentencing scheme. Thus, compensation through restitution is part of the criminal process. Sometimes restitution orders involve large amounts. In the *Cosgaya-Alvarez* case, the court ordered a defendant convicted of murder to pay restitution of more than $100,000 to the victim's survivors, and the appellate court approved the inclusion of an amount to pay the victim's required child support.

Sometimes a restitution order is a direct part of the sentence. Another variation is to have the payment of restitution as a probation condition, perhaps expressed in terms of paying a certain amount each month. Timely and full payment is enforced by the probation officer, who may seek probation revocation if the offender does not pay as ordered.

(3) *The Limits of Restitution as a Practical Remedy.* Restitution presents a number of issues. If the amount of loss is easily determined, the amount of the restitution order is not difficult to set. For example, if the defendant stole a car and destroyed it in an accident, the amount of restitution may be the fair market value of the car. Similarly, if the crime caused the victim to incur medical and hospital bills, the amount of those can be assessed as restitution. Some jurisdictions also add lost wages, the cost of traveling to various criminal hearings, and other tangible losses. Most jurisdictions refuse, however, to order restitution for pain and suffering, loss of life expectancy, or prevention of performance of normal activities. A victim who seeks such damages must resort to a civil suit.

Restitution orders may become meaningless if the defendant cannot pay. The United States Supreme Court has held that indigent defendants may not be incarcerated simply because of an inability to pay various court-ordered costs, such as restitution. *See Bearden v. Georgia*, 461 U.S. 660 (1983); *see generally* Neil P. Cohen, *The Law of Probation and Parole* 11–35 to 11–44 (2d ed. 1999).

[2] *Compensation from Public Funds*

Notes on Crime Victim Compensation Acts and Adversarial Claims Against Government

Another means of compensation for crime victims is to obtain reparations from government resources. The source may be a fund set up to compensate victims, or in special circumstances, it may be an adversarial claim asserted by a suit against the government.

(1) *Crime Victim's Compensation Funds: Coverage, Claims, Administration, and Funding: State v. Jackson*, 384 S.W.3d 208 (Mo. 2012). All American jurisdictions and the federal government maintain funds to compensate some crime victims for at least some of their losses. The focus is virtually always on victims of violent crimes, who may receive payments for such losses as medical, dental, and mental health expenses; lost income; funeral expenses, and even loss of support for dependents of such victims. *See generally* Julie Goldscheid, *Crime Victim Compensation in a Post-9/11 World*, 79 Tul. L. Rev. 167 (2004). Too often these funds are not as helpful as they might be. Many victims do not use the fund because they are unaware of its existence or how to apply for compensation. Moreover, because of limited resources, compensation is ordinarily limited to a specific dollar amount, with an average cap of $35,000, irrespective of the actual amount of harm.

Victims' compensation programs are often funded by court costs assessed in criminal cases. In effect, all convicted criminals who are able to pay must contribute toward restitution of crime victims generally. In the *Jackson* case, *supra*, the court even held that the defendant could be required to pay a cash bond rather than a surety bond, partly for the purpose of ensuring that there would be money to pay required amounts to the state's Crime Victim Compensation Fund.

(2) *Suits against Government and Government Officials.* Another, far more difficult possibility is for a crime victim to sue for damages from a government entity on the theory that the entity somehow caused or contributed to the loss. For example, if a government employee acted irresponsibly in releasing an offender, a lawsuit by the person the released offender injured is a theoretical possibility. *See, e.g., Monroe v. Pape*, 365 U.S. 167 (1961) (police officer acting under color of state law may be sued under 42 U.S.C. § 1983 for violating a citizen's civil rights). But the conditions for recovery are narrow, and such suits are expensive. Doctrines of sovereign and individual immunity may eliminate most suits. Finally, it may be difficult to prove that the entity was legally responsible. *See, e.g., Martinez v. California*, 444 U.S. 277 (1980) (parolee killed decedent but parole authorities immune from suit).

[3] Damages from Third Parties

Notes on Negligent Security Claims and Related Theories

(1) *Theories Underlying Crime Victims' Claims against Premises Owners, Transportation Providers, Manufacturers, and Others.* Crime victims may also explore lawsuits against people other than the offender or the government. One illustration, based on products liability law, may involve a lawsuit against a business that somehow provided the means for the crime. An example is lawsuits against gun manufacturers and distributors for harm inflicted by a criminal who used a handgun. *See, e.g., Ileto v. Glock*, 349 F.3d 1191 (9th Cir. 2003) (permitting shooting victims and family members to sue gun manufacturers, distributors, and dealers for various tort claims based on defendant's use of a gun to harm four people). But in 2005, Congress enacted the Protection of Lawful Commerce in Arms Act, which insulates most gun manufacturers from civil liability in such cases. *See Ileto v. Glock*, 565 F.3d 1126 (9th Cir. 2009) (upholding dismissal of claims against domestic gun manufacturers).

(2) *Negligent Security Claims.* Victims have also brought suit against property owners of locations where the crime occurred. Such a suit may allege that the owner failed to take adequate precautions to prevent the offense and therefore was negligent in providing security. The prototype is a claim by a customer or guest to the effect that a retailer, apartment, or hotel proximately caused a violent crime against the plaintiff by providing security that fell short of reasonable expectation. *See, e.g., Doe v. Gunny's Ltd. Partnership*, 593 N.W.2d 284 (1999) (woman raped in bar's parking garage sued property owner, who was found to have a duty to take precautions against such crimes). *See also* Robin J. Effron, *Event Jurisdiction and Protective Coordination: Lessons from the September 11th Litigation*, 81 S. Cal. L. Rev. 199 (2008) (discussing the complexities of litigating claims by families of 9/11 victims against airlines and airplane manufacturers for alleged negligence that allowed terrorists to hijack aircraft).

[C] Participation (and Influence) in Criminal Proceedings

[1] Victims' Rights Laws

Notes on Victim Participation in Trials: Advice, Presence, Evidence, and Argument

(1) *New Laws, Especially about Sentencing: Ebron v. Commissioner of Correction*, 53 A.3d 983 (Conn. 2012). An important part of the movement to recognize the interests of crime victims is to give them the right to be present at—and sometimes to participate in—criminal justice processes. The *Ebron* case, supra, resulted in a holding that, under a state constitutional provision requiring an opportunity for the victim to "participate meaningfully" in the defendant's sentencing, even a guilty plea pursuant to a plea bargain must be delayed and made contingent on the court's hearing from the victim.

(2) *The Historic Problem: Poor Treatment of Victims.* The experience of the authors of this book has included contact with victims and witnesses before Victims' Rights laws were adopted. It was not uncommon, in some jurisdictions, for victims and witnesses to be subpoenaed repeatedly—as frequently as ten to twenty times—only to be informed, after spending hours sitting, that their cases were not reached for trial and that they would need to return. Prosecutors had no duty, and only very limited time, to inform witnesses of processes or developments. A negotiated plea might end the matter with no notice to anyone but the court, lawyers, and defendant. Restitution was not routinely sought. Crime victims had no recognized right to be heard by the court on matters concerning their personal safety, their interests in the disposition of the case, or the impact of the crime upon them. Lest this picture seem more bleak than it is, it should be added that prosecutors did often consult victims, attend to their needs, and notify them of developments, as a matter of concern rather than of duty, as time permitted, and so did some courts. But the systematic protection of these interests that exists today was lacking.

In fact, prior to such laws, victims had no greater right than any citizen to attend a criminal proceeding. In some respects, their rights were less than that of the casual citizen. Because of the evidence rule that witnesses could be kept out of the courtroom during the testimony of other witnesses, the crime victim—often viewed as simply a witness—could be barred from attending most of the trial. Moreover, too often they were not notified of court dates, not consulted on prosecutorial decisions, and not afforded an opportunity to speak at some hearings.

(3) *Typical Protections of Victims and Witnesses under Modern Laws.* The new provisions vary markedly among the jurisdictions. Many begin with a general statement about the victim's right to be treated with fairness, respect, and dignity. Some include respect for the victim's privacy. They then give crime victims some or all of the following rights, which the victim may (or may not) have standing to enforce in court:

1. To be notified of their rights under the victims' rights laws.

2. To be notified of the date, time, and location of various court proceedings, such as the trial, sentencing, and plea hearings, probation revocation, post-conviction relief hearing, and parole release proceeding.

3. To attend various proceedings. In many jurisdictions, this protection includes the right to be present during the entire trial, including the testimony of other witnesses. It may also extend to the victim's close relatives.

4. To address the court on the issue of the appropriate sentence. Ordinarily, this right includes giving the court or jury a "victim's impact statement" informing the court of how the crime affected the victim's life. Some jurisdictions give the defendant the right to cross-examine the victim after the statement.

5. To be consulted by the prosecution about the case.

6. To be notified when the defendant escapes or is released from custody.

7. To a timely resolution of the criminal matter.

Problem 14A (Victims' Rights): Is More Better?

The above list does not include every possible involvement by the crime victim. If you were a legislator who wanted to strike an appropriate balance that protected the rights of both the victim and the defendant and also respected the values inherent in the jurisdiction's criminal justice system, would you add any of the following to the list?

1. The victim's right to provide input to the prosecutor about which, if any, charges to bring (ordinarily this is left to the prosecutor's discretion). [Before you say yes, consider that the resources consumed by this right would be extensive, in comparison to the existing regime. Can you see why?]

2. The victim's right to have the defendant prosecuted (*i.e.* giving the victim, not the prosecutor, the right to have the case processed through the criminal justice system to trial).

3. The victim's right to have the charges dismissed (particularly relevant in domestic violence cases) or to refuse to testify. [Consider whether some victims might be made worse off by having this right. Many jurisdictions insist on prosecuting credible domestic cases, today, even in the absence of victim cooperation. Can you see why this approach might arguably be sound—and better for many victims?]

4. The victim's right to veto any plea bargain that gives the accused a sentence less than the maximum sentence, or in the alternative, the right to be consulted on any plea bargain. *See* Ore. Const. Art 1, § 42 (right to be consulted, upon request, regarding plea negotiations for any violent felony).

5. The victim's right to insist on a trial rather than a guilty plea, to ensure that the defendant's conduct is revealed in a public forum.

6. The victim's right to appeal a sentence deemed too lenient.

7. Restrictions on defense interviews of the victim (perhaps by giving the victim the right to have the prosecutor present during any such interview).

8. The victim's right to sit at the prosecutor's table during the entire trial and all hearings.

9. The victim's right to discover information in the district attorney's file in order to facilitate the victim's civil suit against the defendant.

10. The right to have the victim's interests considered in the decision where the case will be tried (*i.e.*, in what venue).

[2] Hiring a Private Prosecutor

Notes on Special Prosecutors

(1) *What Can the Victim Do If He or She Is Dissatisfied with the Efforts of the District Attorney?* In criminal cases the government is represented by the district attorney. Though the victim is not formally the prosecutor's client, every prosecutor realizes that he or she does, in some ways, represent the interests of the victim. But what if the victim is dissatisfied with that representation or simply wants to have someone else prosecute the case?

A large number of American jurisdictions authorize crime victims to retain a lawyer to assist the public prosecutor with the case. *See generally* John D. Bessler, *The Public Interest and the Unconstitutionality of Private Prosecutors*, 47 Ark. L. Rev. 511 (1994). The regular prosecutor retains control over the case. *See, e.g., Riner v. Commonwealth*, 579 S.E.2d 671 (Va. Ct. App. 2003) (no limit on the percent of work a private prosecutor may do on a case as long as the public prosecutor is in continuous control of the case).

(2) *Beyond Assistance: Special Prosecutors?* A small number of jurisdictions go further, allowing the victim's "private prosecutor" to handle the case as if he or she were the public prosecutor. This hired lawyer makes the ordinary prosecutorial decisions about the case, such as what charges to bring, what plea to accept, and what evidence to present at trial. *See, e.g., Cronan v. Cronan*, 774 A.2d 866 (R.I. 2001) (assault victim hired private lawyer to prosecute; public prosecutor withdrew, and the case was successfully prosecuted by the private prosecutor; practice authorized by law). Obviously, this procedure gives the victim more power in the criminal process. Why do so few states allow it (is this system fair to the defendant and the system of justice)? Consider that in *Cronan*, above, the private prosecution was brought by the wife-victim while she and defendant-husband were involved in a difficult divorce. Does this practice make sense?

[D] Dealing with Crime Victims' and Survivors' Emotional Needs

Notes on Formal Support Programs

(1) *A Changing Landscape.* There is no doubt that many crime victims suffer both physically and mentally because of the crime. Traditionally the criminal justice system handled the victim's mental and emotional needs informally. Some law enforcement and prosecution agencies trained their personnel or trained staff to deal with such needs. Today, however, the landscape has changed. Many jurisdictions have adopted formal, funded programs designed to be more sensitive to the victims' non-financial needs.

(2) *Victim-Witness Coordinators and Advocates; The Alaska Example.* One approach is for a prosecutor's office to employ personnel whose responsibilities specifically include assisting crime victims. This approach may entail such activities as assisting victims in applying for compensation, informing them of proceedings and the status of their cases, referring them to counseling or other resources, and generally being available when the victim needs to talk with someone from the prosecution's office.

One of the most innovative approaches is Alaska's Office of Victim's Rights, a law firm that represents the interests of victims throughout the state. A primary responsibility is ensuring that victims receive the rights given them by the state constitution and statutes. State law gives these lawyers the right to appear in court on behalf of the victim. *See generally* Stephen E. Branchflower, *The Alaska Office of Victims' Rights: A Model for America*, 21 Alas. L. Rev. 259 (2004).

(3) *Victim and Survivor Support Groups.* Another innovation is the formation of victims' support groups. Often there are group sessions where victims share their stories with one another, meetings for the same purpose, or "telephone pals" available to talk to a crime victim who is "having a bad day." Some such groups take an active role in promoting the interests of crime victims, perhaps by monitoring court proceedings or advocating changes in the law.

(4) *Programs Leading to Prompt Resolution: Should Victims and Survivors Be Entitled to a Speedy Trial?* A common complaint of crime victims is that the criminal process may take a long time to reach a final resolution. As noted above, some victims' rights developments are designed to ensure that the victim is kept informed about the status of the case and has an opportunity to be present and participate in many facets. Another approach is an effort to speed the process on the theory that the victim deserves a prompt resolution.

Some jurisdictions attempt to reduce delay by including in their victims' rights laws language giving the victim a right to a prompt resolution of the crime. *See, e.g.,* Ariz. Const. art II, § 2.1(A)(10) (crime victim has right to speedy trial or disposition and prompt and final conclusion of the case); S.C. Const. art I, § 24(11) (prompt and final conclusion of the case).

[E] Protecting the Victim's Privacy and Safety

[1] Protecting the Victim's Privacy Interests

Notes on Privacy-Related Issues

(1) *A Crime as a "Public Event"—and the Victim's Contrary Interests.* Crime victims not only suffer the direct consequences of a robbery or rape but also may have to endure other intrusions into their privacy and safety. Some legal developments attempt to alleviate at least some of these concerns.

In some ways a crime becomes a public event, perhaps reported by the media, resolved in the public crucible of the criminal process. While the public and the democratic system may gain by this openness, some crime victims feel that it invades their privacy and adds additional harm to that precipitated directly by the offender. The legal system has made some efforts to balance the important privacy concerns of the victim and the public and defendant's interests in a public proceeding.

(2) *Excluding the Public from Proceedings.* Crime victims, including those who have suffered sexual assaults, often prefer that all or part of the criminal proceedings be conducted without the public and press being present. While both the defendant and the public have a right to have open proceedings, in narrowly tailored situations the law allows closure of at least some proceedings. *See Richmond Newspapers, Inc. v. Virginia*, 448 U.S. 555 (1980) (public and press have First Amendment right to attend criminal proceedings, absent overriding public interest in closure); *Globe Newspaper Co. v. Superior Court*, 457 U.S. 596 (1982) (overturning state statute requiring trial judges to exclude the press and public from the courtroom during testimony by minor sex crime victims; case-by-case exclusion to protect minor crime victims may satisfy First Amendment). Some victim's rights provisions even give victims standing to challenge decisions opening such trials to the public. *E.g., State in Interest of K.P.*, 709 A.2d 315 (N.J. Super. Ct. Ch. Div. 1997) (victim has standing under New Jersey victim's rights law to oppose a newspaper's petition to open a sexual assault trial).

(3) *Protecting Victims' and Witnesses' Personal History from Public Disclosure.* Crime victims may resent criminal proceedings that require them to disclose personal facts. A good example is a rape trial in which the defense seeks to intimidate and impeach the victim by inquiring into her sexual history. In recent years, some evidence rules have been adopted to reduce unnecessary intrusions. *See, e.g.,* Fed. R. Evid. 412 (federal rape-shield law). For a noteworthy holding, see the *N.G.* case, discussed in the Notes in § 14.02[A], above, in which the trial judge ordered the victim to list all health care providers over the previous 20 years and sign a release of her psychiatric records; the state supreme court reversed this order.

(4) *A Right to Refuse to Cooperate with Discovery by Defendant or Defense Counsel?* Ethically a prosecutor may not ask a crime victim to refrain from discussing

the case with defense counsel, but the rules also provide that a victim need not have such discussions. The victim is free to choose whether to cooperate with defense requests to interview the victim.

Some of the Victim's Rights laws specifically recognize the victim's right to refuse to discuss the crime with the defense. *E.g.*, Ariz. Const. Art 2, §2.1. They may also authorize the victim to refuse to comply with defense discovery requests. *E.g.*, Ariz. Const. Art 2, §2.1; Ore. Const. Art 1, §42 (right to refuse an interview, deposition, or other discovery request by defense).

[2] Protecting the Victim's Safety

Notes on Protection and Notification

(1) *A Right to Be Protected (Does It Exist in Reality?)* Too often crime victims feel—or actually experience—threats to their safety. This problem has been most publicized in domestic violence and organized crime cases, but it is a phenomenon that extends to other cases and victims as well. Some of the Victim's Rights provisions specifically address this issue by giving the victim the right to be free of intimidation, harassment, or abuse during the criminal justice process. *E.g.*, Ariz. Const. Art 2, §2.1 (reasonably protected from accused throughout criminal justice process); Ill. Const. Art.1, §8.1(7) (same). Other provisions guarantee the right to a safe environment in certain settings. *E.g.*, Cal. Const. Art 1, §28 (safe schools). Crime survivors often feel, however—and sometimes correctly—that these protections are merely theoretical, not addressed to their individual circumstances. In fact, few jurisdictions can "provide protection" of the kind imagined in some television or motion picture dramas; it is impossible for them routinely to delegate around-the-clock police officers to perform the task.

A related approach is to make public safety a consideration in the decision whether to release the defendant from custody pending trial or other proceedings. *E.g.*, Cal. Const. Art 1, §28.

(2) *Notification of Release or Escape.* Similarly, some locales give the victim the right to be notified when the defendant is released from prison or other custodial situations (or when the defendant escapes). *E.g.*, Alas. Const. Art. 1; Mich. Const. Art. 1, §24(1) (information about release of accused).

[F] Changing Evidence, Procedure, and Crime Definition

Notes on Victims' and Survivors' Interests in Law Revision

(1) *The Crime Victim's View of the Law—and Interest in Changing It.* One common reaction of crime victims is to seek to change the future public response to crime. Thus, the victim may become a lobbyist (or at least a member of an organization that lobbies), on the impulse that "I want to prevent what happened to me [or my loved one] from happening to someone else."

In some instances, victim lobbying is persuasive. Mothers against Drunk Driving has lobbied for improved drunk driving laws that arguably target more precisely the conditions that should produce conviction for this offense (which was taken much less seriously fifteen to twenty years ago). As another illustration, victim-related lobbying led to amendment of the California Constitution to broaden admissibility of relevant evidence, including the defendant's prior convictions. *See* Cal. Const. Art. 1, § 28.

(2) *Countervailing Forces: Will Victim's Organizations Push the Balance Too Far in One Direction?* In some states, in the not-too-distant past, the most potent lobbying force has been the local association of criminal defense attorneys. Public prosecutors were underfunded and outnumbered. Victims' rights groups have changed this balance. The question arises: will these groups become too successful, so that the balance shifts excessively in one direction?

(3) *Appropriate Lobbying Roles: Changing Procedures That Provide Little Safety from an Overreaching State but That Impede Sound Law Enforcement; Redefining Crimes for Greater Precision and Consistency with Policy; Seeking Proportional Sentencing.* Some of the best kinds of lobbying efforts have altered processes that provide little real protection to defendants' legitimate interests but that seriously impede sound adjudication. For example, victim's lobbying groups have successfully advocated legislation reversing overly exacting appellate analysis of indictments: the practice of focusing on minor errors in stock phrases. The errors made no practical difference in the quality of notice given to the defendants (or courts or juries), and were not even objected to by defense counsel at trial, yet resulted in appellate reversal of convictions. In such a situation, arguably, the defendant has only the hope of a windfall escape from legitimate conviction, and victim lobbyists thus reduce arbitrariness in the adjudicatory process — or so they would see it. Victims also have produced crime definitions with greater precision and congruence with policy, as in the case of intoxicated driving laws that define intoxication not merely in terms of functional impairment, but also in terms of specific blood alcohol content.

The problem is that people disagree vigorously about exactly which criminal laws provide so little protection of legitimate civil libertarian interests, and cause such significant arbitrariness in adjudication, as to merit this kind of revision. For example, a state legislature considering alteration of its sexual assault law to allow conviction upon negligent failure to recognize nonconsent, as opposed to recklessness or knowledge, may be urged by victim's rights groups to make the change. But others would oppose this revision.

(4) *Is the Ability of the Victim's Rights Movement to Alter the Balance a Self-Limiting Power?* One consideration that may restrain concerns about these issues involves the ultimate objectives of victim's rights groups. For example, the authors of this book are unaware of any victim's lobbyist who has called for watering down the burden of proof beyond a reasonable doubt. Victims presumably have no interest

in facilitating conviction to the point of distorting the system so as to convict the wrong people, leaving the real perpetrators free to continue committing crimes. At some point, therefore, it can be argued that the persuasive power of the victim's lobby is self-limiting. There remains real disagreement between the two camps about whether, say, admitting certain kinds of evidence will lower the proof burden or otherwise skew the balance. Do you think, however, that this argument, that the victim's rights lobby may be more prone to self-limitation than some other lobbies, has any merit?

[G] Striking the Proper Balance

Notes on the Conflict Between the Interests of the Victim and of the Accused

(1) *Provisions That Explicitly Recognize the Limits of Victim's Rights.* While making efforts to accommodate the important interests of crime victims, we must remember that the defendant also has rights that must be respected. Sometimes the interests of victims and defendants conflict. Moreover, values other than protection of the defendant's rights may also conflict with the victim's rights. For example, in one state, the separation of powers doctrine has persuaded a court to invalidate a victim's rights provision shortening time limits for filing for postconviction relief. *State ex rel. Napolitano v. Brown*, 982 P.2d 815 (Ariz. 1999).

Some victim's rights provisions recognize this potential conflict and state explicitly that the defendant's rights should not be compromised by the victim's rights. *See, e.g.*, Fla. Const. Art 1, § 16 (b) (victim's right to be informed, present, and heard is recognized "to the extent that these rights do not interfere with the constitutional rights of the accused"); Ore. Const. Art 1, § 42 (1) (victim's rights provision designed "to ensure that a fair balance is struck between the rights or crime victims and the rights of criminal defendants").

(2) *How Often Do Victim's Rights Laws Infringe Unconstitutionally on Defendants' Rights?* When courts are faced with the conflict between the rights of the victim and those of the accused, most decisions seem to find that the accused's rights are not violated by the new protections accorded the victim. *See, e.g., State v. Gonzales*, 892 P.2d 838 (Ariz. 1995) (assault-robbery victim's presence in court room during jury selection, in accordance with victim's rights law, did not violate accused's constitutional rights); *Gore v. State*, 599 So. 2d 978 (Fla. 1992) (finding no due process violation when victim's stepmother was permitted to remain in courtroom during trial, as allowed by victim's rights law). But there are exceptions. *See, e.g., State ex rel. Romley v. Superior Court*, 836 P.2d 445 (Ariz. Ct. App. 1992) (denying defendant access to victim's medical records, when victim's rights act barred discovery of such records, could violate defendant's Due Process rights if such records are essential to the presentation of his self-defense claim).

§ 14.03 Conviction by Guilty Plea

[A] The Methods and Realities of Plea Agreements

Notes on Settlement: Plea Bargaining, Why and How

(1) *Trial Is the Unusual Exception in America Today.* As the materials below show, the overwhelming majority of cases are resolved by settlement, both on civil and on criminal dockets. In 2012, for example, 97 percent of all federal offenders pled guilty. U.S. Sentencing Commission, *Overview of Federal Criminal Cases: Fiscal Year 2012*, at 4.

(2) *The Real Decisionmakers Often Are the Defendant, Defense Attorney, and Prosecutor.* Each of these three actors can autonomously prevent their joint encounter from being resolved by settlement. Often, the actor who insists on trial is the defendant, either with or against the advice of counsel. The prosecutor also can insist on trial by refusing to settle for less than the maximum in a serious case — or by creating conditions under which the defendant believes a better result will come from trial. Consider the following case.

NEWMAN v. UNITED STATES, 382 F.2d 479 (D.C. 1967). Newman and Anderson were indicted for housebreaking and petty larceny. Negotiations between the government and Anderson's counsel led to his guilty plea and sentence for lesser included misdemeanors, but the government declined to consent to the same settlement with Newman. He failed to appear for trial, became a fugitive, was apprehended, tried and convicted, and received a sentence of 2 to 6 years. The court, through Judge (later Chief Justice) Burger, rejected Newman's claim that he was denied due process and equal protection:

> Few subjects are less adapted to judicial review than the exercise by the Executive of . . . discretion in deciding when and whether to institute criminal proceedings, or what precise charge shall be made, or whether to dismiss a proceeding once brought. . . .

> To say that the United States Attorney must literally treat every offense and every offender alike is to delegate him an impossible task; of course this concept would negate discretion. Myriad factors can enter into the prosecutor's decision. Two persons may have committed what is precisely the same legal offense but the prosecutor is not compelled by law, duty or tradition to treat them the same as to charges. [If, for example,] one played a lesser and the other a dominant role, one the instigator and the other a follower, the prosecutor can and should take such factors into account; no court has any jurisdiction to inquire into or review his decision. . . .

Notes and Questions

(1) *Settlement Based on a Race to the Courthouse.* Imagine that the United States Attorney settles with one defendant: the one who is the first to confess and implicate the other. This defendant pleads to a reduced charge. The other defendant offers to plead guilty to the same lesser offense, but the government refuses. The majority's opinion appears to permit this differential treatment. Can you explain this conclusion (and also, evaluate why the race-to-the-courthouse scenario could merit differential treatment)?

(2) *What if the Settlement Offer Is to Dismiss as to One Defendant if the Other Pleads Guilty?* Sometimes, in nonviolent cases in which it is difficult to discern which of multiple defendants is most culpable, a prosecutor will offer to settle by dismissal of other defendants if any one pleads guilty. This practice, too, appears permissible under the *Newman* holding. The justification appears to be that settlement is preferable for both sides to trial and that the defendants' choice is likely to be affected by their relative culpability. Consider the case in the following note.

(3) *No Settlement Unless All Defendants Plead Guilty: People v. Henzey*, 24 A.D.2d 764 (N.Y. App. Div. 1965). The court in this case upheld the discretion of the District Attorney to refuse to recommend lesser convictions for any of four defendants unless all four pled guilty:

> Appellant's contention is that the District Attorney's refusal to consent to a reduced plea from her younger brother unless she pleaded guilty to a reduced charge was a form of coercion depriving her of her constitutional rights. We shall assume *arguendo* that her motive, sole or primary, in pleading guilty was to protect her younger brother from the hazard of a first degree murder conviction with its concomitant possible severe sentence. Nevertheless, no threats were made against her or her brother and her plea of guilty was not induced by threats or coercion, but was her voluntary act and reasoned choice. . . . The judgment of conviction may not be set aside in the situation presented herein.

(4) *The Prevalence of, and Lawyering Strategies Involved in, Settlement.* Great nations resolve disputes without war, by negotiation, and children do the same on the playground. In the criminal law, it is well known that most indictments are resolved by negotiation and settlement, just as they are in civil cases. This does not mean that lawyering work, and hard work at that, is not needed. Sometimes a settlement by plea requires more work by the lawyers than a trial.

(5) *Defendants Who Insist on Pleading Guilty Even if Defense Counsel Advises Otherwise.* This situation is actually fairly common: "My client just doesn't have the stomach for trial." The reason may be fear of the unknown, unwillingness to have twelve strangers hear the sordid details in public, avoidance of anxiety, delay, and heartache, a wish to avoid exposing friends or associates to the need to testify,

wanting not to testify oneself, consciousness of guilt, a combination of all these reasons, or something else. Students sometimes express incredulity at this phenomenon, but one does not sense the pressure of the situation without being a part of it.

[B] The Case Against Plea Bargaining

Scott v. United States

419 F.2d 264 (D.C. Cir. 1969)

BAZELON, CHIEF JUDGE:

Vincent Scott was convicted of robbery under 22 D.C. Code § 2901 (1967) and sentenced to prison for five to fifteen years. [As the court puts it, Scott's claim "was that his co-defendant suggested and executed the crime, while he declined the invitation to participate and resolutely looked the other way." Under the evidence, this defense was improbable, and neither the jury nor the judge believed Scott.] The proceedings preceding his conviction were, we conclude, free from error. The events surrounding his sentencing, however, present thorny questions concerning what factors the trial judge may properly consider at that stage. We affirm the conviction, but remand for a resentencing in accordance with the principles announced in this opinion.

I . . .

[T]he trial judge explained in some detail the reasons for which the sentence was imposed. He stated repeatedly throughout the hearing that he did not believe the exculpatory testimony the appellant had given at trial. And at one point the judge indicated that he was influenced as well by the fact that the appellant had insisted upon a trial in the first place: "Now the Court didn't believe your story on the stand, the Court believes you deliberately lied in this case. If you had pleaded guilty to this offense, I might have been more lenient with you." . . . He went on, "I hope sometime I hear some defendant say, 'Judge, I am sorry, I am sorry for what I did.' That is what I have in mind." . . .

[The court of appeals holds that the judge's consideration of the defendant's failure to express remorse during the sentencing hearing is error because it denied the defendant the privilege against self-incrimination.]

Since a resentencing will be necessary, two other considerations the trial judge relied upon in sentencing the appellant require comment. The first problem arises from the judge's repeated statements that he believed the appellant had committed perjury on the witness stand in denying that he had participated in the robbery. There are two arguments why this belief would properly influence the choice of a sentence: (1) that additional punishment should be imposed for the independent substantive offense of perjury; (2) that the commission of perjury reflected adversely upon the appellant's prospects for rehabilitation, and therefore justified a lengthier sentence for the crime of robbery.

The first argument deserves emphatic rejection. The Government could if it wished prosecute the appellant for perjury.* . . .

As for the second argument, the peculiar pressures placed upon a defendant threatened with jail and the stigma of conviction make his willingness to deny the crime an unpromising test of his prospects for rehabilitation if guilty. . . .

. . . The stark import of [the trial judge's] comment is that the defendant paid a price for demanding a trial. . . .

And yet, despite the startling incongruity, empirical evidence supports the proposition that judges do sentence defendants who have demanded a trial more severely. At least one Court of Appeals has taken approving "judicial notice of the fact that trial courts quite generally impose a lighter sentence on pleas of guilty than in cases where the accused pleaded not guilty but has been found guilty by a jury." An advisory committee of the American Bar Association has concluded that "it is proper for the court to grant charge and sentence concessions to defendants who enter a plea of guilty . . . when the interest of the public in the effective administration of criminal justice would thereby be served." . . .

Repentance has a role in penology. But the premise of our criminal jurisprudence has always been that the time for repentance comes after trial.** The adversary process is a fact-finding engine, not a drama of contrition in which a prejudged defendant is expected to knit up his lacerated bonds to society.

. . . There is other, and better, evidence of such repentance. The sort of information collected in presentence reports provides a far more finely brushed portrait of the [defendant] than do a few hours or days at trial. . . .

The second argument for differential sentencing is necessity. Most convictions, perhaps [more than] 90 per cent in some jurisdictions, are the product of guilty pleas. Unless a large proportion of defendants plead guilty, the argument runs, the already crowded dockets in many jurisdictions would collapse into chaos. . . . Ergo, differential sentences are justified for those who plead guilty and those who plead innocent.

When approached from this perspective, the problem inevitably becomes entwined with that of plea bargaining. . . . Its format may vary. The prosecutor may agree to reduce the charge in exchange for a guilty plea [Eds. note: "count" bargaining], or he may agree to recommend a lighter sentence ["sentence" bargaining]. . . .

Thus, to the extent that the appellant here received a longer sentence because he pleaded innocent, he was a pawn sacrificed to induce other defendants to plead guilty. Since this is so, to consider the price he paid for the exercise of his right without regard for the process of which it is but one instance would be to ignore reality. . . .

---

* This reasoning no longer is prevalent. As Chapter Nine, on Sentencing, explains, recommended enhancements for obstruction of justice are provided by the Federal Sentencing Guidelines, including perjury offered by the defendant at trial. — Eds.

** Again, this reasoning no longer is prevalent. — Eds.

In this case the trial judge did not bargain with the defendant. Indeed he did not even point out that he might be more lenient with a defendant who pleaded guilty until after trial. But in so stating at the sentencing hearing he announced to all future defendants the guidelines in his court room. We cannot approve of these guidelines for the same reasons that we could not condone actual plea bargaining by a trial judge. . . . [W]e cannot ignore the impact of such a policy on the appearance of justice to criminal defendants and their ability to choose wisely between a plea of guilty and an exercise of their right to trial. [Reversed and remanded for resentencing.]

Notes and Questions

(1) *What Did the Trial Judge Do Wrong?* The trial judge was not wrong in using "differential sentencing," according to the court of appeals. In other words, it was not wrong to sentence more leniently after a guilty plea. What was wrong was that the judge allegedly participated in plea bargaining. But the judge did not plea bargain regarding this defendant, because he did not mention his policies until after the defendant's (proper) trial and conviction. What, then, merited the court of appeals' criticism? The trial judge "announced to all future defendants the guidelines in his courtroom." In thus accurately stating his policies, the trial judge created an adverse impact on future defendants' "ability to choose wisely between a plea of guilty and an exercise of their right to a trial."

How does a trial judge "impair" defendants' choices by accurate announcement of his policies? The court of appeals appears to attempt to have it both ways: to approve what it calls "differential sentencing" but at the same time to condemn it (or at least discourage public recognition of it). Is this what is happening?

(2) *Repentance, Perjury, and Guilty Pleas: The Federal Sentencing Guidelines Firmly Disagree with This Court.* Current wisdom runs counter to this court's remarks about repentance as demonstrated by guilty pleas. Acceptance of responsibility is a factor that reduces a Guideline Sentence, and it may be shown in part by guilty plea. Likewise, the Guidelines encourage the judge to enhance sentences because of perjury at trial. *See* Chapter 9.

[C] The Pressure of the Numbers: Docketed Cases and Available Court Time

One of the clear trends in American criminal cases is the decline of jury trials. For example, in 2009–2010 Florida Circuit Courts disposed of about 200,000 cases. What approximate percent of those do you think were resolved by a jury trial?

  a. 25%   b. 18%   c. 14%   d. 5%   e. 2%

The answer is (e), about 2%. Are you surprised that the percentage is so low? It reflects one of the most significant trends in American law: the so-called "disappearing jury trial." By contrast, in Florida in 1986–87, the rate was 50% higher (3.1%). A larger study of state courts found a similar trend. In 1976, 8.5% of criminal dispositions were by trial (both jury and non-jury), while in 2002 the percent was only $3.3%. *Report of the Special Committee to Study the Decline in Jury Trials* (Florida, Final Report 2011). Still another study of 23 state courts found a 15% decline in criminal jury trials between 1976 and 2002. T. Munsterman & S. Strickland, Jury News (National Center for State Courts, Court Manager, vol. 19, issue 2).

Problem 14B: Would You Go to Trial?

Assume Guthrie, age 24, was arrested for beating his girlfriend and threatening her with a knife. Guthrie had been paroled from prison a month earlier. He claims to be innocent of the charges. The case is a "he said, she said" one where the victim-girlfriend's version of the event differs markedly from Guthrie's, who maintains his girlfriend attacked him with a knife and he grabbed the knife and used it to keep her away while he ran from the room.

The prosecutor offers a deal for two years in prison plus a probation term. Under state law, a person convicted of certain crimes, including serious assaults, who had recently been released from prison could be sentenced to a mandatory life sentence requiring service of as many as fifty years in prison.

You are defense counsel who believes both Guthrie and the girlfriend may be credible witnesses. Would you recommend that your client take the two-year offer or risk the possibility of a life sentence after a guilty verdict at trial? *See Sentencing Shift Gives New Leverage to Prosecutors*, N.Y. Times, Sept. 26, 2011 (discussing the Guthrie case).

Notes and Questions

(1) *Why So Few Jury Trials?* Which of the following statements do you think are true, and which are related to the reasons for the small number of jury trials in criminal cases? (a) Our society provides too few judges, courts, public defenders, and prosecutors to try many more criminal cases, causing these actors to use their influence to obtain a large number of guilty pleas. (b) Judges' time is disproportionately consumed by other matters, including pretrial issues. (c) Clients are risk-averse. (d) Attorneys are risk-averse. (e) The expense of litigation makes settlement rational. (f) Settlement is rational in most cases even apart from the expense of litigation because judges impose a "trial penalty" (a harsher sentence) on those defendants who elect to be tried and are nevertheless convicted. (g) Trends in sentencing toward mandatory and longer sentences give the prosecutor more bargaining power to induce defendants to plead guilty.

(2) *Why Does One Side or the Other Decline to Settle and Insist on the (Unusual) Resolution of a Trial in a Given Case?* Which of the following do you think are true and related to the reasons why a given criminal case might succumb to (the unusual) resolution of being tried? (a) One side has a stubborn lawyer. (b) One side has a stubborn client. (c) The lawyer or the client on one side remains ignorant of the

factors that would lead to an accurate assessment of the value of the case. (d) Our society sends the message that it is ethically superior to try the case than to settle.

(3) *To What Conclusions about Your Role as a Litigator or Trial Lawyer Do Your Analyses of the Questions above Lead?* One possible conclusion is that the typical student in your class who becomes a trial lawyer is actually not going to try very many criminal cases. Consider what other conclusions can be drawn about the meaning of these data to the practitioner.

United States Sentencing Commission Guidelines Manual (2018)
Chapter 1: Introduction, Authority, and General Application Principles

§ 4(c) *Plea Agreements.*

. . . Some commentators on early Commission guideline drafts urged the Commission not to attempt any major reforms of the plea agreement process on the grounds that any set of guidelines that threatened to change pre-guidelines practice radically also threatened to make the federal system unmanageable. Others argued that guidelines that failed to control and limit plea agreements would leave untouched a "loophole" large enough to undo the good that sentencing guidelines would bring.

The Commission decided not to make major changes in plea agreement practices in the initial guidelines, but rather to provide guidance by issuing general policy statements concerning the acceptance of plea agreements. . . .

The Commission expects the guidelines to have a positive, rationalizing impact upon plea agreements for two reasons. First, the guidelines create a clear, definite expectation in respect to the sentence that a court will impose if a trial takes place. In the event a prosecutor and defense attorney explore the possibility of a negotiated plea, they will no longer work in the dark. Second, the guidelines create a norm to which courts will likely refer when they decide whether . . . to accept or to reject a plea agreement or recommendation.

Some Other Considerations About Settlement: Notes and Questions

(1) *How Much Judicial Courtroom Time Is Spent, on Average, on a Felony Case?* One interesting mental exercise for understanding settlement is to imagine the mean (or "average") amount of courtroom judicial time allocated to felony cases in a state court. Given the necessary statistics, one can figure this average by dividing the total minutes of court time by the number of cases handled. Imagine a metropolitan system in which twelve (12) judges each spend 200 courtroom days in a year at five (5) courtroom hours (of 50 minutes each) per day to dispose of 30,000 felony indictments. The total number of courtroom minutes for all twelve judges is $12 \times 5 \times 50 \times 200 = 720,000$, which when divided by 30,000 yields twenty-four (24) minutes per case.

Notice that 24 minutes is the mean, or "average." If a robbery case is tried for a week in a given judge's court, it will occupy $5 \times 5 \times 60 = 1500$ minutes, meaning that it has required more than sixty (60) times the average amount of judicial courtroom time. If the average is 24 minutes, this trial means that there must be many cases that occupy much less time than 24 minutes; many probably occupy less than five (5) minutes.

(2) *Jury Trials as a Scarce, Precious Resource, with Settlement as the Norm: The Reality of the Criminal Justice System.* Whatever may be your position as a political philosopher on these issues, they should help you to see two attitudes that necessarily must characterize judges and others who have responsibility for making the criminal justice system work (and who do not have the luxury of imagining reality away). (a) Although the system and personnel within it may seek to preserve the right to jury trial, they necessarily must come to regard settlement (usually by dismissal or guilty plea) as the norm—rather than adjudication. (b) Similarly, a jury trial is a scarce, precious resource, one that cannot be squandered.

And as a corollary, a third attitude usually develops: (c) The disposition of a case by guilty plea or dismissal, some people believe, is approximately as likely to reflect a just outcome as is a jury trial, particularly given the ability of attorneys to predict average outcomes and the vagaries of the jury trial process itself. In other words, some people believe that a system with settlement as the norm, and with trials as a rare event, does justice as well as if there were more trials. Are these attitudes understandable—and are they appropriate?

[D] Rules for Safeguarding Guilty Pleas and Plea Agreements

Notes on Rules Governing Guilty Pleas

(1) *The Court's Colloquy with the Defendant before Accepting a Guilty Plea: Fed. R. Crim. P. 11.* Federal Rule of Criminal Procedure 11 requires the judge to cover many specific points with the defendant before accepting a guilty plea. First, the court must "address the defendant personally in open court" and ensure that the defendant understands the crime and sentence range, the right to counsel, the right to jury trial, and other matters of law. Second, Rule 11 requires the judge to ensure that the plea is voluntary and "not the result of force or threats or promises" other than a plea agreement. Third, the court must obtain disclosure of any plea agreement, and if the court does not follow the agreement, afford the defendant an opportunity to withdraw the plea. Finally, the court must make whatever inquiry is necessary to ascertain that there is a "factual basis" for inferring guilt of the crime at issue.

(2) *The Necessary Detail: United States v. Medina-Roman,* 376 F.3d 1 (1st Cir. 2004). The *Medina-Roman* case appears in Chapter 11 on Complicity and Multiple-Party offenses, above. There, the defendant sought to withdraw her guilty plea because of inadequate admonishments by the trial court. Although the court of appeals upheld the conviction, it did so only after an exhaustive analysis of the court's colloquy with the defendant as compared to the elements of the crime. *See also State v. Ayres,*

2013 N.J. Super. Unpub. LEXIS 205 (N.J. App. Jan. 31, 2013) (holding defendant could not withdraw his guilty plea, but only after reviewing the record to confirm defendant had been informed that the plea would waive his right to appeal).

(3) *State Procedures.* Many states have similar processes for guilty pleas. See below.

(4) *A Guilty Plea Is Really a Trial.* This statement may seem surprising, since a guilty plea is consensual. The record of the plea hearing, however, must conform rigorously to the requirements imposed by law. Consider the case that follows.

Tullos v. State

698 S.W.2d 488 (Tex. App. 1985)

BENAVIDES, JUSTICE.

Appellant, without a plea agreement, pled guilty to two indictments charging him with two aggravated assaults. The trial court assessed punishment at six years in each case. We affirm the judgment of the trial court in 13–85-089-CR, and reverse the judgment in 13–85-090-CR and remand for the entry of acquittal.

Briefly stated, the evidence shows that appellant stabbed Michael Smith in the back with a scratchawl, an icepick-like instrument used to mark sheet metal. When Michael cried out, his father, Horace Smith, came to his aid with a hammer. Appellant shot Horace in the hip with a handgun.

The indictment in cause 13–85-090-CR alleged that appellant used a deadly weapon, "to wit a scratchawl, to threaten Michael A. Smith, with imminent bodily injury by use of the said deadly weapon. . . ." Appellant alleges that the evidence is insufficient to show that he threatened Michael Smith and that he is entitled to an acquittal. We agree.

Although appellant pled guilty to this offense, the State is still required to introduce sufficient proof to support the guilty plea. Tex. Code Crim. Proc. Ann. art. 1.15 (Vernon 1977). [I]f the State fails to introduce sufficient evidence to support the guilty plea in a felony case, the accused is entitled to an acquittal. *Thornton v. State,* 601 S.W.2d 340 (Tex.Crim.App.1980).

In the present case, the State introduced ample evidence to show that appellant stabbed Michael Smith in the back. It introduced no evidence, however, to show that appellant threatened Michael Smith. Evidence of actual bodily injury is insufficient to support the threat allegation. *McGowan v. State,* 664 S.W.2d 355 (Tex.Crim.App.1984). As in McGowan, the victim here was stabbed from behind. No threats were made before the stabbing and appellant fled immediately afterward. . . .

The State argues that appellant waived his challenge to the sufficiency of the evidence because he testified at both the guilt and punishment phases of trial and admitted his guilt. . . . Generally, if an accused testifies at either the guilt or punishment phase of trial and admits that he committed the acts alleged in the indictment, he is foreclosed from challenging the sufficiency of the evidence. *DeGarmo v. State*, 691 S.W.2d 657 (Tex.Crim.App.1985). The accused's admission of guilt must, however, conform to the allegations in the indictment. . . .

[Here,] Appellant never admitted threatening Michael Smith. The evidence is therefore insufficient to support the State's burden of proof. . . . Appellant's first ground of error in 13–85-090-CR is sustained.

Appellant does not challenge the sufficiency of the evidence to support the conviction in cause no. 13–85-089-CR for the aggravated assault on Horace Smith; rather, . . . the sole point of error . . . alleges that appellant was improperly admonished regarding the range of punishment that might be assessed. [State rules of criminal procedure require various admonitions, including that of the sentence range.] The court instructed appellant that he was subject to confinement for any term of years not more than ten nor less than two, and that, in addition, the court could assess a fine not to exceed $10,000.00. This was error. Aggravated assault is a felony of the third degree. Thus, the maximum fine would be $5,000.00, not $10,000.00. Tex. Penal Code Ann. § 12.34(b) (Vernon 1974). Nevertheless, we overrule appellant's grounds of error complaining of the admonishment he received. No fine was imposed and there is no showing that appellant was harmed by the trial court's admonishment.

The judgment of the trial court in cause no. 13–85-090-Cr is REVERSED and REMANDED to the trial court for an entry of acquittal. The judgment of the trial court in cause no. 13–85-089-CR is AFFIRMED.

Notes and Questions

(1) *What Proceedings Are Required for a Bargained Guilty Plea in Federal Court, and What Is Meant by a "Factual Basis" for Such a Plea?* Consider Fed. R. Crim. P. 11. One requirement is assurance of a "factual basis" for the plea. What is meant by a "factual basis" (proof beyond a reasonable doubt, or some information about all the elements, or even information proving a closely related crime)? Would the *Tullos* guilty-plea conviction have been affirmed in federal court?

(2) *"How Can the State Lose a Guilty Plea?" The Requirement of Supporting Evidence.* As the *Tullos* case indicates, in some jurisdictions, a plea of guilty is like a trial. In fact, it *is* a trial, requiring admissible evidence proving all elements. It is not required, however, that all of it be oral or by question and answer. A written stipulation, signed by the defendant, typically supplies the proof in some states. But as *Tullos* shows, it is entirely possible for the state to lose!

(3) *Withdrawal upon the Court's Refusal to Follow a Plea Bargain.* Note the provision in Federal Rule 11 governing the court's nonacceptance of a plea bargain provides for the right of withdrawal of the plea by the defendant. Many states have similar rules. Are these good rules?

§ 14.04 Competencies Needed for the Practice of Criminal Law

Notes on Competencies, Strategies, and Simulation Exercises

(1) *Lawyering Competencies and Strategies.* Lawyers do not confine themselves to reading court opinions or doing legal research (or even spend much time that way). What do they do, then? DeCotiis & Steele, below, observed lawyers who went about their daily tasks. Although they found that lawyers did very little traditional writing, lawyers did exercise a separate competency that DeCotiis & Steele call (a) "document preparation." Lawyers also spend time on (b) client relations, (c) negotiating, (d) advice and consultation, (e) courthouse activities, (f) continuing education, and (g) practice management.

(2) *The Lawyering Problems throughout This Book: Developing the Strategy Aspect.* Decotiis & Steele's article has influenced the Simulation Exercises that appear in this book. If lawyers do not spend much time reading cases, but instead they prepare documents, negotiate, relate to clients, and advise and counsel, then it would seem that reading cases is not alone enough to prepare you for practice. The Simulation Exercises in this book expose you to document preparation, negotiating, client relations, and counseling, as well as to substantive knowledge. The aim is to enable you to understand strategies — the strategies of practice, of real lawyering. Now, consider DeCotiis & Steele's article.

Thomas A. Decotiis & Walter W. Steele, *The Skills of the Lawyering Process: A Critique Based on Observation*

40 Texas Bar Journal 483 (June 1977)*

... Curiously, at the very time when law schools are undertaking to provide more training in lawyering skills than ever before, the legal profession is increasing its complaints about the insufficiency of available skills training in formal legal education. However good their intentions may be, law schools cannot provide relevant instruction in the skills of lawyering until these skills have been accurately identified and defined and their use in practice determined.

Unfortunately, ... no systematic data or procedures exist which can be used to distinguish successful from unsuccessful practice. ...

Despite the call for more research, only two recent articles have appeared that report on attempts to analyze and evaluate lawyering skills. ... In each case ... [lawyers] were asked to rank, according to importance to successful law practice, a predetermined list of lawyering skills set forth in the questionnaire. One of the researchers made the following seminal comment about the impact of his findings on law school curriculum.

---

* Reprinted with permission from the Texas Bar Journal.

Interpersonal skills such as interviewing and counseling were ranked as highly important to the practice of law. Understanding human behavior was also ranked among the top five skills. Time spent in interviewing and counseling was shown to be comparable to that spent in legal research and drafting documents. . . . Whatever the reason has been for failing to implement the skills courses, results of the survey would suggest an urgent need for their implementation. . . .

The present study is a step towards understanding the legal profession; it adds to the knowledge gained by previous studies that asked lawyers to rank in order a fixed list of skills. . . .

Method

The decision was made to use observers who would be aware of those skills which might conceivably be used by practicing attorneys, and who would have some prior knowledge of what the representation of clients requires. Five advanced law students who had participated in clinical programs were selected as observers.

These students were trained in the techniques of behavior observation and description in a one-week training program that consisted of a series of mini-seminars on the skills of observing and describing job behavior. . . .

Five local attorneys, knowledgeable of the local bar membership, were asked to nominate potential participants. . . . [E]ach member of the advisory panel was asked to submit the names of attorneys who were considered by them to be "good general practitioners" in firms of one to five members in Dallas County, Texas. . . .

The attorneys were observed on a random basis during normal office hours. The total observation time was 200 hours. . . . Each attorney was asked to avoid unnecessary conversation with the observer, and to continue his normal work routine in the observer's presence. . . .

. . . The first step in analyzing these data was to identify the distinct activities or task areas of attorney practice. . . . Subsequently the notes were categorized in terms of perceived similarity of content. The result was the identification of seven areas of lawyer activity: (a) rapport building, (b) advice and consultation, (c) document preparation, (d) negotiation, (e) courthouse functions, (f) continuing legal education, and (g) practice management.

The task of categorizing the research data, as described above, led to what may be our most significant and unexpected finding: the general practice of law does not encompass an extremely wide range of activities even though several different skills may be applied within each of the seven categories of activity identified. In other words, although general practice seems to involve a [few] activities, each lawyer uses a wide range of skills while engaging in any one activity.

Lawyer Activities

By way of illustrating the content of the seven categories of activity, some typical events that occurred during the observation period are described below.

Rapport Building. Lawyers spend a great deal of time and effort building rapport with their various constituencies. As might be expected, much of the rapport building activity involves interpersonal skills. For example, a lawyer may speak briefly with a client, telling the client where to meet him the next day. Similarly, a lawyer may encourage clients to call him at home in the evening should he or she have any questions or comments. The purpose of these behaviors is to make the client feel that his or her attorney is working and available. Another public lawyers must interact with is other lawyers. A lawyer may exchange, for example, information with another lawyer by telephone. Typically, such exchanges are much more jovial and light in manner than are client interactions.

Still other publics with whom lawyers interact and build rapport include witnesses and courthouse personnel. In both instances, rapport is built through the exchange of pleasantries and showing of interest in the person in an unpretentious manner. In one instance, this approach resulted in the courtroom personnel showing a lawyer how to file a specific document with the court. In another instance, a lawyer was able to persuade a nurse to read the latest medical report on a client to him by phone.

The rapport building events and skills described above involved different attorneys at different times, yet there is a common theme that runs through them; specifically, the attorneys were pleasant and personable, or kind and considerate when appropriate. . . . [T]he observations about joviality, et cetera, were uniform, leading to the conclusion that the observed attorneys were exercising some learned skills . . . . Apparently, they learned the truth of the saying that "it is easier to catch bears with honey than with a club" early in their careers. . . .

Advice and Consultation. Some of the attorneys observed seemed to be more concerned than others about their skill in communication with clients. Nevertheless, all the attorneys observed were highly rated for their ability to advise and consult using methods designed to facilitate and maximize the flow of information between the attorney and the client.

The observations indicate that the majority of all interpersonal contact between attorney and client is not for the purpose of the client providing information to the attorney, but rather for the purpose of the attorney transmitting information to the client. In fact, it appears that attorneys do a remarkable amount of teaching, using clients as students—attorneys do not merely tell the client what to do next. Rather, the client is *taught* and coached on what to do in detail. For example, the lawyer will outline a possible strategy for the client and then inform the client of the arguments and problems inherent in the strategy and situations that will be encountered. In another instance, a lawyer advised a client about the possible steps to take in order to collect an outstanding judgment, telling him the whole story, but generally leaving the decision to the client. . . .

Almost all attorney-client communication observed was structured by the attorneys. Clients were not generally encouraged to express their feelings. However, the consultation process was invariably solicitous of the client's right to make his own choices from among the alternatives presented by the attorney. The attorney assured an intelligent choice by the client by repetition and review of possible alternatives and frequent iteration of the consequences of each alternative, frequently using hypothetical examples to illustrate points.

Document Preparation. . . . [L]egal documents are an essential part of any law practice. . . . For example, some attorneys had prior-prepared motions for discovery and interrogatories from [formbooks] and other cases and . . . modified them to fit the facts of the current situations. Or as one observer noted, an attorney might use the same divorce information form in all divorce cases without variation because it provides for all of the necessary information except the clients' property. Another attorney talked about where to find a good form for a motion and decided to look in the files his partner had collected. These files came from previous motions the other attorney in the office had drawn, as well as from other attorneys in previous cases.

. . . [S]ince attorneys relied heavily on "canned" documents, they were alert to the necessity of making minor alterations in the document to meet the particular needs of a specific situation. In this way the documents were continually improved and modified. The fact that more time is spent by attorneys collecting existing documents rather than drafting original documents does not discredit practitioners and may, in fact, indicate effective practice. Obviously, a document that has evolved through several attorneys and lawsuits is much more apt to be complete and mechanically accurate than an original document drafted after only a few hours study.

The attorney's proclivity to hoard and then to cannibalize forms raises some interesting questions for legal education. Should law schools concentrate, as they do now, on *drafting skills;* or should law schools concentrate on the function of a particular document in the overall scheme of things? For example, instead of asking students to draft a will based on a particular set of facts, would it be more useful to ask students to change a pre-drafted will to meet the needs presented by a new client?

Negotiation. The most highly developed skill in the practice of law is negotiation between attorneys in the representation of their respective clients. . . . Attorneys have developed a special set of intra-professional rules, an implicit understanding of the limits of the negotiation process. These unwritten "rules" allow each attorney virtually unlimited freedom to manipulate, move and countermove to gain an advantage. As a consequence, behavior that might appear dishonest to a layman is an art form to the professional. . . . [An] example involved an attorney returning a call to another attorney and "playing dumb" by asking the other attorney questions, the answers to which were already known by the first attorney. . . . In still another example, the observed attorney made a conciliatory statement to opposing counsel (*i.e.,* "His doing what he did got you and me fighting when we shouldn't be") in order to establish rapport and to get the other attorney to talk so as to find out what the strategy of the other side will be. These negotiations are always done in a manner that shows high regard for the feelings of the individuals he negotiates with and for the egos of those he may be talking about. . . .

Courthouse Activities. Many attorneys engaged in the general practice of law spend a great deal of time in the courthouse or in preparing to go to the courthouse. Given that activity in the courthouse is often characterized as the epitome of law practice, it should be useful to know more about what attorneys actually do there. Our observers found that most of the activity at the courthouse is clerical in nature . . . , with some notable exceptions related to trial itself. . . .

With the exception of trial, which is a rare occurrence in relative terms, most courthouse activity consists of low-key discussion with other attorneys and with the various legal functionaries who are housed in the courthouse. . . .

Continuing Legal Education. Continuing legal education (CLE) as a classification of work performed in the practice of law, was defined as all efforts made by attorneys to learn something new about law or lawyering skills. Therefore, research necessitated by a particular case was classified as CLE as well as attending any formal program specifically designed for continuing legal education. As defined, CLE turned out to be a major part of an attorney's daily life, although the majority of the CLE appeared to be very informal.

For example, an attorney discussed with his partner the best way to organize client files. Or, an associate was researching case precedents and engaged in general conversations about several possible lines of argument. As another example, during a lunch break, one of the attorneys stopped by another attorney's office to ask a basic question about the trial record in a current case and his opinion as to the law. . . .

It should be noted that the attorneys observed did not personally do any conventional legal research during the observation period. The reasons cited for this omission are that the work is very time consuming, prohibitively costly to clients, and, perhaps more important, any such research is most often done by clerks or junior associates.

Practice Management. Practice management groups all those activities related to the operation of the attorney's practice itself, as distinguished from activities related to the management of a particular case. We found practice management to be the only activity of the seven discussed in which the activities of the attorneys observed were not homogeneous. . . . [E]ach attorney appears to have his [or her] own style.

. . . A great deal of time appeared to be spent by the attorneys in consultation with secretaries. Curiously, the attorneys seemed much more capable of defining tasks and responsibilities to be delegated to other attorneys in the firm than they were at defining tasks and responsibilities to be delegated to secretaries.

Many of the attorneys made efficient use of dictating equipment, using it not only to transcribe documents, but also as an efficient method of communication with their secretaries about other matters. Furthermore, the attorneys were quite explicit and detailed about the instructions they gave regarding format and content of whatever they were dictating. Nevertheless, many of the attorneys seemed to be almost inordinately obsessed with the task of proofreading and re-editing every instrument that had been previously so laboriously and meticulously dictated. Few attorneys seemed willing to trust a secretary's judgment about the accuracy of any typewritten work. . . .

Conclusion . . .

Although some people may characterize the practice of law as a bookish profession, we find that most lawyers do very little reading, except for proofreading. The tendency to verbalize everything is so strong that even a lawyer's continuing legal education is done on an informal, verbal, tutorial basis, rather than in a more traditional book-and-pencil style. . . .

Perhaps, the most significant finding in the observers' notes is that attorneys in the general practice of law do not employ a large variety of skills. The most predominant skill is the ability to manipulate people and situations, and the insight that goes with this ability. . . .

Finally, our observers were most impressed with the lawyers' desire to be efficient managers of time. [But] they were not seen as particularly effective time managers. . . . This is not surprising in the light of the fact that law office management is generally ignored in law school. . . .

In summary we might say that lawyers are very much a product of their formal education. They work well with legal doctrine and they have a facility for making factual analysis. Obviously, these skills are acquired in law school. Conversely, lawyers lack insights into business management skills, a topic that is just as obviously ignored in law school.

. . . Those who claim that some of the lawyering skills are best taught on the job seem to be ignoring the fact that we know very little about what lawyering skills are and consequently we simply cannot give an honest, thoughtful answer to the question of what part of the lawyering process is best left to law school and what part to practice. . . . Lawyers of the future must be taught more than the law — they must also be taught how to practice the law in a functional and economic way.

Notes and Questions

(1) *"Document Preparation," Not "Expository Writing."* DeCotiis & Steele imply that lawyers do very little expository writing of papers like those you wrote in college English. Instead, they do "document preparation." The difference is that many legal documents are functional, not expository. Their preparation usually involves cannibalizing existing documents, often referred to as "forms." The authors say that starting with an existing form may be "good practice," as opposed to writing the document from scratch. The implication is that using forms not only may save time, but it may also produce a better document. Why?

Also, the competencies involved in "document preparation" are different from those for "expository writing." But document preparation requires a high level of intellect. What are the document-preparation competencies that differ from skills for expository writing, and why do they involve a high level of intellect? Notice that in adapting a document form, the lawyer needs to understand not only what the words say, but what concealed advantages or dangers lurk within future applications of those words. And the lawyer must thoroughly understand the client's goals, which the adaptation is intended to serve.

(2) *Reading, Writing, and Research: Very Little.* DeCotiis & Steele conclude that general practice lawyers do little conventional reading (except proofreading) or legal research. Legal research is one of the few competencies systematically taught in law school, but general practitioners evidently think that research is a low-level skill. Why might there be such a difference in emphasis between lawyers and law schools about this?

(3) *Are Lawyers Bad Managers?* DeCotiis & Steele suggest that lawyers are bad managers of their practices. They suggest that lawyers' educations may be one reason, in that law students are not taught much about management. And yet, anyone familiar with lawyer malpractice or discipline knows that most of the most serious client complaints result from lawyers' neglect of office procedures. Why, then, do law schools not emphasize practice management?

(4) *Other Important Competencies: Negotiation, Rapport-Building, Counseling, and Continuing Legal Education.* Negotiation is the lawyer's "most highly developed skill." Can people be taught to improve their negotiating skills, and if so, does law school teach them adequately? Consider that question for the other listed competencies: rapport building, counseling, and continuing legal education.

(5) *Updating DeCotiis & Steele.* This article was published in 1977. The world has changed since then. For example, many lawyers prepare documents on computers without secretaries. A great deal of communication is done by e-mail. Consider what would change if Decotiis and Steele's observations were replicated today. Would you expect their fundamental conclusions to hold up? (Probably so. For this book, five lawyers were interviewed after reading DeCotiis and Steele, and their feedback indicates that the article still is remarkably accurate today.)

Appendix A

Excerpts from the Model Penal Code

Part I. General Provisions
Article 1. Preliminary . . .

§ 1.02. Purposes; Principles of Construction.

(1) The general purposes of the provisions governing the definition of offenses are:

(a) to forbid and prevent conduct that unjustifiably and inexcusably inflicts or threatens substantial harm to individual or public interests;

(b) to subject to public control persons whose conduct indicates that they are disposed to commit crimes;

(c) to safeguard conduct that is without fault from condemnation as criminal;

(d) to give fair warning of the nature of the conduct declared to constitute an offense;

(e) to differentiate on reasonable grounds between serious and minor offenses.

(2) The general purposes of the provisions on sentencing, applicable to all official actors in the sentencing system, are:

(a) in decisions affecting the sentencing of individual offenders:

(i) to render sentences in all cases within a range of severity proportionate to the gravity of offenses, the harms done to crime victims, and the blameworthiness of offenders;

(ii) when reasonably feasible, to achieve offender rehabilitation, general deterrence, incapacitation of dangerous offenders, restitution to crime victims, preservation of families, and reintegration of offenders into the lawabiding community, provided these goals are pursued within the boundaries of proportionality in Subsection (a)(i);

(iii) to render sentences no more severe than necessary to achieve the applicable purposes in Subsections (a)(i) and (a)(ii); and

(iv) to avoid the use of sanctions that increase the likelihood offenders will engage in future criminal conduct.

(b) in matters affecting the administration of the sentencing system:

   (i) to preserve judicial discretion to individualize sentences within a framework of law;

   (ii) to produce sentences that are uniform in their reasoned pursuit of the purposes in Subsection (2)(a);

   (iii) to eliminate inequities in sentencing across population groups;

   (iv) to ensure that adequate resources are available for carrying out sentences imposed and that rational priorities are established for the use of those resources;

   (v) to ensure that all criminal sanctions are administered in a humane fashion;

   (vi) to promote research on sentencing policy and practices, including the effects of criminal sanctions on families and communities; and

   (vii) to increase the transparency of the sentencing and corrections system, its accountability to the public, and the legitimacy of its operations as perceived by all affected communities.

§ 1.05. All Offenses Defined by Statute; Application of General Provisions of the Code.

(1) No conduct constitutes an offense unless it is a crime or violation under this Code or another statute of this State. . . .

§ 1.12. Proof Beyond a Reasonable Doubt; Affirmative Defenses; Burden of Proving Fact When Not an Element of an Offense; Presumptions.

(1) No person may be convicted of an offense unless each element of such offense is proved beyond a reasonable doubt. In the absence of such proof, the innocence of the defendant is assumed.

(2) Subsection (1) of this Section does not:

   (a) require the disproof of an affirmative defense unless and until there is evidence supporting such defense; or

   (b) apply to any defense that the Code or another statute plainly requires the defendant to prove by a preponderance of evidence.

(3) A ground of defense is affirmative, within the meaning of Subsection (2)(a) of this Section, when:

   (a) it arises under a section of the Code that so provides; or

   (b) it relates to an offense defined by a statute other than the Code and such statute so provides; or

   (c) it involves a matter of excuse or justification peculiarly within the knowledge of the defendant on which he can fairly be required to adduce supporting evidence.

(4) When the application of the Code depends upon the finding of a fact that is not an element of an offense, unless the Code otherwise provides:

(a) the burden of proving the fact is on the prosecution or defendant, depending on whose interest or contention will be furthered if the finding should be made; and

(b) the fact must be proved to the satisfaction of the Court or jury, as the case may be. . . .

Article 2. General Principles Of Liability

§ 2.01. Requirement of Voluntary Act; Omission as Basis of Liability; Possession as an Act.

(1) A person is not guilty of an offense unless his liability is based on conduct that includes a voluntary act or the omission to perform an act of which he is physically capable.

(2) The following are not voluntary acts within the meaning of this Section:

(a) a reflex or convulsion;

(b) a bodily movement during unconsciousness or sleep;

(c) conduct during hypnosis or resulting from hypnotic suggestion;

(d) a bodily movement that otherwise is not a product of the effort or determination of the actor, either conscious or habitual.

(3) Liability for the commission of an offense may not be based on an omission unaccompanied by action unless:

(a) the omission is expressly made sufficient by the law defining the offense; or

(b) a duty to perform the omitted act is otherwise imposed by law.

(4) Possession is an act, within the meaning of this Section, if the possessor knowingly procured or received the thing possessed or was aware of his control thereof for a sufficient period to have been able to terminate his possession.

§ 2.02. General Requirements of Culpability.

(1) *Minimum Requirements of Culpability.* Except as provided in Section 2.05, a person is not guilty of an offense unless he acted purposely, knowingly, recklessly or negligently, as the law may require, with respect to each material element of the offense.

(2) *Kinds of Culpability Defined.*

(a) *Purposely.*

A person acts purposely with respect to a material element of an offense when:

(i) if the element involves the nature of his conduct or a result thereof, it is his conscious object to engage in conduct of that nature or to cause such a result; and

(ii) if the element involves the attendant circumstances, he is aware of the existence of such circumstances or he believes or hopes that they exist.

(b) Knowingly.

A person acts knowingly with respect to a material element of an offense when:

(i) if the element involves the nature of his conduct or the attendant circumstances, he is aware that his conduct is of that nature or that such circumstances exist; and

(ii) if the element involves a result of his conduct, he is aware that it is practically certain that his conduct will cause such a result.

(c) Recklessly.

A person acts recklessly with respect to a material element of an offense when he consciously disregards a substantial and unjustifiable risk that the material element exists or will result from his conduct. The risk must be of such a nature and degree that, considering the nature and purpose of the actor's conduct and the circumstances known to him, its disregard involves a gross deviation from the standard of conduct that a law-abiding person would observe in the actor's situation.

(d) Negligently.

A person acts negligently with respect to a material element of an offense when he should be aware of a substantial and unjustifiable risk that the material element exists or will result from his conduct. The risk must be of such a nature and degree that the actor's failure to perceive it, considering the nature and purpose of his conduct and the circumstances known to him, involves a gross deviation from the standard of care that a reasonable person would observe in the actor's situation.

(3) *Culpability Required Unless Otherwise Provided.* When the culpability sufficient to establish a material element of an offense is not prescribed by law, such element is established if a person acts purposely, knowingly or recklessly with respect thereto.

(4) *Prescribed Culpability Requirement Applies to All Material Elements.* When the law defining an offense prescribes the kind of culpability that is sufficient for the commission of an offense, without distinguishing among the material elements thereof, such provision shall apply to all the material elements of the offense, unless a contrary purpose plainly appears.

(5) *Substitutes for Negligence, Recklessness and Knowledge.* When the law provides that negligence suffices to establish an element of an offense, such element also is established if a person acts purposely, knowingly or recklessly. When recklessness suffices to establish an element, such element also is established if a person acts purposely or knowingly. When acting knowingly suffices to establish an element, such element also is established if a person acts purposely.

(6) *Requirement of Purpose Satisfied if Purpose Is Conditional.* When a particular purpose is an element of an offense, the element is established although such purpose is conditional, unless the condition negatives the harm or evil sought to be prevented by the law defining the offense.

(7) *Requirement of Knowledge Satisfied by Knowledge of High Probability.* When knowledge of the existence of a particular fact is an element of an offense, such knowledge is established if a person is aware of a high probability of its existence, unless he actually believes that it does not exist.

(8) *Requirement of Wilfulness Satisfied by Acting Knowingly.* A requirement that an offense be committed wilfully is satisfied if a person acts knowingly with respect to the material elements of the offense, unless a purpose to impose further requirement appears

(9) *Culpability as to Illegality of Conduct.* Neither knowledge nor recklessness or negligence as to whether conduct constitutes an offense or as to the existence, meaning or application of the law determining the elements of an offense is an element of such offense, unless the definition of the offense or the Code so provides.

(10) *Culpability as Determinant of Grade of Offense.* When the grade or degree of an offense depends on whether the offense is committed purposely, knowingly, recklessly or negligently, its grade or degree shall be the lowest for which the determinative kind of culpability is established with respect to any material element of the offense.

§ 2.03. Causal Relationship Between Conduct and Result; Divergence Between Result Designed or Contemplated and Actual Result or Between Probable and Actual Result.

(1) Conduct is the cause of a result when:

(a) it is an antecedent but for which the result in question would not have occurred; and

(b) the relationship between the conduct and result satisfies any additional causal requirements imposed by the Code or by the law defining the offense.

(2) When purposely or knowingly causing a particular result is an element of an offense, the element is not established if the actual result is not within the purpose or the contemplation of the actor unless:

(a) the actual result differs from that designed or contemplated, as the case may be, only in the respect that a different person or different property is injured or affected or that the injury or harm designed or contemplated would have been more serious or more extensive than that caused; or

(b) the actual result involves the same kind of injury or harm as that designed or contemplated and is not too remote or accidental in its occurrence to have a [just] bearing on the actor's liability or on the gravity of his offense.

(3) When recklessly or negligently causing a particular result is an element of an offense, the element is not established if the actual result is not within the risk of which the actor is aware or, in the case of negligence, of which he should be aware unless:

(a) the actual result differs from the probable result only in the respect that a different person or different property is injured or affected or that the probable injury or harm would have been more serious or more extensive than that caused; or

(b) the actual result involves the same kind of injury or harm as the probable result and is not too remote or accidental in its occurrence to have a [just] bearing on the actor's liability or on the gravity of his offense.

(4) When causing a particular result is a material element of an offense for which absolute liability is imposed by law, the element is not established unless the actual result is a probable consequence of the actor's conduct.

§ 2.04. Ignorance or Mistake.

(1) Ignorance or mistake as to a matter of fact or law is a defense if:

(a) the ignorance or mistake negatives the purpose, knowledge, belief, recklessness or negligence required to establish a material element of the offense; or

(b) the law provides that the state of mind established by such ignorance or mistake constitutes a defense.

(2) Although ignorance or mistake would otherwise afford a defense to the offense charged, the defense is not available if the defendant would be guilty of another offense had the situation been as he supposed. In such case, however, the ignorance or mistake of the defendant shall reduce the grade and degree of the offense of which he may be convicted to those of the offense of which he would be guilty had the situation been as he supposed.

(3) A belief that conduct does not legally constitute an offense is a defense to a prosecution for that offense based upon such conduct when:

(a) the statute or other enactment defining the offense is not known to the actor and has not been published or otherwise reasonably made available prior to the conduct alleged; or

(b) he acts in reasonable reliance upon an official statement of the law, afterward determined to be invalid or erroneous, contained in (i) a statute or other enactment; (ii) a judicial decision, opinion or judgment; (iii) an administrative order or grant of permission; or (iv) an official interpretation of the public officer or body charged by law with responsibility for the interpretation, administration or enforcement of the law defining the offense.

(4) The defendant must prove a defense arising under Subsection (3) of this Section by a preponderance of evidence. . . .

§ 2.05. When Culpability Requirements Are Inapplicable to Violations and to Offenses Defined by Other Statutes; Effect of Absolute Liability in Reducing Grade of Offense to Violation.

(1) The requirements of culpability prescribed by Sections 2.01 and 2.02 do not apply to:

(a) offenses which constitute violations, unless the requirement involved is included in the definition of the offense or the Court determines that its application is consistent with effective enforcement of the law defining the offense; or

(b) offenses defined by statutes other than the Code, insofar as a legislative purpose to impose absolute liability for such offenses or with respect to any materials thereof plainly appears.

(2) Notwithstanding any other provision of existing law and unless a subsequent statute otherwise provides:

(a) when absolute liability is imposed with respect to any material element of an offense defined by a statute other than the Code and a conviction is based upon such liability, the offense constitutes a violation; and

(b) although absolute liability is imposed by law with respect to oe or more of the material elements of an offense defined by a statute other than the Code, the culpable commission of the offense may be charged and proved, in which event negligence with respect to such elements constitutes sufficient culpability and the classification of the offense and the sentence that may be imposed therefor upon conviction are determined by Section 1.04 and Article 6 of the Code.

§ 2.06. Liability for Conduct of Another; Complicity.

(1) A person is guilty of an offense if it is committed by his own conduct or by the conduct of another person for which he is legally accountable, or both.

(2) A person is legally accountable for the conduct of another person when:

(a) acting with the kind of culpability that is sufficient for the commission of the offense, he causes an innocent or irresponsible person to engage in such conduct; or

(b) he is made accountable for the conduct of such other person by the Code or by the law defining the offense; or

(c) he is an accomplice of such other person in the commission of the offense.

(3) A person is an accomplice of another person in the commission of an offense if:

(a) with the purpose of promoting or facilitating the commission of the offense, he

(i) solicits such other person to commit it, or

(ii) aids or agrees or attempts to aid such other person in planning or committing it, or

(iii) having a legal duty to prevent the commission of the offense, fails to make proper effort so to do; or

(b) his conduct is expressly declared by law to establish his complicity.

(4) When causing a particular result is an element of an offense, an accomplice in the conduct causing such result is an accomplice in the commission of that offense if he acts with the kind of culpability, if any, with respect to that result that is sufficient for the commission of the offense.

(5) A person who is legally incapable of committing a particular offense himself may be guilty thereof if it is committed by the conduct of another person for which he is legally accountable, unless such liability is inconsistent with the purpose of the provision establishing his incapacity.

(6) Unless otherwise provided by the Code or by the law defining the offense, a person is not an accomplice in an offense committed by another person if:

(a) he is a victim of that offense; or

(b) the offense is so defined that his conduct is inevitably incident to its commission; or

(c) he terminates his complicity prior to the commission of the offense and

(i) wholly deprives it of effectiveness in the commission of the offense; or

(ii) gives timely warning to the law enforcement authorities or otherwise makes proper effort to prevent the commission of the offense.

(7) An accomplice may be convicted on proof of the commission of the offense and of his complicity therein, though the person claimed to have committed the offense has not been prosecuted or convicted or has been convicted of a different offense or degree of offense or has an immunity to prosecution or conviction or has been acquitted.

§ 2.07. Liability of Corporations, Unincorporated Associations and Persons Acting, or Under a Duty to Act, in Their Behalf.

(1) A corporation may be convicted of the commission of an offense if:

(a) the offense is a violation or the offense is defined by a statute other than the Code in which a legislative purpose to impose liability on corporations plainly appears and the conduct is performed by an agent of the corporation acting in behalf of the corporation within the scope of his office or employment, except that if the law defining the offense designates the agents for whose conduct the corporation is accountable or the circumstances under which it is accountable, such provisions shall apply; or

(b) the offense consists of an omission to discharge a specific duty of affirmative performance imposed on corporations by law; or

(c) the commission of the offense was authorized, requested, commanded, performed or recklessly tolerated by the board of directors or by a high managerial agent acting in behalf of the corporation within the scope of his office or employment.

(2) When absolute liability is imposed for the commission of an offense, a legislative purpose to impose liability on a corporation shall be assumed, unless the contrary plainly appears. An unincorporated association may be convicted of the commission of an offense if:

(a) the offense is defined by a statute other than the Code that expressly provides for the liability of such an association and the conduct is performed by an agent of the association acting in behalf of the association within the scope of his office or employment, except that if the law defining the offense designates the agents for whose conduct the association is accountable or the circumstances under which it is accountable, such provisions shall apply; or

(b) the offense consists of an omission to discharge a specific duty of affirmative performance imposed on associations by law.

(3) As used in this Section:

(a) "corporation" does not include an entity organized as or by a governmental agency for the execution of a governmental program;

(b) "agent" means any director, officer, servant, employee or other person authorized to act in behalf of the corporation or association and, in the case of an unincorporated association, a member of such association;

(c) "high managerial agent" means an officer of a corporation or an unincorporated association, or, in the case of a partnership, a partner, or any other agent of a corporation or association having duties of such responsibility that his conduct may fairly be assumed to represent the policy of the corporation or association.

(4) In any prosecution of a corporation or an unincorporated association for the commission of an offense included within the terms of Subsection (1)(a) or Subsection (3)(a) of this Section, other than an offense for which absolute liability has been imposed, it shall be a defense if the defendant proves by a preponderance of evidence that the high managerial agent having supervisory responsibility over the subject matter of the offense employed due diligence to prevent its commission.

(5) This paragraph shall not apply if it is plainly inconsistent with the legislative purpose in defining the particular offense.

(6) (a) A person is legally accountable for any conduct he performs or causes to be performed in the name of the corporation or an unincorporated association or in its behalf to the same extent as if it were performed in his own name or behalf.

(b) Whenever a duty to act is imposed by law upon a corporation or an unincorporated association, any agent of the corporation or association having primary responsibility for the discharge of the duty is legally accountable for a reckless omission to perform the required act to the same extent as if the duty were imposed by law directly upon himself.

(c) When a person is convicted of an offense by reason of his legal accountability for the conduct of a corporation or an unincorporated association, he is subject to the sentence authorized by law when a natural person is convicted of an offense of the grade and the degree involved.

§ 2.08. Intoxication.

(1) Except as provided in Subsection (4) of this Section, intoxication of the actor is not a defense unless it negatives an element of the offense.

(2) When recklessness establishes an element of the offense, if the actor, due to self-induced intoxication, is unaware of a risk of which he would have been aware had he been sober, such unawareness is immaterial.

(3) Intoxication does not, in itself, constitute mental disease within the meaning of Section 4.01.

(4) Intoxication that (a) is not self-induced or (b) is pathological is an affirmative defense if by reason of such intoxication the actor at the time of his conduct lacks substantial capacity either to appreciate its criminality [wrongfulness] or to conform his conduct to the requirements of law.

(5) Definitions. In this Section unless a different meaning plainly is required:

(a) "intoxication" means a disturbance of mental or physical capacities resulting from the introduction of substances into the body;

(b) "self-induced intoxication" means intoxication caused by substances that the actor knowingly introduces into his body, the tendency of which to cause intoxication he knows or ought to know, unless he introduces them pursuant to medical advice or under such circumstances as would afford a defense to a charge of crime;

(c) "pathological intoxication" means intoxication grossly excessive in degree, given the amount of the intoxicant, to which the actor does not know he is susceptible.

§ 2.09. Duress.

(1) It is an affirmative defense that the actor engaged in the conduct charged to constitute an offense because he was coerced to do so by the use of, or a threat to use, unlawful force against his person or the person of another, that a person of reasonable firmness in his situation would have been unable to resist.

(2) The defense provided by this Section is unavailable if the actor recklessly placed himself in a situation in which it was probable that he would be subjected to duress. The defense is also unavailable if he was negligent in placing himself in

such a situation, whenever negligence suffices to establish culpability for the offense charged.

(3) It is not a defense that a woman acted on the command of her husband, unless she acted under such coercion as would establish a defense under this Section. [The presumption that a woman acting in the presence of her husband is coerced is abolished.]

(4) When the conduct of the actor would otherwise be justifiable under Section 3.02, this Section does not preclude such defense. . . .

§ 2.11. Consent.

(1) *In General.* The consent of the victim to conduct charged to constitute an offense or to the result thereof is a defense if such consent negatives an element of the offense or precludes the infliction of the harm or evil sought to be prevented by the law defining the offense.

(2) *Consent to Bodily Injury.* When conduct is charged to constitute an offense because it causes or threatens bodily injury, consent to such conduct or to the infliction of such injury is a defense if:

(a) the bodily injury consented to or threatened by the conduct consented to is not serious; or

(b) the conduct and the injury are reasonably foreseeable hazards of joint participation in a lawful athletic contest or competitive sport or other concerted activity not forbidden by law; or

(c) the consent establishes a justification for the conduct under Article 3 of the Code.

(3) *Ineffective Consent.* Unless otherwise provided by the Code or by the law defining the offense, assent does not constitute consent if:

(a) it is given by a person who is legally incompetent to authorize the conduct charged to constitute the offense; or

(b) it is given by a person who by reason of youth, mental disease or defect or intoxication is manifestly unable or known by the actor to be unable to make a reasonable judgment as to the nature or harmfulness of the conduct charged to constitute the offense; or

(c) it is given by a person whose improvident consent is sought to be prevented by the law defining the offense; or

(d) it is induced by force, duress or deception of a kind sought to be prevented by the law defining the offense. . . .

§ 2.13. Entrapment.

(1) A public law enforcement official or a person acting in cooperation with such an official perpetrates an entrapment if for the purpose of obtaining evidence of the

commission of an offense, he induces or encourages another person to engage in conduct constituting such offense by either:

(a) making knowingly false representations designed to induce the belief that such conduct is not prohibited; or

(b) employing methods of persuasion or inducement that create a substantial risk that such an offense will be committed by persons other than those who are ready to commit it.

(2) Except as provided in Subsection (3) of this Section, a person prosecuted for an offense shall be acquitted if he proves by a preponderance of evidence that his conduct occurred in response to an entrapment. The issue of entrapment shall be tried by the Court in the absence of the jury.

(3) The defense afforded by this Section is unavailable when causing or threatening bodily injury is an element of the offense charged and the prosecution is based on conduct causing or threatening such injury to a person other than the person perpetrating the entrapment.

Article 3. General Principles Of Justication

§ 3.01. Justification an Affirmative Defense; Civil Remedies Unaffected.

(1) In any prosecution based on conduct that is justifiable under this Article, justification is an affirmative defense.

(2) The fact that conduct is justifiable under this Article does not abolish or impair any remedy for such conduct that is available in any civil action.

§ 3.02. Justification Generally: Choice of Evils.

(1) Conduct that the actor believes to be necessary to avoid a harm or evil to himself or to another is justifiable, provided that:

(a) the harm or evil sought to be avoided by such conduct is greater than that sought to be prevented by the law defining the offense charged; and

(b) neither the Code nor other law defining the offense provides exceptions or defenses dealing with the specific situation involved; and

(c) a legislative purpose to exclude the justification claimed does not otherwise plainly appear.

When the actor was reckless or negligent in bringing about the situation requiring a choice of harms or evils or in appraising the necessity for his conduct, the justification afforded by this Section is unavailable in a prosecution for any offense for which recklessness or negligence, as the case may be, suffices to establish culpability.

§ 3.03. Execution of Public Duty.

(1) Except as provided in Subsection (2) of this Section, conduct is justifiable when it is required or authorized by:

(a) the law defining the duties or functions of a public officer or the assistance to be rendered to such officer in the performance of his duties; or

(b) the law governing the execution of legal process; or

(c) the judgment or order of a competent court or tribunal; or

(d) the law governing the armed services or the lawful conduct of war; or(e) any other provision of law imposing a public duty.

(2) The other sections of this Article apply to:

(a) the use of force upon or toward the person of another for any of the purposes dealt with in such sections; and

(b) the use of deadly force for any purpose, unless the use of such force is otherwise expressly authorized by law or occurs in the lawful conduct of war.

(3) The justification afforded by Subsection (1) of this Section applies:

(a) when the actor believes his conduct to be required or authorized by the judgment or direction of a competent court or tribunal or in the lawful execution of legal process, notwithstanding lack of jurisdiction of the court or defect in the legal process; and

(b) when the actor believes his conduct to be required or authorized to assist a public officer in the performance of his duties, notwithstanding that the officer exceeded his legal authority.

§ 3.04. Use of Force in Self-Protection.

(1) *Use of Force Justifiable for Protection of the Person.* Subject to the provisions of this Section and of Section 3.09, the use of force upon or toward another person is justifiable when the actor believes that such force is immediately necessary for the purpose of protecting himself against the use of unlawful force by such other person on the present occasion.

(2) Limitations on Justifying Necessity for Use of Force.

(a) The use of force is not justifiable under this Section:

(i) to resist an arrest that the actor knows is being made by a peace officer, although the arrest is unlawful; or

(ii) to resist force used by the occupier or possessor of property or by another person on his behalf, where the actor knows that the person using the force is doing so under a claim of right to protect the property, except that this limitation shall not apply if:

(A) the actor is a public officer acting in the performance of his duties or a person lawfully assisting him therein or a person making or assisting in a lawful arrest; or

(B) the actor has been unlawfully dispossessed of the property and is making a re-entry or recaption justified by Section 3.06; or

(C) the actor believes that such force is necessary to protect himself against death or serious bodily injury.

(b) The use of deadly force is not justifiable under this Section unless the actor believes that such force is necessary to protect himself against death, serious bodily injury, kidnapping or sexual intercourse compelled by force or threat; nor is it justifiable if:

(i) the actor, with the purpose of causing death or serious bodily injury, provoked the use of force against himself in the same encounter; or

(ii) the actor knows that he can avoid the necessity of using such force with complete safety by retreating or by surrendering possession of a thing to a person asserting a claim of right thereto or by complying with a demand that he abstain from any action that he has no duty to take, except that:

(A) the actor is not obliged to retreat from his dwelling or place of work, unless he was the initial aggressor or is assailed in his place of work by another person whose place of work the actor knows it to be; and

(B) a public officer justified in using force in the performance of his duties or a person justified in using force in his assistance or a person justified in using force in making an arrest or preventing an escape is not obliged to desist from efforts to perform such duty, effect such arrest or prevent such escape because of resistance or threatened resistance by or on behalf of the person against whom such action is directed.

(c) Except as required by paragraphs (a) and (b) of this Subsection, a person employing protective force may estimate the necessity thereof under the circumstances as he believes them to be when the force is used, without retreating, surrendering possession, doing any other act that he has no legal duty to do or abstaining from any lawful action.

(3) *Use of Confinement as Protective Force.* The justification afforded by this Section extends to the use of confinement as protective force only if the actor takes all reasonable measures to terminate the confinement as soon as he knows that he safely can, unless the person confined has been arrested on a charge of crime.

§ 3.05. Use of Force for the Protection of Other Persons.

(1) Subject to the provisions of this Section and of Section 3.09, the use of force upon or toward the person of another is justifiable to protect a third person when:

(a) the actor would be justified under Section 3.04 in using such force to protect himself against the injury he believes to be threatened to the person whom he seeks to protect; and

(b) under the circumstances as the actor believes them to be, the person whom he seeks to protect would be justified in using such protective force; and

(c) the actor believes that his intervention is necessary for the protection of such other person.

(2) Notwithstanding Subsection (1) of this Section:

(a) when the actor would be obliged under Section 3.04 to retreat, to surrender the possession of a thing or to comply with a demand before using force in self-protection, he is not obliged to do so before using force for the protection of another person, unless he knows that he can thereby secure the complete safety of such other person; and

(b) when the person whom the actor seeks to protect would be obliged under Section 3.04 to retreat, to surrender the possession of a thing or to comply with a demand if he knew that he could obtain complete safety by so doing, the actor is obliged to try to cause him to do so before using force in his protection if the actor knows that he can obtain complete safety in that way; and

(c) neither the actor nor the person whom he seeks to protect is obliged to retreat when in the other's dwelling or place of work to any greater extent than in his own.

§ 3.06. Use of Force for Protection of Property.

(1) *Use of Force Justifiable for Protection of Property.* Subject to the provisions of this Section and of Section 3.09, the use of force upon or toward the person of another is justifiable when the actor believes that such force is immediately necessary:

(a) to prevent or terminate an unlawful entry or other trespass upon land or a trespass against or the unlawful carrying away of tangible, movable property, provided that such land or movable property is, or is believed by the actor to be, in his possession or in the possession of another person for whose protection he acts; or

(b) to effect an entry or re-entry upon land or to retake tangible movable property, provided that the actor believes that he or the person by whose authority he acts or a person from whom he or such other person derives title was unlawfully dispossessed of such land or movable property and is entitled to possession, and provided, further, that:

(i) the force is used immediately or on fresh pursuit after such dispossession; or

(ii) the actor believes that the person against whom he uses force has no claim of right to the possession of the property and, in the case of land, the circumstances, as the actor believes them to be, are of such urgency that it would be an exceptional hardship to postpone the entry or re-entry until a court order is obtained. . . .

(3) *Limitations on Justifiable Use of Force.*

(a) *Request to Desist.* The use of force is justifiable under this Section only if the actor first requests the person against whom such force is used to desist from his interference with the property, unless the actor believes that:

(i) such request would be useless; or

(ii) it would be dangerous to himself or another person to make the request; or

(iii) substantial harm will be done to the physical condition of the property that is sought to be protected before the request can effectively be made.

(b) *Exclusion of Trespasser.* The use of force to prevent or terminate a trespass is not justifiable under this Section if the actor knows that the exclusion of the trespasser will expose him to substantial danger of serious bodily injury.

(c) *Resistance of Lawful Re-entry or Recaption.* The use of force to prevent an entry or re-entry upon land or the recaption of movable property is not justifiable under this Section, although the actor believes that such re-entry or recaption is unlawful, if:

(i) the re-entry or recaption is made by or on behalf of a person who was actually dispossessed of the property; and

(ii) it is otherwise justifiable under Subsection (1)(b) of this Section.

(d) *Use of Deadly Force.* The use of deadly force is not justifiable under this Section unless the actor believes that:

(i) the person against whom the force is used is attempting to dispossess him of his dwelling otherwise than under a claim of right to its possession; or

(ii) the person against whom the force is used is attempting to commit or consummate arson, burglary, robbery or other felonious theft or property destruction and either:

(A) has employed or threatened deadly force against or in the presence of the actor; or

(B) the use of force other than deadly force to prevent the commission or the consummation of the crime would expose the actor or another in his presence to substantial danger of serious bodily injury. . . .

(5) *Use of Device to Protect Property.* The justification afforded by this Section extends to the use of a device for the purpose of protecting property only if:

(a) the device is not designed to cause or known to create a substantial risk of causing death or serious bodily injury; and

(b) the use of the particular device to protect the property from entry or trespass is reasonable under the circumstances, as the actor believes them to be; and

(c) the device is one customarily used for such a purpose or reasonable care is taken to make known to probable intruders the fact that it is used. . . .

§ 3.07. Use of Force in Law Enforcement.

(1) *Use of Force Justifiable to Effect an Arrest.* Subject to the provisions of this Section and of Section 3.09, the use of force upon or toward the person of another is justifiable when the actor is making or assisting in making an arrest and the actor believes that such force is immediately necessary to effect a lawful arrest.

(2) Limitations on the Use of Force.

(a) The use of force is not justifiable under this Section unless:

(i) the actor makes known the purpose of the arrest or believes that it is otherwise known by or cannot reasonably be made known to the person to be arrested; and

(ii) when the arrest is made under a warrant, the warrant is valid or believed by the actor to be valid.

(b) The use of deadly force is not justifiable under this Section unless:

(i) the arrest is for a felony; and

(ii) the person effecting the arrest is authorized to act as a peace officer or is assisting a person whom he believes to be authorized to act as a peace officer; and

(iii) the actor believes that the force employed creates no substantial risk of injury to innocent persons; and

(iv) the actor believes that:

(A) the crime for which the arrest is made involved conduct including the use or threatened use of deadly force; or

(B) there is a substantial risk that the person to be arrested will cause death or serious bodily injury if his apprehension is delayed.

(3) Use of Force to Prevent Escape from Custody. The use of force to prevent the escape of an arrested person from custody is justifiable when the force could justifiably have been employed to effect the arrest under which the person is in custody, except that a guard or other person authorized to act as a peace officer is justified in using any force, including deadly force, that he believes to be immediately necessary to prevent the escape of a person from a jail, prison, or other institution for the detention of persons charged with or convicted of a crime.

(4) Use of Force by Private Person Assisting an Unlawful Arrest.

(a) A private person who is summoned by a peace officer to assist in effecting an unlawful arrest, is justified in using any force that he would be justified in using if the arrest were lawful, provided that he does not believe the arrest is unlawful.

(b) A private person who assists another private person in effecting an unlawful arrest, or who, not being summoned, assists a peace officer in effecting an unlawful arrest, is justified in using any force that he would be justified in using if the arrest were lawful, provided that (i) he believes the arrest is lawful, and (ii) the arrest would be lawful if the facts were as he believes them to be. . . .

§ 3.09. Mistake of Law as to Unlawfulness of Force or Legality of Arrest; Reckless or Negligent Use of Otherwise Justifiable Force; Reckless or Negligent Injury or Risk of Injury to Innocent Persons.

(1) The justification afforded by Sections 3.04 to 3.07, inclusive, is unavailable when:

(a) the actor's belief in the unlawfulness of the force or conduct against which he employs protective force or his belief in the lawfulness of an arrest which he endeavors to effect by force is erroneous; and

(b) his error is due to ignorance or mistake as to the provisions of the Code, and other provision of the criminal law or the law governing the legality of an arrest or search.

(2) When the actor believes that the use of force upon or toward the person of another is necessary for any of the purposes for which such belief would establish a justification under Sections 3.03 to 3.08 but the actor is reckless or negligent in having such belief or in acquiring or failing to acquire any knowledge or belief which is material to the justifiability of his use of force, the justification afforded by those Sections is unavailable in a prosecution for an offense for which recklessness or negligence, as the case may be, suffices to establish culpability.

(3) When the actor is justified under Sections 3.03 to 3.08 in using force upon or toward the person of another but he recklessly or negligently injures or creates a risk of injury to innocent persons, the justification afforded by those Sections is unavailable in a prosecution for such recklessness or negligence towards innocent persons. . . .

§ 3.11. Definitions.

In this Article, unless a different meaning plainly is required:

(1) "unlawful force" means force, including confinement, that is employed without the consent of the person against whom it is directed and the employment of which constitutes an offense or actionable tort or would constitute such offense or tort except for a defense (such as the absence of intent, negligence, or mental capacity; duress; youth; or diplomatic status) not amounting to a privilege to use the force. Assent constitutes consent, within the meaning of this Section, whether or not it otherwise is legally effective, except assent to the infliction of death or serious bodily injury.

(2) "deadly force" means force that the actor uses with the purpose of causing or that he knows to create a substantial risk of causing death or serious bodily injury. Purposely firing a firearm in the direction of another person or at a vehicle in which another person is believed to be constitutes deadly force. A threat to cause death or serious bodily injury, by the production of a weapon or otherwise, so long as the actor's purpose is limited to creating an apprehension that he will use deadly force if necessary, does not constitute deadly force.

(3) "dwelling" means any building or structure, though movable or temporary, or a portion thereof, that is for the time being the actor's home or place of lodging.

Article 4. Responsibility

§ 4.01. Mental Disease or Defect Excluding Responsibility.

(1) A person is not responsible for criminal conduct if at the time of such conduct as a result of mental disease or defect he lacks substantial capacity either to appreciate the criminality [wrongfulness] of his conduct or to conform his conduct to the requirements of law.

(2) As used in this Article, the terms "mental disease or defect" do not include an abnormality manifested only by repeated criminal or otherwise antisocial conduct.

§ 4.02. Evidence of Mental Disease or Defect Admissible When Relevant to Element of the Offense [; Mental Disease or Defect Impairing Capacity as Ground for Mitigation of Punishment in Capital Cases].

(1) Evidence that the defendant suffered from a mental disease or defect is admissible whenever it is relevant to prove that the defendant did or did not have a state of mind that is an element of the offense.

[(2) Whenever the jury or the Court is authorized to determine or to recommend whether or not the defendant shall be sentenced to death or imprisonment upon conviction, evidence that the capacity of the defendant to appreciate the criminality [wrongfulness] of his conduct or to conform his conduct to the requirements of law was impaired as a result of mental disease or defect is admissible in favor of sentence of imprisonment.]

§ 4.03. Mental Disease or Defect Excluding Responsibility Is Affirmative Defense; Requirement of Notice; Form of Verdict and Judgment When Finding of Irresponsibility Is Made.

(1) Mental disease or defect excluding responsibility is an affirmative defense.

(2) Evidence of mental disease or defect excluding responsibility is not admissible unless the defendant, at the time of entering his plea of not guilty or within ten days thereafter or at such later time as the Court may for good cause permit, files a written notice of his purpose to rely on such defense.

(3) When the defendant is acquitted on the ground of mental disease or defect excluding responsibility, the verdict and the judgment shall so state. . . .

Article 5. Inchoate Crimes

§ 5.01 Criminal Attempt.

(1) *Definition of Attempt.* A person is guilty of an attempt to commit a crime if, acting with the kind of culpability otherwise required for commission of the crime, he:

(a) purposely engages in conduct that would constitute the crime if the attendant circumstances were as he believes them to be; or

(b) when causing a particular result is an element of the crime, does or omits to do anything with the purpose of causing or with the belief that it will cause such result without further conduct on his part; or

(c) purposely does or omits to do anything that, under the circumstances as he believes them to be, is an act or omission constituting a substantial step in a course of conduct planned to culminate in his commission of the crime.

(2) *Conduct That May Be Held Substantial Step Under Subsection (1)(c).* Conduct shall not be held to constitute a substantial step under Subsection (1)(c) of this Section unless it is strongly corroborative of the actor's criminal purpose. Without negativing the sufficiency of other conduct, the following, if strongly corroborative of the actor's criminal purpose, shall not be held insufficient as a matter of law:

(a) lying in wait, searching for or following the contemplated victim of the crime;

(b) enticing or seeking to entice the contemplated victim of the crime to go to the place contemplated for its commission;

(c) reconnoitering the place contemplated for the commission of the crime;

(d) unlawful entry of a structure, vehicle or enclosure in which it is contemplated that the crime will be committed;

(e) possession of materials to be employed in the commission of the crime, that are specially designed for such unlawful use or that can serve no lawful purpose of the actor under the circumstances;

(f) possession, collection or fabrication of materials to be employed in the commission of the crime, at or near the place contemplated for its commission, if such possession, collection or fabrication serves no lawful purpose of the actor under the circumstances;

(g) soliciting an innocent agent to engage in conduct constituting an element of the crime.

(3) *Conduct Designed to Aid Another in Commission of a Crime.* A person who engages in conduct designed to aid another to commit a crime that would establish his complicity under Section 2.06 if the crime were committed by such other person, is guilty of an attempt to commit the crime, although the crime is not committed or attempted by such other person.

(4) *Renunciation of Criminal Purpose.* When the actor's conduct would otherwise constitute an attempt under Subsection (1)(b) or (1)(c) of this Section, it is an affirmative defense that he abandoned his effort to commit the crime or otherwise prevented its commission, under circumstances manifesting a complete and voluntary renunciation of his criminal purpose. The establishment of such defense does not,

however, affect the liability of an accomplice who did not join in such abandonment or prevention.

Within the meaning of this Article, renunciation of criminal purpose is not voluntary if it is motivated, in whole or in part, by circumstances, not present or apparent at the inception of the actor's course of conduct, that increase the probability of detection or apprehension or that make more difficult the accomplishment of the criminal purpose. Renunciation is not complete if it is motivated by a decision to postpone the criminal conduct until a more advantageous time or to transfer the criminal effort to another but similar objective or victim.

§ 5.02. Criminal Solicitation.

(1) *Definition of Solicitation.* A person is guilty of solicitation to commit a crime if with the purpose of promoting or facilitating its commission he commands, encourages or requests another person to engage in specific conduct that would constitute such crime or an attempt to commit such crime or would establish his complicity in its commission or attempted commission.

(2) *Uncommunicated Solicitation.* It is immaterial under Subsection (1) of this Section that the actor fails to communicate with the person he solicits to commit a crime if his conduct was designed to effect such communication.

(3) *Renunciation of Criminal Purpose.* It is an affirmative defense that the actor, after soliciting another person to commit a crime, persuaded him not to do so or otherwise prevented the commission of the crime, under circumstances manifesting a complete and voluntary renunciation of his criminal purpose.

§ 5.03. Criminal Conspiracy.

(1) *Definition of Conspiracy.* A person is guilty of conspiracy with another person or persons to commit a crime if with the purpose of promoting or facilitating its commission he:

(a) agrees with such other person or persons that they or one or more of them will engage in conduct that constitutes such crime or an attempt or solicitation to commit such crime; or

(b) agrees to aid such other person or persons in the planning or commission of such crime or of an attempt or solicitation to commit such crime.

(2) *Scope of Conspiratorial Relationship.* If a person guilty of conspiracy, as defined by Subsection (1) of this Section, knows that a person with whom he conspires to commit a crime has conspired with another person or persons to commit the same crime, he is guilty of conspiring with such other person or persons, whether or not he knows their identity, to commit such crime.

(3) *Conspiracy with Multiple Criminal Objectives.* If a person conspires to commit a number of crimes, he is guilty of only one conspiracy so long as such multiple crimes are the object of the same agreement or continuous conspiratorial relationship.

(4) Joinder and Venue in Conspiracy Prosecutions.

(a) Subject to the provisions of paragraph (b) of this Subsection, two or more persons charged with criminal conspiracy may be prosecuted jointly if:

(i) they are charged with conspiring with one another; or

(ii) the conspiracies alleged, whether they have the same or different parties, are so related that they constitute different aspects of a scheme of organized criminal conduct.

(b) In any joint prosecution under paragraph (a) of this Subsection:

(i) no defendant shall be charged with a conspiracy in any county [parish or district] other than one in which he entered into such conspiracy or in which an overt act pursuant to such conspiracy was done by him or by a person with whom he conspired; and

(ii) neither the liability of any defendant nor the admissibility against him of evidence of acts or declarations of another shall be enlarged by such joinder; and

(iii) the Court shall order a severance or take a special verdict as to any defendant who so requests, if it deems it necessary or appropriate to promote the fair determination of his guilt or innocence, and shall take any other proper measures to protect the fairness of the trial.

(5) Overt Act. No person may be convicted of conspiracy to commit a crime, other than a felony of the first or second degree, unless an overt act in pursuance of such conspiracy is alleged and proved to have been done by him or by a person with whom he conspired.

(6) Renunciation of Criminal Purpose. It is an affirmative defense that the actor, after conspiring to commit a crime, thwarted the success of the conspiracy, under circumstances manifesting a complete and voluntary renunciation of his criminal purpose.

(7) Duration of Conspiracy. For purposes of Section 1.06(4):

(a) conspiracy is a continuing course of conduct that terminates when the crime or crimes that are its object are committed or the agreement that they be committed is abandoned by the defendant and by those with whom he conspired; and

(b) such abandonment is presumed if neither the defendant nor anyone with whom he conspired does any overt act in pursuance of the conspiracy during the applicable period of limitation; and

(c) if an individual abandons the agreement, the conspiracy is terminated as to him only if and when he advises those with whom he conspired of his abandonment or he informs the law enforcement authorities of the existence of the conspiracy and of his participation therein.

§ 5.04. Incapacity, Irresponsibility or Immunity of Party to Solicitation or Conspiracy.

(1) Except as provided in Subsection (2) of this Section, it is immaterial to the liability of a person who solicits or conspires with another to commit a crime that:

(a) he or the person whom he solicits or with whom he conspires does not occupy a particular position or have a particular characteristic that is an element of such crime, if he believes that one of them does; or

(b) the person whom he solicits or with whom he conspires is irresponsible or has an immunity to prosecution or conviction for the commission of the crime.

(2) It is a defense to a charge of solicitation or conspiracy to commit a crime that if the criminal object were achieved, the actor would not be guilty of a crime under the law defining the offense or as an accomplice under Section 2.06(5) or 2.06(6) (a) or (6)(b).

§ 5.05. Grading of Criminal Attempt, Solicitation and Conspiracy; Mitigation in Cases of Lesser Danger; Multiple Convictions Barred. . . .

(3) *Multiple Convictions.* A person may not be convicted of more than one offense defined by this Article for conduct designed to commit or to culminate in the commission of the same crime. . . .

Part II. Definition Of Specific Crimes . . .
Article 210. Criminal Homicide

§ 210.0. Definitions.

In Articles 210–213, unless a different meaning plainly is required:

(1) "human being" means a person who has been born and is alive;

(2) "bodily injury" means physical pain, illness or any impairment of physical condition;

(3) "serious bodily injury" means bodily injury which creates a substantial risk of death or which causes serious, permanent disfigurement, or protracted loss or impairment of the function of any bodily member or organ;

(4) "deadly weapon" means any firearm or other weapon, device, instrument, material or substance, whether animate or inanimate, which in the manner it is used or is intended to be used is known to be capable of producing death or serious bodily injury.

§ 210.1. Criminal Homicide.

(1) A person is guilty of criminal homicide if he purposely, knowingly, recklessly or negligently causes the death of another human being.

(2) Criminal homicide is murder, manslaughter or negligent homicide.

§ 210.2. Murder.

(1) Except as provided in Section 210.3(1)(b), criminal homicide constitutes murder when:

(a) it is committed purposely or knowingly; or

(b) it is committed recklessly under circumstances manifesting extreme indifference to the value of human life. Such recklessness and indifference are presumed if the actor is engaged or is an accomplice in the commission of, or an attempt to commit, or flight after committing or attempting to commit robbery, rape or deviate sexual intercourse by force or threat of force, arson, burglary, kidnapping or felonious escape.

(2) Murder is a felony of the first degree [but a person convicted of murder may be sentenced to death, as provided in Section 210.6].

§ 210.3. Manslaughter.

(1) Criminal homicide constitutes manslaughter when:

(a) it is committed recklessly; or

(b) a homicide which would otherwise be murder is committed under the influence of extreme mental or emotional disturbance for which there is reasonable explanation or excuse. The reasonableness of such explanation or excuse shall be determined from the viewpoint of a person in the actor's situation under the circumstances as he believes them to be.

(2) Manslaughter is a felony of the second degree.

§ 210.4. Negligent Homicide.

(1) Criminal homicide constitutes negligent homicide when it is committed negligently.

(2) Negligent homicide is a felony of the third degree.

§ 210.5. *Causing or Aiding Suicide.*

(1) *Causing Suicide as Criminal Homicide.* A person may be convicted of criminal homicide for causing another to commit suicide only if he purposely causes such suicide by force, duress or deception.

(2) *Aiding or Soliciting Suicide as an Independent Offense.* A person who purposely aids or solicits another to commit suicide is guilty of a felony of the second degree if his conduct causes such suicide or an attempted suicide, and otherwise of a misdemeanor. . . .

Article 211. Assault, Reckless Endangering, Threats

§ 211.0. Definitions.

In this Article, the definitions given in Section 210.0 apply unless a different meaning plainly is required.

§ 211.1. Assault.

(1) *Simple Assault.* A person is guilty of assault if he:

(a) attempts to cause or purposely, knowingly or recklessly causes bodily injury to another; or

(b) negligently causes bodily injury to another with a deadly weapon; or

(c) attempts by physical menace to put another in fear of imminent serious bodily injury.

Simple assault is a misdemeanor unless committed in a fight or scuffle entered into by mutual consent, in which case it is a petty misdemeanor.

(2) *Aggravated Assault.* A person is guilty of aggravated assault if he:

(a) attempts to cause serious bodily injury to another, or causes such injury purposely, knowingly or recklessly under circumstances manifesting extreme indifference to the value of human life; or

(b) attempts to cause or purposely or knowingly causes bodily injury to another with a deadly weapon.

Aggravated assault under paragraph (a) is a felony of the second degree; aggravated assault under paragraph (b) is a felony of the third degree.

§ 211.2. Recklessly Endangering Another Person.

A person commits a misdemeanor if he recklessly engages in conduct which places or may place another person in danger of death or serious bodily injury. Recklessness and danger shall be presumed where a person knowingly points a firearm at or in the direction of another, whether or not the actor believed the firearm to be loaded.

§ 211.3. Terroristic Threats.

A person is guilty of a felony of the third degree if he threatens to commit any crime of violence with purpose to terrorize another or to cause evacuation of a building, place of assembly, or facility of public transportation, or otherwise to cause serious public inconvenience, or in reckless disregard of the risk of causing such terror or inconvenience.

Article 212. Kidnapping And Related Offenses, Coercion

§ 212.0. Definitions.

In this Article, the definitions given in Section 210.0 apply unless a different meaning plainly is required.

§ 212.1. Kidnapping.

A person is guilty of kidnapping if he unlawfully removes another from his place of residence or business, or a substantial distance from the vicinity where he is found, or if he unlawfully confines another for a substantial period in a place of isolation, with any of the following purposes:

(a) to hold for ransom or reward, or as a shield or hostage; or

(b) to facilitate commission of any felony or flight thereafter; or

(c) to inflict bodily injury on or to terrorize the victim or another; or

(d) to interfere with the performance of any governmental or political function.

Kidnapping is a felony of the first degree unless the actor voluntarily releases the victim alive and in a safe place prior to trial, in which case it is a felony of the second degree. A removal or confinement is unlawful within the meaning of this Section if it is accomplished by force, threat or deception, or, in the case of a person who is under the age of 14 or incompetent, if it is accomplished without the consent of a parent, guardian or other person responsible for general supervision of his welfare.

§ 212.2. Felonious Restraint.

A person commits a felony of the third degree if he knowingly:

(a) restrains another unlawfully in circumstances exposing him to risk of serious bodily injury; or

(b) holds another in a condition of involuntary servitude.

§ 212.3 False Imprisonment.

A person commits a misdemeanor if he knowingly restrains another unlawfully so as to interfere substantially with his liberty. . . .

Article 213. Sexual Offenses
[under revision]

§ 213.0. Definitions.

In this Article, unless a different meaning plainly is required:

(1) the definitions given in Section 210.0 apply;

(2) "Sexual intercourse" includes intercourse per os or per anum, with some penetration however slight; emission is not required;

(3) "Deviate sexual intercourse" means sexual intercourse per os or per anum between human beings who are not husband and wife, and any form of sexual intercourse with an animal.

§ 213.1. Rape and Related Offenses.

(1) *Rape.* A male who has sexual intercourse with a female not his wife is guilty of rape if:

(a) he compels her to submit by force or by threat of imminent death, serious bodily injury, extreme pain or kidnapping, to be inflicted on anyone; or

(b) he has substantially impaired her power to appraise or control her conduct by administering or employing without her knowledge drugs, intoxicants or other means for the purpose of preventing resistance; or

(c) the female is unconscious; or

(d) the female is less than 10 years old.

Rape is a felony of the second degree unless (i) in the course thereof the actor inflicts serious bodily injury upon anyone, or (ii) the victim was not a voluntary social companion of the actor upon the occasion of the crime and had not previously permitted him sexual liberties, in which cases the offense is a felony of the first degree.

(2) *Gross Sexual Imposition.* A male who has sexual intercourse with a female not his wife commits a felony of the third degree if:

(a) he compels her to submit by any threat that would prevent resistance by a woman of ordinary resolution; or

(b) he knows that she suffers from a mental disease or defect which renders her incapable of appraising the nature of her conduct; or

(c) he knows that she is unaware that a sexual act is being committed upon her or that she submits because she mistakenly supposes that he is her husband.

§ 213.2. Deviate Sexual Intercourse by Force or Imposition.

(1) *By Force or Its Equivalent.* A person who engages in deviate sexual intercourse with another person, or who causes another to engage in deviate sexual intercourse, commits a felony of the second degree if:

(a) he compels the other person to participate by force or by threat of imminent death, serious bodily injury, extreme pain or kidnapping, to be inflicted on anyone; or

(b) he has substantially impaired the other person's power to appraise or control his conduct, by administering or employing without the knowledge of the other person drugs, intoxicants or other means for the purpose of preventing resistance; or

(c) the other person is unconscious; or

(d) the other person is less than 10 years old.

(2) *By Other Imposition.* A person who engages in deviate sexual intercourse with another person, or who causes another to engage in deviate sexual intercourse, commits a felony of the third degree if:

(a) he compels the other person to participate by any threat that would prevent resistance by a person of ordinary resolution; or

(b) he knows that the other person suffers from a mental disease or defect which renders him incapable of appraising the nature of his conduct; or (c) he knows that the other person submits because he is unaware that a sexual act is being committed upon him.

§ 213.3. Corruption of Minors and Seduction.

(1) *Offense Defined.* A male who has sexual intercourse with a female not his wife, or any person who engages in deviate sexual intercourse or causes another to engage in deviate sexual intercourse, is guilty of an offense if:

(a) the other person is less than [16] years old and the actor is at least [four] years older than the other person; or

(b) the other person is less than 21 years old and the actor is his guardian or otherwise responsible for general supervision of his welfare; or

(c) the other person is in custody of law or detained in a hospital or other institution and the actor has supervisory or disciplinary authority over him; or

(d) the other person is a female who is induced to participate by a promise of marriage which the actor does not mean to perform.

(2) *Grading.* An offense under paragraph (a) of Subsection (1) is a felony of the third degree. Otherwise an offense under this section is a misdemeanor.

§ 213.4. Sexual Assault.

A person who has sexual contact with another not his spouse, or causes such other to have sexual contact with him, is guilty of sexual assault, a misdemeanor, if:

(1) he knows that the contact is offensive to the other person; or

(2) he knows that the other person suffers from a mental disease or defect which renders him or her incapable of appraising the nature of his or her conduct; or

(3) he knows that the other person is unaware that a sexual act is being committed; or

(4) the other person is less than 10 years old; or

(5) he has substantially impaired the other person's power to appraise or control his or her conduct, by administering or employing without the other's knowledge drugs, intoxicants or other means for the purpose of preventing resistance; or

(6) the other person is less than [16] years old and the actor is at least [four] years older than the other person; or

(7) the other person is less than 21 years old and the actor is his guardian or otherwise responsible for general supervision of his welfare; or

(8) the other person is in custody of law or detained in a hospital or other institution and the actor has supervisory or disciplinary authority over him.

Sexual contact is any touching of the sexual or other intimate parts of the person for the purpose of arousing or gratifying sexual desire.

§ 213.5. Indecent Exposure.

A person commits a misdemeanor if, for the purpose of arousing or gratifying sexual desire of himself or of any person other than his spouse, he exposes his genitals under circumstances in which he knows his conduct is likely to cause affront or alarm.

§ 213.6. Provisions Generally Applicable to Article 213.

(1) *Mistake as to Age.* Whenever in this Article the criminality of conduct depends on a child's being below the age of 10, it is no defense that the actor did not know the child's age, or reasonably believed the child to be older than 10. When criminality depends on the child's being below a critical age other than 10, it is a defense for the actor to prove by a preponderance of the evidence that he reasonably believed the child to be above the critical age.

(2) *Spouse Relationships.* Whenever in this Article the definition of an offense excludes conduct with a spouse, the exclusion shall be deemed to extend to persons living as man and wife, regardless of the legal status of their relationship. The exclusion shall be inoperative as respects spouses living apart under a decree of judicial separation. Where the definition of an offense excludes conduct with a spouse or conduct by a woman, this shall not preclude conviction of a spouse or woman as accomplice in a sexual act which he or she causes another person, not within the exclusion, to perform.

(3) *Sexually Promiscuous Complainants.* It is a defense to prosecution under Section 213.3 and paragraphs (6), (7) and (8) of Section 213.4 for the actor to prove by a preponderance of the evidence that the alleged victim had, prior to the time of the offense charged, engaged promiscuously in sexual relations with others.

(4) *Prompt Complaint.* No prosecution may be instituted or maintained under this Article unless the alleged offense was brought to the notice of public authority within [3] months of its occurrence or, where the alleged victim was less than [16] years old or otherwise incompetent to make complaint, within [3] months after a parent, guardian or other competent person specially interested in the victim learns of the offense.

(5) *Testimony of Complainants.* No person shall be convicted of any felony under this Article upon the uncorroborated testimony of the alleged victim. Corroboration may be circumstantial. In any prosecution before a jury for an offense under this Article, the jury shall be instructed to evaluate the testimony of a victim or complaining witness with special care in view of the emotional involvement of the witness and the difficulty of determining the truth with respect to alleged sexual activities carried out in private.

Article 220. Arson, Criminal Mischief, and Other Property Destruction

§ 220.1. Arson and Related Offenses.

(1) *Arson.* A person is guilty of arson, a felony of the second degree, if he starts a fire or causes an explosion with the purpose of:

(a) destroying a building or occupied structure of another; or

(b) destroying or damaging any property, whether his own or another's, to collect insurance for such loss. It shall be an affirmative defense to prosecution under this paragraph that the actor's conduct did not recklessly endanger any building or occupied structure of another or place any other person in danger of death or bodily injury.

(2) *Reckless Burning or Exploding.* A person commits a felony of the third degree if he purposely starts a fire or causes an explosion, whether on his own property or another's, and thereby recklessly:

(a) places another person in danger of death or bodily injury; or

(b) places a building or occupied structure of another in danger of damage or destruction.

(3) *Failure to Control or Report Dangerous Fire.* A person who knows that a fire is endangering life or a substantial amount of property of another and fails to take reasonable measures to put out or control the fire, when he can do so without substantial risk to himself, or to give a prompt fire alarm, commits a misdemeanor if:

(a) he knows that he is under an official, contractual, or other legal duty to prevent or combat the fire; or

(b) the fire was started, albeit lawfully, by him or with his assent, or on property in his custody or control.

(4) *Definitions.* "Occupied structure" means any structure, vehicle or place adapted for overnight accommodation of persons, or for carrying on business therein, whether or not a person is actually present. Property is that of another, for the purposes of this section, if anyone other than the actor has a possessory or proprietary interest therein. If a building or structure is divided into separately occupied units, any unit not occupied by the actor is an occupied structure of another. . . .

§ 220.3. Criminal Mischief.

(1) *Offense Defined.* A person is guilty of criminal mischief if he:

(a) damages tangible property of another purposely, recklessly, or by negligence in the employment of fire, explosives, or other dangerous means listed in Section 220.2(1); or

(b) purposely or recklessly tampers with tangible property of another so as to endanger person or property; or

(c) purposely or recklessly causes another to suffer pecuniary loss by deception or threat.

(2) *Grading.* Criminal mischief is a felony of the third degree if the actor purposely causes pecuniary loss in excess of $5,000, or a substantial interruption or impairment of public communication, transportation, supply of water, gas or power, or other public service. It is a misdemeanor if the actor purposely causes pecuniary

loss in excess of $100, or a petty misdemeanor if he purposely or recklessly causes pecuniary loss in excess of $25. Otherwise criminal mischief is a violation. . . .

Article 221. Burglary and other Criminal Intrusion

§ 221.0. Definitions.

In this Article, unless a different meaning plainly is required:

(1) "occupied structure" means any structure, vehicle or place adapted for overnight accommodation of persons, or for carrying on business therein, whether or not a person is actually present.

(2) "night" means the period between thirty minutes past sunset and thirty minutes before sunrise.

§ 221.1. Burglary.

(1) *Burglary Defined.* A person is guilty of burglary if he enters a building or occupied structure, or separately secured or occupied portion thereof, with purpose to commit a crime therein, unless the premises are at the time open to the public or the actor is licensed or privileged to enter. It is an affirmative defense to prosecution for burglary that the building or structure was abandoned.

(2) *Grading.* Burglary is a felony of the second degree if it is perpetrated in the dwelling of another at night, or if, in the course of committing the offense, the actor:

(a) purposely, knowingly or recklessly inflicts or attempts to inflict bodily injury on anyone; or

(b) is armed with explosives or a deadly weapon.

Otherwise, burglary is a felony of the third degree. An act shall be deemed "in the course of committing" an offense if it occurs in an attempt to commit the offense or in flight after the attempt or commission.

(3) *Multiple Convictions.* A person may not be convicted both for burglary and for the offense which it was his purpose to commit after the burglarious entry or for an attempt to commit that offense, unless the additional offense constitutes a felony of the first or second degree.

§ 221.2. Criminal Trespass.

(1) *Buildings and Occupied Structures.* A person commits an offense if, knowing that he is not licensed or privileged to do so, he enters or surreptitiously remains in any building or occupied structure, or separately secured or occupied portion thereof. An offense under this Subsection is a misdemeanor if it is committed in a dwelling at night. Otherwise it is a petty misdemeanor.

(2) *Defiant Trespasser.* A person commits an offense if, knowing that he is not licensed or privileged to do so, he enters or remains in any place as to which notice against trespass is given by:

(a) actual communication to the actor; or

(b) posting in a manner prescribed by law or reasonably likely to come to the attention of intruders; or

(c) fencing or other enclosure manifestly designed to exclude intruders.

An offense under this Subsection constitutes a petty misdemeanor if the offender defies an order to leave personally communicated to him by the owner of the premises or other authorized person. Otherwise it is a violation.

(3) *Defenses.* It is an affirmative defense to prosecution under this Section that:

(a) a building or occupied structure involved in an offense under Subsection (1) was abandoned; or

(b) the premises were at the time open to members of the public and the actor complied with all lawful conditions imposed on access to or remaining in the premises; or

(c) the actor reasonably believed that the owner of the premises, or other person empowered to license access thereto, would have licensed him to enter or remain.

Article 222. Robbery

§ 222.1. Robbery.

(1) *Robbery Defined.* A person is guilty of robbery if, in the course of committing a theft, he:

(a) inflicts serious bodily injury upon another; or

(b) threatens another with or purposely puts him in fear of immediate serious bodily injury; or

(c) commits or threatens immediately to commit any felony of the first or second degree.

An act shall be deemed "in the course of committing a theft" if it occurs in an attempt to commit theft or in flight after the attempt or commission.

(2) *Grading.* Robbery is a felony of the second degree, except that it is a felony of the first degree if in the course of committing the theft the actor attempts to kill anyone, or purposely inflicts or attempts to inflict serious bodily injury.

Article 223. Theft and Related Offenses

§ 223.0. Definitions.

In this Article, unless a different meaning plainly is required:

(1) "deprive" means: (a) to withhold property of another permanently or for so extended a period as to appropriate a major portion of its economic value, or with intent to restore only upon payment of reward or other compensation; or (b) to dispose of the property so as to make it unlikely that the owner will recover it.

(2) "financial institution" means a bank, insurance company, credit union, building and loan association, investment trust or other organization held out to the public as a place of deposit of funds or medium of savings or collective investment.

(3) "government" means the United States, any State, county, municipality, or other political unit, or any department, agency or subdivision of any of the foregoing, or any corporation or other association carrying out the functions of government.

(4) "movable property" means property the location of which can be changed, including things growing on, affixed to, or found in land, and documents although the rights represented thereby have no physical location; "immovable property" is all other property.

(5) "obtain" means: (a) in relation to property, to bring about a transfer or purported transfer of a legal interest in the property, whether to the obtainer or another; or (b) in relation to labor or service, to secure performance thereof.

(6) "property" means anything of value, including real estate, tangible and intangible personal property, contract rights, choses-in-action and other interests in or claims to wealth, admission or transportation tickets, captured or domestic animals, food and drink, electric or other power.

(7) "property of another" includes property in which any person other than the actor has an interest which the actor is not privileged to infringe, regardless of the fact that the actor also has an interest in the property and regardless of the fact that the other person might be precluded from civil recovery because the property was used in an unlawful transaction or was subject to forfeiture as contraband. Property in possession of the actor shall not be deemed property of another who has only a security interest therein, even if legal title is in the creditor pursuant to a conditional sales contract or other security agreement.

§ 223.1. Consolidation of Theft Offenses; Grading; Provisions Applicable to Theft Generally.

(1) *Consolidation of Theft Offenses.* Conduct denominated theft in this Article constitutes a single offense. An accusation of theft may be supported by evidence that it was committed in any manner that would be theft under this Article, notwithstanding the specification of a different manner in the indictment or information, subject only to the power of the Court to ensure fair trial by granting a continuance or other appropriate relief where the conduct of the defense would be prejudiced by lack of fair notice or by surprise.

(2) Grading of Theft Offenses.

(a) Theft constitutes a felony of the third degree if the amount involved exceeds $500, or if the property stolen is a firearm, automobile, airplane, motorcycle, motor boat, or other motor-propelled vehicle, or in the case of theft by receiving stolen property, if the receiver is in the business of buying or selling stolen property.

(b) except that if the property was not taken from the person or by threat, or in breach of a fiduciary obligation, and the actor proves by a preponderance of the evidence that the amount involved was less than $50, the offense constitutes a petty misdemeanor.

(c) The amount involved in a theft shall be deemed to be the highest value, by any reasonable standard, of the property or services which the actor stole or attempted to steal. Amounts involved in thefts committed pursuant to one scheme or course of conduct, whether from the same person or several persons, may be aggregated in determining the grade of the offense.

(3) *Claim of Right.* It is an affirmative defense to prosecution for theft that the actor:

(a) was unaware that the property or service was that of another; or

(b) acted under an honest claim of right to the property or service involved or that he had a right to acquire or dispose of it as he did; or

(c) took property exposed for sale, intending to purchase and pay for it promptly, or reasonably believing that the owner, if present, would have consented.

(4) *Theft from Spouse.* It is no defense that theft was from the actor's spouse, except that misappropriation of household and personal effects, or other property normally accessible to both spouses, is theft only if it occurs after the parties have ceased living together.

§ 223.2. Theft by Unlawful Taking or Disposition.

(1) *Movable Property.* A person is guilty of theft if he unlawfully takes, or exercises unlawful control over, movable property of another with purpose to deprive him thereof.

(2) *Immovable Property.* A person is guilty of theft if he unlawfully transfers immovable property of another or any interest therein with purpose to benefit himself or another not entitled thereto.

§ 223.3. Theft by Deception.

A person is guilty of theft if he purposely obtains property of another by deception. A person deceives if he purposely:

(1) creates or reinforces a false impression, including false impressions as to law, value, intention or other state of mind; but deception as to a person's intention to perform a promise shall not be inferred from the fact alone that he did not subsequently perform the promise; or

(2) prevents another from acquiring information which would affect his judgment of a transaction; or

(3) fails to correct a false impression which the deceiver previously created or reinforced, or which the deceiver knows to be influencing another to whom he stands in a fiduciary or confidential relationship; or

(4) fails to disclose a known lien, adverse claim or other legal impediment to the enjoyment of property which he transfers or encumbers in consideration for the property obtained, whether such impediment is or is not valid, or is or is not a matter of official record.

The term "deceive" does not, however, include falsity as to matters having no pecuniary significance, or puffing by statements unlikely to deceive ordinary persons in the group addressed.

§ 223.4. Theft by Extortion.

A person is guilty of theft if he purposely obtains property of another by threatening to:

(1) inflict bodily injury on anyone or commit any other criminal offense; or

(2) accuse anyone of a criminal offense; or

(3) expose any secret tending to subject any person to hatred, contempt or ridicule, or to impair his credit or business repute; or

(4) take or withhold action as an official, or cause an official to take or withhold action; or

(5) bring about or continue a strike, boycott or other collective unofficial action, if the property is not demanded or received for the benefit of the group in whose interest the actor purports to act; or

(6) testify or provide information or withhold testimony or information with respect to another's legal claim or defense; or

(7) inflict any other harm which would not benefit the actor.

It is an affirmative defense to prosecution based on paragraphs (2), (3) or (4) that the property obtained by threat of accusation, exposure, lawsuit or other invocation of official action was honestly claimed as restitution or indemnification for harm done in the circumstances to which such accusation, exposure, lawsuit or other official action relates, or as compensation for property or lawful services.

§ 223.5. Theft of Property Lost, Mislaid, or Delivered by Mistake

A person who comes into control of property of another that he knows to have been lost, mislaid, or delivered under a mistake as to the nature or amount of the property or the identity of the recipient is guilty of theft if, with purpose to deprive the owner thereof, he fails to take reasonable measures to restore the property to a person entitled to have it.

§ 223.6. Receiving Stolen Property.

(1) *Receiving.* A person is guilty of theft if he purposely receives, retains, or disposes of movable property of another knowing that it has been stolen, or believing that it has probably been stolen, unless the property is received, retained, or disposed with purpose to restore it to the owner. "Receiving" means acquiring possession, control or title, or lending on the security of the property.

(2) *Presumption of Knowledge.* The requisite knowledge or belief is presumed in the case of a dealer who:

(a) is found in possession or control of property stolen from two or more persons on separate occasions; or

(b) has received stolen property in another transaction within the year preceding the transaction charged; or

(c) being a dealer in property of the sort received, acquires it for a consideration which he knows is far below its reasonable value.

"Dealer" means a person in the business of buying or selling goods including a pawnbroker.

§ 223.7. Theft of Services

(1) A person is guilty of theft is he purposely obtains services which he knows are available only for compensation, by deception or threat, or by false token or other means to avoid payment for the service. "Services" includes labor, professional service, transportation, telephone or other public service, accommodation in hotels, restaurants or elsewhere, admission to exhibitions, use of vehicles or other movable property. Where compensation for service is ordinarily paid immediately upon the rendering of such service, as in the case of hotels and restaurants, refusal to pay or absconding without payment or offer to pay gives rise to a presumption that the service was obtained by deception as to intention to pay.

(2) A person commits theft if, having control over the disposition of services of others, to which he is not entitled, he knowingly diverts such services to his own benefit or to the benefit of another not entitled thereto.

§ 223.8. Theft by Failure to Make Required Disposition of Funds Received.

A person who purposely obtains property upon agreement, or subject to a known legal obligation, to make specified payment or other disposition, whether from such property or its proceeds or from his own property to be reserved in equivalent amount, is guilty of theft if he deals with the property obtained as his own and fails to make the required payment or disposition. The foregoing applies notwithstanding that it may be impossible to identify particular property as belonging to the victim at the time of the actor's failure to make the required payment or disposition. An officer or employee of the government or of a financial institution is presumed:

(i) to know any legal obligation relevant to his criminal liability under this Section, and (ii) to have dealt with the property as his own if he fails to pay or account upon lawful demand, or if an audit reveals a shortage or falsification of accounts.

§ 223.9. Unauthorized Use of Automobiles and Other Vehicles.

A person commits a misdemeanor if he operates another's automobile, airplane, motorcycle, motorboat, or other motor-propelled vehicle without consent of the owner. It is an affirmative defense to prosecution under this Section that the actor reasonably believed that the owner would have consented to the operation had he known of it.

Article 224. Forgery and Fraudulent Practices

§ 224.0. Definitions.

In this Article, the definitions given in Section 223.0 apply unless a different meaning plainly is required.

§ 224.1. Forgery

(1) *Definition.* A person is guilty of forgery if, with purpose to defraud or injure anyone, or with knowledge that he is facilitating a fraud or injury to be perpetrated by anyone, the actor:

(a) alters any writing of another without his authority; or

(b) makes, completes, executes, authenticates, issues or transfers any writing so that it purports to be the act of another who did not authorize that act, or to have been executed at a time or place or in a numbered sequence other than was in fact the case, or to be a copy of an original when no such original existed; or

(c) utters any writing which he knows to be forged in a manner specified in paragraphs (a) or (b).

"Writing" includes printing or any other method of recording information, money, coins, tokens, stamps, seals, credit cards, badges, trade-marks, and other symbols of value, right, privilege, or identification.

(2) *Grading.* Forgery is a felony of the second degree if the writing is or purports to be part of an issue of money, securities, postage or revenue stamps, or other instruments issued by the government, or part of an issue of stock, bonds or other instruments representing interests in or claims against any property or enterprise. Forgery is a felony of the third degree if the writing is or purports to be a will, deed, contract, release, commercial instrument, or other document evidencing, creating, transferring, altering, terminating, or otherwise affecting legal relations. Otherwise forgery is a misdemeanor. . . .

§ 224.5. Bad Checks.

A person who issues or passes a check or similar sight order for the payment of money, knowing that it will not be honored by the drawee, commits a misdemeanor. For the purpose of this Section as well as in any prosecution for theft committed by means of a bad check, an issuer is presumed to know that the check or order (other than a post-dated check or order) would not be paid, if:

(1) the issuer had no account with the drawee at the time the check or order was issued; or

(2) payment was refused by the drawee for lack of funds, upon presentation within 30 days after issue, and the issuer failed to make good within 10 days after receiving notice of that refusal.

§ 224.6. Credit Cards.

A person commits an offense if he uses a credit card for the purpose of obtaining property or services with knowledge that:

(1) the card is stolen or forged; or

(2) the card has been revoked or cancelled; or

(3) for any other reason his use of the card is unauthorized by the issuer.

It is an affirmative defense to prosecution under paragraph (3) if the actor proves by a preponderance of the evidence that he had the purpose and ability to meet all obligations to the issuer arising out of his use of the card. "Credit card" means a writing or other evidence of an undertaking to pay for property or services delivered or rendered to or upon the order of a designated person or bearer. An offense under this Section is a felony of the third degree if the value of the property or services secured or sought to be secured by means of the credit card exceeds $500; otherwise it is a misdemeanor.

§ 224.7. Deceptive Business Practices.

A person commits a misdemeanor if in the course of business he:

(1) uses or possesses for use a false weight or measure, or any other device for falsely determining or recording any quality or quantity; or

(2) sells, offers or exposes for sale, or delivers less than the represented quantity of any commodity or service; or

(3) takes or attempts to take more than the represented quantity of any commodity or service when as buyer he furnishes the weight or measure; or

(4) sells, offers or exposes for sale adulterated or mislabeled commodities. "Adulterated" means varying from the standard of composition or quality prescribed by or pursuant to any statute providing criminal penalties for such variance, or set by established commercial usage. "Mislabeled" means varying from the standard of truth or disclosure in labeling prescribed by or pursuant to any statute providing criminal penalties for such variance, or set by established commercial usage; or

(5) makes a false or misleading statement in any advertisement addressed to the public or to a substantial segment thereof for the purpose of promoting the purchase or sale of property or services; or

(6) makes a false or misleading written statement for the purpose of obtaining property or credit; or

(7) makes a false or misleading written statement for the purpose of promoting the sale of securities, or omits information required by law to be disclosed in written documents relating to securities.

It is an affirmative defense to prosecution under this Section if the defendant proves by a preponderance of the evidence that his conduct was not knowingly or recklessly deceptive. . . .

Article 230. Offenses Against the Family

§ 230.1. Bigamy and Polygamy.

(1) *Bigamy*. A married person is guilty of bigamy, a misdemeanor, if he contracts or purports to contract another marriage, unless at the time of the subsequent marriage:

(a) the actor believes that the prior spouse is dead; or

(b) the actor and the prior spouse have been living apart for five consecutive years throughout which the prior spouse was not known by the actor to be alive; or

(c) a Court has entered a judgment purporting to terminate or annul any prior disqualifying marriage, and the actor does not know that judgment to be invalid; or

(d) the actor reasonably believes that he is legally eligible to remarry.

(2) *Polygamy*. A person is guilty of polygamy, a felony of the third degree, if he marries or cohabits with more than one spouse at a time in purported exercise of the right of plural marriage. The offense is a continuing one until all cohabitation and claim of marriage with more than one spouse terminates. This section does not apply to parties to a polygamous marriage, lawful in the country of which they are residents or nationals, while they are in transit through or temporarily visiting this State.

(3) *Other Party to Bigamous or Polygamous Marriage.* A person is guilty of bigamy or polygamy, as the case may be, if he contracts or purports to contract marriage with another knowing that the other is thereby committing bigamy or polygamy. . . .

Article 240. Bribery and Corrupt Influence

§ 240.0. Definitions.

In Articles 240–243, unless a different meaning plainly is required:

(1) "benefit" means gain or advantage, or anything regarded by the beneficiary as gain or advantage, including benefit to any other person or entity in whose welfare he is interested, but not an advantage promised generally to a group or class of voters as a consequence of public measures which a candidate engages to support or oppose;

(2) "government" includes any branch, subdivision or agency of the government of the State or any locality within it;

(3) "harm" means loss, disadvantage or injury, or anything so regarded by th e person affected, including loss, disadvantage or injury to any other person or entity in whose welfare he is interested;

(4) "official proceeding" means a proceeding heard or which may be heard before any legislative, judicial, administrative or other governmental agency or official authorized to take evidence under oath, including any referee, hearing

examiner, commissioner, notary or other person taking testimony or deposition in connection with any such proceeding;

(5) "party official" means a person who holds an elective or appointive post in a political party in the United States by virtue of which he directs or conducts, or participates in directing or conducting party affairs at any level of responsibility;

(6) "pecuniary benefit" is benefit in the form of money, property, commercial interests or anything else the primary significance of which is economic gain;

(7) "public servant" means any officer or employee of government, including legislators and judges, and any person participating as juror, advisor, consultant or otherwise, in performing a governmental function; but the term does not include witnesses;

(8) "administrative proceeding" means any proceeding, other than a judicial proceeding, the outcome of which is required to be based on a record or documentation prescribed by law, or in which law or regulation is particularized in application to individuals.

§ 240.1. Bribery in Official and Political Matters.

A person is guilty of bribery, a felony of the third degree, if he offers, confers or agrees to confer upon another, or solicits, accepts or agrees to accept from another:

(1) any pecuniary benefit as consideration for the recipient's decision, opinion, recommendation, vote or other exercise of discretion as a public servant, party official or voter; or

(2) any benefit as consideration for the recipient's decision, vote, recommendation or other exercise of official discretion in a judicial or administrative proceeding; or

(3) any benefit as consideration for a violation of a known legal duty as public servant or party official.

It is no defense to prosecution under this section that a person whom the actor sought to influence was not qualified to act in the desired way whether because he had not yet assumed office, or lacked jurisdiction, or for any other reason. . . .

Article 241. Perjury and Other Falsification in Official Matters

§ 241.0. Definitions.

In this Article, unless a different meaning plainly is required:

(1) the definitions given in Section 240.0 apply; and

(2) "statement" means any representation, but includes a representation of opinion, belief or other state of mind only if the representation clearly relates to state of mind apart from or in addition to any facts which are the subject of the representation.

§ 241.1. Perjury.

(1) *Offense Defined.* A person is guilty of perjury, a felony of the third degree, if in any official proceeding he makes a false statement under oath or equivalent affirmation, or swears or affirms the truth of a statement previously made, when the statement is material and he does not believe it to be true.

(2) *Materiality.* Falsification is material, regardless of the admissibility of the statement under rules of evidence, if it could have affected the course or outcome of the proceeding. It is no defense that the declarant mistakenly believed the falsification to be immaterial. Whether a falsification is material in a given factual situation is a question of law.

(3) *Irregularities No Defense.* It is not a defense to prosecution under this Section that the oath or affirmation was administered or taken in an irregular manner or that the declarant was not competent to make the statement. A document purporting to be made upon oath or affirmation at any time when the actor presents it as being so verified shall be deemed to have been duly sworn or affirmed.

(4) *Retraction.* No person shall be guilty of an offense under this Section if he retracted the falsification in the course of the proceeding in which it was made before it became manifest that the falsification was or would be exposed and before the falsification substantially affected the proceeding.

(5) *Inconsistent Statements.* Where the defendant made inconsistent statements under oath or equivalent affirmation, both having been made within the period of the statute of limitations, the prosecution may proceed by setting forth the inconsistent statements in a single count alleging in the alternative that one or the other was false and not believed by the defendant. In such case it shall not be necessary for the prosecution to prove which statement was false but only that one or the other was false and not believed by the defendant to be true.

(6) *Corroboration.* No person shall be convicted of an offense under this Section where proof of falsity rests solely upon contradiction by testimony of a single person other than the defendant. . . . .

§ 241.5. False Reports to Law Enforcement Authorities.

(1) *Falsely Incriminating Another.* A person who knowingly gives false information to any law enforcement officer with purpose to implicate another commits a misdemeanor.

(2) *Fictitious Reports.* A person commits a petty misdemeanor if he:

(a) reports to law enforcement authorities an offense or other incident within their concern knowing that it did not occur; or

(b) pretends to furnish such authorities with information relating to an offense or incident when he knows he has no information relating to such offense or incident. . . .

Article 242. Obstructing Governmental Operations, Escapes . . .

§ 242.2. Resisting Arrest or Other Law Enforcement

A person commits a misdemeanor if, for the purpose of preventing a public servant from effecting a lawful arrest or discharging any other duty, the person creates a substantial risk of bodily injury to the public servant or anyone else, or employs means justifying or requiring substantial force to overcome the resistance.

§ 242.3. Hindering Apprehension or Prosecution.

A person commits an offense if, with purpose to hinder the apprehension, prosecution, conviction or punishment of another for crime, he:

(1) harbors or conceals the other; or

(2) provides or aids in providing a weapon, transportation, disguise or other means of avoiding apprehension or effecting escape; or

(3) conceals or destroys evidence of the crime, or tampers with a witness, informant, document or other source of information, regardless of its admissibility in evidence; or

(4) warns the other of impending discovery or apprehension, except that this paragraph does not apply to a warning given in connection with an effort to bring another into compliance with law; or

(5) volunteers false information to a law enforcement officer.

The offense is a felony of the third degree if the conduct which the actor knows has been charged or is liable to be charged against the person aided would constitute a felony of the first or second degree. Otherwise it is a misdemeanor.

§ 242.4. Aiding Consummation of Crime.

A person commits an offense if he purposely aids another to accomplish an unlawful object of a crime, as by safeguarding the proceeds thereof or converting the proceeds into negotiable funds. The offense is a felony of the third degree if the principal offense was a felony of the first or second degree. Otherwise it is a misdemeanor.

§ 242.5. Compounding.

A person commits a misdemeanor if he accepts or agrees to accept any pecuniary benefit in consideration of refraining from reporting to law enforcement authorities the commission or suspected commission of any offense or information relating to an offense. It is an affirmative defense to prosecution under this Section that the pecuniary benefit did not exceed an amount which the actor believed to be due as restitution or indemnification for harm caused by the offense. . . .

Article 250. Riot, Disorderly Conduct, and Related Offenses. . . .

§ 250.2. Disorderly Conduct.

(1) *Offense Defined.* A person is guilty of disorderly conduct if, with purpose to cause public inconvenience, annoyance or alarm, or recklessly creating a risk thereof, he:

    (a) engages in fighting or threatening, or in violent or tumultuous behavior; or

    (b) makes unreasonable noise or offensively coarse utterance, gesture or display, or addresses abusive language to any person present; or

    (c) creates a hazardous or physically offensive condition by any act which serves no legitimate purpose of the actor.

"Public" means affecting or likely to affect persons in a place to which the public or a substantial group has access; among the places included are highways, transport facilities, schools, prisons, apartment houses, places of business or amusement, or any neighborhood.

(2) *Grading.* An offense under this section is a petty misdemeanor if the actor's purpose is to cause substantial harm or serious inconvenience, or if he persists in disorderly conduct after reasonable warning or request to desist. Otherwise disorderly conduct is a violation.

§ 250.4. Harassment.

A person commits a petty misdemeanor if, with purpose to harass another, he:

    (1) makes a telephone call without purpose of legitimate communication; or

    (2) insults, taunts or challenges another in a manner likely to provoke violent or disorderly response; or

    (3) makes repeated communications anonymously or at extremely inconvenient hours, or in offensively coarse language; or

    (4) subjects another to an offensive touching; or

    (5) engages in any other course of alarming conduct serving no legitimate purpose of the actor.

§ 250.5. Public Drunkenness; Drug Incapacitation.

A person is guilty of an offense if he appears in any public place manifestly under the influence of alcohol, narcotics or other drug, not therapeutically administered, to the degree that he may endanger himself or other persons or property, or annoy persons in his vicinity. An offense under this Section constitutes a petty misdemeanor if the actor has been convicted hereunder twice before within a period of one year. Otherwise the offense constitutes a violation.

§ 250.6. Loitering or Prowling.

A person commits a violation if he loiters or prowls in a place, at a time, or in a manner not usual for law-abiding individuals under circumstances that warrant alarm for the safety of persons or property in the vicinity. Among the circumstances which may be considered in determining whether such alarm is warranted is the fact that the actor takes flight upon appearance of a peace officer, refuses to identify himself, or manifestly endeavors to conceal himself or any object. Unless flight by the actor or other circumstance makes it impracticable, a peace officer shall prior to any arrest for an offense under this section afford the actor an opportunity to dispel any alarm which would otherwise be warranted, by requesting him to identify himself and explain his presence and conduct. No person shall be convicted of an offense under this Section if the peace officer did not comply with the preceding sentence, or if it appears at trial that the explanation given by the actor was true and, if believed by the peace officer at the time, would have dispelled the alarm. . . .

Appendix B

The Personal Dimension of Lawyering—Or "Can a Criminal Lawyer Be Competent, Diligent, Professional, Successful, and Altrustic . . . and Also Live a Full Life?"

SYNOPSIS

§ B.01 Why We Have Included This (Unusual) Appendix

[A] A Disclaimer

This Appendix is Subject to Disagreement, Contains Controversial Opinions, and Requires Individualized Adaptation to Your Personal Circumstances. It is inherently difficult to describe the job satisfactions and dissatisfactions of criminal lawyers. To say what clients are "like," or to identify what to watch out for in your dealings with judges, obstreperous opponents, or (for that matter) alcohol, obviously will result in some ill-fitting advice. Nevertheless, the effort may be worthwhile. During the 1990's, for example, the State of California decided to require—not to suggest, but to *require*—every single practicing lawyer to undertake regular instruction in substance abuse avoidance, stress reduction, and office management. The life of a lawyer can be very hard if one does it the wrong way but very satisfying if done right; and our goal in this Appendix is to help you confront the consequences of the choices you must make.

[B] The Depth of Lawyer Dissatisfaction — and the Good News

(1) *Lawyer Dissatisfaction Is Surprisingly Prevalent: An ABA Survey Showed That Only Three In Five Would Choose the Profession if They Had It to Do Over Again.* One ABA survey of lawyers showed that a high percentage would not even enter the profession if they had the choice to make again. ABA Journal, Sept. 1986, at 44 (reporting that only 59.4%, or three out of five, said they would choose a legal career again). Furthermore, those three-fifths obviously shared the same dissatisfactions as those who would reject the profession: Only about a third (34%) reported no significant complaints about their choice. Other surveys, too, have shown large percentages of lawyer discontent. *See, e.g.,* Grimes, *Are There Too Many Lawyers (And Are They Happy?)*, Hous. Lawyer, Sept.-Oct. 1990, at 6 (43% of lawyers "wouldn't do it again"); *Smell the Roses: Lawyers, a Troubled Group, Told How to Improve Their Lives*, ABA Journal, Oct. 1991, at 43 (reporting "alarming" dissatisfaction, with 24 percent of lawyers disclosing "depression" symptoms; Jefferson, *But What Role for the Soul?*, ABA Journal, Dec. 1991, at 60 (reporting on study concluding that

"[l]awyers have the highest depression rates of any group in the workplace," "more than twice the rate in the general population"; comparing rate for physicians, who virtually "aren't depressed at all").

(2) *Updating Lawyer Dissatisfaction: It's Just as Bad, or Worse: Jeena Cho, Changing Course,* ABA J., Aug. 2019, at 266. "I think about walking out of my job all the time, but I have no idea what I'd do. All I know how to be is a lawyer." Ms. Cho says, "This is something I hear frequently from the lawyers I work with." And she adds, "I often see that these feelings of discontent were there for a long time."

(3) *The Good News.* The same surveys also showed, however, that most lawyers were basically content with the profession they had chosen. Again, these lawyers clearly share many of the same problems. What distinguishes those who are content from those who are dissatisfied?

(4) *A Variety of Causes That, Unfortunately, Are Built into the System.* Lawyers complain about opposing counsel, whom they see as "dumb," or "pushy," or "sneaky." (See below.) They also are disappointed in judges, possibly because the societal image of judges is inflated. Clients are unappreciative, uncooperative, and enthralled with unrealistic expectations; partners or employers are exploitative; and the adversary system produces constant stress, injustice and oppression. There is no time for the lawyer's own concerns — not for hobbies, not even for errands. *Cf* ABA Journal, Sept. 1986, at 44; ABA Journal, Oct. 1991, at 42–43.

[C] Justice O'Connor's View (But It Calls for Skepticism)

(1) *Justice O'Connor's View, Expressed in 1999: Reports Say That "More than Half" of Lawyers Call Themselves Dissatisfied — Houston Chronicle, May 24, 1999, at 8A.* In a speech at American University's Washington College of Law on May 23, 1999, Justice Sandra Day O'Connor reportedly cited surveys concluding that "more than half the country's lawyers" say that they are dissatisfied at work. She mentioned such irritants as money, public perceptions of lawyers, and frustration at lack of social worth in lawyers' work. Her reported solution: civility, and devoting more time to pro bono work. Justice O'Connor particularly emphasized providing more legal services to the poor as a means of reducing frustration. *See also* Sandra Day O'Connor, *Professionalism,* 78 Ore. L. Rev. 385, 386, 390–391 (1999) (speech at University of Oregon Law School, citing a RAND study concluding that "only half would choose to become lawyers if they had to do it over," and repeating the call for pro bono services as part of a solution).

(2) *Skepticism About Justice O'Connor's Proposed Solution.* Many lawyers, having been involved extensively in pro bono work, are skeptical of Justice O'Connor's proposed solution. These lawyers advocate pro bono work for its own sake, but they caution that the work should not be viewed as decreasing frustration or stress. In some circumstances it may have the opposite effect. There are other solutions to dissatisfaction, and we'll develop them in this appendix.

[D] Life, Law Practice, and Law School: How Much Correlation Between Your Preparation and the Real World?

(1) *Decotiis & Steele, The Skills of the Lawyering Process*, 40 Tex. B.J. 483 (1977). These two researchers observed five general practitioners of high reputation to find how they spent their time on a day-to-day basis. The results were surprising. The lawyers did very little reading, "except proofreading." They also did very little expository writing, except for short letters, although they did exercise a different kind of skill that the researchers called "document preparation" (which differed from writing because it normally involved the "cannibalizing" of clauses from existing documents, although it required a high degree of experience, knowledge and judgment). As for legal research (the only skill other than appellate opinion analysis that universally is taught to all law students), these practitioners avoided it as a low-level endeavor. They hired others, such as law clerks, to do their research. The most highly developed skill: negotiation. The lawyers also were adept at interviewing and at explaining the legal system and legal choices to others (such as clients).

(2) *The Implications: Practice Requires a Greater Adjustment than You Might Expect, and Career Choices Are More Difficult — Cf. Biehl, Things They Didn't Teach You in Law School*, ABA Journal, Jan. 1989, at 52. Thus, law school may provide an idealized view of the profession — one in which the more prosaic and the more seamy side is underexplored. New lawyers also sometimes are surprised about the persistence of their practice deficiencies. Finally, since law school course content does not correspond to the daily tasks of lawyering, new lawyers lack a basis for career choices (or for daily choices that a career presents, such as whether to accept a given criminal client or not). The point, however, is not that there is something "wrong" with the material selected for teaching in law school. The ability to analyze an appellate decision is essential, because one must appreciate legal analysis before knowing how to go about "fact gathering." Rather, the point is that there are aspects of the legal profession that law school does not aspire to teach.

[E] Coping with a Changing Lawyer Marketplace

(1) *Are There Really "Too Many" Lawyers?: See "Will 'Happy Days' Be Here Again"?*, Law Office Management & Administration Report, July 1991, at 16–17. This Report describes a "stabilizing" legal market "in which carefully managed firms not guilty of overreaching and excessive optimism can survive." The "high salary standards and competition for lawyers [w]ill undoubtedly continue to crumble in the [future]." And, the supply of new associates "will favor the employer," since "more professionals will be looking for jobs than are available." But at the same time, there is good news. The Report emphasizes that it "isn't forecasting negatives in the extreme, or 'doom and gloom'." The profession is undergoing a restructuring that will alter it. "[T]he future legal environment won't be made up of 'unhappy' days; they simply won't be the same."

(2) *The Solutions: Flexibility about Professional Prospects and Careful Study of New Market Conditions.* Criminal law will continue to grow slightly, keeping its approximate percentage of the practice. The Report points out some of the ways in which law practice will be changing. Environmental litigation, intellectual property, and bankruptcy may grow, while commercial litigation, merger and acquisition work, and representation of housing and building developers will shrink. Clients will be attempting to cut their costs, with legal fees among the first expenses they will try to reduce; therefore, alternatives to straight hourly charges—new billing techniques—will be in demand. *See also* Morgan, *Value Billing in this Technological Age*, 53 Tex. B.J. 216 (1990); Morgan, *How to Draft Bills Clients Rush to Pay*, Legal Economics, July-Aug. 1985, at 22. Support staff and technology investments will be reduced—meaning that the future lawyer will expend less on secretarial assistance and computer support. In summary, you will need to consider these matters more than your predecessors did, you will need to be more flexible, and you can maximize opportunities by studying market conditions carefully. But if you do so, and if you have the makeup of a lawyer, you can develop sound prospects of finding job satisfaction in the field.

§ B.02 Law Practice in Human Terms: The "Down Side"

This Section Gives You the Bad News First, Then the Good News. The materials that follow may appear unrelentingly gloomy. For three reasons, they are not. First, if you anticipate these problems, you will be able to avoid them. Second, we plan to offer solutions when they are available (and often, even for the most serious problems, they are). Third, remember the disclaimer, above: There are two sides to this picture, and we plan to give you the "up" side, also, after we finish with the "down" side.

Problem A

A CAUTIONARY TALE ABOUT A FAST-LANE DIVORCE, adapted from Hous. Chronicle, Sept. 20, 1994, at 4A (New York Times report). "When [wife] surrendered her two sons to her former husband's custody 11 days ago, it was the climactic act in a cautionary tale of two-career couples in the 1990's.

"To [wife], 43, a counsel to [the United States Senator who chairs the Senate Judiciary Committee], and [to] the feminist legal groups rallying around her, the decision by a Washington judge to award custody to the father is chilling evidence of a judicial backlash against professional women.

"[But] her former husband, . . . 48, the assistant executive director of the American Federation of Television and Radio Artists, [sees the matter differently].

"The battle lines were drawn after a July decision by Judge Harriet Taylor of the District of Columbia Superior Court.

"In a sharply worded opinion, . . . [Judge] Taylor painted [wife] as a driven work-aholic who seldom arrived home before dinner and [husband] as a doting father who put his children first.

"In her opinion [Judge] Taylor quotes friends and relatives of [husband's], as well as a baby-sitter who said [wife] often ate dinner alone and very late at night, 'while sitting on the kitchen floor, with her plate on the floor, talking on the telephone or writing while she was eating.' Friends of [husband] described [wife] as working even during her children's birthday parties, of 'barking orders,' and of being 'very tightly wound.'

"Taylor said [wife] was 'more devoted and absorbed by her work and her career than anything else in her life, including her health, her children, and her family.'"

(1) *First Question: Why Did This Sad Divorce Decision Occur?* Consider the following hypotheses as reasons for this result.

(1) Has wife's training made her take on counterproductive behaviors? [Before you reject this hypothesis, wait to read Problem B, below, which considers whether law school engenders certain personality characteristics.]

(2) Is wife the victim of gender bias?

(3) Did wife's decision to combine a legal career with a family create the problem?

(4) Was wife's decision to take on a particularly all-consuming position inconsistent with being a good custodial mother (or for that matter, for a man, a good custodial father)?

(5) Could wife have handled the balance by changing some of her behaviors or circumstances?

(6) Are all of the above possibly true (or partially true)?

(7) Are there other possibilities that you can think of?

(2) *Second Question. Can a Lawyer Avoid This Sort of Outcome?* Consider the following possibilities as a means of avoiding a similarly unfortunate result in your own life and career.

(1) Good time management (as you will see below, some people consider this the single biggest factor within a lawyer's control).

(2) Stress management.

(3) Business management.

(4) Effective dealings with other lawyers, and with the people on your side.

(5) Finding a position that fits your life and personality.

(6) Avoiding dysfunctional dependencies (on drugs or on work).

(7) Recognizing what the problems are.

(8) Other possibilities that you may recognize.

[A] Institutional Causes of Lawyer Dissatisfaction (and Solutions)

[1] *Time: How Lawyers Measure, Manage and Use It*

(1) *Time, and Keeping "Time Records": The Negative Psychological Effects*—Hecht, *Lawyer's Life Governed by the Tick of the Clock*, Nat'l L.J., April 21, 1986, at 17, col 1. The evidence strongly indicates that lawyers who keep time records are more effective than lawyers who do not. (Time records are the only accepted billing method for major areas of practice.) Even contingent-fee lawyers need to record time regularly because "reasonable" attorney's fees so frequently are part of the recovery, and government or corporate employers often require time keeping by their in-house lawyers as a means of efficient resource allocation. But a new lawyer who never has experienced the negative personal effects of dividing her professional life into tenths of an hour is in for a shock. For example, one lawyer who left the practice says she felt "worn away in six-minute increments." Jefferson, above, ABA Journal, Dec. 1991, at 60. Interruptions become intolerable because they sidetrack the lawyer's record keeping; the learning curve with unfamiliar law becomes a source of frustration (and so does the series of short telephone calls that the lawyer did not immediately memorialize); and at the end of the day, the lawyer faces gaps that are impossible to reconstruct. The temptation toward "padding" is enormous. But perhaps the worst effect surfaces when the lawyer's spouse or friend calls to discuss this evening, or just to talk. At that point, the lawyer's values turn upside down. Glancing continuously at her watch, the lawyer struggles with the question: "How am I going to bill this time?," while attempting in frustration to end the conversation!

(2) *Time as "Stock in Trade": Not Enough Time for Avocations, People, or Even Personal Errands*—*See Id.; See Also* Blodgett, *Time and Money: A Look at Today's Lawyer*, ABA Journal, Sept. 1986, at 47. Timekeeping leads to another problem. The focus is not how valuable is the time the lawyer has spent, or even whether it was effective; and it certainly is not whether the lawyer has enough time left for personal pursuits. Lawyer billable hours have increased. *See* Jefferson, above, ABA Journal, Dec. 1991, at 60 ("As overhead went up through the Eighties, firms kept upping the number of hours people were required to bill. . . . That's how we ended up with this 2500 hour-a-year rat race"). Many lawyers who once were avid pleasure-readers virtually stop reading non-law books, and many have little time for hobbies, avocations, or personal friends. Not only is it difficult to find time to take an art class, the lawyer cannot even find time for car repairs, exercise, or necessary personal errands. And this problem may be getting worse instead of better. *See Look at the Time*, ABA Journal, December 1989, at 88 (reporting that many firms now insist on posting all lawyers' time daily, rather than weekly); Jefferson, above, at 64 (to bill 1,900 or 2,000 hours a year, "[Y]ou're probably going to be in the office at least 10 hours a day." [What if you try to bill 2,500?]).

(3) *Deadlines and the Court Management Revolution.* Statutes of limitations and time limits for post-trial motions have long existed, and pretrial cutoffs have existed

for some time. In transactional practice, analogous deadlines have the same effect. These deadlines have always meant that a lawyer with (say) 200 active matters needs to be alert to the calendar, and many lawyers have suffered the experience of time-barring a client's rights by inadvertence. But today, the consequences of inadvertent noncompliance have increased exponentially with the court management revolution, which includes such innovations as differential case management, staging and fast-tracking, and with modern transactional contracts, which feature multiple "contingency periods" or options. The ultimate result: The criminal lawyer must spend much more time managing calendar systems. And worst of all, the lawyer inevitably feels a twinge in the stomach while locking the office door to leave for the night. The lawyer fears that a glitch in the time management system will cause a clients' rights to be "adjudicated" by deadline when the clock strikes midnight.

(4) *The Solution: Short-Term Time Management, Long-Term Time Management, and Vigorous Self Discipline*—Hanson, *Laughing All the Way Home: A "Tickler" System That Works*, 29 Tex. B.J. 568 (1966). Numerous systems are on the market for time keeping. Initial negotiation with the client of how billing should be submitted is essential. When the client's demands for billing detail become excessive, the lawyer should consider declining the representation or altering the fee arrangement to reflect increased costs. As for deadline management, many lawyers keep "double entry tickler systems," and the lawyer should also set up a device called a "perpetual calendar" because some deadlines may span as much as ten years (*e.g.*, execution on an existing judgment). [These are paper-and-pencil systems for low-tech lawyers. Increased technology may not be the trend.] Finally, the lawyer must use rigorous self-discipline about time. *See also* Brill, *How Planning Your Priorities Will Improve Your Pleasure and Profitability*, 44 Tex. B.J. 1360 (1981). Careful attention to selection and refusal of representation, attention to the quality of results from different kinds of efforts, reservation of time for non-billable matters, and (perhaps most importantly) insistence upon time for exercise, family, friends and avocations, are all important.

(5) *But Time Also Involves Cancellations, Washouts, Unexpected Events, and Chaos: The Paradox of Time Management.* Yet efficient time management is not enough. You must have patience, too. A settlement conference that you had scheduled for this morning washes out because the "Rambo" lawyer on the other side instructed his client not to appear, and the two conflicting transactional meetings that you had scheduled for two o'clock this afternoon both canceled. You must adjust quickly if you are to avoid wasting your "stock in trade." Here is the paradox: You must be rigorous in insisting on time management, but at the same time you must be flexible. You must be able to tolerate the frustration of your time plans. Again, self-discipline is a key attribute.

[2] The Dark Side of the Practice of Criminal Law

(1) *Failure and Loss—it Occurs Frequently: Can You Deal With It?* A trial is a zero-sum game. Logically, one side has to lose what the other side wins. And it is

difficult to overstate how bad it feels to some lawyers to lose a jury trial. Almost always, the losing lawyer perceives the loss as an injustice; the defeat is public; it may be published in trial reports in many jurisdictions; the fact that it actually is the loss of the client, who trusted the lawyer, makes matters worse; all too often, the lawyer identifies something that "could have been done" to avoid disaster; and sometimes, the opposing (winning) lawyer has seemed to be obstreperous, condescending, and (occasionally) sleazy. Personal commitment works against the good lawyer, here: It elevates the defeat to a personal rejection. In fact, some lawyers, after losing a jury trial, actually experience the stages of grief that are associated with much more serious losses: denial ("the judge will give me a new trial"); anger ("the other side's witnesses didn't tell the truth and the judge didn't let me show that"); self-negotiation ("I could have hired a metallurgy expert—but then, maybe that wouldn't have made any difference either"); and finally, acceptance ("well, I'll take it as a learning experience.")

Transactions can have the same effect. A transaction that did not close can make the lawyer feel a personal defeat. And a transaction that turns bad for the client and causes a loss is worse. But it happens, and it's not infrequent in the real world.

(2) *The Vince Lombardi Approach: "Winning [Is] the Only Thing."* "Winning isn't everything; it's the only thing," said legendary Green Bay Packer Coach Vince Lombardi. (From Lombardi's standpoint, that astounding statement probably made sense: Instilling into young professional football players an instinctive rejection of anything associated with failure probably motivated them to win, but it did so at a high cost, because of the inevitability of some losses).

(3) *How Effective Will You Be After Law School in Dealing With Losses or Failures?* Imagine that your professor asks, "Now, this lawyer lost the case. What could he have done to win it?" Or, "How should the lawyer have written this contract to win?" (As though the lawyer could control both the client and the other party.) These are useful questions to expose the impact of substantive law choices. But you should not misunderstand the professor's question as an indication that all losses are the fault of lawyers. You should not infer that favorable verdicts result from sheer lawyer cleverness uninfluenced by the case facts. Furthermore, you should not assume that the result was predictable, because litigation and transactions often are chaotic. (Thus, chances are good that any given "solution" was foreclosed by events not contained in the casebook—which, reflects only a tiny fraction of the lawyering by the parties.) Above all, you should avoid assuming that the lawyer "lost" the case through misfeasance. Quite possibly, two skillful lawyers battled vigorously to a close victory for one of them, and there are many choices that "could" have made a difference—just as Lombardi's Packers could have lost to any other team on a given Sunday.

(4) *Dealing with Frequent Losses in Criminal Cases: Do a Good Job Anyway.* In some areas of practice, lawyers lose trials much more often than they win them. "We lose 90 percent of the time, so if you're a person who hates to lose, you're going to have a lot of dissatisfaction," says one public defender who nevertheless is happy with her job. Jefferson, above, at 64. The point is that frequent failures and losses are

inherent in the law, and law school may not prepare you for them. Living a satisfying life requires learning to deal with them on your own. Lawyers, lik e other people, can and should get satisfaction from doing the job well: We guarantee effort, but not results.

(5) *The Opposite Problem—Oppression of Innocent People:* Benson, *Why I Quit Practicing Law,* Newsweek, Nov. 4, 1991, at 10. In this remarkable essay, former Colorado lawyer Sam Benson describes the instant when he realized he was going to quit. He was weary of what he saw as trickery and deception; he did not like pushy lawyers and clients; but his most significant source of discontent was the oppression that was inevitable in law practice. "Most of all," he writes, "I was tired of the misery my job caused other people." The problem is that most professional codes require lawyers to represent their clients' legitimate interests. Many if not most lawyers interpret this command as requiring them to advocate both facts and law just short of ethical limits, and unfortunately, says Benson, "they may be right." The result is the criminal lawyer as a "hired gun" who thinks only about winning cases or making transactions one-sided without actually breaking enforceable rules, not about avoiding oppression of innocent people or solving problems cooperatively. Benson adds: "A nice guy does not usually make a good attorney in the adversarial system." [Do you think Benson's description is too starkly pessimistic? (We do, at least in some respects—Ed.) Even if so, isn't it clear that a person who makes his living as a criminal lawyer in the real world regularly will be subject to a perceived "duty to oppress"?]

(6) *Truthtelling, Falsification, and "Zealous" Advocacy: Do the Difficulty of Line-Drawing and the Infrequency of Detection Lead to Cynical Toleration?* In one (real) case, an interrogatory asked, "Identify all photographs of the relevant event." The responding lawyer (who later became president of a major bar association) had a professionally-produced videotape of the entire event—but he answered, with technical correctness, "I know of none." Under applicable discovery rules, it is difficult to argue that this response was anything other than proper. In transactions, lawyers sometimes see themselves pushing the envelope in similar ways. In another case, the interrogatory asked, "Identify all depictions of the product's packaging," and the responding lawyer attempted to justify a similar "no" answer by the argument that the photographs in his possession were not technically "depictions." [One of the authors of this book, as co-counsel, insisted on a "yes" answer, which actually is the answer that the other co-counsel would have arrived at anyway.] The trouble is that the difference between these two definitional problems turns on matters of degree, about which argument is possible in both cases. And often, even looser standards of "reasonableness" or the like govern the propriety of an argument.

(7) *The Mushiness of Standards—and the Result:* Burke, *"Truth in Lawyering": An Essay on Lying and Deceit in the Practice of Law,* 38 Ark. L. Rev. 1 (1984). These circumstances breed cynicism as lawyers see others define terms aggressively and succeed at it. Their own experience calls for similar kinds of self-serving interpretation—with only a blurred line, representing vague matters of degree, demarcating

what is forbidden. The result? "For years we have 'winked, blinked, and nodded' at blatant if not outrageous lying and deception in pleading, negotiating, investigating, testifying and bargaining. [W]e have come to accept, in fact, to expect, a certain amount of lying and deception . . . , "according to Professor Burke, above. But perhaps the worst news is that Professor Burk e sees lawyers' codes of ethics, as well as the rules of evidence and procedure, as "largely responsible" for this ethical confusion. [Are these conclusions justified? Probably, many lawyers would disagree with some of what Professor Burke says, but his essay is valuable even if only to demonstrate the moral conflict.] And, consider: "[I]t is easy to tell a lie, but harder to tell only one. . . . [A]fter the first lies, [o]thers come more easily." S. Bok, *Lying: Moral Choice in Public and Private Life* 25 (1978); *see also* Tuohy & Warden, *The Fall from Grace of a Greylord Judge*, ABA Journal, Feb. 1989, at 60.]

(8) *Injustice: Its Incidence and Its Effects.* Injustice, or least perceived injustice, is a frequent condition in the law, especially in Criminal Law. The object, after all, is resolving disputes or producing compromise in transactions, and that is a messy business. To avoid becoming consumed by stress, the lawyer must avoid feeling responsible for every injustice that happens to occur. But the trouble is, the lawyer also must prevent this attitude from subtly developing into toleration of (or willing participation in) those injustices. And that is not as easy as it sounds.

(9) *The Spectre of Malpractice—and the Situations in Which You are "Damned If You Do and Damned If You Don't."* A beginning lawyer perceives the testimony of an opposing party as willful perjury and believes that his duty is to expose it. After several months of vigorous effort, he is sanctioned under Federal Rule 11 for an amount in the hundreds of thousands of dollars because the court found the allegation unreasonable. [This example is taken from a real case, or at least is taken from the "real" version given by the lawyer.] Situations like this one, in which you are "damned if you do and damned if you don't," occur sometimes. *See also Costly Errors*, ABA Journal, June 1989, at 28.

(10) *Solutions ("Am I Insured for This?")*—Cross, *The Spectre of the Malpractice Suit*, Legal Advocate, Mar. 1979, at 3, col. 1. How can the lawyer avoid disaster in these problem situations? Experience is helpful, as is hard work; the humility of a lawyer who recognizes that she is not omniscient may be even more important, because it helps her to recognize the impending disaster. But even competent, ethical lawyers make mistakes, especially in today's climate, with occasionally disastrous losses to their clients, and with the spectre of malpractice liability more real today than ever. As for malpractice insurance, it is only a partial solution. It is sufficiently expensive so that lawyers in less lucrative practices may determine that they cannot afford it. Increasingly, too, malpractice insurers are insisting on "claims made" policies, covering only claims that are asserted against the insured during the policy period. If the act of malpractice or the loss occurred in an earlier year and the lawyer no longer is insured, there is no coverage under such a policy. And since the annual application requires disclosure of prior conduct that might give rise to claims, the insurer may be in a position to refuse the coverage. *See also* Lynch,

The Insurance Panic for Lawyers, ABA Journal, July 1986, at 42; *Lawyers' S & L Malpractice*, ABA Journal, Nov. 1989, at 24.

[3] Transactional Practice Raises the Same Problems

(1) *Even if You Say, "I'll Never Be a Criminal Lawyer or a Trial Lawyer," You Should Not Assume That You Are Exempt from These Problems.* It is natural to say to yourself, "Since I'm not going to be a criminal lawyer, or any kind of trial lawyer, I won't have to worry about these problems." In the first place, some of your transactions will end up in litigation. Second, there are other transactions that will involve frequent threats of, and stomach-acid efforts to avoid, litigation. Third and most importantly, transactional practice itself involves the same stressors as litigation.

(2) *Transactional Practice Involves Deadlines, Management Issues, Confrontation, Contentiousness, Opposing Lawyers, and Difficult Clients, Just as Criminal or Civil Litigation Does.* Time management can be even more difficult for transactional lawyers than for litigators, because the day gets chopped up by emergency calls and client requests more frequently and because transactional lawyers bill by time expended more than criminal or civil litigators, who often use other billing methods. As this book shows, every transaction involves multiple deadlines, which the lawyer must properly calendar and address. Decisions in ambiguous circumstances, such as a question whether to insist upon curing a defect that creates marginal risk, or whether to terminate for breach, or whether to discontinue a closing, are frequent, and they carry large potential liability without clearly correct alternatives. Transactional clients sometimes can be even more difficult than litigation clients. Imagine, for example, representing a client who uses strong-arm and aggressive tactics on the other potential contracting party, and presumably uses them also on his own attorneys. Or, imagine representing the other party, who is dealing with an opponent like that. The practice often puts a transactional lawyer in high-pressure situations, in which the lawyer faces a damned-if-you-do-and-damned-if-you-don't decision. In fact, negotiators on the other side often exploit (or create) these situations. And there is plenty of contentiousness in transactional practice, with some lawyers readily accusing other lawyers of dishonesty or the like. There are no statistics that tell us whether this happens more in litigation than in transactional practice, but it happens too often in both. Dealing with uncooperative or incompetent lawyers, parties, lending officers, title examiners, surveyors, or inspectors, is a complaint in transactional practice as well. Long hours, crash-basis lawyering that compresses complex transactions into emergencies that cannot be competently handled, and too-soon termination dates, all make trouble for the transactional lawyer just as comparable issues do for criminal or civil litigators.

(3) *The Point Isn't That Transaction Practice Is Unpleasant.* On the contrary, transactional work can be deeply satisfying. The point, instead, is simply that ignoring these problems creates difficulty for transactional lawyers, just as it does for litigators. And likewise, proper attention to these issues can make the practice satisfying.

[4] People Problems, Part I: The People on Your Side

(1) *Clients Who Are Difficult or Uncooperative:* James W. McElhaney, *Difficult Clients,* ABA J., July 2004, at 30. This article identifies several kinds of clients to avoid: high-maintenance personalities, micromanagers, manipulators, the obsessed, etc. *See also* Hecht, Nat'l L.J., Mar. 9, 1987, at II, col. 2. "The case may be good. . . . But what can you do when the client doesn't help you represent him [or her?]" Hecht identifies "four categories" of uncooperative clients: (1) the "Never-in Nellie," who is never in and who "never returns your phone calls" (send the client a "please call me" letter after three attempts), (2) "the great Houdini," who is reachable on the telephone but "never appears for depositions, contract signings, court dates and the like," (3) "Mal Content," who "disagrees with everything you do and, if that isn't enough, despises you" (solution: "don't even try" to please this client), and (4) "Double-Dealing Debbie," who generates second opinions herself (or obtains them from dubious sources) and asks questions like "Why didn't you raise the defense of collateral estoppel?" The result may be that "your Rolaids bill" exceeds the fee you earn. Hecht suggests: first, transferring these clients to a colleague; second, telling the client that the case is "flawed (even if it isn't)(?!)" to make the client feel a degree of responsibility; and third, making the client "an adversary." This last solution is accomplished by a lengthy series of letters warning the client that "unless x is provided, the case may be dismissed." Hecht's conclusion: "At least estate attorneys do not have these problems since their clients [n]ever utter a complaint, since they are dead. Lucky guys." [What do you think of this advice—is it ethical? And if so, is it unduly cynical?]

(2) *"Cases and Clients That Should Be Turned Down,"* in J. Foonberg, *How to Start and Build a Law Practice,* 5 1–54 (1976). Foonberg's ostensibly cynical (but more often sensible) advice is that the beginning lawyer should refuse employment in certain situations, including: (1) "When you are the second or third lawyer on the case (earlier lawyers may have had honest differences but often they indicate a. a nonmeritorious case[;] b. an uncooperative client[; or] c. a nonpaying client"); (2) "'hurt feeling' cases" such as cases of libel, brawls, or assault and battery (which have arguably wrongful conduct, but "nominal damages"); (3) "landlord-tenant cases (unless you are paid in full in advance)," in which "each side wants to use the lawyer for revenge if he can use the lawyer for free." In addition, Foonberg recommends against acceptance of (4) criminal cases unless paid in full in advance (a client who is in prison does not earn much, Foonberg points out), (5) bankruptcy cases unless the lawyer is prepaid in full ("It was embarrassing when my client amended his bankruptcy schedules to include the unpaid balance of the fee due me"), (6) clients who "use your telephones, secretary and offices to do their business" (this client, he says, somehow always ends up being "trouble"), and the like. For (7) cases totally without merit, Foonberg's solution is, "Tell your client the truth."

(3) *"Firing the Client:" The Solution of Withdrawal.* Some commentators recommend liberal use of the withdrawal option for serious problem clients, unless

withdrawal is impractical or unethical (*e.g.*, it would prejudice the client's case). *See* Foonberg, above, at 102; *cf* Hecht, above, at 14. Often, conflict or nonpayment makes the client avoid the lawyer; in that situation, a "due process trail" of letters may be necessary to avoid prejudicing the client and to protect the lawyer.

(4) *"The Client's Curve of Gratitude."* Foonberg reproduces this "curve," which is similar to the Bell curve familiar to statisticians. The curve begins with the day the complaint is served on the client, who recognizes that he is in trouble: "I didn't know those pulleys I sold [and didn't check] were defective and would be used in a jet airplane which crashed." The curve reaches its topmost point on the day when the lawyer's hard work produces a favorable settlement on the courthouse steps: "No other lawyer could have done what he did. I owe him my business, my career, everything." Mysteriously, the curve turns downward, until, ten weeks later, the client considers the lawyer "crazy if he thinks I'm going to pay" and, even tually, decides to complain to the bar association and sue the lawyer "for malpractice." Foonberg's message is simple. The lawyer should insist on payment in advance (or bill monthly and take steps to collect). For reasons that involve the client's welfare as well as his own, Foonberg implies that the sensible lawyer never lets the client get "too far ahead" of him (*i.e.*, too much in debt to the lawyer).

(5) *Fee Disputes.* A large percentage of complaints or grievances presented by clients to disciplinary boards originate in fee disputes. A partial solution lies in the nearly universal advice that the attorney insist upon a written fee agreement in every case (which is more difficult that it might appear). Another partial solution is the practice of regular billing and collection, which tends to ensure that disputes are confronted early.

(6) *Clients in Divorce, Personal Injury and Criminal Cases: A Special Problem*—Buchmeyer, *How to Avoid Grievance Complaints*, 47 Tex. B.J. 162 (1983). Consider the following client dilemma. The only sensible course is for your client to accept insurance policy limits of $20,000, even though he is horribly disfigured, because his case is weak on liability and there is no defendant who even approaches solvency. Naturally, the client objects to the proposed settlement. But assuming that trial absolutely cannot produce more money and that a zero verdict is a real possibility, your duty is to persist in your advice. Here is the point: If you must overcome strong client resistance, watch out, even though there is no other alternative. In this area of practice (personal injury)—and in divorce and criminal law—clients make disciplinary complaints at a much higher rate than in other areas. In these areas, lawyers deal almost invariably with unsophisticated clients who are unfamiliar with the litigation system and have unrealistic expectations of it. Buchmeyer points out that these "target" areas of practice account for more than 70% of client grievances filed, though they total less than 30% of all law practice. (Incidentally, Buchmeyer convincingly refutes the hypothesis that there is a lesser standard among these practitioners.) The solutions: consider declining representation; don't promise the moon; help your client to confront the weaknesses in the case; don't coerce settlement; seek another lawyer's assistance in explaining the problems to the client when necessary;

and treat the client with respect. *See also* Grasso, *Defensive Lawyering: How to Keep Your Clients from Suing You*, ABA Journal, Oct. 1989, at 98.

(7) *Pick Your Mentor Carefully for Courage, Time Availability, and Willingness to Give Support: The Problems of Co-Counsel, Employers and Supervisors.* In addition to trouble with opposing counsel, lawyers often have trouble with counsel who ostensibly are on the same side. To take a situation that (we hope) is infrequent, if a superior is mendacious, it can be surprisingly difficult for a beginning lawyer to avoid entanglement in ethical violations or sanctionable conduct. The beginner's inexperience makes her uncertain of her ground and her subordinate position makes her eager to please. Sometimes, the problem is even worse than that: The superior who lacks integrity also lacks courage and takes steps to ensure that the subordinate rather than the superior is the one in the compromised position. The solution: Pick your mentors with care. Look for the time availability that will let you obtain guidance (although this quality is not as abundant as one might hope). Look to see whether she takes the responsibility herself rather than placing it on subordinates. And, finally, look for integrity.

Problem B

MILGRAM'S EXPERIMENTS WITH AUTHORITY AND OBEDIENCE. The social psychology of authority and obedience has produced some disturbing results. Stanley Milgram's authority experiment is a classic example. Milgram set up a phony "experimenter" in an official-looking white lab coat, who actually was a stooge, and who instructed subjects to administer electrical "shocks" to a strapped-down "learner" whenever the learner made errors. The scale began at "15 Volts- 'Slight' Shock" and went through 150 Volts ("'Strong' Shock") to 450 Volts.

But in reality, there were no shocks, and the learner also was a stooge, who both erred intentionally and gasped in pain at the lower settings. At 120 volts, the stooge playing the part of the learner protested that the shocks were painful; at 150, the stooge (through a voice recorder) shouted "Get me out of here! . . . I refuse!" But if the subject faltered, the experimenter responded firmly that "the experiment requires that you go on." At "180 volts," the learner shouted that he "couldn't stand" the pain; at 300, responses stopped, and the experimenter told the subject to treat a non-response as a wrong answer. Most subjects who "prematurely" terminated this charade were highly agitated, and so were those who continued, protesting all the way, to 450 volts. The white-jacketed "experimenter" simply told the subject that "the experiment requires you to continue."

Astonishingly, more than 60 percent of the subjects continued to the top of the scale, hearing increasingly agonized cries. Milgram's conclusion was that "ordinary people" were sufficiently obedient to authority that they could be engaged in a "terribly destructive process."

(1) *First Question: What Significance Does This Have for Lawyers?* A new lawyer will encounter many authority figures, ranging from clients to judges to

employers to partners. Does Milgram's experiment demonstrate that these authoritative people might succeed to a surprising degree in inducing the new lawyer to behave dysfunctionally?

(2) *Second Question: What Factors or Behaviors Increase or Decrease the Likelihood That an Authority Can Induce Bad Behavior in You?* Milgram's experiments also showed some of the factors that affected obedience to commands to shock. Obedience increased (a) when the authority (the white-coated "experimenter") had high status, (b) when there was no disobeying role model, (c) when the experimenter was physically close, (d) when the victim was distant, and (e) when the subject was depersonalized (*e.g.,* when the subject wore a mask). Other experiments have shown that conformity increases (f) when the subject has no clear commitment against the suggestion, (g) when the subject belongs to a culture that values conformity, (h) when a sizable group is the authority, and (i) when the correctness or wrongness of the suggested behavior is ambiguous. What do these factors suggest about how you can avoid being led into destructive behavior by the people on your side?

[5] People Problems, Part II: The Other Participants

(1) *Disappointments With Judges and Courts: Report of the State Judicial Qualification Commission,* 58 Tex. B.J. 1095 (1991). The public impression of judges is that they are selfless and scholarly. Courtroom etiquette reinforces the natural tendency to hold judges in esteem. Perhaps for that reason, judges often are sources of attorney disappointment. First, in today's disposition-oriented climate, docket pressures often motivate judges to become abusive, to cut *off* arguments, to refuse relief, and to treat disputants like feuding children even when they have honest differences requiring adjudication. (Thus, the above report notes one judge who "used profanity and became personally abusive toward a defendant when the judge lost his temper in the course of a judicial proceeding.") Second, sometimes the judge acts energetically and with good motives, but with an unfortunate disassociation from rules and consequences: "In an effort to avoid further conflict between the parties, a judge heard evidence from each party outside the presence of the other party, thereby failing to allow cross-examination." Another judge "personally conducted a field investigation concerning a case pending in his court, which included surveillance of the defendant's home and interviewing the defendant's neighbors." *Id.* Third, judges sometimes abuse their positions: "A judge telephoned a member of a law firm, which had other cases pending in the judge's court, to inquire into the progress of a civil matter, on behalf of a friend who had an interest in that civil matter." *Id.* Fourth, judges sometimes have garden-variety prejudices. These kinds of disappointing conduct occur in every state and are especially troublesome when the judge cannot be removed. Often, the inexperienced lawyer is helpless to counteract judicial misbehavior. *See also, e.g.,* Gilbert, *Difficult Judges: How to Survive Them,* California Litigation, Winter 1991, at 3 (contending that even if the judge acts in a blatantly sexist manner toward you or your client in front of the jury, "a quick lesson on the evils of sexism may hurt rather than help your client"); Smolin,

Thirteen Deadly Sins: How Lawyers Irritate Judges, California Litigation, Winter 1991 at 11 (the "greatest" deadly sin, according to this article: "boring the judge").

(2) *Opposing Counsel Who Are Uncooperative, Unresponsive or Incompetent.* A competent lawyer dealing with a counterpart who simply does not understand the process can experience great difficulty. Unless the trial judge has the time, the experience, and the fortitude to impose sanctions, dealing with such an adversary can be maddeningly frustrating. Often, the judge chooses forbearance, rather than visitation of the sins from the opposing lawyer's ignorance on his client—although the judge perhaps should be aware that this forbearance visits them instead on the competent lawyer's client. The only solution, then, is patience.

(3) *The Difficult Problem of the "Rambo" Lawyer.* Imagine the following scenario. Your client has cancelled a potentially profitable meeting to be present for his deposition, and you have taken several hours to prepare him. The Rambo litigator on the other side, of course, set it up by notice without calling you beforehand. Together with your client, you wait . . . and you wait. After almost an hour, you call Rambo's office, only to hear an unconcerned receptionist explain that Rambo is vacationing at a distant ski resort. Surprise: You have just experienced one of Rambo's favorite tactics, which is to notice depositions and not show up. (You can file a motion for sanctions, but don't place inordinate faith in it: Rambo knows how to stop just short of conduct that will truly invoke sanctions. He will have an excuse, which perhaps will involve a telephone call in which he left a message with "someone" in your office cancelling the deposition.) *See* James W. McElhaney, *Difficult Clients*, ABA J., July 2004, at 30 (saying that there are whole "firms" composed of "Rambo lawyers").

(4) *The Varieties of Rambo Tactics:* Lynn, *Handling the Obstructionist Lawyer*, in University of Houston, *Advanced Civil Discovery* (D. Crump ed. 1990). Rambo's client declines to answer deposition questions about documents, because he "doesn't know what the word 'document' means." When you define it as any paper he uses in his business, he again will demur, feigning ignorance of what the word "business" means. This conduct is not accidental but results from Rambo's instructions to the client. When it comes to pushing, Rambo knows how to draft an interrogatory that will require you to assemble information from every one of your client's 10,000 installations. Rambo knows how to set depositions on five days' notice, to force your hand in attending them, and to threaten a motion for sanctions if you insist on terminating at 3:00 p.m. for a previous engagement. Rambo is abusive to your client, repeatedly calling the client (or you) a "liar" during the deposition. And opposing parties or lawyers in transactions can be similar.

(5) *What Can You Do, In the Real World, About the Rambo Lawyer?:* Cardwell, *Dealing With Rambo Lawyers*, in University of Houston, *Advanced Civil Discovery* (D. Crump ed. 1991). First, slow down. Painstaking care and patience pay off. There may be no way to avoid the additional dollars that Rambo will cost your client, in that all other alternatives may cost even more. Second, avoid trying to out-Rambo Rambo. Most of us are not as good at it as Rambo is, and your inept imitations will give Rambo his best arguments for avoiding sanctions (or for imposing sanctions

on you; remember, motions for sanctions are another favorite arrow in Rambo's quiver). Third, proceed methodically but with perseverance. Fourth, advise your client of the reasons you have chosen this course and of the need for perseverance. Fifth, do not file a grievance at the first slight opportunity. You invite the judge or disciplinary board (who, after all, does not assume that Rambo is Rambo) to treat your complaints as the initiation of a childish squabble, diminishing the credibility of later, more serious motions. Finally, document the offending behavior carefully, and grieve the matter only when the conduct is egregious, persistent, and indisputably provable to the neutral observer. Invite compliance by Rambo in the meantime. If you must present a motion for sanctions, handle it with professional restraint. Remember, as far as this motion is concerned, you're the prosecutor, the "heavy," and you must avoid overstatement.

(6) *Avoid Confusing "Negotiating Behavior" with Malfeasance or Rambo Tactics.* Consider these scenarios: Your opponent identifies internal investigative documents but declines to produce them on a marginal claim of work product. Or: In an antitrust case, your opponent seeks documents relevant to "every meeting" participated in by your client's bidding agent over a ten-year period. Or: Your opponent communicates the insurance adjuster's settlement offer of $5,000 for your client's paraplegic injuries. Pause before you react to this conduct; in each instance, it may be the opening of a normal course of negotiation. If the work product claim is "marginal," that still means it is subject to reasonable argument, and your adversary may be able to make reciprocal concessions with you during discovery. The $5,000 offer represents the opening of a channel of communication, and you are perfectly at liberty to respond with your demand of $10 million. The distinction between negotiation and Rambo tactics is important, but it often eludes beginning lawyers. *See also, e.g., In re Snyder,* 472 U.S. 634 (1985) (even if opponent is rude or lacks professional courtesy, a single incident may not invoke sanctions).

Problem C

ENTRAPMENT IN ESCALATION: THE DOLLAR AUCTION. One psychological trap that has generated significant research is the "dollar auction." An auctioneer announces that he will exchange a $1 bill for a payment from the highest bidder. The catch is that the next-highest bidder also must pay his or her bid. Therefore, as the bidding closes in on $1, players scramble to avoid becoming the next-highest bidder, a phenomenon that often sends the bids up to amounts exceeding $1.

There are three crucial junctures in the dollar auction: the second bid (which means that there now is going to be a loser), the first bid over 50 cents (which means that the auctioneer will profit from the players), and, of course, the "magic moment" (the first bid that exceeds $1). Why would anyone bid more than $1 for a dollar? The answer may lie in the "Concorde fallacy," as it is called, which takes its name from the supersonic airliner produced by a British-French consortium, in which costs escalated dramatically. Even after it would have been apparent to an objective observer that the economically sound strategy was to cut and run, both governments increased their levels of commitment because they had "too much invested to withdraw."

A similar psychological trap has been observed in dollar auction experiments, with astonishing results. Experimenters typically give subjects sums ranging from $2.50 to $20 to bid, and often the escalation continues until the limit is reached. In fact, that is a common outcome: subjects given $20 bid until their entire $20 is gone. In some experiments, the subjects have become distraught to the point of crying. This "entrapment" phenomenon occurs in high percentages of experiments.

(1) *Does the Entrapment-in-Escalation Phenomenon Reflect a Change in Motivation and Does it Explain Escalating Litigation Discourtesy?* One group of experimenters surveyed subjects during dollar-auction play and found that a change in motivation develops the initial economic motivation, which is to obtain something of value at a bargain price, gives way to a competitive urge that obscures the actor's initial economic goals. This change accompanies entrapment in escalation. Does this factor explain why it is difficult, in contentious transactions, to avoid becoming entrapped yourself in escalating nastiness?

(2) *The Dollar Auction and the Uneconomical, Yet Unresolvable Dispute.* It sometimes happens that parties to a lawsuit or transaction spend more in preparation than the amount at issue and still find themselves unable to resolve the matter short of a termination that will more than double the losses of each. Likewise, sometimes labor and management are unable to end a strike that has produced losses far exceeding any possible gains. The historical arms race between the United States and the former Soviet Union displayed the same characteristics. Can you explain how these phenomena are related to the dollar auction? Also, consider whether mediation might reduce the losses in some of these cases.

[6] Business Management in the Criminal Law Practice

(1) *Law Practice Management (and the Impact of Money Concerns).* Imagine that your client has suffered an adverse jury verdict in a case with clear error. But the likelihood of reversal is less than 25%. The posting of an appeal bond (at a premium of 10%), plus the costs of preparing the record, printing briefs, and attorney's fees for the appeal, exceed any expectancy of gain that might result from reversal. Many lawyers suffer severe frustration with these kinds of money-driven dispositions. But don't let it get to you: Much of the decisionmaking in lawyering is economically determined, and the only solutions are anticipation of these bottlenecks—and acceptance.

(2) *The Costs of Accomplishing Even Small Steps Seems Inordinately Large.* Filing and serving a subpoena may seem easy, but the number of steps required in some instances to serve even a non-evasive out-of-state defendant can be formidable. Courts often reject pleadings for noncompliance, which means wasted (and expensive, non-billable) effort. The costs of taking depositions in another city readily can exceed $5,000, and experts in a personal injury case may well exceed $50,000

(which the lawyer, as a practical matter, must advance). In a transaction, inspections, regulatory costs, etc., can balloon and frustrate expectations. The solution is not to take these steps for granted and to deal with clients accordingly.

(3) *Money in the Criminal Law Practice.* One partner practices law diligently, billing thousands of hours over the year. Another partner has frequent 3-hour lunches and bills a fraction of the first partner's production—but this partner is the "rainmaker," the one who has the clients. How should these two clients divide the pie? This question, and others like it, are what partnership dissolutions are made of. The truth may well be that both partners have something valuable to offer, and each needs the other. [In declining economic times, the calculus becomes even more difficult, because there is no attractive way to allocate a shrinking pie.] The best solution is to recognize the problem, to avoid egocentrism when recognizing the other partner's worth, and to negotiate without attributing motives.

(4) *Management Systems (and Criminal Lawyers' Aversion to Them): See Special Bar Journal Section [on Professional Management]: An Introduction,* 53 Tex. B.J. 204 *et seq.* (1990). The values of slipsheet timekeeping, form freezers, personnel management, and other organizational devices are clear. They become obscured, however, by deadlines and daily production needs. Furthermore, lawyers' educations contain little that concerns office management—and, indeed, the every-case-is-unique approach of the Socratic dialogue tends to depreciate the value of management, which is concerned with efficient handling of repetitive problems. The solution is to have the self-discipline to implement office systems by setting aside the time to do so.

[B] The Personal Costs of the Lawyer's Life—and Solutions
[1] Stress

(1) *What Stress Is and What It Does:* Finney, *The Stressful Workplace,* Management Digest, in Newsweek, Nov. 4, 1991, at A-6. Stress is caused partly by external stimuli, such as conflicting demands, unreasonable expectations, unclear directions, and frequent frustrations or "hassles." Additional causes of stress, ironically, are self-imposed: They include poor self-image, anger, impatience and intolerance. Finally, there are life change stressors, which the Holmes-Rahe "Social Readjustment Rating Scale" measures (in this scale, the death of a spouse is the highest stressor, at 100 points, with divorce, promotion, intercity moves, and other life events occupying lower ratings; the cumulative total over a period of time is what indicates disadvantageous stress). Dysfunctional stress interferes with relationships as well as job performance. Ultimately, it leads to physical diseases, including gastrointestinal disorders, hypertension, and heart disease. *See also* Biehl, *Calm Yourself,* ABA J., Oct. 1989, at 122.

(2) *What Conditions are Correlated With Dysfunctional Stress?: A Multiple-Choice Test.* Which of the following is most likely to produce conditions of dysfunctional stress?

(a) Learning that a friend who lives in a distant city has died.

(b) Hearing from a lawyer who recently opposed you in a case that he has referred a client to you.

(c) Receiving an adverse jury verdict in a case in which you expended a large effort and which will result in a substantial prison sentence for the client.

(d) After running behind and missing meetings all day because you are trying to prepare for a hearing early tomorrow morning, having the temporary secretary tell you that the computer lost the only copy of the brief you must file tomorrow.

(e) Learning that you did not make partner this year.

The above source suggests that the correct answer is (d). Repetitive, cumulative assaults by life's smaller hassles, according to consistent research, often creates more dysfunctional stress than a single (even very serious) event. *See* Management Digest, above. But big events also cumulate with "hassle"-type stressors.

(3) *"But Wait—Those 'Stress-Producing Conditions' Are Exactly What Law Practice Inevitably Produces!"* Exactly. That's the point. Lawyers are particularly prone to stress because they are constantly in ambiguous, conflicted, acrimonious, irritating, unjust and often humiliating situations. It is for this reason that California has required every practicing lawyer to take regular instruction in stress reduction (see above)—and it also is why this section is in this book.

(4) *But Some Stress is "Good," Some People Thrive on It, and Even Dysfunctional Stress Has. Its Uses.* Exciting, interesting experiences often are stressful. Most people would find a stress-free existence to be intolerably boring. (See below.) And even dysfunctional stress has its uses; without the stress of confronting a jury trial or transactional deadline together with you, your client might never evaluate the settlement offer that is the best alternative. [Incidentally, the Rambo litigator is unethical and unpleasant, but Rambo's no fool; Rambo knows about stress, and uses it.]

(5) *A Multiple-Choice Test About Stressor Effects.* Lawyer Brown and Lawyer Green both are handling large dockets of difficult criminal cases. Brown seems to thrive on it, while Green is becoming depressed and frustrated. Why?

(a) Brown went to a more prestigious law school.

(b) Brown is older.

(c) Brown functions happily under stress while Green does not.

(d) Brown is more motivated by money.

(e) Brown took a practice course in law school.

Undoubtedly, you have guessed that the answer is (c). Some individuals enjoy a work environment that others would find dysfunctionally stressful. If Brown were deprived of the excitement he gets at work, he might seek his stress by skydiving or gaming in Las Vegas.

(6) *Dealing with Stress: Some Solutions.* Replacing a negative self-image with a positive one is a major solution to harmful stress. Another solution is to ensure that you reserve time each day for relaxation and exercise. *See id.; cf.* Evans, *Ten Commandments for Lawyers' Health*, Nat'l L.J., Aug. 24, 1987, at 13 (suggesting a positive outlook, perspective, maintenance of creativity, avoidance of anger, organization, diet, exercise, avoiding smoking, daily escape, and attention to one's body, as the "Ten Commandments" for avoiding stress). *See also* Becky Gillespie, *Hunting Happy,* ABA J., Aug 2011, at 40 ("[T]he 'lawyer personality' may play a role . . . . Attorneys are . . . self-selected for introversion and . . . more pessimistic than the general population. . . . After all, . . . it's good to think about worst-case scenarios when you're writing contracts").

Problem D

THE EXECUTIVE MONKEY EXPERIMENT. The famous "executive monkey" experiment paired two monkeys, both of which were subject to a series of electric shocks, but one of which, the executive monkey, controlled the timing of each shock. The difference in manifestations of stress between the two monkeys was dramatic. This was so even though there was no difference in the number or intensity of the shocks. Photographs clearly show the executive monkey, which differed only in having the ability to determine when the shocks occurred, as relatively relaxed. The other monkey, which was unable to control the shocks, remained rigidly anxious.

Question: Given that a criminal lawyer often is subject to unpleasant stimuli delivered unpredictably by deadlines, adversaries, clients, and employers and cannot very well control his or her schedule, what does the executive monkey experiment suggest about the resultant stress?

[2] Secondary Effects: Substance Abuse and Dysfunctional Personal Relationships

(1) *Substance Abuse: Alcohol and Beyond* — Crowley, *Recognizing and Dealing with Dependency and Co-dependency,* 53 Tex. B.J. 234 (1990). Attorneys exhibit high rates of alcohol abuse. Some surveys have reported astounding alcohol usage by attorneys. *See also* Becky Gillespie, *Hunting Happy,* ABA J., Aug. 2011, at 40 ("high rates of alcoholism, depression, and suicide"). The temptation to seek this avenue as a relief from stress is as prevalent as it is counterproductive. Likewise, abuse of drugs other than alcohol is more serious among lawyers than among many other groups. *See also Fighting Back from Drugs,* ABA Journal, Mar. 1989, at 15; Wharton, *The Disease of Addiction,* 52 Tex. B.J. 286 (1989); Doot, *Disease of Chemical Dependence, id.* at 283.

(2) *Effects of Stress, Time Management, and Contentiousness on the Lawyer's Personal Relationships: Divorce, Children and Friends.* Lawyers often have days that they feel have been consumed entirely in fighting with other people. (After all, one of the main things a lawyer has to offer to a client is the ability to induce a third person

or entity to do something that that person otherwise would not do.) It is difficult for human beings to "turn off" this kind of behavior immediately upon leaving the job, and therefore, lawyers tend to extend their arguments to spouses, children, and friends. Thus, "battles in the boardroom" become "battles in the bedroom." Likewise, the difficulties that lawyers have in reserving time for personal obligations lead to neglect of spouses, children and friends. Among the results: a high divorce rate for the legal profession. The solution? Again, it is self-discipline, good time management, stress control, professional counseling when one can benefit from it—and an awareness of the problem in the first place.

Problem E

DSM-IV AND THE OBSESSIVE-COMPULSIVE PERSONALITY DISORDER: CAN LAW SCHOOL INDUCE SOME DYSFUNCTIONAL CHARACTERISTICS? The American Psychiatric Association's Diagnostic and Statistical Manual of Mental Disorders is known as "DSM" for short. Under the heading, "Obsessive-Compulsive Disorder," the fourth edition (DSM-IV) sets forth the following diagnostic criteria:

301.4 Obsessive-Compulsive Personality Disorder

A pervasive pattern of preoccupation with orderliness, perfectionism, and mental and interpersonal control, at the expense of flexibility, openness, and efficiency, beginning by early adulthood and present in a variety of contexts, as indicated by four (or more) of the following:

(1) is preoccupied with details, rules, lists, order, organization, or schedules to the extent that the major point of the activity is lost

(2) shows perfectionism that interferes with task completion (e.g., is unable to complete a project because his or her own overly strict standards are not met)

(3) is excessively devoted to work and productivity to the exclusion of leisure activities and friendships (not accounted for by obvious economic necessity)

(4) is overconscientious, scrupulous, and inflexible about matters of morality, ethics, or values (not accounted for by cultural or religious identification)

(5) is unable to discard worn-out or worthless objects even when they have no sentimental value

(6) is reluctant to delegate tasks or to work with others unless they submit to exactly his or her way of doing things

(7) adopts a miserly spending style toward both self and others; money is viewed as something to be hoarded for future catastrophes

(8) shows rigidity and stubbornness

Other sources suggest that, in moderation, some measure of these characteristics may be functional (perhaps in a lawyer, for example). Excessive manifestation of these behaviors, however, has unpleasant results and may drive to distraction anyone close to such a person.

(1) *Can Law School "Nudge" You Toward These Characteristics in a Dysfunctional Way?* No one is suggesting that everyone who emerges from law school is clinically obsessive-compulsive (or even a significant percentage) or that your professors are setting out to "teach" you how to be dysfunctional. But doesn't DSM's list display a striking coincidence with some of what law school seems to inculcate, such as "preoccup[ation] with details, rules, lists, order," etc. that often departs from the "major point" (the just outcome), or "excessive devot[ion] to work and productivity"?

(2) *How Can You Maintain "Good" Compulsiveness (Meticulous Professionalism) but Keep It in Balance?* Certainly, no one is saying that a law school education is a bad thing, either! In context, concentration on rules and devotion to work are good things. Maybe the meticulous professional simply is bound to appear a little obsessive at times. But how can you ensure that your compulsivity won't get out of balance?

[3] *Lack of Significance in One's Work*

(1) *There Are Boring Jobs in the Law, and Boring Parts of Any Job.* Criminal Law courses should not mislead you into concluding that beginning lawyers spend the bulk of their time trying cases before juries. On the contrary, they spend relatively little time in trial and much more with business matters, meetings, or document analyses (or sifting through the results)—which are much less exciting tasks. Like any endeavor, criminal lawyering is composed in large percentage of tasks that are neither interesting nor inherently valuable in isolation.

(2) *The Deeper Problem of Lack of Significance.* Benson's explanation, cited above, of his reasons for quitting the practice of law indicates a deeper kind of dissatisfaction than intermittent boredom. Benson, *Why I Quit Practicing Law*, Newsweek, Nov. 4, 1991, at 10. Many lawyers are not only bored and stressed, but convinced that their efforts do not matter. Sometimes, this perception results from the enormous costs in proportion to perceived gains. Because many matters take years to resolve, our system creates the impression that legal problems do not "turn," and that the paper shuffling associated with it is ineffective to resolve real issues.

(3) *The Solutions: Information, Flexibility, Persistence.* The solution to this problem is to learn as much as possible about any job you consider, including what lawyers who do it really do on a daily basis, *before* accepting the position. A second solution is to avoid prejudice about what you really would like to do. Sometimes, a law student who seems to have the soul of a poet thrives in a large competitive law firm, finding that the interests served ultimately benefit society, and that the lawyer's own abilities are well utilized. Sometimes such a lawyer even finds caring mentors in that "impersonal" law firm. On the other hand, it is surprising how often a law student who seems drawn to prestige and financial rewards is happier in the district attorney's office—or in a solo practice, or in a setting that more explicitly claims to serve the public interest. Likewise, another attorney may be astounded to find that a corporate legal department offers a better combination of lifestyle

and professional interest. *Cf.* Machlovitz, *Lawyers Move In-House*, ABA Journal, May 1989, at 66 (reporting, counterintuitively, that the buildup of corporate legal departments may mean not only that that is where jobs are, but also a better quality of life for many lawyers). Thus, a full exploration of the alternatives, without prejudice, pays enormous dividends later in life. Third, it is inadvisable to forsake a chosen path at the first sign of boredom or conflict, because those conditions are unavoidable in any legal career. Finally, persistent conviction that one's work lacks significance should lead, as it did in Benson's case, to a decision to change it.

§ B.03 The "Up" Side: Positive Reasons for Practicing Law

[A] "Good" Stress: Challenge and Adventure

(1) *Practicing Law Can Involve "Good" Stress — Or, Work That Is Interesting and Exciting.* In explaining the significance of his work, one personal injury lawyer asks: "Where else could I depose a safety expert from [a major automobile manufacturer], and make him answer my questions about defects in the way his company designs cars?" Short of election to Congress (and perhaps not even then), he is right. There are few other positions offering such an opportunity to deal with issues of significance, and, indeed, to have such interesting experiences. Even in matters that themselves seem to be devoid of significance, issues about an obscure security interest provision in the UCC can be fantastically interesting, when they affect real people.

(2) *Interest and Excitement as the Number One Reason Given by Lawyers for Entering the Profession*, ABA Journal, Sept. 1986, at 44. People go to law school because they think it will be interesting. "Roughly three in five lawyers (58.4%) said they studied law because the subject interested them, and more than half (58.1%) did so in the expectation that their work as lawyers would be interesting." This reason — interest and excitement — was mentioned by more lawyers in this survey than income potential (46.3%), prestige (43.1%), or the desire to improve society (23.4%). In fact, the "interesting subject matter" motivation prevailed over wanting to "see justice done" (21.6%) by more than 2 to 1. Therefore, you should seek work that interests you, whether it is criminal law, bankruptcy, environmental litigation (where lawyers go to court infrequently), personal injury defense in a small-to-medium sized firm (where trial work is much more frequent), or something else.

[B] Service

(1) *A High Proportion of Civic Activities:* Blodgett, *Time and Money: A Look At Today's Lawyer*, ABA Journal, Sept. 1, 1986, at 47. Today's lawyer "would like to spend more time with his [or her] family yet willingly assumes a host of duties and civic activities." These activities include not only *pro bono* litigation, but serving upon

local boards of directors of hospitals and other nonprofit organizations. It appears that these kinds of organizations value lawyers because of their organizational ability, practical approach to getting things done, and dedication to service.

> Lawyers make things work. They may do it in a variety of ways. They may do it by sabbaticals and periodic service in government. They may do it by commissions and boards and special roles. They may do it solely iii their community or in their church, or in fund-raising or legislative activities, reforms or programs within the system. They certainly serve the public interest day in and day out by guaranteeing due process and protecting the rights and liberties of our citizens.

Civiletti, *Projecting Law Practice in the 1990's*, Nat'l L.J., Aug. 10, 1987, at 22.

(2) *Public Service Through Service to Clients.* Furthermore, civic efforts are not the only way in which lawyers are of service. The plaintiff's attorney who deposed the safety expert, above, provided a service to his client, and in the traditional manner, thereby indirectly served the larger public by advocating safer products—as did his counterpart on the defense side, who advocated products that were functional and affordable. As Civiletti says, lawyers "make things work" as well as preserving values such as due process—and they do it by doing their jobs.

(3) *Service to a Legal System That "Works" Overall and That Is a Part of Democratic Government, Even Though It Miscarries in Some Cases.* Every society must have a system of dispute resolution that has public confidence. It is an essential part of the "glue" that allows the society to function. Our own legal system reflects such deeply held values as the individual's right to be heard before an impartial decision-maker subject to a neutral body of norms applicable to all. The criminal lawyer plays an indispensable role in that system. Thus, the lawyer contributes to the function of our democracy and to a system that "works," at least in the overall sense—even when the particular case is only of routine importance and even though the system has imperfections.

[C] Financial Rewards

(1) *Personal Wealth.* In 1986, "[t]he median income of lawyers [was] $64,448 and the average income [was] $104,625. Lawyers [had] an average household income of $121,913". As for investment portfolios, "[t]he median was $69,079, and the average was $300,340." The picture is that of a profession in which members work hard (perhaps too hard) and in which earnings do not exceed those of some ot her professions, but in which the financial rewards are significant. Blodgett, above, ABA J. at 47–51.

(2) *Independence and Self-Development.* But these financial factors understate a separate, additional advantage: The lawyer has greater independence than many other workers. "Today's lawyer is a hardworking entrepreneur." *Id.* A lawyer in a very large firm has the prospect of setting up a one-person firm, still with significant

earnings almost from the beginning, with little lead time. The dues that lawyers pay, as they struggle with time pressures, adversaries and stress, give them a freedom that is unusual.

[D] The Profession—And the Fellowship of Other Lawyers

(1) *A Profession With a History:* Trevathan, *No More Lawyer-Bashing*, Hous. Lawyer, Nov. 1991, at 11. "Our 'ancestors' include Cicero, Patrick Henry, Justice Louis D. Brandeis and Oliver Wendell Holmes"—to which, we could add Sir Thomas More and Abraham Lincoln.

(2) *The Fellowship of Other Lawyers.* As one California lawyer put it: "If I scored big in the lottery, I'd still keep practicing law." Blodgett, above, ABA Journal at 48. Lawyers make wonderful company to work with or to know socially. Even the less professional and altruistic members of the profession tend, at least, to be interesting.

[E] It's Up to You

The Point of This Appendix. The point is that the choices you make in how you select your career, the organization in which you undertake it, the way you manage it, and the ways you balance it with your personal life, all will make a difference in whether you can find the elusive path to combining competence, ethics, altruism and success with a full life as a lawyer. And you can enhance the quality of your choices by careful examination and self-discipline. You will have to live with the consequences, but you can make them turn out positively. It's up to you.

Index

I

J